CW00663754

1 MONTH OF
FREE
READING

at

www.ForgottenBooks.com

By purchasing this book you are eligible for one month membership to ForgottenBooks.com, giving you unlimited access to our entire collection of over 1,000,000 titles via our web site and mobile apps.

To claim your free month visit:

www.forgottenbooks.com/free928151

* Offer is valid for 45 days from date of purchase. Terms and conditions apply.

ISBN 978-0-260-10308-6
PIBN 10928151

This book is a reproduction of an important historical work. Forgotten Books uses state-of-the-art technology to digitally reconstruct the work, preserving the original format whilst repairing imperfections present in the aged copy. In rare cases, an imperfection in the original, such as a blemish or missing page, may be replicated in our edition. We do, however, repair the vast majority of imperfections successfully; any imperfections that remain are intentionally left to preserve the state of such historical works.

Forgotten Books is a registered trademark of FB &c Ltd.
Copyright © 2018 FB &c Ltd.
FB &c Ltd, Dalton House, 60 Windsor Avenue, London, SW19 2RR.
Company number 08720141. Registered in England and Wales.

For support please visit www.forgottenbooks.com

B

AGRICULTURE, RURAL DEVELOPMENT, FOOD AND DRUG ADMINISTRATION, AND RELATED AGENCIES APPROPRIATIONS FOR 1994

4.AP6/1:
G8/994/PT.5

HEARINGS

BEFORE A

SUBCOMMITTEE OF THE
COMMITTEE ON APPROPRIATIONS
HOUSE OF REPRESENTATIVES

ONE HUNDRED THIRD CONGRESS

FIRST SESSION

SUBCOMMITTEE ON AGRICULTURE, RURAL DEVELOPMENT, FOOD AND DRUG ADMINISTRATION, AND RELATED AGENCIES

RICHARD J. DURBIN, Illinois *Chairman*

JAMIE L. WHITTEN, Mississippi	JOE SKEEN, New Mexico
MARCY KAPTUR, Ohio	JOHN T. MYERS, Indiana
RAY THORNTON, Arkansas	BARBARA F. VUCANOVICH, Nevada
ROSA L. DeLAURO, Connecticut	JAMES T. WALSH, New York
DOUGLAS "PETE" PETERSON, Florida	
ED PASTOR, Arizona	
NEAL SMITH, Iowa	

ROBERT B. FOSTER, TIMOTHY K. SANDERS, and CAROL MURPHY, *Staff Assistants*

PART 5

AGRICULTURAL PROGRAMS

Printed for the use of the Committee on Appropriations

SUPERINTENDENT OF DOCUMENTS

AGRICULTURE, RURAL DEVELOPMENT, FOOD AND DRUG ADMINISTRATION, AND RELATED AGENCIES APPROPRIATIONS FOR 1994

HEARINGS

BEFORE A

SUBCOMMITTEE OF THE

COMMITTEE ON APPROPRIATIONS

HOUSE OF REPRESENTATIVES

ONE HUNDRED THIRD CONGRESS

FIRST SESSION

SUBCOMMITTEE ON AGRICULTURE, RURAL DEVELOPMENT, FOOD AND DRUG ADMINISTRATION, AND RELATED AGENCIES

RICHARD J. DURBIN, Illinois *Chairman*

JAMIE L. WHITTEN, Mississippi
MARCY KAPTUR, Ohio
RAY THORNTON, Arkansas
ROSA L. DeLAURO, Connecticut
DOUGLAS "PETE" PETERSON, Florida
ED PASTOR, Arizona
NEAL SMITH, Iowa
JOE SKEEN, New Mexico
JOHN T. MYERS, Indiana
BARBARA F. VUCANOVICH, Nevada
JAMES T. WALSH, New York

ROBERT B. FOSTER, TIMOTHY K. SANDERS, and CAROL MURPHY, *Staff Assistants*

PART 5

AGRICULTURAL PROGRAMS

Printed for the use of the Committee on Appropriations

U.S. GOVERNMENT PRINTING OFFICE

67-751 O WASHINGTON : 1993

COMMITTEE ON APPROPRIATIONS

WILLIAM H. NATCHER, Kentucky, *Chairman*

JAMIE L. WHITTEN, Mississippi,
Vice Chairman
NEAL SMITH, Iowa
SIDNEY R. YATES, Illinois
DAVID R. OBEY, Wisconsin
LOUIS STOKES, Ohio
TOM BEVILL, Alabama
JOHN P. MURTHA, Pennsylvania
CHARLES WILSON, Texas
NORMAN D. DICKS, Washington
MARTIN OLAV SABO, Minnesota
JULIAN C. DIXON, California
VIC FAZIO, California
W. G. (BILL) HEFNER, North Carolina
STENY H. HOYER, Maryland
BOB CARR, Michigan
RICHARD J. DURBIN, Illinois
RONALD D. COLEMAN, Texas
ALAN B. MOLLOHAN, West Virginia
JIM CHAPMAN, Texas
MARCY KAPTUR, Ohio
DAVID E. SKAGGS, Colorado
DAVID E. PRICE, North Carolina
NANCY PELOSI, California
PETER J. VISCLOSKY, Indiana
THOMAS M. FOGLIETTA, Pennsylvania
ESTEBAN EDWARD TORRES, California
GEORGE (BUDDY) DARDEN, Georgia
NITA M. LOWEY, New York
RAY THORNTON, Arkansas
JOSÉ E. SERRANO, New York
ROSA L. DELAURO, Connecticut
JAMES P. MORAN, Virginia
DOUGLAS "PETE" PETERSON, Florida
JOHN W. OLVER, Massachusetts
ED PASTOR, Arizona
CARRIE P. MEEK, Florida

JOSEPH M. McDADE, Pennsylvania
JOHN T. MYERS, Indiana
C. W. BILL YOUNG, Florida
RALPH REGULA, Ohio
BOB LIVINGSTON, Louisiana
JERRY LEWIS, California
JOHN EDWARD PORTER, Illinois
HAROLD ROGERS, Kentucky
JOE SKEEN, New Mexico
FRANK R. WOLF, Virginia
TOM DELAY, Texas
JIM KOLBE, Arizona
DEAN A. GALLO, New Jersey
BARBARA F. VUCANOVICH, Nevada
JIM LIGHTFOOT, Iowa
RON PACKARD, California
SONNY CALLAHAN, Alabama
HELEN DELICH BENTLEY, Maryland
JAMES T. WALSH, New York
CHARLES H. TAYLOR, North Carolina
DAVID L. HOBSON, Ohio
ERNEST J. ISTOOK, JR., Oklahoma
HENRY BONILLA, Texas

FREDERICK G. MOHRMAN, *Clerk and Staff Director*

AGRICULTURE, RURAL DEVELOPMENT, FOOD AND DRUG ADMINISTRATION, AND RELATED AGENCIES APPROPRIATIONS FOR 1994

THURSDAY, FEBRUARY 18, 1993.

ECONOMIC RESEARCH SERVICE

WITNESSES

KEITH J. COLLINS, ACTING ASSISTANT SECRETARY FOR ECONOMICS

JOHN E. LEE, JR., ADMINISTRATOR, ECONOMIC RESEARCH SERVICE

STEPHEN B. DEWHURST, BUDGET OFFICER, DEPARTMENT OF AGRICULTURE

Mr. DURBIN. I want to apologize for being late. It turns out I have a conflict with the Whip's meeting Thursday mornings. I will do my best to reschedule it in the future. We would like to welcome, on behalf of the Economic Research Service, Mr. Keith Collins, Acting Assistant Secretary for Economics; Dr. John Lee, the Administrator of ERS; and, of course Steve Dewhurst is back with us again.

Your statement will be included, in its entirety, in the record. Please proceed, and we would appreciate it if you would summarize or highlight your statement.

ECONOMIC AGENCIES

Mr. COLLINS. We are delighted to be back so soon. Today we have the heads of our Economic Agencies to discuss their programs.

I have no statement to make but I would perhaps for the benefit of the many young people in the room start by just reading a short quote, and it is a quote that always makes me feel good. It is one that is probably familiar to you. It comes from the 130-year-old statutory language that created the Department of Agriculture and defined its mission, and it reads like this.

It is, and I quote "hereby established, a Department of Agriculture, designs and duties of which shall be to acquire and diffuse among the people of the United States useful information on subjects connected with agriculture in the most general and comprehensive sense of the word."

Mr. DURBIN. Wasn't it a President from Springfield, Illinois, who said that?

Mr. COLLINS. Indeed it was. And in fact that was a paraphrase from a speech that George Washington made in his farewell address to the Nation, which called for the creation of a board on agriculture.

The USDA's mission has changed dramatically since 1862, but the agencies you will hear from this morning are still involved in that fundamental mission of acquiring and diffusing information.

The first agency you will hear from is the Economic Research Service. Dr. John Lee on my right is the Administrator of the Economic Research Service. Their charge is to provide information and analysis on world and U.S. agriculture and rural people and rural communities. And Dr. Lee will tell you more.

ERS MISSION AND PROGRAM

Dr. LEE. Thank you.

Good morning, Mr. Chairman, Members of the committee. It is a pleasure for me to have the opportunity to be here today and talk to you about the Economic Research Service. With your permission, I would like to submit the written statement for the record and make a few comments that excerpt from that.

Mr. DURBIN. Fine. Go ahead.

Dr. LEE. Since we don't have a specific budget at this point to talk about, what I would like to do is talk a little bit about who we are. Since there are a number of new Members on the committee, and if I could talk a bit about the mission and purpose and content of what we do in the Economic Research Service.

The mission of the Economic Research Service is to provide to policymakers, farmers, and other people the economic information they need to make decisions to improve the performance of agriculture, performance as it is affected by policies being made by the Congress or USDA, decisions that are being made by individual farmers or by consumers, whoever. Our job is to get the information coming out of our research and analysis out there to the people who use it, wherever they are, so that they can make better decisions and thereby improve the performance of the sector and improve the well-being of all the people associated with it.

We do that through a variety of programs and things that we do, and I will talk a bit about those. We are unique. There is no other research organization that has responsibility for addressing comprehensive economic problems facing agriculture, the food industry, natural resources, and rural America from a national perspective.

Together with our sister agencies, the National Agricultural Statistics Service and the World Agricultural Outlook Board, we provide the information base on which the Nation's food and fiber system operates.

Our small staff is stretched thin across a broad front of issues that are critical to national policy making, to management of Federal programs, to the ongoing operation of America's food and agriculture business. While the influence of what ERS does is pervasive, the agency itself is not very highly visible to the public, and many people don't know that we exist or what we are about.

We have a staff of 669 full-time employees in four major research program divisions: 459 of these people are economists, mostly agricultural economists, and 35 are other social scientists. Those 459 economists are about 45 percent of the Department's famous 1,000 economists. We have other staff, clerks, and support staff. We also provide 113 people to other agencies of the Department, mainly our Economics Management Staff, which is our central support staff.

ERS BUDGET

We have a budget in fiscal 1993 of $58.7 million. That is the same budget we had in fiscal 1992. We have made some small downsizing adjustments to take care of pay increase and other inflationary costs, as we have been doing somewhat over the 1980s. We are accustomed to downsizing. We have about 200 people fewer today than when I became administrator in 1981, and that was about 200 people fewer than they had in the agency in the decade prior to that.

Nevertheless, we feel like we have handled that downsizing very well, that we are very efficient, and we probably are able to do more and do it better today with the staff we have, partly because of the upgrading of the skills of the staff, than was able to be done earlier.

ERS SITUATION AND OUTLOOK ANALYSIS

If I might talk a moment about the programs, one of the things we do is put out what is called commonly in the trade, situation and outlook analyses. That is designed to provide intelligence and analysis of current conditions, both near term and longer term, in agricultural markets and food markets. This analysis explains what the market situation is, why the markets are what they are, and what the prospects are for the future.

This information is very widely used and is sort of a bread-and-butter kind of information for us. The Department of Agriculture uses ERS's situation and outlook analysis to monitor and adjust the operation of farm programs. For example, the setting of commodity loan rates, the setting of acreage production percentages, begins with the ERS's analyses of crop prospects for the year in question.

In every State and in every county of the United States, there are extension agents who are using ERS's situation and outlook reports this month and every month. Many of the States have been cut back on their extension staffs, in particular their State level specialists, who once did their own analysis of market prospects within the States. Now the States depend primarily very heavily on ERS analyses that they can tailor to local conditions.

So we do service those people out in the universities and the county extension offices and State offices. As I said, this is more critical now that they have had cutbacks in staff.

Many farm magazines and newspapers and other media feature outlook material that comes basically out of ERS analysis. You pick up your favorite farm magazine, there will be a page in there that says, soybeans or corn or wheat or whatever, that will contain some situation and outlook analysis. Regardless of whose name is on the byline there, the fundamental analysis came out of ERS.

I was coming up in the elevator the other morning and mentioned that I was coming to the hearings, I asked the young lady standing on the elevator with me, "Do you happen to have in your office any clips or anything like that that you know of people drawing on what we do, whether or not our name is associated with the article?" She came back a few minutes later and had this big pile. I said, "You must have been anticipating this kind of request."

But it is simply a reflection that, again, this information is pervasively used whether or not our name is associated with it. Farm and commodity organizations also depend very heavily on ERS's analysis of production, consumption, price, and export forecasts.

The program is unique in another way. We not only look at individual commodities but also we put those things together in a way so we have an integrated picture of the whole farming sector so we can look at things like the farm income, like the well-being of the sector. We also look at the longer term. We put together analyses that draw in the best expertise we have on foreign countries, on individual commodities, on farm income, on environmental issues.

Those people bring their expertise and their analytic capabilities together, and we put together five-year and 10-year, longer-term prospects. And those longer-term prospects underlie the department's budgeting process, has improved that budgeting process and makes better estimates for the longer term-future. That is used in analysis related to the GATT, to the NAFTA, and things like the 1990 farm bill discussions. That basic starting point, that basic underlying baseline is the point of departure for departmental analyses. That comes out of the ERS program.

SERVICE TO OTHER AGENCIES

The agency also provides a lot of direct service to the other agencies, particularly the program agencies of the Department of Agriculture. For example, last year, just as a few samples, we were involved in developing profitable farm practices that would go into the water quality initiative. We conducted a large multi-year grain quality study for the Federal Grain Inspection Service to look at the cost and benefits of improving the quality of grain. That has been a big controversial issue.

We have been doing regulatory impact analyses of food labeling proposals, providing analytical backup to the implementation of Endangered Species Act, conducting interagency studies to look at grazing fees—impact of grazing fees on use of public lands and estimating what those fees probably should be.

We did a series of studies on looking at ethanol and other kinds of alternative uses of agricultural products. And we have done a number of other studies for other agencies. Our analysis, for example, is used to set beef import quotas. We estimate how much commercial butter and cheese is displaced by the food donation programs. So it is pervasive, people throughout the department drawing on our analyses to carry out their work.

Our work is also heavily used by the Congressional Research Service, GAO, and the Office of Technology Assessment as they respond to congressional requests. We get many, many dozens of calls from those offices for backup to support what they are doing for you.

INFORMATION TO POLICY MARKETS

As I said, we also are directly servicing the decision-making process of the Secretary. Secretaries of Agriculture now have a broader array of programs they have to manage, much broader than was the case 100 years ago.

ERS has the unique responsibility of fulfilling the Department's economic needs to undergird all of those programmatic decisions of the department, particularly the economic information needs. We are the only ones who have the capacity to develop the basic information and to assess the impacts on farmers, on consumers, on the environment, on rural people, and the overall economy in a comprehensive, objective and timely manner.

A couple of examples. I mentioned the commodity situation and outlook work already. But in the area of food safety, we support FSIS and APHIS rulemaking with economic analysis of benefit and cost and the distribution of the effects of the rulemaking processes.

We assist in developing research information to respond to the concern of the public about chemical and microbial contamination. Our assistance ranges from estimating the economic impact of changes in poultry inspection to analyzing the effects of the Department's new food safety strategies.

We cooperate with the National Agricultural Statistics Service and the Agricultural Marketing Service to collect information on the use of agrochemicals in food production and marketing, and we are responsible for doing follow-up cost-benefit analysis.

We provide assistance in the area of domestic food assistance and nutrition, for example, in doing cost-benefit analysis of nutrition labeling—and a whole host of programs in that area now.

And in rural development, the Secretary has the statutory authority to lead Federal rural development efforts. The capacity to generate research information to help the Secretary shape Federal rural development efforts exists mainly within ERS.

I should say also that the Governors Association and the regional rural development groups out in the country also look primarily to ERS as the information base for their actions in the area of rural development. That means we play a critical role here in underlying any strategic efforts that are developed in this area.

In the area of water quality and pesticide use, we play a critical role.

Trade strategies: The GATT and the NAFTA, we are the only source in the U.S. Government of in-depth trade policy analysis on economic information from foreign countries. As a result, we play a key role in providing analysis of strategic options to U.S. officials involved in trade negotiations. There was some discussion of that by Mr. Collins a couple of days ago.

In the area of food aid and development assistance, our analysis of the agricultural and food service in the Soviet Union has been useful to the government to sort out what our policy should be toward the former Soviet Union, and the same thing is true in Africa as they face droughts. Basically ERS people provide estimates and work directly with AID in the process. These are just some examples of some of the things that we do in servicing the department, and the public.

ERS FUNDED SURVEYS

We do fund some surveys in addition to the funds that the National Agricultural Statistics Service has relating to farm cost and returns. That is the data that provides us the estimates of farm income, of cost of production, and of estimates of the well-being and financial vulnerability of farmers in the farm sector.

Our data provides the only survey on prices of farmland, for example, and we have Post Farmgate Pesticide and Chemical Use Surveys and Water Quality Surveys that provide data on the impact of regulations on chemical use.

ERS ECONOMIC INDICATORS

We have a host of economic indicators, things we publish, like the cost of production, land values, earnings for non-metro people and rural people, food consumption, world trade.

There are several dozen basic economic indicators that are regularly calculated and published by the Economic Research Service, and these are widely used. They are used by the administration, by the Congress, and by agencies that service you. These indicators in effect constitute a great deal of what the American people feel that they know about American agriculture. The numbers that are commonly used, how many people are fed by one farmer, et cetera. All these things come out of the USDA and ERS analyses.

ERS RESEARCH PROGRAM

We have a research program. That provides the backup for the staff analyses and for the economic indicators. At one time that constituted half of our resources, doing research to feed the part that goes into the outreach and into direct use. As the demand for specific analysis and staff work and situation outlook work has grown, and our staff has shrunk in size, now only about 30 to 35 percent, roughly a third of our staff, are there building the future capital to feed that outreach process.

ERS AND UNIVERSITIES

We do, though, link up with what is going on in the universities so that we don't duplicate anything they are doing, so that we are in contact with the work that is being done at the University of Illinois and Purdue and all the other places. We know those people; our people are reviewing their work. We not only know their work so we don't duplicate it, but we draw on that work as we do staff work and other kinds of analysis. We also try to influence what they do.

ERS AND INTERNATIONAL ORGANIZATIONS

Moreover, we have strong linkages with international research organizations so that, for example, we can leverage our own resources. To give you an example, we are quite interested in what is happening to changing productivity in a number of countries in the world that compete with us, or that might be importers. What we have done is work with the research groups, the economic research groups in those countries, show them how to calculate these estimates, and then let them use their resources to do it and provide the results to us. That way we leverage our resources many times over. We do that in many areas of research, out in the universities and other places. We are trying to make the most effective use of our own resource, and it also keeps us in touch with these major research centers around the United States and around the world so we have the benefit of what they do.

Again, I appreciate this opportunity to expound, too long, I know, on the work of the Economic Research Service. You might gather, I am sort of gung-ho, enthusiastic about our agency. I think it is a great outfit. I feel a little bit like a company commander who has been in combat with his troops. I have been there with them, and they are a hell of a good gang, and they are a hard-working group.

ERS AND APPROPRIATIONS SUBCOMMITTEE

We are very happy to work with Members of this committee. And as we face the future and make priority decisions, we appreciate the input of this group. We need that to guide what we would do. Please do not hesitate to call on us for any information or assistance we can provide.

I have ascertained that your offices will be regularly provided copies of some of the key periodicals such as Agricultural Outlook, which is a monthly publication, and the other key ones that provide information, for example, on what is happening in rural areas, rural conditions and that sort of thing. We have a one-page flyer that we send to your offices each week that lists all of our recent analyses and reports that your staff can ask for, and we will be more than happy to send them.

Thank you very much.

[CLERK'S NOTE.—Mr. Collins' biography appears on page 46. The Administrator's statement appears on pages 47 through 61. The budget justifications, which were received on May 10, 1993, appear on pages 62 through 85.]

BUDGET CUTS

Mr. DURBIN. Thank you.

We just received word this morning of the proposal in the President's budget for some reductions in spending to your agency. Are you prepared at this time to comment on those proposals?

Dr. LEE. Mr. Chairman, I have heard that rumor. I have not seen the budget. The only thing I would say is that if what I have heard is so, it will be a major cut. However, we are prepared to take a look at what we would do with an agency approximately 25 percent smaller than what we are now, and to sort out the priorities.

We will approach that the same way we approached downsizing in the past, and that is to sort out what is really most essential to American agriculture and this committee, the Department of Agriculture, and these are things we will focus on and do them as well as we can.

Mr. DURBIN. How will a 25-percent reduction affect the mission of your agency?

Dr. LEE. It would reduce the amount of economic information and analysis we provide.

COMPUTER CAPABILITY

Mr. DURBIN. Perhaps after you have had time to analyze the President's proposals, we might have you back to talk about the changes you envision.

The next question is just one of my own curiosities. How would you assess the computer capability of your agency at this moment?

Dr. LEE. It is in reasonably good shape. We have gradually shifted over to a linked PC-based system so that we have been able to get off of the large scale—mainly off of the large-scale computers in Kansas city and other places so we don't have to pay these charges. That has greatly increased our efficiency and enabled individual researchers to draw information from data pools wherever they exist within the agency.

It has been very difficult because we have had to take money out of salaries because we have had no funds specifically allocated for that purpose. We had hoped to get a shot in the arm, assistance on that. That is not in the cards, so we will continue to do the best we can with the resources we have. But I think we are in reasonably good shape in that regard.

CROP INSURANCE REPORT

Mr. DURBIN. Over the course of the last couple of years, last two fiscal years, there have been continuing references to a report which ERS is doing on reforming crop insurance. In fact, at last year's hearing, it is my understanding you told us the report was in its final stages. Has it reached its final stage?

Dr. LEE. Yes, sir. That report is done and was submitted to the—I think we sent a copy to OMB.

Mr. COLLINS. I don't think it has been published yet, but it is complete and clear.

Mr. DURBIN. We have been waiting with bated breath for three fiscal years.

Dr. LEE. We finished a preliminary study earlier and this is the final study. That study has been completed, as Mr. Collins says it has been cleared, and I will go back and check on the progress of it, and we will get it to you.

Mr. DURBIN. It will probably end up in paperback before we see the hard-bound version. If you could send it up, we would appreciate it.

Dr. LEE. We will send each Member of the committee a copy.

[CLERK'S NOTE.—The information is too lengthy for reprint. A copy is retained in Committee files.]

FOOD SAFETY

Mr. DURBIN. During last year's hearing, you discussed the redirection of $1.7 million of existing funds to enhance your work in the Department's Food Safety Initiative. At that time, you were in the process of determining where this amount was going to come from. Has this redirection of funds taken place? If so, tell us specifically where this money came from.

Dr. LEE. We were able to redirect nearly that amount. The base program in FY 1992 was $1.15 million and the FY 1993 program is

$2.71 million, representing an increase of $1.56 million from internal redirection. This was achieved by "taxing" other program areas based on relative priorities at the margin. One-third was raised by reducing natural resource and production agriculture inputs programs, one-fourth by reducing commodity analysis programs, one-fourth by reducing rural development research and economic indicators of the farm sector programs, and one-sixth by reducing international trade programs.

PESTICIDE DATA PROGRAM

Mr. DURBIN. What was the total amount your agency spent on the pesticide data program in fiscal year 1992 and what do you plan to spend in fiscal year 1993?

Dr. LEE. In FY 92, ERS spent $1.873 million on the Pesticide Data Program (PDP); planned spending in FY 93 is unchanged. I will provide background information on the PDP for the record.

[The information follows:]

The Pesticide Data Program (PDP) provides pesticide residue and use data that will help determine risk assessments, set pesticide tolerances, and assess the economic impact of alternative pest management strategies. This database will permit Federal agencies to respond quickly and effectively to food safety concerns. ERS's role in the Program (with NASS) is to assist in the design and collection of pesticide use data. ERS participates in developing the Vegetable Chemical Use and Economic Surveys, the Fruit and Nut Surveys, and the Cropping Practice Surveys.

ERS works jointly with NASS to develop and provide statistically reliable state level estimates of agricultural chemical usage on food crops; collect economic input data linking chemical use with economic characteristics of U.S. farms; and coordinate Pesticide Data Program activities with the Environmental Protection Agency (EPA) and the Food and Drug Administration (FDA) to meet their needs for risk assessments, tolerance setting, and focused residue sampling.

ERS works with the Agricultural Marketing Service (AMS) to link pesticide residue sampling data with farm and marketing pesticide use data to identify potential risk-reducing strategies.

Within the Pesticide Data Program, ERS is also responsible for analyzing the effects of alternative pest control strategies on crop yields and food quality; evaluating changes in production costs associated with alternative pest control practices; estimating the demand for food quality characteristics; establishing the relationship between production and marketing practices and pesticide residue levels; and assessing the economic impact of alternative pest control policies on consumers.

ERS's efforts have focused on the production aspects of pest management. ERS's research has examined the demand for and adoption of pest control practices by producers. We have looked at the demand for conventional practices, alternative practices recommended and subsidized by the SCS and ASCS under the Agricultural Conservation Program (ACP) and the Water Quality Incentive Program (WQIP) and the demand for new and innovative strategies. Using data from the PDP, ERS has examined the determinants of the adoption of alternative pest management strategies by vegetable growers. We have examined the demand for agricultural chemicals and the substitutability of the chemicals with other (management) practices in the Corn Belt. We have also examined the relationship between cotton production, chemical use and water quality.

Planned efforts using the PDP data include identifying factors that influence the adoption of alternative production and pest management practices; measuring the productivity of pesticides on major field crops, fruits and vegetables; and determining the geographic distribution of pesticide use, their environmental impacts and economic consequences of pesticide use change.

FOOD SAFETY SEMINAR

Mr. DURBIN. In 1991 you initiated a Food Safety Seminar Series to bring in outside researchers to discuss their methodology and findings, to foster interaction with others working on food safety, and to communicate current food safety research. Did you continue this series in 1992?

Dr. LEE. Yes, we continued the ERS Food Safety Seminar Series through 1992 and the series will continue through 1993. I will provide for the record a list of seminars held in 1992.

[The information follows:]

"Food Safety: Property Rights and Risks to Subpopulations," by Richard Williams Jr. of the FDA.

"Cosmetic Impacts, Pesticide Risks and Produce Quality: How Are They Relevant to Consumers Decisions?" Young Sook Eom, Clark University and V. Kerry Smith, North Carolina State University.

"Valuing Food Safety Using the Contingent Valuation Method," Jordan Lin, University of Florida.

"Valuing Consumer Benefits When They Hold Misperceptions About Risks," David Lynch, Mary Washington College.

NUTRITION EDUCATION AND MONITORING

Mr. DURBIN. Update the Committee on your activities regarding nutrition education and monitoring.

Dr. LEE. ERS analyzes factors affecting food expenditures, food consumption, food choices and nutrition. This information is used by the food industry to help understand market trends and changes. Recently, we have conducted research to measure the impact of diet/health awareness on food choices and nutrient intake. This information is needed to evaluate nutrition education efforts to modify food choices and dietary practices. Research has also been undertaken to assess the implications for agriculture if consumers made adjustments in their diets to follow the Dietary Guidelines.

ERS is working closely with other USDA agencies to improve the evaluation of nutrition education programs.

In the area of nutrition monitoring, ERS is responsible for one of the five major nutrition monitoring components of the National Nutrition Monitoring System established by Congress in the National Nutrition Monitoring and Related Research Act of 1990. ERS develops estimates of supply, use, and per capita consumption for over 200 agricultural commodities. This information is published annually in "Food Consumption, Prices, and Expenditures." This information is used by the Human Nutrition Information Service to calculate the nutrient content of the nation's food supply.

FOOD SUPPLY ESTIMATES

Mr. DURBIN. Dr. Lee, from this information, can you tell us what have been the trends over the years?

Dr. LEE. In 1991, Americans used an average of 112 pounds of red meat, 58 pounds of poultry, and 15 pounds of fish and shellfish (equivalent boneless) per capita. That's 20 pounds less red meat, 24 pounds more poultry, and 3 pounds more seafood per capita than in 1970.

Annual per capita use of eggs declined 25 percent between 1970 and 1991, from 309 eggs to 231.

The aging of the baby boomers brought a 5.5-gallon decline since 1970 in annual per capita use of beverage milk to 25.7 gallons in 1990. The trend toward lower fat milks was pronounced; in 1970, per capita use was 25.4 gallons of whole milk and 5.8 gallons of lowfat or skim; by 1990, its use was 10.5 gallons of whole milk and 15.2 gallons of lowfat and skim. However, Americans used 1 percent more milkfat per person in 1990 than in 1970 because of their yen for cheese (per capita use rose 13.3 pounds during 1970-90, to 24.7 pounds) and cream products (per capita use rose 2.2 pounds, to 7.1 pounds).

Per capita use of soft drinks increased 75 percent during the same period, to 42.5 gallons in 1990, and per capita use of beer increased 30 percent, to 24 gallons.

Growing interest in healthy eating and convenience, significant growth in in-store and retail bakeries, the mainstreaming of ethnic foods, and a host of new products spurred a 36-percent increase in annual per capita use of flour and cereal products from 1970-1990.

Per capita use of fresh potatoes declined 26 percent from 1970 to 1990, while consumption of frozen potatoes nearly doubled, to 25 pounds per person (retail weight) in 1990. 1990 was the first year in which, on a farm-weight basis, use of potatoes for freezing surpassed fresh market use. In contrast, total per capita use of 16 other major commercial fresh vegetables in 1990 was 25 percent above the 1970 level. Fresh fruit use gained similarly.

Total per capita use of caloric sweeteners increased 18 pounds (dry basis), or 15 percent, during 1970-91, from 121 pounds to 139 pounds. By 1991, low-calorie use was about 24 pounds per person in sugar-sweetness equivalent, accounting for about 15 percent of overall sweetener use, compared with 5 percent in 1970.

FOOD CONSUMPTION, PRICES, AND EXPENDITURES REPORT

Mr. DURBIN. Please submit a copy of the latest report for the record.

Dr. LEE. I am pleased to submit a copy of "Food Consumption, Prices, and Expenditures, 1970-90" (Statistical Bulletin No. 840, August 1991).

[CLERK'S NOTE.—The report is too lengthy for reprint. A copy is retained in Committee files.]

WIC FOOD BASKET COSTS

Mr. DURBIN. In last year's hearing, you described some work you were doing in helping FNS develop a model for forecasting and monitoring WIC food basket costs. What is the status of this effort?

Dr. LEE. A statistical model for forecasting WIC food basket costs has been developed and evaluated. A draft report detailing this effort was completed and sent out by the Food and Nutrition Service (FNS) for public comment. Currently, ERS and FNS are revising the report to address the concerns raised in the public comments. A final report will be delivered to Congress in the third quarter of FY 1993.

AGRICHEMICAL DATABASE

Mr. DURBIN. What is the status of the reestablishment of an agrichemical database?

Dr. LEE. In 1990 and 1991, ERS supported NASS in the collection of chemical use information on 8 major field crops, 25 vegetable, and 15 fruit, nut and berry crops. Over 40,000 personal interviews, representing over 210,000 cropland acres, were conducted to obtain detailed usage of pesticides, fertilizers, and related practices. This database provides state level estimates of acres treated, application rates, and number of treatments per acres for each nutrient and pesticide active ingredient applied to the crop. The database also contains timing and method of application information along with information on related practices such as tillage, crop rotation, and scouting.

The 1992 surveys include the annual surveys of field crops and an expanded survey of vegetables. The 1992 vegetable survey was expanded from 4 states in 1990 to 14 states in 1992 and will represent almost all commercial vegetable crops produced in the U.S. Plans for 1993 include continuation of the annual survey and a repeat survey of fruit, nut, and berry crops.

I will provide for the record a list of reports based on the agrichemical data base which have been released.

[The information follows:]

USDA, *Agricultural Chemical Usage, 1990 Field Crops Summary*, National Agricultural Statistics Service and Economic Research Service, AgCh 1(91), March 1991.

USDA, *Agricultural Chemical Usage, 1990 Vegetables Summary*, National Agricultural Statistics Service and Economic Research Service, AgCh 1(91), June 1991.

USDA, *Agricultural Chemical Usage, 1990 Vegetables Summary*, California, National Agricultural Statistics Service and Economic Research Service, AgCh 1(92), June 1992.

USDA, *Agricultural Chemical Usage, 1991 Field Crops Summary*, National Agricultural Statistics Service and Economic Research Service, AgCh 1(92), March 1992.

USDA, *Agricultural Chemical Usage, 1991 Fruits and Nuts Summary*, National Agricultural Statistics Service and Economic Research Service, AgCh 1(92), June 1992.

USDA, *Agricultural Chemical Usage, 1992 Field Crops Summary*, National Agricultural Statistics Service and Economic Research Service, AgCh 1(93), Planned for release March 18, 1993.

HISTORY OF USDA SINCE 1961

Mr. DURBIN. The "History of the Department of Agriculture Since 1961" was expected to be released in fiscal year 1992. Has this document been released, what type of information does it contain, how many copies were printed, what was the cost to produce this document, how many have been sold, and what is the sales price?

Dr. LEE. The "History of the Department of Agriculture Since 1961" has not been released, but it is nearly completed. It is a book-length history of the Department covering its institutional history and programs. The expected printing will be 5,000 copies. Printing cost estimates have ranged from $25,000 to $50,000 with a projected sales price of between $13 and $20 per copy.

RURAL DEVELOPMENT COUNCILS

Mr. DURBIN. As a result of the President's Rural Development Initiative of 1990, eight State Rural Development Councils have been created to better plan and manage rural development in each state. Do all states plan to establish these Councils?

Dr. LEE. As of February 19, 1993, 28 States have joined the original eight by signing a Memorandum of Understanding (MOU) with the Department of Agriculture—the first step in establishing a State Rural Development Council. Eight other States and three territories are in the process of scheduling a meeting to sign MOUs. Thus, 44 States and three territories currently have Councils or are working toward establishing them.

Mr. DURBIN. How effective have they been in promoting and developing our rural areas?

Dr. LEE. As most Councils are still in the process of getting underway, it is too early to draw any clear conclusions about their success in promoting rural development. Even the eight Councils that have been functioning for over two years have invested most of their energies to date in the process of organizing collaborative partnerships among the Federal, State, local and tribal governments and the private sector and have not yet had much impact on rural development action programs. Nonetheless, an assessment conducted by researchers at the University of Southern California (USC) in 1991 concluded that the eight pilot Councils were beginning to establish the foundation for a more comprehensive, cooperative, and effective approach to rural development. Currently, ERS has a cooperative agreement with USC to conduct a more comprehensive and detailed assessment of the State Council efforts over the next 18 months.

DATA PRODUCT SALES

Mr. DURBIN. Last year you provided the Committee with a list of all data base products available through user fees, the number of requests made for each product, and the sales price for fiscal years 1990–1991. Please provide this same information for fiscal year 1992.

Dr. LEE. I will submit the requested information about our data products for the record.

[The information follows:]

ECONOMIC RESEARCH SERVICE
Standard Data Product Sales, FY 1992

Stock Number and Title		User Fee	Orders FY1992
86003	Dry Beans & Peas	$45	7
86005	Policy Impact Codes		
	A--1974 nonmetro definition	25	4
	B--1983 nonmetro definition	25	10
86010	Farm Real Estate Values	25	16
86012	Fertilizer Use & Price Statistics	25	13
86013	PL480 & Other Concessional Exports	25	6
86014	Food, Beverages, & Tobacco Expenditures		
	A--5.25″ disks	85	0
	B--3.5″ disks	35	8
86015	Rural Fire Protection	25	1
86016	Farm Machinery Statistics	35	8
87011	Agricultural Outlook Yearbook	45	9
87012	Value of Land & Buildings Per Acre	45	10
87013	Feed Grain Data by States	55	9
87014	Farm & Ranch Irrigation, 1984	35	1
87015B	Foreign-owned Agricultural Land	25	2
87017	U.S. & State Agricultural Profiles	45	1
88002	Fresh Fruit Prices & Marketing Spreads	35	6
88003	USSR Grain Harvesting Progress	25	4
88004	USSR Grain Seeding Progress	25	2
88006	Weather in U.S. Agriculture		
	A--All States & Farm Regions	95	6
	B--17 Western States	45	0
	C--21 Central States	45	0
	D--20 Northeastern States	45	0
	E--17 Southern States	45	0
	F--10 Farming Regions	35	0
88007	Feed Grain Yearbook		
	A--5.25″ disks	45	18
	B--3.5″ disk	25	2
88008	Wheat Yearbook		
	A--5.25″ disks	45	9
	B--3.5″ disk	25	3
88009	Fresh Veg. Prices & Marketing Spreads	35	7
88010	National Financial Summary		
	A--5.25″ disks	45	1
	B--3.5 ″ disk	25	5
88011	Plant Protection & Quarantine Data	35	3
88012	State Financial Summary		
	A--5.25″ disks	95	0
	B--3.5″ disks	35	11
88013	Rural Development		
	A--5.25″ disks	65	0
	B--3.5″ disks	35	11

Stock Number and Title		User Fee	Orders FY1992
88014	Census of Agriculture County Profiles		
	A--Northeast	130	1
	B--North Central	130	1
	C--South	130	2
	D--West	130	1
88015	Caribbean Fruits & Vegetables		
	A--5.25" disks	65	2
	B--3.5" disks	25	5
88016	USSR Agricultural Trade		
	A--1986	35	1
	B--1987	35	2
	C--1988-89	35	2
88017	Dynamics of Land Use Change, 1970's	35	2
88018	Dynamics of Land Use Change, 1960's		
	A--North & East	25	1
	B--Southeast	35	1
	C--West	45	2
	D--Pacific	45	1
88019	U.S.-USSR Bilateral Trade	25	4
88020	USSR Grain Production	45	16
88021	Exchange Rates	35	9
88022	Geographic Distribution of Federal Funds	130	0
88023	USSR Trade Compendium	75	6
89001	Rice Yearbook	25	18
89002	Oil Crops Yearbook	25	16
89003	Major Land Uses	25	8
89004	Cotton & Wool Yearbook	25	9
89005	Feed Manufacturing	55	7
89006	U.S. Broiler Industry	25	11
89007	Poultry & Egg Statistics		
	A--5.25" disks	105	2
	B--3.5" disks	45	12
89009	East European Agriculture	35	1
89010	Ag. Statistics of the European Community	45	2
89011	Vegetable Yearbook	45	17
89012	Asia/Near East Agricultural Trade	45	1
89013	Rural Public Water Systems	35	1
89014	Cash Receipts	25	5
89015	Food Consumption		
	A--5.25" disks	55	0
	B--3.5" disk	25	16
89016	State-level Wheat Statistics	35	4
89017	Trade Liberalization	65	5
89018	Tobacco Industry	25	5
89019	Sugar & Sweetener Yearbook	35	10
89020	Agricultural Statistics of E. Europe & USSR	55	6
89021	Rural/Urban Continuum Codes	25	14
89022	Fruit & Nut Yearbook	55	6
89023	Irrigation Production Data System	45	6

Stock Number and Title		User Fee	Orders FY1992
89024	World Agriculture: Trends & Indicators		
	A--North America	25	9
	B--Central America	45	7
	C--The Caribbean	45	7
	D--South America	55	23
	E--Western Europe	65	6
	F--Eastern Europe & USSR	45	7
	G--Sub-Saharan Africa	135	6
	H--North Africa & Middle East	05	6
	I--South Asia	45	3
	J--Southeast Asia & Pacific Islands	65	4
	K--East Asia & PRC	45	6
	L--Australia & New Zealand	25	4
	M--EC-12	55	7
	N--World & Regional Data	55	6
89025	Costs of Production	25	17
89026	Production & Efficiency Statistics	35	7
89027	USSR Grain Production & Procurement	25	7
89028	PS&DView	25	79
89029	U.S. Watermelon Industry	35	1
89030	U.S. Trade, 1978-87	135	3
89031	Conservation Reserve Program Statistics	65	5
89032	Dairy Yearbook	25	23
89D01	USDA Outlays	25	7
90001	Agricultural Water Use	25	5
90002	Livestock & Dairy Costs of Production	45	22
90003	USSR Oilseeds	65	3
90004	Soil Depletion Estimates Model	25	6
90005	Food Spending in American Households		
	A--5.25" disks	55	0
	B--3.5" disks	35	9
90006	Price Spreads for Beef & Pork	25	9
90007	U.S./Pacific Rim Agricultural Trade	45	3
90008	U.S. Monthly Cash Receipts	25	3
90009	Producer & Consumer Subsidy Equivalents	55	7
90010	China: Basic Social & Economic Indicators	25	4
90011	China: Grain Statistics	35	11
90012	China: Fibers & Oilseeds Statistics	25	6
90013	China: Miscellaneous Crop Statistics	25	4
90014	China: Livestock Statistics	25	8
90015	China: Agricultural Inputs	25	5
90016	China: Agricultural Prices	25	5
90017	China: Cost of Agricultural Production	35	6
90019	China: International Agricultural Trade	25	9
90020	China: Rural Banking & Finance	25	2
90021	China: Income & Consumption	25	5
90022	U.S. Farm Income	35	4
90023	Structural Change in U.S. Agriculture	35	4

Stock Number and Title		User Fee	Orders FY1992
90024	Greenhouse & Nursery Statistics		
	A--5.25" disks	85	0
	B--3.5" disks	35	5
90025	Cash Rents for U.S. Farmland	25	6
91001	World Agricultural Trade Flows		
	A--Food Grains	45	6
	B--Feed Grains	65	4
	C--Soybean Products	55	5
	D--Rape & Sunflower Seed & Oil	45	3
	E--Tropical Oils	65	0
	F--Nonfood Oilseed Products	75	0
	G--Peanut, Maize, & Olive Oil	55	0
91002	Americans & Food		
	A--Single Copy	25	4
	B--Educational Discount (10 copies)	40	2
	C--Educational Discount (50 copies)	75	1
91003	U.S. Food Expenditures	25	8
91004	World Red Meat & Poultry Consumption	25	11
91006	U.S. Sugar Statistical Compendium	25	17
91007	U.S. Live Cattle Imports	35	8
91008	Agricultural Commodity Output	25	5
91010	U.S. Agricultural Trade	25	7
91011	Potato Statistics	35	13
91012	Beef Packer Analyzer	25	14
91013	Farm Sector Balance Sheet	25	12
91014	U.S. Vegetable and Melon Production		
	A--Sweet corn, snap beans, broccoli	65	6
	B--Leafy green vegetables	65	2
	C--Potatoes, root vegetables	65	1
	D--Tomatoes, peppers, and cucumbers	65	6
	E--Melons	35	3
	F--Dry beans and peas	45	2
91015	U.S. Fruit, Nut, and Berry Production		
	A--Tree fruits	75	2
	B--Subtropical fruits	25	1
	C--Citrus fruits	25	1
	D--Tree nuts	25	1
	E--Berries	45	0
91016	U.S. Greenhouse and Nursery Production	85	4
91017	WATI/TS-View	45	33
91018	High-Value Export Indexes	35	6
92001	U.S. Corn and Soybean Weather/Prod. Models	25	11
92002	Farm Real Estate Taxes	25	2
92003	Farm Sector Balance Sheet by Sales Class	25	5
92004	U.S. Vegetable and Melon Farms	55	3
92005	U.S. Fruit, Nut, and Berry Farms	55	0
92006	U.S. Greenhouse and Nursery Farms	55	1
92007	CALC	25	1

Stock Number and Title		User Fee	Orders FY1992
92008	Weather in U.S. Agriculture		
	A--5.25" disks	105	0
	B--3.5" disks	35	13
92010	Tomato Statistics	35	0
92011	SWOPSIM Database		
	A--World Model Data (33 countries/regions)	35	1
	B--Aggregate of 92011A (11 countries/regions)	25	1
	C--European Model (37 countries/regions)	35	0
	D--W. Hemisphere Model (38 countries/regions)	35	0
	E--Asia & Pacific Rim (37 countries/regions)	35	0
	F--Africa Model (38 countries/regions)	35	0
92012	SWOPSIM '92	25	2
92013	State-level Costs of Production	25	0
92014	Agricultural Statistics of the Former Soviet Republics	25	0
92015	Tobacco Yearbook	25	0
92016	Processed Food Trade	25	0
92017	Acid Rain	25	0
92018	Ozone	55	0
		Total Orders	1,063

GLOBAL FOOD ASSESSMENT REPORT

Mr. DURBIN. Your Agriculture and Trade Analysis Division produces an annual global food assessment report which includes analysis of food aid needs for certain countries. Tell us the results of your 1992 assessment.

Dr. LEE. USDA's Economic Research Service in its annual "Global Food Assessment" reported a significantly higher level of global food needs for 1992/93 than for the previous year. The report projected total needs of 60 developing countries calculated on the basis of meeting the United Nations' minimum nutritional standard at 27 million tons of grain with 15.5 million tons needed for Sub-Saharan Africa. These estimates took into account these countries' domestic food production and financial capacity to import food.

Foods needs calculated on the basis of maintaining per capita consumption at a constant 5-year average amounted to 16 million tons of grain. Both estimates are far greater than food aid receipts of 12 million tons in 1991/92. Nearly 10 million tons were needed in the 36 countries of Sub-Saharan Africa to maintain the current consumption level. The needs of Sub-Saharan Africa were estimated at nearly 60 percent above those of the previous year.

Ethiopia was the country with the largest food aid need of 1.6 million tons. Somalia and the Sudan, with fewer people, had food aid needs of under half a million tons each. Somalia needs were about 70 kilograms of grain on a per capita basis to maintain its historic consumption level.

Last year's drought situation in Southern Africa resulted in serious food shortages and a much larger amount than usual of food aid. These Southern Africa countries required a very large increase in food aid needs totaling 4 million tons, almost 4 times the food aid received in 1991/92. Drought reduced grain production by nearly 50 percent. Output of corn, the region's staple crop, dropped 60 percent. The region's traditional surplus producers, South Africa and Zimbabwe, commercially imported corn in large quantities. One-third of Southern Africa's population was affected by the drought, with the food situation most critical in Malawi, Zimbabwe, and Mozambique.

In West Africa, lower crop output occurred in most countries, especially for those along the coast where rainfall was below normal. Food aid needs for 1992/93 were 1.7 million tons. Although substantial carryover stocks existed from 1991's good harvest, many countries in the region lacked the financial resources necessary to transfer these stocks to the low-income groups.

In North Africa, needs were greatest in Morocco where drought caused grain output to fall sharply from the record 1991 crop.

Food aid needs for the 11 Latin American countries included in the report were estimated at 2.5 million tons of grain for 1992/93. This quantity was 30 percent above last year's receipts.

The six countries of South Asia imported an estimated 5 million tons of grains commercially, allowing the region to replenish depleted stocks. Food aid needs for 1992/93 were estimated at 2.6 million tons, about the same level as average receipts during the last 5 years.

U.S. FOOD COMPANIES IN EC

Mr. DURBIN. Last year you provided the Committee with a list of all U.S. food companies located in the EC. Has this list changed? If so, how?

Dr. LEE. Certainly the top 10 U.S. food companies in the EC have not abandoned the EC and to our knowledge neither have any of the other U.S. food companies nor are they likely to. The changes that have occurred are due to ranking U.S. food companies by amount of sales. We do know that U.S. food companies have expanded their operations in the EC. I am submitting a table that indicates the degree of U.S. food companies' EC expansion since the EC accounts for about 75 percent of U.S. food companies sales abroad. The table indicates that U.S. food company affiliates in foreign countries with sales over $250 million increased their sales by 23 percent from 1991 to 1992.

An update of the list of companies we provided last year is not possible because each company would have to be interviewed directly. Company annual reports do not distinguish overseas sales by region.

[The information follows:]

TOTAL U.S. FOOD SALES FROM SELECTED FOREIGN OPERATIONS

[$US 1,000]

Company name	Foreign sales 1991–1992	Foreign sales 1990–1991	Percent change
Philip Morris/GF-Kraft	9,297,000	7,388,000	25.8
Coca Cola	7,401,314	6,260,000	18.2
MM/Mars	4,000,000	2,362,500	69.3
CPC	3,880,600	3,458,900	12.2
Pepsico	3,571,600	3,071,000	16.3
Heinz	2,378,965	2,305,802	3.2
Kellogg's	2,375,600	2,137,600	11.1
Sara Lee	2,210,503	1,935,401	14.2
Quaker Oats	1,867,900	1,652,900	13.0
Archer Daniels Midland	1,854,836	1,935,401	−4.2
Campbell Soup	1,774,000	1,747,850	1.5
Ralston Purina	1,700,000	1,600,050	6.2
Con Agra	1,687,400	520,918	223.9
Dole	1,436,000	1,016,690	41.2
Borden	1,350,881	1,220,488	10.7
RJR/Nabisco	1,200,000	669,990	79.1
Anheuser Busch	830,328	608,016	36.6
General Mills	776,400	375,185	106.9
Multifoods	500,800	447,351	11.9
Wm. Wrigley	421,057	433,701	−2.9
Hershey's	332,718	207,067	60.7
W.R. Grace	329,400	136,980	140.5
Pet Inc.	308,567	409,904	−24.7
McCormick	290,000	256,500	13.1
Totals	51,775,869	42,158,794	22.8

Source ERA database

Mr. DURBIN. Where did last year's list come from?

Dr. LEE. The original list was part of a one-time study that was done in 1989–90. Information came from a firm-level data based developed through North Central Regional Project NC–194 coordinated at Ohio State University. It would require significant resources to repeat the study. While we can update the list of firms that have affiliates in the EC and can indicate the total EC sales of all such affiliates, with a two-year lag, EC sales by individual firm affiliate are not available.

EC'S PLAN ON FOOT AND MOUTH DISEASE

Mr. DURBIN. What is the status of the EC's plan to eradicate foot-and-mouth disease within its borders?

Dr. LEE. The European Community's (EC) commitment to eradicate foot-and-mouth disease (FMD) and other serious livestock diseases within its borders is intended to facilitate the free movement of animals and animal products within the borders of the EC pursuant to forming a single European market. The last outbreak of FMD in the EC was in 1989.

The EC has prohibited vaccination for FMD in an effort to bring all member states to a level of FMD control approaching that practiced in the United Kingdom, Denmark, and Ireland. These countries, forgoing the use of FMD vaccine, have eradicated infected animals to control FMD. The last vaccination for FMD in the EC occurred in August 1991 in Italy.

All member states of the EC accept one another as free of FMD. The EC accepts the concept of "regionalization" and has proposed specific measure for managing FMD. Regionalization in the EC means that in the event of an FMD outbreak, an area surrounding the outbreak would be isolated and the disease eradicated without interrupting trade between disease-free areas. The areas affected by a disease outbreak would be defined geographically and epidemiologically and would not necessarily conform to political borders. The EC will apply the regionalization concept to third countries as well. Regionalization is also an objective of the current GATT round and NAFTA.

The United States has been free of FMD since 1929 and, to protect this status, rigorously regulates imports of live ruminants and swine and the fresh, chilled, and frozen meat thereof, from countries not explicitly recognized as FMD-free. To date, the United States recognizes only the United Kingdom, Denmark, and Ireland as FMD-free EC member states. USDA's Animal and Plant Health Inspection Service published proposals in the U.S. Federal Register on October 19, 1992, to recognize Spain, and, on January 5, 1993, to recognize the Netherlands as FMD-free. A legislative moratorium has delayed action to Spain's application and comments are being taken on the Netherlands's application until March 8, 1993. France has applied to the United States to be recognized as FMD-free, but a proposal has not yet been published. Japan is expected to follow he U.S. lead in recognizing the FMD-free status of EC member states.

Spain, the Netherlands, and France, if declared FMD-free by the United States, would have special restrictions imposed on shipments of fresh, chilled, and frozen meat of ruminants and swine destined for the United States, similar to restrictions imposed on shipments from the United Kingdom and Denmark. Special restrictions are imposed on some countries recognized by the United

States as FMD-free because they: supplement their national meat supply by importing fresh, chilled, or frozen meat of ruminants or swine from countries infected with FMD or rinderpest; have a common land border with such countries; or import ruminants or swine from such countries under conditions less restrictive than would be acceptable for importation into the United States.

EC'S UNIFIED MARKET

Mr. DURBIN. Please give us an update on the status of the EC's plan to create a single unified market and how it affects U.S. products.

Dr. LEE. To date there has not been any substantial effect on U.S. food and agricultural exports to the EC as a result of the virtual elimination of internal EC borders on January 1, 1993. As expected, the EC largely completed adoption of all directives that would affect the rules and regulations affecting agricultural production and trade by January 1, 1993. Also, as expected, implementation of EC rules and regulations at the member state level has lagged—only 72 percent of the directives had been implemented into all member states' national legislation by the January 1 deadline. Consequently, much of the regulation of intra- and extra-EC trade is being done on an *ad hoc* basis.

The EC is planning on evaluating the status of the Single Market in July of this year. The EC has also stated that food imports into the EC will have to meet EC health and safety standards by June of this year but this will not be done systematically at external borders. Inspections are carried out at the retail level and have not cause any problems for U.S. imports nor are any expected.

The United States has met with the EC on a regular basis on health and safety issues and it is still not clear whether U.S. exports of food and agricultural products will have any problems. If there are problems they will likely occur in the pesticide tolerance area where the EC has prepared two lists of tolerances that will be imposed sequentially. The first list is in the EC Council and probably will not be adopted until summer. The next list has not been proposed yet but has been drafted. In preparing and adopting the lists the EC takes into account EC and non-EC agricultural practices and adopts the strictest level that is non-toxilogical.

Other areas of interest to the United States include regulations of food additives and organic food definitions. Food additive regulations have been proposed but have not been adopted at the EC level and are not expected to be adopted until 1994. The EC has adopted an organic food law and has given the United States a grace period of one year in order to be in compliance.

COMMISSION ON AGRICULTURAL WORKERS REPORT

Mr. DURBIN. The Commission on Agricultural Workers was scheduled to release a final report by November 6, 1992. Has this report been released, and if so, what were its findings and recommendations?

Dr. LEE. The Commission on Agricultural Workers released its final report on February 18, 1993. I am providing you with a copy of the Executive Summary which describes the Commission's findings and recommendations.

[CLERK'S NOTE.—The summary is too lengthy for reprint. A copy is retained in committee files.]

AGRICHEMICAL USE

Mr. DURBIN. Please update the Committee as to what you are doing and what conclusions you are making in the area of water quality problems associated with agrichemical use.

Dr. LEE. ERS contributes to USDA's Water Quality Program in several ways. I will describe the contributions, in detail, for the record.

[The information follows:]

The Chemical Use Surveys, conducted annually by NASS with funding and assistance from ERS, collect data used to identify state level chemical use and to assess long-term trends in chemical usage. This is the only database of its kind, and is in great demand by policy makers in USDA, EPA, other Federal agencies, and States. The Area Study Surveys (conducted in cooperation with NASS, USGS, and SCS) are designed to provide the information needed to understand the impact of chemicals on the Nation's waters and on U.S. farmers. Using the Area Studies, ERS will evaluate the economic and environmental effects of several water quality related policies to provide legislators and the public with the information needed under the Coastal Zone Management Act and under the Clean Water Act.

The data collection efforts contribute to the ERS research program. ERS researchers are currently evaluating the potential economic impacts of various economic and regulatory instruments designed to improve water quality. For example, ERS is evaluating the economic impacts on the agriculture sector of alternative management options for the herbicide atrazine, which is widely found at various levels in surface waters in the midwest. A ban on atrazine in the midwest would reduce farm income. Ongoing research is evaluating management strategies that would mitigate the need for further controls on atrazine use and/or economic losses to producers if controls are imposed.

ERS is evaluating point-nonpoint trading to improve water quality. Current research is identifying waterbodies that would benefit from point-nonpoint trading. Several coastal watersheds have been identified (based on several economic and physical factors) as candidates for successful trading programs to meet the requirements of the 1990 Amendments to the Coastal Zone Management Act.

ERS is developing a method to identify U.S. cropland vulnerable to high nitrogen leaching. An index was developed to account for the susceptibility of groundwater, preliminary estimates indicate that states with the most acres of cropland susceptible to nitrogen leaching to groundwater are Illinois, Texas, California, Indiana, and Ohio.

ERS research shows that the implementation of a national tax on fertilizer use will not result in a significant reduction in the use of nitrogen fertilizer. Taxing fertilizer use in only those regions most vulnerable to groundwater contamination (targeted tax) results in an increase in nitrogen use and soil erosion in untaxed regions as commodity production shifts away from taxed regions to untaxed regions.

Other research indicates that environmental damage to surface and groundwater posed by cotton farming may be reduced, with only limited effects on yield and prices, if restrictions on agrichemical use or production are applied to those limited areas most vulnerable to water quality problems. The study highlights the importance of targeting pollution-prevention programs to attain the most cost-effective environmental goals.

ERS is also conducting research on the costs and benefits of USDA's water quality program, which is based on education, technical assistance, research, and cost-sharing. This research will provide policymakers with information on the effects of water-related policies on farm income, prices, trade, and Government costs.

WATER QUALITY PROGRAM RESEARCH

Mr. DURBIN. When do you expect to have the costs and benefits of USDA's water quality program research complete?

Dr. LEE. Several research products are underway or planned. A preliminary evaluation of the economic and water quality impacts of the Hydrologic Unit Area and Demonstration projects has been completed. The report is preliminary because the full effects of these programs have yet to be realized, and only 5 of the 90 projects were studied. A second research project, studying the effectiveness of water quality practice demonstration projects, will be completed in 1993. An economic study of incentive programs for water quality-improving practices will be completed by 1994. The Area Study project and ERS research on technology adoption is providing data for the development of economic/water quality models of agriculture in a number of agriculture regions of the U.S. An economic evaluation of water quality policies in the western Corn Belt will be completed by 1994, and an evaluation of the water quality program for the entire U.S. in 1995.

MINNESOTA FARM SURVEY

Mr. DURBIN. The National Agricultural Statistics Service—NASS—collected data on on-farm chemical use and farm financial characteristics in Minnesota. Have you completed analysis of the information? What did you find?

Dr. LEE. The Chemical Use and Farm Finance Survey—CUFFS—is a pilot study designed to test procedures for a new comprehensive multi-purpose chemical use and economic survey. The Water Quality and Food Safety Initiatives have required the collection of a wide variety of chemical use and related cropping practice data as well as economic data. The pilot survey addresses new and existing data needs by integrating both sample design and data collection in an attempt to improve data quality, minimize respondent burden, and increase the cost effectiveness of our data collection efforts. ERS has not yet received the data because NASS is still analyzing various sampling methods and performing statistical tests to determine the accuracy and reliability of the CUFFS relative to the other survey instruments it may replace.

ERS and NASS have prepared an extensive set of criteria that CUFFS must satisfy before we proceed with CUFFS on a broader scale. Preliminary results from NASS's testing suggest that CUFFS is as accurate as previous survey instruments.

ENVIRONMENTAL PROTECTION AGENCY

Mr. DURBIN. Please tell the Committee what work you did in fiscal year 1992 and what you have ongoing in fiscal year 1993 related to findings of the Environmental Protection Agency.

Dr. LEE. ERS provides significant resources and personnel to evaluate the impact of proposed EPA actions on farmers through the National Agricultural Pesticide Impact Assessment Program NAPIAP. Separate, but related activities that ERS is involved in are the Pesticide Data Program—PDP—and the Water Quality Program. The PDP provides pesticide use and residue data for fruits, nuts and vegetables and are designed to help determine risk assessments, set pesticide tolerances and assess the economic impact of alternative pest and nutrient management strategies. ERS coordinates with NASS on the design, collection and analysis of these data. ERS is also involved in the Water Quality Program that involves coordination with NASS for the collection of pesticide use and economic data for field crops. These data are used for an accounting of total pesticide and fertilizer use by farmers nationally and by states or regions and evaluating the economic impact of altering the pesticide and nutrient management strategies of producers.

ERS's role in NAPIAP is to assess the economic impact of EPA actions regarding pesticides on farmers and agricultural production. The work performed and findings for FY 1992 involved assessments of restrictions on atrazine, the effects of banning certain pesticides on cotton, the effects of EBDC fungicide bans and the banning of the miticide propargite.

The estimates of the economic impacts of pesticide bans or other controls provided by NAPIAP include the effect of the next best alternative pest control option. Specifically, biologists indicate the next best option to a regulated chemical product and the expected yield loss (or change) associated with that alternative product. ERS estimates the change in the associated production costs. If a regulation effects a major crop where expected supply changes may effect prices, those impacts are also estimated. The reports issued by ERS present the economic analyses of EPA proposed regulations and also discuss the next best options as indicated by the biologists. ERS's role is to examine the economic viability of those options. That assessment is fundamental for the estimation of the benefits and costs of proposed regulatory actions.

For FY 1993, assessments have been or are being made on chlorpyrifos, diazinon, fungicides on leafy green vegetables, methyl bromide and 2,4-D. NAPIAP is currently considering the initiation of several assessments this fiscal year that may require ERS participation in future fiscal years. These include the pesticides Carbaryl Telone (1,3-D) and commodity impacts (of major pesticides and groups of pesticides) for potatoes and Rice. I will provide information for the record on the specific findings or efforts for FY 1992 and FY 1993:

[The information follows:]

FY 1992

Atrazine.—Examined the impacts of restrictions on atrazine and triazine herbicide use in corn and sorghum production in the Mississippi Valley. The annual economic losses would be $80 million if preemergence atrazine rates were restricted to 1.5 pounds active ingredient per acre and postemergence rates were restricted to 1 pound, $320 million if preemergence applications were banned and postemergence rates restricted to 1 pound, $810 million if atrazine were banned, and $1.2 billion if atrazine and all other triazine herbicides were banned. "The Effects of Restricting or Banning Atrizine Use to Reduce Surface Water Contamination in the Upper Mississippi River Basin: A Summary," prepared by NAPIAP, June 26, 1992.

Cotton.—Examined the economic effects of banning 48 individual pesticides and 9 major groups of pesticides. Annual economic losses of banning pyrethroid insecticides, seed treatment fungicides, or all desiccants and defoliants would be about $600 million per year. Banning other major groups would cause losses in the $100 to $400 million range, while the losses of banning individual materials would typically be much less than $100 million. Craig Osteen, "Potential Economic Effects of Banning Cotton Pesticides," in *The Importance of Pesticides and Other Pest Management Practices in U.S. Cotton Production,* prepared by NAPIAP, unpublished draft. Craig Osteen, Ron Davis, and Kent Smith, "Potential Economic Effects of Banning Cotton Pesticides: Preliminary Results of the USDA/State Cotton Assessment." *Proceedings of the 1992 Beltwide Cotton Conferences.*

The cotton assessment helped NAPIAP to quickly estimate the economic loss of cancelling arsenic acid, a desiccant, in response to an EPA proposal. The estimated loss w

Fungicides: Examined effects of banning EBDC fungicides (maneb, mancozeb, and metiram) and chlorothanil on beans, carrots, celery, cucumbers, lettuce, onions, sweet corn, tomatoes, and potatoes. Annual economic losses would be $210 million for EBDSs and $68 million for chlorothanil. Walter Ferguson, L. Joe Moffitt, and Michael Davis. "Short-Run Welfare Implications of Restricting Fungicide Use in Vegetable Production," *Journal of Agribusiness*, Spring 1992, Vol. 10.

Propargite: Estimated the annual economic loss of banning this miticide on 21 crops to be about $240 million. In addition, the report estimated the annual loss of having no miticide on almonds, apples, corn, cotton, and grapes to be $740 million. Craig Osteen, "Economic Effects of Banning Propargite" in the *Biological and Economic Assessment of Propargite.* Unpublished Draft.

FISCAL YEAR 1993

Chlorpyrifos: Estimated the annual economic impact of banning the use of this insecticide on more than 40 crops to be about $100 million. Martin Shields and Craig Osteen, "Estimating Economic Impacts" in *The Biologic and Economic Assessment of Chlorypyrifos*, prepared by NAPIAP, revisions required before completion.

Diazinon: Examine the impacts of banning the use of this insecticide on over 50 crops. Assessment in progress.

Fungicides on Leafy Green Vegetables: Examine the impacts of banning the use of important fungicides in the production of lettuce, spinach, collards, kale, mustard greens, and turnip greens. Assessment in progress.

Methyl Bromide: Estimated the annual economic loss of banning the use of methyl bromide for soil fumigation in the production of 21 crops to range from $850 million to $1.1 billion. Walter Ferguson, "The Economic Effects of Banning Methyl Bromide for Soil Fumigation," in *The biologic and Economic Assessment of Methyl Bromide,* prepared by NAPIAP, unpublished draft.

2,4-D: Recently initiated assessment to examine the effects of banning the use of this herbicide on more than 40 crops. To be completed in fiscal year 1994.

ERS also participants on the Minor Use Working Group. The Working Group's function is to examine actions that impact minor use crops and share information and research regarding those actions. ERS conducts and brings to the group informed analysis of the effects of regulatory actions on minor use crops.

FUNDS EXPENDED ON EPA STUDIES

Mr. DURBIN. What funds were expended in fiscal year 1992 and what do you expect to spend in fiscal year 1993 in this area?

Dr. LEE. The funds expended on these activities in fiscal year 1992 were $500,000: this same amount is budgeted for fiscal year 1993.

PRICES SPREAD BETWEEN FARMER AND CONSUMER

Mr. DURBIN. Please bring the Committee up to date on your study of the Price Spread Between the Farmer and the Consumer. What did you spend in fiscal year 1992 and what do you expect to spend in fiscal year 1993 on this study?

Dr. LEE. In 1992, the spread between prices consumers pay for food and farm prices of commodities accounted for 74 cents of each dollar consumers spent for food in retail food stores. The price spread represents all charges and profit made by marketing firms involved in processing and distributing foods.

In 1992, there was a 2.0 percent increase in the price spread, a substantially smaller increase than in recent years. This was likely due to consumers' increasing price sensitivity that forced food companies to limit price increases, and lower inflation that held down costs. About half of total food marketing costs are for labor. Such costs rose moderately because of increases in hourly earnings for employees, which closely approximated increases for workers in other industries plus escalating costs for employee benefits, particularly health insurance. In addition to labor, food marketing firms incurred higher costs for transportation, electric power, advertising, repairs and other services. Many food manufacturers and retail food chains earned lower profits margins in 1992.

Farm prices of food commodities averaged 2.5 percent lower, due in large measure to lower hog, egg, and orange prices. The farm value share of the food dollar spent at foodstores averaged 26 percent, down from 27 percent a year earlier. Farm value shares varied widely among a group of 41 food products. As might be expected, the farm share is higher for animal products than for crops because animal products generally require more inputs and thus have higher farm values. For example, the farm share was 57 percent for Choice beef, 51 percent for broiler chicken, and 43 percent for fresh milk. Costs tend to be the highest for prepared foods while the farm value of the commodities used in them is relatively low. For example, the farm share was 26 percent for peanut butter, 13 percent for potato chips, 7 percent for bread, and 5 percent for corn-flake cereal. Farm shares are reported in an Agricultural Information Bulletin, "Food Costs * * * From Farm to Retail in 1992".

The Economic Research Service spent $542,000 on farm-to-retail price spread research in 1992. We expect to spend $562,000 in 1993.

FEES FROM PUBLICATIONS SALES

Mr. DURBIN. Update the table that appears on page 148 of last year's hearing record, listing fees collected from sales of publications to include 1992 actuals.

Dr. LEE. I will be happy to update that table for the record.

[The information follows:]

Fiscal Year 1988	49,000
Fiscal Year 1989	140,000
Fiscal Year 1990	312,000
Fiscal Year 1991	338,000
Fiscal Year 1992	327,000

OTHER USDA AGENCIES

Mr. DURBIN. In your statement you say that in addition to the 669 full-time and 40 part-time employees you have, ERS appropriations also fund staff in other USDA agencies, specifically, the Economics Management Staff, the Office of Energy, and the Economic Analysis Staff. Where are each of these offices located within the Department and what does each do?

Dr. LEE. All three of these agencies are located in the Washington, D.C. USDA complex and answer to the Assistant Secretary for Economics.

The Office of Energy, OE, was created by the Secretary of Agriculture. The OE serves as the focal point for all USDA energy and energy related matters. The office coordinates Departmentwide energy policy and reviews and evaluates all USDA energy and energy related programs. OE serves as the Department representative at hearings, conferences, and other contacts with respect to energy and energy related matters including liaison with other government agencies. OE functions include: developing Departmental energy policy and coordinating the Secretary's biofuels and new uses initiative as well as other energy programs; briefing the Secretary, Deputy Secretary, Assistant Secretary for Economics, and other Department officials on all energy and biofuels related activities that could potentially affect agriculture or rural America; economic and policy analysis of regulations that affect energy supply and demand in the agricultural sector; participation in the regulatory process; and coordination of biofuels energy research. In addition, OE is responsible for the development, implementation and management of a Departmental Biofuels Action Plan as well as analyzing, evaluating, and developing energy policies and strategies. The OE has a staff of 7.

The Economic Analysis Staff has established by the Secretary to advise and assist the Assistant Secretary for Economics in fulfilling his responsibility for economic policy review and analysis in the Department. ERS funds one-half of the 7 employees in EAS. The other one-half is funded by the National Agricultural Statistics Service. EAS funds include: Policy development—developing, organizing, coordinating, and synthesizing economic and statistical analyses for use as a basis for planning short- and intermediate-range agricultural policy; Policy analysis—conducting economic and statistical analyses in order to evaluate domestic and foreign agricultural problems and issues crossing agency lines, calling attention to effects of utilizing particular courses of action under varying situations and recommending alternative actions; Policy evaluation—reviewing and evaluating recommendations submitted to USDA agencies, task forces, and study groups for their policy implication and impact upon the agricultural economy, and providing continuous information on the performance of farm programs; Legislative analysis—analyzing legislative proposals concerning domestic and foreign agricultural issues for policy implications and developing amendments to legislative proposals to further short- and intermediate-range policy objectives; Agricultural labor regulation—carrying out statutory responsibilities, in conjunction with other agencies to develop farm labor regulations including those related to the Seasonal Agricultural Worker, SAW, program, the Replenishment Agricultural Worker, RAW, program, and the H-2A program, as provided by the Immigration Reform and Control Act; and finally the EAS represents the Assistant Secretary in meetings with agriculture, industry, and consumer groups to discuss the economic impact of existing and proposed department programs and policies. The EAS provides ERS with a direct link to the Department's policy process by serving as a conduit for ERS policy analyses and by interpreting results of ERS research and analysis in the context of specific policy divisions.

The Economics Management Staff, EMS, provides management and administrative support services to those agencies reporting to the Assistant Secretary of Economics. These services include budget development and execution, personnel management and organizational analysis, procurement and property management, records and space management, financial liaison and review functions, and production and editing of ERS publications. EMS has 172 staff, 106 of whom are funded by ERS. The remainder are funded by the National Agricultural Statistics Service and the World Agricultural Outlook Board.

STATE OF THE AGRICULTURAL ENVIRONMENT REPORT

Mr. DURBIN. When do you expect to publish the State of Agricultural Environmental Report?

Dr. LEE. This report is in the planning stage and decisions regarding contents and publication timetable will be made soon.

FEDERAL GRAIN INSPECTION SERVICE STUDY

Mr. DURBIN. Your statement mentions a multi-year study you are conducting for the Federal Grain Inspection Service to determine the costs and benefits of improving the quality of grains and oilseeds for export. What is the status of this study?

Dr. LEE. Reports on the benefits and costs to the domestic market and the export market are in final stages of review. Reports for corn and soybeans are in preparation. The preliminary finding of the wheat reports is that costs of cleaning all wheat for export would exceed benefits; however, strategies that would improve transmission of information on importers' desires for clean wheat in specific niche markets might merit further consideration.

ETHANOL

Mr. DURBIN. Describe, for the record, the work you are doing in the area of ethanol.

Dr. LEE. ERS economists are addressing several topics on the economics of ethanol. A recently published report, Hohmann, Neil and C. Matthew Rendleman. "Emerging Technologies in Ethanol Production." USDA, ERS, Agricultural Information Bulletin, No. 663 addressed technological change and its effect on production costs. Additional research is focusing on the environmental effects of ethanol blended fuels, the impacts of increased ethanol production on the agricultural sector and rural employment, and the interaction of agricultural and trade policies on the corn gluten feed market, an ethanol byproduct. These reports will be published in fiscal year 1993.

ERS also provides funding for the USDA Office of Energy, OE. OE staff have participated in every aspect of the regulatory activities related to oxygenated fuels and reformulated gasoline programs mandated by the Clean Air Act Amendments of 1990, CAA. OE and ERS staff are working together on issues involving the "complex model" proposed by EPA for certifying reformulated gasoline as part of the CAA program. OE staff continue to work with EPA to develop additional proposals to improve the rules EPA announced last October for reformulated gasoline that contain the "ethanol compromise." In addition, OE and ERS staff have cooperated on the analysis of several energy tax proposals that affect ethanol such as the ethanol prorata tax provision in the National Energy Policy Act of 1992. OE has coordinated ethanol economic analysis and scientific evaluation of research within USDA and with EPA, the Department of Energy, the ethanol industry, and agricultural groups. This activity focuses on increasing ethanol's market opportunities and identifying and supporting promising new technologies for expanding ethanol production and consumption.

NUTRITION EDUCATION PROGRAMS

Mr. DURBIN. Tell us about the alternative nutrition education programs you are evaluating.

Dr. LEE. ERS has engaged in a cooperative effort with other Departmental agencies to formulate an evaluation framework to guide program planning. This framework builds upon and complements existing evaluation efforts in the program agencies by providing a consistent set of objective measures that enhance evaluation of program costs and program impact on nutrition knowledge, skills, awareness and behavior. This framework is being used for evaluating new nutrition education efforts, such as the project developed jointly by the Extension Service and the Food and Nutrition Service to provide improved nutrition education to WIC clients.

Also, ERS is developing a prototype evaluation of a targeted nutrition education program, "Great Beginnings", designed by the University of New Hampshire Cooperative Extension for pregnant and parenting teens who are also clientele of the USDA's WIC Program. This nutrition education program was developed in cooperation with FNS, which asked for our assistance in developing and implementing an evaluation process.

The evaluation strategy we devised for the "Great Beginnings" program expands upon previous methods by including assessments on three components: nutrition knowledge, diet quality, and anthropometric/health measures on both mother and child. In addition, the evaluation will include pre and post tests and both control and treatment groups. The "Great Beginnings" program is an excellent project for a prototype evaluation because it typifies many of the intensive education programs targeted to high risk groups. This project provides an important piece of analysis by examining the feasibility of a multifaced program evaluation and establishing a model for future impact evaluations.

FOOD STAMP BENEFITS

Mr. DURBIN. You have provided analysis of food stamp cash-out and electronic benefits transfer for the Food and Nutrition Service. What were your findings and recommendations to FNS?

Dr. LEE. Recent ERS research on a cash-only Food Stamp Program, FSP, has focused on measuring how such a change would affect food expenditures of current FSP participants. The methodology and data used by ERS are different from the experimental design employed by FNS in their San Diego and Alabama cash-out demonstration projects. However, both the ERS and FNS studies find that food spending declines between 0 and 12 percent.

Current FSP research at ERS involves measuring the changes in participation levels when the coupon based method of delivering FSP benefits is altered to either a cash or Electronic Benefit Transfer, EBT, system. The change in program participation depends on how the delivery mechanism affects a potential recipient's direct and indirect cost of participation. This work will be completed in fiscal year 1993.

RURAL DEVELOPMENT ADMINISTRATION

Mr. DURBIN. Explain in further detail your involvement in the establishment of a strategy development program in the Rural Development Administration.

Dr. LEE. ERS information and analysis on rural conditions, trends, and development strategies is relied upon heavily by the staff of the Rural Development Administration, RDA, as they build a strategy development program. ERS information is provided to RDA continuously through both formal and informal channels. Since RDA's inception, ERS has taken steps to insure that its research program complements RDA's mission. For example, over the past year, ERS and RDA have been engaged in a joint effort—along with the Aspen Institute—to develop a "rural development strategy research agenda." The effort is an attempt to have major users and providers of rural development strategy research come to common understanding on what constitutes the highest priority rural research activities.

NAFTA COMMODITY ANALYSIS

Mr. DURBIN. You were a member of the Department's NAFTA Task Force and provided analysis of the effects of alternative trade policy provisions on 31 commodities, assessing the costs and benefits for states and regions, the environment, farm workers, food safety, and farm income. For the record, provide a brief summary of your analysis for those commodities.

Dr. LEE: As our analysis shows, NAFTA will result in net gains for both the United States and Mexico. The agreement insures that the growth in U.S. agricultural exports to Mexico will continue due to greater market access in the future.

Mexico's growing population, 92 million, is becoming more urban and represents a significant market for U.S. agricultural products. Improved economic activity resulting from the agreement will boost income one half to one percent annually and stimulate demand. In addition, Mexico's comparative advantages suggest it will continue to be a net importer of food and fiber. These points and greater market access assures continued opportunities for growth in U.S. agricultural exports.

NAFTA will lead to efficiency gains in both Mexico and the U.S. as producers respond to market opportunities. U.S. agriculture will benefit from trade creation, slightly higher agricultural export prices, and increases in economic efficiency and productivity gains. Because the Mexican share of U.S. farm exports and imports is relatively small, about 5–10 percent, and because the trade barriers in general are already relatively small between the two countries, the total quantitative effects of the free trade agreement on U.S. agriculture will also be limited.

By the end of the transition period, an additional $2.0 to $2.5 billion per year of added exports to Mexico are expected. Grains and meats are estimated to account for the majority of the expansion in U.S. agricultural exports. Our analysis indicates that imports from Mexico will be about $0.5 to $0.6 billion higher. Winter fruits and vegetables will constitute most of that increase.

By the end of the transition period, annual U.S. agriculture cash receipts are expected to increase by about 3 percent. More trade will also expand employment in related areas of processing, transportation, and marketing.

I will submit for the record additional analysis of the commodity effects of NAFTA.

[The information follows:]

Wheat.—The United States is a major supplier of wheat to Mexico. Mexico's imports have been variable, and are equal to about 2 percent of U.S. wheat exports. NAFTA will increase Mexican incomes leading to growth in wheat demand over the long run. The agreement is expected to increase U.S. wheat exports to Mexico by about 20 percent by the end of the transition period and to lead to slightly higher U.S. wheat prices.

Coarse Grains.—The United States is a major exporter of coarse grains to Mexico, but imports are limited by tariffs and licenses. NAFTA assures the United States a 2.5 million metric ton duty-free quota for corn that will increase by 3 percent each year. Mexico's 215 percent over-quota tariff for corn will be phased out over the 15-year transition period. Tariffs on other coarse grains will be reduced at more rapid rates and imports will expand accordingly. By the end of the transition period, annual U.S. corn exports are expected to be 60 percent higher than otherwise and industry revenues for corn and sorghum will likely increase by about $450-$500 million due to the NAFTA.

Rice.—The United States is the major exporter of rice to Mexico and the U.S. rice industry will benefit from expanded trade under NAFTA. Mexican rice tariffs will be reduced to zero over a 10-year transition period under the NAFTA. U.S. rice prices and exports will be greater than without a NAFTA. By the end of the transition period, U.S. rice exports will likely increase 10 to 20 percent and revenues will increase about $10 to $20 million.

Oilseeds.—The United States is also the major exporter of oilseeds to Mexico and NAFTA will benefit the U.S. oilseed industry. U.S. exports to Mexico should increase moderately because of NAFTA. Under NAFTA, higher prices and production are expected to add $400-$500 million to U.S. soybean industry revenues by the end of the transition period.

Cotton.—U.S. cotton exports to Mexico are expected to increase under NAFTA. NAFTA will gradually remove all import barriers between the countries. Income growth and textile trade opportunities under NAFTA are likely to increase Mexican cotton textile production and demand. The United States, the world's largest cotton exporter and close by, is likely to be the major supplier of the increase in Mexican cotton mill demand.

Seeds.—Benefits for the seed industry under NAFTA will depend on Mexico's changing production patterns and reduction in trade barriers. With the NAFTA, most U.S. seed exports will enter Mexico duty-free immediately.

Sugar.—Under NAFTA, the United States and Mexico will gradually reduce barriers to sugar trade between the two countries and harmonize border protection with the rest of the world. During the 15-year transition period, any additional access to the U.S. market beyond Mexico's current 7,258 metric ton quota will be conditioned on Mexico becoming a new surplus producer of sugar. Mexico is currently a large net importer of sugar. The United States has exported substantial refined sugar to Mexico in recent years and the sugar re-export program will remain in place.

Peanuts.—The United States will enhance its role as a major supplier of peanuts to Mexico under the NAFTA. U.S. exports of peanuts to Mexico will likely increase in response to higher Mexican incomes. By the end of the transition period, U.S. exports to Mexico are expected to increase to about 19,000 metric tons, an 8-percent increase above levels expected in the absence of the NAFTA. Mexico has been a net importer of peanuts in the past and there is little reason to expect Mexico to become a significant supplier of peanuts to the United States.

Tobacco.—The United States ships almost no tobacco to Mexico because of restrictive import tariffs and licenses. NAFTA will increase U.S. exports by removing these restrictive barriers to U.S. exports and increasing Mexican incomes. U.S. and Mexican tariffs for tobacco will be reduced over the 10-year transition period.

Dry Beans.—Mexico has been an important market for the U.S. dry bean industry. Eliminating Mexican import licenses and phasing out tariffs under the NAFTA will expand U.S. exports to Mexico and result in somewhat higher U.S. dry bean prices.

Vegetables and Melons.—Under NAFTA, U.S. exports of some vegetables will increase as trade barriers are reduced and income growth occurs in Mexico. In addition to the usual winter fresh vegetables, Mexico will supply a wider range of vegetables year round to the U.S. market. Improved Mexican access to Canadian markets and the continued phaseout of Canadian tariffs on U.S. exports will moderate the potential effect of phasing out U.S. tariffs for Mexico bilaterally.

Noncitrus Fruit.—U.S. fruit exports to Mexico have increased since 1986 reflecting Mexico's lower tariffs and a reduction in the number of commodities subject to licensing regulations. NAFTA will further increase U.S. exports of peaches, pears, and apples by reducing barriers and stimulating income growth in Mexico. Mexican tariffs on pears, plums, and apricots will be phased out over 5 years, while tariffs on peaches and apples will be phased out over 10 years and the tariff on fresh strawberries will be eliminated immediately. The phaseout of Canadian tariffs under the U.S.-Canada Free Trade Agreement will continue to help increase U.S. exports of some fruits.

Grapes.—NAFTA is not expected to have a significant effect on the U.S. grape industry. Most of Mexico's fresh grape exports to the United States enter duty free. Exports of U.S. grapes to Mexico are expected to increase slightly due to the 10-year phaseout of the Mexican tariff during the June 1 to October 14 period, a major harvesting season for U.S. fresh grapes.

Citrus.—NAFTA will provide improved export opportunities for U.S. fresh oranges in Mexican markets, especially for high quality fruit in urban areas. U.S. tariff reductions for fresh oranges will be matched by Mexico. U.S. frozen concentrated orange juice (FCOJ) exports from Mexico will be subject to a tariff-rate quota and the over-quota tariff will be phased out over 15 years. U.S. imports of FCOJ are expected to increase 3 to 4 percent but increased exports from Mexico will come partly at the expense of other exporters, including Brazil. U.S. imports of fresh limes are expected to increase.

Tree Nuts.—U.S. exports of almonds, hazelnuts, pistachios, and walnuts are likely to increase under NAFTA. U.S. imports of Mexican pecans may increase. Under NAFTA, Mexican and U.S. tariffs on all major tree nuts will be eliminated immediately.

Greenhouse and Nursery.—NAFTA will have a relatively small effect on the U.S. greenhouse and nursery industry. Mexico has the potential to increase exports of nursery products to the United States. However, NAFTA only restores Mexico's competitive position relative to its major competitors, Colombia, Bolivia, Ecuador, and Peru.

Pork.—Under NAFTA, U.S. exports of pork and hogs to Mexico are expected to double by the end of the transition period compared to no NAFTA. Export growth will result from the elimination of Mexican tariffs and increased growth in Mexican incomes. U.S. pork exports to Mexico, however, will remain small relative to U.S. pork production. By the end of the transition period, U.S. hog and pork prices will likely rise a little, adding $150–$200 million in revenue to the industry.

Beef.—NAFTA will increase trade in both live cattle and beef between the United States and Mexico The U.S. Meat Import Law will no longer apply to Mexican beef exports to the United States. Due to the size of Mexican imports and exports relative to the U.S. market, NAFTA will have small effects on total U.S. cattle production and prices. By the end of the transition period, U.S. cattle prices will rise $0.50 to $1.00 per hundredweight (about 1 percent) which will create an added $200 to $400 million in revenue for the industry.

Dairy.—The U.S. dairy industry will benefit from the NAFTA because Mexico's population and income growth are projected to outpace its dairy production growth for many years. Mexican imports of U.S. milk powder are expected to grow by about 20,000 metric tons by the end of the transition period due to the NAFTA. That is 36 million additional dairy export sales at current world prices. Other dairy product exports will also increase faster than without NAFTA. Exports of all dairy products under NAFTA could increase $200–$250 million. Dairy trade rules with respect to U.S.-Canada and Mexico-Canada are unchanged under the NAFTA.

Hides and Skins.—Under NAFTA, U.S. exports of hides and skins to Mexico are expected to increase gradually as a result of expected income gains from stronger economic growth and greater demand for higher quality leather products in Mexico. U.S. exports to Mexico were about 11 percent of the total U.S. export value of hides and skins during 1991. Nearly 90 percent of U.S. hides and skins moving into Mexico have no tariffs, so the removal of the 10 percent tariff on sheep, hog, and some other skins will be modest benefits for the U.S. industry.

Poultry.—Mexico has been a rapidly growing market for U.S. poultry despite high Mexican tariffs and import licensing. NAFTA will likely increase U.S. exports of poultry and poultry products to Mexico. Higher Mexican incomes under NAFTA will likely stimulate additional sales of poultry products, but imports of lower-prices U.S. grain will help lower Mexican feed costs and boost poultry production.

Eggs.—NAFTA is expected to increase U.S. egg exports to Mexico which has been a variable market for U.S. eggs. U.S. exports to Mexico increased 37 percent between 1990 and 1991 despite import licensing. Higher Mexican incomes under NAFTA will likely stimulate additional demand for eggs. However, lower priced U.S. grain imports will offset declines in Mexican producer prices for eggs and lead to increased egg production.

Sheep.—Mexico has been a variable market for the U.S. cull sheep breeding stock and mutton. NAFTA will likely increase U.S. exports to Mexico. Higher Mexican incomes under the NAFTA will likely stimulate demand for sheep meat, increasing the salvage value of cull sheep.

ERS DATA COSTS

Mr. DURBIN. How much did you spend in fiscal years 1991 and 1992 to purchase data and how much do you plan to spend in fiscal year 1993?

Dr. LEE. We spent $16 million in fiscal year 1991, $7 million in fiscal year 1992, and we plan to spend $5.5 million in fiscal year 1993. Most of the funds are transferred to NASS for collection of data on farm income, costs of production, and pesticide use.

ECONOMIC INDICATORS

Mr. DURBIN. Your agency develops a series of indicators depicting agricultural and rural conditions, many of which are mandated by Congress. For the record, please provide a list of all indicators that are mandated, as well as a list of those that aren't.

Dr. LEE. I will provide that information for the record.

[The information follows:]

INDICATORS MANDATED BY CONGRESS

Cost of production estimates for wheat, corn, sorghum, barley, oats, cotton, and dairy.

Foreign ownership of U.S. agricultural land.

Market basket statistics.

INDICATORS REQUIRED FOR MANDATED PROGRAMS

Cost of production for tobacco, sugar, peanuts, rice, and soybeans.

Net Farm Income estimates prepared for the United States and each State—these data are supplied to the Bureau of Economic Analysis, Department of Commerce, for use in preparing estimates of Gross Domestic Product and Personal Income.

OTHER INDICATORS PROVIDED BY ERS

Food and Fiber.—
- Employment and Value Added by the U.S. Food and Fiber System.
- Farm Income and Related Estimates.
- Farm Sector Balance Sheet.
- Food Spending by Americans.
- Total Food Expenditures.
- U.S. Food Supply Statistics.

International.—
- Food Aid Needs Estimates.
- Producer and Consumer Subsidy Equivalents.
- U.S. Agricultural Trade.
- Value-Weighted Quantity Indexes for Agricultural Exports.
- World Agriculture Trends and Indicators.
- The World Economy and Exchange Rates.
- World Trade in Selected Agricultural Commodities.

Resources and Technology.—

Agricultural Land Values and Real Estate Transfers.
Agricultural Production and Efficiency.
Cash Rents and Grazing Rates.
Farm Inputs and Cropping Practices.
Farm Real Estate Taxes.
Major Land Uses in the United States.
Rural Development and Rural People.—
Characteristics of Hired Farmworkers.
Economic and Social Structure of Nonmetro Counties.
Farm and Rural Population Estimates.
Macroeconomic Indicators.
Nonmetro Employment and Unemployment.
Off-Farm Income.
Operating Statistics of Banks.
Poverty in Nonmetro Areas.

Mr. DURBIN. Thank you.

Mr. Skeen?

1993 BUDGET

Mr. SKEEN. Thank you.

Refresh my memory, what was your budget last year, 59 million?

Dr. LEE. Fifty-eight point seven.

Mr. SKEEN. How many personnel?

Dr. LEE. The authority is for 842 total, that's the money funds. We are under our ceiling. We have about 113 of those people go to support agencies and other groups that we fund with those funds. So about 649 actually in ERS.

FOOD SAFETY SEMINARS

Mr. SKEEN. I appreciate the work that you do, in particular the database that you put together, as it applies to food safety programs. I also understand that you have been running food safety seminars, or does another agency within USDA run them.

Dr. LEE. We have been conducting some internally. I am not aware of external seminars on food safety that we have been——

Mr. SKEEN. It is my understanding that you used to run food safety seminars, or did you discontinue that program? We will clear that mystery up.

Dr. LEE. I apologize, but I am a little stumped by that. I don't recall that we have done that. We have participated——

Mr. SKEEN. Somewhere this rogue information has come about. I was just curious.

Dr. LEE. I will check into that and——

RISK ANALYSIS

Mr. SKEEN. What I am getting at is we hear a lot about pesticide problems and so forth and you have been accumulating a great deal of data.

Dr. LEE. Yes.

Mr. SKEEN. You do the economic analysis. Do you do the risk analysis as well?

Dr. LEE. Yes. We have studies going on on how to measure the risk and do the risk analysis, as well as trying to get some handle on what the consuming public is willing to pay——

Mr. SKEEN. I also wanted to know if you are heavily involved in risk analysis. We are long on information about pesticides and we can detect minute parcels or parts per billion of various chemicals in pesticides, but we are short on risk analysis.

Dr. LEE. One of the things that the current program, or the department of which we are a part in this area is trying to do is collect—trying to get at risk in a combination of the work that the three agencies are doing. ERS and the National Agricultural Statistics Service are collecting data on use of pesticides and the instance of pesticide use throughout agriculture, particularly in the food safety area in fruits and vegetables. The Agricultural Marketing Service is looking at the residue, monitoring the residues that end up on that food. And the Human Nutrition Information Service is looking at food consumption to say what the consumption aspect of that is. So you can combine all of that and get what the ingestion risk might be, what exposure humans have.

I would say at this time it does appear that from the preliminary data, they are not finding very many residues, and when they do, they are not beyond the tolerances. They are just of some particular chemical that may not be registered for that particular commodity. And those are at very low levels.

Mr. SKEEN. Does your data help establish those levels?

Dr. LEE. No, sir, we don't get into the establishment of tolerance as such. That is done primarily in the EPA.

FOOD STAMP DATA

Mr. SKEEN. Do you work with FSIS, the Food Safety Information Service?

Dr. LEE. Yes, we do, very closely.

Mr. SKEEN. You have been doing a comparison on effectiveness of alternative programs within the food stamp, the WIC and the lunch programs. Is that a major responsibility for the department?

Dr. LEE. It has come back more recently. We did some of this work back in the 1970s. We weren't doing much of it in the early 1980s, but in the last three years we have been doing considerably more. We have been trying to evaluate the effectiveness of educational programs, and that is a very difficult task. We are working on doing that and we have just brought a couple of staff on board who are experts in doing that.

We are also looking at such things as impacts of, for example, cashing out food stamps as opposed to coupons. We have done some work and have some results in that area.

Mr. SKEEN. But you do collect data in that regard?

Dr. LEE. We don't collect a lot of data in that area. We use the data that the program agencies and the surveys that come out of other places——

Mr. SKEEN. Then you do an economic analysis?

Dr. LEE. Yes, sir.

ERS PRIORITIES

Mr. SKEEN. Before we cut all these programs, I wanted to try and establish some sort of line of priorities. It is going to take a great deal of in-depth analysis of the department itself.

Dr. LEE. Yes, sir.

Mr. SKEEN. It will be very interesting when we get a budget to see what this Agency will identify as its priorities.

Dr. LEE. We will have to do a lot of hard work on that.

Mr. SKEEN. Are you going to make recommendations to us?

Dr. LEE. Certainly. We will first be trying to sort it out based on all the user input that we can get, and then obviously we will be talking to whichever Assistant Secretary we answer to at that time. And we will be happy to provide the results of where we come out to this committee, and get your input into the process.

Mr. SKEEN. We would also like to have some justifications on the priorities, and the ones that you cut. I would like to hear why you cut them. That would be very interesting. I think it would be illuminating to the administration as well.

Thank you.

Mr. DURBIN. Thank you.

Mr. Thornton?

Mr. THORNTON. Thank you, Mr. Chairman.

I would like to explore and pursue further Mr. Skeen's questioning with regard to the establishment of priorities. How are priorities now set within ERS?

Dr. LEE. They are set in a planning process that incorporates input from several places. We look at, first of all, any feedback or sense of the Congress that might come back in appropriations language, as well as in our basic responsibility or charges. And sometimes there are specific suggestions in that appropriation language. We give those top priority, of course.

USERS ADVISORY BOARD

We get input from a group called the Users Advisory Board. That is a group that has been established by the Congress——

Mr. THORNTON. It was established in 1977, part of Section 13 of the farm bill of that year, I believe. I happened to write that provision.

Dr. LEE. In fact, I met yesterday with that group, and went over much of what we discussed here this morning with them. They annually make recommendations and we take those recommendations into account in our planning process.

We have specific feedback from the department that comes not so much from instructions on what needs to be done, but rather from signals that come out of the frequency of demand for various kinds of analysis to undergird programs.

So we look at the programs, we look at what else they need, and we take that into account. We also read the newspapers and are sensitive to what the public issues are in the areas that are encompassed by the Department of Agriculture. Then we sit down and we look at all of those issues, the resources we have, and figure out the things in that group that we would be irresponsible not to do, and do all that we can with the resources that we can cover.

There seems to be a growing demand for economic analysis and information, and that is a constant challenge to us. But that is our process and we go through an annual planning process that takes into account all of these signals, and then we incorporate those back internally.

So we are constantly—and each year we go through, we are dropping something that may be important but it is less important than what seems to be coming along.

ERS INFORMATION TO EXTENSION AGENTS

Mr. THORNTON. However, judgments are made as to the importance of different factors. I notice that you have many services which relate directly to the department, furnishing information to the extension agents for dissemination to farmers, for example. I would assume that would be a high priority?

Dr. LEE. Yes, sir, that is a high priority.

GRAIN AND OILSEEDS EXPORT STUDY

Mr. THORNTON. The thing I am concerned more about is—well, yesterday we had some questioning about the advantages of the Federal Grain Inspection Service, and it appears that you determined, or did a study to determine, the costs and benefits of improving the quality of grains and oilseeds for export.

It seems that that may have answered a question that we had yesterday in Committee as to what the advantages and disadvantages were for spending money to inspect our grain. Is that correct, or are you familiar with that?

Dr. LEE. Yes, it turns out to be a very complicated study, that the answers don't call easy, and there are a lot of different views on that. We have forthcoming soon the results of that study, which will be made public soon. That includes not only economic analysis, cost and benefits, internally here, and getting the views of our own people, but we sent teams to each major importing country, including also some competing exporters, to get their view, and we incorporated—we have some 1600 pages, I think, some huge amount of text of studies that come out of getting the views of people who buy our grain in other countries, and we are now incorporating that into our final analysis.

So when we get through with this, it may not make the question of whether or not to spend money any easier, but we will have as definitive information as is currently available.

COMMERCIAL BUTTER AND CHEESE SALES

Mr. THORNTON. On the other hand, you have situations where you provide proposals or analyze proposals relating to labeling and how much commercial butter and cheese sales will be displaced by the Food and Nutrition Service's food donation programs. How did those projects come about?

Dr. LEE. Those were direct requests from the agencies. The agencies have to make those decisions, and they come to us——

PRIORITIES FOR ERS

Mr. THORNTON. This is the point I am asking. When the agency makes the request, how is it reviewed and how is it prioritized?

Dr. LEE. First of all, it tends to come through the Office of the Assistant Secretary or the Secretary, and when that happens, we obviously give it high priority.

Mr. THORNTON. If it comes from your boss, I think I understand, it has a high priority.

Dr. LEE. It has a high priority. Also we do feel that if people have real honest-to-God decisions to make, that is very critical for us—that is a high priority for us to use the expertise we have to help them make the best possible decision, at least to give them the economic analysis, whatever other factors they have to take into account. We do feel it is very important that we provide that kind of service to other agencies.

We have done that basically without any reimbursement. When they call, we respond because we feel it is our duty to do so. If we are considerably smaller in the future, we may have to prioritize, if you will, those kinds of requests, because there are more requests from the agencies than we can fulfill.

Mr. THORNTON. Would there be opportunities to use user fees or something parallel to that?

Dr. LEE. That certainly is something we propose to talk about within the department, yes.

If I might, Mr. Thornton——

Mr. THORNTON. Please, go ahead.

Dr. LEE. This may be the right place to say, the agency faces somewhat of a dilemma in that who we are and what we should be doing is perceived very differently by different audiences.

Mr. THORNTON. Yes.

Dr. LEE. I am sure that the Congress, in providing funding for the Economic Research Service views that you are funding a service that has a responsibility to provide information to the public and to the farmers, to other people who need that information. And we try to fulfill that mission.

At the same time, I expect that many in the department feel very strongly that our first duty is as a staff group to the department, and may not be conscious of or aware of the public service responsibilities that we have. So we are constantly trying to balance our mission and what we do from among the various perceptions of what we should be doing.

In addition, we get feed back directly from users. We go around the country and talk to cattlemen, the farmers, the commodity groups, the environmental groups, all the people who feel like we should be providing information for public use. So we try to balance those demands and those expectations the best we can.

Mr. THORNTON. Thank you very much.

I yield back.

Mr. DURBIN. Thanks, Mr. Thornton.

Mr. Pastor?

UNIVERSITIES AND ERS

Mr. PASTOR. I am sorry I am late and didn't have a chance to hear your comments. I am reading through them hurriedly. How much of the research that you do should be transferred or encouraged by universities so that basically your function would cease?

Dr. LEE. That is a very important question, because we have such limited resources, and also the States have been—virtually all the States have been going through a downsizing process at the university departments, and we have very close interaction with them, not only with professional associations but in terms of linkages.

Each area of work in the ERS, for example, if you are researching livestock or doing environmental research, one of the responsibilities of the people doing that work is that they are in touch with anything significant going on, not only in the U.S. universities but private research organizations and international institutions.

We make a very deliberate effort first of all to get all we can out of what they are doing so that we are not duplicating anything. We are trying to do only what other people are not doing or cannot do by virtue of the fact that we have some unique advantages, and in some cases disadvantages, and also then trying to influence what they do so that it contributes to our mission, so that we are trying to influence their priorities as much as possible to help us address national priorities.

Mr. PASTOR. What can we do to encourage universities to do more research, influence the direction of the research?

Dr. LEE. Well, I think overall we are getting small and they are getting smaller, and the other thing is that in universities, more and more they are being held accountable by their State legislators and others to move from the esoteric to the practical. So the agricultural economists in the States I talk to frequently say that there is more and more of a return, with their smaller and smaller staff, to doing things of more practical value to their farmers, State legislators, and the people there.

The one thing unique about ERS is that we have the opportunity, for example, in putting together a comprehensive baseline on which to do analysis. Individual States may have experts that might be as good as or even better on some particular aspect, but no State has a large enough staff—first of all, they don't have the databases there and they don't have a large enough staff to put together a critical mass, such that they could take a comprehensive look at the agricultural sector or do a comprehensive analysis of the impact of some proposed policy or environmental rule or whatever it may be.

When we do analysis, we try to do a very complete analysis looking at the impacts not only on the farmers but the distributional effects, impacts on the rural economy, et cetera, and we can draw our experts in to do that.

So there are certain things we have a unique advantage in doing by virtue of being in one place and having a critical mass and having huge databases at our disposal. We do make those databases available to people out in the State so they can do more, but they don't have the resources to do what we can do.

ERS AND NASS

Mr. PASTOR. How much of an overlap is there between your organization and the National Agricultural Statistics Service?

Dr. LEE. Zero, because we don't conduct any surveys in ERS. The National Agricultural Statistics Service does all the survey work for the USDA and they do that work with their own funds and augmented by some funds that we contribute to them. For example, in the pesticide area we augment their funds by giving them additional funds.

We also augment a small expenditure survey they once had with some additional funds so that we now have more comprehensive information on farm income, on cost of production, on the well-being of people out in the farm sector.

There is absolutely no overlap there, nor with the third speaker coming up, the World Agricultural Outlook Board. ERS does the basic analysis, research to back up that analysis, on situation and outlook for the department. But there are many other agencies in the department who by virtue of the work they do—for example, ASCS and their commodity people working on programs there, have a lot of expertise. They know a lot about what is happening in the markets.

What the World Agricultural Outlook Board does is bring all those people together to review our reports and our analysis by a peer review committee. It is like bringing the best expertise together in the department so that when we put out something, we have tapped all that best expertise and we are speaking with one voice.

Mr. PASTOR. Is it possible that sometimes as you conduct research and develop databases, you and other USDA agencies may be duplicating your efforts?

Dr. LEE. I don't think in—now, which agency are you talking about?

Mr. PASTOR. The one that is going to follow you.

Dr. LEE. No, sir. We are sister agencies and we do our planning jointly. We know exactly what their plans are. We don't collect any data independently of them. We do obtain some data from the Census, but also work with the Census. They don't duplicate what the Census does or what any other agency does. They do it all for us and we get the data from them.

Mr. PASTOR. Can you foresee the possibility of combining these two agencies to make them more effective, allowing their administration and some of the services to be combined?

Dr. LEE. That is certainly a possibility. I would say that right now, we think we achieve the benefits of being combined by the fact that we have a joint planning process, we sit down and work together. We have very good, cordial working relations.

When they go out to train their people to do surveys that are valuable to us, we send people out to work with them to tell them why they are valuable so they can tell the farmers. I don't think there would be any efficiencies gained. That was done 1977 to 1981, ERS and NASS at that time, they were called the Statistical Reporting Service. We were combined into one agency, called Economics and Statistics Service. We worked together. That could be done again.

I don't think there are any particular efficiencies to be gained by that, but—and hopefully no inefficiencies. It might add another layer of management on top, but I hope not.

Mr. PASTOR. I kind of hope not.

SURVEY TRAINING

Taking your example, they send somebody out to do the survey training, and then you send somebody out there to talk to the farmer. So now we have two people going out there.

Dr. LEE. We don't do that.

Mr. PASTOR. I just heard you say that.

Dr. LEE. They have training schools—for example, doing surveys, you can talk about getting financial information from farmers, that gets fairly sensitive. They want to know, why do you want that information, what are you going to do with it? So ERS people go to the training schools, and sometimes on a pretest, not a large number, just a few people, and they help explain to those enumerators who are being trained what this information is being used for by the department, by the Congress, and why it is important that farmers cooperate and volunteer that information. So when the enumerators get asked that, they can explain that.

We only go when requested, when we are needed to assist in the training process. We don't send people out duplicating what they send out.

Mr. PASTOR. I yield back.

Mr. DURBIN. Thank you, Mr. Pastor.

Mr. Walsh?

Mr. WALSH. Thank you, Mr. Chairman.

ERS SUGGESTIONS ON BUDGET CUTS

First of all, my ears really perked up when I heard you say there is a report from the President on the proposed budget cuts, and obviously we would all love to get a look at those as quickly as possible.

For the Administrator, the question on running up against what the Chairman has said, were you asked as Administrator of this department for your suggestions on how you might make some cuts in your department by the administration or by the transition team?

Dr. LEE. Well, annually we are involved in submitting a budget and sending it forward. I have to say I have heard this morning that there is a proposed budget cut. I have not actually seen a budget for USDA—for ERS at this point.

Mr. WALSH. Were you folks asked for your ideas on how you might meet a certain goal in terms of cutting your budget?

Dr. LEE. We haven't been, no, sir.

Mr. WALSH. You have not? Okay.

When we all see these, as the Chairman suggested, you will be able to come back and give us an idea of how you are going to achieve those cuts?

Dr. LEE. Certainly. I would be happy to do that.

ERS PUBLICATION SALES

Mr. WALSH. You mentioned that you had a pretty good stack of publications there that use the services, the reports that you folks produce. Do the publishers of those publications pay you for that service?

Dr. LEE. No. Our information is—we view ourselves as an information wholesaler, not a retailer, and we make our publications available free to the media and to the Congress. Everyone else pays.

Mr. WALSH. Give me an example of who else would pay for that?

Dr. LEE. There are hundreds of consulting groups here in town that use our publications regularly. They repackage them and sell them for very high prices.

Mr. WALSH. So it embellishes what they sell to their customers?

Dr. LEE. Yes. And there are analysts all over the country who are commodity analysts servicing farmers or whoever that use our publications. We sell about $220,000 worth a year.

Mr. WALSH. So your revenue is $220,000?

Dr. LEE. I think that is the number, yes, something like that. We operate——

Mr. WALSH. Could you make more money from all the publication services you are providing?

Dr. LEE. I think the guidelines specify we are only allowed to charge the cost of publishing and distributing. So we can charge for the printing and postage but we can't charge for the research that backs it up.

Mr. WALSH. Is there value there that those individuals who buy it now would be willing to pay for if the law didn't require that you sell it at cost?

Dr. LEE. I think certainly some would. It is always a market test. We can raise the price and see what happens to demand. But I presume that certainly some people who get a very high return from what they pay for those publications would be willing to do so.

Our concern about that would be that there are also a large number of people who provide public service, who would not have the benefit of those publications. One of the things we feel that is important is that for the effective operation of a free market, it is very important that all of the participants in that market have an equal access to information.

One of the justifications of a public information service, as we are, is that it enables—it empowers all the people who are participants in the marketplace to be on an equal footing. And we would hate to be in a situation where only people who could afford to pay high prices for the information get access to it.

There are many ways that people get this information. Many private services, for example, provide computer-type services, data is available through computers. Many farmers subscribe to computer data services, and call up data daily on their computer screens. Our data is put out by that—through many of these private services. They would probably be willing to pay more. But I can't really answer as to what the market would bear.

Mr. WALSH. I am just trying to get a general feeling of whether the information would be worth more than what you are providing it for.

You are providing raw data based on statistical analysis that you have done. Are you adding value to that statistical data?

Dr. LEE. Yes, sir. The raw data is collected by the statistical service, and what we do with our data and research is to add value to that data. We have a large number of data products.

For example, the database that backs up various kinds of indicators in series that we have published, we have the historical and background data for those available on tapes and on disk, and we make those available again at the cost of reproducing them. We have huge sales of those data. So many people are purchasing those data for their own use now, and we make those available.

Sometimes we not only do the data that we have added value to, but we may add some of the raw data in there if it makes it convenient for the users. Our attempt is to be as user friendly as possible and to get as many people having access to our information as possible.

FOREIGN COMPANIES AND ERS DATA

Mr. WALSH. Do you have foreign companies interested in this data?

Dr. LEE. Yes, in fact, in December I was part of a team reviewing a program that is the equivalent of the ERS in the Netherlands. They have a very fine service there.

Mr. WALSH. Do they sell their data?

Dr. LEE. They don't. They do research. But I asked them where they got their data, and they said, "We buy data from ERS." I was surprised that they were operating off our database.

Most of our data is sold to companies and universities and others who are conducting research.

ERS PESTICIDE AND FOOD SAFETY STUDIES

Mr. WALSH. Just a couple of other questions. Do you do economic analysis of pesticide fertilizer applications in terms of some of these programs that were discussed in the farm bill such as integrated pest management? Did you do those analyses?

Dr. LEE. Yes, we do. Congress provided funds to the National Agricultural Statistics Service and to ERS. The National Agricultural Statistics Service use those funds now under two programs: the Food Safety Program and the Water Quality Program. The Food Safety Program is primarily focused on fruits and vegetables, the fruits that might have pesticide residues; has water quality, we are interested in broad acre crops where there are large applications of pesticides that might find their way into the groundwater.

We have data on pesticide use, rates of applications, the circumstances surrounding those applications—for example, what kind of pesticides are used, what kind of soil—and the general economics of the situation, so we can do analysis of impacts, for example, of various kinds of proposals that might be aimed toward reducing pesticide contamination; taxing fertilizer, or regulations of various kinds, or other kinds of market incentives that might put on farmers. We have the complete set of information surrounding pesticide use and the rates of application to do that kind of analysis.

Mr. WALSH. Do any of the land grant colleges do that sort of analysis also?

Dr. LEE. There is certainly some done and we are very much in contact with those people. We share our data and our analysis with them, and they share their analysis with us.

Mr. WALSH. Thank you, Mr. Chairman.

Mr. DURBIN. Mr. Myers?

NUTRITION EDUCATION EVALUATION

Mr. MYERS. The mission of your agency is to provide economic and other social science information and analysis for improving the performance of agriculture in rural America.

Please explain how the evaluation and monitoring of USDA's nutrition education program, a project which was undertaken last year by ERS, meets your mission.

Dr. LEE. As a research service agency, ERS supports the functions of the Department of Agriculture; this includes providing analytical support for evaluating USDA's food assistance and nutrition education programs which account for over one-half of the Department's budget. ERS's expanded role in nutrition evaluation has placed more emphasis on looking at a broader array of performance measures, including economic costs and benefits. USDA support for nutrition education has increased from $132.2 million in FY 1986 to $195.8 million in FY 1992, an increase in nominal terms of approximately 47 percent; in real dollars this represents an increase of approximately 19 percent. As money for nutrition education increases, it becomes increasingly important for USDA to assess program effectiveness objectively to help assure that tax dollars are being used effectively.

When we refer to the performance of agriculture, we interpret the word agriculture broadly to include all aspects of the industry: resources, manufactured inputs, farm production, processing, and marketing and distribution, including food and nutrition programs.

ERS INFORMATION TO THE PUBLIC

Mr. MYERS. Your agency provides information as a service to the general public. How does this information differ from that offered to the public by the Extension Service and other USDA agencies?

Dr. LEE. Some of the information offered to the public by the Extension Service and other USDA agencies comes directly from ERS. ERS produces information from research and analysis; the Extension Services helps to deliver that information to users around the country. As I mentioned in my formal statement, in every State and nearly every county of the United States, extension agents use the ERS situation and outlook reports each month, with adjustments to reflect State and local conditions to brief farmers and agribusiness people. In general, however, ERS information is different from that offered by other USDA agencies—not different answers to the same question or different forecasts of the same variable, but different in nature and content. For example, NASS provides the public with estimates of crop area, yield, and production, and ERS provides the public with an analysis of what those estimates imply for future prices. Many USDA agencies provide the public with statistics on their programs; ERS provides the public with analysis of what those statistics mean. But most important of all, ERS provides information not available elsewhere: indicators and trends for the agricultural sector as a whole, analysis of trade policies of foreign governments and their implications for U.S. agricultural trade, costs and benefits of alternative programs to conserve resources, costs and benefits of restricting the use of chemicals and pesticides in food production and marketing, and analysis of alternative programs to stimulate growth in rural areas, as examples.

EMPLOYEES OUTSIDE OF WASHINGTON, D.C.

Mr. MYERS. Are any of your employees located outside of Washington? If so, please indicate the number of employees and where they are located.

Dr. LEE. ERS does not have any employees permanently located outside of Washington, D.C. Currently, two employees are serving temporary assignments outside the United States, one in Sofia, Bulgaria, and the other in Kazakhstan. Both are serving as advisors to the ministries of agriculture in the respective countries, as part of the U.S. effort to assist emerging democracies.

Mr. DURBIN. Thanks for your testimony today, Dr. Lee.

Thanks, Mr. Collins.

[CLERK'S NOTE.—Mr. Collins' biography follows:]

BIOGRAPHY OF KEITH J. COLLINS

Mr. Collins is Acting Assistant Secretary for Economics and Director, Economic Analysis Staff, U.S. Department of Agriculture (USDA). The Economic Analysis Staff is responsible for economic analysis of farm programs, regulations, and legislative proposals. He was previously a Deputy Division Director in the Economic Research Service, USDA. Mr. Collins, a member of the Senior Executive Service, received the Presidential Rank Award in 1990.

Mr. Collins, a native of Connecticut, holds degrees from Villanova University and the University of Connecticut and a Ph.D. in economics and statistics from North Carolina State University. He has been employed by USDA for 16 years.

[The prepared statement follows:]

ECONOMIC RESEARCH SERVICE

Statement of John E. Lee, Jr., Administrator, before the Subcommittee on Agriculture, Rural Development, Food and Drug Administration, and Related Agencies.

Mr. Chairman and members of the committee, I am pleased to appear before you to describe the mission, programs, and activities of the Economic Research Service.

Mission

The mission of the Economic Research Service is to provide policymakers, farmers, and others the economic information they need to make decisions that improve the performance of agriculture and the rural economy. We do this with a multifaceted program that includes short-term analyses in response to requests from the Secretary of Agriculture and others, analysis of situation and outlook for agricultural markets, analysis and publication of ongoing indicators of performance and well-being of agriculture and the people associated with it, and longer term, problem-oriented research on issues high on the public agenda.

ERS is unique. There is no other research organization that has responsibility for addressing comprehensive economic problems facing agriculture, the food industry, natural resources, and rural America from a national perspective. Together with our sister agency, the National Agricultural Statistics Service, we provide the economic information base on which the Nation's food and agricultural system operates.

Our small staff is stretched thin across a broad agenda of issues and services that are critical to national policymaking, management of Federal programs, and the ongoing operation of America's food, agricultural, and rural businesses. While the influence of what ERS does is pervasive, the agency is not highly visible to the public.

Organization and Staffing

ERS has 669 full-time employees organized into four program divisions—agriculture and rural economy (134), agriculture and trade analysis (143), commodity economics (177), and resources and technology (124)—a data services center (60) and my office (31), which includes a number of miscellaneous agencywide services such as facilities management, library, EEO counselor, international programs staff, information resource management staff, program planning and evaluation staff, and data and staff analysis coordinators. Of the 669 full-time employees, 459 are economists (mostly agricultural economists), 35 are other social scientists, and the remainder are in various support occupations, including 55 computer specialists, 49 clerks, and 42 secretaries/office managers. ERS also has 40 part-time employees, some in most of the above capacities. The

ERS appropriation also funds staff in other USDA agencies: 104 full-time and 4 part-time in the Economics Management Staff (which provides personnel, procurement, budget, and publication support to ERS), 5 full-time in the Office of Energy, and 4 full-time in the Economic Analysis Staff. All ERS staff and the publications division of the Economics Management Staff work at 1301 New York Avenue NW, Washington, D.C., in leased space.

FY 1993 Budget

ERS's FY 1993 appropriation is $58.7 million, unchanged from FY 1992. In order to absorb the increased salary costs and inflation in nonsalary expenditures, ERS has had to further reduce its staff. We are, nevertheless, proceeding with the high priority programs that we are committed to carry out in FY 1993, and attempting to minimize the adverse affect of absorbing the increased costs of doing business by increasing the efficiency of the remaining staff.

Programs

ERS Develops Information on Current and Future Market Conditions

ERS's so-called "situation and outlook" program is designed to provide intelligence and analysis of current conditions and both near- and long-term developments in food and agricultural markets. This analysis explains what the market situation is, why the markets are what they are, and what the prospects are for the future. More important than our forecasts are our explanations of the supply and demand forces that drive the outlook, so that users of the ERS work are in a better position to apply their own judgment about potential market developments.

The use of ERS situation and outlook analyses is pervasive:

• The Department uses ERS situation and outlook analyses to monitor and adjust the operation of farm programs. For example, the setting of commodity loan rates and Acreage Reduction Program percentages begins with ERS analyses of crop prospects for the year in question.

• In every State and nearly every county of the United States, extension agents use the ERS situation and outlook reports each month, with adjustments to reflect State and local conditions to brief farmers and agribusiness people. The availability of ERS's commodity outlook reports to State extension specialists is now more critical than ever since most States have been forced by their own budget cutbacks to eliminate their own analysts.

• Many farm magazines have pages that feature analysis of prospects for individual commodities. Almost always, the underlying analyses for those pages come from ERS publications.

• Farm and commodity organizations are heavily dependent on ERS's analysis of production, consumption, price, and export prospects.

The ERS situation and outlook program is unique in another way: the intelligence and analyses are integrated into a comprehensive view of the agricultural sector—from wheat prices to farm income to program participation—ensuring consistency across the different subject areas.

ERS also has the lead role in USDA's effort to provide longer term analyses of agricultural prospects and trends. ERS coordinates most of the analysis and conducts underlying research on long-term factors affecting U.S. and global agriculture. Our data and analysis are used as the Department's benchmark for measuring the impact of various policy, financial, technological, and resource-use scenarios. For example, the many scenarios analyzed during the 1990 Farm Bill debates and as part of the GATT and NAFTA negotiations were done by ERS staff using the ERS baseline. The baseline also provides the basis for the Department's 5-year budget projections, for evaluating loan applications in the Farmers Home Administration, and for many other policy purposes.

Each year, ERS publishes approximately 150 situation and outlook reports on nearly 30 different topics. These include costs of production, inputs, international (foreign countries and global), domestic crops, livestock, poultry, specialty products, productivity, marketing margins, farm income, and macroeconomic data. And a new effort is underway to develop an annual "State of the Agricultural Environment" report. Paid subscriptions and reprints account for about 220,000 reports annually.

ERS Provides Service to other Agencies

Our analysts are continually participating in and contributing to a significant number of departmental priority activities or simply providing a service to other agencies. Last year, for example, ERS was involved in: developing profitable farm practices that meet the goals of the Water Quality Initiative; conducting a large, multiyear study for the Federal Grain Inspection Service to determine the costs and benefits of improving the quality of grains and oilseeds for export; doing a regulatory impact analysis of food labeling proposals; providing analytical backup to implementation of the Endangered Species Act; conducting an interagency study to update cost data for determining grazing fees on public lands; preparing a series of reports on ethanol; doing several research projects for the Agricultural Stabilization and Conservation Service on commodity program operations; and analyzing dozens of regulatory proposals ranging from labeling to food inspection. We also produce the estimates used in setting beef import quotas; and we estimate how much commercial butter and cheese sales will be displaced by the Food and Nutrition Service's food donation programs.

ERS data and analyses are heavily used by the Congressional Research Service, General Accounting Office, and Office of Technology Assessment as they respond to congressional requests.

ERS Provides Essential Information for Policymaking and Program Management

ERS provides the Secretary of Agriculture and other policy officials with accurate and timely information and analysis as inputs to Departmental decisionmaking. The Department has a broadening array of responsibilities covering food assistance, nutrition, food safety, international trade, and rural development, as well as continuing to operate traditional farm programs and provide market information. ERS has the unique responsibility of fulfilling the Department's information needs in all of these areas. Only ERS has the capacity to develop basic information and assess impacts on farmers, agribusiness, consumers, rural people, the environment, and the overall economy in a comprehensive, objective, and timely manner. For example:

Commodity Market Data and Analysis—ERS provides data collection and analysis on supply, demand, and price of all major farm commodities. This information is used to develop the official Departmental outlook estimates that underlie policy assessment. These activities also provide a "level playing field" for farmers and other market participants by ensuring that basic information is available to all.

Food Safety—ERS supports FSIS and APHIS rule making with economic analysis of benefits and costs and distributions of effects. It also assists in developing research information to respond to the public's concern about chemical and microbial contamination. ERS assistance ranges from estimating the economic impact of changes in poultry inspection to analyzing the impacts and likely effectiveness of the Secretary's new food safety strategy. ERS is also collaborating with the National Agricultural Statistics Service and the Agricultural Marketing Service to collect information on the use of agrochemicals in food production and marketing, and is responsible for doing followup cost/benefit analyses.

Domestic Food Assistance and Nutrition—ERS played an important role, working with the Food Safety and Inspection Service, in conducting the cost/benefit analysis of nutrition labeling. ERS is now heavily involved in evaluating alternative nutrition education programs. ERS is the lead agency for major parts of the new USDA 10-year Nutrition Monitoring Plan, and is working closely with the Human Nutrition Information Service to improve food survey data used to support the Department's nutrition and food assistance programs. The agency also provides analyses for the Food and Nutrition Service of longer term program options such as food stamp cash-out and electronic benefit transfers.

Rural Development—The Secretary has statutory authority to lead Federal rural development efforts. This requires him to collaborate with many other agencies whose programs affect the well-being of rural people and viability of rural communities. The capacity to generate research information to help the Secretary shape Federal rural development efforts exists mainly within ERS. That capacity has made ERS research information and staff support a critical resource in USDA-led Federal initiatives; for example, formation and funding of state rural development councils, and establishment of a strategy development program in the Rural Development Administration. Moreover, ERS plays a key role for the Secretary in assuring that initiatives undertaken by others—the National Governor's Association; General Accounting Office, Office of Technology Assessment, and the Congressional Research Service; private foundations; and international organizations—have access to a factual assessment of current rural conditions and a research-based analysis of future opportunities and challenges.

Water Quality and Pesticide Use—ERS plays a critical role in USDA water quality efforts, performing analyses and evaluating policy options to weigh the potential costs and benefits to farmers and other citizens. ERS cooperates with National Agricultural Statistics Service to collect national data on current levels and trends in chemical use. These survey data are the only reliable source of information to assist the Department in assessing the impact of chemicals on the Nation's water quality and strategies to improve water quality. Similarly, ERS and National Agricultural Statistics Service data, and ERS research capacity, underpin USDA assessments of alternative pest control strategies—especially the likely effects on crop yields, farmers' costs and returns, and food quality and price.

Trade Strategies—GATT and NAFTA—ERS is the only source in the U.S. Government of in-depth agricultural trade policy and economic information on foreign countries. As a result, ERS staff have played a key role in providing analyses of strategic options to U.S. officials involved in trade negotiations. Many of the positions adopted by the United States were recommended by USDA, and were selected because of the ERS analyses of potential impacts. As a member of USDA's NAFTA Task Force, ERS analyzed the effects of alternative trade policy provisions on 31 commodities, assessing the costs and benefits for States and regions, the environment, farm workers, food safety, and farm income. ERS was the principal contributor to several major GATT and NAFTA analyses released by

USDA during 1991 and 1992. We expect a continued high level of activity as the negotiations continue.

Food Aid and Development Assistance—ERS analyses of the agricultural and food situation in the former U.S.S.R. helped the U.S. Government focus U.S. assistance on facilitating basic reform in institutions and legal structures, not just food aid. These analyses formed the basis for coordinated assistance by the industrial nations, meeting real aid needs, while not blocking fundamental restructuring in agriculture and other sectors. Similarly, ERS is the main source of information on the agricultural supply and demand situation for the Africa Bureau of the U.S. Agency for International Development, which uses the ERS information to provide benchmarks required by the Congress for the Development Fund for Africa. In cases of serious drought and famine, ERS is the agency turned to for reliable information about the extent and likely scale of food aid needs.

This is only a sample of the policy issues where ERS plays a key role in informing departmental decisionmaking.

ERS-Funded Surveys Provide Important Data Not Available Elsewhere

ERS funds surveys each year on farm costs and returns, farmland values, natural resources, and water quality. The surveys are conducted in response to mandates and information requests from different sectors of the government. For example, the Farm Costs and Returns Survey is congressionally mandated and provides data for estimating farm income, costs of production of major commodities, and the financial condition of farm operators. The Postfarmgate Pesticide and Chemical Use Survey and Water Quality Survey provide essential data for estimating the impacts of chemical use and regulations on agriculture. The Land Values Survey provides the only data on prices of farmland. By providing an unbiased and highly regarded pool of information, the various surveys further the quality of data available not only to ERS analysts but agricultural producers, public policymakers, university researchers, agribusiness decisionmakers, and associations concerned with rural and environmental issues.

ERS Develops Indicators that Provide a Comprehensive Picture of Agricultural and Rural Conditions

ERS produces a host of economic and social indicators on such diverse topics as agricultural land values, the costs of production for major crop and livestock enterprises, nonmetro earnings, per-capita food expenditures, and world trade in agricultural commodities. In the aggregate, these indicators describe the status and major trends over time of the food and agricultural system, natural resources, and the rural economy.

ERS collects a small amount of the data directly; other data are purchased or acquired from other sources, primarily the National Agricultural Statistics Service. Even for data from other sources, ERS adds considerable value to the data through interpreting them, correcting them, and putting them in publications and electronic data bases that make them more accessible to public and private decisionmakers.

Major users of the indicators are Congress (which has mandated many of the indicators) and the Administration, which uses the data to help formulate, administer, implement, and evaluate agricultural and rural programs and policies. However, the indicators are also used by a wide range of nongovernmental sources, including agricultural and food producers, university researchers, rural bankers, and agribusiness decisionmakers. By contributing to a better public understanding of ongoing events in the agricultural sector and rural areas, the indicators serve the interests of domestic and global producers and consumers alike. The indicators constitute much of what people think they know about U.S. agriculture and the rural economy.

ERS's Research Program Serves as the Analytical Foundation for all other Program Activities

The ERS research program generates the knowledge base for all the other functions—staff analysis, economic and social indicators, and situation and outlook. The research, which covers a broad range of themes, is designed to gain a better understanding of the conditions of different economies, market systems, and sectors, and the underlying relationships between policies and events and the resulting outcomes.

For example, the agricultural sector is affected by trade, environmental, and macroeconomic policies. Agricultural producers in the United States use pesticides in the production of commodities. If pesticide use is restricted to protect the environment (i.e., water quality, human and/or wildlife safety), then the producer's cost structure changes. The mix of commodities and how they are produced, the competitiveness of U.S. commodities in international markets, farm income, consumer prices, Federal outlays, and rural well-being may or may not be affected, but policymakers need to know whichever is the case. Similarly, agricultural and trade policies have an impact on the environment and the rural community.

ERS attempts to use research produced by universities and other organizations, and great care is taken to avoid duplication of research done by others.

Closing Remarks

I appreciate the support that this Committee has given ERS and look forward to continue working with you and your staffs to ensure that ERS is addressing the highest priority issues and making the best possible use of the funds entrusted to it, through you, by the U.S. taxpayer. All members of this Committee will be provided key ERS publications and other available information. Please do not hesitate to call on us for information and assistance.

Thank you. I will be happy to respond to your questions.

ECONOMIC RESEARCH SERVICE

Purpose Statement

The Economic Research Service (ERS), was established in 1961 principally under the authority of the Agricultural Marketing Act of 1946 (7 U.S.C. 1621-1627).

ERS's mission is to provide economic and other social science information and analysis for improving the performance of agriculture and rural America

ERS produces such information as a service to the general public and to help Congress and the administration develop, administer, and evaluate agricultural and rural policies and programs. ERS monitors, analyzes, and forecasts U.S. and world agricultural production and demand for production resources, agricultural commodities, and food and fiber products. ERS also measures the costs of and returns to agricultural production and marketing; evaluates the economic performance of U.S. agricultural production and marketing; and estimates the effects of government policies and programs on farmers, rural residents and communities, natural resources, and the public. In addition, ERS produces economic and other social science information about the organization and institutions of the U.S. and world agricultural production and marketing systems, natural resources, and rural communities.

ERS-produced information is made available to the public through research monographs, situation and outlook reports, standardized data products in electronic media, professional and trade journals (including The Journal of Agricultural Economics Research), magazines (including Agricultural Outlook, Food Review, Rural Conditions and Trends, and Rural Development Perspectives), radio, television, newspapers, and frequent participation of ERS staff at various public forums.

ERS has four program divisions--Commodity Economics, Agriculture and Trade Analysis, Resources and Technology, and Agriculture and Rural Economy--that carry out the four principal functions of ERS: research, situation and outlook analysis, staff analysis, and development of economic and statistical indicators. Research and economic and statistical indicators provide the knowledge base and the data base for the situation and outlook and staff analysis functions. The products of the situation and outlook analysis function are periodic reports that analyze the current situation and forecast the short-term outlook for major agricultural commodities, agricultural exports, agricultural finance, agricultural resources, and world agriculture. Staff analysis entails assessments of issues requiring policy decisions by the administration and Congress.

ERS is located in Washington, D.C. As of September 30, 1992, ERS had 773 permanent, full-time employees and 57 part-time employees.

ECONOMIC RESEARCH SERVICE

Available Funds and Staff-Years

1992 Actual and Estimated, 1993 and 1994

Item	1992 Actual Amount	1992 Actual Staff-Years	1993 Estimated Amount	1993 Estimated Staff-Years	1994 Estimated Amount	1994 Estimated Staff-Years
Economic Research Service	$58,930,000	775	$58,925,000	764	$51,461,000	751
Obligations under Other USDA appropriations:						
Agricultural Marketing Service for study of marketing of U.S. agricultural products	311,921	3	206,000	2	140,000	1
Animal and Plant Health Inspection Service for support of Great Plains Council and grasshopper project (passthru)	43,946	--	9,000	--	35,000	--
Agricultural Research Service for support of Great Plains Council (passthru)	9,803	--	9,000	--		
Agricultural Cooperative Service for agricultural food marketing consortium	10,000	--				
Cooperative State Research Service for: study of sustainable agriculture and new uses	120,438	2	109,000	1	225,000	2
Extension Service for: support of Great Plains Council (passthru)	8,946	--	9,000	--		
Farmers Home Administration for personnel details and wastewater needs data	93,051	--	83,000	--		
Federal Crop Insurance Corporation for support of the insurance program	200,000	--	--	--	--	--
Federal Grain Inspection Service for grading and price impact studies	246,721	3	275,000	3		
Food and Nutrition Service for study of WIC program	18,500	--	--	--		

Item	1992 Actual		1993 Estimated		1994 Estimated	
	Amount	Staff-Years	Amount	Staff-Years	Amount	Staff-Years
Foreign Agricultural Service for international trade studies (passthru)	28,334	--	16,000	--		
Forest Service for support of Great Plains Council (passthru)	10,689	--	9,000	--		
Office of Energy for personnel detail and support of marketing and food safety	69,918	1				
Packers & Stockyards for concentration study	127,500	1				
Rural Development Administration for the support of state councils (passthru)	1,736,348	--	4,000,000	--	5,750,000	--
Soil Conservation Service for support of Great Plains Council (passthru)	8,946	--	9,000	--		
Miscellaneous reimbursements	18,297	--	13,000	--	--	--
Total, Other USDA Appropriations	3,063,358	10	4,747,000	6	6,150,000	3
Total, Agriculture Appropriations	61,993,358	785	63,672,000	770	57,611,000	754
Other Federal Funds:						
Department of Defense for grain transportation	25,556	--	--	--	--	--
Council of Economic Advisors for personnel detail	96,071	1	--	--	--	--
Commission on agricultural workers for analysis of wages and employment	10,000	--	--	--		
Environmental Protection Agency for studies on pesticide residues and water control	39,500	--	--	--		
Office of International Cooperation and Development for personnel details and food aid studies	2,266,788	14	2,916,000	19	294,000	4
Total, Other Federal Funds	2,437,915	15	2,916,000	19	294,000	4

Item	1992 Actual Amount	Staff-Years	1993 Estimated Amount	Staff-Years	1994 Estimated Amount	Staff-Years
Non-Federal Funds:						
Miscellaneous Contributed Funds from publications and data sales, and other private organizations	497,468	1	400,000	1	389,000	1
North Carolina State University for personnel detail	279,688	3	300,000	3	456,000	3
Texas A&M for a study of regional implications of farm programs	68,000	--	37,000	--	--	--
Total, Non-Federal Funds	845,156	4	737,000	4	845,000	4
Total, Economic Research Service	$65,276,429	804	67,325,000	793	58,750,000	762

ECONOMIC RESEARCH SERVICE

Permanent Positions by Grade and Staff-Year Summary

1992 and Estimated 1993 and 1994

ES-6	1	1	1
ES-5	1	1	1
ES-4	4	4	4
ES-2	1	2	2
ES-1	1	--	--
Senior Level	1	1	1
GS/GM-15	56	56	56
GS/GM-14	127	127	126
GS/GM-13	204	204	201
GS-12	117	117	114
GS-11	45	45	44
GS-10	2	2	2
GS-9	37	37	37
GS-8	20	20	20
GS-7	50	50	50
GS-6	43	43	42
GS-5	46	46	45
GS-4	12	12	11
GS-3	4	4	4
GS-2	1	1	1
Total Permanent Positions			
Unfilled Positions end-of-year			
Total, Permanent Employment, end-of-year			
Staff-Years:			
Ceiling			

ECONOMIC RESEARCH SERVICE

CLASSIFICATION BY OBJECTS

1992 and Estimated 1993 and 1994

	1992	1993	1994
Personnel Compensation:			
Headquarters	36,093,932	37,096,000	36,206,000
Field	--	--	--
11 Total personnel compensation	36,093,932	37,096,000	36,206,000
12 Personnel benefits	6,634,669	6,819,000	6,655,000
13 Benefits for former personnel	5,326	5,000	20,000
Total Pers. Comp & Benefits	42,733,927	43,920,000	42,881,000
Other Objects:			
21 Travel	880,947	817,000	485,000
22 Transportation of things	78,935	74,000	20,000
23.3 Communications, utilities, and misc. charges	699,941	648,000	822,000
24 Printing and reproduction	418,975	389,000	400,000
25 Other services	10,967,900	10,216,000	6,203,000
26 Supplies and materials	986,407	909,000	350,000
31 Equipment	2,105,910	1,952,000	300,000
Total other objects	16,139,015	15,005,000	8,580,000
Total direct obligations	58,872,942	58,925,000	51,461,000
Position Data:			
Average Salary, ES positions	$102,600	$105,000	$105,000
Average Salary, GM/GS positions	$46,108	$46,236	$46,483
Average Grade, GM/GS positions	11.2	11.2	11.2

ECONOMIC RESEARCH SERVICE

The estimates include appropriation language for this item as follows (new language underscored; deleted matter enclosed in brackets):

For necessary expenses of the Economic Research Service in conducting economic research and service relating to agricultural production, marketing, and distribution as authorized by the Agricultural Marketing Act of 1946 (7 U.S.C. 1621-1627), and other laws, including economics of marketing; analyses relating to farm prices, income and population, and demand for farm products, use of resources in agriculture, adjustments, costs and returns in farming, and farm finance; research relating to the economic and marketing aspects of farmer cooperatives; and for analysis of supply and demand for farm products in foreign countries and their effect on prospects for United States exports, progress in economic development and its relation to sales of farm products, assembly and analysis of agricultural trade statistics and analysis of international financial and monetary programs and policies as they affect the competitive position of United States farm products, [$58,720,000] <u>$51,461,000</u>; of which $500,000 shall be available for investigation, determination and finding as to the effect upon the production of food and upon the agricultural economy of any proposed action affecting such subject matter pending before the Administrator of the Environmental Protection Agency for presentation, in the public interest, before said Administrator, other agencies or before the courts: *Provided*, That this appropriation shall be available to continue to gather statistics and conduct a special study on the price spread between the farmer and the consumer: *Provided further*, That this appropriation shall be available for employment pursuant to the second sentence of section 706(a) of the Organic Act of 1944 (7 U.S.C. 2225): *Provided further*, That this appropriation shall be available for analysis of statistics and related facts on foreign production and full and complete information on methods used by other countries to move farm commodities in world trade on a competitive basis.

ECONOMIC RESEARCH SERVICE

Appropriation Act, 1993	$58,720,000
Budget Estimate, 1994	51,461,000
Decrease in Appropriation	-7,259,000

Adjustments in 1993:

Appropriation Act, 1993	58,720,000	
Office of the Secretary Transfer a/	+205,000	
Adjusted base for 1993		58,925,000
Budget Estimate, Current Law 1994		51,461,000
Decrease from adjusted 1993		-7,464,000

a/ The transfer from the Office of the Secretary is to provide technical support for the development of new uses for agricultural commodities including a strong emphasis on alternative fuels. On a comparable basis, the full annual cost of for this activity is $205,000 for 1993 and $205,000 for 1994.

Summary of Increases and Decreases
(On basis of adjusted appropriation)

Item of Change	1993 Estimated	Pay Costs	Other Changes	1994 Estimated
Economic Analysis and Research	$58,925,000	+$979,000	-$8,443,000	$51,461,000

Project Statement
(On basis of adjusted appropriation)

Project	1992 Actual		1993 Estimated		Decrease	1994 Estimated	
	Amount	Staff-Years	Amount	Staff-Years		Amount	Staff-Years
Economic Analysis and Research	$58,872,942	775	$58,925,000	764	(1) -$7,464,000	$51,461,000	751
Unobligated Balance	57,058	--	--	--	--	--	--
Total available or estimate	58,930,000	775	58,925,000	764	-7,464,000	51,461,000	751
Transfer from Secretary's Office	-210,000	-2	-205,000	-2			
Total, Appropriation	58,720,000	773	58,720,000	762			

EXPLANATION OF PROGRAM

he appropriation for the Economic Research Service funds the following activity:

--Economic analysis and research--This activity includes research, situation nd outlook analysis, staff analysis, and development of economic and statistical ndicators in the four major program areas--commodity economics, agriculture and rade analysis, resources and technology, and agriculture and rural economy.

JUSTIFICATION OF INCREASES AND DECREASES

1) A net decrease of $7,464,000 for economic analysis and research, consisting of:

(a) An increase of $405,000, which reflects a 2.7-percent increase in nonsalary costs.

Need for Change. These funds are necessary to offset increased operating costs. Continued absorption of these increased operating costs will severely affect the quality and quantity of our program.

Nature of Change. This increase will be used to maintain a current level of services associated with inflation which will affect critical parts of our program.

(b) An increase of $979,000 for absorbed fiscal year 1993 pay costs .

(c) A decrease of $10,000 for FTS 2000 funding ($90,000 available in fiscal year 1993).

This decrease reflects lower long distance telecommunications prices due to price redeterminations in the FTS 2000 contracts.

(d) A decrease of $395,000 for rice modeling ($395,000 available in fiscal year 1993).

Need for Change. This reduction is part of a governmentwide effort to reduce the Federal deficit by control of discretionary spending.

Nature of Change. This decrease would terminate ERS funding of a project at the Universities of Arkansas and Missouri to expand the capability of their commodity policy modeling system to conduct analysis on the consequences of value-added exports. This project was funded by ERS in fiscal years 1992 and 1993, for a cumulative total of $790,000.

(e) A decrease of $50,000 for the Western Livestock Marketing Information Program ($50,000 available in fiscal year 1993).

Need for Change. This reduction is part of a governmentwide effort to reduce the Federal deficit by control of discretionary spending.

Nature of Change. This decrease would terminate the ERS contribution to the funding of this regional information project. ERS has contributed $50,000 annually to this project since fiscal year 1979, for a cumulative total of $750,000.

(f) A decrease of $8,393,000 for economic analysis and research ($58,390,000 million available in fiscal year 1993.

Need for Change. ERS will realize $8.4 million in program savings in fiscal year 1994 through a combination of improved program efficiencies, consolidation of staff around issues and subject matters most essential to the Department's policymaking needs, reductions in areas where problems of the 1980's have diminished, and reduction of data purchases and support services. This reduction is part of a governmentwide effort to reduce the Federal deficit by control of discretionary spending.

For fiscal year 1994 through 1997, the budget includes a total savings of about $59 million. This is a 22-percent reduction from current activities and will be accomplished through further staff reductions and a refocusing of analyses on the Department's most essential issues.

Nature of Change. Specific program reductions and efficiencies will be determined at a later date. However, examples of possible reductions include:

- Reduction in cooperative research with land-grant and other universities. Efforts could be made to continue critical joint research with in-kind contributions by both parties.

- Reduction in survey funding and data purchases. With the farm sector in improved financial condition relative to the mid-1980's, ERS could drop much of the detailed analysis of financially vulnerable farmers and other well-being measures. Cost-of-production data could be dropped for commodities not mandated by the Congress.

- Reduction in analysis of decisions before the Administrator of the Environmental Protection Agency that pertain to use of agricultural pesticides. ERS is mandated in its appropriation language to review the actions of the Administrator of EPA as to their effect on the production of food and upon the agricultural economy. The Department now has a National Agricultural Pesticide Impact Assessment Program process that can draw on universities for analytical assistance.

- Major reduction in travel related to training and participation in State and regional constituent meetings. Travel related to requests for assistance to other agencies could be funded by requestors.

- Reduction in commodity research and market analysis. A reduced staff could focus on the most critical commodities and realize further savings by reducing frequency and depth of situation and outlook reports. Reduced number of printed reports could be partly offset with more fee-driven electronic dissemination of analyses and data.

- Reduction in analyses of farm credit, finance, and structural issues. Improved farm financial conditions, compared to the 1980's, may reduce the urgency of some of this work, including the annual report to the Congress on the status of family farms.

- Savings from streamlining economic analysis related to international trade, farm and food marketing, environment, global change, energy, and new crop uses are possible.

- Savings from increased efficiencies and reduced support activities, including ADP, manuscript editing, and personnel management. More work can now be done with desktop publishing. With a smaller staff and no hiring for several years, the number of personnel specialists could be reduced.

ECONOMIC RESEARCH SERVICE
GEOGRAPHIC BREAKDOWN OF OBLIGATIONS AND STAFF-YE
1992 and Estimated 1993 and 1994

	1992		1993	
	Amount	Staff-Years	Amount	Staff-Years
Alabama	81,000	- -	- -	- -
Arizona	6,525	- -	- -	
Arkansas	319,355	- -	26,000	- -
California	155,360	- -	46,000	- -
Colorado	8,943	- -	9,000	- -
Connecticut	131,245	- -	50,000	- -
Delaware	8,500	- -	- -	- -
District of Columbia	56,664,706	775	58,350,000	764
Florida	82,000	- -	43,000	- -
Hawaii	15,000	- -	- -	
Illinois	40,000	- -	- -	
Indiana	138,952	- -	36,000	- -
Iowa	57,500	- -	- -	
Kentucky	103,948	- -	58,000	- -
Louisiana	5,000	- -	17,000	- -
Maryland	37,400	- -	- -	
Massachusetts	27,650	- -	15,000	- -
Michigan	27,000	- -	16,000	- -
Minnesota	76,745	- -	17,000	- -
Missouri	135,645	- -	61,000	- -
Montana	79,602	- -	60,000	- -
Nebraska	7,500	- -	- -	
New York	146,204	- -		- -
New Mexico	20,500	- -	- -	- -
North Carolina	56,000	- -	- -	- -
Ohio	17,500	- -	85,000	- -
Oklahoma	43,500	- -	- -	
Oregon	55,018	- -	- -	
Pennsylvania	17,000	- -	- -	
Tennessee	20,000	- -	- -	
Texas	162,020	- -	36,000	- -
Virginia	46,124	- -	- -	- -
Wisconsin	79,500	- -	- -	- -
Subtotal, Available or Estimate	58,872,942	775	58,925,000	764
Unobligated balance	57,058	- -	- -	- -
Total, Available or Estimate	58,930,000	775	58,925,000	764

ECONOMIC RESEARCH SERVICE

STATUS OF PROGRAM

The Economic Research Service (ERS) performs work under one appropriation item--economic analysis and research. Current activities and selected examples of recent progress are described briefly below.

ECONOMIC ANALYSIS AND RESEARCH

Current Activities: ERS carries out its economic analysis and research in four program divisions, whose programs and plans for 1993 are highlighted below.

1. The Commodity Economics Division (CED) carries out a program of analysis designed to improve the public's understanding of U.S. and world markets for agricultural products. This entails activities in three major areas, including: commodity supply, demand, and price monitoring and forecasting; analysis of the structure, conduct, and performance of the major national and international commodity markets; and analysis of national and international commodity marketing—from the U.S. producer through domestic and foreign consumers and from the foreign producer of imported products through to the U.S. consumer.

   In 1993, CED plans to analyze commodity developments and disseminate results through regular situation and outlook reports, special reports as market developments warrant, yearbooks, presentations, and responses to public information requests; conduct research on the structure, operation, and performance of the major commodity markets in alternative policy settings; conduct research on investment and competition in the food marketing industries in the United States and abroad; expand research efforts on food safety, food assistance, and nutrition education; continue analytic support for trade negotiations and agreements; provide technical assistance in the development of situation and outlook programs for Eastern Europe and Taiwan; respond to requests for special studies and analyses, including congressionally mandated studies of commodity policy and program issues; and develop and maintain data bases and models to improve analyses, forecasts, and projections.

2. The Agriculture and Trade Analysis Division (ATAD) is a major source of expertise, data, models, and research information about the agricultural economies and policies of foreign countries and the agricultural trade and development relationships between foreign countries and the United States. The major mission of ATAD is to provide analyses of the global and regional trade implications of the changing agricultural, technological, economic, and policy environments. The topics covered by ATAD include agricultural and trade policies and their relationship to the economic, technical, and political factors affecting agricultural trade among countries; economic and agricultural market structure, efficiency, and production systems of foreign countries; technical production systems of foreign countries; and foreign governments' production, consumption, macroeconomic, and trade policies.

   In 1993, ATAD plans to examine the trade implications of environmental policies and food safety regulations in other countries; develop and analyze a global baseline projection system for world agriculture; analyze and update measures of support for agriculture in key countries; evaluate potential preferential trade agreements among countries in the Western Hemisphere, Europe, and Asia; examine the economic implications of political restructuring in Central and Eastern Europe, the former Soviet Union, and some developing countries; and assess food aid needs of foreign countries.

3. The Resources and Technology Division (RTD) conducts economic analyses of agricultural resource and technology issues. RTD's integrated research, staff analysis, and situation and outlook activities assess the economic costs of agricultural production on the environment as well as the costs to agriculture of policies and programs seeking to mitigate environmental effects. RTD analyzes the impacts of national and global developments, domestic and international policies and programs, and macroeconomic variables on the use and value of land, water, capital assets, and other agricultural resources, and assesses the possible impacts of proposed or anticipated policy and program changes on agricultural production decisions; studies the economics of environmental and health risk reduction, including the demand for risk reduction, appropriate production strategies for supplying risk reductions, costs and benefits of policy alternatives, and the trade implications of environmental and food safety regulations; estimates supply, demand, and price relationships, substitutability, and productivity of resources, including capital equipment, fertilizer, pesticides, energy, land, and water; evaluates public policies and programs that affect technology and productivity, the adoption and transfer of new technologies, the economic impacts of regulating agricultural practices and inputs, and the economics of sustainable agricultural systems; and analyzes the environmental benefits and costs associated with agricultural activities, especially the impacts on water quality.

   In 1993, RTD plans to be heavily involved in USDA initiatives on food safety, water quality, and global climate change. RTD will participate in cross-division activities on trade and the environment and on food safety. Other high priority issues to be addressed in 1993 include ethanol and biofuels, economic impacts of the Endangered Species Act implementation, and geographic information systems. The 1993 program covers nonmarket evaluation of environmental amenities, including air and water quality, wetlands, productivity, global change, and food safety; economics of environmental and health risk, including pesticides, food safety, and global change; policy evaluation and benefit-cost analysis, including water quality; ethanol; trade, environment, food safety, and agriculture tradeoffs; conservation provisions; land and water policies; technology research, development, and adoption, including agricultural research; water quality initiative; global change initiative; food safety initiative; and productivity, environment, and trade. These areas of emphasis are supported by an ongoing program of research, staff analysis, and situation and outlook activities. In situation and outlook reports, RTD will continue to publish the latest information on land use and values, farm real estate taxes, foreign ownership, water availability and use, irrigation development, cropping practices, soil conservation activities and program participation, and supply, demand, and prices of manufactured inputs including fertilizer, pesticides, energy, and farm machinery.

4. The Agriculture and Rural Economy Division (ARED) conducts a national program of research and analysis related to agricultural and rural conditions and trends and identifies and evaluates public and private sector actions and policies that affect the sector and rural areas. ARED's agenda is shaped by the changing economic and demographic structures of agriculture and rural America. Its program covers: the industrial transformation of the rural economy; interconnections between agriculture and the rural economy and the Nation's economy; differences in performance between urban and rural economies; financial performance of the farm sector and its components; effects of international economic and financial integration on the rural economy; migration and population change; changes in rural and agricultural labor markets and labor conditions; and the implications of the evolving structures of farming, credit, and finance for rural people, businesses, communities, and banks.
   In 1993, as part of its research to better understand the agricultural sector and its relationship to the national and regional economies, ARED

plans to publish the annual "Status of the Family Farm" report for the first time using time series data from the Farm Costs and Returns Survey that will provide an annual farm-based profile of the sector and provide projections of the future structure of the U.S. farm sector in to the next decade; use the Farm Costs and Returns Survey to research the financial performance and viability of farm businesses from both an enterprise and whole-farm perspective; analyze the relationship of economic performance and well-being of the farm operator household to the operator's farm business and the rural areas in which the farm is located; use the Department of Commerce 1982 national input/output table to update ARED models of widely used estimates of the components of the food and fiber system and of the effects of agricultural exports on the U.S. economy; incorporate disaggregated household data into the input/output and computable general equilibrium models to permit analysis of the distribution among households of the effects of policy changes; study the relationship of national interest rates and employment to the agricultural and rural economies to improve the public's understanding of the relationship of the sector and the broader rural economy to the national economy; analyze the effects of changes in farm production on several prototypical farming areas, placing special emphasis on the interrelationship between farming and farm-related sectors and the overall local economy; improve understanding of the evolution of the rural economy, the process of local economic development, and the potential of government strategies to affect that process in order to improve the well-being of rural people and communities; publish a monograph providing an updated profile of rural America with particular emphasis on the ways in which changes in rural families, jobs, and income over the last decade varied according to regional location, remoteness from major urban centers, and the nature of local economies; examine the skills of the rural work force and the demand for those skills in local labor markets, particularly in manufacturing; study the dimensions of rural manufacturing to adapt to increasingly competitive global markets; complete research on the extent to which structural adjustments in response to markets and regulatory developments affect the profitability of rural financial institutions and, in turn, the flow of credit to rural farm and nonfarm businesses; assess the effectiveness of diverse rural development strategies under varying local conditions with the creation of USDA's Rural Development Administration and the establishment of State Rural Development Councils in many States; provide a historical perspective on several dimensions of the evolving agricultural sector and rural America and associated Federal policies and programs; and complete a history of rural development policies and continue work on an oral history of USDA designed to capture and record the experiences of major figures involved in the formulation and implementation of departmental policies and programs over several decades.

Selected Examples of Recent Progress: Recent accomplishments under this appropriation item are cited below, by program division.

Commodity Economics Division:

1. Nutrition education evaluation. ERS economists worked closely with other USDA agencies involved in nutrition education to develop evaluation strategies to assess the cost and impact of USDA activities. Preliminary evidence suggests that nutritionally aware individuals have altered their consumption of foods in response to health concerns but have not been more successful in altering their nutrient intake.

2. Microbial food safety. ERS expanded its economic analysis of microbial contamination in food. ERS completed a survey and began data analysis on the cost of Campylobacter, a foodborne contaminant that causes most human illnesses. A survey instrument on the economics of farm management procedures to control salmonella enteritidis in eggs was designed and data collection started on several Pennsylvania farms. ERS staff participated in

USDA's Food Safety Task Force by developing 1994 budget initiatives, conducting briefings on the economics of food safety, conducting a benefit/cost analysis of irradiating poultry, and conducting economic reviews of other proposed rule changes. ERS analysts also expanded research on the conceptual foundations of risk and uncertainty and its relationship to consumer behavior and market performance. ERS research clarified the meaning of risk aversion used in models, demonstrated how risk information concepts can be rigorously incorporated into models, and analyzed the pitfalls of using standard expected utility theory to model food choices involving both risk and taste.

3. Estimating the effects of shifting to a more sustainable agriculture. ERS economists assembled and coordinated a 16-member steering committee to design the Sustainable Agriculture Economic Impact Study. The committee determined that not enough is known on the farm/ranch-level to support analysis on a more aggregate level. About 75 percent of the study budget will fund 6 projects that focus on estimating the farm/ranch-level effects of a more sustainable agriculture in specific rural places. These farm/ranch-level projects are quite diverse, but the lead researchers will provide estimates of a common set of indicators. These estimates, along with data from other sources, will serve as inputs into the regional/national modeling framework. The remaining study funds will go to build that framework. Indicators include measures of economic costs and returns, soil erosion, and chemical leaching. Some projects will also investigate social issues such as the impact on land tenure and off-farm employment.

4. Industrial uses of agricultural materials. ERS economists have expanded their research program on industrial uses of farm products by examining the production, processing, marketing, and uses of new and traditional crops for industrial raw materials. New crops include kenaf, industrial rapeseed, crambe, meadowfoam, jojoba, and lesquerella. This work will help farmers expand their markets and create jobs in farm States. ERS economists are writing a series of reports on industrial crops with other USDA analysts and university staff. Each report presents the crop's current agronomic status, commercialization, and market potential. In 1992, *Lesquerella as a Source of Hydroxy Fatty Acids for Industrial Products* was released. Reports are planned on kenaf, milkweed, jojoba, and meadowfoam.

5. Regulatory rules reviewed in AMS, APHIS, ASCS, FAS, FCIC, FGIS, FSIS, OICD, and P&SA. A review of USDA regulations, conducted at the request of the President, involved individual agency study teams each including staff from USDA's OBPA, OGC, and ERS. Each rule reviewed required an economic impact analysis. Over the period of the review, 30 ERS analysts worked on teams reviewing regulations. The reviews resulted in regulation changes either during the review period or after. Examples range from the requirement that FCIC collect Social Security numbers from applicants as a way of identifying applicants previously engaged in fraudulent claims, to the rule approving irradiation of poultry. The former rule required minimal review although it may have significant effect on the efficiency of a program. The second rule required a benefit/cost analysis that incorporated previously published ERS research. Numerous other rules received analysis ranging from quantitative benefit/cost to qualitative economic assessment of effects.

6. Sugar and sweetener policy work. ERS made major contributions in modeling and analyzing domestic and world sugar and sweetener supply, demand, price, and trade, and used this information to assist with policy decisions such as setting the U.S. sugar quota, study options for the North American Free Trade Agreement, and project impacts of various GATT scenarios. ERS analysts assisted in forecasting the probability that USDA would need to trigger the standby marketing allotments for sugar called for in the 1990 farm legislation. Options analyzed included that of extending the sugar

quota year. ERS analysts engaged in a wide range of research and analysis on the domestic sugar industry, conducted annual studies of the costs of production of sugarbeets and sugarcane and of the costs of sugar processing, maintained a cost-of-production data base, provided key information for calculation of beet and cane sugar loan rates and sugarcane and sugarbeet support prices, and assisted the Polish Ministry of Agriculture with developing a situation and outlook reporting system for sugar and sweeteners.

7. North America Free Trade Agreement (NAFTA). ERS produced general economic information concerning U.S./Mexico commodity production, trade, and border measures, including tariff and non-tariff barriers, and several major multi-commodity analyses of the effects of alternative proposals. ERS analysis showed the biggest impacts in absolute and in relative terms to be on the Mexican markets, both in terms of exports and imports. Mexico depends on the United States for 75 percent of its imports or exports. For the United States, the relative impacts of NAFTA on production and prices for most commodities are less than a 2-percent change. Impacts on trade can be quite small on total U.S. trade for the commodity, while showing significant increases in trade with Mexico. In some cases, U.S. exports could double in 15 years over what would be expected without NAFTA. The biggest gainers for the United States will be grains, meats, protein meals, and deciduous fruits. Mexico gains primarily in citrus and some winter vegetables.

8. GATT negotiations. As the multilateral GATT negotiations on agricultural and trade policies intensified, ERS researchers evaluated the impact of numerous scenarios, involving a wide variety of U.S. and foreign country policy adjustments, on U.S. farm commodity sectors, farm income, and food prices. The range of issues spanned philosophical approaches to agricultural and trade policy, technical relationships, and structural adjustments. ERS analyses included the effects on U.S. commodities of lower U.S. and foreign "clean" and "dirty" tariff equivalents and higher minimum access provisions, reductions in the EEP, extension of the CRP and changes in EC land use, and changes in the composition of EC feed ingredients. Other analyses included the impact of a GATT agreement and EC CAP reform on total world grain trade and world prices.

9. Nutrition labeling. ERS analysts worked closely with USDA's FSIS to provide economic analysis of the USDA initiative. ERS staff worked with EAS, OBPA, FSIS, and OMB to revise the final regulatory impact analysis and developed a supplemental analysis addressing particular OMB concerns. The preliminary analysis indicated FSIS would explore a small business exemption and would assess its prior label approval process. ERS staff served on an interagency prior label approval task force and participated in small business forums in Kansas City, Atlanta, and San Francisco; worked with OMB and FSIS to address OMB concerns about a proposed questionnaire for gathering labeling cost data; and, at the request of FSIS, worked with FDA to obtain tabulations of the number and volume of FSIS-regulated products from grocery store scanner data. ERS staff worked on estimates and prepared an options paper for the Office of the Secretary analyzing the parameters of the small business exemption.

10. Situation and outlook and policy analysis technical assistance programs. ERS economists are assisting government agencies in Eastern Europe to establish economic information systems to support both private and public decisionmaking. A lack of timely and easily accessible data is hampering the shift to market-oriented agriculture in the region. The ERS project is a cross-divisional effort funded by the SEED II Act (Support for Emerging European Democracies). ERS staff conducted intensive training sessions on the role of ERS and USDA in supporting market operations and decisionmaking for representatives from Czechoslovakia. ERS analysts worked with teams from Poland, Hungary, and Czechoslovakia on techniques for analyzing

commodity markets and on developing and institutionalizing a program of regularly scheduled situation and outlook reports for critical commodities. In Poland, reports were published on grains, oilseeds, dairy, red meat, poultry, sugar, potatoes, and inputs. An outlook conference was held in Poland to highlight the situation and outlook program. Grains and red meats reports were published in Hungary, while in Czechoslovakia, reports were published on grains and dairy. These reports are intended to provide the information base for government policymaking and to help overcome the lack of information available to farmers and other private decisionmakers. ERS staff also provided assistance in analyzing the economic consequences of alternative agricultural programs and policies. Policy decisionmakers from Poland and Hungary participated in an agricultural policy workshop in Washington, D.C. A series of workshops were held in the respective countries for mid-level analysts to address commodity supply, demand and price analysis, macroeconomics, agricultural intervention policies, and price stabilization programs. ERS also provided a resident policy adviser to the Bulgarian Ministry of Agriculture.

riculture and Trade Anal sis Division:

1. Reform in Central and Eastern Europe. ERS's work on Central and Eastern Europe in 1992 proceeded on two parallel and mutually reinforcing fronts: intensive involvement in the Central Europe institution building project and continued monitoring and analysis of the reform process in the region. ERS staff are working with the agricultural ministries of Central Europe to develop and institutionalize the capacity to conduct sound economic analysis to support government decisionmaking and to help farmers and agribusinesses in the rapidly emerging private sectors make informed decisions on production and marketing. ERS staff worked with in-country counterparts to initiate a series of situation and outlook reports, and provided training in how to do policy-oriented economic analysis. ERS research on Central and Eastern Europe focused on the long-term effects of economic reform, EC association, and eventual membership in the EC. ERS analysts assisted USDA's FAS in analyzing the effects of the EC association agreements on U.S. trade and the effects of different sectoral policies on the agricultural sector of Hungary.

2. Economic reform and agriculture in the former USSR. ERS analysis showed that reforming the economies of the former Soviet Union countries is a daunting challenge. The countries lack the institutional and legal structures crucial for well-operating market economies. Therefore, the most serious problems in the agricultural sectors are linked to shortcomings in the functioning of the overall economies. Food shortages are primarily the result of macroeconomic imbalances and inflationary pressure that has severely weakened the ruble as an effective means of exchange. The dysfunction of money hindered the flow of goods, resulting in localized shortages of food and other goods. Property rights and private property are essential institutional and legal foundations for market economies. The obstacles to privatization and competition are greater in the former USSR than those experienced by developed or developing countries because of the pervasiveness of public ownership in all aspects of the economies. The wide extent of public ownership in the former USSR means that almost no parallel markets exist to help set a value on the state's assets. The large price and subsidy distortions in the past mean that a firm or farm's past performances is often not a good indicator of its future value. Another problem for large- scale privatization is the lack of private sector funds to purchase and invest. Even the emerging private farms remain squeezed between input and marketing monopolies.

3. Reform of agricultural policy in the European Community. ERS analysis on CAP reform included: an examination of the reform proposals, that often contained many loopholes; an examination of the production, consumption, and

trade effects of CAP reform on EC grains, oilseeds and livestock; an examination of the extent to which the reforms would meet the commitments contained in the agricultural text of the Uruguay Round, particularly commitments on import access, export subsidies, and internal support; a comparison of U.S. and EC programs and the possibility of fraud and other forms of noncompliance; and adjustments to either the EC's CAP reform proposals and/or the agricultural text of the Uruguay Round, which would allow the EC to meet the terms of a GATT agreement.

4. Agricultural reform in the People's Republic of China. Expanded institutional contacts and better statistics bolstered ERS research program on China. ERS staff presented research results at a conference in Beijing. One objective of the conference was to get critique by Chinese scholars. ERS studies evaluated the effects of alternative Chinese policies on crop production and distribution patterns and trade. Preliminary results indicate that maintaining self-sufficiency would increase trade between regions in China but decrease international trade. However, domestic production costs would increase substantially. On the other hand, if China liberalized trade, wheat and coarse grain imports and rice exports would increase. Preliminary results also indicate that if China encouraged greater feedgrain self-sufficiency by the year 2000 while liberalizing trade, it would have to promote greater consumption of poultry and less of pork. Unilateral policy reform would lead to a decline in self-sufficiency but an increase in real income. In another study, China's food consumption patterns were projected to the year 2000 drawing on Taiwan's experience. The results indicated that by the end of the century, China's demand for coarse grains would greatly exceed domestic supply. Other studies examined China's changing land tenure system, the elasticity of demand for agricultural goods, and agricultural sustainability.

5. Future of agricultural markets in Japan. ERS projections to 2000 for Japan, the leading overseas farm market for U.S. agricultural exports, indicate the likelihood of important changes in that agricultural market in the next decade. Areas of uncertainty include policy reform, demographic change, environmental constraints, and macroeconomic change. ERS analysis forecasts that consumption of livestock products in Japan will continue to grow in the coming decade, but all the increase will come from imports; expansion in domestic production will stall and even decline because of increased imports and competition; and domestic livestock industries will have difficulty adjusting to the increased competition because of high costs of production—resulting in part from inefficiencies in input supply industries and environmental constraints. The future of the rice sector will depend on how policies are changed in response to internal forces and international forces through the GATT. Even in the absence of policy reform, rice consumption and production in Japan are projected to decline during the 1990's. While dietary composition will change with more meats and less rice, total per capita caloric intake is expected to rise only slightly. Important changes also are expected in food processing and food services with rising incomes and greater female workforce participation.

6. Food strategies and market liberalization in Africa. ERS conducted a study of food security policies during the 1980's of Kenya, Tanzania, and Zimbabwe. These countries are representative of many countries in sub-Saharan Africa with respect to socioeconomic, financial, and agricultural characteristics. In the 1980's, many African countries implemented policy reforms proposed by international organizations and foreign donors designed to remove agricultural production constraints and stimulate economic growth. The reforms involved reducing government intervention, raising consumer prices, and lowering input subsidies. The prescriptions were the same for countries with different marketing infrastructure, capacities to use improved technology, and research, extension, and credit institutions. Trade opportunities differ greatly among countries because of different

financial conditions, terms of trade, and export potential. The ERS study found that in the three countries studied, policy changes led to higher farm-level commodity prices. However, input subsidies were removed, leading to higher input prices and partially offsetting the production-expanding effects of increased producer prices. A medium-term projection of market liberalization effects on producers and consumers indicated that policy reforms alone are insufficient to balance domestic food production and population growth. Food imports are expected to grow for commodities such as rice and wheat. More secure domestic food supplies depend heavily on further development of resources, institutions, and growth-oriented policies.

7. North America Free Trade Agreement (NAFTA). ERS researchers and other U.S. and Mexican government agencies and universities prepared background information and developed analytical capacity to measure the impacts of various proposals. ERS research focused on agricultural impacts, including the identification and description of government institutions and policies, estimates of producer and consumer support levels, and quantitative analysis of the effects of removing barriers on trade among the three countries. ERS preliminary findings show that reducing government barriers to trade will provide net benefits and expand agricultural trade to all three countries. The agreement ensures that the growth in U.S. agricultural exports to Mexico will continue due to greater market access in the future. More important, it prevents the countries experiencing increased imports from returning to the protectionist policies of the early 1980's. Freer trade among the countries would expand and redistribute income among commodity sectors within and among countries. By the end of the transition period, an additional $1.5 billion to $2.0 billion per year of added U.S. exports are likely. Grains and meats are estimated to account for the majority of the expansion in U.S. agricultural exports. In addition, higher exports would lead to an increase of 2 to 3 percent in U.S. agricultural market revenue for crops and livestock. More trade would expand employment in related areas of processing, transportation, and marketing. Increased horticultural exports from Mexico to the United States and Canada would benefit Mexican horticultural producers and assure U.S. and Canadian consumers with stable supplies of high quality, offseason commodities.

Resources and Technology Division:

1. Agricultural chemical data base. Public policy initiatives indicate a growing need for an agricultural chemical use data base to research water quality, food safety, endangered species, farm worker safety, and other agricultural and resource policy issues. New funding, along with coordinated ERS planning, has strengthened the primary data collection to provide more reliable fertilizer and pesticide use estimates, to cover more commodities, and to provide a richer research data base for analyzing economic and environmental policy issues. Surveyed commodities now cover most major field crops (corn, soybean, wheat, cotton, rice, potatoes, sorghum, and peanuts) and some 35 vegetable, fruit, berry, and nut crops. In addition, special chemical use and farm financial surveys have been conducted in 8 drainage basins (Columbia River Basin, Central Nebraska Basin, Indiana's White River Basin, Lower Susquehanna Basin, Albemarle-Pamlico Drainage, Georgia-Florida Coastal Plain, Iowa/Illinois River Basins, and Snake River in Idaho) in association with the Soil Conservation Service's National Resources Inventory and U.S Geological Survey's National Water Quality Assessment. These results, along with plans for additional sites, offer ERS researchers the opportunity to link chemical use, production and pest management practices, resource properties, farm financial characteristics, and water quality information for in-depth analysis.

2. Research on technological change. ERS economists are assessing the determinants of technological change in agriculture and analyzing the

effects of the adoption of new technologies and practices. Recent research has explored the impact of innovation costs, price expectations, price uncertainty, and environmental policies on the rate and direction of technical progress. The results suggest that price expectations and variability will impact innovation, output, and input use. These impacts could affect a country proceeding with trade liberalization or a transition to a market economy. Preliminary results indicate that environmental policies discourage some types of research investment but encourage others. Reduction in innovation costs (for example, through research and development tax credits or the increased supply of scientists) unambiguously increases the rate of research investment. Further ERS research shows that the rate of return to public agricultural research is higher than that for private agricultural research. Factors affecting the adoption of two types of technological advance have been analyzed. Biotechnologies hold the promise to improve the quality of the Nation's food supply, but field test regulations and uncertainty about property rights will have a negative effect on the diffusion of biotechnology innovations. ERS economists have also analyzed the adoption of technologies designed to reduce contamination by agricultural chemicals. The use of integrated pest management practices and low-volume irrigation systems is expected to decrease the loading and transport of pesticides and fertilizers. ERS research has shown that the adoption of these technologies will depend on farm profitability. Financial incentives may be necessary to induce adoption and reach environmental goals in some areas. Natural resource conditions faced by farmers will affect the choice of technology and the impact that technology adoption will have on profits, agricultural output, chemical use, and environmental quality.

3. Ethanol: economic and policy issues. ERS economists addressed selected topics on the economics of ethanol, including technological change and its effect on production costs, environmental effects of ethanol blended fuels, impacts of increased ethanol production on the agricultural sector and rural employment, and the interaction of agricultural and trade policies on the corn gluten feed market. ERS research indicates that the estimated cost savings associated with near-term technologies range from $0.05 to $0.07 per gallon of ethanol, while long-term technologies could reduce costs by an additional $0.04 to $0.08 per gallon. Converting cellulose from other plants and organic waste is expected to significantly lower ethanol production costs. Using ethanol blended fuels rather than conventional gasoline can help reduce certain types of air pollution. This would create economic benefits by reducing the health care costs associated with exposure to polluted air. Increasing ethanol production from an expected 1.2 billion to 2.0 billion gallons per year also is estimated to increase total farm income by about $170 million, while expanding ethanol production to 5 billion gallons per year is estimated to increase total farm income by $1.0 billion. Increasing ethanol production to 2 billion gallons per year is also estimated to create direct and indirect jobs from ethanol processing, temporary jobs from construction, and jobs from added crop production. The profitability of ethanol depends on sales of corn gluten feed (CGF), a coproduct of ethanol production. Since 1981, the coproduct credit for CGF has ranged from $0.20 to $0.33 per gallon of ethanol. Because 90 percent of total US CGF production is exported to the European Community (EC), EC farm policies will be an important determinant of CGF demand. If the US expands ethanol production, there will be additional downward pressure on CGF prices. However, an expansion in ethanol production also increases the US corn price, which implicitly raises the CGF price floor (CGF prices are not likely to fall significantly below the US corn price).

4. Estimating water quality benefits. ERS researchers reviewed practical approaches and theoretical foundations for estimating the economic value of changes in water quality. Knowledge of the benefits and costs to water users is required for a complete assessment of policies to create incentives for water-quality-improving changes in agricultural production. The types

of water uses affected by changes in water quality include recreation, commercial fisheries, navigation, municipal water treatment and use, and water storage. Estimating the economic effects of changes in water quality on water users is complicated by the lack of organized markets for environmental quality. There are no observed prices with which to measure value. Instead, a number of methods exist for deriving welfare measures by making use of information contained in the behavior of water users. These methods include revealed preference, contingent valuation and averting behavior, and changes in production costs. Each of these methods was reviewed, including theoretical framework, application, and data requirements.

5. Drought and reallocations of irrigation water supplies. As the drought in the western United States completes its sixth year in some locations, ERS economists continue to monitor the severity and extent of the drought. Information on consequences of the drought helps USDA estimate impacts in commodity markets and formulate drought response strategies. The California drought motivated legislation to provide more water for fish and wildlife needs. The Central Valley Project Improvement Act, as proposed, will alter irrigation water supplies from the Federally-financed Central Valley Project in California. Initial estimates indicate that the combination of State law governing water allocations and physical infrastructure result in an uneven distribution of the impacts, with some producers not affected and others severely impacted. The impacts on any producer depends in large part on the availability of water from other sources. The aggregate impact on California agriculture depends on the extent of crop substitution and the ability to substitute for reduced surface water supplies. Possible substitutes for reduced surface water supplies at the farm level include groundwater, improved water management, improved application technology, and purchasing water from a market, depending on availability and price.

6. Research on trade and the environment. ERS researchers investigated the effect of freer agricultural trade between the United States and Mexico on agricultural environmental quality in Mexico. Preliminary results indicate that, although Mexico has some pressing environmental concerns, it does not appear that the North American Free Trade Agreement will significantly worsen or improve the quality of Mexico's agri-environment beyond what would be expected without trade reform. While some subsectors, such as horticulture, are expected to grow more rapidly and potentially contribute to increased environmental degradation, the reduction in input subsidies and irrigation credits will tend to ameliorate any negative effects of increased production. Freer-trade-induced increases in livestock production in Mexico are not likely to contribute to further deforestation, primarily because the estimated increases in production are small and because land already under grain production could be used for livestock production. ERS economists also conducted a cross-country comparison of the effects of agricultural support, as measured by the producer subsidy equivalent (PSE), on agricultural intensification and extensification. Intensification results in greater use of fertilizer and pesticides in a given area, contributing to the pollution of ground and surface water and creating consumer and worker safety concerns. Extensification results in land-use change with potential loss of wild plant and animal life, and increased risk of water pollution and soil degradation caused by agricultural runoff. Agricultural protection contributes to intensification, but changes in agricultural support may not be significantly correlated with land area in the short- to medium-run time frame.

Agriculture and Rural Economy Division:

1. Macroeconomics and agriculture. The health of the agricultural sector is heavily dependent on developments in the general economy, especially those that affect national growth, inflation, and interest rates. ERS economists

developed analyses to better explain the way national interest rates affect the interest rates banks charge farmers for short-term loans. Although changes in national interest rates were found to be an important factor in agricultural rates, other factors, such as the size and financial health of the lending bank and the overall indebtedness of the farm sector, also were important. ERS economists also developed models to predict movements in long-term government interest rates. These rates are important determinants of long-term agricultural interest rates and useful in predicting growth and employment in the overall economy. ERS research shows that movements in foreign interest rates are important determinants of U.S. long-term interest rates.

2. Rural employment conditions. ERS analysis of rural employment conditions was enhanced in two ways. First, ERS developed the capacity to seasonally adjust quarterly rural employment data that allows labor market trends to be tracked with greater timeliness. Second, ERS analysis further developed the links between national and rural employment conditions. These advances were used to track rural employment conditions and analyze why rural labor markets were less adversely affected than urban areas by the 1990 recession and the subsequent period of slow and uneven growth. Following the 1981-82 recession, rural unemployment remained higher than the national average until the end of the decade. However, the 1990 recession affected metropolitan employment more severely, and the rural unemployment rate is now near the national average. The relatively strong rural performance is probably due, at least in part, to the low value of the dollar in international markets, which is particularly beneficial to exporters in rural areas. Rural areas have almost twice the share of jobs in export-sensitive-goods-producing industries than do urban areas. Rural unemployment tends to be less sensitive to high real interest rates than is urban unemployment.

3. Rural-urban manufacturing productivity gap. Manufacturing is one of the key sectors in most rural communities accounting for nearly 25 percent of wage and salary income and 17 percent of all jobs. ERS analysis of previously unpublished Census of Manufacturing data for 1977-87 showed that output per worker was lower in rural industries than in urban industries in both years and the gap in productivity increased over the ten years. While some of the productivity gap can be attributed to less capital per worker, agglomeration economies were also important. The presence of agglomeration economies means that a given combination of capital and labor is more productive in larger than smaller areas. The effect of agglomeration economies on productivity was weaker in 1987 than in 1977, contributing to a small increase in the rural share of both employment and output, largely in lower productivity industries. This increase in lower productivity industries in rural areas apparently more than offset the effect of the weakening of agglomeration economies, resulting in the widening of the rural-urban productivity gap.

4. Rural development strategies research. ERS analysts completed several interrelated studies as part of a significant research effort on the use and effectiveness of various rural development strategies employed by Federal, State, and local governments. ERS research on individual rural strategies focused on assessing the viability of each strategy for promoting rural development under a variety of conditions. Specific studies focused on enterprise zones, self-development efforts, multi-community collaboration, and retiree recruitment as rural development strategies. Research findings indicate that each of these individual strategies may be effective under certain conditions; for instance, self-development is found to be useful as a supplement to other rural development approaches in a community faced with a crisis but with an ability to tap outside financial resources. Evidence suggests that no strategy for rural development should be dismissed automatically as inappropriate, but, on the other hand, there is no magic

formula that will produce rural development in all places under any conditions.

5. Measuring loan repayment capacity of farm businesses. ERS economists developed new estimates of commercial farm operators' use of debt repayment capacity, defined as the maximum amount of debt supportable by that portion of a farm's net cash income available for loan payments. This enhanced ERS's capability to monitor how expected changes in farm income, use of debt, and level of interest rates may affect farmers ability to meet their debt obligations. Using estimates of farm income, assets, and liabilities, the maximum amount of commercial farm operator debt that could be supported by annual net cash income available for principal and interest payments was estimated for 1970-92. Comparing actual farm debt with the estimate of maximum feasible amount of debt indicated the extent to which farmers had used their available credit capacity. Results showed that debt repayment capacity use rose from 29 percent of available capacity in 1970 to more than 95 percent in 1981. Use of available capacity began to recede in 1981, but still remained above 82 percent through 1984. Although income available for debt coverage was rising during the 1970's and early 1980's, it did not increase enough to offset the principal and interest payments required on a rising volume of farm debt. This result lends credence to previous assertions that inability to meet debt repayment obligations from cash flows was a contributing factor to the farm financial crisis of the mid-1980's. Since the mid-1980's, the use of debt repayment capacity has returned to a level more like that of the mid-1970's. This reflects an increase in the amount of income available for debt coverage, a reduction in the amount of debt outstanding, and a reduction in the interest rates charged on that debt. For 1992, although the amount of income available for debt coverage is projected to decline by more than $2 billion and the level of debt outstanding to increase by $1 billion, the drop in interest rates will be sufficient to leave debt capacity use at 41 percent, about the same level as in the mid-1970's.

6. Structure of the farm sector. ERS researchers completed the first pilot report of a new series that will allow annual monitoring of major structural and financial characteristics of farms and the farm sector from USDA's Farm Costs and Returns Survey. Researchers analyzed the changes in the structure of commercial (over $40,000 in sales) farms over the 1987-89 period. Major structural characteristics (organization, production, and land use) remained stable over the period, but financial variables measuring income and wealth status fluctuated on a year-by-year basis. Net farm incomes and net farm cash incomes increased during 1987-89. Studies of the causes of farm structural change focused on how farmers acquire ownership or control of land over their lifetimes. Young farmers rely heavily on renting to acquire farmland. As the farmer becomes established, more capital is available for land purchases and dependence on rented land diminishes. In later years preceding retirement, the farmer often scales back by renting fewer acres. Acquisition of farmland from family members is an important source of ownership for young farmers, but most land owned by young farmers, is purchased from nonrelatives. The capital outlay needed to enter farming is substantial, however the amount can be over estimated because young farmers generally farm less land than more experienced farmers and they rent most of the land they farm. The option of renting as a means for acquiring farmland allows young entrepreneurs to begin farming with a modest amount of capital and debt.

7. Agricultural employment analyzed. ERS researchers completed work in support of USDA's responsibilities under the Immigration Reform and Control Act (IRCA). Because there were no forecasts of shortages of workers on U.S. farms during 1989-93, no foreign workers were needed under IRCA's Replenishment Agricultural Workers Program. ERS research found that IRCA had no significant effects on farm employment or wages at the U.S. or

regional levels. The farm work force did not diminish nor did it increase because of IRCA's Special Agricultural Worker program. Research on employment in agriculture-related industries focused on red meat and poultry processing and on fuel ethanol production. A regional input/output analysis showed local employment impacts to be 75 percent higher for areas specializing in poultry processing than in red meat processing. Increasing annual ethanol production to 2 billion gallons (doubling current production) is also estimated to create direct and indirect jobs from ethanol processing, temporary jobs from construction, and jobs from added crop production. For a typical Corn Belt production area, a new 100 million gallon ethanol plant would create 1,240 local jobs—perhaps as a much as a 1.2-percent addition to local employment.

8. Financial well-being of farm operator households. ERS researchers developed detailed information on the financial well-being of farm operator households based on Farm Costs and Returns Survey data. In 1990, the average household income for farm operator ~~households from all~~ sources was $39,000, which is comparable to the average U.S. household. About 90 percent of farm operator households received some income from off-farm sources, and many operators spent the majority of their work effort in off-farm occupations. A substantially larger percentage of farm operator households than all U.S. households were in lower income categories. On the other hand, another important indicator of financial well-being, net worth, shows that most farm operator households have significant net worth. Nearly three-quarters of U.S. farms are small farms, with gross sales of less than $50,000. These farms typically lose money, but their operators earn more income off the farm than other farm operator households. Operators of small farms are more likely to be older and have a nonfarm major occupation than are other operators. As farm size increases, average net farm incomes increase significantly. Household incomes also increased as the educational attainment of farm operators increased. Educational attainment was strongly associated with the participation in off-farm employment of both farm operators and their spouses.

THURSDAY, FEBRUARY 18, 1993.

NATIONAL AGRICULTURAL STATISTICS SERVICE

WITNESSES

KEITH J. COLLINS, ACTING ASSISTANT SECRETARY FOR ECONOMICS, DEPARTMENT OF AGRICULTURE

DONALD M. BAY, ACTING ADMINISTRATOR AND DEPUTY ADMINISTRATOR FOR OPERATIONS, NATIONAL AGRICULTURAL STATISTICS SERVICE

RICHARD D. ALLEN, DEPUTY ADMINISTRATOR FOR PROGRAMS, AND CHAIRPERSON OF THE AGRICULTURAL STATISTICS BOARD, NATIONAL AGRICULTURAL STATISTICS SERVICE

FRED S. BARRETT, DIRECTOR, STATE STATISTICAL DIVISION, NATIONAL AGRICULTURAL STATISTICS SERVICE

STEPHEN B. DEWHURST, BUDGET OFFICER, DEPARTMENT OF AGRICULTURE

Mr. DURBIN. Our next panel is from the National Agricultural Statistics Service. Mr. Collins remains at the table, with Mr. Dewhurst. Joining them are, Donald Bay, Acting Administrator and Deputy Administrator for Operations; Richard Allen, Deputy Administrator for Programs and Chairperson of the Agricultural Statistics Board; and Fred Barrett, Director of the State Statistical Division.

Mr. Bay.

OPENING STATEMENT

Mr. BAY. Thank you, Mr. Chairman, Members of the Subcommittee. I appreciate this opportunity to appear before you and discuss the National Agricultural Statistics Program. I would like to summarize the comments that were submitted to the Committee, if I may be permitted to do that.

Mr. DURBIN. Please do. It would be most appreciated.

Mr. BAY. The National Agricultural Statistics Service, or NASS, as we have become known recently, has developed over the past 130 years. We do trace back to Abraham Lincoln, Springfield, Illinois, Mr. Chairman.

Mr. DURBIN. You know that makes points with me.

Mr. SKEEN. He knew that.

Mr. BAY. During this long period of 130 years, we have developed what we feel like is a very admirable program of providing accurate, timely, and, most importantly, impartial statistics about the Nation's agriculture and the entire food industry.

The Crop and Livestock Estimating Program is carried out as a State/Federal cooperative program to minimize costs, eliminate duplication, and reduce the burden on those that report to us—farmers and agricultural businesses. The States provide resources to support local estimates, county estimates, and special State programs.

This past year, NASS celebrated, with the State Departments of Agriculture, 75 years of the State and Federal cooperative program, with a special celebration in Madison, Wisconsin, where it all started.

Today, all 50 States operate under cooperative agreements, and over half of our field offices are collocated with their State cooperators.

Although State budgets have come under tremendous pressure recently, we have been very fortunate that the priority for agricultural statistics has remained uppermost in most States' budgets, and we have maintained strong support from our State cooperators.

Let's look at the basic program of NASS statistics. We feel like we provide a level playing field for those who are producers, processors, and consumers in the food chain, with our estimates that cover over 120 different crops and 45 different livestock poultry items.

NASS data are also used to help administer the farm program. Our price estimates, which many of you know, come under great scrutiny because they are used for computing deficiency payments. Crop production and stocks data are used as part of the supply statistics by the World Board that help the Department develop the set-aside requirements.

The crop yield and price data are used to administer disaster programs. Some of you are familiar with the Minnesota/Wisconsin price estimates that are used as part of the Dairy Price Program.

Recently, and it has already been discussed by Dr. Lee, NASS has become very much involved with collecting environmental statistics since the beginning of the Food Safety and Water Quality Programs. We now have current, reliable pesticide usage information available for all major field crops, and most fruits and vegetables produced in the United States.

Recently, a representative of the Food and Drug Administration was in a meeting at the USDA and commented that in 1988, the U.S. Congress passed a law requiring other countries that exported food to the United States to provide statistics on what chemicals were being applied to those crops. He said it was rather embarrassing because they would often come back to FDA and say, "where are the figures for the United States on their food commodities that they export?" And the U.S. did not have them. Today, because of the reports that we now have, the Food and Drug Administration is able to provide figures on what chemicals are applied to most food commodities that we export.

NASS has been a leader in developing improved methods for collecting agricultural statistics through a very strong statistical research program. The diversity and specialization that exists today in agricultural production complicates the sampling procedures required to produce accurate estimates.

Think about it. Years ago, when we had many more farms and they were very similar in nature, a very small sample survey of farms collecting information on milk production and corn and soybeans and other crops that they produced was all that was needed to have good estimates of year-to-year change.

Today, with the specialization that we face, there are many more commodities being produced in the United States, which is evident in the supermarket, and when you estimate most of these commodities, you have to get information from certain large producers, or your figures are not credible. This has really changed the nature of how we operate—we can't go out and do small random surveys of all farmers and be able to handle today's estimates. We have to structure our surveys to the specific commodities that we are estimating.

NASS does considerable survey work for other USDA agencies. We do work for ERS and many other agencies within the Department, and also work with the EPA and do some survey work for them.

We provide technical assistance on a reimbursable basis to a number of foreign countries, most recently Poland and Bulgaria, in trying to help them develop their agricultural statistics in this transition period.

Finally, NASS holds hearings every year around the country to find out what our data users and the people who report to us are interested in, what changes we need to make, and what we can eliminate, and what we should add. These meetings are very useful to us to keep our program relevant in today's changing world.

That completes my summary. I would be happy to take any questions.

[CLERK'S NOTES.—Mr. Bay's biography appears on page 114. Mr. Barrett's biography appears on page 115. The Acting Administrator's prepared statement appears on pages 116 through 121. The budget justifications, which were received on May 10, 1993, appear on pages 122 through 140.]

ORGANIZATION AND EFFICIENCY

Mr. DURBIN. Mr. Bay, let me follow up on a question that Mr. Pastor asked Dr. Lee. Tell me what your thoughts are on the difference in mission between your agency and the Economic Research Service. Is there any way to bring these agencies together, or other related agencies, so that we eliminate any kind of overlap and perhaps have a more efficient operation?

Mr. BAY. Well, Mr. Chairman, I was here when we were combined with ERS in 1977 through 1981. From NASS's standpoint, it took about a million dollars of our program money to support the additional hierarchy that was established to bridge those two organizations together.

Mr. DURBIN. So you had a third group created.

Mr. BAY. Yes, a third group was created to bridge them together. In fact, we took a budget cut to be separated back out as a separate agency, as a savings. There was a savings of $768,000.

Mr. DURBIN. We sure have a way about us when it comes to becoming more efficient.

Let me ask you this, aside from the fact that there was a new administrative layer created, what about the missions of the two agencies? Are they consistent? Can they work in the same room? Do they complement one another?

AGENCY MISSION

Mr. BAY. We collect the basic statistics, and they enhance the value of those statistics by doing the analysis and providing them to the public in such a way that it means more to the users. But it really is two steps. And they are not that much involved in the basic surveys.

You know, we put out over 400 reports a year, and we cooperate directly with ERS on very few of those. Of course, there is cooperation with ERS on the environmental and the farm income surveys. Most of that cooperation, we do for them on a reimbursable basis, not as a joint effort, but as a service to them like we service other agencies within USDA.

PESTICIDE DATA PROGRAM

Mr. DURBIN. At last year's hearing, you stated that you were planning to conduct a marketing channel survey, jointly funded by you and ERS, which would collect chemical use data on commodities between the farm and retail outlets. Were you able to begin this survey? What have you discovered?

Mr. BAY. A pilot survey to determine chemical usage on grapefruit after leaving the orchard was conducted during 1992 and a published report is to be released by ERS about April 1, 1993. Similar surveys covering other commodities were intended to be part of the 1993 Pesticide Data Program but were not begun because they were not funded in FY 1993.

Mr. DURBIN. Under the pesticide use data program, you alternate chemical use surveys annually between vegetables and fruits and nuts. In fiscal year 1991, you conducted a chemical use survey in five States, which produce 80 percent of the entire country's vegetable supply. You are scheduled to do this survey again during fiscal year 1993. Will you expand the survey to include more States and/or additional crops?

Mr. BAY. The Vegetable Chemical usage survey for fiscal year 1993 will include 14 States—AZ, CA, FL, GA, IL, MI, MN, NJ, NY, NC, OR, TX, WA, WI—and 30 commodities. Results are to be published in June 1993.

Mr. DURBIN. Specifically, what other agencies use the data you collect through the pesticide data program and how do they use this information?

Mr. BAY. The Environmental Protection Agency uses the pesticide usage data for reviews associated with re-registration of chemicals.

The Agricultural Marketing Service uses the pesticide use data to help determine which chemicals residue tests need to be included on specific fruits and vegetables.

The U.S. Geological Survey uses pesticide usage data in determining the relationship between water quality and agricultural chemical usage in different geographical regions throughout the country.

The Economic Research Service analyzes pesticide usage and cultural practice data to determine the impact various regulations and production practices will have on the economics of crop production.

The Extension Service uses the NASS pesticide usage data as an important input to the National Agricultural Pesticide Impact Assessment Program.

The Food and Drug Administration uses NASS chemical usage data to identify specific pesticides to test for in its laboratory analyses. FDA can now provide U.S. data that conforms to the data the United States requires from other countries under the Pesticide Monitoring Act of 1988.

Mr. DURBIN. What is the status of the implementation of the agricultural pesticide use information data base?

Mr. BAY. All pesticide use reports published by NASS are available in electronic media. The pesticide use data base has been populated with most of the results of the FY 1991 surveys. All 1991 and 1992 pesticide data should be loaded and a menu of standard retrieval selections created by the end of calendar year 1993.

MINNESOTA-WISCONSIN MILK PRICE SERIES

Mr. DURBIN. What is the status of the Department-wide Minnesota-Wisconsin competitive milk price series and what is your role in this issue?

Mr. BAY. NASS continues to collect data on the average prices paid to producers for manufacturing Grade B milk in Minnesota and Wisconsin. NASS agreed to continue providing the Minnesota-Wisconsin, M-W, price estimates for AMS until an alternative survey or pricing system could be put in place. AMS is studying alternatives to the M-W price series and has asked NASS to conduct a price survey of Grades A & B milk used for manufacturing in Minnesota and Wisconsin. AMS is close to issuing an initial recommended alternative to the M-W price series. AMS expects to announce a final decision this summer after reviewing comments on the initial proposal. The only NASS role is to collect the price information AMS specifies.

INTERNATIONAL ASSISTANCE

Mr. DURBIN. Last year you provided the Committee with a table showing the breakout of technical assistance provided to other countries for fiscal year 1991. Would you please provide us with a similar table for fiscal year 1992?

Mr. BAY. I will provide a table listing the countries involved in our technical assistance efforts for the record.

[The information follows:]

NATIONAL AGRICULTURAL STATISTICS SERVICE INTERNATIONAL TECHNICAL ASSISTANCE FISCAL YEAR 1992

[Dollars in Thousands]

Country—Type of Assistance	Resources	
	Amount	Staff-years
Bulgaria—Short-term statistical consulting	17	0.2
Cameroon—Long-term statistical consulting	76	.7
Colombia—Short-term statistical consulting	7	.1
Egypt—Short- and long-term statistical consulting	143	1.3
Honduras—Long-term statistical consulting	36	.3
Hungary—Short-term statistical consulting	3	.1
Kenya—Short-term statistical consulting	7	.1
Morocco—Short-term statistical consulting	23	.3
Nicaragua—Short-term statistical consulting	4	.1
Pakistan—Short- and long-term statistical consulting	188	1.7
Poland—Short-term statistical consulting	19	0.2

Mr. DURBIN. Have any of the newly independent States of the former Soviet Union requested any assistance?

Mr. BAY. The agency has received an official request for assistance from Armenia. There have been informal comments from statistical agency personnel of several other states of the former Soviet Union indicating help will be needed in developing agricultural data systems to meet new situations in their countries, but no official requests have been received as of this date.

RESTRICTED USE PESTICIDES

Mr. DURBIN. Mr. Bay, section 1491 of the 1990 Farm Bill requires that all certified applicators of restricted use pesticides maintain records of usage. I understand an agreement between you and EPA has been worked out and that you planned to conduct a pilot study of restricted use pesticide applicators in the State of New Hampshire during fiscal year 1992. What is the status of this project?

Mr. BAY. The pilot study was conducted in Arizona rather than New Hampshire because Arizona had been included in earlier fruit and vegetable chemical use surveys conducted by NASS. This historical survey data will be used to make comparisons to applicator records required by the State. The Arizona Department of Agriculture, AMS, and NASS are cooperating on this study.

The study will also provide information on current pesticide records, including formats used, whole farm usage information, and how different certifications are recorded.

Mr. DURBIN. What has EPA done with respect to this provision?

Mr. BAY. EPA and NASS established a Memorandum of Understanding which specified that NASS would be responsible for providing reports of agricultural restricted use pesticides and EPA would be responsible for reports of non-agricultural restricted use pesticides. It was our understanding that EPA planned to begin a survey of non-agricultural applicators in 1992.

Mr. DURBIN. These reports were to be made annually to Congress. Has a report been submitted to date? If so, what did it say?

Mr. BAY. A NASS report of restricted use pesticides used in agriculture was provided to Congress and other data users last December. The report contained a summary of federally restricted use pesticides applied on the major fruits, nuts, vegetables, and field crops in the United States. The summary included pesticide rates, application rates, acres treated, and number of applications by chemical by crop for the years 1990 and 1991. The report extracted information on restricted use pesticides from the other NASS agricultural chemical usage reports.

LIST FRAME COVERAGE BY AREA FRAME SURVEY

Mr. DURBIN. What were the results of the area frame survey you conducted in fiscal year 1992?

Mr. BAY. One of the many important by-products of the area frame survey is that it measures the incompleteness of the NASS farm list. The survey conducted in 1992 indicated that the NASS farm list now covers 81 percent of all land in farms.

The opportunity and effort expended in recent years to improve the NASS list frame has paid dividends not just in greater coverage, but also in the removal of duplication, which can be even more detrimental to survey results than lack of coverage. The more complete and accurate a list, the greater the sampling efficiency, which improves data quality and lowers survey costs. To that effect, NASS is working closely with the Agricultural Stabilization and Conservation Service (ASCS) in a major list improvement effort.

STATE/INDUSTRY MATCHING FUNDS

Mr. DURBIN. If a state and/or industry wants you to conduct a specific survey, are they required to provide matching funds?

Mr. BAY. NASS has only limited funds available to match with other organizations to conduct special fruit tree inventory surveys. Otherwise, State and/or industry special survey requests would require full reimbursement to NASS. In addition, for NASS to undertake special surveys, they would need to meet NASS statistical standards, provide useful information not already available, and individual reported data would remain confidential and the property of NASS.

TECHNICAL ASSISTANCE TO ACS

Mr. DURBIN. Did you provide technical assistance to ACS during fiscal year 1992 for their data processing conversion efforts? Will this assistance continue into fiscal year 1993?

Mr. BAY. ACS has successfully converted their mainframe based system to local personal computers. The agreement for fiscal year 1992 included reimbursement of $20,000 for technical assistance during the conversion. Since the conversion is now complete we do no expect to provide additional technical assistance to ACS in the futture.

REMOTE SENSING

Mr. DURBIN. The Delta Remote Sensing Project uses satellite data to estimate specific crop acreage. This project was initiated in 1991 in the Mississippi Delta regions of Arkansas and Mississippi, and was expected to be expanded to include Louisiana in 1992. Did this in fact occur?

Mr. BAY. Yes, Louisiana was added in 1992, which completed the project for the three Delta States.

Mr. DURBIN. Last year, you stated that the sampling efficiency gain from this project was four times better when compared to using ground survey only data. Is using satellite data more cost-efficient when compared to the benefits?

Mr. BAY. When optimum satellite coverage is available and linked with accurate ground survey data, such as in 1991, the benefits are cost-efficient compared to other alternatives and a four-fold increase in the degree of precision is attainable. However, efficiency gains can change as the extent of cloud cover during key Landsat satellite passes varies considerably from year to year.

Mr. DURBIN. Do you plan to expand the use of remote sensing to other States?

Mr. BAY. We do not plan to expand the use of Landsat remote sensing to other States at this time. Since there has been a delay in the planned launch of Landsat 6 until August 1993, the satellite data coverage for 1993 may be quite limited. We are limiting the project to the State of Arkansas for 1993, using it as a State level prototype. We will add the use of the National Oceanic and Atmospheric Administration's Advanced Very High Resolution Radiometer data to the project this year. Prospects for its coverage remain excellent.

Mr. DURBIN. What is your relationship with the World Agricultural Outlook Board with regards to satellite imaging?

Mr. BAY. The World Agricultural Outlook Board coordinates the Department's remote sensing activities by chairing the Remote Sensing Coordination Committee. NASS is an active member of the committee and thus shares knowledge and techniques with other USDA agencies.

SHEEP AND GOAT PREDATOR LOSS SURVEY

Mr. DURBIN. You perform a special survey on the number and economic values of sheep and lambs killed by predators. What is the cost of this survey and how is this information used?

Mr. BAY. We did conduct a survey of sheep and lamb losses due to predators as part of our January 1991 Livestock Survey and the results were published in the Sheep and Goat Predator Loss Report released on April 24, 1991.

This study was undertaken at the request of the Animal Damage Control Unit in the Animal Plant and Health Inspection Service APHIS. Funding of $120,000 was provided to NASS through a reimbursable agreement. This information documents the extent, location, and magnitude of wildlife damage and is used by APHIS to better target its control and technical assistance programs.

LAN INSTALLATION

Mr. DURBIN. Have you completed the installation of LAN's in all field offices?

Mr. BAY. Yes, in February 1992, NASS installed the last field office LAN. In July 1992, we installed the Washington, D.C. LAN. By March 1993, NASS expects to interconnect all LAN's together in a Wide Area Network.

Mr. DURBIN. How has the installation of the LAN's affected your use of the Martin Marietta mainframe?

Mr. BAY. Initially, mainframe usage increased because LAN's provided all field offices with improved on-line access to maintain their list universe. However, some recent offsetting savings in mainframe processing were captured by converting several mainframe systems to run on the LAN. NASS staff are actively reviewing other systems that might be transferred from the mainframe.

NASS is also in the initial phase of developing a prototype of a LAN-based client/server data base management system. If successful, the new data base management system will provide the capability to significantly reduce mainframe usage by converting our major farm lists to the LAN environment.

HISTORICAL ESTIMATES DATA BASE

Mr. DURBIN. What is the status of the completion of loading all historical estimates into a data base?

Mr. BAY. One of the goals of NASS is to maintain all published estimates in a data base in order to answer public inquiries for historical data. Currently, State and U.S. level data for 82 commodities have been loaded to the Published Estimates Data Base. Some series date back to 1866. Loading all remaining historical series will require another year to complete. File formats are being restructured for some commodities to simplify data loading and extracting.

County-level data are available for the years 1972–91 for 16 farm commodities. The county data files were reviewed extensively last year for data validity. The preparation and loading of these data takes place in the spring, following the year of production.

DISCONTINUED REPORTS

Mr. DURBIN. Did you discontinue any reports during fiscal year 1992, and do you plan to discontinue any reports during fiscal year 1993. If so, please list these reports for the record, showing the frequency of the report, the total number of copies printed each year, and the reason for discontinuing.

Mr. BAY. NASS discontinued the "Sugar Market Statistics" report in fiscal year 1992. Responsibility for compiling and issuing this report shifted from NASS to ASCS. NASS had been printing and issuing the report four times each year, printing 6,100 copies annually.

During fiscal year 1993, NASS will discontinue the monthly "Celery" report. We had been printing 11,600 copies of the "Celery" report annually. In the future, celery data will be published in our periodic "Vegetables" reports. The preliminary "Farm Production Expenditures" report will be discontinued, saving the printing of 1,300 copies. We will reduce the frequency of two other reports this fiscal year. The "Farm Labor" report will change from monthly to quarterly, saving the printing of 16,800 copies. The "Vegetables" report will be reduced from 14 to 6 issues, saving the printing of 7,900 copies. These reports were eliminated to permit NASS to stay within its fiscal year 1993 funding authority.

USER FEES

Mr. DURBIN. Please list for the record all reports that are on a user fee basis and indicate the fee for each report.

Mr. BAY. Reports are available for a fee from NASS Headquarters and the State offices. Farmers and other respondents to our surveys, news media, congressional offices, and other Federal agencies receive requested reports without charge. I will provide, for the record, order forms which list the Agricultural Statistics Board publications and associated fees.

[The information follows:]

National Agricultural Statistics Service Order Form

Periodical Title	Order #	1 Year	2 Years	3 Years
Field Crop Reports				
Crop Production (monthly plus annual *Summary* plus annual *Prospective Plantings* and *Acreage* and *Winter Wheat and Rye Seedings*)	PCP	__ $42	__ $82	__ $122
Crop Progress (weekly, April through November)	PCR	__ $41	__ $80	__ $119
Grain Stocks (quarterly)	PGS	__ $17	__ $32	__ $47
Hop Stocks (March and September)	PHS	__ $13	__ $24	__ $35
Peanut Stocks and Processing (monthly)	PPS	__ $22	__ $42	__ $62
Potato Stocks (6 issues plus annual *Potatoes*)	PPO	__ $18	__ $34	__ $50
Rice Stocks (quarterly)	PRS	__ $15	__ $28	__ $41
Cotton Ginnings (13 issues plus *Annual*)	PCG	__ $25	__ $48	__ $71
Fruit, Nut, and Vegetable Reports				
Almond Production (annual)	ZAL	__ $7	__ $12	__ $17
Cherry Production (annual)	ZCP	__ $7	__ $12	__ $17
Citrus Fruits (annual)	ZCF	__ $10	__ $18	__ $26
Cranberries (annual)	ZCR	__ $10	__ $18	__ $26
Hazelnut Production (annual)	ZFP	__ $7	__ $12	__ $17
Noncitrus Fruits and Nuts (2 issues)	PNF	__ $14	__ $26	__ $38
Pistachio Production (annual)	ZPP	__ $7	__ $12	__ $17
Walnut Production (annual)	ZWP	__ $7	__ $12	__ $17
Vegetables (5 issues plus annual *Summary*)	PVG	__ $18	__ $34	__ $50
Livestock Reports				
Cattle (2 issues plus monthly *Cattle on Feed*)	PCT	__ $22	__ $42	__ $62
Hogs and Pigs (quarterly)	PHP	__ $15	__ $28	__ $41
Livestock Slaughter (monthly plus annual *Summary*)	PLS	__ $27	__ $52	__ $77
Meat Animals: Production, Disposition, and Income (annual)	ZMA	__ $10	__ $18	__ $26
Sheep and Goats (annual plus *Wool and Mohair* and 3 issues of *Sheep and Lambs on Feed*)	ZSG	__ $18	__ $34	__ $50
Poultry Reports				
Broiler Hatchery (weekly)	PBH	__ $52	__ $102	__ $152
Egg Products (monthly)	PEP	__ $21	__ $40	__ $59
Eggs, Chickens, and Turkeys (monthly plus *Hatchery Production* and *Layers and Egg Production, Poultry: Production and Value* and *Turkeys*)	PEC	__ $35	__ $68	__ $101
Turkey Hatchery (monthly)	PTH	__ $21	__ $40	__ $59
Poultry Slaughter (monthly)	PPY	__ $22	__ $42	__ $62
Dairy Reports				
Dairy Products (monthly plus *Summary*)	PDP	__ $25	__ $48	__ $71
Milk Production (monthly plus annual *Milk Production, Disposition, and Income*)	PMP	__ $22	__ $42	__ $62
Price and Expenditure Reports				
Agricultural Prices Monthly (monthly)	PAP	__ $28	__ $54	__ $80
Agricultural Prices Annual (annual)	ZAP	__ $12	__ $22	__ $32
Farm Production Expenditures (July and August)	PFP	__ $14	__ $26	__ $38
Crop Values (annual)	ZCV	__ $11	__ $20	__ $29
Prices Received, Minnesota-Wisconsin Manufacturing Grade Milk (annual)	ZPR	__ $10	__ $18	__ $26

SUBTOTAL (please add to total on other side of order form) ______

National Agricultural Statistics Service Order Form

Periodical Title	Order #	1 Year	2 Years	3 Years
Other Reports				
Agricultural Chemical Usage (March and June)	PCU	__ $17	__ $32	__ $47
Catfish Processing (monthly plus Catfish Production)	PCP	__ $25	__ $48	__ $71
Cold Storage (monthly plus *Summary* and *Capacity of Refrigerated Warehouses*)	PCS	__ $27	__ $52	__ $77
Farm Labor (quarterly)	PFL	__ $15	__ $28	__ $41
Farm Numbers and Land in Farms (annual)	ZFL	__ $10	__ $18	__ $26
Floriculture Crops (annual)	ZFC	__ $12	__ $22	__ $32
Honey (annual)	ZHO	__ $10	__ $18	__ $26
Trout Production (annual)	ZTP	__ $10	__ $18	__ $26
NASS Historical Data				
Cattle: Final Estimates 1984-88	SB-798	__ $11		
Chickens and Eggs: Final Estimates 1984-87	SB-801	__ $11		
Citrus Fruits: Final Estimates 1981-82 Crop, 1986-87 Crop	SB-796	__ $ 8		
Crop Values: Final Estimates 1982-87	SB-818	__ $11		
Farm Employment and Wage Rates: 1910-90	SB-822	__ $14		
Farms and Land in Farms: Final Estimates 1979-87	SB-792	__ $ 4		
Field Crops: Final Estimates 1982-87	SB-783	__ $11		
Hogs and Pigs: Final Estimates 1983-87	SB-797	__ $ 8		
Meat Animals, Production, Disposition and Income: Final Estimates 1983-87	SB-805	__ $ 8		
Milk: Final Estimates 1983-87	SB-802	__ $11		
Noncitrus Fruit and Nuts: Final Estimates 1982-87	SB-809	__ $11		
Potatoes and Sweetpotatoes: Final Estimates 1982-87	SB-799	__ $ 8		
Poultry Production and Value: Final Estimates 1984-87	SB-806	__ $ 8		
Rice Stocks: Final Estimates 1978-88	SB-795	__ $ 8		
Sheep and Goats: Final Estimates 1984-88	SB-800	__ $ 8		
Stocks of Grains, Oilseeds and Hay: Final Estimates 1983-88	SB-794	__ $11		
Vegetables: Final Estimates 1982-87	SB-814	__ $11		

Subtotal from above	
Subtotal from other side	
Add 25% for shipment to foreign addresses (includes Canada)	
ORDER TOTAL	

Mail to: ERS-NASS
341 Victory Drive
Herndon, VA
22070

- Use purchase orders, checks drawn on U.S. banks, cashier's checks, or international money orders specifying U.S. funds.
- Make payable to ERS-NASS.
- 25-percent discount on 25 or more copies of a single report to a single address (Note: No refunds on bulk-discounted copies).

☐ Check here for a free subscription to *Reports*, a quarterly catalog describing the latest in NASS and ERS releases.

Payment method:

☐ Bill me. ☐ Enclosed is $ ________.

Credit card orders:

☐ MasterCard ☐ Visa Total charges $________.

Credit card number ☐☐☐☐☐☐☐☐☐☐☐☐☐☐☐☐ Expiration date ☐☐

Name ____________________

Organization ____________________

Address ____________________

____

City, State, Zip ____________________

Daytime phone ____________________

For *fastest* service, call our toll-free order desk at 1-800-999-6779
(in the U.S. and Canada; other areas, please call 703-834-0125).

CONSULTANTS

Mr. DURBIN. Have you employed any consultants during the past year, and if so, for what purposes?

Mr. BAY. NASS employed one contractor during fiscal year 1992. Synex Corporation conducted an evaluation and test of various client/server data based platforms and additional front end software tools. Synex is also developing a prototype of this relational data base system to run NASS's list frame on the LAN's.

COOPERATIVE AGREEMENTS

Mr. DURBIN. Would you please list for the record all cooperative agreements that were signed during fiscal year 1992, indicating the amount of each agreement as well as a description of the purpose of the agreement?

Mr. BAY. I will submit, for the record, a list of NASS Cooperative Agreements during fiscal year 1992.

[The information follows:]

COOPERATOR	AMOUNT	PURPOSE
National Association of State Departments of Agriculture	$18,000,000	Data Collection
Washington Department of Agriculture	45,000	Crop Reporting Services
Pennsylvania Department of Agriculture	11,500	Assistance in Dissemination of Crop and Livestock Reports
Michigan Department of Agriculture	5,000	Assistance in Dissemination of Crop and Livestock Reports
Nebraska Department of Agriculture	40,000	Assistance in Dissemination of Crop and Livestock Reports
New Mexico Department of Agriculture	4,500	Assistance in Dissemination of Crop and Livestock Reports
North Carolina Department of Agriculture	13,700	Assistance in Dissemination of Crop and Livestock Reports
Alabama Department of Agriculture	10,000	Assistance in Dissemination of Crop and Livestock Reports
Idaho Department of Agriculture	47,000	Assistance in Dissemination of Crop and Livestock Reports
Louisiana Department of Agriculture and Forestry	63,000	Assistance in Dissemination of Crop and Livestock Reports
Oklahoma Department of Agriculture	27,000	Assistance in Dissemination of Crop and Livestock Reports
Texas Department of Agriculture	20,000	Assistance in Dissemination of Crop and Livestock Reports
Maryland Department of Agriculture	40,400	Assistance in Dissemination of Crop and Livestock Reports
Oregon Department of Agriculture	10,000	Assistance in Dissemination of Crop and Livestock Reports
Colorado Department of Agriculture	3,000	Assistance in Dissemination of Crop and Livestock Reports
University of Houston - Clear Lake	50,000	Crop Acreage Research
Minnesota Department of Agriculture	30,000	Assistance in Dissemination of Crop and Livestock Reports

COOPERATOR	AMOUNT	PURPOSE
Illinois Department of Agriculture	42,000	Assistance in Dissemination of Crop and Livestock Reports
Iowa Department of Agriculture	16,000	Assistance in Dissemination of Crop and Livestock Reports
Kansas State Board of Agriculture	13,500	Assistance in Dissemination of Crop and Livestock Reports
Kentucky Department of Agriculture	10,000	Assistance in Dissemination of Crop and Livestock Reports
Tennessee Department of Agriculture	62,371	Crop Reporting Services
Virginia Department of Agriculture and Consumer Services	8,000	Crop Reporting Services
Georgia Department of Agriculture	48,000	Crop Reporting Services
Southern University	9,000	Cooperative Study Program
West Virginia Department of Agriculture	22,000	Crop Reporting Services
Wisconsin Department of Agriculture	50,000	Crop Reporting Services
New York Department of Agriculture	13,500	Crop Reporting Services
University of California	636,000	Computer Assisted Survey Services
Utah Department of Agriculture	4,500	Crop Reporting Services
Minnesota Department of Agriculture	70,000	Assistance in Dissemination of Crop and Livestock Reports
Purdue University, Agricultural Experiment Station	10,800	Crop Reporting Services
Louisiana State University	8,000	Crop Reporting Services
North Carolina State University	2,000	Weather and Crop Report Program
Hawaii Department of Agriculture	3,300	Crop Reporting Services

COOPERATOR	AMOUNT	PURPOSE
North Carolina Department of Agriculture	20,000	Computer Services
North Carolina Department of Agriculture	92,200	Crop Reporting Services
Mississippi Department of Agriculture	71,200	Crop Reporting Services
Maine Department of Agriculture	6,000	Crop Reporting Services
California Department of Food and Agriculture	50,000	Crop Reporting Services
University of Arkansas	30,500	Crop Reporting Services
University of Alaska, Cooperative Extension Service	11,106	Crop Reporting Services
American Statistical Association	140,000	Statistical Sampling
Iowa State University	50,000	Water Quality Survey
New Mexico State University	15,000	Indian Resource Development Program
New Jersey Department of Agriculture	90,000	Crop Reporting Services
New Mexico Department of Agriculture	4,000	Cooperative Study Program
Missouri Department of Agriculture	4,500	Crop Reporting Services
Total:	20,033,577	

FIELD USE OF LAPTOP COMPUTERS

Mr. DURBIN. What is the status of the project in California where electronic calipers and laptop computers are used to record and store almond measurements at the point of collection?

Mr. BAY. Data Collection, on a research basis, using calipers and laptop computers to record almond measurements, went smoothly in 1992. Experience from this project, coordinated with other research efforts using laptops, has helped to demonstrate the technical feasibility of using laptop computers for data collection in the field. We are in the process of testing a higher level integrated and interactive software package that should determine the scope of future activities.

CATFISH EXPORTS

Mr. DURBIN. How much processed catfish was exported in fiscal year 1992 and to whom?

Mr. BAY. Farm-raised processed catfish exported during calendar year 1992 totaled 221,000 pounds, 49 percent above the 148,000 pounds exported during 1991. Of the total exported during 1992, 33 percent went to Germany, 28 percent to the United Kingdom, 16 percent to Japan, 5 percent to Mexico, and the remaining 18 percent to all other countries.

FTS2000 COSTS

Mr. DURBIN. Please update the table that appears on page 214 of last year's hearing record regarding FTS2000 costs to include the 1992 actuals and the 1993 estimates.

Mr. BAY. NASS continues to benefit from the FTS2000 contract. Actual fiscal year 1992 expenditures were below last year's estimate because data communications did not switch to FTS2000 until August 1, 1992. The estimated increase in fiscal year 1993 reflects expected additional FTS2000 costs for data transmission following the successful installation of the data network last summer.

[The information follows:]

[Dollars in thousands]

Media	Fiscal year	Costs
FTS2000	1989	$1,382
FTS2000	1990	1,231
FTS2000	1991	678
FTS2000	1992	562
FTS2000	1993	(Est.) 830

FARMS AND LAND IN FARMS

Mr. DURBIN. What is the total number of farms operating in the U.S. and what is the acreage of land being farmed compared to total U.S. acreage?

Mr. BAY. The number of U.S. farms as of June 1, 1992, was 2,096,000. Land in farms totaled 980 million acres, which includes cropland, pasture, woodland that is part of the farm, and other land including the farmstead. The total land area in the United States is 2.27 billion acres.

DISASTER PAYMENT CALCULATIONS

Mr. DURBIN. In your opening statement, you say that you provide ASCS with data on crop yields and average market prices for 120 crops to be used for computation of disaster payments, but that there are over 1,000 other crops covered for which no official statistics exist. How are disaster payments calculated for those crops?

Mr. BAY. NASS is not specifically involved in the determination of the prices used for calculating disaster payments for these 1,000+ other crops you referenced. ASCS must rely on producer reported information or "expert" opinions if official estimates are not available.

ASSISTANCE TO CENSUS OF AGRICULTURE

Mr. DURBIN. How many NASS personnel are being used for the Census of Agriculture?

Mr. BAY. NASS currently has one person detailed full-time as a liaison with the Agriculture Division of the Bureau of the Census. Later this year, each State office will provide two senior agricultural statisticians to the Agriculture Division for at least one week. These NASS statisticians will use their State knowledge and experience to identify possible omissions or duplications before the results of the census are published. A similar review process has been utilized by the Census Bureau for at least the last eight Agricultural Censuses.

REIMBURSABLE SURVEYS

Mr. DURBIN. Provide a list, for the record, of all surveys done on a reimbursable basis.

Mr. BAY. I will provide, for the record, a list of all survey work done on a reimbursable basis in FY 1992.

[The information follows:]

NATIONAL AGRICULTURAL STATISTICS SERVICE
Reimbursable Surveys FY 1992

Source	Project
Agricultural Marketing Service	Milk Price Data
Animal and Plant Health Inspection Service	National Animal Health Monitoring System
Animal and Plant Health Inspection Service	Animal Damage Control
Agricultural Stabilization and Conservation Service	Feed Grain County Estimates
Economic Research Service	Cropping Practices
Economic Research Service	Farm Costs and Returns
Economic Research Service	Farm and Rural Land market
Economic Research Service	Land Use Data
Economic Research Service	Land Values
Economic Research Service	Water Quality Service
Economic Research Service	Area Studies
Economic Research Service	Chemical Use and Farm Financial Survey
Economic Research Service	Post Harvest Survey
Economic Research Service	Wool Stocks
Federal Crop Insurance Corporation	County Estimates
Forest Service	Grazing Fees
World Agricultural Outlook Board	Wool and Mohair
Environmental Protection Agency	Environmental Monitoring and Assessment Program
Department of Interior, Bureau of Land Management	Grazing Fees
Department of Labor, Bureau of Labor Statistics	Immigration Reform and Control Act
State Departments of Agriculture	Crop reporting services

SHEEP ON FEED SURVEY

Mr. DURBIN. Included in last year's appropriation were funds to conduct a sheep-on-feed report. Provide the Committee with a status of this report, including total cost, industry support, type of information provided, how the information is used and by whom.

Mr. BAY. The sheep-on-feed program developed though consultation with industry leaders will include an expanded January 1 survey plus new March 1 and November 1 sheep-on-feed surveys. The expanded January 1 survey has been completed and data collection and processing costs were $46,000. It is estimated that the March 1 and November 1 surveys will cost an additional $33,000. Although the total annual cost may exceed the $63,000 appropriation for this year, these expenses are expected to be within the appropriated funding once start-up costs are eliminated. The first report was issued on January 1, 1993, showing inventory of sheep and lambs on feed for the slaughter market by three weight groups. This report included the 16 major lamb feeding States that account for about 85 percent of the U.S. total. Separate estimates were provided for those in dry-lot and on pasture. These data are important to data users in forecasting sheep and lamb slaughter and to the sheep industry to maintain orderly marketing patterns.

Mr. DURBIN. Does the industry contribute any funding for these surveys?

Mr. BAY. The sheep industry does not contribute any funding for the sheep on feed survey program. The surveys are done entirely with appropriated funds.

Mr. DURBIN. Thank you very much.

Mr. Skeen?

Mr. SKEEN. Thank you, Mr. Chairman.

Mr. Bay, I understand that you stress the timeliness of your responses.

Mr. BAY. Yes, sir.

RESPONSE BURDEN

Mr. SKEEN. You have been doing some work to address response burdens for agricultural producers. How does that work?

Mr. BAY. We have tried to integrate a lot of our surveys into single surveys to reduce the burden. We have also tried to model data where we can. You know we try to avoid going to the same person 12 times a year and asking them the same questions.

Mr. SKEEN. Having been in agriculture 30 years, I can tell you it gets a little onerous. You feel compelled to respond to the statistical inquiries, but then if you get a multitude of forms, we want to just toss them, and forget about them.

Mr. BAY. We try to rotate our samples as frequently as we can to try to avoid that. There are certain operations that are large or unique and if you are going to make an estimate on that particular commodity and have reliable statistics, you almost have to contact those operations and find out what they have.

Mr. SKEEN. Do you have good cooperation?

Mr. BAY. We have excellent cooperation.

Mr. SKEEN. Do you receive suggestions from agriculture producers on how to incorporate savings and cut down on the response time on your statistical inquires?

Mr. BAY. We get lots of suggestions from the public on how things could be done.

Mr. SKEEN. They are not a bashful group.

Mr. BAY. No, they are not.

STATE COOPERATION

Mr. SKEEN. You cooperate with 45 States' statistical offices.

Mr. BAY. Those 45 offices are our offices.

Mr. SKEEN. They are your offices, but you also cooperate with the State Departments of Agriculture.

Mr. BAY. That is correct.

STATE FUNDING

Mr. SKEEN. I know they are under economic stress as well. How are States keeping up with their part of the contribution?

Mr. BAY. Very well. For example, we had one State that really got in trouble about three years ago, and we actually increased our assistance for that State because they felt like it was temporary. Now they have come back with their State funding so that we are able to continue that cooperative relationship.

Overall, we are receiving close to the same amount, which is around $12 million a year.

Mr. SKEEN. Twelve million dollars?

Mr. BAY. Right.

Mr. SKEEN. Would you give me a State by State——

Mr. BAY. We will put that in the record.

Mr. SKEEN. I would kind of appreciate having that.

[The information follows:]

The following is a list of State Cooperator funding in support of NASS and the agricultural statistics program in each State for 1990-1991 based on each State's respective fiscal year. These figures represent the sum total of value amounts applied for staff, office space, communications, survey work, vehicle use, etc.

STATE	COOPERATOR FUNDING 1990-91	1991-92
	($000)	
Alabama	74.6	73.9
Alaska	46.0	45.5
Arizona	46.7	47.3
Arkansas	49.4	66.9
California	1,668.5	1,384.1
Colorado	79.5	82.0
Delaware	29.5	29.7
Florida	1,191.7	1,378.4
Georgia	197.3	104.2
Hawaii	560.6	642.5
Idaho	44.4	39.5
Illinois	478.5	575.6
Indiana	192.8	184.5
Iowa	443.7	369.9
Kansas	283.1	285.9
Kentucky	165.2	155.5
Louisiana	90.8	90.8
Maryland	188.8	195.3
Michigan	330.6	458.3
Minnesota	416.4	307.7
Mississippi	200.5	225.3
Missouri	79.5	105.8
Montana	100.6	109.0
Nebraska	148.1	168.5
Nevada	22.7	22.7
New Hampshire	5.4	8.0
New Jersey	75.0	116.8
New Mexico	55.1	57.2
New York	975.2	995.2
North Carolina	1,686.2	1,770.0
North Dakota	72.6	73.4
Ohio	78.7	37.4
Oklahoma	170.0	175.9
Oregon	36.5	65.0
Pennsylvania	337.7	328.5
South Carolina	100.6	115.1
South Dakota	19.5	20.3
Tennessee	238.6	211.3
Texas	469.0	432.6
Utah	23.4	23.6
Virginia	134.6	110.9
Washington	153.3	164.7
West Virginia	100.2	114.2
Wisconsin	395.1	385.5
Wyoming	27.1	26.6
TOTAL	12,283.3	12,381.0

DATA COLLECTION COSTS

Mr. SKEEN. Last year you proposed an increase in the budget for data collection costs, covering part-time workers. Are you going to ask for that increase again?

Mr. BAY. I haven't seen the budget for NASS yet.

Mr. SKEEN. We haven't either. But I would be interested in knowing if you receive an increase because it has been a very important part of your statistical analysis in States like New Mexico with regard to part-time help.

RESTRICTED USE OF PESTICIDES

You have a Memorandum of Understanding with the EPA on restricted use of pesticides; is that correct?

Mr. BAY. That is correct.

Mr. SKEEN. How is that relationship working, with EPA?

Mr. BAY. I think it is working very well. They have commented at various hearings and meetings that they now use our data as the source of pesticide usage information.

Mr. SKEEN. They are not duplicative?

Mr. BAY. No.

Mr. SKEEN. Do they depend on your analysis or your data?

Mr. BAY. They have a monitoring program that you may be familiar with. It is called EMAP, which is being developed to collect or monitor the environment in all eco areas. There are seven eco areas. We are working with them in a cooperative relationship on the agricultural eco areas so there is no duplication.

Mr. SKEEN. How many other agencies use it?

Mr. BAY. We had a list——

Mr. SKEEN. A great number?

Mr. BAY. Yes, because we do it with a lot of land-grant universities.

Mr. SKEEN. How about other Federal agencies?

Mr. BAY. We do it with ASCS. We signed a Memorandum of Understanding recently with them. We do it a lot with ERS.

OVERPAYMENTS TO FARMERS

Mr. SKEEN. Over the past few years we have had some lengthy discussions with you about overpayments. The Inspector General was concerned that your agency needed to improve its data collection efforts. What has been the resolution on that?

Mr. BAY. The resolution was that the overpayment charge was primarily because of definitional differences. It wasn't because of a statistical error. We have resolved those definitional differences.

Mr. SKEEN. You have cleaned up all that?

Mr. BAY. We have cleaned it up.

Mr. SKEEN. I thank you.

Thank you, Mr. Chairman.

Mr. DURBIN. Thank you, Mr. Skeen.

Mr. Thornton?

Mr. THORNTON. Thank you, Mr. Chairman.

I want to congratulate you, Mr. Bay, on that excellent testimony.

Mr. Chairman, I don't have any questions of this witness.

Mr. DURBIN. Thank you, Mr. Thornton.

Mr. Walsh?

FARM SAFETY

Mr. WALSH. What, if anything, has NASS done in gathering statistics on farm safety?

Mr. BAY. NASS cooperated through reimbursable agreements in FY 1990 and FY 1991 with the University of Minnesota School of Public Health to conduct a regional Rural Injury Study. The survey collected data from farm households in Minnesota, Wisconsin, North Dakota, South Dakota, and Nebraska about both farm and nonfarm related injuries that occurred to all members of the farm household.

The results of the project are being used to calculate a variety of injury rates and identify potential risk factors that will enable targeting for specific intervention efforts.

Several recent surveys have been undertaken by NASS State Statistical Offices in Kansas, Minnesota, South Carolina, Washington, and Wisconsin to collect farm injury and exposure data identified by the sponsoring State agencies. NASS has been approached to develop national level statistics on farm or rural safety, but no resources have been identified to support this activity.

Mr. DURBIN. Thank you, Mr. Walsh.

Mr. Pastor?

STAFF PROFESSION

Mr. PASTOR. Good morning. If I were to ask what your principal occupation is or the occupation profession of your staff, what would it be?

Mr. BAY. Statisticians.

Mr. PASTOR. Would they be economists, by any chance?

Mr. BAY. Many of our statisticians like myself, at the time we went to school, majored in agriculture and minored in things like economics, but most of us only have bachelor's degrees. We are not really considered economists and we don't have Ph.D.s.

Because of the fact that there wasn't commonly a major in statistics many years ago, many of our older people did major in agricultural economics or agronomy or other agricultural fields. But we have supplemented that education with statistical training for those people, so that we really don't look at them as economists today; we look at them as statisticians.

NASS AND ERS MISSIONS

Mr. PASTOR. I am still not persuaded that the objective of your organization or that of the agency testifying earlier, which is to collect, analyze, and publish information, is needed by the farming community. Would you clarify the difference between your organization and the one appearing before you?

Mr. BAY. Kind of in chronological order, I think. We design surveys, collect the data and analyze them from a statistical standpoint, and then publish that information in a very timely manner, in a manner of 10 days or so from the time the survey was completed. That data then is made available not only to ERS but to all other economists in private industry and so forth to do their own analysis. After they do their analysis, ERS will come out with additional reports which bring into account demand and other economic factors which NASS is not involved in at all.

So I believe we are involved in a piece of the beginning of what ERS does, that of providing them some of the basic statistics that they need to do their analysis, but it is really a separate operation.

Mr. PASTOR. Would there be a benefit, without forming a third administrative function, to combine these two agencies? Basically, I am interested in one issue, how is the information that you produce so different from that developed by ERS and why is it necessary to have two separate entities working on related tasks?

Mr. BAY. I don't believe that the data that we produce are duplicated at all by ERS. They take the data that we produce—for example, another organization, the World Board, which puts out the supply and demand statistics, plugs in our supply figures for the U.S. in their report, and then they do all the other analysis that brings in the world and the demand side. But——

Mr. COLLINS. Do you mind if I——

Mr. BAY. You are getting into two agencies—

Mr. COLLINS. Maybe I can join this discussion, too.

Mr. PASTOR. Please do.

Mr. COLLINS. To pick up on what Don is saying, a lot of the work that is done in ERS focuses on understanding cause and effect in agriculture. It is relationships among agriculture. A lot of what NASS does is to acquire the raw data.

There may be a crops branch in NASS and a crops branch in ERS—entirely different functions, entirely different people. The crops branch in NASS is statisticians concerned with survey design, data collection, proper enumeration, and ultimately their product is by State, area planted, area harvested for each crop, production, and price received by farmers by surveying first buyers and so on.

That might be done by a person who specializes in wheat in NASS. There will be a wheat analyst in ERS who will then take that data to establish a relationship between the price of wheat, corn, milo, and the acreage planted. That estimated relationship will be used to project for 1993 what the wheat acreage and price will be, and from that come up with, say, a projected deficiency payment rate for wheat so that we can announce that rate prior to signup on March 1st.

The range of activities in ERS picks up from the NASS data, primarily establishing the functional relationships among the variables so that you can understand how if something happens in one area of the wheat economy, what the outcome will be in another area. That kind of analysis is really the foundation of policy analysis.

In addition to that, ERS does a wide range of things where they don't use NASS data. They have international trade analysts who use databases from other countries of the world, for example, and collect, compile, and evaluate that data.

A lot of the rural development work that is done, for example, a lot of the food consumption and food nutrition work that is done, really is not dependent upon NASS data. So there are many areas on the economic side unrelated to NASS. Those areas where there is a common point, it is really kind of a sequential thing.

Mr. PASTOR. I thank you for the explanation.

Mr. BAY. Could I just add one additional point here? I think one thing is very important, that NASS is independent of ERS from the standpoint that we are not projecting the future, and therefore we have no tendency to try to make the numbers fit with what we projected.

Mr. PASTOR. You are just collecting current data?

Mr. BAY. We just collect what has happened or what is out there right now. And we feel like to maintain our credibility, that we do not want to get into the forecasting business on prices and things like that.

Mr. PASTOR. Thank you, Mr. Chairman. I yield.

Mr. DURBIN. Thank you, Mr. Pastor.

I appreciate your testimony, Mr. Bay. We will be back in touch with you. Mr. Myers, do you have any questions?

COLLOCATION OF STATE OFFICES

Mr. MYERS. I have been rather quiet. Characteristically, of course.

Of the 24 co-located field offices, is there any effort being made to co-locate the other 21, and is there an economic advantage to do that?

Mr. BAY. It depends on our State cooperative relationship and whether they have space available for collocation.

Also, we are collocated in most of our other States with other USDA agencies. So we are collocated almost everywhere. In some cases, we are collocated with land grant universities. There are a few States that do not have State Departments of Agriculture.

FUNDS APPROPRIATED IN 1993

Mr. MYERS. Your fiscal year 1993 budget request was for $87 million. The Agriculture Appropriations Conference Report contained $81 million for the NASS in 1993. What projects were you unable to fund due to the shortfall?

Mr. BAY. The 1993 appropriation did not include any new initiatives planned for 1993. Therefore, the planned increase in the food safety program to expand chemical use survey coverage to more States, commodities, and in the marketing channel from the farm to the retail market were put on hold. NASS has not been able to provide restricted use pesticide data on livestock, pastures, and on other areas of the farm, as required by section 1491 of the Food, Agriculture, Conservation and Trade Act of 1990. Also NASS had to delay the development and implementation of an enhanced area sampling frame. To absorb pay costs for our staff and enumerators, NASS had to discontinue objective yield work in a few States and reduce the frequency of selected reports.

USDA FIELD OFFICE REORGANIZATION

Mr. MYERS. The NASS statistics program is conducted through 45 field offices throughout the nation. Would any of these offices be among those targeted for consolidation in USDA's proposals?

Mr. BAY. As of this date the USDA review of field office structure for NASS, as well as other similar agencies, has not made any specific recommendations which might affect our 45 field offices.

PESTICIDE DATA COLLECTION

Mr. MYERS. Both NASS and the Economic Research Service are projected to work on a pesticide data collection study this year. How are those two overlapping agencies working?

Mr. BAY. NASS does all the actual data collection and editing of pesticide survey data for both agencies and publishes the basic chemical usage statistics. ERS is provided the detailed farm level micro-data that include the basic chemical use information along with other economic and cultural practice data. These data are necessary to perform comprehensive policy analysis and economic studies on water quality and food safety issues. The survey specifications are developed jointly to create one survey instrument that serves the needs of both agencies. This system has worked well over the past few years without any duplication or overlapping work.

Mr. DURBIN. Thank you.

Mr. Bay, thank you for joining us.

[Mr. Bay's biographical sketch and prepared statement follow:]

BIOGRAPHICAL SKETCH

DONALD M. BAY
Acting Administrator
National Agricultural Statistics Service

Upon receiving his B.S. degree in Agricultural Economics in June 1957, Mr. Bay joined the National Agricultural Statistics Service (NASS) of the U.S. Department of Agriculture (USDA). He served in the Illinois and Tennessee State Statistical Offices prior to being transferred to Washington, D.C. in 1965. During the following 10 years, Mr. Bay was responsible for several national estimating programs including the livestock slaughter, sheep and wool, cattle, cotton, tobacco, peanuts, seed crops, etc.

From 1975 to 1987, he served as State Statistician in charge of the Missouri State Statistical Office. He served as Chairperson of the Missouri Agricultural Leaders Group and the Missouri Food and Agriculture Council. He was a senior staff member of the Missouri Department of Agriculture.

In 1988, he returned to Washington, D.C. to serve as Director of the Estimates Division. He was directly responsible for all of the Agency's estimating and forecasting programs.

In February 1990, he was appointed Deputy Administrator for Operations. This position includes the management responsibility for the State Statistical Division, Research and Applications Division, International Programs Office, and the Program Support Staff.

In April 1992, Mr. Bay became Acting Administrator due to the extended illness of the Administrator.

Mr. Bay has considerable experience with agricultural statistics programs in other countries. Beginning in 1972, he was the project leader of a NASS agricultural statistics development project in Thailand. As a result of this project, Thailand implemented a new area frame sampling program for collecting their annual agricultural statistics which is still being used in 1992. He led a delegation to the People's Republic of China in 1981, after participating in an economic and statistics exchange to China in 1980. He also provided technical assistance to Rwanda and Cameroon in Africa between 1985 and 1987.

Under a World Bank program, Mr. Bay worked with the agricultural statistics program in Brazil in 1990. In 1991, he initiated an agricultural statistics exchange with statisticians in the Ministry of Agriculture in Venezuela. Most recently, Mr. Bay visited Poland and Bulgaria and developed the framework for a more extensive exchange of agricultural statistics programs between the U.S. and these two countries.

February 1993

BIOGRAPHICAL SKETCH

FRED S. BARRETT, JR.
Director
State Statistical Division
National Agricultural Statistics Service

Mr. Barrett is a native of North Carolina where he grew up on a general crop and livestock farm. He is a graduate of North Carolina State University with a B.S. degree in Agricultural Economics.

He began work as a full-time agricultural statistician in our Alabama State Statistical Office in August 1963.

In September 1967 he was transferred to the South Carolina SSO.

In February 1971 he was promoted to a group leader in the Arkansas SSO where he had major responsibility for the data processing operation as well as crop production estimation.

In October 1973 he was transferred to Washington D.C. During the period 1973 to 1978, he had major responsibilities in designing and carrying out the national corn, cotton, and soybean objective yield surveys; multiframe cattle and hog surveys; as well as the June and December surveys. He made significant contributions toward the improvement of the nationwide land area frame and objective yield surveys for the Agency.

In mid-1978, he was detailed to the President's reorganization project of the Federal Statistical Systems and served as Assistant to the Executive Director, Dr. James T. Bonnen, Michigan State University. Following completion of this assignment, he returned to the Agency and was assigned to the Livestock Branch, Estimates Division, and had responsibility for the hog estimates.

In June 1980, he was chosen to lead our research work at the Johnson Space Center in Houston, Texas, as Program Support Supervisor of the Aerospace Remote Sensing Survey Project for Agriculture.

In 1982, he was selected as the State Statistician in charge of the Illinois State Statistical Office, and served in that leadership position until 1990.

In November 1990, he assumed his current position as Director, State Statistical Division in Washington, D.C. Headquarters.

February 1993

NATIONAL AGRICULTURAL STATISTICS SERVICE

Statement of Donald M. Bay, Acting Administrator, before the Subcommittee on Agriculture, Rural Development, Food and Drug Administration, and Related Agencies.

Mr. Chairman and members of the Committee, I appreciate the opportunity to appear before this Committee to discuss the National Agricultural Statistics Service (NASS). This Service exists to provide useful and timely statistics and other information about the Nation's food and agricultural industry.

Especially for the new members of the Committee, I would like to provide a brief historical background of this Service. In 1862 as the first Commissioner of the newly formed Department of Agriculture, Isaac Newton established an initial goal to "collect, arrange, and publish statistical and other useful agricultural information." One year later, in July, the Department's Division of Statistics issued the Nation's first official Crop Production report.

The structure of farming and the agricultural industry has changed dramatically during the succeeding 130 years. However, the need for having accurate, timely, and impartial statistical information on the Nation's agriculture has remained essential for supporting a market economy. The crop, livestock, and other estimates developed and published throughout the year, in cooperation with State Departments of Agriculture, are a major part of the public information available concerning current agricultural conditions.

NASS reports, either directly or indirectly, have an important impact on the entire population since the Nation's food industry affects our nutritional well being and the quality of the environment in which we live. Because of this importance, it is essential that NASS does not compromise the quality or integrity of its surveys.

All reports are made available to the public at previously announced release times. These reports are not only used to assess the supply and demand of agricultural commodities but are used for establishing agricultural policy decisions relating to farm program and disaster legislation, foreign trade, commodity programs, conservation programs, agricultural research, environmental programs, rural development, and many other related activities. NASS data are examined very closely and utilized by farmers, economists, and investors as they make decisions that have considerable economic impact.

Statistical research is conducted to improve the methods and techniques used in collecting and processing agricultural data. For example, NASS has become a leader in the development of the use of satellite imagery to improve agricultural statistics. NASS also performs an expanding number of statistical services for other Federal, State, and producer organizations on a reimbursable basis.

Major Activities of the National Agricultural Statistics Service (NASS)

The primary activities of NASS are the collection, summarization, analysis, and publication of reliable agricultural forecasts and estimates. Farmers, ranchers, and agribusinesses voluntarily respond to a series of nationwide surveys about their crops, livestock, prices, and other agricultural activities each year. Frequent surveys are required due to the perishable nature of many food products. These surveys are supplemented by actual field observations in which various plant counts and measurements are collected. Administrative data from other State and USDA agencies, as well as Census data, are thoroughly analyzed and utilized as appropriate. NASS prepares estimates for over 120 crops and 45 livestock items which are published annually in almost 400 reports. The World Agricultural Outlook Board utilizes NASS data for the U.S. portion of its reports as does the Economic Research Service (ERS) in its Situation and Outlook reports.

The agricultural production and marketing data that are developed and published by NASS include: number of farms and land in farms; acreage, yield, and production of grains, hay, oilseeds, cotton, tobacco, most important fruits and vegetables, floriculture, and other specialty crops; stocks of grains; inventories and production of hogs, cattle, sheep and wool, goats, catfish, trout, poultry, eggs, and dairy products; prices received by farmers; prices paid by farmers for inputs and services; cold storage supplies; agricultural labor and wage rates; agricultural chemical usage; and other data related to the agricultural economy.

The NASS agricultural statistics program is conducted through 45 field offices servicing all 50 States. All field offices operate under cooperative funding and 24 are collocated with their State Departments of Agriculture and/or Land-Grant universities. The joint State-Federal program helps meet the State and local agricultural data needs while minimizing overall costs by eliminating duplication of effort and reducing the reporting burden on farm and ranch operators.

NASS has developed a broad environmental statistics program under the Department's water quality and food safety programs. Until 1991 there was a complete void in the availability of recent, reliable pesticide usage data which was brought to light during the Alar situation. In cooperation with other USDA agencies, the Environmental Protection Agency, and the Food and Drug Administration, NASS has implemented comprehensive chemical usage surveys to correct this information void. In cooperation with ERS, detailed economic and cultural practice information is also collected for the purpose of determining the economics associated with different levels of chemical use.

For the years when a disaster program is authorized, NASS provides the Agricultural Stabilization and Conservation Service (ASCS) detailed data on crop yields and average market prices for the 120 crops for which estimates are available. Although these crop estimates cover a very high percentage of the cultivated land area in the United States, over a thousand other (mostly specialty) crops are currently covered under the disaster program for which there exists no official statistics on average yield or price.

NASS data on prices received by farmers are currently used by ASCS for the computation of deficiency payments provided under the 1990 Farm Bill. A small difference in price can amount to an over/under payment of millions of dollars. For example, a penny difference in the corn price estimate affects the amount paid by $60 million. NASS has instituted survey quality improvements in order to better ensure the accuracy of these price data.

A statistical research program is devoted to improving methods and techniques for obtaining agricultural statistics with an acceptable level of accuracy. The growing diversity and specialization of the Nation's farm universe has greatly complicated procedures to produce the agricultural statistics. The development of sophisticated sampling and survey methodology along with intensive use of computers have enabled NASS to keep up with an increasingly complex agricultural economy.

NASS works very closely with the Census Bureau of the Department of Commerce during the development, collection, and analysis of the Census of Agriculture every 5 years. Key NASS field and headquarters personnel are sworn in as actual Census employees to meet Census security procedures while they assist with detailed analysis to help make the published census data as accurate as possible.

NASS conducts a number of surveys on a reimbursable basis for USDA and other Federal, State, and private agencies or organizations. Conducting surveys and providing other statistical services on a reimbursable basis enables NASS to increase the productivity of its organization. It enables the cooperator to have access to additional technical resources and eliminates duplicate effort, thereby increasing efficiency while reducing respondent burden.

NASS provides consulting services for many USDA agencies on survey methodology, sample design, information resource management, and statistical analysis. This consulting may take a few hours or several years and is provided either gratis or on a fee basis depending on the scope of the project.

Technical assistance in cooperation with other Government agencies is provided on a cost-reimbursable basis to improve agricultural survey programs in other countries. Until recently, this program was primarily aimed at developing countries in Asia, Africa, Middle East and South America. However, a major effort is underway to assist Eastern and Central European countries during their transition period and NASS is prepared to assist the newly independent states of the former Soviet Union upon request. Having accurate information available as demonstrated in the United States is an essential ingredient to facilitate the orderly marketing of farm products in other countries.

NASS annually seeks input on data needs and priorities from the public through regional data user meetings with commodity groups, special briefings during the release of major reports, and numerous individual contacts. The Agency has made many adjustments in its program in response to suggestions by data users. Requests continue for expanded detail, wider geographic coverage, more frequent reports, new data series, and restoration of data series discontinued because of budget restrictions.

This concludes my statement, Mr. Chairman, and I will be happy to respond to your questions.

NATIONAL AGRICULTURAL STATISTICS SERVICE

Purpose Statement

The USDA published its first crop report in 1863, and further strengthened this responsibility in 1905 by creating the Crop Reporting Board (now the Agricultural Statistics Board). Today, the major responsibility for collecting and publishing current statistics on the Nation's agriculture is carried on by the National Agricultural Statistics Service (NASS). These responsibilities were authorized under the Agricultural Marketing Act of 1946 (7 U.S.C. 1621-1627).

NASS's unbiased statistics on agriculture keep all involved with America's biggest industry well informed, help provide the basic foundation necessary to keep agricultural markets stable and efficient, and help maintain a "level playing field."

NASS programs are conducted in the following major areas:

1. Agricultural Estimates. NASS State Statistical Offices regularly survey thousands of operators of farms, ranches, and agribusinesses who voluntarily provide information on a confidential basis. Consolidating these reports with field observations, objective yield measurements, and other data, statisticians then produce State estimates. These estimates are forwarded to NASS headquarters where they are combined and released to the press and public through the Agricultural Statistics Board. Annually, over 400 national reports are complemented with State reports that provide broad coverage of agriculture, including more than 120 crop and 45 livestock items.

2. Statistical Research and Service. Research is conducted to improve the statistical methods and techniques used in developing agricultural statistics. This research is directed toward improved quality and efficiency in sampling, data collection, and forecasting techniques.

3. Work Performed for Others. Services are performed for other Federal and State agencies and private commodity organizations on a reimbursable basis. These services consist primarily of conducting surveys and performing related data collection activities. They also include technical consultation, support, and assistance for international programs under participating agency service agreements.

The National Agricultural Statistics Service maintains a central office in Washington, D.C., and a network of 45 field offices, serving all 50 States, that operate through cooperative agreements with State Departments of Agriculture or universities. As of September 30, 1992, the Service had 1,098 permanent full-time employees and 64 part-time employees, including 392 full-time and 38 part-time employees in Washington, D.C.

NATIONAL AGRICULTURAL STATISTICS SERVICE

Available Funds and Staff-Years

1992 Actual and Estimated, 1993 and 1994

Item	1992 Actual Amount	1992 Actual Staff-Years	1993 Estimated Amount	1993 Estimated Staff-Years	1994 Estimated Amount	1994 Estimated Staff-Years
National Agricultural Statistics Service	$82,641,400	1,046	$81,004,000	1,040	$82,479,000	1,036
Obligations under Other USDA appropriations:						
Agricultural Cooperative Service for data processing	20,000	--	--	--	--	
Agricultural Marketing Service for consulting services and data on pesticides and milk prices	203,900	3	384,000	5	400,000	5
Animal and Plant Hnealth Inspection Service for animal health monitoring system and data on animal damage control	420,000	5	420,000	5	450,000	5
Agricultural Stabilization and Conservation Service (CCC) for data on feed grains, and wool and mohair stocks	100,000	1	110,000	1	100,000	1
Economic Research Service for data on chemical use and farm economics, cropping practices, farm costs and returns, farm and rural markets, land use, land values, farm real estate taxes, post harvest handling practices, water quality, and wool and mohair stocks	4,521,000	57	4,657,000	59	2,898,000	41
Federal Crop Insurance Corporation for acreage and yield production data on insured crops	645,000	9	670,000	9	950,000	15
Forest Service for data on grazing fees	40,000	--	40,000	--	40,000	--
Human Nutrition Information Service for consulting services	100,000	2	100,000	2	100,000	2
Office of Information Resource Management for personnel detail	12,480	--	--	--	--	

Item	1992 Actual Amount	1992 Staff-Years	1993 Estimated Amount	1993 Staff-Years	1994 Estimated Amount	1994 Staff-Years
Office of Operations for personnel detail	6,420	--	--	--	--	
Soil Conservation Service for liaison with 1890 colleges	--	--	65,000	--	65,000	--
World Agricultural Outlook Board for grain report, lockup support and data on wool and mohair stocks	12,566	--	7,000	--	7,000	--
Total, Other USDA Appropriations	6,081,366	77	6,453,000	81	5,010,000	69
Total, Agriculture Appropriations	88,722,766	1,123	87,457,000	1,121	87,489,000	1,105
Other Federal Funds:						
Commerce, Department of, for assistance in research on computer assisted telephone interview techniques, data editing and personnel detail	500,000	1	264,000	1	350,000	1
Environmental Protection Agency for data on agroecosystems and water quality	200,000	3	250,000	3	350,000	5
Interior, Department of, for data on grazing fees	40,000	--	40,000	--	40,000	--
Labor, Department of for assistance in research on computer assisted telephone interview techniques, and for data on seasonal agricultural workers	252,500	--	253,000	--	350,000	--
National Academy of Sciences for personnel detail	41,200	--	16,000	--	--	
Office of International Cooperation and Development (from AID) for training, technical assistance, equipment and personnel detail	705,067	9	424,000	6	600,000	10
Total, Other Federal Funds	1,738,767	13	1,247,000	10	1,690,000	16

Item	1992 Actual Amount	1992 Staff-Years	1993 Estimated Amount	1993 Staff-Years	1994 Estimated Amount	1994 Staff-Years
Non Federal Funds:						
State Agencies for survey work	1,945,058	24	1,800,000	22	1,800,000	22
Misc. Contributed Funds for distribution of crop releases and data on beef, hops, malting barley, milk, oats, fruit, vegetables, wheat, soybeans, wool and mohair stocks, agricultural equipment dealers, farm families, and conducting mailings	220,138	2	250,000	2	243,000	2
Total Non-Federal Funds	2,165,196	26	2,050,000	24	2,043,000	24
Total, National Agricultural Statistics Service	92,626,729	1,162	90,754,000	1,155	91,222,000	1,145

NATIONAL AGRICULTURAL STATISTICS SERVICE

Permanent Positions by Grade and Staff-Year Summary

1992 and Estimated 1993 and 1994

Grade	FY 1992			FY 1993			FY 1994		
	Headquarters	Field	Total	Headquarters	Field	Total	Headquarters	Field	Total
ES-5	3	--	3	3	--	3	3	--	3
ES-4	3	--	3	3	--	3	3	--	3
ES-3	1	--	1	1	--	1	1	--	1
ES-2	1	--	1	1	--	1	1	--	1
ES-1	1	--	1	1	--	1	1	--	1
GS/GM-15..	22	13	35	22	13	35	21	13	34
GS/GM-14..	49	48	97	49	48	97	48	48	96
GS/GM-13..	123	64	187	123	64	187	122	64	186
GS-12	38	89	127	38	91	129	37	91	128
GS-11	21	73	94	21	73	94	20	73	93
GS-10	1	--	1	1	--	1	1	--	1
GS-9	18	85	103	18	85	103	18	84	102
GS-8	21	2	23	21	2	23	21	2	23
GS-7	29	98	127	29	98	127	29	97	126
GS-6	28	95	123	28	95	123	28	95	123
GS-5	23	78	101	23	78	101	22	77	99
GS-4	9	56	65	9	56	65	8	56	64
GS-3	1	4	5	1	4	5	1	4	5
Other Graded Positions	--	1	1	--	1	1	--	1	1
Total Permanent Positions	392	706	1,098	392	708	1,100	385	705	1,090
Total Permanent Employment, end-of-year	392	706	1,098	392	708	1,100	385	705	1,090
Staff-Years Ceiling..	414	748	1,162	412	743	1,155	405	740	1,145

NATIONAL AGRICULTURAL STATISTICS SERVICE

CLASSIFICATION BY OBJECTS

1992 and Estimated 1993 and 1994

	1992	1993	1994
Personnel Compensation:			
Headquarters	$16,596,409	$17,170,000	$17,199,000
Field	22,208,633	22,918,000	23,090,000
11 Total personnel compensation	38,805,042	40,088,000	40,289,000
12 Personnel Benefits ...	8,631,056	8,879,000	8,919,000
13 Benefits for former personnel	2,174	2,000	2,000
Total Personnel Compensation & Benefits......	47,438,272	48,969,000	49,210,000
Other Objects:			
21 Travel	1,519,682	1,504,000	1,542,000
22 Transportation of things	439,750	365,000	375,000
23.3 Communications, utilities and miscellaneous charges..	2,908,235	3,289,000	3,334,000
24 Printing and reproduction	469,047	605,000	620,000
25 Other services	25,233,959	23,269,000	24,277,000
26 Supplies and materials	1,071,781	1,168,000	1,198,000
31 Equipment	3,475,439	1,834,000	1,922,000
42 Insurance Claims and Indemnities	15,259	--	--
43 Interest and dividends	628	1,000	1,000
Total other objects	35,133,780	32,035,000	33,269,000
Total direct obligations .	82,572,052	81,004,000	82,479,000
Position Data:			
Average Salary, ES positions	$102,211	$105,489	$105,489
Average Salary, GM/GS positions	$37,218	$38,608	$38,598
Average Grade, GM/GS positions	9.6	9.6	9.6

NATIONAL AGRICULTURAL STATISTICS SERVICE

The estimates include appropriation language for this item as follows (new language underscored; deleted matter enclosed in brackets):

NATIONAL AGRICULTURAL STATISTICS SERVICE:

For necessary expenses of the National Agricultural Statistics Service in conducting statistical reporting and service work, including crop and livestock estimates, statistical coordination and improvements, and marketing surveys, as authorized by the Agricultural Marketing Act of 1946 (7 U.S.C. 1621-1627) and other laws, [$81,004,000] $82,479,000: Provided, That this appropriation shall be available for employment pursuant to the second sentence of section 706(a) of the Organic Act of 1944 (7 U.S.C. 2225), and not to exceed $40,000 shall be available for employment under 5 U.S.C. 3109.

NATIONAL AGRICULTURAL STATISTICS SERVICE

Appropriations Act, 1993	$81,004,000
Budget Request, 1994	82,479,000
Increase in Appropriation	+ 1,475,000

SUMMARY OF INCREASES AND DECREASES
(On basis of appropriation)

Item of Change	1993 Estimated	Pay Costs	Other Changes	1994 Estimated
Agricultural Estimates........	$77,415,000	$1,049,000	+ $350,000	$78,814,000
Statistical Research and Service	3,589,000	54,000	+ 22,000	3,665,000
Total Available	81,004,000	+ 1,103,000	+ 372,000	82,479,000

PROJECT STATEMENT
(On basis of adjusted appropriation)

Project	1992 Actual Amount	1992 Actual Staff-Years	1993 Estimated Amount	1993 Estimated Staff-Years	Increase or Decrease	1994 Estimated Amount	1994 Estimated Staff-Years
1. Agricultural Estimates	$78,983,052	1,004	$77,415,000	998	+$ 1,399,000 (1)	$78,814,000	994
2. Statistical Research and Service	3,589,000	42	3,589,000	42	+76,000 (2)	3,665,000	42
Unobligated balance	69,348	--	--	--	--	--	--
Total available or estimate	82,641,400	1,046	81,004,000	1,040	+ 1,475,000	82,479,000	1,036
Transfer from Departmental Administration	-40,400						
Total Appropriation	82,601,000						

EXPLANATION OF PROGRAM

The National Agricultural Statistics Service has two major activities, authorized by the Agricultural Marketing Act of 1946, as follows:

-- Agricultural Estimates - This area includes the conducting of scientifically designed surveys; summarizing and analyzing survey data; developing estimates of production, supply, price, and other aspects of the agricultural economy; and issuing official USDA national, State and county estimates and reports relating to acreage, types and production of farm crops, number of livestock on farms, livestock products, stocks of agricultural commodities, value and utilization of farm products, prices received and paid by farmers, agricultural chemical use, and other subjects as required. Estimates are published in about 400 Federal reports each year. All information is made available to the public at scheduled release times, providing the basic, unbiased data necessary to maintain an orderly association between the consumption, supply, marketing, and input sectors of agriculture.

-- Statistical Research and Service - Research is conducted to improve the statistical methods and techniques used in developing agricultural statistics. This research is directed toward better sampling, yield forecasting, and survey techniques. Consulting services in the areas of survey methodology, statistical methodology, and remote sensing technology are provided both gratis and on a reimbursable basis.

GAO Reports:

GAO/RCED-92-175, July 1992, "DATA COLLECTION: Opportunities to Improve USDA's Farm Costs and Returns Survey" (Final Report).

NASS is in general agreement with the findings of this report. All attainable recommendations are expected to be implemented during calendar year 1993.

GAO/IMTEC-92-11, January 1992, "FOOD SAFETY: USDA Data Program Not Supporting Critical Pesticide Decisions" (Final Report).

NASS' Pesticide Usage Surveys have been widely praised, and were singled out in this report as "proceeding on schedule and EPA and FDA officials have expressed satisfaction" with this portion of the Pesticide Data Program.

JUSTIFICATION OF INCREASES AND DECREASES

(I) An increase of $1,399,000 for agricultural estimates consisting of:

(a) An increase of $833,000 which reflects a 2.7 percent increase in non-salary costs.

Need for Change. These funds are necessary to offset increased operating costs. Continued absorption of these increased operating costs will severely affect the quality and quantity of our programs.

Nature of Change. This increase will be used to maintain a current level of services associated with inflation which will affect the critical parts of the program. Examples of cost increases are travel, postal rates, supplies, equipment, maintenance, and ADP related costs.

(b) An increase of $1,049,000 for absorbed fiscal year 1993 pay costs.

(c) A decrease of $245,000 which reflects a 3 percent reduction in administrative expenses from the amount made available for fiscal year 1993 adjusted for inflation.

Need for Change. To promote the efficient use of resources for administrative purposes, in keeping with the President's Executive Order, total USDA baseline outlays for these activities will be reduced by 3 percent in FY 1994, 6 percent in FY 1995, 9 percent in FY 1996, and 14 percent in FY 1997.

Nature of Change. In order to achieve this savings, NASS will carefully monitor travel, training, supply purchases, printing and reproduction costs, and utility usage.

(d) A decrease of $200,000 which reflects the savings due to a staff-year reduction.

Need for Change. The decrease of $200,000 is to support the President's program of reducing Federal full-time equivalent employment by 100,000 by FY 1997.

Nature of Change. These savings will be spread proportionally between the NASS State Statistical Offices and headquarters.

(e) A decrease of $38,000 for FTS 2000 funding.

This decrease reflects lower long distance telecommunications prices due to price redeterminations in the FTS 2000 contracts.

(2) An increase of $76,000 for statistical research and service consisting of:

(a) An increase of $32,000 which reflects a 2.7 percent increase in non-salary costs.

Need for Change. These funds are necessary to offset increased operating costs. Continued absorption of these increased operating costs will severely affect the quality and quantity of our programs.

Nature of Change. This increase will be used to maintain a current level of services associated with inflation which will affect the critical parts of the program. Examples of cost increases are travel, postal rates, supplies, equipment, maintenance, and ADP related costs.

(b) An increase of $54,000 for absorbed fiscal year 1993 pay costs.

(c) A decrease of $10,000 which reflects a 3 percent reduction in administrative expenses from the amount made available for fiscal year 1993 adjusted for inflation.

Need for Change. To promote the efficient use of resources for administrative purposes, in keeping with the President's Executive Order, total USDA baseline outlays for these activities will be reduced by 3 percent in FY 1994, 6 percent in FY 1995, 9 percent in FY 1996, and 14 percent in FY 1997.

Nature of Change. In order to achieve this savings, NASS will carefully monitor travel, training, supply purchases, printing and reproduction costs, and utility usage.

NATIONAL AGRICULTURAL STATISTICS SERVICE
GEOGRAPHIC BREAKDOWN OF OBLIGATIONS AND STAFF-YEARS
1992 and Estimated 1993 and 1994

	1992		1993		1994	
	Amount	Staff Years	Amount	Staff Years	Amount	Staff Years
Alabama........	$860,726	14	$887,000	14	$903,000	14
Alaska.........	138,746	2	139,000	2	142,000	2
Arizona........	664,239	9	648,000	9	660,000	9
Arkansas.......	1,217,968	17	1,182,000	17	1,204,000	17
California.....	3,670,741	36	3,350,000	35	3,411,000	35
Colorado.......	1,237,088	20	1,413,000	20	1,439,000	21
Delaware.......	94,110	1	94,000	1	96,000	1
District of Columbia......	32,233,183	375	30,933,000	373	31,493,000	370
Florida........	1,438,794	19	1,347,000	18	1,372,000	18
Georgia........	1,327,999	17	1,268,000	17	1,291,000	17
Hawaii.........	455,591	8	468,000	8	477,000	8
Idaho..........	1,102,518	15	1,172,000	15	1,193,000	15
Illinois.......	1,657,318	18	1,654,000	18	1,684,000	18
Indiana........	1,132,958	16	1,242,000	16	1,265,000	16
Iowa...........	1,614,775	18	1,495,000	18	1,522,000	18
Kansas.........	1,412,105	17	1,438,000	17	1,464,000	17
Kentucky.......	972,351	15	1,010,000	15	1,028,000	15
Louisiana......	982,218	14	1,017,000	14	1,036,000	14
Maryland.......	842,735	12	797,000	12	812,000	12
Michigan.......	1,521,741	20	1,430,000	20	1,456,000	20
Minnesota......	1,676,948	18	1,572,000	18	1,601,000	18
Mississippi....	1,272,750	15	1,181,000	15	1,203,000	15
Missouri.......	1,307,509	17	1,340,000	17	1,364,000	17
Montana........	747,033	12	793,000	12	807,000	12
Nebraska.......	1,413,385	19	1,534,000	19	1,562,000	19
Nevada.........	224,517	4	233,000	4	237,000	4
New Hampshire..	949,296	15	991,000	15	1,009,000	15
New Jersey.....	761,049	13	752,000	13	766,000	13
New Mexico.....	603,515	8	590,000	8	601,000	8
New York.......	1,370,328	17	1,346,000	17	1,371,000	17
North Carolina.	1,576,739	17	1,371,000	16	1,396,000	16
North Dakota...	970,542	16	1,054,000	16	1,073,000	16
Ohio...........	1,325,941	21	1,344,000	21	1,368,000	19
Oklahoma.......	1,022,540	15	1,075,000	15	1,095,000	15
Oregon.........	1,072,765	15	1,144,000	15	1,165,000	15
Pennsylvania...	1,009,038	16	1,033,000	16	1,052,000	16
South Carolina.	740,685	12	772,000	12	786,000	12
South Dakota...	1,010,087	16	1,062,000	16	1,081,000	16
Tennessee......	1,008,775	14	987,000	14	1,005,000	14
Texas..........	2,703,632	28	2,467,000	27	2,512,000	27
Utah...........	537,642	9	575,000	9	585,000	9
Virginia.......	1,099,343	13	1,021,000	13	1,040,000	13
Washington.....	1,009,176	14	1,162,000	14	1,183,000	14
West Virginia..	507,533	8	522,000	8	532,000	8
Wisconsin......	1,465,291	21	1,451,000	21	1,477,000	21
Wyoming........	608,089	10	648,000	10	660,000	10
Subtotal, Available or Estimate.	82,572,052	1,046	81,004,000	1,040	82,479,000	1,036
Unobligated Balance.....	69,348	--	--	--	--	--
Total, Available or estimate	82,641,400	1,046	81,004,000	1,040	82,479,000	1,036

NATIONAL AGRICULTURAL STATISTICS SERVICE

STATUS OF PROGRAM

The National Agricultural Statistics Service (NASS) administers the United States Department of Agriculture's program of collecting and publishing current national and State agricultural statistics. Statistical data provided by the Service on the Nation's agriculture are essential in making effective policy, production, and marketing decisions.

NASS programs are organized in the following major areas: (1) agricultural estimates, (2) statistical research and service, and (3) work performed for others.

AGRICULTURAL ESTIMATES

Current Activities: Agricultural production and marketing data are collected, summarized, analyzed, and published for a wide range of items including: number of farms and land in farms; acreage, yield, production, and stocks of grains, hay, oilseeds, cotton, potatoes, tobacco, fruits, vegetables, floriculture, and selected specialty crops; inventories and production of hogs, cattle, sheep and wool, goats and mohair, mink, catfish, trout, poultry, eggs, and dairy products; prices received by farmers for products, prices paid for commodities and services, and related indexes; cold storage supplies; agricultural chemical use; and other related areas of the agricultural economy.

Thousands of farmers, ranchers, agribusinesses, and others voluntarily respond to surveys about crops, livestock, and other agricultural activities. These surveys are supplemented by field observations, objective yield counts and measurements, and other data to provide reliable information.

The estimating program is conducted through 45 State Statistical Offices (SSO's) servicing all 50 States. The majority of these SSO's are operated as joint State-Federal offices. The cooperative funding arrangements with State agencies provide for development of additional State and county data to supplement and complement information produced with Federal resources.

Estimates for approximately 120 crops and 45 livestock items are published in almost 400 reports each year through the NASS Agricultural Statistics Board (ASB). All information is made available to the public and news media at scheduled release times. A user fee system covers the costs of maintaining mailing lists, printing, and mailing the releases. Survey respondents, news media, congressional offices, and other Federal agencies are not required to pay for ASB releases.

The principal program goals are to: (1) provide data and services needed for commercially important segments of the agricultural industry; (2) provide statistics necessary for informed government policy development and program implementation, especially statistics mandated by law; (3) increase the accuracy, dependability, and public usefulness of national and State data; (4) conduct program reviews to ensure that statistical information is collected and published in an efficient manner and satisfies user needs; (5) minimize the time between data collection and release; (6) improve information distribution; and (7) reduce survey response burden on individuals and firms.

Selected Examples of Recent Progress: Recent accomplishments under this appropriation item are cited below by project:

Additional estimates and services:

1. Chemical use publication. A new series of NASS publications covering on-farm fertilizer and agricultural chemical use for fruits and nuts was started in 1992. The Agricultural Chemical Usage report, covering 1991 crop fruits and nuts, was issued in July 1992 and provided chemical use data for the 14 major fruit producing States. The data presented in this publication was provided

through the President's Water Quality and Food Safety Initiatives and represented the initial effort to develop a data series on chemical use.

2. Cattle and calf death loss. NASS conducted a special survey to obtain information on the number and economic value of cattle and calf deaths due to predators and disease. The agency published estimates of losses and value by type of predator and disease for major States as well as by region and the United States.

3. Nursery and greenhouse study. An in-depth nursery and greenhouse survey was conducted in Oregon during 1992. Data on acreage in production, gross sales, and other marketing and wage information was published in a September report and generally highlighted the significant size of this industry in Oregon.

4. Additional farm labor data. Starting with the May 1992 Farm Labor report, additional information for selected States was provided on all farm workers, hourly wage rates, field worker wage rates, and field and livestock workers combined wage rates. Annual average wage rates by States were published in the November report.

5. New estimates provided. New State estimates of the number of sheep operations and inventory by size of flock and estimates of livestock slaughter by class were initiated during 1992. In addition, a breakout of cane berries by type of container was added to the monthly Cold Storage report. These new estimates were instituted at the request of data users.

6. New vegetable estimates provided. NASS expanded its coverage of fresh market vegetables starting in January 1992. In the quarterly Vegetables report, forecasts of acreage for harvest were added for eight new vegetable crops. Estimates for an additional seven fresh market and four processed vegetables are provided annually.

7. Minor oilseed estimates expanded. Estimates of acreage, yield, production, and ending stocks of minor oilseeds (canola, rapeseed, safflower, and mustard seed) were added to the existing series of sunflower and flaxseed, starting with the 1991 crop. Sunflower and flaxseed estimates were expanded to all States.

Increasing data accuracy and dependability:

1. Small grain yield update. Because of the lateness of the 1992 small grain crop harvest in the Northern States, NASS conducted a special Yield Update Survey where harvest was not complete by early September. The special survey, conducted the last week of September, recontacted farm operators in the usual small grain annual production survey. Results were used to update small grain production for the October Crop Production report.

2. Cattle on Feed Survey integrated. The Cattle on Feed Survey in the 13 States that account for about 85 percent of the U.S. fed cattle marketings was integrated with the January and July probability cattle surveys. The interim monthly and quarterly surveys will be conducted as follow-on surveys. This reduced respondent burden and provided the base for statistically improved estimates.

Reviewing commodity programs:

1. Friday release date for cattle reports. In response to cattle industry requests, the Cattle, Cattle on Feed, and Livestock Slaughter reports were rescheduled for release on Fridays rather than any other work day to minimize disruption of normal marketing patterns. This action followed a USDA study of livestock marketing patterns, and received additional support from analysts and traders to benefit the broad range of data users.

2. December Hogs and Pigs report. The December Hogs and Pigs report will be issued on the next to last workday of December beginning December 30, 1992. This report had been issued the first week in January and is in response to a Chicago Mercantile request to assist producers and traders in planning end-of-year marketing strategies.

Data handling and user services:

1. Enhanced data user knowledge. Public Data Users Meetings were held at five sites: Atlanta, Georgia; St. Paul, Minnesota; Sacramento, California; Denver, Colorado; and Washington, D.C. The 1992 meetings focused on USDA livestock, dairy, poultry, and cold storage statistics. The meetings provided a forum for the public to review current reports and estimating procedures and to provide suggestions for improving the agricultural statistics program.

2. New systems installed. NASS completed the installation of local area networks (LAN) in all State offices and in headquarters. This provides uniform hardware and software to every NASS employee.

3. List frame data base. A data base was created for the Agency's LAN, providing timely, but limited, access to the NASS List Sampling Frame during survey processing periods. This not only increases productivity during peak work loads, but also reduces costs by removing this particular activity from costly mainframe processing.

4. Published Estimates Data Base (PEDB) expanded. Estimates of prices received for corn, wheat, sorghum, soybeans, peanuts, sweet potatoes, hogs, and sheep were added to the PEDB. Acres, yield, and production estimates for tobacco, sugar beets, sugarcane and milk production were also added. The Agricultural Stabilization and Conservation Service was given access to the PEDB to retrieve estimates electronically.

5. FTS2000. All data communications were converted from the Martin Marietta Computer System to FTS2000 in July 1992. This allows NASS to connect all State offices and headquarters with a wide area network, standardizing data transfers between locations and providing strong central support for State offices.

6. Field Services Section established. The Field Services Section was established in the Colorado State Statistical Office to develop applications for the LAN's. This unit most recently modified, documented, and trained users on a major personal computer system to create county estimates.

STATISTICAL RESEARCH AND SERVICE

Selected Examples of Recent Progress: Recent accomplishments under this appropriation item are cited below by project:

Improving operational programs:

1. Vegetative index for crop condition assessment. A research data base has been constructed of vegetative indices utilizing polar orbiting weather satellite data. The vegetative indices will aid crop analysts in determining the extent of damage from disasters such as droughts, floods, and crop diseases.

2. Analysis of bias in cattle on feed indications. Analysis of 1992 January and July reinterview survey data indicated a level of bias that was attributed to several questionnaire issues. The level of bias in survey indications are being measured for further analysis and interpretation.

3. Precipitation data utilized to improve crop forecasting. The operational use of precipitation data in regional yield forecasting models was initiated in 1992. Study of these data to reflect yield differences between States in early-season forecasting continues.

4. Analysis of nonrespondent characteristics utilized to improve hog survey indications. Analysis of information from 15 previous quarterly surveys indicates that prior knowledge about nonrespondents will allow NASS to properly reflect their impact on current survey indications.

5. Analysis of respondent characteristics help improve the Farm Costs and Returns Survey. Subsampling small operations not on the list of known agricultural operations, improving adjustments about nonrespondents, and adjusting for survey undercoverage will be implemented during 1993. All adjustments are made by size and type of farming operation.

6. Evaluation of using historical acreage information in follow-on surveys. NASS is evaluating the use of previously reported acreage information in computer assisted telephone surveys. Use of prior information will reduce individual respondent burden since it will not have to be obtained in subsequent interviews. This procedure is also expected to improve data quality.

7. Satellite data for crop acreage estimation. Final 1991 crop acreage estimates for rice and cotton were derived using Landsat Thematic Mapper satellite data in three Delta States (Arkansas, Louisiana, and Mississippi). Precision of acreage estimates was more than tripled by using the satellite data.

8. Computer assisted personal interviewing. The complex farm expenditures portion of the Farm Costs and Returns Survey was programmed in a computer assisted personal interview instrument using a laptop computer. Several successful interviews with farm operators were completed this year, demonstrating farmer acceptance of the technology.

9. Computer assisted telephone interviewing (CATI) and interactive editing (IE). NASS staff began an evaluation of a relatively new software package for large scale CATI and IE use. This software was developed by the Netherlands Central Bureau of Statistics, with the product name of "Blaise." The Agency recently processed small national trout, catfish, and cotton ginnings surveys plus several large State surveys in Blaise, avoiding the costly mainframe processing and solidifying its potential for larger scale applications.

Statistical consulting and services:

1. Assistance to the Human Nutrition Information Service (HNIS). Statistical consulting assistance was provided on the sampling design for future HNIS dietary surveys. Advice was also given on the analysis of survey data, the creation of adjustments for survey nonresponse, the development of reasonable measures of survey accuracy, and the estimation of the distribution of usual dietary intakes.

2. Assistance to the Agricultural Marketing Service (AMS). NASS staff provided statistical assistance and advice for the residue testing component of the Pesticide Data Program. This involved revising the sampling procedures of fresh fruit and vegetables selected in the wholesale market and determining statistically correct weighting schemes for linking the survey samples to the total population of interest.

3. Consultation to USDA agencies. In addition to HNIS and AMS, NASS provided statistical consultation and advice to the Agricultural Stabilization and Conservation Service, the USDA Office of Advocacy and Enterprise, and the USDA Equal Opportunity/Civil Rights Critical Element Review Committee.

4. <u>International assistance provided</u>. NASS provided technical assistance and training to improve agricultural statistics programs in a number of foreign countries. Long-term resident assistance was provided in Cameroon, Egypt, Honduras, and Pakistan, while short-term assignments supported work in several other countries, including Bulgaria and Poland. The NASS International Statistics course, conducted in Washington, D.C., trained 18 persons from 8 countries. A modified version of this course was also conducted in Egypt for 22 persons and in Bulgaria for 70 participants.

4. International assistance provided. NASS provided technical assistance and training to improve agricultural statistics programs in a number of foreign countries. Long-term resident assistance was provided in Cameroon, Egypt, Honduras, and Pakistan, while short-term assignments supported work in several other countries, including Bulgaria and Poland. The NASS International Statistics course, conducted in Washington, D.C., trained 16 persons from 8 countries. A modified version of this course was also conducted in Egypt for 22 persons and in Bulgaria for 70 participants.

PASSENGER MOTOR VEHICLES

The 1994 Budget Estimates propose the purchase of 1 additional motor vehicle and the replacement of 3 passenger motor vehicles.

The passenger motor vehicles of the National Agricultural Statistics Service are used (where common carrier or GSA vehicles are not feasible) for necessary field travel in carrying out the mission of the agency. All passenger motor vehicles are located at various field offices.

Additional passenger motor vehicle. The one additional passenger motor vehicle is for the NASS field offices. GSA has gradually closed many of its motor pool facilities making it more difficult for NASS personnel to obtain cars when needed. The use of common carrier is not feasible in carrying out the program of NASS.

Replacement of passenger motor vehicles. Replacement of 3 of the 11 vehicles now in operation is proposed. These 11 vehicles are located in 10 field locations and are necessary to meet the transportation requirements inherent in carrying out the agency's program. The vehicles proposed to be replaced will have passed the minimum replacement standards of 6 years of age or 60,000 miles prescribed by the General Services Administration.

Age and mileage data for motor vehicles on hand as of September 30, 1992, are as follows:

Age Data			Mileage Data		
Age-Year Model	Number of Vehicles	Percent of Total	Lifetime Mileage (thousands)	Number of Vehicles	Percent of Total
1988 or older	6	55	80-100	0	0
1989	4	36	60-80	5	45
1990	0	0	40-60	3	27
1991	0	0	20-40	2	18
1992	1	9	Under 20	1	9
Total	11	100	Total	11	100 a/

a/ Column does not add because of rounding.

THURSDAY, FEBRUARY 18, 1993.

WORLD AGRICULTURAL OUTLOOK BOARD

WITNESSES

KEITH COLLINS, ACTING ASSISTANT SECRETARY FOR ECONOMICS, DEPARTMENT OF AGRICULTURE

JAMES R. DONALD, CHAIRPERSON, WORLD AGRICULTURAL OUTLOOK BOARD

GERALD A. BANGE, DEPUTY CHAIRPERSON, WORLD AGRICULTURAL OUTLOOK BOARD

NORTON D. STROMMEN, CHIEF METEOROLOGIST, WORLD AGRICULTURAL OUTLOOK BOARD

THOMAS W. BICKERTON, REMOTE SENSING COORDINATOR, WORLD AGRICULTURAL OUTLOOK BOARD

STEPHEN B. DEWHURST, BUDGET OFFICER, DEPARTMENT OF AGRICULTURE

Mr. DURBIN. The third panel is from the World Agricultural Outlook Board. With Mr. Collins and Mr. Dewhurst, we have James Donald, Chairperson; Gerald Bange, Deputy Chairperson; Norton Strommen, Chief Meteorologist; and Tom Bickerton, Remote Sensing Coordinator.

Mr. Donald, please proceed. Your testimony will of course be included in its entirety. We would appreciate your summarizing at this point.

OPENING STATEMENT

Mr. DONALD. Thank you very much, Mr. Chairman, members of the committee.

Let me just take about two minutes, perhaps, and tell you what it is that we do and how we do it, and some things we think need to be done. You have heard the discussion here, we have both the side that is doing economic analysis and the side that is collecting data on an international basis. Specifically, one of our missions is putting together world crop production forecasts.

There we are interested in both our competitors and our consumers in world markets. So that is one of our primary functions on the statistical side. To do that, we work through the attachés, and we depend on analysis from ERS.

And the second area is what we call the supply-demand estimates side. In other words, we are looking at markets, we are looking at prices, projecting stocks, and that type thing, establishing balance sheets for the various commodities which we are interested in, both domestic markets and export markets.

We are a very small agency. We have a budget of $2.5 million. So how do we do our work? We do our work through committees, interagency committees. In the department, we are reaching across various agencies, ASCS and ERS, for example. As you heard here, the main analytical support that we get in this interagency process, which the Members of the Board chair, is from the Economic Research Service. They are the analytical or economic research arm of the Department.

The interagency committees include those for Commodity Estimates, for Agricultural Projections, for Climate and Weather and for Remote Sensing. Those are the departmental areas that have members from the various agencies within the department.

Let me mention also, Mr. Chairman, we are responsible for a panel at the Department where we are actually involved in one operational aspect: We have a cooperative agreement with the Department of Commerce's National Weather Service, and we are responsible for monitoring weather developments throughout the world and bringing these into play when we are looking at production forecasts. We are monitoring 8,000 stations at various locations around the world.

Let me just mention briefly two areas where we need to do some work. One area is on the short-term forecasts, for both the export and the domestic market. We need to improve the accuracy of those forecasts. We are making progress. Analytical support from the Economic Research Service has been very critical.

Why do we need to do that? Because farm programs provisions are tied to a number of things that we publish monthly in the World Agricultural Supply and Demand Estimates report, the one publication that we do put out.

The acreage reduction percentages, for example, are based on our projections of stocks in relation to use. So it is very important that we get stocks and use correct.

The other area is longer term projections. We need to put more effort into that area. Those are the projections for commodities that underlie the President's budget when the costs are computed, and they are also the basis for looking at alternative program provisions.

How do we do all this, make these improvements, both for the short term and the long term? The first thing we do is look at the record. How did our forecasts come out, and if they are different from what actually happened, why are they different? So that is the starting place.

That is what we are really beginning to do now, to look at the record and see where we have gone astray and where we can make improvements. Did we miss exports? Did we miss domestic use? Where is it that we went astray? So that is an area where we really need to spend more time.

That concludes my comments. Mr. Chairman. I would be happy to respond to any questions.

[CLERK'S NOTE.—Mr. Donald's prepared statement appears on pages 157 through 164. The budget justifications, which were received on May 10, 1993, appear on pages 165 through 173.]

REMOTE SENSING

Mr. DURBIN. Thank you very much.

I have a series of questions for you that I would really like to save for a more informal setting. It concerns this whole question of remote sensing and changes in the Soviet Union. Perhaps we could find an opportunity to sit down and discuss that.

Mr. DONALD. I would be happy to do that, Mr. Chairman.

Mr. DURBIN. I think it relates to changes in your agency and the world. I will ask one question now. At last year's hearing you were unable to go into any detail about getting more accurate and reliable data from the former Soviet Union or about ground verifying their production estimates because it was too early in the breakup. Would you please update this situation for us?

Mr. DONALD. One of WAOB's primary functions is to coordinate the development of the Department's global production estimates for most major commodities. With respect to the former Soviet Union (FSU), we are finding that there is considerable variation in the quality of production data among commodities and republics. Generally, data must be pieced together and/or supplemented with qualitative judgments. At present, attache coverage is essentially limited to Russia. In Russia and to an even greater extent elsewhere in the FSU, conflicting agricultural production estimates from various sources are common. Thus, analysis of weather and remote sensing data remain a critical element in the development of the Department's estimates for the FSU.

GATT AND NAFTA AGREEMENTS

Mr. DURBIN. What role have you had in the decisions that are being made regarding the GATT and NAFTA agreements? What information are you able to supply the officials negotiating these agreements?

Mr. DONALD. WAOB's commodity analysts have provided commodity expertise to USDA's Uruguay Round and NAFTA negotiators, and has assisted in analyzing the economic implications of various negotiating proposals. The Department's Interagency Agricultural Projections Committee, chaired by WAOB, has furnished negotiators with "baseline" trade forecasts as a starting point for impact analysis.

Assistance to negotiators has been proffered through formal meetings and memoranda as well as informal contacts. WAOB officials have done some independent analysis of the implications of various negotiating proposals, but most of the agency's input has been through contributions to and reviews of reports prepared by other agencies.

SUPPLY AND DEMAND ESTIMATES

Mr. DURBIN. The Secretary, using his transfer authority, transferred two staff-years to the Board in fiscal year 1992 to strengthen supply and demand forecasting. Describe in further detail how these two staff-years were used.

Mr. DONALD. With the budget equivalent of two staff years, the Board was able to make substantial progress on this project. All monthly USDA short-term commodity supply/demand forecasts issued since 1973, numbering approximately 500,000, have been entered into a database. At present, all USDA long-term commodity projections used to develop estimates of program outlays for the President's budget are being prepared for entry into the database. Computer software needed to manage this database in a network environment is being developed under contract.

These data will provide us with a record of our past forecasts and permit us to identify sources of errors. Then, we can take steps to improve the reliability of commodity supply and use estimates.

Mr. DURBIN. Will this transfer take place again in fiscal year 1993?

Mr. DONALD. Yes. The Secretary redirected $170,000 to WAOB in fiscal year 1993 for the purpose of continuing the efforts to strengthen the Department's commodity supply and demand estimates program.

Mr. DURBIN. At last year's hearing you discussed a proposed project to automate your data system for supply and demand estimates. What is the status of this project?

Mr. DONALD. The funds redirected to WAOB in fiscal year 1992 were used for data entry and for staff support through a reimbursable agreement with the Office of Information Resource Management, Fort Collins, Colorado for systems analysis and development. To date, substantial progress has been made on this project. A large historical database of monthly commodity supply/demand estimates and actual outcomes has been created and ADP systems development work is well underway.

Automation is proceeding by commodity group. A system is in place for grains, and is presently used for all grain tables, domestic and foreign, in the monthly World Agricultural Supply and Demand Estimates—WASDE—report. Cotton and sugar modules are being developed now and oilseeds and livestock modules will follow. The WASDE database for U.S. field crops has been made available to the public as part of the user fee program.

Fiscal year 1993 funds are being used for project management, data entry, systems analysis and for on-site technical support.

MAJOR WORLD CROP AREAS AND CLIMATE PROFILES

Mr. DURBIN. The revised publication, "Major World Crop Areas and Climatic Profiles," was expected to be completed by the spring of this year. What is the status of this publication?

Mr. DONALD. Currently, commodity statistics are being compiled to include the most recent set of official data available. Crop calendar information is being re-evaluated to reflect area and varietal changes; maps identifying the concentration of crop areas within a country are being prepared; and, climatic data are being analyzed to reflect any changes in 30-year averages for rainfall and temperature which now cover the period 1961–1990. Further, the publication is expanding to include more crop areas and additional commodities, including coffee and sugarcane. Initial layouts of the draft report have been prepared.

WORKER'S COMPENSATION CLAIM

Mr. DURBIN. What is the status of the worker's compensation claim you have pending? At last year's hearing you estimated the cost of this claim to be approximately $50,000 per year.

Mr. DONALD. The Department of Labor has determined that this individual is disabled as a result of an on-the-job injury. Until this claimant is determined to be fully recovered, the Board is responsible for salary compensation, medical and rehabilitation costs. In fiscal year 1994, Board outlays for this claim will be approximately $50,000 comprised of approximately $41,000 for salary compensation and $9,000 for medical expenses.

INTERGOVERNMENTAL PANEL ON CLIMATE CHANGE

Mr. DURBIN. The Intergovernmental Panel on Climate Change was scheduled to release its revised report in June of 1992. Has this report been released? If so, what did it say?

Mr. DONALD. The revised report from the Intergovernmental Panel on Climate Change has been released. Its basic conclusion, pointing to the possibility for global warming, remains unchanged. That is, with a doubling of carbon dioxide, the potential for warming remains estimated at between 1.5 and 4.5 degrees C.

JOINT AGRICULTURAL WEATHER FACILITY

Mr. DURBIN. Please provide a table showing the annual budget, broken out between the Board and NOAA, for fiscal years 1988 through 1992 actuals and 1993 estimates. Include both dollars and FTEs.

Mr. DONALD. I will provide the requested table for the record.

[The information follows:]

JOINT AGRICULTURAL WEATHER FACILITY—FY 1988–93

[Dollars in thousands]

	WAOB		NOAA		TOTAL	
	Amount	FTE	Amount	FTE	Amount	FTE
1988 actual	$431	8.0	$526	9.0	$957	17.0
1989 actual	472	8.0	531	7.5	1,003	15.5
1990 actual	588	9.0	543	9.5	1,131	18.5
1991 actual	520	7.0	566	9.0	1,086	16.0
1992 actual	567	7.7	547	8.5	1,114	16.2
1993 estimate	585	9.0	550	7.5	1,135	16.5

WORLD AGRICULTURAL SUPPLY AND DEMAND ESTIMATES

Mr. DURBIN. Please provide for the record a copy of the most recent monthly report of "World Agricultural Supply and Demand Estimates."

Mr. DONALD. I will submit a copy of the most recent monthly report of World Agricultural Supply and Demand Estimates for the record.

[CLERK'S NOTE.—The report is too lengthy for reprint. A copy is retained in Committee files.]

Mr. DURBIN. What is the estimated annual cost of this publication?

Mr. DONALD. The current gross annual cost to produce the World Agricultural Supply and Demand Estimates is $15,181, comprised of $5,886 for postage fees, $3,370 for contractual mailing services, and $5,925 for printing. This gross cost is mostly offset by collecting $13,295 in subscription fees.

Mr. DURBIN. What is the subscription level of this report?

Mr. DONALD. There are 1,229 paid subscribers, 629 who receive the report from the Government Printing Office and 600 who receive it through our user-fee subscription program. One year ago, there were 743 paid subscribers, 463 through the Government Printing Office and 280 through the user-fee subscription program.

WEATHER STATISTICS

Mr. DURBIN. During last year's hearing you described for us how an agreement with the Commerce Department to collect daily weather records for over 7,000 stations around the world, dating back to 1977, would improve quantitative modeling of weather/crop relationships. Has this study been completed? If so, how has it helped both farmers and the Department?

Mr. DONALD. The project, initiated and funded by WAOB has been completed. These daily temperature and precipitation reports for 7,000 stations around the world are available both to the Department and to the public.

These data sets provide the most comprehensive global weather records in easily-accessible format to the public for analyzing weather information and determining impacts on agriculture. It will permit the Department to gain further insight into weather/crop yield relationships and to improve the reliability of USDA foreign crop production forecasts.

Also, using this data, WAOB designed a new set of statistical parameters, including freeze dates and precipitation probabilities, to be produced on disk by the National Climatic Data Center. This information will be available once the station inventory has been revised to reflect changes in political boundaries such as countries of the former Soviet Union.

ANALYSTS VISITS TO FORMER SOVIET UNION

Mr. DURBIN. During fiscal year 1991 analysts from the Board were part of two teams that traveled to the Soviet Union. One team focused on the status of the mixed feed industry and the other focused on spring wheat technology and use. Describe for us in further detail what you learned.

Mr. DONALD. The mixed feed team gained excellent insight into Soviet feed milling technology. Basically, former Soviet Union—FSU—countries could be doing much more with the resources they have to deliver quality feed but the incentive to do so is still lacking, although there has been some phasing down of the role of state-run enterprises. Problems in current mixed feed enterprises point to the need to do more on-farm-feed mixing. Greater dependence on feed additives and supplements along with on-farm feed mixing equipment could boost productivity in the FSU. But, unless economic incentives are adjusted to permit more decision making at the local levels, possibilities remain limited.

The spring wheat technology team evaluated the impact of drought on the spring wheat crop, providing valuable information for the USDA estimate of FSU grain production. Decreasing soil fertility and humus content were of major concern throughout the New Lands. Removal of straw after threshing combined with deep tillage contributed greatly to the decrease in soil organic matter.

On the marketing side, major limitations in the grain marketing system included a shortage of trucks, poor road conditions, and large distances between procurement points.

Mr. DURBIN. Were any Board members a part of other teams that traveled abroad during fiscal year 1992?

Mr. DONALD. During fiscal year 1992, WAOB staff traveled abroad as part of several teams. WAOB's cotton analyst participated in a USDA/industry team which visited three republics of the former Soviet Union in early September. The team obtained valuable data and information regarding the cotton situation and near-term outlook in Russia, Uzbekistan, and Turkmenistan.

WAOB's oilseeds analyst participated in travel to India and Indonesia. This team, organized by the Foreign Agricultural Service, gained further insight into the implications for the United States of increased vegetable oil and protein meal production and changing trade patterns in these countries.

RELATIONSHIP WITH ECONOMIC RESEARCH SERVICE

Mr. DURBIN. You rely on the Economic Research Service for analytical support. Describe for us in further detail your relationship with ERS.

Mr. DONALD. WAOB is responsible for coordinating USDA's economic intelligence program. WAOB oversees and clears for consistency the underlying assumptions, data and analytical results relating to domestic and international commodity supply and demand. As a very small agency, WAOB is not responsible for preparing primary economic research on behalf of the Department. This responsibility rests with the Economic Research Service—ERS—the Department's principal economic research arm.

WAOB accomplishes its mission by chairing the Interagency Commodity Estimates Committees, which focus on short-term commodity forecasts, and the Interagency Agricultural Projections Committee which focuses on longer-term cross-commodity relationships and aggregate farm sector projections. Primary analytical support for these committees is provided by ERS. The working relationship between WAOB, ERS and other agencies represented in the interagency process is one of mutual cooperation for the purpose of bringing together the best information and expertise on any given issue.

With respect to the economic outlook, all assumptions, data and preliminary analytical results developed by ERS are reviewed and cleared by interagency committees prior to public release. Thus, WAOB and ERS analysts work very closely through the interagency committees to arrive at consensus forecasts and projections.

DOMESTIC AND INTERNATIONAL ORGANIZATIONS

Mr. DURBIN. You mentioned in your statement three domestic and international organizations in which your agricultural meteorologists participate. Describe for us what each organization does and specifically what your role is with each.

Mr. DONALD. The Office of the Federal Coordinator for Meteorological Services and Supporting Research—OFCM—was established by Congress to ensure no duplication exists in the Nation's operational meteorological programs. The WAOB chief meteorologist represents USDA on the Interdepartmental Committee for Meteorological Services and Supporting Research (ICMSSR) of OFCM and is the alternate on the Federal Committee for Meteorological Services and Supporting Research (FCMSSR) of OFCM. The USDA member works to ensure the needs of the Department are presented within the framework of the Nation's Weather Service Programs.

The National Academy of Science's Board on Atmospheric Sciences and Climate—NAS/BASC—focuses on the cutting edge of basic research in the Atmospheric Sciences. BASC evaluates research at universities and governmental laboratories to ensure the focus is on filling critical gaps in our knowledge base, that the plan for research is scientifically sound and that information on the progress and results are shared between researchers, both nationally and internationally. WAOB's chief meteorologist focuses on the link between science and operations to ensure USDA can take advantage of scientific findings in relation to the Nation's capability to produce food and fiber.

WAOB's chief meteorologist heads the U.S. Delegation to the World Meteorological Organization's Commission for Agricultural Meteorology—WMO/CAgM. The Commission focuses on transfer of knowledge about uses of weather and climate information to improve management of crop production systems around the world. This information is very useful to USDA's agricultural meteorologists. It includes information on type of crops, crop calendars, management practices, etc. which are part of the inputs required to make crop condition and yield potential assessments.

The WAOB chief meteorologist has maintained contact with FAO since 1975 and has helped FAO establish a weather-based crop assessment capability similar to USDA's. FAO has focused intensively on Africa. WAOB and FAO exchange assessment information on a regular basis. FAO tends to focus on less developed countries while WAOB focuses more on major U.S. markets and competitors.

INTERAGENCY COMMITTEES

Mr. DURBIN. How are the Interagency Commodity Estimates Committee and the Interagency Agricultural Projections Committee the same and/or different?

Mr. DONALD. The Interagency Commodity Estimates Committees—ICEC's—develop the Department's short-term and long-term commodity supply/use forecasts and projections. The Separate ICEC's for grains, oilseeds, cotton, sugar, and dairy are chaired by WAOB senior commodity analysts. Each ICEC has standing representatives from the Economic Research Service (ERS), the Foreign Agricultural Service—FAS, the Agricultural Stabilization and Conservation Service—ASCS, and the Agricultural Marketing Service—AMS. Other agencies may be requested to participate in ICEC meetings as appropriate.

The Interagency Agricultural Projections Committee—IAPC—on the other hand, is a single committee which focuses on cross-commodity issues and aggregate farm sector projections. Its purpose is to sharpen the Department's focus on projections for the President's budget and as a base for analysis of alternative government programs. The Department established the IAPC in 1988.

The IAPC furnishes economic and policy assumptions and develops "baseline" projections (including commodity projections for the next 10 years, 5 years beyond the ICEC projections) for commodity-related components of the agricultural sector. IAPC projections provide the data for those USDA agencies with responsibilities requiring the use of such projections. The IAPC is chaired by the Chairperson of WAOB. Permanent members of the IAPC include: AMS, ASCS, Economic Analysis Staff, ERS, FAS, Federal Crop Insurance Corporation, Office of Budget and Program Analysis, and Soil Conservation Service.

Primary analytical support to the IAPC for U.S. and foreign macroeconomics assumptions and U.S. cost of production data is provided by the Economic Research Service, the Department's non-program, economic research arm. All ICEC chairpersons are represented on the IAPC. Any USDA agency may be requested to participate in the IAPC as appropriate.

REPORTS

Mr. DURBIN. Who produces the Crop Production report and how is it different from the Supply and Demand Estimates report?

Mr. DONALD. The Crop Production report is produced by the National Agricultural Statistics Service. The Crop Production report provides domestic crop forecasts only.

The World Agricultural Supply and Demand Estimates—WASDE—report provides forecasts of world supply and demand for grains, oilseeds and cotton; and U.S. supply and demand estimates for red meat, poultry, eggs and milk. Thus, the Crop Production report is limited in scope to agricultural production in the United States, while the WASDE report focuses on the global supply and disappearance of agricultural commodities.

SWEETENER MARKET DATA

Mr. DURBIN. Describe the new publication, Sweetener Market Data, in further detail. Is this a document you publish or does ASCS publish it?

Mr. DONALD. Sweetener Market Data is published by ASCS. It contains monthly data on U.S. sugar stocks, production, use, and trade. All data in the publication are historical, compiled from survey forms completed by all U.S. sugar producers and refiners. Sweetener Market Data replaces the quarterly report Sugar Market Statistics, formerly prepared and published by the National Agricultural Statistics Service (NASS).

The Food, Agriculture, Conservation, and Trade Act of 1990 (FACTA) mandates all U.S. cane sugar refiners, sugar beet processors, and crystalline fructose manufacturers to furnish the Department, on a monthly basis, statistics on imports, distribution, and stocks of sugar and crystalline fructose. The FACTA also directs the Department to use these data to publish, on a monthly basis, composite data on imports, distribution, and stocks of sugar and crystalline fructose. Sweetener Market Data does not contain crystalline fructose statistics because the Department is prohibited from disclosing the operations of individual companies.

USER FEE PROGRAM

Mr. DURBIN. What type of information from the database on U.S. field crops will be offered for sale under the user fee program?

Mr. DONALD. Data currently sold under the user fee program includes selected U.S. crop estimates from the World Agricultural Supply and Demand Estimates Report (WASDE) for U.S. crops from the first issue on September 17, 1973 through no. 272 (November 10, 1992). Prior to issue number 55 (June 9, 1977) the report was known as Agricultural Supply and Demand Estimates. Data offered for sale are those actually published. Updates will follow release of each year's November report. Sugar, livestock and dairy information will be included in the next release.

The crop estimates released cover cotton, rice, long grain rice, short- and medium-grain rice, soybeans, soymeal, soyoil, total feed grains, corn, sorghum, barley, oats, wheat, and wheat by class (hard winter, hard spring, soft red, white, and durum).

GLOBAL WEATHER

Mr. DURBIN. Describe in further detail the new source of global weather products you now have access to through the Navy.

Mr. DONALD. The Joint Agricultural Weather Facility, JAWF, receives vast amounts of daily global temperature and precipitation data from NOAA for global weather monitoring over crop areas. But, the ability to access and display products indicating storm location and intensity or projected storm tracks which may affect crop areas, heretofore, has been unavailable in an automated format.

The Navy's Fleet Numerical Oceanography Center developed a flexible automated system which allows desk top microcomputers to easily define geographical areas of interest and allow selection of required weather data. Data are stored for retrieval by the microcomputer, with capability to zoom into selected geographic areas, and to examine weather data for those areas. This system provides a tailored capability to complement our existing historical and near real-time data with current and forecast weather conditions to maintain high quality global surveillance of agricultural weather.

REMOTE SENSING

Mr. DURBIN. Please list the seven agencies that depend on remote sensing along with a brief summary of how they use the information.

Mr. DONALD. I will provide a brief description of how each of the seven agencies uses remote sensing information for the record.

[The information follows:]

National Agricultural Statistical Service (NASS): NASS uses remote sensing to estimate U.S. crop area and production. Its research is directed at developing accurate methods of forecasting with remote sensing data at costs that are lower than via traditional methods.

Foreign Agricultural Service (FAS): FAS uses satellite data to assess foreign crop conditions; shares these assessments with other Department agencies; and provides remote sensing support to ASCS.

Forest Service (FS): FS uses remote sensing to manage, inventory, and protect 191 million acres of the U.S. National Forest System and more than 600 million acres of forest outside these boundaries.

Agricultural Stabilization and Conservation Service (ASCS): ASCS, a major producer of imagery, uses the remote sensing to monitor U.S. crop program compliance and assesses damage done to crops by drought and other bad-weather phenomena. To support this work, it operates the Aerial Photography Field Office in Salt Lake City, which provides aerial photo contracting for USDA and sells this imagery to 2800 ASCS field offices, other federal agencies, and nonfederal users.

Soil Conservation Service (SCS): SCS uses remote sensing data to monitor soil, water, and natural resource conditions and to conduct resource inventories.

Agricultural Research Service (ARS): ARS conducts research to support remote sensing applications for making crop assessments and monitoring natural resources.

World Agricultural Outlook Board (WAOB): WAOB coordinates Department remote sensing activities. It represents the Department to outside organizations on remote sensing matters; chairs interagency meetings at which USDA remote sensing data needs are identified; organizes Department responses to requests for information and assessments of proposed remote sensing programs and policies; provides for technical and cost information exchange among USDA agencies; and oversees the integration of remote sensing data with information from meteorological and other sources to ensure the timely and accurate preparation of crop production and supply estimates.

OUTLOOK CONFERENCE

Mr. DURBIN. The Board is responsible for putting on the annual outlook conference, which is designed to highlight new developments within the Department. This year's conference, held this past December, was called Agriculture's Changing Horizon. Tell us some specific examples of the message of this conference.

Mr. DONALD. The annual outlook conference provides commodity forecasts for the year ahead and insight into policy developments that affect the outlook. The 60th annual conference, held last December, was attended by 600 members of the public from all facets of agriculture, including 100 farm journalists.

Farm analysts from USDA, industry and universities present detailed farm-and food forecasts for 1993. I will provide some specifics on forecasts for the record.

[The information follows:]

1993 begins with very big supplies of crops from 1992 harvests. Record-shattering yields were recorded for many 1992 crops and production expanded more than use.

Demand will further improve for crops as U.S. and foreign economies recover. This will help to prevent an even bigger buildup in stocks before 1993 harvests and limit the decline in crop prices.

Meat and poultry production is expected to grow 3 percent this year, following similar gains the past two years. Per capita meat supplies could hit 212 pounds per person, compared with 203 pounds in 1991.

Farm income, which has been at a high level since 1990, could drop a little in 1993 as farmers sell more, but at lower prices.

Retail food prices, which rose only 1.2 percent in 1992, could increase 2-4 percent this year. Ample food supplies and slow inflation in food marketing costs will help counteract pressure from stronger demand.

Special sessions focused on the longer term agricultural outlook in light of an increasingly urban and health conscious society and new political and economic realities across the globe.

Studies suggest that the U.S. farm sector will expand to feed growing markets, especially abroad, but will still struggle with the problem of excess capacity to produce.

If budget cuts reduce future participation in farm programs, one analyst suggested, acreage covered by conservation compliance would dwindle.

Several speakers emphasized cooperative alternatives regulating agriculture. New York City is working with upstate dairy farmers to reduce contamination of the City's water sources. California's water bank allowed market forces to reallocate water from farm to urban use.

Even as their numbers decline, farmers are growing more important to our society economically and environmentally. Yet several speakers see growing mistrust between farmers and other Americans. They urge steps to increase mutual understanding.

Mr. DURBIN. Mr. Skeen?

WEATHER FORECASTING

Mr. SKEEN. We are all aware of the important responsibilities of your agency involving weather forecasting and the notification as well as coordination with other agencies in planning for crop disasters, and the like. I do recall that there was an attack in a Washington Post article, a few years back, claiming that your weather predictions came true only 30% of the time. Knowing the Post's reputation, would you give me your impression of your agency's reliability?

I understand your agency assists in the operation of the Joint Agricultural Weather Facility, along with the National Oceanic and Atmospheric Administration and continues to jointly publish with NASS the Weekly Weather and Crop Bulletin.

I'm interested in your elaboration of the specific benefits of these programs to the farmers and crop experts?

Mr. DONALD. USDA does not make weather forecasts. This is the responsibility of the National Weather Service (NWS). USDA agricultural meteorologists convert current weather data and short-term forecasts from NWS into crop impact assessments which are used to alert the Secretary of Agriculture, commodity analysts and, as appropriate, Congress, the White House and the public, including farmers, of developing problems related to weather events around the world. These short-term assessments have proven to be quite reliable, providing important information and helping to stabilize markets for the benefit of farmers and others.

Mr. SKEEN. Will your budget recommendation provide for any improvements in this program for fiscal year 1994?

Mr. DONALD. At this time, the final FY 1994 budget is still being prepared.

FARM CROP PRODUCTION

Mr. SKEEN. Have you noticed any particular patterns and conditions which have affected farm crop production in the last two or three years?

Mr. DONALD. The more normally expected weather patterns during the last two to three years have been interrupted by the periodic occurrence of an El Nino centered in the Pacific and the eruption of Mt. Pinatubo in the Philippines. Both of these events have affected agricultural production, sometimes negatively and sometimes positively, depending on the region in question.

The El Nino in 1991 was weaker than in 1982–83 and produced a significantly different global weather pattern than observed during the 1986–87 El Nino event. There is no clear set pattern of change with the El Nino event, but the occurrence of an El Nino often portends unusual weather somewhere in the world. The eruption of Mt. Pinatubo was the largest volcanic eruption since 1883 and produced highly unusual weather in many parts of the world. Both of these events have affected agricultural production, sometimes negatively and sometimes positively, depending on the region in question.

AUTOMATED DATA SYSTEM FOR SUPPLY AND DEMAND ESTIMATES

Mr. SKEEN. In last year's budget request, you proposed an additional $60 thousand to develop an automated system for supply and demand estimates.

Would you provide for the committee a brief explanation of any progress in these forecasts for the agency and its users?

Mr. DONALD. WAOB's request to develop an automated system for evaluating commodity supply and demand estimates was denied. However, with funds redirected by the Secretary to WAOB and specifically earmarked for this purpose, substantial progress has been made.

WAOB has built an automated data base containing all monthly commodity supply and demand forecasts, including prices, published in the World Agricultural Supply and Demand Estimates report since September 1973. Also using redirected funds, WAOB has acquired managerial and technical services for the project and entered into a reimbursable agreement with USDA's Office of Information Resources Management for on-going ADP systems analysis and software development services. To date a WASDE report module for grains has been developed, modules for sugar and cotton are nearing completion. Oilseeds and livestock modules will be developed this summer and fall.

Mr. DURBIN. Mr. Myers?

WEATHER FORECASTING

Mr. MYERS. We are all aware of the important responsibilities of your agency involving weather forecasting and the notification as well as coordination with other agencies in planning for crop disasters, and the like. I do recall that there was an attack in a Washington Post article, a few years back, claiming that your weather predictions came true only 30% of the time. Knowing the Post's reputation, would you give me your impression of your agency's reliability?

I understand your agency assists in the operation of the Joint Agricultural Weather Facility, along with the National Oceanic and Atmospheric Administration and continues to jointly publish with NASS the Weekly Weather and Crop Bulletin.

I'm interested in your elaboration of the specific benefits of these programs to the farmers and crop experts?

Mr. DONALD. USDA does not make weather forecasts. This is the responsibility of the National Weather Service (NWS). USDA agricultural meteorologists convert current weather data and short-term forecasts from NWS into crop impact assessments which are used to alert the Secretary of Agriculture, commodity analysts and, as appropriate, Congress, the White House and the public, including farmers, of developing problems related to weather events around the world. These short-term assessments have proven to be quite reliable, providing important information and helping to stabilize markets for the benefit of farmers and others.

Mr. MYERS. Will your budget recommendation provide for any improvement in this program for fiscal year 1994?

Mr. DONALD. At this time, the final FY 1994 budget is still being prepared.

FARM CROP PRODUCTION

Mr. MYERS. Have you noticed any particular patterns and conditions which have affected farm crop production in the last two or three years?

Mr. DONALD. The more normally expected weather patterns during the last two to three years have been interrupted by the periodic occurrence of an El Nino centered in the Pacific and the eruption of Mt. Pinatubo in the Philippines. Both of these events have affected agricultural production, sometimes negatively and sometimes positively, depending on the region in question.

The El Nino in 1991 was weaker than in 1982–83 and produced a significantly different global weather pattern than observed during the 1986–87 El Nino event. There is no clear set pattern of change with the El Nino event, but the occurrence of an El Nino often portends unusual weather somewhere in the world. The eruption of Mt. Pinatubo was the largest volcanic eruption since 1883 and produced highly unusual weather in many parts of the world. Both of these events have affected agricultural production, sometimes negatively and sometimes positively, depending on the region in question.

AUTOMATED DATA SYSTEM FOR SUPPLY AND DEMAND ESTIMATES

Mr. MYERS. In last year's budget request, you proposed an additional $60 thousand to develop an automated system for supply and demand estimates.

Would you provide for the committee a brief explanation of any progress in these forecasts for the agency and its users?

Mr. DONALD. WAOB's request to develop an automated system for evaluating commodity supply and demand estimates was denied. However, with funds redirected by the Secretary to WAOB and specifically earmarked for this purpose, substantial progress has been made.

WAOB has built an automated data base containing all monthly commodity supply and demand forecasts, including prices, published in the World Agricultural Supply and Demand Estimates report since September 1973. Also using redirected funds, WAOB has acquired managerial and technical services for the project and entered into a reimbursable agreement with USDA's Office of Information Resources Management for on-going ADP systems analysis and software development services. To date a WASDE report module for grains has been developed, modules for sugar and cotton are nearing completion. Oilseeds and livestock modules will be developed this summer and fall.

INFORMATION DATA AND COLLECTION SYSTEMS

Mr. MYERS. How has the WAOB worked with the former Soviet nations in the last year on information data and collection system? Are the new nations now cooperating with your agency?

Mr. DONALD. Efforts to gather information from nations of the former Soviet Union (FSU) have yielded mixed results depending on the country in question. The most complete official data are available from Russia and Ukraine. USDA attache coverage is limited virtually everywhere and team travel remains difficult. In general, FSU officials have been cooperative but, in many instances, they, too, have had difficulty in obtaining reliable data internally.

WEATHER AND CLIMATE

Mr. MYERS. Your agency is involved in a great deal of weather-based assessment information. How do you integrate this mission with that of the National Oceanic and Atmospheric Association, which is charged with the mission of oceanic and atmospheric research?

Mr. DONALD. There is an Interagency Agreement between the Departments of Commerce and Agriculture which provides for cooperation in the application of weather and climate information to agriculture. The Joint Agricultural Weather Facility (JAWF), established in 1978, is a world agricultural weather information center located in the Department of Agriculture and jointly staffed and operated by NOAA's National Weather Service and USDA's World Agricultural Outlook Board. The JAWF serves as a focal point for the transfer of basic weather data as well as products derived from weather satellites to agencies of USDA involved in crop production estimates.

NOAA provides meteorological expertise for the analysis and interpretation of global weather patterns and data products. This expertise increases the on-site analytical capability for monitoring, briefing and report preparation of global weather conditions in agricultural areas. WAOB agricultural meteorologists work closely with NOAA's on-site meteorologists to evaluate weather's effects on crop conditions and to assess the potential impact on crop yields.

JAWF's mission includes the publication of the Weekly Weather and Crop Bulletin, daily and weekly weather briefings for USDA staff, preparation of daily highlights for the USDA Secretary, weekly briefings to the USDA Secretary, and analytical input to yield estimates in USDA's monthly World Agricultural Supply and Demand Estimates report.

Mr. DURBIN. I would like to thank the three panels for joining us today, and we will be back in touch with you. Obviously there are some questions about organization and function that I would like to really address in a more informal atmosphere. In particular I might bring back Dr. Lee and Mr. Bay, for example, who have had some personal experience with reorganization efforts.

We will be working with Secretary Espy and trying our best to make sure that your function is enhanced and not penalized if there are such changes.

Thank you for joining us today. Again, I apologize for showing up a little late.

[The prepared statement follows:]

WORLD AGRICULTURAL OUTLOOK BOARD

Statement of James R. Donald, Chairperson, before the House Subcommittee on Agriculture, Rural Development, Food and Drug Administration, and Related Agencies

Mr. Chairman and Members of the Committee, it is my pleasure to appear before you today to discuss the work of the World Agricultural Outlook Board.

Overview

The World Agricultural Outlook Board (WAOB) plays a critical role in the U.S. Department of Agriculture's (USDA's) ongoing effort to ensure that its commodity information system responds to today's rapidly changing world. The purpose of the WAOB is twofold: to ensure that USDA's intelligence on both domestic and foreign developments which influence U.S. agriculture is timely, accurate, and objective; and to speed the flow of that information to producers, consumers, policy makers and the general public.

WAOB's main function is to coordinate and review for accuracy and consistency all USDA forecasts and analyses relating to international and domestic commodity supply and demand conditions. As a small agency responsible for coordinating USDA's economic intelligence program, the WAOB is highly dependent for analytical support on other agencies, especially the Economic Research Service, the Department's principal economic research arm.

WAOB is the Department's focal point for weather and climate information and weather-based impact assessments; these monitoring and analytical activities within USDA are coordinated by the WAOB Chairperson. Remote sensing activities in USDA also are coordinated by the WAOB Chairperson. Weather assessments and remote sensing activities are directed at improving the accuracy and timeliness of crop estimates.

USDA representation with respect to economic and meteorological matters is provided by WAOB staff. WAOB economists maintain liaison with counterparts in the Commodity Futures Trading Commission (CFTC) regarding developments in commodity markets. WAOB agricultural meteorologists participate in various domestic and international organizations such as: the Department of Commerce based Office of the Federal Coordinator for Meteorological Services and Supporting Research; the National Academy of Science's Board on Atmospheric Sciences and Climate; and the United Nation's World Meteorological Organization and Food and Agricultural Organization.

Specific Functions and Progress

WAOB chairs USDA's Interagency Commodity Estimates Committees (ICEC's) and seeks to assure that sound information from both domestic and international sources is fully integrated into the analytical process. The ICEC's are composed of representatives from the Economic Research Service (ERS), Agricultural Stabilization and Conservation Service (ASCS), Foreign Agricultural Service (FAS), Agricultural Marketing Service (AMS), and WAOB. All committee members are USDA professionals with responsibility for developing official estimates of supply, utilization, and prices for the major agricultural commodities. It is through these committees that the various USDA agencies work together in a coordinated effort. Development and use of new analytical tools and evaluation of forecasting performance are ongoing responsibilities of each committee.

Also, WAOB chairs the Interagency Agricultural Projections Committee (IAPC), created to sharpen the Department's focus on longer term commodity and aggregate farm sector projections. Macroeconomic and farm program assumptions used by USDA analysts are cleared through the IAPC to assure uniformity within the Department. Analytical results approved by the IAPC provide the data to USDA agencies charged with responsibilities requiring the use of such projections.

WAOB publishes the World Agricultural Supply and Demand Estimates (WASDE) report each month. WASDE presents aggregated global supply and demand data for all major agricultural commodities as well as detailed production, trade, utilization and stocks forecasts for the United States and for principal U.S. competitors and foreign importers. Release is simultaneous with the U.S. Crop Production report. Like the domestic Crop Production report, the WASDE report is viewed by U.S. and international agriculture as a benchmark report.

The Agricultural Statistics Board (ASB) of the National Agricultural Statistics Service (NASS) and the WAOB are co-located in a single lockup facility to maximize security conditions for analysis, compilation and release of world crop data and supply/demand estimates. This physical arrangement with the ASB facilitates interaction between domestic and international analysts.

USDA provides unbiased commodity supply and demand information to all market participants simultaneously and at minimal cost. As commodity prices are impacted less by Government programs and more by market forces, the need for objective and current information becomes even more critical. WAOB recognizes the need for rapid information dissemination and strives to place the WASDE report into the hands of farmers and other users as quickly and effectively as possible. Increasingly, improved technologies are being used to speed the flow of information. WASDE is transmitted electronically upon release at 3 p.m. to a central USDA system that can forward it to all interested users, greatly broadening the potential for report dissemination. A summary of the report placed in USDA's AgNewsFAX system gives ready access to the press and public. Wide advertising of the WASDE report through the Economic Agencies' "Reports" catalog has greatly increased public subscriptions.

Each month, WAOB records highlights of the WASDE report for broadcast on USDA's radio and television satellite network. Also, the report summary is sent electronically to U.S. embassies and trade offices around the world to keep U.S. agricultural attaches, counselors, and trade representatives current with the very latest information on commodity supplies and prices.

Weather, as much as any economic or policy development, continues to be a significant variable underlying agricultural production and prices in the Board's current year assessment work. Consequently, USDA places a high priority on incorporating weather-based assessment information into all analyses. The focal point for this activity is the Joint Agricultural Weather Facility (JAWF), operated jointly by the WAOB and the National Oceanic and Atmospheric Administration of the Department of Commerce. This facility, located in the South Agriculture Building, continually monitors and assesses global weather events and their probable impact on agricultural output. JAWF briefings, reports and special alerts are key inputs to the development of USDA crop yield estimates for both competitors and customers in world markets.

The Weekly Weather and Crop Bulletin (WWCB), USDA's electronic dissemination network, and radio and television are the principal means used by JAWF to disseminate meteorological assessments to the public. JAWF's early warning capability diminishes the likelihood that policy makers, farmers and other participants in the agricultural system will be caught unaware of a foreign crop failure or other significant global weather-related event. The WWCB is widely recognized as a prime source of reliable domestic and international crop and weather information. Summaries of this report are dispatched electronically by FAS to selected foreign posts.

Recent Activities

WAOB improved the monthly World Agricultural Supply and Demand Estimates report, which presents estimates of global supply and use for grains, oilseeds, and cotton and U.S. supply and use estimates for red meat, poultry, eggs, and milk, by expanding coverage to include sugar and by strengthening the analytical data base for forecasting all commodities.

In March 1992, WAOB began publishing a monthly U.S. sugar supply and use balance sheet in the WASDE report. Also, WAOB assisted ASCS in designing Sweetener Market Data, a new publication. These reports provide timely information to policy makers, producers, processors, and the public.

Since July 1992, more comprehensive coverage of all oilseeds and products have been reported in the WASDE report. This improvement was timely in light of the significant shortfall in rapeseed production, particularly in the EC and Canada.

WAOB continued to develop and implement a forecast evaluation system. The primary purpose of this project is to improve commodity forecasts by evaluating past performance. Substantial progress has been made on this project with the support of the Department's leadership and technical assistance provided by USDA's Office of Information Resources Management. All forecasts published in the WASDE report, numbering about 500,000, from the first issue in September 1973 to the current issue have been entered into the evaluation data base. Because of public interest, a portion of the data base on U.S. field crops will be offered for sale under the user fee program for USDA economic publications.

The Department's Interagency Agricultural Projections Committee, under leadership of WAOB, continued a concerted effort to improve USDA's longer term commodity estimates. These projections are used by the Commodity Credit Corporation to develop a budget baseline as well as for analyzing farm program alternatives.

The Joint Agricultural Weather Facility, operated by the WAOB and the National Oceanic and Atmospheric Administration, continued to jointly publish with NASS the Weekly Weather and Crop Bulletin. The WWCB summarizes global weather developments and assesses the potential impact on agricultural production.

WAOB monitored weather conditions at home and abroad to provide both the Executive and Legislative Branches with early warnings concerning potential weather impacts on crop yields. For example, as early-season dryness developed in the Midwest, WAOB evaluated the potential effects on forage availability and on potential crop prospects for use by USDA policy makers, particularly in disaster assistance decisions. Conversely, excessive rains in June delayed corn planting and cool weather slowed crop development raising additional concerns. While worst-case scenarios of summer drought or an early autumn freeze were predicted throughout the season by private-sector forecasters, WAOB maintained objective assessments of actual conditions, tempering the predictions of low crop output. As the season further unfolded during 1992, WAOB's crop assessments proved to be quite accurate.

In the foreign arena, WAOB meteorologists prepared special statements, reports, and briefings providing early alerts of weather conditions affecting crop yield potential in major international crop areas. Notably, weather difficulties in the former Soviet Union, China, Europe, Morocco, Australia, Brazil, Argentina, and Canada were documented.

Through interaction and cooperation with U.S. Navy meteorologists, WAOB gained on-line access to a new source of global weather products for agricultural areas. This enhances JAWF's agricultural weather assessments by improving the ability to anticipate significant foreign weather developments that may impact agriculture up to 72 hours in advance of the actual event.

As part of WAOB's role in climate activities, the Board's Chief Meteorologist represents the United States on the North Atlantic Treaty Organization's "Special Programme on the Science of Global Environmental Change." The panel directs the organization of scientific workshops bringing together the world's leading scientists on global climate and environmental change.

The Board coordinates remote sensing activities at the Department level. Seven USDA agencies depend on remote sensing to assess crop conditions, manage natural resources, and operate farm programs. USDA is the largest purchaser of Landsat imagery among civilian Federal agencies. The Board represented the Department at interagency meetings, provided data to NASA to support negotiations for reduced imagery costs, and contributed information to NASA's Annual Aeronautics and Space Report to the President and several surveys on agency remote imagery requirements.

Consistent with the Board's projections responsibility, WAOB's Chief Meteorologist participated in two conferences focusing on environmental and climate change. At present, the work is in the data collection and discovery phase. Much analysis remains to be done before conclusions can be drawn about weather's impact on agriculture.

Among long-term significant Board projects of the past year, WAOB worked with FAS and ERS to identify data needs and develop revised data series for the 12 countries of the former Soviet Union and the Baltic States. To collect otherwise unavailable information regarding the supply and demand for agricultural commodities, WAOB personnel traveled to the former Soviet Union, China, India, and Indonesia. These data improved the analytical base for forecasting U.S. cotton, vegetable oil, and protein meal exports.

WAOB coordinated USDA's participation in Commodity Futures Trading Commission's weekly closed market surveillance briefings. USDA and the CFTC shared market information as part of an ongoing futures price monitoring activity.

WAOB coordinated and directed USDA's 69th Annual Outlook Conference, "Agriculture's Changing Horizon" (December 1-3, 1992.) The conference featured 31 topical sessions and prominent speakers from the public and private sectors; it attracted an on-site audience of 1,000, including a large press contingent. Plenary sessions of the conference were broadcast nationwide via satellite.

WORLD AGRICULTURAL OUTLOOK BOARD

Purpose Statement

The World Agricultural Outlook Board (WAOB) was created by the Secretary of Agriculture on June 3, 1977, under the authority of the Reorganization Plan No. 2 of 1953. The WAOB serves as the single focal point for the Nation's economic intelligence related to domestic and international food and agriculture, and is responsible for coordination and clearance review of all commodity and aggregate agricultural and food-related data used to develop outlook and situation material within the Department of Agriculture. The WAOB's primary objective is to improve the consistency, objectivity and reliability of outlook and situation material developed in the Department.

WAOB functions include: information dissemination; market surveillance; coordination of assessments of international and domestic agricultural developments; improvement of forecasting techniques; and coordination of weather, climate and remote sensing activities.

The WAOB is located in Washington, D.C. As of September 30, 1992, there were 29 full-time employees and I part-time employee. Budget, personnel, administrative and general managerial support are provided by the Economics Management Staff.

WORLD AGRICULTURAL OUTLOOK BOARD

Available Funds and Staff-Years

1992 Actual and Estimated 1993 and 1994

Item	1992 Actual Amount	1992 Actual Staff-Years	1993 Estimated Amount	1993 Estimated Staff-Years	1994 Estimated Amount	1994 Estimated Staff-Years
World Agricultural Outlook Board	$2,452,000	30	$2,537,000	35	$2,582,000	35
Obligations under Other USDA appropriations:						
Economic Research Service for Annual Outlook Conference	32,292	--	32,300	--	32,300	--
Extension Service for Annual Outlook Conf	21,528	--	21,500	--	21,500	--
Foreign Agricultural Service for Annual Outlook Conference	10,764	--	10,800	--	10,800	--
Total, Other USDA Appropriations	64,584	--	64,600	--	64,600	--
Total, Agriculture Appropriations	2,516,584	30	2,601,600	35	2,646,600	35
Total, World Agricultural Outlook Board	2,516,584	30	2,601,600	35	2,646,600	35

WORLD AGRICULTURAL OUTLOOK BOARD

Permanent Positions by Grade and Staff-Year Summary

1992 and Estimated 1993 and 1994

Grade	1992 Headquarters	1993 Headquarters	1994 Headquarters
ES-5	1	1	1
ES-4	1	1	1
Senior Level	1	1	1
GS/GM-15	9	9	9
GS/GM-14	3	3	3
GS/GM-13	1	3	3
GS-12	4	5	5
GS-11	1	1	1
GS-10	1	1	1
GS-9	1	3	3
GS-7	4	5	5
GS-6	1	1	1
GS-5	1	1	1
Total Permanent Positions	29	35	35
Unfilled Position end-of-year	--	-4	-4
Total, Permanent Employment, end-of-year	29	31	31
Staff-Years	30	35	35
Total	30	35	35

WORLD AGRICULTURAL OUTLOOK BOARD

CLASSIFICATION BY OBJECTS

1992 and Estimated 1993 and 1994

	1992	1993	1994
Personnel Compensation:			
Headquarters	$1,623,582	$1,742,000	$1,781,000
Field	--	--	--
11 Total personnel compensation	1,623,582	1,742,000	1,781,000
12 Personnel benefits	251,876	265,000	271,000
Total pers. comp. & benefits	1,875,458	2,007,000	2,052,000
Other Objects:			
21 Travel	47,663	50,000	42,000
22 Transportation of things	1,380	1,000	1,000
23.3 Communications, utilities, and misc. charges	69,277	69,000	72,000
24 Printing and reproduction	30,440	30,000	32,000
25 Other services	270,752	253,000	263,000
26 Supplies and materials	57,607	52,000	55,000
31 Equipment	86,411	75,000	65,000
43 Interest and dividends	132	--	--
Total other objects	563,662	530,000	530,000
Total direct obligations	2,439,120	2,537,000	2,582,000
Position Data:			
Average Salary, ES positions	$106,000	$109,550	$109,550
Average Salary, GM/GS positions	$33,623	$40,349	$42,224
Average Grade, GM/GS positions	11.1	11.7	11.9

WORLD AGRICULTURAL OUTLOOK BOARD

The estimates include appropriation language for this item as follows (new language underscored; deleted matter enclosed in brackets):

World Agricultural Outlook Board:

For necessary expenses of the World Agricultural Outlook Board to coordinate and review all commodity and aggregate agricultural and food data used to develop outlook and situation material within the Department of Agriculture, as authorized by the Agricultural Marketing Act of 1946 (7 U.S.C. 1622g), [2,367,000] $2,582,000: Provided, That this appropriation shall be made available for employment pursuant to the second sentence of section 706(a) of the Organic Act of 1944 (7 U.S.C. 2225).

WORLD AGRICULTURAL OUTLOOK BOARD

SALARIES AND EXPENSES

Appropriation Act, 1993	$2,367,000
Budget Estimate, 1994	2,582,000
Increase in Appropriation	+215,000

Adjustments in 1993:

Appropriation Act, 1993	$2,367,000	
Office of the Secretary Transfer a/	+170,000	
Adjusted base for 1993		2,537,000
Budget Estimate, Current Law 1994		2,582,000
Increase over adjusted 1993		+45,000

a/ The transfer from the Office of the Secretary is for the Estimates Automation and Evaluation program. On a comparable basis the cost is $170,000 for FY 1993 and $170,000 for FY 1994.

Summary of Increase and Decreases
(On basis of adjusted appropriation)

Item of Change	1993 Estimated	Pay Cost	Other Changes	1994 Estimated
Annualization of FY 1993 Pay Raise..................	--	+$45,000	--	+$45,000
Non pay inflation............		--	+$14,000	+14,000
Administrative overhead reduction.................	--	--	-14,000	-14,000
All Other....................	$2,537,000	--	--	2,537,000
Total Available.............	2,537,000	+45,000	--	2,582,000

Project Statement
(On basis of adjusted appropriation)

Project	1992 Actual Amount	1992 Actual Staff-Years	1993 Estimated Amount	1993 Estimated Staff-Years	Increase	1994 Estimated Amount	1994 Estimated Staff-Years
Commodity and Aggregate and Agricultural and Food Outlook Situation.	$2,439,120	30	$2,537,000	35	+$45,000	$2,582,000	35
Unobligated balance.......	12,880		--		--	--	
Total Available or estimate...	2,452,000	30	2,537,000	35	+45,000	2,582,000	35
Transfer from Secretary's Office.........	-85,000	-1	-170,000	-2	--	--	--
Total appropriation.	2,367,000	29	2,367,000	33			

WORLD AGRICULTURAL OUTLOOK BOARD

EXPLANATION OF PROGRAM

The World Agricultural Outlook Board (WAOB) coordinates and reviews for clearance all commodity and aggregate agricultural and food-related data used to develop outlook and situation material within the U.S. Department of Agriculture. The WAOB provides a focal point for the Nation's economic intelligence relative to domestic and international food and agriculture, with two primary objectives: improving the consistency, objectivity, and reliability of outlook and situation material being disseminated to the public; and integrating and coordinating USDA domestic and international economic information assistance. In a cooperative effort with the National Oceanic and Atmospheric Administration, the WAOB operates the Joint Agricultural Weather Facility which provides a daily review of significant weather developments around the world and their implications for agriculture. The WAOB's functions include market surveillance; coordination of assessments of international and domestic agricultural developments; weather, climate and remote sensing coordination; and forecasting techniques and information dissemination.

JUSTIFICATION OF INCREASES AND DECREASES

(1) An increase of $45,000 for Commodity and Aggregate Agricultural and Food Outlook and Situation consisting of:

(a) An increase of $45,000 for absorbed fiscal year 1993 pay costs.

(b) An increase of $14,000 which reflects a 2.7 percent increase in non-salary costs.

Need for Change. These funds are necessary to offset increased operating costs. Continued absorption of these increased operating costs will severely affect the quality and quantity of our program.

Nature of Change. This increase will be used to maintain a current level of services associated with inflation which will affect the critical parts of the program.

(c) A decrease of $14,000 which reflects a 3 percent reduction in administrative expenses from the amount made available for fiscal year 1993 adjusted for inflation.

Need for Change. To promote the efficient use of resources for administrative purposes, in keeping with the President's Executive Order. Total USDA baseline outlays for these activities will be reduced by 3 percent in FY 1994, 6 percent in FY 1995, 9 percent in FY 1996 and 14 percent in FY 1997.

Nature of Change. In order to achieve this savings, WAOB will carefully monitor travel, training, supply purchases, printing and reproduction costs, utility usage, and curtail its agreements with other Federal agencies.

GEOGRAPHIC BREAKDOWN OF OBLIGATIONS AND STAFF-YEARS
1992 and Estimated 1993 and 1994

	1992		1993		1994	
	Amount	Staff-Years	Amount	Staff-Years	Amount	Staff-Years
District of Columbia	$2,439,120	30	$2,537,000	35	$2,582,000	35
Unobligated Balance	12,880	--	--	--	--	--
Total Available or Estimate.........	2,452,000	30	2,537,000	35	2,582,000	35

WORLD AGRICULTURAL OUTLOOK BOARD

STATUS OF PROGRAM

The World Agricultural Outlook Board (WAOB) coordinates and reviews for clearance all commodity and aggregate agricultural and food-related data used to develop outlook and situation material within the U.S. Department of Agriculture. Prior to the creation of WAOB on June 3, 1977, agricultural outlook and situation data were collected, analyzed and reported by several agencies in USDA. The Board's role is to coordinate and assure the accuracy, timeliness and objectivity of USDA's agricultural outlook and situation analysis. The Board not only directs the compilation and review of critical economic intelligence data, it also makes sure the essential information quickly reaches policy makers and the public, especially the U.S. farmer.

Current Activities: WAOB functions include: information dissemination; market and agricultural weather surveillance; coordination of USDA forecasts of international and domestic agricultural developments; and coordination of weather, climate and remote sensing research activities.

The Board presents weekly briefings of significant agricultural developments to the Secretary and other top officials, supplemented by a daily market intelligence report.

Selected Examples of Recent Progress: As a part of USDA's ongoing economic information program, the WAOB continued to publish the monthly World Agricultural Supply and Demand Estimates report, which provides projections of world and U.S. supply and utilization data for grains, soybeans and cotton; and U.S. estimates for red meat, poultry, eggs and milk. During fiscal year 1992, coverage was expanded to include U.S. refined sugar, U.S. and world oilseeds and more detail for the former Soviet Union. The report also includes forecast reliability tables for selected commodities and parameters.

The Joint Agricultural Weather Facility (JAWF), operated by the WAOB and the National Oceanic and Atmospheric Administration, in cooperation with the National Agricultural Statistics Service, published the Weekly Weather and Crop Bulletin. The JAWF continued to monitor and interpret significant global weather developments and their implications for agriculture. Greater access to U.S. weather observations and advance meteorologic indications enhance the JAWF's ability to monitor weather impacts on agriculture.

During a year highlighted by weather that plagued agriculture, USDA's World Agricultural Outlook Board provided policy makers and the public with early and frequent assessment of how world crops were likely to be affected.

The El Nino weather phenomenon and the eruption of Mount Pinatubo in the Philippines affected global weather patterns during the past year and raised fears of potential impacts on crop production. Heightening concern in the United States were a prolonged wet spring, the sixth year of drought in the far west, and pockets of dryness elsewhere. Summer was unusually cool, delaying crop development. With ending stocks tight last summer, markets were highly tentative about possible crop losses. Hurricane Andrew and an active hurricane season in the Pacific raised additional worries. The World Board responded to numerous inquiries from Government officials, Congress and the press. Based on analysis of past climatic history, the Board correctly counseled early caution against assuming large U.S. crop losses.

Despite the spring flooding and cool summer, the Board released early U.S. projections from May through July that correctly anticipated the actual outcome of bumper U.S. harvests of grains and oilseeds. The global impact of

El Nino and the Mount Pinatubo eruption created great concern for crops abroad, focusing unusual attention on the supply and demand projections for key foreign regions released each month by the Board in the World Agricultural Supply and Demand Estimates report. These pre-season estimates proved to be consistent with forecasts released by the National Agricultural Statistics Service as the season progressed.

WAOB helped conduct or coordinate a number of analyses of trade issues related to the U.S.-EC oilseeds dispute, the Uruguay Round negotiations and the North American Free Trade Area negotiations. On the domestic front, WAOB provided analytical input to a number of farm program decisions.

The Board's oilseeds analyst traveled to India and Indonesia to gain further insight into the implications for the United States of increased vegetable oil and protein meal production and changing trade patterns. The WAOB cotton analyst participated in a team visiting three republics of the former Soviet Union, which revealed that cotton was not moving from producing republics to Russia, where most of the mills are located.

With responsibility for chairing all Interagency Commodity Estimates Committees, the WAOB continued to further advance and focus USDA's economic information system. For the purpose of improving USDA's longer term commodity supply and demand and farm sector projections, WAOB directed the activities of the Interagency Agricultural Projections Committee (IAPC). Twice annually, the IAPC provides a common set of farm program and macroeconomic assumptions to the Interagency Commodity Estimates Committees to assure uniformity in the preparation of interagency projections. The IAPC routinely reviews livestock and crop projections and farm income forecast for internal consistency. These projections underlie Federal budget and USDA farm program planning.

WAOB's Remote Sensing Coordinator facilitated information exchanges on remote sensing projects and activities among USDA agencies to avoid duplication of effort and ensure optimum use of resources. Contacts with private-sector remote sensing specialists were encouraged to resolve data dissemination problems and assure that USDA's information requirements will receive high priority in future satellite systems. Better interchange among agencies and the private sector has resulted in sharing of data and resources and the avoidance of unnecessary costs.

WAOB coordinated USDA's contribution to the annual Aeronautics and Space Report of the President: Fiscal Year 1992 Activities. This recurring project requires contact with and solicitation of significant achievements from the agencies that are dominant in remote sensing.

Existing links with the Commodity Futures Trading Commission were continued under a formal CFTC-USDA agreement to ensure that the futures markets best serve the interests of both farmers and consumers.

WAOB hosted the 68th U.S. Agricultural Outlook Conference held December 3-5, 1991. With a theme "New Opportunities for Agriculture," the Conference featured 30 topical sessions and prominent speakers from the public and private sectors and attracted a large on-site audience and extensive press coverage. All major plenary sessions of the Conference were broadcast nationwide via satellite. Prior to the event, significant links were developed with potential viewers especially at Land Grant and 1890 institutions. These actions greatly enhanced public access to the Conference and understanding of USDA and its programs.

WEDNESDAY, MARCH 24, 1993.

FOOD AND NUTRITION SERVICE

WITNESSES

GEORGE A. BRALEY, ACTING ASSISTANT SECRETARY, FOOD AND CONSUMER SERVICES

ANDREW P. HORNSBY, JR., ACTING ADMINISTRATOR, FOOD AND NUTRITION SERVICE

KENNETH BRESNAHAN, BUDGET OFFICER, FOOD AND NUTRITION SERVICE

STEPHEN B. DEWHURST, BUDGET OFFICER, DEPARTMENT OF AGRICULTURE

Ms. DELAURO. Good morning. I will open the hearing this morning. Chairman Durbin is tied up testifying at another committee, but will be here in about ten or fifteen minutes. So we are going to get underway.

I want to thank you for coming this morning. We are going to hear from the Food and Nutrition Service. Mr. Braley is the Acting Assistant Secretary. If you would like to introduce the other members of the panel who are here with you this morning, and then proceed to making your statement.

Mr. BRALEY. Thank you very much. I am accompanied for the first part of this morning's activities by the Acting Administrator of the Food and Nutrition Service, Andrew Hornsby, to my right. And then to his right is Kenneth Bresnahan, who is our budget officer. And of course, you know the Department's budget officer, Steve Dewhurst, quite well by now.

Ms. DELAURO. I have seen him many times, yes.

Please go ahead.

PREPARED STATEMENT

Mr. BRALEY. If we could proceed with very brief introductory comments. And Mr. Hornsby will have a brief statement. And then we can proceed to questions.

It is my pleasure to appear before the subcommittee to discuss the current fiscal year exceed $38 billion. And that includes a repartment of Agriculture.

The total appropriations for the Food and Nutrition Service in the current fiscal year exceeds $38 billion. And that includes a reserve for the Food Stamp Program should it be necessary to request those funds.

The Food and Nutrition Service provides food assistance to low-income Americans, helping them to achieve adequate and nutritious diets. We estimate that one out of every six Americans is served through the 14 programs that we manage at the Food and Nutrition Service. The Food Stamp Program, of course, is our largest program, and one which is available to all low income and low resource households.

SPECIAL TARGET POPULATIONS

In addition, the agency serves special target populations such as schoolchildren through the Child Nutrition Programs, pregnant and postpartum women, and Infants through the WIC Program, and the Commodity Supplemental Food Program, Native Americans, and senior citizens through various commodity and cash support programs. It is in recognition that these groups are at a particularly high nutritional risk.

During the questioning session, with your permission, as you can see, Mr. Hornsby and I are both acting in our current positions. Mr. Hornsby has an extensive background in the Food Stamp Program. He is normally the Deputy Administrator for Food Stamps. Most of my background in the Food and Nutrition Service has been with the other programs, Child Nutrition, WIC, and the commodities programs. So Mr. Hornsby would probably take the lead in responding to food stamp questions and I will tend to take the lead on the others, if that is okay with you.

And I will conclude my remarks at this point, and ask Mr. Hornsby if he has a brief statement.

[CLERK'S NOTE.—Mr. Braley's prepared statement appears on pages 377 through 379.]

Mr. HORNSBY. Thank you. It is a pleasure to appear before this subcommittee to discuss the operations of food assistance programs administered by the USDA. I would like to introduce some key members of the staff of the Food and Nutrition Service who are here with me.

KEY STAFF MEMBERS

Bonny O'Neil is the Acting Deputy Administrator for the Food Stamp Program. Ron Vogel is the Acting Deputy Administrator for the Special Nutrition Programs. Michael Fishman is the Acting Director of our Office of Analysis and Evaluation. You already met Ken Bresnahan.

Mr. Vogel and Mr. Fishman are appearing before the committee for the first time. And in keeping with the committee policy, we would like to place their biographical sketches into the record at this point.

[CLERK'S NOTE.—Biographies for Mr. Vogel and Mr. Fishman appear on pages 375 and 376.]

Mr. HORNSBY. The mission of the Food and Nutrition Service is to alleviate hunger, and to safeguard the health and well-being of the Nation through the administration of nutrition education and domestic food assistance programs. The Food and Nutrition Service is the federal government's front line agency providing food assistance to the most needy and vulnerable of our citizens.

1993 APPROPRIATIONS

As Mr. Braley mentioned, our fiscal 1993 appropriations for the Food and Nutrition Service total $38.1 billion. I should mention that $2.5 billion of that money is in a food stamp reserve.

We have eight accounts covering fourteen major programs including federal administrative expenses. FNS has allocated 1,979 staff years funded from the Food Program Administration, Food Stamps, and the Child Nutrition accounts. Food and Nutrition Service's eight appropriations account for over half of the budget authority of the USDA.

I am providing this statement for the record. And with your permission, we will submit that for the record, and we will proceed into questions that you may have.

Ms. DeLauro. That is fine. Thank you.

[Clerk's note.—Mr. Hornsby's prepared statement appears on pages 380 through 401. The budget justifications, which were received on May 10, 1993, appear on pages 402 through 570.]

Ms. DeLauro. Are there any other statements?

Mr. Braley. Not at this point.

NATIONAL SCHOOL LUNCH PROGRAM

Ms. DeLauro. Before I get to some food stamp questions, let me ask a couple of questions about the child nutrition programs, if I might.

I am from the State of Connecticut. Our statistics are showing that one out of six youngsters in the State are at risk for hunger. And while we are one of the richest States per capita in the country, we have three of the poorest cities in the country, New Haven, Hartford, and Bridgeport. So these are important programs for us.

I met not too long ago with the providers of child nutrition programs in my state, and with regard to the school lunch and breakfast programs, a number of them have talked to me about the fat intake in these programs. Yet the National School Lunch Act mandates that whole milk be served to children who are participating in the programs.

Is that correct?

WHOLE MILK REQUIREMENT

Mr. Braley. Yes. The authorizing legislation for the school lunch program requires that whole milk be offered as one of the alternatives that are available for children to consume. There is also a requirement that low fat milk be offered.

Ms. DeLauro. Representative Miller has introduced legislation to eliminate the whole milk requirement. What is your opinion of that?

Mr. Braley. The Department has not taken an official position on that particular piece of legislation. There are certainly pros and cons to the current situation that allows children to select low fat milk. But it does provide them with the alternative of whole milk.

Unfortunately, I am not in the position today to comment definitively on what the policy is going to be on that issue from the Department.

FAT INTAKE

Ms. DeLauro. Do you currently do anything to monitor and limit the fat intake of children being served through these programs?

Mr. BRALEY. Yes, we do.

Ms. DELAURO. If you would not mind, I am new to the Committee this year, would you elaborate on that for me?

SCHOOL LUNCH EVALUATION

Mr. BRALEY. Sure. I will be happy to. Stepping back a few years in the school lunch program, we have done fairly extensive evaluations about every ten years of the nutritional quality of school meals. In the early 1980s, we went out and did a major national statistically representative sample of school lunches, and found that in terms of delivering vitamins and minerals, school lunches were very superior to alternative lunches that were available to children, either ones that they brought from home or ones that they left campus to eat.

Since then, the concern about fat and sodium, which we call macro nutrients, has really emerged as an increasing concern. Information that we have right now suggests that school lunches are very similar in terms of fat content to the diets of children of that age, both within and outside of school. So it is an issue that really needs to be addressed, both in and out of school. About 38 to 39 percent of calories in school lunch come from fat, 38 to 39 percent, depending on which studies you look at.

So we do have a way to go in that area. We have efforts under way to look at the meal pattern that is used for the program to see if there are ways to modify it, to encourage lower fat foods. We have lowered the fat and sodium content of many of the commodities that USDA purchases and provides for school lunch programs, and are very active in that regard currently.

But there is clearly more that we need to do. And I think that it needs to be more of a community effort. Not limited to meal programs, but also to getting parents aware of these issues. Getting PTA groups, teachers, and that sort of gathering.

We have a number of demonstration projects going on right now around the country where school districts are trying to lower the fat, and at the same time, to keep kids participating in the program. The big concern is that if we do something too drastic, you may lose some of your customers in the process. We do not want that to happen, while we are in the process of lowering fat and sodium, and other nutrients of concern.

School lunches, in terms of other aspects of nutrition, vitamins, and minerals, and protein, are doing an excellent job, and are better than the alternatives, but we have places to improve.

SCHOOL BREAKFAST PROGRAM

Ms. DELAURO. I applaud the school lunch program. I believe that it is working. I think that it is having a very, very positive effect. In addition to the school lunch program, there is also the breakfast program. What I found when I met with people in my own State is that they are taking advantage of the school lunch program, but the breakfast program is really not utilized to the extent that the lunch program is. I do not know if Connecticut is atypical, or if this is a pattern that is national.

Is there any review of why this is occurring?

Mr. BRALEY. I would be pleased to comment on that. For a lot of years, I have had in my mind—I have worked with these programs for about twenty years now—that about a third of the schools in the lunch program also offered a breakfast, and that the participation was much lower. And I thought that was kind of about as good as we could do.

SCHOOL BREAKFAST EXPANSION

But we have had legislative initiatives, initiatives by advocacy groups, and initiatives by state agencies to expand the breakfast program in recent years. We are now up to a point where half of the schools in the country that have a lunch program also have a breakfast program.

We have been making progress in that regard, but I still think that there is quite a bit more progress to be made. There are obstacles to starting breakfast programs in certain school districts. It can be a facilities issue, or it can be a scheduling issue of getting buses to get kids to school on time for them to have breakfast.

But what we are finding is, where people are interested in adding a breakfast program, ways can be found to do so.

We have been administering a start-up grant program for schools. We are just about to start the fifth year of that program. And we have added breakfast programs in schools that have 600,000 needy children in them just through those start-up grants alone. The last year of those grants will be issued shortly.

Ms. DELAURO. How was the information disseminated on the grant start-up program? How do school districts avail themselves of that information? Do you do a direct outreach?

Mr. BRALEY. We administer these programs through state educational agencies. So our contact is initially with state education agencies. We rely on them to target school districts within the state that do not have a breakfast program that they think might have potential for starting a program. Then the state pulls together a state proposal for us to consider.

I believe to date that we have funded programs one year or another in 38 of the states. So I think that it is fairly widely known that these grants exist, and the majority of states have availed themselves of them in one year or another.

OUTREACH

Ms. DELAURO. Let me turn to outreach efforts. When I met with program leaders in Connecticut, one of the most difficult problems that they face is the lack of funding for outreach. Only half of Connecticut residents who are eligible for food stamps participate in the program, and about three fourths of the eligible senior citizens do not participate.

In the WIC program in Connecticut, about one-third of women, infants, and children age five or under who are eligible do not participate in the program.

Is this a problem in other states as well, and what are you doing in an effort to try to improve outreach efforts?

Mr. BRALEY. Just a brief comment, and then maybe Mr. Hornsby may want to elaborate. We do have some breakfast outreach grants that were funded last year, and there will be some additional activity in that area this year.

As you probably know, too, food stamp participation is at a record level. So a lot of people are coming into the food stamp program now, possibly through outreach efforts from other programs. Once they are in the system, they also avail themselves of food stamp benefits. But I will let Mr. Hornsby elaborate on that.

Mr. HORNSBY. I recall testifying before you with Congressman Downey last year. You expressed some similar interest. It is of great concern to us, that eligible people especially among the elderly, do not avail themselves of the Food Stamp Program.

The Food Stamp Program I think is doing a very good job on outreach, as evidenced by the participation levels. We have a record level number of program participants. Yet we are concerned that obviously needy people still do not avail themselves of the program.

We are about to award some grants to states to assist in outreach efforts. We have some money set aside for that purpose and states are in the process of applying now. We believe this will help states reach other eligible people.

FOOD STAMP TAX OFFSET

Ms. DELAURO. Let me move to some food stamp questions. One big concern is obviously about fraud within the program.

How long do you expect it to take before there is program-wide use of the tax refund offset program? How long will it be before we are really up to speed on that? You talked about this in your testimony.

Mr. HORNSBY. We believe that tax offset will be used program-wide no later than 1997. We hope that we can move a little faster and we are being encouraged on several fronts to move tax offset faster. It has been real encouraging that states are volunteering to come into the federal tax refund offset program. I think that we have 9 states in already. We plan to add about 12 next year. We may have a few hold-outs, but we believe that the law is pretty specific. This is a tool that states will be required to use to collect food stamp debts.

Ms. DELAURO. What is the difficulty in starting?

Mr. HORNSBY. The states have used federal refund tax offsets for collection in child support for several years, and it is fairly easy. Some states have also collected against their state income tax. Those states have experience with it, and are anxious to get into it.

We have had to develop our capacity to manage this. It is not something that we could take on overnight. We have had to manage it with existing staff and existing resources.

We started slow with just two states in the pilot program, and then went to a total of nine, and then going on up to the twenties. But as fast as states want to come on, I think that we can put them.

Ms. DELAURO. These are my last questions, then I will turn to my colleague, Mr. Skeen, to ask questions.

FOOD STAMP TRAFFICKING

How much money was lost last year due to food stamp trafficking?

Mr. HORNSBY. That is a difficult question. We do not have a finite figure on how much food stamp trafficking occurs, or how much is lost to fraud. I would say that I am encouraged by two aspects of the food stamp program. One, three-fourths of all food stamps issued are spent in the nation's supermarkets. The other feature that comforts me is we do a very careful quality control check nationwide on food stamp households.

We pull thousands of food stamp cases, and literally dissect those cases, and determine whether this family is correctly certified for food stamps and are receiving the right amount of benefits. We find a very small percentage that have more or less misrepresented their circumstances.

The vast majority of food stamps are spent by eligible people for eligible food, but we do know and we do receive reports of trafficking. We are most concerned about street level trafficking in and around food stamp issuance offices. We are working with our Office of Inspector General, and with state and local investigative and law enforcement agencies to try to crack down on that and have an impact there.

ELECTRONIC BENEFIT TRANSFER

Ms. DELAURO. What about the electronic benefit transfer program? You did not mention it in terms of dealing with trafficking.

Mr. HORNSBY. That is a good point. I am sorry that I failed to mention that. We have about five or six EBT projects going on nationwide. In Maryland, they will be statewide with EBT in just another month or so. Right now, we are more or less in the demonstration phases. We have had some investigations of trafficking and other activities involving EBT. We found EBT to be a very effective tool to help identify people who are illegally converting their benefits to cash. It is a very effective tool in the investigations that we have had so far.

Plus it cuts down on what I consider street-level trafficking. Often unscrupulous people will wait on the outside of food stamp issuance offices in an attempt to buy food stamp benefits at a discount. And if a person is under some economic pressure for whatever reason, to pay a bill or something, they may sell $80 in food stamps. Normally, they will not get but $40 or $50 back.

With an EBT system, the benefit is virtually like cash, except it only can be used for food. There is no way to convert that benefit on the street. You would have to go into the store to do it.

Ms. DELAURO. In terms of the EBT, how do you handle the mom and pop stores or the farmers markets?

Mr. HORNSBY. In the projects that we have had so far, we have been able to accommodate them. I think that the test is going to be in Maryland statewide, where we will have every eligible retail food store in Maryland hooked up on EBT.

Mr. BRALEY. This includes retailers in rural areas and small ones. Maryland has a pretty good cross-section of urban and rural areas. So that will be a good example for us to see how cost effective that can be.

Ms. DeLauro. Thank you very much.

Mr. Skeen?

Mr. Skeen. Thank you, Madam Chair.

I am sorry about the delay this morning in getting here. Talk about traffic, is there anything that you can do about the Third Street tunnel? If you want to bring Washington to its knees, just plug that one tunnel up. Maybe we can get an electronic transfer or something, so you can get from home to the office without having to go through the traffic situation.

UNIVERSAL SCHOOL LUNCH

Let me continue with a line of questioning that I am particularly interested in, the school lunch program that you deal with.

How has that cooperation been with the states? And if you have any critique to make or criticism to make, I would like to hear them. And particularly, in the area of the so-called universal lunch program that has been proposed in many states.

Mr. Braley. I would be pleased to respond, Congressman Skeen. We have been working very well, I think, with the state agencies and representatives of local school districts on a number of administrative issues. We had an issue that was affecting that relationship for awhile, the coordinated review effort.

Mr. Skeen. It has been a rocky road.

Mr. Braley. It has been for the past few years but I think we are on a better footing now. I think that we put some of those issues behind us last summer with the regulation that we agreed on. I think that we are now getting some experience on the monitoring system.

We appreciate this committee's support for enabling us to have some federal oversight of local operations. That is an ongoing concern.

You raised a question on the universal school lunch program. We have been asked in a Senate resolution last year to take a look at that in terms of how much it would cost, and are there some ways to finance that.

We are in the process of preparing an answer to that Senate Resolution 303. That should be available this summer in time to be looked at as part of the reauthorization. The big obstacle to that, of course, is its cost.

Mr. Skeen. Always.

Mr. Braley. We estimate, and CBO has a similar estimate, of \$6.5 to \$7.5 billion to create a universal school lunch and breakfast program under current rules. Now again, maybe we can find some ways to cut that down a little bit, but it is a very expensive proposition. About half of the money would go to increased subsidies for children who are already in the program. So that is a concern as well. We will have a study available this summer on it, sir.

FAT FREE MILK

Mr. Skeen. I know that it is very difficult dealing with all of the various State regulations that may be in conflict with the general premise. And one is in the utilization of various agricultural products, for example, milk. The old standard was how much butter fat does it have in it, and now we want to get the fat out.

We just completed a little tour of the agricultural research station in the southern region in New Orleans this past weekend, and they have come up with new products that are virtually fat free milk products. Because what we are finding, and I am sure that your nutritional service has been a party to the development of this information, is the fact that more people today drink soda pop than they drink water.

People in general are drinking less milk today than ever before in the history of this country. Women are drinking less of it than men. And they are more susceptible to things like osteoporosis.

How much effect do you have in helping states to get them up-to-date nutritional information?

Mr. Braley. Congressman Skeen, one of the things that we have found in studies of school lunch programs and school breakfast programs in the past is that they do a good job of delivering the milk-related nutrients to kids. Their calcium intakes tended to be higher than children who either ate a brown bag meal or left school and had lunch, and that sort of thing.

The law requires now that we offer both whole milk and a low fat alternative. In many schools, they offer a low fat chocolate milk as well, in order to get more kids to consume the milk. And that is the way that we have dealt with that issue. But fluid milk is a required component of most all of the child nutrition meal service programs.

SCHOOL LUNCH PARTICIPATION

Mr. Skeen. I think that you have done a good job in the elementary schools. But I am a little bit concerned about secondary, and the high school level. Because teenagers seem to have the largest most precipitous drop-off in the intake of nutritional foods. And then they go to the fad foods.

Mr. Braley. The participation rates in lunch programs tend to drop off, too, at that level. Fewer and fewer of the school children participate in the lunch program as they get into junior high or middle school, and on into high school. They sometimes have an open campus where they can leave, or they are more apt to bring meals from home. That is an issue that we have been struggling with frankly for many, many years, in trying to work with local people to make meals even more attractive to the older students.

Mr. Skeen. Is there an element in the universal lunch proposal, which would extend it through the secondary school systems?

Mr. Braley. Again, the proposal, as I have understood it, would be for all systems to provide a free meal to any child that attends that school. Although I think that some people have asked that we look at what it might cost if you just did it at the elementary level. And some of those kinds of issues will be looked at. But the proposal, as we have seen it so far, really would make a lunch free of charge to all of the children up through high school.

MILK FIZZ

Mr. SKEEN. In new products developed by Food and Nutrition, do you have a method of persuasion, through informational services, to initiate the use of new products, such as milk fizz?

Mr. BRALEY. That is a new one on me, I am afraid.

Mr. SKEEN. It tastes pretty good. I had my doubts, too. But it is a great source of calcium, and it is in the popular mode. It is like milk soda pop, if you can imagine that. Or maybe you do not want to imagine it.

LOW-FAT PRODUCTS

Mr. BRALEY. I am not familiar with that particular product. But certainly, through our commodity program in particular, we have tried to introduce lower fat products more consistent with dietary guidelines. Today, we have lower fat beef products, and ground turkey products.

Mr. SKEEN. There is a whole plethora.

Mr. BRALEY. And we are very much involved in that. The school food service industry, through its national convention and state conventions, has industry come in all of the time and present new products. Every year that you go to that conference, you see brand new products. More and more of them are addressing the issues of lower fat, and lower sodium, and cholesterol, and the kinds of things that are of concern today.

FOOD STAMP FRAUD

Mr. SKEEN. On the topic of food stamp fraud. I know that one of the most difficult parts of your whole enforcement program is dealing with the various states. And it varies from one state to another with their ability to track and keep up their end of the bargain as far as the food stamp program.

Would you run a critique on how well you can negotiate these systems in various state programs?

Mr. BRALEY. I think that I will ask Mr. Hornsby if he will comment on that.

Mr. SKEEN. I would like for you to be specific about it.

Mr. HORNSBY. Yes, sir. We probably can submit some state by state data to you.

Mr. SKEEN. I would enjoy having it.

Mr. HORNSBY. Yes, sir. We can do that. Let me just say though that it is mixed. It is like all of the aspects of the food stamp program. States are responsible for correctly certifying households to receive food stamp, and correctly issuing the right amount of food stamps. We do ask that states establish claims.

I was real encouraged during fiscal 1992 that states established more claims than they had previously. I was concerned that with the huge caseload growth that we have had in food stamps in the last couple of years that those resources working on fraud claims and other claims would be drained off into just determining eligibility for households.

We had, I think, about a 3 percent increase in the total dollar amount of claims established, which was encouraging. It showed that states were still committed. Some states do a better job than others. But I worry about the resources that states have to put into that.

Mr. SKEEN. That brings up the other question. In light of their troubles with financing and their appropriation level, it is just as severe I am sure state by state as ours is. Sometimes I think that they are just totally incapable of having the kind of response capability built into their budget. And I am sure that you are closely aware of it state by state.

Am I correct in that assumption?

Mr. HORNSBY. Yes, sir, you are. We can give you that state by state information, and we will do so.

Mr. SKEEN. I would like to have it.

[The information follows:]

FOOD STAMP PROGRAM ACTIVITY - FY 1992

STATE	PERSONS FY 1992	PERSONS PERCENT CHANGE 91-92	ISSUANCE FY 1992	ISSUANCE PERCENT C A GN 91-92	TOTAL ADMIN FEDERAL SHARE FY 1992	ADMIN PERCENT CHANGE 91-92	TOTAL CLAIMS COLLECTED FY 1992	TOT COLL PERCENT CHANGE 91-92	FRAUD CLAIMS COLLECTED FY 1992	FRD COLL PERCENT CHANGE 91-92
CO NNECTICUT	202,265	17.97%	$131,367,477	31.08%	$14,271,913	-2.65%	$405,057	28.53%	$114,663	-18.30%
MAINE	132,509	14.11%	$108,725,439	28.26%	$5,869,522	3.59%	$422,810	12.86%	$106,537	-1.49%
MASSACHUSETTS	428,764	8.04%	$315,469,854	17.17%	$21,655,020	-6.58%	$639,079	5.09%	$248,996	4.27%
NEW HAMPSHIRE	57,704	23.25%	$45,489,072	32.32%	$2,638,396	-.95%	$217,068	6.98%	$122,451	1.78%
NEW YORK	1,885,054	9.87%	$1,586,192,277	22.99%	$135,157,431	7.68%	$5,961,378	21.89%	$1,197,958	18.19%
RHODE ISLAND	87,392	12.63%	$68,998,776	21.66%	$5,343,227	6.95%	$100,000	35.95%	$82,137	50.43%
VERMONT	53,530	12.62%	$36,758,090	22.71%	$3,584,628	-.78%	$110,904	11.08%	$44,539	79.71%
DELAWARE	50,621	23.33%	$42,003,800	29.52%	$3,442,780	11.24%	$208,866	10.84%	$109,587	12.03%
DISTRICT OF COL	82,268	14.44%	$70,026,556	28.62%	$7,816,451	12.81%	$224,165	-2.67%	$132,452	19.02%
MARYLAND	343,207	13.01%	$312,245,858	20.57%	$16,640,974	6.05%	$1,330,149	29.49%	$127,588	19.26%
NEW JERSEY	494,110	12.09%	$433,167,313	18.36%	$47,548,126	1.33%	$5,298,771	33.80%	$2,089,249	10.95%
PENNSYLVANIA	1,137,393	8.11%	$915,576,582	15.59%	$82,203,156	5.38%	$5,580,354	2.93%	$733,765	4.30%
VIRGINIA	495,464	19.81%	$406,059,256	26.55%	$36,321,547	13.03%	$945,454	-8.47%	$236,317	-8.35%
VIRGIN ISLANDS	16,482	12.07%	$18,517,265	19.56%	$2,291,156	11.84%	$147,587	31.19%	$29,434	-8.03%
WEST VIRGINIA	309,606	10.29%	$254,981,517	15. 6%	$6,325,253	.01%	$1,158,835	9.54%	$419,903	10.90%
ABAMA	549,704	9.01%	$450,882,840	14.45%	$29,002,689	2.69%	$3,457,335	87.44%	$1,885,037	90.83%
FLORIDA	1,403,991	36.93%	$1,306,377,821	50.96%	$54,038,979	-.54%	$2,499,468	-12.22%	$971,411	4.40%
GEORGIA	751,028	15.97%	$626,951,373	24. %1	$46,334,675	-.98%	$6,462,474	11.85%	$3,519,215	10.87%
KENTUCKY	528,825	6.54%	$430,470,338	11.31%	$27,136,011	8.63%	$1,319,113	1.27%	$7[illegible],634	-7.12%
MISSISSIPPI	535,921	3.08%	$421,356,589	8.25%	$18,250,668	.74%	$1,098,274	-.37%	$764,213	9.66%
NORTH CAROLINA	596,734	15.39%	$48 ,177,839	22.14%	$30,673,807	3.91%	$1,660,787	-4.10%	$926,414	-5.78%
SOUTH CAROLINA	368,835	12.13%	$297,033,863	24.21%	$18,521,076	-.97%	$2,196,394	72.91%	$810,205	31.34%
TENNESSEE	701,932	15.52%	$561,751,558	22.33%	$32,214,377	11.77%	$2,169,427	2.63%	$1,382,[illegible]81	6.19%
ILLI OIS	1,156,380	5.47%	$1,069,843,950	11.31%	$54,197,646	-2.11%	$9,670,580	18.07%	$440,515	N/A
INDIANA	447,663	19.32%	$372,898,446	26.91%	$21,258,099	6.55%	$1,141,353	-5.79%	$327,548	12.53%
MICHIGAN	994,230	1.62%	$846,004,055	4.72%	$58,305,901	18.01%	$4,336,488	24.82%	$2,926,372	29.09%
MINNESOTA	308,880	7.98%	$234,149,882	15.73%	$22,250,722	.35%	$1,219,351	15.54%	$234,363	22.52%
OHIO	1,250,631	6.77%	$1,102,285,702	12.01%	$57,289,082	20.71%	$2,787,655	-6.79%	$1,578,321	3.77%
WISCONSIN	333,977	13.47%	$235,670,914	13.71%	$22,137,610	17.99%	$1,919,850	3.22%	$383,354	31.70%
ARKANSAS	276,766	7.26%	$207,029,936	13.14%	$13,830,414	1.61%	$938,357	19.72%	$496,[illegible]53	11.03%
LOUISIANA	779,290	5.03%	$677,307,547	13.17%	$31,348,159	9.29%	$1,498,549	6.05%	$669,[illegible]21	9.22%
NEW MEXICO	221,321	17.70%	$181,848,093	23.46%	$10,616,207	.02%	$861,510	15.82%	$101,[illegible]95	-12.46%
OKLAHOMA	346,019	16.18%	$275,498,975	22.84%	$19,294,793	-3.89%	$924,368	20.72%	$267,[illegible]55	17.98%
TEXAS	2,453,608	13.56%	$2,103,319,000	19.89%	$118,840,648	12.10%	$11,020,017	18.97%	$3,154,[illegible]72	8.17%

FOOD STAMP PROGRAM ACTIVITY - FY 1992

STATE	PERSONS FY 1992	PERSONS PERCENT CHANGE 91-92	ISSUANCE FY 1992	ISSUANCE PERCENT CHANGE 91-92	TOTAL ADMIN FEDERAL SHARE FY 1992	ADMIN PERCENT CHANGE 91-92	TOTAL CLAIMS COLLECTED FY 1992	TOT COLL PERCENT CHANGE 91-92	FRAUD CLAIMS COLLECTED FY 1992	FRD COLL PERCENT CHANGE 91-92
COLORADO	259,693	7.87%	$218,640,430	17.04%	$11,159,574	-4.04%	$1,540,803	-4.14%	$739,781	-4.26%
IOWA	192,289	6.95%	$143,337,591	16.32%	$8,449,889	-.52%	$898,209	13.95%	$162,661	8.01%
KANSAS	174,518	11.72%	$132,796,477	17.42%	$7,242,567	8.58%	$642,535	16.75%	$209,123	23.23%
MISSOURI	549,476	12.11%	$447,078,324	17.80%	$23,338,837	5.29%	$2,586,407	-8.87%	$1,335,975	-13.86%
MONTANA	66,288	8.73%	$52,190,852	12.17%	$5,111,135	-20.54%	$252,783	-11.69%	$105,253	3.80%
NEBRASKA	107,342	8.37%	$77,833,529	16.62%	$5,791,166	18.96%	$409,425	28.69%	$100,285	40.95%
NORTH DAKOTA	45,864	12.88%	$34,933,734	23.55%	$3,250,330	12.18%	$269,983	12.01%	$53,656	-4.84%
SOUTH DAKOTA	54,683	4.81%	$42,010,786	9.10%	$3,875,993	6.82%	$136,987	-8.01%	$5 ,050	-10.92%
UTAH	123,198	12.08%	$95,517,459	15.13%	$9,905,323	28.81%	$7 7,245	16.09%	$283,891	.26%
WYOMING	33,434	8.69%	$26,415,882	16.38%	$2,755,331	3.27%	$199,879	-1.04%	$48,327	-17.52%
ALASKA	37,713	24.61%	$41,044,725	20.89%	$7,065,034	11.35%	$253,341	-6.60%	$97,946	-25.47%
ARIZONA	457,099	17.71%	$376,879,876	21.72%	$19,086,109	8.63%	$1,928,285	6.13%	$297,549	-10.82%
CALIFORNIA	2,557,925	15.64%	$1,759,511,436	34.62%	$215,999,440	21.28%	$11,684,111	19.39%	$1,619,652	-.57%
GUAM	19,806	81.92%	$28,229,701	82.16%	$2,270,874	57.14%	$76,151	-18.50%	$28,462	-32.18%
HAWAII	94,265	13.48%	$120,669,426	20.28%	$5,951,517	-22.57%	$964,538	121.89%	$413,510	64.78%
I HO	71,871	10.19%	$53,294,942	13.30%	$4,363,997	7.54%	$383,698	13.59%	$141,263	14.16%
NEVADA	79,740	26.41%	$74,280,784	32.49%	$5,146,615	35.34%	$196,328	.34%	$84,466	-2.43%
OREGON	264,857	10.17%	$226,393,995	15.05%	$15,717,686	6.03%	$2,610,112	19.88%	$716,884	14.81%
WASHINGTON	431,602	12.11%	$343,740,686	23.63%	$29,632,452	10.44%	$2,513,966	13.87%	$408,345	27.84%
UNITED STATES	25,403,766	12.28%	$20,902,238,488	20.55%	$1,462,765,012	8.28%	$108,256,613	14.79%	$34,313,869	13.23%

INSPECTOR GENERAL—FOOD STAMP WORK

Mr. SKEEN. The Inspector General recommendations that they testified to last year about developing and implementing an aggressive error reduction strategy in the states, particularly those with the highest error rates. You testified that 40 percent of investigative resources go to investigating just the food stamp program. I just wondered why.

Is this the largest and biggest problem that you have, the fraud program, which warrants budget dedication?

Mr. HORNSBY. We work hand and glove with the Inspector General's Office. We are pleased that they do devote a significant percentage of their resources to investigating food stamp activities. The 40 percent, I think, has been about the norm of late.

I should mention though, Mr. Skeen, that the food stamp program was over $22 billion last year. It is a huge program. I think that the Inspector General has got to have the resources in the right place to help us.

The Inspector General spends a lot of time on illegal activities involving retail food stores and other businesses who are converting food stamp benefits illegally. We do ask that states take action against those households that are engaging in illegal activity.

Mr. SKEEN. The food stamp traffic, even at the lower level, and I think that Congresswoman DeLauro mentioned it, the mom and pop stores. I know that we have a nationwide system as far as credit card verifications and things of that kind.

ELECTRONIC BENEFIT TRANSFER

A program similar or a parallel program for food stamps, is it feasible? I am sure that it would be feasible for even small operations to have that kind of data response.

Mr. HORNSBY. Yes, sir. I am not sure that I exactly understood the question. Are you talking about the electronic benefits transfer?

Mr. SKEEN. The electronic benefits transfer.

Mr. HORNSBY. Albuquerque, New Mexico is one of our pilot demonstrations. We do believe that that will help us in managing the food stamp program and has a fraud deterrent capability that we do not have now with paper food stamps.

We have been concerned, and have been proceeding fairly cautiously with EBT, because we wanted to make sure that this is a viable system for mom and pop stores across the country and in rural areas, and in farmers markets and other places. So far, all of the signs are very encouraging.

Mr. SKEEN. Thank you for your responses.

And thank you, Mr. Chairman. And welcome back.

Mr. DURBIN. I apologize for not being here earlier.

Mr. SKEEN. I understand. I was just a little bit ahead of you.

Mr. DURBIN. I was attending another hearing at the subcommittee down the hall, and I had to wait my turn to question the witness. I am sorry I could not be here to hear your statement, but I have reviewed your testimony.

PRICE SUPPORT AND PURCHASING

I would like to ask a few questions. The GAO just completed a study on the peanut program and there were a lot of questions raised by it. One of the things that came as a surprise to me was to learn about some of the difficulties you have had with the purchase of peanut butter over the last several years, because of the increases in prices.

During the 1990 crop year, peanut butter prices more than doubled from 81 cents a pound to about $1.78 a pound, in nominal dollars. The report also stated that at some point the USDA food assistance programs have to make a choice as to whether they are going to continue purchasing peanut butter or seek alternative lower-priced products that may not be as high in protein.

Tell me what the situation has been. First, do you agree with GAO's conclusion, and second, what has been your relationship with vendors and providers of peanut butter?

Mr. BRALEY. Mr. Chairman, we do monitor the prices of alternative products for use in our programs quite closely, whether it be school lunch or EFAP, the Emergency Food Assistance Program. I know in the case of the EFAP program, when peanut prices went up significantly, and we could not get peanut butter at a reasonable price, we ended up in one particular year not buying any peanut butter for that program and buying cheese instead. It was a popular item, and also high in protein.

We diminished our school lunch purchases of that particular product when the price went up. We really do that for all products, and look for alternatives and substitutes. Because the money that we have to spend is limited, we want to get as much nutritious food for the dollar as we can.

We are buying peanut butter again now. For the EFAP program, for example, we are making fairly extensive purchases of peanut butter right now. What we buy is largely driven by the price of that product and alternatives to that product.

Mr. DURBIN. And the price of peanut butter is driven by the government program?

Mr. BRALEY. I suspect that there is some relationship there. I am not an expert on the peanut program, so I really cannot comment on that.

Mr. DURBIN. I am just learning about it. It is interesting. The GAO came to a conclusion that our food assistance programs operated through USDA are not really being treated fairly by the folks selling peanut butter in terms of the prices we have to pay as a government purchasing agent being dictated by the so-called support price which the government is also dictating. So the government is raising its own prices, to the ultimate benefit, obviously, of people who are growing peanuts and happen to be enrolled in the program.

Can you tell me whether there are any commodities which are purchased for food assistance programs where you have any kind of special relationship with the providers or vendors in terms of price, other than what the open market price is?

Mr. BRALEY. Well, there are a number of programs for which price support mechanisms are in place. Dairy programs come to mind. There are peanut products and grain products. Fruits and vegetables, and meat and poultry are in another category where there may be some market order activities, but there is not a price floor that is set.

The Department makes decisions about what to purchase in that area based on the market conditions at a particular time.

Mr. DURBIN. What I am driving at is when you sit down and make these decisions, the prices that influence your decision are in many cases the government established price for the commodity. Do you always have to deal, at the retail level, in terms of what you can purchase, or do you get any kind of break through the price support programs for a lower price than one might find if they were buying for some private institution?

COMMODITY PURCHASING PRACTICES

Mr. BRALEY. We do get price breaks on the products that we go out and purchase on the open market. We certainly pay less than retail, even on products where there is a price support mechanism in place. It varies product to product. But we can generally do better than individual school districts can when we are buying for that program, because of the volumes at which we are purchasing, and just the economies of scale of our operation.

But it works a little bit differently for products that have a price support mechanism in place versus those where there is no mechanism, and we are just intervening in the market.

We try to buy products that are in surplus, and where the price is very moderate, and at a time of year when prices are low. We buy in the fall after the fruit and vegetable crops have been harvested, and buy them at a time when supply is abundant, and get a good price, and then distribute them to schools during the course of the year. In that way, we get a better deal. We have been pretty successful at that, I think.

BREASTFEEDING IN WIC

Mr. DURBIN. Let me move to another issue, if I might. The WIC program is trying to encourage breastfeeding among mothers, and I know that this is a national goal as well. What success have we had in that effort?

Mr. BRALEY. We have had some success, not as much as we would like to have. We have been trying to encourage breastfeeding recently. We published a regulation just in the last several months that will enhance the food package that is available to post-partum women who breastfeed their infants.

We do not want to have an incentive to not breastfeed, because of the availability of infant formula through the program. So we have increased the food package for post-partum women who agree to breastfeed. We have not had that in effect long enough to know how effective it will be.

We have also had grants to state and local agencies to do breastfeeding promotion projects, and we have had some success. We are trying to get experiences in certain locations that we can transfer to other places.

We have really taken the lead in sponsoring a breastfeeding promotion consortium of federal, state, and private nonprofit groups who are interested in breastfeeding promotion nationally.

We have hosted meetings of that group, and tried to come up with strategies for increasing breastfeeding. I may be able for the record to give you some specific numbers in terms of where we have been successful in increasing both the rate of breastfeeding and the duration of breastfeeding in the WIC population. I do not have those at hand right at the moment.

Mr. DURBIN. The reason I asked is that in talking about welfare reform, one of the goals of the Administration is to get able-bodied people off of welfare and into school or back to work. One of the concerns I have is that we try to be consistent in our policy when it comes to encouraging mothers to nurse their children, so that we at least provide some period of time after the child is born, perhaps six months or so, where the mother is given that opportunity.

I am trying to determine, and perhaps the statistics you will provide will help me, what success you have had when comparing WIC participants with mothers in similar demographic groups.

Mr. BRALEY. Okay.

Mr. DURBIN. If you would be kind enough to include that with your submission.

Mr. BRALEY. I would be very happy to give you what we have on that. I think we have some information, but it is probably not nationally representative. It may be site-specific, but we would be happy to provide it for the record.

[The information follows:]

A recently-released USDA study that analyzed National Maternal and Infant Health Survey (NMIHS) data found that approximately 36 percent of pregnant women participating in The Special Supplemental Food Program for Woman, Infants, and Children (WIC) initiate breastfeeding, compared with 43 percent of women who are income-eligible for WIC but do not participate, and 64 percent of women whose incomes exceed the limits for WIC. However, WIC participants and income-eligible nonparticipants have comparable rates of breastfeeding initiation and duration, after statistical models control for socioeconomic differences between groups and other factors.

Although WIC participants as a group were less likely to breastfeed than eligible nonparticipants, there was an interesting finding in this study. About 44 percent of participants who reported having been advised to breastfeed at the WIC clinic breastfed, compared with 26 percent of participants who did not report such advice.

About 9 percent of prenatal WIC participants are still breastfeeding at 6 months of age, compared with 12 percent of eligible nonparticipants and 22 percent of women who are not eligible for WIC.

For the nation as a whole, the rate of breastfeeding in the early postpartum period is 52 percent. About 16 percent are still breastfeeding their infants at 6 months of age.

THE WIC BREASTFEEDING REPORT: THE RELATIONSHIP OF WIC PROGRAM PARTICIPATION TO THE INITIATION AND DURATION OF BREASTFEEDING

EXECUTIVE SUMMARY

This study employs descriptive and multivariate statistical techniques to model the determinants of breastfeeding initiation and duration among prenatal WIC participants and nonparticipants using cross-sectional data from the 1988 National Maternal and Infant Health Survey. In contrast to previous research, this study explicitly corrects for unmeasured differences between WIC participants and income-eligible nonparticipants (usually referred to as selection bias), in addition to controlling for other socioeconomic and demographic factors that are frequently found to be associated with breastfeeding, including mothers' and fathers' ages, education, race and family income.

Descriptive analysis revealed that the rate of breastfeeding initiation among women who were not income-eligible was higher than for women who were income-eligible but not participating in WIC. Income-eligible nonparticipants, in turn, had a higher rate of breastfeeding initiation than prenatal WIC participants. Thirty-seven percent of prenatal WIC participants initiated breastfeeding. The mean duration of breastfeeding for these women was 1.19 months.

Although causal relationships cannot be identified using data and methods as these, multivariate analysis revealed a number of statistically significant associations which may provide interesting hypotheses for future research:

- *After controlling for socioeconomic differences, prenatal WIC participants and eligible nonparticipants had comparable rates of breastfeeding initiation.*

- *Although the overall rate of breastfeeding was lower among prenatal WIC participants, those who reported having received advice to breastfeed their babies were more likely to initiate breastfeeding than income-eligible nonparticipants.*

- *Prenatal WIC participants who did not report having received advice to breastfeed were less likely to initiate breastfeeding than income-eligible nonparticipants.*

- *Maternal age, race, education, and location of residence were also associated with the likelihood of initiating breastfeeding.*

- *For women who initiated breastfeeding, neither prenatal WIC participation nor the reported receipt of advice to breastfeed were associated with breastfeeding duration.*

- *Factors associated with the duration of breastfeeding include maternal age, ethnicity, location of residence, and living situation.*

These findings suggest that WIC participation, and WIC nutrition education in particular, may play an important role in womens' infant feeding decisions. However, while encouraging, these findings should not be interpreted as evidence of a causal relationship between WIC participation and breastfeeding. Nor can these data provide support for the effectiveness of any specific method of breastfeeding promotion.

The lack of an association between WIC participation and breastfeeding duration should not be interpreted as evidence that nutrition education and breastfeeding promotion in particular do not, or cannot, increase the duration of breastfeeding.

In the past, most breastfeeding promotion efforts have focused on communicating the benefits of breastfeeding to mothers during the prenatal period. In recent years, there has been increasing recognition of the role of breastfeeding instruction and support during the early postpartum period. Other factors not examined in this analysis may also affect the initiation and duration of breastfeeding.

This analysis was derived from a retrospective cross-sectional survey which does not have sufficient data to explore potential biases that may have affected mothers' responses. For example, WIC clinics in 1988 may have selectively provided breastfeeding advice only to those who expressed an interest in it, and who presumably intended to breastfeed. Alternatively, WIC clinics may have provided breastfeeding advice to all participants, but the receipt of such advice may have been selectively reported only by those who chose to act on it. It is also important to note that this analysis is based on 1988 data. Since then, legislative changes outlined in PL 101-147 have placed renewed emphasis on breastfeeding promotion in the WIC Program.

This study suggests that more research is needed to investigate WIC's role in breastfeeding initiation and duration, and to identify appropriate strategies for approaching each of these distinct breastfeeding promotion objectives.

Mr. DURBIN. When was the Breastfeeding Promotion Act of 1992 enacted into law? What is the cost to implement this legislation? enacted? What is the cost to implement this legislation?

Mr. BRALEY. The Breastfeeding Promotion Act of 1992 enacted on August 14, 1992, calls for the Secretary of Agriculture to implement a campaign to promote breastfeeding as the best method of infant feeding and foster wider public acceptance of breastfeeding in the United States. The law does not provide any Federal funding for the campaign, but authorizes USDA to solicit funds from private sources.

USDA is currently involved in planning for the campaign. However, private funding to implement it has not yet been secured. It is conservatively estimated to cost $3.5 million over a four-year period.

Mr. DURBIN. Is the food package that was being proposed last year for breastfeeding women whose infants do not receive infant formula from the WIC program available?

Mr. BRALEY. A final rule was published in the Federal Register on November 27, 1992. This rule established an enhanced food package for those breastfeeding participants who do not receive infant formula from the WIC program. This food package provides additional foods for mothers in lieu of the standard infant package. State agencies are expected to implement the provisions of this regulation by December 27, 1993. Some States have already begun to offer the new food package. However, specific data on the current availability and use of the new food package are not yet available.

Mr. DURBIN. The Washington Times has reported that more than 120 developing countries have barred the distribution of free or low-cost infant formula to hospitals as part of an effort to promote breastfeeding. Tell us your views on this?

Mr. BRALEY. WIC is interested in improving hospital support of breastfeeding. WIC State agencies work hard to promote breastfeeding among participants through nutrition education during the prenatal period. To ensure success in breastfeeding, it is also necessary to have the appropriate breastfeeding promotion and support services and environment in the hospital upon delivery.

The initiative to bar the distribution of free or low-cost infant formula to hospitals is part of a more general effort to improve hospital breastfeeding promotion and support practices in countries around the world called the Baby Friendly Hospital Initiative. This initiative is co-sponsored by the United Nations Children's Fund and the World Health Organization.

Considering that this initiative was originally developed for application in a global context, several components must be tailored for our country. The notion of barring distribution of free or low-cost infant formula to hospitals is controversial for some U.S. hospitals and health professionals. The research on whether providing complimentary discharge packs with infant formula samples to new mothers discourages breastfeeding is not conclusive; some studies show that it has a significant effect, others show that it does not.

In addition, the main thrust of the Baby Friendly Hospital Initiative is certification of hospitals. In the United States, however, credentialing of hospitals is a private sector endeavor. Therefore, it is likely that the Baby Friendly Initiative will have to be modified for successful U.S. application.

USDA has provided $25,000 to the U.S. Department of Health and Human Services in partial support of a grant to study the feasibility of implementing this initiative in the U.S. and adapt the Baby Friendly concept for implementation in this country. USDA will support the final recommendations of the Working Group, to be composed of select health professional and hospital associations and advocacy groups. These final recommendations will constitute the U.S. Government's position on the domestic Baby Friendly Initiative.

SMOKING CESSATION

Mr. DURBIN. I am aware of at least one WIC clinic that has specifically tried to discourage pregnant women from smoking, and has had some success.

Can you tell me if the WIC program includes information about the dangers of smoking during pregnancy, as well as the dangers of consuming alcohol and drugs in the counseling that is given to pregnant women and new mothers?

Mr. BRALEY. Yes. Mr. Chairman, it is a part of the program at many, many local agencies, and we are promoting that concept throughout the WIC program currently. Many agencies have smoking as a nutritional risk factor to get people into the program during their pregnancy, consider it a risk, and then immediately place a pregnant woman into a smoking cessation module that is available or refer them to another appropriate smoking cessation program locally. That is something we are trying to encourage.

WIC DRUG ABUSE EDUCATION

We work closely with the Centers for Disease Control and Prevention at HHS to develop material on both abuse of alcohol, drugs and smoking. New material has recently been published that we are making available throughout the country. It includes some brochures for participants, video tapes, so that we can incorporate that into the nutrition education activities that are provided through the WIC program.

We have had some success in the demonstration projects that we did jointly again with the Centers for Disease Control, and we are trying to replicate those successes around the country.

Mr. DURBIN. I take it from your testimony that this is being done on a random or partial basis at the moment?

Mr. BRALEY. I would say with the publication of our regulations and the making available of these new materials we should be able to move that throughout the program, though I am sure there are areas that may not take that up immediately. If you have thoughts and suggestions on how we can do more in that area, we would be very happy to consider them.

Mr. DURBIN. Well, I would like to work with you on that, and if it takes some direction or resources from this committee, I think it is money well invested. I was surprised to learn, in speaking to some of the WIC administrators, of the success they have had just by going one on one with the mother and explaining the dangers involved if she continued to smoke during her pregnancy or in the presence of the child after the child was born. I really think that is money well spent.

Mr. BRALEY. Oh, I agree.

Mr. DURBIN. A concern I have, and I am sure you do too, is that there comes a point where Administrators of the program say stop, stop giving us all these wonderful ideas and directives. We do not have enough people or enough time. We have to keep in mind that WIC started off as a nutrition program, and we want to continue that. On the one hand, I do not want to overburden the program operators, but on the other hand, it strikes me that in some of these public health areas they are in a perfect position, maybe the only people in that position, to sit down with that mother and to counsel her and give her some good advice during some critical moments.

IMMUNIZATION RATES

Mr. BRALEY. I think the people that operate the WIC Program at the state and local level are very willing to take on a lot of those responsibilities and not just with regard to smoking and drug abuse. WIC can play a very important role in increasing immunization rates.

Mr. DURBIN. Absolutely.

Mr. BRALEY. We have had some success to date, and can do more in that regard. I think there are a number of areas where WIC can be a real gateway to a lot of other services that are available. The food benefit that is available is often what entices someone into the program.

WIC FULL FUNDING

Mr. DURBIN. Let me talk to you for a moment about the President's goal of full funding of WIC, one which I think virtually everyone shares. A goal to bring all the eligible mothers and children into the program.

Now, I happen to believe, and I am sure most would agree, that it is almost impossible to reach 100 percent participation.

Mr. BRALEY. Yes, sir.

Mr. DURBIN. And it may not even be a good idea to try to achieve that. The last few percentages of nonparticipants may be so expensive to bring into the program that you have to question the worth of the investment.

I am just wondering if you have compared the effort involved, in terms of cost, of increasing priority participants up to higher levels of participation as opposed to the health value of having a broader group involved in the program.

Is that kind of discussion underway?

CHILDREN IN WIC

Mr. BRALEY. We talk about that on an ongoing basis. We have got very positive results for the WIC Program with regard to pregnancy outcome and the cost benefit analysis that has been done in terms of Medicaid cost savings and in terms of getting pregnant women into the program. We have also got some pretty compelling information about older children that needs to be considered. When I say older children, I mean children really up to their fifth birthday, so older children in the WIC sense, but not older children as we might normally think about it. The WIC Program does increase the dietary intake of that group of children for a number of key nutrients, including iron, vitamin C, thiamin, niacin, vitamin B6. We have gotten very positive results for that group in terms of the nutrient density of their diets as a result of being on the WIC Program.

The WIC program has been associated in some research with reductions in the incidents of childhood iron deficiency anemia. Researchers for the Centers for Disease Control cited a major drop in that deficiency as some changes were made in the overall diet, but specifically mentioned the WIC Program as one of the factors in reduction of anemia.

We have some positive indications on cognitive development for older children as well from the national WIC evaluation, and I mentioned before that WIC has been shown to increase immunization rates by getting people into the health care system. Many WIC clinics can provide immunizations right on the spot when people come in for a WIC visit, and many others can refer young children for immunizations elsewhere in the health care system.

WOMEN IN WIC

I do not want to overlook the fact that although we are doing a pretty good job of covering pregnant women at this point in one sense, one area that we can improve on is getting women in the WIC program earlier in their pregnancies. The information we have from a few years ago is that we were, on average, getting women into WIC around their middle trimester. About 24–25 percent come in the first trimester, about half are coming in their second trimester of pregnancy, and the other quarter are coming very late in their pregnancy. We would like to devote more efforts to try to bring pregnant women into the program earlier.

One of the other things we know is that many women have a second child within five years of their first child. If the first child is enrolled in WIC, the chances of getting that woman into the WIC Program at the beginning of her subsequent pregnancy are increased. So we think there are benefits.

I focus a lot on older children in my comments, because that is the group that is largely unserved at this point, though, again, there are certainly some increases in pregnant and postpartum women that we could make as well.

Mr. DURBIN. I think that illustrates the point I am trying to make. To merely say that all of the priority one participants, 100 percent of them, are enrolled may overlook a more important question as to how early in their pregnancy they get involved.

Mr. BRALEY. That is right.

Mr. DURBIN. I am not a doctor, I do not play one on TV either, but from what I have heard and read, timing is critically important in terms of early intervention and early involvement of medical supervision.

I really need to work with you as we move toward this full funding model, to make sure that we are taking these factors into consideration.

Mr. BRALEY. Yes, sir.

Mr. DURBIN. To merely say we have reached 98 percent in every category and to dust our hands off and say the job is done, I think, overlooks some of these very important questions.

Mr. BRALEY. I agree, Mr. Chairman.

WIC PROGRAM SCOPE AND COVERAGE

Mr. DURBIN. Let me ask you this. Someone raised the point, in a meeting I went to earlier, that the Federal government made a commitment to get involved in the nutrition of its citizens. From the WIC program through the food stamp program, we have decided as a nation that we want the American people to have a nutritious diet, and we are going to help them, particularly when they are in a circumstance where they cannot help themselves.

As you take a look at all of the different feeding programs we have under USDA, from WIC, school lunch, food stamps and others, are there gaps in our commitment to nutrition? Are there certain people, deserving people, who are not covered by a program for some reason, or do they move from one program to another with different nutritional standards? Have we integrated the nutritional standards of all the various Federal programs?

Mr. BRALEY. In terms of gaps in availability of programs, there are not big ones that I am aware of. There is always concern whether the levels of benefits are appropriate for this population. These kinds of discussions come up all the time.

CHILD NUTRITION HOMELESS DEMONSTRATIONS

We have been working just recently on a population that perhaps we had overlooked. It is a small population, but an important one. It is the homeless pre-school population. They were not in schools and they were not in child care per se, so they were not receiving any meals service like their older siblings would, or like their counterparts would if their parents were going off to work and the children were in day care. We have been working with state and local cooperators and have developed some innovative ways to try to reach that population while they are in shelter situations and cannot necessarily prepare food like a food stamp household would. So there probably are some fairly small target populations that we are not reaching.

The other question you raised is about the consistency of our nutritional message. I think we try to be consistent, but I think we have to be mindful of the climate in which our various programs operate. WIC is in a clinic environment. You have one-on-one contact with people as they come through that kind of a system, and so we do a lot of nutrition education in that environment. We try to integrate nutrition education into a school environment as well. We do a little bit with food stamps, but the environment of a welfare office or a human services office does not lend itself to the same type of nutrition education and intervention that a WIC clinic does.

I think we are being consistent in our message, but the degree to which each of our programs has a nutrition or nutrition education component does vary some, and a lot of that is by statute.

WHOLE MILK REQUIREMENT

Mr. DURBIN. I understand this question may have been asked earlier, but I want to follow through on it.

If I am not mistaken, Congress has mandated the type of milk that can be used in the School Lunch program.

Mr. BRALEY. Yes, the Congress has mandated that at least two alternatives have to be available, whole milk and a low fat alternative form of milk, and that schools can on their own offer additional types of milk.

Mr. DURBIN. Now, I am trying to determine whether or not that congressional mandate is consistent with the nutritional premises of the program. In other words, absent the mandate, would a nutritionist say it is far more acceptable, more wise, to use 2 percent or other forms of low fat milk in the School Lunch program?

Mr. BRALEY. I think a lot of nutritionists would make that argument, Mr. Chairman. The counter to it is maybe there are some children who would only consume whole milk and might not consume milk if they did not have whole milk available as an alternative.

There is some legislation that has been introduced, two pieces of legislation, to change that provision. I indicated earlier that we have not taken a position on either of those bills at this point from a policy sense, so I cannot speak in support of going one direction or the other on that particular issue.

Mr. DURBIN. Can you give me any other examples where Congress has mandated certain foods or food supplements be used that may be questionable from a nutritional viewpoint in any of the food assistance programs that you are involved in?

Mr. BRALEY. I cannot think of any that is quite as explicit as the whole milk requirement in the School Lunch program.

INFANT FORMULA IN PUERTO RICO SETTLEMENT

Mr. DURBIN. Back to the WIC program, the staff has advised me of a recent action by the Federal Trade Commission, where, in Puerto Rico, they found three infant formula companies that violated the law and antitrust charges were filed against them. Two of them have entered into a consent decree, Mead Johnson and Wyeth, while the third company, Ross Laboratories, has not.

Now, the Mead Johnson and Wyeth consent decree provided that they would give some 3.6 million pounds of infant formula powder or its equivalent in liquid concentrate to the program.

How common or frequent is this? Was this a situation where there was collusion on price or some other type of activity?

Mr. BRALEY. There were, I think, concerns about the way in which bids were being made to provide infant formula in the commonwealth. I do not know the specific circumstances of that situation in Puerto Rico, so I cannot comment on the exact allegations that were made.

Your figures, in terms of the recoveries we made from the two companies that entered into the consent degree, are consistent with the information I have, and that product had a retail value of approximately $25 million. I believe we are still pursuing the third company.

[Additional information follows:]

The Federal Trade Commission (FTC) is currently pursuing litigation against Ross Laboratories. The FTC is nearing the end of the discovery process, which has a deadline of May 1, 1993. No trial date has been set, since the judge assigned to the case recently passed away. A new trial schedule will be established soon.

The FTC entered into a consent decree with the other two infant formula manufacturers for the settlement of 3.6 million pounds of infant formula to USDA. The retail value of this infant formula is estimated to be as large as $25 million. The actual product is being distributed through the Mississippi WIC Program which has a direct distribution system. However, savings to the Mississippi WIC Program due to the settlement are being deducted from the State's grant level and reallocated for the benefit of all State agencies.

Mr. DURBIN. With only three major suppliers of infant formula to the program, it really seems the potential for bid-rigging is high.

What are you doing to investigate that in cases outside of Puerto Rico?

Mr. BRALEY. That would not be a matter that we would investigate in the Food and Nutrition Service. When we have concerns of that nature, we normally inform our Inspector General and they pass that information along to the appropriate investigative agencies.

I know the Federal Trade Commission has been active in the past, and they currently may be, in looking at infant formula pricing issues. I am not up to date at the moment in terms of what FTC is doing in that regard. It is a situation we pay very close attention to because we, through the WIC Program, purchase probably close to 40 percent of the infant formula sold in the United States. We have been very successful, as you know, in reducing the cost of infant formula for the WIC Program through the very successful infant formula rebate program.

[Additional information follows:]

We continually monitor rebates offered by the infant formula manufacturers to insure that bidding practices are conducted competitively and equitably. Recent infant formula rebate contracts awarded by State agencies suggest that bidding has been conducted fairly and equitably, and rebate amounts have been consistent with prior levels. Also, the recent contract award to Carnation from the Western States Contracting Alliance, representing 12 State agencies, allowed a fourth manufacturer to capture a significant portion of the WIC rebate market.

Public Law 102-512, the WIC Infant Formula Procurement Act, enacted on October 24, 1992, has expanded the Food and Nutrition Service's (FNS) authority to penalize infant formula manufacturers found guilty of price-fixing and anti-competitive activities in the infant formula rebate market, as well as to disqualify manufacturers from the WIC Program for up to two years. Manufacturers will be subject to civil penalties of up to $100,000,000 to provide restitution to the program for harm done. The Attorney General of the United States will institute judicial action to collect fines established by the Food and Nutrition Service.

Mr. DURBIN. For the record, provide the Committee a table showing the amount of rebate revenues and the number of participants supported by this amount for each year since it was begun.

Mr. BRALEY. I will provide that information for the record.

[The information follows:]

SPECIAL SUPPLEMENTAL FOOD PROGRAM FOR WOMEN, INFANTS, AND CHILDREN

[Annual total infant formula rebate revenues 1988 to 1992]

Fiscal year	Total rebate revenues [1]	Number of participants supported
1988	$36,000,000	70,000
1989	293,000,000	550,000
1990	505,000,000	870,000
1991	656,000,000	1,100,000
1992 [2]	700,000,000	1,200,000

[1] Total Rebate Revenues rounded to nearest million dollars

[2] Reflects estimated revenues, as actual data for Fiscal Year 1992 is not yet available

Mr. DURBIN. Also, provide a table similar to last year's showing the total rebate savings by State for fiscal years 1991 and 1992.

Mr. BRALEY. I will provide the rebate revenues collected by each WIC state agency in fiscal year 1991. Data is not yet available for fiscal year 1992. The 1992 data will be available in May 1993 and the Food and Nutrition Service (FNS) will submit the information to you at that time.

[The information follows:]

State agency	*(H) Total rebate savings*
NERO:	
Connecticut	$5,940,861
Maine	1,763,007
Massachusetts	10,774,935
New Hampshire	1,302,892
New York	55,378,122
Rhode Island	2,486,835
Vermont	0
Indian Tw	0
Pl Point	0
Seneca Na	5,360
Subtotal	77,652,012
MARO:	
Delaware	1,846,083
District of Columbia	2,702,847
Maryland	10,257,797
New Jersey	13,687,195
Pennsylvania	27,685,239
Puerto Rico	7,632,310
Virginia	9,713,464
V Islands	192,557
W Virginia	3,202,341
Subtotal	76,919,833
SERO:	
Alabama	17,577,461
Florida	38,271,552
Georgia	24,105,813
Kentucky	8,507,338
Mississippi	0
North Carolina	16,496,752
South Carolina	5,044,444
Tennessee	18,966,984
Seminoles	0
Miccosuke	0
Choctaw	0

State agency	(H) Total rebate savings
E. Cherok	13,809
Subtotal	128,984,153
MWRO:	
Illinois	26,429,454
Indiana	13,961,616
Michigan	26,103,675
Minnesota	9,962,657
Ohio	20,018,259
Wisconsin	9,138,062
Subtotal	105,613,723
SWRO:	
Arkansas	9,099,417
Louisiana	13,770,562
New Mexico	2,793,642
Oklahoma	5,858,005
Texas	54,198,838
Acl, Nm	0
8n Pueblo	0
Isleta	0
Santo Dom	0
5 Sandova	11,696
San Felip	0
WCD, ENT	121,932
Choctaw	152,796
Cherokee	557,167
Chickasaw	108,550
Otoe-Miss	42,230
Potawatom	63,005
Zuni	33,840
ITC, OK	19,951
Subtotal	86,831,631
MPRO:	
Colorado	4,737,126
Iowa	4,075,242
Kansas	5,151,295
Missouri	11,132,120
Montana	1,019,249
Nebraska	2,046,710
North Dakota	1,163,913
South Dakota	1,418,169
Utah	857,318
Wyoming	565,174
Shosh/Ara	29,177
Ute Mtn	8,421
Winnebago	23,332
Cheyenne	32,207
Rosebud	65,018
St Rock	35,145
Ft Bertho	23,698
Subtotal	32,383,314
WRO:	
Alaska	866,780
Arizona	7,184,032
California	120,745,398
Guam	197,268
Hawaii	1,731,520
Idaho	1,193,608
Nevada	1,621,116

State agency	(H) Total rebate savings
Oregon	4,402,109
Washington	8,714,225
Itcn	0
Mannilaq	0
Navajos	1,031,371
Itca	360,059
Subtotal	148,047,486
National	656,432,152

Mr. DURBIN. Are there any other commodities purchased in the program where rebates are offered and accepted?

Mr. BRALEY. Currently, we are aware that four WIC state agencies have contracted for rebates for infant cereal. They are Indiana, North Carolina, Texas and New York. California is presently soliciting for an infant cereal rebate.

However, several other state agencies have been unsuccessful with their solicitation for rebates for other supplemental foods such as peanut butter, adult cereals, infant cereal, and infant juice. The U.S. Department of Agriculture, Food and Nutrition Service continues to encourage and promote the purchase of supplemental foods other than infant formula under cost containment procedures.

MILK PRICE BID-RIGGING

Mr. DURBIN. Are you familiar with the bid-rigging case in the School Lunch program involving milk?

Mr. BRALEY. I am indeed.

Mr. DURBIN. You were interviewed on the subject, were you not?

Mr. BRALEY. Yes, I got to see myself on television.

Mr. DURBIN. Quite a treat, I am sure. The latest figures show that some 37 corporations and 41 individuals were convicted. Fines and settlements against companies that supply milk to the program have reached $100 million.

Do you know whether there was a recommendation made that any of these companies or individuals be debarred from participating in the program?

Mr. BRALEY. Let me comment on that. We are going to consider suspension or debarment actions on a case-by-case basis for these companies or anybody else who has a similar history. We have not suspended or debarred any companies to date.

We have worked with the Defense Logistics Agency in working with companies to come up with appropriate monitoring and payment schemes so that they could continue to participate in the program under closer scrutiny by both DLA and USDA.

As I understand the statute on debarment and suspension, it is not intended as a punitive action. It is intended to keep somebody out of the program if you believe you are still at risk of them continuing to engage in bid rigging and that type of illegal activity. So we have not looked at it as a punitive step. But if we have an ongoing concern that a company is going to continue to behave in this manner, we would take a suspension or debarment action.

I attended a procurement conference yesterday in Williamsburg which one of our regions was hosting. We had a presentation there by a senior trial attorney from the Antitrust Division at the Department of Justice, and part of what we were trying to do in that session was sensitize state and local school food service people to what to look for in bid rigging, how to cooperate with investigative agencies, whether it's the state attorney general's office or the Department of Justice. We are doing this because, frankly, a lot of people just are not thinking that way in doing their day-to-day business. Most companies are honest and I think everyone assumes they all are. So we as an agency are trying to sensitize the school food service world to the fact that this is a potential, it has happened a lot, and I was glad for the publicity that that story brought, because I think it should have a chilling effect on other companies who might consider entering into these kinds of arrangements.

Mr. DURBIN. USDA provides cash reimbursements to State agencies for meals served and they in turn purchase commodities. What does FNS do, if anything, to monitor the State agency's procurement process to prevent bid-rigging from occurring?

Mr. BRALEY. Program regulations require State agencies to monitor school food authorities' compliance with the procurement requirements. In addition, we believe that training to heighten an awareness of bid-rigging is needed. In connection with this, Food and Nutrition Service (FNS) has been active in promoting, coordinating, and conducting procurement workshops for State and local agencies participating in the Child Nutrition Programs. A number of FNS Regional Office sponsored procurement workshops have been held over the past few years which have included sessions on recognizing and dealing with noncompetitive industry practices including bid-rigging. FNS is continuing in that effort. This week, for example, our Mid-Atlantic Regional Office conducted a school food service procurement conference in Williamsburg, Virginia for State and local agencies in the Region. Training in noncompetitive industry practices, including bid-rigging, was featured at the conference.

Mr. DURBIN. Do you have established guidelines or regulations that State's must use in the procurement process?

Mr. BRALEY. Program regulations require State agencies and school food authorities to comply with the requirements of the Office of Management and Budget (OMB) Circular A-102, Attachment O, Procurement Standards. Attachment O establishes standards and guidelines for procurement which are designed to ensure that materials and services are obtained efficiently and economically. Attachment O also prohibits Federal agencies from imposing additional procurement requirements or subordinate regulations.

Mr. DURBIN. In addition to cash reimbursements, the Agricultural Marketing Service purchases commodities for the government to be distributed to the schools. What safeguards do they have, if any, to prevent bid-rigging from occurring?

Mr. BRALEY. The Department of Agriculture's purchase announcements require that offerors certify that they are responsible for determining the prices offered and that they further certify, under contracting regulations, that: the prices in the offer have been arrived at independently; the prices will not be disclosed to any other competitor; and no attempt has been made by the offeror to induce any other concern to submit or not to submit offers for the purpose of restricting competition.

Failure to comply with the above regulations will lead to debarment proceedings against an offeror. Under the Federal Acquisition Regulations subpart 9.4, individuals or entities can be suspended or debarred if they are suspected of conducting questionable or illegal activities in connection with government contracts. Such activities would include a violation of Federal antitrust statutes, including those proscribing price fixing between competitors, allocation of customers between competitors, and bid rigging.

Mr. DURBIN. Could these procedures be used by state purchasing agents as well.

Mr. BRALEY. Yes, States should follow the same procedures and should also engage the same proceedings against companies found in violation of the statues when Federal funds are used to acquire products.

Mr. DURBIN. Of those companies found guil y of bid-rigging, how many have been suspended or debarred from participating in the program?

Mr. BRALEY. While the Food and Nutrition Service (FNS) has taken a suspension action against a company found guilty on other charges, we have not yet suspended or debarred any company found guilty of bid-rigging. FNS has worked closely with the Department of Justice (DOJ) to insure that the resolution of individual bid-rigging cases takes into consideration the recovery of local school milk damages either through separate State action or through Federal action. However, in reviewing proposed DOJ settlement agreements in these cases, FNS has insisted that suspension or debarment action not be precluded by the agreements. FNS has also worked closely with the Defense Logistics Agency (DLA) on some of their suspension actions under the Federal Acquisition Regulations (FAR) against dairies involved in bid-rigging on military as well as school milk contracts. In these cases, DLA has negotiated administrative agreements with the firms to lift suspension actions and, through coordination with FNS, safeguards and oversight applicable to school milk contracts were included in the agreements. As a result, FNS determined that further action was not needed in those cases. FNS is reviewing all other cases to determine the necessity for suspension and debarment action; determinations will consider present responsibility of the firms and individuals involved, program impact, and other pertinent information.

Mr. DURBIN. Why aren't more companies barred from the program?

Mr. BRALEY. Under the regulations, Federal agencies have the authority but are not required to take suspension or debarment actions. The regulations specify that such actions are not to be considered punitive but are to be taken to protect the interests of the Federal government and the public. FNS will continue to make determinations regarding the necessity for debarment or suspension action against dairies convicted of bid-rigging. In making these determinations, we will consider only the conviction but the present responsibility of the companies and individuals involved, the potential impact of a debarment or suspension action on local program operations, and any other information that may be pertinent to the determination. FNS has taken positive actions to address noncompetitive industry practices such as bid-rigging. A number of FNS sponsored procurement workshops for State and local agencies have been held over the past few years which have included training on recognizing and dealing with noncompetitive practices. We have invited food and equipment vendors to these workshops so that they can be an integral part of the process. That effort is continuing. We have also negotiated or assisted in negotiating administrative agreements to resolve suspension actions. These agreements in many instances can achieve the safeguards and the oversight necessary to protect the interests of the Federal government and the public without removing the firm from the competitive marketplace.

FOOD STAMP PROGRAM EFFECTIVENESS

Mr. DURBIN. Let me shift to an area that I know my colleague from New Mexico is very interested in, and I am as well, and that is the Food Stamp program.

I have asked different witnesses before this committee to kind of step back for a moment and consider a very basic question.

Is the Food Stamp program the best way to feed poor people in America?

Mr. BRALEY. I think it has been a very, very successful program over the years that it has been around. It strikes a balance between making sure that people get food benefits, earmarking the benefits, but still gives them flexibility to make choices of the types of food as compared to the forerunner of the program, a commodity-based program.

I think, in terms of ensuring that the benefits go to people who need them, food stamps is the appropriate way to go. There may be some technological changes and electronic benefits, and so on, that can shore up some of the weaknesses of the current system's susceptibility to trafficking and fraud and that type of thing. But I think it is appropriate with that kind of a technological change.

Mr. Hornsby, do you want to comment?

FOOD STAMP QUALITY CONTROL

Mr. HORNSBY. Mr. Durbin, that is a good question. I have been around the program 25 years, and it has been in existence, as you know, 32 years, and I think we can make improvements, and it is a constant effort to try to make sure the benefits are going to the right people, in the right amount, and being spent properly.

Before you got here I mentioned that one fact that always comforts me is that 75 percent of all food stamps are spent in supermarkets, and through our quality control program, states, with a verification from us, literally pull a representative sample of every food stamp case in the nation, and it is thousands and thousands of cases, and dissect that case. They determine how many benefits a family got, was it correct, did they have money in the bank, did they have any other thing which would affect their benefit levels. We really have a pretty good picture of who is getting food stamps.

The overwhelming majority of the people are receiving the right amount of benefits, and I think are spending them correctly.

But you know with a $20 billion program it does not take but a little bit of fraud or misappropriation and you have got a big problem.

INSPECTOR GENERAL—FOOD STAMP WORK

Mr. DURBIN. Well, it was interesting when the Inspector General came to testify and told us that approximately half of their people were dedicated to the food stamp program. I think, of the 800 or so employees at OIG, half of them work full time on food stamp fraud. And from what he had to say, they certainly can pay their own way by what they discover in terms of fraudulent behavior, not only by recipients, but certainly by vendors as well.

The reason I asked that threshold question was because I really think it is time for us to sit back and ask, is this the best way? If we had to reinvent the program with the same goal, would we do it the same way?

Now, I know you are experimenting with different ways to approach this, electronic benefit transfer is an example, and it is possible that technology is going to move us forward. I now go through my supermarket at home and items are rung using the bar codes. The day is coming, in fact in some places it has arrived, where when I present my card to pay for the groceries there will be an automatic record of what I purchased and the fact that I purchased it, which will then be sold to companies who will send me coupons to buy more.

If you move to the next generation, it is obvious that we could take this electronic benefit transfer card from a food stamp recipient and match it against what they just purchased to make sure they are purchasing what they are supposed to. That may be over the horizon, but I do not think it is too far over the horizon.

In one of the towns in my State I heard a story about the food stamp recipient who walks into the liquor store and hands over his or her food stamp coupon book and is given 25 cents on the dollar in return. Then they go and gamble in the back of the store. Now, I hope that is a rare situation, if it is true, and I have been told it is. But, this sort of thing obviously does occur, and we should keep in mind that vendors tend to abuse this system too.

So we have caught ourselves in kind of an administrative tangle here, in terms of trying to feed poor people. This brings me back to the basic question. What would be the alternative to this? Would a cash payment be more sensible? Would it—even if it were politically acceptable, would it be more sensible to say we can feed poor people by handing them money, because that is where they are going to go, to buy food?

Mr. HORNSBY. We have had two pilot demonstration projects giving food stamp households cash in lieu of food stamps, one in San Diego and one in Alabama, and they worked pretty well. There was good acceptance on the part of the people. Of course, the driving concern is what do they do with their cash benefit. Does the family benefit? Do they in fact purchase food?

There was a drop in the amount of nutritional food purchased in the two experiments. Now, we have not gotten all of our data in yet, but that research will be finished, I hope, very shortly. We are anxious to see what were the results of giving people cash instead of food stamps, and were benefits diverted to non-food purchases.

I guess I would like to brag about the Food Stamp program a little bit. I do think it works better than the general public believes. I really think our checks, and what the states do to determine that the right people are getting the right amount of food stamps and are spending them properly are basically working reasonably well. The program has demonstrated that it is able to respond to economic downturn, take care of people, and there is a better story there than maybe we have been able to tell.

The Inspector General's office and our own investigators focus only on the bad aspects of the program. That is all they see, and there is another side there. I think the program is working reasonably well.

Mr. SKEEN. Mr. Chairman, if I may.

In connection with the supplementation today in the food programs, I think Puerto Rico has been a big example.

Mr. HORNSBY. Yes, sir.

Mr. SKEEN. And how well has that worked or not worked?

Mr. HORNSBY. As you know, the Congress cashed out the Food Stamp program in Puerto Rico back in 1982.

Mr. SKEEN. We just advocated to send them the money.

Mr. HORNSBY. Right. We gave them a block grant, and they elected to send out checks. Our research shows that the program works reasonably well. In fact, there was an insignificant drop in nutritional intake of food among households in Puerto Rico when we compared what they were doing with their money with what they were doing with the food stamps previously.

We wanted to see if that experience could be translated to the U.S. and that is why we have engaged in these cash out demonstration projects.

Mr. SKEEN. Well, also in the case of Puerto Rico we were supplanting their own agricultural system because everything was coming from the U.S.

Mr. HORNSBY. Yes.

Mr. SKEEN. So that was really part of the problem.

FOOD STAMP TRAFFICKING

Mr. DURBIN. Thank you very much, Mr. Skeen.

Let me ask you about your testimony that suggests that in the last fiscal year trafficking in food stamps occurred in 763 retailer investigations, a 44 percent increase over fiscal year 1991, and a 255 percent increase over fiscal year 1988.

Does this suggest that people who are gaming the system are getting more sophisticated?

Mr. HORNSBY. I think it suggests a couple of things, Mr. Durbin. One thing we did, as a result of this committee providing additional funds to put into what we call a strike force, was to target 3,000 retailers or vendors which had the most indications that they were violating the Food Stamp Program. We collect sales data on all food stores, and we compare that with how many food stamps they take in. Some stores, believe it or not, even report more food stamps than they report sales. So that is a pretty good indication that there is something going on. We work very closely with the OIG on these investigations.

I am told that some retailers do not report accurately to the Internal Revenue Service, and so they are reluctant to tell us correct sales information.

We called it Project 3,000, and we targeted the 3,000 most likely violators, along with the Office of the Inspector General, and went after them.

Mr. DURBIN. What percentage would that 3,000 be of the total number of vendors?

Mr. HORNSBY. We have about 210,000 stores in the program, so that would be——

Mr. DURBIN. One and a half percent.

Mr. HORNSBY. Yes, one and a half percent, right.

We went after those stores, and I think the results you cited were as a result of this committee giving us some funding so we could really intensify our efforts to get the people out of the program who had been violating it. We were real pleased with the results, but we were kind of like shooting fish in a barrel. We were going after the people who we had not had the resources, nor had OIG, to really get out and make a great effort.

We also refocused on trafficking, and I am told, I do not know, that perhaps when there are bad economic times there is more pressure on families to convert benefits to cash. If they are discounting food stamps in certain food stores, then we go in and investigate, and use investigative aides, and we can pretty much tell what is going on in a store.

Mr. DURBIN. How many of those 3,000 vendors were debarred or suspended from participating in the program?

Mr. HORNSBY. I will have to get back to you with those figures. It was several hundred, and some of them are still in process. If I can, I will submit for the record the results of all 3,000 of those investigations.

[The information follows:]

Action on this project began during Fiscal Year 1992, and the final Compliance Branch investigations will conclude by the end of April 1993. The project involved approximately 3,000 stores whose annual redemptions exceeded the amount of annual food sales that had been reported by the firms. In many cases, the food sales data in the Agency's data base was not current.

Project 3,000 relied upon the verification of food sales data as well as investigative activity. For instance, when the food sales update was conducted by the Agency, the decision was made not to investigate approximately 1,400 stores on the list as a result of receiving updated sales information which indicated no compliance problem at these firms. The food sales update also showed that an additional 208 stores no longer existed.

Approximately 1,400 firms on the list were investigated or, in some cases, are still in the process of being investigated. Of that number, 251 had been investigated by Compliance Branch prior to distribution of the Project 3,000 print-out. Eighty-two stores were sent to the Office of Inspector General for investigation.

At the end of Fiscal Year 1992, when the latest status report was prepared on Project 3,000, Compliance Branch had completed investigations of 690 stores from the printout. Three hundred fifty-one cases (51%) disclosed violations while 339 (49%) were negative, in that no program violations occurred. One hundred fifty-seven of the positive cases (44.7%) included evidence of trafficking (the exchange of food stamps for cash), which is a higher percentage of trafficking cases than Compliance Branch had on investigations derived from other sources during Fiscal Year 1992.

Actions are proceeding to remove from the Food Stamp Program all of those firms found trafficking and those firms in which the investigation disclosed other violations severe enough to result in disqualification.

Mr. HORNSBY. Now, a lot of the 3,000 we targeted we did not need to investigate. We had bad sales information. When we reviewed updated sales information it appeared reasonable and we did not have any indication that they were violating program rules.

Mr. DURBIN. Are recipients guilty of fraudulent behavior treated the same as vendors guilty of fraudulent behavior when it comes to suspension or debarment?

Mr. HORNSBY. From the federal level, we have direct responsibility for authorizing retail food stores to accept food stamps, and we focus a lot of our investigative resources on the retailers.

Now, we, through state human service agencies, ask our state counterparts to certify households for food stamps, issue food stamps to them properly, and take responsibility for investigating recipient fraud. We did have a lot of success last year with investigations of recipients and debarment or suspension of people who were found to be violating the Food Stamp Program.

Mr. DURBIN. But are they treated the same? Is a recipient more likely to be disqualified from the program than a vendor if both are guilty of fraudulent behavior?

Mr. HORNSBY. Well, an individual recipient will be disqualified if they misreport their income, that is to say if they lie, and we get a fraud conviction against the individual. However, the states will not disqualify the whole household. So I guess recipients are probably not treated quite as harshly as the retailers.

Mr. DURBIN. Excuse me, did you say they are not treated as harshly?

Mr. HORNSBY. Probably not, no, sir, and I am speaking collectively nationally.

Mr. BRALEY. Mr. Chairman, I have an interesting example of how an EBT arrangement helped us with regard to retailer fraud as well as participant fraud. We had a case that we worked on with the Inspector General in Reading, Pennsylvania, which was the original EBT site, where people were coming in with an EBT card and the store was giving people cash back at a discounted rate, and then running the card through the machine.

As a result of the EBT technology we knew what transactions were being made. The place was staked out. People came out, and you could tell they were not carrying $400 worth of groceries, and yet the computer told us that the transaction had occurred at that point. We took action against the retailer at the federal level, and the state went ahead and took action against about 200 food stamp participants who had committed fraud in that manner. The computer system gave us the kind of record you would need to be able to show that the fraud had actually occurred and tied the fraudulent transactions back to the actual participant.

EBT is not foolproof, but you have got a lot better tools to go after both retailers and individuals who abuse the system.

Mr. HORNSBY. Mr. Durbin, I have got my statements available and I will submit this to you for the record. In fiscal 1992, state agencies conducted over 430,000 recipient fraud investigations, and they conducted 17,000 prosecutions and a number of administrative disqualification hearings. We have seen a dramatic rise in state recipient investigations. In 1981, 30,000 investigations to 430,000 investigations in fiscal 1992, and we believe the result of the enhanced funding contributed to that rise. The Department will pay 75 percent of state and local cost of investigating and prosecuting fraud cases and claims collection activities. So I think it is a pretty impressive number of cases, although I think we could do a lot better with it.

Mr. DURBIN. Can you tell me about a specific case I read where someone accumulated $30,000 worth of food stamp coupons and tried to buy a house with them?

Mr. HORNSBY. Yes, sir. I think that was an Office of Inspector General case. It is a New Jersey case and it is several years old. I do not know the specifics about the case. We can get that information and submit it to you. But I think in the course of dealing with a retailer they found out he also had a real estate license and somebody asked could we buy a house if we get enough food stamps, and he said, well, sure. That was the case, but that is not the norm. Most households do not accumulate $30,000 worth of food stamps. I will provide some additional information for the record.

[The information follows:]

In February 1991, a Camden, New Jersey authorized retailer, who also worked as a real estate broker, sold an Office of Inspector General (OIG) agent a house in Camden in exchange for $30,000 in food stamps. The grocer initially purchased food stamps for cash at his store from the agent. On a subsequent transaction, through his realty connection, he offered to sell the agent a house for food stamps. After consultation with the Justice Department, OIG proceeded with the transaction.

The agent gave the subject a downpayment of $1,000 in food stamps and later gave him the remaining $29,000 in food stamps, at which time the subject gave the agent the keys to the house and told him where to pick up the deed. The subject was arrested, pled guilty at trial, and was sentenced to 8 months in prison. He is currently incarcerated.

SCHOOL BREAKFAST PROGRAM

Mr. DURBIN. Under the school breakfast program there are two reimbursement rates for reduced and free meals served, regular and severe. As I understand it, the difference is for schools that served 40 percent or more of their lunches free or at a reduced price during the second preceding school year. In school year 1991–92 these rates were 92.75 cents for regular meals and 62.75 cents for regular reduced meals compared to 110.25 cents for severe need free meals and 80.25 cents for severe need reduced meals. What are these rates for school year 1992–93?

Mr. BRALEY. The rates for School Year 1992–93 are 94.5 cents for regular free and 64.5 cents for regular reduced price breakfasts as compared with 112.25 cents for severe need free and 82.25 cents for severe need reduced price breakfasts.

Mr. DURBIN. Provide a five-year table showing the number of meals that were reimbursed for each category as well as the number of full price breakfasts served.

Mr. BRALEY. I will provide the information for the record.

[The information follows:]

SCHOOL BREAKFAST PROGRAM MEALS SERVED BY CATEGORY

[Thousand Meals]

	Fiscal Year—				
	1988	1989	1990	1991	1992
Paid	80,538	86,628	94,036	97,795	102,365
Free-Reg	222,285	225,128	227,481	237,067	256,805
Free-Sn	309,237	313,837	348,853	394,510	446,097
Sub Free	531,522	538,965	576,334	631,577	702,902
Red-Reg	14,821	15,982	18,474	21,473	21,418
Red-Sn	15,713	16,883	18,681	21,365	22,232
Sub Reduced	30,534	32,865	37,155	42,838	43,650
Total	642,595	658,458	707,525	772,210	848,917

SUMMER FOOD SERVICE PROGRAM REVIEWS

Mr. DURBIN. During the summer of 1992 you had planned to review all private nonprofit sponsors as well as public sponsors participating in the summer food service program. Did you achieve this goal? What were your findings and recommendations?

Mr. BRALEY. In Fiscal Year 1992 the Agency achieved its goal of reviewing all the private nonprofit sponsors participating in the Summer Food Service Program. Review of public sponsors is the responsibility of participating State agencies except in those States where the program is administered directly by an FNS regional office.

We are currently in the process of analyzing data collected during the 1992 reviews of all private non-profit sponsors. We will make our findings and recommendations available upon completion of our analysis.

Mr. DURBIN. How many sponsors and sites are there participating in the summer food service program?

Mr. BRALEY. For the month of July 1992, there were 2,487 sponsors and 22,771 sites participating in the Summer Food Service Program.

Mr. DURBIN. What was the funding levels in both dollars and staff that were used in fiscal year 1992 to do these reviews and what are your estimates for fiscal year 1993?

Mr. BRALEY. The funding level for Fiscal Year 1992 for reviews of all Summer Food Service Program private nonprofit sponsors was $908,000. Fifteen staff years were devoted to the effort. We expect the 1993 level to be $1,078,000 and 15 staff years.

Mr. DURBIN. Do you perform an annual review of these operations?

Mr. BRALEY. As in 1992, the Agency's 1993 goal is to review all private non-profit sponsors. In those States where the Summer Food Service Program is administered by our Regional Offices, reviews will be conducted of all new and second year public sponsors, and all or a sample of public sponsors that have been in the program more than 2 years. States are required to conduct reviews of new sponsors that administer more than 10 sites. In addition, States conduct reviews of a portion of public sponsors that have been in the program two or more years. In order to eliminate duplication of effort, reviews conducted by FNS count toward State review requirements.

COORDINATED REVIEW EFFORT

Mr. DURBIN. The Coordinated Review Effort was designed to provide a comprehensive review and monitoring of the administration of the National School Lunch program by both the Federal government and State agencies administering the program. As I understand it, FNS conducts management evaluations of each State agency that is responsible for administering the program including a review of the States' compliance with monitoring requirements. Although you conduct some administrative reviews of school food authority operations as part of your management reviews, this part of the coordinated effort is the responsibility of the State agency. The State agency is required to conduct an administrative review of each school food authority at least once during a four year cycle. How do you see this effort—is it achieving the goals it intended; what are its strong points as well as its weak points; are any changes needed in the way it's being carried out; are States in compliance; is a review once every four years enough?

Mr. BRALEY. At the present time, it is too early to assess the effectiveness of the Coordinated Review Effort, CRE. An interim rule published on August 26, 1992, authorized the Food and Nutrition Service, FNS, to approve a State agency's request to delay implementation of CRE from July 1, 1992 to January 1, 1993. In these early stages of implementation, FNS is closely monitoring the system by conducting management evaluations, evaluating local programs through observation of State agency reviews, assisting State agencies in local level reviews, and conducting reviews independently. As information obtained from these activities becomes available, FNS will evaluate the system and identify modifications which may be needed to improve its effectiveness.

It should be noted that under this system, approximately 8,000 schools and 5,000 school food authorities will be reviewed in each of the four years in the review cycle. The overclaims as a result of these reviews will reflect the success and popularity of our intensive training and technical assistance effort of the last few years. The intent of Coordinated Review is not to increase collections, but to increase the accuracy of claims and to respond quickly and effectively in these cases where problems are identified.

Mr. DURBIN. How do the States and the school food authorities view this effort? What feedback have you had from them?

Mr. BRALEY. Although the Food and Nutrition Service is aware that there is criticism of the CRE at both the State and school food authority levels, State and local officials have also informed FNS that the system is having a positive effect. The use of a standardized form, developed in cooperation with State and local officials, has enabled reviewers to evaluate program operations on a consistent basis and target needed corrective action. We have been informed that CRE procedures have identified problems previously undetected. New and ongoing concerns regarding CRE are continuing to be addressed. For example, we are currently negotiating a contract to develop software which will streamline the review process as well as reduce the amount of time needed to complete the review. In addition, FNS is considering a regulation which would provide significant relief to State agencies in the review of free and reduced price meal applications.

Mr. DURBIN. School food authorities have complained for a number of years that the paperwork required to operate child nutrition programs is too cumbersome and resource intensive. Has this initiative alleviated some of these reporting requirements?

Mr. BRALEY. Since the Coordinated Review Effort is a system for State agencies to follow in conducting administrative reviews, it has no direct effect on reporting or recordkeeping at the local level. States review records maintained at the schools to ensure that eligibility for free and reduced price meals is properly documented, that counting of meals and consolidation of claims are correct and that meals served to children contain the components and quantities established for the program. States also rely on observation of the meal service to assess the school's operation of the program. None of these activities add any paperwork at the local level.

The Department has undertaken a number of initiatives to reduce the paperwork burden on local schools. We have implemented Direct Certification, under which schools may certify children for free meals based on direct contact with Food Stamp or Aid to Families with Dependent Children offices. This system reduces the number of actual applications handled, resulting in a substantial decrease in workload at the local level. Moreover, the agreements between school food authorities and State agencies to operate the programs are now permanent and need to be updated only when changes occur, rather than annually as was formerly the case. We have also authorized a number of demonstration projects to test alternatives to the current requirements for eligibility determinations and meal counting and claiming. We will be reviewing the results of these tests to determine if broad changes to current procedures would be feasible. We continue to look for ideas to reduce the paperwork, and we welcome the opportunity to work with Congress to improve these programs.

Mr. DURBIN. How much, in both dollars and staff, did you devote to this effort in fiscal year 1992 and what are your estimates for fiscal year 1993?

Mr. BRALEY. The funding level for Fiscal Year 1992 for implementation of the Coordinated Review Effort and closeout of Federal Review was $4.1 million. Sixty-two staff years were devoted to these efforts. About one-half of the staff and associated dollars are devoted to training and technical assistance efforts, while the remainder is devoted to actual review activities. We expect the 1993 levels to be $4.2 million and 62 staff years.

Mr. DURBIN. How much of State Administrative Expense funds appropriated in fiscal year 1992 did States use towards this effort and how much do they plan to use in fiscal year 1993? Also, do they contribute any State funding to this effort? If so, how much?

Mr. BRALEY. States are provided $4 million specifically for this effort through the State Administrative Expense (SAE) funds allocation formula, and can also spend other SAE funds for reviews. States are not required to report their costs for the Coordinated Review Effort. Therefore, no information is available on how much of the State Administrative Expense funds or State contributions were used to support this effort.

Mr. DURBIN. Required implementation of the Coordinated Review Effort for all States was July 1, 1992. Are all States now operating this system?

Mr. BRALEY. An interim rule published on August 26, 1992, authorized the Food and Nutrition Service to approve a State agency's request to delay implementation of the CRE from July 1, 1992 to January 1, 1993. Forty States implemented CRE prior to January 1993 with the remaining States beginning the 4-year cycle of reviews on January 1, 1993. Although some States will not conduct any CRE reviews during the current school year, the CRE system only requires that all reviews be completed within a 4-year cycle.

DIETARY GUIDELINES

Mr. DURBIN. Preliminary results of a study being conducted by USDA shows that although schools are making progress in improving the fat and salt content of lunches, much improvement still needs to be done. In the 1993 appropriation for Child Nutrition Programs we provided $2,000,000 for dietary guidelines to develop new meal patterns and nutrition education materials for all child nutrition programs. Tell us specifically how this money is being used?

Mr. BRALEY. FNS distributed over 250,000 copies of "Nutrition Guidance for the Child Nutrition Programs", to schools and child care institutions participating in FNS programs. The publication was jointly developed by the United States Department of Agriculture and the Department of Health and Human Services and it will be translated into Spanish and printed for dissemination this Fall. This publication, based on the 1990 revision of the "Dietary Guidelines for Americans" gives guidance to those responsible for preparing meals for children participating in the Child Nutrition Programs.

An interagency agreement for recipe file development and standardization is being negotiated with the Department of Defense. This recipe file will consist of more than 50 recipes. These recipes are chosen to encourage a diet with a wide variety of foods that are low in total and saturated fats and cholesterol and includes new foods in the vegetables, fruits and grains, dairy products, and meat meal alternates. A second phase to the project will consist of printing and disseminating the recipe file to all Child Nutrition Programs. A merchandizing and training component will be developed to introduce the new foods and train school food service workers in preparation techniques. A similar series of activities related to recipes for child care centers participating in the Child and Adult Care Food Program will be initiated.

An alternative method to the current meal pattern for implementing the Dietary Guidelines is being introduced by the Food and Nutrition Service. This method, called Nutrient Standard Menu Planning, would require that school meals meet a specific nutritional standard rather than a food-based meal pattern. A national demonstration project will be initiated and FNS will soon issue an announcement inviting school districts to apply to participate in the project. Training materials are currently being developed and will be printed for distribution to schools participating in the demonstration. Workshops will be conducted at the national, regional and local level to implement the training and the demonstration.

Food Service workers use the United States Department of Agriculture's "Food Buying Guide for Child Nutrition Programs" as a resource for food procurement and quantity requirements. The Food Buying Guide will be revised to include new foods and current yields in an effort to encourage the use of a wide variety of foods.

Current efforts are underway to revise the School Lunch meal pattern to reflect the Dietary Guidelines for Americans and the 1989 Recommended Dietary Allowances. These new meal patterns will be followed with a new "Menu Planning Guide for School Food Service" that will address the five methods needed to fully implement the Dietary Guidelines, namely menu modification, procurement specifications, recipe modifications, preparation techniques and education. A breakout of the $2 million for dietary guidelines will be provided for the record.

[The information follows:]

Reprint current "Food Buying Guide" while developing and distributing new FBG (contract)	$350,000
Develop and publish new School Lunch and Child Care recipes and train local staffs to use them	720,000
Design training program and train school food service personnel participating in national Nutrient Standard Menu Planning Demonstration Project (contract)	470,000
Revise print and distribute new "Menu Planning Guide for School Food Service" (contract)	347,500
Translate, print and distribute Spanish version of "Nutrition Guidance for Child Nutrition" Programs (contract)	112,500
Total	2,000,000

LOW-FAT BEEF PATTIES

Mr. DURBIN. It's a challenge to develop foods that are both nutritious and something kids will eat. USDA has been working on developing low-fat beef patties. Specifications have been written for two low-fat beef patties purchased for the school lunch program. One formulation is beef mixed with oat bran and oat fiber and the other is beef mixed with carrageenan, a seaweed extract. Have these low-fat beef patties been purchased for the 1993 School Year?

Mr. BRALEY. The Department of Agriculture has purchased 171 truckloads, totalling 6,771,400 pounds, of low-fat beef patties for use in the School Lunch Program during the 1993 School Year.

Mr. DURBIN. Include for the record a table showing the amount of regular beef patties and low-fat beef patties purchased and distributed in the school lunch program for school year 1991-92 and school year 1992-93?

Mr. BRALEY. I will be happy to provide a table showing the amount of 100% regular beef patties with vegetable protein product (VPP) and low-fat beef patties purchased and distributed in the school lunch program for school year 1991-92 and school year 1992-93 for the record.

[The information follows:]

BEEF PATTIES DELIVERED FOR SCHOOL YEAR 1992 AND 1993

Commodities	SY 1992 deliveries		SY 1993 deliveries	
	Pounds	Dollars	Pounds	Dollars
Beef patties 100%	9,228,528	$12,671,407	9,187,200	$12,359,985
Beef patties, vegetable protein products	22,048,452	25,049,082	20,869,200	23,310,992
Beef patties lean	3,737,880	6,628,768	6,771,600	10,737,072

100% Beef Patties average 19-20% fat and have no additives.

Patties VPP average 18-19% fat. They are made with at least 80% beef and no more than 20% hydrated soy protein product.

Patties low-fat average less than 10% fat. They are made with 90% beef and a formula of either oat bran products and seasoning or carrageenan (seaweed) and seasoning.

ALTERNATIVE MEAL COUNTING AND CLAIMING

Mr. DURBIN. You currently have 11 pilot projects underway around the country that are testing the feasibility of alternatives to meal counting and claiming procedures. Please bring us up to date on each of these projects. Also, if any new projects have, describe them for us.

Mr. BRALEY. There are 3 types of pilot projects operating in 10 sites: (1) tests of extended application intervals; (2) tests of providing meals at no charge to all students; and (3) tests of direct certification. We originally accepted 12 sites into the pilot program but two have left the demonstration.

San Bernadino, California and Springfield, Oregon, are testing extended application intervals. In these sites, applications for free or reduced price meals are valid for two or three years instead of the current regulatory limit of one year.

Salinas, California; Philadelphia, Pennsylvania; National City, California; Jersey City, New Jersey; and Terrell County, Georgia, are testing universal free programs—that is, they serve meals at no charge to all students and receive free or reduced price Federal reimbursement rates based on the numbers of children eligible for free or reduced price meals. Each of these sites has used a different method to determine what percentage of their students qualify for free and reduced price meals. Although they serve meals at no charge to all students, they prepare claims for reimbursement based on the free and reduced price percentages.

Columbus, Ohio; Lowell, Massachusetts; and the State of Maine are testing direct certification. In these sites, the local or State agency personnel have coordinated with Food Stamp or Aid to Families with Dependent Children (AFDC) offices for documentation that children are members of food stamp households or AFDC assistance units. These children are automatically eligible for free meals or free milk and need not fill out applications.

An interim report based on preliminary data from all sites is currently being prepared. We are scheduled to report to Congress on July 1.

PROCESSED COMMODITY INVENTORY MANAGEMENT SYSTEM

Mr. DURBIN. Mrs. Nelsen testified at last year's hearings that the Processed Commodities Inventory Management System designed to streamline and improve the flow of commodities to schools and summer food service programs will be fully operational for school and fiscal year 1993. Is this the case?

Mr. BRALEY. Yes. Processed Commodities Inventory Management System, PCIMS, became operational in the Agricultural Marketing Service, AMS, last year and in January 1992 at the Agricultural Stabilization and Conservation Service, ASCS. PCIMS became operational in the Food and Nutrition Service in April 1992 and is supporting the flow of commodities to schools and summer food services programs as well as to our other commodity distribution programs. PCIMS is a more automated system than the collection of systems which it replaced. As a result, data entry time has been significantly reduced by eliminating the need to re-key large volumes of data. The benefits of PCIMS include more accurate, consistent and timely information, better analysis of purchase alternatives, and an ability to determine the status of an order and to respond quickly to recipient needs.

Mr. DURBIN. Describe for the Committee how this system operates.

Mr. BRALEY. Acquiring commodities for the Child Nutrition Programs is a joint effort by the AMS, ASCS and the FNS. Initially, FNS receives notification from AMS and the ASCS provides FNS with information on the availability of various commodities. FNS uses PCIMS and the list of commodities provided by AMS and ASCS to survey State Distributing Agencies on commodities needed for their programs. FNS then compiles the orders from the State distributing agencies, and provides delivery orders to AMS and ASCS using the PCIMS system. AMS and ASCS procure the commodities, through PCIMS, based on FNS program needs. ASCS and Federal Grain Inspection Service provide grading and inspection services to ensure contract compliance. ASCS, in addition to procuring certain commodities, coordinates all warehousing and shipping of commodity products as well as all payments to vendors. Most of these transactions, including the accounting functions, take place through the PCIMS system.

The next step towards fully integrating acquisition operations will be to acquire data connections for communication with the States, shipping contractors and warehouse companies through PCIMS.

HOMELESS CHILDREN DEMONSTRATION PROJECT

Mr. DURBIN. Public Law 101-147 authorized the Child Nutrition Demonstration Project for Homeless Children. According to your statement, you now have 33 participating sponsors serving 56 homeless shelters. How many sponsors and/or participants are authorized to partake in these demonstration projects?

Mr. BRALEY. Public Law 101-147 does not specify the number of sponsors which may be authorized to participate in the demonstration project. Instead, the number of the demonstration project sponsors authorized to participate is limited by the amount of funding made available for the demonstration.

Mr. DURBIN. Do you plan to expand this project in fiscal year 1993 or 1994?

Mr. BRALEY. We have announced the availability of the demonstration to new sponsors for participation and have established no deadline for receiving applications. We continue to accept and review applications as received. Provided that there is not a sudden increase in the number or size of sponsors applying, we anticipate being able to approve all eligible applicants for participation in Fiscal Year 1993.

Further expansion of the project in Fiscal Year 1994 is contingent on the number of sponsors participating in the demonstration at the end of Fiscal year 1993 and on the amount of funds available from recovered State Administrative Expense funds.

Mr. DURBIN. How much is authorized for these projects and how much is currently being spent?

Mr. BRALEY. Public Law 101-147 authorized $50,000 to be made available in Fiscal Year 1990 to begin the Child Nutrition Homeless Demonstration project. It authorized $350,000 to expand and carry out the project in each of the Fiscal Years 1991 through 1994, in addition to any amounts made available by the return of unspent State Administrative Expense (SAE) funds. Public Law 102-342 increased the Fiscal Year 1993 authorization to $650,000 and the Fiscal Year 1994 authorization to $800,000.

Public Law 102-512 required that the Department estimate the amount of recoveries to be made during the fiscal year, and make the amount available for the project. This year, the Department estimates that $1.5 million will be returned. It further specified that not less than $1 million and not more than $4 million in SAE Funds be used for the project in each of Fiscal Years 1993 and 1994.

We expect to provide $1,350,000 in reimbursement to sponsors currently participating in the demonstration in Fiscal Year 1993. We anticipate providing an additional $300,000 in Fiscal Year 1993 in reimbursement to sponsors which will begin participation in the project sometime during Fiscal Year 1993; for a total expenditure of $1,650,000 in Fiscal Year 1993.

Mr. DURBIN. Where is the funding to operate this program coming from?

Mr. BRALEY. In Fiscal Year 1993, $650,000 was appropriated and $800,000 is authorized in Fiscal Year 1994 to operate the demonstration program. With the passage of Public Law 102-512, the Food and Nutrition Service was granted the authority to allocate up to $4 million for this program.

Mr. DURBIN. Do you plan to request additional funding for this project in fiscal year 1994?

Mr. BRALEY. Two types of funding will be available in Fiscal Year 1994 for the demonstration projects: $800,000 and the Department's estimate of funds to be recovered or $1 million, whichever is greater. The funds will be made available from a combination of carryover and other funds "that have not been otherwise allocated to the States."

Mr. DURBIN. What have your evaluations of the project shown to date?

Mr. BRALEY. The Agency conducted a study of the homeless shelter demonstration in four shelters in Philadelphia, Pennsylvania. The evaluation covered the period of May 1990 through March 1991. During this 11-month period, the participating shelters served about 65 children on a daily basis. All shelters provided meals to residents prior to the demonstration. However, the demonstration enhanced the quality of meals served to children under the age of 6—by providing more fruits, vegetables, milk, and full strength juice—and freed up resources so that the nutritional value of meals for older children and adults could be improved. A second report summarizing the demonstration in a larger number of shelters is currently in Agency clearance. We expect to release this report later this spring.

Mr. DURBIN. At the end of last year the authorizing committee passed a bill earmarking additional funds for the project. Would you describe the details of this bill and how it affects ongoing child nutrition programs?

Mr. BRALEY. Public Law 102-512 requires the Food and Nutrition Service to allocate $1 million or more for the demonstration early in the fiscal year based on the amount of State Administrative Expense funds anticipated to be recovered from the States later in the fiscal year.

To the extent that funds are used for purposes of the demonstration, there are less funds available to allocate to the States for administration of the Child Nutrition Programs. Such funds are used for special State initiatives.

DEMONSTRATIONS, STUDIES AND REPORTS

Mr. DURBIN. In last year's hearing record you provided the committee with a list of all demonstrations, studies, and reports mandated by P.L. 101-147, as well as the results of those that were completed. Please update the list for us.

Mr. BRALEY. I will include for the record an update for these demonstrations, studies, and reports.

[The information follows:]

Demonstrations, Studies and Reports Mandated By the Child Nutrition and WIC Reauthorization Act of 1989

I. Child Nutrition Programs

Demonstrations

Year Round Food Service to Homeless Preschool Children

This demonstration will provide the Department with information on methods to provide year-round nutrition assistance to preschool children living in homeless shelters.

Completion Date: The first phase of this project demonstrated a food assistance program at four homeless shelters in Philadelphia, Pennsylvania. A report was submitted to Congress in March 1992 summarizing the demonstration at these four shelters. A description of the first phase findings are attached. The demonstration expanded in Fiscal Year 1991 and the Agency is finalizing a second report on the demonstration to include the 1991 expansion sites. To date, through additional expansion efforts, there are 39 sponsors and 60 shelters participating in the demonstration throughout the United States.

Estimated Costs: Operations - Authorized amounts include $50,000 in Fiscal Year 1990, $350,000 for Fiscal Years 1991 and 1992, $650,000 for Fiscal Year 1993, and $800,000 for Fiscal Year 1994. The Agency is also authorized to spend returned state administrative funds for these purposes and will spend an estimated $1 million in Fiscal Year 1993.

Evaluation - $65,000 in Fiscal Year 1990, $110,000 in Fiscal Year 1992.

Efforts to Reduce Barriers to Low-Income Family Day Care Home Child and Adult Care Food Program (CACFP) Participation

This demonstration will test three strategies in six areas/sites to remove barriers to CACFP participation faced by low-income family day care homes.

Completion Date: The year-long demonstrations ended in October of 1991. A report is currently in Agency clearance and will be available this summer.

Estimated Costs: Operations - FNS awarded six grants for a total of $140,000

Evaluation - $70,000

CACFP Private For-Profit Demonstration Projects

This demonstration will examine the impact of modifying eligibility requirements for private, for-profit child care centers on low-income CACFP participation in the States of Kentucky and Iowa. As a result of participating in the demonstration, the child care centers must either lower the child care fees for children with incomes below 185 percent of the poverty level or improve the quality of meals served to children in their care.

Completion Date: The first year of the demonstration ended in October of 1991. A report on the first year of the demonstration will be available this summer. The demonstration will end in Fiscal Year 1994.

Estimated Costs: Operations - $1,000,000 (Fiscal Year 1991)
$2,500,000 (Fiscal Year 1992)

Evaluation - $46,000 for Fiscal Year 1990

Alternate Counting Methods Pilot Projects

This demonstration in 10 sites seeks alternatives to financial accountability systems involved in administering programs under the National School Lunch and Child Nutrition Acts by testing alternative methods for the application process as well as methods to count and claim meals.

Completion Date: Spring 1994

Estimated Costs: Operations - $0

Evaluation - $850,000

Studies and Reports

Child Nutrition Paperwork Reduction Report

In this requirement, USDA reported on the extent to which paperwork required of State and local agencies, schools, and other agencies participating in nutrition programs under the Child Nutrition Act and the Child Nutrition and WIC Reauthorization Act could be reduced. This report was developed in consultation with State and local administrators of child nutrition.

Completion Date: Report submitted to Congress in April of 1991. A description is attached.

Estimated Costs: $50,000 for consultation with State and local administrators.

Nutrition Guidance for Child Nutrition Programs

This publication, developed jointly by the Secretary of Agriculture and the Secretary of Health and Human Services provides nutrition guidance based on the Dietary Guidelines, primarily in the areas of menu planning, meal preparation, and meal supplements for the Child Nutrition Programs.

Completion Date: Publication is completed. The Agency distributed the publication in May of 1992.

Estimated Costs: $900,000 for printing and the dissemination of 450,000 copies of the pamphlet and a poster.

Efforts to Increase Participation in the School Breakfast Program

This report will describe the efforts of the Secretary of Agriculture and all State Educational Agencies to increase participation in the School Breakfast Program. Public Law 101-147 authorized the Food and Nutrition Service to award a series of competitive grants to States to begin breakfast programs in areas of need. The grants are primarily used to buy the necessary equipment to start a program and to fund outreach activities. States are required to report on expenditure activities quarterly and participation activities on a yearly basis for three years. FNS is required to report to Congress in October 1993.

Completion Date: October 1, 1993.

Estimated Costs: Operations - $3,000,000 for Fiscal year 1990
$5,000,000 each year for Fiscal Years 1991-1994

II. WIC Program

Studies and Reports

Estimates of Women, Infants, and Children Eligible for the Special Supplemental Food Program for Women, Infants, and Children (WIC).

This report will produce estimates of persons who are income eligible for WIC at the national, State and county levels based on 1990 Census and other data.

Completion Date: Fiscal Year 1994.

Estimated Costs: A contract was awarded in Fiscal Year 1992.

Nutritional Risk Criteria Used in the Special Supplemental Food Program for Women, Infants and Children (WIC)

This report reviewed the relationship between the nutritional risk criteria and the priority system used in the WIC Program, especially as it affects pregnant women.

Completion Date: Report submitted to Congress in December 1991. A description is attached.

Estimated Costs: $75,000

Appropriateness of Foods Eligible for Purchase Under the WIC Program

This report reviewed the appropriateness of foods eligible for purchase under the WIC Program.

Completion Date: Report submitted to Congress in December 1991. A description is attached.

Estimated Costs: $80,000

The WIC Program Administrative Cost Impact Report

This report reviews the effects of P.L. 101-147 on State and local agencies' costs for nutrition services and administration.

Completion Date: Report submitted to interested members of Congress in November of 1990. A description is attached.

Estimated Costs: $0

III. Summary of Completed Research

Year Round Food Service to Homeless Preschool Children

This demonstration provides year-round nutrition assistance to preschool children living in homeless shelters. The first year report summarizes the demonstration in four homeless shelters in Philadelphia, Pennsylvania. The evaluation covered the period of May 1990 through March 1991. During the nine-month period, the participating shelters served about 65 children on a daily basis. All shelters provided meals to residents prior to the demonstration. However, the demonstration enhanced the quality of meals served to children under the age of 6 (by providing more fruits, vegetables, milk, and full strength juice) and freed up resources so that the nutritional value of meals for older children and adults could be improved.

VI. Summary of Reports

Child Nutrition Paperwork Reduction Report

This report summarizes the extent to which paperwork required of State and local agencies, schools, and other agencies participating in child nutrition programs has been reduced. Of the recommendations submitted to the Department by a Task Force, 34 have been implemented, 10 have been accepted for implementation, 10 will be addressed in future rulemaking, and 11 have been rejected by the Department. In addition, one recommendation has been identified for further consideration.

Nutrition Guidance for Child Nutrition Programs

This publication offers suggestions for planning healthy meals for children and teens.

Nutritional Risk Criteria Used in the Special Supplemental Food Program for Women, Infants, and Children (WIC)

Several recommendations from the National Advisory Council on Maternal, Infant, and Fetal Nutrition on the WIC nutritional risk criteria may be found in the Council's 1992 biennial report. Attached is a copy of the report for the record.

Appropriateness of Foods Eligible for Purchase Under the WIC Program

Several recommendations from the National Advisory Council on Maternal, Infant, and Fetal Nutrition on the appropriateness of the WIC food package may be found in the Council's 1992 biennial report mentioned above.

The WIC Program Administrative Cost Impact Report

This report contains information on grants allocated to WIC State agencies for administration of the WIC Program, the actual expenditures of these grants during Fiscal Year 1990, and notable differences before and after the implementation of P.L. 101-147.

PARTICIPATION LEVELS

Mr. DURBIN. Please update the table that appears on page 90 of last year's hearing record showing the number of outlets and average daily participation for the school lunch, school breakfast, and child and adult care food programs to include fiscal year 1992 as well as the summer food service program.

Mr. BRALEY. I will submit that information for the record.

[The information follows:]

NATIONAL SCHOOL LUNCH, SCHOOL BREAKFAST, AND CHILD AND ADULT CARE FOOD PROGRAMS
Outlets and Average Daily Participation, Fiscal Years 1980 through 1992 1/

Fiscal Year	National School Lunch Program: Outlets (October)	National School Lunch Program: Average Daily Participation	School Breakfast Program: Outlets (October)	School Breakfast Program: Average Daily Participation	Child and Adult Care Food Program — Child Care: Averages of Quarterly: Outlets	Child Care: Attendance	Adult Care: Averages of Quarterly: Outlets	Adult Care: Attendance
1980	94,082	26,607,666	32,816	3,585,445	36,517	659,358		
1981	93,960	25,823,667	35,079	3,810,333	57,625	777,667		
1982	91,151	22,940,445	34,342	3,323,333	68,500	844,875		
1983	90,586	23,185,191	33,534	3,376,969	73,825	909,350		
1984	89,615	23,376,276	33,840	3,428,162	84,250	982,275		
1985	89,546	23,573,475	34,795	3,437,169	93,512	1,046,723		
1986	89,857	23,719,123	35,180	3,497,060	99,256	1,100,543		
1987	90,122	23,938,835	37,161	3,619,679	107,590	1,185,549		
1988	90,608	24,210,022	38,816	3,680,589	120,235	1,255,721	213	6,605
1989	91,493	24,187,218	40,029	3,813,489	135,491	1,358,314	365	10,493
1990	91,325	24,133,381	42,766	4,068,692	152,068	1,472,712	633	17,270
1991	91,620	24,213,249	46,140	4,437,150	168,710	1,618,425	1,031	26,495
1992	92,284	24,832,473	49,973	4,834,206	185,867	1,789,444	1,144	31,573

1/ Outlet data for National School Lunch and School Breakfast Programs are reported only in October. Their ADP, a number estimated by increasing reported ADM (average daily meals) using an absentee factor, is a school year average (Sept-May) of those estimates. The ADP number assumes no absentees -- that all students participating were actually at school that day. Outlets and attendance are reported quarterly for the Child and Adult Care Food Program. The numbers above are averages of those quarterly numbers.

Source: FNS 10 and FNS 52 reports.

Mr. DURBIN. Also, update the tables that appear on pages 92 and 93 to reflect fiscal year 1992 actuals and fiscal year 1993 estimates.

Mr. BRALEY. I will also submit that information for the record.

[The information follows:]

CHILD NUTRITION PROGRAMS
Number and Type of Meals Served
Fiscal Years 1990 through 1994
(Meals in 000's)

Child Nutrition Programs	Fiscal Year	Meals served to children where family income is: below 130% of poverty	130% to 185% of poverty	above 185% of poverty	Total
National School Lunch Program	FY 1990	1,661,596	273,016	2,074,464	4,009,076
	FY 1991	1,748,830	292,517	2,009,927	4,051,273
	FY 1992	1,881,653	284,557	1,925,883	4,092,093
	FY 1993 1/	2,011,615	290,937	1,887,356	4,189,908
	FY 1994 1/	2,043,566	295,558	1,917,340	4,256,464
School Breakfast Program	FY 1990	576,334	37,155	94,036	707,525
	FY 1991	631,577	42,838	97,795	772,210
	FY 1992	702,902	43,650	102,365	848,917
	FY 1993 1/	790,222	46,583	104,587	941,392
	FY 1994 1/	846,506	49,870	112,106	1,008,482
Child and Adult Care Food Program	FY 1990	760,287	43,452	154,386	958,125
	FY 1991	844,477	43,569	163,724	1,051,770
	FY 1992	962,367	45,441	172,962	1,180,770
	FY 1993 1/	1,117,126	50,764	177,571	1,345,461
	FY 1994 1/	1,315,360	54,527	190,512	1,560,399
Summer Food Service Program	FY 1990	91,218			91,218
	FY 1991	96,218			96,218
	FY 1992	105,822			105,822
	FY 1993 1/	117,332			117,332
	FY 1994 1/	126,246			126,246

1/ Projected data.

Source: State-reported data from forms FNS 10, 44, and 418.

CHILD NUTRITION PROGRAMS
Average Daily Participation for
Fiscal Years 1990 through 1994

Child Nutrition Programs	Fiscal Year	Average Daily Participation: below 130% of poverty	130% to 185% of poverty	above 185% of poverty	Total
National School Lunch Program	FY 1990	9,896,149	1,653,937	12,583,295	24,133,381
	FY 1991	10,293,053	1,762,641	12,157,555	24,213,249
	FY 1992	11,226,798	1,728,058	11,677,222	24,632,078
	FY 1993 1/	11,945,314	1,763,640	11,443,349	25,152,303
	FY 1994 1/	12,135,045	1,791,652	11,625,147	25,551,844
School Breakfast Program	FY 1990	3,297,768	219,086	551,838	4,068,692
	FY 1991	3,610,062	251,521	575,567	4,437,150
	FY 1992	4,054,238	260,080	604,553	4,918,871
	FY 1993 1/	4,536,777	276,779	616,341	5,429,897
	FY 1994 1/	4,859,912	296,309	660,651	5,816,872
Child and Adult Care Food Program 2/	FY 1990	1,168,619	66,789	237,304	1,472,712
	FY 1991	1,299,450	67,043	251,933	1,618,425
	FY 1992	1,458,944	68,404	262,096	1,789,444
	FY 1993 1/	1,712,000	77,796	272,128	2,061,924
	FY 1994 1/	2,015,794	83,563	291,960	2,391,317
Summer Food Service Program	FY 1990	1,689,957			1,689,957
	FY 1991	1,839,674			1,839,674
	FY 1992	1,916,359			1,916,359
	FY 1993 1/	2,094,038			2,094,038
	FY 1994 1/	2,253,127			2,253,127

1/ Projected data.
2/ Only total attendance is reported for CACFP, so the categories must be estimated for all years.

CNP STUDIES

Mr. DURBIN. Last year you provided the committee with a list of all ongoing and planned Child Nutrition studies which included a description, estimated completion date, amount obligated to date, and whether or not it was congressionally mandated. Please update this list and be sure to include any studies initiated or planned in fiscal year 1993 as well as the results of those that were completed.

Mr. BRALEY. Several major studies initiated prior to Fiscal Year 1993 are currently ongoing. In addition, the Agency intends to implement five new Child Nutrition studies during Fiscal Year 1993. I will include for the record an updated list of current ongoing and planned Fiscal Year 1993 Child Nutrition studies, as well as the executive summaries of those that were completed in Fiscal Year 1992.

[The information follows:]

<u>Ongoing Child Nutrition Studies</u>

SCHOOL NUTRITION DIETARY ASSESSMENT STUDY

This study examines the nutrient content of the school nutrition programs as offered, selected, and consumed by students. It measures the dietary impact of school nutrition programs and serves to update the National Evaluation of School Nutrition Programs which collected similar consumption data in 1980. The study also assesses the effect of policy changes in the 1980's (offer versus serve, the revised SBP meal pattern, etc.).

Estimated Completion Date: June 1993
Amount Obligated Through Fiscal Year 1992: $2,935,142
Congressionally Mandated: No

ADULT DAY CARE STUDY

This study describes the characteristics of adults and adult day care centers participating in the Child and Adult Care Food Program (CACFP). It also compares participating centers to non-participating centers, and assesses the potential for growth in the CACFP. Finally the study will examine adult dietary intake in participating centers.

Estimated Completion Date: September 1993
Amount Obligated Through Fiscal Year 1992: $987,342
Congressionally Mandated: No

SPECIAL NUTRITION ANALYSIS AND MODELING

The analyses undertaken use existing and newly available nationally representative data, as well as information collected through demonstrations and special projects, to examine research questions concerning the characteristics of program eligible and program participants; the impact of program changes on participation and the institutions that administer the programs; and the impact of demographic and economic trends on participation.

Estimated Completion Date: Fall 1993
Amount Obligated Through Fiscal Year 1992: $718,694
Congressionally Mandated: No

FOOD SERVICE MANAGEMENT COMPANIES

This study examines the range of experiences of SFAs that have contracted with food service management companies and the contractual agreements and oversight responsibilities for food service management company operators. The intent is to learn advantages and disadvantages of this method of providing food service as compared to traditional self-managed operations in order to develop improved guidance and direction to States and SFAs.

Estimated Completion Date: Fall 1993
Amount Obligated Through Fiscal Year 1992: $853,355
Congressionally Mandated: No

CHILD CARE DEMONSTRATIONS

The Child Nutrition and WIC Reauthorization Act of 1989 (P.L. 101-147) mandates the Secretary of Agriculture to implement demonstration projects to: remove or reduce barriers to low-income family day care home participation in the Child and Adult Care Food Program (CACFP); examine the impact of modifying CACFP eligibility requirements for private, for-profit child care centers on low-income CACFP participation; and determine the best means of providing year-round food assistance to preschool children in homeless shelters. The study will collect, analyze, and report data which will enable USDA to evaluate the three demonstrations.

Estimated Completion Date: August 1993
Amount Obligated Through Fiscal Year 1992: $292,343
Congressionally Mandated: Yes; PL 101-147

STUDY OF SCHOOL LUNCH ELIGIBLE NON-PARTICIPANTS

This study will examine why eligible students don't apply for, or eat, free and reduced-price meals. Results of this study should allow the Secretary to assess what more should be done to reach all eligible students. By means of case study methodology, this study will examine the reasons why those income-eligible to participate in the school lunch program fail to do so. Potential barriers (real and perceived) will be examined by directly interviewing non-participant households. The study will also recommend ways to reduce barriers and increase daily participation. This study was recommended by Congress in the 1990 FACT Act pending availability of funds.

Expected Completion Date: Fall 1993
Amount Obligated Through Fiscal Year 1992: $566,373
Congressionally Mandated: Yes; P.L. 101-624

ALTERNATE MEAL COUNTING AND CLAIMING

Formerly known as the Paperwork Reduction Pilot Projects Evaluation, Public Law 101-147 amended the National School Lunch Act to require the Secretary to conduct three pilot programs seeking to simplify and reduce meal counting and claiming requirements in the National School Lunch Program. Ten pilot sites are currently involved in this demonstration. The evaluation design calls for a pretest-posttest case study approach. Baseline data was collected during School Year 1991. Alternative application and meal counting procedures began in School Year 1992. This evaluation requires data collection and analysis in all 10 sites through 1994.

Expected Completion Date: July, 1994
Amount Obligated Through Fiscal Year 1992: $853,996
Congressionally Mandated: Yes; P.L. 101-147

MENU MODIFICATION DEMONSTRATIONS

In order to learn more about the processes and effects of reducing fat and sodium in school meals, in accordance with the Dietary Guidelines for Americans and within current meal patterns, competitive grants were awarded to five school districts to plan and implement changes over a 3-year period. The five grantees are: Denver, Colorado; Chattanooga, Tennessee; San Bernardino, California; Princeton City (Cincinnati), Ohio; and West Baton Rouge, Louisiana. Data collection includes nutritional analysis of menu items, plate waste measures and 24-hour dietary recalls. Analyses will focus on what is offered, selected and consumed by students.

Estimated Completion Date: Spring 1993
Amount Obligated Through Fiscal Year 1992: $508,518
Congressionally Mandated: No

SCHOOL LUNCH AND BREAKFAST COST STUDY

The purpose of this study is to determine the cost to produce reimbursable meals in the National School Lunch Program and the School Breakfast Program. In addition, the study will examine the indirect costs charged to School Food Authorities to produce school meals, and local administrative costs and sources of non-Federal revenue that support meal production.

Estimated Completion Date: Spring 1994
Amount Obligated Through Fiscal Year 1992: $702,173
Congressionally Mandated: Yes; P.L. 101-624

MULTI-USE APPLICATION DEMONSTRATION

The State of West Virginia is testing new methods of providing enhanced services to children in need. To this end, they have developed a multi-use application for free and reduced price National School Lunch Program meals that includes a series of waivers to allow income information to be shared with other agencies that provide services to low-income children. FNS has entered into a cooperative agreement with the West Virginia State

Department of Education to assess whether or not controlled sharing of information has any effect (e.g., presents a barrier or an inducement) on application and participation rates in the National School Lunch Program.

Estimated Completion Date: Fall 1994
Amount Obligated Through Fiscal Year 1992: $50,000
Congressionally Mandated: No

Completed Child Nutrition Studies

COMMODITY LETTER OF CREDIT (CLOC) MODIFICATION EVALUATION

This study examines modifications to the Commodity Letter of Credit (CLOC) System to be implemented in 25 school districts. These modifications are intended to make the CLOC system more responsive to surplus removal goals to support the agricultural community while simultaneously providing flexibility to schools.

Completion Date: June 1992
Amount Obligated Through Fiscal Year 1992: $371,264
Congressionally Mandated: Recommended in Conference Report for P.L. 101-147

CHILD NUTRITION PROGRAM OPERATIONS STUDY

This project enables the Agency to meet its information needs using a "modular" survey which can be repeated periodically. This study is designed to collect data over a three year period on issues that are currently, or likely to be, the focus of the Agency's policy-making process. Topics examined in the first year included program participation, meal prices and meal costs, food distribution issues, claims reimbursement, food service management companies, and training and technical assistance. The second year focused on program participation, meal prices and meal costs, the Buy American provision and commodity processing, CN labeling and technical assistance. The second year also examined the food and nutrient composition of NSLP and SBP meals at three levels: (1) as offered by participating schools, (2) as selected by participating students, and (3) as actually consumed by participating students.

Major issues examined in the third year of the study include: participation in the NSLP and SBP, meal prices, Food Donation Program operations, technical assistance related to the nutritional analysis of meals, use of commercial food service vendors, and implementation of after-school care programs which include food service.

Completion Date: March 1993
Amount Obligated Through Fiscal Year 1992: $1,686,912
Congressionally Mandated: No

CHILD NUTRITION MEAL COST METHODOLOGY STUDY

This is a methodological study to identify an approach for FNS to measure the full cost of meal production for reimbursable meals in the NSLP and SBP. The methodology developed focuses on identifying all costs associated with meal production. A technical assistance manual will be prepared for SFAs interested in using this method.

Completion Date: May 1992
Amount Obligated Through Fiscal Year 1992: $474,833
Congressionally Mandated: No

New Child Nutrition Studies

NSLP SCHOOL DROPOUT STUDY

This study will examine why schools chose not to participate in the National School Lunch Program. The study will include both schools which have recently dropped out of the program and those which are longtime nonparticipants. The final report will include a description of the scope of the dropout/nonparticipation problem; the reasons for and the decision-making process for dropout and nonparticipation; and the characteristics of dropout/nonparticipation schools.

Estimated Completion Date: To be awarded
Amount Obligated Through Fiscal Year 1992: To be awarded
Congressionally Mandated: Yes; P.L. 101-624

STATE AND LOCAL ADMINISTRATIVE COST STUDY

The primary objective of this study is to examine the changes in the responsibilities of State level staff administering the National School Lunch Program and School Breakfast Program and the costs associated with these changes. A survey will be conducted with all State Child Nutrition Directors to examine a number of issues related to the administration of the school lunch and breakfast program including the organization of the State agencies, their functional responsibilities, budget process and fiscal behavior of these State agencies, and the perceptions of State agency officials about the appropriateness of State Administrative Expense (SAE) funding. FNS program data will be used to document changes in the amount of SAE funding over the past several years.

Estimated Completion Date: To be awarded
Amount Obligated Through Fiscal Year 1992: To be awarded
Congressionally Mandated: Yes; P.L. 101-624

UNIVERSAL FREE LUNCH STUDY

The Senate passed a resolution in July of 1992 asking the Secretary of Agriculture to conduct a study of various options for implementing and funding universal school lunch and breakfast programs, i.e., all lunches and breakfasts reimbursed at one rate (with no regard to income status) and served at no charge to students.

Estimated Completion Date: Scheduled to report to Congress October 1, 1993
Amount Obligated Through Fiscal Year 1992: None
Congressionally Mandated: Yes; Senate Resolution 303 (7/92)

SPECIAL NUTRITION ANALYSIS AND MODELING

This contract will provide quick response capability for the Child Nutrition Programs in answering questions posed by legislators or policy makers. This contract will be used for many purposes, including responding to reauthorizations questions and providing cost estimates. Research questions will include characteristics of program eligibles; characteristics of program participants and institutions that administer programs; and the effect of child care expansion legislation. The analyses would use existing data available from national studies, demonstrations or special projects.

Estimated Completion Date: To be awarded
Amount Obligated Through Fiscal Year 1992: To be awarded
Congressionally Mandated: No

CACFP NUTRITION STUDY

This study will examine the nutritional content of the meals offered in family day care homes and centers. It will examine the relationship between the current meal pattern and the nutritional needs of child care participants. Additionally, the nutritional contribution of those meals will be determined. Dietary intake data will be collected to determine the contribution of the meals to children's daily dietary intake. The extent of implementation of the Dietary Guidelines will be examined. Additionally, this study will provide data on the characteristics of participants and institutions participating in the program, with an emphasis on nutrition education initiative activities.

Estimated Completion Date: To be awarded
Amount Obligated Through Fiscal Year 1992: To be awarded
Congressionally Mandated: No

Mr. DURBIN. In looking at last year's list I noticed a study called the Child Nutrition Meal Cost Methodology Study due to be completed in the summer of 1992 and one called the School Lunch and Breakfast Cost Study not yet started. The explanation of both studies describes the same objective. Would you clarify this for me?

Mr. BRALEY. The Meal Cost Methodology Study was conducted to develop a methodology to identify and measure all costs associated with the production of meals in the National School Lunch Program (NSLP) and School Breakfast Program (SBP) and to directly allocate these costs to different school food service activities. A direct measurement approach was pilot tested in 18 school districts. The results of this pilot test indicated that this direct measurement approach is a feasible mechanism for measuring per-meal costs of reimbursable meals in the NSLP and SBP.

The School Lunch and Breakfast Cost Study is using the direct measurement approach developed in the Meal Cost Methodology Study to produce national estimates of the cost of producing school lunches and breakfasts, including indirect and local administrative costs. The study also examines the composition of food service costs by categories like food, labor, and indirect costs, and the variation in meal production costs across the different types of meal production systems like self-preparation and central kitchens used by school districts. A nationally-representative sample of about 100 school districts is participating in this study.

CASH AND CLOC PROGRAMS

Mr. DURBIN. What is the status of the Cash and Commodity Letter of Credit programs that were scheduled to end on September 30, 1992?

Mr. BRALEY. The Child Nutrition Amendments of 1992 (P.L. 102–342) signed into law on August 14, 1992 extended through September 30, 1994 the Cash and Commodity Letter of Credit (CLOC) options to those school districts that were operating under these alternatives. In School Year 1992–93 there are 34 cash pilot sites and 25 CLOC pilot sites.

EDUCATIONAL MATERIALS

Mr. DURBIN. Do you provide training and/or distribute educational materials to school food authorities on the safe handling and preparation of foods served in the child nutrition programs?

Mr. BRALEY. Over the last decade, the Food and Nutrition Service has issued several educational publications to all of the approximately 20,000 school food authorities participating in the Child Nutrition Programs which contain sections outlining safe food handling and food preparation practices. These publications include the "Menu Planning Guide for School Food Service, Facts about USDA Commodities," and "Quantity Recipes for School Food Service." In addition, specifications written for perishable commodities contain an EXHIBIT section which gives school food service personnel advice on how to safely handle, store, and prepare these foods. The Food and Nutrition Service also provides guidance and information to local districts. Two articles were written in late 1992 for the United States Department of Agriculture Commodity Newsletter which covered how to safely handle, store, and prepare low fat ground beef products and information on the types of bacteria that cause food borne illnesses. All school food authorities receive the commodity newsletter.

INFANT FORMULA PROCUREMENT ACT

Mr. DURBIN. Your statement mentions a law, the Infant Formula Procurement Act, which passed last year and requires the Department to solicit bids on behalf of a group of states, if requested to do so. What resources are needed to implement this Act?

Mr. BRALEY. In our estimate, 5.5 additional staff years would be needed to effectively carry out the responsibilities associated with this Act in the FNS national and regional offices. Since we are not requesting additional staff years, existing staff will be reassigned, as necessary, to carry out these responsibilities. FNS staff would be responsible for writing and interpreting cost containment regulations, interpreting public comment and incorporating comments into final regulations. Additional responsibilities include developing the request for proposal, evaluating bids, responding to bid solicitation questions, and all responsibilities associated up to point of contract award. If bids are rejected or State agencies decline to participate, FNS must conduct a resolicitation of bids for any remaining State agencies that are still interested in FNS' solicitation. After contract award, ongoing monitoring of State agencies for compliance with contract provisions throughout the contracting period will be necessary. Currently, we have discontinued several expenditure monitoring activities in order to perform the above tasks.

FNS staff would also carry out the responsibilities related to the provision to reduce the cost of supplemental foods by continuing to promote and encourage state agencies to purchase supplemental foods other than infant formula under cost containment procedures, which may include studying the feasibility of soliciting for rebates for items such as infant cereal and juice, peanut butter, and any other WIC food package item that impacts food package costs. FNS could also more actively pursue projects or innovative ideas that will substantially contain costs regarding the purchase of supplemental foods other than infant formula, and efforts related to program cost containment such as competitive bidding for retail vendor authorization.

Staff would additionally provide miscellaneous support functions such as technical and legal advice on contracting and procurement issues related to the cost containment initiatives. Finally, staffing would be required to provide clerical and administrative support for these functions.

Mr. DURBIN. Have you received any requests to date?

Mr. BRALEY. We recently conducted an informal survey of all WIC State agencies to determine which state agencies were interested in the Food and Nutrition Service conducting bid solicitation and selection for infant formula rebates on their behalf. We received responses from 27 State agencies. Thirteen States indicated that they would be interested; six States indicated an interest if the contract is available when current contracts expire; and eight

States, who were either involved in another multi-State contract or did not think a group solicitation would be cost advantageous to the State agency, said they were not interested at this time.

OPERATION WEED AND SEED

Mr. DURBIN. Please update the Committee on Operation Weed and Seed, an initiative to promote neighborhood revitalization, and the role WIC plays in this program.

Mr. BRALEY. Since the inception of the Weed and Seed initiative, FNS has been active in promoting the inclusion of a variety of our nutrition assistance programs in local community "seeding" strategies.

With respect to the WIC Program, the agency has encouraged states in which "Weed and Seed" sites are located to insure that, upon request from local communities, adequate resources are made available to serve all fully eligible WIC applicants. In addition, several sites, in cooperation with FNS Regional offices, have earmarked administrative funds to "Weed and Seed" communities in order to ensure adequate clinic resources are available to appropriately serve WIC applicants. Notable in this regard were efforts by New Jersey to provide resources to promote WIC enrollments and immunization screening in Trenton's "safe haven" school initiative. Likewise, Massachusetts made resources available to Chelsea to promote WIC outreach and bilingual nutritional services.

However, WIC and other FNS programs are operated pursuant to Federal-State agreements. States are responsible for targeting WIC benefits and resources to their respective communities. Therefore, FNS is unable to provide direct grants to Weed and Seed communities as is the case with many other Federal grant programs. Despite this limitation, the Agency has had no reports from local Weed and Seed communities that FNS programs are not appropriately funded for each community's identified food assistance needs.

WIC STUDIES

Mr. DURBIN. Please update last year's list of all ongoing and planned WIC program studies to include new studies initiated in fiscal year 1992 and those planned for fiscal year 1993 as well as the results of any that were completed.

Mr. BRALEY. I will include for the record the status of those studies that were in progress in Fiscal Year 1992 as well as the seven new WIC Program studies to be initiated in Fiscal Year 1993.

[The information follows:]

Ongoing WIC Program Studies

NATIONAL MATERNAL & INFANT HEALTH SURVEY (1990 FOLLOW-UP)

FNS transferred funds to the National Center for Health Statistics to support this large-scale survey of women and their infants. The survey collected extensive data on medical, behavioral and socioeconomic factors which influence pregnancy and birth outcomes. At FNS's request, questions on WIC participation were included in the survey to increase the usefulness of this rich database for WIC Program analyses. FNS has received a fully documented maternal and provisional health care provider data set. Analyses of the maternal data are currently underway. Follow-up data on the original respondents and their children will be obtained from NCHS in a separate study.

Status: All data sets are expected to be delivered to FNS by Spring 1994.

WIC VENDOR ISSUES STUDY

This study examines the prevalence and magnitude of vendor overcharging in the WIC Program. A national estimate of vendor overcharging will be established through compliance buys from a nationally representative sample of WIC vendors. This estimate will serve as a national baseline from which to assess the effectiveness of WIC State agencies' actions in curbing overcharging. This study also examines characteristics of vendors found to be overcharging in the WIC Program.

Status: Final report is in clearance with release scheduled for Spring 1993.

WIC MODELING AND ANALYTIC PROJECTS (MAP)

This study provides for analyses of new data bases (such as the National Maternal and Infant Health Survey, the 1990 Longitudinal Follow-up) and existing data sources (such as PC88, WIC Income Verification and WIC/Medicaid Cost-Benefit Studies). MAP also has essential quick turnaround, ad hoc analysis capability to answer questions posed by legislators and policy makers on the WIC Program. Some research topics include: participant health status characteristics; State-level eligibility estimates; breastfeeding prevalence and duration; WIC's market share in allowable foods; infant formula prices and market effects of rebates; income verification; and the effect of WIC participation on dietary intake, infant mortality and cost of medical care.

Status: Analysis of various databases is ongoing. Two reports have been released. The Executive Summary of each is included for the record.

WIC DYNAMICS

Increased participation brought on by rebates and more funding, along with other changes, have affected the dynamics of local WIC agency operations. This study will describe the effects of such changes on service to participants and on those who operate the WIC Program. Areas of key interest include the impacts on health care referrals and other links to the medical community and the current status of nutrition education. An understanding of challenges to program integrity, opportunities for greater effectiveness, and participant responses to new conditions are necessary for future program planning and budgeting.

Status: Data collection and analysis is ongoing with a final report scheduled for the second quarter of Fiscal Year 1994.

WYOMING WIC EBT ASSESSMENT

The State of Wyoming pilot tested an off-line "smart card" benefit delivery system from May to December 1991. The test included about 800 WIC participants served out of four food retail stores in the Casper area. FNS and Wyoming entered into a cooperative agreement to gain some insight into effects on each major participating group (i.e., WIC participants, retail vendors, local and State WIC agencies, banks. etc.).

Status: A report showing positive participant attitudes to the "smartcard" was shared with FNS under this agreement. Over the next few years, Wyoming plans to expand smartcard benefit delivery for WIC to five additional counties and to explore combining WIC and food stamp benefits on one card in Natrona County.

WIC PARTICIPANT AND PROGRAM CHARACTERISTICS STUDY

This biennial study, describes WIC participants in April 1990 and April 1992 in two separate reports, using information reported to FNS to provide Congress nationally representative data on WIC State Agencies and WIC participants, including income and nutritional risk characteristics, participation by migrant farmworker households, and other attributes of participants the Secretary considers appropriate.

Status: Project is ongoing. The Executive Summary of the 1990 report is provided for the record.

WIC ELIGIBILITY STUDY II

This study will review the eligibles estimation methodology and produce estimates of persons eligible for the WIC Program at the national, State and county levels. The estimates will include the Congressionally mandated estimate of income eligible women, infants and children. The study will also analyze new national health and nutrition data from the Third National Health and Nutrition Examination Survey to update information on the portion of income eligible persons likely to be at nutritional risk and thus fully eligible for the WIC Program.

Status: A contract was awarded in Fiscal Year 1992.

WIC DIETARY ASSESSMENT VALIDATION STUDY

WIC State agencies have been encouraged to use validated dietary assessment procedures that are based on professionally recognized guidelines and to use a food frequency instrument when dietary risk is the only eligibility factor. Two food frequency questionnaires have been developed for use in determining WIC eligibility for women and children. The primary focus of this study is a validation of the food frequency instruments to assess ability to measure dietary intake, usefulness for the WIC Program, suitability for certain ethnic groups served by the WIC Program, and accurateness and simplicity of scoring.

Status: A contract was awarded in Fiscal Year 1992. Data collection will begin in August 1993.

NUTRITION EDUCATION ASSESSMENT

The purpose of this project is to document the process of nutrition education as it is currently taking place in selected WIC local agencies; to identify factors that may be related to positive nutrition education outcomes; to evaluate the impact of WIC nutrition education on participant knowledge, attitudes, practices and satisfaction with nutrition education; to relate possible changes in these to specific nutrition education formats or inputs; and to identify strategies that are effective in reaching hard-to-serve populations such a low-literacy groups, teenage mothers, and members of different ethnic and cultural groups. The study will collect participant and agency level data on nutrition education impacts in 6 sites. Additional data on nutrition education processes will be collected in up to 24 additional sites.

Status: The contract was awarded in Fiscal Year 1992.

<u>Completed WIC Program Studies</u>

WIC CHILD IMPACT FIELD TEST

This study simultaneously field tested two research designs to assess the effect of WIC on growth and development of infants and children. Data collection measures and procedures were also tested. The Field Test examined several feasibility issues concerning a full-scale WIC child impact study.

Status: The final report for the Field Test was released in March 1992. A copy of the Executive Summary is provided for the record.

WIC INFLATION INDEX

This study developed a new inflation index to use to allocate WIC food grants to the States. The index is based on the foods that are prescribed as part of the WIC food package. The report will include a description of the index model, data sources, and test results.

Status: An interim report was published in August of 1992 for comment. The final report will be submitted to Congress in the third quarter of Fiscal Year 1993. A summary of the report is included for the record.

New WIC Program Studies

STUDY OF WIC PARTICIPANT AND PROGRAM CHARACTERISTICS

Public Laws 99-500 and 99-591 enacted in 1986 require that FNS submit to Congress a biennial report on WIC participant and program characteristics. To satisfy this requirement, FNS developed a prototype system which will routinely collect WIC Program information directly from State WIC agencies, beginning in 1992. This effort will use the prototype to collect data for April 1994 and April 1996. FNS plans to contract for analysis of the data submitted for 1994 and 1996.

Status: Award of the contract for analysis of 1992 and 1994 data is planned in Fiscal Year 1993.

WIC MODEL APPLICATION FORM

A model application form for use by a pregnant woman or child under the age of six for numerous maternal and child assistance programs, such as Medicaid, Head Start, and WIC will be developed. An interagency agreement will be used for an evaluation of whether, and to what extent, states adopt and modify the model application form to suit their individual state and local program requirements and needs. In addition, the evaluation will assess the usefulness of the model form for program access and coordination of services.
Status: Developing interagency agreement for execution during the third quarter of Fiscal Year 1993.

EARLY ENROLLMENT/MISSED OPPORTUNITIES

This study will examine the use of services among low-income pregnant and postpartum women whose infants are enrolled in WIC. Services include AFDC and Medicaid. The study will examine the characteristics of women who enroll early, and characteristics of program coordination that promote enrollment and participation.

Status: Expected contract award in fourth quarter of Fiscal Year 1993.

NUTRITION RISK CRITERIA

This project will catalogue the risk criteria states are using for eligibility. An examination of the criteria would be used to meet the Agency's commitment to the WIC Advisory Council that FNS would work with the National Academy of Sciences on anthropometric and hematological measures based on the best available empirical evidence.

Status: The cooperative agreement is expected to be signed with the National Academy of Sciences in the fourth quarter of Fiscal Year 1993.

INFANT FEEDING PRACTICES

This study addresses the lack of information about infant feeding practices among WIC participants. It will include the circumstances and influences that shape maternal intentions regarding feeding practices during the first year of life. Information will be collected before delivery and after delivery periodically for a specified number of months. The study will address issues such as changes in feeding patterns over time, factors that influence feeding patterns, and relationships between feeding patterns and subsequent health of the infant.

Status: A contract will be awarded during the fourth quarter of Fiscal Year 1993.

WIC MODELING AND ANALYTIC PROJECTS (MAP) II

This contract will provide quick response capability for the WIC Program in answering questions posed by legislators or policy makers. This project will produce an ongoing, regular monograph series on topics such as: (1) trimester of WIC enrollment, (2) use of optional data items (e.g., food package prescriptions), and (3) state and regional variations in nutritional risk.

Status: Award of contract is planned for the third quarter of Fiscal Year 1993.

WYOMING WIC AND FSP SMARTCARD DEMONSTRATION

The State of Wyoming is planning to conduct expanded WIC smartcard benefit delivery in 5 counties, and to demonstrate a combined WIC and Food Stamp Program benefit delivery using smartcards for approximately 2600 households in Natrona County (the site of the earlier WIC smartcard demonstration). The WIC/FSP smartcard demonstration is expected to require approximately 3 years for design, development, and implementation. An FNS evaluation of the combined WIC/FSP smartcard demonstration is planned.

Status: Both Wyoming's Demonstration contract and the FNS Evaluation of Wyoming's EBT Demonstration are planned to be awarded in Fiscal Year 1993.

STUDY OF WIC PARTICIPANT AND PROGRAM CHARACTERISTICS, 1990
EXECUTIVE SUMMARY

WIC PROGRAM OVERVIEW

The Special Supplemental Food Program for Women, Infants and Children (WIC) was established in 1973 by an amendment to the Child Nutrition Act of 1966. The WIC Program, administered by the Food and Nutrition Service (FNS) of the U. S. Department of Agriculture, is designed to provide nutritious supplemental foods to pregnant, postpartum and breastfeeding women, infants and children up through age four. WIC has expanded rapidly since its inception in 1972 as a two-year pilot project. Funding has increased from $20 million in Fiscal Year 1974 to approximately $2.1 billion in Fiscal Year 1990.

Public Laws 99-500 and 99-591 enacted in 1986 require that FNS submit to Congress a biennial report on WIC participant and program characteristics. To satisfy this requirement, FNS is developing a prototype system, starting in 1992, which will routinely collect WIC Program information directly from State WIC Agencies (PC92). Previous FNS data collection efforts in 1984 (PC84) and 1988 (PC88) required either private contractors (in 1984) or WIC Program staff (in 1988) to survey a nationally representative sample of WIC participants.

As has been the case in previous WIC Participant Characteristics reports, PC90 is the product of cooperative effort among local, State and Federal offices administering the WIC Program. Thanks to the commitment of the National Association of WIC Directors (NAWD) to participating in joint planning with FNS, PC90 is only one of many steps in assuring quality and efficiency in meeting the biennial Congressional reporting requirement.

STUDY METHODS

The PC90 survey is a transitional report which builds upon the research designs of PC84 and PC88 while minimizing the participant sample size to conserve research expenditures. Part of the goal of PC90 and future participant characteristics studies is to minimize burden on the WIC Program while fully describing services provided to WIC participants. While PC90 relied on contractor staff to sample data from participant records, PC92 and future characteristics studies will rely on participant data provided directly by States using their ongoing management information systems

- For the first time PC90 used a questionnaire, the Summary of State and Local Programs (SSLP), to gather descriptions of both State and local WIC operations from all State WIC Agencies (rather than surveying a separate small sample of local agencies as in previous studies.)

- Information on 1990 WIC participant characteristics was obtained through abstraction by contractor staff of a nationally representative sample of approximately 2,300 WIC case records.

State Agency Survey

In addition to gathering information on main characteristics of State WIC operations, the Summary of State and Local Programs (SSLP) is both a more efficient and a more fully descriptive way of gaining information on the thousands of widely varying (and often small) WIC local agencies that deliver WIC services across the country. Due to cost constraints, previous studies relied on small sample surveys of WIC local agencies drawn from a limited number of States. While these samples represented WIC participation well, they tended to overrepresent States and local agencies within those States which had large caseloads.

Gathering local agency information at the State level required some adaptation from the way States traditionally report on local agencies. In some States, for example, Arkansas, Delaware, Louisiana, or in many Indian Tribal Organizations, the State and local WIC agency are a single administrative entity. In order to gain a uniform context for describing local agencies, the SSLP asked States in which the State administered local agencies to provide a list of local agencies for a service level most similar to local agencies in other States. For specific health and social service questions, the SSLP defined "local WIC agency" as "the first reporting level below the State agency at which direct WIC Program services are provided to WIC participants".

Using this approach, States were able to describe over 2,000 administrative units at the equivalent of the local agency level (compared to administrative counts which typically address 1,700 local agencies). Therefore, PC90 provides an enlarged and somewhat differently focused picture of WIC services from prior studies in that it reflects a broad awareness held by State Agencies of the configuration of WIC services across the nation.

Another new feature of the SSLP is translation of State-specific codes for recording the nutritional risks of WIC participants into a classification system generated by the Information Committee of the National Association of WIC Directors (NAWD) for use by FNS in analyzing WIC nutritional risks on a national basis. The NAWD classification system describes five broad classes of nutritional risks:

- anthropometric
- biochemical
- clinical/health/medical

- dietary, and
- other.

Similar data collection is planned for PC92 and future reports.

Survey of Participant Records

The major objective of PC90 was to produce reliable national estimates for the month of March, 1990, of the characteristics of each of four categories of WIC participants: pregnant women; breastfeeding and postpartum women; infants; and children. To accomplish this objective, data abstractions were completed on 2,343 WIC participants, with approximately 600 from each of the four WIC participants categories. PC90 was therefore a smaller sample than that used for PC88, which covered five categories of participants and was designed to yield approximately 6,600 participant data abstractions along with personal interviews. While the PC88 data provided exceptionally detailed information on demographic and nutritional risk characteristics of WIC participants, the use of interviews proved far too burdensome for the WIC Program to sustain.

PC90's return to record abstraction as the sole source of participant data is a transitional effort in preparation for a near census of key data items on WIC participants planned for 1992. Data that are already being collected for certification and program management will be combined into a PC92 data base using standardized definitions of the Minimum Data Set developed by the NAWD Information Committee. (Minimum Data Set items are listed in Appendix A of this report.)

PC90 largely focuses on characteristics which will continue to be part of the Minimum Data Set rather than the large array of characteristics which were described in PC88. The transition in 1992 to automated, census-based data is planned to allow State-by-State estimates of key participant features which can assist States as well as national policymakers in assessing the needs of the WIC Program. It will also allow much more detailed description of small groups within the WIC population such as migrants, teens, or Native Americans.

PARTICIPANT CHARACTERISTICS

Participants by Category and Age

The estimated national distribution of WIC participants as of March 1990, is shown in Figure 1. An estimated 4.5 million individuals were enrolled in the WIC Program during that month. The largest single category of participants was children, accounting for nearly half (46 percent) of all WIC participants. Infants were the next largest category (30 percent) and women the smallest group (24 percent). Women were divided between pregnant women (accounting for 13.5 percent of all participants), and postpartum or breastfeeding women (10.4 percent of all participants).

Figure 1

Distribution of WIC Participants by Category

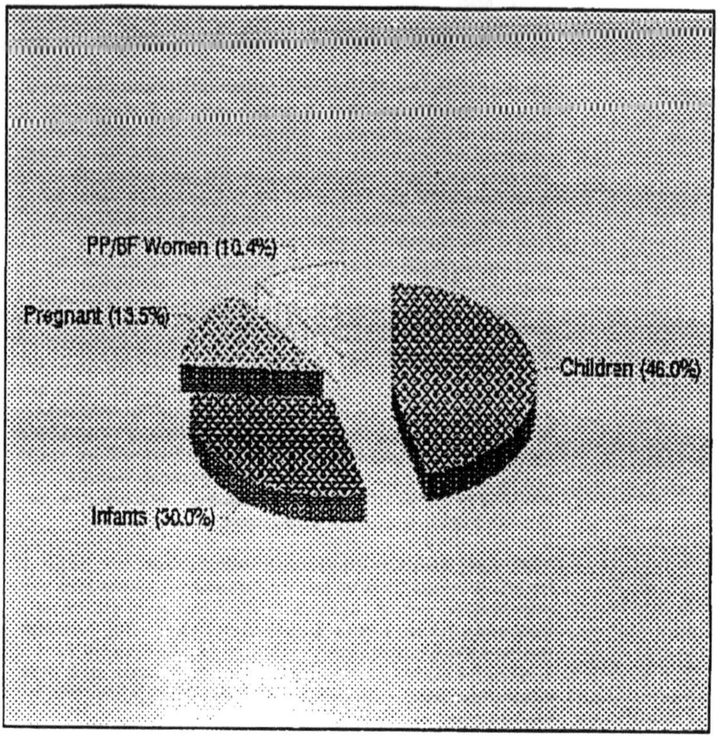

[1]Postpartum and Breastfeeding Women

Source: Study of WIC Participants and Program Characteristics, 1990.

In March 1990, 85 percent of all pregnant women participating in WIC were between the ages of 18 and 34. It is estimated that WIC served about 53 percent of all pregnant women under the age of 18, regardless of income, and about 6.3 percent of pregnant women over the age of 35.

Most WIC infants were enrolled in the Program shortly after birth – over three-quarters of infant participants were ages 0-3 months at the time of certification.

Children appeared to participate less frequently in WIC as age increases, with most children in the 12 to 23 months range (41 percent). Children between their second and third birthdays comprised 27 percent of all children, children between their third and fourth birthdays comprise 21 percent, and those age four years accounted for only about 10 percent of all children participating in WIC.

Migrant Status

One of the areas of particular interest to Congress is the extent to which the WIC Program is able to reach migrant families. While States are required to report migrant participation to FNS, not all States included in the PC90 participant sample recorded migrant status as part of their individual certification records. In March 1990, based on those States that did collect such information, it was estimated that about 35,000 individuals participating in WIC were migrants. This represents less than one percent of all WIC participants.

Race and Ethnicity

For geographic State Agencies in the contiguous United States, whites represented nearly half of all WIC participants (49 percent) in PC90, while blacks comprised over one-fourth (28 percent), and Hispanics about one-fifth (21 percent).

Household Size

In PC90, participating women were found in smaller households than infants and children, with a median size of three persons. The median size of households in PC90 with participating infants and children was four persons.

Health Services

For pregnant women for whom the data were available in local case files, the most commonly recorded source of health care for their current pregnancy was a primary care physician (40 percent). Other frequently listed providers included health departments (17 percent), and hospital outpatient clinics (14 percent). With the exception of hospital outpatient clinics, nearly identical figures were found for infants and children.

Prior Obstetric History and Prior WIC Participation

Local agency case records indicate that more than half of all women participants have had a prior pregnancy, with an average of close to three total pregnancies (including the pregnancy on which their current eligibility is based).

Certification records showed that about one-fourth of all pregnant women had a previous spell of WIC participation; over three-quarters of postpartum and breastfeeding women previously participated in WIC, primarily during the period of pregnancy for the current infant.

Participation for mothers during pregnancy is usual for infants with the mother of more than half of the infants participating in WIC during pregnancy. However, data on the mother's participation in WIC was not available in local agency case records for over 20 percent of the infants. Over one-third of the children were reported as having mothers who had been on WIC during their pregnancies. Information on this topic was also not available for close to half the children. PC88 data showed that over 69 percent of the infants and 71 percent of children on WIC had mothers who had participated in WIC during their pregnancies.

Average Annual Income

Among all WIC participants for whom income was available, annual income averaged $9,002 in 1990. Annual income varied somewhat by participant category, with the families of WIC infants having the lowest income ($8,288), and the families of WIC children having the highest ($9,603). Among women participants, pregnant women had an average annual income of $8,430, while breastfeeding and postpartum women averaged $9,065.

Those WIC participants for whom income was not available were nearly all automatically eligible due to participation in other means-tested programs such as Medicaid, the Food Stamp Program or Aid to Families with Dependent Children.

In the PC88 study of income, for each participant category, the most frequently reported source of income was wages (at 58 percent of participants' families). Thirty-two percent of all WIC participants' families reported receipt of AFDC benefits. Between 63 and 66 percent of WIC participants' households included an adult male. The presence of this adult male resulted in an average income which was approximately $5,000 higher than for other households not containing an adult male. Generally, PC88 data show somewhat higher incomes for WIC participants than in PC90 due to the detailed personal interviews used in PC88.

Poverty Status

In PC90, WIC participants were quite poor, with nearly three-quarters having recorded annual incomes in 1990 of under 100 percent of the OMB poverty level. Case records indicated that one-third have annual incomes less than 50 percent of the official poverty level for their household size.

Those who were automatically income eligible through participation in other means-tested programs were poorer than other WIC participants: 94 percent of the automatically income eligible participants with an income reported in PC90 were at, or below, 130 percent of the OMB poverty guidelines.

Recorded Nutritional Risk Factors

The PC90 abstraction process collected up to three nutritional risks for each sampled participant. For those records with information available, 53 percent had only a single risk factor listed on the certification documents; 22 percent had two risk factors reported, and 18 percent had three risk factors recorded.

Among all women, the most commonly recorded risks were clinical/medical/health risks.

The most common nutritional risks for infants under four months of age were a breastfeeding mother/infant dyad and an infant of a WIC-eligible mother or mother whose medical records indicated that she was at nutritional risk during her pregnancy.

In the files of children and older infants, those aged four months or more, the most common risk recorded was an anthropometric risk.

Anthropometric Measures

In PC90, up to 11 percent of infants were recorded as low in weight for their height, that is, at or below the 10th percentile, while another 20 percent had a high weight for their height, that is, they were above the 90th percentile for this measure. The percent of children at a high weight for height (above the 90th percentile) was greater, 29 percent for children under two years of age, and 24 percent for children two or more years of age.

In PC90 (as in PC84 and PC88) a disproportionate share of WIC infants and children appeared to be overweight when compared to the distribution of weight for height and weight for age for both for infants and children in the U.S. population as a whole.

Birth Weight

Infants whose mothers were on WIC had a slightly higher average birth weight and a lower percentage of birth weights below 2,500 grams. However, these data cannot be used to infer the prenatal effect of WIC on birth outcomes. Other unmeasured factors may explain the observed differences and many infants are enrolled in WIC at birth as a result of their low birth weight.

Looking at birth weight of offspring for pregnant and breastfeeding women, women who were not on WIC showed a lower mean birth weight and were more than twice as likely to have had a low birth weight child. However, as above, these data cannot be used to draw inferences about the effect of WIC. PC92 optional data elements include birth weight and the length of time the mother was on WIC during her pregnancy. Approximately 30 WIC State Agencies have already indicated that they plan to report birth weight in PC92.

Hematological Measurements

PC90 abstracted data on hematological measures from participant records. More WIC clients had recorded hematocrit values than hemoglobin values. Some WIC State Agencies also record erythrocyte protoporphyrin blood values, but these measures were not collected in PC90. However, they will be included in PC92 to the extent that States are able to provide these data.

Using the 1990 State specific WIC criteria, 22 percent of pregnant women were below State standards in 1990 while 16 percent of children were classified as below State standards in 1990. The 1990 modal criteria are stricter than either 1988 or 1990 State-specific criteria for pregnant women and children. The percentages below these modal standards were 17 percent of pregnant women and 14 percent of children. However, more breastfeeding and postpartum women are classified as below State standards using the 1990 State modal criteria (32 percent) as opposed to the 1990 State specific criteria (24 percent).

Generally speaking anemia was far more prevalent in minority groups among the WIC population than among white WIC participants. PC88 reported differences of about the same magnitude in anemia incidence.

WIC Priority Levels

Because the WIC Program cannot serve all eligible applicants, FNS has sought to target WIC funds to the most "nutritionally at-risk" among eligible populations. Federal regulations have created a priority system for WIC applicants that is intended to guide the distribution of benefits at the State and local service delivery levels. This system of seven priority groups, places pregnant and breastfeeding women and infants who are at nutritional risk as the persons most in need of WIC services. Priority VII is permitted, at State option, for previously certified participants who currently have no nutritional risks but who may regress in nutritional or health status without continuation of WIC benefits.

FNS data for May of 1990 show that 93 percent of pregnant women were classified as Priority I and 6 percent were classified as Priority IV. With respect to breast-feeding women, nearly 89 percent were classified as priority I and over 5 percent were classified both to Priority II and Priority IV. The majority of postpartum women (49 percent) were classified as Priority III, while 35 percent were classified as priority IV and almost 10 percent as Priority IV. The majority of infants (49 percent) were classified as Priority II with another 46 percent classified as Priority I. The vast majority of children (77 percent) were classified as Priority III with another 20 percent classified as Priority V.[1]

---

[1]A listing of WIC Priorities appears on page 1-5.

STATE AND LOCAL AGENCY CHARACTERISTICS

Local WIC Agency Sponsorship

Under Federal regulations, any public or private nonprofit health or human service agency that provides health services, either directly or by contracting for such services, is eligible to apply to their respective State Agency to operate a WIC Program. In PC90, over 82 percent of all local agencies operated through a public health agency.[2] Most of these were county sponsored (39 percent of all local agencies) or sponsored by the State Health Department (nearly 14 percent). Only six percent of local WIC agencies were operated through community action agencies and four percent were sponsored by hospitals.

In terms of numbers of participants in the contiguous United States, two-thirds of all participants were served in local WIC agencies operated by public health agencies. For the most part, these were county or district health agencies, accounting for more than half of all WIC participants. The remaining participants were served by hospitals (nearly 8 percent), community action agencies (6 percent), and other nonprofit organizations (10 percent). For about eleven percent of participants, the type of sponsoring agency was unknown.

Local Availability of On-site Health Services

The WIC Program facilitates access to health care in a variety of ways. In PC90, geographic States report that 14 percent of local WIC sponsoring agencies had formal contracts with private physicians to provide health care to WIC participants.

States reported that 73 percent of local WIC sponsoring agencies typically provide pediatric and well-baby care to most or at least some WIC participants. Similar high levels of service provision were reported for family planning (67 percent), obstetrical and gynecologic care, (59 percent) and routine health services (56 percent). Dental care was typically available to most or at least some participants in 36 percent of local agencies. (These services did not include referrals or contracts for services outside of the WIC administrative unit.) Twenty percent of local agencies required most or at least some participants to obtain blood tests from sources other than WIC.

Of the Indian Tribal State Agencies providing information (22 out of 32 Indian State Agencies), 60 percent of local agency sites were reported to provide pediatric care to most or at least some participants. Indian local WIC agency sites were also reported to have similar levels of routine

---

[2]For the purpose of common definition across States, the term "local WIC agency" means the first reporting level, below the State level, at which direct WIC Program services are provided.

health services (59 percent). Family planning was offered to at least some participants by 44 percent of local sites, and obstetrical and gynecologic care by 53 percent. Dental care was offered far more frequently by Indian than by geographic State WIC Agencies. Twenty-five percent provided contracted health care to most participants, and three percent did so for at least some participants. Eleven percent of Indian agencies required most participants to obtain blood tests from some source other than WIC, while another 23 percent required at least some participants to do so.

Access to Social Services

In PC90 for the first time, WIC State Agencies were asked to describe how many of their local WIC sponsoring agencies typically provide certain social services to WIC participants. As with health services, States were asked not to include referrals to other agencies outside the administrative sponsoring unit in which WIC operates. Access to social service programs within WIC sponsoring agencies may cover a wide range of activities. For example, Medicaid benefits may be used for costs of sponsor-offered health services, or, in other cases, direct certification for AFDC or the Food Stamp Program may be accomplished by an on-site social service worker.

Geographic WIC State Agencies reported that 28 percent of local agencies typically provided access to Medicaid services to most or at least some WIC participants. In addition, 12 percent typically offered access to AFDC, 15 percent typically provided access to the Food Stamp Program, and 11 percent offered access to general assistance programs to most or at least some WIC participants. In addition, 19 percent typically provided access to other miscellaneous services.

Local agencies and service sites for Indian WIC State Agencies were far more likely to be involved in providing access to social services than those described by geographic State Agencies. AFDC application was available to most WIC participants in 40 percent of local Indian WIC clinics; general assistance was offered to most or at least some participants in 53 percent of Indian WIC local clinics; Medicaid and the Food Stamp Program each in 44 percent; and child support enforcement and counseling in 34 percent. Access to assisted day care was available to at least some participants in close to one fourth of Indian service sites. Miscellaneous other services were offered to at least some participants by 19 percent of Indian WIC Services Sites.

Local Agency Hours of Operation

PC90 also, for the first time, asked States to describe the hours of operation for local WIC agencies or service sites in their respective jurisdictions.

Geographic WIC State Agencies reported that 42 percent of all local WIC agencies or service sites provide full-time operations to most participants. A small proportion offered extended hours, five percent to most participants and four percent to at least some participants. Part-time operations were available to most participants at 32 percent of local agencies or service sites, and another 10 percent had part-time operations for at least some participants.

Indian WIC State clinics reported that just over half of their service sites offered full-time services to most of their participants; 39 percent offered part-time operations to most participants and 10 percent altogether had extended hours.

State Policies on WIC Eligibility Determination

To be eligible for the WIC Program, applicants must satisfy both income and nutritional risk criteria.

- **Income Eligibility.** In 1990, all States used 185 percent of the non-farm poverty income guidelines established by the Office of Management and Budget and promulgated by the Department of Health and Human Services. (Special exceptions were made for individuals in unusual situations who qualify for Medicaid.)

  WIC applicants can be adjunctively income-eligible for WIC on the basis of their participation in a means-tested public assistance program. In 1990, all States determined WIC income eligibility using categorical eligibility standards for at least one program. Medicaid clients were accepted as income eligible for WIC in 81 percent of reporting States. In addition, AFDC and Food Stamp Program clients were adjunctively income eligible for WIC in 1990 in 73 percent and 59 percent of 44 State Agencies, respectively. Automatic eligibility for WIC was infrequently based on participation for Supplemental Security Income or a free or reduced-price school meal program.

- **Nutritional Risk Assessment.** In addition to demonstrating income eligibility, WIC applicants must be certified by a competent professional (e.g., nutritionist, dietitian, nurse, physician etc.) to be nutritionally at risk because of medical reasons or an inadequate diet.

  For all WIC applicants, except infants under six months, a hematological test must also have been performed as a minimum requirement in determining nutritional risk. WIC State Agencies are responsible for establishing appropriate hemoglobin, hematocrit or other hematologic criteria used within their jurisdictions. A participant is considered eligible for WIC due to nutritional risk if their hemoglobin or hematocrit count is less that the applicable State criterion. Because the normal range for hemoglobin changes considerably throughout childhood, as well as during pregnancy, such changes are usually reflected in the reference criteria. Criteria are also adjusted for altitude, as appropriate. Over one-half of the State WIC Agencies reported hemoglobin and hematocrit nutritional risk eligibility criteria dependent upon a woman's trimester of pregnancy.

States were asked about their policies and methods for obtaining dietary intake information for WIC participants and what methods are routinely used in collecting this information. Sixty WIC State Agencies, serving 81 percent of WIC participants, obtain dietary intake information on all participants.

Food Packages

State and local agencies tailored food packages to meet the nutritional needs of individual WIC clients, and to make adjustments for reasons relating to increasing the administrative efficiency of the WIC Program. Administrative adjustments to WIC food packages include specifying the size of the food package, food brands, and the form of food within a food group.

Almost nine out of ten State Agencies in 1990 issued WIC food instruments using a standard frequency (87 percent) of issuance. Over three-quarters of State Agencies issued food vouchers on a monthly basis (77 percent), and just under half on a bimonthly basis (49 percent). Only eight percent issued WIC vouchers every three months and another eight percent issued food instruments on some other schedule.

Across all categories of WIC participants, the average food package cost reported by State Agencies in the SSLP was $40.05. By participant category, the highest food package cost was for infants, $51.81; the cost for children was $34.02; and for all women it was $36.74. Among pregnant women the mean cost was $38.89, while among breastfeeding and postpartum women it was $33.91. Food package costs varied by region and by State as well as by participant category. The lowest overall average cost was for the Midwest at $37.90, while the Northeast had the highest at $43.37. Several States have notably lower food package costs for infants, presumably, reflecting highly favorable manufacturer rebate agreements for infant formula in some States.

Since the cost outlays reported by State Agencies do not uniformly reflect infant formula rebates, average food package costs for each State are shown as reported in the FNS-498, WIC Monthly Financial and Program Status Report for March, 1990. These figures attribute all applicable infant formula rebates to show the "close out" figure used for administrative purposes and are generally lower than the average food package costs reported by State Agencies in PC90. The national average food package cost including infant formula rebates was $31.01 for March 1990.

STUDY OF THE IMPACT OF WIC ON THE GROWTH AND DEVELOPMENT OF CHILDREN: FIELD TEST

FINAL REPORT

VOLUME I: FEASIBILITY ASSESSMENT

OCTOBER 31, 1991

EXECUTIVE SUMMARY

INTRODUCTION

The Special Supplemental Food Program for Women, Infants and Children (WIC) provides supplemental food, nutrition education, and access to health care services for low-income pregnant, postpartum and breastfeeding women, infants, and children (up to age five) who are at nutritional risk. The Program, administered by the Food and Nutrition Service (FNS) of the U.S. Department of Agriculture, is designed to serve as an adjunct to ongoing prenatal and pediatric health care by operating through a network of local institutions including county health departments, hospitals, and other nonprofit human service organizations.

This report presents the results of an assessment of the feasibility of conducting a longitudinal study of the long-term developmental effects of WIC on infants and children. Two alternative research designs were examined as part of this field test. The first is a quasi-experimental approach that selects two comparison groups from vital statistics records -- 6-month old infants enrolled in WIC and 6-month old income-eligible non-participants. The second design, developed by the Abt project team, is an experimental study that identifies low-income pregnant women and randomly assigns them to either a group that receives WIC benefits, or a non-WIC control group.

An assessment of the results of this field test is intended to provide FNS with information needed to decide whether to proceed with full-scale implementation of either design or some modification of these research proposals. The following discussion provides this assessment in terms of six feasibility questions posed by FNS.

WHICH DESIGN MAXIMIZES THE VALIDITY OF THE ESTIMATED PROGRAM IMPACTS?

In theory, an experimental design will produce more valid estimates of the impact of WIC than the quasi-experimental design. This difference primarily results from one of the major shortcomings of the quasi-experimental design -- the inherent problem of selection bias. No matter how well the WIC and non-WIC infants are matched at the start of the longitudinal study, it is likely that the two groups will have initial differences on a variety of unmeasured characteristics that may be related to their growth and development.

The quasi-experimental design will, if implemented as proposed, produce national estimates of Program impact which cannot be matched by the experimental design. However, this gain in external validity comes at the expense of the internal validity of the estimated impacts. If the estimated effects are questionable to begin with, extrapolating them to all participants may not be a real gain.

The experimental design proposed by the Abt team, on the other hand, offers greater strength in examining the effects of prenatal WIC participation as a result of the random assignment of pregnant women and the collection of baseline data prior to their enrollment in the Program.

Finally, the theoretical strengths of the experimental design may be undermined as a result of certain practical constraints that must be imposed on its implementation. First and foremost, women assigned to the control group may enroll in WIC on their own. This may lead to dilution of the control group if substantial numbers of these women enroll in WIC after random assignment. If implemented as now proposed, the experimental design should reduce the risk of this occurrence, but it will also focus the study on a somewhat unique sample of sites, i.e., new service sites in low WIC penetration areas. If this design approach fails, the study may be seriously compromised.

Second, the random assignment of eligible unserved pregnant women to WIC may lead to a situation where the created treatment group is not comparable to the existing WIC caseload. This situation will require early assessment before a decision can be made to proceed with a long-term longitudinal study.

CAN THE NECESSARY INSTITUTIONAL COOPERATION BE OBTAINED?

Obtaining the approval of a Human Subjects Review Committee to conduct the WIC Child Impact Study is feasible. This will take some time to accomplish, but the study represents a negligible risk to participants and precautions have been built in to both research designs to provide for informed consent and the ethical treatment of all study subjects.

For the quasi-experimental design, the primary hurdle to overcome is obtaining the cooperation of from 25 to 35 State Vital Statistics Directors to provide monthly computer files of birth records. The field test results indicate that this is a feasible, but very time consuming, process. More importantly, it is likely that some States will not cooperate and others will not be able to provide the necessary data in a timely enough manner to allow the study to be implemented. This may require the use of more costly county-based sampling, but if cooperation cannot be achieved for approximately 85 percent of the 100 sampled PSUs (primarily counties or groups of counties) then the goal of achieving national impact estimates will be unattainable. Because achieving this desired level of coverage appears unlikely, this design alternative may not be able to meet one of its primary goals, producing national estimates of the impact of WIC on children.

For the experimental design, cooperation from more different types of institutions will be required. Cooperation will have to be obtained from State and local WIC agencies to establish new service sites and from community-based institutions to recruit WIC-eligible pregnant women. On the positive side, this effort will be concentrated in fewer places which should provide some gains in efficiency.

The field test experience indicates that gaining such cooperation is feasible but much more labor-intensive and time-consuming than anticipated. Consequently, adequate time and resources will have to be dedicated to this activity for implementation of the experiments to be successful.

CAN THE SAMPLE REQUIREMENTS BE MET?

With regard to the quasi-experimental design, the field test demonstrated the need for an important change to the original design proposal. Specifically, a fairly intensive field tracing effort is needed -- about 50 percent of the cases required field tracing. Without this, it is unlikely that an unbiased sampling frame could be developed from which the study sample is later selected. Certain types of individuals will continue to be very difficult to locate, but the procedures adopted for the field test greatly reduce the negative effects of non-response.

With this modification, the field test results indicate that it is generally possible to meet the sampling requirements. The one important exception is low-birthweight babies, especially those not enrolled in WIC. The initial assumptions used to create the sampling plan proved to be incorrect, contributing to a shortfall in the sample for this group. This does not, however, mean that the design is infeasible. The selection process depends upon many assumptions to calculate the number of birth records needed to fulfill the sample requirements. For national implementation, it is recommended that a careful analysis be done to obtain the best estimates possible for the selected PSUs and that the sampling process be monitored throughout the 12-month selection period in order to make adjustments as better information becomes available. This should ensure that the sample requirements are met without incurring unnecessary data collection costs.

Although appropriate sample sizes can be obtained, the field test provides strong evidence that the quasi-experimental design will not yield comparable samples of WIC and non-WIC infants. Any quasi-experimental design is potentially vulnerable to the problem of selection bias. Recognizing this, the design evaluated in this field test included a stratification by birthweight to make the WIC participant and non-participant samples more comparable. The field test indicated, however, that participant and non-participant samples were very different even with this stratification. Furthermore, it appears that statistical procedures are unable to overcome these differences.

With regard to the experimental design, the procedures examined in the field test were found to yield unacceptably high levels of no-shows (treatment group women who failed to enroll in WIC) and crossovers (control group women who enrolled in WIC). If implemented as tested, this design would have been hopelessly undermined by these two events. Consequently, a new experimental design has been developed by the Abt project team which is considered both administratively feasible and likely to provide adequate protection against both events. This depends upon the creation of new service sites in low WIC penetration areas, random assignment from a waiting list, the staggered phase-in of services to meet the needs of women assigned to the treatment group, and a short restriction on re-application by women assigned to the control group.

ARE THE DESIGN LOGISTICS FEASIBLE?

Implementing the quasi-experimental design requires (1) the timely receipt of birth records on a monthly basis, and (2) the successful tracing and screening of birth mothers. As noted above, with the use of intensive field tracing and careful monitoring of the sampling process, this aspect of the design should be feasible. The need to obtain birth records from States within two to three months from the end of a particular birth month will be problematic in certain States. This will lead to a difficult decision for FNS. Either the study will have to accept the exclusion of some States, or provisions will have to be made to abstract birth records on a monthly basis from a large number of local county offices. This latter option will increase study costs, but may be worthwhile if the alternative is the loss of a State such as California, which accounts for a relatively large share of the total WIC caseload.

As noted earlier, implementing the experimental design will involve a considerable effort to gain the cooperation of WIC agencies and local community-based institutions. Although feasible, this logistical requirement will involve a significant effort. The level of effort required for the field test was much greater than anticipated. This led to a number of problems, particularly in interactions with local WIC agencies and obtaining cooperation from recruitment sites.

It also appears that the process of random assignment may have gone somewhat awry (as evidenced by a large difference in the size of the treatment and control samples), although it was not possible to document instances of specific breakdowns. The field test results suggest that a centralized process be used instead of depending on field staff.

The more important logistical issue is the expected level of no-shows and crossovers observed and whether procedures can be implemented to protect the integrity of this research design. As noted above, the design as field tested suffered greatly from both problems leading to a revised design proposal from the Abt project team which is logistically feasible and capable of largely insulating the study from both threats to the validity of the impact estimates.

ARE THE PROPOSED MEASURES FEASIBLE?

The longitudinal study requires a total of seven measurement points at 6-month intervals from the child's 6-month birthday through 42 months of age. Each measurement includes information on: physical development (anthropometric measurements of height, weight, head circumference, and two skinfold measures); presence of anemia and/or iron deficiency through the collection of blood samples; health status and utilization of health care services; dietary intake; socioemotional development; and the home environment. For a subsample of children, cognitive assessments are also recommended. Finally, data are to be collected on the operational characteristics of WIC agencies serving those in the WIC comparison group.

The measurements and their associated data collection procedures have been shown to be feasible. This is not to say that everything worked perfectly, or that problems will not arise during a full-scale study. The planned data collection is exceedingly complex, involving the coordinated actions of large numbers of people. However, with the recommended changes noted in this report -- primarily related to the measurement of dietary intake -- it is considered feasible to collect the required data in a manner that will meet accepted standards for reliability.

An important consideration will be the logistical problems of training the required field staff. In particular, the need to have adequate numbers of young infants and children to serve as test subjects during training and anthropometric standardization. This will be a problem for both research designs, but it will be more severe in the case of the quasi-experimental design because of the substantially larger field staff that is needed.

ARE THE COSTS OF IMPLEMENTATION FEASIBLE?

The estimated cost of the quasi-experimental design is $32.6 million. The estimated cost of the Abt proposed experimental design is about $26.5 million -- $21 million for the evaluation study and $5.5 million to pay the cost of benefits and administrative expenses for the study participants assigned to the WIC treatment group. The variation in cost is due in large part to sample size differences. Adding the optional sibling study to either design would increase costs by about $120,000.

REPORT ON A WIC INFLATION INDEX

The report presents a new inflation index developed by the Economic Research Service (ERS) with the assistance of the Office of Analysis and Evaluation and the Bureau of Labor Statistics, Department of Labor.

FNS is considering the use of the index in the funding formula used to allocate food funds to States in the Special Supplemental Program for Women, Infants, and Children, commonly known as the WIC Program.

In addition to the funding formula, the index could be used to develop WIC budget and participation estimates and monitor WIC food costs.

The report findings include:

Thrifty Food Plan inflation projections do not accurately forecast changes in WIC food costs.

Test results indicate that the WIC index shows promise but needs further development. In particular, FNS and ERS need to improve the model's performance in capturing the effects of infant formula rebates.

The report solicits comments on the WIC index model, both on its construction and its appropriateness for use in the WIC funding allocation formula.

Comments received will help refine and strengthen the index and inform FNS' decision on whether or not to adopt it for use in the funding formula.

FNS intended to publish a notice of the index in the Federal Register. However, because of the regulatory moratorium, FNS will directly distribute the report to a broad audience, including Congress, WIC state agencies, advocacy groups, and economists.

The report is an interim report to Congress. After a public comment period, FNS will send a final report containing the Department's revisions with recommenations and findings to Congress in the third quarter of FY 1993.

WIC STATE ADMINISTRATIVE COSTS

Mr. DURBIN. Describe, in detail, how state administrative costs are derived.

Mr. BRALEY. We recently implemented a new reporting system to collect information on types of activities funded with nutrition services and administrative (NSA) funds at the state and local level. NSA expenditures for the WIC Program are now reported in the following categories:

General Administration.—This category includes all costs generally considered to be overhead or management costs, such as costs associated with program monitoring, prevention of fraud, general oversight and food instrument accountability. Examples include automated data processing costs, which include development costs, bank-related and ongoing operation costs. Also included is WIC administrative salaries/benefits and other costs necessary to conduct outreach, food instrument reconciliation, monitoring and payment, vendor monitoring.

Nutrition Education.—State agencies are required to spend one-sixth of their NSA expenditures on nutrition education activities. Examples include salary/benefits, cost to develop, procure, print and distribute nutrition education materials and costs associated with evaluation and monitoring nutrition education.

Breastfeeding Promotion and Support Activities.—Nationally, $8 million of NSA funds is to be spent on breastfeeding promotion activities. Examples include salary/benefits of WIC staff who plan or conduct educational and other services to promote or support breastfeeding. Also, salary and benefits of peer counselors and individuals hired to undertake home visits and other actions to encourage continuation of breastfeeding. Costs to develop, procure, print and distribute educational materials related to breastfeeding promotion and support, clinic space devoted to breastfeeding, educational and training activities including space set aside for nursing may also be paid for with these monies. In addition, these funds are used to purchase breastfeeding such as breast pumps, breast shells, etc., which directly support the nutrition and continuation of breastfeeding.

Client Services.—This category includes all costs expended to deliver food and other services and benefits. Examples include WIC staff salaries/benefits, medical supplies and equipment necessary to conduct diet and health assessments required in the certification process. Also included is salary and benefits of WIC staff who issue food instruments and explain their use. In addition, WIC staff salary/benefits and other costs necessary to refer client to other health care and social services, to coordinate services with other programs, to participate in activities which promote a broader range of health and social services for participants, such as lead screening, referral for immunizations, and alcohol and drug abuse counseling.

Mr. DURBIN. In a clinic where more than one service is provided, how are administrative costs broken out and charged to different Federal agencies?

Mr. BRALEY. There are two types of administrative costs: indirect costs and direct costs. Indirect costs are those which are not easily identifiable with specific programs or services. Indirect costs often include costs such as rent, utilities, motor pools, and support personnel. These costs are accumulated into indirect cost pools and allocated among the various programs. The costs are allocated based upon a cost allocation plan which has been approved by the cognizant Federal agency. For the WIC Program, the cognizant Federal agency is the Department of Health and Human Services (DHHS). Direct costs are those which are easily identifiable with specific programs or services. Direct costs often include equipment and the personnel costs of employees who provide the various services. Many of these costs are paid entirely by the single, benefiting program. In other cases, costs are allocated among several programs. For example, time studies that record the amount of an employee's time spent on various program activities are often used to allocate his or her salary and benefits among the various programs for which he or she provides services.

Mr. DURBIN. Is there a state administrative matching requirement in the WIC Program?

Mr. BRALEY. There is no state administrative matching requirement in the WIC Program. Nevertheless, a number of States contribute varying amounts of state funds and in-kind services to the Program. However, states are not required to report actual state funds utilized to cover WIC expenditures.

VENDOR MONITORING

Mr. DURBIN. On page 6 of your testimony you discuss vendor management. In fiscal year 1988, OIG performed a national audit were discovered. You go on to say that you intend to issue new, were discovered. You go on to say that you intend to issue new tougher regulations in the spring of 1993, five years after OIG's audit. Why weren't these regulations issued sooner?

Mr. BRALEY. On December 28, 1990, FNS published a proposed rule which was designed to strengthen and improve vendor management and food instrument accountability in the Special Supplemental Food Program for Women, Infants and Children (WIC).

A one hundred and twenty day comment period followed the proposed rule's publication in the Federal Register. Over one thousand responses were received from both the public and Congressional representatives. Many of the comments were very detailed and required a substantial amount of time to analyze. FNS analyzed and collated the comments, discussed refinements and rewrote the proposal. The revised proposed rule underwent comprehensive rewrite to accommodate commenter concerns.

The revised proposed rule entered the formal Department clearance process in February 1992, at the time a government-wide moratorium was imposed on all non-critical regulations. The moratorium has recently been lifted and the revised proposed rule is now being prepared to re-enter formal clearance. We predict that it will be published this summer.

Mr. DURBIN. Tell us what your original proposed regulations were.

Mr. BRALEY. The original proposed rule was developed with input over several years from state agency experts in food delivery.

In addition, suggestions were solicited at two meetings of selected WIC Vendor managers in 1988 and at the 1989 meeting of the National Association of WIC Directors. The proposed rule responded to recommendations made by the Department's Office of the Inspector General (OIG) and Congress, and mandated detailed State agency design standards for managing WIC authorized food vendors.

These included: establishment of mandatory criteria for selection of vendors; permitting state agencies to establish limits on the number of WIC vendors consistent with program needs, strengthening high risk vendor monitoring systems by requiring, for example, requirements for annual compliance buys or inventory audits of the state agency's WIC vendor population, strengthening vendor sanctions by requiring mandatory minimum and maximum disqualification periods, and, streamlining the administrative review process to ensure timely and appropriate consideration of vendors' appeals of State actions.

Other areas of proposed change included improvements in food instrument accountability, requiring identification and follow-up on dual participants quarterly; and, increasing the maximum participant sanction from 3 months to 1 year.

Mr. DURBIN. How does your new proposal differ from the original proposal?

Mr. BRALEY. The revised proposed rule will address the concerns raised by commenters on the December 1990 proposed rule and provide guidelines to state agencies for minimizing fraud and abuse. Major changes respond to commenters' concerns by making the rule more fair and less burdensome and include: revisions to the mandatory vendor selection criteria; revision to the mandatory high-risk vendor monitoring systems; and modifications to the state agency vendor appeal process.

Mr. DURBIN. What were the public and political reactions to your original proposal?

Mr. BRALEY. Comments were received from 105 retail food stores, 26 retailer associations, 77 WIC State and local agencies, over 800 participants, Senator Leahy, and the Alabama Congressional delegation. Retailer associations and retailer food stores were generally critical of the provisions strengthening State agencies' ability to limit the number and geographic distribution of authorized stores, and mandated use of competitive pricing as a selection criteria; although OIG and many state agencies were supportive of these provisions. Comments received from Senator Leahy and the Alabama Congressional delegation were also critical of the proposal. Some of the stated objections were:

Selection criteria: Imposing selection criteria on WIC vendors will give larger vendors an unfair competitive advantage over smaller stores and adversely affect participant access; mandating nonselection because a store has a history of Food Stamp Program (FSP) abuse is unfair; the requirement that grocers demonstrate a "lack of a history of a business-related criminal conviction" will be burdensome, create red tape, and is not cost effective in rural areas because abuse is low.

Authorization: Vendor participation will be discouraged, and paperwork and red tape will be encouraged by: limiting periods for acceptance of applications; requiring the collection of FSP authorization numbers; and by the proposed modifications to the vendor agreement.

Training: Requiring vendors to maintain documentation of training of their employees will cause needless paperwork.

Sanctions: The proposed sanctions: unfairly disqualify vendors for both intentional and unintentional acts; unfairly disqualify innocent vendors for the unfortunate actions of one of their employees; and will adversely affect participant access.

To the extent that commenters were able to offer convincing arguments and evidence, we responded with alterations which will be reflected in the revised proposal.

Mr. DURBIN. For the record, provide a copy of both your original and revised proposal.

Mr. BRALEY. We will provide you with a copy of our original proposal, however, our revised proposal is undergoing final editing in preparation for the formal clearance process.

[CLERK'S NOTE.—The material is too lengthy for reprint. A copy is returned in Committee files.]

Mr. DURBIN. At last year's hearing, Mrs. Nelsen testified that FNS was in the process of collecting $6,000,000 in administrative overcharges and that the OIG was planning to perform follow-up audits to determine if improved controls have been put into place. As I understand it, the proposed regulations to strengthen and improve vendor management and food instrument accountability was delayed due to President Bush's regulatory moratorium. What is the status of these regulations?

Mr. BRALEY. Of the $6,000,000 identified by the ten administrative costs audits conducted by the OIG, FNS billed states for over $3,700,000 in overcharges. To date, over $3,300,000 has been collected. Follow-up audits in this area are on the OIG's work plan for fiscal year 1993.

The proposed regulations to strengthen and improve vendor management and food instrument accountability are being prepared for formal clearance. It is anticipated that these regulations will be published in the summer of 1993.

Mr. DURBIN. Has OIG performed any follow-up audits? If so, what did they find? Have additional overcharges been identified?

Mr. BRALEY. The OIG agreed to delay follow-up audits in this area to allow States adequate time to implement corrective actions. A period of time between the implementation of correct action measures and audit coverage is necessary for the corrective actions to be reflected in states' financial records. Follow-up audits in this area are on the OIG's work plan for fiscal year 1993.

Mr. DURBIN. The WIC Vendor Issues Study was scheduled to be released by December 1992 and it was to include a baseline estimate of dollar loss due to overcharging? Has this data been released?

Mr. BRALEY. The WIC Vendor Issues Study is being conducted for FNS by Aspen Systems Corporation, and is the first nationally representative study of overcharging in the WIC Program. The study report was received on February 26, 1992 and is now undergoing review by the agency before bulk printing. We anticipate distribution of the report later this spring.

REVIEWS FOR EFFICIENCY

Mr. DURBIN. What type of reviews are being conducted at the state level, clinic level, and vendor level to ensure that Federal dollars are being spent efficiently and properly?

Mr. BRALEY. There are state as well as Federal level systems to ensure that Federal dollars are being spent efficiently and properly. State agencies are required to review all local agencies every other year, including at least 20 percent or one clinic site, whichever is greater, to determine if they are functioning efficiently.

On the Federal level, the State Technical Assistance Review (STAR) system has been implemented for reviews of both the state and local level conducted by the FNS Regional Office. The STAR review looks at eleven functional areas: Vendor Management; Nutrition Services; Management Information Systems; Staffing and Organization; Administrative Expenditures; Food Funds Management; Caseload Management; Certification and Eligibility; Food Delivery/Food Instrument Accountability; Monitoring and Audits; and Civil Rights.

Once the review has been conducted, the regional office provides the state agency with its findings, significant observations and other comments, and sends the National office a copy of the document. These findings are summarized in an annual report which provides information on the nature and scope of the deficiencies that have been identified in the WIC Program on a national basis. This process heightens the awareness of the national office to the management of the WIC Program at the state and local level and enables timely feedback to the regional offices.

Review of vendors is primarily a State responsibility. Current regulations require that ten percent of vendors be reviewed annually. As resources permit, FNS Regional Offices will visit vendors to ensure that they clearly understand program requirements.

VENDOR ACTIVITY MONITORING PROFILE

Mr. DURBIN. The Vendor Activity Monitoring Profile, a system used by state agencies to detect vendor abuse, has been used since 1989. Do all states use this system? How is it working? What more needs to be done?

Mr. BRALEY. The Vendor Activity Monitoring Profile (VAMP) consists of two reports that states complete and submit to Headquarters annually. One, the Vendor Summary Report, is mandatory and submitted by all state agencies that have a retail food delivery system. This report contains summary information such as the number of participants served, number of vendors, how many have been designated as high risk, and the aggregate results of investigations conducted.

The Vendor Detailed Report is submitted by states that conduct investigations, or compliance buys, of their vendors. Compliance buys are not mandated at this time. For fiscal year 1992, 48 of the 85 State agencies have submitted Vendor Detailed Reports. These reports contain information about specific vendors, including which ones have been designated as high risk, which high risk indicators were used, how many compliance buys were conducted, and the results of those buys. Information is also included about subsequent penalties such as fines and disqualifications, if the vendor appealed the sanction and the results of the appeal.

VAMP has been useful in tracking vendor monitoring efforts, and has shown the level of states' activity systems, as well as the results of investigations. Many states have developed sophisticated computerized systems and excellent investigation procedures. Other states could make further improvements to their vendor management systems.

Vendor management is staff intensive, and does demand considerable resources for state agencies. However, FNS believes that it is imperative that states maintain, and in some cases, increase their level of effort in vendor monitoring. It is critical that as we move toward WIC full funding, state agencies ensure that food package expenditures are only for authorized foods at the shelf price charged other customers. We are aware that there continues to be vendors that abuse the program, and that is of great concern to us. We fully support and encourage state efforts in identifying and sanctioning abusive vendors.

VENDOR COMPETITIVE BID PROCESS

Mr. DURBIN. The state of Delaware has implemented a vendor competitive bid process in two of its three counties. Would you describe this process in further detail for the record?

Mr. BRALEY. In March 1990, the Delaware WIC Program implemented a unique vendor selection initiative called Selecting Authorized Vendors Efficiently (SAVE). SAVE is a process of selecting and authorizing a predetermined number of vendors who will provide WIC approved foods at competitive prices and allow convenient access to participants.

The initiative limits the number of participating vendors in a service area and saves administrative resources required to authorize, train, and monitor vendors. The State agency also saves food dollars by selecting vendors whose competitive prices will remain stable for the contract period. Vendors are required to submit bids for all WIC authorized foods (except non-contract formula), which are usually below normal shelf prices. In fiscal year 1992, the State agency realized savings of approximately $288,000. These savings reflect the difference between the vendor's current shelf price and bid price for WIC authorized foods.

Delaware used these savings to serve approximately 830 additional participants each month during fiscal year 1992. Regional discretionary administrative funds were provided to the Delaware state WIC Program to assist in the implementation of the SAVE project. Delaware represents the first state in the nation to bring this type of project to fruition.

Mr. DURBIN. What is the status of the New York proposal to initiate a vendor competitive bid process?

Mr. BRALEY. We have provided a special grant to the New York State WIC Program to develop a system for assigning a "Not To Exceed" amount for their Food Instruments. We have received a preliminary draft procedure and software program from New York which will enable other state agencies to monitor the costs charged for food packages by vendors and establish realistic cost ceilings.

As a complement to this project, New York is developing an initiative similar to the Delaware vendor competitive bid process. New York's Bid Based System is designed to assist in evaluating competitive bids submitted, award the best prices, and monitor adherence to contract prices. It is still in the planning and development stage, but New York hopes to have a procedure to test in the near future.

INCOME VERIFICATION ERROR RATE

Mr. DURBIN. What is the national WIC income verification error rate for fiscal year 1992 and how much does this translate into ineligibles served?

Mr. BRALEY. Food and Nutrition Service (FNS) does not collect data to provide annual WIC income verification error rates. The Women, Infant, and Children (WIC) Income Verification Study estimated that in Fiscal Year 1988, the national certification error rate, defined as the percent of participants certified to receive, but not eligible for, WIC benefits, was 5.7 percent of the WIC participants and 5.8 percent of WIC benefits. Using the error rate from the income verification study, we estimate that approximately $150 million in 1992 may have been used to serve WIC participants who were not income eligible. This is equivalent to 5.8 percent of the Fiscal Year 1992 WIC appropriation of $2.6 billion.

It should be noted, however, that the 1988 study was completed prior to the expansion of Medicaid eligibility and adjunctive WIC income eligibility for applicants who are eligible for Medicaid.

These factors have more than likely reduced WIC's income certification error rate.

UNSPENT AND SPENDFORWARD FUNDS

Mr. DURBIN. Please provide a ten-year table showing the total amount of spendforward funds and the amount of unspent funds that were recovered and reallocated.

Mr. BRALEY. As a result of state agencies experiencing difficulty in spending exactly 100 percent of their grants, Public Law 100-356, dated June 28, 1988, authorized state agencies to spendforward not more than five percent of their food grants from one fiscal year to the next. Spendforward authority was effective for fiscal year 1987 closeout. Spendforward totals for fiscal years 1987–1991 will be provided for the record. A spendforward amount for fiscal year 1992 is not yet available.

Totals for unspent funds, excluding spendforward funds, for fiscal years 1982–1992 will also be provided for the record. Each fiscal year, unspent funds are recovered and reallocated to State agencies.

[The information follows:]

United States Department of Agriculture, Food and Nutrition Service—Special Supplemental Food Program for Women, Infants and Children (WIC)

[Fiscal Years 1982-1992]

Total Unspent Funds:	
1982	$68,962,000
1983	54,969,000
1984	27,022,000
1985	36,489,000
1986	34,040,000
1987 [1]	11,808,000
1988 [1]	9,252,000
1989 [1]	25,608,000
1990 [1]	28,072,000
1991 [1]	73,382,000
1992 [2]	56,877,343

[1] Figures are net of spendforward amounts.
[2] Estimate.

[Fiscal Years 1987-1991]

Total Spendforward:	
1987	$7,322,438
1988	18,893,644
1989	24,997,867
1990	26,646,077
1991	27,429,625

MODEL APPLICATION FORM

Mr. DURBIN. What is the status of the model application form that was developed with the Department of Health and Human Services? How many States use this new form?

Mr. BRALEY. As required by Public Law 101–239, the Omnibus Budget Reconciliation Act of 1989, the model application form was published in the *Federal Register* on December 9, 1991. The model application form was developed by an Interagency Workgroup comprised of program representatives and legal counsel. In addition to the Special Supplemental Program for Women, Infants and Children (WIC), the other programs included in the joint form are the

Maternal and Child Health Block Grant, Medicaid, Migrant and Community Health Centers, Grants for the Homeless, and Head Start. The *Federal Register* Notice and model application form have been disseminated to state program representatives responsible for administering the programs included in the form, as further required by the legislation. In a subsequent letter to state program representatives, states were provided with additional technical guidance on the development of a joint application form. Copies of the Notice and form were also disseminated to all Healthy Start and Pediatric AIDS grantees and to interested Congressional committee staff. In addition, a letter was sent to each state governor, which was signed jointly by the Secretary of Agriculture and the Secretary of Health and Human Services, to inform them of the model application form and encourage their support in state efforts to develop a joint application. Numerous national meetings, such as the Surgeon General's Healthy Children Ready to Learn Conference, state association meetings, and regional workshops have and continue to be used as forums to promote the model application form and showcase state-designated joint applications.

We are aware that many state program representatives have reviewed and analyzed the model form to determine how such a form could be utilized at the state level. A survey was undertaken by the Interagency Workgroup in the Spring of 1992 to determine the extent to which states were using or in the process of developing joint application forms. This survey found that 13 states were using a joint application form and 16 states were working on the development of a joint form. At the time, this survey did not focus on specifically determining how many of the states' efforts were based on the model application form. However, we are in the process of developing an interagency agreement with the Maternal and Child Health Bureau, DHHS, to support a jointly-funded contract which will evaluate the extent to which the states have adopted or adapted for local program use the model application form.

Mr. DURBIN. At this time last year the Department was considering developing specific policy and guidance on food substitutions or additions to the WIC food packages for the program's culturally diverse populations. What is the status of this initiative?

Mr. BRALEY. The Department is continuing to explore the issues surrounding this matter. It is our intention to obtain extensive information, from both the public and private sectors, about the cultural food patterns of the WIC population before policy decisions are made. Therefore, we are currently developing a Notice of Solicitation of Public Comment to be published in the *Federal Register*. This Notice will gather valuable public comments on the various issues regarding the accommodation of cultural food patterns in the WIC Program.

WIC COUNSELING AND NUTRITION EDUCATION

Mr. DURBIN. What type of counseling and nutrition education do you provide to clients? Provide us with specific examples.

Mr. BRALEY. The two goals of WIC nutrition education are to: stress the relation between proper nutrition and good health with special emphasis on the nutritional needs of participants; and assist the participant in achieving a positive change in food habits, resulting in improved health status. WIC regulations require that at a minimum each WIC participant must be provided the opportunity to receive two nutrition education contacts per certification period. Nutrition education contacts may be provided via individual counseling or group sessions.

During the WIC eligibility screening process, health data in the form of, height, weight, blood work for determining iron-deficiency anemia, health history and dietary intake information are collected, recorded and evaluated as part of the applicant's nutrition assessment to identify qualifying nutritional risk factors. Both FNS and state agency guidance to local WIC clinics advises them to tailor the content of the nutrition education provided to the nutritional needs of the participant. Typically, the content of WIC nutrition education relates to the participant's nutrition risk conditions (e.g., anemia, underweight, or inadequate diet) identified during his/her nutrition assessment and/or relates to the participant's category of eligibility such as pregnant, breastfeeding or nonbreastfeeding postpartum woman, infant or child.

The first of two required nutrition education contacts routinely occurs when a participant is screened for WIC eligibility and is delivered via an individual counseling session. The second nutrition education contact usually occurs one or more months afterwards within the participant's certification period and is typically delivered via a group session unless the participant is identified to be at high risk.

Most WIC state agencies have established policies and procedures to assist local WIC staff in identifying high-risk participants. This group of WIC participants has more serious nutritional risk conditions, requiring in the majority of cases more individualized nutrition counseling on a one-to-one basis. Many WIC clinics offer high-risk participants nutrition education on a basis that is more frequent than twice a certification. When WIC clinics cannot provide the type of follow-up services needed, they routinely refer these clients to appropriate health professionals or facilities that can.

The Anti-Drug Abuse Act of 1988 (P.L. 100-690) and the Child Nutrition and WIC Reauthorization Act of 1989 (P.L. 101-147) define the role of the WIC Program in providing drug abuse prevention information and referrals. As a result, the provision of drug abuse prevention information is integrated into WIC's nutrition education component. If during the WIC eligibility screening process, a pregnant woman is suspected to be an abuser of drugs or other harmful substances, WIC has a responsibility to refer this client for an in-depth evaluation by a professional trained in drug and other harmful substance abuse assessment, counseling and treatment.

There is a wide range of WIC nutrition education provided to participants which varies not only by the content but by the methods used to teach the participant. Examples of actual nutrition education activities developed by State and local WIC agencies which are cited in FNS-267 *The WIC Exchange: Ideas To Help Nutrition Educators Help Clients* and the respective WIC agency will be provided for the record.

[The information follows:]

THE WIC EXCHANGE: IDEAS TO HELP NUTRITION EDUCATORS HELP CLIENTS

A mock grocery store was organized for clients to practice shopping for nutritious foods. (Winfield-Moody Health Center, IL and Cortland County WIC Program, NY)

"Breakfast With the Easter Bunny" taught WIC children and their parents about the importance of starting each day with a nutritious meal. As a memento, each child was also given a photo of himself/herself with the Easter Bunny to take home. (Hamilton City Clinic, OH)

A "WIC Shower" was organized to provide group nutrition education to pregnant clients. (Windham WIC Program, CT

"A Bite of WIC" was offered to WIC Clients to a low-income housing site. It included a cooking demonstration, taste testing, recipe pamphlets, nutrition and dental education, prizes from local merchants, and voucher pickup. (Seattle-King County Department of Public Health, WA)

A puppet show video, "Adventures of Sir Good Food," was developed to provide nutrition education to children without having to use staff time at each session to operate the puppets. (Nebraska WIC Program)

"WIC Jeopardy" was designed to be played with two teams of clients who are asked to select from a game board with categories, such as WIC foods, WIC vouchers, etc. The highest scoring team wins donated prizes. (Finger Lakes WIC Program, NY)

Mr. DURBIN. The 1993 appropriation for the Extension Service included $3,530,000 to expand nutrition education efforts in the WIC population. Do you coordinate your nutrition education efforts with the Extension Service? Describe your working relationship to us.

Mr. BRALEY. Yes, the Food Nutrition Service (FNS) coordinates WIC nutrition education efforts with the Extension Service (ES). A specific project that we have been working on over the past two years is the ES/WIC Nutrition Education Initiative. The purpose of this initiative is to supplement or enhance WIC's basic nutrition education component for the "neediest" WIC participants. State Cooperative Extension System (CES) institutions will be required to closely coordinate with WIC state/local agencies during all phases of this initiative.

Two categories of projects, competitive and non-competitive, are being funded and will operate concurrently. FNS and ES Headquarters staff have been working together since Spring 1992 to develop the requirements. FNS and ES Headquarters staff are also currently serving on a Technical Review Panel.

In 1992 FNS hosted a meeting of state and local WIC and CES representatives to develop the requirements and guidelines for implementing the ES/WIC nutrition education initiative. The representatives also shared information about coordinated activities at the state and local level. In general, coordinated efforts include joint development and distribution of nutrition education materials to provide a consistent message to participants, serving together on state/local nutrition or advisory councils to achieve common goals, coordinated nutrition education sessions at WIC clinic sites, and shared training and continuing education of staff.

WIC FULL FUNDING

Mr. DURBIN. The President's initiative to fully fund the WIC program is an initiative that I personally support wholeheartedly and if you look at the funding history of the program you'll see that it is one that this Committee strongly supports. A concern that I have, and others on the Committee may share in this concern, is that regardless of how good or how beneficial a program is, providing large increases to the program every year doesn't necessarily make it a better program. In fact, it may do just the opposite and become an inefficient and wasteful program. A recent article in the Washington Post questions the expansion of the Head Start program. An IG report has found that centers have been given so much money so fast that they cannot spend it. Even its founder has warned that it is expanding too fast. Has USDA done a study of the WIC program to determine an annual rate of expansion that would provide the most effective and efficient use of money?

Mr. BRALEY. We share your concern that efforts to expand the WIC program to serve all eligible women, infants, and children should not affect the program's effectiveness and efficiency. We are aware that while some WIC State agencies have the capacity to absorb caseload increases, others may not be able to easily add more participants. Phasing in WIC full funding, as proposed by the President, would allow USDA to manage program growth while maintaining the quality and integrity of the WIC program.

The Food and Nutrition Service (FNS) is currently sponsoring a study, the WIC Dynamics Study, to determine the effects of recent WIC participation increases on WIC local agency operations. The study will provide information about measures which need to be taken by state and local WIC agencies to accommodate caseload increases. The study is also collecting data which will provide some information about the capacity of local health care delivery systems to accept increased referrals of WIC participants for maternal and child health services.

The WIC Dynamics Study is currently in the date collection phase. FNS expects to have a final report ready for release by the second quarter of fiscal year 1994.

Mr. DURBIN. What control measures are used to monitor the states ability to increase participation in an efficient way and to make sure that those most in need are being served?

Mr. BRALEY. The funds allocation formula first provides funds to support prior year participation levels. Once appropriated funds are allocated based on prior fiscal year grant levels, additional funds are allocated, in part, to state agencies serving less than their equitable share of eligibles as compared to other state agencies. Recovered unspent funds are also allocated to state agencies most in need.

A new reporting system became effective in October 1992, which provides detailed actual and projected monthly participation and expenditure data for each state. This information is used to monitor state agencies' progress in maintaining their projected participation and appropriate expenditure levels. The Food and Nutrition Service also works closely with state agencies throughout the fiscal year to provide technical assistance in caseload and resource management.

Mr. DURBIN. Depending upon who you are talking to, the total population that is eligible to participate in the WIC program at any given time is different. The Department establishes an income eligibility range and a set of nutritional risk criteria to be used by the states. When the states submit their annual plan of operation to FNS they have the flexibility to set income and nutritional risk criteria within these guidelines. These eligibility criteria can be changed annually or more often with FNS approval. Full funding of the program is a moving target. Have you explored the option of establishing one set of eligibility criteria for all states to follow?

Mr. BRALEY. A uniform set of eligibility criteria would ensure equal geographical access to WIC. However, establishing one set of criteria for all states is a technically complex and politically sensitive task which must be coordinated with the WIC and medical communities. FNS is currently considering a cooperative agreement with the National Academy of Sciences to conduct a scientific review of the nutritional risk criteria used in the WIC Program. We believe that the Academy has a unique ability to assemble the Nation's most eminent scholars and experts to provide advice, guidance and objectivity to USDA in developing WIC nutritional risk criteria based on best available empirical data.

FNS does periodically collect state data and identify a model set of nutritional risk criteria used by the 51 geographical WIC state agencies. The FNS regional office staff routinely work with states that are using more liberal criteria to encourage them to voluntarily change their criteria to be more consistent with the model set.

WIC PROGRAM MONITORING ACTIVITIES

Mr. DURBIN. How much did you spend in fiscal year 1992 in monitoring the administration of the WIC program? How much do you plan to spend in fiscal year 1993?

Mr. BRALEY. Diring fiscal year 1992 our FNS regional offices conducted management evaluation reviews in 33 WIC State agencies and 68 WIC local agencies. Our review guidance covers 11 functional areas of program management. They are: Vendor Management; Nutrition Services; Management Information Systems; Staffing and Organization; Administrative Expenses; Food Funds Management; Caseload Management; Certification and Eligibility; Food Delivery/Food Instrument Accountability; Monitoring and Audits; and Civil Rights.

For fiscal year 1992, the 7 FNS Regional Offices submitted plans which estimated an effort of about 17 staff years for conducting the reviews noted above. At the National office, about one staff year was expended preparing a national summary of fiscal year 1991 review findings and conducting a national training session for regional staff on conducting reviews. Assuming an average salary and benefit cost of $47,070 per staff year, the cost for those reviews was $847,260.

In fiscal year 1993 we have selected 29 state agencies for review. Review expenditures in fiscal year 1993 should approximate expenditures for fiscal year 1992.

It is important to note that our efforts only pertain to on-site reviews in state agencies. Other monitoring activities occur using financial, participation, and vendor report data submitted by state agencies for in-office analysis.

Mr. DURBIN. During last year's hearing we discussed with then Secretary Madigan WIC participation and he provided us with a table showing the WIC eligibility and participation rate estimates for 1990. Would you please update this table for us?

Mr. BRALEY. FNS' estimates are average numbers of women, infants, and children who were fully eligible each month in 1991 to participate in the WIC Program. The Congressional Budget Office, using a different data base and methodology, has projected that 9.6 million persons would be fully eligible in fiscal year 1994. Our estimate is not a projection, but is based on historical data for calendar year 1991. I will provide an updated table for the record.

[The information follows:]

SPECIAL SUPPLEMENTAL FOOD PROGRAM FOR WOMEN, INFANTS AND CHILDREN (WIC); ELIGIBILITY AND COVERAGE ESTIMATES, 1991 UPDATE—U.S. AND OUTLYING AREAS

	1991 Eligible (000)	CY 1991 Partic. (000)	1991 Coverage (%)	1990 Eligible (000)	CY 1990 Partic (000)	1990 Coverage (%)
Pregnant Women	819	730	90	765	659	85
Postpartum & Breastfeeding	876	425	50	818	381	45
Infants	1,762	1,603	90	1,646	1,444	90
Children	5,173	2,296	45	4,950	2,063	40
Total	8,630	5,054	60	8,178	4,548	55

Based on the March 1992 Current Population Survey (CPS), FNS estimates that 8.6 million women, infants and children were fully eligible for the WIC Program in 1991, a 5.5 percent increase over the number eligible in 1990. A significant increase in WIC average monthly participation (over 500,000) allowed overall program coverage to increase to about 60 percent in 1991 from about 55 percent in 1990 despite the increase in the number of WIC eligible persons. (Coverage estimates are rounded to the nearest 5 percent).

Coverage of pregnant women increased to about 90 percent in 1991 from about 85 percent in 1990 because of the 10.7 percent increase in participation. Coverage of postpartum and breastfeeding women increased from 45 percent to about 50 percent and children from about 40 percent to about 45 percent due to participation increases of 11.6 percent and 11.3 percent respectively. Coverage of infants remained about 90 percent in 1991 despite the 11 percent increase in infant participation.

A total of 10.6 million women, infants and children fell below the WIC income eligibility limit in 1991, a 5.4 percent increase over the number income eligible in 1990. The March 1992 CPS uses income information from the prior year capturing the continuation through 1991 of the recession that began in July 1990. The increase in WIC income eligible persons was less than the 6.3 percent increase between 1990 and 1991 of the number of persons below poverty reported by Census. Census identified a U.S. poverty rate of 14.2 percent in 1991, up 5.2 percent from the 13.5 percent rate in 1990.

The estimate of 8.6 million WIC eligible persons in 1991 assumes that about 4 out of 5 income eligible persons are also at nutritional risk and thus fully eligible for the WIC Program. The estimates of pregnant, postpartum and breastfeeding women are based on the count of infants from the CPS and relationships found in the 1980 Decennial Census. These estimates do not factor in the effect of Medicaid adjunct eligibility. Assumptions about counts of women and the effect of Medicaid adjunct eligibility are currently being analyzed using data from the 1990 Decennial Census. Assumptions about percentages of income eligible persons at risk will be reanalyzed when new national health and nutrition survey data become available.

These eligibility and coverage estimates are for 1991 and do not factor in changes in participation or eligibles that have occurred since 1991. WIC participation has continued to grow; in FY 1992 WIC participation averaged 5.4 million women, infants and children per month (as of August 1992). The recession also continued throughout FY 1992 with higher unemployment rates and Food Stamp participation than in 1991; therefore it is likely that the number of WIC eligibles has also increased. Estimates of program coverage rates for 1992 cannot be made until 1992 income data become available.

Mr. DURBIN. Former Secretary Madigan also told us that when census data became available, FNS would be able to provide the number of WIC eligibles by state as well as national estimates. Is this data available?

Mr. BRALEY. The data are not currently available, but we should be able to provide State as well as county-level estimates of the number of persons that qualify for Women, Infant, and Children (WIC) based on income this summer. We have worked very closely with the Bureau of the Census to obtain special extract files and a contractor is currently analyzing the data to prepare the estimates.

FOLIC ACID

Mr. DURBIN. The Public Health Service has recently recommended, through the coordinated efforts of CDC, FDA, HRSA, and NIH, that all women of childbearing age who are capable of becoming pregnant should consume 0.4 mg of folic acid per day for the purpose of reducing their risk of having a pregnancy affected with spina bifida or other neural tube defects. In view of this finding, what could be done through WIC to ensure women in the program receive this daily recommended amount?

Mr. BRALEY. The Public Health Service based its recommendation on findings from studies which have concluded that, when consumed in adequate amounts beginning several weeks before conception and continuing during the early weeks of pregnancy, folic acid will reduce the risk of having a child with a serious neural tube defect. The new Public Health Service recommendation is about twice the level of the current Recommended Dietary Allowances (RDAs) for non-pregnant and lactating women, and is the same for pregnant women.

The current WIC food packages were designed with consideration of the RDAs for five targeted nutrients—protein, calcium, iron and vitamins A and C. Although folic acid is not a target WIC nutrient at this time, the WIC food packages can be tailored by nutritionists to provide sufficient folic acid to satisfy the dietary needs of pregnant, lactating, and postpartum non-breastfeeding women, consistent with the current RDAs. WIC food packages for pregnant or breastfeeding women can provide such folic acid-rich foods as orange and grapefruit juice, dried beans and peas or peanut butter and cereals fortified with folic acid. Many WIC cereals contain .4 mg of folic acid per 1-ounce serving.

FNS testified at the Food and Drug Administration's Food Advisory Committee Meeting of the Subcommittee on Folic Acid. Once final recommendations are implemented through a change in RDAs, FNS will, in alignment with the new RDAs, consider the impact of those revisions on WIC food packages. In the meantime, WIC will continue to provide existing folic acid-rich foods in the packages. Further, WIC nutrition education can appropriately address the need for a well-balanced diet which includes folic acid and can identify good sources in addition to WIC foods. Currently, FNS is encouraging state agencies to work closely with local agencies to assist participating women in choosing WIC and other foods that are rich in folic acid.

Mr. DURBIN. How many mothers in the program have more than one child while enrolled in WIC?

Mr. BRALEY. The 1988 Study of Women, Infants, and Children (WIC) Participant and Program Characteristics identified the number of WIC participants in households of WIC recipients. Among WIC women surveyed, 19 percent were in households containing three or more members receiving WIC benefits. Among breastfeeding or postpartum women, about one-third in each group reported three or more WIC participants in their households. On average, there were 1.8 WIC participants in each household.

This information shows the number of WIC participants in a household at a particular point in time. We do not have longitudinal data that would allow us to determine how many women and children participate in WIC over a longer time period. However, we do have data regarding size of family/economy unit of WIC participants in 1984, 1988, and 1990. I will provide this information for the record.

[The information follows:]

TABLE 3.6
Size of Family/Economic Unit of WIC Participants in 1984, 1988, and 1990 by Category: Percent Distribution

	Women							Infants			Children		
	Pregnant			Breastfeeding and Postpartum Women	Total Women								
Size of family/Economic Unit	1990	1988	1984	1990	1990	1988	1984	1990	1988	1984	1990	1988	1984
1	15.2	6.0	16.0	0.0	8.6	3.7	8.7	0.0	0.0	1.3	0.0	0.0	0.3
2	26.4	23.7	22.4	15.6	21.5	17.9	18.3	16.3	7.9	18.9	11.6	7.4	10.9
3	21.6	25.8	21.5	26.0	23.5	25.9	26.3	29.1	26.8	24.8	22.4	20.7	22.2
4	17.3	18.8	19.8	25.7	20.9	21.4	22.6	21.8	23.9	26.1	27.5	29.9	30.1
5	9.8	11.8	6.9	14.2	11.7	13.9	10.7	15.1	21.4	13.3	17.9	19.8	18.0
6+	9.7	14.0	13.4	18.5	13.8	17.3	13.4	17.7	20.1	15.6	20.7	22.4	18.4
Median	3.3	3.5	3.0	4.0	3.6	3.8	3.0	3.8	4.3	4.0	4.1	4.4	4.0
Mean	3.1	3.6	3.3	4.1	3.5	3.9	3.6	4.0	4.4	4.1	4.2	4.5	4.3

SOURCE: Studies of WIC Participant and Program Characteristics, 1990 and 1988.

COMMODITY SUPPLEMENTAL FOOD PROGRAM

Mr. DURBIN. Were any new CSFP sites approved in the 1993 caseload allocation?

Mr. BRALEY. No new Commodity Supplemental Food Program (CSFP) sites were approved in the 1993 caseload allocation.

Mr. DURBIN. Were any additional elderly participants served in fiscal year 1992 over fiscal year 1991?

Mr. BRALEY. September elderly participation for fiscal year 1992 was 145,414 compared to 114,736 for the same month of the previous year. This addition of 30,678 elderly participants marks a 26.7 percent increase in one year. Current CSFP regulations permit states with guidance to allow a reasonable increase in elderly par- and children caseload slots for service to the elderly. We provide States with guidance to allow a reasonable increase in elderly participation while still preserving adequate resources to serve women, infants and children. This dramatic one-year increase is the result of that process.

Mr. DURBIN. Please update the tables that appear on pages 142 and 143 of last year's hearing record showing caseload levels to include fiscal year 1992 actual caseload and fiscal year 1993 requests and authorized levels.

Mr. BRALEY. The updated tables will be provided for the record.

[The information follows:]

COMMODITY SUPPLEMENTAL FOOD PROGRAM
WOMEN, INFANTS AND CHILDREN CASELOAD

STATES	FISCAL YEAR 1989			FISCAL YEAR 1990			FISCAL YEAR 1991		
	STATES' REQUEST FOR EXPANSION CASELOAD	TOTAL AUTHORIZED CASELOAD	** CASELOAD USED	STATES' REQUEST FOR EXPANSION CASELOAD	TOTAL AUTHORIZED CASELOAD	** CASELOAD USED	STATES' REQUEST FOR EXPANSION CASELOAD	TOTAL AUTHORIZED CASELOAD	** CASELOAD USED
New Hampshire	*	2,478	2,342	1,500	2,342	2,342	0	2,650	2,650
New York	0	10,068	5,840	3,000	6,077	6,043	6,991	12,120	11,120
D.C.	*	4,772	4,645	0	5,712	5,360	0	5,360	5,896
Kentucky	2,000	4,204	3,488	0	3,672	3,469	500	3,969	3,384
N. Carolina	0	738	674	0	674	564	500	564	564
Tennessee	5,000	18,371	17,755	0	18,083	16,960	3,000	19,960	15,496
Illinois	1,645	11,334	11,334	2,666	11,334	10,422	2,666	13,088	12,564
Michigan	8,000	46,469	44,889	12,000	52,463	48,984	18,000	57,093	57,093
Minnesota	8,123	2,788	2,788	8,212	2,974	2,974	8,212	5,948	5,472
Red Lake	0	554	554	46	651	564	0	564	620
Louisiana	5,916	27,992	27,188	10,003	29,317	27,960	11,468	35,402	33,592
New Mexico	8,451	10,000	6,315	0	6,315	6,315	3,685	10,000	10,000
Colorado	0	14,410	14,410	1,050	16,638	14,932	0	16,638	18,302
Iowa	0	1,987	1,566	0	1,672	1,623	0	1,623	1,755
Kansas	*	2,943	2,712	3,842	2,751	2,610	3,838	5,361	3,238
Nebraska	2,898	7,694	6,294	0	6,510	6,180	1,500	7,680	5,127
South Dakota	0	1,373	1,232	0	1,232	1,104	0	1,104	927
Arizona	1,642	5,510	5,510	1,490	6,298	5,840	15,490	12,138	11,138
California	2,083	4,925	4,907	400	4,907	4,731	0	9,638	9,638
Oregon	2,071	929	649	0	701	701	274	975	975
Texas	0	0	0	0	0	0	10,000	0	0
Ohio	0	0	0	32,112	0	0	32,112	0	0
Pennsylvania	0	0	0	0	0	0	3,000	0	0
TOTALS	47,829	179,539	165,092	76,321	180,323	169,678	121,236	221,875	209,551

* NOT ON FILE AND DID NOT REACH 90% OF THEIR CASELOAD
** INDICATES HIGHEST OF FOLLOWING MEASURES: FISCAL YEAR AVERAGE PARTICIPATION, FOURTH QUARTER AVERAGE PARTICIPATION, OR SEPTEMBER PARTICIPATION. THE HIGHEST MEASURE IS THEN USED IN DETERMINING CASELOAD FOR THE NEXT FISCAL YEAR.

COMMODITY SUPPLEMENTAL FOOD PROGRAM
WOMEN, INFANTS AND CHILDREN CASELOAD

STATES	FISCAL YEAR 1992: STATES' REQUEST FOR EXPANSION CASELOAD	FISCAL YEAR 1992: TOTAL AUTHORIZED CASELOAD ***	FISCAL YEAR 1992: ** CASELOAD USED	FISCAL YEAR 1993: STATES' REQUEST FOR EXPANSION CASELOAD	FISCAL YEAR 1993: TOTAL AUTHORIZED CASELOAD
New Hampshire	750	2,327	2,327	0	2,327
New York	9,000	21,120	21,120	7,500	21,120
D.C.	1,000	6,289	5,900	0	5,900
Kentucky	0	3,384	3,278	0	3,278
N. Carolina	500	564	483	0	483
Tennessee	0	15,496	14,910	2,500	14,910
Illinois	1,436	17,000	15,606	1,394	15,606
Michigan	12,875	64,312	62,266	6,800	62,266
Minnesota	8,212	8,906	7,567	0	7,567
Red Lake	0	620	607	0	607
Louisiana	0	31,416	30,434	5,000	30,434
New Mexico	10,000	17,711	16,991	0	16,991
Colorado	1,740	18,937	18,108	0	18,108
Iowa	81	1,836	1,792	0	1,792
Kansas	2,123	4,519	3,845	0	3,845
Nebraska	1,000	5,127	4,875	600	4,875
South Dakota	0	927	807	0	807
Arizona	10,862	18,750	18,750	3,000	18,750
California	2,000	12,138	12,138	5,000	15,494
Oregon	250	1,225	1,225	175	1,225
Texas	10,000	0	0	10,000	0
Ohio	32,112	0	0	32,112	0
Pennsylvania	3,000	0	0	3,000	0
TOTALS	106,941	252,604	243,029	77,081	246,385

** INDICATES HIGHEST OF FOLLOWING MEASURES: FISCAL YEAR AVERAGE PARTICIPATION, FOURTH QUARTER AVERAGE PARTICIPATION, OR SEPTEMBER PARTICIPATION. THE HIGHEST MEASURE IS THEN USED IN DETERMINING CASELOAD FOR THE NEXT FISCAL YEAR.

*** REPRESENTS INITIAL CASELOAD EXPANSION OF 61,327 SLOTS AND SUBSEQUENT EXPANSION OF 3,500 SLOTS AND CONVERSION OF 18,536 SLOTS TO ELDERLY.

COMMODITY SUPPLEMENTAL FOOD PROGRAM
ELDERLY CASELOAD

	FISCAL YEAR 1989			FISCAL YEAR 1990			FISCAL YEAR 1991		
STATES	STATES' REQUEST FOR EXPANSION CASELOAD	TOTAL AUTHORIZED CASELOAD	** CASELOAD USED	STATES' REQUEST FOR EXPANSION CASELOAD	TOTAL AUTHORIZED CASELOAD	** CASELOAD USED	STATES' REQUEST FOR EXPANSION CASELOAD	TOTAL AUTHORIZED CASELOAD	** CASELOAD USED
New Hampshire	0	0	0	0	0	0	9,000	0	0
New York	0	0	0	0	0	0	1,000	1,000	0 *
D.C.	3,458	10,000	7,621	0	8,489	8,489	0	8,489	8,489
Kentucky	2,000	3,225	3,225	2,500	3,236	3,186	2,000	3,386	3,386
N. Carolina	597	1,674	1,514	0	1,702	1,527	1,000	1,527	1,522
Tennessee	5,000	12,046	11,345	5,000	11,704	11,359	2,000	12,359	12,359
Illinois	2,955	2,955	2,955	3,045	3,381	3,101	2,619	3,625	3,625
Michigan	0	32,855	32,732	9,000	33,911	32,363	16,000	32,363	32,363
Minnesota	0	0	0	0	0	0	7,000	0	0
Red Lake	0	0	0	0	0	0	0	0	0
Louisiana	10,237	24,478	24,478	15,001	24,478	24,478	15,001	25,478	25,417
New Mexico	0	0	0	0	0	0	0	0	0
Colorado	0	4,828	4,828	2,000	5,634	5,188	0	5,188	5,188
Iowa	500	5,164	4,615	0	4,743	4,571	0	4,571	4,369
Kansas	0	0	0	0	0	0	625	0	0
Nebraska	10,803	9,962	7,963	0	8,575	8,575	3,000	9,575	9,394
South Dakota	0	0	0	0	0	0	0	0	0
Arizona	1,500	2,920	2,791	1,080	3,071	3,071	18,209	4,071	3,955
California	600	3,000	2,687	0	2,726	2,707	300	2,707	2,700
Oregon	0	0	0	0	0	0	0	0	0
TOTALS	37,650	113,107	106,754	37,626	111,650	108,615	77,754	114,339	112,767

* ALTHOUGH NEW YORK DID NOT UTILIZE THE ELDERLY CASELOAD IT IS PROTECTED FOR A SECOND CASELOAD CYCLE.
** INDICATES HIGHEST OF FOLLOWING MEASURES: FISCAL YEAR AVERAGE PARTICIPATION, FOURTH QUARTER AVERAGE PARTICIPATION, OR SEPTEMBER PARTICIPATION. THE HIGHEST MEASURE IS THEN USED IN DETERMINING CASELOAD FOR THE NEXT FISCAL YEAR.

COMMODITY SUPPLEMENTAL FOOD PROGRAM
ELDERLY CASELOAD

	FISCAL YEAR 1992			FISCAL YEAR 1993	
STATES	STATES' REQUEST FOR EXPANSION CASELOAD	TOTAL AUTHORIZED CASELOAD ***	** CASELOAD USED	STATES' REQUEST FOR EXPANSION CASELOAD	TOTAL AUTHORIZED CASELOAD
New Hampshire	9,000	1,402	1,402	9,000	1,402
New York	500	0	0	0	0
D.C.	1,000	9,425	9,401	500	9,401
Kentucky	2,000	3,915	3,915	2,200	3,915
N. Carolina	0	1,722	1,519	0	1,519
Tennessee	5,000	12,688	12,688	2,500	12,688
Illinois	2,375	7,000	6,202	798	6,202
Michigan	12,800	40,348	39,694	15,650	39,694
Minnesota	17,000	2,367	2,367	17,000	2,367
Red Lake	0	0	0	0	0
Louisiana	25,000	31,422	31,422	25,000	31,422
New Mexico	0	2,289	2,285	5,000	2,285
Colorado	1,294	6,622	6,037	1,000	6,037
Iowa	291	4,660	4,214	0	4,214
Kansas	625	1,171	1,171	829	1,171
Nebraska	3,000	10,123	10,123	2,400	10,123
South Dakota	0	0	0	0	0
Arizona	17,929	7,534	6,781	7,716	6,781
California	500	3,029	3,029	500	3,029
Oregon	0	0	0	0	0
TOTALS	98,314	145,717	142,250	90,093	142,250

** INDICATES HIGHEST OF FOLLOWING MEASURES: FISCAL YEAR AVERAGE PARTICIPATION, FOURTH QUARTER AVERAGE PARTICIPATION, OR SEPTEMBER PARTICIPATION. THE HIGHEST MEASURE IS THEN USED IN DETERMINING CASELOAD FOR THE NEXT FISCAL YEAR.

*** REPRESENTS INITIAL 4,568 EXPANSION SLOTS AND SUBSEQUENT APPROVAL OF 9,146 EXPANSION SLOTS AND 18,236 CONVERSION SLOTS FROM WOMEN, INFANTS AND CHILDREN.

TEXAS, OHIO AND PENNSYLVANIA WOULD NOT BE ELIGIBLE FOR ELDERLY CASELOAD UNTIL THE SECOND YEAR OF OPERATION.

WIC REFERRALS

Mr. DURBIN. Many of the women, infants, and children that participate in the program are referred from the WIC program. As WIC moves closer and closer to full funding what do you see happening to this program?

Mr. BRALEY. The full funding estimate of the Congressional Budget Office and the increases in the President's Budget assumed constant participation in CSFP by women, infants, and children. As the WIC program moves toward full funding, we would expect decreases in participation by women, infants and children in CSFP.

FOOD STAMP PARTICIPATION LEVEL

Mr. DURBIN. Your fiscal year 1993 participation estimates were based on a revised forecasting model. The 1993 budget request is based on an estimated participation of 25.8 million. Your statement says that participation in 1993 will be 27.3 million. Obviously, your revised forecasting model is not working. What do you attribute this increase to result from?

Mr. BRALEY. In December 1991, Food Stamp Program participation for fiscal year 1993 was forecast at a monthly average of 25.803 million persons. This forecast was based on projected unemployment conditions provided to the Agency by the Office of Management and Budget (OMB).

Since then, actual unemployment has been about one half of a percentage point higher than OMB projected. OMB has responded to this by upwardly revising their projection of fiscal year 1993 unemployment levels. This accounts for about 500,000 of the higher participation estimate. Our revised projected fiscal year 1993 Food Stamp Program participation of 27.300 million persons reflects actual current caseloads and the new, higher levels of anticipated unemployment, as well as continued improvement in our forecasting methods.

The Food and Nutrition Service, in an effort to provide the most accurate program forecasts possible, bases its projections on the best available forecasts of future national economic conditions. Over time, as more and better information about national economic trends becomes available, OMB updates its projections of future economic conditions. Commensurate adjustments to Agency projections of program performance are to be expected.

Mr. DURBIN. Your proposed increase for benefit costs in fiscal year 1993 was only $999,524. Mrs. Nelson testified last year that this was based on a maximum benefit level increase from $370 in fiscal year 1992 to $371 in fiscal year 1993 and a decrease in the unemployment rate from 6.80 percent to 6.58 percent. Although the maximum benefit level would have been reduced to $368 due to lower food costs, the Authorizing Committee passed a bill last year requiring you to keep the level at $370 so this assumption still holds true. But the unemployment rate did not fall to 6.58 percent; in fact it remains up near 7.0 percent. How has this affected the benefit costs to the program?

Mr. BRALEY. The cost of Food Stamp Program benefits tends to change over time as the number of participants rises or falls. Changes in participation can result from a number of factors, including fluctuations in the economy, changes in program rules, and changes in household behavior. Our annual budget submissions reflect our best estimates of future participation levels based on what we know about current participation and on the economic indicators generated by the Office of Management and Budget available at the time.

Participation in the Food Stamp Program is at record levels now because the anticipated economic recovery has not been as strong or as fast as hoped. There may also be some underlying social changes that have increased participation. Because the unemployment rate remains unacceptably high, more people are eligible for and participating in the program this year than we had originally predicted. We now believe that benefits in 1993 will cost about $1.5 billion more than in 1992. Despite this increase, we are confident that sufficient funds have been appropriated in 1993 to cover all program costs.

RESERVE

Mr. DURBIN. Have you used any of the $2.5 billion reserve that was provided in the 1993 appropriation?

Mr. BRALEY. No, the Food and Nutrition Service (FNS) has not used any of the reserve provided for fiscal year 1993. Our current estimates indicate that we will return that entire amount to the Treasury.

FOOD STAMP ADMINISTRATIVE COSTS

Mr. DURBIN. Please describe for the Committee how both State and Federal administrative costs for the food stamp program are derived and the controls used to monitor these costs.

Mr. BRALEY. Administrative costs for the Food Stamp program are shared between the Federal government and each state. The cost of administrative activities such as certification of households, issuance of food stamps, quality control and fair hearings are shared equally between the Federal and state governments. Federal funding in excess of 50 percent is available for certain categories of activity, including fraud prevention and automated certification systems development.

A comprehensive system of financial controls over state expenditures for food stamp administrative cost is in place. In order for states to claim costs to the Federal government, those costs must be deemed allowable under OMB Circular A–87, *Cost Principles for State and Local Governments,* as well as under Food Stamp Program regulations. The actual monitoring of compliance with Federal financial requirements takes several forms. Since Food Stamps is a major program, it is audited annually as part of each state's single audit in accordance with OMB Circular A–128, *Audits of State and Local Governments.* USDA's Office of Inspector General may elect to conduct program compliance audits of one or more states. In addition, FNS regional offices routinely conduct expenditure validation reviews of Food Stamp administrative costs as part of their state oversight responsibility.

OVERPAYMENT ERROR RATE

Mr. DURBIN. What is the overpayment error rate measured by your quality control system for fiscal year 1992?

Mr. BRALEY. Unfortunately, official error rates for fiscal year 1992 will not be available until June 30, 1993. We will furnish them after that time.

Mr. DURBIN. Please provide for the record a ten-year table showing the overpayment error rate.

Mr. BRALEY. The overpayment error rates for the most recent ten years; fiscal years 1982 through 1991, will be provided for the record.

[The information follows:]

Fiscal Year	*Overpayment Error Rate*
1982	9.54
1983	8.32
1984	8.59
1985	8.27
1986	8.09
1987	7.58
1988	7.41
1989	7.25
1990	7.34
1991	6.96

LOW-ERROR RATES

Mr. DURBIN. Update the table that appears on page 149 of last year's hearing record showing the states and enhanced funding received for low-error rates to include fiscal years 1991 and 1992.

Mr. BRALEY. In 26 instances, states received up to 10 percent enhanced administrative funding totalling $27,843,545 for achieving low error rates during fiscal years 1986 through 1991. A list of the states and amounts received by fiscal year for the record will be provided for the record.

[The information follows:]

Fiscal year	Number of states	States	Total enhanced funding
1986	3	Nevada North Dakota South Dakota	$1,175,006
1987	4	Hawaii Nevada North Dakota South Dakota	2,173,455
1988	2	Nevada South Dakota	985,962
1989	7	Alabama Hawaii Kentucky Montana Nevada North Dakota South Dakota	7,150,142
1990	5	Alabama Hawaii Kentucky North Dakota South Dakota	6,936,616
1991	5	Alabama Hawaii Kentucky North Dakota South Dakota	9,422,364
Totals	26		27,843,545

Data for fiscal year 1992 is not included since the qualifying states and amounts for this and subsequent years will not be known until nine months after the year for which they qualify.

DEBARMENT

Mr. DURBIN. Those who receive food stamps can be disqualified from the program as a result of fraudulent behavior. Are vendors also barred from the program if they abuse the system?

Mr. BRALEY. Yes, retailers are disqualified from program participation for violating program regulations, including the sale of ineligible items, trafficking (cash for coupons) cash change violations and accepting stamps from other authorized retailers, or unauthorized retailers and individuals. Disqualification periods range from 6 months to permanent debarment depending on the seriousness of the violations.

Mr. DURBIN. How many retailers were barred from the program in fiscal year 1992?

Mr. BRALEY. In fiscal year 1992, 916 retailers were disqualified from participating in the program as a result of violations which were uncovered in FNS and OIG investigations. In addition, 203 retailers were assessed a civil money penalty.

TAX-OFFSET PROGRAM

Mr. DURBIN. One of the projects you are currently working on to collect monies owed due to fraud and erroneous information is through tax offsets. You estimate that program-wide use of tax offsets would result in at least $25 million per year in collections. You started this project in fiscal year 1992 with two states and plan to expand this to 21 states in fiscal year 1994. How much did you spend in fiscal year 1992 on this project and how much do you plan to spend in fiscal years 1993 and 1994?

Mr. BRALEY. We will provide the information requested in a chart that identifies estimated increased FNS Administrative costs and projected collections for 1992-1994.

[The information follows:]

Year	Number of states	Collections from federal tax refund offset	FNS administrative costs
1992	2	$3,500,000	$308,000
1993	9	9,000,000	698,000
1994	21-23	25,000,000	940,000

Mr. DURBIN. How much has been recovered to date?

Mr. BRALEY. The Financial Management Service, Department of the Treasury prepares weekly accumulative reports of all Federal agency collections. The most recent report we have (March 19, 1993) indicates that the total collections for this Agency, since it began participation in 1992, is $9.04 million.

Mr. DURBIN. What would it cost to go nationwide with this program?

Mr. BRALEY. At the continued rate of implementation, we estimate that it would cost approximately $940,000 in increased FNS administrative costs for fiscal year 1994, and project $1.13 million for fiscal year 1995, $1.31 million for fiscal year 1996, and $1.46 million for fiscal year 1997. It is anticipated that all participating Food Stamp state agencies would begin operating the Program by the close of 1997. Gradual implementation allows FNS the opportunity to work with State agencies with recipient claims accounting systems which need strengthening before participating in the Program.

1992 RESERVE

Mr. DURBIN. How much of the fiscal year 1992 reserve was returned to the Treasury?

Mr. BRALEY. The total amount returned to the Treasury from the Food Stamp Program was about $640 million, of which about $583 million was from the reserve.

WELFARE REFORM PROJECTS

Mr. DURBIN. Please provide an update for the Committee on each of the welfare reform projects you currently have underway.

Mr. BRALEY. An overview of the welfare reform projects currently in operation will be provided for the record.

[The information follows:]

Maryland: The Maryland Primary Prevention Initiative

Summary: The Maryland demonstration encourages increased parental responsibility and preventative health care. Aid to Families with Dependent Children (AFDC) benefits are reduced if school age children do not attend school regularly or do not receive required health services. The State agency received a food stamp waiver to exclude an annual $20 special needs allowance payment that is provided to AFDC households complying with required health checkups.

Implementation/Project Area: The Statewide project was implemented in 1992 and will operate for five years.

Virginia: Virginia Incentive to Advance Learning --VITAL--

Summary: The demonstration targets families of children in grades six, seven and eight in three schools. Incentives -- increased AFDC grants-- are provided to encourage school attendance and extensive counseling services are available to the AFDC families. The State agency received a food stamp waiver to exclude the increased AFDC grant amount as income in food stamp calculations.

Implementation/Length of Demonstration: The project was implemented in the cities of Norfolk and Richmond and Chesterfield County in 1992 and will operate for two years.

Michigan: To Strengthen Michigan Families

Summary: The Michigan demonstration expands eligibility to working and two-parent families, modifies work requirements and strengthens child support provisions. The State agency received a food stamp waiver to exclude, as income and resources, all income earned by dependent children, up to age 19, who are AFDC recipients and students.

Implementation/Project Areas: The Statewide project was implemented October 1, 1992 and will operate for five years.

Utah: Utah Single Parent Employment Project --SPED--

Summary: The Utah SPED project will target AFDC recipients with intensive work requirements designed to transform the AFDC program from a maintenance into an employment program. Exemptions from work requirements will be waived to assign participants to "self-sufficiency" activities. Participants who complete assigned activities will receive incentive payments while those who fail to complete the activities will have their AFDC benefits reduced. Waivers are provided to streamline the eligibility requirements between the AFDC and Food Stamp programs. Households receiving both AFDC and Food Stamp benefits will have the option of receiving food stamp benefits in cash.

Implementation/Project Area: The project will be implemented in one county in early 1993 and will last no longer than 5 years. The State may include additional counties to the project provided the Federal agencies are advised three months ahead of time.

Alabama: Avenues to Self-Sufficiency through Employment and Training --ASSETS--

Summary: The project consolidates AFDC, Food Stamps, and Medicaid. Eligibility criteria for all programs is simplified and handled by a single caseworker, i.e., case management. The project provides food stamp benefits in cash, standardizes benefits, intensifies employment and training activities, enhances child support enforcement activity, and extends Medicaid eligibility. Participation is mandatory.

Implementation/Project Area: The project operates in three counties which were phased in between May 1990 and January 1991. The project is expected to end January 1995.

New York: New York Child Assistance Program --CAP--

Summary: CAP is an assistance program available to recipients of AFDC with earnings and child support orders as an alternative to AFDC. Child assistance payments are made to eligible custodial parents, and are based on household size, and reduced by a portion of the income earned. Food stamp benefits are cashed out under CAP in keeping with the basic concept of CAP, as a non-welfare program designed to give low-income wage earners responsibility for management of their own financial resources. CAP recipients are exempt from food stamp work registration and employment and training requirements.

Implementation/Project Area: Implementation was completed in phases between October 1988 and April 1989. Due to delays in the implementation, the project was extended to end April 1994. CAP operates in seven counties.

Ohio: Ohio Transition to Independence

Summary: The demonstration is an initiative designed to help AFDC recipients become self-sufficient through employment. Two food stamp waivers were approved: the first allowed the State to develop a standard deduction for self-employment business expenses of in-home day care providers; the second waived the $62 monthly bonus incentive for meeting Learning, Earning and Parenting (LEAP) school attendance requirements as household income for food stamp computation.

Implementation/Project Area: The project was implemented in January 1989 and currently operates Statewide.

Washington: Washington Family Independence Program--WFIP--

Summary: WFIP replaces AFDC and Food Stamp benefits for families with children. All benefits are provided in the form of cash. Increased work incentives are reflected in benefit levels which rise with attachment to the work force. Extensive employment and training activities are available to clients, as well as a variety of other supportive services, e.g., child care and transitional benefits. Participation is voluntary.

Implementation/Project Area: The project was implemented in July 1988 and will end June 1993. The project operates in 15 Community Services Offices.

Mr. DURBIN. Also, provide an update on the Disqualified Recipient System, the Software Renewal Project and the State Cooperative Data Exchange project.

Mr. BRALEY. The information will be provided for the record.

[The information follows:]

Disqualified Recipient System

Mandated by Congress, the comprehensive, on-line, menu-driven Disqualified Recipient Subsystem (DRS) has been designed, developed, and tested. The design provides for both pre-certification and post-certification searches of a national database to ensure proper assessment of penalties for intentional Food Stamp Program violations. DRS also includes voice technology whereby caseworkers can query the DRS database directly by telephone.

FNS has entered into a reimbursable agreement with the Social Security Administration for the use of its File Transfer Management System (FTMS) for the DRS transmissions. The sharing of the FTMS electronic highway is an effective use of resources and obviates the need for FNS to acquire telecommunications software and bandwidth for the DRS operation.

FNS will shortly be announcing the operation of DRS via *Federal Register* notice for the first series of States that have matching agreements in place. The DRS database currently has 146,182 disqualification actions on 140,339 violators representing 12 States.

Software Renewal Program

FNS has been successful with its Software Renewal Program (SRP) and as a result, the information architecture to support the Agency's critical program mission and immense fiduciary responsibility has been dramatically enhanced. Software modernization accomplishments under the SRP include the implementation of: Food Stamp Program Integrated Information System (FSPIIS); Special Nutrition Programs Integrated Information System (SNPIIS); Agency Financial Management System (AFMS); and National Data Bank (NDB) System.

The databases primarily consist of program and financial reports received from State agencies and other reporting points for the FNS suite of programs. All report data is available for on-line display as menu selection items. This includes retrieval for 2,836 food stamp project areas for such data as number of households, number of persons, and whether participants are also AFDC recipients.

As a part of the SRP, Coupon Requisition and Inventory Management Subsystem (CRIMS) (developed and implemented as part of FSPIIS) provides the Agency a comprehensive, automated system to support the requisition, distribution, and inventory management of food coupons. CRIMS was used last year in the wake of Hurricanes Andrew and Iniki, and Typhoon Omar, to process orders in one day. Prior to CRIMS, the processing would have required a week. The CRIMS also provides enhanced capabilities for serial number tracking—a feature popular with the OIG.

Currently under development are the coupon Printer Accountability Subsystem (PAS) and the Store Tracking and Redemption Subsystem (STARS). Once implemented, both will provide improved vendor management, program accountability, and management information. STARS is an extension of an earlier Agency initiative, the Redemption Accountability Program (RAP).

The newly implemented AFMS provides the Agency with greatly improved automated accounting and budgeting support to bring the Agency in compliance with JFMIP, Treasury, OMB, and CFO Act requirements. Currently under development as part of Phase 2 is the grants management subsystem. Still awaiting funding under Phase 2 are the budget formulation, administrative funds management, and an Executive Information System (EIS).

The National Data Bank (NDB) System was designed to integrate the most commonly used FNS program and financial data into one official data based for analysis and controlled public release.

The Benefit/Cost Study for the Software Renewal Program (FSPIIS, SNPIIS, AFMS, and NDB) projects a favorable benefit to cost ratio of 2.98 over the systems' life cycle.

State Cooperative Data Exchange

Software to support on-line State Cooperative Data Exchange (SCDEX) functions has been developed and is scheduled for pilot testing in April and May, 1993. As enhancements to the Food Stamp Program Integrated Information System (FSPIIS) and the Special Nutrition Programs Integrated Information System (SNPIIS), these functions will provide users at FNS State agencies with the ability to enter this information directly into FSPIIS and SNPIIS and allow FNS users to review and approve the data entered by the States. Additionally, on-line SCDEX functions will allow State agency users to access program information on-line and print management reports.

On-line SCDEX represents the initial stage of FNS' *Cooperative Data Sharing* in which State agencies will interact directly with FNS' automated systems. In later stages, batch (full EDI) SCDEX functions will provide for data files to be transmitted from the State agency computer systems to the FSPIIS and SNPIIS data bases at the National Computer Center in Kansas City. In the long term it is expected that virtually all data required of organizations which participate in FSP and SNP will be entered through one of these methods—effecting paperless reporting.

NUTRITION EDUCATION

Mr. DURBIN. Included in the fiscal year 1993 appropriation for the food stamp program was $500,000 for a nutrition education initiative. Would you tell us specifically how this money is being used?

Mr. BRALEY. The Food Stamp Nutrition Education Grants will develop creative approaches to providing nutrition education by enhancing food stamp participants' abilities and skills in meal planning, budgeting food money, and purchasing and preparing foods.

The grants will support the development, implementation and evaluation of innovative community-based nutrition education programs directed toward Food Stamp Program participants.

We expect to award these grants through a full and open competition among state food stamp agencies, cooperative extension service agencies, and public and private non-profit organizations. We expect to award 7 to 10 projects before the end of this year. Each project will operate for up to 2 years.

Mr. DURBIN. Mrs. Nelson testified last year that the food stamp program makes available an unlimited amount of funds for nutrition education on a 50/50 match by the States. Would you describe this program in further detail?

Mr. BRALEY. Section 272.2(d)(2) of the Food Stamp Regulations allows States the option to develop Nutrition Education Plans.

Food Stamp Program 50–50 administrative matching funds are provided for state initiated nutrition education plans that are conducted exclusively for the benefit of food stamp applicants and participants. In fiscal year 1992 states spent about $1.2 million of their Federal matching funds on nutrition education activities.

Mr. DURBIN. Seven states have used this option. Please provide a list of the states and a brief description of how money was used?

Mr. BRALEY. In fiscal year 1992 seven States had nutrition education plans approved by the Food and Nutrition Service (FNS): New Hampshire, New York, Ohio, Minnesota, Wisconsin, Oklahoma, and Washington. There is great diversity in the food stamp population targeted and the methodology of the nutrition plans initiated by the states. The plans cover such activities as meal planning, food purchasing, budgeting food stamps, storage and sanitation of food, increasing nutrition knowledge, networking with community agencies and organizations, and providing informational materials.

As a specific example, New Hampshire has prepared a series of lessons called "Great Beginnings." These lessons provide practical nutrition and wellness information to pregnant teens and teen parents who, as a group, are at high risk of having underweight babies.

In fiscal year 1993 two additional states, Maine and Oregon, have nutrition education plans.

Mr. DURBIN. Why don't more states use this program?

Mr. BRALEY. States have the option to develop nutrition education plans. We do not know the reasons why more states do not use this program. USDA encourages states do expend more effort on nutrition education and, as authorized, will match administrative funding on a 50/50 basis. The Department often receives letters pointing out the poor purchasing habits of food stamp recipients. More nutrition education could ameliorate this problem and the diets, and perhaps health of food stamp recipients, could be improved.

QUALITY CONTROL

Mr. DURBIN. At this time last year, one quality control case against Massachusetts was pending a decision from the U.S. District Court. What is the status of this case?

Mr. BRALEY. On April 6, 1992, the United States District Court for the District of Massachusetts upheld the Food and Nutrition Service's (FNS) $1,323,864 quality control (QC) billing action against the Commonwealth of Massachusetts for the April 1982 through September 1982 reporting period. The Court found that the statistical system used by FNS was reasonable and deferred to the agency's expertise in selecting the statistical system to be used.

The Commonwealth appealed the District Court's decision to the United States Court of Appeals for the First Circuit. On January 22, 1993, the U.S. Court of Appeals upheld the statistical methodology adopted by FNS as the basis for QC liabilities. The Court determined that the system adopted by FNS for calculating errors and penalties was not an irrational one that was arbitrarily conceived, profoundly flawed or operated in a wholly capricious manner.

On February 4, 1993, the Commonwealth filed a motion requesting that the First Circuit Court of Appeals reconsider its decision. We are awaiting a decision on this motion.

Mr. DURBIN. For fiscal years 1986 to 1991, state agencies have agreed to settle $300 million in outstanding quality control liabilities. What was the total states were liable for versus how much was actually collected?

Mr. BRALEY. For fiscal years 1986 to 1991, states overissued almost $5.6 billion dollars in Food Stamp benefits. Based on over and underissuance error rates which exceeded the error tolerance level, the Food and Nutrition Service assessed potential liabilities of $300 million for this same period.

Under the terms of the January 19, 1993 settlement agreement, states agreed to invest approximately $45 million into payment accuracy improvements over the next five years. The settlement of these liabilities will provide States with additional resources for improving payment accuracy and administration of the Food Stamp Program.

Two States—Vermont and the Virgin Islands—chose to pay settlement claims rather than investing in program improvements. A total of $7,017 was collected as a result of this decision.

Mr. DURBIN. How many cases do you have for fiscal year 1992?

Mr. BRALEY. Unfortunately, official error rates for fiscal year 1992 will not be available until June 1993. We will furnish them after that time.

For fiscal years 1990 and 1991, eleven states were in a position of liability because of their error rate performance. Based on potential increases in fiscal year 1992 error rates it is possible that there may be more states facing liabilities. The exact number of states, however, will not be available until June.

Mr. DURBIN. You also state that states will invest almost $45 million to improve payment accuracy over the next five years. How much in total do states spend in improving error rates?

Mr. BRALEY. The Food and Nutrition Service does not collect specific information on states' expenditures for error reduction activities. However, we do know that the Federal share of administrative costs for certification activities was $760 million in fiscal year 1991. This amount includes expenditures relating to eligibility determinations which would reflect error reduction activities.

Mr. DURBIN. Two states have chosen to pay settlements as opposed to investing in improvements. Why is this?

Mr. BRALEY. Under the agreed upon terms, Vermont and the Virgin Islands owed $6,262 and $755, respectively. Considering the small amount owed, states decided that direct payment was more cost-effective than investing in improvements.

Both states will continue to engage in corrective action efforts aimed at improving payment accuracy.

ELECTRONIC BENEFIT TRANSFER

Mr. DURBIN. The final rule for Electronic Benefit Transfer or EBT allowing states to implement EBT as an operational alternative was to be effective April 1, 1992. Was this date met?

Mr. BRALEY. The final EBT rule was published on April 1, 1992, effective immediately.

Mr. DURBIN. How many state agencies are operating an EBT system and how many are in the planning stages?

Mr. BRALEY. There are currently 5 states with operating EBT systems for food stamps: Pennsylvania—Reading; New Mexico—San Bernalillo County—Albuquerque; Minnesota—Ramsey County—St. Paul; Maryland—Baltimore County; soon to be statewide; and Ohio—Dayton.

According to our information, there are approximately 25 other states that are in the process of implementing, developing, or planning for the implementation of EBT systems. Of these, the furthest along are: Iowa—plans to implement food stamp EBT late Spring; New Jersey—contractor is developing EBT system; South Carolina—reviewing contractor proposals; and Texas—has issued a request for proposals.

Mr. DURBIN. I understand that as of April, Maryland will be operating statewide in providing benefits through the use of EBT. Does this mean coupons will no longer be used in Maryland?

Mr. BRALEY. In June, not April, coupons will be virtually eliminated in Maryland. A two month delay has occurred because of a backlog in training clients in Baltimore City. The Food Nutrition Service (FNS) requires that all clients receive Electronic Benefit Training (EBT) before their benefits are issued by EBT. After all clients are on EBT the only coupons retained by the state will be for converting EBT balances for clients who are moving out of Maryland.

Some leftover coupons are probably still in the possession of Maryland clients. Also, clients from bordering states will probably bring coupons into Maryland stores. Stores that are authorized by FNS in Maryland must accept paper or EBT benefits.

PROPOSED FOOD STAMP INCREASE

Mr. DURBIN. The President's fiscal year 1994 proposal includes $603 million for the food stamp program and $7.0 billion over the next four years to increase benefits and help offset the effects of the proposed energy tax on low-income households. Specifically, how will this increase be used to offset the proposed energy tax?

Mr. BRALEY. The concurrent resolution on the budget for fiscal year 1994 recently passed by the House of Representatives would provide $585 million in fiscal year 1994 outlays and $7.505 billion in outlays over the next five years to fund increases in the Food Stamp Program. While the details of our proposals are still under discussion, we do note that the House Budget Committee's report accompanying the concurrent budget resolution indicates the increases would allow funding of the Mickey Leland Childhood Hunger Relief Act. The Senate Budget Committee's report suggests proposals to increase benefits for nearly all households, provide relief for high shelter costs, and relax the treatment of vehicles in the asset test. Whatever is included in the final package will result in low income households receiving more food assistance than under current law. This additional assistance will, when added to increases in the Earned Income Tax Credit (EITC) and Low-Income Energy Assistance Program (LIEAP), help to offset any adverse financial impacts from the proposed energy tax.

LIMITING ADMINISTRATIVE COSTS

Mr. DURBIN. The Secretary testified that beginning April 1, 1994, all state welfare administrative expenses would be limited to a 50-percent match with Federal funds. As I understand it, food stamp administrative expenses are currently at that level. Please explain this in further detail.

Mr. BRALEY. The President is seeking to eliminate enhanced funding for certain activities in the Food Stamp, Aid to families with Dependent Children and Medicaid programs. Within the Food Stamp Program, this includes anti-fraud investigations which is now funded at 75 percent, some data processing system development which is funded at 63 percent, and verification of the documented alien status of applicants through the Systematic Alien Verification for Entitlements systems which is now funded at 100 percent. Under the president's proposal, each of these higher rates would be reduced to 50 percent.

FOOD STAMP CASH-OUT PROJECTS

Mr. DURBIN. When do you expect to have a final analysis on the food stamp cash-out projects being conducted in Alabama and San Diego, California?

Mr. BRALEY. In January 1993, FNS released two reports on the effects of food stamp cash-out on participating households in San Diego, California and on participating households and administrative costs in Alabama. In the summer of 1993, FNS will release a report on the effects of cash-out on administrative costs, program participation and food retailers in San Diego, California. The Executive Summaries of each report will be provided for the record.

[The information follows:]

EXECUTIVE SUMMARY

This Executive Summary describes the impacts of the San Diego Food Stamp Cash-Out Demonstration on the food-purchasing and food-use patterns of Food Stamp Program (FSP) recipients. Under the demonstration, which is taking place in San Diego County, California, food stamp recipients receive their program benefits as checks, rather than as the traditional food coupons.

This report is the first of two that will present findings from the San Diego evaluation. This report focuses on the impacts of cash-out on food stamp recipients; the second, which will be prepared after additional experience with full cash-out has been accumulated, will consider effects on administrative costs, program participation, the vulnerability of the issuance system to fraud, and the operations of food retailers in San Diego County.

POLICY CONTEXT

The debate about how benefits should be paid out under the FSP has been of long standing. Advocates of the current coupon system argue that coupons are a direct and inexpensive way to ensure that food stamp benefits are used to purchase food. Coupon advocates contend that, despite some evidence of fraud and benefit diversion under the current system, the unauthorized use of food stamps is relatively limited. In addition, they contend that coupons provide some measure of protection to food budgets from other demands on limited household resources.

Advocates of cashing out the FSP argue that the current system limits the food-purchasing choices of recipients and places a stigma on participation. Moreover, they cite the cumbersome nature and cost of coupon issuance, transaction, and redemption.

The current debate about the desirability of one form of benefit over the other is limited by the paucity of available empirical evidence comparing coupon and cash food benefits. The U.S. Department of Agriculture, Food and Nutrition Service (FNS) conducted two studies in the early 1980s: (1) the Supplemental Security Income/Elderly Demonstration, and (2) the Puerto Rico Nutrition Assistance Program (NAP) evaluation. Although both studies produced valuable findings, they examined cash-out as applied to highly atypical food stamp populations--in the first instance, to elderly participants in the program, and, in the second, to the extremely-low-income Puerto Rico food stamp caseload. Thus, the results of these studies could not be reliably generalized to the broader food stamp caseload.

Therefore, it is important to obtain additional information about the effects of cash-out, so as to better inform the policy debate. The San Diego Food Stamp Cash-Out Demonstration has been designed to allow a rigorous evaluation of the effects of cash-out. The San Diego demonstration is one of four tests of the cash-out approach that FNS has undertaken since 1989. The other three are (1) the Washington State Family Independence Program (FIP), (2) the Alabama Avenues to Self-Sufficiency through Employment and Training Services (ASSETS) Demonstration, and (3) the Alabama "Pure" Cash-Out Demonstration.

The Washington State FIP and the Alabama ASSETS demonstrations are testing cash-out in conjunction with other changes in the welfare systems in those states. However, the Alabama "Pure" Cash-Out Demonstration, like the San Diego demonstration, is testing cash-out without any other changes. Comparisons of the latter two evaluations, when the results of both are available, will, therefore, be of particular interest.

THE DEMONSTRATION AND ITS SETTING

The San Diego Food Stamp Cash-Out Demonstration was implemented in two stages. During the first stage, which extended from July of 1989 through August of 1990, a randomly selected sample of 20 percent of the food stamp caseload in San Diego County was cashed out. During the second stage, which began in September of 1990, cash-out was extended to the full caseload.

San Diego County is the southernmost county in California. The western half of the county, which contains most of the county's population (and most of the food stamp caseload), includes San Diego City and is highly urbanized. Overall, the county contains approximately 2.4 million persons, 175,000 of whom received food stamps in a typical month in 1991.

A relatively high proportion of the food stamp caseload in San Diego (88 percent) receives Aid to Families with Dependent Children (AFDC) assistance. This proportion, which is far higher than that for the national food stamp caseload, reflects principally two factors: First, Supplemental Security Income (SSI) recipients in California receive food stamp benefits as part of their SSI benefits and do not apply for food stamps separately. Thus, many elderly and disabled people who would be part of the food stamp caseload in most other states are not directly included in the program in California, making the proportion of AFDC cases higher. Second, during the time covered by the evaluation, California had one of the most generous AFDC payment levels in the nation. As a result, households who would not have qualified for AFDC assistance in many other states were eligible for AFDC in California.

Because AFDC income is relatively high, food stamp benefit levels, relative to household income, are lower in San Diego than they are in many parts of the country. The percentage of food stamp benefits as compared with overall household income plus food stamp benefits is 12 percent in the San Diego food stamp caseload, compared with 23 percent nationally.

It is important that these aspects of the FSP in San Diego County be kept in mind when assessing the evaluation findings reported in this summary. They also highlight the importance of considering the San Diego findings jointly with the results of the other cash-out evaluations, which are under way.

RESEARCH QUESTIONS AND OUTCOME VARIABLES

The findings presented in this report address the following research questions:

What are the effects of cash-out on the value of purchased and nonpurchased food used at home?

The regular coupon-based FSP provides benefits that can legally be used to purchase only non-restaurant food. This earmarking is intended to further the program's stated objective of "raising the levels of nutrition among low-income households," by encouraging household purchases of food for home use. Thus, the program's direct impact is expected to be on the amounts of food purchased for home use. The analysis reported here examines the effects of cash-out on the value of purchased food used at home in order to obtain direct evidence as to whether cash-out alters the means (that is, food purchases) through which the program is expected to affect nutrition.

The principal measure in the study of the value of purchased food used at home is based on detailed survey data on the value of purchased food used at home by households during the seven days that preceded a survey conducted for the evaluation. In parts of the analysis, this measure is adjusted for differences in household size and composition by dividing the value of food used by the number of "adult male equivalent" (AME) persons in the household. This measure states household size in terms of the number of adult males that would be expected to consume the same amount of food as that consumed by the household, given its age and gender composition. A second adjustment measure, "equivalent nutrition units" (ENU), further adjusts household size to control for differences between households in the percentages of meals that household members eat from the home food supply.

The analysis also examines effects on the money value of *all* food used at home. Although food coupons and food checks only *directly* affect purchased food, cash-out might have effects on nonpurchased food, as well, by making households more likely or less likely to make use of food received through direct government food programs, food received as gifts, or home-grown food. Therefore, it is important to assess not only effects on purchased food, but also effects on all food used at home.

The principal outcome variable for the analysis of the value of all food used at home is drawn from the same survey as the outcome variables described above. The dollar values of nonpurchased food were estimated by using imputed prices based on prices of similar items in the data for purchased foods.

What are the effects of cash-out on nutrient availability?

To the extent that the value of food used at home is altered by cash-out, this alteration may be associated with changes in the nutrients available to members of the household. Average levels of nutrient availability are examined in comparison with recommended dietary allowances (RDA) for key nutrients for members of the household.

Does cash-out lead to households running out of food?

Critics of the cash-out approach have been concerned that, under cash-out, households might spend their benefits on other goods and services soon after receiving the benefits and, consequently, might run out of food by the end of the month. It is important to assess whether this has happened. The analysis is based largely on survey responses to questions about the adequacy of the food available to the household in the month preceding the survey.

Does cash-out lead households to switch to food purchased and used away from home?

In general, coupon benefits cannot be used in restaurants. However, cash benefits may be used to purchase food in any location. Therefore, it is of interest to consider whether cash-out leads households to switch their food expenditures from food used at home to food purchased away from home. This issue is examined by analyzing both the absolute value of food purchased away from home and the share of all food expenditures from food used away from home.

Does cash-out result in switches to or away from other expenditure categories?

To the extent that cash-out affects expenditures for food, it is of interest to examine what other types of consumption items may also be affected. To examine this issue, the study has analyzed changes in the shares of consumption expenditures for all major categories of goods and services.

What are the attitudes of program participants toward cash-out?

A full assessment of the cash-out approach must consider how program participants perceive cash-out. Of particular interest are their attitudes toward the relative flexibility of cash-out and to potential problems in food budgeting created by the use of checks. We use the survey data to examine these issues.

What experiences have clients had when cashing food stamp checks?

It is important to assess whether the value of food stamp benefits to program participants is significantly eroded by any fees that clients may have to pay in order to cash their checks. We use the survey data to examine this and other possible difficulties in the check-cashing process.

RESEARCH DESIGN

During the first year of the cash-out demonstration, the cash-out policies were implemented only for a randomly selected sample of 20 percent of the San Diego food stamp caseload. For much of the analysis of the impacts of cash-out reported in this summary, data obtained during this period of limited cash-out were used to make comparisons between check recipients and coupon recipients. Because the cash-out participants during this period were selected randomly, we can expect them to have similar characteristics to the coupon recipients, except for statistical sampling error. Therefore, any systematic differences observed between the groups can be attributed to cash-out.

This report is based largely on data obtained from an in-person survey of approximately 600 check recipients and 600 coupon recipients that was conducted between May and August of 1990. The survey obtained detailed information on household composition and income receipt. It also collected very extensive data on the foods used by each household during the seven days preceding the interview. In the survey, respondents were also asked questions about their households' attitudes toward and experiences with cash-out. The survey attained an overall response rate of 78 percent: 79 percent for coupon recipients, and 77 percent for check recipients.

To supplement this survey information, we also draw in this report on information obtained during two focus group discussions with FSP participants. The discussions were held in San Diego County with participants who had previously received their benefits as coupons, but whose benefit form had been converted to checks. The focus groups enabled us to explore issues related to client experiences with cash-out in greater depth than was possible in the structured survey.

FINDINGS

The following sections summarize the key findings of the study concerning each of the research questions highlighted previously.

Effects on the Money Value of Food Used at Home

The evidence from the household survey suggests that cash-out had a relatively small, but statistically significant, downward impact on household food use. The weekly value of purchased food used at home (the measure of food use that is most directly affected by the FSP) was $5.17, or 7.5 percent, lower for check recipients than for coupon recipients (Table 1). This difference is statistically significant at the 95 percent confidence level. When the measure is scaled by ENUs, which adjusts for differences in household composition and differences in the numbers of meals eaten at home, the relative magnitude of the estimated effect is essentially unchanged. In this case, the estimated effect is a reduction of $2.42 per ENU, or 6.8 percent.

We found similar results for the weekly value of *all* food used at home, including both purchased and nonpurchased food received through food-assistance programs or as gifts. The money value of all food used at home by check-recipient households is 6.6 percent lower than that used by coupon-recipient households.

Taken together, these findings strongly suggest that cash-out reduced the effectiveness of the FSP in stimulating food use. The resultant reductions in the value of food used at home ranged from 5 percent to 8 percent.

Of particular concern is whether cash-out affects food use by food stamp recipients who tend to use relatively low amounts of food and who, therefore, are presumably at greatest nutritional risk. To examine this issue, we compared food use for different quartiles of households, as defined by their food use per ENU. The results indicate that cash-out had no discernable effect on the use of food at home per ENU by households that are in the lower end of the distribution of food use.

TABLE 1

MONEY VALUE OF FOOD USED AT HOME

	Mean Value		Difference in Means		
	Check	Coupon	Absolute	Percentage	t-Statistic
Money Value of Purchased Food Used at Home (dollars per week)					
For the overall household	63.94	69.11	-5.17	-7.48	2.09††
Per equivalent nutrition unit for energy[a]	33.28	35.70	-2.42	-6.78	2.45††
Money Value of all Food Used at Home (dollars per week)					
For the overall household	68.00	72.82	-4.82	-6.62	1.88††
Per equivalent nutrition unit for energy[a]	35.95	37.63	-1.68	-4.46	1.62†

SOURCE: Evaluation of the San Diego Food Stamp Cash-Out Demonstration, household survey, weighted tabulations.

[a]Household size in "equivalent nutrition units" is an adjusted measure of household size that takes into account differences in food energy requirements among households with different compositions in terms of the ages, genders, and pregnancy and lactation statuses of household members. In addition, this measure takes into account the percentages of meals eaten at home by household members, as well as meals served by the households to guests.

†Statistically significant at the 90 percent confidence level, one-tailed test.
††Statistically significant at the 95 percent confidence level, one-tailed test.

Recipients of food stamp checks in San Diego reduced their food costs by cutting back on the overall quantity of food used and by shifting their purchases from higher-priced food groups to lower-priced food groups. These savings were partially offset by the tendency of check recipients to use foods from specific food groups that were higher priced than those used by coupon recipients.

Nutrient Availability

The reductions in the money value of food used at home resulting from cash-out were accompanied by decreases in the amounts of food energy and protein contained in the food that was used (Table 2). These reductions, although relatively small (roughly 5 percent each), are statistically significant.

When assessing these findings, it is important to note that underconsumption of food energy and protein is not considered to be a health problem for most Americans. Ninety-seven percent of the sample was estimated to be attaining the RDA of protein; this percentage was essentially unchanged by cash-out. Thus, the reduction in the average availability of protein does not appear to be a problem.

However, for food energy, the percentage of households attaining the RDA was about 5 percentage points lower for check than for coupon recipients (69 percent versus 74 percent), and the difference is statistically significant. This finding suggests that the demonstration had an adverse effect on the consumption of food energy for some households.

The evaluation also examined the effects of the demonstration on the use of seven micronutrients that are regarded as potentially problematic from a public health perspective (Table 2). The effects of cash-out on nutrient availability were found to be generally small and insignificant. Statistically significant negative effects on nutrient availability were estimated for two of the seven micronutrients, with the estimated effects ranging from 4 percent to 4.5 percent. The demonstration had no statistically significant effects on the percentages of households attaining the RDA for any of the seven micronutrients.

The limited impacts of cash-out on the availability of the micronutrients may reflect the greater "nutrient efficiency" of the foods used by check recipients. The ratio of the availability of the micronutrients to the availability of food energy was higher for cash-out recipients for six of the seven micronutrients studied; however, only one of these differences is statistically significant at the 90 percent confidence level. Some participants in the focus group discussions, which we have referred to previously, indicated their belief that checks helped them to purchase food more economically. The participants felt that the checks did so by allowing them to shop at stores that generally do not accept food stamp coupons, such as farm stands and large discount stores.

Impacts on Households Running Out of Food

Cash-out did not increase the incidence of acute shortages of food in households. Indeed, as shown in Table 3, the percentage of households that reported having insufficient amounts of food at some point during the month preceding the survey was 4 percentage points higher for *coupon* recipients than for check recipients (31 percent versus 27 percent). However, this difference is not statistically significant.

TABLE 2

NUTRIENT AVAILABILITY PER EQUIVALENT NUTRITION UNIT
(Nutrient Levels as a Percentage of the RDA)

	Mean Value		Difference in Means		
Nutrient	Check	Coupon	Absolute	Percentage	t-Statistic
Food Energy	133.58	140.00	-6.42	-4.59	1.76††
Protein	249.34	263.08	-13.73	-5.22	1.98††
Vitamin A	210.92	214.40	-3.49	-1.63	0.38
Vitamin C	265.51	276.14	-10.63	-3.85	0.75
Vitamin B_6	154.96	161.56	-6.59	-4.08	1.38†
Folate	225.38	230.54	-5.15	-2.24	0.54
Calcium	118.25	123.72	-5.47	-4.42	1.36†
Iron	163.43	160.61	2.82	1.76	0.49
Zinc	119.60	123.73	-4.13	-3.33	1.21

SOURCE: Evaluation of the San Diego Food Stamp Cash-Out Demonstration, household survey, weighted tabulations.

RDA = recommended dietary allowance.

†Statistically significant at the 90 percent confidence level, one-tailed test.
††Statistically significant at the 95 percent confidence level, one-tailed test.

TABLE 3

RESPONDENT REPORTS OF THE ADEQUACY OF AVAILABLE FOOD
(During Previous Month)

	Mean Value		Difference in Means		
	Check	Coupon	Absolute	Percentage	t-Statistic
Respondents Reporting Household Did Not Have "Enough" Food Some Days	26.88	30.90	-4.02	-13.01	1.50
Respondents Reporting Household Members Had to Skip Meals	17.77 ·	21.63	-3.86	-17.85	1.64
Respondents Reporting Household Made Use of Food Banks or Food Pantries	9.86	6.66	3.20	48.05	1.97 **
Respondents Reporting Household Used Surplus Commodities	8.03	5.20	2.82	54.23	1.87 *

SOURCE: Evaluation of the San Diego Food Stamp Cash-Out Demonstration, household survey, weighted tabulations.

*Statistically significant at the 90 percent confidence level, two-tailed test.
**Statistically significant at the 95 percent confidence level, two-tailed test.

As indicated in Table 3, this finding is based on an interview question that asked respondents if they had always had "enough" food during the month. We do not know exactly how respondents interpreted the concept of "enough" food. However, it is interesting that substantial numbers of households believed that they had not had "enough" food on one or more days during the month, even though Table 2 shows the average caloric content of the food used to substantially exceed the relevant RDAs. This difference may reflect several factors. First, although average caloric availability might have exceeded the RDAs, substantial numbers of households were below the RDAs. Second, households that were well above the RDAs for the month as a whole might have been below them at certain times during the month. Third, there may be discrepancies between households' self-definitions of "enough" and the RDAs.

Coupon recipients were also somewhat more likely than check recipients to report that one or more household members had to skip meals during that month because food was unavailable. Again, however, the difference is not statistically significant.

One way that check recipients avoided acute food shortages was by making somewhat greater use than coupon recipients of food pantries and food banks. Approximately 10 percent of check recipients reported having used these food sources in the month preceding the survey, compared with 7 percent of coupon recipients. The difference is statistically significant.

Check recipients were also were more likely than coupon recipients to participate in government commodity distribution programs. Eight percent of check recipients used surplus commodities, compared with approximately 5 percent of coupon recipients, a statistically significant difference.

Impacts on the Purchase of Food Used Away from Home

Cash-out did not have any significant effect on the purchase of food used away from home. Contrary to expectations, the weekly expenditures for food prepared and used away from home were actually lower for check recipients than for coupon recipients ($3.00 per AME versus $3.48 per AME); however, the difference is not statistically significant. Similarly, check recipients reported eating a slightly lower percentage of their meals away from home, but the difference is not statistically significant. These results suggest that the reductions that we have reported in the money value of food used at home did not result from a shift to meals purchased outside of the home.

Impacts on Other Types of Consumption

The reductions in the money value of food used at home resulting from cash-out were accompanied by a decrease of 1.6 percentage points in the share of total household expenditures allocated to food (Table 4). In three expenditure categories--housing, medical costs, and education--the increases in expenditure shares were statistically significant.

Participant Attitudes Toward Cash-Out

Virtually all members of the focus groups preferred checks to coupons. The major reasons cited for this preference were: no stigma is associated with receiving and using check benefits, check

TABLE 4

DISTRIBUTION OF EXPENDITURES, BY EXPENDITURE CATEGORY
(Entries Are Percentages of Total Expenditures in Each Category)

	Mean Value		Difference in Means		
Expenditure Category	Check	Coupon	Absolute	Percentage	t-Statistic
All Food	32.38	33.95	-1.57	-4.62	-2.11††
Food used at home	29.87	31.18	-1.31	-4.20	-1.80††
Food used away from home	2.51	2.77	-0.27	-9.75	-0.94
Shelter	51.42	49.42	2.00	4.01	2.02††
Housing	43.89	42.37	1.52	3.59	1.49†
Utilities	7.53	7.05	0.48	6.81	1.19
Medical	0.85	0.43	0.42	97.67	2.43††
Transportation	6.37	6.45	-0.08	-1.24	-0.14
Clothing	3.97	4.35	-0.38	-8.74	-1.04
Education	0.49	0.32	0.17	53.13	1.65††
Dependent Care	0.63	0.87	-0.24	-27.59	-1.11
Recreation	2.31	2.52	-0.21	-8.33	-0.77
Personal Items	1.58	1.69	-0.11	-6.51	-0.98
Total	100.00	100.00			

SOURCE: Evaluation of the San Diego Food Stamp Cash-Out Demonstration, household survey, weighted tabulations.

†Statistically significant at the 90 percent confidence level, one-tailed test.
††Statistically significant at the 95 percent confidence level, one-tailed test.

benefits promote a feeling of self-esteem, checks allow increased flexibility in purchasing decisions, checks make it possible to shop at a wider range of stores, and checks make shopping and budgeting easier.

Survey respondents were asked a series of open-ended questions about the aspects of check and of coupon issuance that they thought were good and bad. The advantage of checks most commonly cited by check recipients in the survey was that checks could be used to purchase items other than food. This advantage was mentioned by 42 percent of check respondents (Table 5). The other two advantages that were mentioned by more than 10 percent of respondents were that check benefits allow recipients to shop at a wider range of food stores, and that checks make it possible to avoid embarrassment when using food assistance.

Coupon recipients tended to cite as an advantage of coupon issuance the fact that coupons ensured that food benefits were spent on food. Fifty-five percent of the coupon recipients who responded to the survey mentioned this characteristic. A related advantage of coupons, that they make it possible to budget food expenses better, was mentioned by 10 percent of coupon recipients.

Check-Cashing Experiences of Participants

Thirty-eight percent of check recipients cashed their food checks at a supermarket, grocery, or other food store, and another 35 percent cashed or deposited them at a bank (Table 6). Most of these establishments did not charge fees for cashing FSP checks. However, 19 percent of check recipients used check-cashing agencies, which did charge fees.

The majority of recipients (63 percent) paid no fee to cash their checks. Most of the rest (29 percent of recipients) paid a fee of $5 or less. Eight percent paid a fee that was higher than $5.

CONCLUSIONS

The potential impact of cash-out on the ability of the FSP to target its benefits specifically to food has been a central component of the policy debate about the desirability of this policy alternative. Opponents of cash-out have been concerned that issuing benefits in the form of checks would greatly weaken the program's impacts on food use; proponents have felt that the purchase of food would remain a high priority for recipients, even without the specific linkages to food purchases provided by coupons.

The evidence from the San Diego Cash-Out Demonstration suggests that, in San Diego County, cash-out reduced food expenditures more than its proponents had hoped, but less than its critics had feared. Statistically significant decreases in the value of food used at home were observed, but these differences were relatively small--on the order of 6 percent to 8 percent. Similarly, evidence showed that the availability of food energy and protein decreased, but the effects were relatively small.

In making an overall assessment of cash-out, it is important to remember that effects on food use by FSP recipients, although very important, are only one of several criteria against which this policy alternative must be judged. Effects on administrative costs, program participation, the operations of food retailers, and the vulnerability of the issuance system to fraud are other potentially important factors. The concluding chapter of this report summarizes how we will address these issues in a subsequent report.

TABLE 5

MOST COMMONLY MENTIONED ADVANTAGES OF CHECKS AND COUPONS

	Percentage of Respondents Mentioning Advantage
Advantages of Checks[a]	
Can be used for items other than food	42.1
More choices of food stores	19.0
Do not feel embarrassed	16.2
Advantages of Coupons[b]	
Make sure benefits spent on food	55.4
Can budget food expenses better	10.1

SOURCE: Evaluation of the San Diego Food Stamp Cash-Out Demonstration, household survey, weighted tabulations.

[a]Sample limited to check recipients.

[b]Sample limited to coupon recipients.

TABLE 6

CHECK-CASHING EXPERIENCES OF CHECK RECIPIENTS

Check-Cashing Experience	Percentage of Respondents
Place Where Check Is Usually Cashed or Deposited	
Supermarket or grocery store	31.0
Other food store	6.9
Bank	34.7
Check-cashing outlet	19.3
Other	8.1
Fee Paid to Have Check Cashed	
$0	63.3
$0.01 to $2.00	23.0
$2.01 to $5.00	6.0
$5.01 to $10.00	5.0
$10.01 or more	2.6

SOURCE: Evaluation of the San Diego Food Stamp Cash-Out Demonstration, household survey, weighted tabulations.

EXECUTIVE SUMMARY

The Alabama Food Stamp Cash-Out Demonstration took place in 12 of Alabama's 67 counties during the period May through December, 1990. Under the demonstration, a small percentage of randomly selected food stamp recipients received their program benefits in the form of checks, rather than in the traditional coupon form. This report describes the impacts of the demonstration on the food-purchasing and food-use patterns of Food Stamp Program (FSP) recipients. It also describes the planning and implementation of the demonstration and assesses the impacts of cash-out on the costs of administering the FSP.

POLICY CONTEXT

The form of the benefits provided under the FSP has been an issue of long-standing debate. Advocates of the current coupon system argue that coupons are a direct and inexpensive way to ensure that food stamp benefits are used to purchase food. They contend that, despite some evidence of fraud and benefit diversion under the current system, the unauthorized use of food stamps is relatively limited. In addition, they contend that coupons provide some measure of protection to food budgets from other demands on limited household resources.

Advocates of cashing out food stamp benefits argue that the current system limits the food-purchasing choices of recipients and places a stigma on participation in the program. Moreover, they cite the cumbersome nature and cost of coupon issuance, transaction, and redemption.

The current debate about the desirability of one form of food stamp benefit over the other is limited by the paucity of available empirical evidence comparing coupon and cash food benefits. The U.S. Department of Agriculture, Food and Nutrition Service (FNS) conducted two studies in the early 1980s: (1) the evaluation of the Supplemental Security Income/Elderly Cash-Out Demonstration, and (2) the evaluation of Puerto Rico's Nutrition Assistance Program. Although both studies produced useful findings, they examined cash-out as applied to highly atypical food stamp populations--in the first instance, to elderly participants in the program, and, in the second, to participants in Puerto Rico, whose incomes are very low relative to those of participants in the mainland United States. Thus, the results of those studies could not be reliably generalized to the broader food stamp caseload.

Therefore, it is important to obtain additional information about the effects of cash-out, so as to better inform the policy debate. The Alabama Food Stamp Cash-Out Demonstration has been designed to allow a rigorous evaluation of the effects of cash-out. The Alabama demonstration is one of four tests of the cash-out approach that FNS has undertaken since 1989. The other three are: (1) the Washington State Family Independence Program (FIP), (2) the Alabama Avenues to Self-Sufficiency through Employment and Training Services (ASSETS) Demonstration, and (3) the San Diego Food Stamp Cash-Out Demonstration.

The Washington State FIP and the Alabama ASSETS demonstrations are testing cash-out in conjunction with other changes in the welfare systems in those states. However, the Alabama Food Stamp Cash-Out Demonstration, like the San Diego demonstration, is testing cash-out without any other changes. Therefore, it is of particular interest to compare the latter two evaluations. This report provides a number of such comparisons.

THE TIMING OF THE DEMONSTRATION

The Alabama Food Stamp Cash-Out Demonstration was implemented in two urban and ten rural counties in May of 1990. In those counties, approximately 4 percent of the existing caseload and 4 percent of new cases that entered the FSP over the course of the demonstration were randomly selected to receive benefits in the form of checks. December of 1990 was the last month in which cash benefits were issued under the demonstration. As of the date of this report, Alabama continues to issue cash benefits to food stamp recipients in three counties under the separate ASSETS Demonstration.

THE SETTING OF THE DEMONSTRATION

Alabama has a population of 4 million people. On average, those people are more likely to reside in rural areas than is true for the population of the United States as a whole. In addition, residents of Alabama are more likely to be unemployed or to have low incomes than is the case nationwide; Alabama's unemployment rate is one-third higher, and its average per capita income is 20 percent lower, than are those of the United States as a whole.

Alabama's low-income population depends heavily on food stamps. In 1989, 11 percent of the residents of Alabama received food stamps; only six states and the District of Columbia had higher proportions of residents receiving food stamps. At $146 in July of 1989, the average household food stamp benefit in Alabama was 10 percent higher than the $135 average in the United States as a whole. This difference is due, in part, to low levels of cash assistance benefits in Alabama. General Assistance is not available in Alabama, and Aid to Families with Dependent Children (AFDC) provides low benefit levels; in 1990, Alabama's maximum monthly AFDC payment of $118 for a three-person family was the lowest in the nation. Compared with food stamp households nationwide, a higher proportion of food stamp households in Alabama earn income, but the average amount of earned income is relatively low. In addition, food stamp households in Alabama are 60 percent more likely than food stamp households nationwide to be elderly.

These characteristics of Alabama and of those of its residents who are served by the FSP should be kept in mind when assessing the findings from the Alabama Food Stamp Cash-Out Demonstration and when attempting to generalize from those findings to other areas of the United States. The many large differences between food stamp households in Alabama and elsewhere (including other rural states and states with low AFDC benefits) suggest that the Alabama findings might generalize poorly to many other states. These factors highlight the importance of considering the Alabama findings jointly with the findings from the other contemporaneous cash-out evaluations.

RESEARCH QUESTIONS AND OUTCOME VARIABLES: RECIPIENT IMPACTS

This report addresses questions pertaining to the impacts of cash-out on recipients of food stamp benefits and on the administration of the FSP. The research questions and methodologies pertaining to the impacts of cash-out on food stamp recipients are identical in the evaluations of the Alabama and San Diego Food Stamp Cash-Out Demonstrations. They are as follows:

Does cash-out lead to reductions in the money value of food used at home? The regular coupon-based FSP provides benefits that, in general, can legally be used to purchase food only at authorized outlets, and to purchase only those items that are eligible under program regulations. This earmarking of benefits is intended to further the stated objective of the FSP of "raising the levels of nutrition among low-income households" by encouraging recipient households to purchase food for use at home. Thus, the program's direct impact is expected to be on the amounts of food purchased for use at home. The analysis presented in this report examines the effects of cash-out on the money value of purchased food used at home in order to obtain direct evidence as to whether cash out reduces the means (that is, the use of purchased food at home) through which the FSP is expected to affect nutrition.

The principal outcome measure in the analysis of the money value of purchased food used at home is based on detailed survey data on the use of food at home by households during the seven days that preceded a survey conducted as part of the evaluation. In some components of the analysis, we adjust this measure for differences in household size and composition by dividing the money value of food used by the number of "adult male equivalent" (AME) persons in the household. This measure states a household's size in terms of the number of adult males that would be expected to consume the same amount of food as the household would be expected to consume, given its age and gender composition. We also use a second adjusted measure of household size, the number of "equivalent nutrition units" (ENUs), which further adjusts a household's size to control for the percentage of all meals that its members eat from the home food supply.

The analysis also examines effects on the money value of *all* food used at home, including both purchased food and nonpurchased food. Although spending food coupons and food checks can *directly* affect the use of purchased food only, cash-out might have *indirect* effects on the use of nonpurchased food by making households more likely to use food received through government commodity distribution programs, food received from food pantries or other charitable organizations, food received as gifts from friends and relatives, or home-produced food. Therefore, it is important to assess not only the effects of cash-out on purchased food used at home, but also its effects on all food used at home.

The outcome measures for the analysis of the money value of all food used at home are drawn from the same survey as were the outcome measures described previously. They include measures adjusted for household age and gender composition, as well as for the percentage of meals eaten at home. We estimated the dollar value of nonpurchased food used by a household by using imputed prices; the imputed prices were the average values of the reported prices of similar food items that had been purchased by the households participating in the survey.

Does cash-out lead to reductions in the nutrients available to household members? To the extent that cash-out leads to reductions in the use of food at home, there might be associated reductions in the nutrients available to household members. For both check households and coupon households, we examine the average levels of nutrient availability in relation to the recommended dietary allowances (RDAs) for key nutrients.

Does cash-out lead households to run out of food? Critics of food stamp cash-out have been concerned that, under this form of benefit issuance, households might spend their benefits on nonfood products and services and, consequently, might run out of food by the end of each month. It is important to assess whether households ran out of food in the Alabama Food Stamp Cash-Out Demonstration. The analysis is based largely on the reported perceptions of respondents to the household survey regarding the adequacy of the food available to their households in the month preceding the survey.

Does cash-out lead households to switch to food purchased and used away from home? In general, coupon benefits cannot be used in restaurants. However, cash benefits can be used to purchase food in any location. Therefore, it is of interest to consider whether cash-out leads households to switch their food expenditures from food used at home to food purchased and used away from home. We examine this issue by analyzing both the money value of food purchased away from home and the share of all food expenditures accounted for by food used away from home.

Does cash-out result in shifts of spending to nonfood consumption categories? To the extent that cash-out leads to reduced expenditures for food, it might lead to increased expenditures for other types of consumption items. To examine this issue, the study analyzes the shares of expenditures for all major categories of consumer goods and services.

What are the attitudes of program participants toward cash-out? A full assessment of the cash-out approach to food stamp benefit issuance must consider how program participants perceive check benefits relative to coupon benefits. Of particular interest are participants' attitudes toward the relative flexibility of check benefits and toward the potential food-budgeting problems created by the use of checks. We use survey and focus group data to examine these issues.

What experiences have clients had when cashing food stamp checks? It is important to assess whether the value of food stamp benefits to program participants is significantly eroded by any fees that clients might have to pay in order to cash their checks. We use the survey data to examine this and other possible difficulties in the check-cashing process.

RESEARCH QUESTIONS AND OUTCOME VARIABLES: ADMINISTRATIVE OUTCOMES

The Alabama demonstration provided cash benefits to only four percent of the food stamp caseload in 12 out of 67 counties, whereas the San Diego demonstration provided cash benefits to all food stamp recipients after an initial period of providing cash benefits to 20 percent of the caseload. As a consequence of these design differences, the San Diego demonstration can support a more comprehensive analysis of the impacts of cash-out on administrative outcomes. This report addresses the following research questions pertaining to the impacts of cash-out in Alabama on FSP administrative outcomes.

What tasks and staff were involved in planning and implementing the Alabama Food-Stamp Cash-Out Demonstration? Analyzing the process of planning, implementing, and operating cash-out in Alabama aids in understanding the demonstration's impact on recipient behaviors, administrative costs, and losses. The process analysis also aids in assessing the degree to which the Alabama experience can be generalized to other states, and the potential usefulness of the demonstration experience for developing future policy. This analysis is based on Alabama Department of Human Resources documents and on interviews with program staff.

Does switching from coupons to checks reduce benefit-issuance costs? If so, do the savings accrue to the state government or to the federal government? A major impetus behind the interest in food stamp cash-out is an expected savings in administrative costs through the streamlining of benefit issuance. Switching from coupons to checks eliminates or reduces some issuance activities and costs, but creates or increases others. We use time estimates provided by program staff and data on other resources used in issuance to estimate the savings and cost increases, identify the levels of government at which the savings and costs occur, and arrive at an overall picture of the impacts of cash-out on issuance costs at the federal and state levels of government.

Does switching from coupon issuance to check issuance reduce or increase the incidence or amount of benefit loss, and in what specific areas? Loss of benefits can occur through theft during coupon production, shipment, and storage; overissuances due to clerical error; and excessive issuance due to the fraudulent use of authorization-to-participate cards. We assess the impact of the Alabama Food Stamp Cash Out Demonstration on these types of losses by examining program data on reported losses, supplemented with narrative material from focus group discussions with FSP participants. Our findings include estimates of the amounts of loss borne by the state and federal governments, food stamp recipients, and third parties, and of how those losses changed under cash-out.

DATA COLLECTION

The findings on recipient impacts that we present in this report are based largely on data obtained from an in-person survey of 1,255 check recipients and 1,131 coupon recipients that we conducted between August and November of 1990. Of the responding households, 48 percent resided in the demonstration's two urban counties, and 52 percent resided in the demonstration's ten rural counties, thus closely approximating the 46 percent/54 percent urban/rural distribution of the entire food stamp caseload in Alabama.

The recipient survey obtained detailed information on household composition and income receipt. It also collected very extensive data on the foods used by each household during the seven days preceding the interview. In the survey, respondents were also asked questions about their households' attitudes toward and experiences with cash-out. The survey attained a response rate of 78 percent (80 percent among check recipients; 76 percent among coupon recipients) for the questions on household composition, income, and attitudes, and a rate of 75 percent (78 percent among check recipients; 73 percent among coupon recipients) for the questions on food use.

To supplement the recipient survey data, we also draw on information obtained during four focus group discussions with FSP participants. The discussions were held in one urban site (the city of Birmingham, in Jefferson County) and in one rural site (the town of Fayette, in Fayette County) with participants who had previously received their benefits as coupons, but whose benefit form had been converted to checks. Two sessions were held at each site, one with elderly program participants, and one with nonelderly participants. The focus groups enabled us to explore issues related to client experiences with cash-out in greater depth than was possible in the structured survey.

The findings on administrative outcomes that we present in this report are based on information obtained through in-person and telephone interviews with county-level and state-level FSP staff in Alabama, telephone interviews with representatives of advocacy groups, a mail survey of FSP staff who had handled check-issuance problems, and data compiled or tabulated by FSP staff. We supplement these sources with information obtained from program procedures manuals, official periodic reports on program operations, and other material. Some information was obtained from the focus group discussions with FSP participants. Federal-level issuance costs were obtained from an evaluation of a demonstration of the electronic transfer of food stamp benefits (Kirlin et al., 1990).

FINDINGS FROM THE ANALYSIS OF RECIPIENT IMPACTS

The evaluation of the Alabama Food Stamp Cash-Out Demonstration has produced little evidence of any effect of cash-out on food stamp recipients in Alabama. For almost all outcome measures corresponding to the study's research questions on recipient impacts, the difference in mean values between check recipients and coupon recipients is small in an economic or nutritional sense and is not significantly different from zero in a statistical sense. This section summarizes the key findings of the study concerning each of the previously highlighted research questions on recipient impacts.

The money value of food used at home. The evidence from the household survey indicates that cash-out did not lead to a reduction in the money value of food used at home. As shown in Table 1, the mean weekly value of purchased food used at home (the measure of food use that is most directly affected by the FSP) is $54.85 for coupon recipients and $55.46 for check recipients. The 1 percent difference in mean values is not statistically significant. This finding of no reduction in the money value of food used at home under cash-out holds regardless of whether the outcome measure includes only purchased food or includes all food used at home, and regardless of whether the measure is scaled by ENUs to adjust for differences in household composition and differences in the percentage of meals eaten at home.

There is no evidence from this study that the absence of negative impact of cash-out on the money value of food used at home by all food stamp households is masking a negative impact on the subset of food stamp households that are at greatest nutritional risk. A comparison of check and coupon households in the lower tail of the cumulative distribution of the money value of food used at home per ENU revealed that cash-out had virtually no effect on the use of food by those households.

Nutrient availability. For food energy, protein, and seven micronutrients that are regarded as potentially problematic from a public health perspective, the estimated effects of the demonstration on availability from food used at home are small, ranging from 0 percent to 3 percent, and mixed in sign (Table 2). These small and statistically insignificant differences between check and coupon recipients support the conclusion that cash-out did not result in a reduction in nutrient availability. Data from the demonstration on the percentages of households for which the availability of these nutrients equals or exceeds the RDAs also support this conclusion. For example, the availability of food energy from food used at home was less than the RDA for 20 percent of both check and coupon households.

Running out of food. Cash-out did not increase the incidence of perceived shortages of food in households. Indeed, as shown in Table 3, the percentage of households that reported not having enough food during the month preceding the survey is 3 percentage points lower for check recipients than for coupon recipients (16 percent versus 19 percent). The interview question on which this finding is based asked whether respondents had always had "enough" food during the preceding month. We do not know exactly how respondents interpreted this concept. However, it is interesting to note that the percentages of check and coupon households that reported having not "enough" food are roughly equivalent to the percentages for which the availability of food energy from food used at home was less than the RDA.

Respondent reports on the skipping of meals by household members due to insufficient food also are consistent with the conclusion that cash-out did not increase the incidence of shortages of food. Again, check recipients were somewhat less likely than coupon recipients to report that one or more household members skipped meals during the month preceding the survey because food was unavailable.

TABLE 1

MONEY VALUE OF FOOD USED AT HOME
(In Dollars per Week)

	Mean Value		Difference in Means		
	Check	Coupon	Absolute	Percentage	t-Statistic
Money Value of Purchased Food Used at Home					
For the overall household	55.46	54.85	0.61	1.13	0.43
Per equivalent nutrition unit[a]	33.43	33.66	-0.23	-0.69	0.31
Money Value of all Food Used at Home					
For the overall household	60.31	59.54	0.77	1.29	0.50
Per equivalent nutrition unit[a]	36.25	36.41	-0.16	-0.44	0.21

SOURCE: Evaluation of the Alabama Food Stamp Cash-Out Demonstration, household survey.

NOTE: In this study, critical values of the t-statistic for a two-tailed test (for example, a test of the hypothesis that cash-out caused a *change* in food use) are 1.960 (95 percent confidence) and 1.645 (90 percent confidence); for a one-tailed test (for example, a test of the hypothesis that cash-out caused a *reduction* in food use), they are 1.645 (95 percent confidence) and 1.282 (90 percent confidence).

One-tailed statistical tests for lower money value of purchased food and all food used at home by check recipients were performed on the check-coupon differences shown in this table. None of the differences is statistically significant at the 90 percent confidence level or higher.

[a]Household size in "equivalent nutrition units" is an adjusted measure of household size that takes into account differences in recommended levels of food energy among households with different compositions in terms of the age, gender, and pregnancy and lactation statuses of household members. In addition, this measure takes into account the percentage of meals eaten at home by household members, as well as meals served by the household to guests.

TABLE 2

NUTRIENT AVAILABILITY
PER EQUIVALENT NUTRITION UNIT
(Nutrient Levels as a Percentage of the RDA)

Nutrient	Mean Value		Difference in Means		
	Check	Coupon	Absolute	Percentage	t-Statistic
Food Energy	162.19	161.46	0.73	0.45	0.22
Protein	258.18	258.99	-0.81	-0.31	0.15
Vitamin A	227.32	229.71	-2.39	-1.04	0.26
Vitamin C	250.63	255.40	-4.77	-1.87	0.60
Vitamin B_6	157.59	157.30	0.29	0.19	0.09
Folate	223.94	221.69	2.25	1.02	0.39
Calcium	121.34	117.61	3.73	3.18	1.23
Iron	183.99	183.87	0.12	0.06	0.02
Zinc	127.28	128.87	-1.59	-1.23	0.56

SOURCE: Evaluation of the Alabama Food Stamp Cash-Out Demonstration, household survey.

NOTE: One-tailed statistical tests for lower availability of nutrients among check recipients were performed on the check-coupon differences shown in this table. None of the differences is statistically significant at the 90 percent confidence level or higher.

RDA = recommended dietary allowance.

TABLE 3

RECIPIENTS' PERCEPTIONS OF THE ADEQUACY
OF THE HOUSEHOLD FOOD SUPPLY
(During Previous Month)

	Percentage of Respondents		Difference in Percentages		
	Check	Coupon	Absolute	Percentage	t-Statistic
Respondents Reporting Household Did Not Have Enough Food	16.02	18.57	-2.55	-13.74	1.64
Respondents Reporting Household Member Skipped Meals Due to Insufficient Food	8.21	9.90	-1.69	-17.12	1.44

SOURCE: Evaluation of the Alabama Food Stamp Cash-Out Demonstration, household survey.

NOTE: One-tailed statistical tests for lower perceptions of food adequacy among check recipients were performed on the check-coupon differences shown in this table. None of the differences is statistically significant at the 90 percent confidence level or higher.

The household survey provides little evidence that check recipients were more likely than coupon recipients to avoid shortages of food by relying more heavily than coupon recipients on nonpurchased food or on government food-assistance programs. Both groups of recipients reported that they used home-produced food and food that they had received as a gift or as a payment-in-kind that had an average money value of about $4.75 per household per week. Check and coupon households also reported similar rates of participation in most government food-assistance programs. However, check recipients did report that they participated in government commodity-distribution programs during the month preceding the survey at a greater rate (20 percent) than did coupon recipients (17 percent). This difference is statistically significant at the 95 percent confidence level.

The purchase of food used away from home. Cash-out did not lead to an increase in the purchase of food used away from home, such as restaurant meals. Contrary to expectations, the mean weekly expenditure for food prepared and used away from home was slightly lower for check recipients than for coupon recipients ($3.29 versus $3.50, for the overall household). Similarly, check recipients reported eating a slightly lower percentage of their meals away from home.

Other types of consumption expenditures. One of the basic concerns about food stamp cash-out is that it might lead recipient households to shift their spending away from food used at home and to food used away from home and nonfood goods and services. Table 4 shows the percentage shares of total expenditures that households in the demonstration allocated to broad categories of consumer goods and services. This table shows that, relative to coupon recipients, check recipients did not allocate a smaller percentage of their total expenditures to food used at home, nor did they allocate a greater percentage to food used away from home. Among the nonfood consumption categories, the only category for which check recipients reported a significantly larger expenditure share than coupon recipients is the utilities component of shelter expenses. Check recipients reported allocating 1.1 percentage points more of their total consumption expenditures to utilities. Further investigation would be required to determine if this difference was actually caused by cash-out.

Participant attitudes toward cash-out. Virtually all benefit recipients who participated in the focus group discussions preferred checks to coupons. The major reasons given for this preference were: checks can be used to purchase nonfood items, such as paper products; receiving checks by mail is more convenient than picking up coupons in-person at the food stamp office; and check benefits promote the self-esteem of recipients.

The respondents to the household survey were asked a series of open-ended questions about the aspects of check and of coupon issuance that they thought were good and bad. The advantage of checks most commonly cited by check recipients was that checks can be used to purchase items other than food. Forty-three percent of the check recipients who responded to the survey mentioned this characteristic of checks (Table 5). It is not necessarily the case that these respondents actually used their check benefits to buy nonfood items. The second most commonly mentioned advantage of checks was that they eliminate the need to go to the food stamp issuance office. The frequent mention of this characteristic reflects the fact that, in Alabama, food stamp coupons are typically issued over-the-counter at food stamp offices, whereas food stamp checks were issued by mail. Sixteen percent of check recipients mentioned the elimination of the need to go to the food stamp office to pick up their benefits as an advantage of checks.

Coupon recipients tended to cite as an advantage of coupon issuance the fact that coupons ensure that benefits are spent on food. Thirty-eight percent of the coupon recipients who responded to the survey mentioned this characteristic of coupons. Thirteen percent of coupon recipients mentioned a related advantage, that coupons make it possible to budget food expenses better. In

TABLE 4

EXPENDITURE SHARES, BY CONSUMPTION CATEGORY
(Entries Are Percentages of Total Expenditures in Each Category)

	Mean Percentage Share of Total Expenditures		Difference in Means		
Consumption Category	Check	Coupon	Absolute	Percentage	t-Statistic
All Purchased Food	43.31	43.43	-0.12	-0.27	0.15
Food at home	41.34	41.27	0.07	0.17	0.09
Food away from home	1.98	2.17	-0.19	-8.77	0.94
All Shelter	33.98	32.80	1.18	3.59	1.53 †
Housing	14.16	14.04	0.12	0.89	0.21
Utilities	19.82	18.76	1.06	5.61	1.88 ††
Medical	4.70	4.43	0.27	5.96	0.66
Transportation	8.28	8.60	-0.32	-3.72	0.72
Clothing	5.23	5.62	-0.39	-6.97	1.08
Education	1.02	1.26	-0.24	-18.85	1.91
Dependent Care	0.62	0.81	-0.19	-23.78	1.37
Recreation	1.47	1.61	-0.14	-8.47	0.89
Personal Items	1.39	1.43	-0.04	-3.16	0.42
Total	100.00	100.00			
Mean Total Expenditure	$633.05	$632.49			

SOURCE: Evaluation of the Alabama Food Stamp Cash-Out Demonstration, household survey.

NOTE: One-tailed statistical tests for lower expenditure shares for "all purchased food" and for "(purchased) food at home" and for greater expenditure shares for other consumption categories among check recipients were performed on the check-coupon differences shown in this table.

†Statistically significant at the 90 percent confidence level, one-tailed test.
††Statistically significant at the 95 percent confidence level, one-tailed test.

TABLE 5

MOST COMMONLY MENTIONED ADVANTAGES OF CHECKS AND COUPONS

	Percentage of Respondents Mentioning Advantage
Advantages of Checks[a]	
Can be used for items other than food	42.9
Do not have to go to issuance office	16.2
More choices of food stores	5.7
Do not feel embarrassed	5.3
Does not involve standing in line for a long time	5.3
More convenient/easier to spend	5.3
Advantages of Coupons[b]	
Make sure benefits spent on food	37.8
No sales taxes charged	25.8
Can budget food expenses better	12.6

SOURCE: Evaluation of the Alabama Food Stamp Cash-Out Demonstration, household survey.

[a]Sample limited to check recipients.

[b]Sample limited to coupon recipients.

Alabama, state and county sales taxes are charged on all cash purchases of food, including purchases made with the proceeds of food stamp checks. Despite the fact that the state augmented the check benefits to offset the sales tax, 26 percent of coupon recipients cited the absence of sales taxes on coupon purchases of food as an advantage of coupon issuance. It is likely that many coupon recipients were unaware of the sales tax offset that was added to the check benefit amounts.

Check-cashing experiences. Seventy-three percent of check recipients cashed their food checks at a supermarket, grocery, or other food store, and another 23 percent cashed or deposited them at a bank (Table 6). Most of these establishments did not charge fees for cashing food stamp checks. Fewer than 1 percent of check recipients used check-cashing outlets, which did charge fees.

The vast majority of check recipients (91 percent) paid no fee to cash their food stamp checks. Most of those who did pay a fee paid $1 or less (57 percent of fee payers).

FINDINGS FROM THE ANALYSIS OF ADMINISTRATIVE OUTCOMES

The evaluation of the Alabama Food Stamp Cash-Out Demonstration provides findings on the lessons learned during the planning and implementation of the demonstration, and on the impact of cash-out on administrative costs and benefit losses. This section summarizes the key findings of the study concerning each of the previously highlighted research questions on administrative outcomes.

The planning and implementation of cash-out. A number of Alabama officials, most notably the Commissioner of the Alabama Department of Human Resources (DHR), were eager to implement a cash-out demonstration. Most of their efforts to achieve that goal occurred in the context of the ASSETS welfare reform demonstration; however, those efforts also made feasible the implementation of "pure cash-out"–the Alabama Food Stamp Cash-Out Demonstration. To garner public support for these demonstrations, the Commissioner and other high-level DHR staff participated in legislative hearings on welfare reform, attended meetings with FSP and public housing staff, and presided over informational meetings on cash-out and welfare reform for retail trade associations, county DHR directors, civic groups, and advocacy groups.

One key issue that had to be resolved before cash-out could be implemented was how to compensate check recipients for state and county sales taxes, which are levied on cash purchases of food, but not on coupon purchases of food. DHR resolved this issue by allocating its own funds to be used to augment the food stamp benefit of each check recipient by 7 percent, the approximate amount of the sales tax. This recurring monthly cost made DHR sensitive to the duration of the demonstration.

The development of the computer software that was an integral component of the check-issuance system was a major challenge in implementing the demonstration. This work absorbed considerable resources, primarily in the form of labor hours by the staff of DHR and a DHR contractor. The software development required more labor hours and more calendar time than was originally anticipated, which was one reason why the implementation of cash-out was delayed by four months, from January to May of 1990. The development of the software was complicated by two factors: (1) Alabama was implementing two related demonstration programs simultaneously ("pure cash-out" and ASSETS), and (2) some modifications to the cash-out automated system, which had been made before the evaluator of the pure cash-out demonstration was hired, had to be changed to fit the needs of the evaluation. With the exception of the modifications to the automated system, cash-out was implemented very smoothly. In addition to the systematic groundwork laid by the Commissioner,

TABLE 6

CHECK-CASHING EXPERIENCES OF CHECK RECIPIENTS

Check-Cashing Experience	Percentage of Respondents
Place Where Check Is Usually Cashed	
Supermarket, grocery store, or other food store	73.3
Bank	23.4
Check-cashing outlet	0.3
Other	3.0
Was a Fee Charged to Cash Check?	
Yes	9.2
No	90.8
Amount of Check-Cashing Fee, if Fee Was Charged[a]	
$0.01 to $1.00	56.9
$1.01 to $5.00	38.8
$5.01 or more	4.3

SOURCE: Evaluation of the Alabama Food Stamp Cash-Out Demonstration, household survey.

[a]The statistics given in this section of the table are based on the fee amounts that were reported by the 116 households that reported paying a fee to cash their food stamp checks.

an important factor in the ease of implementation was the training provided by DHR to its county and state staff. A DHR staff trainer who was well-informed about cash-out worked full-time to ensure that all relevant DHR staff had a good working knowledge of cash-out and of its associated new procedures.

We estimate that the labor and associated costs of planning and implementing cash-out were $183,000, with the majority of that amount going to software development. This estimate includes fringe benefits, but does not include overhead. It also includes the cost of contracted services and products.

Issuance costs. We found that costs were indeed lower under check issuance than under coupon issuance. Overall, check issuance cost $1.03 per case-month, or about one-half the cost of coupon issuance, which was $2.05 per case-month. Columns A and B of Table 7 show that issuance costs incurred at the federal level ($0.51 per case-month under coupon issuance) were eliminated under check issuance. Issuance costs incurred at the county and state levels were $1.54 per case-month under coupon issuance, but were only $1.03 per case-month under check issuance. The federal government pays 100 percent of issuance costs incurred at the federal level, as well as 50 percent of the costs incurred at the county and state levels. This allocation of responsibility for the payment of issuance costs is reflected in Columns C-E of Table 7, which show that three-quarters of the savings in issuance costs resulting from cash-out accrued to the federal government and one-quarter accrued to the state government.

Benefit losses. Food stamp cash-out in Alabama virtually eliminated several types of benefit losses that had been borne by either the state or the federal government under coupon issuance. However, these types of losses are quite small under coupon issuance, thus precluding the possibility that cash-out might achieve substantial cost savings in this area.

One type of loss, losses and thefts in the mail, increased significantly under cash-out. This increase was due largely to the increased use of mail issuance under the demonstration. Under coupon issuance in Alabama, most issuances are made on an over-the-counter basis, which is a relatively secure (although expensive) form of issuance. The mail issuance of coupons is generally restricted to small benefit amounts. Under cash-out, food stamp benefit checks were sent to program participants through the mail, an issuance mode that is substantially more vulnerable to losses. Costs resulting from checks being lost or stolen in the mail and then fraudulently cashed averaged $0.14 per case-month under cash-out. Because the average mailed benefit amount is substantially lower under coupon issuance than under check issuance, the mail loss of benefits is much lower ($0.05 per mail-issuance case-month) under coupon issuance than under check issuance. This difference should not be interpreted as evidence that coupons are more secure than checks when issued through the mail.

Overall, the analysis implies that issuance-system vulnerabilities increased as a result of cash-out. This increase occurred primarily because of the issuance of food stamp checks by mail, rather than because of the change in the form of benefit. Thus, the additional costs arising from the loss and theft of food stamp checks in the mail is less a cost of cash-out than it is of the change in the mode of delivering benefits to clients. The costs resulting from the loss and theft of benefit checks in the mail were borne by the third parties, such as banks and stores, that cashed the fraudulent checks. (Under the regular coupon-issuance system, the federal government bears the cost of replacing benefits that have been lost in the mail.)

TABLE 7

COUPON-ISSUANCE AND CHECK-ISSUANCE COSTS PER CASE-MONTH, BY LEVEL OF GOVERNMENT AT WHICH COSTS ARE INCURRED AND PAID
(In Dollars)

	Costs Incurred		Costs Paid		
	Coupon Issuance (A)	Check Issuance (B)	Coupon Issuance (C)	Check Issuance (D)	Savings (E=C-D)
Federal Government	0.51	0.00	1.28	0.515	0.765
State/County Government	1.54	1.03	0.77	0.515	0.255
Total	2.05	1.03	2.05	1.030	1.020

SOURCE: Evaluation of the Alabama Food Stamp Cash-Out Demonstration.

NOTE: The amounts shown under "Costs Paid" reflect federal sharing of 50 percent of costs incurred at the state and county levels.

It is likely that losses borne by food stamp clients declined under cash-out, because the FSP replaced checks that were lost or stolen before being endorsed and cashed, whereas the FSP will not replace lost or stolen coupons. In addition, check recipients were less likely to be subject to possible overcharging of food stamp recipients by some food retailers.

CONCLUSIONS

The potential impact of cash-out on the ability of the FSP to target its benefits specifically to food has been a central component of the policy debate about the desirability of this policy alternative. Opponents of cash-out have been concerned that issuing benefits in the form of checks would greatly weaken the program's impact on food use, whereas proponents have felt that the purchase of food would remain a high priority for recipients, even without the specific linkage to food purchases provided by coupons. Proponents have also argued that cash-out would lower the cost of administering the FSP and the cost of benefit losses.

The evidence from the Alabama Food Stamp Cash-Out Demonstration indicates that, in Alabama, cash-out did not result in lower expenditures for food or in reductions in the amount of nutrients provided by food used at home. The differences between check and coupon recipients in the mean values of these and other outcome variables are 3 percent or less and are mixed in sign. For none of the major outcome variables are the check-coupon differences in mean values statistically significant.

The impact of cash-out on the cost of administering the FSP is also relevant in assessing this policy alternative. We found that the cost of issuing benefits was 50 percent lower under check issuance than under coupon issuance. Costs incurred at the combined county and state levels declined, while costs incurred at the federal level were eliminated. Considering federal sharing of costs incurred at the county and state levels, three-quarters of the savings from the reduced issuance costs accrued to the federal government, and one-quarter accrued to the state government.

The impact of cash-out on benefit losses is also an important policy issue. The costs to the federal and state governments from losses during the production, shipment, and storage of coupons, and from the overissuance of benefits, declined or were eliminated under cash-out. The costs to food stamp recipients associated with the theft and loss of coupons also declined or were eliminated. However, the greater security of checks was more than offset by a higher use of mail issuance, which is more vulnerable than over-the-counter issuance to loss, and by a higher average mailed benefit amount. These two factors resulted in an increase in the per-case-month cost of mail loss that exceeded the decrease in the per-case-month cost of other types of losses for which we have data. The increased cost of benefit loss was borne by third parties, such as banks and stores. Thus, under cash-out, the state and federal governments and food stamp recipients experienced reductions in costs associated with benefit losses, but third parties experienced increases in costs from such losses.

Finally, all of these results from the Alabama demonstration must be considered in light of the somewhat different findings obtained in evaluating the San Diego Food Stamp Cash-out Demonstration. In San Diego, cash-out was observed to have a small but statistically significant negative impact on the value of food purchased for home use and on several other outcome variables. (Administrative findings for San Diego are not yet available.) This finding suggests that the impacts of cash-out may depend on the context and way in which this alternative form of issuance is implemented.

RECIPIENT CLAIMS

Mr. DURBIN. Provide a table showing the total amount of recipient claims and the actual amount collected for fiscal year 1988 through fiscal year 1992.

Mr. BRALEY. I will provide the information in table form for the record.

[The information follows:]

FOOD STAMP RECIPIENT CLAIMS

	1988	1989	1990	1991	1992
Amount of Claims Established [1]	$181	$197	$193	$216	$223
Amount of Claims Collected [1]	$71	$73	$84	$94	$109

[1] Above figures are in millions of dollars

OVERPAID BENEFITS

Mr. DURBIN. On page seven of your statement you say that over $1.9 billion in benefits issued were the result of errors. How much of this is the result of caseworker or participant mistakes and how much is the result of outright fraud?

Mr. BRALEY. Our quality control data for fiscal year 1991, the most recent official data that is available, shows that approximately $1.21 billion in benefits were overpaid. Our estimates are that 23 percent, $276 million, of the total overissuance may be attributable to willful client misrepresentation of information, i.e., possible fraud. In addition, 32 percent, $384 million, can be traced to some non-fraud-related mistakes by the client, whereas 45 percent, $540 million, of the errors can be attributable to some state agency failure in processing the case information.

Mr. DURBIN. What are you doing as an agency to reduce this number?

Mr. BRALEY. The Regions have worked with the states for years on an ongoing effort to control error rates. Through regional leadership efforts, state agencies are encouraged to undertake payment accuracy efforts which have taken the form of conferences, newsletters and seminars and implementation of proven error reduction methods.

Funds are provided through the State Exchange Program which go to support travel between state agencies to allow for the observation of successful payment accuracy efforts. The Agency also compiles and distributes TARGET (Techniques to Achieve Realistic Goals and Enhanced Teamwork), a periodically updated publication which helps share effective practices and assists with caseload management. These funds also have allowed the Agency to support state efforts to develop technical assistance projects such as "The Road to Enhanced Funding" which describes those practices which have proven successful, and can be shared with other state agencies, and outlines the process for receiving funding.

Further, the Agency is about to award $300,000 in competitive grant money to states to assist in error reduction demonstration projects, chosen both for their potential effectiveness and for the possibility of their use in other sites.

States who have low error rates are eligible for enhanced funding. For fiscal year 1991, 5 states received a total of $9.4 million for maintaining combined error rates below 6 percent. Automation has been a significant factor in improving the ability of State agencies to compare information provided by applicants against data available from state and Federal income and resource data.

After analysis of the latest availability Quality Control information, we intend to actively pursue the collection of penalty fines assessed against those states with unacceptably high error rates. It is critical that in a program where benefit amounts are 100% federally funded, error reduction be made a priority through fiscal responsibility. At the same time, the Agency has offered the reinvestment program which allows the option for the development of management practices that are intended to help improve payment accuracy by using the funds which would have been paid to satisfy fines incurred by the state.

Mr. DURBIN. Provide a table showing the overpayment error rate, the underpayment error rate, and the total for fiscal years 1988 to 1992.

Mr. BRALEY. Fiscal year 1992 official error rates are not available until June 30, 1993. The overpayment, underpayment, and total error rat for fiscal years 1988 through 1991 will be provided for the record. e

[The information follow:]

	Overpayment rate	Underpayment rate	Total
Fiscal Year:			
1988	7.41	2.52	9.93
1989	7.25	2.53	9.78
1990	7.34	2.47	9.81
1991	6.96	2.35	9.31

Mr. DURBIN. Please update the table that appears on page 158 of last year's hearing record showing the overpayment error rate, the dollar amount associated with this rate and the amount recovered to include fiscal year 1991. Also, footnote any discrepancies.

Mr. BRALEY. The updates on the overpayment error rate will be provided for the record.

[The information follows:]

	Overpayment error rate (percent)	Estimated overpayment	Recovered (claims collected)
Fiscal year:			
1980	9.51	$791,082,618	$0
1981	9.90	1,013,137,756	1,455,048.00
1982	9.54	905,764,366	[1] 1,672,702.50
1983	8.32	894,504,311	1,058,141.20
1984	8.59	902,320,084	588,503.00
1985	8.27	847,502,397	299,390.00
1986	8.09	840,024,012	[2] 0
1987	7.58	742,792,841	[2] 0

	Overpayment error rate (percent)	Estimated overpayment	Recovered (claims collected)
1988	7.41	825,622,613	[2] 0
1989	7.25	846,913,050	[2] 0
1990	7.34	1,036,960,425	[2] 0
1991	6.96	1,206,458,734	[2] 7,017.00
Total		10,853,083,207	5,050,801.70

[1] The only outstanding QC liability is a sanction in the amount of $1,323,884 owed by the State of Massachusetts for April—September 1982. The State agency has been billed; collection is pending a decision on rehearing of a U.S. Court of Appeals decision upholding the sanction.

[2] States have agreed to invest almost $45 million in program improvements as a result of settling $300 million in outstanding quality control liabilities for Fiscal Years 1986–1991. Because it is an investment of State funds, it is not included in the dollar value of claims recovered. The $7,017 represents a cash payment by the two States which chose to pay the settlements as opposed to investing in program improvements.

PARTICIPATION AND UNEMPLOYMENT RATES

Mr. DURBIN. Update the table that appears on page 159 of last year's hearing record showing food stamp participation and unemployment rates to include fiscal year 1992.

Mr. BRALEY. The information will be provided for the record.

[The information follows:]

HISTORICAL FOOD STAMP DATA—AVERAGE MONTHLY PARTICIPATION AND UNEMPLOYMENT RATE

	Participants	Civilian unemployment rate (percent)
Fiscal year:		
1982	21,717,393	9.11
1983	21,624,639	10.12
1984	20,853,631	7.33
1985	19,899,052	7.25
1986	19,429,101	7.05
1987	19,113,129	6.48
1988	18,645,291	5.63
1989	18,764,433	5.28
1990	20,086,124	5.38
1991	22,624,627	6.48
1992	25,403,766	7.31

TRAFFICKING

Mr. DURBIN. You testified that trafficking identified through retailer investigations has increased 44 percent over fiscal year 1991 and 255 percent over fiscal year 1988. These increases are staggering. What do you attribute it to?

Mr. BRALEY. There is no evidence that trafficking has increased. The number of Food and Nutrition Service (FNS), Compliance Branch retailer investigations which found evidence of food stamp trafficking increased 44 percent over fiscal year 1991 and 255 percent over fiscal year 1988. We attribute these increases to several factors.

Prior to fiscal year 1989, the Compliance Branch concentrated its investigative efforts on uncovering evidence of the sale of ineligible items for food stamps by stores. We conducted the vast majority of our cases based on an automated violation prone profile which successfully identified stores subject to such violations. However, most of these firms were small stores with very low food stamp redemptions.

We subsequently determined that our investigative efforts would better serve the program if we refocused our attention to uncovering trafficking violations. Therefore, FNS investigators began a concerted effort to make contacts with State and local program, investigative and regulatory officials to develop intelligence on stores suspected of trafficking. These contacts have proven to be a very successful source of leads for trafficking investigations. We also assigned a priority to investigating stores on which the FNS Field Offices received information of possible trafficking.

We have instructed investigators to spend more time in the development of cases where trafficking is suspected. Twelve senior investigator positions were established and additional training has been provided for them at the Federal Law Enforcement Training Center.

In fiscal year 1992 we conducted a project involving a series of investigations based on FNS automated data showing firms with grossly excessive redemption activity compared to total food sales reported to FNS. This project was successful in focusing our activity on stores trafficking in fiscal year 1992 and continues in fiscal year 1993.

Finally, there has been a slight increase in the number of Compliance Branch investigators. In fiscal year 1988, we had 47 investigators on board; at the end of fiscal year 1992 we had 51 investigators on board.

The combination of the above factors, along with the invaluable experience gained by Compliance Branch investigators in trafficking investigations, has resulted in the increases described above. This focusing on trafficking has resulted in a reduction in the overall number of retailer investigations conducted annually—from 8454 in fiscal year 1988 to 4848 in fiscal year 1992. We believe the attention to stores that are seriously diverting food stamp benefits from their intended nutritional purpose—by exchanging cash for stamps at a discount—has been a much more effective use of FNS investigative resources.

Mr. DURBIN. Describe for us the pilot projects you have planned for fiscal year 1994 to identify effective detecting investigative and sanctioning techniques against street trafficking.

Mr. BRALEY. We are planning to have funding available for a maximum of seven projects to address the serious problem of street trafficking. We will seek several State or local food stamp agency proposals which have innovative ideas for working with State or local law enforcement agencies to investigate street trafficking at issuance sites or other high trafficking areas. We will also be seeking in these same proposals methods which address trafficking by recipients, buyers who purchase food stamps on the street, and authorized retail food stores through prosecution or disqualification.

Both the Food and Nutrition Service (FNS) and State investigative resources are insufficient to pursue street trafficking. Therefore, state and local law enforcement agencies will be enlisted in this struggle. Street trafficking is extremely damaging, diverting large amounts of food stamp benefits from their intended purpose, affecting the nutritional well being of recipients, and eroding public support for the Food Stamp Program.

Mr. DURBIN. What do you estimate the total level of trafficking within the program to be?

Mr. BRALEY. We do not have an estimate of the total level of trafficking with the Food Stamp Program. Trafficking is by definition an illegal act, which involves recipients, authorized retailers, and in many instances, unauthorized third parties. Consequently, we have no effective way to determine its full magnitude.

The vast majority of recipients who receive food stamps are eligible for those benefits and receive the proper amount, and 75 percent of all food stamps spent are redeemed through supermarkets where there is little evidence of trafficking. Therefore, we do not believe the Food Stamp Program is fraught with trafficking. However, we are aware from our own investigative activity, that of the Office of Inspector General and various State agencies, and from media reports that trafficking is a significant problem. That is why we continue to concentrate our retailer investigative efforts in this area, and are soliciting the help of State agencies and State and local law enforcement officials in addressing this problem.

Mr. DURBIN. When will the Store Trafficking Authorization and Redemption Subsystem, which stores all data on retailers and records their redemptions of food stamps through the banking and Federal Reserve systems, be operational?

Mr. BRALEY. FNS should complete testing of the system this Summer with training to follow soon thereafter. We anticipate nationwide implementation of this system sometime this Fall.

IRM PLAN

Mr. DURBIN. Your agency has a five-year Information Resources Management Plan at a cost of over $77 million. What is the status of this plan? What has been accomplished to date?

Mr. BRALEY. The Food and Nutrition Service (FNS) publishes a five-year Information Resources Management Long Range Plan, which is updated annually. The $77 million represents the Agency's projected needs to develop new and enhance existing automated systems during fiscal years 1992-1996. The $77 million does *not* reflect actual funds available. In the first 2 years of the plan, approximately $12 million was funded for the development of program-specific automated systems.

Over $27 million of the $77 million projected in the 5-year Plan is directed at the Agency's infrastructure needs—the hardware and operations software that support all employees in the day-to-day efficient operation of the Agency. Based on actual appropriations for fiscal year 1992, over $900,000 became available for infrastructure needs. Work continues on the plan as funds are made available.

Availability of administrative funding affects the timing of these investments. Ongoing investment in appropriate computer infrastructure is particularly important for FNS since it is accountable for over one-half of the entire USDA budget through 14 separate food assistance programs. Over one-third of the FNS inventory of computer hardware will be over 8 years old in fiscal year 1994, and most of the remaining two-thirds will be over 5 years old. As equipment becomes obsolete or replacement parts become too expensive, agency employees can no longer do their jobs as efficiently. Time and money is wasted, and program integrity may suffer. The same is true when microcomputer software cannot be replaced by updated or new versions and the old versions are no longer supported by vendors. Information on accomplishments to date will be provided for the record.

[The information follows:]

Systems implemented	Purpose
Food Stamp Coupon Requisition and Inventory Management Subsystem (CRIMS); Implementation FY 1992 and FY 1993.	Improves coupon inventory accountability and support of the shipping function for 1,406 shipping points; allows on-line serial number tracking for OIG investigation of fraudulent coupon uses.
Processed Commodity Inventory Management System (PCIMS); Implemented FY 1992 and work continues..	Triagency system (FNS, ASCS, AMS) provides single database to track flow of food requisitions from earliest identification through product delivery; improves accountability and reconciliation.
Disqualified Recipients Subsystem	Mandated by Congress. Allows States to check FNS data to identify disqualified recipients and prevent repeat abusers from obtaining benefits; estimated annual savings per year $.5 million.
Cooperative Data Sharing	Promotes sharing of information with other Federal and State organizations to accomplish program oversight; states can directly enter and access information, send large batch files directly to FNS (60,000 reports received annually); assists in identifying fraudulent claimants and collecting overpayments via the tax offset initiative.
Agency Financial Management System (AFMS).	Upgrade to FNS's financial management operations to enhance oversight of $38.5 billion in FY 1993 funds.

HOMELESS PROVISION OF FARM BILL

Mr. DURBIN. The 1990 Farm Bill directed that restaurants be authorized to accept food stamps from homeless persons by February 1, 1992. How is this provision being implemented? How are restaurants being authorized and monitored?

Mr. BRALEY. In early March 1992, all State agencies were informed of the provision in the 1990 Farm Bill allowing them to contract with restaurants to provide meals in exchange for food stamps from homeless persons. An interested restaurant must obtain such a contract from the State agency and must then apply for authorization to accept food stamps at the local Food and Nutrition Service field office in its area. Local FNS field offices then authorize qualified restaurants and monitor their participation in the Program. A total of 136 restaurants are authorized to accept food stamps. Some of these restaurants serve the elderly and disabled. We do not collect separate data on restaurants serving homeless persons, but there has been as increase of 41 restaurants authorized since February 1992, the effective data of the homeless provision.

STAGGERED MONTHLY ISSUANCE ON INDIAN RESERVATIONS

Mr. DURBIN. The Farm Bill also included a provision allowing staggered monthly issuance on Indian reservations. A large number of negative comments to the proposed regulation prompted a delay in its implementation and a Comptroller General report on the need for the provision. What is the status of this issue?

Mr. BRALEY. The staggered issuance provision was published as a proposed regulatory amendment on May 20, 1991, and the comments which the Department of Agriculture (USDA) received from State agencies and Native American organizations were not favorable. After our proposed rulemaking, Congress delayed implementation of the provision (Section 908a of the Food, Agriculture, Conservation, and Trade Act Amendments) until April 1, 1993. Congress also requested the General Accounting Office (GAO) to examine whether prices at authorized grocery stores serving reservations are increased during times of the month when food stamps are issued. GAO was asked to examine whether or not eligible households living on reservations preferred to have their issuance of food stamps staggered. On November 25, 1992, the GAO issued Letter Report Number B-251277 which contained a summary of comments from 13 State agencies and two national Indian organizations. The report contained no new information about pricing-raising at grocery stores, but did contain the same general objections to staggered issuance which had been received by the Department in response to the proposed rule.

On April 1, 1993, legislation was enacted which again delayed implementation of staggered issuance on Indian reservations, from April 1, 1993, until January 31, 1994. Prior to that date, Congress will convene a joint hearing involving the committees on Agriculture and Indian Affairs to examine more closely the participation in the Food Stamp Program of the American Indian and Alaskan Native.

WELFARE SIMPLIFICATION AND COORDINATION ADVISORY COMMITTEE

Mr. DURBIN. Did the Welfare Simplification and Coordination Advisory Committee meet during fiscal year 1992? If so, what were their findings and recommendations?

Mr. BRALEY. Two of the Advisory Committee's four meetings were held in fiscal year 1992; the others were held in fiscal year 1993. The meeting schedule was: April 30 and May 1 in Arlington, Virginia; August 26-28 in Seattle, Washington; January 7-9 in Charlotte, North Carolina; and March 11-13 in Wilmington, Delaware.

The findings and recommendations of the Committee will be presented in a report to Congress and the relevant Federal agencies by July 1, 1993.

COMPLIANCE BRANCH

Mr. DURBIN. Update the table that appears on page 175 of last year's hearing record showing the staff and funding level of your Compliance Branch to include fiscal year 1992 actuals.

Mr. BRALEY. The information requested will be submitted for the record.

[The information follows:]

Fiscal year	Investigator staff years	Total compliance branch staff years	Total expenditures
1991	43	64	$3,105,877
1992	44.51	66.16	3,765,289
1993 [1]	51	59	3,900,000
1994 [1]	51	59	3,900,000

[1] Estimated

INCREASED AUTHORITY

Mr. DURBIN. The Farm Bill increased your authority to penalize violators in the food stamp program. Final regulations to implement these changes were published in February of 1992 and at last year's hearing there was not sufficient time to evaluate the use of these new provisions. Now that they have been in effect over a year, how have they worked?

Mr. BRALEY. The final rulemaking implementing the penalties included in the Farm Bill was published on February 3, 1992, and provided for increased civil money penalties for trafficking in food coupons; permanent disqualification from the Food Stamp Program for accepting food coupons in exchange for firearms, ammunition, explosives or controlled substances; fines for the acceptance of loose coupons of denominations not authorized to be used in changemaking; and fines against unauthorized persons who illegally accept or redeem food coupons. In addition, the rule provided for increased criminal penalties against persons who unlawfully issue, redeem, use, transfer, acquire, alter or possess food coupons or food stamp benefit access devices. In order to capitalize on the deterrent value that these provisions offer, a notice to all authorized retailers and wholesalers alerting them to the new penalties was issued shortly thereafter.

We have little information to date by which to judge the effectiveness of these particular provisions. However, we believe that any increase in the penalties associated with Food Stamp Program noncompliance is very helpful in the enforcement of program requirements and in maintaining program integrity.

ADMINISTRATION FOR CHILDREN AND FAMILIES

Mr. DURBIN. What is the mission of the Administration for Children and Families and where is it located?

Mr. BRALEY. The Administration for Children and Families is part of the Department of Health and Human Services. It is the focal point of that Department's efforts to provide services to children and families.

Major programs administered by the agency include Head Start, Aid to Families with Dependent Children, Child Support Enforcement, Job Opportunities and Basic Skills Training, Adoption Assistance, Foster Care, Child Welfare Services, Social Services Block Grant, Child Care and Development Block Grant, Maternal and Child Health Block Grant, and child abuse programs.

NUTRITION ASSISTANCE FOR PUERTO RICO

Mr. DURBIN. The block grant provided the Commonwealth of Puerto Rico is intended to cover 100 percent of benefits and 50 percent of administrative expenses. Describe for the Committee how administrative expenses are derived?

Mr. BRALEY. Administrative costs of the Puerto Rico Nutrition Assistance Program (NAP) block grant are those associated with the certification of individual households for the program, issuance of benefits to eligible households, and all other functions necessary to operate the block grant in conformance with legislative and regulatory requirements. These administrative costs are monitored and accounted for by the Puerto Rico Department of Social Services which receives 50 percent reimbursement from the block grant for these administrative costs.

Mr. DURBIN. Is this program reviewed and/or monitored by FNS? If so, how? If not, why not?

Mr. BRALEY. Puerto Rico's Nutrition Assistance Program is monitored through annual reviews or more frequently as needed, by Food and Nutrition Service's Caribbean Area Office (CAO) under the supervision of our Mid-Atlantic Regional Office. Some examples include Civil Rights reviews, financial validation closeout reviews and financial benefit reviews that are conducted annually.

Mr. DURBIN. When do you expect the Cattle Tick Eradication project to be complete?

Mr. BRALEY. The Department has not requested any funds for this project in 1994 in the Nutrition Assistance to Puerto Rico.

Mr. DURBIN. The Commonwealth initiated an approved special project in 1988, the Special Wage Incentive Program. This program's goal was to bring industry and jobs to 31 targeted low-income municipalities by subsidizing the wages of NAP recipients employed by approved industries. Due to the poor initial response, Puerto Rico expanded coverage to the entire Commonwealth and all private business sectors. Was this expansion approved by FNS?

Mr. BRALEY. Expansion of the Special Wage Incentive Program (SWIP) from the originally targeted 31 low-income municipalities to an islandwide program was approved by FNS on February 21, 1991.

Mr. DURBIN. With expansion to all of Puerto Rico and all private business sectors, what is the new purpose of the project?

Mr. BRALEY. The purpose of the Special Wage Incentive Program (SWIP) under the expanded islandwide program remains the same as originally proposed: to bring industry and jobs to the Commonwealth while concurrently assisting Nutrition Assistance Program (NAP) recipients to enhance their income to the point where they require little or no public assistance.

Mr. DURBIN. Provide a table of the annual cost of this project since its inception.

Mr. BRALEY. The information will be provided for the record.

[The information follows:]

SPECIAL WAGE INCENTIVE PROGRAM

Fiscal year	Administrative costs	Benefit costs	Total [1]
1988	0	0	0
1989	32,206	68,769	100,975
1990	55,464	616,616	672,080
1991	238,202	2,400,130	2,728,430
1992 [2]	643,379	8,791,878	9,435,257
Total	969,341	11,967,401	12,936,742

[1] Federal share of program costs.
[2] Preliminary figures.

Mr. DURBIN. Are any other special projects ongoing or planned?

Mr. BRALEY. No other special projects are authorized in Puerto Rico under the block grant, and to our knowledge, no other such projects are being planned at this time.

Mr. DURBIN. What were the findings and recommendations of the GAO report which studied the nutritional needs of the citizens of Puerto Rico and potential alternatives to providing nutrition assistance?

Mr. BRALEY. The July 21, 1992 General Accounting Office (GAO) report found that about 20 percent fewer people were receiving food assistance under the Nutrition Assistance Program (NAP) than would have received assistance under the Food Stamp Program (FSP) in fiscal year 1990 because the NAP's criteria are more restrictive than are those in the FSP. For the same reason, those receiving NAP benefits are receiving less assistance than they would have received if the FSP had been continued. No current islandwide nutrition studies are available to assess the specific nutritional impacts of having replaced the FSP with the NAP or the current nutrition conditions of the general Puerto Rico population. Food assistance alternatives, such as restoring the FSP in the Commonwealth or adjusting NAP benefits and eligibility criteria would increase program assistance levels and participation in Puerto Rico. These changes would also increase program costs, however.

THE EMERGENCY FOOD ASSISTANCE PROGRAM

Mr. DURBIN. What commodities do you plan to distribute in fiscal year 1993? Please separate those purchased with appropriated funds and those acquired through normal price support and surplus removal programs.

Mr. BRALEY. The commodities purchased with appropriated funds received through the Hunger Prevention Act of 1988 and the Farm Credit and Associations Safety and Soundness Act of 1992 were: Canned Applesauce, Canned Orange Juice, Canned Peaches, Canned Pears, Raisins, Canned Peas, Canned and Dry Beans, Canned Pork, Peanut Butter, Rice, Canned Apple Juice, Canned Fruit Cocktail, Canned Green Beans, and Canned Tuna.

The same products will be distributed during fiscal year 1993. Corn Meal and peanut butter were the only items acquired through price support. None of the items were surplus removal products.

Mr. DURBIN. Please provide a table showing the amount of commodities purchased with appropriated funds and the amount of commodities donated to the program for each year since the program began.

Mr. BRALEY. A table will be provided for the record.

[The information follows:]

COST OF TEFAP COMMODITIES

[Data Rounded to Thousands]

Fiscal year	Entitlement	Bonus
1982	0	179,461
1983	0	973,940
1984	0	1,030,291
1985	0	972,872
1986	0	845,796
1987	0	845,695
1988	0	537,206
1989	120,000	135,164
1990	119,573	118,921
1991	119,998	89,305
1992	119,310	85,128

Sources: 1982–88: Public Information Data Base (PIDB). 1989–92: Food Orders (data provided by Food Distribution Division for Budget "Green Sheets") Costs include anticipated adjustment.

Mr. DURBIN. Update the list that appears on page 181 of last year's hearing record showing the amount of administrative funds returned to the U.S. Treasury to include fiscal year 1992.

Mr. BRALEY. The updated table will be provided for the record.

[The information follows:]

Fiscal Year:	
1992	$1,000
1991	1,397,639
1990	2,212,657
1989	6,029,196
1988	2,304,618
1987	1,000,000

Mr. DURBIN. Describe in detail how this program is monitored by your agency including what controls are in place to verify the integrity of the program.

Mr. BRALEY. Several methods are available to monitor the Emergency Food Assistance Program. First, Regional Offices of the Food and Nutrition Service (FNS) have the responsibility to conduct management evaluations of State program administration. Last year, comprehensive management evaluation guidance was developed for this program to promote more uniform, in-depth coverage during evaluations. Agency Headquarters systematically review the results of management evaluations to identify needs for changes in program requirements, intensified technical assistance to States, and increased Federal oversight. An automated data processing system was developed last year to facilitate this analysis.

In addition, independent oversight activities complement FNS' management evaluations. The Department's Office of the Inspector General (OIG) may initiate program audits and investigations in connection with its independent responsibility to ensure program integrity, or undertake such actions in response to requests from the FNS, which, in turn, may derive from State requests or whistleblower complaints.

The Food and Nutrition Service also carefully monitors State commodity orders to ensure that States do not exceed their allocations.

Mr. DURBIN. How does this appropriation differ from the $32 million appropriated under the Food Donations Program for soup kitchens?

Mr. BRALEY. The Hunger Prevention Act of 1988 (P.L. 100–435) authorized appropriations for the Food Donations Program for Soup Kitchens. The law stipulated that these funds were to be used to purchase commodities primarily for soup kitchens which prepare meals for the homeless and food banks which serve such soup kitchens. The Emergency Food Assistance Program, on the other hand, is intended primarily to provide commodities for household distribution to low-income and unemployed persons. However, the Emergency Food Assistance Act of 1983 specifically lists soup kitchens among eligible institution types. Therefore, although the primary emphasis of these programs differs, they have shared target populations from the outset.

P.L. 100–435 acknowledged the kinship between the two programs by authorizing states to use Emergency Food Assistance Program administrative funds for administration of the Food Donations Program for Soup Kitchens. The Food, Agriculture, Conservation, and Trade Act Amendments of 1991 (P.L. 102–237) increased states' ability to fully utilize their commodity allocations in the latter program by establishing a priority system that requires commodities not needed by soup kitchens to be made available for household distribution to the needy. Thus each of these programs provides commodities for both household distribution and meal preparation for the needy. Indeed, households may receive commodities under both programs from the same distribution site.

Mr. DURBIN. How much of the $50 million in TEFAP administrative funds are used for the commodities to soup kitchens and food banks program?

Mr. BRALEY. States are required to pass on 40 percent of Administrative funds to total agencies administering The Emergency Food Assistance Program (TEFAP) and match, in-cash or in-kind, funds retained for State level administration. The annual appropriation of $50 million for program administration between 1983 and 1991 was reduced to $45 million for fiscal years 1992 and 1993. We have heard concerns from States and local distributing agencies that the administrative funds are insufficient to support TEFAP operations. States are not required to report whether, and if so to what extent, they share TEFAP administrative funds with the Soup Kitchen/Food Bank Program. Although some states identify funds sharing in their State distribution plan, complete data is not available to address your question, and we believe that funds sharing is not particularly widespread.

FOOD DONATIONS PROGRAMS

Mr. DURBIN. The 1993 appropriation made funding available for two fiscal years as opposed to one. This was done to improve program administration and allow funds returned to FNS from ASCS because a contract to purchase food had not been awarded to be reallocated. How has this provision affected the program?

Mr. BRALEY. This two year appropriation was made available for the Food Distribution Program on Indian Reservations and the Nutrition Program for the Elderly. Since it was effective beginning with Fiscal Year 1993 and six months still remain in this fiscal year, there has not been sufficient time to assess the impact. However, the two-year appropriation will enhance the Agency's ability to respond to these programs' needs and ensure that the delivery of benefits to recipients are not delayed at the beginning of each new fiscal year.

Mr. DURBIN. Does it affect more than just non-awarded contracts to purchase commodities?

Mr. BRALEY. Yes, it does affect more than just non-awarded contracts. This two year appropriation will enable us to more effectively plan all purchases for both programs and ensure that recipients receive program benefits in a timely and consistent manner.

Mr. DURBIN. Describe in detail the administrative costs of each of the programs in this account including how they are derived, states' costs, and how they are reviewed and monitored.

Mr. BRALEY. Among the programs and functions in this account, separately identified administrative funding is available only for the Food Distribution Program on Indian Reservations and food assistance to the nuclear-affected islands.

Our request for administrative funding for the Food Distribution Program on Indian Reservations is based on the cost of prior operations, including an adjustment for inflation, and the anticipated addition of new administering agencies. Administering agencies incur costs primarily for storage, handling, and transportation of program commodities, certification of households, and recordkeeping and reporting. Necessary and reasonable costs include capital expenditures for equipment, such as fork lifts, freezer and refrigeration units, and trucks.

Each year, Food and Nutrition Service Regional Offices receive administrative funding allocations with which to negotiate line-item administrative budgets with each administering agency. These budgets include operating expenses and, as appropriate, capital expenditures. Regulations require that administering agencies contribute 25 percent of program administrative costs in cash or in kind, except that the Food and Nutrition Service (FNS) can allow matching at a lesser percentage with justification. Given the irreducible basic administrative costs and the significant number of small Indian Tribal Organizations administering the program, it has proven necessary to allow numerous exceptions to the 25-percent requirement. FNS Regional Offices monitor administering agency expenditures against budgets throughout the fiscal year. We also retain a small portion of available administrative funding to cover vital unanticipated needs that may arise during the year.

Mr. DURBIN. Please update the table that appears on page 186 of last year's hearing record showing FDPIR participation levels to include fiscal year 1992.

Mr. BRALEY. The updated table will be provided for the record.

[The information follows:]

FDPIR participation levels—average monthly participation

Fiscal year:	*Persons*
1986	144,952
1987	145,679
1988	137,771
1989	141,120
1990	138,313
1991	129,869
1992	118,535

Mr. DURBIN. Also, provide a similar table showing participation levels for the elderly feeding program.

Mr. BRALEY. The table will be provided for the record.

[The information follows:]

NPE meals served—annual totals

Fiscal year:	*Meals*
1986	228,244,565
1987	232,128,489
1988	240,421,065
1989	243,347,090
1990	245,650,349
1991	244,598,985
1992	244,827,118

Mr. DURBIN. Were any new tribes accepted into the program during fiscal year 1992?

Mr. BRALEY. In Fiscal Year 1992, Umatilla in Oregon joined the Food Donations Program on Indian Reservations (FDPIR). The estimated participation of this tribe is 500.

Mr. DURBIN. Are there any requesting participation in fiscal year 1993?

Mr. BRALEY. While no new tribes have submitted official requests for participation in the program, we have been advised by our regional offices that seven tribes have requested preapplication forms. In addition, the Yanton Sioux and Oglala Sioux, which participated under the umbrella of the South Dakota State distributing agency, requested approval to administer their own programs. Approval was granted.

Mr. DURBIN. At this time last year you were intending to propose rules to address three issues—the 10,000 population limit; Native American children in a household with no Native American adult, and foster children. What is the status of these issues?

Mr. BRALEY. Upon examination of current regulatory provisions, it was determined that issues associated with the treatment of foster children and foster care payments could be addressed through a policy memorandum. On January 24, 1992, a policy memorandum was issued to all FNS regional offices for dissemination to Indian Tribal Organizations and State agencies. The policy set forth allows households to classify foster children as either household members or as boarders. Payments for foster children are considered income only when the foster children are classified as household members. This policy ensures that households that care for foster children is not adversely affected as a result of receiving foster care payments which are provided for the sole purpose of caring for the foster children.

With regard to redefining "urban place," we had planned to use the 1990 Census data to evaluate whether the current 10,000 population limit remains appropriate. The data proved to be insufficiently delineated for our purposes. However, we can under current regulations continue to address the issue by granting waivers to the 10,000 limit as appropriate for urban areas in all States except Oklahoma. Therefore, a rule has been drafted which would extend the Department's waiver authority to urban areas in Oklahoma. In the meantime, we do not intend to withdraw program services from areas in Oklahoma which may have grown beyond the 10,000 limit as a result of the 1990 Census simply because waiver authority is not yet explicitly established. Rather, we will address each such case after the rulemaking process has been completed.

The Department also intends to amend current regulations so that income-eligible households located near reservations and including Indian children, but lacking an Indian adult, can participate in the program. Such households would be eligible even if the children were not members of the tribe(s) on the reservation.

Officials of the new administration, as appointed, will be reviewing these regulations.

Mr. DURBIN. How much did you spend in fiscal year 1992 for inventory restoration?

Mr. BRALEY. We spent approximately $11 million in fiscal year 1992 to restore the inventory from the effects of the Americold fire. Approximately $9 million was spent to replace food that could not be saved. $1.8 million was spent for reconditioning and related costs for food that could be salvaged (valued at $8.4 million).

We spent an additional $23 million in fiscal year 1992 to replenish inventories to recover from the effects of disaster assistance and to have sufficient inventory on hand as the reconditioning process was underway.

Mr. DURBIN. What is the level of commodities kept in inventory?

Mr. BRALEY. Our goal is to maintain a four to five month inventory supply for use in the Commodity Supplemental Food Program (CSFP) and Food Distribution Program on Indian Reservations (FDPIR). The overall volume of inventory should therefore average 65 million pounds monthly. The current inventory is approximately 75 million pounds of commodities. However, fluctuations in inventories do occur because of our purchasing schedule which is designed to meet price support and surplus removal needs as well as obtain commodities at a low cost. Depending on the commodity, purchases are scheduled yearly, quarterly or monthly.

Mr. DURBIN. Please update the table that appears on page 189 of last year's hearing record showing the amount of funds made available to the Freely Associated States and Palau to reflect fiscal year 1993 actuals.

Mr. BRALEY. I will provide this information for the record.

[The information follows:]

Funds available to the Freely Associated States and Palau

Fiscal Year:	*Amounts*
1993	$895,000
1992	581,000
1991	979,000
1990	1,010,000
1989	530,000
1988	704,000
1987	1,610,000

Mr. DURBIN. What is the status of the authorization for this program?

Mr. BRALEY. The authorization for special assistance to the nuclear-affected islands was extended through fiscal year 1993 by Public Law 102–247 Omnibus Insular Arms Act of 1992, enacted February 24, 1992.

Mr. DURBIN. Did these islands receive any food assistance under the Disaster Feeding Program in fiscal year 1992? If so, how much?

Mr. BRALEY. Food assistance received by the Federated States of Micronesia and the Republic of the Marshall Islands under the Disaster Feeding Program for fiscal year 1992 was: Federated States of Micronesia (Yap, Chuuk and Pohnpei) Approximate value of food purchases: $3.3 million; and Republic of the Marshall Islands (Ujae, Lae, MIli, Jaluit, Arno, and Ailinglaplap) Approximate value of food purchases: $1.4 million

ELDERLY FEEDING PROGRAM

Mr. DURBIN. This Committee has been receiving a number of calls and letters requesting a supplemental appropriation for the Elderly Feeding program. As I understand it, the authorizing committee finally got around to reauthorizing the program for fiscal years 1992 and 1993 after we passed the fiscal year 1993 appropriations bill. In this reauthorization, the per meal reimbursement rate was increased retroactively to the beginning of fiscal year 1992. There was enough unused money in fiscal year 1992 to cover the increase, which is probably why they made it retroactive, but the 1993 appropriation, which was based on current rates, is not enough to cover the adjusted increase. Would you tell us how much would be needed in fiscal year 1993 to provide the authorized level?

Mr. BRALEY. Based on an estimate of 247 million meals, an additional $10.5 million would be needed in fiscal year 1993 to reimburse at the authorized rate of 62.06 cents.

Mr. DURBIN. Is the Administration going to request this amount in a supplemental?

Mr. BRALEY. There are no plans to do so at this time.

FOOD PROGRAM ADMINISTRATION

Mr. DURBIN. For the record, please provide a detailed description of what your responsibilities are with respect to each program administered by FNS and what are the responsibilities of the staff in each program.

Mr. BRALEY. The Administrator is responsible for the planning, direction, coordination and control of the overall operations of the programs of the Food and Nutrition Service (FNS). These programs include, but are not limited to, Food Stamp, School Lunch, School

Breakfast, Child Care, Special Milk, Food Distribution, Special Assistance Programs, and related activities primarily directed toward low-income families, and defense mobilization programs in connection with food management.

The Deputy Administrators for the Food Stamp and Special Nutrition Programs are responsible for implementing program statutes through promulgation of regulations and instructions under their jurisdictions. They provide training and assistance to State agencies, assure proper funds allocation and control, conduct program monitoring and evaluation, develop program policy and provide policy oversight.

The Deputy Administrator for Financial Management is responsible for accounting, budget, grants management and program information functions for all FNS programs, including oversight of the Agency's administrative review process both at FNS headquarters and five outstationed sites located throughout the Nation.

The Deputy Administrator for Management is responsible for personnel activities, civil rights and employment opportunity, information resource management, procurement, property and general administrative services.

Seven Regional Administrators are responsible for supervising 81 field locations (field and satellite) and 3 Regional Office Administered Programs (ROAP) offices whose mission is to ensure compliance in the Food Stamp Program and provide various review and support services for the other food assistance programs. Each Regional Administrator provides leadership and direction in implementing FNS program policy, develops operational planning and strategy, maintains cooperative working relationships with State agencies, and executes State corrective actions when necessary.

NATIONAL ADVISORY COUNCIL ON COMMODITY DISTRIBUTION

Mr. DURBIN. The National Advisory Council on Commodity Distribution met in February of 1992 and developed 18 recommendations. Provide a list of the recommendations as well as a brief description of your response to each.

Mr. BRALEY. The National Advisory Council on Commodity Distribution developed a total of 17 recommendations for their February 1992 Report to Congress. A summary of those recommendations and USDA's response to each recommendation will be provided for the record.

[The information follows:]

<u>Recommendation #1 - Specifications</u>. The Council recognized that USDA frozen beef products purchased by USDA using the current USDA specifications enable recipient agencies to meet the recommended dietary guidelines for fat when these products are used in program meals. The Council recommended continued use of these specifications.

USDA response. USDA is continuing to purchase frozen beef products under the specifications reviewed by the Council. These offer schools a variety of options for product selection to fit into their meal patterns. USDA continues to review the specifications for improvement, particularly those for the lowfat beef.

<u>Recommendation #2 - Processed Commodities</u>. The Council recommended that products and specifications be as user-friendly as possible with consideration given to reprocessing high-volume foods at the Federal level. The Council also encouraged the expansion of the State Option Contract (SOC) Program and USDA's reprocessing of surplus-removal bonus products.

USDA response. USDA is continuing to consider adding new products under the SOC Program. This year, chicken nuggets and chicken patties were available under SOC. USDA is also planning to test pork patties and salsa for possible inclusion into the program next year. USDA believes that the SOC Program is an excellent product development tool which can be used to provide recipient agencies with the kinds of products they wish to serve in their child nutrition meal programs.

<u>Recommendation #3 - Dietary Guidelines</u>. The Council encouraged USDA to continue its thrust to provide nutritious meals to recipients by continuing to provide commodity foods which will help to achieve this goal.

USDA response. USDA is committed to implementation of the dietary guidelines. The Food and Nutrition Service is in the process of developing recipes and guidance which will assist the schools in implementation of these guidelines.

Recommendation #4 - Nutrition Education. The Council commended USDA for the nutrition education initiatives presented in the 1993 budget and recommended that Congress appropriate the funds for these initiatives to include activities targeted to the population served by the Food Distribution Programs.

USDA response. USDA has developed a series of 12 nutrition and health fact sheets for distribution to households participating in the Food Distribution Program on Indian Reservations. The fact sheets address health problems prevalent in the native American population such as diabetes and heart disease. Monthly distribution began in January 1993.

Recommendation #5 - Ethnic and Regional Preferences. The Council commended USDA for its efforts to provide products that meet ethnic and regional preferences and recommended that these efforts be continued.

USDA response. USDA intends to continue current efforts to developing end product specifications tailored to the ethnic and regional preferences of program participants.

Recommendation #6 - Timing of Commodity Purchases. USDA should continue to explore alternative funding methods to make more commodity products available to recipient agencies at the beginning of the school year. Providing the Commodity Credit Corporation with authority to advance funds to USDA's Food and Nutrition Service (FNS) that would be repaid after FNS receives its appropriations is one alternative the Council recommends to Congress.

USDA response. The Food and Nutrition Service (FNS) is attempting to obtain advanced first quarter funding in order to purchase commodities to ensure delivery at the beginning of the school year. One of the methods under consideration is to provide the Commodity Credit Corporation the authority to advance funds as the Council reommends. This proposal would require legislation.

Recommendation #7 - Unitization of Shipments. The Council recommended that all shipments of USDA foods coming into initial receiving points within States be unitized with special transportation needs taken into account by program. Palletization is preferred.

USDA response. Most commodities being delivered this school year are being unitized (palletized or shrink wrapped). The only items not being unitized are those products (light weight items such as frozen french fries and potato rounds) typically not unitized in the industry. USDA is considering all the options available to industry in attempting to deliver commodities to the distributing agencies to ensure easy handling.

Recommendation #8 - Processing Agreements. The Council recommended that USDA expedite the promulgation of regulations allowing for a 1-year processing agreement with two 1-year possible extensions. The Council also recommended that the first renewal extension be effective for school year 1993-1994.

USDA response. USDA is working with regulations which would allow processing agreements to be in effect for 1 year, plus two 1-year extensions, providing that any changes in the contract provisions, and product data schedules, bond amounts, etc., be updated annually. These proposed regulations regulations are currently under review by the Office of Management and Budget.

Recommendation #9 - Food Service Management Companies. The Council reaffirmed its support for ensuring that companies such as food service management companies performing processing functions in a central commissary or plant are not exempt from the processing regulations.

USDA response. USDA is working on regulations which would require food service management companies performing processing functions in a central commissary or plant setting to be subject to the processing requirements stipulated by the State and National Commodity Processing Programs' regulations.

Recommendation #10 - Commodity Letter-of-Credit (CLOC) Sites. The Council recommended discontinuation of the CLOC/cash pilot programs and continued its strong support of the commodity distribution programs. The Council also recommended that efforts by USDA should be focused on ensuring that all federally funded programs purchase foods in compliance with the "Buy America" provisions.

USDA response. USDA continues to support the discontinuation of the CLOC/cash pilot programs; however, CLOC has been legislatively extended through school year 1995. USDA published an interim rule on July 21, 1988, containing "Buy American" provisions required by the Commodity Distribution Reform Act of 1987. This rule contained provisions which require schools to purchase domestic food items with any Federal funds.

Recommendation #11 - Transportation Issues. The Council urged USDA to address those transportation issues which were identified through a task force in order to ensure improved service to program recipients.

USDA response. The Transportation Task Force, comprised of representatives from USDA's Food and Nutrition Service, Agricultural Marketing Service and Agricultural Stabilization and Conservation Service and State distributing agencies, recently responded to the identified transportation concerns by updating FNS Instruction 709-5, Shipment and Receipt of Foods.

Recommendation #12 - Commodity Foods Newsletter. The Council commended USDA for publication of the Commodity Foods newsletter and encourages its continued publication with at least 3 issues per year, including one issue targeted to the non-school commodity programs.

USDA response. USDA continues to publish the Commodity Foods newsletter. The next issue, which will concentrate on The Emergency Food Assistance Program and the Nutrition Program for the Elderly, is scheduled for publication in June 1993.

Recommendation #13 - State Advisory Councils. The Council recommended that in order to improve the effectiveness of State Advisory Councils, USDA should develop guidelines for meaningful and effective State councils, addressing the structure of councils and appropriate content of council meetings to include frequency of meetings, communications, and alternate means of soliciting council input.

USDA response. USDA has developed the guidance and presented it at the Food Distribution National Advisory Council meeting held March 16-17, 1993. USDA will next furnish the draft guidance to States and the FNS regional offices for comment prior to finalizing the guidance.

Recommendation #14 - The Food Distribution Program on Indian Reservations (FDPIR). The Council recommended that USDA amend the current FDPIR regulation (7 CFR Part 254) to reestablish USDA waiver authority for cities and towns in Oklahoma with populations in excess of 10,000.

USDA response. This regulation has been drafted and will be submitted for formal clearance in the near future.

Recommendation # 15 - The Emergency Food Assistance Program (TEFAP) and the Soup Kitchen/Food Bank Program. The Council encouraged USDA to make purchases for TEFAP and the Soup Kitchen/Food Bank Program that will provide maximum volume of products for distribution.

USDA response. For Fiscal Year 1993, food banks will receive applesauce, orange juice, peaches, pears, raisins, green beans, peas, canned and dry beans, canned pork, apple juice and fruit cocktail. Soup kitchens will receive applesauce, fruit cocktail, pears, pineapple, corn, green beans, peas, tomato juice, canned pork, frozen ground beef, cut up chicken and nonfat dry milk. Additionally, the Farm Credit Banks and Associations Safety and Soundness Act of 1992 appropriated 42.3 million dollars for additional purchases for TEFAP distribution. Furthermore, under the President's economic recovery program, a request has been made for an additional $23.5 million to purchase even more food for this program. This request is currently being considered by Congress.

<u>Recommendation #16 - Commodity Supplemental Food Program (CSFP)</u>. The Council recommended that USDA expedite the proposed regulations to allow State agencies to allocate slots in CSFP between the Women, Infants, and Children (WIC) Program and the elderly to make optimum use of commodities.

USDA response. USDA has a proposed rule currently being developed which would consider a single caseload allocation allowing States flexibility to serve any categorically eligible applicant. Current authority allows States to convert unused Women, Infant and Children slots to serve the elderly population. However, States must make this decision within 90 days after receiving their caseload allocation.

<u>Recommendation #17 - Federal Food Safety Program</u>. The Council recommended that a Federal Food Safety Program be implemented providing national uniform tolerances regarding pesticides. The program should establish regulations on the basis of sound scientific evidence together with improvements in monitoring and testing.

USDA response. The Environmental Protection Agency establishes limits on pesticides in food and the Food and Drug Administration monitors products for compliance. This testing applies to all products except meat and poultry which are monitored by the Food Safety and Inspection Service of USDA. These Federal agencies are continally working to assure the wholesomness and safety of the nation's food supply.

Mr. DURBIN. Does the Council plan to meet in fiscal year 1993?

Mr. BRALEY. The National Advisory Council on Commodity Distribution recently met in March 1993. During this meeting, Council members continued their discussions on ways to improve commodity distribution. This meeting resulted in the development of recommendations that will be included in the Council's annual report to Congress.

The current membership of this Council expired with the March 1993 meeting. The Department of Agriculture will begin the nomination and selection process for new Council members shortly. We do not anticipate holding the next Council meeting until the first quarter of fiscal year 1994.

WIC DIETARY ASSESSMENT STUDY

Mr. DURBIN. What is the status of the WIC Dietary Assessment Study?

Mr. BRALEY. The recently competed WIC Dietary Assessment Study was the first of two studies aimed at providing improved methods of dietary assessment for use in WIC clinics.

The purpose of the initial study was to develop appropriate food frequency questionnaires for screening diets of women and children 1-5 years of age. The final report of the study, *Dietary Assessment Methodology for Use in the Special Supplemental Food Program for Women, Infants and Children (WIC)*, was submitted to the Food and Nutrition Service (FNS) by the Harvard School of Public Health in July 1991.

The follow-up study calls for the validation of the Harvard food frequency questionnaires (FFQ) and an existing set of food frequency questionnaires against a reference standard to determine which set of FFQ's has the greater validity relative to the standard. A contract for the WIC Dietary Assessment Validation Study was awarded by FNS in September 1992. A final report is expected by September 1994.

PROCESSED COMMODITIES INVENTORY MANAGEMENT SYSTEM

Mr. DURBIN. At last year's hearing, you told us that the Processed Commodities Inventory Management System, which has been in development since 1984, was undergoing final testing. Bring us up to date, including what the final cost was.

Mr. BRALEY. The Processed Commodities Inventory Management System (PCIMS), a system that serves the Agricultural Marketing Service, the Agricultural Stabilization and Conservation Service and the Food and Nutrition Service, became operational in FNS in April 1992 and is performing the day to day operations it was designed to do. Although the basic system is in place and is operational it is going through a period of changes and corrections to bring it to a point of maximum efficiency. This is common for a system of this size and complexity. The dollar amount paid to the contractors by the three Agencies from December 1983 through February 1993 was $47,726,757.

WELFARE REFORM PROJECTS

Mr. DURBIN. Last year you provided the Committee with a list and brief summary of all welfare reform projects you had underway or were being planned. Update this list for us, and be sure to include the results of completed projects, as well as a list of new ones planned for 1994.

Mr. BRALEY. The Department of Health and Human Services (DHHS) or the Food and Nutrition Service (FNS) has the lead for approving welfare reform projects. All projects are approved on the condition that they are cost neutral to the Federal Government. The information will be provided for the record.

[The information follows:]

Welfare Reform Projects Planned for Fiscal Year 1994

Minnesota: Minnesota Family Investment Plan (MFIP)

Summary: MFIP will consolidate Aid To Families With Dependent Children (AFDC), General Assistance for families, and Food Stamps to form a single program with one set of rules and with benefits issued as a cash grant. MFIP will encourage, support, and reward families engaged in activities leading to self-support.

Implementation/Project Area: The project is scheduled for implementation in April 1994 and will operate for 5 years. Participation will be capped at 6000 households.

Food Stamp Program Waivers Approved/Implemented in Fiscal Year 1993

Maryland: The Maryland Primary Prevention Initiative

Summary: The Maryland demonstration encourages increased parental responsibility and preventative health care. Families AFDC benefits are reduced if school-age children do not attend school regularly or do not receive required health services. The State agency received a food stamp waiver to exclude an annual $20 special needs allowance payment that is provided to AFDC households complying with required health checkups.

Implementation/Project Area: The Statewide project was implemented in 1992 and will operate for five years.

Virginia: Virginia Incentive to Advance Learning (VITAL)

Summary: The demonstration targets families of children in grades six, seven and eight in three schools. Incentives, such as increased AFDC grants, are provided to encourage school attendance and extensive counseling services are available to the AFDC families. The State agency received a food stamp waiver to exclude the increased AFDC grant amount as income in food stamp calculations.

Implementation/Length of Demonstration: The project was implemented in the cities of Norfolk and Richmond and Chesterfield County in 1992 and will operate for two years.

Michigan: To Strengthen Michigan Families

Summary: The Michigan demonstration expands eligibility to working and two parent families, modifies work requirements and strengthens child support provisions. The State agency received a food stamp waiver to exclude as income and resources, all income earned by dependent children, up to age 19, who are AFDC recipients and students.

Implementation/Project Areas: The Statewide project was implemented October 1, 1992 and will operate for five years.

Utah: Utah Single Parent Employment Project (SPEP)

Summary: The Utah SPEP project will target AFDC recipients with intensive work requirements designed to transform the AFDC program from a maintenance into an employment program. Exemptions from work requirements will be waived to assign participants to "self-sufficiency" activities. Participants who complete assigned activities will receive incentive payments while those who fail to complete the activities will have their AFDC benefits reduced. Waivers are provided to streamline the eligibility requirements between the AFDC and Food Stamp programs. Households receiving both AFDC and Food Stamp benefits will have the option of receiving food stamp benefits in cash.

Implementation/Project Area: The project will be implemented in one county in early 1993 and will last no longer than 5 years. The State may include additional counties to the project provided the Federal agencies are advised three months ahead of time.

__Ongoing Welfare Reform Projects__

Alabama: Avenues to Self-Sufficiency through Employment and Training (ASSETS)

Summary: The project consolidates AFDC, Food Stamps, and Medicaid. Eligibility criteria for all programs is simplified and handled by a single caseworker --i.e., case management--. The project provides food stamp benefits in cash, standardizes benefits, intensifies employment and training activities, enhances child support enforcement activity, and extends Medicaid eligibility. Participation is mandatory.

Implementation/Project Area: The project operates in three counties which were phased in between May 1990 and January 1991. The project is expected to end January 1995.

New York: New York Child Assistance Program --CAP--

Summary: CAP is an assistance program available to recipients of AFDC with earnings and child support orders as an alternative to AFDC. Child assistance payments are made to eligible custodial parents, based on household size, and reduced by a portion of the income earned. Food stamp benefits are cashed out under CAP in keeping with the basic concept of CAP as a non-welfare program designed to give low-income wage earners responsibility for management of their own financial resources. CAP recipients are exempt from food stamp work registration and employment and training requirements.

Implementation/Project Area: Implementation was completed in phases between October 1988 and April 1989. Due to delays in the implementation, the project was extended to end April 1994. CAP operates in seven counties.

Ohio: Ohio Transition to Independence

Summary: The demonstration is an initiative designed to help AFDC recipients become self-sufficient through employment. Two food stamp waivers were approved for Ohio's Transition to Independence program: the first allowed the State to develop a standard deduction for self-employment business expenses of in-home day care providers; the second waived the $62 monthly bonus incentive for meeting Learning, Earning and Parenting (LEAP) school attendance requirements as household income for food stamp computation.

Implementation/Project Area: The project was implemented in January 1989 and currently operates Statewide.

Projects Scheduled to End in Fiscal Year 1993

Washington: Washington Family Independence Program (WFIP)

Summary: WFIP replaces AFDC and Food Stamp benefits for families with children. All benefits are provided in the form of cash. Increased work incentives are reflected in benefit levels which rise with attachment to the work force. Extensive employment and training activities are available to clients, as well as a variety of other supportive services (e.g., child care and transitional benefits). Participation is voluntary.

Implementation/Project Area: The project was implemented in July 1988 and will end June 1993. The project operates in 15 Community Services Offices.

ACCOUNTS RECEIVABLE INFORMATION

Mr. DURBIN. Please update the table that appears on page 107 of last year's hearing record, showing accounts receivable information, to include fiscal year 1992.

Mr. BRALEY. The updated table will be provided for the record.

[The information follows:]

Food and Nutrition Service
STATUS OF RECEIVABLES
(In thousands of dollars)

	1992 Estimate		1993 Estimate	
	Number	Amount	Number	Amount
Change in Receivables:				
1. Receivables, start of year	1,207	700,578	1,331	772,419
2. New receivables	1,924	364,955	2,399	395,132
3. Receivables collected	-1,211	-140,083	-1,352	-172,069
Income tax refund offset	(-2)	(-3,448)	(-9)	(-9,000)
Litigation	-16)	(-998)	(-18)	(-1,043)
Private collection agencies	(-62)	(-26)	(-101)	(-55)
4. Write-offs	-139	-818	-141	-858
5. Other adjustments	-450	-152,213	-616	-227,829
6. Receivables, end of year	1,331	772,419	1,421	786,795
Status of Receivables:				
1. Delinquent receivables, end of year	1,195	760,304	1,275	771,059
2. Loan loss estimate	0	0	0	0
Guaranteed loans:				
1. Total amount outstanding	0	0	0	0
2. Participation by Federal government	0	0	0	0
3. Guaranteed loans terminated	0	0	0	0
4. Loans repurchased	0	0	0	0
5. Recoveries from liquidation of collateral	0	0	0	0

Mr. DURBIN. Provide a list of all legislation enacted in fiscal year 1992 affecting FNS programs. Include a description of the legislation, how it will affect the program, and any costs associated with its implementation.

Mr. BRALEY. A summary of the legislation for each program will be provided for the record.

[The information follows:]

CHILD NUTRITION PROGRAMS

Four separate pieces of legislation which affected the Child Nutrition Programs were enacted during Fiscal Year 1992. The first of these was Public Law 102-342 which increased the amount of funding required to be spend on the homeless demonstration projects to $650,000 in Fiscal Year 1993 and $800,000 in Fiscal Year 1994, made public entities eligible for the demonstration and required notification of States of the availability of the projects. These provisions have the overall effect of increasing the size of the demonstration. Such an increase will have a significant impact in the areas of staffing and travel funds.

A second provision found in Public Law 102-342 changed the eligibility requirements for Title XX centers participating in the Child and Adult Care Food Program (CACFP) to allow such centers to participate when 25 percent of their licensed capacities are made up of children receiving Title XX benefits. This provision will in some cases facilitate the participation of these centers in the CACFP both with respect to their ability to get onto the program as well as the month-to-month determination of their eligibility status. Its enactment had a cost of less than $1 million associated with it.

Public Law 102-375 expanded the group of individuals eligible for benefits under the adult day component of the CACFP by adding those persons who are enrolled in a participating adult day care center and living in a group arrangement in the community. This provision simply codified program policy previously implemented and, therefore, had no costs associated with its implementation.

During Fiscal Year 1992, Congress enacted into law Public Law 102-337, which amended the National School Lunch Act to correct a technical flaw in Public Law 101-147 pertaining to the National Food Service Management Institute. This technical amendment clarified the Department's authority to maintain the Institute through a cooperative agreement or a grant agreement. There were no costs associated with its implementation.

Finally, Public Law 102-512 revised the funding formula for State Administrative Expense funds to permit the Agency to use $1 million of Homeless Demonstration Project funds at the beginning of the fiscal year. The enactment of this provision has the potential for a very significant increase in the size of the demonstration. Combined with the increase in funding resulting from the enactment of Public Law 102-342 discussed above, this provision will have serious implications for staffing and technical assistance/monitoring costs.

<u>Food Stamp Program</u>

The following items of legislation that affect the Food Stamp Program were approved in Fiscal Year 1992:

P.L. 102-237, the Food, Agriculture, Conservation, and Trade Act Amendments of 1991 (approved December 13, 1991) had no overall cost. The provisions of the legislation:

- Expanded eligibility to receive food stamps and to use them to purchase meals provided by group living arrangements to all individuals who meet the Food Stamp Act's definition of "disabled".

- Limited categorical eligibility for General Assistance (GA) recipients to those receiving benefits from programs that have income limits at least as stringent as the food stamp gross income test.

- Denied categorical eligibility to recipients of GA programs that provide one-time emergency payments that cannot be provided for more than one continuous month. This restriction does not apply to GA programs that require monthly certification, but provide on-going nonemergency payments for more than a single month in at least some instances.

- Expanded the income exclusion for educational income by excluding income either used for or made available (i.e., earmarked) by the school, institution, program, or other grantor for: tuition, mandatory fees (including the rental or purchase of equipment, material, and supplies related to pursuing the course of study involved), books, supplies, transportation, and miscellaneous personnel expenses (other than living expenses).

- Provided a food stamp income exclusion for amounts necessary for the fulfillment of a plan for achieving self-support (PASS) under Title XVI of the Social Security Act. (The Farm Bill approved in Fiscal Year 1991 provided a resource exclusion for such funds.)

- The income exclusion for PASS accounts was effective upon enactment unless (1) a State agency had information that a household member had a PASS account (in which case, the effective date for such a household was October 1, 1990) or (2) there was a fair hearing on the subject of a denied income exclusion for a PASS account (in which case, the effective date was the date of the fair hearing request). State agencies were not required to do file searches unless the question of an income exclusion for PASS accounts had been raised with the State agency prior to enactment.

- Expanded the definition of an inaccessible resource: one whose sale or other disposition is unlikely to produce any significant amount of funds for the support of the household.

- Prohibited the Department from requiring State agencies to require verification of the value of inaccessible resources unless the State agency determines that the information provided by the household is questionable.

- Excluded all of the resources of recipients of AFDC; SSI; and the SSI substitutes.

- Included as income the portion of a transitional housing vendor payment that equals 50% of AFDC's maximum shelter allowance only if the shelter allowance to be paid is calculated separately from amounts for other household needs.

- Required the publication of outcome-based performance standards for the Employment and Training (E&T) Program (including improvements in education levels) by 12 months after the publication of final outcome-based performance standards for the Job Opportunities and Basic Skills (JOBS) training programs.

- Deleted the specific requirements now in the Food Stamp Act on the content of outcome-based E&T performance standards, referring only to service to individuals with greater barriers to employment and volunteers.

- Required the new standards and the interim standards to meet the current effort required by the regulations for E&T components; i.e., 12 hours a month for two months.

- Prohibited the Department from requiring E&T participation of more than 10 percent of nonexempt work registrants in Fiscal Years 1992 and 1993 and 15 percent in Fiscal Years 1994 and 1995.

- Postponed implementation of required staggered issuance and exemptions from monthly reporting for households on Indian reservations until April 1, 1993. Required final regulations by December 1, 1992.

- Required the General Accounting Office (GAO) to report to Congress by 180 days after enactment on its findings about the difficulties experienced by residents on Indian reservations in obtaining food stamp benefits, using food stamps, and purchasing food economically with food stamps.

- Required that the GAO study include actions at the Federal, State or local level that could remedy problems on Indian reservations.

- Required GAO to consult with tribes, State agencies, and other appropriate parties.

- Corrected one place in the Food Stamp Act where the term "allotments" was not replaced with "benefits" to cover areas where food stamp benefits are provided electronically rather than in coupon form.

- Prohibited prorating during certification periods except during the initial month.

- Gave households who have claims made against them because of inadvertent household errors 10 days to select alternate means of paying the claims before allotment reduction is used. (Effective upon enactment)

- Required the Department to commence operating the vehicle exclusion limit demonstration project by January 1, 1993. Solicitation of requests to participate in the demonstration projects were required by May 1, 1992.

- Made a technical amendment to the Homeless Eligibility Clarification Act of 1986 so that restaurants could be authorized as retail food stores to accept food stamps from homeless people. (Retroactive to October 1, 1990)

- The effective date for provisions not otherwise specified was February 1, 1992.

P.L. 102-265, Technical Correction to Food Stamp Act of 1977 Relating to Income Exclusions (approved March 26,1992), which corrected a technical error in P.L. 102-237 so that blind SSI recipients can have their PASS accounts excluded as income, just as other SSI recipients do. This legislation had no cost associated with its implementation.

P.L. 102-325, the Higher Education Amendments of 1992 (approved July 23, 1992), which provided a blanket exclusion for food stamp purposes for assistance received under the Higher Education Act or under Bureau of Indian Affairs student assistance programs and for loans provided under the Tribal Development Student Assistance Revolving Loan Program. The food stamp cost of this legislation was $25 million.

P.L. 102-351 (approved August 26, 1992), which prevented a reduction in the adjusted cost of the Thrifty Food Plan in Fiscal Year 1993. The estimated cost associated with the implementation of this legislation is $386 million.

Food Distribution Programs

Public Law 102-237, the Food, Agriculture, Conservation, and Trade Act Amendments of 1991, was enacted December 13, 1991. Section 921 of the Act amended the Agriculture and Food Act of 1981 to extend the Elderly Commodity Processing Demonstrations through Fiscal Year 1994. Section 922 of the Act amended the Hunger Prevention Act of 1988 to establish a three-tiered priority system for the distribution of section 110 commodities to soup kitchens and food banks. The Act also gave the Secretary the authority to settle and adjust claims arising under the Emergency Food Assistance Act of 1983, and section 110 of the Hunger Prevention Act. No costs are associated with implementation of this Act.

Public Law 102-375, the Older Americans Act Amendments of 1992, was enacted September 30, 1992. Section 310 of the law reauthorized the Nutrition Program for the Elderly through Fiscal Year 1995. In addition, the law retroactively increased the Fiscal Year 1992 per-meal reimbursement rate from $.5676 to $.61 and established a level of assistance for succeeding fiscal years equal to the greater of $.61 per meal, adjusted annually for inflation, or the current appropriation divided by the number of meals served in the preceding year. The law also requires that final reimbursement claims be adjusted to use the full program appropriation each year. The rate increase for Fiscal Year 1992 cost $10,386,382. Based on our estimate of the number of meals to be served this year, the Fiscal Year 1993 cost should be $2,595,147.

Public Law 102-342, the Child Nutrition Amendments of 1992, was enacted August 14, 1992. Section 301 of the law amended the National School Lunch Act to extend the demonstration projects for Cash in Lieu of Commodities (CASH)/Commodity Letter of Credit (CLOC) through Fiscal Year 1994. Section 410 amended the Commodity Distribution Reform Act and WIC Amendments of 1987 to reauthorize the National Advisory Council on Commodity Distribution through Fiscal Year 1996. For Fiscal Year 1993, costs to convene the legislatively-mandated semiannual meetings of the National Advisory Council on Commodity Distribution and prepare the Council's annual report to Congress will be approximately $70,000.

WIC Program

Authorization

Public Law 102-342, the Child Nutrition Amendments of 1992, was enacted on August 14, 1992. This legislation establishes a WIC Breastfeeding Promotion Program "...to promote breastfeeding as the best method of infant nutrition, foster wider public acceptance of breastfeeding in the United States, and assist in the distribution of breastfeeding equipment to breastfeeding women." It also authorizes the Department to accept donations or support from outside sources to support the effort since no funds were specifically appropriated for this program. Implementation costs are expected to be approximately $3 to 5 million, the bulk of which will be supported by funds solicited from the private sector. FNS will also incur travel, research and staff costs which, without additional resources, will have to be sustained through a redirection of priorities within FNS.

In addition, this legislation adds homelessness and migrancy as nutritional risk criteria for WIC Program eligibility. No significant implementation costs are associated with this provision.

WIC Farmers' Market Nutrition Program

Public Law 102-314, the WIC Farmers' Market Nutrition Act of 1992, was enacted on July 2, 1992. This law authorized the creation of the WIC Farmers' Market Nutrition Program (FMNP) to accomplish two goals: (1) to provide fresh, nutritious, unprepared foods (such as fruits and vegetables) from farmers' markets to women, infants and children who are nutritionally at risk; and (2) to expand the awareness and use of farmers' markets by consumers. Previous to this legislation, the Department was authorized to establish farmers' market demonstration projects. These projects were authorized in certain areas of 10 States: Connecticut, Iowa, Maryland, Massachusetts, Michigan, New York, Pennsylvania, Texas, Vermont, and Washington. These areas continue to be authorized under the newly created FMNP. The $3 million appropriated for the FMNP for Fiscal Year 1993 along with unspent funds from the previous fiscal year will sustain the current 10 States. FNS will incur administrative costs such as program implementation, training, and monitoring costs which, without additional resources, will have to be sustained through a redirection of priorities within FNS.

In addition, Public Law 102-512, the WIC Infant Formula Procurement Act of 1992, was enacted on October 24, 1992. This law includes several provisions. First, it requires the Department to establish procedures for the solicitation and selection of infant formula bids on behalf of State agencies. If requested by State agencies, it requires the Department to solicit infant formula rebate contracts on their behalf. Second, it imposes civil money penalties of up to $100 million per year or disqualification of infant formula manufacturers that price-fix or engage in related anti-competitive activities. Third, it requires State agencies to include in their Fiscal Year 1994 State Plans a description of the methods that will be used to reduce the purchase of low-iron infant formula for infants on the program for whom such formula has not been prescribed by a physician or other appropriate health professional. We estimate that FNS will need 5.5 additional staff years at its headquarters and regional offices to negotiate with WIC State agencies, develop the bid request, and select the winning bid.

BENEFITS AND ADMINISTRATIVE COSTS

Mr. DURBIN. In your statement you say that over 99 percent of the total appropriation for FNS is for benefit payments or grants to states for administrative costs. Tell us what percent of the total and what the dollar value is for each, benefits and state administrative costs.

Mr. BRALEY. The costs associated with benefits and state administrative costs are $36.0 billion and $2.5 billion, respectively. Benefits represent approximately 93 percent of the total appropriation and administrative costs are approximately 6 percent.

STAFF LEVELS

Mr. DURBIN. FNS has almost 2,000 staff years associated with it. This is less than two percent of the entire workforce for USDA. Tell us, Mr. Braley, is this enough considering your agency administers over $38 billion in various programs? Do you have enough personnel to effectively manage these programs?

Mr. BRALEY. The Food and Nutrition Service (FNS) is allocated 1,979 staff years for fiscal year 1993. This represents a reduction in Agency size of roughly one-third since 1980. It is true the agency employs less than two percent of the USDA workforce. State and local level employees are generally responsible for the operation of our various programs. Nevertheless, growth in the size and number of our programs over the past decade, as well as the increase in legislative activity in these programs, has made it more difficult to maintain adequate program guidance and oversight. Within the current budget climate, however, the Agency is prepared to effectively undertake the most critical aspects of our mission within the resource levels we have requested.

FINANCIAL MANAGEMENT SYSTEM

Mr. DURBIN. When will your new financial management system be complete?

Mr. BRALEY. The new financial management system was designed to be developed and implemented in two phases. Phase 1 was completed in September 1992 with the installation of a new core accounting system incorporating the standard general ledger and all Joint Financial Management Improvement Program, Treasury and OMB requirements.

The second phase, begun in September 1992, ties the remaining major financial functions into the core accounting system so that all major financial functions are integrated in one set of related databases, as directed by instruction pursuant to the CFO Act. Integration allows for the control by management of financial transactions across the range of financial functions (e.g. comparing budget projections to obligations to outlays by transaction code).

The second phase has four component parts: grants management which covers payments to grantees through Treasury and the Federal Reserve; budget formulation which ties account balances electronically to the formulation process; administrative funds management which allows us to both project and account for such funds, and; performance measurement which can track the cost of doing business along with performance measures.

All work to date has been completed within budget. To date only the grants management part of Phase 2 has been funded. Pending availability of funds, the budget, administrative funds and performance measurement work can proceed in fiscal year 1994 with full operation in fiscal year 1995.

CFO ACT

Mr. DURBIN. How much did you spend in fiscal years 1991 and 1992 to comply with the requirements of the CFO Act and what are your estimates for fiscal year 1993?

Mr. BRALEY. The Food and Nutrition Service (FNS) established a CFO-type organization in 1977 led by a Deputy Administrator for Financial Management. Prior to passage of the CFO Act, FNS had already started work on many of the components of the CFO Act including installation of an integrated Agency Financial Management System (AFMS) to ensure accurate accounting and budget data, pursuit of Electronic Benefits Transfer (EBT) to improve cash management and getting into the Federal Tax Refund Offset Program (FTROP) to improve debt management. The AFMS is an off-the-shelf software package for a core accounting system which was installed October 1, 1992. Costs for AFMS have been primarily for modification, installation, and training. Costs for EBT were for the development of a settlement service and reconciliation which will allow FNS to support large scale EBT operations by paying retailers accounts daily electronically within the same time frames that commercial debit card transactions now occur across the country.

STUDIES

Mr. DURBIN. You state that over $19 million will be spent on ten congressionally mandated studies and one non-mandated study. Briefly describe each of these and the cost associated with them.

Mr. BRALEY. I will include for the record a brief description and the costs associated with each of the 10 mandated studies. In addition to these congressionally mandated studies, we also have numerous nonmandated studies. These include EBT, control of food stamp trafficking, reducing barriers to good nutrition among food stamp program participants, use of nutrient standards in the National School Lunch Program, assessment of nutritional content of meals in the Child and Adult Care Food Program, and the Infant Feeding Study.

[The information follows:]

FOOD STAMP COMPETITIVE NUTRITION EDUCATION GRANTS AND OUTCOME EVALUATION

Recognizing that low-income families need access to nutrition education as well as food assistance, Congress appropriated up to $500,000 in FY 1993 to provide competitive grants to one or more State cooperative extension services who shall administer the grants in coordination with other State or local agencies serving low-income people. The grants will include a requirement for evaluations of the outcome of nutrition education interventions.

Cost: $500,000

FOOD STAMP RESOURCE TESTS FOR LICENSED VEHICLES

This study will evaluate the impact of exempting one vehicle per household from the fair market value test for countable assets.

Cost: Unknown at this time

Food Stamp Outreach Grants and Evaluation

Congressional action on the 1993 appropriation for the Food Stamp Program included $1,000,000 to fund grants for outreach to hard-to-reach eligible populations. The evaluation will focus on success in reducing barriers to participation, increases in program participation, administrative effectiveness, program efficiency, and the adequacy of administrative resources.

Cost: $1,000,000.

WIC PARTICIPANT AND PROGRAM CHARACTERISTICS STUDY

This biennial study, planned to describe WIC participants in April 1993, will use information reported to FNS to provide Congress data on local WIC agencies and WIC participants, including income and nutritional risk characteristics, participation by migrant farmworker households, and other attributes of participants.

Cost: Unknown at this time

School Lunch and Breakfast Cost Study

The purpose of this study is to determine the cost to produce reimbursable meals in the National School Lunch Program and the School Breakfast Program. In addition, the study will examine the indirect costs charged to School Food Authorities to produce school meals, and local administrative costs and sources of non-Federal revenue that support meal production.

Cost: $1,542,316

NSLP School Dropout Study

This study will examine why schools chose not to participate in the National School Lunch Program. The study includes both schools which have recently dropped out of the program and those which are longtime nonparticipants. The final report will include a description of the scope of the dropout/nonparticipant problem; the reasons for and the decision-making process for dropout and nonparticipation; and the characteristics of dropout/nonparticipant schools.

Cost: To be awarded in Fiscal Year 1993.

State Administrative Cost Study

The primary objective of this study is to examine the changes in the responsibilities of State level staff administering the National School Lunch Program and School Breakfast Program and the costs associated with these changes. A survey will be conducted with all State Child Nutrition Directors to examine a number of issues related to the administration of the school lunch and breakfast programs, including the organization of the State agencies, their functional responsibilities, budget process and fiscal behavior of State agencies, and the perceptions of State agency officials about the appropriateness of State Administrative Expense (SAE) funding. FNS program data will be used to document changes in the amount of SAE funding over the past several years.

Cost: To be awarded in Fiscal Year 1993.

Paperwork Reduction Pilot Projects Evaluation

Public Law 101-147 amended the National School Lunch Act to require the Secretary to conduct three pilot programs seeking to simplify and reduce paperwork burden in the National School Lunch Program by improving application an meal counting processes. Ten pilot sites are currently involved in this demonstration. The evaluation design calls for a pretest-posttest case study approach. Baseline data was collected during School Year 1991. Alternative application and meal counting procedures began in School Year 1992. This evaluation requires data collection and analysis in all 10 sites through 1994.

Cost: $853.996.

Study of School Lunch Eligible Non-Participants

This study examines why some eligible students don't apply for, or eat, free and reduced-price meals. Results of this study should allow the Secretary to assess what more should be done to reach all eligible students. By means of case study methodology, this study will examine the reasons why those income-eligible to participate in the school lunch program fail to do so. Potential barriers (real and perceived) will be examined by directly interviewing nonparticipant households. The study will also recommend way to reduce barriers and increase daily participation.

Cost: $566,373

UNIVERSAL FREE LUNCH STUDY

The Senate passed a resolution in July of 1992 asking the Secretary of Agriculture to conduct a study of various options for implementing and funding universal school lunch and breakfast programs, i.e., all lunches and breakfasts reimbursed at one rate (with no regard to income status) and served at no charge to students. FNS will merge data from a variety of research projects such as the Evaluation of the Paperwork Reduction Pilot Projects, the School Nutrition Dietary Assessment Study, the child Nutrition Program Operations Study, and the Farm Bill studies to answer the questions posed by the Senate.

Cost: Federal staff costs only.

Mr. DURBIN. Are any of these studies duplicating research already done by Federal or non-Federal entities?

Mr. BRALEY. Virtually all of the studies that FNS is conducting are topics that are unique and do not duplicate research completed by other researchers. However, there are two issues where Congress has required research from both FNS and the General Accounting Office (GAO). We have been in contact with GAO to reduce the amount of overlap where possible.

The first assignment that GAO has begun is an examination of the costs to produce a school lunch and a comparison with Federal reimbursement rates. GAO is reexamining data collected in the Food and Nutrition Service's Child Nutrition Program Operations Study. The Food and Nutrition Service is currently conducting the School Lunch and Breakfast Study required by P.L. 101-624. We are collecting data from a representative sample of school districts to produce a national estimate of the cost of producing reimbursable meals in the NSLP and SBP, including indirect and local administrative costs.

The second assignment undertaken by GAO is to identify and rank factors which have led schools to drop out of the National School Lunch Program. Based on the requirements of the Farm Bill, the Food and Nutrition Service is about to embark on a similar study that would examines schools that have dropped out or have never participated in the NSLP. Many of the same issues are expected to be examines.

Mr. DURBIN. You have a number of reports coming out over the next few months. Please send this Committee a copy of all reports issued by your agency.

Mr. BRALEY. It is normal procedure to provide a copy of all reports to the Chairman and Ranking Minority Member of the Committee. We will be glad to continue this policy. A list of reports that are expected to be released in the next six months will be provided for the record.

[The information follows:]

Special Nutrition Dietary Assessment Study.
Adult Day Care Study.
Study of Food Service Management Companies in School.
Nutrition Programs.
Menu Modification Demonstration Grants: Evaluation Results.
CACFP For-Profit Center Demonstration Final Report.
Low-Income Family Day Care Home Demonstration.
Child Nutrition Homeless Shelter Demonstration Year 2. Final Report.
Paperwork Reduction Pilot Projects Interim Report.

The Impacts of the State-Initiated EBT Demonstration on the Food Stamp Program.
Administrative Costs and Retailer Impacts in the San Diego Cashout Demonstration.
Characteristics of New Applicants for Food Stamps.
A Profile of the Motor Vehicle Assets.

Mr. DURBIN. Mr. Skeen, do you have any other questions?

Mr. SKEEN. No, Mr. Chairman.

Mr. DURBIN. Well, I thank you very much for your testimony. We have quite a responsibility in dealing with the appropriations for your services. The Subcommittee is going to do its best to continue to give you the resources to make sure that these programs have their integrity maintained and enhanced. I thank you for your testimony this morning.

Ronald J. Vogel
Biography

Mr. Ronald J. Vogel is the Associate Deputy Administrator for Special Nutrition Programs, Food and Nutrition Service (FNS), U.S. Department of Agriculture. He is specifically responsible for programs managed within FNS' Child Nutrition Division, which includes the National School Lunch Program, the School Breakfast Program, Special Milk Program, the Child and Adult Care Food Program and the Summer Food Service Program. He is also responsible for programs managed within FNS' Food Distribution Division. Previously, Mr. Vogel was Director of the Supplemental Food Programs Division. Programs under his director included WIC and the Commodity Supplemental Food Program (CSFP). Mr. Vogel was also Director of the Program Information Division for Financial Management, a Food Program Specialist within the Office of Regional Operations, and a Program Specialist for the Office of Analysis and Evaluation. Mr. Vogel was employed as an evaluation specialist in the private sector for six years before joining the Federal Government in 1981. He obtained his undergraduate degree from the University of Virginia and his postgraduate degree from Duke University.

In 1991, Ron received the Department's Superior Service Award in the category of food assistance "for outstanding contributions in promoting better health and nutrition for the needy women and young children."

Biography of Michael E. Fishman

Michael E. Fishman became the Acting Director of Office of Anlaysis and Evaluation in November 1992. Mr. Fishman joined the Office of Analysis and Evaluation on September 20, 1992 as Associate Director.

Prior to coming to FNS, Mr. Fishman served as the Director of the Division of Income Security Policy in the Office of the Assistant Secretary for Planning Evaluation at the Department of Health and Human Services in Washington, DC. In this capacity, he was involved with many social service programs including: Aid to Families With Dependent Children (AFDC); Job Opportunities and Basic Skills Program (JOBS); Child Support Enforcement Program; Old Age, Survivors, and Disability Insurance (OASDI); Supplemental Security Income (SSI); Low Income Home Energy Assistance (LIHEAP); Community Services Block Grant (CSBG); and Refugee Assistance.

In his 20-year career with the Department of Health and Human Services, Mr. Fishman has served in the Office of Human Development Services and the Office of Assistant Secretary for Planning and Evaluation at the national and regional office level. He received his Master's Degree in Psychology from Antioch College in Seattle, Washington, and is pursuing his Doctoral Degree in Public Administration at the University of Southern California, Public Affairs Center, Washington, DC.

For Release only by the
House Committee on Appropriations

UNITED STATES DEPARTMENT OF AGRICULTURE
Food and Nutrition Service

Statement by George Braley, Acting Assistant Secretary, for Food and Consumer Services
Before the Subcommittee on Agriculture, Rural Development, Food and Drug Administration and Related Agencies

Thank you, Mr. Chairman. It is my pleasure to appear before this subcommittee to discuss the current operations of food assistance programs of the United States Department of Agriculture (USDA). David Rust, Acting Administrator for the Human Nutrition Information Service, and Andrew Hornsby, Acting Administrator for the Food and Nutrition Service, are here with me today.

The total appropriations enacted for the current Fiscal Year exceed $38 billion, including the reserve for the Food Stamp Program. The Human Nutrition Information Service operates with $10.8 million and the Food and Nutrition Service operates with over $38.5 billion.

HUMAN NUTRITION INFORMATION SERVICE

The Human Nutrition Information Service (HNIS) conducts applied research in support of the USDA's mission to promote the health and well-being of Americans through improved nutrition. HNIS contributes to this mission through national food consumption surveys, food composition research, and nutritional education programs. HNIS' accomplishes these tasks by conducting the national food intake and food consumption surveys, gathering data on the nutrition composition of food which it maintains for all to use in the National Nutrient Data Bank, and by providing information about a wide range of nutrition issues. The work of HNIS assumes new importance in light of the general public's increasing concern about nutrition, pesticide residues, and the safety of food additives. The Agency provides leadership for USDA in the National Nutrition Monitoring and Related Research Program and in the development and promotion of the Dietary Guidelines for Americans. The food guide pyramid, which visually portrays the dietary guidelines is the best known product of HNIS' nutrition education efforts.

Current appropriations support the Continuing Survey of Food Intakes by Individuals, a major national survey designed to track changes in food consumption patterns of individuals, redesign and maintenance of the National Nutrient Data Bank, the updating of the Dietary Guidelines for Americans, and a wide range of activities authorized by Public Law 101-445, the National Nutrition Monitoring and Related Research Act of 1990.

FOOD AND NUTRITION SERVICE

The Food and Nutrition Service provides food assistance to low-income people, helping them to achieve adequate and nutritious diets. We estimate that one out of every six Americans is served through the fourteen programs managed by the Food and Nutrition Service. The Food Stamp Program is, of course, our largest program--one which is available to all low-income, low-resource households. In addition, Agency programs target special groups, such as pregnant and post-partum women, infants, school children, Native Americans and the elderly, recognizing that these groups are at high nutritional risk.

Our presentations today will provide an overview of the missions of these agencies, their organizational structures, and a review of current operations in the Department's food assistance programs. We will also note issues which we believe to be of interest to this committee, and of course we will be happy to answer your questions about these matters.

With your permission, Mr. Chairman, I would now like to ask Mr. Rust and Mr. Hornsby to make their presentations. Afterwards, we will be pleased to answer any questions the Committee may have. Thank you.

For Release only by the
House Committee on Appropriations

UNITED STATES DEPARTMENT OF AGRICULTURE
Food and Nutrition Service

Statement of Andrew P. Hornsby Jr., Acting Administrator
Food and Nutrition Service
Before the Subcommittee on Agriculture, Rural Development, Food and Drug Administration and Related Agencies

Thank you Mr. Chairman. It is a pleasure to appear before this subcommittee to discuss the operations of food assistance programs administered by the United States Department of Agriculture (USDA). I would like to introduce key members of the staff of the Food and Nutrition Service appearing with me: Bonny O'Neil, the Acting Deputy Administrator for the Food Stamp Program, Ron Vogel, Acting Deputy Administrator for the Special Nutrition Programs, Michael Fishman, Acting Director of our Office of Analysis and Evaluation and Kenneth Bresnahan, our Budget Director. Mr. Vogel and Mr. Fishman are appearing before the committee for the first time. In keeping with committee policy, I would like to place their biographical statements into the record at this point.

THE MISSION OF THE FOOD AND NUTRITION SERVICE

The mission of the Food and Nutrition Service (FNS) is to alleviate hunger and to safeguard the health and well-being of the Nation through the administration of nutrition education and domestic food assistance programs. The Food and Nutrition Service is the Federal Government's front-line agency providing food assistance to the most needy and vulnerable of our citizens.

Established in 1969 to administer the domestic food assistance and nutrition education programs of the USDA, FNS works in partnership with State and local governments to perform its mission.

SIZE AND ORGANIZATION OF FNS

Fiscal Year 1993 appropriations for the Food and Nutrition Service total $38.5 billion, in eight accounts covering fourteen major programs, including federal administrative expenses. FNS is allocated 1,979 staff years funded from the Food Program Administration, Food Stamp and Child Nutrition accounts.

The Food and Nutrition Service's eight appropriations account for over half of the budget authority of the USDA. Over two-thirds of the total appropriations are used to fund the Food Stamp Program. Over 99 percent of the total appropriations are used for recipient benefit payments or grants to States for their administration of the programs. Less than one percent of the total amounts appropriated pays for direct federal administrative expenses, including salaries and benefits, travel, program research and evaluation, information technology and the cost of printing, distributing and redeeming food stamps. The Food and Nutrition Service employs less than two percent of the people who work for the USDA.

About one-third of FNS employees are stationed at the headquarters office in Alexandria, Virginia. These staff are engaged primarily in program policy and regulatory development, program research and evaluation, Food Stamp Program compliance activity, information resources management, financial management and certain other centralized administrative support functions. The other two-thirds of the staff are located at seven regional offices and 81 field offices nationwide. These personnel work closely with State and local cooperators to implement and monitor the programs, as well as working with retailers who seek authorization to redeem food stamps.

I will provide for the record a copy of the current agency organization chart and geographic staff allocation.

THE BUDGET OVERVIEW

As I mentioned earlier, for Fiscal Year 1993, the Food and Nutrition Service appropriation totaled about $38.5 billion, including reserves. This was an increase of about $5.4 billion above the Fiscal Year 1992 appropriated level. The most significant changes occurred in the mandatory programs and are driven by changes in the economy and other technical factors.

THE WIC PROGRAM

We appreciate the consistent support that this Committee has shown for the Special Supplemental Food Program for Women, Infants, and Children (WIC). For Fiscal Year 1993, the appropriation totals $2.86 billion compared to $2.6 billion appropriated for Fiscal Year 1992. With this funding, WIC's average monthly participation will increase to about 5.9 million, an increase of about 500,000 from the Fiscal Year 1992 average.

FULL FUNDING FOR WIC

As you know, President Clinton's Economic Stimulus package includes a request for $75 million in additional Fiscal Year 1993 appropriations, to begin working immediately toward fully funding this program by the end of Fiscal Year 1996. The additional funds, if available by April 1, would enable States to reach as many as 300,000 additional participants each month, and would raise the average program participation to 6 million for the year. According to the Congressional Budget Office (CBO), the cost of fully funding the program in Fiscal Year 1994 would be $1 billion over current services. The Fiscal Year 1994 Budget proposes further program expansion with the goal of serving all eligible persons by September 1996. CBO has estimated that at that time 9.3 million persons will be eligible and that 7.5 million will apply.

Proposed appropriations language for Fiscal Year 1993 would allow the Secretary to waive regulations governing the funding allocation formula to ensure that these funds can be used most effectively.

WIC INFANT FORMULA REBATES

Infant formula rebates negotiated by States and manufacturers are a critical component of the cost effectiveness of the WIC Program. WIC Infant formula rebate revenues for Fiscal Year 1993 are projected to be over $800 million and will support nearly 1.3 million participants, about one-fifth of projected WIC participation. Public Law 102-512, The Infant Formula Procurement Act, requires the USDA to conduct bid solicitations for infant formula rebates on behalf of a group of States, if requested to do so. Through expanded multi-State bidding it is expected that even greater savings would accrue to the WIC Program. The new law must be implemented by April 1993.

BREASTFEEDING PROMOTION

USDA has traditionally played a significant role in promoting and supporting breastfeeding among WIC participants. Also, in recent years USDA has actively undertaken a number of new initiatives in further support of this important health practice, including sponsorship of a Breastfeeding Promotion Consortium (BPC) of health professional, government and advocacy organizations mutually interested in breastfeeding. At the Consortium's recommendation, USDA has developed a national campaign to promote breastfeeding among the general public and others who influence a woman's decision on how to feed her infant.

IMMUNIZATION PROMOTION

For the last two years, USDA has worked very closely with the Centers for Disease Control and Prevention (CDC) to increase immunization rates among preschool-age WIC participants. Numerous activities are occurring at all levels of program operation to promote timely immunization. These various strategies seem to be having a positive effect.

WIC VENDOR MANAGEMENT

During Fiscal Year 1988, the Office of the Inspector General (OIG) performed a national audit of WIC State agency vendor monitoring systems. The major findings of the audit dealt with the inadequacy of State agency Automated Data Processing systems to detect and analyze vendor redemption data for probable abuse; weak State agency vendor selection practices; limited Federal staff resources to oversee State agency operations; the need to standardize vendor sanctions nationwide; and the need for improved information sharing on vendor abuse between the Food Stamp and WIC Programs.

In response to these findings, FNS proposed new more clearly defined and stringent regulations. These regulations define State responsibility in the area of vendor selection, training, monitoring, investigative reviews, and vendor sanctions. Over 1,000 comments were received on the proposal. Due to significant public and political reaction to the proposed rulemaking, a new proposal was developed. As WIC moves toward full funding, maintaining high standards for program integrity will become even more important. Therefore, we intend to issue the new, tougher regulations in the Spring of 1993.

FOOD STAMP PROGRAM

The Food Stamp Program operates with a Fiscal Year 1993 appropriation of $28 billion, including reserve funding, to ensure that funds are available to meet increases in program needs and $1.051 billion in Nutrition Assistance for Puerto Rico. Our projections suggest that:

- o The rate of unemployment will average 7.1 percent in 1993 and the seasonally adjusted average number of unemployed persons in Fiscal Year 1993 will be about 9.15 million;

- o Average monthly program participation will rise to 27.3 million in 1993;

- o the average monthly benefit for 1993 will be $68.24 per person.

The program is expected to operate within current funding for the remainder of the fiscal year.

As part of his *"Vision of Change for America"*, President Clinton has proposed an increase in benefit payments, in part to help offset the cost of the proposed energy tax to food stamp households and to raise benefits for these households.

FOOD STAMP PROGRAM ERROR REDUCTION

Food stamps issued in error last year exceeded $1.9 billion. We must continue to pursue improved payment accuracy rates as a high priority activity. In Fiscal Years 1992 and 1993, increased participation has overburdened State agencies already suffering under diminished fiscal and personnel resources.

In an attempt to assist State efforts to improve payment accuracy, FNS has expanded its program efforts in two significant ways. First, in Fiscal Year 1993, FNS will be awarding about $300,000 in grants to State and local agencies to implement and test effective and replicable error reduction procedures. Projects chosen for funding will demonstrate innovative as well as cost effective methods which can be implemented immediately with minimal expense. In response to widely published announcements of the grant program, we have received a significant number of promising proposals and will make the final awards in April of this year. In addition, as a result of our emphasis on payment accuracy, each of our regional offices is conducting Error Reduction Conferences which provide a forum for the exchange of effective ideas and methods. Finally, through the use of our State Exchange project, FNS continues to support the interchange between State and local agencies of proven methods to reduce certification and issuance errors.

SETTLEMENT OF FOOD STAMP LIABILITIES

FNS recently agreed with 26 State agencies to settle $300 million in outstanding food stamp error rate liabilities for Fiscal Years 1986 - 1991. States agreed to invest almost $45 million in payment accuracy improvements over the next five years. FNS' offer of resolution of these liabilities was made so that Federal and State attention could remain focused on program management rather than on a lengthy court appeals process.

Most of the States affected submitted acceptable investment plans by

February 19, 1993. The plans reflect a broad spectrum of corrective action activities, such as increased client contact in the form of front-end verification, quality assurance reviews, enhanced automation, expanded staff/client training, and targeting of cases with high error probabilities. Two States chose to pay settlement claims rather than investing.

The settlement of these older claims will not compromise future action by FNS to agressively pursue collection of quality control sanctions.

FOOD STAMP TAX OFFSET EXPANSION

We are working now to strengthen the agency's debt collection methods. One method being tested collects the amount of overissued food stamp benefits from Federal income tax refunds of individuals who received such excess benefits because of fraud or providing erroneous information. These individuals are no longer participating in the program. In Fiscal Year 1992, the first year of the test, we collected more than $3 million in offsets in the two States involved. Voluntary payments provided an additional $400,000. Within our current funding we have added seven States for 1993, and collections, both offsets and voluntary payments, are higher than expected. We plan to add another 12 States in 1994, which would bring in a total of 21 States. While the amount of collections to the Federal government are substantial in relation to the cost of the effort, starting up the program is resource intensive. We plan to expand the program to the maximum extent that resources permit. We estimate that program-wide use of tax offset would result in at least $25 million worth of collections per year. There is currently more than $600 million in debt for overissued food stamp benefits due to fraud and erroneous information, and a significant portion of this could be collected through Federal income tax offset.

FOOD STAMP TRAFFICKING

FNS investigators have focused their efforts on retailers who purchase food stamps for cash at a discount. Last fiscal year, trafficking occurred in 763 retailer investigations, a 44 percent increase over Fiscal Year 1991, and a 255 percent increase over Fiscal Year 1988. Limited additional funding permitted us to increase the number of investigators on board at the beginning of this year from 42 to 50. Therefore, a further increase in trafficking investigations is expected. An initiative begun last year to promote the civil prosecution of trafficking retailers by U.S. Attorneys resulted in settlements for over $250,000 in fines. We have already exceeded this level so far this year and expect this activity to result in over $1 million in settlements in FY 1993. FNS is also taking actions to expand the activity of States, primarily State and local law enforcement units, against trafficking between recipients and buyers in the streets. We are planning a limited number of pilot projects for FY 1994 to identify effective detection, investigation and sanctioning techniques against street trafficking. FNS carefully coordinates its efforts with the Office of the Inspector General to ensure that trafficking investigations are effectively conducted.

RETAILER REAUTHORIZATION

FNS began a major initiative in Fiscal Year 1992 to collect current information and reauthorize the 213,000 retailers which support the Food Stamp Program. Resources had not been available and data on these stores had not been updated since the early 1980s, resulting in a deterioration of our ability to monitor store compliance. Funding in Fiscal Years 1992 and 1993 has enabled the Agency to remove stores which had closed or were no longer eligible, collect information on new store owners and obtain current sales information, which is the key to monitoring program compliance. By maintaining current data on stores, limited resources can be targeted to follow up on those which present the greatest threat to program integrity.

ELECTRONIC BENEFIT TRANSFER

Electronic Benefit Transfer (EBT) has the potential to reduce benefit diversions, including trafficking. Selling or trading benefits through a third party is expected to be more difficult with EBT because of the need for a system access terminal, the recipient's EBT card and personal identification number to determine the amount of benefits to sell. EBT also enhances control of trafficking by providing an audit trail that supports both detection and prosecution of benefit diversions.

Today, there are approximately 200,000 food stamp households and 3,750 retailers using EBT. Over $400 million in program benefits will be provided through EBT in Fiscal Year 1993. Maryland will be operating Statewide as of April 1993, and there are also EBT systems currently operating in Reading, Pennsylvania, Bernalillo County, New Mexico, Ramsey County, Minnesota, and Dayton, Ohio. An additional 25 States have expressed interest in EBT and are in the process of planning or developing their systems. Federal staff continue to work with States by providing technical assistance and review of system documentation. We are also pursuing a standard system for settlement and reconciliation of EBT payments with the Department of Treasury and the Federal Reserve. A standard settlement system, as currently operated by the Federal Reserve for the food coupon redemption system, would be necessary for large-scale inter-State EBT operations.

FOOD STAMP PROGRAM INTEGRITY THROUGH INFORMATION MANAGEMENT

The Agency is implementing new automated systems in Fiscal Year 1993 which are critically important to program and financial integrity. The Store Tracking, Authorization and Redemption Subsystem (STARS) is the automated system which stores all data on retailers and records their redemptions of food stamps through the banking and Federal Reserve systems. The Disqualified Recipient System (DRS) will give States access to a nation-wide list of persons who have defrauded the Food Stamp Program. It will help keep these persons off the program for the proper disqualification period, even if they move to a different State.

PROGRAM CONFORMITY AND SIMPLIFICATION

We are active on a number of fronts to achieve greater conformity among federal public assistance programs and the Food Stamp Program, as well as to simplify administrative requirements. For example, FNS is providing staff support to the Welfare Simplification and Coordination Advisory Committee. The eleven member Committee has met three times to discuss how interactions between Food Stamps, Aid to Families with Dependent Children (AFDC), Medicaid and public housing programs can be streamlined. A report to Congress and the Federal agencies containing recommendations for change will be released on July 1 of this year.

In addition, FNS has been actively working with the Administration for Children and Families to assist the American Public Welfare Association task force on program coordination in developing recommendations for areas in which consistency in requirements for the AFDC and Food Stamp Programs could be achieved through regulations or legislation.

EMPLOYMENT AND TRAINING DEMONSTRATIONS

Demonstration projects testing improved conformity between the Food Stamp Employment and Training Program (E&T) and the Job Opportunities and Basic Skills Program (JOBS) of AFDC are being conducted in 49 project areas. Beginning this year and lasting up to four years, the projects allow States to waive the food stamp E&T regulations and substitute JOBS regulations in their place. Demonstration sites are in the States of Missouri, Georgia, South Dakota, Texas and Hawaii.

NUTRITION ASSISTANCE FOR PUERTO RICO

The appropriation for Fiscal Year 1993 for the Food Stamp Program also includes $1.051 billion for Nutrition Assistance for Puerto Rico, the full amount authorized by the Food, Agriculture, Conservation, and Trade (FACT) Act of 1990. The Program provides cash benefits and administrative funds for a food assistance program tailored to the needs of low-income households in Puerto Rico.

CHILD NUTRITION PROGRAMS

For the Child Nutrition Programs, we have an appropriation of $6.8 billion for Fiscal Year 1993. These funds are required to meet the payments authorized under current law for subsidies to all children and for providing free and reduced price lunches, breakfasts and snacks to eligible children in schools, child and adult care centers and through Summer Food Service Programs.

HEAD START EXPANSION

As part of his proposal to expand Head Start, the President requested supplemental appropriations for the Child and Adult Care Food Program. The request for $56 million will cover the increased meals and snacks that will be served to the participants of the proposed new Head Start summer program. The Fiscal Year 1994 Budget also incorporates an increase for this purpose.

IMPACT OF MILK BID-RIGGING ON PROGRAM OPERATIONS

We share the concerns expressed by this committee regarding bid-rigging of milk supplies to local schools operating our feeding programs. According to the Department of Justice's (DOJ) Antitrust Division, as of February 1, 1993, 79 criminal cases involving school milk bid-rigging had been filed against 43 corporations and 55 individuals in the southeast, midwest, and Texas. To date, 37 corporations and 41 individuals have been convicted, and fines imposed total approximately $35 million. Twenty-three individuals have been sentenced to serve time in jail. Federal civil damages in excess of $7 million have also been imposed. Thirty-four grand juries in 23 States continue to investigate the milk industry. FNS has worked with DOJ since 1989 on these cases.

However, the actual direct damages resulting from milk bid-rigging fall on local schools. The recovery of these damages and their return to the local schools has been our primary concern in the resolution of these cases. FNS has worked closely with the DOJ to insure that proposed settlement actions presented to us for concurrence take into consideration the recovery of local school milk damages either through separate State action or through the Federal legal actions. Since the return to local schools of those damages only occurs when recovery is through State action, FNS has concurred with a strategy for these cases which reserves the recovery of direct damages to the

States and focuses DOJ's efforts on criminal and civil penalty actions. To date, we are aware of State civil actions which have recovered over $50 million in local school damages from over 20 corporations. State civil actions are also pending against at least 4 other corporations.

FNS will continue to make determinations regarding the necessity for debarment or suspension action against dairies convicted of bid-rigging. In making these determinations, we will consider the present responsibility of the companies and individuals involved, the potential impact of such actions on local program operations, and any other information that may be pertinent to the determination.

SCHOOL BREAKFAST PROGRAM START-UP GRANTS

As you know, the Agency has been actively pursuing expansion of the School Breakfast Program through the use of special start-up grants. As one means of encouraging schools to operate breakfast programs, Public law 101-147 established a five-year series of competitive grants to help defray start-up costs. As envisioned in the statute, these grants cover nonrecurring costs and are targeted to schools attended by a significant number of low income students. In the first four years, $18 million in grants were awarded for over 2,800 schools with nearly 580,000 needy students in 38 different States. For the Fiscal Year 1994 grants totalling $5 million, 38 States submitted proposals totalling over $7.1 million. We are in the process of evaluating these proposals and expect to make awards later this Spring.

HOMELESS DEMONSTRATION PROJECTS

The Homeless Demonstration Project, authorized by Public Law 101-147 to determine the best means for providing food service to homeless children under the age of 6 in emergency shelters, is now in its third year of operation. Since the beginning of the Project, we have solicited sponsors on three separate occasions and now have 33 participating sponsors serving 56 homeless shelters. We are continuing to accept applications and anticipate adding additional shelters to the Project.

COMMODITY SUPPLEMENTAL FOOD PROGRAM

For Fiscal Year 1993, the appropriation is $94.5 million. This amount supports caseload allocations of about 246,000 women, infants and children and 141,000 elderly. For Fiscal Year 1993, USDA will donate 4 million pounds of nonfat dry milk and 9 million pounds of cheese, as required by the FACT Act of 1990, to supplement food purchased with funds directly appropriated to the program.

FOOD DONATIONS PROGRAMS FOR SELECTED GROUPS

An appropriation of $256.5 million supports the programs for the Food Distribution Program on Indian Reservations (FDPIR), Nutrition Program for the Elderly (NPE), Commodities for Soup Kitchens, the remaining support for the nuclear affected islands as well as Palau and disaster assistance. NPE meals are currently reimbursed at a rate of 57.8 cents, the maximum rate that can be paid within the appropriation to support the estimated Fiscal Year 1993 service of 247 million meals. We are closely monitoring program participation, and will adjust the rate if conditions warrant.

THE EMERGENCY FOOD ASSISTANCE PROGRAM

Overall funding for this program is $207.3 million, which includes $162.3 million for the purchase of commodities authorized by law, and $45 million to assist States with administrative expenses. This includes $42.3 million provided by the Congress through the Farm Credit Safety Act of 1992.

President Clinton has also asked for an additional $23.5 million in Fiscal Year 1993 for the Emergency Food Assistance Program. Appropriations language will permit USDA to deliver these commodities to States through December 1993, thus eliminating a service gap caused by the need to wait each year for annual appropriations before beginning the purchase cycle. The Fiscal Year 1994

TEFAP budget will also contain increases in discretionary funding for this important program.

SPECIAL MILK PROGRAM

We are operating this program with a $14.9 million appropriation. About $7 million is available in funds carried forward from Fiscal Year 1992 to support overall estimated federal obligations of $20.0 million.

FOOD PROGRAM ADMINISTRATION

Critical to achievement of sound program management are the administrative funds of the Agency. For Fiscal Year 1993, appropriations total $103.5 million, the same as Fiscal Year 1992. This level has required the agency to implement a hiring freeze and to defer some expenditures for maintenance and improvement of automated program and financial systems.

We recognize that all government agencies must take aggressive action to improve management and administrative practices in order to reduce unnecessary spending. We are working very hard to achieve this goal without jeopardizing our mission to safeguard the interests of our program recipients and the taxpayers who pay the bills.

FINANCIAL MANAGEMENT INITIATIVES

As you know, the Chief Financial Officers (CFO) Act of 1990 requires federal agencies to perform a number of actions, including: creating integrated financial systems over a five year period; producing annual audited financial statements; developing systematic performance measurement; and improving management reporting. FNS has made significant progress in all of these areas.

In October 1992 we implemented the first phase of a new financial management system which, when completed, will provide a single, integrated data base and accounting system for all FNS accounting and financial reporting operations. This systems development effort, which was begun five years ago, is one of the few in the federal government which has come in on time and on budget. Although this effort has required--and will require for the next several years--significant resources from our salary and expenses budget, we believe that a smaller level of effort would not permit the data integrity, accountability, and reporting capabilities required for major federal programs like the Food Stamp Program and WIC. When compared with the size of the annual, and growing, budget authority for which FNS is responsible, the amount of resources expended and needed in the future for our integrated financial management system represents a very large benefit with an immediate payback.

FNS has produced financial statements for the past six years. FNS issued its first Annual Report for Fiscal Year 1991 that included the most recent

Financial Statements and our first publication of program performance measures as required by the CFO Act. These statements were audited by the General Accounting Office (GAO) in Fiscal Years 1987 and 1988 and by the USDA in Fiscal Years 1991 and 1992. We have also improved our financial management operations in a wide number of areas in response both to GAO and OIG audits and to our internal management controls and CFO Act 5-year plan action items. These actions include improved training programs for our financial management personnel, the systems development effort which has resulted so far in implementation of the first phase of our new integrated financial management system, and in improved internal controls and data integrity throughout the agency.

RESEARCH AND EVALUATION

During Fiscal Year 1993, FNS expects to spend slightly over $19 million on program research, demonstrations and evaluation studies. These funds will support ten Congressionally-mandated or requested projects including Competitive Nutrition Education Grants, Resource Tests for Licensed Vehicles, Food Stamp Outreach Grants, WIC Participant and Program Characteristics, a School Breakfast and Lunch Meal Cost Study, a National School Lunch Program (NSLP) School Drop Out Study, a State Administrative Cost Study, Paperwork Reduction Pilot Projects, School Lunch Eligible Nonparticipants, and a Universal Free Lunch Study.

Additional areas of research include EBT, control of food stamp trafficking, reducing barriers to good nutrition among food stamp program participants, use of nutrient standards in the National School Lunch Program (NSLP), assessment of nutritional content of meals in the Child and Adult Care Food Program (CACFP), and the Infant Feeding Project.

We have several significant reports coming out over the next few months. As I mentioned earlier, this year marks the culmination of our research on demonstrations of cash-out of the Food Stamp Program. We released results from the San Diego and Alabama "pure" demonstrations on January 19, 1993. We expect reports very soon from the Washington State Family Independence Program and Alabama ASSETS demonstrations. A report on administrative costs and retailer impacts in San Diego will also be available shortly. In other areas, we expect to release a report on the impacts of EBT in New Mexico and Minnesota in the next few months. Also, we expect to release the results of a study on the nutrient content and dietary impact of the NSLP, as well as a national study on the adult day care component of CACFP.

That summarizes the current operations of the Food and Nutrition Service. I will be happy to answer the Committee's questions.

FOOD AND NUTRITION SERVICE

Purpose Statement

The Food and Nutrition Service (FNS) was established August 8, 1969, by Secretary's Memorandum No. 1659 and Supplement 1 pursuant to the authority contained in 5 U.S.C. 301 and the Reorganization Plan No. 2 of 1953.

The Food and Nutrition Service administers food assistance programs which provide access to a more nutritious diet for persons with low incomes and which encourage better eating patterns among the nation's children. The programs are:

Food Stamp Program. Food stamps are issued to eligible low-income households to enable them to obtain a better diet by increasing their food purchasing power. The program is a Federal-State partnership with the Federal Government paying the full cost of food stamps. The Federal Government also funds over half of the expenses incurred by the States to administer the program, including recipient household certification, food coupon issuance and employment and training activities for recipients. Funds for this program are provided by direct appropriation.

Nutrition Assistance for Puerto Rico. This program provides grant funds to the Commonwealth of Puerto Rico to operate a food assistance program specifically tailored to the needs of its low-income citizens provided that the program assures assistance for the most needy persons in the jurisdiction. Puerto Rico has established eligibility standards and administrative mechanisms approved by FNS to assist low-income households with cash grants, rather than food stamps or coupons. This assistance is intended to supplement recipients' income to help them purchase food for an adequate diet. A small portion of the grant is also used to stimulate local food production and distribution activities through a Tick Eradication Program. Another small portion is used to fund a Special Wage Incentive Program for Nutrition Assistance Program recipients. Funds for this program are provided by direct appropriation.

Child Nutrition Programs. The purpose of the Child Nutrition Programs -- the National School Lunch, School Breakfast, Summer Food Service and Child and Adult Care Food Programs -- is to assist State and local governments in providing food services for children in public and nonprofit private schools, child care institutions, certain adult day care centers, and summer recreation programs. FNS provides the States with cash and additional commodities on a per meal basis to offset the cost of food service and cash to offset a portion of State administrative expenses, sponsor administrative expenses and technical assistance. FNS also administers the various Child Nutrition Programs directly in cases where the State has chosen not to administer the programs. In addition to the cash and commodity assistance provided for all meals, substantially higher cash rates are paid as special assistance for meals served free or at a reduced price to children from low income families. Funds for these programs are provided by direct appropriation and by transfer from section 32.

Special Milk Program. The Special Milk Program provides funding for milk service in some kindergartens, as well as in schools, nonprofit child care centers and camps which have no other federally assisted food programs. Milk is provided to children either free or at a low cost depending on their family income level. The Food and Nutrition Service provides cash subsidies to State administered programs and directly administers the program in the States which have chosen not to administer the program. Funds for this program are provided by direct appropriation.

Commodities for Soup Kitchens. This program provides for the purchase and distribution of commodities to soup kitchens and food banks. Commodities are distributed to the States which, in turn, provide them to public and charitable institutions that maintain an established feeding operation to provide food to needy homeless persons on a regular basis as an integral part of their activities. In instances when these commodities cannot be used by these organizations, States provide such commodities to food banks that maintain an established operation involving the provision of food or edible commodities to food pantries, soup kitchens, hunger relief centers or other food or feeding centers that provide meals or food to needy persons on a regular basis as an integral part of their normal activities. Funds for this program are provided by direct appropriation.

The Emergency Food Assistance Program (TEFAP). The Emergency Food Assistance Program helps States to relieve situations of hunger and distress by making available surplus foods from USDA farm support program inventories. In addition to surplus commodities, USDA also purchases and distributes to States foods that are high in nutrient density, easily and safely stored and are convenient to use and consume. The program also provides funds to States to aid in the intrastate storage and distribution of these foods. The allocation of both commodities and administrative expense grants to the States is based on a formula which considers the States' unemployment level and the number of persons with incomes below the poverty level. Funds for this program are provided by direct appropriation.

Food Program Administration. This account funds Federal personnel compensation, benefits and other operating expenses of the Food and Nutrition Service. FNS administers the Food Stamp, Child Nutrition, Special Supplemental Food and other programs described above in a Federal-State partnership in which State agencies and local entities directly operate most programs. FNS implements program statutes through promulgation of regulations and instructions. FNS staff provide training and assistance to State agencies, assure proper funds allocation and control, conduct program monitoring and evaluation, and develop program policy.

Agency headquarters are in Alexandria, Virginia. Regional offices are at seven locations: Boston, Massachusetts; Robbinsville, New Jersey; Atlanta, Georgia; Chicago, Illinois; Dallas, Texas; Denver, Colorado; and San Francisco, California. On September 30, 1992, FNS employed 1,907 full time permanent and 56 part time and temporary employees, of which 639 were in the headquarters office and 1,324 in the field. Of the field total, 894 employees were stationed in seven regional offices and the balance in six Food Stamp Compliance offices; one computer support center in Minneapolis, Minnesota; five Administrative Review offices; and 84 field offices. Funds for these activities are provided by direct appropriation.

Special Supplemental Food Program for Women, Infants and Children (WIC). The purpose of the WIC Program is to improve the health of low-income pregnant, breastfeeding and postpartum women, infants and children up to their fifth birthday. This is achieved by providing food packages designed to supplement each participant's diet with foods that nutritional research indicates are typically lacking in the WIC target population and by providing eligible recipients with nutrition education, including information about breastfeeding, and access to health services. In addition to paying the full cost of the food packages, appropriated funds are provided to States for administrative and nutrition services costs for the program. The WIC Farmers' Market Nutrition Program (FMNP) is also funded from the WIC appropriation. The FMNP is designed to accomplish two major goals: 1) to improve the diets of WIC (or WIC-eligible) participants by providing them with coupons to purchase fresh, nutritious, unprepared foods, such as fruits and vegetables, from farmers' markets; and 2) to increase the awareness and use of farmers' markets by low-income households. Although directly related to the WIC Program, most of the current FMNP operations are administered by State Departments of Agriculture rather than the State WIC agencies. Funds for the WIC program are provided by direct appropriation.

Commodity Supplemental Food Program (CSFP). The first priority of the CSFP is to provide food packages designed to improve the health of low-income pregnant, breastfeeding and postpartum women, infants and children up to their sixth birthday, a target population similar to that of the WIC Program. The next priority of CSFP is to provide supplemental food packages to improve the health of the low-income elderly; i.e., persons 60 years of age or older. The foods are purchased directly by the Department of Agriculture and distributed through State and local agencies to eligible women, infants, children and the elderly. The Food and Nutrition Service provides cash assistance to distributing agencies to offset their operating expenses at a rate of 20 percent of appropriated funding. Funds to purchase commodities and pay expenses for this program are provided by direct appropriation and may be supplemented by commodities purchased under farm program authorities and distributed at no charge against the funds appropriated.

Food Donations Programs for Selected Groups

Food Distribution Program on Indian Reservations (FDPIR). This program provides nutrition assistance to low-income American Indians living on or near reservations who choose not to participate in the Food Stamp Program. Through monthly distribution from local warehouses, participating Indians receive a variety of commodities to help maintain a healthy diet. Participating agencies can order food items according to households' preferences. They also receive information on proper nutrition, food storage, sanitary food preparation methods and suggestions for use of the commodities. Funds to purchase commodities and pay expenses for this program are provided by direct appropriation and may be supplemented by commodities purchased under farm program authorities and distributed at no charge against the funds appropriated.

Nutrition Program for the Elderly. This program provides cash and commodities to States for distribution to local organizations that prepare meals served to elderly persons in congregate settings or delivered to their homes. The program promotes good health through nutrition assistance and by reducing the isolation experienced by the elderly. USDA's role in this program is to supplement the Department of Health and Human Services' funding for programs for the elderly with cash and commodities on a per meal basis for each meal served to an elderly person. Funds for this program are provided by direct appropriation.

Nutrition Education and Training (NET) Program

The NET program provides children, through child care and schools, with opportunities to acquire the knowledge, skills, attitudes and behaviors necessary to make healthful food choices. NET develops nutrition education programs and instructs food service workers and teachers in nutrition and health. While planning nutrition education activities, USDA identified a special need to provide nutrition education to child care and preschool providers to 1) improve the conformity of USDA subsidized meals with the Dietary Guidelines and 2) enable providers to use nutrition education curricula with preschool children in order to promote nutritious food selection. FNS estimates that about $10 million will be needed to maintain the current level of effort for NET. This NET funding is an important component of the comprehensive multi-year initiative to implement the Dietary Guidelines for Americans in the Child Nutrition Programs by the year 2000, and is needed to reach the diverse population of child care and preschool providers.

Food Stamp Program Nutrition Education

USDA also recognizes a special need for reaching limited resource adults with nutrition education. These adults need information on basic nutrition, food selection and food handling communicated in a way that is sensitive to their income and education levels and cultural preferences. Food stamps help assure that recipients have the purchasing power to acquire an adequate diet, but recipients still have little margin for shopping error. Nutrition knowledge could make a real difference. The Food Stamp Program will continue to provide States with 50-50 matching funds for nutrition education activities. In 1993, FNS initiated a two-year grant program for development and demonstration of culturally relevant and cost effective nutrition education programs for Food Stamp Program participants who do not currently receive other nutrition education. In 1994, USDA will continue the demonstration grant program at the 1993 level of $0.5 million. FNS will work closely with the Extension Service to encourage development of educational models and materials that can be replicated in other locations. These will complement similar grants being funded through the Extension Service for $4.0 million. The FNS grants were authorized by the FACT Act. In 1994, FNS will also coordinate with the USDA Human Nutrition Information Service and Extension Service to update, reprint and distribute revised FNS publications for Food Stamp Program households, low literacy adults, and the elderly, to include the current Dietary Guidelines and associated graphic, the Food Guide Pyramid.

Special Supplemental Food Program for Women, Infants and Children (WIC)

WIC provides the largest single source of Federal nutrition education funding, reaching over 5 million pregnant, breastfeeding and postpartum women, infants and young children at critical times in physical growth and mental development each month. In addition to continuing the required level of nutrition education within the WIC Program, FNS will work more closely with the Extension Service in providing intensive nutrition education to the neediest WIC participants, and in evaluating the effectiveness of this effort. A major goal of WIC nutrition education is to improve WIC breastfeeding rates. These efforts will also complement the Surgeon General's goal of increasing "to at least 75 percent the proportion of mothers who breastfeed their babies at hospital discharge and to at least 50 percent the proportion who continue breastfeeding until their babies are 5 to 6 months old" (Healthy People 2000, No.2, 11).

Nutrition Education through the Food Distribution Program on Indian Reservations (FDPIR)

Nutrition education has traditionally been integral to FDPIR. However, past efforts in this area have proven inadequate in view of the continued high incidence of diet-related health conditions, such as hypertension, diabetes, and obesity among the Native American population. FNS is intensifying efforts in this area through the

USDA Nutrition Education Activities

In 1994 USDA will continue its efforts to enhance nutrition education activities towards the goal of using education to achieve better nutrition. The USDA nutrition education focus seeks to favorably alter the food consumption behavior and promote the nutritional well-being of all Americans with a particular emphasis on educating and informing (1) children, their parents and care providers on the importance of good eating habits; (2) low-income adults on ways to improve their diets, food purchasing habits, and food handling; and (3) individuals in the general public who seek to improve their diets.

The USDA budget request supports five areas of investment to achieve this objective:

1) enhance ongoing nutrition education programs for target groups;

2) increase professional and consumer access to nutrition information to promote informed choice;

3) expand nutrition monitoring to implement the 10 year plan for nutrition monitoring and related research;

4) improve evaluation of nutrition education activities to measure outcomes including behavioral changes; and

5) increase basic nutrition research as an investment to strengthen the research base for nutrition program activities and nutrition monitoring.

The Food and Nutrition Service continues to play a major role in this initiative, along with seven other USDA agencies. FNS activities are well aligned with the objective of the initiative for reaching children and low-income adults, with children having the primary focus. In summary, the FNS proposals are for continued funding and increased effectiveness of WIC nutrition education, continued matching funds for State nutrition education for Food Stamp assistance, and training for implementation of the Dietary Guidelines for Americans in the $6 billion Child Nutrition Programs. In addition, FNS will continue working closely with the Extension Service in their efforts to provide additional nutrition education to the most needy WIC participants.

<u>Dietary Guidelines Implementation</u>

The USDA initiative will provide the assistance to Child Nutrition Programs needed to improve meals and follow the Dietary Guidelines for Americans. The nation's Health Objectives for the Year 2000, established by the Department of Health and Human Services (DHHS) with USDA concurrence on the nutrition objectives, established a target for this decade: "increase, to at least 90 percent, the proportion of school lunch and breakfast services and child care food services with menus that are consistent with the nutrition principles in the <u>Dietary Guidelines for Americans</u>" (<u>Healthy People 2000</u>, No.2, 17, page 126). As a first step toward meeting this objective, USDA and DHHS, developed and disseminated to all Child Nutrition Program cooperators a publication entitled <u>Building for A Future: Nutrition Guidance for the Child Nutrition Programs</u>. This publication will serve as a basis for revisions of USDA meal patterns and menu planning guides. It will also guide the development of new recipes and commodity specifications. For school nutrition programs, a short term goal is to provide all school districts in the country with access to the necessary tools to meet the Dietary Guidelines for Americans in school meals. FNS will use the 1994 funding to provide training and technical assistance to proceed with this effort and to develop possible alternatives to the current meal pattern system.

use of FDPIR administrative funds specifically earmarked for nutrition education. These funds are allocated among regions using a participation-based formula. Regions, in turn, use their allocations for direct provision of nutrition education to Indian Tribal Organizations and their program participants, or for competitive grants to Indian Tribal Organizations. This funding is intended to stimulate innovative approaches to the specific nutrition education needs and cultural sensitivities of Native Americans.

FOOD AND NUTRITION SERVICE
Available Funds and Staff-Years
1992 Actual and Estimated, 1993 and 1994

Item	1992 Actual Amount	1992 Actual Staff Years	1993 Estimated Amount	1993 Estimated Staff Years	1994 Estimated Amount
Food Stamp Program..........	$22,649,975,000	23	$27,064,357,000	25	$30,148,655,0
Nutrition Assistance for Puerto Rico...........	(a) 1,013,000,000		(b) 1,051,000,000		1,091,000,0
Child Nutrition Programs:					
Appropriation............	1,393,223,000		2,592,098,000		2,848,744,0
Transfer from Section 32 and other accounts.....	4,775,092,000		4,290,455,000		4,710,185,0
Total - Child Nutrition Programs........	(c) 6,168,315,000	125	6,882,553,000	127	7,558,929,0
Special Milk Program........	(d) 23,011,000		(e) 14,898,000		20,277,0
Special Supplemental Food Program..............	(g) 2,600,000,000		(h) 2,935,000,000		3,287,220,0
Commodity Supplemental Food Program..............	(i) 90,000,000		94,500,000		94,500,0
Food Donations Programs for Selected Groups...........	265,437,000		256,513,000		244,413,0
The Emergency Food Assistance Program........	165,000,000		188,481,000		209,455,(
Temporary Assistance P.L. 102-552.............	0		42,329,000		
Food Program Administration	103,535,000	1,809	[j] 103,535,000	1,822	105,201,(
Total, Food and Nutrition Service Funds.............	33,078,273,000	1,957	38,633,166,000	1,974	42,759,650,(
Obligations under other USDA Appropriations:					
Human Nutrition Information Service for Administrative Support....................	250,000	5	259,000	5	259,
Farmers Home Administration..	47,095		3,000		15,
Agricultural Stabilization and Conservation Service..	31,070				
Soil Conservation Service...	12,364				
Miscellaneous Reimbursements	8,566				
Total, Other USDA Appropriations............	349,095	5	262,000	5	274,

FOOD AND NUTRITION SERVICE
Available Funds and Staff-Years
1992 Actual and Estimated, 1993 and 1994

Item	1992 Actual		1993 Estimated		1994 Estimated	
	Amount	Staff Years	Amount	Staff Years	Amount	Staff Years
Other Federal Funds:						
Army Audit Agency for Health and Building Management Services	7,824					
Total, Other Federal Funds	7,824	0	0	0	0	0
Total, Food and Nutrition Service	33,078,629,919	1,962	38,633,428,000	1,979	42,759,924,000	1,979

[a] Excludes $10,825,000 in funds transferred to APHIS for Tick Eradication.
[b] Excludes $10,825,000 in funds transferred to APHIS for Tick Eradication.
[c] Excludes $68,517,687 in unobligated balances and $47,833,939 in recoveries of PY obligations and transfer of $100,000,000 from the Food Stamp Program.
[d] Excludes $4,772,623 in unobligated balances and $645,262 in recoveries of PY obligations.
[e] Excludes $5,379,187 in unobligated balances.
[f] Excludes $254,187 in unobligated balances.
[g] Excludes $2,672,135 in unobligated balances and $73,381,806 in recoveries of PY obligations.
[h] Excludes $2,647,148 in unobligated balances.
[i] Excludes $6,109,462 in unobligated balances and $259,883 in recoveries of PY obligations.
[j] Excludes $4,258 in unobligated balances.

FOOD AND NUTRITION SERVICE

Permanent Positions by Grade and Staff-Year Summary

1992 and Estimated 1993 and 1994

	1992			1993			1994		
	Headquarters	Field	Total	Headquarters	Field	Total	Headquarters	Field	Total
ES-6	1	0	1	1	0	1	1	0	1
ES-5	1	0	1	1	0	1	1	0	1
ES-4	4	6	10	4	6	10	4	7	11
ES-3	2	0	2	2	1	3	2	0	2
ES-2	1	1	2	1	0	1	1	0	1
ES-1	3	0	3	3	0	3	3	0	3
GS/GM-15	21	7	28	21	7	28	21	7	28
GS/GM-14	63	35	98	63	35	98	63	35	98
GS/GM-13	141	81	222	143	81	224	143	81	224
GS-12	165	249	414	168	253	421	168	253	421
GS-11	119	541	660	122	547	669	122	547	669
GS-10	1		1	1		1	1		1
GS-9	33	67	100	34	70	104	34	70	104
GS-8	8	7	15	8	7	15	8	7	15
GS-7	59	65	124	60	67	127	60	67	127
GS-6	41	54	95	41	54	95	41	54	95
GS-5	34	112	146	35	114	149	35	114	149
GS-4	18	31	49	18	32	50	18	32	50
GS-3	2	5	7	2	5	7	2	5	7
GS-2	4	2	6	4	2	6	4	2	6
GS-1	0	0	0	0	0	0	0	0	0
Ungraded Positions	4	0	4	4	0	4	4	0	4
Total Permanent Positions........	725	1,263	1,988	736	1,281	2,017	736	1,281	2,017
Unfilled Positions end-of-year.......	-17	-29	-46	-5	-49	-54	-3	-48	-51
Total, Permanent Employment, end-of-year...........	708	1,234	1,942	731	1,232	1,963	733	1,233	1,966
Staff-Years........	712	1,297	2,009	716	1,263	1,979	716	1,263	1,979

FOOD AND NUTRITION SERVICE

CLASSIFICATION BY OBJECTS

(dollars in thousands)

	Actual 1992	Estimated 1993	Estimated 1994
Personnel Compensation:			
Headquarters	30,790	31,538	32,516
Field	47,300	48,568	49,290
11 Total personnel compensation	78,090	80,106	81,805
11.1 Full-time permanent	74,576	76,781	78,446
11.3 Other than full-time permanent	2,451	2,616	2,636
11.9 Special personal services	1,063	709	723
12 Personnel benefits	14,391	13,807	14,036
13 Benefits for former personnel	66	42	44
Total pers. compensation and benefits	92,547	93,955	95,885
Other objects:			
21 Travel	4,466	4,512	4,300
22 Transportation of things	3,836	5,301	5,403
23.1 Rental payments to GSA			
23.2 Rental payments to others	391	427	425
23.3 Communications, utilities and misc. charges	2,856	3,693	3,623
24 Printing and reproduction	45,354	49,059	50,028
25.1 Consulting services	47,088	51,016	64,262
25.2 Other services	5,125	7,688	8,298
26 Supplies and materials (incl. commodities)	505,574	588,253	572,067
31 Equipment	5,454	1,640	1,684
32 Land and structures			
41 Grants, subsidies and contributions	32,328,703	34,899,669	36,964,907
42 Insurance claims and indemnities	7		
43 Interest and dividends	1		
Total other objects	32,948,855	35,611,258	37,674,997
Total direct obligations	33,041,402	35,705,213	37,770,882
Position Data:			
Average Salary, ES positions	100,863	101,084	101,368
Average Salary, GM/GS positions	39,885	41,475	41,533
Average Grade, GM/GS positions	10.35	10.34	10.34

31-11

FOOD AND NUTRITION SERVICE

Reports of Audits and Investigations of National Significance Received during Fiscal Year 1992

Program/Activity Reviews	Report Number	Date Issued	Subject
Reports from the Office of the Inspector General			
Food Stamp	27600-8-CH	03-31-92	Food Stamp Program: Authorizing and Monitoring of Retailers
Food Stamp	27013-47-TE	09-10-92	SAVE System Cost Effectiveness
Food Stamp	27019-69-CH	09-30-92	Quality Control Activities
Food Stamp	27002-24-HY	09-02-92	Compliance Branch Controls Over Cash and Food Stamp Coupon Inventories
Financial Management	27070-2-HY	08-10-92	Financial statements FY'91
Reports from the General Accounting Office			
Food Donations	RCED-92-62	12-09-91	Homelessness: Policy and Liability Issues in Donating Prepared Food
Food Donations	RCED-92-67	12-31-91	Processing of USDA Commodities Donated to the National School Lunch Program
Food Stamp	HRD-92-92	09-25-92	Better Coordination of Food Stamp Services for Social Security Clients
Food Stamp	RCED-92-114	07-21-92	Nutritional Conditions and Program Alternatives in Puerto Rico
WIC	HRD-92-18	04-07-92	Federal Investments like WIC Can Produce Savings
Food Stamp	AFMD-92-63	08-06-92	OMB's High Risk Program: Benefits Found but Greater Oversight Needed
Food Stamp	IMTEC-92-29	05-27-92	Ineffective Federal Oversight Permits Costly Automated System Problems in Welfare Programs

FOOD AND NUTRITION SERVICE

Food Assistance Table
Budget Authority under Current Law
(Dollars in Thousands)

	1992 Estimate	1993 Estimate	1994 Estimate	Change 1993-1994
A. Child Nutrition Programs:				
1. Program grants to States:				
a. School Lunch Program	3,782,968	4,110,794	4,327,236	216,442
b. School Breakfast Program	801,191	891,163	980,352	89,189
c. Child Care and Adult Care Food Program	1,089,627	1,326,811	1,638,773	311,962
d. Summer Food Service Program	202,927	230,394	254,612	24,218
e. State administrative expenses	69,108	77,086	86,738	9,652
TOTAL, Cash payments to States	5,945,821	6,636,248	7,287,711	651,463
2. Commodities to States (including cash in lieu of commodities):				
a. FNS commodities	203,254	225,029	245,706	20,677
b. AMS Section 32 commodities	400,000	400,000	400,000	0
c. CCC bonus commodities	0	0	0	0
d. AMS bonus commodities	0	0	0	0
TOTAL, Commodities to States	603,254	625,029	645,706	20,677
3. Nutrition studies and education:				
a. Nutrition studies and surveys, section 6(a)(3)	3,835	3,835	3,939	104
b. Nutrition education and training, section 19	10,000	10,000	10,270	270
c. Child Nutrition Federal Review System	4,083	3,780	3,843	63
d. Food Service Management Institute	1,322	1,661	1,706	45
e. Dietary Guidelines	0	2,000	2,054	54
TOTAL, Nutrition studies and education	19,240	21,276	21,812	536
Section 17(p) Demos	0	0	3,700	3,700
TOTAL, Child Nutrition Programs	6,568,315	7,282,553	7,958,929	676,376
LESS: AMS Section 32 commodities	400,000	400,000	400,000	0
CCC bonus commodities	0	0	0	0
AMS bonus commodities	0	0	0	0
TOTAL, FNS Child Nutrition Account	6,168,315	6,882,553	7,558,929	676,376
B. Special Milk Program: Cash Payments	23,011	14,898	20,277	5,379
C. Special Supplemental Food Program (WIC):				
1. Cash grants to States	2,595,000	2,930,000	3,282,220	352,220
2. Studies and evaluations	5,000	5,000	5,000	0
TOTAL, FNS Special Supplemental Food Program Account	2,600,000	2,935,000	3,287,220	352,220

Continued on next page

FOOD AND NUTRITION SERVICE

Food Assistance Table
Budget Authority under Current Law
(Dollars in Thousands)

	1992 Estimate	1993 Estimate	1994 Estimate	Change 1993-1994
D. Commodity Supplemental Food Program (CSFP):				
1. Commodities for supplemental food	72,000	75,600	75,600	
2. Payments to distributing agencies for administration	18,000	18,900	18,900	0
3. Special administrative funds	0	0	0	0
4. CCC donations	0	0	0	0
SUBTOTAL, Commodity Supplemental Food Program (CSFP)	90,000	94,500	94,500	0
LESS: CCC Donations	0	0	0	0
TOTAL, FNS CSFP Account	90,000	94,500	94,500	0
E. Food Stamp Program:				
1. Benefit costs	19,526,638	22,880,127	23,409,031	528,904
2. State administrative costs	1,538,117	1,588,976	1,634,079	45,103
3. Other program costs	86,670	95,254	106,545	11,291
4. Benefit Reserve	1,498,550	2,500,000	5,000,000	2,500,000
5. Excess state error liabilities	0	0	-1,000	-1,000
6. Fed. Tax Refund Program	0	0	0	0
7. Adjustments in expired accounts	0	0	0	0
TOTAL, FNS Food Stamp Program Account	22,649,975	27,064,357	30,148,655	3,084,298
F. Nutrition Assistance for Puerto Rico	1,013,000	1,051,000	1,091,000	40,000

Continued on next page

FOOD AND NUTRITION SERVICE

Food Assistance Table
Budget Authority under Current Law
(Dollars in Thousands)

	1992 Estimate	1993 Estimate	1994 Estimate	Change 1993-1994
G. Food Donations Programs:				
1. Food Distribution Program on Indian Reservations:				
a. Commodities in lieu of food stamps..............	64,495	63,157	50,596	-12,561
b. Distributing agency administrative costs........	17,450	18,444	18,905	461
c. Section 32 bonus commodities....................	0	0	0	0
d. Section 416 bonus commodities...................	0	0	0	0
TOTAL, Food Distribution Program on Reservations......	81,945	81,601	69,501	-12,100
LESS: Bonus commodities............................	0	0	0	0
TOTAL, FNS Food Distribution Program on Indian Reservations Account...........	81,945	81,601	69,501	-12,100
2. Nutrition Program for the Elderly:				
a. Commodities.....................................	9,918	9,367	9,358	-9
b. Cash in lieu of commodities.....................	141,574	133,545	133,554	9
c. Section 32 Bonus Commodities....................	0	0	0	0
d. Section 416 Bonus Commodities...................	0	0	0	0
TOTAL, Nutrition Program for the Elderly..............	151,492	142,912	142,912	0
LESS: Bonus Commodities............................	0	0	0	0
TOTAL, FNS Nutrition Program for the Elderly Account..........................	151,492	142,912	142,912	0
3. Commodities for Soup Kitchens......................	32,000	32,000	32,000	0
TOTAL, FNS Food Donations Programs Account...............	265,437	256,513	244,413	-12,100
H. The Emergency Food Assistance Program (TEFAP):				
1. FNS Commodities....................................	120,000	143,481	163,240	19,759
2. CCC Bonus Commodities..............................	0	0	0	0
3. TEFAP Administrative Expense.......................	45,000	45,000	46,215	1,215
TOTAL, The Emergency Food Assistance Program...............................	165,000	188,481	209,455	20,974
LESS: Bonus Commodities............................	0	0	0	0
TOTAL, FNS TEFAP Account..................................	165,000	188,481	209,455	20,974
I. Temporary Assistance P.L. 102-552: Commodities.......	0	42,329	0	-42,329

Continued on next page

FOOD AND NUTRITION SERVICE

Food Assistance Table
Budget Authority under Current Law
(Dollars in thousands)

	1992 Estimate	1993 Estimate	1994 Estimate	Change 1993-1994
J. Bonus Commodities to Other Outlets:				
1. Charitable Institutions				
a. Section 32 commodities..........................	0		0	0
b. Section 416 commodities..........................	0		0	0
2. Summer Camps				
a. Section 32 commodities..........................	0	0	0	0
b. Section 416 commodities..........................	0	0	0	0
3. Disaster Feeding				
a. Section 32 commodities..........................	0	0	0	0
b. Section 416 commodities..........................	0	0	0	0
TOTAL, Bonus Commodities to Other Outlets................	0	0	0	0
K. Food Program Administration:				
1. Child nutrition/Special Milk........................	27,416	27,416	27,857	441
2. Supplemental feeding................................	11,409	11,409	11,593	184
3. Food stamp..	57,949	57,949	58,881	932
4. Cash and commodity subsidies........................	6,761	6,761	6,870	109
TOTAL, Food Program Administration......................	103,535	103,535	105,201	1,666
GRAND TOTAL, Food Assistance.............................	33,478,273	39,033,166	43,159,650	4,126,484
LESS: Section 32 commodities for Child Nutriton......	400,000	400,000	400,000	0
AMS bonus commodities..........................	0	0	0	0
CCC bonus commodities..........................	0	0	0	0
TOTAL, FNS Accounts......................................	33,078,273	38,633,166	42,759,650	4,126,484

FOOD AND NUTRITION SERVICE

Food Assistance Table
Program Level under Current Law
(Dollars in Thousands)

	1992 Estimate	1993 Estimate	1994 Estimate	Change 1993-1994
A. Child Nutrition Programs:				
1. Program grants to States:				
a. School Lunch Program	3,870,098	4,131,424	4,328,214	196,790
b. School Breakfast Program	801,191	891,163	980,352	89,189
c. Child Care and Adult Care Food Program	1,089,627	1,326,811	1,638,773	311,962
d. Summer Food Service Program	202,927	230,394	254,612	24,218
e. State administrative expenses	68,766	79,932	86,738	6,806
TOTAL, Cash payments to States	6,032,609	6,659,724	7,288,689	628,965
2. Commodities to States (including cash in lieu of commodities):				
a. FNS commodities	203,254	224,051	245,706	21,655
b. AMS Section 32 commodities	400,000	400,000	400,000	0
c. CCC bonus commodities	84,396	84,396	84,396	0
d. AMS bonus commodities	37,765	37,765	37,765	0
TOTAL, Commodities to States	725,415	746,212	767,867	21,655
3. Nutrition studies and education:				
a. Nutrition studies and surveys, section 6(a)(3)	3,829	3,835	3,939	104
b. Nutrition education and training, section 19	10,000	10,000	10,270	270
c. Child Nutrition Federal Review System	4,111	4,241	3,843	-398
d. Food Service Management Institute	1,322	1,661	1,706	45
e. Dietary Guidelines	0	2,000	2,054	54
TOTAL, Nutrition studies and education	19,262	21,737	21,812	75
Section 17(p) Demos	:	0	3,700	3,700
TOTAL, Child Nutrition Programs	6,777,286	7,427,673	8,082,068	654,395
LESS: AMS Section 32 commodities	400,000	400,000	400,000	0
CCC bonus commodities	84,396	84,396	84,396	0
AMS bonus commodities	37,765	37,765	37,765	0
TOTAL, FNS Child Nutrition Account	6,255,125	6,905,512	7,559,907	654,395
B. Special Milk Program: Cash Payments	21,587	20,023	20,531	508
C. Special Supplemental Food Program (WIC):				
1. Cash grants to States	2,667,449	2,968,647	3,291,220	322,573
2. Studies and evaluations	5,027	5,000	5,000	0
TOTAL, FNS Special Supplemental Food Program Account	2,672,476	2,973,647	3,296,220	322,573

Continued on next page

31-17

FOOD AND NUTRITION SERVICE

Food Assistance Table
Program Level under Current Law
(Dollars in Thousands)

	1992 Estimate	1993 Estimate	1994 Estimate	Change 1993-1994
D. Commodity Supplemental Food Program (CSFP):				
1. Commodities for supplemental food.	.78,109	75,600	75,600	0
2. Payments to distributing agencies for administration.	18,257	18,900	18,900	0
3. Special administrative funds.	0	0	0	0
4. CCC donations.	21,833	22,653	22,084	-569
SUBTOTAL, Commodity Supplemental Food Program (CSFP)..	118,199	117,153	116,584	-569
LESS: CCC Donations.	21,833	22,653	22,084	-569
TOTAL, FNS CSFP Account.	96,366	94,500	94,500	0
E. Food Stamp Program:				
1. Benefit costs.	20,899,531	22,397,394	23,409,031	1,011,637
2. State administrative costs.	1,483,392	1,588,976	1,634,079	45,103
3. Other program costs.	84,832	94,124	106,545	12,421
4. Benefit Reserve.	0	0	0	0
5. Excess state error liabilities.	0	0	0	0
6. Fed. Tax Refund Program.	0	0	0	0
7. Adjustments in expired accounts.	0	0	0	0
TOTAL, FNS Food Stamp Program Account.	22,467,755	24,080,494	25,149,655	1,069,161
F. Nutrition Assistance for Puerto Rico.	1,002,175	1,040,175	1,091,000	50,825

Continued on next page

FOOD AND NUTRITION SERVICE

Food Assistance Table
Program Level under Current Law
(Dollars in Thousands)

	1992 Estimate	1993 Estimate	1994 Estimate	Change 1993-1994
G. Food Donations Programs:				
1. Food Distribution Program on Indian Reservations:				
a. Commodities in lieu of food stamps	64,219	63,157	50,596	-12,561
b. Distributing agency administrative costs	17,548	18,444	18,905	461
c. Section 32 bonus commodities	0	0	0	0
d. Section 416 bonus commodities	1,491	1,491	1,491	0
TOTAL, Food Distribution Program on Reservations	83,258	83,092	70,992	-12,100
LESS: Bonus commodities	1,491	1,491	1,491	0
TOTAL, FNS Food Distribution Program on Indian Reservations Account	81,767	81,601	69,501	-12,100
2. Nutrition Program for the Elderly:				
a. Commodities	9,271	9,367	9,358	-9
b. Cash in lieu of commodities	134,448	133,545	133,554	9
c. Section 32 Bonus Commodities	832	832	832	0
d. Section 416 Bonus Commodities	577	577	577	0
TOTAL, Nutrition Program for the Elderly	145,128	144,321	144,321	0
LESS: Bonus Commodities	1,409	1,409	1,409	0
TOTAL, FNS Nutrition Program for the Elderly Account	143,719	142,912	142,912	0
3. Commodities for Soup Kitchens	32,000	32,000	32,000	0
TOTAL, FNS Food Donations Programs Account	257,486	256,513	244,413	-12,100
H. The Emergency Food Assistance Program (TEFAP):				
1. FNS Commodities	120,000	143,481	163,240	19,759
2. CCC Bonus Commodities	89,305	89,305	89,305	0
3. TEFAP Administrative Expense	44,999	45,000	46,215	1,215
TOTAL, The Emergency Food Assistance Program	254,304	277,786	298,760	20,974
LESS: Bonus Commodities	89,305	89,305	89,305	0
TOTAL, FNS TEFAP Account	164,999	188,481	209,455	20,974
I. Temporary Assistance P.L. 102-552: Commodities	0	42,329	0	-42,329

Continued on next page

FOOD AND NUTRITION SERVICE

Food Assistance Table
Program Level under Current Law
(Dollars in Thousands)

	1992 Estimate	1993 Estimate	1994 Estimate	Change 1993-1994
J. Bonus Commodities to Other Outlets:				
1. Charitable Institutions				
a. Section 32 commodities	15,155	15,155	15,155	0
b. Section 416 commodities	80,032	80,032	80,032	0
2. Summer Camps				
a. Section 32 commodities	308	308	308	0
b. Section 416 commodities	2,471	2,471	2,471	0
3. Disaster Feeding				
a. Section 32 commodities	1,552	1,552	1,552	0
b. Section 416 commodities	1,015	1,015	1,015	0
TOTAL, Bonus Commodities to Other Outlets	100,533	100,533	100,533	0
K. Food Program Administration:				
1. Child nutrition/Special Milk	27,484	27,487	27,930	443
2. Supplemental feeding	11,438	11,439	11,623	184
3. Food stamp	58,091	58,098	59,035	937
4. Cash and commodity subsidies	6,777	6,777	6,887	110
TOTAL, Food Program Administration	103,790	103,801	105,475	1,674
GRAND TOTAL, Food Assistance	33,778,491	36,443,027	38,508,139	2,065,112
LESS: Section 32 commodities for Child Nutriton	400,000	400,000	400,000	0
AMS bonus commodities	55,612	55,612	55,612	0
CCC bonus commodities	281,120	281,940	281,371	569
TOTAL, FNS Accounts	33,041,759	35,705,475	37,771,156	2,065,681

FOOD AND NUTRITION SERVICE

Food Assistance Table
Outlays under Current Law
(Dollars in Thousands)

	1992 Estimate	1993 Estimate	1994 Estimate	Change 1993-1994
A. Child Nutrition Programs:				
1. Program grants to States:				
a. School Lunch Program	3,759,731	4,117,436	4,300,348	182,912
b. School Breakfast Program	792,786	878,163	968,133	89,970
c. Child Care and Adult Care Food Program	1,080,689	1,296,086	1,596,033	299,947
d. Summer Food Service Program	198,516	224,005	251,346	27,341
e. State administrative expenses	72,739	76,367	84,519	8,152
TOTAL, Cash payments to States	5,904,461	6,592,057	7,200,379	608,322
2. Commodities to States (including cash in lieu of commodities):				
a. FNS commodities	203,254	224,051	245,706	21,655
b. AMS Section 32 commodities	400,000	400,000	400,000	0
c. CCC bonus commodities	0	0	0	0
d. AMS bonus commodities	0	0	0	0
TOTAL, Commodities to States	603,254	624,051	645,706	21,655
3. Nutrition studies and education:				
a. Nutrition studies and surveys, section 6(a)(3)	3,835	3,835	3,939	104
b. Nutrition education and training, section 19	10,000	10,000	10,270	270
c. Child Nutrition Federal Review System	4,111	4,241	3,843	-398
d. Food Service Management Institute	1,322	1,661	1,706	45
e. Dietary Guidelines	0	2,000	2,054	54
TOTAL, Nutrition studies and education	19,268	21,737	21,812	75
Section 17(p) Demos	0	0	3,700	3,700
TOTAL, Child Nutrition Programs	6,526,983	7,237,845	7,871,597	633,752
LESS: AMS Section 32 commodities	400,000	400,000	400,000	0
CCC bonus commodities	0	0	0	0
AMS bonus commodities	0	0	0	0
TOTAL, FNS Child Nutrition Account	6,126,983	6,837,845	7,471,597	633,752
B. Special Milk Program: Cash Payments	19,178	20,365	20,410	45
C. Special Supplemental Food Program (WIC):				
1. Cash grants to States	2,541,654	2,899,744	3,263,156	363,412
2. Studies and evaluations	3,036	8,337	5,000	-3,337
TOTAL, FNS Special Supplemental Food Program Account	2,544,690	2,908,081	3,268,156	360,075

Continued on next page

FOOD AND NUTRITION SERVICE

Food Assistance Table
Outlays under Current Law
(Dollars in Thousands)

	1992 Estimate	1993 Estimate	1994 Estimate	Change 1993-1994
D. Commodity Supplemental Food Program (CSFP):				
1. Commodities for supplemental food..................	78,080	73,437	75,600	2,163
2. Payments to distributing agencies for administration....................	17,499	22,069	18,900	-3,169
3. Special administrative funds.......................	0	0	0	0
4. CCC donations......................................	0	0	0	0
SUBTOTAL, Commodity Supplemental Food Program (CSFP)..	95,579	95,506	94,500	-1,006
LESS: CCC Donations................................	0	0	0	0
TOTAL, FNS CSFP Account...............................	95,579	95,506	94,500	-1,006
E. Food Stamp Program:				
1. Benefit costs......................................	20,110,088	22,420,629	23,378,581	957,952
2. State administrative costs.........................	1,610,773	1,585,884	1,630,109	44,225
3. Other program costs................................	82,992	94,380	98,654	4,274
4. Benefit Reserve....................................	0	0	0	0
5. Excess state error liabilities.....................	0	0	-1,000	-1,000
6. Fed. Tax Refund Program............................	0	0	0	0
7. Adjustments in expired accounts....................	0	-598,274	0	598,274
TOTAL, FNS Food Stamp Program Account....................	21,803,853	23,502,619	25,106,344	1,603,725
F. Nutrition Assistance for Puerto Rico..................	995,806	1,043,488	1,090,675	47,187

Continued on next page

FOOD AND NUTRITION SERVICE

Food Assistance Table
Outlays under Current Law
(Dollars in Thousands)

	1992 Estimate	1993 Estimate	1994 Estimate	Change 1993-1994
G. Food Donations Programs:				
1. Food Distribution Program on Indian Reservations:				
a. Commodities in lieu of food stamps..............	58,831	61,782	52,983	-8,799
b. Distributing agency administrative costs........	16,385	18,226	18,817	591
c. Section 32 bonus commodities....................	0	0	0	0
d. Section 416 bonus commodities...................	0	0	0	0
TOTAL, Food Distribution Program on Reservations......	75,216	80,008	71,800	-8,208
LESS: Bonus commodities............................	0	0	0	0
TOTAL, FNS Food Distribution Program on Indian Reservations Account...........	75,216	80,008	71,800	-8,208
2. Nutrition Program for the Elderly:				
a. Commodities.....................................	11,742	7,587	9,304	1,717
b. Cash in lieu of commodities.....................	125,036	147,626	133,608	-14,018
c. Section 32 Bonus Commodities....................	0	0	0	0
d. Section 416 Bonus Commodities...................	0	0	0	0
TOTAL, Nutrition Program for the Elderly..............	136,778	155,213	142,912	-12,301
LESS: Bonus Commodities............................	0	0	0	0
TOTAL, FNS Nutrition Program for the Elderly Account..........................	136,778	155,213	142,912	-12,301
3. Commodities for Soup Kitchens......................	32,108	32,000	32,000	0
TOTAL, FNS Food Donations Programs Account...............	244,102	267,221	246,712	-20,509
H. The Emergency Food Assistance Program (TEFAP):				
1. FNS Commodities....................................	120,000	143,481	163,240	19,759
2. CCC Bonus Commodities..............................	0	0	0	0
3. TEFAP Administrative Expense.......................	45,378	47,211	45,881	-1,330
TOTAL, The Emergency Food Assistance Program...............................	165,378	190,692	209,121	18,429
LESS: Bonus Commodities............................	0	0	0	0
TOTAL, FNS TEFAP Account.................................	165,378	190,692	209,121	18,429
I. Temporary Assistance P.L. 102-552: Commodities.......	0	42,329	0	-42,329

Continued on next page

FOOD AND NUTRITION SERVICE

Food Assistance Table
Outlays under Current Law
(Dollars in Thousands)

	1992 Estimate	1993 Estimate	1994 Estimate	Change 1993-1994
J. Bonus Commodities to Other Outlets:				
1. Charitable Institutions				
a. Section 32 commodities..........................	0	0	0	0
b. Section 416 commodities..........................	0	0	0	0
2. Summer Camps				
a. Section 32 commodities..........................	0	u	0	0
b. Section 416 commodities..........................	0	0	0	0
3. Disaster Feeding				
a. Section 32 commodities..........................	0	0	0	0
b. Section 416 commodities..........................	0	0	0	0
TOTAL, Bonus Commodities to Other Outlets...............	0	0	0	0
K. Food Program Administration:				
1. Child nutrition/Special Milk........................	26,723	28,985	27,522	-1,463
2. Supplemental feeding................................	11,121	12,062	11,454	-608
3. Food stamp..	56,484	61,263	58,172	-3,091
4. Cash and commodity subsidies........................	6,589	7,147	6,786	-361
TOTAL, Food Program Administration......................	100,917	109,457	103,934	-5,523
GRAND TOTAL, Food Assistance............................	32,496,486	35,417,603	38,011,449	2,593,846
LESS: Section 32 commodities for Child Nutriton......	400,000	400,000	400,000	0
AMS bonus commodities..........................	0	0	0	0
CCC bonus commodities..........................	0	0	0	0
TOTAL, FNS Accounts.....................................	32,096,486	35,017,603	37,611,449	2,593,846

FOOD AND NUTRITION SERVICE

Food Assistance Table
Budget Authority at the Recommended Level
(Dollars in Thousands)

	1992 Estimate	1993 Estimate	1994 Estimate	Change 1993-1994
A. Child Nutrition Programs:				
1. Program grants to States:				
a. School Lunch Program	3,782,968	4,110,794	4,327,236	216,442
b. School Breakfast Program	801,191	891,163	980,352	89,189
c. Child Care and Adult Care Food Program	1,089,627	1,326,811	1,638,773	311,962
d. Summer Food Service Program	202,927	230,394	254,612	24,218
e. State administrative expenses	69,108	77,086	86,738	9,652
TOTAL, Cash payments to States	5,945,821	6,636,248	7,287,711	651,463
2. Commodities to States (including cash in lieu of commodities):				
a. FNS commodities	203,254	225,029	245,706	20,677
b. AMS Section 32 commodities	400,000	400,000	400,000	0
c. CCC bonus commodities	0	0	0	0
d. AMS bonus commodities	0	0	0	0
TOTAL, Commodities to States	603,254	625,029	645,706	20,677
3. Nutrition studies and education:				
a. Nutrition studies and surveys, section 6(a)(3)	3,835	3,835	3,939	104
b. Nutrition education and training, section 19	10,000	10,000	10,270	270
c. Child Nutrition Federal Review System	4,083	3,780	3,843	63
d. Food Service Management Institute	1,322	1,661	1,706	45
e. Dietary Guidelines	0	2,000	2,054	54
TOTAL, Nutrition studies and education	19,240	21,276	21,812	536
Section 17(p) Demos	0	0	3,700	3,700
TOTAL, Child Nutrition Programs	6,568,315	7,282,553	7,958,929	676,376
LESS: AMS Section 32 commodities	400,000	400,000	400,000	0
CCC bonus commodities	0	0	0	0
AMS bonus commodities	0	0	0	0
TOTAL, FNS Child Nutrition Account	6,168,315	6,882,553	7,558,929	676,376
B. Special Milk Program: Cash Payments	23,011	14,898	20,277	5,379
C. Special Supplemental Food Program (WIC):				
1. Cash grants to States	2,595,000	2,930,000	3,282,220	352,220
2. Studies and evaluations	5,000	5,000	5,000	0
TOTAL, FNS Special Supplemental Food Program Account	2,600,000	2,935,000	3,287,220	352,220

Continued on next page

FOOD AND NUTRITION SERVICE

Food Assistance Table
Budget Authority at the Recommended Level
(Dollars in Thousands)

	1992 Estimate	1993 Estimate	1994 Estimate	Change 1993-1994
D. Commodity Supplemental Food Program (CSFP):				
1. Commodities for supplemental food..................	72,000	75,600	75,600	
2. Payments to distributing agencies for administration....................	18,000	18,900	18,900	0
3. Special administrative funds........................	0	0	0	0
4. CCC donations.......................................		0	0	0
SUBTOTAL, Commodity Supplemental Food Program (CSFP)..	90,000	94,500	94,500	0
LESS: CCC Donations................................	0	0	0	0
TOTAL, FNS CSFP Account...............................	90,000	94,500	94,500	0
E. Food Stamp Program:				
1. Benefit costs.......................................	19,526,638	22,880,127	23,409,031	528,904
2. State administrative costs..........................	1,538,117	1,588,976	1,614,079	25,103
3. Other program costs.................................	86,670	95,254	106,545	11,291
4. Benefit Reserve.....................................	1,498,550	2,500,000	5,000,000	2,500,000
5. Excess state error liabilities......................	0	0	-1,000	-1,000
6. Fed. Tax Refund Program.............................	0	0	0	0
7. Adjustments in expired accounts.....................	0	0	0	0
TOTAL, FNS Food Stamp Program Account.....................	22,649,975	27,064,357	30,128,655	3,064,298
F. Nutrition Assistance for Puerto Rico..................	1,013,000	1,051,000	1,091,000	40,000

Continued on next page

FOOD AND NUTRITION SERVICE

Food Assistance Table
Budget Authority at the Recommended Level
(Dollars in Thousands)

	1992 Estimate	1993 Estimate	1994 Estimate	Change 1993-1994
G. Food Donations Programs:				
1. Food Distribution Program on Indian Reservations:				
a. Commodities in lieu of food stamps	64,495	63,157	50,596	-12,561
b. Distributing agency administrative costs	17,450	18,444	18,905	461
c. Section 32 bonus commodities	0	0	0	0
d. Section 416 bonus commodities	0	0	0	0
TOTAL, Food Distribution Program on Reservations	81,945	81,601	69,501	-12,100
LESS: Bonus commodities	0	0	0	0
TOTAL, FNS Food Distribution Program on Indian Reservations Account	81,945	81,601	69,501	-12,100
2. Nutrition Program for the Elderly:				
a. Commodities	9,918	9,367	9,358	-9
b. Cash in lieu of commodities	141,574	133,545	133,554	9
c. Section 32 Bonus Commodities	0	0	0	0
d. Section 416 Bonus Commodities	0	0	0	0
TOTAL, Nutrition Program for the Elderly	151,492	142,912	142,912	0
LESS: Bonus Commodities	0	0	0	0
TOTAL, FNS Nutrition Program for the Elderly Account	151,492	142,912	142,912	0
3. Commodities for Soup Kitchens	32,000	32,000	32,000	0
TOTAL, FNS Food Donations Programs Account	265,437	256,513	244,413	-12,100
H. The Emergency Food Assistance Program (TEFAP):				
1. FNS Commodities	120,000	143,481	163,240	19,759
2. CCC Bonus Commodities	0	0	0	0
3. TEFAP Administrative Expense	45,000	45,000	46,215	1,215
TOTAL, The Emergency Food Assistance Program	165,000	188,481	209,455	20,974
LESS: Bonus Commodities	0	0	0	0
TOTAL, FNS TEFAP Account	165,000	188,481	209,455	20,974
I. Temporary Assistance P.L. 102-552: Commodities	0	42,329	0	-42,329

Continued on next page

FOOD AND NUTRITION SERVICE

Food Assistance Table
Budget Authority at the Recommended Level
(Dollars in Thousands)

	1992 Estimate	1993 Estimate	1994 Estimate	Change 1993-1994
J. Bonus Commodities to Other Outlets:				
1. Charitable Institutions				
a. Section 32 commodities..........................	0	0	0	0
b. Section 416 commodities.........................	0	0	0	0
2. Summer Camps				
a. Section 32 commodities..........................	0	0	0	0
b. Section 416 commodities.........................	0	0	0	0
3. Disaster Feeding				
a. Section 32 commodities..........................	0	0	0	0
b. Section 416 commodities.........................	0	0	0	0
TOTAL, Bonus Commodities to Other Outlets...............	0	0	0	0
K. Food Program Administration:				
1. Child nutrition/Special Milk........................	27,416	27,416	27,858	442
2. Supplemental feeding................................	11,410	11,410	11,593	183
3. Food stamp..	57,949	57,949	58,881	932
4. Cash and commodity subsidies........................	6,760	6,760	6,869	109
TOTAL, Food Program Administration......................	103,535	103,535	105,201	1,666
GRAND TOTAL, Food Assistance............................	33,478,273	39,033,166	43,139,650	4,106,484
LESS: Section 32 commodities for Child Nutriton......	400,000	400,000	400,000	0
AMS bonus commodities..........................	0	0	0	0
CCC bonus commodities..........................	0	0	0	0
TOTAL, FNS Accounts.....................................	33,078,273	38,633,166	42,739,650	4,106,484

FOOD AND NUTRITION SERVICE

Food Assistance Table
Program Level at the Recommended Level
(Dollars in Thousands)

	1992 Estimate	1993 Estimate	1994 Estimate	Change 1993-1994
A. Child Nutrition Programs:				
1. Program grants to States:				
a. School Lunch Program	3,870,098	4,131,424	4,328,214	196,790
b. School Breakfast Program	801,191	891,163	980,352	89,189
c. Child Care and Adult Care Food Program	1,089,627	1,326,811	1,638,773	311,962
d. Summer Food Service Program	202,927	230,394	254,612	24,218
e. State administrative expenses	68,766	79,932	86,738	6,806
TOTAL, Cash payments to States	6,032,609	6,659,724	7,288,689	628,965
2. Commodities to States (including cash in lieu of commodities):				
a. FNS commodities	203,254	224,051	245,706	21,655
b. AMS Section 32 commodities	400,000	400,000	400,000	0
c. CCC bonus commodities	84,396	84,396	84,396	0
d. AMS bonus commodities	37,765	37,765	37,765	0
TOTAL, Commodities to States	725,415	746,212	767,867	21,655
3. Nutrition studies and education:				
a. Nutrition studies and surveys, section 6(a)(3)	3,829	3,835	3,939	104
b. Nutrition education and training, section 19	10,000	10,000	10,270	270
c. Child Nutrition Federal Review System	4,111	4,241	3,843	-398
d. Food Service Management Institute	1,322	1,661	1,706	45
e. Dietary Guidelines	0	2,000	2,054	54
TOTAL, Nutrition studies and education	19,262	21,737	21,812	75
Section 17(p) Demos	0	0	3,700	3,700
TOTAL, Child Nutrition Programs	6,777,286	7,427,673	8,082,068	654,395
LESS: AMS Section 32 commodities	400,000	400,000	400,000	0
CCC bonus commodities	84,396	84,396	84,396	0
AMS bonus commodities	37,765	37,765	37,765	0
TOTAL, FNS Child Nutrition Account	6,255,125	6,905,512	7,559,907	654,395
B. Special Milk Program: Cash Payments	21,587	20,023	20,531	508
C. Special Supplemental Food Program (WIC):				
1. Cash grants to States	2,667,449	2,968,647	3,291,220	322,573
2. Studies and evaluations	5,027	5,000	5,000	0
TOTAL, FNS Special Supplemental Food Program Account	2,672,476	2,973,647	3,296,220	322,573

Continued on next page

FOOD AND NUTRITION SERVICE

Food Assistance Table
Program Level at the Recommended Level
(Dollars in Thousands)

	1992 Estimate	1993 Estimate	1994 Estimate	Change 1993-1994
D. Commodity Supplemental Food Program (CSFP):				
1. Commodities for supplemental food..................	78,109	75,600	75,600	
2. Payments to distributing agencies for administration....................	18,257	18,900	18,900	0
3. Special administrative funds........................	0	0	0	0
4. CCC donations..	21,833	22,653	22,084	-569
SUBTOTAL, Commodity Supplemental Food Program (CSFP)..	118,199	117,153	116,584	-569
LESS: CCC Donations.................................	21,833	22,653	22,084	-569
TOTAL, FNS CSFP Account..............................	96,366	94,500	94,500	0
E. Food Stamp Program:				
1. Benefit costs..	20,899,531	22,397,394	23,409,031	1,011,637
2. State administrative costs..........................	1,483,392	1,588,976	1,614,079	25,103
3. Other program costs.................................	84,832	94,124	106,545	12,421
4. Benefit Reserve......................................	0	0	0	0
5. Excess state error liabilities......................	0	0	0	0
6. Fed. Tax Refund Program.............................	0	0	0	0
7. Adjustments in expired accounts.....................	0	0	0	0
TOTAL, FNS Food Stamp Program Account..................	22,467,755	24,080,494	25,129,655	1,049,161
F. Nutrition Assistance for Puerto Rico.................	1,002,175	1,040,175	1,091,000	50,825

Continued on next page

FOOD AND NUTRITION SERVICE

Food Assistance Table
Program Level at the Recommended Level
(Dollars in Thousands)

	1992 Estimate	1993 Estimate	1994 Estimate	Change 1993-1994
G. Food Donations Programs:				
1. Food Distribution Program on Indian Reservations:				
a. Commodities in lieu of food stamps	64,219	63,157	50,596	-12,561
b. Distributing agency administrative costs	17,548	18,444	18,905	461
c. Section 32 bonus commodities	0	0	0	0
d. Section 416 bonus commodities	1,491	1,491	1,491	0
TOTAL, Food Distribution Program on Reservations	83,258	83,092	70,992	-12,100
LESS: Bonus commodities	1,491	1,491	1,491	0
TOTAL, FNS Food Distribution Program on Indian Reservations Account	81,767	81,601	69,501	-12,100
2. Nutrition Program for the Elderly:				
a. Commodities	9,271	9,367	9,358	-9
b. Cash in lieu of commodities	134,448	133,545	133,554	9
c. Section 32 Bonus Commodities	832	832	832	0
d. Section 416 Bonus Commodities	577	577	577	0
TOTAL, Nutrition Program for the Elderly	145,128	144,321	144,321	0
LESS: Bonus Commodities	1,409	1,409	1,409	0
TOTAL, FNS Nutrition Program for the Elderly Account	143,719	142,912	142,912	
3. Commodities for Soup Kitchens	32,000	32,000	32,000	0
TOTAL, FNS Food Donations Programs Account	257,486	256,513	244,413	-12,100
H. The Emergency Food Assistance Program (TEFAP):				
1. FNS Commodities	120,000	143,481	163,240	19,759
2. CCC Bonus Commodities	89,305	89,305	89,305	0
3. TEFAP Administrative Expense	44,999	45,000	46,215	1,215
TOTAL, The Emergency Food Assistance Program	254,304	277,786	298,760	20,974
LESS: Bonus Commodities	89,305	89,305	89,305	0
TOTAL, FNS TEFAP Account	164,999	188,481	209,455	20,974
I. Temporary Assistance P.L. 102-552: Commodities	0	42,329	0	-42,329

Continued on next page

FOOD AND NUTRITION SERVICE

Food Assistance Table
Program Level at the Recommended Level
(Dollars in Thousands)

	1992 Estimate	1993 Estimate	1994 Estimate	Change 1993-1994
J. Bonus Commodities to Other Outlets:				
1. Charitable Institutions				
a. Section 32 commodities..........................	15,155	15,155	15,155	0
b. Section 416 commodities..........................	80,032	80,032	80,032	0
2. Summer Camps				
a. Section 32 commodities..........................	308	308	308	0
b. Section 416 commodities..........................	2,471	2,471	2,471	0
3. Disaster Feeding				
a. Section 32 commodities..........................	1,552	1,552	1,552	0
b. Section 416 commodities..........................	1,015	1,015	1,015	0
TOTAL, Bonus Commodities to Other Outlets................	100,533	100,533	100,533	0
K. Food Program Administration:				
1. Child nutrition/Special Milk........................	27,484	27,487	27,930	443
2. Supplemental feeding...............................	11,438	11,439	11,623	184
3. Food stamp..	58,091	58,098	59,035	937
4. Cash and commodity subsidies........................	6,777	6,777	6,887	110
TOTAL, Food Program Administration.......................	103,790	103,801	105,475	1,674
GRAND TOTAL, Food Assistance.............................	33,778,491	36,443,027	38,488,139	2,045,112
LESS: Section 32 commodities for Child Nutriton......	400,000	400,000	400,000	0
AMS bonus commodities..........................	55,612	55,612	55,612	0
CCC bonus commodities..........................	281,120	281,940	281,371	569
TOTAL, FNS Accounts......................................	33,041,759	35,705,475	37,751,156	2,045,681

31-32

FOOD AND NUTRITION SERVICE

Food Assistance Table
Outlays at the Recommended Level
(Dollars in Thousands)

	1992 Estimate	1993 Estimate	1994 Estimate	Change 1993-1994
A. Child Nutrition Programs:				
1. Program grants to States:				
a. School Lunch Program	3,759,731	4,117,436	4,300,348	182,912
b. School Breakfast Program	792,786	878,163	968,133	89,970
c. Child Care and Adult Care Food Program	1,080,689	1,296,086	1,596,033	299,947
d. Summer Food Service Program	198,516	224,005	251,346	27,341
e. State administrative expenses	72,739	76,367	84,519	8,152
TOTAL, Cash payments to States	5,904,461	6,592,057	7,200,379	608,322
2. Commodities to States (including cash in lieu of commodities):				
a. FNS commodities	203,254	224,051	245,706	21,655
b. AMS Section 32 commodities	400,000	400,000	400,000	0
c. CCC bonus commodities	0	0	0	0
d. AMS bonus commodities	0	0	0	0
TOTAL, Commodities to States	603,254	624,051	645,706	21,655
3. Nutrition studies and education:				
a. Nutrition studies and surveys, section 6(a)(3)	3,835	3,835	3,939	104
b. Nutrition education and training, section 19	10,000	10,000	10,270	270
c. Child Nutrition Federal Review System	4,111	4,241	3,843	-398
d. Food Service Management Institute	1,322	1,661	1,706	45
e. Dietary Guidelines	0	2,000	2,054	54
TOTAL, Nutrition studies and education	19,268	21,737	21,812	75
Section 17(p) Demos	0	0	3,700	3,700
TOTAL, Child Nutrition Programs	6,526,983	7,237,845	7,871,597	633,752
LESS: AMS Section 32 commodities	400,000	400,000	400,000	0
CCC bonus commodities	0	0	0	0
AMS bonus commodities	0	0	0	0
TOTAL, FNS Child Nutrition Account	6,126,983	6,837,845	7,471,597	633,752
B. Special Milk Program: Cash Payments	19,178	20,365	20,410	45
C. Special Supplemental Food Program (WIC):				
1. Cash grants to States	2,541,654	2,899,744	3,263,156	363,412
2. Studies and evaluations	3,036	8,337	5,000	-3,337
TOTAL, FNS Special Supplemental Food Program Account	2,544,690	2,908,081	3,268,156	360,075

Continued on next page

31-33

FOOD AND NUTRITION SERVICE

Food Assistance Table
Outlays at the Recommended Level
(Dollars in Thousands)

	1992 Estimate	1993 Estimate	1994 Estimate	Change 1993-1994
D. Commodity Supplemental Food Program (CSFP):				
1. Commodities for supplemental food	78,080	73,437	75,600	2,163
2. Payments to distributing agencies for administration	17,499	22,069	18,900	-3,169
3. Special administrative funds	0	0	0	0
4. CCC donations	0	0	0	0
SUBTOTAL, Commodity Supplemental Food Program (CSFP)	95,579	95,506	94,500	-1,006
LESS: CCC Donations	0	0	0	0
TOTAL, FNS CSFP Account	95,579	95,506	94,500	-1,006
E. Food Stamp Program:				
1. Benefit costs	20,110,088	22,420,629	23,378,581	957,952
2. State administrative costs	1,610,773	1,585,884	1,611,869	25,985
3. Other program costs	82,992	94,380	98,654	4,274
4. Benefit Reserve	0	0	0	0
5. Excess state error liabilities	0	0	-1,000	-1,000
6. Fed. Tax Refund Program	0	0	0	0
7. Adjustments in expired accounts	0	-598,274	0	598,274
TOTAL, FNS Food Stamp Program Account	21,803,853	23,502,619	25,088,104	1,585,485
F. Nutrition Assistance for Puerto Rico	995,806	1,043,488	1,090,675	47,187

Continued on next page

31-34

FOOD AND NUTRITION SERVICE

Food Assistance Table
Outlays at the Recommended Level
(Dollars in Thousands)

	1992 Estimate	1993 Estimate	1994 Estimate	Change 1993-1994
G. Food Donations Programs:				
1. Food Distribution Program on Indian Reservations:				
a. Commodities in lieu of food stamps..............	58,831	61,782	52,983	-8,799
b. Distributing agency administrative costs........	16,385	18,226	18,817	591
c. Section 32 bonus commodities....................	0	0	0	0
d. Section 416 bonus commodities...................	0	0	0	0
TOTAL, Food Distribution Program on Reservations......	75,216	80,008	71,800	-8,208
LESS: Bonus commodities............................	0	0	0	0
TOTAL, FNS Food Distribution Program on Indian Reservations Account...........	75,216	80,008	71,800	-8,208
2. Nutrition Program for the Elderly:				
a. Commodities.....................................	11,742	7,587	9,360	1,773
b. Cash in lieu of commodities.....................	125,036	147,626	133,552	-14,074
c. Section 32 Bonus Commodities....................	0	0	0	0
d. Section 416 Bonus Commodities...................	0	0	0	0
TOTAL, Nutrition Program for the Elderly..............	136,778	155,213	142,912	-12,301
LESS: Bonus Commodities............................	0	0	0	0
TOTAL, FNS Nutrition Program for the Elderly Account..........................	136,778	155,213	142,912	-12,301
3. Commodities for Soup Kitchens......................	32,108	32,000	32,000	0
TOTAL, FNS Food Donations Programs Account...............	244,102	267,221	246,712	-20,509
H. The Emergency Food Assistance Program (TEFAP):				
1. FNS Commodities....................................	120,000	143,481	163,240	19,759
2. CCC Bonus Commodities..............................	0	0	0	0
3. TEFAP Administrative Expense.......................	45,378	47,211	45,881	-1,330
TOTAL, The Emergency Food Assistance Program...............................	165,378	190,692	209,121	18,429
LESS: Bonus Commodities............................	0	0	0	0
TOTAL, FNS TEFAP Account..................................	165,378	190,692	209,121	18,429
I. Temporary Assistance P.L. 102-552: Commodities.......	0	42,329	0	-42,329

Continued on next page

31-35

FOOD AND NUTRITION SERVICE

Food Assistance Table
Outlays at the Recommended Level
(Dollars in Thousands)

	1992 Estimate	1993 Estimate	1994 Estimate	Change 1993-1994
J. Bonus Commodities to Other Outlets:				
1. Charitable Institutions				
a. Section 32 commodities..........................	0	0	0	0
b. Section 416 commodities.........................	0	0	0	0
2. Summer Camps				
a. Section 32 commodities..........................	0	0	0	0
b. Section 416 commodities.........................	0	0	0	0
3. Disaster Feeding				
a. Section 32 commodities..........................	0	0	0	0
b. Section 416 commodities.........................	0	0	0	0
TOTAL, Bonus Commodities to Other Outlets................	0	0	0	0
K. Food Program Administration:				
1. Child nutrition/Special Milk.......................	26,723	28,985	27,522	-1,463
2. Supplemental feeding...............................	11,121	12,062	11,454	-608
3. Food stamp...	56,484	61,263	58,172	-3,091
4. Cash and commodity subsidies.......................	6,589	7,147	6,786	-361
TOTAL, Food Program Administration.......................	100,917	109,457	103,934	-5,523
GRAND TOTAL, Food Assistance.............................	32,496,486	35,417,603	37,993,209	2,575,606
LESS: Section 32 commodities for Child Nutriton......	400,000	400,000	400,000	0
AMS bonus commodities..........................	0	0	0	0
CCC bonus commodities..........................	0	0	0	0
TOTAL, FNS Accounts......................................	32,096,486	35,017,603	37,593,209	2,575,606

FOOD AND NUTRITION SERVICE

The estimate includes appropriation language for this item as follows (new language underscored; deleted matter enclosed in brackets):

State Child Nutrition [Programs] Payments (Including Transfers of Funds):

For necessary expenses to carry out the National School Lunch Act
1 (42 U.S.C. 1751-1769b), and the applicable provisions other than sections 3 and 17 of the Child Nutrition Act of 1966 (42 U.S.C. 1773-1785, and 1788-1789); [$6,826,553,000] $7,443,929,000 to remain available through September 30, [1994] 1995, of which [$2,536,098,000] $2,733,744,000 is hereby appropriated and [$4,290,455,000] $4,710,185,000 shall be derived by transfer from funds available under section 32 of the Act of August 24, 1935
2 (7 U.S.C. 612c): Provided, That $3,700,000 of these funds shall be available to continue demonstration projects under section 17(p) of the National School Lunch Act: Provided further That funds appropriated for the purpose of section 7 of the Child Nutrition Act of 1966 shall be allocated among the States but the distribution of such funds to an individual State is contingent upon that State's agreement to participate in studies and surveys of programs authorized under the National School Lunch Act and the Child Nutrition Act of 1966, when such studies and surveys have been directed by the Congress and requested by the Secretary of Agriculture: Provided further, That if the Secretary of Agriculture determines that a State's administration of any program under the National School Lunch Act or the Child Nutrition Act of 1966 (other than section 17), or the regulations issued pursuant to these Acts, is seriously deficient, and the State fails to correct the deficiency within a specified period of time, the Secretary may withhold from the State some or all of the funds allocated to the State under section 7 of the Child Nutrition Act of 1966 and under section 13(k)(1) of the National School Lunch Act; upon a subsequent determination by the Secretary that the programs are operated in an acceptable manner some or all of the funds withheld may be allocated: Provided further, That only final reimbursement claims for service of meals, supplements, and milk submitted to State agencies by eligible schools, summer camps, institutions, and service institutions within sixty days following the month for which the reimbursement is claimed shall be eligible for reimbursement from funds appropriated under this Act. States may receive program funds appropriated under this Act for meals, supplements, and milk served during any month only if the final program operations report for such month is submitted to the Department within ninety days following that month. Exceptions to these claims or reports submission requirements may be made at the discretion of the Secretary: Provided further, That up to [$3,780,000] $3,843,000 shall be available for independent verification of school food service claims: Provided further, That [$1,661,000] $1,706,000 shall be available to provide financial and other assistance to operate the Food Service Management Institute. (Agriculture, Rural Development, Food and Drug Administration, and Related Agencies Appropriations Act, 1993.)

The first change makes funds provided available through September 30, 1995.

The second change designates discretionary funds for demonstration projects.

CHILD NUTRITION PROGRAMS

Appropriations Act, 1993	$6,826,553,000
Budget Estimate, 1994	7,443,929,000
Increase in Appropriations	+617,376,000

SUMMARY OF INCREASES AND DECREASES
(On basis of appropriation)

Item of Change	1993 Estimated	Pay Cost	Other Changes	1994 Estimated
School lunch program	$4,110,794,000	--	+$216,442,000	$4,327,236,000
School breakfast program	891,163,000	--	+89,189,000	980,352,000
Child and adult care food program	1,273,160,000	--	+255,286,000	1,528,446,000
Summer food service program	230,394,000	-17,518	+24,235,518	254,612,000
State administrative expenses	77,086,000	+77,274	+9,574,726	86,738,000
Commodity procurement a/	222,680,000	--	+18,353,000	241,033,000
Coordinated Review Effort	3,780,000	+68,748	-5,748	3,843,000
Nutrition studies and surveys	3,835,000	--	+104,000	3,939,000
Nutrition education and training	10,000,000	--	+270,000	10,270,000
Food Service Management Institute	1,661,000	--	+45,000	1,706,000
Dietary Guidelines	2,000,000	--	+54,000	2,054,000
Section 17(p) Demos	--	--	+3,700,000	3,700,000
Total Appropriation	6,826,553,000	+128,504	+617,247,496	7,443,929,000

a/ In addition, $400.0 million is available for entitlement commodity procurement from Section 32.

PROJECT STATEMENT
(On basis of appropriation)

Project	1992 Actual Amount	SYs	1993 Estimated Amount	SYs	Increase or Decrease	1994 Estimated Amount	SYs
1. Cash payments to States							
(a) School lunch:							
(1) Above 185% of poverty	$302,501,000		$337,085,000		+$17,829,000	$354,914,000	
(2) 130-185% of poverty	378,126,000		390,526,000		+20,654,000	411,180,000	
(3) Below 130% of poverty	3,102,340,404		3,383,183,000		175,959,000	3,561,142,000	
Total, School Lunch1/	3,782,967,404		4,110,794,000		(2) 216,442,000	4,327,236,000	
(b) School Breakfast program							
(1) Above 185% of poverty	19,229,000		21,388,000		+2,140,000	23,528,000	
(2) 130-185% of poverty	32,849,000		36,538,000		+3,656,000	40,194,000	
(3) Below 130% of poverty	749,113,471		833,237,000		+83,393,000	916,630,000	

PROJECT STATEMENT
(On basis of appropriation)

Project	1992 Actual Amount	SYs	1993 Estimated Amount	SYs	Increase or Decrease	1994 Estimated Amount	SYs
Total, School Breakfast.....	801,191,471		891,163,000		+89,189,000	980,352,000	
(c) Child and adult care food program							
(1) Meal Service:							
(a) Above 185% of poverty.	465,968,000		559,127,000		+98,562,000	657,689,000	
(b) 130-185% of poverty.	33,360,000		37,454,000		+9,099,000	46,553,000	
(c) Below 130% poverty	576,810,596		657,950,000		+144,629,000	802,579,000	
Subtotal.......	1,076,138,596		1,254,531,000		+252,290,000	1,506,821,000	
(2) Audit expense.....	13,489,000		18,629,000		2,996,000	21,625,000	
Total, Child and Adult Care Food Program..	1,089,627,596		1,273,160,000		(4) +255,286,000	1,528,446,000	
(d) Summer Food Service Program.....	202,926,601	33	230,394,000	35	(5) +24,218,000	254,612,000	35
(e) State Admin. expenses....	69,108,000	30	77,086,000	30	(6) +9,652,000	86,738,000	30
2. Commodity Procurement							
(a) Commodities	162,768,852		177,899,200		+14,230,100	192,129,300	
(b) Cash-in-lieu of commodities	40,485,076		44,780,800		+4,122,900	48,903,700	
Total, Commodity procurement2/.	203,253,928		222,680,000		(7) +18,353,000	241,033,000	
3. Coordinated Review2/.....	4,083,000	62	3,780,000	62	(8) +63,000	3,843,000	62
4. Nutrition Studies and Education2/..							
(a) Nutrition Studies and Surveys......	3,835,000		3,835,000		+104,000	3,939,000	
(b) Nutrition Ed and training	10,000,000		10,000,000		+270,000	10,270,000	
(c) Food Service Management Institute...	1,322,000		1,661,000		+45,000	1,706,000	
(d) Dietary Guidelines..	--		2,000,000		+54,000	2,054,000	

PROJECT STATEMENT
(On basis of appropriation)

Project	1992 Actual Amount	SYs	1993 Estimated Amount	SYs	Increase or Decrease	1994 Estimated Amount	SYs
Total, Nutrition Studies and Education	15,157,000		17,496,000		(9) +473,000	17,969,000	
Section 17(p) Demos.2/	--		--		(10) +3,700,000	3,700,000	
Transfer from Food Stamps	-100,000,000		--		--	--	
Total, Appropriation	6,068,315,000	125	6,826,553,000	127	617,376,000	7,443,929,000	127
Economic Stimulus			56,000,000		-56,000,000		
Investment Proposal					+115,000,000	115,000,000	
Total, Pres. Budget			6,882,553,000		+676,376,000	7,558,929,000	

PROJECT STATEMENT
(On basis of available funds)

Project	1992 Actual Amount	SYs	1993 Estimated Amount	SYs	Increase or Decrease	1994 Estimated Amount	SYs
1. Cash payments to States							
(a) School lunch:							
(1) Above 185% of poverty	$317,348,000		$338,777,000		+$16,137,000	$354,914,000	
(2) 130-185% of poverty	367,659,000		392,485,000		+18,695,000	411,180,000	
(3) Below 130% of poverty1/	3,185,090,459		3,400,162,817		+161,957,183	3,562,120,000	
Total, School Lunch	3,870,097,459		4,131,424,817		(2) +196,789,183	4,328,214,000	
(b) School Breakfast program							
(1) Above 185% of poverty	19,229,000		21,388,000		+2,140,000	23,528,000	
(2) 130-185% of poverty	32,849,000		36,538,000		+3,656,000	40,194,000	
(3) Below 130% of poverty	749,113,471		833,237,000		+83,393,000	916,630,000	
Total, School Breakfast	801,191,471		891,163,000		(3) +89,189,000	980,352,000	
(c) Child and adult care food program:							
(1) Meal Service							
(a) Above 185% of poverty	465,968,000		559,127,000		+98,562,000	657,689,000	
(b) 130-185% of poverty	33,360,000		37,454,000		+9,099,000	46,553,000	

PROJECT STATEMENT
(On basis of available funds)

Project	1992 Actual Amount	SYs	1993 Estimated Amount	SYs	Increase or Decrease	1994 Estimated Amount	SYs
(c) Below 130% poverty	576,810,596		657,950,000		+144,629,000	802,579,000	
Subtotal	1,076,138,596		1,254,531,000		+252,290,000	1,506,821,000	
(2) Audit expense	13,489,000		18,629,000		2,996,000	21,625,000	
Total, Child and Adult Care Food Program	1,089,627,596		1,273,160,000		(4) +255,286,000	1,528,446,000	
(d) Summer Food Service Program	202,926,601	33	230,394,000	35	(5) +24,218,000	254,612,000	35
(e) State Admin. expenses	68,765,863	30	79,932,000	30	(6) +6,806,000	86,738,000	30
2. Commodity Procurement							
(a) Commodities	162,768,852		177,362,000		+15,464,400	192,826,400	
(b) Cash-in-lieu of commodities	40,485,076		44,340,000		+3,866,600	48,206,600	
Total, Commodity procurement 2/	203,253,928		221,702,000		(7) +19,331,000	241,033,000	
3. Coordinated Review 2/	4,111,215	62	4,241,000	62	(8) -398,000	3,843,000	62
4. Nutrition Studies and Education 2/							
(a) Nutrition Studies and Surveys	3,828,801		3,835,000		+104,000	3,939,000	
(b) Nutrition Ed and training	9,999,712		10,000,000		+270,000	10,270,000	
(c) Food Service Management Institute	1,322,000		1,661,000		+45,000	1,706,000	
(d) Dietary Guidelines	--		2,000,000		+54,000	2,054,000	
Total, Nutrition Studies and Education	15,150,513		17,496,000		(9) +473,000	17,969,000	
Section 17(p) Demos. 2/	--		--		(10) +3,700,000	3,700,000	
TOTAL, Obligations	6,255,124,646	125	6,849,512,817	127	+595,394,183	7,444,907,000	127
Recovery of prior year Obligations	-47,833,939		-1,500,000		+1,500,000	--	
Unobligated Bal Available Start-of-year	-68,517,687		-22,437,817		+21,459,817	-978,000	
Available End-of-year	+22,437,817		+978,000		-978,000		
Expiring	+7,104,163						
Transfer from Food Stamps	-100,000,000		--		--	--	

31-41

PROJECT STATEMENT
(On basis of available funds)

Project	1992 Actual Amount	SYs	1993 Estimated Amount	SYs	Increase or Decrease	1994 Estimated Amount	SYs
Total, Appropriation.	6,068,315,000		6,826,553,000		617,376,000	7,443,929,000	
Economic Stimulus......			56,000,000		-56,000,000		
Investment Proposal......					+115,000,000	115,000,000	
Total, President Budget........			6,882,553,000		+676,376,000	7,558,929,000	

1/ Fiscal Year 1992 includes the transfer of $100,000,000 from the Food Stamp Program.

2/ Fiscal Year 1994 amounts include a request of $12,678,000 in discretionary additions to the mandatory baseline.

EXPLANATION OF PROGRAM

Overview of Program Development. The Child Nutrition Programs, authorized by the National School Lunch Act (NSLA) and the Child Nutrition Act of 1966, subsidize meals served to children in schools and in a variety of other institutions. The Child Nutrition Programs have their origins in commodity distribution programs operated in the 1930's. In 1946, the NSLA established the National School Lunch Program "to safeguard the health and well-being of the Nation's children and to encourage the domestic consumption of nutritious agricultural commodities."

In 1966, Congress expanded the availability of Federal food assistance for children by providing for a pilot breakfast program, which was made a permanent program in 1975. Meal service was extended to pre-school age children in child care in 1968. In 1969, Congress made provisions to assist feeding programs in serving meals for free or at a reduced price to children who met certain income eligibility guidelines. A Summer Food Service Program was initiated in 1968 to serve low income children while school was out of session. The Child Nutrition and WIC Reauthorization Act of 1989 (P.L. 101-147) reauthorized the Summer Food Service Program, State Administrative Expenses, the Commodity Distribution Program and the Nutrition Education and Training Program through 1994.

Eligibility and Benefits. A general description of eligibility for and benefits of the programs follows:

1. Cash Payments to States. The programs are operated under an agreement entered into by State agencies and the Department. Funds are made available by letters of credit to State agencies for use in reimbursing participating schools and other institutions. Sponsors make application to the State agencies and, if approved, are reimbursed on a per-meal basis in accordance with the terms of their agreements and the rates prescribed by law. The reimbursement rates are adjusted annually to reflect changes in the Consumer Price Index for Food Away From Home as provided for in Section 11 of the NSLA.

   (a) National School Lunch Program (NSLP). Assistance is provided to the States for the service of lunches and snacks to children in participating schools and institutions, regardless of household income. Additional assistance is provided to the States for serving lunches and snacks free or at a reduced price to needy children. States must match a portion of the Federal cash grant. Schools which, in the second previous school year, served at least 60 percent of their lunches at free or reduced prices receive an additional two cents per meal in assistance.

(b) School Breakfast Program (SBP). Federal reimbursement is based on the number of breakfasts served to children from low, lower or upper income families. Schools that served at least 40 percent of their lunches at free or reduced prices in the second preceding year and had unusually high preparation costs which exceeded regular breakfast per meal reimbursement, receive higher subsidies in both the free and reduced price categories. FNS also provides expansion grants as authorized by P.L. 101-147, the Child Nutrition and WIC Reauthorization Act of 1989.

(c) Child and Adult Care Food Program (CACFP). Nonprofit child care centers and family and group day care homes receive subsidies for meals served to preschool and other children. Profit-making child care centers receiving compensation under Title XX of the Social Security Act may participate in the program if 25 percent of the children enrolled are Title XX participants. Certain adult day care centers are also eligible for participation in this program if they provide meals to persons 60 years or older or to adults who are functionally impaired. They must be nonprofit unless they receive compensation under Title XIX or Title XX of the Social Security Act for at least 25 percent of their enrollees. The Child and Adult Care Food Program provides reimbursement to State agencies at varying rates for breakfasts, lunches, suppers and meal supplements. Two percent of total CACFP obligations from the second preceding year are provided for audits and administrative reviews of CACFP institutions. Under the Regional Office Administered Program (ROAP), the Office of the Inspector General contracts with Certified Public Accounting firms for audits of the child care institutions directly administered by FNS. FNS may use some of these funds not needed for audits for administrative reviews of child care sponsors for which the regional office is responsible. As authorized in Public Law 101-147, FNS will, through the end of Fiscal Year 1994, continue to administer grants to homeless shelters to determine the most effective way of providing meals to homeless children under the age of six.

(d) Summer Food Service Program. Meals served free to children in low-income neighborhoods during the summer months are supported on a per-meal basis by Federal cash subsidies to State agencies. Funds are also provided for related State and local administrative expenses.

The Child Nutrition and WIC Reauthorization Act of 1989 added a new section (q) to Section 13 of the NSLA which requires the Secretary to "establish a system under which the Secretary and States shall monitor the compliance of private nonprofit organizations." In recognition of the

vulnerability of this class of summer program sponsors to program abuse, 1/2 of 1 percent of the funds appropriated are authorized to carry out this function.

The Food and Nutrition Service will monitor high risk sponsors using federal reviewers during the summer months. This strategy will enable each of the seven regional offices to concentrate on these sponsors during the periods of operation. Headquarters staff will provide support for the review guides and resource planning. Nationally consistent review procedures will be used in all regional office reviews. All materials will be made available to State Agencies administering the program to assure consistent procedures. The goal will be to perform a review of every private nonprofit sponsor/site in the program. Priority for review will be given to the largest sponsors and sites and to those sponsors and sites identified "at risk" due to past problems. Reviews will be coordinated with State Agencies to the maximum extent practical. State plan and sponsor agreement information will be used to identify sponsors for review. Follow-up reviews and corrective action will be carefully coordinated with State Agencies.

(e) State Administrative Expenses. These funds may be used for State employee salaries, benefits, support services and office equipment. The total amount of State Administrative Expenses available for allocation to States is equal to 1.5 percent of Federal cash program payments for the National School Lunch, School Breakfast, Child and Adult Care Food and Special Milk Programs in the second previous fiscal year. Some States are prohibited by law and some States choose not to administer the programs in private schools and institutions. In these States, FNS directly administers the programs through its regional offices.

2. Commodity Procurement. Entitlement commodities and cash-in-lieu thereof required under section 6(e) of the National School Lunch Act (NSLA) are provided from two sources: funds appropriated to the Child Nutrition Programs and funds available to the Agriculture Marketing Service (AMS) under section 32 of the Act of August 24, 1935. Commodities are purchased for distribution to the School Lunch, Child and Adult Care Food and Summer Food Service Programs. The minimum, or "entitlement" commodity support rate for all school lunch and child care center lunches and suppers served is mandated by section 6(e) of the National School Lunch Act and is adjusted annually on July 1 to reflect changes in the Producer Price Index for Food Used in Schools and Institutions.

Section 32. This authority provides for purchase of perishable non-price support commodities when it is necessary to stabilize market conditions. Within the constraints of market conditions seasonality of crops, and other factors, these purchases are planned so that commodities are delivered to schools on a regular basis throughout the year. The typical commodities purchased include meat, poultry, fish, fruits and vegetables.

Section 6(e) of the National School Lunch Act. Although market considerations play a role, this authority can be used to purchase price support and non-price support commodities based on recipient need and preference. Section 6(e) funds are used to provide schools with some of the perishable foods, such as meat, as well as non-perishable price support commodities (grains, oil, and peanut products) that they need. In addition, section 6(e) funds are used to provide cash-in-lieu of commodities when authorized by law. The areas currently receiving cash-in-lieu of commodities are Kansas, the sites which participated in the study of alternatives to commodity donation and which received commodity assistance in the form of cash-in-lieu of commodity letters of credit, adult care centers and child care centers which may elect to receive all of their commodity entitlement in cash.

Bonus Commodities. In addition to entitlement commodities, when supplies permit, "bonus" commodities are provided to schools and institutions. Outlets can obtain as much of some bonus commodities as they can use without waste; other bonus commodities are offered on a limited basis. Commodities are purchased by AMS and the Commodity Credit Corporation (CCC) and then donated to FNS for distribution. The two sources of bonus commodities are the Price Support Program and the Surplus Removal Program.

Price Support Program. When the Commodity Credit Corporation (CCC) acquires significant inventories of price support commodities, section 416 of the Agricultural Act of 1949 authorizes the CCC to donate commodities from its inventory to schools and other institutions. During Fiscal Year 1992, the Department donated butter, honey, flour and corn meal.

Surplus Removal Program. Under the provisions of Section 32, funds are available for emergency surplus removal purchases.

The Secretary of Agriculture determines when perishable commodities such as fruits and vegetables should be purchased and donated to schools and institutions under this surplus removal authority.

3. Coordinated Review Effort

FNS conducts NSLP program reviews in cooperation with State agencies in the National School Lunch Program to evaluate the accuracy of local and State meal service data, and provides training and technical support to schools to help improve local program administration and accountability. The Coordinated Review Effort replaces the Federal Review System and the State-conducted Assessment, Information, and Monitoring System (AIMS).

State training and transition activities occurred during the first quarter of Fiscal Year 1993 with actual reviews beginning before January. Fiscal Year 1994 will mark the first full year of Coordinated Review with all phases fully implemented.

4. Nutrition Studies and Education

(a) Nutrition Studies and Surveys. Section 6(a)(3) of the NSLA authorizes the use of Child Nutrition Program funds for nutrition studies and surveys. The purpose of these studies and surveys is to provide descriptive and evaluative information about the programs in order to make informed decisions and improve program operations.

(b) Nutrition Education and Training (NET). This program, established in 1977 by P.L. 95-166, the National School Lunch Act and Child Nutrition Amendments of 1977, has provided funds to State agencies for the development of comprehensive nutrition education and information programs for children participating in or eligible for school lunch and related Child Nutrition Programs. NET provides direct educational benefits to children. The program goals for NET include the instruction of educators and students in the fundamentals of nutrition and training of school food service personnel in nutrition and food service management to help build good food habits. Nutrition education resources and curricula are identified, developed and disseminated through NET.

(c) Food Service Management Institute (FSMI). A Food Service Management Institute has been established in Mississippi to provide instruction for educators and school food service personnel in nutrition and food service management.

(d) Dietary Guidelines. This funding will continue to provide support to schools and child care providers in implementing the Dietary Guidelines for Americans in food service operations. The request will fund meal pattern analysis and assessment, menu planning technical aids, recipe development and training, and assistance to State and local food service operators.

State/Federal Responsibilities. The Child Nutrition Programs are operated through a State/Federal partnership under agreements signed by State educational, agricultural, social service or health agencies and FNS. Through this Federal/State partnership, FNS has agreements with 85 State agencies. There are over 20,000 School Food Authorities which oversee the activities of over 92,000 schools, over 50 percent of which offer both lunch and breakfast. Typical Summer Food Service Program sponsors include School Food Authorities and local county or municipal governments. Currently there are over 2,800 sponsors for the Summer Food Service Program and over 11,000 sponsors of the Child and Adult Care Food Program (CACFP). There are currently over 191,000 child care centers and family day care homes participating in the CACFP.

FNS provides cash reimbursements for meals served by type and ensures that appropriate commodities are delivered on a timely basis. FNS also provides funds to help defray State administrative expenses. FNS also promulgates rules implementing the programs as defined by statute, including specifying nutritional requirements for the meals (i.e., meal patterns), meal counting and reporting procedures to ensure confidentiality of free and reduced price meal recipients while assuring accurate counts; requirements for cash and facilities management; and other administrative requirements.

JUSTIFICATION OF INCREASES AND DECREASES

The Fiscal Year 1994 request for the Child Nutrition Programs reflects an increase of $617,376,000.

(1) A decrease of $340,000 for administrative efficiency.

Need for Change. To promote the efficient use of resources for administrative purposes, in keeping with the President's Executive Order, total USDA baseline outlays for these activities will be reduced by 3 percent in Fiscal Year 1994, 6 percent in Fiscal Year 1995, 9 percent in Fiscal Year 1996, and 14 percent in Fiscal Year 1997.

Nature of Change. In order to achieve this savings, the Child Nutrition Programs will reduce non-salary administrative costs from Fiscal Year 1993 levels adjusted for inflation by $65,000 in the Summer Food Service Program, by $258,000 in Commodity Procurement, and by $17,000 in the Coordinated Review Effort by limiting travel and other administrative expenses.

(2) An increase of $216,442,000 in the appropriation for the School Lunch Program ($4,110,794,000 budgeted in 1993). On the basis of available funds, there is an increase of $196,789,183 ($4,131,424,817 available in 1993).

Need for Change. The total number of school lunches is expected to increase by 72 million in Fiscal Year 1994 due to increased school enrollment and an increase in the number of children applying for free meals. The number of free meals is projected to increase by 1.7% in Fiscal Year 1994. The projected rise in reimbursement rates on July 1 reflecting increases in the Consumer Price Index (CPI) for Food Away from Home contributes to the need for increased funding.

Nature of Change. A funding level of $4,327,236,000 will be needed in Fiscal Year 1994 for the School Lunch Program. This funding level will provide full reimbursement for meal service currently projected for Fiscal Year 1994.

School Lunch Program. Funding for the National School Lunch Program excluding commodities, is projected at $4.3 billion in Fiscal Year 1994. This represents an increase of about 5 percent over the 1993 level of $4.1 billion.

Total meals are projected to increase by about 1.7 percent over the Fiscal Year 1993 level.

School Lunch Program
Program Performance Data

	1992 Actual	1993 Estimate	1994 Estimate	Change
Meals served (millions):				
Above 185% of poverty-------	1,925	1,885	1,917	+32
130%-185% of poverty--------	285	291	296	+5
below 130% of poverty-------	1,880	2,009	2,044	+35
	4,090	4,185	4,257	+72
Average participation: (millions)	24.5	25.0	25.5	+.5
Average subsidy per meal (cents):				
Above 185% of poverty-------	16.1	16.3	16.9	+.6
130%-185% of poverty--------	110.8	113.9	118.4	+4.5
Below 130% of poverty-------	150.9	154.1	158.5	+4.4
Commodities----------	14.0	14.0	14.0	--
PROGRAM TOTAL (million)-----	$3,870	$4,131	$4,327	+196

(3) An increase of $89,189,000 in the appropriation for the School Breakfast Program ($891,163,000 available in 1993).

Need for Change. An increase of 67 million meals is projected for Fiscal Year 1994. This increase is due in part to School Breakfast Program expansion grants awarded in previous years and which are funded at $5 million in 1994.

The projected rise in reimbursement rates on July 1 reflecting increases in the CPI for Food Away from Home contributes to the need for increased funding.

Nature of Change. An appropriation of $980,352,000 will be needed in Fiscal Year 1994 for the School Breakfast Program.

School Breakfast Program. The requested level of funding for the School Breakfast Program is projected at $980.4 million for Fiscal Year 1994. This is an increase of about 10 percent over the current services estimate for Fiscal Year 1993. The number of meals projected for Fiscal Year 1994 is 1,008 million. This represents an increase of 7 percent over the 1993 level. Expansion grants amounting to $5 million a year are being made available to States for Breakfast outreach programs. The total number of outlets increased by about 8.8 percent between Fiscal Year 1991 and Fiscal Year 1992.

School Breakfast Program
Program Performance Data

	1992 Actual	1993 Estimate	1994 Estimate	Change
Meals served (millions):				
Above 185% of poverty---	102	105	112	+7
130%-185% of poverty----	44	47	50	+3
Below 130% of poverty---	702	790	846	+56
	848	942	1,008	+66

Average participation (millions)----------	5.1	5.6	6.0	+.4

School Breakfast Program
Program Performance Data

	1992 Actual	1993 Estimate	1994 Estimate	Change
Average subsidy per meal (cents):				
Paid------------------	18.6	18.9	19.3	+.4

School Breakfast Program
Program Performance Data

	1992 Actual	1993 Estimate	1994 Estimate	Change
Reduced price:				
Regular--------------	63.4	65.2	67.7	+2.5
Severe need----------	80.7	82.8	85.8	+3.0
Free:				
Regular--------------	93.2	95.0	97.6	+2.6
Severe need----------	110.6	112.7	115.7	+3.0
PROGRAM TOTAL (millions)	$801	$891	$980	+89

(4) An increase of $255,286,000 in the appropriation for the Child and Adult Care Food Program ($1,273,160,000 available in 1993).

Need for Change. The current request projects an increase of 269 million meals for Fiscal Year 1994 in child care centers, family day care homes and adult day care centers.

The rise in reimbursement rates on July 1 reflecting increases in the CPI for Food Away from Home will contribute to the need for increased funding.

Nature of Change. An appropriation level of $1,528,446,000 will be needed in Fiscal Year 1994 to provide full reimbursement for meals served in the Child and Adult Care Food Program.

The effect of the President's investment proposal providing expanded funding for Head Start programs will increase the appropriation request for this program by $110,327,000 in fiscal year 1994. This amount will fully fund an additional 106.5 million meals which will be served in child care centers.

Child and Adult Care Food Program. The funding estimate for the Child and Adult Care Food Program in Fiscal Year 1994, including the President's investment proposal, is $1.639 billion excluding commodities. This represents an increase of 24 percent over the adjusted fiscal year 1993 level of $1.327 billion for 1993.

Child and Adult Care Food Program
Program Performance Data

	1992 Actual	1993 Estimate	1994 Estimate	Change
Meals served (millions):				
Centers				
Above 185% of poverty---	173	178	190	+12

130%-185% of poverty---	45	51	55	+4
below 130% of poverty--	351	471	623	+152
	569	700	868	+168
Family Day Care Homes--	612	699	799	+100
Average subsidy per meal (cents):*				
Above 185% of poverty--	16.1	16.3	16.8	+.5
130%-185% of poverty--	85.8	88.4	91.9	+3.4
Commodities------------	14.0	14.0	14.0	--
Below 130% of poverty---	115.8	118.3	121.9	+3.4
Family Day Care Homes-	108.2	110.7	113.8	+3.1
PROGRAM TOTAL (millions)	$1,090	$1,327	$1,647	+313

*Rates are a blend of all reimbursement levels within an income category.

(5) A net increase of $24,218,000 in the appropriation for the Summer Food Service Program ($230,394,000 appropriated in 1993). The increase consists of:

(a) A net increase of $130,544 which includes an inflationary increase of 195,544 and a 3 percent reduction in administrative expenses of $65,000 from the amount made available for Fiscal Year 1993 adjusted for inflation.

(b) A net decrease of $17,518 for pay cost which reflects presidential cost cutting initiatives, including an increase for inflation of $70,649 and a reduction of $88,167.

(c) An increase of $24,104,974 in grants to States for the Summer Food Service Program.

Need for Change. An increase of 8.9 million meals is projected for Fiscal Year 1994 for a total of 126.2 million meals. The projected rise in the reimbursement rate on January 1 reflecting increases in the CPI for Food Away from Home will contribute to the need for increased funding.

Nature of Change. An appropriation of $254,612,000 will be needed in the Summer Food Service Program in Fiscal Year 1994 to provide full reimbursement for meals served and continuation of program operations.

The Summer Food Service Program estimate of $255 million for Fiscal Year 1994 provides for an increase of about 11 percent over the 1993 level.

Federal Reviews of private nonprofit sponsors and sites are conducted every summer. An estimated 300 private nonprofit sponsors and 600 sites will be reviewed by Federal personnel in FY 1993.

Summer Food Service Program
Program Performance Data

	1992 Actual	1993 Estimate	1994 Estimate	Change
Meals served (millions):				
Summer Food Program-----	105.3	117.3	126.2	+8.9

Average subsidy per meal (cents):				
Summer rates :				
Lunch----------------	201.0	205.5	211.3	+5.8
Breakfast------------	112.0	114.5	117.5	+3.0
Supplements----------	32.8	34.0	35.5	+1.5
PROGRAM TOTAL (millions)------	$202.9	$230.4	$254.6	+24.2
Reviews (SY)	15	15	15	--
Direct Administration (SY)	18	20	20	--

(6) A net increase of $9,652,000 in the appropriation for State Administrative Expenses ($77,086,000 available in 1993). The increase consists of:

(a) An increase of $77,274 for pay costs which will provide for the effects of inflation.

(b) An increase of $9,574,726 for State administrative expenses.

Need for Change. The increase is due to the rise in meal service in Fiscal Year 1992 which is the base year for grant formulation.

Nature of Change. An appropriation of $86,738,000 will be needed in Fiscal Year 1994 for State Administrative Expenses. Each State will receive a grant of at least one percent of the funds expended by the State during Fiscal Year 1992 with a minimum grant of $100,000. The funds available above the basic grant will be allocated to the States to improve program administration.

State Administrative Expenses. State Administrative Expense funds are used for State employee salaries, benefits, support services and office equipment. The total amount of State Administrative Expenses available for allocation to States is equal to 1.5 percent of Federal cash program payments for the National School Lunch, School Breakfast, Child and Adult Care Food and Special Milk Programs in the second previous fiscal year. Some States are prohibited by law and some States choose not to administer the programs in private schools and institutions. In these States, FNS directly administers the programs through its regional offices. In Fiscal Year 1994, approximately $1.9 million of the estimated $86.7 million in State Administrative Expense funds will be applied to FNS costs of directly operating Child Nutrition Programs in eight States. This amount will support a total of 30 staff years.

(7) A net increase of $18,353,000 in the appropriation for Commodity Procurement ($222,680,000 available in 1993). The increase consists of:

(a) A decrease of $258,000 which reflects a 3 percent reduction in administrative expenses from the amount made available for Fiscal Year 1993 adjusted for inflation.

(b) An increase of $18,611,000 for commodity procurement activities.

Need for Change. Overall Federal entitlement commodity support will increase by $18.4 million in Fiscal Year 1994 as required by law. This increase includes funds for Federal program administrative costs related to USDA tri-agency commodity procurement, the Processed Commodity Inventory Management System (PCIMS), as well as funds for ADP systems. Additional development funds in the amount of $2.5 million dollars are required to maintain and enhance PCIMS in Fiscal Year 1994. The majority of this amount will be used to pay the FNS share of system enhancements to connect State agencies to the Federal system, and provide for other modifications to tighten USDA control of the 8 different appropriation accounts that fund the commodity programs. State connectivity will expand program automation by allowing electronic input of commodity orders at the State level and electronic access to reports that are currently available to States only in hard copy.

Nature of Change. An appropriation of $241,033,000 will be needed to fund all aspects of commodity procurement.

Commodities. The FNS commodity activity includes funding for food as well as for administrative costs associated with purchasing, distributing and tracking child nutrition commodities. In Fiscal Year 1994, $470,000 is budgeted for Agricultural Marketing Service administrative costs resulting from commodity purchasing and shipping activities. Administrative costs budgeted for the Agricultural Stabilization and Conservation Service total $1,475,000. Computer support costs for the Software Renewal Project, State connectivity, and NCC processing total $1.3 million. Funding is also included for the operation of PCIMS which was developed to provide more accurate information on commodity purchases, allocation and payments. The current estimate for 1994 shows a slight change in the projected commodity reimbursement rate based on a forecast of the Producer Price Index.

Commodity Cost Data
($ millions)

	1992 Actual	1993 Estimate	1994 Estimate
School Lunch:			
CN Appropriation:			
Commodity Purchases----	171.0	185.4	191.5
Administrative Costs			
Computer Support-------	0.9	.6	1.3
AMS Admin-------------	0.1	.4	.5
ASCS Admin------------	0.8	1.4	1.5
PCIMS-----------------	1.0	1.6	2.5
Section 32 Commodities-	400.0	400.0	400.0
School Lunch Total-----	573.8	589.4	597.3
Child and Adult Care Commodities/Cash----	28.6	34.7	42.4
Summer Food Service Commodities	0.9	..	1.6
TOTAL COMMODITY COSTS	$603.3	$625.0	$641.3

(8) A net increase of $63,000 in the appropriation for the Coordinated Review Effort ($3,780,000 appropriated in 1993). The change consists of:

(a) A decrease of $5,792 which includes an inflationary increase of 11,208 and a 3 percent reduction in administrative expenses of $17,000 from the amount made available in Fiscal Year 1993 adjusted for inflation.

(b) A net increase of $68,748 for pay costs which reflects presidential cost cutting initiatives including an inflationary increase of $170,183 and a reduction of $101,435.

Need for Change. The Coordinated Review Effort (CRE) was authorized by P.L. 101-147, the WIC and Child Nutrition Reauthorization Act of 1989.

CRE replaces the Federal Review System and the State-conducted Assessment, Information, and Monitoring System (AIMS) with a unified review system. Federal personnel will work with State and local personnel to conduct management evaluations and local reviews to ensure that meals are being counted and claimed accurately and to provide technical assistance when necessary.

Nature of Change. An appropriation of $3,843,000 will be needed in Fiscal Year 1994 to fund the Coordinated Review Program.

(9) An increase of $473,000 in the appropriation for Nutrition Education, Nutrition Studies and Surveys, the Food Service Management Institute and the Dietary Guidelines. ($17,496,000 available in 1993).

Need for change. This amount represents a increase of $104,000 in studies and surveys and an increase of $270,000 for the Nutrition Education and Training program; an increase of $45,000 for the Food Service Management Institute; and an additional $54,000 for Dietary Guidelines. These increases maintain the current level of operations.

Nature of change. An appropriation of $17,969,000 will be needed to fund these programs in Fiscal Year 1994.

Nutrition Studies and Education is authorized in Section 6(a)(3) of the National School Lunch Act for necessary surveys and studies of the requirements for food service programs. The 1994 current law request of $3.9 million will be used to fund an extensive study of the nutritional impact of the Child and Adult Care Food Program and to support research to assist in implementation of the Dietary Guidelines.

Nutrition Education and Training. The requested funding level of $10.3 million for the Nutrition Education and Training Program is within the level authorized in Section 19(1)(2) of the Child Nutrition Act of 1966.

Food Service Management Institute. The current services request includes a level of $1.7 million for maintenance of operations at the food Service Management Institute, which was authorized by Public Law 101-147.

Dietary Guidelines

This funding will continue to provide support to schools and child care providers in implementing the Dietary Guidelines for Americans in food service operations. The request maintains the current level of $2.0 million for meal pattern analysis and assessment, menu planning technical aids, recipe development and training and assistance to State and local food service operators.

(10) An appropriation of $3,700,000 to fund Section 17(p) demonstration projects.

Need for Change. The National School Lunch Act authorizes two statewide demonstration projects under which private for-profit organizations providing non-residential day care services qualify for inclusion in the program. P.L. 102-342 reauthorized this demonstration, subject to the availability of appropriations.

Nature of Change. A funding level of $3,700,000 will be needed to fully fund the program in Fiscal Year 1994.

Child Nutrition Programs
Summary of Investment Proposal

SUMMARY OF INCREASES AND DECREASES - INVESTMENT PROPOSAL

	1994		
Item of Change	Base Request	Investment Proposal	Total Request
School Lunch Program.....	4,327,236,000		4,327,236,000
School Breakfast Program..	980,352,000		980,352,000
Child and Adult Care Food Program................	1,528,446,000	110,327,000	1,638,773,000
Summer Food Service Program	254,612,000		254,612,000
State Administrative Expenses................	86,738,000		86,738,000
Commodity Procurement a/..	241,033,000	4,673,000	245,706,000
Coordinated Review Effort.	3,843,000		3,843,000
Nutrition Studies and Surveys.................	3,939,000		3,939,000
Nutrition Education and Training................	10,270,000		10,270,000
Food Service Management Institute...............	1,706,000		1,706,000
Dietary Guidelines........	2,054,000		2,054,000
Section 17(p) Demos.......	3,700,000		3,700,000
Total Appropriation.......	7,443,929,000	115,000,000	7,558,929,000

a/ In addition, $400.0 million is available for entitlement commodity procurement from Section 32.

Explanation of Investment Proposal

The additional funding will provide meal reimbursement and commodity assistance for the additional meals generated by the President's proposal to provide additional funding to expand Head Start enrollment.

Proposed Language

In addition to funding already provided, $115,000,000 for necessary expenses of the Child Nutrition Programs.

CHILD NUTRITION PROGRAMS

STATUS OF PROGRAM

Child Nutrition Programs

The National School Lunch and Child Nutrition Acts as amended, authorize a number of food service programs for children in schools and other institutional settings. These programs include the National School Lunch, School Breakfast, Child and Adult Care Food and Summer Food Service Programs. In addition, the Child and Adult Care Food Program provides for food service for certain impaired adults. The Acts also authorize funding to help States pay the administrative expenses associated with these programs, for a Nutrition Education and Training Program and for the costs of certain nutrition studies and surveys. Funds are also provided for the continued support of a Food Service Management Institute, the Processed Commodity Inventory Management System (PCIMS) and the computer support activities which aid in transition from contractor to FNS in-house maintenance of Special Nutrition Programs software renewal systems.

The Food and Nutrition Service (FNS) is responsible for the nationwide administration of the Child Nutrition Programs. Cooperating State agencies administer the programs in public schools and institutions. A number of State agencies administer the programs for nonprofit private schools and institutions as well. However, some States are prohibited by law and some States choose not to administer the programs in private schools and institutions. In these States, FNS directly administers the programs through its regional offices. Nonetheless, under the Omnibus Reconciliation Act of 1981, P.L. 97-35, no State which administered the Child Nutrition Programs since October, 1980 can request that FNS administer them.

National School Lunch Program

States are reimbursed on the basis of the number of meals served to children in participating schools at reimbursement rates which vary according to family need. Children from families which meet certain income guidelines can qualify for free or reduced price lunches. Income eligibility for free meals is set at or below 130 percent of the Federal income poverty guidelines and eligibility for reduced price meals is set at between 130 and 185 percent. For the period July 1, 1992 to June 30, 1993, a child from a family of four with an annual income of $18,135 or less will be eligible for free meals, and for reduced price meals if the family income is no more than $25,808.

On an average school day in Fiscal Year 1992, an estimated 24.5 million children participated in the National School Lunch Program, compared to an estimated 24.2 million children in Fiscal Year 1991. The total number of participating schools and residential child care institutions increased from about 91,600 in Fiscal Year 1991 to about 92,300 during Fiscal Year 1992.

Per-meal reimbursement rates for meals served are revised on July 1 of each year. For the period July 1, 1992 to June 30, 1993, the cash reimbursement rates are as follows: section 4 rate paid for all eligible meals is $.1625; section 11 free rate is $1.5325; section 11 reduced price rate is $1.1325. The cash reimbursement per free or reduced price meal is the sum of section 4 and section 11 reimbursement rates. In addition, the commodity assistance rate is $0.14 for all eligible meals. School food authorities which served 60 percent or more free and reduced price lunches during the second preceding year receive increased assistance at the rate of $.02 per meal served. The following table compares the lunches served in the three income categories for Fiscal Years 1991 and 1992.

	FY 1991	FY 1992	Percent Change
Number of lunches served (millions):			
Upper income	2,010	1,925	-4.2
Lower income	292	285	-2.4
Low income	1,749	1,882	+7.6
Total Lunches	4,051	4,092	1.0

The Interim Coordinated Review Effort rule - National School Lunch Program, School Breakfast Program, Special Milk Program - was published on August 26, 1992. This interim rule revised the Coordinated Review Effort to: 1) establish an effective date of July 1, 1992 (or January 1, 1993 with demonstration of good cause) for implementation; 2) cap the number of multi-site residential child care institutions to be reviewed; 3) allow States flexibility in follow-up review periods; 4) allow limitations of fiscal liabilities, provided corrective action occurs, and, when determined to be in the best interest of the program, establish an administrative appeal procedure.

School Breakfast Program

This program, initially authorized as a two-year pilot program under the Child Nutrition Act of 1966, was made permanent in October 1975. For each breakfast served, schools are reimbursed at established free, reduced price and paid meal rates. Schools which serve 40 percent or more of their lunches during the second preceding school year at the reduced price and/or free rates are eligible for "severe need" assistance calculated at established rates.

The income eligibility guidelines for the School Breakfast Program are the same as those for the National School Lunch Program. The School Breakfast Program is available to the same schools and institutions as the National School Lunch Program

In Fiscal Year 1992, school breakfasts were available to approximately 22 million children daily in schools and institutions. Between October 1991 and October 1992, the number of schools and institutions participating in the breakfast program increased by about 9 percent. The average number of children eating breakfasts daily increased from an estimated 4.4 million in Fiscal Year 1991 to an estimated 4.9 million in Fiscal Year 1992. In Fiscal Year 1992, 849 million breakfasts were served as compared to 772 million in Fiscal Year 1991.

The rates in effect from July 1, 1992 to June 30, 1993, follow: paid rate - $.1875; regular reduced price rate - $.6450; regular free rate - $.9450; severe need reduce price rate - $.8225; severe need free rate - $1.1225.

The Child Nutrition and WIC Reauthorization Act of 1989 (P.L. 101-147) authorized $ million in Fiscal Year 1990 and $5 million in Fiscal Years 1991-1994 for startup grants for new School Breakfast Programs (SBP) serving low-income children. For Fiscal Year 1992, grants were awarded to school districts in 25 States and for Fiscal Year 1993, 27 States will receive grant funds. Eighteen million dollars in start-up grants have been awarded to schools in 38 states. Grants were awarded on the basis of need, number of children to be added to the program, and feasibility and cost-effectiveness of States' proposals. Most of this 1992 grant money was spent by school districts for capital expenditures, though some funds went to train food service workers and to publicize the new programs. A final rule on program outreach in the School Breakfast Program was published on July 2, 1991. State agencies are now required to (1) provide information to school boards and public officials concerning the enhanced benefits and availability of the Program and (2) direct special informational efforts annually toward selected nonparticipating schools with a substantial low-income enrollment.

Summer Food Service Program

The Summer Food Service Program, authorized under section 13 of the National School Lunch Act, provides funds for food service for needy children during summer vacation. Service institutions eligible to participate in this program are limited to those serving children from areas in which poor economic conditions exist. Furthermore, these institutions must be public or private non-profit schools, other public entities, sites serving homeless children, colleges and universities that operate the National Youth Sports Program, private non-profit organizations that meet certain criteria and residential camps. Meals are served free to all participants ages 1-18 and are limited to lunch and either breakfast or a supplement, except in summer camps and migrant programs which may serve breakfast, lunch, supper and a supplement to each participant daily.

In addition to cash support, commodities are distributed to summer program sponsors that are schools and/or prepare their own meals or obtain them from schools. Funds are also made available to conduct health inspections and to defray State and local administrative costs.

In the summer of 1992, FNS administered the program in six States. The balance of the program was operated by State agencies. During July, the peak month of program operations, approximately 1.9 million children participated in the program. Over the course of the summer, an estimated 106 million meals were served at an estimated cost of $203 million.

Child and Adult Care Food Program

Authorized under section 17 of the National School Lunch Act, the Child and Adult Care Food Program provides cash and commodities or cash-in-lieu of commodities for food service for children in non-residential child care centers and family day care homes and for chronically impaired adults and persons 60 years of age or older who are enrolled in adult day care centers. The centers must be either nonprofit facilities, or for-profit centers with at least 25 percent of their enrollment receiving Title XX funds. As part of a demonstration project, homeless children under age 6 are also eligible for the program if they reside in approved emergency shelters. Adult day care centers may also participate if 25 percent of their enrollment receives Title XIX funds. Providers must be licensed or approved according to Federal, State or local standards. In addition, funds are made available to the States for audit expenses associated with the administration of the Child and Adult Care Food Program.

In Fiscal Year 1992, average daily attendance was approximately 1.8 million participants in the Child and Adult Care Food Program, as compared to 1.6 million in Fiscal Year 1991. The number of meals served increased by 12.3 percent from 1.05 billion meals in Fiscal Year 1991 to about 1.18 billion meals in Fiscal Year 1992.

Commodity Procurement

The commodity subsidy for the National School Lunch, and Child and Adult Care Food Programs is authorized by section 6(e) of the National School Lunch Act and is based on a "rate per meal" concept; while section 13(h) authorizes commodity assistance for the Summer Food Service Program. For Fiscal Year 1992, schools, day care centers, and residential institutions were authorized to receive an average of 14.0 cents worth of commodities for each lunch or supper. USDA also provides commodities which are acquired through the price support and surplus removal programs. Therefore, schools and institutions receive both the commodities under the rate per meal subsidy, called "entitlement" commodities, and the commodities which USDA acquires through agricultural programs and donates to schools, called "bonus" commodities.

In Fiscal Year 1992, food and cash, in lieu of commodities valued at $724.4 million, was provided for the National School Lunch, Child and Adult Care Food and Summer Food Service Programs. This amount includes $122 million of food given to States from Commodity Credit Corporation (CCC) inventories and section 32 surplus removal operations. An additional $40.5 million in cash-in-lieu of commodities was distributed for child care food programs, which may opt for commodities or cash, to the State of Kansas, and to sites which participated in the study of alternatives to commodity donation and received their commodity assistance in the form of cash-in-lieu of commodities or Commodity Letters of Credit. For the school programs, excluding Kansas and the school districts which participated in the study, 100 percent of the authorized commodity subsidy in school year 1992 was provided through food donations.

In Fiscal Year 1992, the value of the cash/commodity entitlement was computed to be $599.0 million for the National School Lunch, Summer Food and Child and Adult Care Food Programs. As with the cash subsidy, this amount was the product of the estimated number of total meals times the commodity rate for the National School Lunch and Child and Adult Care Food Programs, with a fixed amount for the Summer Food Service Program. Public Law 101-147 included a new provision for annual reconciliation of commodity assistance or cash-in-lieu of commodities provided to each State. The commodity entitlement will now be based on the meal data from the preceding school year.

For Fiscal Year 1992, commodity assistance to Child Nutrition Programs (including commodities, cash-in-lieu of commodities and administrative costs) totaling $602.3 million was funded by using $399.0 million from section 32 funds and $203.3 million from Child Nutrition Programs appropriated funds. Section 6(e) funds are used to provide cash-in-lieu of commodities when authorized by law. The areas currently receiving cash-in-lieu of commodities are the State of Kansas, the sites which participated in the study of alternatives to commodity donation and which received commodity assistance in the form of cash-in-lieu or Commodity Letters of Credit, and nonresidential child care institutions electing to receive their commodity entitlements in cash. Funding is also included for the Processed Commodity Inventory Management System which integrates the commodity purchasing, tracking, shipping and payments for the commodity activities of FNS, AMS and ASCS. This new computerized system will provide greater efficiency, increased accuracy, and more timely and improved reporting capabilities for all users.

Commodity Donations

In addition to commodities purchased to fulfill the Child Nutrition Programs' entitlement, commodities that are acquired by USDA through its agricultural programs may be donated to schools and other institutions when available in inventory in sufficient quantities. There are two types of agricultural programs through which commodities are acquired: the price support program and the surplus removal program.

Price Support. During Fiscal Year 1992, the Department donated the following products under the Price Support Program: butter, cornmeal and flour. Section 416 bonus donations to the Child Nutrition Programs were estimated at $84.4 million in Fiscal Year 1992.

Surplus Removal Program. In Fiscal Year 1992, about $37.8 million in section 32 bonus commodities were delivered to schools and other eligible child nutrition outlets under the Surplus Removal Program authority. The following table shows the type and value of commodities purchased or donated and the amount of cash-in-lieu of commodities allocated in Fiscal Year 1992.

Value of Commodities in the Child Nutrition Programs

Fiscal Year 1992

		Value ($ in millions)
Financed with funds appropriated to FNS:		
	Meats, poultry fruit and vegetables.........	47.9
	Grains, oils, peanut products...............	112.1
Subtotal:	Entitlement commodities.....................	160.0
	Kansas and Freely Associated States.........	7.4
	Child and Adult Day Care Food Program.......	25.7
	Study: Alternatives to Commodity Donations..	7.4
Subtotal:	Cash in lieu of entitlement commodities.....	40.5
	AMS & CCC reimbursement.....................	.9
	Processed Commodity Inventory Management System......................................	1.0
	Update Commodity System Computer Software...	.9
Subtotal:	Cash for Administrative Expenses............	2.8
TOTAL: All FNS funds......................................		203.3

Fiscal Year 1992		Value ($ in millions)
Financed with funds appropriated to CCC or AMS and "donated" to FNS:		
	Meat, poultry, fish, fruits and vegetables (AMS)	399.0
	CCC commodities	0.0
Subtotal:	Entitlement Commodities	399.0
	Butter, cornmeal, flour, and honey	84.4
	Fruits and vegetables (AMS)	37.8
Subtotal:	Bonus Commodities	122.2
TOTAL:	Entitlement commodities and cash-in-lieu	599.5
TOTAL:	Bonus commodities	122.2
TOTAL:	Administrative expenses	2.8
GRAND TOTAL		724.5

State Administrative Expenses

FNS makes funds available to the States for program administration and for supervision and technical assistance in local school districts and child care institutions. The Fiscal Year 1992 appropriation was $69.1 million for State Administrative Expenses. An additional $1.4 million was made available from recoveries and carryover for a total funding level of $70.5 million.

Of this amount $59.6 million was allocated to States under the basic legislative formulas for program administration, an additional $9.5 million was made available to States to supplement the basic formulas, and $1.1 million was redistributed to States for justified administrative needs through the reallocation process. Of the amounts allocated to the States for their program administration, $42.7 million was for administration of the school food programs, $23.3 million was for the administration of the Child and Adult Care Food Program, and $3.1 million was for the administration of the Food Distribution Program.

Funds for State Administrative Expenses are available to the States for obligation for two years--the year of appropriation and the following year. Thus, States can carry over these funds from the first year into the second year. As of September 30, 1992, the amount of funds carried over at the State level from Fiscal Year 1992 into Fiscal Year 1993 was about $12.6 million, an amount equal to 18.2 percent of the Fiscal Year 1992 appropriation for State Administrative Expenses. Public Law 101-147 limits the State agency carry-over funding for State Administrative Expenses to 25 percent of the funds made available to the State agency during Fiscal Year 1991 and 20 percent of the amounts made available in each succeeding fiscal year. These recovered funds are to be used to provide food service in homeless demonstration projects authorized through Fiscal Year 1994. In accordance with section 7(a)(5)(B)(i)of the Child Nutrition Act of 1966, as amended by P.L. 102-512, at least $1 million but not more than $4 million is to be allocated for this purpose in Fiscal Years 1993 and 1994. Any funds remaining after the allocation to the homeless demonstration projects are to be allocated to State agencies with a demonstrated need for additional administrative funds.

Child Nutrition Program Research

Agency research priorities for Fiscal Year 1992 included a study to determine the actual costs to produce a school lunch and breakfast, and a study to evaluate the effects of a multi-use school lunch application on lunch participation rates. The Agency also continued a dietary assessment of Child Nutrition Programs and studies of food service management companies and the Adult Day Care component of the Child and Adult Care Food Program. In addition, the Agency continued a number of Congressionally mandated demonstrations, studies, and reports including demonstrations to increase low income participation in the Child and Adult Care Food Program and to serve children in homeless shelters; and studies of alternative counting procedures to reduce paperwork in the National School Lunch Program.

Studies completed during Fiscal Year 1992 include:

- Child Nutrition Program Operations Study--Second Year Report. This three-year panel study was designed to provide descriptive data on Child Nutrition Program characteristics from a nationally representative sample of 1,740 School Food Authorities (SFAs). The second year of the study also included direct observation of a representative sample of participating students in 20 purposively-selected SFAs to examine food and nutrient composition of school lunches and breakfasts. The second year report, released in June 1992, examined participation in National School Lunch Program and School Breakfast Program, meal prices and meal costs, Food Donation Program operations, Child Nutrition labeling, technical assistance, and food and nutrient composition of National School Lunch Program and School Breakfast Program meals. This study provided current program information on participation, labeling, meal prices, costs, training, and technical assistance.

- Commodity Letter of Credit (CLOC) Modification Demonstration Evaluation. This study examined the effectiveness of modifications made to the CLOC program intended to make the CLOC system more responsive to the surplus removal goals to support the agricultural community. The primary focus of the evaluation was on farm impact issues. Issues related to the domestic origin of products, the level of entitlement benefits and the administrative burden on local school districts were also examined. Twenty-five CLOC sites and 25 matching commodity sites participated in the demonstration. The study results indicate almost no difference in the commodity acquisition or use practices of school food authorities using commodity letters of credit or commodities.

- Child Nutrition Homeless Shelter Demonstration--Year One. The purpose of this demonstration was to examine the impact of a food assistance program for children under age six in four homeless shelters. This demonstration was mandated by P.L. 101-147, the "Child Nutrition and WIC Reauthorization Act of 1989". This study found that the demonstration enhanced the quality of meals for children under age 6 and freed up resources in shelters so that meals for older children and adults could be improved.

Coordinated Review Effort

FNS conducts National School Lunch Program (NSLP) reviews in cooperation with State agencies in the National School Lunch Program to improve State and school management of the program and to evaluate the accuracy of local and State meal service data, and provides training and technical support to schools to help improve local program accountability. In Fiscal Year 1992, 485 schools and 80 school food authorities were reviewed which resulted in 57 claims being established for a total of $1.5 million. The training aspect consisted of: 1) 16 multi-state coordinated sessions for Federal and State employees; 2) accountability training for States and school food authorities through the development of training packages on major aspects of school lunch and breakfast programs; and 3) development of technology transfer materials which were distributed to 20,000 school food authorities. The Coordinated Review System replaces the Federal Review System and the State-conducted Assessment, Information, and Monitoring System (AIMS). State training and transition activities will occur during the first quarter of Fiscal Year 1993 with actual reviews beginning in January. Fiscal Year 1994 will mark the first full year of Coordinated Review with all phases fully implemented.

Nutrition Education and Training Program

The Nutrition Education and Training (NET) Program is authorized by section 19 of the Child Nutrition Act. The program provides funds for training school food service personnel in food service management, instructing teachers in nutrition education and teaching children about the relationship of nutrition to health in order to assist them in making wise food choices.

In Fiscal Year 1992, $10 million was allocated among the States for the NET Program. Final Fiscal Year 1991 State agency reports show that approximately 87 thousand school food service personnel, 103 thousand teachers, and 4.0 million children participated in NET funded projects. In Fiscal Year 1993, $10.0 million has been allocated to States for this program.

National Commodity Processing Program (NCP)

Using broad CCC authorities and specific Congressional authorities of Public Law 98-8, the Emergency Food Assistance Act, Public Law 99-198, the Food Security Act of 1986, and Public Law 100-237, the Commodity Distribution Reform Act and WIC Amendments of 1987, and the FACT Act of 1990, the Department distributes surplus agricultural commodities from the Commodity Credit Corporation to various outlets using processing agreements with private companies. The NCP Program is authorized through September 30, 1995. Under NCP, the Food and Nutrition Service enters directly into agreements with private food processors to convert specifically designated surplus commodities into a variety of finished end products. Processors holding agreements with FNS sell these products at reduced prices to recipient agencies eligible to receive surplus donated commodities. The price reductions reflect the value of donated ingredients contained in the end product.

To ensure program integrity, there is a management information system centralized at the Kansas City Computer Center. This system is an integrated data base capable of storing and editing data and generating management reports for the NCP Program. In this system, data on the more than 30,000 registered recipient agencies, processors, end products, sales and inventory balances are maintained. This computerized management information system has been recognized by private industry and State governments as a model of good management.

In addition to claims determined through evaluation of data contained in the management information system, the Office of Inspector General (OIG) has conducted audits of several companies participating in the NCP Program. Based on the results of these audits, additional claims have been issued. As a result of all these monitoring activities, FNS has recovered in excess of $6.2 million since the program began in Fiscal Year 1982.

The Processed Commodity Inventory Management System (PCIMS).

The Processed Commodity Inventory Management System (PCIMS) is a tri-agency computer system that supports the Food Distribution Programs of the Department. The Food and Nutrition Service (FNS), the Agricultural Marketing Service (AMS) and the Agricultural Stablilization and Conservation Service (ASCS) use the system to carryout their functions relative to commodity program administration.

PCIMS functions include procurement and delivery of commodities; order processing; entitlement and payment tracking; as well as fund accounting and control for 11 different commodity programs.

SPECIAL MILK AND CHILD NUTRITION PROGRAMS
FINANCING FOR FISCAL YEAR 1992

State or Territory	Special Milk Program	School Lunch	School Breakfast	State Admin. Expenses	Commodities and Cash in Lieu of Commodities	Child And Adult Care	Summer Food Service	NET	Total Program Contribution
Alabama	$34,789	$86,687,650	$16,448,948	$1,579,703	$16,181,375	$19,042,657	$4,973,120	$159,069	$145,107,311
Alaska	5,515	10,447,379	1,274,264	319,823	1,074,251	4,045,806	17,468	62,500	17,247,006
Arizona	200,219	61,026,039	14,732,106	1,053,262	10,217,169	15,996,152	2,790,942	123,135	106,141,024
Arkansas	36,508	46,436,197	13,291,765	1,031,471	9,158,234	12,547,511	1,988,624	92,131	84,582,441
California	931,721	484,216,772	108,515,633	7,699,753	67,028,576	132,215,989	12,042,944	1,101,896	813,653,287
Colorado	136,767	37,435,175	4,544,800	937,898	7,502,828	20,803,305	1,449,730	120,622	72,931,125
Connecticut	626,262	28,556,974	4,888,420	627,322	5,912,855	10,518,131	1,755,015	111,057	53,996,036
Delaware	45,526	6,991,739	1,498,469	325,045	1,747,115	5,401,787	1,481,169	62,500	17,553,350
District of Columbia	17,202	11,396,165	2,825,868	321,645	1,627,518	1,843,132	326,423	62,500	18,420,453
Florida	119,070	204,236,566	49,020,379	2,915,017	34,119,278	36,734,719	17,589,772	414,210	345,169,011
Georgia	47,123	131,127,794	30,204,812	2,002,631	26,354,494	22,629,799	6,414,124	250,780	219,031,557
Hawaii	12,056	15,646,656	2,834,949	378,418	4,216,419	3,931,106	339,008	62,500	27,421,112
Idaho	193,060	17,050,929	1,751,022	347,555	3,152,423	2,699,767	444,714	62,500	25,701,969
Illinois	2,940,438	154,591,892	18,891,641	2,489,936	27,439,447	37,038,754	8,968,377	435,265	252,795,750
Indiana	372,561	63,845,171	6,347,070	1,089,938	17,588,191	13,437,295	1,738,348	212,760	104,631,334
Iowa	244,915	35,632,022	4,112,313	750,048	10,704,302	12,295,081	918,615	106,621	64,763,917
Kansas	322,211	34,052,090	3,198,192	916,605	8,253,463	27,069,506	660,132	92,523	74,564,722
Kentucky	242,009	73,347,241	20,813,697	1,163,630	14,702,403	11,605,796	2,253,172	140,928	124,268,876
Louisiana	75,416	116,425,946	30,973,958	1,944,250	18,282,825	23,030,699	5,446,013	188,463	196,367,570
Maine	138,238	14,142,675	1,967,190	436,114	2,795,047	7,214,674	459,928	62,500	27,216,366
Maryland	399,261	48,371,616	8,884,587	1,060,068	9,250,352	19,238,960	2,325,091	165,722	89,695,657
Massachusetts	526,464	53,224,744	10,994,440	1,397,483	10,713,975	29,053,209	2,225,696	196,102	108,332,113
Michigan	1,377,879	96,682,830	8,752,907	1,894,988	20,674,308	38,297,776	4,806,428	357,379	172,844,495
Minnesota	1,048,219	48,457,317	5,994,615	1,703,294	13,242,804	49,809,643	1,985,806	167,583	122,409,281
Mississippi	11,643	84,023,856	21,139,719	1,554,721	13,138,801	17,911,478	4,777,872	114,539	142,672,629
Missouri	573,586	68,447,221	12,712,499	1,278,335	14,281,550	19,071,546	2,879,004	188,143	119,431,884
Montana	58,060	11,400,636	1,277,926	419,779	2,611,733	5,284,098	340,012	62,500	21,454,744
Nebraska	241,314	20,630,000	2,009,287	639,603	5,546,885	15,025,548	432,977	62,500	44,588,114
Nevada	85,550	11,528,070	2,589,416	273,407	2,250,237	2,537,288	370,481	62,500	19,696,949
New Hampshire	214,212	8,317,689	943,908	390,932	2,655,904	2,373,116	322,355	62,500	15,280,616
New Jersey	1,085,815	77,431,628	8,140,192	1,377,682	14,686,184	20,473,974	5,899,583	261,847	129,356,905
New Mexico	16,026	35,686,143	6,289,748	887,771	4,876,974	18,225,158	6,360,110	63,889	72,405,819
New York	1,557,939	270,016,666	54,651,454	3,049,149	41,770,810	63,714,350	37,799,747	631,471	473,191,586
North Carolina	122,036	107,463,883	28,931,834	1,752,446	21,585,462	24,389,786	3,890,842	233,646	188,369,935
North Dakota	69,101	9,051,270	828,521	406,416	2,454,935	8,678,583	367,262	62,500	21,918,588
Ohio	1,119,175	125,592,057	23,275,516	2,166,154	26,412,259	34,283,554	3,403,884	408,748	216,661,347
Oklahoma	133,180	55,225,182	13,895,698	1,120,039	10,963,552	14,522,599	1,521,745	120,181	97,502,176
Oregon	265,159	32,797,905	5,359,476	702,678	7,083,000	14,566,964	803,558	103,279	61,682,019
Pennsylvania	819,939	122,980,601	16,332,492	1,983,347	28,168,264	32,334,442	11,856,816	415,096	214,890,997
Rhode Island	115,020	9,676,803	1,133,785	361,330	1,480,676	2,579,571	1,020,441	62,500	16,430,126
South Carolina	26,825	72,139,243	18,304,108	1,077,808	12,036,708	11,466,080	6,651,952	134,793	121,837,517
South Dakota	49,164	12,931,493	2,088,339	506,782	2,880,229	4,485,950	923,912	62,500	23,928,369
Tennessee	41,474	79,820,901	21,160,643	1,324,036	16,609,205	13,214,305	2,761,491	177,997	135,110,052
Texas	104,896	376,208,138	100,990,739	5,806,313	58,344,379	84,387,639	10,208,958	703,396	636,754,458
Utah	87,850	29,546,511	1,829,222	691,164	7,280,815	19,796,263	1,337,941	89,637	60,659,403
Vermont	154,017	5,045,814	637,105	303,707	4,319,256	3,202,895	107,767	62,500	13,833,061
Virginia	264,453	72,120,128	15,268,439	830,210	23,603,707	16,173,484	2,657,938	212,363	131,130,723
Washington	300,108	54,847,041	10,840,694	1,205,481	10,549,957	28,382,249	1,915,947	176,666	108,218,143
West Virginia	25,410	31,214,841	11,159,158	626,731	9,012,425	5,414,362	850,662	65,956	58,369,545
Wisconsin	1,950,178	53,060,454	3,957,726	1,006,678	13,868,577	15,187,504	1,289,072	187,545	90,507,734
Wyoming	18,405	6,422,889	671,191	296,975	1,639,224	3,244,279	129,037	62,500	12,484,500
American Samoa	0	0	0	0	0	0	0	62,500	62,500
Freely Associated States	0	0	0	0	0	0	0	3,960	3,960
Guam	0	1,852,749	637,447	201,328	366,129	45,401	0	62,500	3,165,554
N. Mariana Islands	0	0	0	0	34,758	0	0	0	34,758
Puerto Rico	0	108,078,363	23,342,350	1,412,517	12,099,923	511,010	4,021,091	143,602	149,608,856
Virgin Islands	8,967	3,067,112	104,044	231,270	87,485	500,122	354,709	62,500	4,416,209
Indian Tribes	0	0	0	0	0	0	0	0	0
DOD Army/AF/USMC/NAVY	0	3,359,281	0	0	2,781,196	0	0	0	6,140,477
AMS/ASCS/PCIMS Admin. Exp	0	0	0	0	2,774,817	0	0	0	2,774,817
Undistributed	1,973,898	30,083,309	18,026,750	495,177	4,270,434	31,142,744	4,268,776	-288	90,260,800
TOTAL	$21,586,829	$3,870,097,459	$801,191,471	$68,765,863	$724,466,101	$1,089,627,596	$202,926,601	$9,999,712	$6,788,661,632

NOTE: Data is based on obligations as reported September 30, 1992. Commodities are based on preliminary food orders for fiscal year 1992. Totals may not add due to rounding.

CHILD NUTRITION PROGRAMS
Quantity and Value of Commodities

School or Fiscal Year 1992

ENTITLEMENT COMMODITIES	Thousands of Pounds	Thousands of Dollars
SECTION 6/32 TYPE:		
APPLE SLICES, CANNED	11,782	$4,920
APPLES, FRESH	5,668	1,913
APPLESAUCE, CANNED	21,967	6,420
BEANS, DRY	3,594	694
BEANS, DRY CANNED	18,918	3,956
BEANS, GREEN, CANNED	31,386	8,138
BEANS, GREEN, FROZEN	2,563	909
BEANS, REFRIED, CANNED	4,766	1,441
BEANS, VEGETARIAN	22,700	5,469
BEEF PATTIES, FRZ	9,262	12,732
BEEF PATTIES, FRZ W/VPP	22,177	25,193
BEEF PATTIES, EXTRA LEAN	3,830	6,810
BEEF, FROZEN GROUND	88,938	115,473
BEEF, CANNED N/J	612	906
BEEF, FRZ GRD COARSE-PROCESS	9,072	11,759
CHICKENS, CHILLED BULK	14,611	7,274
CHICKENS, FROZEN, CUT-UP	60,454	33,257
CHICKENS, FRZ BREADED	3,988	4,596
CHICKENS, NUGGETS FRZ SOC	468	241
CHICKENS, DICED FRZ	9,921	22,107
CORN, CANNED	26,444	7,781
CORN, FROZEN	7,694	3,083
EGGS, WHOLE FROZEN	12,044	5,966
HAM, FRZ COOKED BONELESS	6,652	9,641
MIXED FRUIT	12,376	6,473
PEACHES, CLING CANNED	14,293	7,135
PEACHES, FREESTONE CND	5,876	2,916
PEACHES, FREESTONE FRZ SLICED	8,697	5,377
PEARS, BOSC FRESH	403	116
PEARS, DICED	8,584	3,529
PEARS, HALVES	10,431	4,548
PEARS, SLICED	10,513	4,474
PEARS, D'ANJOU FRESH	3,717	1,134
PEAS, GREEN CANNED	7,129	2,196
PEAS, GREEN FROZEN	7,607	2,910
PINEAPPLE, CANNED	6,543	3,194
PLUMS, CANNED PURPLE	2,204	734
PLUMS, CANNED PITTED	689	275
PORK, CANNED W/NJ	720	923
PORK, FRZ GROUND	16,947	15,349
PORK, FRZ GRD COARSE-PROCESS	2,020	1,986
POTATO ROUNDS, FROZEN	33,865	9,060
POTATOES, DEEP FRY	2,961	725
POTATOES, OVEN FRY	28,061	6,863
SWEET POTATOES, MASHED	768	334
SWEET POTATOES, SYRUP	7,131	2,694
TOMATO PASTE, CANNED	17,167	6,759
TOMATOES, CANNED	7,682	2,365
TOMATOES, CRUSHED	16,496	5,208
TUNA	5,607	6,522
TURKEY ROASTS, FROZEN	13,221	18,637
TURKEY, FROZEN GROUND	7,847	5,978
TURKEY, FROZEN WHOLE	10,949	7,551
TURKEY,CHILLED, BULK	9,821	5,870
TURKEY, FRZ GROUND BURGERS	756	809
VEGETABLES, MIXED FROZEN	5,655	2,721
Total Section 6/32 Type	686,254	$446,041

continued on the next page

CHILD NUTRITION PROGRAMS
Quantity and Value of Commodities

School or Fiscal Year 1992 Page 2 of 2

ENTITLEMENT COMMODITIES	Thousands of Pounds	Thousands of Dollars
SECTION 416-TYPE:		
CHEESE, CHEDDAR	9,538	$10,673
CHEESE, MOZZARELLA	11,531	15,589
CHEESE, PROCESS	33,630	47,105
GRITS, CORN	362	52
MACARONI	5,879	1,353
NFD, MILK	6,441	5,804
OATS, ROLLED	3,026	580
OIL, SALAD DRESSING SOC	267	59
OIL, SOYBEAN	7,634	1,882
OIL, VEGETABLE	25,841	8,397
PEANUT BUTTER	9,394	7,890
PEANUT GRANULES	124	113
PEANUTS, ROASTED	1,569	1,507
RICE, BROWN	60	10
RICE, MILLED	18,361	3,516
SHORTENING, LIQUID VEG	5,066	1,725
SHORTENING, VEGETABLE	12,029	4,736
SPAGHETTI, ENRICHED	4,896	1,062
WHEAT, ROLLED	298	57
Total Section 416-Type	155,946	$112,110
Anticipated Adjustment		894
Total Commodity Entitlement	842,199	$559,045

BONUS COMMODITIES		
SECTION 32-TYPE:		
ALMOND BUTTER	5,709	$6,659
ASPARAGUS, CANNED	987	681
ASPARAGUS, FROZEN	80	100
CATFISH, FILLET STRIPS FRZ	252	733
DATE PIECES	1,581	919
PORK CANNED, W/NJ	3	5
RAISINS	6,078	3,242
RASPBERRY PUREE, FROZEN	100	84
SALMON, PINK CANNED	1,929	3,219
TOMATOES, CRUSHED	4,985	1,574
TOMATO PASTE, CANNED	2,516	974
TOMATOES, CANNED	3,481	1,041
TURKEY, COMMERICAL PACK	17,775	10,434
TURKEY ROASTS, FRZ	4,373	5,606
WALNUTS, ENGLISH PIECES	1,532	2,494
Total Section 32 Type	51,382	$37,765
SECTION 416-TYPE:		
BUTTER	56,457	57,529
BUTTER PATTIES	1,010	1,567
CORNMEAL	6,756	767
FLOUR	199,459	24,397
FLOUR, BAKERY MIX SOC	664	137
Total Section 416 Type	264,345	$84,396
Total Bonus Commodities	315,727	$122,161
TOTAL - ALL COMMODITIES	1,157,927	$681,206
CASH IN LIEU OF COMMODITIES	0	40,485
AMS/ASCS/PCIMS ADMIN.EXPENSES	0	2,775
GRAND TOTAL	1,157,927	$724,466

Source: Preliminary food orders for school or fiscal year 1992.

Note: Due to rounding, the individual entries may not add to the totals shown.

31g-13

SCHOOL LUNCH PROGRAM
SCHOOLS, ENROLLMENT AND PARTICIPATION

FISCAL YEAR 1992

STATE OR TERRITORY	NUMBER OF SCHOOLS	ENROLLMENT (000)	PEAK PARTICIPATION (000)
Alabama	1,316	731	567
Alaska	381	100	43
Arizona	1,116	609	356
Arkansas	1,161	432	310
California	8,528	4,992	2,268
Colorado	1,356	551	290
Connecticut	1,024	437	220
Delaware	183	99	59
District of Columbia	178	82	47
Florida	2,650	1,912	1,149
Georgia	1,810	1,120	927
Hawaii	264	182	148
Idaho	527	213	135
Illinois	4,053	1,711	955
Indiana	2,136	982	610
Iowa	1,739	510	396
Kansas	1,670	466	313
Kentucky	1,512	673	523
Louisiana	1,686	817	691
Maine	740	209	106
Maryland	1,343	750	352
Massachusetts	2,062	844	429
Michigan	3,681	1,590	745
Minnesota	1,985	774	505
Mississippi	893	514	420
Missouri	2,427	867	557
Montana	668	151	88
Nebraska	965	274	197
Nevada	330	178	83
New Hampshire	473	176	90
New Jersey	2,518	1,338	513
New Mexico	748	319	183
New York	5,562	2,759	1,577
North Carolina	1,964	1,106	750
North Dakota	497	122	94
Ohio	4,026	1,856	953
Oklahoma	1,840	598	370
Oregon	1,264	431	246
Pennsylvania	3,693	1,735	979
Rhode Island	378	137	61
South Carolina	1,067	636	458
South Dakota	574	142	106
Tennessee	1,621	844	592
Texas	5,996	3,326	2,091
Utah	725	446	221
Vermont	361	93	48
Virginia	1,854	1,006	589
Washington	1,787	865	395
West Virginia	989	327	184
Wisconsin	2,305	809	480
Wyoming	386	96	59
American Samoa	0	0	0
Freely Associated States	0	0	0
Guam	47	34	19
N. Mariana Islands	0	0	0
Puerto Rico	2,975	577	489
Virgin Islands	61	26	16
Indian Tribes	0	0	0
DOD Army/AF/USMC/NAVY	191	101	46
TOTAL	92,284	42,696	25,095

NOTE: These data are based in part on preliminary data submitted by State and local agencies and are subject to change as revised reports are received. Totals may not add due to rounding.

31g-14

SCHOOL LUNCH PROGRAM
THOUSANDS OF LUNCHES SERVED

FISCAL YEAR 1992

STATE OR TERRITORY	TOTAL LUNCHES SERVED			
	PAID	REDUCED PRICE	FREE	TOTAL
Alabama	41,549	6,419	42,705	90,673
Alaska	3,221	707	2,951	6,879
Arizona	22,511	4,354	30,862	57,727
Arkansas	23,212	3,587	22,725	49,523
California	109,490	24,586	258,218	392,295
Colorado	24,764	3,918	16,982	45,664
Connecticut	20,279	2,336	13,285	35,901
Delaware	5,636	497	3,277	9,409
District of Columbia	1,359	370	6,333	8,063
Florida	73,634	14,708	103,673	192,016
Georgia	81,702	10,126	62,720	154,548
Hawaii	16,281	1,610	5,178	23,068
Idaho	12,525	2,352	7,230	22,108
Illinois	64,934	8,842	79,057	152,833
Indiana	67,475	5,180	27,758	100,413
Iowa	43,770	4,106	14,043	61,919
Kansas	31,180	4,372	14,053	49,605
Kentucky	41,974	5,730	35,358	83,061
Louisiana	41,866	7,800	59,178	108,843
Maine	8,999	1,470	6,497	16,965
Maryland	30,337	4,219	22,772	57,327
Massachusetts	38,933	3,337	25,428	67,698
Michigan	60,624	6,359	46,919	113,902
Minnesota	52,002	6,036	19,403	77,441
Mississippi	20,620	5,172	43,853	69,645
Missouri	52,040	5,573	31,649	89,262
Montana	8,089	1,298	5,058	14,445
Nebraska	20,478	3,012	8,103	31,593
Nevada	8,114	998	5,369	14,481
New Hampshire	10,193	894	3,328	14,414
New Jersey	42,958	5,815	37,551	86,324
New Mexico	8,784	2,838	18,099	29,720
New York	95,838	17,661	137,836	251,334
North Carolina	63,823	9,957	50,480	124,260
North Dakota	8,940	1,223	3,632	13,796
Ohio	88,124	8,611	59,823	156,558
Oklahoma	27,301	6,082	25,615	58,998
Oregon	21,220	3,070	15,253	39,543
Pennsylvania	93,142	10,202	56,670	160,015
Rhode Island	3,889	600	4,930	9,420
South Carolina	33,974	4,985	35,958	74,917
South Dakota	9,493	1,743	5,491	16,727
Tennessee	51,757	5,666	38,390	95,813
Texas	133,974	22,379	193,673	350,026
Utah	24,598	5,198	11,393	41,188
Vermont	4,217	484	2,255	6,957
Virginia	58,556	6,224	32,777	97,557
Washington	34,152	5,329	25,419	64,900
West Virginia	14,768	2,586	15,260	32,614
Wisconsin	49,191	5,033	23,126	77,350
Wyoming	6,066	845	2,623	9,535
American Samoa	0	0	0	0
Freely Associated States	0	0	0	0
Guam	1,814	183	799	2,796
N. Mariana Islands	0	0	0	0
Puerto Rico	5,736	6,752	58,218	70,706
Virgin Islands	647	358	1,477	2,482
Indian Tribes	0	0	0	0
DOD Army/AF/USMC/NAVY	5,129	768	940	6,836
Anticipated Adjustment...				
TOTAL	1,925,883	284,557	1,881,653	4,092,093

NOTE: These data are based in part on preliminary data submitted by State and local agencies and are subject to change as revised reports are received. Totals may not add due to rounding.

31g-15

SCHOOL BREAKFAST PROGRAM
SCHOOLS, ENROLLMENT, AND PARTICIPATION

FISCAL YEAR 1992

STATE OR TERRITORY	NUMBER OF SCHOOLS AND INSTITUTIONS	ENROLLMENT (000)	PEAK PARTICIPATION (000)
Alabama	865	446	117
Alaska	144	27	5
Arizona	814	443	92
Arkansas	996	357	100
California	4,008	2,671	595
Colorado	471	216	32
Connecticut	284	88	29
Delaware	166	88	10
District of Columbia	170	80	17
Florida	2,286	1,529	302
Georgia	1,167	688	204
Hawaii	236	162	24
Idaho	299	138	12
Illinois	1,377	695	129
Indiana	577	460	41
Iowa	806	208	30
Kansas	365	111	18
Kentucky	1,136	504	144
Louisiana	1,449	705	219
Maine	328	86	15
Maryland	957	472	56
Massachusetts	1,019	399	72
Michigan	717	256	49
Minnesota	757	304	40
Mississippi	683	468	148
Missouri	1,239	437	85
Montana	205	45	8
Nebraska	196	61	12
Nevada	230	127	18
New Hampshire	176	66	7
New Jersey	654	420	46
New Mexico	484	221	46
New York	3,393	1,624	308
North Carolina	1,707	1,098	190
North Dakota	113	53	7
Ohio	1,414	525	122
Oklahoma	1,263	156	96
Oregon	625	216	33
Pennsylvania	1,258	1,310	95
Rhode Island	121	35	6
South Carolina	736	396	116
South Dakota	224	44	12
Tennessee	1,333	648	153
Texas	5,702	3,194	642
Utah	175	91	9
Vermont	144	37	5
Virginia	1,368	594	113
Washington	1,265	593	68
West Virginia	953	324	68
Wisconsin	383	278	24
Wyoming	87	28	4
American Samoa	0	0	0
Freely Associated States	0	0	0
Guam	39	30	6
N. Mariana Islands	0	0	0
Puerto Rico	2,397	207	182
Virgin Islands	12	5	1
Indian Tribes	0	0	0
DOD Army/AF/USMC/NAVY	0	0	0
Anticipated Adjustment	0	0	0
TOTAL	49,973	24,466	4,981

NOTE: These data are based in part on preliminary data submitted by State and local agencies and are subject to change as revised reports are received. Totals may not add due to rounding.

31g-16

SCHOOL BREAKFAST PROGRAM
THOUSANDS OF BREAKFASTS SERVED

FISCAL YEAR 1992

STATE OR TERRITORY	TOTAL BREAKFASTS SERVED					
		REDUCED PRICE		FREE		
	PAID	REGULAR	SEVERE NEED	REGULAR	SEVERE NEED	TOTAL
Alabama	2,328	919	117	12,231	3,591	19,185
Alaska	183	33	46	352	343	958
Arizona	1,471	311	465	3,653	9,489	15,389
Arkansas	2,767	793	178	9,113	3,318	16,168
California	5,508	679	2,245	12,881	84,267	105,580
Colorado	834	207	65	2,799	1,451	5,357
Connecticut	997	60	223	1,331	2,940	5,552
Delaware	254	41	30	601	764	1,689
District of Columbia	120	5	71	223	2,296	2,715
Florida	4,439	515	1,742	6,766	36,366	49,829
Georgia	5,883	829	1,446	6,973	18,946	34,077
Hawaii	1,507	363	0	2,066	11	3,946
Idaho	435	137	5	1,483	182	2,242
Illinois	1,681	658	0	19,540	0	21,879
Indiana	1,085	192	138	3,296	2,576	7,288
Iowa	1,501	260	85	1,816	1,732	5,393
Kansas	620	149	129	1,148	1,643	3,689
Kentucky	4,265	319	1,200	2,635	14,835	23,255
Louisiana	3,828	1,115	633	16,465	12,428	34,468
Maine	583	111	57	1,096	655	2,503
Maryland	954	227	510	1,669	5,977	9,336
Massachusetts	1,244	198	130	5,754	4,697	12,025
Michigan	765	35	169	461	7,261	8,691
Minnesota	1,081	248	164	2,123	3,200	6,817
Mississippi	2,275	1,317	41	20,807	451	24,891
Missouri	2,677	422	364	3,836	7,318	14,617
Montana	247	56	52	505	619	1,480
Nebraska	302	60	84	441	1,300	2,187
Nevada	699	70	63	915	1,369	3,116
New Hampshire	589	52	8	426	361	1,436
New Jersey	873	233	152	4,010	3,606	8,873
New Mexico	729	452	3	6,258	40	7,482
New York	5,362	508	2,389	4,059	43,126	55,443
North Carolina	4,289	801	1,358	7,878	17,376	31,703
North Dakota	382	43	24	366	335	1,150
Ohio	1,817	72	586	1,071	19,382	22,928
Oklahoma	2,736	706	812	4,713	7,147	16,114
Oregon	770	100	180	1,091	3,617	5,758
Pennsylvania	2,427	232	510	2,354	11,887	17,409
Rhode Island	50	14	0	1,146	46	1,256
South Carolina	2,347	189	878	1,991	13,741	19,146
South Dakota	289	94	62	529	1,297	2,270
Tennessee	4,661	948	578	9,288	9,593	25,067
Texas	11,971	2,111	2,790	25,150	64,937	106,959
Utah	283	78	94	391	1,165	2,011
Vermont	230	24	28	183	351	816
Virginia	4,083	1,181	74	13,674	907	19,919
Washington	1,640	270	322	3,579	6,173	11,783
West Virginia	3,363	171	794	1,301	7,766	13,395
Wisconsin	459	142	24	1,265	2,340	4,230
Wyoming	138	27	39	162	404	770
American Samoa	0	0	0	0	0	0
Freely Associated States	0	0	0	0	0	0
Guam	357	12	59	73	406	907
N. Mariana Islands	0	0	0	0	0	0
Puerto Rico	2,156	2,626	0	22,860	0	27,642
Virgin Islands	34	3	16	13	64	130
Indian Tribes	0	0	0	0	0	0
DOD Army/AF/USMC/NAVY	0	0	0	0	0	0
Anticipated Adjustment	0	0	0	0	0	0
TOTAL	102.365	21,418	22,232	256,805	446,097	848,917

NOTE: These data are based in part on preliminary data submitted by State and local agencies and are subject to change as revised reports are received. Totals may not add due to rounding.

31g-17

SUMMER FOOD SERVICE PROGRAM
NUMBER OF SITES, PARTICIPATION AND MEALS SERVED

FISCAL YEAR [illegible]

STATE OR TERRITORY	NUMBER OF SITES	PARTICIPATION (JULY) (000)	TOTAL MEALS SERVED (000)
Alabama	614	46	2,204
Alaska	2	0	4
Arizona	256	22	1,447
Arkansas	134	14	1,019
California	1,297	122	6,360
Colorado	151	16	664
Connecticut	240	18	820
Delaware	326	16	770
District of Columbia	46	6	232
Florida	1,436	193	9,734
Georgia	1,014	68	3,200
Hawaii	32	4	170
Idaho	39	3	322
Illinois	1,144	65	4,567
Indiana	221	15	864
Iowa	100	7	509
Kansas	65	6	368
Kentucky	329	23	1,073
Louisiana	436	54	3,088
Maine	45	3	259
Maryland	546	29	1,300
Massachusetts	305	20	1,316
Michigan	925	48	2,542
Minnesota	282	14	992
Mississippi	285	43	2,332
Missouri	376	22	1,568
Montana	37	3	195
Nebraska	76	6	274
Nevada	55	3	196
New Hampshire	43	2	166
New Jersey	934	62	3,577
New Mexico	598	44	2,960
New York	2,163	359	20,857
North Carolina	524	48	2,051
North Dakota	18	3	173
Ohio	569	36	1,972
Oklahoma	157	12	833
Oregon	80	10	423
Pennsylvania	1,828	101	6,966
Rhode Island	162	9	567
South Carolina	1,144	69	3,388
South Dakota	91	6	489
Tennessee	497	31	1,786
Texas	1,026	112	5,983
Utah	77	11	634
Vermont	16	1	46
Virginia	484	30	1,381
Washington	322	17	977
West Virginia	237	9	436
Wisconsin	218	17	841
Wyoming	17	1	61
American Samoa	0	0	0
Freely Associated States	0	0	0
Guam	0	0	0
N. Mariana Islands	0	0	0
Puerto Rico	449	35	670
Virgin Islands	118	5	199
Indian Tribes	0	0	0
DOD Army/AF/USMC/NAVY	0	0	0
Anticipated adjustment			
TOTAL	22,586	1,919	105,822

NOTE: These data are based in part on preliminary data submitted by State and local agencies and are subject to change as revised report: are received. Totals may not add due to rounding.

31g-18

CHILD AND ADULT CARE FOOD PROGRAM
PARTICIPATION AND MEALS SERVED

FISCAL YEAR 1992

ATE OR TERRITORY	NUMBER OF CENTERS/ HOMES	PARTICIPATION PEAK MONTH (000)	TOTAL MEALS SERVED: CHILD CARE AND ADULT CARE CENTERS: PAID (000)	REDUCED PRICE (000)	FREE (000)	TOTAL (000)	FAMILY DAY CARE HOMES (000)	TOTAL (000)
ma	2,546	29	1,638	450	8,607	10,695	9,145	19,840
a	647	6	1,236	185	430	1,850	1,590	3,440
na	2,819	31	3,912	1,331	7,534	12,778	7,280	20,058
sas	1,475	18	2,114	552	5,436	8,103	6,349	14,451
ornia	24,094	219	11,658	5,926	29,940	47,524	86,879	134,403
ado	5,156	37	3,764	685	3,393	7,842	16,681	24,523
cticut	2,566	20	1,427	623	2,091	4,142	6,284	10,426
are	1,116	10	849	186	1,462	2,497	3,474	5,971
ict of Columbia	249	5	693	418	1,220	2,331	386	2,717
da	3,286	65	4,364	1,482	27,043	32,889	6,467	39,356
ia	3,411	41	1,562	619	8,340	10,520	12,580	23,100
i	827	30	5,077	652	1,375	7,103	1,290	8,393
	392	6	474	72	516	1,062	2,556	3,619
ois	6,788	61	6,689	1,762	13,127	21,578	21,584	43,162
na	2,151	55	4,791	798	5,520	11,109	9,955	21,064
	2,764	25	4,153	477	2,793	7,423	8,021	15,444
s	6,256	52	3,862	547	2,469	6,877	23,276	30,153
cky	1,169	31	6,284	1,086	7,625	14,995	1,899	16,894
iana	5,256	32	1,163	424	8,911	10,498	11,641	22,139
	1,629	13	645	167	1,035	1,826	6,422	8,248
and	4,601	34	3,326	507	4,275	8,108	13,550	21,658
chusetts	7,232	46	2,936	1,321	7,610	11,867	18,016	29,883
gan	7,967	54	5,296	1,405	9,576	16,277	25,700	41,977
sota	11,871	85	3,558	480	2,799	6,837	46,620	53,457
ssippi	2,486	35	932	574	11,425	12,931	5,918	18,849
uri	2,917	37	3,850	745	6,101	10,697	14,040	24,737
na	1,127	11	698	137	1,011	1,846	4,442	6,287
ska	3,437	31	3,142	289	2,572	6,003	13,293	19,295
a	706	8	611	194	609	1,414	1,598	3,012
ampshire	461	5	1,033	197	608	1,838	1,377	3,216
ersey	2,249	39	4,768	2,556	11,726	19,050	4,437	23,488
exico	4,670	30	2,549	642	3,743	6,933	11,866	18,799
ork	6,916	126	8,453	4,183	38,148	50,785	14,078	64,863
Carolina	2,825	46	9,604	1,704	14,835	26,143	6,931	33,074
Dakota	2,034	17	849	106	625	1,580	7,892	9,472
	6,312	73	8,689	1,260	10,281	20,230	19,764	39,994
oma	1,976	29	4,069	713	8,075	12,857	4,848	17,705
n	3,788	25	1,793	260	1,942	3,996	11,292	15,287
ylvania	4,376	71	6,472	2,759	12,937	22,168	12,817	34,985
Island	379	7	490	198	1,468	2,157	826	2,982
Carolina	892	20	1,272	700	6,367	8,339	3,161	11,500
Dakota	803	8	996	165	776	1,936	3,433	5,369
ssee	1,586	28	2,146	711	7,764	10,602	5,647	16,249
	11,611	127	7,153	2,054	26,148	35,355	52,832	88,187
	3,650	40	4,099	556	3,593	8,247	13,920	22,167
nt	909	7	397	112	387	895	2,921	3,817
nia	3,826	29	3,582	754	3,907	8,243	10,351	18,594
ngton	6,118	41	4,962	689	4,682	10,333	21,431	31,763
Virginia	1,178	10	1,725	158	2,068	3,951	2,333	6,285
nsin	3,723	42	5,999	639	4,659	11,297	9,812	21,109
ng	809	7	791	152	551	1,494	2,481	3,975
can Samoa	0	0	0	0	0	0	0	0
y Associated States	0	0	0	0	0	0	0	0
	5	0	204	18	2	223	0	223
riana Islands	0	0	0	0	0	0	0	0
o Rico	97	1	92	35	259	386	180	566
n Islands	8	0	72	67	426	544	0	544
n Tribes	0	0	0	0	0	0	0	0
rmy/AF/USMC/NAVY	0	0	0	0	0	0	0	0
TAL	188,320	1,955	172,962	45,441	350,801	569,204	611,566	1,180,770

These data are based in part on preliminary data submitted by State and local agencies and are subject to change as revised reports are received. Totals may not add due to rounding.

FOOD AND NUTRITION SERVICE

The estimates include appropriation language for this item as follows (new language underscored; deleted matter enclosed in brackets):

Special Milk Program:

For necessary expenses to carry out the Special Milk Program, as authorized by section 3 of the Child Nutrition Act of 1966 (42 U.S.C. 1772), [$14,898,000] $20,277,000, to remain available through September 30, [1994] 1995. Only final reimbursement claims for milk submitted to State agencies within sixty days following the month for which the reimbursement is claimed shall be eligible for reimbursement from funds appropriated under this Act. States may receive program funds appropriated under this Act only if the final program operations report for such month is submitted to the Department within ninety days following that month. Exceptions to these claims or reports submission requirements may be made at the discretion of the Secretary.

This change makes the appropriation available until September 30, 1995.

SPECIAL MILK PROGRAM

Appropriations Act, 1993	$14,898,000
Budget Estimate, 1994	20,277,000
Increase in Appropriation	+5,379,000

SUMMARY OF INCREASES AND DECREASES
(On basis of appropriation)

Item of Change	1993 Estimated	Other Change	1994 Estimated
Cash payments to States	$14,898,000	+$5,379,000	$20,277,000

PROJECT STATEMENT
(On basis of appropriation)

Project	1992 Actual	1993 Estimated	Increase or Decrease	1994 Estimated
1. Cash payments to States:				
(a) Paid milk (>130% poverty)	$21,239,153	$13,676,000	+4,899,000	$18,575,000
(b) Free milk (<130% poverty)	1,771,847	1,222,000	+480,000	1,702,000
Total, Appropriation	23,011,000	14,898,000	+5,379,000(1)	20,277,000

PROJECT STATEMENT
(On basis of available funds)

Project	1992 Actual	1993 Estimated	Increase or Decrease	1994 Estimated
1. Cash payments to States:				
(a) Paid milk (>130% poverty)	$19,934,641	$18,360,000	+469,187	$18,829,187
(b) Free milk (<130% poverty)	1,652,188	1,663,000	+ 39,000	1,702,000
Total, obligation	21,586,829	20,023,000	+508,187	20,531,187
Unobligated balances				
Recovery of prior obligations	-645,262	—	—	—
Unobligated balances				
Available, start of year	-4,772,623	-5,379,187	+5,125,000	-254,187
Available, end of year	+5,379,187	+254,187	-254,187	—
Expiring	+1,462,869			
Total, Appropriation	23,011,000	14,898,000	+5,379,000(1)	20,277,000

EXPLANATION OF PROGRAM

Overview of Program Development. Originally designed to support milk prices while encouraging children to drink more milk, the Special Milk Program was first funded by the Commodity Credit Corporation in 1955. The Agricultural Act of 1961 authorized the first direct appropriation for the Program. The Special Milk Program is now authorized by Section 3 of the Child Nutrition Act of 1966, as amended.

<u>Eligibility</u>. Eligible institutions include public and private nonprofit schools of high school grade or under, summer camps, and similar institutions that do not participate in another meal service program authorized by the Child Nutrition Act or the National School Lunch Act. In addition, children in split session kindergarten programs in public or private non-profit schools who do not have access to the meal service programs operating in those schools may participate in the Special Milk Program.

<u>Benefits</u>. The program provides institutions with subsidies for half-pints of milk served to children. In Fiscal Year 1993, approximately 179 million half-pints of milk will be served in the Special Milk Program. These include about 167 million half-pints served to children whose family income is above 130 percent of poverty and about 12 million half pints served free to children whose family income is at or below 130 percent of poverty. During Fiscal Year 1993, the average full cost reimbursement for milk served to needy children is expected to be 14.33 cents for each half-pint. Milk served to non-needy children is estimated to be reimbursed at 11.00 cents for each half pint. The cash reimbursement rate for non-needy children is adjusted annually on July 1.

<u>State/Federal Responsibilities</u>. The program is operated through a partnership under agreements signed by State educational, social service or health agencies and the Food and Nutrition Service. State agencies administer the program through local school food authorities or other institutions. FNS provides cash reimbursements for milk served to eligible children and also provides funds for State administrative expenses relating to the program.

<u>JUSTIFICATION OF INCREASES AND DECREASES</u>

(1) <u>An increase of $5,379,000 is requested in the appropriation for the Special Milk Program ($14,898,000 appropriated in 1993). On the basis of available funds, there is an increase of $508,187 ($20,023,000 available in 1993).</u>

<u>Need for change</u>. The increase in funds reflects the current estimate of funds needed to maintain the program in Fiscal Year 1994 due to adjustments for inflation and program participation. Fiscal Year 1994 will be funded in part by the availability of unobligated carryover funds at the start of the fiscal year.

<u>Nature of change</u>. An appropriation level of $20,277,000 plus carryover of funds from Fiscal Year 1993 estimated at $.3 million will be needed in Fiscal Year 1994 to provide reimbursement for milk served in the Special Milk Program. Participation continues to grow at a low level. Reimbursement rates for both paid and free milk are also expected to grow at a low level in Fiscal Year 1994.

	1992 Estimate	1993 Estimate	1994 Estimate
Half-pints served (thousands)			
Paid (above 130% of poverty)	164,475	166,907	170,245
Free 130% of poverty or below)	10,534	11,603	11,835
Total	175,009	178,510	182,080
Reimbursement Rates (cents)			
Paid	11.00	11.00	11.06
Free	14.16	14.33	14.38

31g-19

31g-34

SPECIAL MILK PROGRAM

STATUS OF PROGRAM

The Special Milk Program, as authorized by section 3 of the Child Nutrition Act of 1966, helps schools and institutions not otherwise participating in a federally subsidized meal service program provide milk to children at a low price or free of charge in order to encourage children to drink more milk.

Program Operations. The program is administered in most States by the State educational agency. Where the States are prohibited by their laws from disbursing funds to private schools and institutions, or in instances where State agencies are unwilling to operate the program, the Food and Nutrition Service (FNS) administers the program directly through its regional offices. However, pursuant to P.L. 97-35, no State which administered the Special Milk Program for private schools and institutions since October 1980 may turn over administration of the program to FNS. During Fiscal Year 1992, FNS directly administered the Special Milk Program in seven States.

Program funds are made available to State agencies for use in providing payments to eligible outlets for milk served to children under the program. Participating schools and institutions that charge for any milk served under the program must agree to use the payments to reduce the cost of milk to the children. When local officials elect to serve free milk to needy children, the half-pint reimbursement rate for such milk is based on the average cost of all milk served in the eligible outlet under the program including local level distribution costs. All other milk served under the program is reimbursed at the per half-pint rate established annually by the Secretary. States also receive funds to offset the costs of administering the Special Milk Program from the Child Nutrition Programs appropriation.

For the period July 1, 1992 to June 30, 1993, the reimbursement rate for milk served to children from families with income above 130 percent of poverty is 11.0 cents per half-pint. During Fiscal Year 1992, the average reimbursement to cover the cost of milk in eligible outlets serving free milk to needy children at or below 130 percent of poverty, including local level distribution costs, was about 14.16 cents per half-pint.

During Fiscal Year 1992, the total number of half-pints served was 192.9 million including 181.2 million paid half-pints and 11.7 million free half-pints.

31g-20

SPECIAL MILK PROGRAM
NUMBER OF PARTICIPATING OUTLETS AND OBLIGATIONS BY STATE

FISCAL YEAR 1992

STATE OR TERRITORY	OUTLETS				OBLIGATIONS 1/
	SCHOOLS	NON-RESIDENTIAL CHILD CARE INSTITUTIONS	SUMMER CAMPS	TOTAL	
Alabama	10	3	15	28	$34,789
Alaska	2	0	3	5	5,515
Arizona	58	2	28	88	200,219
Arkansas	9	0	11	20	36,508
California	315	16	183	514	931,721
Colorado	118	1	31	150	136,767
Connecticut	340	3	26	369	626,262
Delaware	15	0	0	15	45,526
District of Columbia	8	0	0	8	17,202
Florida	51	0	39	90	119,070
Georgia	4	0	13	17	47,123
Hawaii	4	0	1	5	12,056
Idaho	150	0	40	190	193,060
Illinois	991	7	54	1,052	2,940,438
Indiana	226	0	48	274	372,561
Iowa	150	15	78	243	244,915
Kansas	424	0	9	433	322,211
Kentucky	160	4	16	180	242,009
Louisiana	14	0	11	25	75,416
Maine	8	0	25	33	138,238
Maryland	217	0	45	262	399,261
Massachusetts	233	42	82	357	526,464
Michigan	746	0	179	925	1,377,879
Minnesota	527	79	127	733	1,048,219
Mississippi	2	0	12	14	11,643
Missouri	362	1	42	405	573,586
Montana	54	0	8	62	58,060
Nebraska	912	0	11	923	241,314
Nevada	10	17	4	31	85,550
New Hampshire	53	11	83	147	214,212
New Jersey	364	0	17	381	1,085,815
New Mexico	11	0	6	17	16,026
New York	778	0	231	1,009	1,557,939
North Carolina	55	0	34	89	122,036
North Dakota	65	0	25	90	69,101
Ohio	368	2	0	370	1,119,175
Oklahoma	155	0	17	172	133,180
Oregon	279	0	33	312	265,159
Pennsylvania	570	15	108	693	819,939
Rhode Island	132	1	9	142	115,020
South Carolina	15	2	9	26	26,825
South Dakota	30	0	6	36	49,164
Tennessee	5	1	17	23	41,474
Texas	29	1	34	64	104,896
Utah	85	0	6	91	87,850
Vermont	113	2	18	133	154,017
Virginia	159	2	25	186	264,453
Washington	121	0	62	183	300,108
West Virginia	10	0	16	26	25,410
Wisconsin	283	125	131	539	1,950,178
Wyoming	9	3	9	21	18,405
American Samoa	0	0	0	0	0
Freely Associated States	0	0	0	0	0
Guam	0	0	0	0	0
N. Mariana Islands	0	0	0	0	0
Puerto Rico	0	0	0	0	0
Virgin Islands	2	0	0	2	8,967
Indian Tribes	0	0	0	0	0
DOD Army/AF/USMC/NAVY	0	0	0	0	0
Anticipated Adjustment	0	0	0	0	1,973,898
TOTAL	9,811	355	2,037	12,203	$21,586,829

1/ Obligations as reported September 30, 1992.

NOTE: These data are based in part on preliminary data submitted by State and local agencies and are subject to change as revised reports are received.

31g-21

SPECIAL MILK PROGRAM
HALF-PINTS OF MILK SERVED

FISCAL YEAR 1992

STATE OR TERRITORY	AVERAGE SERVED DAILY			TOTAL SERVED FY 92		
	FREE (000)	PAID (000)	TOTAL (000)	FREE (000)	PAID (000)	TOTAL (000)
Alabama	0	1	1	1	314	316
Alaska	0	1	1	0	50	50
Arizona	1	7	8	139	1,638	1,778
Arkansas	0	1	1	57	258	315
California	2	36	38	321	8,051	8,373
Colorado	0	5	5	65	1,159	1,224
Connecticut	3	27	30	452	5,104	5,556
Delaware	0	3	3	9	403	411
District of Columbia	0	1	1	2	154	156
Florida	0	5	5	9	1,071	1,080
Georgia	0	1	1	80	324	404
Hawaii	0	1	1	1	109	109
Idaho	1	8	9	84	1,646	1,730
Illinois	6	143	149	949	25,494	26,443
Indiana	2	14	16	268	3,038	3,306
Iowa	1	9	10	180	1,992	2,172
Kansas	2	15	17	376	2,441	2,816
Kentucky	2	10	12	293	1,818	2,111
Louisiana	0	3	3	0	686	686
Maine	1	4	5	209	985	1,193
Maryland	0	19	19	25	3,597	3,622
Massachusetts	2	21	23	297	4,398	4,696
Michigan	8	52	60	1,474	10,605	12,079
Minnesota	0	42	42	42	9,474	9,517
Mississippi	0	0	0	46	46	92
Missouri	1	28	29	206	4,946	5,152
Montana	0	3	3	68	439	507
Nebraska	2	10	12	352	1,734	2,087
Nevada	0	4	4	9	765	775
New Hampshire	0	5	5	39	1,897	1,936
New Jersey	5	52	57	690	8,971	9,661
New Mexico	0	1	1	13	129	142
New York	3	69	72	521	13,484	14,005
North Carolina	0	4	4	4	1,105	1,108
North Dakota	0	3	3	43	572	615
Ohio	4	44	48	745	9,203	9,948
Oklahoma	1	6	7	131	1,040	1,171
Oregon	1	9	10	237	2,101	2,339
Pennsylvania	4	30	34	665	6,587	7,252
Rhode Island	1	3	4	228	748	976
South Carolina	0	1	1	0	244	244
South Dakota	0	2	2	41	394	435
Tennessee	0	1	1	1	375	377
Texas	0	3	3	4	948	952
Utah	0	3	3	8	788	796
Vermont	1	6	7	177	1,169	1,346
Virginia	0	12	12	67	2,317	2,384
Washington	1	11	12	127	2,563	2,690
West Virginia	0	1	1	17	208	226
Wisconsin	4	90	94	726	16,783	17,508
Wyoming	0	1	1	0	167	167
American Samoa	0	0	0	0	0	0
Freely Associated States	0	0	0	0	0	0
Guam	0	0	0	0	0	0
N. Mariana Islands	0	0	0	0	0	0
Puerto Rico	0	0	0	0	0	0
Virgin Islands	1	0	1	41	28	69
Indian Tribes	0	0	0	0	0	0
DOD Army/AF/USMC/NAVY	0	0	0	0	0	0
Anticipated Adjustment	0	0	0	1,129	16,662	17,791
TOTAL	60	831	891	11,668	181,223	192,890

NOTE: These data are based in part on preliminary data submitted by State and local agencies and are subject to change as revised reports are received. Totals may not add due to rounding.

FOOD AND NUTRITION SERVICE

The estimates include appropriation language for this item as follows (new language underscored; deleted matter enclosed in brackets):

Special Supplemental Food Program for Women, Infants, and Children (WIC):

For necessary expenses to carry out the special supplemental food program as authorized by section 17 of the Child
1 Nutrition Act of 1966 (42 U.S.C. 1786), [$2,860,000,000] $2,937,220,000 to remain available through September 30, [1994] 1995 of which up to $3,000,000 may be used to carry
2 out the farmer's market coupon [demonstration project] program: Provided, That until revised allocation regulations have been issued, the Secretary may waive regulations governing allocations
3 as necessary to ensure funds are received by States most in need.

The first change makes the appropriation available until September 30, 1995.

The second change recognizes the status of the Farmer's Market Coupon Program, which was authorized as a permanent program by Public Law 102-314, enacted on July 2, 1992.

The third change provides for the waiver of existing allocation rates to ensure the distribution of funds to those States furtherest from full funding.

SPECIAL SUPPLEMENTAL FOOD PROGRAM FOR WOMEN, INFANTS, AND CHILDREN (WIC)

Appropriations Act, 1993	$2,860,000,000
Budget Estimate, 1994	2,937,220,000
Increase in Appropriations	77,220,000

SUMMARY OF INCREASES AND DECREASES
(On basis of adjusted appropriation)

Item of Change	1993 Estimated	Other Changes	1994 Estimated
Special Supplemental Food Program (WIC)	$2,860,000,000	+$77,220,000	$2,937,220,000

PROJECT STATEMENT
(On basis of adjusted appropriation)

Project	1992 Actual	1993 Estimated	Increase or Decrease	1994 Estimated
Spec. Supplemental Food Program (WIC):				
(a) Grants to States for supplemental food	$1,949,355,372	$2,145,764,000	+$55,716,000	$2,201,480,000
(b) Costs for nutrition svcs and admin.	642,644,628	706,236,000	+21,504,000	727,740,000
(c) Farmers' Market Projects.....	3,000,000	3,000,000	--	3,000,000
(d) Program eval. projects.......	5,000,000	5,000,000	--	5,000,000
Total, Appropriation	2,600,000,000	2,860,000,000	+77,220,000	2,937,220,000
Economic Stimulus..		75,000,000	-75,000,000	
Investment Proposal			+350,000,000	350,000,000
Total, President's Budget...........		2,935,000,000	(1) +352,220,000	3,287,220,000

PROJECT STATEMENT
(On basis of available funds)

Project	1992 Actual	1993 Estimated	Increase or Decrease	1994 Estimated
Special Supplemental Food Program (WIC)				
(a) Grants to States for Supplemental food...............	$1,998,336,867	$2,175,363,148	+$33,064,852	$2,208,428,000
(b) Costs for nutrition services and administration	666,112,289	715,284,000	+14,508,000	729,792,000
(c) Farmers' Market Project.........	3,000,000	3,000,000	--	3,000,000
(d) Program evaluation projects........	5,026,674	5,000,000	--	5,000,000
TOTAL, Obligations	2,672,475,830	2,898,647,148	+47,572,852	2,946,220,000

PROJECT STATEMENT
(On basis of available funds)

Project	1992 Actual	1993 Estimated	Increase or Decrease	1994 Estimated
Recovery of prior obligations..........	-73,381,806	-45,000,000	45,000,000	--
Unobligated balances				
Avail., start of year	-2,672,135	-2,647,148	-6,352,852	-9,000,000
Avail., end of year	+2,647,148	+9,000,000	-9,000,000	--
Expiring............	+930,963	--	--	--
Total, Appropriation.	2,600,000,000	2,860,000,000	+77,220,000	2,937,220,000
Economic Stimulus....		75,000,000	-75,000,000	
Investment Proposal..			+350,000,000	350,000,000
Total, President's Budget..............		2,935,000,000	+352,220,000	3,287,220,000

EXPLANATION OF PROGRAM

Overview of Program Development. The Special Supplemental Food Program for Women, Infants and Children (WIC) is authorized by section 17 of the Child Nutrition Act of 1966, as amended. The program was established as a two-year pilot project under Public Law 92-433. Public Law 96-499, enacted on December 5, 1980, extended the program authorization through September 30, 1984. The authorization was extended through 1989 by Public Laws 99-500 and 99-591, the School Lunch and Child Nutrition Amendments of 1986. Public Law 101-147, the Child Nutrition and WIC Reauthorization Act of 1989, authorizes the program through September 30, 1994.

Eligibility. Funds are made available to local health clinics or other service sites through State departments of health and to Indian Tribal Organizations to provide supplemental foods to low-income pregnant, postpartum and breastfeeding women, to infants, and to children up to five years of age who are determined by competent professionals (physicians, nutritionists, nurses and other health officials) to be at nutritional risk.

Benefits. The WIC Program is intended to promote good health among mothers and their children by encouraging breastfeeding, providing nutrition education referrals to health services, and supplement recipients' existing diets with food packages designed to provide foods rich in nutrients often lacking in the diets of the WIC Program target population. The authorised supplemental foods are iron-fortified infant formula, infant cereal, milk, cheese, eggs, iron-fortified breakfast cereal, fruit or vegetable juice which contains vitamin C, dry beans and peas, and peanut butter. For women who exclusively breastfeed, a special package which includes tuna and carrots is available.

The WIC program encourages breastfeeding in an effort to raise breastfeeding rates toward the U.S. Surgeon General's goal, which is to increase to at least seventy five percent the proportion of mothers who breastfeed their babies in the early postpartum period and to at least fifty percent the proportion who continue breastfeeding until their babies are 5 to 6 months old. USDA has added an enhanced food package offering more types and quantities of foods to women who breastfeed their infants and receive no infant formula through the WIC Program.

There are three general types of delivery systems for WIC foods: (1) retail purchase in which participants obtain supplemental foods through retail stores; (2) home delivery systems in which food is delivered to the participant's home; and (3) direct distribution systems in which participants pick up food from a distribution outlet. WIC benefits are free of charge to all participants. Expansion of cost containment measures, especially infant formula rebates, and increases in appropriated funds have allowed the number of people who can be served by the program to increase.

State/Federal Responsibilities. The program is administered in a Federal/State partnership in which FNS provides cash grants to States for food and administrative expenses. States develop operating plans which, after consideration of public comment and FNS approval as required by statute and Federal regulations, define how the State will implement the program for the year. States then enter into written agreements with local agencies and allocate administrative money to local health care agencies and clinics where

WIC programs are administered. In retail purchase States, the local clinics prescribe food packages by providing participants "food instruments" each month which the participants exchange for foods at approved retail grocery stores. The form of the food instruments varies from State to State; they may be vouchers or checks. Where food instruments are checks, retailers deposit them in a bank before their expiration date. Vouchers must be submitted to a State or local WIC agency before their expiration date and the retailers are paid within 60 days. The States are responsible for monitoring retailers and assuring the integrity of the redemption system. Presently, over 47,000 retailers are authorized to participate in the program.

FNS provides funds for the cost of the food packages and the costs of administering the program, including nutrition education and health care referrals. Food funds are allocated to States for food costs on the basis of a funding formula which takes into consideration previous funding, benefit targeting, inflation and each state's number of income eligible persons, low weight births, and infant mortality rates. Administrative funds are allocated among the States for costs for nutrition services and administrative costs associated with the WIC Program. These costs include certifying participant eligibility, food delivery and warehousing, monitoring, nutrition education, breastfeeding promotion, health care coordination and referral, drug abuse education, financial management, systems development and operations, clinic operations and administration by State agencies. Slightly more than one-sixth of these administrative funds must be used for breastfeeding promotion and support and nutrition education activities. Up to one-half of one percent of sums appropriated, not to exceed $5 million, may be made available for evaluation of program performance.

<u>State Food Cost Containment Initiatives to Expand Participation</u>. The Commodity Distribution Reform Act and WIC Amendments of 1987, P.L. 100-237, the Rural Development, Agriculture and Related Agencies Appropriations Act of 1989, P.L. 100-460, and the Child Nutrition and WIC Amendments Reauthorization

Act, P.L. 101-147, require State agencies with retail food delivery systems to use a single supplier competitive bidding system or a system with equal savings for the procurement of infant formula. Savings from these efforts are to be used to expand program participation. Further, since increasing participation would increase administrative costs, P.L. 101-147 authorized administrative funding based on a per participant allocation, annually adjusted for the increased costs of providing State and local services.

The total amount of savings from rebates for Fiscal Year 1992 is estimated at more than $700 million, supporting an average 1,200,000 participants each month. For Fiscal Year 1993, savings are projected at over $800 million, and will support over 1,300,000 participants each month.

P.L. 101-147 permits State agency fiscal year spend forward authority from the second year of implementation of an approved cost-containment system in an amount equal to 3 percent of the States' food grant, and 5% of the food grant in the first year. P.L. 101-147 also permits State agencies with approved cost containment systems to use funds from the first quarter of a fiscal year to cover obligations incurred during the fourth quarter of the preceding year.

<u>Farmer's Market Nutrition Program (FMNP)</u>

The Hunger Prevention Act of 1988, P.L. 100-435, authorized FNS to award grant funds for up to ten three-year demonstration projects to provide WIC participants with coupons that can be redeemed for fresh, unprepared foods at authorized farmers' markets. The following States were selected through a competitive grant application process to administer the projects: Connecticut, Iowa, Maryland, Massachusetts, Michigan, New York, Pennsylvania, Texas, Vermont, and Washington. A permanent WIC Farmers' Market Nutrition Program (FMNP) which allows additional States to participate in the program, subject to appropriation, was authorized by WIC Farmers' Market Nutrition Act of 1992, Public Law 102-314, enacted on July 2, 1992. The FMNP grandfathers in the States which participated in the earlier demonstration project. In Fiscal Year 1993 $3.0 million will be allocated to these States based on the same pro rata share of available funds as they received in Fiscal Year 1992.

<u>JUSTIFICATION OF INCREASES AND DECREASES</u>

(1) <u>A net increase of $77,220,000 in the appropriation for WIC ($2,860,000,000 appropriated in 1993). On the basis of available funds there is an increase of $47,572,852 ($2,898,647,148 available in 1993). The appropriations increase consists of:</u>

(a) An increase of $55,716,000 in State WIC food grants ($2,145,764,000) budgeted in 1993.

Need for Change. This increase will fund inflationary increases in the cost of WIC foods. The investment proposal together with this increase will serve about 6.4 million at-risk pregnant women, infants and children each month, the most vulnerable members of the low-income population.

Nature of Change. Including the Economic Stimulus for Fiscal Year 1993 and the Investment Proposal, the average monthly cost per person will rise from $31.02 in Fiscal Year 1993 to $32.03 in Fiscal Year 1994. Program participation will rise from 6.0 million to 6.4 million persons per month.

(b) An increase of $21,504,000 in the cost of nutrition education and administrative services ($706,236,000 budgeted in 1993).

Need for Change. This increase will fund inflationary increases in the cost of providing WIC nutrition education and counseling, State ADP systems development, and other administrative services. The investment proposal together with this increase will fund about 6.4 million at-risk pregnant women, infants and chldren each month in 1994.

Nature of Change. Including the Economic Stimulus for Fiscal Year 1993 and the Investment Proposal, the monthly adminstrative grant per participant will rise from $10.18 to $10.43 per month.

Special Supplemental Food Program (WIC)
Summary of Investment Proposals

SUMMARY OF INCREASES AND DECREASES - INVESTMENT PROPOSAL

Item of Change	1994 Base Request	1994 Investment Proposal	1994 Total Request
Special Supplemental Program (WIC):			
(a) Grants to States for supplemental food................	$2,201,480,000	+$268,451,000	$2,469,931,000
(b) Costs for nutrition services and administration......	727,740,000	+81,549,000	809,289,000
(c) Farmers' Market Projects............	3,000,000	---	3,000,000
(d) Program evaluation projects............	5,000,000	--	5,000,000
Total Available..........	2,937,220,000	+350,000,000	3,287,220,000

Explanation of Investment Proposal

The additional funding will support the Administration's commitment in the long-term investment plan to full funding for WIC so that it serves all eligible women, infants, and children.

Proposed Language

In addition to funding already provided, $350,000,000 for necessary expenses of the Special Supplemental Food Program (WIC).

Special Supplemental Food Program for Women, Infants and Children, (WIC)

	1992 Actual	1993 Estimate	1994 Estimate	Change
Average Participation per month (in millions) 1/...................	5.4	6.0	6.4	+0.4
Average Cost per person per month				
Food Costs..........................	$30.17	$31.02	$32.03	+$1.01
Administrative Cost...............	10.20	10.18	10.43	+.25
Total	40.37	41.20	42.46	+$1.26
Program level ($ in millions):				
Current Law........................	$1,998.4	$2,175.3	$2,208.4	+$33.1
Economic Stimulus..................	--	57.5	--	-57.5
Investment Proposal...............	--	--	268.3	+268.3
Food Costs......................	1,998.4	2,232.8	2,476.7	+$243.9
Current Law........................	666.1	715.3	729.8	+$14.5
Economic Stimulus..................	--	17.5	--	-17.5
Investment Proposal...............	--	--	81.7	+81.7
State and local administrative costs............................	666.1	732.8	811.5	+$78.7
Farmers' Market Projects..........	3.0	3.0	3.0	--
Program evaluation projects.......	5.0	5.0	5.0	--
Total 2/...........................	$2,672.5	$2,973.6	$3,296.2	+$322.6

1/ A portion of the estimated participation is supported by anticipated recoveries from previous year.

2/ Includes estimated recoveries and reallocated funds.

SPECIAL SUPPLEMENTAL FOOD PROGRAM FOR WOMEN, INFANTS AND CHILDREN (WIC)

STATUS OF PROGRAM

The Special Supplemental Food Program for Women, Infants and Children (WIC) provides nutritious supplemental foods to low income pregnant, postpartum, and breastfeeding women, to infants, and to children up to their fifth birthday, who are determined by competent professionals (physicians, nutritionists, nurses, and other health officials) to be at nutritional risk.

The Food and Nutrition Service makes funds available to participating State agencies which in turn distribute the funds to participating local agencies. Participating State agencies may be State health departments or Indian tribes which are recognized by either the Department of Health and Human Services' Indian Health Service or by the Department of the Interior. State and local agencies use WIC funds to pay the costs of specified supplemental foods provided to WIC participants, and to pay specified administrative costs, including the cost of nutrition education and health care referrals.

Program Participation and Costs

An average of 5.4 million persons participated each month in Fiscal Year 1992. The monthly costs of the food package varied among the individual States, with an average monthly cost of $30.17 nationwide. In addition to food costs, approximately 24 percent of the funds appropriated were available for State program administrative costs. In Fiscal Year 1992, these costs averaged $10.20 per person per month for a total monthly cost per person of $40.37.

Benefit Targeting

During Fiscal Year 1992, State agencies continued reporting nutritional risk priority data on participants. This data provides information on the results of State agency targeting efforts. Strong emphasis has been placed on service to high risk persons. High risk persons are placed in Priorities I - III, and are considered to be most in need of the WIC program benefits due to nutrition-related medical conditions. The Priority I group consists of pregnant and breast-feeding women and infants with certain medical conditions. Priority II consists of infants of women who actually participated in WIC or infants of women who would have been eligible to participate as Priority I participants during their pregnancies. Also, women who are breastfeeding Priority II infants may be classified as Priority II. Priority III is composed of children with certain medical conditions and some high-risk postpartum women. Analysis of the priority data collected for Fiscal Year 1991 disclosed that Priorities I, II and III account for 30.75, 16.35 and 34.82 percent, respectively, of the national WIC caseload. Thus, over 81 percent of all persons enrolled in WIC are in the three highest risk groups.

Cost Containment Initiatives

General. In an effort to use their food grants more efficiently, all geographic WIC State agencies and most Indian Tribal State agencies have implemented cost containment activities. Savings generated by competitive bidding, rebate, home delivery or direct distribution systems allow State agencies to provide benefits to more participants at no additional food cost. The most successful cost containment strategy has been to obtain rebates on infant formula. By the end of Fiscal Year 1992, 74 State agencies had contracts with infant formula companies to receive rebates for each can of infant formula purchased with WIC funds. Rebate savings to these State agencies for Fiscal Year 1992 are projected to be over $750 million.

Legislation. The Child Nutrition and WIC Reauthorization Act of 1989, enacted November 10, 1989, codified the provisions of Public Law 100-460 (an appropriations act which expired September 30, 1989) which required WIC State agencies to explore the feasibility of implementing one of four acceptable cost containment initiatives: competitive bidding, rebates, home delivery, or direct distribution. Such cost containment initiatives were to focus primarily on the acquisition of infant formula, and on other foods supplied by the WIC Program, if practicable. It also required most WIC State agencies with retail purchase food delivery systems to pursue and implement competitively bid single source infant formula rebate contracts, unless a State agency can demonstrate to FNS' satisfaction that an alternative arrangement will produce equal or greater food cost savings. On October 24, 1992, Public Law 102-512 was signed for the Infant Formula Procurement Act. This legislation amends the Child Nutrition Act of 1966 to enhance competition among infant formula for the WIC Program. The major provisions of this act are that (1) the U.S. Department of Agriculture, Food and Nutrition Service staff will conduct bid solicitation/selection for multi-State (two or more States) infant formula rebate contracts; and (2) to disqualify and/or impose civil penalties of up to $100 million per year for infant formula manufacturers that price-fix or engage in related anti-competitive activities. The WIC Program currently has five multi-State infant formula rebate contracts, involving 20 WIC geographic State agencies and three WIC Indian State agencies.

WIC Vendor Management

During Fiscal Year 1988, the Office of the Inspector General (OIG) performed a national audit of WIC State agency vendor monitoring systems, vendor compliance activities, the reconciliation process, efforts to detect and prevent dual participation, and overall FNS/State agency monitoring. The major findings of the audit dealt with (1) the inadequacy of State agency ADP systems to detect and analyze vendor redemption data for probable abuse; (2) weak State agency vendor selection practices; (3) limited Federal staff resources to oversee State agency operations; (4) the need to standardize vendor sanctions nationwide; and (5) the need for improved information sharing on vendor abuse between the Food Stamp and WIC Programs.

The corrective action plan developed in response to the audit has resulted in the initiation of several projects. The Vendor Futures Group, consisting of regional, headquarters, and State representatives was convened to discuss proposed regulations addressing the deficiencies found in the audit. A National Vendor Meeting was held in December 1988 to provide technical assistance to States on identifying and taking action against abusive vendors. An FNS Instruction was developed and distributed in December 1988 to facilitate the sharing of information between State agencies and FNS on joint WIC/Food Stamp vendors. A Vendor Management Analysis Profile reporting system was established to monitor State actions against abusive vendors. Proposed regulations addressing the deficiencies outlined in the audit were discussed at the February 1990 meeting of the National Association of WIC State Directors. The proposed rule was published December 28, 1990. Over 1,000 comments were received on the proposal. A final rule is expected to be published during calendar year 1993. A national comprehensive management evaluation guide to ensure a uniform approach to review of State agency operational areas has been developed as well as a format for improved reporting of State agency vendor management data to FNS.

WIC Program Research

Agency research priorities for Fiscal Year 1992 included a study to examine the effect of prenatal WIC participation on the incidence of very low birthweight, the development of a resource guide to assist State and local WIC staff to carry out self-initiated evaluation projects, and the development of a WIC Inflation Index to be used to estimate WIC participation and to monitor WIC food prices. The Index is still under development, and comments are currently being solicited from interested parties. A final report on the WIC Index will be sent to Congress in Fiscal Year 1993. The Agency also continued work on comparative analyses of WIC participants and nonparticipants health care use, breastfeeding patterns, and birth outcomes using data from the 1988 National Maternal and Infant Health Survey (NMIHS), a comparative analysis of infant mortality among Medicaid beneficiaries according to WIC participation status during pregnancy, State by State estimates of WIC eligibles using Current Population Survey (CPS) data, and measurement of vendor abuse. In addition, the Agency continued work on the congressionally-mandated, biennial reports on WIC Participant and Program characteristics (PC). The report, PC90, has been completed, and PC92 is underway.

WIC Very Low Birthweight Study. This study extends the original WIC Medicaid analysis by examining whether participation in WIC is also associated with a decrease in the incidence of very low birthweight (that is, birthweight less than 1,500 grams). The study found that WIC participation was associated with a significantly lower incidence of very low birthweight, and corresponding savings in Medicaid costs. The estimated reductions in the prevalence of very low birthweight attributable to WIC ranged from 27 percent in Florida to 55 percent in South Carolina, with intermediate values of 39 percent in Texas, and 45 percent in North Carolina. On average, States saved $12,093 to $15,385 for each very low weight birth prevented.

WIC Evaluation Resource Guide. The purpose of the resource guide was to assist State and local WIC staffs in carrying out self-initiated evaluations of their WIC Programs. The guide includes a primer on program evaluation, examples of State and local WIC evaluations, and potential resources for further technical assistance. This report has been widely distributed within the WIC community and FNS continues to receive numerous requests for copies.

Interim Report on the Development of a WIC Inflation Index. This report, which was sent to Congress in August 1992, presents information on a WIC inflation index which is still under development. FNS has requested comments from interested parties on work to date and will provide a final report to Congress in Fiscal Year 1993. If an appropriate index can be developed it would replace the Thrifty Food Plan index currently used in the WIC funding formula and could also be used in the development of WIC participation estimates and to monitor WIC food prices.

Reviews of WIC Nutritional Risk Criteria and Food Packages

P.L. 101-147 required the Department to conduct reviews on the relationship between nutritional risk and the participant priority system, especially as it affects pregnant women; and the appropriateness of the components of the WIC food packages, particularly with regard to the provision of protein, calcium, iron and other nutrients critical to participants and the nutrient density of foods. Federal Register notices were published (September 14, 1990 and October 24, 1990, respectively) announcing the reviews and soliciting input from State and local agency directors, nutrition experts, and members of the general public concerning the issues under review. A preliminary report was provided to Congress on September 27, 1990. An ad hoc meeting of 12 members of the National Advisory Council on Maternal, Infant and Fetal Nutrition was held in June 1991 to discuss the technical papers developed by the University of Arizona and Pennsylvania State University respectively, for the nutritional risk criteria and food package reviews. An interim report was provided to Congress on July 1, 1991. These papers were then revised and used to form the agenda of a full Council meeting in September 1991. A final report was submitted to Congress by the Council on December 31, 1991, which included its recommendations regarding the review topics. Largely as a result of the nutritional risk criteria review and the subsequent Council report, legislation was enacted on August 14, 1992 (Public Law 102-342) that includes homelessness and migrancy as predisposing nutritional risk criteria for the WIC Program. A proposed rule implementing this recent legislation is expected to be published in FY 1993. The rule will address the relative priority of this condition vis-a-vis other nutritional risk criteria.

WIC Farmers' Market Nutrition Program

The Hunger Prevention Act of 1988 (Public Law 100-435), enacted on September 19, 1988, authorized up to 10 Farmers' Market Coupon Demonstration Projects for a 3-year period. Congress appropriated up to $3 million for Fiscal Year 1992 which enabled the projects to continue operations. The WIC Farmers' Market Nutrition Act of 1992, P.L. 102-314, was enacted July 2, 1992 and reauthorized the projects through Fiscal Year 1994.

States selected to administer the projects are as follows: Connecticut, Iowa, Maryland, Massachusetts, Michigan, New York, Pennsylvania, Texas, Vermont, and Washington. Eight of the projects are administered by State Departments of Agriculture and two (Texas and Washington) are administered by State Departments of Health. Four projects use State funds to serve other categories, such as elderly persons, in addition to WIC participants. Such persons are served with State matching funds, rather than with Federal grant funds.

P.L. 100-435 also mandated an evaluation of the Farmers' Market Coupon Demonstration Project, which was conducted in two phases. Phase one examined the general management and accountability of the projects during their first season in 1989, and indicated that the projects were generally well-run, particularly in the areas of accountability, benefit delivery, and overall project management. The coupon redemption rate (70 percent) was relatively low. The purpose of the Impact Evaluation (Phase two of the project) was to ascertain the impact of the Project on (1) the women who received the coupons, and (2) participating farmers in order to assess the project's effectiveness in accomplishing the legislative goals. The surveys also measured the self-reported food consumption and purchasing patterns of WIC coupon recipients and sales and food purchases at participating farmers' markets compared with appropriate control groups. Findings from the impact evaluation suggest that the project had a modest positive effect on farmers' incomes, and on the consumption o fruits and vegetables by women participating in the WIC Program. The evaluation also found that participants who received nutrition education alone, without farmers' market coupons, increased their consumption of fresh fruits and vegetables about the same amount as those who received the coupons, thus highlighting the potential impact of nutrition education. The results of both phases of the evaluation were submitted in a report to Congress in April 1991.

P.L. 102-314, enacted on July 2, 1992 transformed the Farmers' Market Coupon Demonstration Project (FMCDP) into the WIC Farmers' Market Nutrition Program (FMNP). The Fiscal Year 1993 appropriation for the program was $3 million. State agencies initially selected to participate in the FMCDP automatically become State agencies under the new program, except that Michigan's program is now administered by the State Department of Health. New State agencies will be added to the FMNP on a competitive basis, contingent upon the availability of funds.

Drug Abuse Prevention

The Anti-Drug Abuse Act of 1988 (P.L. 100-690), and the Child Nutrition and WIC Reauthorization Act of 1989 (P.L. 101-147), expanded the role of the WIC Program by adding drug abuse prevention information and referral activities. For the WIC Program, P.L. 100-690 defines drug abuse as: the provision of information concerning the dangers of drug abuse; the referral of partici who are suspected drug abusers to drug abuse clinics, treatment programs, counselors, or other drug abuse professionals; and the provision of materials developed by the Secretary. Congress directed USDA to conduct a study with respect to the appropriate methods of drug abuse education in the WIC Program. This study was published and copies were sent to Congress in January 1990. Findings from this study and advice of both governmental and private drug abuse prevention experts are being used to define the role WIC should and is able to play in providing drug abuse information and referrals FNS has established a continuing dialogue with DHHS' Office for Substance Abuse Prevention to collaborate on establishing policies and designing materials.

A proposed rule implementing the mandates of P.L. 100-690 and P.L. 101-147 was published in March 1990. Comments have been analyzed and a final rule is expected to be published in Fiscal Year 1993 A brochure in English and a poster in English and Spanish, warning participants about the dangers o alcohol and other drug use during pregnancy and breastfeeding, were distributed to WIC State agencies in January 1991. FNS has developed a resource manual and videotape, which were made available in Fiscal Year 1992, to assist local agency staff in meeting the drug abuse information and referral requirements. The videotape will have a companion piece which will outline effective interviewing, screening and referral techniques. FNS has also developed a videotape for participants which was also available in Fiscal Year 1992. The videotape will have a companion leader's guide for WIC professionals to use in counseling participants.

Breastfeeding Promotion Efforts

The WIC program promotes breastfeeding as the best form of nutrition for infants through the provision of support and encouragement to new mothers and through nutrition education during pregnancy. In addition, breastfeeding WIC mothers receive a larger food package and, if otherwise eligible, are able to stay on WIC for a longer period of time than non-breastfeeding postpartum women. By law, States are required to expend at least $8 million of WIC administrative funding for breastfeeding promotion and support; each State is required to spend its proportionate share. Many States spend more than their minimum requirements on this effort. USDA has several special initiatives under way. First and foremost, USDA has developed a Breastfeeding Promotion Consortium to join together government and private health interests in an overall cooperative venture to share ideas to promote breastfeeding in the U.S. The Consortium, which is comprised now of almost 30 professional and government organizations meets semi-annually. In October 1991, USDA provided a total of $90,000 in grants to eight local agencies to develop and evaluate incentives for breastfeeding. The projects are using privately donated items such as diaper bags, nursery items, and breastfeeding aids to promote breastfeeding among participants, and evaluate the impact of incentives on the incidence and duration of breastfeeding among recipients. In addition, the Secretary transmitted to Congress a legislative proposal dated November 8, 1991 to authorize USDA conduct a national information campaign and education program on breastfeeding, to solicit, accept, utilize, and administer contributions for this cause, and to enter into cooperative agreements to carry out the promotional, educational and informational purposes of the legislation. The legislative proposal, also known as the Breastfeeding Promotion Act of 1992, was signed into law on August 14, 1992, as an amendment to the Child Nutrition Act of 1966 (P.L. 102-342).

SPECIAL SUPPLEMENTAL FOOD PROGRAM (WIC)
PARTICIPATION AND PROGRAM FINANCING

FISCAL YEAR 1992

STATE OR TERRITORY	NUMBER OF CLINICS PROVIDING BENEFITS 2/	AVERAGE MONTHLY PARTICIPATION				PROGRAM GRANT (000)
		WOMEN	INFANTS	CHILDREN	TOTAL	
Alabama	120	26,533	35,821	55,877	118,231	57,430
Alaska 1/	212	3,013	3,526	5,234	11,773	8,035
Arizona 1/	152	19,421	26,530	33,293	79,244	46,559
Arkansas	124	19,639	21,392	37,344	78,375	36,219
California	556	185,738	236,536	112,330	534,604	266,359
Colorado 1/	119	12,207	13,055	26,352	51,614	25,208
Connecticut	81	9,061	13,351	39,216	61,628	33,239
Delaware	16	3,023	4,225	7,166	14,414	6,654
District of Columbia	16	3,493	5,635	7,048	16,176	7,842
Florida 1/	258	55,855	73,937	110,276	240,068	106,254
Georgia	275	34,268	55,755	99,930	189,953	84,232
Hawaii	15	4,687	6,155	7,355	18,197	15,854
Idaho	64	6,571	7,652	14,201	28,424	16,128
Illinois	248	36,134	69,062	99,040	204,236	107,172
Indiana	161	29,923	38,227	61,770	129,920	56,620
Iowa	139	9,211	11,902	55,339	76,452	26,206
Kansas	168	10,992	13,376	25,168	49,536	23,029
Kentucky	151	20,634	28,280	51,673	100,587	50,121
Louisiana	120	31,692	36,219	61,443	129,354	67,960
Maine 1/	113	5,382	5,961	14,306	25,649	13,478
Maryland	108	17,853	24,295	28,637	70,785	31,748
Massachusetts	107	16,949	26,000	49,983	92,932	43,765
Michigan	252	35,011	54,001	86,028	175,040	84,914
Minnesota	263	14,126	19,608	47,531	81,265	36,543
Mississippi 1/	141	21,585	31,003	56,850	109,438	50,058
Missouri	263	22,789	30,929	43,602	97,320	51,998
Montana	82	3,182	4,282	10,540	18,004	10,058
Nebraska 1/	113	6,752	7,620	15,191	29,563	14,761
Nevada 1/	47	3,860	6,225	6,867	16,952	9,051
New Hampshire	186	3,357	4,509	10,394	18,260	9,027
New Jersey	457	25,462	33,674	65,751	124,887	58,836
New Mexico 1/	113	9,608	12,824	20,558	42,990	22,950
New York 1/	563	69,770	111,302	191,482	372,554	195,013
North Carolina 1/	191	37,824	47,010	69,700	154,534	73,228
North Dakota 1/	104	3,741	3,836	10,482	18,059	9,059
Ohio	294	49,172	78,911	101,131	229,214	106,426
Oklahoma 1/	179	17,441	22,989	32,964	73,394	38,226
Oregon	113	17,275	14,675	28,212	60,162	27,283
Pennsylvania	399	31,055	53,766	135,528	220,349	105,588
Rhode Island	23	3,162	5,326	9,500	17,988	10,271
South Carolina	135	26,960	31,045	45,300	103,305	50,210
South Dakota 1/	96	4,714	5,022	11,548	21,284	11,575
Tennessee	154	30,863	51,264	39,068	121,195	58,020
Texas	610	108,375	129,794	228,083	466,252	192,072
Utah	65	12,132	13,325	24,760	50,217	26,895
Vermont	61	3,325	2,943	8,418	14,686	7,699
Virginia	156	16,929	31,940	54,674	103,543	52,491
Washington	220	22,416	30,671	20,095	73,182	38,867
West Virginia	69	8,173	12,235	22,062	42,470	23,358
Wisconsin	220	13,198	23,985	43,430	80,613	40,125
Wyoming 1/	41	2,709	2,772	5,235	10,716	5,619
American Samoa	0	0	0	0	0	0
Freely Associated States	0	0	0	0	0	0
Guam	5	807	1,071	1,754	3,632	3,068
N. Mariana Islands	0	0	0	0	0	0
Puerto Rico	113	32,762	46,384	53,567	132,713	105,903
Virgin Islands	7	1,015	1,693	3,662	6,370	5,223
Indian Tribes	0	0	0	0	0	0
DOD Army/AF/USMC/NAVY	0	0	0	0	0	0
Undistributed	0	0	0	0	0	-76
TOTAL	9,038	1,221,829	1,683,526	2,506,948	5,412,303	$2,664,449 3/

1/ Includes Indian Agencies.
2/ Number of clinics reported for FY 1992.
3/ Excludes $5,026,674 for evaluations, and $3,000,000 for Farmers' Market Projects.

NOTE: These data are based in part on preliminary data submitted by State and local agencies and are subject to change as revised reports are received. Totals may not add due to rounding.

FOOD AND NUTRITION SERVICE

The estimates include appropriation language for this item as follows (new language underscored; deleted matter enclosed in brackets):

Commodity Supplemental Food Program:

For necessary expenses to carry out the Commodity Supplemental Food Program as authorized by section 4(a) of the Agriculture and Consumer Protection Act of 1973 (7 U.S.C. 612c (note)), including not less than $8,000,000 for the projects in Detroit, New Orleans, and Des Moines, $94,500,000, to remain available through September 30, [1994] 1995: Provided, That none of these funds shall be available to reimburse the Commodity Credit Corporation for commodities donated to the program.

This change makes the appropriation available through September 30, 1995.

COMMODITY SUPPLEMENTAL FOOD PROGRAM

Appropriations Act, 1993..................	$94,500,000
Budget Estimate, 1994.....................	94,500,000
Change in Appropriation..................	--

SUMMARY OF INCREASES AND DECREASES
(On basis of appropriation)

Item of Change	1993 Estimated	Other Changes	1994 Estimated
Commodity Supplemental Food Program	$94,500,000	$ --	$94,500,000

PROJECT STATEMENT
(On basis of appropriation)

Project	1992 Actual	1993 Estimated	Increase or Decrease	1994 Estimated
Commodity Supplemental Food Program (CSFP)				
Commodities........	$72,000,000	$75,600,000		$75,600,000
Administrative costs	18,000,000	18,900,000	--	18,900,000
Total, Appropriation.	90,000,000	94,500,000	--	94,500,000

PROJECT STATEMENT
(On basis of available funds)

Project	1992 Actual	1993 Estimated	Increase or Decrease	1994 Estimated
Commodity Supplemental Food Program (CSFP)				
Commodities............	$78,109,000	$75,600,000		$75,600,000
Administrative costs...	18,257,203	18,900,000	--	18,900,000
Total Obligations	96,366,203	94,500,000	--	94,500,000
Recovery of prior year obligations	-259,883	--	--	--
Unobligated balances...				
Available, start of year	-6,109,462	--		
Available, end of year.		--	--	--
Expiring..............	+3,142			
Total, Appropriation...	90,000,000	94,500,000	--	94,500,000

EXPLANATION OF PROGRAM

Overview of Program Development. Instituted in November 1968 through Public Law 90-463, the Commodity Supplemental Food Program (CSFP) is now authorized by section 4(a) of the Agriculture and Consumer Protection Act of 1973, as amended. The elderly component of CSFP was initiated by the Agriculture and Food Act of 1981, P.L. 97-98, which provided for pilot projects for low-income elderly persons in Polk County, Iowa and in Detroit, Michigan. These projects began operations in September, 1982 and a pilot project in New Orleans, Louisiana, began after authorization by P.L. 97-370, December 18, 1982. The Food Security Act of 1985, P.L. 99-198, provided that funds available beyond those needed to serve women, infants, and children could be used to serve elderly persons beyond those participating in the original pilot project sites. The program was reauthorized through Fiscal Year 1995 by the Food, Agriculture, Conservation and Trade Act of 1990 (FACT), P.L. 101-624. This law increased administrative funding from 15 percent to 20 percent of funds appropriated, discontinued administrative funding based on the value of donated commodities, and allowed establishment of elderly-only sites.

Eligibility and Benefits. This program provides foods purchased by USDA to infants and children up to age six and to pregnant, postpartum and breastfeeding women and senior citizens who have low incomes and are residing in approved project areas. The foods are provided by the Department of Agriculture for distribution through State agencies and are intended to supplement food acquired by recipients with their own money, the Food Stamp Program, or other resources. The authorized commodities are iron-fortified infant formula and cereal, adult cereals, canned juice, evaporated milk and/or nonfat dry milk, canned vegetables or fruits, canned meat or poultry or tuna, egg mix, dehydrated potatoes, rice or pasta, and peanut butter or dry beans. Elderly participants are eligible to receive all commodities except iron-fortified infant formula and infant cereal.

CSFP participants sometimes receive "bonus" commodities in addition to the basic food package. As required by P.L. 101-624, 9 million pounds of cheese will be provided as a bonus commodity in Fiscal Years 1993 and 1994, if available, through the Commodity Credit Corporation (CCC) inventory.

When an excess of appropriate commodities are held in CCC inventory, they may be donated by CCC without charge to the CSFP appropriation and used to fulfill part of the entitlement. Such donated commodities are referred to as "free foods." In both Fiscal Years 1993 and 1994, a total of 4 million pounds each year of nonfat dry milk will be donated to this program as required by P.L. 101-624 to the extent that the CCC inventory levels permit. Since free foods are not charged against the CSFP appropriation, funds that are saved can be made available for participant service.

State/Federal Responsibilities. The CSFP is operated as a State/Federal partnership under agreements signed by State health care or agricultural agencies and the Food and Nutrition Service. The Federal government provides all commodities distributed to participants through the program. Under current law, States are given 20 percent of the Federal funds appropriated to cover administrative costs. Allowable costs include nutrition education, warehousing, food delivery, participant certification, and other costs associated with State and local administration of the program.

	FY 1992 Actual	FY 1993 Estimate	FY 1994 Estimate	Change
Caseload (in thousands):				
women, infants, children ..	252	246	246	--
CSFP/Elderly	146	142	127	-15
Avg. Participation (in thousands)				
women, infants, children ..	222	246	246	--
CSFP/Elderly	120	141	127	-14
Program Level ($ in millions)				
Distributed food costs ...	$66.2	$75.1	$75.0	-0.1
Inventory Restoration				
Americold fire 1/.......	3.6			
Disaster and other losses	1.8			
Inventory change.........	6.2			
Total..................	11.6			
State and local admin. costs	18.3	18.9	18.9	
Commodity Administrative Cost & PCIMS	.3	.5	.6	+0.1
Total	$96.4	$94.5	$94.5	--
Average food cost per person per month:				
Entitlement	$18.10	$18.10	$18.75	+$0.65
FNS funded	(17.21)	(17.22)	(17.86)	(+0.64)
Free substitute (donated).............	(.89)	(.88)	(.89)	(+0.01)
Bonus (donated)	3.62	3.56	3.62	+0.06
Average per person total commodities	$21.72	$21.66	$22.37	+$0.71
Elderly:				
Entitlement	$15.53	$15.52	$15.77	+$0.25
FNS funded	(14.29)	(14.30)	(14.53)	(+0.23)
Free substitute(donated).	(1.24)	(1.22)	(1.24)	(+0.02)
Bonus (donated)	4.48	4.41	4.48	+0.07
Average per person total commodities	$20.01	$19.93	$20.25	+$0.32

1/ Approximately $3.6 million was spent in Fiscal Year 1992 from the effects of the Americold fire. The Americold warehouse stores commodities for the Food Distribution Program on Indian Reservations (FDPIR) and the Commodity Supplemental Food Program (CSFP). Approximately 40% of the destroyed commodities are associated with FDPIR.

COMMODITY SUPPLEMENTAL FOOD PROGRAM (CSFP)

STATUS OF PROGRAM

Commodity Supplemental Food Program (CSFP)

The Commodity Supplemental Food Program provides federally purchased commodities and administrative funds to States which distribute the commodities to low-income pregnant, postpartum, and breastfeeding women, infants, and children up to age 6 and persons 60 years of age and older residing in the service areas. The quantity and varieties of commodities are determined by the Secretary of Agriculture.

Program Caseload

In Fiscal Year 1992 there were 20 State agencies operating the program. Sixteen of the State agencies also serve elderly participants. In Fiscal Year 1992, available funds supported caseload allocations of 252,604 women, infants and children and 145,717 elderly. The average monthly participation in Fiscal Year 1992 was about 222,453 women, infants and children, and about 120,086 elderly.

Food Package

Six USDA purchased food packages are provided as benefits according to the following age or categories of participants: (1) infants - birth through 3 months; (2) infants - 4 through 12 months; (3) children - 1 to 6 years; (4) pregnant and breastfeeding women; (5) non-breastfeeding postpartum women; and (6) the elderly. The food packages reflect the health and nutritional requirements of participant categories.

CSFP participants receive monthly food packages which include: juice, hot or cold cereal, nonfat dry milk, evaporated milk, egg mix, dry beans or peanut butter, canned fruits or vegetables, canned meat, tuna or poultry, and dehydrated potatoes, rice or pasta. Infants receive formula and rice cereal. In Fiscal Year 1992, participants also received, as bonus foods, cheese, butter, honey, cornmeal, and nonfat dry milk. The Commodity Credit Corporation provided 9,000,000 pounds of cheese and 4,000,000 pounds of nonfat dry milk as required by P.L. 101-624, the FACT Act.

31g-29

COMMODITY SUPPLEMENTAL FOOD PROGRAM
Quantity and Value of Commodities

By Commodity, Fiscal Year 1992

ENTITLEMENT COMMODITIES	Pounds	Dollars
SECTION 6/32 TYPE:		
APPLE JUICE, CANNED	16,587,194	$5,151,095
APPLESAUCE, CANNED	4,126,632	1,560,254
BEANS, DRY	2,634,744	660,769
BEANS, GREEN, CANNED	2,673,109	757,049
BEEF, CANNED W/NJ	2,627,119	4,079,920
BEEF, MEATBALL STEW	662,175	520,211
CARROTS	1,350,192	408,845
CHICKEN, CANNED BONED	750,553	1,499,305
CORN, CANNED, CREAM STYLE	301,776	108,382
CORN, CANNED, WHOLE KERNEL	977,304	341,608
EGG MIX	4,620,384	8,462,406
FRUIT COCKTAIL, CANNED	1,322,352	804,306
GRAPE JUICE, CANNED	7,430,114	2,558,459
GRAPEFRUIT JUICE, CANNED	3,118,470	835,956
ORANGE JUICE, CANNED	23,580,663	7,291,050
PEACHES, CLING CANNED	1,789,392	1,099,144
PEARS, CANNED	1,004,328	479,628
PEAS, GREEN CANNED	1,525,272	498,596
PINEAPPLE JUICE, CANNED	4,941,114	1,551,746
PINEAPPLE, CANNED	1,780,230	966,811
PLUMS, CANNED, PURPLE	190,752	83,890
PORK, CANNED, W-NJ	1,285,798	1,793,007
POTATOES, DEHYDRATED	1,243,368	580,359
POTATOES, WHOLE	648,768	201,088
POULTRY, CANNED BONED	1,019,178	1,768,010
SPINACH, CANNED	595,016	203,547
SWEET POTATOES, SYRUP	580,752	227,286
TOMATO JUICE, CANNED	1,412,995	282,360
TOMATOES, CANNED	1,289,544	380,130
TUNA, CHUNK	1,369,388	2,132,020
Total Section 6/32 Type	93,438,676	$47,287,237
SECTION 416-TYPE:		
CEREAL, DRY CORN	2,202,753	$2,622,976
CEREAL, DRY RICE	1,548,135	1,697,753
CEREAL, INFANT RICE	469,590	657,719
CEREAL, DRY OATS	894,684	1,047,629
CEREAL, WHEAT	58,476	78,416
FARINA	3,777,627	1,358,742
FORMULA, INFANT	7,628,303	4,578,931
MACARONI	2,011,728	503,291
MILK, EVAPORATED	25,573,280	11,597,498
MILK, NFD	5,920,736	6,170,591
OATS, ROLLED	513,756	100,947
PEANUT BUTTER	3,695,136	3,354,430
RICE, MILLED	3,948,672	800,964
SPAGHETTI	771,288	191,365
Total Section 416-Type	59,014,164	$34,761,252
Anticipated Adjustment		-3,676,489
AMS/ASCS Admin. Expenses		263,000
Total Commodity Entitlement	152,452,840	$78,109,000

BONUS COMMODITIES		
SECTION 416-TYPE:		
BUTTER	3,811,428	$3,551,674
CHEESE PROCESS	9,000,000	12,119,400
CORNMEAL	8,923,700	1,039,706
HONEY	1,255,104	953,498
NFD MILK	4,000,000	4,168,785
Total Section 416 Type	26,990,232	$21,833,063
Total Bonus Commodities	26,990,232	$21,833,063
GRAND TOTAL (Entitlement & Bonus)	179,443,072	$99,942,063

SOURCE: Preliminary food orders for fiscal year 1992.

31g-30

COMMODITY SUPPLEMENTAL FOOD PROGRAM
PROJECTS, PARTICIPATION AND FOOD COST

FISCAL YEAR 1992

STATE OR TERRITORY	PROJECTS	AVERAGE MONTHLY PARTICIPATION (FNS-153) WOMEN	INFANTS	CHILDREN	ELDERLY	TOTAL	FOOD VALUE IN DOLLARS 1/
ARIZONA	10	2,833	0	12,752	4,648	20,233	3,050,227
CALIFORNIA	2	1,551	1,148	8,765	2,975	14,439	2,313,027
COLORADO	7	3,649	3,174	11,286	5,289	23,398	4,453,540
DISTRICT OF COLUMBIA	1	881	788	4,231	9,067	14,967	2,514,676
ILLINOIS	1	2,244	1,884	10,268	4,688	19,084	3,219,784
IOWA	1	357	106	1,329	4,214	6,006	964,341
KANSAS	3	1,017	0	2,509	258	3,784	654,448
KENTUCKY	1	501	304	2,399	3,603	6,807	1,175,024
LOUISIANA	1	4,922	3,703	21,611	25,924	56,160	10,061,522
MICHIGAN	8	9,945	7,048	42,383	34,458	93,834	16,872,100
RED LAKE, MINN	1	108	105	386	0	599	115,306
MINNESOTA	2	1,106	413	4,430	538	6,487	1,184,616
NEBRASKA	7	735	219	3,920	9,720	14,594	2,218,422
NEW HAMPSHIRE	3	891	0	1,523	419	2,833	474,890
NEW MEXICO	5	1,629	1	11,017	190	12,837	2,257,985
NEW YORK	2	2,716	1,904	10,497	0	15,117	3,036,515
NORTH CAROLINA	2	55	39	388	1,519	2,001	292,549
OREGON	1	33	27	1,008	0	1,068	199,597
SOUTH DAKOTA	1	74	57	675	0	806	168,077
TENNESSEE	4	2,328	1,336	11,245	12,576	27,485	4,243,590
AMS/ASCS Admin. Exp.	0	0	0	0	0	0	263,000
ANTICIPATED ADJUSTMENT	0	0	0	0	0	0	18,375,764
TOTAL	63	37,575	22,256	162,622	120,086	342,539	$78,109,000

1/ Total value of entitlement foods.

NOTE: These data are based in part on preliminary data submitted by State and local agencies and are subject to change as revised reports are received.

Food and Nutrition Service

The estimates include appropriation language for this item as follows (new language underscored; deleted matter enclosed in brackets):

Food Stamp Program:

For necessary expenses to carry out the Food Stamp Act (7 U.S.C.
1,2 2011 -[2029] 2027 and 2029), [$28,115,357,000] $29,545,655,000
[; of which $2,500,000,000 shall be available only to the
extent an official budget request, for a specific dollar amount,
is transmitted to the Congress]: Provided, That funds provided
3 herein shall remain available through September 30, [1993] 1994,
in accordance with section 18 (a) of the Food Stamp Act:
Provided further, That up to 5 per centum of the foregoing
amount may be placed in reserve to be apportioned pursuant to
4 [Section 3679 of the Revised Statutes, as amended] 31 U.S.C.
1512, for use only in such amounts and at such times as may
become necessary to carry out program operations: Provided
further, That funds provided herein shall be expended in
accordance with section 16 of the Food Stamp Act: Provided
further, That this appropriation shall be subject to any
work registration or work fare requirements as may be required
by law[: Provided further, That $345,000,000 of the funds
provided herein shall be available after the Secretary has
employed the regulatory and administrative methods available
to him under the law to curtail fraud, waste, and abuse in the
program [: Provided further, That $1,051,000,000 of the
foregoing amount shall be available for Nutrition Assistance for
5 Puerto Rico as authorized by U.S.C. 2028, of which $10,825,000
shall be transferred to the Animal and Plant Health Inspection
Service for the Cattle Tick Eradication Project]. For making
6 after May 31 of the current fiscal year, benefit payments to
individuals under the Food Stamp Act for unanticipated costs
incurred for the current fiscal year, such sums as may be
necessary. For necessary expenses to carry out the Food Stamp
7 Act (7 U.S.C 2011-2027,2029), for the first quarter of fiscal
year 1995, $6,250,000,000 to remain available through September
30, 1995.

The first change removes the U.S.C. reference applicable to nutrition Assistance to Puerto Rico; appropriations for this activity are requested in a separate account.

The second change deletes language identifying the reserve as a contingency.

The third change makes the appropriation available through September 30, 1994.

The fourth change updates a reference to 31 U.S.C. 1512.

The fifth change deletes the provision applicable to Nutrition Assistance to Puerto Rico. Appropriations for this activity are requested in a separate account.

The sixth change provides for indefinite appropriations after May 31, 1994 for unanticipated benefit needs for Fiscal Year 1994. This will give Food Stamps the same treatment as AFDC, Medicaid and SSI.

<u>The seventh change</u> provides for advance appropriations for the first quarter of Fiscal Year 1995. Advance appropriations are requested to ensure continuous funding for the program at the beginning of the fiscal year. This will give Food Stamps the same treatment as AFDC, Medicaid and SSI.

FOOD STAMP PROGRAM - CURRENT LAW

Appropriations Act,1993..........................	$27,064,357,000
Budget Estimate, 1994............................	29,545,655,000
Increase in the Appropriation....................	+2,481,298,000

FOOD STAMP PROGRAM - PROPOSED LEGISLATION

Budget Estimate, Current Law 1994................	$29,545,655,000
Change due to Proposed Legislation...............	-20,000,000
Net Request, President's 1994 Budget Request.....	$29,525,655,000

SUMMARY OF INCREASES AND DECREASES-CURRENT LAW
(On basis of appropriation)

Item of Change	1993 Estimated	Other Changes	1994 Estimated
Benefits:			
Total, Benefits Cost .a/......	$22,880,127,000	-75,096,000	$22,805,031,000
State Admin. Costs.........	1,428,456,000	+42,880,000	1,471,336,000
Employment and Training......	160,520,000	+2,223,000	162,743,000
Other program costs........	95,254,000	+11,291,000	106,545,000
Contingency reserve......	2,500,000,000	+2,500,000,000	5,000,000,000
Total, Appropriation	27,064,357,000	+2,481,298,000	29,545,655,000

a/ This Fiscal Year 1994 estimate includes a net of $15.1 million in collections from the Federal Tax Offset Project.

PROJECT STATEMENT
(On basis of appropriation)

Project	1992 Actual Amount	SYs	1993 Estimated Amount	SYs	Increase or Decrease	1994 Estimated Amount	SYs
Benefits:							
Correct benefits a/	$18,159,773,000		$21,324,278,000		-23,445,000	$21,300,833,000	
Erroneous benefits.	1,366,865,000		1,555,849,000		-50,651,000	1,505,198,000	
Total, Benefits costs	19,526,638,000		22,880,127,000		(1) -74,096,000	22,806,031,000	
Administrative costs:							
State Administration	1,272,875,000		1,321,076,000		+38,036,000	1,359,112,000	
Anti-fraud..........	82,057,000		84,929,000		+6,208,000	91,137,000	
ADP Development.....	25,557,000		22,451,000		-1,364,000	21,087,000	
Subtotal, Administrative costs	1,380,489,000		1,428,456,000		(2) +42,880,000	1,471,336,000	
Employment & Training	157,628,000		160,520,000		(3) +2,223,000	162,743,000	
Other Program Costs.:							
Food Stamp production and redemption.....	65,998,000		73,066,000		(a) 10,796,000	83,862,000	
Computer support Systems.b/.........	1,270,000		1,457,000		(b) +39,000	1,496,000	
Certification of SSI recipients for food stamps............	3,805,000		4,000,000		(c) +80,000	4,080,000	

PROJECT STATEMENT
(On basis of appropriation)

Project	1992 Actual Amount	SYs	1993 Estimated Amount	SYs	Increase or Decrease	1994 Estimated Amount	SYs
Retailer redemption. & monitoring system	1,849,000		2,000,000		(d) +40,000	2,040,000	
Recipient and cooperative services.b/	1,379,000		1,071,000		(e) +30,000	1,101,000	
Research, evaluation & demo projects..b/	9,869,000		10,600,000		(f) +286,000	10,886,000	
Retailer Integrity.b/	2,000,000	12	1,950,000	12	(g) +9,000	1,959,000	12
Electronic Benefit Transfer.b/........	500,000	11	610,000	13	(h) -3,000	607,000	13
Nutrition, Education Initiative.b/......	--		500,000		(i) +14,000	514,000	
Subtotal, Other Program Costs......	86,670,000	23	95,254,000	25	(4) +11,291,000	106,545,000	25
Total, Administrative costs.........	1,624,787,000		1,684,230,000		+56,394,000	1,740,624,000	
Benefit Reserve.....	1,498,550,000		2,500,000,000		(5) +2,500,000,000	5,000,000,000	
Transfer to Other Accounts..........	100,000,000						
Error Liabilities...			--		(6) -1,000,000	-1,000,000	
Total, Appropriation	22,749,975,000	23	27,064,357,000	25	+2,481,298,000	29,545,655,000	25
Proposed Legislation	--		--		-20,000,000	-20,000,000	
Investment Proposal					+603,000,000	+603,000,000	
Total, President's Budget.............					+3,064,298,000	30,128,655,000	25

a/ This Fiscal Year 1994 estimate includes a net of $15.1 million in collections for the Federal Tax Offset Project.

b/ Fiscal Year 1994 amounts include a request of $10,628,000 in discretionary additions to the mandatory baseline.

PROJECT STATEMENT
(On basis of available funds)

Project	1992 Actual Amount	SYs	1993 Estimated Amount	Sys	Increase or Decrease	1994 Estimated Amount	Sys
Benefits:							
Correct benefits a/	$18,997,672,658		$20,874,371,000		+426,396,000	$21,300,833,000	
Erroneous benefits.	1,901,857,219		1,523,023,000		-17,759,000	1,505,198,000	
Total, Benefits costs	20,899,529,877		22,397,394,000		(1) +408,637,000	22,806,031,000	
Administrative costs:							
State Administration	1,245,920,714		1,321,076,000		+38,036,000	1,359,112,000	
Anti-fraud..........	75,916,796		84,929,000		+6,208,000	91,137,000	
ADP Development.....	15,752,836		22,451,000		-1,364,000	21,087,000	
Subtotal, Adminstrative costs	1,337,590,346		1,428,456,000		(2) +42,880,000	1,471,336,000	
Employment & Training	145,802,167		160,520,000		(3) +2,223,000	162,743,000	
Other Program Costs.:							
Food Stamp production and redemption.....	64,700,942		71,936,000		(a) 11,926,000	83,862,000	
Computer support Systems.b/.........	1,109,575		1,457,000		(b) +39,000	1,496,000	
Certification of SSI recipients for food stamps.............	3,696,000		4,000,000		(c) +80,000	4,080,000	
Retailer redemption. & monitoring system	1,849,000		2,000,000		(d) +40,000	2,040,000	
Recipient and cooperative services.b/	996,185		1,071,000		(e) +30,000	1,101,000	
Research, evaluation and demo projects.b/	10,229,246		10,600,000		(f) +286,000	10,886,000	
Retailer Integrity.b/	1,801,645	12	1,950,000	12	(g) +9,000	1,959,000	12
Electronic Benefit Transfer.b/........	449,691	11	610,000	13	(h) -3,000	607,000	13
Nutrition, Education Initiative.b/......	--		500,000		(i) +14,000	514,000	
Subtotal, Other Program Costs......	84,832,284	23	94,124,000	25	(4) +12,421,000	106,545,000	25
Total, Administrative costs.........	1,568,224,797		1,683,100,000		+57,524,000	1,740,624,000	

PROJECT STATEMENT
(On basis of available funds)

Project	1992 Actual Amount	SYs	1993 Estimated Amount	SYs	Increase or Decrease	1994 Estimated Amount	SYs
Total, Obligations..	22,467,754,674		24,080,494,000		+466,161,000	24,546,655,000	
Unobligated balances:							
Available, start of year...........	-765,554,476		-308,000,000		+308,000,000	-0-	
Available, end of year...............	308,000,000		--				
Unob. Bal. Expir..c/	639,774,802		3,291,863,000		(5) +1,708,137,000	5,000,000,000	
Total Available or Estimate...........	22,649,975,000		27,064,357,000		+2,482,298,000	29,546,655,000	
Error Liabilities...			--		(6) -1,000,000	-1,000,000	
Transfer to Other Accounts..........	100,000,000						
Total, Appropriation	22,749,975,000	23	27,064,357,000	25	+2,481,298,000	29,545,655,000	25
Proposed Legislation	--		--		-20,000,000	-20,000,000	
Investment Proposal					+603,000,000	+603,000,000	
Total, President's.. Budget.............					+3,064,298,000	30,128,655,000	25

a/ This Fiscal Year 1994 estimate includes <u>a net of $15.1 million in collections for the Federal Tax Offset Project</u>.

b/ Fiscal Year 1994 amounts include a request of $10,628,000 in discretionary additions to the mandatory baseline.

c/ Includes Fiscal Year 1993 contingency reserve of $2.5 billion and $.792 billion unobligated balance expiring.

EXPLANATION OF PROGRAM

Overview of Program Development. The Food Stamp Program, which is authorized through September 30, 1995 by the Food, Agriculture, Conservation and Trade Act of 1990 (FACT), P.L. 101-624, helps individuals and families with low incomes obtain a more nutritious diet.

The program was initiated on a pilot basis in 1961 and established as a permanent program in 1964. The Food Stamp Program enables low-income households to obtain better diets by supplementing the funds they have to spend on food with food stamps which may be used for purchasing food items at authorized food stores. The Food Stamp Program evolved from the Commodity Distribution to Needy Families Program established in 1936. Commodities purchased for farm assistance purposes were made available for distribution to needy individuals through various Federal, State, and local welfare organizations. In 1961, the basic emphasis of commodity donations changed significantly when an Executive Order expanded the program's objectives from removing surpluses to also encompass raising the quantity and improving the quality of foods distributed. Beginning in that year a food stamp pilot project was undertaken in a number of States.

The Food Stamp Act of 1964 authorized a permanent Food Stamp Program which would gradually supplant commodity distribution. The program was implemented in most counties by 1969, although it was not until Fiscal Year 1975 that the Food Stamp Program expanded to all counties nationally. The Food Stamp Program is currently in operation in all 50 States, the District of Columbia, the Virgin Islands and Guam.

<u>Eligibility and Benefits</u>. Eligible participants are entitled to food stamp allotments based on their household size and net income after certain deductions. Food stamps increase the food purchasing power of eligible households and thus enable them to attain a better diet than would have been possible without the assistance.

<u>Benefit Costs</u>. The cost of food stamps is paid by the Federal Government and is called "benefit" costs. Benefits are paid to program recipients as follows:

1. Food coupons/stamps are the most common method utilized and are issued on a monthly basis to eligible recipients.

2. Electronic Benefit Transfer (EBT) is the major alternative method of providing program participants with the value of the coupons used to make food purchases. EBT projects are currently operating in parts of Pennsylvania, Minnesota, Maryland, Ohio, and New Mexico and are planned in other States. Under this system each household recipient is issued a plastic benefit card with a magnetic stripe or a computer chip to make food purchases; no cash or food coupons are involved. At the store, the recipient presents his/her card and enters a unique personal identification number into a terminal that immediately debits the household's account for the amount of purchase at a centralized computer or on the computer chip. The grocer's account at a designated bank is credited for the same amount by a financial institution. Federal funds are shifted from the Federal Reserve to the financial institution to complete the settlement process. In Fiscal Year 1992, regulations were promulgated as required by statute to make EBT available as an operational alternative nationwide.

   The Financial Management Service of the Department of the Treasury has included, in its FY 1994 request, funds for the development of an EBT Prototype which is the first step toward development of a nationwide EBT system. Phase one of the project, funded with FY 1993 funds, will provide a technical and cost analysis of alternative system models. Phase two, to be funded with FY 1994 and FY 1995 funds, will provide for the implementation and evaluation of the prototype. The coordination of benefit delivery is expected to demonstrate economies of scale, resolve disparities in operational policy among agencies, and demonstrate the successful cooperation of Federal and State agencies, the private sector, and consumer groups for the implementation of a major payment system. The prototype is an effort to test the feasibility of providing benefits for multi-Federal programs including direct Federal payments on a single card and will encompass both issuance and settlement.

   While no funds are being requested in this budget submission for the EBT Prototype itself, the Food and Nutrition Service has designated staff and travel resources to support project operations. This Department fully supports the Financial Management Service's request for funds to support the EBT Prototype project. Settlement and reconciliation are essential components of any EBT system configuration, whether a stand-alone Food Stamp System or a multi-program effort such as the prototype.

3. Cash-out and some welfare reform projects enable participants to use cash in lieu of coupons to make their food purchases. Cash-out projects are currently operating in California, Minnesota, and Vermont. Allotments are issued to recipient households in the form of a check. Welfare Reform projects are currently underway in Alabama, Washington, and New York. A project in Utah is planned for 1993. Generally, the projects consolidate AFDC, General Assistance

for families and food stamps to form a single unified program with one set of rules and with benefits issued in the form of one cash grant to families. It is estimated that approximately $600-800 million in benefits will be issued through these alternate methods in Fiscal Year 1993.

The Thrifty Food Plan is a model plan for achieving a nutritionally adequate diet. As required by law, the food stamp allotments for the various household sizes are revised October 1 of each year to reflect changes in the cost of the Thrifty Food Plan as of the prior June. P.L. 102-351, a Bill To Prevent a Reduction In The Adjusted Cost Of The Thrifty Food Plan During Fiscal Year 1993, prevents the maximum allotment from falling below the 1992 maximum allotment in Fiscal Year 1993. The maximum benefit for a family of four is 103 percent of the value of the estimated plan. In Fiscal Year 1993 the new legislation continues the Fiscal Year 1992 levels, which were greater than 103 percent of the cost of the June 1992 Thrifty Food Plan.

State Administration. All direct and indirect administrative costs incurred for certification of households, issuance of food stamps, quality control and fair hearing efforts are shared by the Federal Government and the States on a 50-50 basis. Under current law, enhanced Federal funding is available for one ADP system development per State. Proposals approved before November 28, 1990 will be matched at 75 percent; proposals approved after that date will be supported at 63 percent in Fiscal Year 1992 and subsequent years. State agencies can also receive at least 75 percent funding or more for fraud prevention related activities. For States with low error rates, the normal 50 percent Federal share of State administrative costs can be increased up to a maximum of 60 percent, depending on the extent to which the State's error rate falls below 6 percent. In order to receive this incentive funding, States must also meet a standard set by the Secretary for the rate of improper denials or terminations. State agencies are held liable when their rate of overissuances and payments to ineligible households plus their rate for underissuance exceeds the lowest national performance measure ever announced plus one percent. Liabilities are based on the level of State issuance and the extent to which the State's error rate exceeds a tolerance level.

Employment and Training Program (E&T). States are required to implement an employment and training program for the purpose of assisting members of households participating in the Food Stamp Program in gaining skills, training or experience that will increase their ability to obtain regular employment. In Fiscal Year 1993, the Department will provide States 100 percent Federal grants totaling $75 million, of which $15 million will be based on State agency performance in placing participants into E&T programs. Additional funds will be spent by State agencies and matched by the Federal government to administer E&T programs.

Other Program Costs. In addition to State administrative and employment and training expenses, other program costs borne by the Federal Government include:

(1) the printing and transporting of food stamps to State agencies; processing and destruction of redeemed food stamps by Federal Reserve Banks; settlement and reconciliation services to support EBT operations.

(2) the computer support systems;

(3) the certification of SSI/Social Security recipients for participation in the Food Stamp Program by the district offices of the Social Security Administration;

(4) the redemption and monitoring systems;

(5) recipient and cooperative services including funds for printing other than stamps, State Exchange and collection of Quality Control liabilities and other claims;

(6) research, evaluation and demonstration projects authorized under Section 17 of the Food Stamp Act of 1977;

(7) retailer integrity;

(8) electronic benefit transfer; and

(9) nutrition education grants.

State/Federal Responsibilities. The Food Stamp Program is a Federal-State partnership in which the States administer the program at the service delivery level. Households apply for food stamps at their local State welfare offices. State workers use uniform nationwide rules promulgated by the Food and Nutrition Service to determine and certify which households are eligible, to calculate the size of each household's allotment, and to monitor and recertify recipient eligibility. Food stamps are typically dispensed on a monthly basis through local banks or the mail.

Each State must have an Employment and Training (E&T) program to help able-bodied individuals in food stamp households gain skills and experience that will help them obtain regular employment.

The Quality Control System encourages payment accuracy by establishing fiscal incentives based on State performance in benefit determinations. State agencies with high error rates are assessed liabilities, while enhanced administrative funding is provided to States with low error rates.

FNS funds 100 percent of the cost of food stamps redeemed. FNS also funds over 50 percent of State administrative costs for the program. FNS is responsible for authorizing and monitoring stores participating in the program. Approximately 213,000 stores are authorized to redeem food stamps.

After recipients use their food stamps to purchase food at stores, the stores redeem the food stamps at banks. The banks, in turn, redeem the food stamps at their regional Federal Reserve Bank, and the Federal Reserve Bank seeks reimbursement from the FNS appropriation directly from the U.S. Treasury. FNS also monitors the redemption process on an ongoing basis.

JUSTIFICATION OF INCREASES AND DECREASES

(1) A decrease of $74,096,000 in the appropriation for Benefit Costs, including the effects of the FACT Act ($22,880,127,000 budgeted in 1993). On the basis of available funds, there is an increase of $408,637,000 ($22,397,394,000 budgeted in 1993). The appropriation decrease consists of:

(a) A decrease of $23,445,000 for properly issued benefits ($21,324,278,000 budgeted in 1993). On the basis of available funds, there is an increase of $426,396,000 ($20,874,371,000 available in 1993).

Need for Change. In Fiscal Year 1994, program participation is expected to decrease from 27.3 million per month in Fiscal Year 1993 to 27.2 million in Fiscal Year 1994. The Fiscal Year 1994 estimate includes $603 million, in part to offset increased costs associated with the Administration's proposed new energy tax.

Nature of Change. A comparison of key program workload and cost indicators based on OMB and mid-session economic indicators for Fiscal Year 1992 through 1994 is presented on the following page.

	FY 1992 Actual	FY 1993 Estimate	FY 1994 Estimate
Average participation (000)	25,403	27,300	27,242 2/
Average unemployment rate (percent)	7.30	7.15	6.70
Average number of unemployed persons (000)	9,250	8,600	8,100
Thrifty Food Plan	$360.60	$355.50	$367.60
Maximum Allotment 1/	$370.00	$370.00	$378.00
Average benefit per person per month	$ 68.57	$ 68.24 1/	$ 69.62

1/ P.L. 102-351 continues the 1992 value of the maximum allotment through Fiscal Year 1993.

2/ Does not include the proposed increase in benefits to offset the effects of the proposed energy tax.

(b) A decrease of $50,651,000 for erroneous benefits ($1,555,849,000 budgeted in Fiscal Year 1993). On the basis of available funds, there is a decrease of $17,759,000 ($1,523,023,000 available in 1993).

Need for Change. The overpayment error rate is projected to decline from 6.8 percent in Fiscal Year 1993 to 6.6 percent in Fiscal Year 1994. Although the dollar value for overall benefits cost is expected to increase, the amount of erroneously issued benefits is expected to decrease slightly.

Nature of Change. A comparison of overpayment error rates and erroneous benefits follows:

	FY 1992 Actual	FY 1993 Estimate	FY 1994 Estimate
Amount of erroneous benefits ($ millions)	$1,902	$1,523	$1,505
Overpayment Error rate	0.070	0.068	0.066

(2) An increase of $42,880,000 in the appropriation for State Administrative costs, including the effects of the FACT Act ($1,428,456,000 budgeted in 1993).

Need for Change. Based on the most recent economic projections, moderate rates of inflation between 1993 and 1994 are expected to increase the cost of providing food stamp benefits.

Nature of Change. This increase reflects the application of a projected rate of inflation of 2.6 percent to the Fiscal Year 1993 base level for costs shared by State and local agencies and the Federal Government. The requested increase also provides an additional $12 million for incentive payments to States and includes additional funds to States for State level anti-trafficking efforts.

(3) An increase of $2,223,000 in the appropriation for the Employment and Training Program ($160,520,000 available in 1993).

Need for Change. The increase is necessary to provide matching funds for participant reimbursements and State administrative costs to carry out the Employment and Training Program.

Nature of Change. Public Law 99-195 mandates the Secretary to allocate funds among the States to carry out the Employment and Training Program. This level of funding will enable the Department to provide States $75 million authorized for 100 percent federally-funded grants, additional matching funds for participant reimbursements and matching funds for additional State administrative costs to assist them in providing employment and training services.

(4) A net increase of $11,291,000 in the appropriation for Other Program Costs, including the effects of the FACT Act ($95,254,000 budgeted in Fiscal Year 1993). On the basis of available funds, an increase of $12,421,000 ($94,124,000 available in 1993).

Need for Change. Increases in other program costs are primarily attributed to increases associated with higher program benefit payments and the rates of inflation projected between 1993 and 1994, increased emphasis on program integrity and the need for settlement and reconciliation services to support large scale Electronic Benefit Transfer (EBT) systems.

Nature of Change.

(a) Food Stamp Production and Redemption:

An increase of $327,000 in the appropriation for printing of stamps ($45,187,000 appropriated in Fiscal Year 1993). Increased benefit costs in Fiscal Year 1993 resulted in the need for additional printing funds in Fiscal Year 1993. This projection is based on current production costs. An increase of $103,000 in the appropriation for shipping of stamps ($5,160,000 budgeted in Fiscal Year 1993).

An increase of $10,366,000 in the appropriation for the processing of redeemed stamps ($22,719,000 budgeted in Fiscal Year 1993). The FY 1994 amount includes $10.0 million to be used to develop an adequate settlement and reconciliation services system to support the growing Electronic Benefit Transfer (EBT) operation. The specifications for an EBT settlement and reconciliation service are currently being developed. The current EBT funding mechanisms - Letters of Credit - do not accommodate EBT-type transactions, nor do they provide for easy reconciliation of benefits issued and redeemed. It is hoped that the settlement and reconciliation services will eliminate these problems.

Currently, five States have operational EBT systems and 26 others are either planning or developing systems. The April 1, 1992 EBT regulations state that FNS the Treasury Department, and the Department of Health and Human Services recognize that the current Federal settlement process needs improvement to be able to support large scale EBT. FNS regional offices now reconcile site settlement data with the Federal settlement data. EBT expansion will place a severe strain on these offices. FNS is currently developing specifications for these settlement and reconciliation services to be implemented in Fiscal Year 1994.

(b) An increase of $39,000 for the cost of computer support systems ($1,457,000 budgeted in Fiscal Year 1993). The projected need for Fiscal Year 1994 includes funding for the Integrated Quality Control Project, the Disqualified Recipient System, and other program systems.

(c) An increase of $80,000 in the appropriation for the cost of certification of Supplemental Security Income recipients for Food Stamps ($4,000,000 budgeted in Fiscal Year 1993).

(d) An increase of $40,000 in the appropriation for the cost of the retailer redemption and monitoring system ($2,000,000 budgeted in Fiscal Year 1993). These funds are used to cover the printing and distribution cost of the redemption certificates used by retail stores in order to redeem their food stamps through the banking system.

(e) An increase of $30,000 in the appropriation for recipient and cooperative services ($1,071,000 budgeted in Fiscal Year 1993). The $1,101,000 projected ned for Fiscal Year 1994 includes $514,000 for printing other than stamps, $369,000 for the State Exchange Project and $218,000 for Food Stamp Program litigation costs and collection of claims.

(f) An increase of $286,000 in the appropriation for research, evaluation and demonstration projects ($10,600,000 budgeted in Fiscal Year 1993). These funds support FNS' research agenda in several areas including welfare reform, coordination and simplifications, evaluation of program effectiveness operations and integrity, and nutrition education and monitoring.

(g) An increase of $9,000 in the appropriation for retailer integrity ($1,950,000 budgeted in Fiscal Year 1993). This increase would continue the retailer data base update. The funds also support twelve (12) staff years and associated costs for retailer compliance. These staff are used for:

- o pre-authorization visits to high risk/marginal stores in urban areas;
- o reviewing data from various "high-risk" profiles and conducting preliminary inquiries prior to referring cases for investigation; and
- o coordinating with State regulatory and investigative offices to increase (a) information sharing, (b) store investigations, (c) recipient trafficking investigations, and (d) prosecutions under State law.

(h) A decrease of $3,000 in the appropriation for the EBT project authorized by the Fiscal Year 1993 Appropriations Act ($610,000 budgeted in 1993). This decrease is the result of presidential administrative cost cutting initiatives.

(i) An increase of $14,000 in the appropriation for the Nutrition Education Initiative ($500,000 budgeted in Fiscal Year 1993). These grants will develop creative approaches to providing nutrition education by enhancing food stamp participant's abilities and skills in meal planning, budgeting food money, and purchasing and preparing foods.

(5) An increase of $2,500,000 in the appropriation for Benefit Reserve ($2,500,000,000 appropriated in Fiscal Year 1993).

Need for Change. This increase will provide a total reserve of $5.0 billion to be used if economic or other circumstances cause an unforeseen increase in required program payments.

Nature of Change. The additional $2,500,000,000 will ensure the availability of sufficient funds and avoid the need for supplemental appropriations or benefit reductions if actual benefit requirements exceed preliminary budget estimates.

(6) A decrease of $1,000,000 for the collection for State error liabilities.

Food Stamp Program
Summary of Investment Proposals

SUMMARY OF INCREASES AND DECREASES - INVESTMENT PROPOSAL

	1994		
	Base Request	Investment Proposal	Total Request
Benefits	$22,805,031,000	+$603,000,000	$23,408,031,000
State Admin. Costs.......	1,471,336,000	---	1,471,336,000
Employment and Training....	162,743,000		162,743,000
Other Program Costs.......	106,545,000		106,545,000
Contingency Reserve.....	5,000,000,000	--	5,000,000,000
Total, Available..	29,545,655,000	+603,000,000	30,148,655,000

Explanation of Investment Proposal

The additional $603 million will provide increased benefits, in part, to offset increased costs associated with the Administration's proposed new energy tax.

Proposed Language

In addition to funding already provided, $603,000,000 for necessary expenses of the Food Stamp Program.

Food Stamp Program
Summary of Proposed Legislation
(Dollars in Thousands)

Summary of Increases and Decreases - Proposed Legislation

Reduce Enhanced Administrative match Rates to 50 Percent: This proposal reduces to 50 percent the administrative match rates in three program areas that are currently matched at higher rates: Automated Data Processing development (from 63 percent); intentional Program violation investigations, prosecutions, and administrative disqualification hearings (from 75 percent); and verification of the documented alien status of applicants through the Systematic Alien Verification for Entitlements system (from 100 percent). The change in match rates would be effective on April 1, 1994. The proposal is estimated to save $20 million in Fiscal Year 1994 and $40 million in Fiscal Years 1995 through 1998.

FOOD STAMP PROGRAM

STATUS OF PROGRAM

The Food Stamp Program (FSP) supplements the food purchasing power of low-income households by issuing coupons redeemable for food at authorized retail stores. In addition to benefit costs, the Food Stamp appropriation provides for State administrative costs, and other program costs such as printing and distribution of food stamps and funds for grants to States for Employment and Training Program activities.

Fiscal Year 1992 saw the continuation of major efforts to improve the management of the Food Stamp Program. Attention remained focused on reducing Federal costs through improving program management and decreasing the instances of error, fraud, and abuse in the program while continuing to respond to the needs of low-income persons, in terms of both benefits and service. These program management improvements were the product of numerous administrative actions taken by the Food and Nutrition Service (FNS). Increased emphasis was also placed on Electronic Benefit Transfer (EBT), the Employment and Training Program to assist food stamp recipients to become more independent, and efforts to conform program requirements to those of programs with similar participants. Finally, significant activity resulted from FNS' operation of emergency disaster Food Stamp programs in six disaster-affected areas.

Program Participation

Participation during Fiscal Year 1992 averaged 25.4 million persons per month. Total benefit costs for Fiscal Year 1992 were $20.9 billion for an average monthly benefit of $68.57 per person. In Fiscal Year 1991, monthly participation averaged 22.629 million persons and monthly benefits averaged $63.89 per person. Monthly unemployment averaged 6.5 percent in Fiscal Year 1991 and 7.3 percent in Fiscal Year 1992.

Food Stamp participation data for Fiscal Year 1992 indicates that program activity increased significantly for the third consecutive year. Average monthly participation grew by 2.8 million persons, 12.3 percent above Fiscal Year 1991. Average participation has risen by 6.6 million persons or 35.4 percent, in comparison to Fiscal Year 1989.

Fiscal Year 1992 growth represents the continuation of participation trends that began to emerge in the program early in the third quarter of Fiscal Year 1989. Our research attributes the start of this trend to a variety of reasons, and no single explanation predominates the others. The most important factors were the expansion of the Medicaid Program, the slackening of economic growth, and legislative and other changes intended to improve access to the program.

Characteristics of Food Stamp Households

The Food Stamp Program serves the nation's most needy households. The following information is derived from the Summer 1991 Characteristics of Food Stamp Households Report:

- The average household size is 2.6 persons.

- The average gross monthly income per food stamp household is $472 (the annual equivalent of $5,664); the average net income is $261 a month -- $3,132 a year.

- 9 percent of households have zero gross income and 20 percent have zero net income.

- 40 percent of all households have gross incomes of less than $400 per month (the annual equivalent of $4,800).

- 77 percent own no countable assets, and an additional 18 percent own no countable assets of $500 or less.

- Average countable assets per household were $74, but for households with elderly members the average was $184.

- Slightly over half (52.2 percent) of food stamp recipients are children, while 7 percent are elderly.

- Food stamp recipients who are able to work are doing so or are meeting the program's work requirements in other ways.

- 7 percent of all heads of households are employed full-time.

- 20 percent of households have earned income.

- 36 percent of non-elderly adult participants are registered for work through the Food Stamp Program or are subject to the work requirements of the Aid to Families with Dependent Children program.

Significant Regulations and Notices Issued in Fiscal Year 1992

Monthly Reporting and Retrospective Budgeting Amendments and Mass Changes - This final rule, published December 4, 1991, included provisions of P.L. 101-624, the Food, Agriculture, Conservation, and Trade Act of 1990 (the FACT Act) which gave State agencies the option to retrospectively budget households not subject to monthly reporting, added households residing on Indian reservations to the categories of households exempt from monthly reporting, and eliminated the requirement that the Secretary of Agriculture prescribe the standards for monthly report forms. In addition, the rule provided numerous technical changes to the food stamp monthly reporting and retrospective budgeting system.

Categorical Eligibility and Application Provisions of the FACT Act - This final rule, published December 4, 1991, amended food stamp regulations to implement three provisions of the FACT Act. These provisions revised requirements for the placement of certain information on the food stamp application form, required a combined food stamp and General Assistance (GA) application form in States that have a Statewide GA application form, and extended categorical eligibility to recipients of GA from certain State or local programs.

Deduction and Disaster Provisions from the FACT Act - This final rule, published December 4, 1991, provided requirements for a standard shelter expense estimate to be used in lieu of verification for homeless households with shelter costs and provided for issuance of food stamp benefits to replace food lost in disasters.

Miscellaneous Provisions of the FACT Act and Food Stamp Certification Policy - This final rule, published December 4, 1991, addressed provisions of the FACT Act which provided Supplemental Security Income (SSI) applicants or recipients with the same information at the social security office as social security applicants or recipients receive, expanded the type of group homes not considered institutions, increased the minimum benefits for one and two-person households, and clarified requirements for verification of medical expenses. The rule also implemented a provision of the Omnibus Budget Reconciliation Act of 1990 which removed the requirement for a single application for SSI and food stamps. The rule also expanded the criteria for eligibility of aliens to include certain elderly or disabled aliens admitted under temporary status and clarified which payments received under the Job Training Partnership Act would be counted as income for food stamp purposes.

Income Exemption for Homeless Households in Transitional Housing - This proposed rule, published February 3, 1992, addressed provisions of the FACT Act which would allow an income exclusion for households living in transitional housing. The exclusion would be equal to half of the maximum shelter allowance provided under an Aid to Families with Dependent Children State plan with a shelter component to families living in permanent housing.

Food Stamp Allotment, Income Eligibility Standards, and Deduction Updates - On August 26, 1992, the Department announced that maximum food stamp allotments for the 48 States, the District of Columbia, Guam, and the Virgin Islands would be held steady at their Fiscal Year 1992 levels. The maximum allotments for these areas were scheduled to drop as a result of the decrease in the cost of the June 1992 Thrifty Food Plan (TFP). However, P.L. 102-351, enacted August 26, 1992, amended the Food Stamp Act to prohibit a reduction in the maximum allotments based on the lower cost of the TFP for June 1992. Because of this amendment, the maximum monthly allotment for a four-person household in the 48 States and the District of Columbia (D.C.) remains $370. The maximum monthly allotment for a four-person household in Guam remains $546, and in the Virgin Islands it remains $476. The maximum monthly allotments for Hawaii and Alaska did increase, however. The maximum allotment for a family of four in Hawaii increased by $3 to $609. The maximum allotment for a family of four increased by $2 to $477 in Urban Alaska, by $2 to $608 in Rural I Alaska, and by $4 to $741 in Rural II Alaska. The new levels were announced by the Department on August 19, 1992.

The Department announced the new income eligibility standards and the deduction updates for the 48 States and D.C., Alaska, Hawaii, Guam, and the Virgin Islands on August 3, 1992. The income eligibility standards were based on the income poverty guidelines published by the Department of Health and Human Services. The net income eligibility standard for the 48 States and D.C. increased from $1,117 a month to $1,163, and the gross income eligibility standard increased from $1,452 to $1,512. The standard and shelter deduction increases were based on certain changes in the Consumer Price Index for All Urban Consumers. The standard deduction increased from $122 to $127. The maximum amount for the excess shelter deduction increased from $194 to $200. The homeless household shelter deduction increased from $128 to $132.

Standards for Approval and Operation of Food Stamp Electronic Benefit Transfer Systems - This Electronic Benefit Transfer (EBT) proposed rule was published December 13, 1991 and the final rule was published April 1, 1992. The rule allows on-line EBT as an operational alternative, requires cost neutrality relative to the State agency's paper issuance costs, requires currently-operating demonstration projects to conform to the regulatory requirements within a two-year period, and provides the procedures and standards to be followed for an on-line system. In addition to six demonstration sites, 20 other States have expressed interest in, or begun the process of obtaining approval for, operational EBT.

Hunger Prevention Act of 1988 Provisions for Good Cause Relief From Quality Control Error Rate Liabilities - On September 28, 1992, a final rule was published which implemented portions of the Hunger Prevention Act of 1988 pertaining to good cause relief from quality control claims against State agencies. The rule: 1) excludes errors caused by incorrect Federal policy guidance as a basis for good cause relief since a rule published in Fiscal Year 1991 excluded such errors from the calculation of error rates; 2) provides that if a good cause request is insufficient, the Secretary will use a formula similar to one used in the past to determine waiver amounts; 3) provides for further adjustments in the good cause waiver amount based on a State's recent error rate history; and 4) requires that the Secretary's determination be final and not subject to appeal.

318-54

Food Stamp Program: Quality Control Claims Adjustments for State Agency Investments - On January 24, 1992, this final rule was published to provide a settlement tool by which States can invest money that would otherwise be paid to FNS for a quality control liability into program management activities that are intended to improve payment accuracy.

Information on Persons Disqualified from the Food Stamp Program - On January 3, 1992, the Department issued a notice announcing FNS' plans to implement a USDA-maintained, limited access nationwide data bank of information on individuals who have been disqualified from participation in the Food Stamp Program. The data base will be composed only of data supplied by State agencies. Utilizing new software, this data base is the successor to an older data base of information on disqualified individuals. FNS will maintain this information and will make it available to the various State agencies administering the Food Stamp Program for program enforcement purposes.

Food Stamp Quality Control Review Handbook (FNS 310)

The Quality Control Review Handbook (FNS 310) was revised to reflect changes in the Food Stamp Program certification regulations, to respond to requests for clarification and expansions, and to incorporate State agency suggestions for streamlining review procedures.

Waivers

In Fiscal Year 1992, requests for waivers of regulatory provisions continued at a high rate. Of the 183 requests for waivers, FNS approved 143 and denied 40. Waivers were primarily designed to reduce the workload of eligibility workers, including waivers to use telephone interviews, extend certification periods, simplify recertification procedures, use standard amounts for certain self-employment expenses, extend the time limit for action on computer matches, and modify recipient claims requirements.

Disasters

During Fiscal Year 1992, FNS operated the emergency disaster Food Stamp Program in six disaster-affected areas: Los Angeles, California following civil unrest; Dade County, Florida following the destruction of Hurricane Andrew; Iberia and St. Mary Parish and portions of Assumption, St. Martin and Terrebone Parishes, Louisiana which were also damaged by Hurricane Andrew; Shasta County, California following forest fires; Guam after it was struck by Typhoon Omar; and Kauai, Hawaii following Hurricane Iniki. Participation and cost totals for the disasters are:

FOOD STAMP PROGRAM DISASTER ASSISTANCE

State	Households	Benefits
California (Los Angeles)	20,214	$ 4,094,961
Florida	206,735	72,724,656
Louisiana	108,400	26,139,264
California (Shasta County)	70	13,625
Guam	21,460	12,226,855
Hawaii	9,712	4,218,973
TOTAL	366,591	$119,418,334

P.L. 102-368 enacted in September 1992 appropriated an additional $400 million in benefits for disaster issuance in Fiscal Years 1992 and 1993.

Court Suit Activity in the Food Stamp Program

During Fiscal Year 1992, 46 court suits were filed against the Food Stamp Program. Twelve of these court suits were filed against USDA. There are presently 166 active cases, excluding quality control (QC) and retail/wholesale suits. Major issues involved in litigation during the year were the treatment of HUD utility payments as income, failure of State agencies to process applications in a timely manner and late payment interest charges.

Litigation continues regarding the quality control system and the resultant liabilities. The only case pending as of Fiscal Year 1992 is against the State of Massachusetts in the amount of $1,323,864.

In April 1992, the United States District Court, District of Massachusetts, entered an order awarding FNS the full amount of the billing. This Federal court decision is the first judicial review of QC sampling by FNS and the first to confirm the sampling methodology. Although the case focused upon the sampling system used by FNS in Fiscal Year 1982, a substantially similar sampling system has been adopted to implement the provisions of the Hunger Prevention Act of 1988 for Fiscal Year 1986 and subsequent years. Massachusetts has appealed this decision to the United States Court of Appeals for the First District and the case is currently pending oral arguments.

Program Management Improvement Initiatives

The Food Stamp Program continued the joint Federal-State effort begun in 1983 to reduce errors and fraud and to increase program efficiency.

The focus of the effort is to coordinate the exchange of information among States and provide technical assistance. In Fiscal Year 1992, the following efforts were pursued in support of local level management improvement initiatives:

FNS supported a broad range of initiatives by its regional offices and State cooperating agencies. These initiatives included conferences sponsored by FNS and State agencies on topics in the areas of payment accuracy, Electronic Benefit Transfer (EBT) and corrective action. In addition, the national and regional office staff participated in a number of public interest group meetings.

In Fiscal Year 1992, FNS continued to place emphasis on the need for States to make food stamp payment accuracy a high priority. FNS actively supported State efforts towards this goal. This support included encouraging States to share resources by forming joint partnerships with other State and local agencies. States effectively shared common problems and approaches to improving payment accuracy through these partnerships. FNS also provided technical assistance to State and local offices. This assistance included the publication of TARGET, a catalog of practices aimed at improving program management and payment accuracy.

Helping States fund payment accuracy efforts was also emphasized in Fiscal Year 1992. FNS' efforts included continuing to provide enhanced administrative funding to States who met specific error rate goals. For Fiscal Year 1992, this meant a total of $9,422,364 in enhanced administrative funding was provided to five States - Alabama, Kentucky, North Dakota, South Dakota and Hawaii. Also, in January 1992, FNS published the Investment rule. This rule provides additional avenues for States to fund payment accuracy efforts. Under the provisions of this rule, funds that would have been paid to FNS to resolve QC claims liabilities can be invested in State program management activities that are intended to improve payment accuracy. No State has yet agreed to participate in the investment option.

The State Exchange Project, an important component of the management improvement initiative, is based on the premise that State and local agencies can often best solve their problems by sharing in the experience of other State and local agencies.

State Exchange funding was first provid... in 1983 to reimburse State agency officials for the cost of visiting anoth... State agency with known expertise in a particular area. In Fiscal Year 1992, $329,000 in State Exchange funding was allocated for State agencies.

Food Stamp Program staff continued to work with the Administration for Children and Families and the American Public Welfare Association to develop recommendations for achieving greater consistency between the requirements of the Aid to Families with Dependent Children program and food stamps. FNS also continued the Concerned Partners effort initiated in March 1991 to assist State agencies in coping with increased caseloads.

Demonstration Projects Using Electronic Benefit Transfer (EBT) Technology

Under the April 1, 1992 final EBT Regulation, currently operating on-line demonstration projects must conform to this regulation within a two-year period. There are four on-line demonstration projects: Reading, Pennsylvania; Albuquerque, New Mexico; Ramsey County, Minnesota; and Maryland. Maryland has been approved to expand Statewide and will be fully expanded by the end of April 1993. As the first Statewide system, it is the subject of an extensive evaluation. The final evaluation report is expected in May 1994.

Although New Jersey was approved as a demonstration project before the final regulation was published, it will have to conform to the EBT regulation. Iowa was approved as a demonstration project and will remain a demonstration project to test voluntary participation of clients and assignment, rather than client selection, of Personal Identification Numbers.

A "smart card" or off-line demonstration project is operating in Dayton, Ohio. This project is not affected by the final EBT regulation, which only applies to on-line systems. This project was fully implemented in June 1992 and will operate until March 1, 1993. Wyoming has a small "smart card" project for the Special Supplemental Food Program for Women, Infants and Children in Casper. The State has been granted approval to include food stamps in this off-line project.

Massachusetts Quarterly Demonstration Project

In 1992, the Department approved this project which allows Massachusetts to issue food stamp benefits Statewide on a quarterly basis to SSI elderly and disabled recipients who receive $10.00 in monthly food stamp benefits. Project operations began in July 1992 and will end in July 1995.

Welfare Simplification and Coordination Advisory Committee

In March 1992, the Secretary appointed 11 people to serve on a new committee that will study ways to simplify and coordinate the efforts of the Federal government's welfare programs. The Committee is chaired by the former Commissioner of the Tennessee Department of Human Services, and brings together experts in the field of public assistance programs.

The Committee is authorized by the FACT Act which requires the submission of a report to Congress by July 1, 1993. The Committee's mission is to examine the policies and procedures of the Food Stamp, Aid to Families with Dependent Children, medical assistance, and housing programs, and identify those barriers that make it difficult to apply for and obtain benefits from more than one program. The Committee's report must also include recommendations for simplifying and coordinating the various programs to remove these barriers.

Collection of Claims Against Recipients

State agencies are required to establish claims against households which receive more benefits than they are entitled to receive. Two categories of claims cover household failure to report information about their circumstances. These categories are intentional program violation (IPV) and inadvertent household error claims. A third category of claims covers State agency administrative errors. As an incentive for collecting claims, State agencies can retain 25 percent of collections of IPV Claims and 10 percent of collections of inadvertent household error claims. In Fiscal Year 1991, State agencies collected $94 million in recipient claims.

In Fiscal Year 1991, the Department initiated a test of collecting IPV and inadvertent household error claims from Federal income tax refunds. The first collections were made during Calendar Year 1992. Including voluntary payments, collections total about $3.5 million. In its first year, this test involved two States, Alabama and California. Seven States will be added in 1993.

Error Rate Liability System and Enhanced Funding

For Fiscal Year 1991, the combined payment error rate, which combines overpayments and underpayments, was 9.31 percent. The combined payment error rate was 9.80 percent in Fiscal Year 1990.

During Fiscal Year 1991, five State agencies qualified for approximately $9.4 million in enhanced funding made available by statute because they achieved low error rates.

The Hunger Prevention Act of 1988 affected the Food Stamp Program's quality control system. Among the provisions contained in the Act are revisions in the definition of payment error, changes in error rate tolerances, and changes in the method used to calculate the claims against States that exceed error rate tolerances. The legislation made these changes retroactive to Fiscal Year 1986.

To establish a State's liability using methods currently available, FNS has developed error rate estimates, tolerances and claims for each of the States for Fiscal Years 1986 through 1991. From these estimates, fourteen States will face claims totalling $45.8 million for Fiscal Year 1986, ten States and $42.6 million for Fiscal Year 1987, eight States and $34.8 million for Fiscal Year 1988, eight States and $56.4 million for Fiscal Year 1989, eleven States and $64.7 million for Fiscal Year 1990, and eleven States will face claims totalling $56.0 million for FY 1991.

Employment and Training Program

The Food Security Act of 1985, P.L. 99-198, required all State agencies to establish an Employment and Training (E&T) Program for food stamp work registrants and other recipients who volunteer to participate.

The intent of the E&T Program, as stated in the legislation is to "assist members of households participating in the Food Stamp Program in gaining skills, training or experience that will increase their ability to obtain regular employment." The E&T Program began on April 1, 1987.

There are three categories of Federal funding. In Fiscal Year 1991, the following amounts were spent in each category: (1) State agencies spent $72.68 million of the $75 million allotted in 100 percent federally funded grants; 2) $49.96 million in Federal funding was spent to match additional administrative costs incurred by the States; and 3) $16.09 million was the Federal share of the cost of reimbursing participants for transportation and dependent care expenses incurred in fulfilling their E&T obligations. In Fiscal Year 1992, State agencies planned to spend $75 million in 100 percent federal funding, $62.25 million in Federal funds for additional administrative costs, and $22.25 million in participant reimbursements for transportation and dependent care. In Fiscal Year 1992, State agencies counted 1,453,369 (annualized) mandatory placements into E&T components, and sent 466,646 (annualized) Notices of Adverse Action to individuals who failed to comply with the requirements. State agencies plan to make 1,260,647 million mandatory placements in Fiscal Year 1993 and expect to send 431,231 Notices of Adverse Action.

Optional Workfare

Optional workfare programs, which operate separately from Employment and Training programs, require able-bodied recipients to perform work in public service jobs for their food stamp allotments. In Fiscal Year 1992, 12 communities were operating Optional Workfare Programs.

E&T/JOBS Conformance Demonstration Projects

On March 27, 1992, FNS published a Notice announcing its intention to conduct a project to demonstrate the effectiveness of conforming the Food Stamp Employment and Training (E&T) Program and the AFDC Job Opportunities and Basic Skills (JOBS) Program.

The FACT Act authorized the Secretary of Agriculture to waive the employment and training requirements of the Food Stamp Act to permit up to 60 project participants to operate their E&T programs on the same terms and conditions under which they operate their JOBS programs. The Fiscal Year 1992 Budget provided $3,000,000 to support the demonstrations and evaluations over the life of the project.

A Technical Review Panel, composed of representatives from USDA and DHHS, was established to evaluato the technical merit of each of the 16 proposals submitted--based on criteria established in the Notice--and recommend a competitive range for proposals to the FNS Board of Awards.

FNS selected five agencies to participate in the E&T/JOBS Conformance demonstration project. Cooperative agreements were negotiated with:

1. Georgia Department of Human Services
2. Hawaii Department of Human Services
3. Missouri Department of Social Services
4. South Dakota Department of Social Services
5. Texas Department of Human Services

Compliance Branch Investigative Activity

In Fiscal Year 1992, the Compliance Branch, to strengthen its efforts against retailer fraud and abuse, created a Strike Force of 12 senior investigators, to concentrate primarily on trafficking cases. During Fiscal Year 1992, with an increased emphasis on detecting trafficking, the Compliance Branch found trafficking occurring in 763 investigations, an increase of 232 (approximately 45 percent) over Fiscal Year 1991. A major initiative during Fiscal Year 1992 involved the promotion of Federal civil prosecution of Compliance Branch trafficking cases under the Federal False Claims Act. A national conference was conducted by the Compliance Branch in June 1992, with 46 Assistant United States Attorneys, representing 26 States, in attendance. As a result of this conference and efforts by area Compliance Branch supervisors, civil prosecutive actions were initiated in 12 U. S. District Courts on 88 Compliance Branch investigations. Forty-eight settlements totaling $255,445 have already been negotiated with violating retailers. As there are hundreds of Compliance Branch trafficking cases available for similar action in more than 60 districts, this initiative has high potential for cost savings for Fiscal Year 1993 and beyond.

A second major initiative involved an analysis of approximately 3,000 authorized firms in the FNS retailer data base on which food stamp redemptions exceeded reported sales. Nearly 1,000 of these firms were identified for investigation by the Compliance Branch and investigations were initiated during Fiscal Year 1992.

Compliance Branch investigators participated with the Department's Office of the Inspector General in criminal investigations of 66 trafficking cases during Fiscal Year 1992, and worked with State law enforcement officers in Florida and Michigan.

The Compliance Branch investigated 4,848 stores in Fiscal Year 1992. Of those stores investigated, 1,951 or 40 percent revealed violations of program regulations. Violations serious enough to warrant disqualification or civil money penalties were uncovered in 1,433 stores, or 30 percent of the total investigated. Stores with less serious violations received an official warning letter, a record of which is maintained as part of their file on program participation.

Retailer Reauthorizations

The FACT Act provided for the periodic reauthorization of all food stores participating in the Food Stamp Program. This reauthorization process includes: determining the continued eligibility of stores, as well as updating the retailer data base with information regarding store characteristics, ownership and related identifying information, sales information and key eligibility factors. This database is the primary tool used by FNS to monitor over 212,000 firms and identify potential violators for investigation. Thus, it is critical that information on stores be updated at least once every two years.

In Fiscal Year 1992, FNS made final determinations on 45 percent of the authorized firms. As a result 85,000 firms were reauthorized to participate in the Food Stamp Program and over 10,000 were withdrawn because they no longer met authorization criteria or failed to cooperate and provide information to make a determination.

FNS plans to complete this first biennial reauthorization cycle in Fiscal Year 1993 and begin a new cycle in Fiscal Year 1994.

Expedited Service Cash-Out Demonstration Projects

In 1990, the Department gave approval to Minnesota and Vermont to implement projects which provide cash benefits to households eligible for expedited service. In Minnesota, an expedited service household receives 25% of its first month benefits in cash; the remainder is in coupons. Vermont provides the full first month allotment in cash. Minnesota implemented its project in September 1990. Vermont implemented its project in July 1991.

"Welfare Reform" Demonstration Projects

The authority to conduct demonstration projects designed to test program changes that might increase the efficiency of the program and improve the delivery of food stamp benefits is limited to projects that do not restrict eligibility or reduce benefits. Exceptions can be made in the case of projects that pay the average value of allotments by household size in the form of cash.

In Fiscal Year 1992, welfare reform demonstrations involving food stamp waivers operated in Alabama, Washington, Maryland, Ohio, and New York. Additional projects in Michigan and Utah were approved in Fiscal Year 1992. All but Michigan, Ohio, and Maryland include food stamp cash-out. A separate cash-out only project continues to operate in San Diego County, California.

Pursuant to P.L. 101-202, which authorized the food stamp portion of the Minnesota Family Investment Plan, Minnesota has proposed a welfare reform demonstration project scheduled for implementation in early 1994. Project participants will receive food assistance in the form of cash, unless they request food coupons. Fiscal Year 1992 activities included reviewing the State's request for proposal and approving waivers.

318-40

Anti-Fraud Funding for State Agencies

In Fiscal Year 1992, $82.1 million was available to State agencies for anti-fraud activity. Anti-fraud funding is designed to cover not less than 75 percent of State agencies' costs in the area of investigation and prosecution of fraud cases and the collection of fraud claims. In Fiscal Year 1992, a total of 50 State agencies were approved for 75 percent enhanced funding. Of these, 36 State agencies had agreements with State or local prosecutors to facilitate the prosecution of cases and the imposition of food stamp disqualifications. During Fiscal Year 1991, the last year for which we have complete data, approximately 34,000 persons were disqualified from the program as a result of prosecutions, and 46,000 were disqualified through administrative hearings.

FOOD STAMP PROGRAM
SUMMARY OF BENEFIT COSTS, PARTICIPATION AND STATE ADMINISTRATIVE FUNDING

FISCAL YEAR 1992

STATE OR TERRITORY	AVERAGE PARTICIPATION IN THOUSANDS		BENEFIT VALUE OF STAMPS ISSUED (000)	AVERAGE MONTHLY BENEFIT PER PERSON	STATE ADMINISTRATIVE FUNDING (000)
	PERSONS	HOUSEHOLDS			
Alabama	550	208	450,883	$68.35	27,976
Alaska	38	12	41,045	90.70	5,868
Arizona	457	166	376,880	68.71	17,630
Arkansas	277	102	207,030	62.34	13,830
California	2,558	958	1,758,937	57.31	200,744
Colorado	260	102	218,640	70.16	10,795
Connecticut	202	86	131,367	54.12	14,272
Delaware	51	19	41,994	69.13	3,580
District of Columbia	82	38	70,025	70.93	7,816
Florida	1,404	553	1,306,395	77.54	52,284
Georgia	751	288	626,951	69.57	46,194
Hawaii	94	39	121,647	107.54	7,896
Idaho	72	26	53,295	61.79	4,364
Illinois	1,156	488	1,069,844	77.10	53,932
Indiana	448	160	372,898	69.42	16,055
Iowa	192	76	143,338	62.12	8,412
Kansas	175	68	132,745	63.39	7,240
Kentucky	529	197	430,470	67.83	27,136
Louisiana	779	278	665,586	71.20	30,882
Maine	133	58	108,725	68.38	5,807
Maryland	343	147	312,253	75.82	15,438
Massachusetts	429	183	315,407	61.30	16,183
Michigan	994	405	845,987	70.91	41,336
Minnesota	309	128	234,150	63.17	16,157
Mississippi	536	196	421,357	65.52	18,236
Missouri	549	214	447,078	67.80	22,983
Montana	66	25	52,144	65.55	5,183
Nebraska	107	43	77,834	60.42	5,723
Nevada	80	36	74,281	77.63	5,635
New Hampshire	58	25	45,489	65.69	2,873
New Jersey	495	201	433,227	72.99	46,764
New Mexico	221	77	181,834	68.47	10,777
New York	1,885	855	1,586,192	70.12	134,271
North Carolina	597	236	461,178	64.40	30,689
North Dakota	46	18	34,934	63.47	3,250
Ohio	1,251	529	1,102,489	73.46	52,706
Oklahoma	346	135	275,900	66.51	19,285
Oregon	265	114	226,394	71.23	15,670
Pennsylvania	1,137	495	915,577	67.08	80,665
Rhode Island	87	38	68,999	65.79	5,214
South Carolina	369	133	297,034	67.11	18,455
South Dakota	55	19	41,981	63.98	3,875
Tennessee	702	280	561,752	66.69	32,156
Texas	2,454	891	2,103,306	71.43	118,583
Utah	123	44	95,517	64.61	9,905
Vermont	54	23	36,758	57.22	3,642
Virginia	495	206	406,058	68.30	36,143
Washington	432	178	343,741	66.37	22,266
West Virginia	310	117	254,982	68.63	6,325
Wisconsin	334	123	235,671	58.80	22,138
Wyoming	33	12	26,416	65.84	2,745
American Samoa	0	0	0	.00	0
Freely Associated States	0	0	0	.00	0
Guam	20	5	28,230	118.78	965
N. Mariana Islands	0	0	0	.00	0
Puerto Rico	0	0	0	.00	0
Virgin Islands	16	5	18,517	93.62	2,244
Anticipated Adjustment	0	0	0	.00	-53,606
TOTAL	25,404	10,059	$20,891,360	$68.53	$1,337,590

NOTE: These data are based in part on preliminary data submitted by State and local agencies subject to change as revised reports are received, and may differ from budgetary information appearing elsewhere in these notes. Totals may not add due to rounding.

31g-42

FOOD STAMP PROGRAM
FIRMS AUTHORIZED TO RECEIVE AND REDEEM FOOD STAMPS

Fiscal Year 1992

STATE OR TERRITORY	RETAILERS	WHOLE-SALERS	MEALS/ WHEELS	COMM DINE	ALCOHOL, DRG TREAT & COMB TREAT	PRIVATE REST	GROUP LIV	HOMELESS MEAL/ BATTERED WOMEN & CHILDREN	TOTAL
Alabama	5,455	6	1	28	9	0	2	1	5,502
Alaska	525	2	4	4	2	0	0	0	537
Arizona	2,190	11	21	29	10	0	0	2	2,263
Arkansas	2,987	4	8	37	6	1	0	0	3,043
California	16,460	45	5	16	112	0	2	5	16,645
Colorado	1,865	6	26	25	8	0	0	5	1,935
Connecticut	1,707	7	13	8	10	0	0	0	1,745
Delaware	509	0	4	4	1	0	0	0	518
District of Columbia	580	0	4	2	2	0	0	0	588
Florida	11,254	28	30	74	39	4	15	7	11,451
Georgia	6,950	3	12	74	4	0	0	6	7,049
Hawaii	1,076	11	2	4	9	19	0	0	1,121
Idaho	788	0	10	13	0	0	1	1	813
Illinois	7,061	17	57	61	11	0	0	11	7,218
Indiana	3,199	6	27	15	1	2	1	2	3,253
Iowa	1,966	1	24	12	0	0	0	1	2,004
Kansas	1,576	4	10	15	12	0	0	1	1,618
Kentucky	5,521	4	3	8	1	0	0	0	5,537
Louisiana	6,326	21	17	43	3	0	1	8	6,419
Maine	2,033	4	12	40	6	1	4	1	2,101
Maryland	3,374	15	19	19	17	0	2	2	3,448
Massachusetts	4,091	7	34	12	20	13	1	0	4,178
Michigan	8,104	7	17	54	10	1	0	0	8,193
Minnesota	3,220	6	62	27	6	1	0	3	3,325
Mississippi	4,833	1	7	11	0	0	0	0	4,852
Missouri	3,920	0	26	70	0	0	0	3	4,019
Montana	839	0	6	25	0	0	0	0	870
Nebraska	1,039	1	1	5	1	0	0	0	1,047
Nevada	550	7	2	11	4	0	0	2	576
New Hampshire	858	3	5	5	3	0	1	0	875
New Jersey	5,267	16	45	33	18	0	4	0	5,383
New Mexico	1,255	1	11	14	1	0	0	0	1,282
New York	14,265	21	85	141	65	108	4	7	14,696
North Carolina	7,456	4	43	75	10	0	1	3	7,592
North Dakota	630	1	39	41	0	0	1	2	714
Ohio	7,537	5	50	65	9	1	0	1	7,668
Oklahoma	3,176	12	9	25	6	0	0	0	3,228
Oregon	2,492	2	15	19	8	2	0	5	2,543
Pennsylvania	10,778	25	115	89	41	1	1	9	11,059
Rhode Island	834	3	3	5	3	0	1	0	849
South Carolina	4,619	3	12	55	7	0	0	2	4,698
South Dakota	669	0	7	16	0	1	0	0	693
Tennessee	5,840	11	15	28	13	0	4	4	5,915
Texas	15,931	33	17	60	26	0	6	16	16,089
Utah	852	7	7	9	12	0	0	2	889
Vermont	778	3	6	1	2	0	0	0	790
Virginia	5,805	9	13	35	14	0	0	1	5,877
Washington	3,351	3	26	41	3	0	0	3	3,427
West Virginia	2,849	0	20	45	0	0	0	2	2,916
Wisconsin	2,838	5	20	30	0	2	0	3	2,898
Wyoming	339	0	3	1	0	1	0	1	345
Guam	211	1	0	0	0	0	0	0	212
Virgin Islands	189	0	1	2	0	0	0	0	192
TOTAL	208,817	392	1,031	1,581	545	158	52	122	212,698

SUMMARY OF QC LIABILITIES AND ENHANCED FUNDING

QC PERIOD	NAT'L GOAL/ TOLERANCE (%)	ENHANCED FUNDING NUMBER OF STATES	ENHANCED FUNDING AMOUNT AWARDED	LIABILITY NUMBER OF STATES	TOTAL INITIAL LIABILITIES	QC COLLECTIONS	OUTSTANDING AND POTENTIAL LIABILITIES
Oct 1980 - Mar 1981	12.60	7	$ 1,406,436	14	$ 16,709,031	$0	$0
Apr 1981 - Sept 1981	12.60	8	$ 5,288,070	12	$ 12,256,197	$1,372,228	$0
Oct 1981 - Mar 1982	13.05	6	$ 2,488,142	12	$ 9,072,985	$1,574,522.56	$0
Apr 1982 - Sept 1982	13.05	7	$ 2,700,139	9	$ 6,811,989	$0	$1,323,864 **
FY 1983	9.00*	1	$ 383,252	12	$ 12,628,093	$1,058,131.20	$0 ***
FY 1984	7.00*	2	$ 744,601	36	$ 81,350,280	$ 558,503	$0 ***
FY 1985	5.00*	3	$ 1,108,245	48	$201,168,802	$ 299,390	$0 ***
FY 1986	11.39	3	$ 1,175,006	14	$ 45,848,754	$0	$ 45,848,754 ****
FY 1987	11.27	4	$ 2,173,455	10	$ 42,592,970	$0	$ 42,592,970 ****
FY 1988	10.97	2	$ 985,962	8	$ 34,775,467	$0	$ 34,775,467 ****
FY 1989	10.80	7	$ 7,150,142	8	$ 56,428,400	$0	$ 56,428,400 ****
FY 1990	10.80	5	$ 6,936,616	11	$ 64,727,769	$0	$ 64,727,769 ****
FY 1991	10.31	5	$ 9,422,364	11	$ 55,953,052	$0	$ 55,953,052 ****
TOTALS			$41,962,430		$640,323,789	$4,862,774.76	$301,650,276

* Excludes underissuance error rates.

** Outstanding liability. State agency has been billed; pending a decision from the U.S. Court of Appeals.

*** Enactment of the 1990 Farm Bill eliminated all remaining outstanding balances for Fiscal Years 1983 through 1985.

**** A tentative settlement for Fiscal Years 1986-1991 was reached with State agencies on January 19, 1993. Under the agreement, State agencies would invest 15% of their total liability amounts in program operational improvements specifically intended to reduce errors measured by the Quality Control System; the remainder of the liability would be waived.

THE FOOD AND NUTRITION SERVICE

The estimates include appropriation language for this item as follows (new language underscored; deleted matter enclosed in brackets):

Nutrition Assistance for Puerto Rico:

For necessary expenses for the Commonwealth of Puerto Rico for nutrition assistance as authorized by 7 U.S.C. 2028, $1,091,000,000.

This change provides a separate appropriation for Nutrition Assistance for Puerto Rico. Comparable language was deleted from the appropriation for the Food Stamp Program.

NUTRITION ASSISTANCE FOR PUERTO RICO

Appropriations Act, 1993	$ 1,051,000,000
Budget Estimate, 1994	1,091,000,000
Increase in Appropriations..............................	+40,000,000

SUMMARY OF INCREASES AND DECREASES
(On basis of appropriation)

Item of Change	1993 Estimated	Other Changes	1994 Estimated
Nutrition Assistance for Puerto Rico.......	$1,051,000,000	+$40,000,000	$1,091,000,000

PROJECT STATEMENT
(On basis of adjusted appropriation)

Project	1992 Actual	1993 Estimated	Increase or Decrease	1994 Estimated
Nutrition Assistance for Puerto Rico...	$1,013,000,000	$1,051,000,000	+$40,000,000	$1,091,000,000

EXPLANATION OF PROGRAM

Overview of Program Development. Authorized by section 116(a) of the Omnibus Budget Reconciliation Act of 1981 (P.L. 97-35), a grant for nutrition assistance to Puerto Rico was implemented July 1, 1982. The Food, Agriculture, Conservation and Trade Act of 1990 (FACT), P.L. 101-624, enacted November 28, 1990, reauthorized appropriations through Fiscal Year 1995.

Eligibility. This grant, which replaced the Food Stamp Program in Puerto Rico, gives the Commonwealth broad flexibility to establish a food assistance program that is specifically tailored to the needs of its low-income households. In Fiscal Year 1994, Puerto Rico will continue its system of providing cash benefits to households which meet eligibility standards of the Nutrition Assistance Program. These eligibility standards are similar to those of the Food Stamp Program.

Benefits. In addition to the provision of direct benefits to the needy, a portion of the grant may be used to fund up to 50 percent of the costs of administering the program.

State/Federal Responsibilities. The Commonwealth must submit its annual plan of operation to the Secretary for approval. The Food and Nutrition Service provides a grant award to the Commonwealth to operate the Program in accordance with its approved plan. The grant is intended to cover 100 percent of the cost of program benefits, 50 percent of the cost of administrative expenses and support for approved special projects up to the limit of the amount available by appropriation.

JUSTIFICATION OF INCREASES AND DECREASES

An increase of 40,000,000 in the appropriation for Nutrition Assistance for Puerto Rico ($1,051,000,000 available in 1993).

Need for change. This request reflects the authorization level provided in the FACT Act.

Nature of change. This level will permit the continuation of the Nutrition Assistance Program in a manner consistent with prior years.

NUTRITION ASSISTANCE FOR PUERTO RICO

STATUS OF PROGRAM

As required by P.L. 97-35, the Omnibus Budget Reconciliation Act of 1981, the Food Stamp Program in the Commonwealth of Puerto Rico was replaced with a block grant effective July 1, 1982.

For Fiscal Year 1992, $1.002 billion in grant funds were provided to Puerto Rico. The Nutrition Assistance Program served an average of 1.48 million persons per month. Total benefit costs are estimated at $971 million, or about $54.76 per person per month. Administrative costs are estimated at $29,614 million, or $7.67 per person, for a total federal program cost per person of $56.43 per person per month. One special project, tick eradication, was budgeted at a cost of $10.825 million. Congress mandated that $10.825 million be transferred to the Animal and Plant Health Inspection Service for use by Puerto Rico in operating this program in Fiscal Year 1992. The objective of the Tick Eradication Project is to carry out appropriate treatment and control activities directed toward the enhancement of livestock productivity through the island-wide eradication of ticks. The Commonwealth is also operating a Special Wage Incentive Program, budgeted at $20 million of the Federal grant for Fiscal Year 1993, which provides wage subsidies to employers hiring Nutrition Assistance Program recipients.

<u>Selected Examples of Recent Progress</u>:

Puerto Rico submits its proposed annual budget plan in July for the fiscal year beginning on the following October 1. That plan identifies the costs of benefits, administration and other projects. Actual costs of these components for 1990 and 1991 and projections for 1992 as contained in the approved budget plan for 1992 are as follows:

	1990 Actual	1991 Actual	1992 Preliminary Final
	($ in thousands)		
Benefits costs	$894,371	$935,394	$972,561
Administrative costs ..	25,881	27,017	29,614
Cattle Tick Eradication Project	9,601	10,825	10,825
Total, Federal funds ..	929,853	973,236	1,013,000
State Administrative costs	25,881	27,017	29,614
Total program costs ...	$955,734	$1,000,253	$1,042,614

From its inception, the Food Stamp Program in Puerto Rico served a much higher proportion of total population than was true of the U.S. as a whole, due to the significantly lower living standards in Puerto Rico. This continues to be the case under the block grant program:. 1.48 million or 43.5 percent of Puerto Rico's total estimated population of 3.4 million people participated in the program in 1992. Monthly participation and estimates for 1990, 1991 and 1992 are as follows:

318-45

	1990 Actual	1991 Actual	1992 Preliminary Final
Average number of persons (millions)	1.48	1.49	1.48
Average number of households	479,334	494,142	500,169
Average household size	3.09	3.02	2.96
Average benefits per household ...	$156	$158	$162

In Fiscal Year 1992 Puerto Rico spent an estimated $29.6 million of Federal money administrative activities, and an equivalent amount of State funds since there is a 50:50 matching requirement for these costs.

Federal Responsibilities. FNS provides funds intended to cover 100 percent of the benefit costs and 50 percent of the administrative costs of the program as appropriated by Congress. FNS must review and approve the Commonwealth's annual plan and monitor program operations to assure program integrity, etc. These monitoring activities include reviewing financial reports such as the SF-269, on-site management reviews of selected program operations and reviewing news reports on program activities.

FOOD AND NUTRITION SERVICE

The estimates include appropriation language for this item as follows (new language underscored; deleted matter enclosed in brackets):

Food Donations [Programs] for Selected Groups:

For necessary expenses to carry out section 4(a) of the Agriculture and Consumer Protection Act of 1973 (7 U.S.C. 612c (note)), section 4(b) of the Food Stamp Act (7 U.S.C. 2013 (b)), and section 311 of the Older Americans Act of 1965, as amended (42 U.S.C. 3030a), [$224,513,000] $212,413,000 to remain available through
1 September 30, [1994] 1995. For necessary expenses to carry out section 110 of the Hunger Prevention Act of 1988, $32,000,000.

This change would make the appropriation available until September 30, 1995.

FOOD DONATIONS PROGRAMS FOR SELECTED GROUPS

Appropriations Act, 1993	$256,513,000
Budget Estimate, 1994	244,413,000
Decrease in Appropriations	-12,100,000

SUMMARY OF DECREASES
(On basis of appropriation)

Item of Change	1993 Estimated	Other Changes	1994 Estimated
Food Distribution Program on Indian Reservations: ...	$81,601,000	-$12,100,000	$69,501,000
Nutrition Program for the Elderly....................	142,912,000	—	142,912,000
Commodities for Soup Kitchens...................	32,000,000	—	32,000,000
Total Available...........	256,513,000	-12,100,000	244,413,000

PROJECT STATEMENT
(On basis of appropriation)

Project	1992 Actual	1993 Estimated	Increase or Decrease	1994 Estimated
1. Food Distribution Program on Indian Reservations:				
Commodities in lieu of food stamps...........	$64,495,000	$63,157,000	-$12,561,000	$50,596,000
Distributing agencies expenses..............	17,450,000	18,444,000	+461,000	18,905,000
Subtotal, Food Distribution Program on Indian Reservations	81,945,000	81,601,000	(1) -12,100,000	69,501,000
2. Nutrition Program for the Elderly:				
Commodities.........	9,918,000	9,367,000	-9,000	9,358,000
Cash in Lieu of commodities........	141,574,000	133,545,000	+9,000	133,554,000
Subtotal, Nutrition Program for the Elderly	151,492,000	142,912,000	(2) —	142,912,000
3. Commodities for Soup Kitchens:...........	32,000,000	32,000,000	—	32,000,000
Total, Appropriation....	265,437,000	256,513,000	-12,100,000	244,413,000

PROJECT STATEMENT
(On basis of available funds)

Project	1992 Actual	1993 Estimated	Increase or Decrease	1994 Estimated
1. Food Distribution Program on Indian Reservations:				
Commodities in lieu of food stamps	$64,219,054	$63,157,000	-$12,561,000	$50,596,000
Distributing agencies expenses..............	17,547,989	18,444,000	+461,000	18,905,000
Subtotal, Food Dist. Program on Indian Reservations.........	81,767,043	81,601,000	(1) -12,100,000	69,501,000
2. Nutrition Program for the Elderly:				
Commodities	9,271,000	9,367,000	-9,000	9,358,000
Cash in Lieu of commodities	134,447,620	133,545,000	+9,000	133,554,000
Subtotal, Nutrition Program for the Elderly	143,718,620	142,912,000	— (2)	142,912,000
3. Commodities for Soup Kitchens:	32,000,000	32,000,000	—	32,000,000

PROJECT STATEMENT
(On basis of available funds)

Project	1992 Actual	1993 Estimated	Increase or Decrease	1994 Estimated
Total Obligations..........	257,485,663	256,513,000	—	244,413,000
Unobligated balances				
Recovery of prior year obligations...............	—	—	—	—
Unobligated balances....	—			
Available, start of year	—	—	—	—
Available, end of year..	—		—	—
Expiring................	+7,951,337		—	—
Total, Appropriation.......	265,437,000	256,513,000	-12,100,000	244,413,000

EXPLANATION OF PROGRAM

Food Donations Programs for Selected Groups includes funds for: the Food Distribution Program on Indian Reservations (FDPIR); the continuation of food assistance to the Republic of Palau; the Nutrition Program for the Elderly; and commodity purchases for soup kitchens and food banks authorized by the Hunger Prevention Act of 1988 (Public Law 100-435).

Food Distribution Program on Indian Reservations (FDPIR)

Overview of Program Development. The Food Stamp Act of 1977 authorized the distribution of agricultural commodities to eligible needy persons residing on or near Indian reservations or in the Pacific Islands. FDPIR was provided as an alternative to the Food Stamp Program for Indian households in rural areas where the Food Stamp Program was not readily available or where food stores were inconveniently located. The Act stipulates that a food distribution program may be established on an Indian reservation if an Indian Tribal Organization (ITO) requests the program. If the ITO is capable of administering the program, it may do so in lieu of administration by a State agency. P.L. 97-98 authorized low-income Indian households residing in Oklahoma to participate in the program. The Program has been reauthorized through Fiscal Year 1995 by the Food, Agriculture, Conservation and Trade Act of 1990 (FACT), P.L. 101-624.

The Compact of Free Association Act of 1985 (P.L. 99-239), as amended by the Palau Compact of Free Association Act (P.L. 99-658), terminated the Trusteeship Agreement with the Federated States of Micronesia and the Marshall Islands and established them as Freely Associated States. For transition purposes, food assistance continued through Fiscal Year 1989 but at reduced levels, except in the nuclear affected zones of Bikini and Enewetak, as prescribed by these laws. Food assistance for Palau will continue at normal levels until a compact is in effect for that area.

Eligibility and Benefits. Household eligibility for FDPIR is determined by income and resources in a manner similar to that used for Food Stamp Program eligibility. Recipients must reside on or near a participating reservation, or reside within a stipulated service area in Oklahoma. In areas where both FDPIR and Food Stamps are available, no household may participate simultaneously in both programs, although they may switch from one program to the other. The entitlement commodities made available to the distributing agencies include canned meats and fish, fruits, vegetables and juice, flour, rice, pasta, cornmeal, dairy products, honey, cereal, oil and shortening. To the extent that surplus price-support commodities are available and can be used without waste, the Commodity Credit Corporation (CCC) donates them for use in this program.

State/Federal Responsibilities. The FDPIR is operated through a partnership between State distributing agencies or Indian Tribal Organizations and the Food and Nutrition Service. The grantee agency is responsible for certifying recipient eligibility, local warehousing and transportation of commodities, distribution of commodities to recipient households, and program integrity.

The Federal Government pays 100 percent of the cost of commodities distributed through the program. In addition, cash payments are made to administering agencies to assist them in meeting the administrative expenses incurred in operating a food distribution program. In Fiscal Year 1993, the Federal Government expects to pay about 80 percent of distributing agencies' administrative expenses. Included among these costs are local warehousing and transportation of commodities, utilities, salaries and equipment.

NUTRITION PROGRAM FOR THE ELDERLY

Overview of Program Development. Food assistance for the Nutrition Program for the Elderly is authorized by Titles III and VI of the Older Americans Act of 1965 (OAA). The Older Americans Act Amendments of 1987 (P.L. 100-175) reauthorized the program through Fiscal Year 1991. The program was most recently reauthorized on September 30, 1992 by P.L. 102-375. The cash and commodities provided are used in preparing meals which are served in senior citizen centers and similar settings or delivered to the home-bound elderly. These meals are the focal point of the nutrition projects for the elderly which have the dual objectives of promoting better health and reducing the isolation of old age.

The Nutrition Program for the Elderly is administered by the U.S. Department of Health and Human Services (DHHS). USDA supplements DHHS programs for the elderly with commodities and/or cash in lieu of commodities for meals served under the provisions of Title III, section 311(a), Grants for State and Community Programs on Aging, and Title VI, Grants for Indian Tribes, of the OAA, as amended.

Eligibility and Benefits. Commodities or cash in lieu of commodities are distributed through State agencies to the local meal sites at a specific rate per meal set by law. P.L. 102-375 established an indexed meal reimbursement rate based on the Consumer Price Index. The legislatively stipulated rate is 62.06 cents per meal for Fiscal Year 1993. However, actual reimbursement for meals served is limited by the appropriation level set by Congress. Most States elect to take all of their subsidies in cash, and some States choose to receive a combination of cash and commodities. The commodities made available to the Nutrition Program for the Elderly are generally the same as those provided to schools under the Child Nutrition Programs. In addition to the 62.06 cent per meal entitlement, States or Indian tribes which elect 20 percent of their benefits in commodities are eligible to receive such bonus commodities as USDA can make available.

Although originally a program to distribute nutritious USDA purchased commodities to senior citizen meal sites, the program has evolved primarily into a cash subsidy program. Approximately 94 percent of program resources are distributed to meal providers in cash.

State/Federal Responsibilities. State Agencies on Aging designate area Agencies on Aging to plan and coordinate the program through local outlets. The State Agencies on Aging and Indian Tribal agencies request USDA-donated foods, cash in lieu of foods, or a combination of both to use in providing meals to the elderly at various sites.

State Agencies on Aging and Indian Tribal Organizations that receive commodities obtain them primarily from the State distributing agency that provides USDA foods to schools for the National School Lunch Program.

COMMODITY PURCHASES FOR SOUP KITCHENS.

Overview of Program Development. USDA continues to provide surplus commodities to soup kitchens and food banks as it has in the past. Section 110 of the Hunger Prevention Act of 1988 mandated the purchase and distribution of commodities to soup kitchens and food banks in Fiscal Years 1989 through 1991. In addition, the FACT Act, P.L. 101-624 authorizes appropriations of $40 million for Fiscal Years 1992-1995 for this purpose.

Eligibility. Commodities are distributed to the States which, in turn, provide them to public and private nonprofit charitable institutions that maintain an established feeding operation to provide food to needy homeless persons and to food banks which serve such institutions. In instances when the States's full commodity allocation cannot be used by these organizations, States provide such commodities may be made available to food banks for distribution to needy households and to organizations that serve meals to predominantly needy persons.

Benefit. USDA provides commodities to States for local distribution to soup kitchens and food banks. USDA anticipates the purchase in Fiscal Year 1993 of the following commodities for these outlets: nonfat dry milk, and the following canned foods: mixed fruit, pineapple, peas, applesauce, tomato juice, corn, green beans, chicken, pork and/or beef. A State may use part of its grant for administrative expenses under the Emergency Food Assistance Program to cover administrative expenses associated with Section 110 commodities.

State/Federal Responsibilities. Within the States, distribution to soup kitchens and food banks and payments for storage and distribution are the responsibility of State Distributing Agencies. States are responsible for requesting commodities only in quantities that can be efficiently utilized by soup kitchens and food banks and managing the distribution of commodities to local organizations. States are also responsible for ensuring that soup kitchens and food banks comply with all Federal program regulations and requirements.

JUSTIFICATION OF INCREASES AND DECREASES

(1) A decrease of $12,100,000 in the appropriation for the Food Distribution Program on Indian Reservations and in the Pacific Islands ($81,601,000 appropriated in Fiscal Year 1993):

(a) A decrease of $12,561,000 in the appropriation for commodities in lieu of food stamps ($63,157,000 available in Fiscal Year 1993).

Need for Change. The net decrease in appropriation consists of:

— A decrease of $12,610,000 in commodity purchases;

— An increase of $49,000 in commodity administrative costs.

Due to lower than expected participation in prior years, federal and grantee inventories have increased. Excess inventories will be utilized to offset the need for commodity purchases in Fiscal Year 1994.

Nature of Change. The requested funds along with existing inventories will be sufficient to cover the slight increase in participation to 125,854 in the Food Donations Program on Indian Reservations.

(b) An increase of $461,000 in the appropriation for distributing agencies' administrative expenses ($18,444,000 available for Fiscal Year 1993).

Need for Change. The funding level for distributing agencies' administrative expenses is based on the cost of prior year operations, including an adjustment for inflation. An estimate of $150,000 is included to provide nutrition education materials to recipients.

Nature of Change. An appropriation of $18,905,000 will be needed for administrative expenses in Fiscal Year 1994.

Food Distribution Program on Indian Reservations
Program Performance Data

Indian Reservations	FY 1992 Actual	FY 1993 Estimate	FY 1994 Estimate	Change
Average monthly participation 1/	121,410	119,875	125,854	+5,979
Average monthly food package:				
FNS purchased..................	$30.93	$31.60	$33.01	+$1.41
CCC bonus commodities..........	3.40	3.50	3.39	-$ .11
Total monthly food package	$34.33	$35.10	$36.40	+$1.30
Inventory Activity:				
Americold fire 2/..............	7,378,238			
Inventory change...............	9,259,185	16,972,600		-16,972,600
Total	$16,637,423	16,972,600	—	-16,972,600

Food Distribution Program on Indian Reservations
Program Performance Data

Indian Reservations	FY 1992 Actual	FY 1993 Estimate	FY 1994 Estimate	Change
Annual value of FNS purchased commodities 3/..................	$44,833,451	$45,261,400	$49,624,000	+4,362,600
Indian Administration Cost.......	17,547,989	18,444,000	18,905,000	+461,000
Disaster and other losses 4/.....	2,516,180	500,000	500,000	—
Commodity Administrative Cost and PCIMS.....................	232,000	423,000	472,000	+ 49,000
TOTAL FNS COST..................	81,767,043	81,601,000	69,501,000	-12,100,000
CCC bonus commodities...........	4,832,000	4,910,000	5,068,000	+158,000
GRAND TOTAL.....................	86,599,043	86,511,000	74,569,000	-11,942,000

1/ Includes 2,875 for participation in Palau for all years.

2/ Approximately $7.4 million was spent in FY 1992 from the effects of the Americold fire. The Americold warehouse stores commodities for the Food Distribution Program on Indian Reservations (FDPIR) and the Commodity Supplemental Food Program (CSFP). Approximately 60 percent of the destroyed commodities are associated with FDPIR.

3/ Includes $527,000 in 1992 and $581,000 in 1993 and 1994 for the nuclear-affected islands.

4/ Disaster assistance was provided for victims of civil unrest in Los Angeles, victims of typhoons in Guam, Federated States of Micronesia, and the Marshall Islands.

Nutrition Program for the Elderly

Meals served (millions)	245	247	247
Rate per meal (cents)	61.00	57.80	57.80

31g-46

FOOD DONATIONS PROGRAMS FOR SELECTED GROUPS

STATUS OF PROGRAMS

In Fiscal Year 1992 the Food Donations Programs for Selected Groups continued to provide direct assistance to needy persons through the Food Distribution Program on Indian Reservations (FDPIR), the Needy Family Program, the Nutrition Program for the Elderly (NPE) and Commodities for Soup Kitchens.

Food Distribution Program on Indian Reservations (FDPIR)

The Food Distribution Program on Indian Reservations implements the requirements of Public Laws 95-113 and 97-98 to allow Indian Tribal Organizations (ITOs) to operate a food distribution program. This program is an alternative to the Food Stamp Program for eligible households living on or near an Indian reservation or Indians residing in Oklahoma.

In 1986 FNS conducted a review of the FDPIR food package contents and nutrition education components. Some recommendations for improving the nutritional content of the food package were implemented prior to this year. The improvements were generally well received and the food package changes have been incorporated into commodity purchases. The improved food package has lower sugar, fat and salt content, and increased portions of fruits and vegetables. These changes were made to address the diet-related health problems of Native Americans. Commodity recipes and fact sheets have been distributed and a series of 12 fliers covering important aspects of nutrition and health was developed in Fiscal Year 1992 to be distributed during Fiscal Year 1993.

In Fiscal Year 1992, two additional Tribes entered FDPIR. At the close of Fiscal Year 1992, 88 Indian Tribal Organizations (ITOs) and 6 States operated the FDPIR on 238 Indian reservations. Participation in the FDPIR reached a monthly average of about 118,500 participants. Foods valued at approximately $64 million were purchased for donation through FDPIR. In addition, foods valued at $1.5 million were donated to FNS without charge to FDPIR from section 32 surplus removal and section 416 price support activities to meet basic food needs.

Needy Family Program

The Needy Family Program provided commodities for distribution to eligible households living in Palau. A cash grant for the administrative costs associated with the distribution of commodities was also provided.

Pursuant to P.L. 99-239, P.L. 99-658, and their Compacts of Free Association, the program was phased out for the Marshall Islands and the Federated States of Micronesia during a three year transition period ending in Fiscal Year 1989. Certain islands in nuclear-affected zones will continue to receive USDA commodities and administrative funds through Fiscal Year 1997, as authorised by P.L. 102-247, enacted February 24, 1992. Funds to continue this program into the current fiscal year were appropriated. The former Trust Territories that ratified the Compact of Free Association continue to be eligible for emergency assistance from the Department for a 15-year period after implementation of the Compact pursuant to the Disaster Relief Act. Until the Compact of Free Association for Palau is implemented, Palau continues to receive assistance under normal program rules.

Disaster Feeding Program

The Federal Emergency Management Agency is generally responsible for coordinating disaster assistance under the Disaster Relief and Emergency Assistance Act. The Act specifically assigns certain responsibilities relating to disaster food assistance to the Secretary of Agriculture. Other duties have been assigned to the Secretary by Executive Order. These responsibilities include using, pursuant to the authority of the Act, funds appropriated under Section 32 to purchase food commodities for assistance in major disasters or emergencies when other food supplies are not readily available. Food assistance purchases under Section 32 for disasters in Fiscal Year 1992 totalled approximately $13 million (as shown below) in addition to funds of $3.6 million.

Location	Disaster/ Emergency	Approx. Value of Commodity Purchases
Hawaii	Hurricane Iniki	$1,500,000
Guam	Typhoon Omar	$ 275,000
Florida/ Louisiana	Hurricane Andrew	$5,000,000
California	Civil unrest in Los Angeles	$2,000,000
Pacific Islands*	Typhoons and Draught	$4,225,000
TOTAL		$13,000,000

*Federated States of Micronesia (Chuuk, Yap, & Pohnpei States) and the Marshall Islands (Ujae, Lae, Mili, Jaluit, Arno and Ailinglaplap Atolls)

Nutrition Program for the Elderly

The United States Department of Agriculture supplements the Department of Health and Human Services (DHHS) programs for the elderly with cash and commodities for meals served under the provisions of Title III (Grants for State and Community Programs on Aging) and Title VI (Grants for Indian Tribes) of the Older Americans Act of 1965 (OAA), as amended.

These DHHS programs provide elderly persons with nutritionally sound meals served through meals-on-wheels programs or in senior citizen centers and similar settings where the elderly participate in social and rehabilitative activities. These meals often provide the focal point for activities which have the dual objectives of promoting better health and reducing the isolation that may occur in old age.

As required by the amendments to the Older Americans Act, P.L. 102-375, signed on September 30, 1992, the Department provided reimbursement for over 244 million meals at the rate of .61 cents per meal in Fiscal Year 1992. The State agencies distributed commodities and/or cash to local elderly nutrition centers. The commodities made available to the Nutrition Program for the Elderly (NPE) were similar in variety to those provided to schools under the Child Nutrition Programs. From the total entitlement funding provided in 1992, $9.3 million was made in the form of commodities and $134.4 million was cash reimbursement. In addition $1.4 million was provided without charge to NPE from section 32 surplus removal and section 416 price support activities. The balance of FNS's FY 1992 appropriated funds for NPE will be made available based on final meal counts.

Soup Kitchens/Food Banks

Pursuant to the Hunger Prevention Act of 1988, Public Law 100-435, $32 million was appropriated to purchase, process, and distribute commodities to soup kitchens and food banks, with priority given to institutions which prepare meals for the homeless.

Commodities were allocated to the States based on a formula which considers the unemployment rate in each State and the number of persons in each State with incomes below the poverty level, as compared to nationwide figures.

In Fiscal Year 1992, approximately 51.7 million pounds of commodities valued at the full $32 million appropriation were purchased and made available to States for distribution to soup kitchens and food banks. The commodities that were made available were canned pork or poultry, rice, non-fat dry milk, orange juice, canned corn, dry beans, canned green beans, canned peaches, canned peas, canned applesauce, and frozen ground beef and chicken.

31g-49

FOOD DISTRIBUTION PROGRAM ON INDIAN RESERVATIONS
AND THE NEEDY FAMILY PROGRAM

PARTICIPATION AND FUNDING
FISCAL YEAR 1992

STATE OR TERRITORY	AVERAGE MONTHLY PARTICIPATION	FOOD COSTS 1/	ADMINISTRATIVE FUNDING
Arizona	21,867	$8,049,204	$2,769,607
California	5,265	1,983,949	646,745
Colorado	608	193,622	94,597
Florida	418	119,155	57,092
Idaho	1,792	615,282	244,755
Iowa	123	38,694	18,970
Kansas	453	163,698	91,820
Michigan	1,831	666,115	363,463
Minnesota	3,922	1,442,756	720,035
Mississippi	695	197,591	109,449
Montana	5,570	2,182,801	1,252,001
Nebraska	1,825	678,554	218,173
Nevada	1,417	509,076	175,426
New Mexico	7,121	2,142,363	911,421
New York	698	208,860	142,542
North Carolina	648	240,355	85,075
North Dakota	5,597	2,199,250	806,730
Oklahoma	34,417	13,251,916	3,127,589
Oregon	1,225	434,455	130,104
South Dakota	11,761	4,645,680	1,848,180
Utah	434	134,130	80,841
Washington	4,475	1,654,811	677,082
Wisconsin	3,644	1,247,886	648,747
Wyoming	1,482	555,123	240,727
Freely Associated States	1,247	8,901	52,666
AMS/ASCS Admin. Expenses	0	232,000	0
Undistributed	0	20,422,827	2,034,152
TOTAL	118,535	$64,219,054	$17,547,989

1/ Includes values for entitlement foods but not for bonus commodities.

NOTE: These data are based in part on preliminary data submitted by State and local agencies and are subject to change as revised reports are received.

FOOD DISTRIBUTION PROGRAM ON INDIAN RESERVATIONS AND FOR DISASTER FEEDING
Quantity and Value of Commodities

By Commodity, Fiscal Year 1992

ENTITLEMENT COMMODITIES	Indian Reservations		Disaster Feeding	
	Pounds	Dollars	Pounds	Dollars
SECTION 6/32 TYPE:				
APPLE JUICE, CANNED	4,263,099	$1,340,109	190,008	$63,310
APPLESAUCE, CANNED	3,692,928	1,410,861	235,800	90,086
BEANS, DRY	3,688,968	942,207	461,808	118,711
BEANS, GREEN, CANNED	2,675,509	759,697	130,200	35,310
BEANS, VEGETARIAN	2,546,520	627,772	0	0
BEEF, CANNED W/NJ	1,745,690	2,711,683	0	0
BEEF, FROZEN GROUND	0	0	72	95
CARROTS	1,677,864	508,852	0	0
CHICKEN, CANNED BONED	869,493	1,736,901	0	0
CHICKEN, DICED FROZEN	0	0	4,800	10,527
CORN, CREAM STYLE	737,544	262,813	0	0
CORN, WHOLE KERNEL	1,593,096	556,957	0	0
EGG MIX	2,076,408	3,817,552	0	0
FRUIT COCKTAIL, CANNED	2,162,112	1,306,511	0	0
GRAPE JUICE, CANNED	1,938,647	683,315	0	0
GRAPEFRUIT JUICE, CANNED	1,892,434	496,515	0	0
MEAT, LUNCHEION CANNED	1,509,705	1,849,879	0	0
MEATBALL STEW	421,291	320,467	0	0
MIXED FRUIT	0	0	37,000	19,351
ORANGE JUICE, CANNED	7,141,673	2,165,213	261,995	83,802
PEACHES, CLING CANNED	3,050,472	1,817,413	0	0
PEARS, CANNED	1,470,480	720,621	0	0
PEAS, DRY SPLIT	2,200	530	0	0
PEAS, GREEN CANNED	1,630,800	527,524	0	0
PINEAPPLE CANNED	2,622,900	1,413,596	0	0
PINEAPPLE JUICE	2,192,992	687,638	0	0
PLUMS, CANNED, PURPLE	326,736	134,205	38,336	12,758
PORK, CANNED W/NJ	958,427	1,282,635	252,126	317,679
POTATOES, DEHYDRATED	1,468,512	688,221	0	0
POTATOES, WHOLE	897,936	277,040	0	0
POULTRY, CANNED BONED	839,578	1,444,791	0	0
PRUNES, DRIED	898,752	864,364	0	0
RAISINS	1,317,456	782,576	0	0
SALMON, PINK CANNED	976,203	1,618,046	0	0
SPINACH, CANNED	495,559	167,778	0	0
SWEET POTATOES, SYRUP	375,192	144,440	0	0
SYRUP, CORN	1,067,086	325,533	0	0
TOMATO JUICE, CANNED	1,740,419	347,056	0	0
TOMATO PASTE, CANNED	0	0	83	32
TOMATO SAUCE	1,858,508	536,702	126,000	35,810
TOMATOES CANNED	1,998,480	589,157	168,000	47,476
TUNA, CHUNK LIGHT-WATER	1,282,233	2,028,834	373,414	597,888
Total Section 6/32 Type	68,103,902	$37,896,004	2,279,642	$1,432,835
SECTION 416-TYPE:				
CEREAL, DRY CORN	1,145,353	1,368,819	0	0
CERAL, DRY OATS	500,676	691,342	0	0
CEREAL, DRY RICE	795,839	890,531	90,685	101,676
CEREAL, DRY WHEAT	1,080	561	0	0
CEREAL, INFANT RICE	0	0	74,730	99,638
CEREAL, INSTANT OATMEAL ENR	0	0	72,000	75,358
CEREAL, WHEAT	56,484	77,318	0	0
CHEESE PROCESS	3,883,350	5,382,059	186,000	268,811
CHEESE, MOZZARELLA	0	0	2,064	2,551
CORNMEAL	42,650	4,983	0	0
FARINA	908,019	325,037	19,404	6,974
FLOUR	9,567,790	1,556,015	172,800	30,741
FORMULA, INFANT	0	0	565,665	897,451
HONEY	1,836	1,410	0	0
MACARONI	2,241,240	560,844	163,200	42,824
MILK, EVAPORATED	8,633,400	3,892,580	0	0
MILK, NFD	3,090,792	3,276,890	211,200	220,113
OATS, ROLLED	1,640,916	323,931	0	0
OIL, VEGETABLE	955,435	419,883	73,920	24,534
PEANUT BUTTER	2,634,240	2,504,916	235,200	198,771
PEANUTS, ROASTED	891,828	992,314	0	0
RICE, BROWN	0	0	21,000	3,284
RICE, MILLED	3,628,800	731,031	758,125	158,398
SHORTENING, VEGETABLE	1,204,092	480,355	138,960	54,792
SPAGHETTI, ENRICHED	2,013,528	484,193	20	4
WHEAT, ROLLED	189,900	36,740	0	0
Total Section 416-Type	44,027,248	$24,001,752	2,784,973	$2,185,920
Undistributed		2,089,298		
AMS/ASCS Admin. Expenses		232,000		
Total Commodity Entitlement	112,131,150	$64,219,054	5,064,615	$3,618,755

continued on the next page

31g-51

FOOD DISTRIBUTION PROGRAM ON INDIAN RESERVATIONS AND FOR DISASTER FEEDING
Quantity and Value of Commodities

By Commodity, Fiscal Year 1992

BONUS COMMODITIES	Indian Reservations		Disaster Feeding	
	Pounds	Dollars	Pounds	Dollars
SECTION 32-TYPE:				
BEANS, DRY PINTO	0	0	200,040	51,550
Total Section 32 Type	0	$0	200,040	$51,550
SECTION 416-TYPE:				
BUTTER	1,167,264	$1,009,700	0	0
CORNMEAL	2,304,300	269,865	0	0
HONEY	280,764	211,808	0	0
FORMULA INFANT	0	0	197,370	98,685
Total Section 416 Type	3,752,328	$1,491,373	$197,370	$98,685
Total Bonus Commodities	3,752,328	$1,491,373	397,410	$150,235
GRAND TOTAL (Entitlement & Bonus)	115,883,478	$65,710,427	5,462,025	$3,768,990

SOURCE: Preliminary food orders for fiscal year 1992.

31g-52

NUTRITION PROGRAM FOR THE ELDERLY
MEALS SERVED AND PROGRAM COSTS

FISCAL YEAR 1992

STATE OR TERRITORY	MEALS SERVED		FNS PROGRAM COSTS a/
	AVERAGE DAILY	TOTAL FY 1992	
Alabama	14,453	3,815,483	2,327,445
Alaska	1,998	527,577	321,822
Arizona	10,352	2,733,002	1,667,131
Arkansas	14,180	3,743,508	2,283,540
California	76,097	20,089,710	12,254,723
Colorado	8,100	2,138,295	1,304,360
Connecticut	10,999	2,903,792	1,771,313
Delaware	3,397	896,756	547,021
District of Columbia	5,282	1,394,465	850,624
Florida	42,207	11,142,563	6,796,963
Georgia	13,207	3,486,613	2,126,834
Hawaii	3,711	979,627	597,572
Idaho	5,058	1,335,301	814,534
Illinois	32,627	8,613,432	5,254,194
Indiana	16,396	4,328,574	2,640,430
Iowa	17,267	4,558,413	2,780,632
Kansas	15,486	4,088,207	2,493,806
Kentucky	13,444	3,549,322	2,165,086
Louisiana	19,257	5,083,833	3,101,138
Maine	4,192	1,106,743	675,113
Maryland	15,295	4,037,782	2,463,047
Massachusetts	28,238	7,454,876	4,547,474
Michigan	39,010	10,298,768	6,282,248
Minnesota	19,033	5,024,748	3,065,096
Mississippi	11,404	3,010,538	1,836,428
Missouri	23,910	6,312,202	3,850,443
Montana	7,499	1,979,749	1,207,647
Nebraska	9,421	2,487,092	1,517,126
Nevada	4,623	1,220,433	744,464
New Hampshire	4,786	1,263,606	770,800
New Jersey	21,670	5,720,977	3,489,796
New Mexico	10,547	2,784,454	1,698,517
New York	91,659	24,197,894	14,760,715
North Carolina	18,702	4,937,356	3,011,787
North Dakota	6,138	1,620,463	988,482
Ohio	30,919	8,162,508	4,979,130
Oklahoma	18,694	4,935,101	3,010,412
Oregon	10,970	2,896,141	1,766,646
Pennsylvania	45,750	12,078,121	7,367,654
Rhode Island	4,648	1,227,059	748,506
South Carolina	9,200	2,428,774	1,481,552
South Dakota	6,836	1,804,831	1,100,947
Tennessee	13,795	3,641,872	2,221,542
Texas	62,802	16,579,793	10,113,674
Utah	5,816	1,535,467	936,635
Vermont	3,085	814,554	496,878
Virginia	12,783	3,374,655	2,058,540
Washington	13,502	3,564,599	2,174,405
West Virginia	9,138	2,412,561	1,471,662
Wisconsin	23,215	6,128,750	3,738,538
Wyoming	4,536	1,197,451	730,445
American Samoa	0	0	0
Freely Associated States	0	0	0
Guam	1,355	357,695	218,194
N. Mariana Islands	409	108,087	65,933
Puerto Rico	10,276	2,712,945	1,654,896
Virgin Islands	0	0	0
Indian Tribes	b/	b/	0
DOD Army/AF/USMC/NAVY	0	0	0
AMS/ASCS Admin. Expenses.	0	0	59,000
Anticipated Adjustment	0	0	-5,684,920
TOTAL	927,374	244,827,118	143,718,620

a/ Includes entitlement commodities and cash in lieu thereof.
b/ Data combined with that for the appropriate State.

NOTE: Data for Title III and VI Programs are based in part on preliminary data submitted by the States and local agencies and are subject to change as revised reports are received. Totals may not add due to rounding.

NUTRITION PROGRAM FOR THE ELDERLY
Quantity and Value of Commodities

School or Fiscal Year 1992

ENTITLEMENT COMMODITIES	Pounds	Dollars
SECTION 6/32 TYPE:		
APPLE SLICES, CANNED	90,558	$37,818
APPLES, FRESH	1,935	653
APPLESAUCE, CANNED	417,801	121,064
APRICOTS, CANNED	130,289	62,031
BEANS, DRY	79,219	16,566
BEANS, GREEN, CANNED	364,496	97,290
BEANS, GREEN, FROZEN	55,500	19,691
BEANS, REFRIED, CANNED	1,932	585
BEANS, VEGETARIAN	19,157	4,615
BEEF PATTIES, FRZ	7,200	8,247
BEEF, FROZEN GROUND	890,424	1,160,654
CHICKENS, FRZ BREADED	42,000	48,212
CHICKENS, DICED FRZ.	127,280	287,362
CHICKEN, QUARTERS	360,000	197,452
CHICKENS, FROZEN, CUT-UP	624,000	339,735
CORN, CANNED, LIQUID	204,437	58,185
EGGS, WHOLE FROZEN	55,400	26,576
HAM, FRZ COOKED BONELESS	128,800	179,067
MIXED FRUIT	389,800	203,865
PEACHES, CLING CANNED	372,920	186,256
PEACHES, FREESTONE CND	18,520	9,190
PEACHES, FREESTONE FRZ SLICED	95,780	54,678
PEARS, D'ANJOU FRESH	2,475	755
PEARS, DICED	120,240	49,430
PEARS, HALVES	393,480	171,557
PEARS, SLICED	74,000	31,494
PEAS, GREEN CANNED	129,480	39,880
PEAS, GREEN FROZEN	19,800	7,574
PINEAPPLE, CANNED	38,160	18,626
PLUMS, CANNED PURPLE	57,422	19,110
PLUMS, CANNED PITTED	38,295	15,264
PORK, FRZ GROUND	230,292	208,032
POTATO ROUNDS, FROZEN	5,220	1,266
POTATOES, OVEN FRY	2,970	721
SWEET POTATOES, MASHED	123,246	53,562
SWEET POTATOES, SYRUP	106,143	40,101
TOMATO PASTE, CANNED	103,051	39,891
TOMATOES, CANNED	128,406	38,406
TOMATOES, CRUSHED	33,356	10,530
TUNA	65,218	75,958
TURKEY ROASTS, FROZEN	583,208	889,979
TURKEY, FROZEN GROUND	323,800	247,664
TURKEY, FROZEN WHOLE	100,400	69,305
Total Section 6/32 Type	7,156,110	$5,148,897

continued on the next page

31g-54

NUTRITION PROGRAM FOR THE ELDERLY
Quantity and Value of Commodities

School or Fiscal Year 1992 Page 2 of 2

ENTITLEMENT COMMODITIES	Thousands of Pounds	Thousands of Dollars
SECTION 416-TYPE:		
CHEESE, CHEDDAR	677	$773
CHEESE, MOZZARELLA	1,613	2,244
CHEESE, PROCESS	222,720	316,636
FLOUR	1,800	218
MACARONI	6,500	1,630
OATS, ROLLED	2,700	457
OIL, SOYBEAN	17,780	4,465
OIL, VEGETABLE	21,761	7,040
PEANUT BUTTER	3,713	3,120
PEANUT, ROASTED	6,480	6,070
RICE, MILLED	20,900	4,283
SHORTENING, VEGETABLE	15,294	5,069
SPAGHETTI, ENRICHED	5,980	1,226
Total Section 416-Type	327,918	$353,231
Anticipated Adjustment		3,709,872
AMS/ASCS Admin. Expenses		59,000
Total Commodity Entitlement	7,484,028	$9,271,000
BONUS COMMODITIES		
SECTION 32-TYPE:		
ALMOND SLIVERS	525	$357
ASPARAGUS, CANNED	62,303	42,991
BEANS, DRY PINTO	36,936	7,723
BEANS, VEGETARIAN	36,936	8,898
CHICKENS, FRZ BREADED	99,960	55,348
HAM, FRZ COOKED BONELESS	156,920	233,827
POTATOES, FLAKED DEHYDRATED	7,500	4,100
RAISINS	6,000	3,200
SALMON, PINK CANNED	108,900	181,634
STRAWBERRIES, IQF FRZ	85,020	87,571
TOMATOES, CRUSHED	35,486	11,203
TOMATO PASTE, CANNED	20,810	8,056
TOMATOES, CANNED	74,779	22,367
TURKEY, COMMERICAL PACK	236,680	139,387
TURKEY ROASTS, FRZ	20,000	25,514
Total Section 32 Type	988,755	$832,176
SECTION 416-TYPE:		
BUTTER	486,540	$466,752
CORNMEAL	154,200	18,622
FLOUR	691,253	92,031
Total Section 416 Type	1,331,993	$577,405
Total Bonus Commodities	2,320,748	$1,409,581
TOTAL - ALL COMMODITIES	9,804,776	$10,680,581
CASH IN LIEU OF COMMODITIES		134,447,620
GRAND TOTAL	9,804,776	$145,128,201

Source: Preliminary food orders for school or fiscal year 1992.

Note: Due to rounding, the individual entries may not add to the totals shown.

31g-55

SOUP KITCHENS AND FOOD BANKS
Quantity and Value of Commodities

By Commodity, Fiscal Year 1992

ENTITLEMENT COMMODITIES	Pounds	Dollars
SECTION 6/32 TYPE:		
APPLESAUCE, CANNED	4,905,600	1,840,076
BEANS, DRY	38,400	12,600
BEANS, GREEN CANNED	9,602,250	3,258,374
BEEF, FRZ GROUND	1,108,800	1,448,043
CHICKEN, CANNED BONED	36,540	72,992
CHICKEN, FRZ CUT-UP	1,960,000	1,050,441
CORN, WHOLE KERNEL	7,761,600	3,062,346
ORANGE JUICE, CANNED	9,921,800	3,385,200
PEACHES, CLING CANNED	1,881,600	1,272,432
PEACHES, FREESTONE CND	470,400	318,108
PEAS. GREEN CANNED	3,494,400	1,456,798
PORK, CANNED, W-NJ	3,889,944	4,958,715
POULTRY, CANNED BONED	3,178,980	6,117,320
Total Section 6/32 Type	48,250,314	$28,253,445
SECTION 416-TYPE:		
NFD MILK	3,037,584	3,392,409
RICE, MILLED	378,000	78,133
Total Section 416 Type	3,415,584	$3,470,542
Anticipated Adjustment		47,013
AMS/ASCS Admin. Expenses		229,000
Total Commodity Entitlement	51,665,898	32,000,000

SOURCE: Preliminary food orders for fiscal year 1992.

SURPLUS COMMODITY DONATIONS TO
CHARITABLE INSTITUTIONS AND SUMMER CAMPS

STATUS OF PROGRAM

Under section 416 price support and section 32 surplus removal authorities, commodities are acquired by the Commodity Credit Corporation (CCC) and the Agricultural Marketing Service (AMS) and are made available at no cost to the Surplus Commodity Donations Program administered by FNS.

Commodities are distributed to nonprofit charitable institutions serving needy persons and to summer camps for children. To be eligible, an institution must be nonprofit and serve meals on a regular basis. Among the charitable institutions receiving donated commodities are: homes for the elderly, hospitals that offer general and long term health care, soup kitchens, meals-on-wheels programs and orphanages that do not participate in any of the Child Nutrition Programs. Similar rules apply to both institutions and summer camps. Those camps participating in the Summer Food Service are not eligible to receive commodities through this program. The Charitable Institutions and Summer Camp Program is one of FNS' largest outlets for commodities bought under farm program authorities and can absorb products during the summer when schools, the largest outlet, cannot.

In Fiscal Year 1992, foods valued at $118.1 million were distributed to charitable institutions. An additional $2.9 million in food was distributed to summer camps.

31g-57

SUMMER CAMPS AND CHARITABLE INSTITUTIONS
Quantity and Value of Commodities

By Commodity, Fiscal Year 1992

ENTITLEMENT COMMODITIES	Summer Camps		Charitable Institutions	
	Pounds	Dollars	Pounds	Dollars
SECTION 6/32 TYPE:				
MEAT, LUNCHEON CANNED	0	$0	126,000	154,035
PORK, CANNED W/NJ	0	$0	162,690	235,233
Total Section 6/32 Type	0	$0	288,690	$389,268
SECTION 416-TYPE:				
GRITS, CORN	12,950	$1,894	2,159,350	$288,446
MACARONI	883,480	212,488	11,819,220	2,787,098
OATS, ROLLED	234,824	43,440	5,188,608	948,645
OIL, SALAD DRESSING SOC	1,052	80	95,222	24,993
OIL, SOYBEAN	37,544	8,673	6,955,593	1,669,357
OIL, VEGETABLE	857,981	268,743	23,274,133	7,312,666
PEANUT BUTTER	851,450	711,865	16,646,090	13,999,305
PEANUT GRANULES	4,200	3,902	576,534	587,770
PEANUTS, ROASTED	207,624	201,762	5,360,736	5,313,050
RICE, BROWN	0	0	357,000	55,836
RICE, MILLED	257,050	48,895	14,086,425	2,667,550
SHORTENING, LIQUID VEG	235,158	76,744	4,201,699	1,378,869
SHORTENING, VEGETABLE	497,988	199,649	15,057,036	5,611,315
SPAGHETTI, ENRICHED	380,660	86,671	7,905,380	1,783,051
WHEAT, ROLLED	4,500	968	661,500	110,341
Total Section 416-Type	4,466,461	$1,865,774	114,344,526	$44,538,292
Total Commodity Entitlement	4,466,461	$1,865,774	114,633,216	$44,927,560
BONUS COMMODITIES				
SECTION 32-TYPE:				
ALMOND SLIVERS	0	0	316,950	215,813
ASPARAGUS, CANNED	0	0	1,274,425	879,361
ASPARAGUS, FROZEN	0	0	240,120	300,486
BEANS, DRY PINTO	0	0	1,010,948	219,400
BEANS, VEGETARIAN	0	0	253,855	61,155
BEANS, REFRIED	0	0	62,244	18,860
CATFISH, PAN READY WHOLE	0	0	2,490,400	4,482,720
CHICKENS, FRZ DRUMSTICKS	0	0	347,800	163,188
CHICKENS, FRZ BREADED - SOC	0	0	4,260,240	2,358,895
CHICKENS, FRZ THIGHS	0	0	250,680	150,634
DATE PIECES	0	0	361,440	210,106
HAM, FRZ COOKED BONELESS	0	0	1,321,200	1,968,724
PORK, CANNED W/NJ	0	0	3,722,213	4,977,142
RAISINS 30#	9,750	5,200	1,364,400	727,638
RASPBERRY PUREE, FROZEN	0	0	40,089	33,803
SALMON, PINK CANNED	0	0	2,690,935	4,484,076
STRAWBERRIES, IQF FROZEN	0	0	532,560	548,537
TOMATO PASTE, CANNED	4,162	1,611	2,165,402	858,891
TOMATOES, CANNED	202,420	74,645	3,926,173	1,302,800
TOMATOES, CRUSHED	32,310	10,200	2,697,115	851,478
TURKEY, COMMERICAL PACK	133,190	77,896	3,833,376	2,252,923
TURKEY ROASTS, FRZ	0	0	40,000	51,216
WALNUTS, ENGLISH PIECES	0	0	244,140	397,560
Total Section 32 Type	381,832	$169,552	33,446,705	$27,515,406
SECTION 416-TYPE:				
BUTTER	809,696	754,017	36,508,386	34,892,956
BUTTER PATTIES, SOC	0	0	169,680	263,427
CORNMEAL	72,180	8,627	5,593,750	635,200
FLOUR	951,350	123,804	77,909,680	9,853,840
FLOUR, BAKERY MIX SOC	1,170	103	147,600	14,619
Total Section 416 Type	1,834,116	$886,551	120,329,096	$45,660,042
Total Bonus Commodities	2,215,948	$1,056,103	153,775,801	$73,175,448
GRAND TOTAL (Entitlement & Bonus)	6,682,409	$2,921,877	268,409,017	$118,103,008

SOURCE: Preliminary food orders for fiscal year 1992

31 8-58

SUMMER CAMPS AND CHARITABLE INSTITUTIONS
Value of Surplus Commodity Donations

Fiscal Year 1992

State or Territory	Summer Camps	Charitable Institutions	TOTAL
Alabama	$13,429	$2,032,071	$2,045,500
Alaska	0	307,643	307,643
Arizona	74,558	2,258,953	2,333,511
Arkansas	21,070	1,022,225	1,043,295
California	0	14,019,952	14,019,952
Colorado	24,782	1,343,612	1,368,394
Connecticut	46,872	975,135	1,022,007
Delaware	680	454,425	455,105
District of Columbia	0	646,043	646,043
Florida	57,226	4,863,927	4,921,153
Georgia	61,934	3,169,374	3,231,308
Hawaii	2,821	350,952	353,773
Idaho	26,258	775,613	801,871
Illinois	68,357	4,366,897	4,435,254
Indiana	132,283	1,848,555	1,980,838
Iowa	26,643	1,664,675	1,691,318
Kansas	0	1,106,371	1,106,371
Kentucky	4,649	1,384,946	1,389,595
Louisiana	27,878	3,484,422	3,512,300
Maine	44,954	599,317	644,271
Maryland	47,080	2,835,289	2,882,369
Massachusetts	60,758	3,108,771	3,169,529
Michigan	133,201	4,386,536	4,519,737
Minnesota	90,880	2,623,031	2,713,911
Mississippi	19,126	1,440,974	1,460,100
Missouri	93,415	3,487,509	3,580,924
Montana	0	492,757	492,757
Nebraska	18,451	953,933	972,384
Nevada	1,125	861,175	862,300
New Hampshire	123,375	459,738	583,113
New Jersey	37,715	2,309,929	2,347,644
New Mexico	8,293	369,925	378,218
New York	415,625	11,930,172	12,345,797
North Carolina	47,271	2,127,350	2,174,621
North Dakota	13,922	561,050	574,972
Ohio	17,062	4,431,605	4,448,667
Oklahoma	49,637	1,603,008	1,652,645
Oregon	68,123	1,149,651	1,217,774
Pennsylvania	210,236	4,650,393	4,860,629
Rhode Island	0	331,141	331,141
South Carolina	26,543	2,156,114	2,182,657
South Dakota	6,943	419,158	426,101
Tennessee	17,462	1,961,371	1,978,833
Texas	154,013	9,099,727	9,253,740
Utah	72,225	615,686	687,911
Vermont	24,548	344,659	369,207
Virginia	100,072	898,279	998,351
Washington	188,127	2,450,358	2,638,485
West Virginia	23,583	466,908	490,491
Wisconsin	173,935	2,068,175	2,242,110
Wyoming	9,470	333,904	343,374
American Samoa	0	0	0
Freely Associated States	0	0	0
Guam	0	1,251	1,251
N. Mariana Islands	0	0	0
Puerto Rico	35,267	481,754	517,021
Virgin Islands	0	16,619	16,619
Indian Tribes	0	0	0
DOD Army/AF/USMC/NAVY	0	0	0
Undistributed	0	0	0
TOTAL	$2,921,877	$118,103,008	$121,024,885

SOURCE: Preliminary food orders for fiscal year 1992

FOOD AND NUTRITION SERVICE

The estimates include appropriation language for this item as follows (new language underscored; deleted matter enclosed in brackets):

The Emergency Food Assistance Program:

For necessary expenses to carry out the Emergency Food Assistance Act of
1983, as amended, [$45,000,000] $46,215,000: Provided That, in accordance with
section 202 of Public Law 98-92, these funds shall be available only if the
Secretary determines the existence of excess commodities. For purchases of
commodities to carry out the Emergency Food Assistance Act of 1983, as amended,
1 [$120,000,000] $123,240,000: Provided, That notwithstanding section 214(h) of
that Act, commodities purchased with these funds may be delivered to States
through December 31, 1994.

The change allows comodities purchased in Fiscal Year 1994 to be delivered through the first quarter of Fiscal Year 1995 to ensure a steady flow of food to food banks throughout the year.

THE EMERGENCY FOOD ASSISTANCE PROGRAM

Appropriation Act, 1993	$165,000,000
Budget Estimate, 1994	169,455,000
Change in Appropriation	+4,455,000

SUMMARY OF INCREASES
(On basis of adjusted appropriation)

Item of Change	1993 Estimated	Other Change	1994 Estimated
The Emergency Food Assistance Program Total Available	$165,000,000	+$ 4,455,000	$169,455,000

PROJECT STATEMENT
(On basis of adjusted appropriation)

Project	1992 Actual Amount	1993 Estimated Amount	Increase or Decrease	1994 Estimated Amount
Administrative Costs	$44,999,380	$45,000,000	+1,215,000 (1)	$46,215,000
Commodity Procurement	120,000,000	120,000,000	+3,240,000 (2)	123,240,000
Total Obligations	164,999,380	165,000,000	+4,455,000	169,455,000
Unobligated Balance Expiring	620			
Total Appropriation	165,000,000	165,000,000		169,455,000
Economic Stimulus		23,481,000	-23,481,000	
Investment Proposal			+40,000,000	+40,000,000
Total, President's Budget		188,481,000	20,974,000	209,455,000

EXPLANATION OF PROGRAM

Overview of Program Development. The Emergency Food Assistance Program (TEFAP) evolved from the Special Dairy Distribution Program which began December 11, 1981, with the release of 30 million pounds of cheese. The program has the dual goal of reducing the government held commodity surpluses and providing emergency food assistance to low-income individuals and households. TEFAP was formally authorized in 1983 by Section 204 of Public Law 98-8 including the provision of funds to State and local agencies to share some of the cost of intrastate distribution of the commodities. Public Law 98-92 appropriated funds for Fiscal Year 1983 and authorized funds through Fiscal Year 1985 for costs of storage and intrastate distribution of Commodity Credit Corporation commodities donated to needy individuals by States. Public Law 100-77 authorized funds through Fiscal Year 1988 for this purpose.

For Fiscal Years 1989 and 1990, the Hunger Prevention Act of 1988 authorized $50 million for continued support of State administrative activities and $120 million for the purchase and distribution of additional commodities that were high in nutrient content, as well as safely and easily stored and used. The purchased commodities were in addition to commodities that could be made available from USDA inventories. These activities were reauthorized by the FACT Act of 1990, P.L. 101-624. Specific authorizations for appropriation of funds for commodity purchases were included for Fiscal Years 1991-1995.

Eligibility. Commodities are distributed to the States which, in turn, provide them to low-income and unemployed persons, according to income-based eligibility criteria set by the States. States are allocated commodities based on a formula which considers the number of persons in each State below the poverty level (60 percent) and the number of persons unemployed (40 percent).

Benefit. USDA provides commodities and cash subsidies for State and local expenses incurred for storage and distribution of USDA donated commodities. USDA will distribute surplus butter and cornmeal in Fiscal Year 1993. In addition, funds have been provided by direct appropriation so that USDA may also purchase foods high in nutrient density specifically for distribution via TEFAP. The additional foods USDA plans to purchase in Fiscal Year 1993 include canned peas, green beans, applesauce, orange juice, pork, and beef, as well as peanut butter, raisins, rice, and dry bagged beans.
In Fiscal Year 1993, a total of $45 million in administrative funds will be distributed by the Food and Nutrition Service (FNS) to States through grants. Allocation of administrative funds to States is based on the same formula used to allocate commodities to States (the number of persons in each State below the poverty level and the number of unemployed persons).

State/Federal Responsibilities. The Emergency Food Assistance Program operates as a Federal/State partnership under agreements entered into between FNS and State agencies. Once the foods are made available to States, the overall organization and administration of the program become the responsibilities of State agencies. Each State is responsible for selecting emergency feeding organizations to distribute the commodities and for determining the eligibility of persons to participate. The frequency of the distributions, as well as the quantities of commodities to be distributed to local areas, are also determined by each State distributing agency.

State administrative costs are subsidized by the Federal government. However, by statute, States must pass down at least 40 percent of their administrative funding to local organizations. State distributing agency costs include contracted services such as warehousing and delivery of commodities.

State distributing agencies coordinate the activities of emergency feeding organizations, which in turn serve distribution sites nationwide. Typical distribution sites include churches and community action agencies; many sites have other principal purposes unrelated to food distribution. They are staffed largely by volunteers.

The Federal government pays 100 percent of the costs of surplus commodities donated to States, plus the cost of purchased commodities and provides grants of administrative funds. USDA also pays for processing the commodities into household size packages, and shipping them to locations within the states.

P.L. 102-552 Temporary Assistance

Section 515 of the Farm Credit Banks and Associations Safety and Soundness Act of 1992, P.L. 102-552, provides for a one year funding increase for commodity distribution from an amount equal to the expected receipts to the Treasury from repayments of debts owed by the Farm Credit System (FCS). This assistance is available for Fiscal Year 1993 and is estimated at $42,329,000 according to the calculation by the Office of Management and Budget as required by P.L. 102-552. These funds will be used to purchase, process and distribute additional commodities through the same channels that USDA uses for the Emergency Food Assistance Program.

JUSTIFICATION OF INCREASES AND DECREASES

(1) An increase of $1,215,000 in the appropriation for Administrative Costs ($45,000,000 available in 1993).

Need for Change. To provide States with increased funds to administer the projected growth in The Emergency Food Assistance Program.

Nature of Change. An increase of $1,215,000 consists of a 2.7 percent inflationary increase to support commodity distribution in Fiscal Year 1994.

(2) An increase of $3,240,000 in the appropriation for Commodity Procurement ($120,000,000 available in 1993).

Need for Change. This increase will provide for additional commodity distribution to program participants, thereby enhancing the Nation's fight against hunger.

Nature of Change. The $3,240,000 increase consists of a 2.7 percent inflationary increase applied to the 1993 base of $120 million.

In addition to the funding needed to support current program efforts, the President's proposed investment of another $40 million will provide additional assistance in the fight against hunger.

The Emergency Food Assistance Program
Summary of Investment Proposals

SUMMARY OF INCREASES AND DECREASES - INVESTMENT PROPOSAL

	1994		
	Base Request	Investment Proposed	Total Request
Administrative Costs...	$46,215,000	—	$46,215,000
Commodity Procurement..	123,240,000	+40,000,000	163,240,000
Total Available........	169,455,000	+40,000,000	209,455,000

Explanation of Investment Proposal

The increase of $40 million will provide funds for additional commodities and enable the Emergency Food Assistance Program to provide additional assistance in the fight against hunger.

Proposed Language

In addition to funding already provided, $40,000,000 for necessary expenses of the Emergency Food Assistance Program.

THE EMERGENCY FOOD ASSISTANCE PROGRAM
STATUS OF PROGRAM

Funds for The Emergency Food Assistance Program (TEFAP) are provided to States to help finance State and local costs associated with the transportation, processing, storage and distribution of donated commodities. A total of $204.4 million in bonus and purchased commodities were provided for Fiscal Year 1992 for household distribution.

Current Activities

TEFAP commodities and funds for intrastate distribution are allocated to the States based on a formula which considers the unemployment rates in the States and the number of persons in each State with incomes below the poverty level. During Fiscal Year 1992, $165 million was appropriated for Commodities and Administrative Funding.

Bonus commodities totaling over 240 million pounds and valued at $85.1 million were donated to the States during Fiscal Year 1992 by the USDA. These commodities included butter, cornmeal, and flour, and wheat. The additional commodities purchased and donated for household distribution include milled rice, pears, applesauce, canned poultry, canned green beans, canned corn, canned tomatoes, canned pork, raisins, and peanut butter. They totaled over 159 million pounds and were valued at $119.3 million. Both donated and purchased commodities are distributed to the needy through the combined efforts of Federal, State, and local governments, private voluntary organizations and volunteer ad hoc efforts.

Once donated foods are made available to States, the overall organization and administration of the program becomes the responsibility of State agencies. Each State is responsible for selecting emergency feeding organizations to distribute the commodities and for determining the eligibility of persons to participate.

Fiscal Year 1992 TEFAP Summary
(millions)

	Dollars	Pounds
State Administrative Funding	$44.9	--
Commodities		
Bonus Commodities	85.1	240.2
Commodity Procurement	119.3	159.0
AMS/ASCS Administration	.7	--
Total	$250.0	399.2

31g-60

THE EMERGENCY FOOD ASSISTANCE PROGRAM
Bonus and Entitlement Commodity Donations

Fiscal Year 1992

State or Territory	Pounds of Food	Value in Dollars
Alabama	8,545,278	4,462,278
Alaska	558,980	249,250
Arizona	4,708,280	2,477,420
Arkansas	5,935,812	2,950,583
California	43,432,766	22,519,250
Colorado	4,352,464	2,218,500
Connecticut	3,083,420	2,015,600
Delaware	981,578	547,641
District of Columbia	1,216,688	733,750
Florida	18,071,101	9,424,420
Georgia	7,665,961	4,314,760
Hawaii	801,846	438,870
Idaho	1,781,850	859,675
Illinois	19,210,120	9,688,925
Indiana	7,483,670	3,816,584
Iowa	3,571,836	1,816,450
Kansas	3,205,524	1,595,240
Kentucky	6,916,962	3,125,990
Louisiana	9,593,784	5,028,325
Maine	1,922,229	1,025,450
Maryland	7,008,014	3,522,225
Massachusetts	9,896,731	4,827,275
Michigan	16,221,038	8,273,800
Minnesota	5,195,582	2,570,550
Mississippi	6,941,808	3,611,250
Missouri	8,771,120	4,196,875
Montana	1,212,902	576,725
Nebraska	1,721,700	896,950
Nevada	1,242,920	640,250
New Hampshire	1,601,518	831,675
New Jersey	11,702,204	5,917,300
New Mexico	2,712,176	1,432,375
New York	30,959,317	15,872,225
North Carolina	10,448,704	5,224,750
North Dakota	999,684	480,530
Ohio	16,110,668	8,196,350
Oklahoma	5,767,458	2,903,250
Oregon	4,612,782	2,199,250
Pennsylvania	17,785,112	9,247,753
Rhode Island	1,230,294	691,267
South Carolina	4,579,002	2,059,126
South Dakota	1,145,634	530,350
Tennessee	8,976,918	4,862,632
Texas	30,151,981	14,973,967
Utah	1,954,998	1,041,162
Vermont	1,148,013	622,758
Virginia	7,876,272	3,843,691
Washington	6,563,784	3,385,216
West Virginia	4,246,536	2,725,860
Wisconsin	5,909,394	3,123,212
Wyoming	639,666	350,088
American Samoa	0	0
Freely Associated States	0	0
Guam	118,800	43,692
N. Mariana Islands	126,000	26,044
Puerto Rico	10,363,260	5,305,626
Virgin Islands	268,019	123,238
Indian Tribes	0	0
DOD Army/AF/USMC/NAVY	0	0
AMS/ASCS Admin. Expenses	--	682,000
Anticipated Adjustment	0	0
TOTAL	399,250,158	205,120,248

SOURCE: Preliminary food orders for fiscal year 1992

31g-61

THE EMERGENCY FOOD ASSISTANCE PROGRAM
Administrative Expense Funding

Fiscal Years 1992-1993

State or Territory	Actual 1992	Estimated 1993
Alabama	$946,334	$868,410
Alaska	78,494	81,405
Arizona	499,776	685,575
Arkansas	580,021	510,615
California	4,955,097	5,468,715
Colorado	459,540	518,805
Connecticut	468,008	402,300
Delaware	113,380	87,660
District of Columbia	140,000	123,120
Florida	2,174,969	2,321,955
Georgia	1,186,440	1,135,575
Hawaii	118,483	119,295
Idaho	175,744	158,490
Illinois	2,061,261	1,992,870
Indiana	851,446	786,870
Iowa	385,304	381,600
Kansas	346,273	318,195
Kentucky	872,905	751,995
Louisiana	1,047,561	1,074,735
Maine	239,427	177,075
Maryland	702,567	633,915
Massachusetts	1,145,008	915,660
Michigan	1,813,838	1,713,960
Minnesota	608,067	571,455
Mississippi	790,612	712,710
Missouri	949,874	861,210
Montana	144,744	148,185
Nebraska	192,425	188,100
Nevada	144,899	176,220
New Hampshire	166,384	141,750
New Jersey	1,189,784	1,139,265
New Mexico	321,324	346,770
New York	3,247,860	3,205,035
North Carolina	1,214,188	1,071,000
North Dakota	101,188	99,945
Ohio	1,708,136	1,804,545
Oklahoma	584,910	580,185
Oregon	452,340	479,880
Pennsylvania	2,055,671	1,873,575
Rhode Island	175,869	164,025
South Carolina	666,996	632,925
South Dakota	83,104	107,730
Tennessee	1,036,437	904,320
Texas	3,121,328	3,650,895
Utah	226,060	227,205
Vermont	97,043	82,665
Virginia	944,553	906,075
Washington	704,604	728,730
West Virginia	420,293	437,175
Wisconsin	653,734	650,160
Wyoming	58,408	64,080
American Samoa	0	0
Freely Associated States	0	0
Guam	18,340	16,065
N. Mariana Islands	9,084	7,965
Puerto Rico	1,529,124	1,773,225
Virgin Islands	20,761	18,135
Indian Tribes	0	0
DOD Army/AF/USMC/NAVY	0	0
Undistributed	-1,000	0
TOTAL	$44,999,000	$45,000,000

31g-62

THE EMERGENCY FOOD ASSISTANCE PROGRAM
Quantity and Value of Commodities

By Commodity, Fiscal Year 1992

ENTITLEMENT COMMODITIES	Pounds	Dollars
SECTION 6/32 TYPE:		
APPLESAUCE	16,027,200	$5,940,895
BEANS, GREEN, CANNED	10,936,800	3,228,722
CORN, WHOLE KERNEL	9,273,600	3,503,304
PEARS, CANNED	7,998,408	4,375,168
PORK, CANNED W/NJ	35,261,622	45,115,477
POULTRY, CANNED BONED	328,860	627,164
RASINS	7,566,720	4,807,423
TOMATOES, CANNED	18,785,424	6,825,467
Total Section 6/32 Type	106,178,634	$74,423,620

ENTITLEMENT COMMODITIES	Pounds	Dollars
SECTION 416-TYPE:		
PEANUT BUTTER	52,584,480	$44,851,555
RICE MILLED	252,000	34,725
Total Section 416-Type	52,836,480	$44,886,280
AMS/ASCS Admin. Expenses		682,000
Anticipated Adjustment		0
Total Commodity Entitlement	159,015,114	119,991,900

BONUS COMMODITIES	Pounds	Dollars
SECTION 416-TYPE:		
BUTTER	65,042,244	$61,653,693
CORN, YELLOW #2	604,800	81,648
CORNMEAL	48,325,200	5,664,952
FLOUR	125,650,800	17,482,643
WHEAT	612,000	245,412
Anticipated Adjustment	0	0
Total Section 416-Type	240,235,044	85,128,348
GRAND TOTAL (Entitlement & Bonus)	399,250,158	$205,120,248

SOURCE: Preliminary food orders for fiscal year 1992

FOOD AND NUTRITION SERVICE

The estimates include appropriation language for this item as follows (new language underscored; deleted matter enclosed in brackets):

Food Program Administration:

For necessary administrative expenses of the domestic food programs funded under this Act, [$103,535,000] $105,201,000; of which $5,000,000 shall be available only for simplifying procedures, reducing overhead costs, tightening regulations, improving food stamp coupon handling, and assistance in the prevention, identification, and prosecution of fraud and other violations of law: Provided, That this appropriation shall be available for employment pursuant to the second sentence of section 706(a) of the Organic Act of 1944 (7 U.S.C. 2225), and not to exceed $150,000 shall be available for employment under 5 U.S.C. 3109.

31-92

FOOD PROGRAM ADMINISTRATION

Appropriations Act, 1993	$103,535,000
Budget Estimate, 1994	105,201,000
Increase in Appropriation	+1,666,000

SUMMARY OF INCREASES
(On basis of appropriation)

Item of Change	1993 Estimated	Pay Cost	Other Changes	1994 Estimated
Salaries and Expenses	$103,535,000	+$1,732,000	-$66,000	$105,201,000

PROJECT STATEMENT
(On basis of appropriation)

Project	1992 Actual Amount	1992 Actual Staff Years	1993 Estimated Amount	1993 Estimated Staff Years	Increase	1994 Estimated Amount	1994 Estimated Staff Years
1. Child Nutrition/ Special Milk	$27,389,000	479	$27,416,000	483	+$441,000	$27,857,000	483
2. Supplemental Feeding	11,398,000	199	11,409,000	201	+184,000	11,593,000	201
3. Food Stamp	57,891,971	1,013	57,949,000	1,019	+932,000	58,881,000	1,019
4. Food Donations	6,754,000	118	6,761,000	119	+109,000	6,870,000	119
Unobligated balance lapsing	102,029	--	--	--	--	--	--
Total, appropriation	103,535,000	1,809	103,535,000	1,822	+1,666,000[1]	105,201,000	1,822

EXPLANATION OF PROGRAM

The Food Program Administration (FPA) appropriation funds Federal salaries and expenses necessary for the Food and Nutrition Service (FNS) to administer the U.S. Department of Agriculture's (USDA) domestic food assistance programs.

Overview. FNS was established August 8, 1969 to administer the domestic food assistance programs. The program goals are to provide needy persons with access to a more nutritious diet, to improve the eating habits of the nation's children, and to help America's farmers by providing an outlet for the distribution of foods purchased under farmer assistance authorities.

USDA began food distribution programs more than fifty years ago and used a variant of the current Food Stamp Program in the 1930's. Over the years, the programs shown in the following table were established and are currently in operation. Most FNS programs are operated in a Federal/State partnership, with State and local agencies administering the program at the actual service delivery level. The general complexity of the programs and the number of State entities that FNS must work with are key factors influencing FPA costs.

Year Begun	Program Name	Number	Types of Non-federal Partners
1946	National School Lunch Program (NSLP)	58	State Education Agencies
		55	Food Distribution Agencies (Also, 20,400 School Food Authorities)
1955	Special Milk Program		(Essentially the same as NSLP)
1961	Food Stamp Program	53	State Agencies
		213,000	Food Retailers
		10,000	Financial Institutions
		37	Federal Reserve Banks
1965	Nutrition Program for the Elderly	57	State Agencies
1966	School Breakfast Program		(Essentially the same as NSLP)
1968	Child and Adult Care Food Program	54	State Agencies
1969	Summer Food Service Program	53	State Agencies
1969	Commodity Supplemental Food Program	20	State Agencies
1972	Special Supplemental Food Program for Women, Infants, and Children (WIC)	86	State Agencies (Also, 47,000 Food Retailers)
1976	Food Distribution Program on Indian Reservations	6	State Agencies
		88	Indian Tribes
1981	The Emergency Food Assistance Program	55	State Agencies
1982	Nutrition Assistance Program for Puerto Rico and Northern Marianas	2	State Agencies
1983	National Commodity Processing Program	11	Food Processors
1988	Soup Kitchen/Food Bank Program	55	State Agencies
1988	Farmers Market Nutrition Program	10	State Agencies

Responsibilities. FNS is responsible for paying the benefit costs and for paying a part of State administrative expenses for most food assistance programs. Depending upon how States have chosen to administer their part of the Federal/State partnership, FNS may work with the State department of human services, department of health, department of education, department on aging, department of agriculture, and/or State level commissions or other administrative units. When State law prohibits a State from disbursing program funds or where no State agency has assumed administrative responsibility, FNS assumes operation of the programs. In some programs, Indian tribal organizations function as State administering agencies.

FNS plans and coordinates the purchase and distribution of commodities to State agencies for use in domestic food assistance programs.

FNS implements program statutes through promulgation of regulations and instructions. FNS staff provide training and assistance to State Agencies, assure proper funds allocation and control, conduct program monitoring and evaluation, assure program integrity, develop program policy, and provide policy oversight.

Organization. Administrative functions of FNS are managed by an Administrator, two Associate Administrators and four Deputy Administrators. Each Deputy Administrator is responsible for management of program or administrative functions, as follows:

-- Food Stamp Program - program planning, development and oversight related to the Food Stamp Program including retail store compliance and monitoring investigations through field locations.

-- Special Nutrition Programs - program planning, development and oversight for Child Nutrition, Supplemental Food Programs, Food Donations Programs, National Commodity Processing and nutrition and technical services.

-- Financial Management - accounting, budget, grants management and program information functions for all FNS programs, including oversight over the Agency's administrative review process both at FNS headquarters and five outstationed sites located throughout the country.

-- Management - personnel, civil rights and equal employment opportunity, information resource management, management information, procurement, property and general administrative services.

Also at Headquarters are two staff offices:

-- Office of Analysis and Evaluation - policy research and analysis, legislative analysis, budget planning and regulatory review across programs, and special studies and evaluations.

-- Office of Governmental Affairs and Public Information - liaison with Congress, liaison with media and the public, and informational support of FNS programs.

Program operations are managed through seven regional offices, each directed by a regional administrator, incorporating 81 field locations (field and satellite) and 3 ROAP offices (2 seasonal). These offices maintain direct contact with State agencies which administer the FNS programs and also conduct on-site management reviews of State operations and the 213,000 retailers authorized to accept food stamps.

For Fiscal Year 1993, FNS will concentrate on improving program administration and operations within existing law. The agency believes that greater emphasis on all aspects of program integrity and efficiency will result in improved benefit delivery to recipients. Major areas of emphasis in the administration of FNS programs include:

<u>Food Stamp Program</u>

-- Continue implementation of the Food, Agriculture, Conservation and Trade Act of 1990, P.L. 101-624, which reauthorized the Food Stamp and Commodity Distribution Programs.

-- Continue development of procedures to increase coordination of services among the Aid to Families with Dependent Children, Medicaid, Supplemental Security Income Programs, and the Food Stamp Program.

-- Implementation of a long-term multi-pronged strategy to increase and enhance enforcement actions including the conclusion of reauthorization of retailers project begun in Fiscal Year 1992, and to provide program modifications which will help deter food stamp trafficking.

-- Food Stamp Program quality control reviews, to assess the States' liabilities due to excessive error rates in issuance of benefits, and the determination of enhanced funding for States with low error rates.

-- Continuation of current demonstration projects testing the impact of Electronic Benefit Transfer technology on the Food Stamp issuance, redemption and reconciliation process, and application of EBT technology for use in WIC.

Special Nutrition Program

-- Continue implementation of The Commodity Distribution Reform Act, P.L. 100-237, which mandated food distribution program enhancements which will make the system more responsive to recipient agencies.

-- Special Nutrition Program activities to improve program integrity, accountability, and quality control particularly for the school, child and adult care food programs, and the WIC program.

-- Continued implementation of required child nutrition program regulations and operation of the grants established under Public Law 101-147, Child Nutrition and WIC Reauthorization Act.

-- Continued operation of the demonstration project to evaluate the participation of proprietary child care centers in the Child and Adult Care Food Program.

-- Continued operation and expansion of the demonstration project to evaluate the feasibility of providing Federal child nutrition funding for meals served to children in homeless shelters.

-- Continued operation of the demonstration project to evaluate various alternative methods for accounting for meals served in schools participating in the National School Lunch Program.

-- Evaluation and issuance of a report to the Congress on the demonstration project established to test various strategies to reduce barriers to participation in the Child and Adult Care Food Program by family day care homes located in low-income areas.

-- Increased information-sharing with States and local school food authorities on the process and benefits of "direct certification"; i.e., allowing direct communication from food stamp and AFDC offices regarding a child's eligibility to participate in lieu of a separate school lunch application.

-- Publish final regulations for direct certification of free meal eligibility in the National School Lunch Program.

-- Development, in coordination with the Department of Health and Human Services, of dietary guidelines for use in Child Nutrition Programs.

-- Development of a training initiative that, building in experiences from the National School Lunch Program and Summer Food Service Program training efforts, involves State agencies in priority setting and in the development of effective, high quality training material.

-- Continue technology transfer efforts in the National School Lunch Program and School Breakfast Program through Best Practice Awards.

-- Continued development of the Coordinated Review System to ensure that it effectively reduces over-counting and claiming problems in the Special Nutrition Programs with special emphasis on integrating Federal and State level reviews to ensure effective resource utilization.

-- Implementation of WIC vendor management improvement initiatives and proposed and final regulations to strengthen the integrity of vendor selection, training, monitoring and sanctioning.

-- Active participation by WIC and other FNS programs in the Surgeon General's Healthy Children Ready to Learn initiative follow up activities.

-- Continued active promotion of Breastfeeding for WIC participants, which include meetings of the USDA-sponsored Breastfeeding Promotion Consortium, the development of a public education campaign, and the conduct of eight breastfeeding incentive demonstration grants. Additionally, implementation of final regulatory changes including administrative support and enhancement of food packages for breastfeeding women on WIC.

-- Cooperation with the Healthy Start initiative, by offering technical assistance, support and advice as requested to grantee cities to permit the optimal use of Federal assistance, especially WIC, to grantees to support their efforts to reduce infant mortality.

-- Continued enhancement of the Processed Commodity Information Management System (PCIMS) which established one database for three USDA Agencies to use to manage the Commodity Programs and makes the programs more responsive to recipient agencies.

-- Implementation of the Farmers Market Nutrition Program, including grant awards, training, and issuance of interim regulations.

-- Coordination of WIC with Even Start and Head Start to foster improved services to participants.

-- Implementation of Public Law 102-512, the WIC Infant Formula Procurement Act of 1992 through regulations, Federal solicitation of infant formula rebate bids and evaluation of this Law's impact on food costs.

Financial Management

-- Implementation of the Chief Financial Officers Act (CFO) to review all financial management functions to ensure that core functions are appropriately placed and delegations of authority and policies are updated.

-- Development of the grants management subsystem to the Agency Financial Management System. This will include systems for grant awards, letter of credit, and regional accounting activities.

-- Continue to cooperate with the U.S. Treasury Financial Management Service to ensure State compliance with the implementation provisions of the Cash Management Improvement Act of 1990.

-- Continuation of an overall strategy to improve the accounting and collection of debts including expansion of the Federal Tax Refund Offset Program from pilot status to operational status. Nine State agencies will participate for tax year 1992. The agency will offer the training and developmental support for an additional 16 State agencies in 1993 so that they may participate in tax year 1993.

Management

-- Implementation of the Store Tracking and Authorization Redemption Subsystem (STARS), WIC Information System Enhancements (WISE), and Disqualified Recipient Subsystem (DRS) under the software Renewal Program to improve vendor management, program administration, and management of disqualified recipients.

-- Coordination with the Department of Health and Human Services to implement General Accounting Office recommendations relevant to approval process for automation of State systems.

-- Development and offering of Agencywide ethics training, as mandated by regulation.

-- Improvement of research contract statement of work guidance, provision of training, and change of existing contract to apply the recent GAO-mandated funding restrictions on the use of contract options.

JUSTIFICATION OF INCREASES AND DECREASES

(1) A net increase of $1,666,000 for salaries and benefits and other expenses consisting of:

(a) An increase of $1,732,000 for salaries and benefits which reflects the annualization of the Fiscal Year 1993 pay raise.

(b) A net decrease of $66,000 for travel and other operation expenses consisting of:

(i) An increase of $474,000 which reflects a 2.7 percent increase in non-salary costs.

(ii) A decrease of $491,000 for administrative efficiency.

Need for Change. To promote the efficient use of resources for administrative purposes, in keeping with the President's Executive Order, total USDA baseline outlays for these activities will be reduced by 3 percent in Fiscal Year (FY) 1994, 6 percent in FY 1995, 9 percent in FY 1996, and 14 percent in FY 1997.

Nature of Change. In order to achieve this savings, FNS will limit travel and other administrative expenses to those essential to Agency missions.

(iii) A decrease of $49,000 for FTS funding. This decrease reflects lower long distance telecommunications prices due to price redeterminations in the FTS 2000 contracts.

FOOD PROGRAM ADMINISTRATION

STATUS OF PROGRAM

The Food Program Administration appropriation provides Federal operating expenses for administering the food assistance programs of the Food and Nutrition Service (FNS). Included under this account are the Food Stamp, Child Nutrition, Special Milk, Special Supplemental Food Program for Women, Infants, and Children (WIC), Commodity Supplemental Food, and Food Donations Programs for Selected Groups Programs. Also included are Nutrition Assistance for Puerto Rico, Surplus Commodity Donations activities, and National Commodity Processing. Major administrative activities of the FNS staff during Fiscal Year 1992 are as follows:

Food Stamp Program

The Food Stamp Program is in operation in all 50 States, the District of Columbia, the Virgin Islands and Guam. Its purpose is to give low income households access to a better diet by increasing their food purchasing power. The State agencies are responsible for certifying eligible households and issuing the food stamps. The major activities performed by FNS include: developing policies and procedures for the administration of the program, providing technical assistance to State agencies, reviewing State agency quality control activities, determining the effectiveness and efficiency of State agency administration, reviewing and approving planning documents for electronic benefit transfer issuance systems, and allocating employment and training funds to the State agencies. In addition, FNS directly authorizes the retail and wholesale firms which are approved to accept food stamps; controls the printing of food stamps and the distribution to State agencies; maintains fiscal accountability for food stamps issued to participants; and, in cooperation with the Federal Reserve System, establishes processes for the redemption and destruction of food stamps.

During Fiscal Year 1992, FNS performed the following principal Food Stamp Program administrative activities:

- Continued work on several demonstration projects directed toward program simplification and testing alternative systems for issuing food stamp benefits.

- Issued 14 proposed and final regulations and 10 general notices.

- Acted upon 183 waiver requests, approving 143 and denying 40. Waivers of the regulations were requested in order to provide State agencies maximum flexibility to administer the program more effectively and efficiently.

- Coordinated the exchange of information on program management initiatives among State agencies by funding interstate exchange of expertise.

- Continued litigation and other action on quality control sanctions; continued litigation on other program issues.

- Approved 53 Employment and Training (E&T) Program State plans, allotted Federal funds for employment and training activities, and provided State agencies with guidance on E&T Program operations.

- Distributed reports on Compliance Branch investigations of retailers authorized to accept food stamps from recipients. The Compliance Branch sends these reports of its investigations of retail food stores to FNS regional offices, for appropriate administrative sanction actions, or to the Department's Office of Inspector General when it is determined that the potential for criminal prosecution exists.

- Investigated 4,848 stores for violations. Of this number, 1,951 of the stores were found to be violating Food Stamp Program regulations (40 percent), 1,433 (30 percent) of which disclosed violations serious enough to warrant disqualification or other sanction action by FNS. The remaining 518 violating firms received official warning letters.

Nutrition Assistance for Puerto Rico

For Fiscal Year 1992, Puerto Rico budgeted: $970.55 million in benefits to clients participating in its Nutrition Assistance Program; $31.625 million (Federal funds) to administer the program; and $10.825 million for the Commonwealth's Tick Eradication special project, for a total Federal budgeted expenditure of $1.013 billion.

Child Nutrition and Special Milk Programs

The Child Nutrition Programs--the National School Lunch, School Breakfast, Summer Food Service and Child and Adult Care Food Programs--serve nutritious meals to needy and other children attending eligible schools, child care institutions, and summer recreational programs. FNS works primarily through State agencies, providing cash and commodities for use in preparing and serving meals. FNS furnishes administrative and program assistance to State agencies and participating schools and institutions. FNS also develops the policies, procedures and standards used in administering the programs and determining eligibility.

The FNS regional offices directly administer the National School Lunch and School Breakfast Programs for residential child care institutions and private schools where the State educational agency does not disburse funds. FNS regional offices also directly administer the Summer Food Service Program and the Child and Adult Care Food Program for nonresidential child care institutions where no State agency has assumed administrative responsibility. Because of the great number and small size of individual centers and sponsors of day care homes participating in States directly administered by FNS Regional Offices, adequate review of participating sponsors requires extensive FNS staff resources. The Summer Food Service Program also continues to place heavy demands on Federal personnel due to the short term of the program and because FNS must directly administer the program in six States.

In Fiscal Year 1992, FNS directly administered the National School Lunch and School Breakfast Programs for private schools in four States, private residential child care institutions in five States, and public residential child care institutions in two states. In addition, FNS operated the Child Care Food Program in two States (Virginia and New York) and the Summer Food Service Program in six States (New York, Virginia, Georgia, Michigan, Missouri and California).

During Fiscal Year 1992, the Federal administration of the Child Nutrition Programs included these principal activities:

- Conducted a pilot demonstration project to determine the best means of providing year round food assistance to homeless preschool children in shelters. The project was mandated by the Child Nutrition and WIC Reauthorization Act of 1989, P.L. 101-147; and in accordance with the reporting language, the project was initiated with the Archdiocese of Philadelphia, and was expanded to include 20 other organizations nationally. Public Law 102-342, enacted on August 14, 1992 authorized increased funding for the project and made public organizations eligible for it.

- Conducted two statewide demonstration projects to test eligibility changes in the Child and Adult Care Food Program. Under this project private for-profit centers may participate if they serve a minimum of 25 percent free or reduced price meals to children. The project is examining nutritional improvements, fees charged to low income children, numbers of additional low income children served, budgetary impact of the eligibility change, and effectiveness of State outreach methods. Pursuant to P.L. 101-147, Kentucky and Iowa were the States selected for these projects.

- Held two national task force sessions of local, state and federal program managers to develop Coordinated Review implementation materials and a national implementation training session.

- Published an interim rule to modify implementation of a coordinated Federal/State review system for the National School Lunch Program.

- Conducted demonstrations in twelve school districts testing alternatives to current requirements governing determinations of eligibility for free and reduced price meals, and counting and claiming of those meals for reimbursement. This initiative was authorized under P.L. 101-147.

- Solicited proposals from States for grants to defray nonrecurring costs associated with starting up the School Breakfast Program. Awarded $5 million to 31 States for the third year.

The Special Milk Program provides cash to States to subsidize milk served to children in eligible nonprofit schools, child care centers, summer camps and similar institutions that do not participate in other Child Nutrition Programs and in certain schools with split session kindergartens. FNS directly administers the program for outlets in States which do not disburse funds to some participants, and for other outlets where no State agency has assumed administrative responsibility. During Fiscal Year 1992, FNS directly administered the Special Milk Program for private schools, summer camps and other institutions in six States.

Special Commodity Initiatives

FNS, in cooperation with the Agricultural Marketing Service and the Agricultural Stabilization and Conservation Service, initiated a long-term project called the Special Commodity Initiative to improve the distribution and quality of commodities in Child Nutrition Programs. Projects for 1992 included:

- Implementing changes in operations and procurement systems to improve predictability of commodity deliveries.

- Continuing the nutrition improvement efforts on the review of current specifications to obtain the lowest possible fat, salt and/or sugar levels while maintaining acceptability, functionality and consistency with dietary guidelines.

- Offering new commodities, such as turkey burgers, 10-percent beef patties, and catfish fillet strips to schools.

- Continuing the integration of the computer system activities of the three agencies to provide greater efficiency, increased accuracy and timeliness, and improved reporting capabilities of all users.

- Increased unitization (placing on pallets and stretch wrapping) of commodities.

Special Supplemental Food Program for Women, Infants, and Children (WIC)

The WIC Program provides nutritious supplemental foods, nutrition education, and health care referrals through local health clinics to low income pregnant, postpartum, and breastfeeding women, and to infants and children up to five years of age who are found to be at "nutritional risk." FNS provides grant funds to State Departments of Health and others to permit the issuance of supplemental food instruments to eligible participants and pays for specified administrative costs including the cost of nutrition education. FNS also develops the policies, procedures, and standards used in administering the program and monitors State agency operations. In Fiscal Year 1992, the WIC Program was administered by 85 State agencies, including 50 States, 31 Indian agencies and the District of Columbia, Puerto Rico, Guam and the Virgin Islands.

In Fiscal Year 1992, FNS conducted the following principal activities:

- Issued congressionally mandated reports to Congress on a) State agency administrative funding patterns; b) paperwork reduction; c) preliminary report on nutrition risk and food package reviews; and d) monthly financial reports discussing inflation trends and State expenditure patterns.

- Conducted one meeting of the National Advisory Council on Maternal, Infant and Fetal Nutrition.

- Planned and conducted a nationwide technical assistance meeting for WIC State and local program operators on automation strategies and future application.

- Issued a study of WIC cost effectiveness showing that prenatal WIC participation is associated with Medicaid savings, increases in birthweight, and lower incidence of pre-term birth.

- Issued final regulations to facilitate service delivery to homeless persons.

- Provided technical assistance to States in the use of a model application form developed with the Department of Health and Human Services for use in one-stop shopping efforts for programs such as WIC, Medicaid, Head Start and other programs serving a similar low income maternal and child health population.

- Cooperated with DHHS on a number of maternal and child health promotions, including Healthy Start and Healthy Children Ready to Learn.

- Cooperated with the Centers for Disease Control in a major collaborative effort to promote immunizations among the WIC population. Assisted CDC in the development of a video promoting immunizations.

- Held one meeting of the Breastfeeding Consortium, a USDA-established collaborative effort which brings together almost 30 professional health organizations and government agencies on a regular basis to discuss breastfeeding promotion strategies.

Commodity Supplemental Food Program (CSFP)

The Commodity Supplemental Food Program provides supplemental food to low income pregnant, postpartum and breastfeeding women, infants, children up to age six and the elderly. The foods are purchased directly by the Department of Agriculture and are distributed through State and local agencies. The major activities performed by FNS include: determination of the quantity of food required and allocation of commodities to meet the requirements; interagency coordination of commodity purchases; program monitoring and review; and allocation of funds to States for administrative costs. During Fiscal Year 1992, the Commodity Supplemental Food Program was operated through 20 State agencies.

Food Donations Programs for Selected Groups

Commodity programs which provide direct assistance to persons in need include: the Food Distribution Program on Indian Reservations, the Nutrition Program for the Elderly, and Soup Kitchen/Food Banks assistance.

- Food Distribution Program on Indian Reservations (FDPIR)

  FNS acquires and distributes agricultural commodities to needy persons and families on Indian reservations through FDPIR provided they do not receive food stamps. Cash assistance is also provided to help finance the administrative cost of operating the program.

  The Food Stamp Act of 1977, which requires that a food distribution program be operated on Indian reservations that request it, also allows the Indian reservations to run FDPIR provided they meet specified administrative criteria. FNS provides the training and other assistance as needed.

  Training and other assistance provided to new reservations are primarily directed toward basic program operations, while the assistance given to more experienced reservations concentrates on the enhancement of program management.

- Nutrition Program for the Elderly

  The Nutrition Program for the Elderly provides commodities and cash-in-lieu of commodities for meals served in senior citizen centers and similar settings where participants can also receive social and rehabilitative services. The management and operation of this program is in the Administration on Aging (AOA) of the Department of Health and Human Services (DHHS). The meals served are the focal point for the nutrition projects which have the dual objectives of promoting better health and reducing the isolation that may occur in old age.

  The activities performed by FNS are receiving and processing States' orders for commodities and providing the commodities and cash-in-lieu of commodities.

- Soup Kitchen/Food Banks

  Pursuant to the Hunger Prevention Act of 1988, Public Law 100-435, $32 million was appropriated for Fiscal Year 1992 to purchase, process, and distribute commodities to soup kitchens and food banks. In Fiscal Year 1992, approximately 51.7 million pounds of commodities valued at $32 million were purchased and made available to States for distribution to soup kitchens and food banks.

Surplus Commodity Donations to Charitable Institutions and Summer Camps

The Surplus Commodity Donations Program provides commodities to nonprofit charitable institutions serving needy persons and to summer camps for children. These commodities are provided under section 416 Commodity Credit Corporation price support operations and section 32 surplus removal activities. Among the charitable institutions receiving donated commodities are homes for the elderly, hospitals, soup kitchens, meals-on-wheels programs, and orphanages that do not participate in one of the Child Nutrition Programs. FNS works through State agencies to provide these commodities. FNS furnishes administrative and program assistance to the cooperating State agencies and also develops the policies, procedures and standards used in administering the programs and determining eligibility.

Emergency Food Assistance Program

FNS allocates administrative funds and commodities to States based on the number of unemployed persons and the number of persons with incomes below the poverty level within each State. During Fiscal Year 1992, FNS distributed $45 million for administration and $120 million worth of commodities were purchased and donated. In addition, $85.1 million worth of surplus commodities from the Commodity Credit Corporation were donated.

Nutrition and Technical Services Support of Program Operations

The Nutrition and Technical Services staff provides technical support to FNS programs in the areas of nutrition science, nutrition education, food service management, and food/science technology. Nutritionists and food technologists at the Agency headquarters provide assistance and information to State and local agencies administering FNS programs.

During Fiscal Year 1992, food service and nutrition education accomplished the following:

- The revised publication, Nutrition Guidelines for the Child Nutrition Programs, was printed and distributed to 375,000 program cooperators. An additional 100,000 copies were printed due to continued demand.

- Continued to provide oversight and direct assistance services to the National Food Service Management Institute. Participated in Board meetings, provided technical assistance in development of Fiscal Year 1993 Statement of Work and in the upcoming reorganization of the contractual support to the Institute.

- Approved approximately 5,600 Child Nutrition labels. Initiated conversion of program to new software.

- Drafted interim regulation to approve the use of the Protein Digestibility Corrected Amino Acid Score method to determine protein quality of enriched macaroni products with fortified protein used in the Child Nutrition Programs.

- Issued criteria to all States for use in reviewing development of dietary guidance for Child Nutrition Programs to be endorsed/distributed by USDA.

- Provided on-going technical assistance to the Food Distribution Division reviewing commodity specifications and State Operation Commodity contracts. Made joint presentation with Agricultural Marketing Service and Food Safety and Inspection Service at commodity distribution meeting.

- Initiated development of nutrient based menu planning option for National School Lunch Program. Drafted discussion papers for approval of the Secretary outlining proposed actions, policy considerations and technical requirements.

- Planned and conducted a strategic planning conference for the Nutrition Education and Training Program (NET). The conference brought together representatives from programs in child nutrition, health, and education, and professional organizations to develop a draft document including strategic direction statement, objectives, strategies, and tactics for implementing NET.

- Developed a five year plan for nutrition education materials development in the Food Stamp Program.

- Developed request for proposals for a validation study of dietary assessment instruments appropriate for use in WIC.

- Developed poster, pamphlet and factsheets for use in promoting breastfeeding for children participating in the Child and Adult Care Food Program.

- Developed request for proposals for the Secretary's Nutrition Education Initiatives for WIC and Food Stamp Programs.

Regional Operations

Along with its headquarters in Alexandria, Virginia, FNS maintains seven regional offices, 81 field locations (field and satellite) and 3 ROAP offices (2 seasonal).

In addition, there are six Food Stamp Compliance offices, five outstationed Administrative Review Offices and one computer support center in Minneapolis which report directly to headquarters.

The regional offices supervise the 81 field locations whose mission is to ensure compliance in the Food Stamp Program and provide various review and support services for the other food assistance programs. Each regional office provides leadership and direction in implementing FNS program policy, develops operational planning and strategy, maintains cooperative working relationships with State agencies, and executes State corrective actions when necessary. A regional office or field office may also directly administer programs for schools and residential child care institutions where State educational agencies do not administer the program, as well as programs in child care institutions and summer program sites where no State agency has assumed administrative responsibility. Because of its location, the Caribbean Area office (a field office in Puerto Rico) performs many Regional office functions including all the on-site review work for Puerto Rico and the Virgin Islands. Similarly the Hawaii field office does the same for the Pacific Islands.

The regional office sites and the States currently in each region are as follows:

Northeast Region

Boston, Massachusetts

Connecticut	New York
Maine	Rhode Island
Massachusetts	Vermont
New Hampshire	

Mid Atlantic Region

Robbinsville, New Jersey

Delaware	Puerto Rico
District of Columbia	Virginia
Maryland	Virgin Islands
New Jersey	West Virginia
Pennsylvania	

Southeast Region

Atlanta, Georgia

Alabama	Mississippi
Florida	North Carolina
Georgia	South Carolina
Kentucky	Tennessee

Midwest Region

Chicago, Illinois

Illinois	Minnesota
Indiana	Ohio
Michigan	Wisconsin

Southwest Region

Dallas, Texas

Arkansas	Oklahoma
Louisiana	Texas
New Mexico	

Mountain Plains Region

Denver, Colorado

Colorado	Nebraska
Iowa	North Dakota
Kansas	South Dakota
Missouri	Utah
Montana	Wyoming

Western Region

San Francisco, California

Alaska	Nevada
American Samoa	Northern Marianas
Arizona	Oregon
California	Freely Associated States
Guam	
Hawaii	Washington
Idaho	

Financial Management Initiatives

During Fiscal Year 1992, FNS executed the following financial management initiatives:

- Increased its oversight of the development of Electronic Benefit Transfer (EBT) projects. Through the use of electronic funds payment systems, FNS hopes to improve services to recipients and grantees, improve cash management, reduce vulnerability to fraud, waste and abuse, and efficiently provide state-reported data on participation rates and costs of these operations.

- Continued to stress the importance of promptly paying all invoices for goods and services. During Fiscal Year 1992 FNS processed over 2,000 invoices, but had only a minimal amount of interest penalty assessed.

- Continued to strengthen and innovate the agency's debt collection methods to increase our collections of delinquent debts, using the most promising of the new methods to be employed, The Federal Tax Refund Offset Program, which permits Federal Agencies to offset delinquent debts against individuals. During Fiscal Year 1992, a total of over $3 million was collected from two states, California and Alabama.

- Continued development of the Agency's Work Measurement System, producing a revised Work Measurement System (WMS) Version 2.0. The revised system incorporated many modifications suggested by agency managers and staff, and it represents a substantial improvement over the version tested during Fiscal Year 1991.

- Continued the development and implementation of the Automated Financial Management System (AFMS). AFMS will upgrade and modernize FNS's financial management operations, thereby enhancing its management and oversight of $36 billion in Fiscal Year 1993 Federal funding.

<u>Debt Management</u>

Debts owed to FNS arise from several sources, such as:

- Audits, investigations and management evaluations of State and local agencies and nonprofit institutions which receive funding from FNS.

- Investigations of retailers and wholesalers participating in the Food Stamp Program, including assessment of civil penalties for program abuse and recoveries for improper redemption of food stamps.

- Losses of commodities which were transferred to commercial food processors prior to being shipped to States and losses of commodities distributed to States.

- Food Stamp coupons lost from State and local inventories, and losses resulting from State coupon issuances by mail.

- Claims against Food Stamp recipients for improper benefits.

- Claims against State agencies for erroneous issuances of food stamp coupons, and for error rates in State food stamp coupon issuance.

- Claims against school food authorities for meals charged inappropriately.

Highlights of Debt Management
Fiscal year 1991 - Fiscal Year 1992
($ Millions)

Debt Management (Excluding Food Stamp Recipient Claims):	1991	1992
Accounts receivable, ending balance	$ 37.6	$ 47.9

Collections	34.9	33.4
Litigation	20.4	21.4
Past Due	2.9	2.8
<u>Food Stamp Recipient Claims:</u>		
Accounts receivable, ending balance	661.3	722.4
Collections	64.3	106.1

Debt collection accomplishments include:

- Collection agency referrals increased 25 percent from the previous year to $2 million.

- New receivables billed of $59.2 million were almost 20 percent greater than Fiscal Year 1991.

- The outstanding balance at the end of the year contained 15 percent more claims in current status than the year before.

- Food Stamp recipient claims collected increased 56 percent over new claims established during the year.

<u>Information Resources Management (IRM) Initiatives</u>

During Fiscal Year 1992 FNS continued to update its technologies and systems in support of Agency goals. Major activities included:

- Purchase of additional microcomputers for FNS headquarters, regional and field office staff.

- Completion of the sixth year of the Software Renewal Program (SRP) which involves the redesign and integration of all FNS program and financial systems. The SRP is scheduled to be completed in Fiscal Year 1993, except for the later phases of the Agency Financial Management System (AFMS). However, some funding will still be required in subsequent fiscal years for contractor support to assist FNS in maintenance of the SRP Systems and for transitional services for eventual operation and maintenance by FNS.

- During Fiscal Year 1992 development continued on the Store Tracking and Redemption Subsystem (STARS) and the Disqualified Recipients Subsystem (DRS). Both of these allow tracking across State lines to prevent store owners re-establishing themselves in another State, or in the DRS, to prevent disqualified recipients from filing for benefits in another State. Both DRS and STARS have been designed to radically reduce program fraud and abuse. Additional functionality to further enhance program accountability will be added during Fiscal Years 1993 and 1994.

- For Special Nutrition Programs Part 2 of the Grantee Management Subsystem was completed and the Evaluate Performance/Analysis Subsystems development continued. The Evaluate Performance/Analysis Subsystems include capabilities for tracking management evaluations, commodity surveys, food complaints, audit status and results, and other special evaluation initiatives.

- Implementing major tasks of the Text Information Management System (TIMS), including conducting training for Headquarters personnel and the Southeast Regional Office personnel.

- Implementation of the Processed Commodities Inventory Management System occurred in four stages (two of which involved FNS) in Fiscal Year 1992. Commodities purchased by the Agricultural Stablization and Conservation Service were implemented in November 1991 and commodities purchased by Agricultural Marketing Service were added beginning in March 1992. The implementation has brought to light several hundred problems that are categorized and prioritized for correction as they are identified. Work to resolve these problems is a major on-going task within FNS. This work will require contractor assistance and the pace with which we are identifying problems indicates that this work will continue through Fiscal Year 1994.

- Implementation of the Expanded Food Stamp Redemption and Accountability Program at the FNS Minneapolis Computer Support Center and Store Update Project, an effort to reauthorize stores eligible to accept Food Stamps.

- Establishment of the Interagency Agreement with Social Security Administration (SSA) to use their Network Data Mover for State Connectivity (Electronic Data Interchange). FNS currently receives more than 60,000 annual reports from States and other reporting points. This effort will allow for electronic reporting and exchange of data with States and other reporting/receiving points through use of SSA's facilities. Testing a similar sharing of SSA's facilities with Disqualified Recipients System (DRS) data began. State agencies are being phased into DRS during Fiscal Year 1992-1993.

- Continued our approach to Long Range IRM Planning by correlating the technology plan to the Agency's program mission and the budget process.

Work Force Diversity Initiative

The Agency's Work Force Diversity Task Team, which represents all parts of the organization reviewed Agency progress during Fiscal Year 1992 and made recommendations for a Fiscal Year 1993 Work Force Diversity Action Plan. Some of the Agency's accomplishments during Fiscal Year 1992 were:

- Developed and implemented a structured mentor/protege program.

- Employed 20 summer intern students, including 10 from the 1890 Black land grant colleges and universities.

- Employed 24 cooperative education students, including 14 minority students.

- Developed an exit interview feedback system designed to help retain the representative diversity the Agency now employs.

- Received approval from the Office of Personnel Management to abolish the Agency's major job series, GS-120, Food Assistance Program Specialist. These positions will be primarily classified in two more general administrative series, GS-301, Miscellaneous Administrative and Program Analysis Series and GS-343, Management and Program Analysis Series. This will enable a wider recruitment of diverse groups and greater opportunity for advancement in other agencies.

- Revised the career ladder for regional office positions to help retain the capable and diverse employees who have been departing the Agency.

- Evaluated recruitment efforts in order to determine the most effective way of reaching a diverse group of employment applicants.

- Employed 13 individuals with disabilities during FY 1992.

WEDNESDAY, MARCH 24, 1993.

HUMAN NUTRITION INFORMATION SERVICE

WITNESSES

GEORGE BRALEY, ACTING ASSISTANT SECRETARY, FOOD AND CONSUMER SERVICES

DAVID RUST, ACTING ADMINISTRATOR, HUMAN NUTRITION INFORMATION SERVICE

ELLEN HARRIS, DIRECTOR OF NUTRITION MONITORING DIVISION

ALANNA MOSHFEGH, POLICY COORDINATOR

BETTY WARFIELD, ACTING CHIEF, BUDGET AND FINANCE

STEPHEN B. DEWHURST, BUDGET OFFICE, DEPARTMENT OF AGRICULTURE

OPENING REMARKS

Mr. DURBIN. Next we will have the Human Nutrition Information Service. Mr. Braley is returning along with David Rust, the Acting Administrator, Ellen Harris, Alanna Moshfegh, Betty Warfield and Steve Dewhurst.

Mr. BRALEY. Mr. Chairman, if I might, just a brief introductory comment.

Mr. DURBIN. Sure.

Mr. BRALEY. And then turn it over to Mr. Rust, who is the Acting Administrator of the Human Nutrition Information Service.

The Human Nutrition Information Service conducts applied research in support of USDA's mission to promote the health and well being of Americans through improved nutrition. HNIS contributes to this mission through national food consumption surveys, food composition research and nutrition education programs.

I think the most recent visible example of the excellent work that is done by HNIS is the food guide pyramid which has become extremely popular both within government and in the private sector as well.

I will now ask Mr. Rust to make his statement.

Mr. RUST. Mr. Chairman, I am accompanied this morning by Ms. Betty Warfield, who is the Director of our Budget and Finance Office; and as you mentioned, by Ellen Harris, who is the Director of our Nutrition Monitoring Division; and Alanna Moshfegh, who is our policy coordinator.

Ms. Warfield, Dr. Harris, and I are appearing today before you for the first time. At the pleasure of the Committee, I would like to submit our biographical data for the record.

As its name implies, HNIS is an information service organization responsible for conducting applied research in three broad areas: Food consumption—what Americans eat; food composition—the nutrient content of these foods; and nutrition education—helping Americans to make informed food choices. These activities enable

HNIS to make a direct and ongoing contribution to the U.S. Department of Agriculture's overarching mission of ensuring the health and well-being of the American population through improved nutrition.

The information HNIS collects, analyzes, and disseminates is essential to support the development of sound public policies by agencies across USDA and throughout the federal government.

Mr. Chairman, I inserted in my testimony a chart which visually displays the linkages between the work of HNIS and other federal agencies, private sector organizations, and the general public. I will not elaborate on it, but I thought that this visual display did a better job of explaining how the data we produce feeds all the way across the Department and through other agencies than we could do in our testimony.

As we near the end of the second quarter of fiscal year 1993, we are operating well within our appropriated funds. There are, however, two fiscal year 1993 issues that I would like to bring to the subcommittee's attention.

First, when we formulated our fiscal year 1993 budget request, we expected to spend between 2.8 and $3 million on the Continuing Survey of Food Intakes by Individuals. This is our major survey activity underway at this time. The Office of General Counsel has determined that we cannot expend any fiscal year 1993 funds on this contract. The basis of their decision is that fiscal year 1993 dollars were not needed to support this contract. Thus, there was no bona fide need for these funds. As a result, funds for the data collection that is to begin in January of 1994 cannot be obligated as originally planned.

The second issue I would like to bring to your attention, Mr. Chairman, is that in our fiscal year 1993 budget request last year, the Administrator of HNIS asked this Subcommittee for $455,000 to cover the cost of moving this agency to a new location. The lease on our current location in Hyattsville, Maryland expires in July of 1993 and we now expect to move to our new offices in the District of Columbia at about that time.

We estimate that no more than $750,000 will be needed to cover the non-GSA moving expenses. Sufficient funds are available to us to cover these costs, because funds originally intended for the CSFII, our continuing surveys, cannot be obligated in this fiscal year.

Our six most essential priorities for fiscal year 1994, are as follows.

Our most important priority is the Continuing Survey of Food Intakes by Individuals 1994 through 1996. The General Accounting Office and the Congress have asked us to continually survey the population to determine the status of nutrition. The total projected cost of this contract for the work currently planned is $14 million over four fiscal years. We are currently in the developmental phase of this contract and expect to begin the first full year of data collection in the second quarter of fiscal year 1994. The projected cost of the work to be funded in fiscal year 1994 is $4.2 million.

Our second priority is planning the household food consumption survey for 1996. Every 10 years since 1936 USDA has conducted a major national food consumption survey. Now that the individual food intake is measured through the CSFII, the household food consumption survey will focus exclusively on collecting household data.

Our third priority is continuing support for the activities of the 10-Year Comprehensive Plan for nutrition monitoring. As you may be aware, Mr. Chairman, the 10-Year Comprehensive Plan was submitted to Congress in January of 1993, and it now will govern the activities of 22 federal departments and agencies in nutrition monitoring over the next decade.

Our fourth priority is supporting jointly with the Department of Health and Human Services the updating of the Dietary Guidelines for Americans. This is due to be completed in 1995.

Our number five priority is using survey data and the developing of a food grouping system to better ascertain levels of exposure to pesticide residues.

And, finally, modernizing the nutrient data bank and expanding our food composition research.

In closing, Mr. Chairman, let me stress once again that we are a small agency with an essential role in helping USDA meet its responsibilities to promote the health and well-being of the American population through improved nutrition. Fiscal year 1994 will be a very productive year for the agency, and we are determined to deliver quality work in a timely manner to our customers at USDA, our other federal agencies, private sector organizations and the general public.

Mr. Chairman, I will be happy to answer any questions you or any member of the committee may have.

[CLERK'S NOTE.—Biographies for Mr. Rust, Dr. Harris and Ms. Warfield appear on pages 626 through 628. The Acting Administrator's prepared statement appears on pages 629 through 643. The budget justifications, which were received on May 10, 1993, appear on pages 644 through 656.]

Mr. DURBIN. Thank you very much, Mr. Rust.

Let me ask you this. Is the data collected by your agency unique in the Federal government?

Mr. RUST. We believe so. We have three major surveys. They really have a dual mission. One is to determine what people are eating, what households are buying, what kind of consumer decisions Americans are making with regard to food and nutrition, and their knowledge levels about food and nutritional issues. We relate those findings not just to the health, but also back to the production side of the Department in terms of the data's value to the field of agriculture, and what changes are occurring that may have implications for the agricultural industry over the years ahead. So I think we have a two-pronged approach which is different than the surveys which are conducted by the Department of Health and Human Services.

USES AND USERS OF HNIS SURVEY DATA

Mr. DURBIN. Is it not true that the Food Marketing Institute, the Market Research Corporation, the Food and Drug Administration, and USDA's Economic Research Service collect similar data on a more timely basis than your agency?

Mr. RUST. They collect different data than my agency. Sometimes they release it in a more timely way and sometimes not. We have had a bit of a problem, if I may be candid. Mr. Chairman, we had a great deal of difficulty with the last Nationwide Food Consumption Survey, which was conducted in the mid 1980s.

We had a very poor response rate. We had great difficulty with our contractor at that time, and we kind of got behind the 8 ball in some respects. The agency was unable to handle that data, justify that data, put that data in a usable form and get it out. I think that may have given us a reputation for getting our data out in a very slow and ineffective manner.

If you look at the survey we conducted before that, we were releasing some of the data within six months after the data was collected, which is far faster than is normal in surveying.

If I may make another comment about the plethora of surveys. We believe that each one of them is different and the data may well be needed. But I would also point out to you that the Office of Management and Budget, and all of us enjoy very much criticizing the Office of Management and Budget, but in this particular instance they really do review all questionnaires. They review all surveys very carefully, and have been meticulous in identifying and avoiding potential areas of duplication.

Mr. DURBIN. Briefly describe for us the type of information you collect in your surveys, the type of information that is collected by the Economic Research Service, as well as the type of information that is collected by the National Center for Health Statistics. How do these surveys and the data they provide differ?

Mr. RUST. HNIS collects three types of information. First, information is collected on food used by households and the cost of that food through the Household Food Consumption Survey, HFCS. Much of food consumption takes place within households. The amounts and the types of food people eat are dependent on what the household buys and what it can afford to buy. Since the Food Stamp Program is targeted to households, it is important to have baseline data on household food patterns. Information from this survey is also used for developing the Thrifty Food Plan which is the legal standard for benefits in the Food Stamp Program. No other national survey collects data similar to the HFCS.

Second information is collected on food eaten by individuals at home and away from home through the Continuing Survey of Food Intake by Individuals, CSFII. This type of information tells us the dietary status of the population as a whole and how specific groups, such as low-income individuals, are faring nutritionally. Information from this survey is vital for developing nutrition guidance such as the Dietary Guidelines for Americans. We need to know how good diets are before we can design programs for improvement.

Both of the these types of information differ considerably from the food supply or disappearance data provided by the Economic Research Service, ERS. ERS food supply data shows food available for consumption by the U.S. civilian population. It is derived from data on production, imports and exports, military use, and inventories. It does not tell us what food households are actually able to buy nor what individuals are actually eating. The food supply data are available on a per capita basis only; they are not available for various population groups. For example, ERS data can tell us if there are enough foods in the food supply to provide iron for the population, but it cannot tell us which groups, such as children or low-income elderly, are not getting enough iron. Also, ERS data covers only foods in the food supply; HNIS provides the data to estimate the nutrient content of the food supply.

The National Center for Health Statistics, NCHS, collects information on the dietary intake of individuals in its National Health and Nutrition Examination Survey, NHANES. This information is somewhat similar to that collected in the CSFII. However the purposes of the surveys differ. The CSFII is food oriented and its purpose is to find out what foods we eat so that nutrition education, food guidance, food assistance programs, food safety, and food production can be targeted in the most approximate way. The purpose of the NHANES survey is to assess the health status of the population through physical examinations of survey participants and a single day's dietary data is a small part of that survey. NCHS does not publish or provide information on food consumption and the NHANES survey captures only one day of dietary intake data which is not adequate for estimating usual intakes of the population. The HNIS surveys include multiple days of dietary intake for this purpose. HNIS and NCHS are working hard to coordinate the surveys so that together we can provide more comprehensive information than either agency could provide in a single survey.

The third type of information HNIS collects is knowledge and attitudes about diet and health through the Diet and Health Knowledge Survey, DHKS. This type of information is used to improve our understanding of factors that affect food choices. Information from the DHKS can be used with the CSFII to link an individual's knowledge and attitudes to his or her dietary behavior since information is collected from the same individuals. This is the first national survey to do this.

The Food and Drug Administration, FDA, conducts a Health and Diet Survey in which it asks about health-related knowledge and behavior, such as have you had your blood cholesterol checked? Have you changed your diet to reduce risk of heart disease. The Department of Agriculture's DHKS asks about food intake-related knowledge and behavior, such as trim fat from meat? Do you use lowfat or regular food products? The DHKS also includes information on attitudes about dietary guidelines, a subject not covered by the FDA survey. Some questions on the surveys are similar and we are working with FDA to facilitate this because comparability will enhance the usefulness of both surveys. A major difference in the two surveys is that USDA's DHKS survey provides information linking knowledge and attitudes with dietary behavior; the FDA survey does not.

Mr. DURBIN. If the USDA stopped its food consumption survey, in what way would the data from these other agencies be inadequate?

Mr. RUST. I think in a number of ways. For instance, you mentioned the Economic Research Service. They use our data, they bring in other data that they have, but they use our data. They do not really duplicate our data.

Our work supports a wide range of activities. In talking about the Food Stamp Program, our data provides the Food and Nutrition Service with the basis for setting the food stamp allotment. The Thrifty Food Plan, for instance, is based on data that we compiled. The Environmental Protection Agency and the Food and Drug Administration are working very closely with us at the present time to try to determine what types and quantities of foods we eat so as to determine what the pesticide residue levels are. So in a real sense, and I use this chart as a way of visualizing it, our data flows through those programs into the work of these other agencies. It really becomes the basis for many policy determinations.

Mr. DURBIN. Can you tell me what reports or articles have been published over the past five years that are dependent on your survey data?

Mr. RUST. May I do that for the record?

The answer is quite a few. We issue a number of reports on each of our surveys, and there have been a number of journal articles on our surveys. I would be glad to provide a listing of those for the record.

Mr. DURBIN. If you would separate those paid for by HNIS and those paid for by others, I would appreciate it.

Mr. RUST. Yes, sir.

[The information follows:]

I. REPORTS FROM NATIONWIDE FOOD SURVEYS (NFCS and CSFII)

A. Survey Reports:

1. Nationwide Food Consumption Survey, 1987-88.

* Lutz, S.M., et al. 1992. Changes in Food Consumption and Expenditures in American Households During the 1980's. U.S. Department of Agriculture, Economic Research Service and Human Nutrition Information Service. Statistical Bulletin No. 849.

Guenther P.M., and B.P. Perloff. 1990. Effects of Procedural Differences Between 1977 and 1987 in the Nationwide Food Consumption Survey on Estimates of Food and Nutrient Intakes: Results of the USDA 1988 Bridging Study. U.S. Department of Agriculture. Report No. 87-M-1.

Guenther P.M., and K.S. Tippett (eds). 1993. Evaluation of Nonresponse in the Nationwide Food Consumption Survey 1987-88. Report No. 87-M-2. (In press).

U.S. Department of Aggiculture, Human Nutrition Information Service.
** Food and Nutrient Intakes by Individuals in the United States, 1 Day, 1987-88. Report No. 87-I-1. (In press).

U.S. Department of Aggiculture, Human Nutrition Information Service. Food Consumption and Dietary Levels of Households in the United States, 1987-88. Report No. 87-H-1. (In preparation).

2. Continuing Survey of Food Intakes by Individuals-NFCS, CSFII:

1986 Series

Report No. 86-1:	Women 19-50 Years and Their Children 1-5 Years, 1 Day, 1986. Issued January, 1987.
Report No. 86-2:	Low-Income Women 19-50 Years and Their Children 1-5 Years, 1 Day, 1986. Issued April, 1987.
Report No. 86-3:	Women 19-50 Years and Their Children 1-5 Years, 4 Days, 1986. Issued September, 1988.
Report No. 86-4:	Low-Income Women 19-50 Years and Their Children 1-5 Years, 4 Days, 1986. Issued January, 1989.

1985 Series

Report No. 85-1:	Women 19-50 Years and Their Children 1-5 Years, 1 Day, 1985. Issued November, 1985.
Report No. 85-2:	Low-Income Women 19-50 Years and Their Children 1-5 Years, 1 Day, 1985. Issued August, 1986.
Report No. 85-3:	Men 19-50 Years, 1 Day, 1985. Issued november, 1986.
Report No. 85-4:	Women 19-50 Years and Their Children 1-5 Years, 4 Days, 1985. Issued August, 1987.
Report No. 85-5:	Low-Income Women 19-50 Years and Their Children 1-5 Years, 4 Days, 1985. Issued March, 1988.

* Jointly or cooperatively funded
** Funded outside Human Nutrition Information Service

B. Administrative Reports:

1989

Human Nutrition Information Service. 1989. Analysis of Nonresponse to the 1986 Continuing Survey of Food Intakes by Individuals. HNIS Adm. Rep. No. 386.

Human Nutrition Information Service. 1989. Machine Readable Data Sets on Composition of Foods and Results from Food Consumption Surveys. HNIS Adm. Rep. No. 378.

1987

Human Nutrition Information Service. 1987. Manual of Food Codes in Numerical Order for the Household Food Consumption Phase of the Nationwide Food Consumption Phase of the Nationwide Food Consumption Survey 1987. HNIS Adm. Rep. No. 383.

Human Nutrition Information Service. 1987. Research Methodology. Proceedings of a Symposium Held at the 71st Annual Meeting of the Federation of American Societies for Experimental Biology, April 1, 1987. HNIS Adm. Rep. No. 382.

Human Nutrition Information Service. 1987. Manual of Food Codes and Weights for Use in Household Food Consumption Phase of the Nationwide Food Consumption Survey. HNIS Adm. Rep. No. 381.

C. Agricultural Experiment Station Bulletins:

1991

McNaughton, J.P., et al. 1991. Food Choices and Diet Quality for Women with Different Levels of Beef Intake. State College, MS: Mississippi State University, Mississippi Agricultural and Forestry Experiment Station, Technical Bulletin No. 177.

1990

McNaughton, J.P., et al. 1990. Beef and Pork Consumers: Socioeconomic, Personal, and Lifestyle Characteristics. State College, MS: Mississippi State University, Mississippi Agricultural and Forestry Experiment Station, Technical Bulletin No. 172.

1989

Eastwood, D.B., and S.C. Morse. 1989. A Theoretical and Empirical Investigation of the Hedonic Price Equation for Foods. Knoxville, TN; The University of Tennessee, Agricultural Experiment Station, Station Bulletin No. 666.

1986

** McCracken, V.A., and J.A. Brandt. 1986. Analysis of Economic and Socio-Demographic Factors Affecting the Consumption of Food Away From Home. West Lafayette, IN: Purdue University, Agricultural Experiment Station, Station Bulletin No. 480.

** McCracken, V.A., and J.A. Brandt. 1986. Methodological Considerations in Estimating Household Demand Models with Incomplete Data. West Lafayette, IN: Purdue University, Agricultural Experiment Station, Station Bulletin No. 481.

** McCracken, V.A., and J.A. Brandt. 1986. The Value of Household Time and the Demand for Food Away-From-Home. West Lafayette, IN: Purdue University, Agricultural Experiment Station, Station Bulletin No. 485.

D. Research Reports, Technical Bulletins:

1989

* Federation of American Societies for Experimental Biology, Life Sciences Research Office. 1989. Nutrition Monitoring in the United States: An Update Report on Nutrition Monitoring. Prepared for the U.S. Department of Health and Human Services and U.S. Department of Agriculture. DHHS Publication No. (PHS) 89-1255.

Pao, E.M., K.E. Sykes and Y.S. Cypel. 1989. USDA Methodological Research for Large-Scale Dietary Intake Surveys, 1975-1988. U.S. Dept. of Agriculture, Human Nutrition Information Service, Home Economics Research Report No. 49.

1988

* Price, D.W. 1988. Estimating Food Use by Age, Sex and Household Size. Pullman, WA: Washington State University, College of Agriculture and Home Economics, Research Bulletin XB1002.

II. PERIODICAL ARTICLES FROM THE NATIONWIDE FOOD CONSUMPTION SURVEY DATA

1992

Cleveland, L.E., A.J. Escobar, S.M. Lutz, S.O. Welsh. 1993. Method for identifying differences between existing food intake patterns and patterns that meet recommendations. J. Am. Dietetic Assoc. (selected as the continuing education articale for registered dietitians)

Basiotis, P.P., et al. 1992. Dietary Intakes and Selected Characteristics of Women Ages 19-50 Years and Their Children Ages 1-5 Years by Reported Perception of Food Sufficiency. Journal of Nutrition Education 24 (1):33-38

** Blaylock, J.R., Blisard N.W. 1992. U.S. Cigarette Consumption: The case of Low - Income Women. American Journal of Agricultural Economics 74 (3) 698-705

* Popkin, B.M., et al. 1992. Dietary Changes in Older Americans. American Journal of Clinical Nutrition 55(5):823-30.

* Murphy, S.P., et al. 1992. Demographic and Economic Factors Associated with Dietary Quality for Adults in the 1987-88 NFCS. Journal of the American Dietetic Association, Forthcoming 1992

* Thompson, E.F., et al. 1992. Sources of Fiber and Fat in Diets of US Women Aged 19 to 50: Implications for Nutrition Education and Policy. American Journal of Public Health 82(5):695-702.

** Johnson, Rachel k., Helen Smiciklas, et al. 1992. Maternal Employment and the Quality of Young Children's Diets: Empirical Evidence Based on the 1987-1988 Nationwide Food Consumption Survey. Pediatrics 90(2):245-249.

1991

** Cook, C.M., et al. 1991. Incorporating Subsistence into a Probit Analysis of Houshold Nutrition Levels. Southern Journal of Agricultural Economics 23(1):195-202.

** Devaney, B., and R. Moffitt. 1991. Dietary Effects of the Food Stamp Program. American Journal of Agricultural Economics 73(1):202-211.

** Ershow, A.G., et al. 1991. Intake of Tapwater and Total Water by Pregnant and Lactating Women. American Journal of Public Health 81(3):328-334.

** Levedahl, J.W. 1991. The Role of Functional Form in Estimating the Effect of a Cash-Only Food Stamp Program. The Journal of Agricultural Economics Research 43(2)Spring:11-19.

Tippett, K.S., and H.A. Riddick. 1991. What Are We Eating? Cereal Foods World 36(9):797-799.

** Wright, H.S., et al. 1991. The 1987-88 Nationwide Food Consumption Survey: An Update on the Nutrient Intake of Respondents. Nutrition Today 26(3): 21-27

1990

** Berner, L.A., et al. 1990. Calcium and Chronic Disease Prevention: Challenges to the Food Industry. Food Technology 44(3):50-70.

** Davis, M.A., et al. 1990. Living Arrangements and Dietary Quality of Older U.S. Adults. Journal of the American Dietetic Association 90(12): 1667-1672.

* Guilkey, D.K., et al. 1990. The Distribution of Food Consumption Over a Year: A Longitudinal Analysis. American Journal of Agricultural Economics 72(4):891-900.

* Haines, P.S., et al. 1990. Methods of Patterning Eating Behaviors of American Women. Journal of Nutrition Education 22(3):124-132.

** Heien, D., and C.R. Wessells. 1990. Demand Systems Estimation with Microdata: A Censored Regression Approach. Journal of Business and Economics Statistics 8(3):365-371.

Krebs-Smith, S.M., et al. 1990. Contributions of Food Groups to Intakes of Energy, Nutrients, Cholesterol, and Fiber in Women's Diets: Effect of Method of Classifying Food Mixtures. Journal of the American Dietetic Association 90(11):1541-1546.

Larkin, F.A., et al. 1990. Dietary Patterns of Women Smokers and Non-Smokers. Journal of the American Dietetic Association 90(2):230-237.

** Moser-Veillon, P.B. 1990. Zinc: Consumption Patterns and Dietary Recommendations. Journal of the American Dietetic Association 90(8): 1089-1093.

* Murphy, S.P., et al. 1990. Factors Influencing the Dietary Adequacy and Energy Intake of Older Americans. Journal of Nutrition Education 22(6):284-291.

Pao, E.M., et al. 1990. Dietary Intake -- Large Scale Survey Methods. Nutrition Today 25(6):11-17.

Perloff, B.P., et al. 1990. Dietary Intake Methodology II. USDA's Nutrient Data Base for Nationwide Dietary Intake Surveys. Journal of Nutrition 120(11s):1530-1534.

Rizek, R.L., and E.M. Pao. 1990. Dietary Intake Methodology I. USDA Surveys and Supporting Research. Journal of Nutrition 120(11s): 1525-1529.

Tippett, K.S., et al. 1990. Food and Nutrient Intakes of Low-Income Women and Children, in Metro/Nonmetro Areas, 1985/86. Family Economics Review 3(1):12-15.

1989

American Dietetic Association. 1989. What Are You Eating? ADA Courier 28(12):6.

Basiotis, P.P., et al. 1989. Sources of Variation in Energy Intake by Men and Women as Determined from One Year's Daily Dietary Records American Journal of Clinical Nutrition 50(3):448-453.

** Devaney, B., and T. Fraker. 1989. The Effect of Food Stamps on Food Expenditures: An Assessment of Findings from the Nationwide Food Consumption Survey. American Journal of Agricultural Economics 71(1):99-104.

Guenther, P.M., and G. Ricart. 1989. Effects of Eating at Food Service Establishments on the Nutritional Quality of Women's Diets. Topics in Clinical Nutrition 4(2):41-45.

Krebs-Smith, S.M., and L.D. Clark. 1989. Validation of a Nutrient Adequacy Score for Use with Women and Children. Journal of the American Dietetic Association 89(6):775-783.

Krebs-Smith, S.M., et al. 1989. Mean Proportion and Population Proportion: Two Answers to the Same Question? Journal of the American Dietetic Association 89(5):671-676.

** National Dairy Council. 1989. Breakfast Consumption Patterns of U.S. Children and Adolescents. Nutrition News 52(2):7.

Perloff, B.P. 1989. Analysis of Dietary Data. American Journal of Clinical Nutrition 50(5):1128-1132.

* Popkin, B.M., et al. 1989. Food Consumption Changes of Adult Women Between 1977 and 1985. American Journal of Agricultural Economics 71(4):949-959.

* Popkin, B.M., et. al. 1989. Food Consumption Trends of U.S. Women: Patterns and Determinants Between 1977 and 1985. American Journal of Clinical Nutrition 49(6):1307-1319.

Rizek, R.L., and K.S. Tippett. 1989. Women's Food Consumption: Diets of American Women in 1985. Food and Nutrition News, National Live Stock and Meat Board 61(1):1-4.

1988

Cleveland, L.E., and R.L. Kerr. 1988. Development and Uses of the USDA Food Plans. Journal of Nutrition Education 20(5):232-238.

Enns, C.W., and P.M. Guenther. 1988. Women's Food and Nutrient Intakes Away From Home, 1985. Family Economics Review 1(1):9-12.

Guenther, P.M., and G. Ricart. 1988. Effect of Eating at Foodservices on the Nutritional Quality of Women's Diets. In Dietetics in the 90's. Role of the Dietitian/Nutritionist: Proceedings of the 10th International Congress of Dietetics. ed. M.F. Moyal, pp. 92-102. Paris, France: John Libbey Eurotext Ltd.

* Haines, P.S., et al. 1988. Modeling Food Consumption Decisions as a Two-Step Process. American Journal of Agricultural Economics 70(3):543-552.

Hama, M.Y., and H.A. Riddick. 1988. Nationwide Food Consumption Survey 1987. Family Economics Review 1(2):24-27.

Hama, M.Y., and W.S. Chern. 1988. Food Expenditure and Nutrient Availability in Elderly Households. Journal of Consumer Affairs 22(1):3-19.

** Heien, D., and C.R. Wessells. 1988. The Nutritional Impact of the Dairy Price Support Program. Journal of Consumer Affairs 22(2):201-219.

** Heien, D.M., and C.R. Wessells. 1988. The Demand for Dairy Products: Structure, Prediction, and Decomposition. American Journal of Agricultural Economics 70(2):219-228.

** Morgan, K.J. 1988. Socioeconomic Factors and Food Usage Patterns. Family Economics Review 1(1):19-25.

* Norum, P.S. 1988. Factors Affecting Productivity in Nutrient Consumption Journal of Consumer Studies and Home Economics 12(1):71-85.

Peterkin, B.B., et al. 1988. Nationwide Food Consumption Survey, 1987. Nutrition Today 23(1):18-24.

Sims, L.S. 1988. Contributions of the US Department of Agriculture. American Journal of Clinical Nutrition 47(2):329-332.

Tippett, K.S., and S. Cristofar. 1988. Dietary Intakes By Employment Status. Family Economics Review 1(4):11-13.

1987

** Akin, J.S., et al. 1987. Determinants of Nutrient Intake of the Elderly. Journal of Applied Gerontology 6(3):227-258.

Basiotis, P.P., et al. 1987. Food Stamps, Food Costs, Nutrient Availability and Nutrient Intake. Journal of Policy Modeling 9(3):383-404.

Basiotis, P.P., et al. 1987. Number of Days of Food Intake Records Required to Estimate Individual and Group Nutrient Intakes with Defined Confidence. Journal of Nutrition 117(9):1638-1641.

** Blaylock, J.R. 1987. Evaluating Food Plans and Poverty Thresholds. Applied Economics 19:1341-1352.

** Blaylock. J.R., and D.M. Smallwood. 1987. Intrahousehold Time Allocation: The Case of Grocery Shopping. Journal of Consumer Affairs 21(2):183-201.

Cleveland, L.E., and A.B. Pfeffer. 1987. Planning Diets to Meet the National Research Council's Guidelines for Reducing Cancer Risk. Journal of the American Dietetic Association 87(2):162-168.

Cronin, F.J., et al. 1987. Developing a Food Guidance System to Implement the Dietary Guidelines. Journal of Nutrition Education 19(6):281-302.

Enns, C.W. 1987. Comparison of Nutrient Intakes by Male vs. Female Heads of Households. Journal of the American Dietetic Association 87(11): 1551-1553.

** Harris, E.W., and E. Randall. 1987. The Influence of Head of Household Structure on the Dietary Quality of Food Available for Consumption Inside U.S. Households 1977-78. Ecology of Food and Nutrition 20(2):109-120.

* Johnson, S.R. 1987. Variability, Reliability, and Validity of Dietary Survey Data. Cereal Foods World 32(2):186-190.

Krebs-Smith, S.M., et al. 1987. The Effects of Variety in Food Choices on Dietary Quality. Journal of the American Dietetic Association 87(7):897-903.

** Lee, J.-Y. 1987. The Demand for Varied Diet with Econometric Models for Count Data. American Journal of Agricultural Economics 69(3):687-692.

** McCracken, V.A., and J.A. Brandt. 1987. Household Consumption of Food-Away-From-Home: Total Expenditure and by Type of Food Facility. Journal of Agricultural Economics 69(2):274-284.

* Morgan, K.J., and B.P. Goungetas. 1987. Cereal Food Usage: Impact of Socioeconomic and Demographic Characteristics. Cereal Foods World 32(6):433-438.

* Morgan, K.J., et al. 1987. Collection of Food Intake Data: An Evaluation of Methods. Journal of the American Dietetic Association 87(7):888-896.

* Morgan, K.J., et al. 1987. Variability of Food Intakes. American Journal of Epidemiology 126(2):326-335.

* Murphy, S.P. 1987. Use of National Survey Data Bases for Nutrition Research. Clinical Nutrition 6(5):208-218.

Peterkin, B.B., and L.S. Sims. 1987. Diets of American Women: How They Relate to Standards. Abstract No. 3992. Federation Proceedings 46(3):1001

Peterkin, B.B., et al. 1987. When, Where, With Whom and What Older Americans Eat. Gerodontics 3(1):14-19.

* Rathje, W.L., and E.E. Ho. 1987. Meat Fat Madness: Conflicting Patterns of Meat Fat Consumption and Their Public Health Implications. Journal of the American Dietetic Association 87(10):1357-1362.

** Reis, C.P., et al. 1987. Impact of Commercial Eating on Nutrient Adequacy. Journal of the American Dietetic Association 87(4):463-468.

** Riley, Jr., A.M. 1987. Breads and Pastas in the U.S. Diet. Cereal Foods World 32(7):460-464.

Tippett, K.S., and H.A. Riddick. 1987. Diets of American Women by Income, Spring 1977 and Spring 1985. Family Economics Review 1987(1):10-17.

** Zabik, M.E. 1987. Impact of Ready-to-Eat Cereal Consumption on Nutrient Intake. Cereal Foods World 32(3):234-239.

* Jointly or cooperatively funded
** Funded outside Human Nutrition Information Service

QUALITY OF SURVEY DATA

Mr. DURBIN. Some have questioned your survey methodology, asking people to remember and report what they ate. And they say that this methodology produces data so flawed that it is dangerous. Your survey is thought to underreport food intake by about 20 percent. There was an article written recently in The Journal of American Dietetics Association by Dr. Mertz. I believe it was published in December, 1992. The article concluded that if Americans ate as little food as HNIS reported, the population would be severely underweight and malnourished. This, of course, looking at me as a good example, is not true. More than 25 percent of the population is overweight. It also concludes that the inaccuracies in your survey methodology are dangerous because the EPA and the FDA use the data to estimate potential pesticide or carcinogen risk from consumption of food. Obviously if food intake is understated and underreported, the risk is going to be underestimated.

Can you respond to this criticism?

Mr. RUST. I would like to ask Dr. Harris to address that issue.

Dr. HARRIS. Collecting adequate dietary information from individuals is a recognized problem in the area, because you are asking people to recall to the best of their ability, and HNIS recognizes this problem as an ongoing issue with data collection in food consumption surveys.

We are currently sponsoring research at the University of Maryland to try to get at some aspects of this problem, and find ways to better assist respondents at estimating their portion sizes. We are particularly interested in respondents who fall in the young child category or proxy respondents who have to respond for children or the elderly.

Mr. DURBIN. I am out of my element here. I am not a statistician, nor do I know how to even start to conduct such a survey. But obviously, Dr. Mertz and others have concluded that the survey methodology which you are using, even if you could repair it by this University of Maryland approach, is not going to do the job. Frankly, they believe there is such a gross discrepancy between what people consume and what they report to you on the survey that the net result is not very valuable in terms of science, and may be dangerous in terms of what conclusions are extrapolated from it.

What you are telling me is, you know that you have a problem and are trying to find ways to repair the survey data.

Dr. HARRIS. Well, we are trying to find ways of better collecting information, not repairing the data that we have collected so far. I think throughout the years nutritionists and other people in the food consumption area have recognized that there are limitations to the data. We are constantly working at trying to find better ways of collecting that information.

In our survey, because it is collected within the home, there are opportunities for the respondent to show the interviewer what exactly a cup or a serving of food might mean. We have food guide measurements, but oftentimes someone may say I drank a cup of something. It could be eight ounces, but it also could be 20 ounces. So we are looking at all kinds of ways of trying to get at better information. We would certainly respond to any input from people like Dr. Mertz to help us collect better information.

Mr. DURBIN. We are spending an awful lot of money on this survey, and it seems to me that there are some really basic flaws in what we are trying to do. We are asking people to remember what they ate, only to find out that they are underreporting it, which is what most of us do when asked.

There is another concern I have, and it came out in a 1991 GAO report, about the data that is being collected. The GAO report looked at the survey done in 1987 and 1988. The survey, incidentally, cost the taxpayers $8 million, not counting several years of staff work. The data produced from the survey were so bad they are distributed with a warning label attached. The response rate for the survey was 34 percent.

Are you familiar with this GAO report?

Dr. HARRIS. I most certainly am, sir.

Mr. DURBIN. It does not speak very well for your survey or your approach.

Dr. HARRIS. I think it speaks of an agency that has collected information for a number of years not responding with the times in terms of updated ways of managing the survey. It speaks of a contractor who, quite frankly, probably got lazy in the management of the survey. Since that time the agency has tried to respond in a very positive way by drawing on the services of the Census Bureau and taking a very hard look at how we conduct surveys and working at doing a better job.

Mr. DURBIN. What were the response rates for the surveys conducted in 1989, 1990, and 1991?

Dr. HARRIS. For 1989, the response rate is in the high 50s. I do not know the exact number right now, but I can get that to you for the record.

[The information follows:]

The CSFII is a complex survey designed to collect national information on the dietary intakes of U.S. households and their members. CSFII 1989–1991 included two independent samples; a "basic" or all-income sample and a low-income sample. Participation rates were somewhat higher than what I had originally indicated to the Committee. Participation by households for 1989 was 63 percent for the basic sample and 73 percent for the low-income sample; for 1990, 62 percent for the basic sample and 69 percent for the low-income sample and; for preliminary 1991 results, 64 percent for basic and 74 percent for low-income. If the basic and low-income samples are combined then the response rates by household participation become 68 percent in 1989, 66 percent in 1990 and 67 percent in 1991.

Mr. DURBIN. What is considered acceptable in this type of a survey to draw conclusions about the eating habits of the population that are meaningful?

Dr. HARRIS. I think you get different responses in terms of what is concerned acceptable. People look hard at anything that is less than 50 percent, because that means that you are talking about less than a majority. When I was in graduate school, we were taught in survey methodology courses that response rates that exceed 70 percent were acceptable.

Mr. DURBIN. I have been told that you need responses around 70 to 75 percent to really say that you have a picture of what the consumption habits are of the American population. Can you tell me if response rates got any better in 1990 or 1991?

Dr. HARRIS. It got better as a result of the 1987-1988 survey. We recognized that there was a problem in the management of the survey, and the agency got together with the contractor and was very aggressive in implementing corrective actions in managing the survey. As a result, you see increases in the response rate. We think a lot of it is related to the contractor managing the survey better.

SURVEY CONTRACTORS

Mr. DURBIN. Who chose the contractor?

Dr. HARRIS. It is a competitive bid where contractors submit proposals. The agency writes a request for proposal. Contractors submit proposals, and then they are technically evaluated by a panel of staff people from within and outside the agency.

Mr. DURBIN. Has the contractor changed over the years?

Dr. HARRIS. Right now there is a new contractor for the survey that is supposed to start in 1994.

Mr. RUST. The previous contractor had had a number of sequential contracts with our agency, but they are no longer doing the survey.

Mr. DURBIN. How much money did we give them before we asked them to leave?

Mr. RUST. The aggregate?

Mr. DURBIN. Yes.

Mr. RUST. I would have to submit that for the record.

[The information follows:]

We have searched the records as far back as they are still available to us. The contractor, National Analysts, conducted a number of studies and surveys for HNIS and its predecessor agency. With the records we have access to, we can track cost data back to the 1965-66 Household Food Consumption Survey. The aggregate cost of all contracts with National Analysts, involving this agency, since 1965 is $26.7 million. We will continue to search for additional records and we will provide the committee with any additional cost information we find.

Mr. RUST. The previous CSFII cost about six or seven million dollars, I think. That was for the three years, 1989, 1990 and 1991.

Mr. DURBIN. And the data is basically worthless?

Mr. RUST. No.

Dr. HARRIS. No, not the CSFII.

Mr. RUST. Not the CSFII.

The worthless one, as you are describing it, was the Nationwide Food Consumption Survey 1987-88. When you look at that data, it is still the best data available in a number of those categories from that period of time, and it is much more widely used outside of government than it is inside.

Mr. DURBIN. But is the data accurate?

Mr. RUST. The answer is—I do not know that we can answer that precisely. The findings and the patterns are sufficiently consistent with other survey work that has been done by us and by others in previous years that we are willing to say that they are accurate enough to use. We put a disclaimer on all of that data and make certain that people understand the response rate problem. And as an agency, we do not duck responsibility for the management of that survey.

COST OF THE NATIONWIDE FOOD CONSUMPTION SURVEY 1987–88

Mr. DURBIN. This survey information which you do not use and put a disclaimer on, how much did that cost the taxpayers?

Dr. HARRIS. The 1987–1988 survey cost?

Mr. DURBIN. The one you have a disclaimer attached to.

Dr. HARRIS. But I have to add, we put a disclaimer on that to let data users know that there were problems with data collection. But as Mr. Rust said, within our agency and outside of the agency there are some uses of that data. ERS, the Economic Research Service, has used the 1987–1988 data.

Mr. DURBIN. How much did the survey cost? Do you know?

Dr. HARRIS. About $8 million.

Mr. DURBIN. What are you doing to rectify the problems so that in 1997–98 the survey will produce statistically accurate data?

Mr. RUST. We are taking several steps to assure that surveys conducted by HNIS will produce accurate and timely data. I will provide the details for the record.

[The information follows:]

(1) The decennial Nationwide Food Consumption Survey (NFCS) has been discontinued. The NFCS included the collection of two types of information—household use of food and individual intake—which required a heavy respondent burden. The average length of the interview was almost 3 hours, and many people refused to participate after being informed of the requirements of the survey. In the future, information on the two components of the survey will be collected in two separate surveys: the Continuing Survey of Food Intakes by Individuals and the Household Food Consumption Survey.

(2) The 1994-96 Continuing Survey of Food Intakes by Individuals has been redesigned to replace the individual intake component of the NFCS. A fixed price contract for this survey was awarded to Westat, Inc. of Rockville, MD following competitive bidding. (This is a different contractor than the one which did the NFCS.) Every facet of the survey has been thoroughly examined and redesigned if necessary. In particular, procedures for improving response rates have been established. HNIS has put in place strong management and quality control procedures both as part of the contract and in its in-house operations to assure that the survey provides accurate data in a timely manner. Unlike work with the NFCS where there were few meetings with the contractor and limited monitoring on our part, we are meeting on a regular basis with Westat to review progress of the survey and we have several staff with assigned responsibilities for monitoring the survey contract. We have developed an in-house tracking system to monitor the status of the interviews. We also have a new food coding system, designed by the University of Texas, that will improve the efficiency of our technical support systems, leading to improved quality and timeliness of the results. The Census Bureau has been involved in the design of the survey, in conducting research leading to improvements in the questionnaire, and in suggesting better management procedures.

(3) The Household Food Consumption Survey, which will be conducted in 1996, replaces the household use of food component of the NFCS. We are working closely with the Census Bureau to plan, design, and execute the survey and to plan for disseminating the results on a timely basis. HNIS, with input from the Census Bureau, is drafting a detailed Statement of Work to prepare for the survey. It is probable that the Census Bureau will collect the data.

Mr. DURBIN. Provide a table showing the cost of the Nationwide Food Consumption Survey for each of the last six decades.

Mr. RUST. All the surveys prior to the 1987–88 survey were conducted by a unit within the Agricultural Research Service or its predecessor agencies which subsequently became part of HNIS in 1981. We have located information on the last three Nationwide Food Consumption Surveys (NFCS). I will provide that information for the record.

[The information follows:]

Human Nutrition Information Service—Nationwide Food Consumption Survey

	Millions
1965/1966	$3.7
1977/1978	[1] 7.8
1987/1988	7.6

[1] Contract included Alaska, Hawaii and Puerto Rico.

Surveys in the three prior decades (1936–1957/58) were reported as a single line item on Budget Documents and Explanatory Notes. The cost of the NFCS was not separately identified in these documents. The NFCS appears to have been included in broad budget categories such as "Special Research," "Nutrition and Consumer Use Research," etc. It may not be possible to reconstruct the exact cost of the early surveys. However, we will continue to research and investigate these historical documents. As we are able to locate more informaton on the costs of these surveys, we will make that information available to the Committee.

Mr. BRALEY. Mr. Chairman, if I could interject just an observation here.

Mr. Rust and Dr. Harris are both doing a good job of defending this survey in the past, but I would like you to know just for your own information that neither of them were in the agency when this work was done, and so they are both new to the Human Nutrition Information Service since that survey was conducted.

The other thing, in the short time I have been in the acting assistant secretary position and being involved with HNIS, there is a very significant amount of coordination that goes on among USDA and other federal agencies on who should be doing what, what surveys should go into the field at what time, and whose responsibility it is to ask certain questions. I think that area of work is rather well coordinated from my own observation now. But there was a very serious problem with that earlier survey, and, frankly, a lot of the money was probably not well spent.

TIMELY RELEASE OF SURVEY DATA

Mr. DURBIN. Well, that is fair, and I am glad you put that in the record.

But I do want to know who is going to take responsibility for the fact that many believe this survey and its methodology is still fatally flawed, and that the number of responses is still not representative of the American population. The information from these surveys are being used to draw conclusions in many different agencies that are very important to the health of the people of this country. It just strikes me that we are struggling to reach the point of having a professional survey, and we are spending millions of dollars and still have not quite reached that goal. This raises a question in my mind if we ever will.

Let me ask you this. Can you demonstrate that you are going to be releasing the data in a timely fashion from the surveys conducted in 1989, 1990 or 1991? Have any of these been published?

Mr. RUST. The 1989 data tape was released last November. The 1990 data tape will be released in May of this year. And the 1993 data tape will be released by the end of this calendar year. Excuse me. That's the 1991 data tape. And we have picked up the tempo on releasing data.

Mr. Chairman, I can understand your frustration. I came over from HHS, and one of the things that I was specifically asked to look at were the same issues that you are referring to today. Ellen is also new to our agency. We have a very new management team, for the most part, at HNIS. We are as concerned by the problems with the surveys as you are.

Let me tell you what I can promise you as the Associate Administrator of the agency and as the Acting Administrator for the time being. We have approached this new contract completely differently than we did before. As I mentioned in my testimony, we expect this one to cost $14 million. It is almost twice what we spent on CSFII in 1989, 1990 and 1991. We have a fixed-price contract. We have a brand new contractor. We have a management team in place that is completely new and unrelated to the group that ran the previous ones. We have a new division chief in Ellen. We have set specific goals that we are going to use to run this survey and run it tightly. We have response rate requirements in the contract for the contractor to meet. We are on their case almost on a daily basis. They are located in Rockville, Maryland, so they are physically close enough for us to have almost daily interplay with them. They want to do this survey right. We want them to do it right. We are in touch with them on a regular basis to make sure that this is as good a survey as you possibly can get for this amount of money.

If I can add just a generic comment. All surveys right now are having difficulty with response rates. There are reasons for that: fear of crime, fear of government intrusion, fear of big brother, more women in the work place. The principal respondent to a questionnaire like this is the principal meal preparer in the home.

Fifteen years ago, 20 years ago, 30 years ago, it was relatively easy to visit the house during the day. The woman was there. She knew this data. She could respond to this data. It is more and more difficult to get that data now. The more you ask us to get and the more the other agencies ask us to get, the more of a burden it becomes. The more of a burden it becomes, the less response you get. So we are constantly trying to balance societal changes and demands for additional data with something the American people will cooperate with and do.

Mr. DURBIN. Data from the 1989 survey was released in 1992 and data from 1990 will be released this year. What takes so long to release this data?

Mr. RUST. Data collection for the 1989 survey began in April 1989 and was completed, on schedule, in May 1990. However, data tapes were not received from the contractor until September 1991. At that time HNIS staff still needed to review and weigh the data and to prepare it for public release in machine readable form. The final 1989 data were released in November 1992, about 2½ years after the completion of the data collection, but 14 months after receipt of data from the contractor. The 1991 survey was completed in May 1992 and we expect data release in fall of 1993, about 1½ years after the survey was completed, and about 11 months after receipt of data from the contractor. We agree that these times are long. In order to improve the timeliness of data release, we have changed how and when data is received from the contractor.

In previous surveys, HNIS has not had access to the data until data collection and contractor processing was completed. At that point there was a considerable amount of additional data processing to do in-house, including reviewing the data for quality and accuracy, weighing the data, and preparing it in machine readable form. These takes delayed the release of the data. CSFII 1994-96 procedures have been designed so that processing will take place on an ongoing basis. Although some procedures, such as weighing of the data and putting it in machine readable form, will still need to be completed after the survey is finished. We anticipate being able to release the data much sooner after completion of the survey.

Mr. DURBIN. How useful is data that is three years old when it is released?

Mr. RUST. Food consumption patterns change slowly over time. We believe that data from the 1989-91 CSFII will reflect recent trends on the dietary status of the population when it is released. It is still the most recent data available. HNIS is committed to the more timely release of data from CSFII 1994-96. We have taken a number of steps in the new contract, in systems improvements, and in the commitment of the agency itself to insure a much more timely release of data from future surveys.

Food consumption data have many uses. I will provide a few examples for the record:

[The information follows:]

Numerous questions in the CSFII 1994-96 have been added for the Environmental Protection Agency and Food and Drug Administration. For example, this survey provides the only data on the amounts and sources of household water consumption, on fresh fish caught by individuals, and on food handling practices related to washing and peeling fruits and vegetables. These questions will be used in estimating pesticide residues.

CSFII is the only survey to capture information on foods eaten away from home and their nutritional content. While many other surveys provide information on the number of people eating out they do not provide information on the nutrient content of food away from home.

The CSFII 1985/86 was used to provide the baseline data used in setting the DHHS Healthy People Objectives for the Year 2000. CSFII 1994-96 will provide us information on the progress of the population in meeting these objectives.

The Food and Drug Administration used the NFCS 1987-88 data to update their Total Diet Study and for input into their work on food labeling.

HNIS uses information from all surveys to design nutrition education programs and to target specific population groups for intervention. The Food Guide Pyramid was developed based on food consumption patterns.

HNIS uses the survey data to design the USDA food plans; the Thrifty Food Plan is the legal basis for the Food Stamp Program.

University researchers working under cooperative agreement with the USDA have used the CSFII and NFCS data to conduct studies on: the characteristics that influence whether individuals use nutrition labeling and the effects of label use on dietary quality; the impact of increased consumption of food-away-from home on diets; the differences between diets of smokers and non-smokers; and the relationship of exercise and TV watching to diet and body weight.

The Food and Nutrition Service uses data from HNIS surveys to support evaluation of the effectiveness of FNS programs in achieving their nutritional objectives. HNIS surveys provide the only information on multiprogram participation by households linked with food consumption in those households.

The Federal Trade Commission has used NFCS data on fiber consumption to prosecute a case on false advertising of breakfast cereals.

Industry uses the data to develop and produce the foods Americans want.

Drug companies have used CSFII/NFCS data to help determine the levels of different vitamins to add to their multivitamin supplements.

In conclusion, for the past decade, USDA food consumption survey data have provided detailed information available on the food and nutrient intakes of Americans. While it would be desirable for USDA survey data to be available more rapidly and USDA is developing new methods and new managerial systems to expedite data processing, the examples of applications of the data that I have provided indicate the usefulness of USDA food consumption surveys.

A list of selected references follows:

1. Life Sciences Research Office, Federation of American Societies for Experimental Biology. Nutrition Monitoring in the United States—An Update Report on Nutrition Monitoring. DHHS Pub. No. (PHS) 89-1255. Washington: U.S. Government Printing Office, 1989. Prepared under contract for the U.S. Department of Agriculture and the U.S. Department of Health and Human Services.

2. Popkin, B.M., P.S. Haines, K.C. Reidy. Food Consumption Trends of U.S. Women: Patterns and Determinants Between 1977 and 1985. American Journal of Clinical Nutrition. 49:1307–1319, 1989. Conducted under Cooperative Agreement with HNIS.

3. Popkin, B.M., P.S. Haines, R.E. Patterson. Dietary Changes Among Older Americans, 1977-87. American Journal of Clinical Nutrition. 55-823-830, 1992.

4. Department of Health and Human Services. Healthy People 2000: National Health Promotion and Disease Prevention Objectives. DHHS Pub. No. (PHS) 91-50212. Washington: U.S. Government Printing Office, 1991.

5. Pennington, J.A.T. The Food and Drug Administration's Total Diet Studies—Results and Revisions. Journal of the American Dietetic Association. 92:A-17, 1992.

6. Welsh, S.O., J. Fox, J.F. Guthrie, and L. Cleveland. Characteristics of Nutrition Label Users and Implications for Label Education. Speech presented at the Fall, 1992 Meeting of the National Exchange for Food Label Education. Washington, DC, September 16, 1992.

7. Haines, P.S., D.W. Hungerford, B.M. Popkin, and D.K. Guikey. Eating Patterns and Energy and Nutrient Intakes of U.S. Women. Journal of the American Dietetic Association, 92:698–707, 1992. Conducted under cooperative Agreement with HNIS.

8. Larkin, F.A., P.P. Basiotis, H.A. Riddick, K.E. Sykes, and E.M. Pao. Dietary Patterns of Women Smokers and Non-Smokers. Journal of the American Dietetic Association. 90:230–237. Conducted by Dr. Frances Larkin, Visiting Scientist, in collaboration with HNIS.

9. Riddick, H.A. Body Mass Index, Television Viewing, Physical Activity and Diets of Females Age 10 to 49 in USDA's Continuing Survey of Food Intakes by Individuals. Paper accepted for presentation at the Annual Meeting of the Federation of American Societies for Experimental Biology. New Orleans, LA, March 1993.

10. Johnson, R.K. H. Smiciklas-Wright, A.C. Crouter, and F.K. Willits. Maternal Employment and the Quality of Young Children's Diets: Empirical Evidence based on the 1987–88 Nationwide Food Consumption Survey. Pediatrics. 90:245–249, 1992.

Mr. DURBIN. Will you conduct a CSFII survey in fiscal year 1993?

Mr. RUST. No. The next CSFII is scheduled for the three-year period of 1994–96. During 1993 HNIS and its contractor are developing and testing new procedures and methodologies. A pilot study for the survey will be conducted in April and May of 1993 in 10 locations throughout the country. The intent of this pilot is to test the administration of the questionnaires and all survey procedures, including in-house data processing. The actual survey will begin in January 1994.

The extensive preparatory activities now underway (including the pilot study) are largely new to this survey and they represent the careful steps HNIS is taking to insure the quality and timeliness of CSFII 1994–96.

Mr. DURBIN. What will be the cost to do the survey?

Mr. RUST. The cost of the CSFII 1994–96 will be approximately $14 million. The contract for this survey has been awarded to Westat, Inc. of Rockville, MD. The cost includes about $1.13 million for start-up and development costs by the contractor and about $4.2, $3.9, and $4.2 million for data collection in 1994, 1995, and 1996, respectively. I will provide a detailed description of the services included for the record.

[The information follows:]

The preparation of survey materials (training manuals, introductory letters, questionnaires, survey publicity);

Survey staff—interviewers, food coders, data reviewers, supervisors, and other support staff including recruitment and training;

Development of data entry software and data tracking system;

Actual conduct of pilot study and survey—listing, contracting and screening housing units, interviewing respondents (These procedures, necessary to assure a survey that is a representative of the U.S. population, are very expensive);

Coding and entry of data, and transmitting data from Contractor to HNIS;

Preparation of survey operations reports; and

Travel for contractor to meet with HNIS and to conduct the survey nationwide.

Mr. DURBIN. Mr. Rust, your agency was established in Octover of 1981. Prior to this, the work was performed within the Agricultural Research Service. Researchers have said that they have been battling problems at USDA for a decade, that the data provided is not as good as it should be. In view of this and your poor track record on conducting surveys, maybe we should transfer the analytical work on foods to agencies better equipped to handle these functions. Specifically, the food composition and analysis work to the Agricultural Research Service and the survey and statistical analysis to the National Agricultural Statistics Service. Tell us, Mr. Rust, what do you think?

Mr. RUST. I believe that it would be extremely inefficient to separate the food composition work and the survey work done by HNIS. The purpose of the surveys is to measure the dietary status of the population. To do this requires collecting information on what people eat and then applying nutrient values to that food. Those nutrient values come from HNIS's National Nutrient Data Bank (NNDB). In turn, the decisions about which foods need improved nutrient data comes, in part, from information in the surveys on what people are eating. Those foods (and nutrients) that are major parts of peoples' diets or that are linked to health problems receive priority.

The survey collection and the NNDB are linked by numerous technical support systems (food coding systems, nutrient database systems, and special data processing/management systems) that could not be easily separated; some, if not all, would require duplication if the surveys were put into a different agency than the NNDB. For example, for the 1994 CSFII the food coding system comprises a data base of approximately 6,700 different foods with descriptions, weights of common measures, accompanying recipes, and yield (after cooking) data. This coding system links the food intake data collected in the survey with the nutrient values in the NNDB. Products that enter the market place during the survey periods may be reported in the survey and must be incorporated into the food coding and nutrient databases. Changes in food formulation must also be monitored and entered into the system.

The HNIS work in food composition is very different from the ARS work. The food composition and analysis work done in HNIS is aimed at compiling as much information as is available from industry, from private or government laboratories, or other sources on the nutrients in foods. Such information is then aggregated and becomes part of a complex system of computer programs which store all available nutrient data and other descriptive information such as growing area, methodology, processing, and season. Such information is used in food intake surveys, for nutrition education programs, to facilitate the labeling of foods, and to develop guidelines for food assistance programs. In contrast, the Nutrient Composition Laboratory (NCL) of the Agricultural Research Service was established 20 years ago to support the work of HNIS and its predecessor agency in generating nutrient data. However, the NCL research program has focused on the development and improvement of methods for the chemical analysis of foods; they have supplied very little actual nutrient data to us. HNIS has had to get its nutrient data from extramural contracts with universities and independent laboratories. In addition to the difficulty created by not having the survey collection and nutrient data work in the same agency as indicated above, moving the HNIS work to ARS would require a complete redefining of the ARS mission from basic to applied research.

Moving HNIS survey work to National Agricultural Statistics Service (NASS) would also be inefficient. Although NASS has considerable experience conducting surveys of farm operations, it has little experience with household based surveys and none with food consumption surveys. Consequently, most of the sampling expertise of NASS would be of limited use and would have to be contracted out. Also, conducting food surveys requires expertise of many types of professionals in addition to statisticians. For example, HNIS employs numerous nutritionists, home economists, economists, food technologists, and chemists to staff the various technical systems required by the survey, to develop and improve the methodology on dietary intake, and to manage the survey.

HNIS was created precisely because the organization arrangements in place at that time were unable to provide the appropriate data in a timely manner. I do not believe that reassigning these key functions will solve the problem. The solution lies in making HNIS perform its responsibilities correctly and that is exactly what the agency's new senior managers are committed to doing.

Mr. DURBIN. The agency also came under criticism last year for its presentation of the four basic food groups in a pyramid and the Secretary stopped the release of the new model to conduct further studies. Some modifications were made and the new food pyramid was released. What has been the overall reaction to the display?

Mr. RUST. HNIS began work in 1988 to develop a new graphic presentation and brochure to explain the research-based food guide we developed in the early 1980's to help people put the Dietary Guidelines for Americans into practice. This food guide differs from the Basic Four which was developed in the 1950's by recommending amounts of different types of food to eat for a total diet that is both adequate in protein, vitamins, and minerals, and moderate in fat, saturated fat, cholesterol, added sugars, and sodium. The new food guide categorizes foods into six groups: five major groups that provide important amounts of vitamins and minerals, and a sixth group that provides mainly calories from fat and added sugars. The food guide and the pyramid illustration show the recommended proportions of these foods in a healthful diet. During development the Pyramid graphic and the information in the brochure were peer-reviewed by nutrition educators and tested with the primary target audience of average adults. Before releasing the new graphic the Secretary wished to conduct more studies to be sure the new graphic would also be understood by children and low-income adults, populations that are major beneficiaries of USDA food programs. A study of graphic alternatives was conducted in 1991. The pyramid graphic was found to be more effective than the other graphics tested, including circles, shopping carts, and bowls. The results were consistent for children, low-income groups, and for the various educational and ethnic groups tested. In April, 1992, USDA released the new Food Guide Pyramid and explanatory booklet with the added confidence that the new graphic would have wide applicability across the many population groups served by USDA.

The new Food Guide Pyramid has been very well received. Every major news channel covered its release. It has been adopted by the professional community—the American Dietetic Association is using it as its National Nutrition Month theme; the Society for Nutrition Education has featured it in children's T.V. programming; software systems, video, card games and several curriculum guides have been developed; the American Academy of Pediatrics and the Food Marketing Institute have featured it in a joint education program; it has been included in textbooks; and a recent survey by the Wheat Industry Council indicated that an unprecedented 25 percent of the population has already heard about the Food Guide Pyramid.

Within USDA, the Food Guide Pyramid is being used extensively. The 32-page bulletin explaining the Food Guide in detail has been widely distributed to the professional community including USDA's Cooperative Extension System and is available to the public through the Consumer Information Center at a cost of $1.00. HNIS and the Food Marketing Institute released a condensed version of the bulletin that has been widely distributed to the professional community and grocery stores. HNIS is featuring the Pyramid in materials for three special audiences—teens through a teaching kit developed for health educators; an educational bulletin for low-literacy audiences; and a bulletin for the elderly developed with DHHS's National Institute on Aging. The Food and Nutrition Service has incorporated the Food Guide Pyramid into the nutrition assistance programs. Copies of the Pyramid have been sent to local schools, child care centers, and each WIC clinic.

Mr. Durbin. Public Law 101-445, the National Nutrition Monitoring and Related Research Act of 1990, requires the Secretaries of the U.S. Department of Agriculture (USDA) and the Department of Health and Human Services (DHHS) to establish and implement a comprehensive plan for the coordinated National Nutrition Monitoring and Related Research Program. As I understand it, both Departments have established a ten-year implementation plan for this program. At last year's hearing, we were told that the plan was in final clearance. Would you provide the Committee with a brief but thorough description of the overall program and its goals?

Mr. Rust. The National Nutrition Monitoring and Related Research Program (NNMRRP) is composed of interconnected Federal and State activities that provide information about dietary and nutritional status of the United States population; conditions existing in the United States that affect the dietary and nutritional status of individuals; and relationships between diet and health.

There are five components of the nutrition monitoring portion of the NNMRRP that are measured by national surveys and surveillance systems. They are: nutrition and related health measurements; food and nutrient consumption; knowledge, attitudes, and behavior assessments; food composition and nutrient data bases; and food supply determinations.

Research conducted in support of the measurement components make up the related research portion of the NNMRRP. In addition, an important mission of the NNMRRP is information exchange and dissemination among policy makers; Federal, State, and local agencies; the food industry; the health community; consumer interest groups; academicians; and professional organizations.

Overall policy direction and coordination for the NNMRRP is provided by the Interagency Board for Nutrition Monitoring and Related Research. The Board is co-chaired by the USDA Assistant Secretary for Food and Consumer Services and the DHHS Assistant Secretary for Health and includes members from 22 Federal agencies that conduct nutrition monitoring or related research and are major users of nutrition monitoring data, and a liaison from the National Nutrition Monitoring Advisory Council. The Board is responsible for enhancing the effectiveness and productivity of Federal nutrition monitoring efforts by improving the planning, coordination, and communication among member agencies. We will provide copies of publications and brochures that were produced in 1992.

[CLERK'S NOTE.—The publications and brochures provided will be retained in the files of the Committee.]

Mr. DURBIN. Also, provide us with a description of the goals and objectives for each year of the Ten-Year Plan, including the cost associated with each year. Be sure to differentiate the costs and requirements of USDA and DHHS.

Mr. RUST. The primary goal of the Ten-Year Comprehensive Plan is to establish a comprehensive nutrition monitoring and related research program by collecting quality data that are continuous, coordinated, timely, and reliable; using comparable methods for data collection and reporting of results; conducting relevant research; and efficiently and effectively disseminating and exchanging information with data users. The Plan is divided into National and State and local objectives and activities to implement the primary goal. The National objectives include: providing for a comprehensive NNMRRP through continuous and coordinated data collection; improving the comparability and quality of data across the NNMRRP; and improving the research base for nutrition monitoring. The State and local objectives include: developing and strengthening State and local capacity for continuous and coordinated nutrition monitoring data collection that complements national nutrition surveys; improving methodologies to enhance comparability of NNMRRP data across Federal, State, and local levels; and improving the quality of State and local nutrition monitoring data.

Implementation of the objectives are delineated in 68 specific activities in the Ten-Year Plan. Each activity has a timeline for completion of the ten-year life of the Plan.

The costs associated with the Ten-Year Plan for specific USDA activities will require about 20 to 40 percent increase in funding above current levels to meet the goals that have been set for a comprehensive NNMRRP.

DIETARY GUIDELINES

Mr. DURBIN. Eight bulletins on using the Dietary Guidelines were targeted for publication in the fall of 1992. Have these bulletins been released?

Mr. RUST. These eight bulletins have not yet been released. The eight bulletins comprise a set of bulletins entitled *Dietary Guidelines and Your Diet,* HG 253 1-8. The set contains one bulletin on each guideline, and an overview bulletin. HNIS technical staff completed their work on the bulletins in June, 1992, in hope of having them available in the fall. However, editing of the final manuscripts and layouts by agency and Departmental Public Affairs staffs was delayed by the large volume of work to be completed during the summer months. Editorial changes to the bulletin set were reviewed and incorporated into the final layouts by the design contractor in September and the bulletins were prepared in final color form on computer disk during October. The completed bulletins with all design, text, and layout on computer disk were submitted to USDA's Office of Public Affairs. Other agencies were invited to participate in the print order. A contract for printing will be let by the Government Printing Office in April 1993. The anticipated release date for the publications is June 1993.

Mr. DURBIN. The Act mandates the review and approval of all dietary guidance materials developed by the Federal government. What is the status of an MOU agreement between USDA and DHHS to carry out this review?

Mr. RUST. The Memorandum of Understanding (MOU) agreement between USDA and DHHS which outlines general procedures for review of dietary guidance for the general population or identified population subgroups is in final negotiation between the two Departments. There is agreement on all but one issue. The unresolved issue involves whether or not dietary guidance for the general public, but directed to health professionals comes under review by the MOU. USDA's position is that any dietary guidance for the general public should come under review whether it is directed to health professionals, Extension Service nutrition specialists, or directly to the media or consumers. DHHS believes that any material targeted to health professionals should not be subject to review, except information for direct distribution to the general public. At issue is whether review should cover all information that may become available for the public indirectly through interpretation by health professionals, or just the material which is directed to the public. Discussions for final approval of the MOU between the two Departments relative to this issue will be resumed when our new policy officials are appointed and confirmed. USDA's Dietary Guidance Working Group (DGWG) and DHHS's Committee on Dietary Guidance (DCDG) are reviewing dietary guidance materials from both Departments as though a MOU were in place. USDA's committee has been reviewing its own materials and sending its materials to DHHS for review since the Committee was established in 1986. Likewise, DCDG reviews DHHS materials and forwards them to USDA for review.

NATIONAL NUTRITION MONITORING ADVISORY COUNCIL

Mr. DURBIN. The Act also requires the establishment of a nine-member advisory council. Who serves on the council?

Mr. RUST. The members of the National Nutrition Monitoring Advisory Council will be provided for the record.

[The information follows:]

Suzanne S. Harris, Ph.D.; Executive Director, Human Nutrition Institute; International Life Sciences Institute; Washington, D.C.

Charles H. James, III, M.B.A.; President and Chief Executive Officer; C.H. James and Company; Charleston, West Virginia.

Shiriki K. Kumanyika, Ph.D., R.D., M.P.H.; Associate Professor and Associate Director for Epidemiology; Center for Biostatistics and Epidemiology; Pennsylvania State College of Medicine; Hershey, Pennsylvania.

Helen E. Lee, M.S.; Lecturer, Foothill College; Los Altos Hills, California.

Sue Greig, M.S., R.D.; Kansas State University; Manhattan, Kansas.

Sheryl Lee, M.P.H., R.D.; Chief, Office of Nutrition Services; Arizona Department of Health Services; Mesa, Arizona.

Marlene E. Marschall, M.A., R.N.; Commissioner of Health, Minnesota; Department of Health; Minneapolis, Minnesota.

Lynn Parker, M.S.; Director, Child Nutrition Programs and Nutrition Policy; Food Research and Action Center; Washington, D.C.

Note: The following member of the Council resigned in March, 1993. David Call, Ph.D.; Dean, College of Agriculture and Life Sciences; Cornell University, Ithaca, New York.

Five members are appointed by the President and four members by the leadership of Congress. They serve staggered terms.

Mr. DURBIN. The council met in February 1992 and issued its first report in December 1992. What were the findings and recommendations of this meeting?

Mr. RUST. The Council met three times in 1992. The meeting dates were February 26–27, July 15–16, and September 24–25, 1992. The first meeting was devoted to orientation of the Council and updating them on the current activities in nutrition monitoring. The second meeting was held in conjunction with the quarterly meeting of the Interagency Board for Nutrition Monitoring and Related Research. Council members were invited guests to the Interagency Board meeting. At their second meeting, the Council defined major areas in nutrition monitoring and related research that they would focus on. At the third meeting, the Council invited two experts in nutrition monitoring from private industry and academia to address food composition data bases and monitoring high-risk population groups.

The annual report of the Council submitted to the Secretaries of USDA and DHHS provided an overview of the activities of the Council during its first year of operation and identified six priority areas that the Council identified to serve as a focus for their future activities and its evaluation of the Nutrition Monitoring and Related Research Program. Two specific recommendations were given in the report. The first was to recommend that the Secretaries take whatever steps were necessary to obtain formal approval and transmittal of the Ten-Year Plan to Congress. The Ten-Year Plan was transmitted to Congress on January 14, 1993. The second recommendation was that a process for deciding the overriding priorities for the Program across agencies be articulated and implemented.

NATIONAL NUTRIENT DATA BANK

Mr. DURBIN. Have you begun to upgrade the National Nutrient Data Bank this fiscal year as planned?

Mr. RUST. The timeline for the upgrade in this fiscal year will be provided for the record.

[The information follows:]

March 31, 1993—Request for Contract sent to Contract Management Branch, FNS; May 30, 1993—Request for Proposals sent to Prospective Bidders; July 1, 1993—Technical Review Panel meets September 30, 1993—Contract Award.

The Nutrient Data Research Branch (NDRB), Nutrition Monitoring Division, of the Human Nutrition Information Service (HNIS) initiated the upgrade (redesign) of the Nutrient Data Bank System (NDBS). As part of the process, an outside consultant reviewed the current system and provided recommendations for the redesign. The next step was a Needs Assessment Report prepared by the staff at NDRB.

The purpose of the redesign is to assure that we take full advantage of existing technology in our mission to provide representative values on the composition of food in the U.S. food supply. An upgrade at this time is necessary to support expanding research activities requiring accurate data bases on the composition of foods. The new system will be required ot support the Nationwide Food Consumption Surveys, the Food Grouping System, activities within the 10-Year Comprehensive Plan for the National Nutrition Monitoring and Related Research Program, nutrition education activities, and other research projects such as the Child Nutrition Program Data Base, and Trend Analysis of Nutrient Intakes.

The internal needs assessment report was evaluated by a data bank users group formed from users of our nutrient data in various government agencies—Food and Drug Administration (FDA), National Institutes of Health (NIH), and National Center for Health Statistics (NCHS) at Department of Health and Human Services (DHHS), Nutrient Composition Laboratory (NCL) and National Program Staff (NPS) of Agriculture Research Service (ARS), and appropriate contracting and computer system analysts from agencies in USDA. The data bank users group will have ongoing input throughout the process; with some members being asked to serve on the technical review panel.

A draft request for contract has been prepared and details the design, development and implementation of the upgraded nutrient data bank system over a minimum period of 3 years. Work on this upgrade throughout the process will be facilitated by an outside consultant working with our staff and input from data bank users in and outside of government. Working groups are established for developing information needed by the contractor, for participation in the technical review of proposals, and guiding the stepwise design process.

Mr. DURBIN. What type of information is included in this data bank?

Mr. RUST. The Nutrient Data Bank System, NDBS, is a computerized system which includes detailed descriptors of foods such as growing location, processing, date of analysis; extensive nutrient values for these foods; factors to calculate specifics such as calories or serving sizes; documentation needed by various users, such as data by brand names or by analytical methods; and formulation procedures to calculate values of complex multi-ingredient foods.

Information in the data bank also includes the representative values for the nutrient composition of the U.S. food supply. These values result from collecting, entering, verifying, aggregating, and reporting data compiled from a wide variety of sources. The data sources include scientific literature, the food industry, academia, other government agencies, and agency sponsored contracts.

The NDBS is used to produce the data published in USDA's Agriculture Handbook No. 8, Composition of Foods . . . Raw, Processed,

Prepared. These data are released through a computerized Bulletin Board which provides a ready source of information about nutrient data releases and makes available nutrient data files quickly and inexpensively. These files include the Standard Reference Data Base (Agriculture Handbook No. 8), annual supplements, and files of additional nutrients such as selenium and carbohydrate fractions.

The NDBS is archival and holds the information on nutrient composition of foods over time, making possible the assessment of changes in nutrient intake and eating habits over time. The NDBS is the most comprehensive source of nutrient data in the world.

CONTINUING SURVEY USERS' GROUP

Mr. DURBIN. The Continuing Survey Users' Group is a group made up of representatives from a number of agencies within the Federal government who use the information obtained from your surveys. Did this group meet fiscal year 1992? What were their findings and recommendations?

Mr. RUST. The Continuing Survey Users' Group, CSUG, includes representatives from 14 Federal agencies. The group met formally three times in fiscal year 1992. I will provide detailed information for the record.

[The information follows:]

1. On December 12, 1991, HNIS presented its recommendations for modification of the 1991 Continuing Survey of Food Intakes by Individuals (CSFII) questionnaires and requested formal written comments from CSUG representatives.

Written comments were received from the Food and Drug Administration (FDA) and the National Center for Health Statistics (NCHS) of the Department of Health and Human Services (DHHS); the Food and Nutrition Service (FNS), Cooperative States Research Service (CSRS) and Economic Research Service (ERS) of the Department of Agriculture. All comments received were given careful review and incorporated into the Pilot Study questionnaires based on the value of the information to be obtained and respondent burden. HNIS solicited and incorporated comments from the Environmental Protection Agency (EPA) on questions relating to water and fish intake. HNIS continues to consult with CSUG representatives as necessary or as requested on questionnaire issues of concern to these agencies.

2. On January 23, 1992, HNIS presented the proposed CSFII 1994-96 sample design and data collection methods. The sample design included two days of food intake data collection. Formal written comments from CSUG representatives were requested.

Written comments requesting a third day of food intake data collection were received from FDA and EPA. NCHS provided written comments on comparability issues between the CSFII and the National Health and Nutrition Examination Survey (NHANES). Survey comparability is acknowledged as an area requiring long-term discussions between HNIS and NCHS.

HNIS met with EPA on an ongoing basis during the development of the CSFII 1994-96 contract regarding EPA's request for a larger sample and a third day of food intake data collection. As a result of EPA and FDA requests, options for the third day and two additional samples of 5,000 and 10,000 persons were added to the CSFII contract.

However, the Office of Management and Budget (OMB) did not approve the option for the collection of a third day of food intake data, stating that an additional day of data was inappropriate for the required statistical analyses and would impact negatively on response rates. OMB's statement corroborated Iowa State University research sponsored by HNIS demonstrating that two days of food intake data were the minimum number needed for calculating distributions of usual intake.

As of this date, EPA has not provided the funds needed to exercise its additional sample options. HNIS has received no funds from any Federal CSFII data users to support survey activities.

3. At an April 2, 1992 meeting, HNIS presented its recommendations for modification of the 1991 DHKS questionnaire and requested formal written comments from CSUG representatives.

Written comments were received from FDA, NCHS, CSRS, and ERS. EPA did not provide written comments. However, HNIS solicited and then received written comments from EPA. Comments were given careful review and incorporated based on the value of the information to be obtained and respondent burden. HNIS continues to work closely with FDA on a series of food labeling questions for the DHKS questionnaire.

4. Data users also were encouraged to provide input during the session entitled "Future CSFII—Your Opportunity for Input" at the Nutrition Monitoring: USDA/HNIS Resources Conference, held on November 7-8, 1991, in Bethesda, MD.

CONTRACTS

Mr. DURBIN. Please provide the Committee with a list of all extramural contracts, including the cost of each, that were used in fiscal year 1992 as well as those ongoing in fiscal year 1993.

Mr. RUST. HNIS extramural contracts that were ongoing in 1992 or 1993 will be provided for the record.

[The information follows:]

Continuing Survey of Food Intakes by Individuals and the Diet and Health Knowledge Survey. Contract with Westat, Inc., Rockville, MD. $1.13 million funded in FY 1992 for survey development costs. Options for survey collection are scheduled for funding in 1994 ($4.2 million), 1995 ($3.9 million), and 1996 ($4.2 million).

Statistical and Methodological Research Related to Analysis of Food Consumption Surveys. Cooperative Agreement with Iowa State University. Five year project 1992 through 1996. The 1992 cost was $170,000 and the 1993 cost was $195,000.

Improving Children's Dietary Intake Reporting. Cooperative Agreement with the University of Maryland. Funded in FY 1991 for $75,000. Terminates in 1993.

Analysis of the Importance of Socioeconomic, Demographic, Personal and Health-related Factors. Cooperative Agreement with Washington State University. Funded in FY 1987 for $197,000. Completed in January 1993.

An Analysis of Variations in Food Consumption Across Household Types and Over Time. Cooperative Agreement with Cornell University. Funded in FY 1987 for $254,000. Ends in 1993.

Relationship of Nutritional Knowledge and Attitudes to Dietary Behavior. Cooperative Agreement with University of North Carolina. Funded in FY 1990 for $224,000. Ends in 1994.

Research Support Agreement with University of Texas School of Public Health. Four year project 1990 through 1993. The 1992 cost was $198,000 and the 1993 cost was $212,339.

Continued Monitoring of the Nutrient Content of Selected Key Foods. Contract with University of Georgia. The 1992 cost was $70,463 and the 1993 cost was $65,383.

Monitoring of Fatty Acids and Sterols. Contract with University of Maryland. The 1992 cost was $68,979.

Development/Verification of Nutrient Retention Values in Foods Prepared by Different Cooking Methods. Contract with Hazleton Laboratories America, Inc. The 1992 cost was $62,518.

Nutrient Content of Ethnic and Geographic Specific Foods. Contract with Southern Testing and Research Labs, Inc. The 1992 cost was $74,814 and the 1993 cost was $72,700.

Monitoring Contents of Lipid Components of Ethnic and Geographic Specific Foods. Contract with University of Maryland. The 1992 cost was $62,152 and the 1993 cost was $52,500.

Nutrient Data Bank System Redesign. Contract to be funded in 1993 for $165,184 with options scheduled for funding in 1994 and 1995.

Development of Quality Assurance Reference Materials for Nutrient Data Contracts. Purchase order with National Food Processors Association Washington, DC. The 1992 cost was $11,860. To be funded in 1993 for $8,000.

Advisory and Assistance Services for Nutrient Data Research Branch by Dr. Loretta Hoover. Purchase order with University of Missouri. The 1992 cost was $24,999.

Total Dietary Fiber in Selected Foods. Purchase order with Southern Testing Laboratories, Inc. The 1992 cost was $11,224.

Design and Formative Evaluation of Revised Bulletins HG 232 (1-7): *Dietary Guidelines and Your Diet* and One Overview Bulletin. Contract with Porter Novelli. Awarded 9/28/90; completed 10/29/92. $134,000 FY 90 funds.

Reaching Pregnant Adolescents with Nutrition Messages. Cooperative Agreement with University of Tennessee-Knoxville. Awarded 9/30/91; estimated completion date 5/24/93. $98,752 FY 91 funds.

"Evaluation of HNIS' Dietary Guidelines Teaching Kit for Home Economics Teachers." Contract with Dr. C. Byrd-Bredbenner. Awarded 5/1/92; completed 12/31/92. $21,032 FY 92 funds.

Dietary Status and Eating Patterns, Cooperative Agreement with the University of North Carolina, Chapel Hill. The contract ran from September 29, 1989 to December 30, 1992, with a total cost of $203,699.

Evaluation of the Usefulness of Theories of Behavior Change for Analyzing Data Obtained from the 1989-91 Diet and Health Knowledge Survey/Continuing Survey of Food Intakes by Individuals, Purchase Order with Elizabeth Colavito, nutrition technician. The contract ran from September 28, 1992 to January 31, 1993 for a total cost of $1,800.

Economic Factors Affecting Household Food Consumption Behavior, Cooperative Agreement with the University of California-Berkeley; The project ran from September 30, 1987 to February 28, 1993, with a total cost of $248,309.00.

Exploration of an Approach to Adjustment of the 1987-88 NFCS to account for Nonresponse. Cooperative Agreement with the University of Arizona. The project ran from October 29, 1988 to December 31, 1992, with a total cost of $170,275.00.

FOOD PLANS

Mr. DURBIN. HNIS determines the cost of four USDA family food plans, including the Thrifty Food Plan which is used to determine the level of food stamps benefits. How often are these plans revised?

Mr. RUST. The USDA family food plans are *revised* periodically to take into account new information on foods costs, food composition, food consumption patterns, and nutritional needs. These revisions occur about every ten years and are linked to USDA food consumption surveys which provide data on food costs and consumption patterns. The last revision was in 1983 based on the 1977-78 Nationwide Food Consumption Survey. The revision before that was in 1975 based on the 1965-66 Nationwide Food Consumption Survey Data. Data from the 1987-88 Nationwide Food Consumption Survey were to be used as the basis to revise the 1983 food plans, but were not because of concerns about the low response rate and the representativeness of the data.

Between revisions the costs of the food plans are *updated* monthly to adjust for fluctuations in the base prices of the foods from the household survey. These base prices are updated by applying percentage changes in the prices of the food or a similar food priced monthly by the Bureau of Labor Statistics (BLS). The costs of the food plans are reflective of a market basket, a fixed collection of quantities of 2400 different foods divided into 31 food groups. BLS data represent the food groups in the market basket, but do not reflect the percentage changes in food prices for all 2400 foods. BLS reports on approximately 100-200 foods and these are used to estimate the costs of the food plans.

Mr. DURBIN. For the record, please provide the most recent food plans.

Mr. RUST. I will provide copies of the thrifty food plan, low-cost plan, moderate-cost plan, and liberal cost plan for the record. Quantities of food for 31 food groups are expressed in pounds for a week by sex and age.

I will also submit HNIS report 329, "Cost of Food at Home Estimated for Food Plans at Four Cost Levels, February 1993 U.S. Average" for the record.

The cost of the USDA family food plans are updated monthly to adjust for fluctuations in the prices of the foods. The cost is updated using data on changes in prices of foods provided to us by the Bureau of Labor Statistics.

[The information follows:]

Table 1.--Thrifty food plan: Quantities of food for a week[1] by sex and age

Food group	Unit	Child: 1-2 years	Child: 3-5 years	Child: 6-8 years	Child: 9-11 years	Male: 12-14 years	Male: 15-19 years	Male: 20-50 years	Male: 51 years and over	Female[2]: 12-19 years	Female[2]: 20-50 years	Female[2]: 51 years and over
Vegetables, fruit:												
Potatoes (fresh weight)	lb	0.47	0.82	1.04	1.11	1.29	2.22	1.50	1.55	1.27	1.16	0.90
High-nutrient vegetables	lb	.52	.67	1.05	1.17	1.65	1.08	1.61	1.52	1.14	1.91	2.28
Other vegetables	lb	.60	.70	.97	1.25	1.35	1.15	1.86	1.33	1.08	2.68	2.03
Mixtures, mostly vegetable; condiments	lb	.01	.02	.05	.07	.02	.06	.11	.06	.07	.08	.01
Vitamin-C-rich fruit[3]	lb	1.19	1.24	1.32	1.62	1.08	1.17	1.13	1.00	2.02	1.73	1.35
Other fruit[3]	lb	.97	.92	1.61	1.86	1.11	1.04	1.20	1.41	1.30	.93	1.37
Grain products:												
Whole-grain/high-fiber breakfast cereals	lb	.44[4]	.33	.17	.24	.38	.27	.17	.13	.30	.12	.17
Other breakfast cereals	lb	.30[4]	.27	.19	.26	.05	.12	.21	.12	.39	.19	.27
Whole-grain/high-fiber flour, meal, rice, pasta	lb	.11	.14	.12	.11	.20	.22	.15	.21	.16	.15	.18
Other flour, meal, rice, pasta	lb	.88	1.23	1.85	1.73	2.15	2.34	1.81	1.87	1.32	1.81	1.32
Whole-grain/high-fiber bread	lb	.09	.10	.09	.11	.15	.17	.24	.21	.21	.34	.29
Other bread	lb	.38	.65	1.01	1.27	1.68	1.33	1.85	1.33	1.04	.59	.29
Bakery products, not bread	lb	.06	.10	.42	.58	.19	.43	.56	.30	.36	.12	.10
Grain mixtures	lb	.08	.06	.07	.11	.02	.13	.23	.15	.31	.37	.19
Milk, cheese, cream:												
Milk, yogurt[5]	qt	3.42	3.06	3.39	4.17	3.99	3.91	2.00	1.63	4.36	2.37	2.17
Cheese	lb	.04	.05	.08	.11	.11	.11	.13	.12	.27	.29	.32
Cream, mixtures mostly milk	lb	.15	.15	.34	.30	.10	.24	.41	.26	.35	.03	.26
Meat and alternates:												
Lower-cost red meats, variety meats	lb	.93	.69	.70	.92	1.20	1.49	1.40	1.73	1.75	1.60	1.95
Higher-cost red meats, variety meats	lb	.15	.11	.13	.19	.18	.26	.39	.54	.20	.35	.55
Poultry	lb	.35	.48	.64	.70	.90	.90	.96	.71	.20	.95	.70
Fish, shellfish	lb	.02	.02	.02	.03	.03	.02	.04	.04	.04	.04	.04
Bacon, sausage, luncheon meats	lb	.18	.32	.31	.24	.26	.27	.56	.49	.24	.45	.45
Eggs	no.	3.00	2.90	1.90	2.60	2.20	3.10	4.10	4.30	4.10	4.40	4.10
Dry beans, peas, lentils (dry weight)[6]	lb	.27	.18	.18	.24	.59	.58	.45	.59	.35	.41	.43
Mixtures, mostly meat, poultry, fish, egg, legume	lb	.05	.06	.01	.01	.02	.03	.13	.15	.20	.13	.15
Nuts (shelled weight), peanut butter	lb	.09	.24	.13	.15	.37	.14	.17	.22	.09	.28	.08
Other foods:												
Fats, oils	lb	.14	.33	.58	.67	.73	.93	.76	.60	.22	.28	.21
Sugar, sweets	lb	.10	.36	.78	.87	1.20	.95	1.01	.76	.31	.21	.22
Soft drinks, punches, ades (single-strength)	lb	.39	.57	.65	.87	.87	1.51	1.17	.32	1.12	.40	.38
Coffee, tea	lb	.00	.00	.00	.00	.00	.00	.02	.02	.00	.02	.01
Seasonings	lb	.01	.01	.02	.02	.03	.08	.07	.03	.05	.05	.01

[1]Quantities are for food as purchased or brought into the household from garden or farm. Food is for preparation of all meals and snacks for a week. About 5 percent of the edible parts of food above quantities needed to meet caloric needs is included to allow for food assumed to be discarded as plate waste, spoilage, etc.

[2]Pregnant and lactating females usually require added nutrients and should consult a doctor for recommendations about diet and supplements.

[3]Frozen concentrated juices are included as single-strength juice.

[4]Cereal fortified with iron is recommended.

[5]Quantities of dry and evaporated milk and yogurt included as the amount of fluid whole milk having the same calcium content.

[6]Count one pound of canned dry beans--pork and beans, kidney beans, etc.--as 0.33 pound.

Table 2. Low-cost food plan: Quantities of food for a week[1] by sex and age

Food group	Unit	Child 1-2 years	Child 3-5 years	Child 6-8 years	Child 9-11 years	Male 12-14 years	Male 15-19 years	Male 20-50 years	Male 51 years or more	Female[2] 12-19 years	Female[2] 20-50 years	Female[2] 51 years or more
Vegetables, fruit:												
Potatoes (fresh weight)	lb	0.50	0.73	1.16	1.28	1.55	1.88	1.97	1.71	1.19	1.19	1.11
High-nutrient vegetables	lb	.55	.50	.86	.98	1.30	1.34	1.91	2.00	1.19	1.86	2.17
Other vegetables	lb	.82	.88	1.20	1.41	1.41	1.54	2.12	2.19	1.54	2.30	2.04
Mixtures, mostly vegetable; condiments	lb	.06	.10	.14	.17	.18	.20	.29	.30	.15	.24	.15
Vitamin-C-rich fruit[3]	lb	1.51	1.43	1.79	1.94	2.03	2.16	1.62	1.75	1.76	1.79	1.91
Other fruit[3]	lb	1.97	1.58	2.30	2.44	2.07	1.45	1.98	2.21	1.81	1.53	2.19
Grain products:												
Whole-grain/high-fiber breakfast cereals	lb	.35[4]	.27	.31	.35	.36	.28	.14	.22	.33	.21	.31
Other breakfast cereals	lb	.38[4]	.26	.33	.38	.39	.31	.16	.25	.36	.23	.22
Whole-grain/high-fiber flour, meal, rice, pasta	lb	.11	.07	.08	.09	.10	.10	.11	.10	.09	.09	.12
Other flour, meal, rice, pasta	lb	.86	.83	1.04	1.17	1.32	1.34	1.40	1.34	.95	1.01	.83
Whole-grain/high-fiber bread	lb	.12	.17	.22	.26	.31	.39	.42	.30	.28	.30	.25
Other bread	lb	.41	.79	1.08	1.28	1.52	1.95	2.08	1.45	1.19	1.24	.84
Bakery products, not bread	lb	.09	.36	.62	.75	.96	.85	.86	.71	.44	.46	.19
Grain mixtures	lb	.15	.20	.18	.30	.33	.34	.29	.13	.23	.22	.14
Milk, cheese, cream:												
Milk, yogurt[5]	qt	3.41	3.23	4.26	4.69	5.02	4.86	2.49	2.07	4.64	1.85	2.16
Cheese	lb	.17	.17	.20	.19	.22	.30	.36	.28	.34	.34	.35
Cream, mixtures mostly milk	lb	.13	.44	.57	.69	.67	.75	.51	.50	.65	.34	.55
Meat and alternates:												
Lower-cost red meats, variety meats	lb	.71	.52	.60	.74	.99	1.23	1.65	1.23	1.13	1.57	1.67
Higher-cost red meats, variety meats	lb	.37	.38	.47	.57	.79	.94	.86	1.04	.70	.95	1.21
Poultry	lb	.42	.43	.63	.67	.85	.77	.94	.98	.83	.91	.95
Fish, shellfish	lb	.09	.07	.14	.11	.16	.14	.25	.23	.17	.21	.19
Bacon, sausage, luncheon meats	lb	.15	.39	.48	.51	.58	.57	.34	.58	.29	.41	.21
Eggs	no.	3.34	3.26	2.50	2.99	3.02	2.97	3.38	3.93	3.82	4.23	4.02
Dry beans, peas, lentils (dry weight)[6]	lb	.22	.09	.12	.15	.20	.19	.27	.19	.24	.34	.14
Mixtures, mostly meat, poultry, fish, egg, legume	lb	.08	.08	.11	.15	.19	.20	.22	.15	.16	.17	.16
Nuts (shelled weight), peanut butter	lb	.09	.20	.20	.22	.20	.22	.14	.08	.11	.07	.04
Other foods:												
Fats, oils	lb	.09	.27	.43	.50	.55	.54	.68	.54	.25	.32	.26
Sugar, sweets	lb	.15	.46	.57	.62	.74	.77	.84	.83	.43	.35	.43
Soft drinks, punches, ades (single-strength)	lb	1.53	1.96	2.72	3.25	3.35	4.63	3.67	1.19	3.96	3.33	.96
Coffee, tea	lb	.01	.00	.00	.00	.01	.01	.02	.12	.03	.15	.11
Seasonings	lb	.02	.02	.03	.04	.04	.05	.04	.04	.03	.03	.03

[1]Quantities are for food as purchased or brought into the household from garden or farm. Food is for preparation of all meals and snacks for a week. About 10 percent of the edible parts of food above quantities needed to meet caloric needs is included to allow for food assumed to be discarded as plate waste, spoilage, etc.

[2]Pregnant and lactating females usually require added nutrients and should consult a doctor for recommendations about diet and supplements.

[3]Frozen concentrated juices are included as single-strength juice.

[4]Cereal fortified with iron is recommended.

[5]Quantities of dry and evaporated milk and yogurt included as the amount of fluid whole milk having the same calcium content.

[6]Count one pound of canned dry beans--pork and beans, kidney beans, etc.--as 0.33 pound.

Table 3. Moderate-cost food plan: Quantities of food for a week[1] by sex and age

Food group	Unit	Child				Male				Female[2]		
		1-2 years	3-5 years	6-8 years	9-11 years	12-14 years	15-19 years	20-50 years	51 years or more	12-19 years	20-50 years	51 years or more
Vegetables, fruit:												
Potatoes (fresh weight)	lb	0.68	0.81	1.34	1.90	1.69	2.17	2.11	1.81	1.31	1.31	1.03
High-nutrient vegetables	lb	.78	1.00	.88	1.48	1.33	1.55	2.22	2.17	1.56	2.51	2.76
Other vegetables	lb	1.06	.81	1.38	1.82	1.65	2.11	2.51	2.76	1.86	2.71	2.52
Mixtures, mostly vegetable; condiments	lb	.10	.13	.17	.22	.21	.24	.32	.34	.20	.29	.23
Vitamin-C-rich fruit[3]	lb	1.60	1.92	2.61	2.47	2.10	2.32	2.26	2.15	1.96	2.22	2.51
Other fruit[3]	lb	1.98	2.19	2.32	2.44	2.88	2.42	1.99	3.12	1.81	1.91	2.78
Grain products:												
Whole-grain/high-fiber breakfast cereals	lb	.53[4]	.24	.35	.42	.42	.38	.19	.22	.41	.23	.23
Other breakfast cereals	lb	.43[4]	.26	.38	.47	.46	.43	.21	.25	.42	.24	.17
Whole-grain/high-fiber flour, meal, rice, pasta	lb	.07	.06	.07	.07	.09	.08	.11	.10	.06	.08	.11
Other flour, meal, rice, pasta	lb	.81	.81	.87	.86	1.19	1.03	1.53	1.38	.86	1.10	.85
Whole-grain/high-fiber bread	lb	.11	.19	.25	.31	.34	.50	.46	.34	.30	.32	.26
Other bread	lb	.41	.82	1.07	1.34	1.52	2.18	2.02	1.48	1.24	1.27	.87
Bakery products, not bread	lb	.21	.53	.76	.65	.78	.86	.93	.80	.59	.53	.31
Grain mixtures	lb	.14	.18	.26	.46	.43	.46	.30	.15	.32	.25	.18
Milk, cheese, cream:												
Milk, yogurt[5]	qt	3.79	3.58	4.72	5.16	6.07	5.38	2.62	1.93	5.09	1.89	2.24
Cheese	lb	.18	.18	.29	.21	.26	.46	.39	.40	.38	.44	.40
Cream, mixtures mostly milk	lb	.28	.34	.71	.99	1.08	.75	.59	.61	.70	.25	.58
Meat and alternates:												
Lower-cost red meats, variety meats	lb	.51	.60	.85	1.11	1.36	1.19	1.48	1.37	1.12	1.60	1.58
Higher-cost red meats, variety meats	lb	.46	.64	.90	1.17	1.43	1.35	1.60	1.46	1.04	1.35	1.50
Poultry	lb	.57	.59	.82	1.00	1.15	.74	1.12	1.03	.94	1.06	1.03
Fish, shellfish	lb	.10	.16	.22	.29	.40	.36	.41	.51	.41	.41	.56
Bacon, sausage, luncheon meats	lb	.26	.42	.59	.50	.26	.72	.50	.43	.32	.24	.22
Eggs	no.	3.64	3.40	2.52	3.08	2.42	2.73	3.10	3.83	3.23	4.37	4.12
Dry beans, peas, lentils (dry weight)[6]	lb	.10	.07	.16	.21	.20	.18	.23	.20	.24	.35	.19
Mixtures, mostly meat, poultry, fish, egg, legume	lb	.08	.10	.14	.16	.17	.23	.29	.19	.17	.19	.17
Nuts (shelled weight), peanut butter	lb	.05	.13	.18	.15	.28	.13	.16	.04	.06	.03	.02
Other foods:												
Fats, oils	lb	.11	.30	.31	.46	.52	.57	.65	.62	.28	.36	.29
Sugar, sweets	lb	.17	.49	.60	.68	.79	.84	.92	.91	.42	.47	.44
Soft drinks, punches, ades (single-strength)	lb	1.57	2.37	2.86	3.69	3.90	4.84	3.73	1.06	4.26	3.71	1.18
Coffee, tea	lb	.01	.01	.01	.03	.02	.05	.22	.24	.05	.22	.21
Seasonings	lb	.02	.03	.04	.05	.05	.06	.06	.05	.04	.04	.03

[1]Quantities are for food as purchased or brought into the household from garden or farm. Food is for preparation of all meals and snacks for a week. About 20 percent of the edible parts of food above quantities needed to meet caloric needs is included to allow for food assumed to be discarded as plate waste, spoilage, etc.

[2]Pregnant and lactating females usually require added nutrients and should consult a doctor for recommendations about diet and supplements.

[3]Frozen concentrated juices are included as single-strength juice.

[4]Cereal fortified with iron is recommended.

[5]Quantities of dry and evaporated milk and yogurt included as the amount of fluid whole milk having the same calcium content.

[6]Count one pound of canned dry beans--pork and beans, kidney beans, etc.--as 0.33 pound.

Table 4. Liberal food plan: Quantities of food for a week[1] by sex and age

Food group	Unit	Child 1-2 years	Child 3-5 years	Child 6-8 years	Child 9-11 years	Male 12-14 years	Male 15-19 years	Male 20-50 years	Male 51 years or more	Female[2] 12-19 years	Female[2] 20-50 years	Female[2] 51 years or more
Vegetables, fruit:												
Potatoes (fresh weight)	lb	0.70	0.78	1.13	1.48	1.57	2.44	2.06	1.74	1.20	1.18	1.10
High-nutrient vegetables	lb	.78	.81	1.24	1.22	1.57	1.78	2.79	2.77	1.89	3.90	2.81
Other vegetables	lb	1.03	.87	1.47	1.61	2.08	2.04	3.02	3.14	2.00	3.72	2.89
Mixtures, mostly vegetable; condiments	lb	.10	.11	.18	.19	.24	.29	.49	.36	.19	.34	.28
Vitamin-C-rich fruit[3]	lb	1.68	2.28	2.32	3.26	2.79	3.08	2.72	2.50	2.21	2.47	2.63
Other fruit[3]	lb	3.24	2.47	2.68	3.38	2.54	2.29	2.44	3.02	2.09	2.15	3.13
Grain products:												
Whole-grain/high-fiber breakfast cereals	lb	.53[4]	.25	.32	.37	.51	.48	.27	.19	.45	.20	.24
Other breakfast cereals	lb	.54[4]	.26	.34	.40	.56	.52	.30	.21	.46	.20	.17
Whole-grain/high-fiber flour, meal, rice, pasta	lb	.05	.06	.09	.09	.08	.10	.11	.11	.07	.09	.09
Other flour, meal, rice, pasta	lb	.85	.89	1.26	1.35	1.20	1.40	1.48	1.54	.93	1.22	.81
Whole-grain/high-fiber bread	lb	.13	.20	.25	.33	.45	.52	.60	.43	.34	.21	.28
Other bread	lb	.45	.76	.94	1.26	1.71	1.94	2.22	1.61	1.24	1.38	.86
Bakery products, not bread	lb	.29	.62	.81	.64	.95	.98	.91	.97	.55	.56	.41
Grain mixtures	lb	.23	.29	.34	.38	.46	.43	.35	.18	.42	.31	.15
Milk, cheese, cream:												
Milk, yogurt[5]	qt	4.14	3.64	5.05	5.13	6.12	5.30	2.46	1.87	5.44	2.05	2.42
Cheese	lb	.23	.24	.41	.38	.34	.50	.45	.41	.43	.45	.45
Cream, mixtures mostly milk	lb	.17	.57	.61	.77	.69	.33	.19	.68	.96	.15	.76
Meat and alternates:												
Lower-cost red meats, variety meats	lb	.60	.54	.98	1.07	1.21	1.23	1.46	1.35	1.15	1.95	1.36
Higher-cost red meats, variety meats	lb	.61	.73	1.13	1.44	1.66	1.65	2.00	1.80	1.42	1.64	1.69
Poultry	lb	.38	.79	.89	1.18	1.06	1.08	1.17	1.20	.89	1.28	1.31
Fish, shellfish	lb	.22	.26	.27	.36	.38	.34	.74	.77	.66	.91	.89
Bacon, sausage, luncheon meats	lb	.18	.53	.51	.62	.68	.70	.36	.43	.27	.19	.22
Eggs	no.	3.51	2.72	2.48	3.73	2.87	3.11	3.55	3.84	3.86	3.90	4.27
Dry beans, peas, lentils (dry weight)[6]	lb	.07	.13	.14	.20	.26	.17	.30	.20	.26	.27	.16
Mixtures, mostly meat, poultry, fish, egg, legume	lb	.10	.13	.15	.19	.31	.26	.19	.21	.24	.28	.19
Nuts (shelled weight), peanut butter	lb	.03	.20	.26	.22	.21	.26	.21	.04	.03	.01	.06
Other foods:												
Fats, oils	lb	.10	.25	.34	.48	.56	.65	.82	.68	.34	.43	.30
Sugar, sweets	lb	.20	.47	.71	.84	.89	.94	1.06	1.01	.43	.48	.67
Soft drinks, punches, ades (single-strength)	lb	1.68	3.20	3.14	4.10	4.84	5.95	4.46	1.46	5.07	3.83	1.28
Coffee, tea	lb	.01	.01	.02	.02	.05	.07	.24	.28	.05	.26	.26
Seasonings	lb	.03	.03	.04	.05	.07	.07	.07	.05	.05	.04	.04

[1]Quantities are for food as purchased or brought into the household from garden or farm. Food is for preparation of all meals and snacks for a week. About 30 percent of the edible parts of food above quantities needed to meet caloric needs is included to allow for food assumed to be discarded as plate waste, spoilage, etc.

[2]Pregnant and lactating females usually require added nutrients and should consult a doctor for recommendations about diet and supplements.

[3]Frozen concentrated juices are included as single-strength juice.

[4]Cereal fortified with iron is recommended.

[5]Quantities of dry and evaporated milk and yogurt included as the amount of fluid whole milk having the same calcium content.

[6]Count one pound of canned dry beans--pork and beans, kidney beans, etc.--as 0.33 pound.

Cost of Food at Home Estimated for Food Plans at Four Cost Levels, February 1993, U.S. Average[1]

SEX-AGE GROUPS	COST FOR 1 WEEK				COST FOR 1 MONTH			
	Thrifty plan	Low-cost plan	Moderate-cost plan	Liberal plan	Thrifty plan	Low-cost plan	Moderate-cost plan	Liberal plan
FAMILIES								
FAMILY OF 2[2]:								
20-50 years	$50.30	$63.60	$78.40	$97.70	$217.70	$275.70	$339 50	$423 00
51 years and over	47.50	61.10	75.30	90.20	206.00	264.80	326.50	390.70
FAMILY OF 4: Couple, 20-50 years and children–								
1-2 and 3-5 years	73.10	91.60	111.90	137.70	316.90	396 90	484.60	596.40
6-8 and 9-11 years	83.80	107.60	134.40	162.10	363.10	466.40	582.30	702.10
INDIVIDUALS[3]								
CHILD:								
1-2 years	13.20	16.20	18.90	22.90	57.40	70.10	81.90	99.30
3-5 years	14.20	17.60	21.70	26.00	61.60	76.20	94.10	112.60
6-8 years	17.40	23.30	29.10	34.00	75.40	101.00	126.20	147.20
9-11 years	20.70	26.50	34.00	39.30	89.80	114.80	147.50	170.40
MALE:								
12-14 years	21.60	30.00	37.40	43.90	93.40	130.00	162.20	190.40
15-19 years	22.30	31.00	38.50	44.60	96.60	134.20	167.00	193.30
20-50 years	24.00	30.80	38.40	46.60	103.90	133.50	166.20	201.70
51 years and over	21.70	29.20	36.00	43.20	94.10	126.70	156.00	187.10
FEMALE:								
12-19 years	21.70	26.00	31.50	38.10	93.90	112.60	136.70	165.30
20-50 years	21.70	27.00	32.90	42.20	94.00	117.10	142.40	182.80
51 years and over	21.50	26.30	32.50	38.80	93.20	114.00	140.80	168.10

[1]Assumes that food for all meals and snacks is purchased at the store and prepared at home Estimates for the thrifty food plan were computed from quantities of foods published in *Family Economics Review*, 1984, No. 1. Estimates for the other plans were computed from quantities of foods published in *Family Economics Review*, 1983, No 2 The costs of the food plans are estimated by updating prices paid by households surveyed in 1977-78 in USDA's Nationwide Food Consumption Survey USDA updates these survey prices using information from the Bureau of Labor Statistics. "CPI Detailed Report", table 4, to estimate the costs for the food plans.

[2]Ten percent added for family size adjustment. See footnote 3

[3] The costs given are for individuals in 4-person families For individuals in other size families, the following adjustments are suggested 1-person--add 20 percent; 2-person--add 10 percent, 3-person--add 5 percent, 5- or 6-person--subtract 5 percent, 7- (or more) person--subtract 10 percent.

HNIS(Adm) 329
Issued March 1993

PESTICIDE DATA PROGRAM

Mr. DURBIN. Your role in the Pesticide Data Program is to provide data on food consumption in a form that will allow the population's exposure to residues to be assessed. Ms. Ritchko testified last year that your agency was working with EPA and FDA in developing a Food Grouping System. This system would take data collected from surveys on the amount and type of food items consumed and translate this information back to the agricultural products which they are composed of. What is the status of this system including the total cost of development and operation?

Mr. RUST. The purpose of the Food Grouping System is to increase the usefulness of food consumption data collected in national surveys. Information on food is collected the way people eat it—as separate items such as a piece of chicken, or as mixtures such as pizza. Before the Food Grouping System, pizza would have been totally classified as a grain product and we would not know how much of the food was actually cheese, tomatoes, or flour. The Food Grouping System allows us to translate the information on consumption of pizza and other mixtures into data on consumption of the specific ingredients, or even further to the level of raw agricultural commodities. The utility of the Food Grouping System presently is limited because of lack of automation. However, we are moving forward with plans to automate the system to further increase its utility for meeting the research and public policy data needs of USDA, FDA, EPA, and other Government agencies.

Work has continued on the development of the databases required for the system. We have completed databases for estimating ingredient consumption for the 1987 NFCS and 1989 CSFII and are currently updating them to permit estimating ingredients for the 1990 and 1991 CSFII's. We are awaiting information from EPA on their requirements for grouping raw agricultural commodities before finalizing the commodities databases. We are also preparing data processing specifications for use in development of the automated system.

We have begun using the Food Grouping databases in limited applications to meet data requirements for USDA and other agencies. These projects have served to test and refine our specifications and processes before expending the funds on the automated system. They have also reinforced the need for the data produced by the system, as well as the requirement that the system be automated in order to take advantage of its full potential and to track and document its various applications.

During Fiscal Year 1992, HNIS received final approval from the Department's Office of Information Resource Management to develop the automated Food Grouping System. To facilitate development of the automated Food Grouping System, we have entered into an interagency agreement with GSA. Planning phases have been completed, and procurement is in process at this time.

We have expended $1,039,000 to plan, develop, and operate the Food Grouping System for Fiscal Years 1990 through 1993. This includes staff time, as well as contracts to plan the automated system. An additional $686,000 has been set aside with GSA for the current procurement.

Mr. DURBIN. The Agricultural Marketing Service has been testing the pesticide residue levels of foods at the consumer's table and has determined that at this level there is not a residue problem. In review of this finding, how necessary is it to develop this Food Grouping System?

Mr. RUST. The Food Grouping System will improve HNIS ability to provide the agricultural community, nutritionists, and public policy administrators with detailed information on what Americans are eating as described in response to the previous question. With regard to pesticide residues, as long as the Government is involved in regulating pesticide use or in estimating potential risk from pesticide residues or other components of foods, there will be a need for the Food Grouping System. The Government needs this mechanism in place and ready to use without delay if the need should arise in the future to assess the risk associated with any pesticide or other possible contaminant.

Even through the Agricultural Marketing Service data may indicate there is not a residue problem at this time, there are many other uses which make development and operation of the Food Grouping System worthwhile. I mentioned earlier that we had begun to use Food Grouping System data files and processes. Even though our work is limited because we presently lack automation, we have begun to see far reaching benefits.

For example, in December 1992 we developed an ingredient consumption data set on grain products for FDA, using Food Grouping databases and the NFCS 1987–88 consumption data. This included not just grain products that were consumed by themselves, but also included data for grains that were consumed as parts of mixed foods, such as the bread crust from a pizza. FDA requested these data to estimate the potential impact that would result if grains were fortified with folate. I would like to quote from a letter we subsequently received from Dr. Elizabeth A. Yetley, Acting Director of the Office of Special Nutrition at FDA, "...We would like to again express our appreciation for the impressive efforts of your staff to respond to a critical need for information by our agency. We look forward to future collaborative efforts."

We have other examples of how these data are being used. We are providing commodity intake data to the USDA Economic Research Service for their use in a Pesticide Regulation Impact Study. Also, Food Grouping data will be used to support activities in the 10-Year Plan for Nutrition Monitoring and Related Research. It will be used to monitor the Year 2000 Health Objectives to increase the intake of fruits, vegetables, and grains. The National Cancer Institute recently requested Food Grouping data on vegetable and fruit intake for assessment of their "Strive for Five" project. They also requested a breakdown on the intake of grains. Preliminary work indicates Food Grouping data will be especially useful in assessing how well Americans are meeting the Dietary Guidelines. Based on our own limited use of Food Grouping data, the requests we have received from other Government agencies, and the inquiries we have begun to receive from the nutrition research community, we believe there is tremendous potential for the Food Grouping System to enhance the traditional research for which national food consumption data are used.

Mr. Chairman, even if the Food Grouping System is not needed to support the regulation of pesticides, HNIS has found that its development is necessary to support the other work of the agency.

Mr. DURBIN. Please update the table that appears on page 30 of last year's hearing record showing the amount spent on the pesticide data program to include fiscal year 1993.

Mr. RUST. The information you requested will be provided for the record.

[The information follows:]

Fiscal year	Budgeted amount	Funds obligated FGS planning and development	Staff years
1990		$225,000	1.5
1991	$500,000	500,000	5.0
1992	500,000	500,000	6.0
1993	500,000	500,000	5.0

NUTRITION EDUCATION AND PREGNANT TEENAGERS

Mr. DURBIN. Your agency initiated a nutrition education research study in 1991 to assess the needs of pregnant teenagers? What is the status of this study?

Mr. RUST. The purpose of the research was to identify elements that are successful or unsuccessful in communicating nutrition information to this hard to reach audience. A cooperative agreement to assess the nutrition education needs of pregnant adolescents and develop prototype materials for this audience was awarded to the University of Tennessee Knoxville on September 28, 1991. This 18 month project will be completed by May 24, 1993. All research has been completed and the final report is being prepared.

The project was conducted in three phases. In phase 1, a needs assessment was conducted by literature review and workshop discussions with nutrition and health professionals who work with pregnant teenagers. In phase 2, focus groups were conducted with a total of 92 pregnant or postpartum teens, including both blacks and whites, and rural and urban participants, who discussed their nutrition information needs and interests, and reacted to samples of available materials in print or video format. Results indicated that teens preferred a video format with teenage actresses over print materials. Teens wanted messages related to eating for the baby's health and messages about food rather than specific nutrients. In phase 3, these results were used to develop a 10-minute prototype videotape with these messages. The videotape was shown to 116 pregnant or postpartum teens in focus groups or individual interviews. Evaluation methods allowed girls to describe their reactions in their own words. Analysis of the transcribed sessions showed that the teens could identify the intended messages, understood the content and like the presentation style. They scored the video very positively. The final report of this study will comprehensively summarize information from the needs assessment, development of the prototype, and evaluation results, and make recommendations for appropriate revisions to the prototype. HNIS will review the results of the study along with Food and Nutrition Service (FNS) and Extension Service (ES) nutritionists involved with the Women, Infants, and Children (WIC) and Expanded Food and Nutrition Education Program (EFNEP) programs and make revisions and plans for final production and distribution of the videotape to programs serving pregnant teenagers. Distribution of this tape will begin before the end of 1993. We will make a copy of the tape available to the Committee as soon as it becomes available.

Mr. DURBIN. Haven't there been studies done in the past on the educational needs to improve the nutrition of pregnant teenagers by some Federal or non-Federal entity?

Mr. RUST. At the time we began this research there was great interest in improving the nutrition of pregnant teenagers in order to improve the health of their infants. While there was general consensus on nutritional needs and healthful eating patterns for teens during pregnancy, little information was available about nutrition topics of most interest to the teens themselves, or ways to deliver the information that would be most appealing and useful to them. Nutrition education research over the last decade has shown that qualitative market research methods such as focus groups and indepth interviews can provide rich descriptive data on comprehension, acceptance and perceived usefulness of nutrition materials and can indicate modifications that can make the information more responsive to audience needs. Rather than develop a new publication that would contain accurate nutrition information but might be unappealing and ineffective with the pregnant teens, HNIS undertook this cooperative research project with nutrition educators at the University of Tennessee, who have considerable experience in working with teenagers, especially pregnant and postpartum teens. Part of the project involved a literature review and workshop with nutrition and health professionals to assess their views on information materials needed for pregnant teens. This review also considered the results of an informal assessment of WIC nutritionists conducted by FNS. Thus, the materials produced should be useful to nutrition educators as well as helpful and appealing to their clientele. The final report for the project, which will describe the needs assessment, the literature review, the concepts tested in the prototype, and the results, should also be helpful to others who develop nutrition information for this audience.

DIETARY GUIDANCE WORKING GROUP

Mr. DURBIN. The Dietary Guidance Working Group is a group which coordinates all activities within USDA related to providing dietary guidance to Americans. Who is represented on this group and how often do they meet?

Mr. RUST. The Dietary Guidance Working Group (DGWG) was formed in 1986. The Working Group reviews all USDA publications and materials that contain dietary guidance information to ensure that guidance is consistent with the Dietary Guidelines for Americans and is consistent and supportive across USDA agencies and the Federal Government. Another major function of the Group is to help coordinate nutrition activities through information exchange among nutrition education specialists in the USDA agencies that provide guidance to their clientele. The group has also been reviewing dietary guidance materials from the U.S. Department of Health and Human Services (DHHS) since 1991. The group, which meets monthly, is composed of representatives from 10 USDA agencies and a DHHS liaison. A list of current members will be provided for the record.

[The information follows:]

DIETARY GUIDANCE WORKING GROUP; SUBCOMMITTEE FOR HUMAN NUTRITION; RESEARCH AND EDUCATION COMMITTEE; U.S. DEPARTMENT OF AGRICULTURE

LIST OF MEMBERS

Susan Welsh, Chairperson; Director, Nutrition Education Division; Human Nutrition Information Service.

Jacqueline Dupont; National Program Leader for Human Nutrition; Agricultural Research Service.

Elizabeth Crosby; Home Economist; Agricultural Marketing Service.

Melvin Mathias; Natural Resources, Food and Social Sciences; Cooperative State Research Service.

David Smallwood; National Economics Division; Economic Research Service.

Jan Singleton; Nutrition; Extension Service.

Elaine McLaughlin; Nutrition, Science & Education Branch; Nutrition & Technical Services Division, Food and Nutrition Service.

Cheryl Wade; Chief, Nutrition Branch; Food Ingredient Assessment Division, Food Safety and Inspection Service.

Carole Davis; Chief, Guidance & Education Research Branch; Nutrition Education Division, Human Nutrition Information Service.

Sally Katt; Chief, Special Programs Division; Office of Governmental and Public Affairs.

Sandra Fascinoli; Coordinator, Food and Nutrition Information Center; National Agricultural Library.

U.S. DEPARTMENT OF HEALTH AND HUMAN SERVICES LIAISON

Elena Carbone; Marilyn Stephenson; Nutrition Research Associate; Office of Disease Prevention and Health Promotion; Department of Health and Human Services.

Mr. DURBIN. When did they meet last and what were their findings and recommendations?

Mr. RUST. At the last monthly meeting of the Dietary Guidance Working Group discussions included reviews of nutrition education materials that were underway or expected in the future. The Committee reviews departmental publications to insure that they are consistent with the Dietary Guidelines for Americans. The content of the 1993 Yearbook of Agriculture and the review of chapters to be handled by the Group were discussed. The yearbook is targeted to the consumer and will offer nutrition guidance to help people make healthier food choices. It will also give general information on such aspects of nutrition as research, food consumption, production, food safety, government programs, and the international scene. The yearbook will be published later this year.

Mr. DURBIN. Thank you, Mr. Rust.

Mr. Skeen?

FUNDING OF HNIS SURVEYS

Mr. SKEEN. Thank you, Mr. Chairman. I think we got into a very significant discussion on the work of this agency. I understand your difficulty, but I understand too that you have been very diligent in trying to come up with a system that gives you better oversight over that kind of information, as reflected in last year's request for additional funding.

Mr. RUST. Yes, sir.

Mr. SKEEN. You were not allowed to use some of that money. Am I not correct?

Mr. RUST. That is correct.

Mr. SKEEN. Does this constitute an overall increase in the agency budget to rectify some of the errors that you have had in the past?

Mr. RUST. It is a little hard to respond to that until the President's budget is finalized.

Mr. SKEEN. Well, it is hard for us to come up with a budget until we get one.

Mr. RUST. Indeed.

Mr. SKEEN. I understand your problem and you understand ours.

Mr. RUST. I understand your problem exactly, Mr. Chairman. Let me say——

Mr. SKEEN. I am trying to get a focal point on where we are going to go. You know, we are talking about the relevancy of all this information.

Mr. RUST. I think perhaps the Chairman was alluding to NHANES, the National Health and Nutrition Examination Survey that is conducted by the Department of Health and Human Services.

Mr. SKEEN. How about the manufacturers?

Mr. RUST. If you were to look at that study, both in terms of size and cost, I suspect you will find that it is a $100 million or $120 million survey over three or four years, when you look at all of the in-kind support that is put into it by NIH and others.

People participating in NHANES get a free physical examination. They get $50 or more in cash.

Mr. SKEEN. Those who participate in the——

Mr. RUST. And so they get a participation rate at a certain level, somewhere in the 70 percent range even with all of that. We struggle with a much different kind of survey. We are struggling to do it right, and we are struggling to get information which is not only health-related, but also gives us information about family incomes, food, food purchasing patterns and so forth which are necessary for the Economic Research Service, the Agricultural Research Service and other agencies to use.

If you want to improve the quality of these surveys, then we are going to have to be funded at a level that gives us and the contractor the tools it takes to go out there and get accurate information.

SELECTION AND OVERSIGHT OF SURVEY CONTRACTORS

Mr. SKEEN. What we are interested in is how much oversight and control do you have over the contractor? Evidently you have had very little in the past.

How many people are involved in the contracting of this?

Mr. RUST. How many people are we trying to survey?

Mr. SKEEN. No, no, no.

How many contractors are in this business? When you open up a bid about how many respondents do you get for the contracts?

Mr. RUST. There were two.

Mr. SKEEN. Two?

Mr. RUST. There were two actual bids submitted for this survey.

Mr. SKEEN. So it is not a large bidding process and there are not a lot of companies involved.

Mr. RUST. Well, it was open, it was open very broadly.

Mr. SKEEN. Oh, it was opened broadly?

Mr. RUST. It was opened broadly, and we even had an opportunity where potential contractors could come in and talk. We had certain days set aside where people could come in and get a better idea of what we expected.

Both of the would-be contractors that ultimately did bid did in fact come in and have those discussions, went back and did submit bids, but only two——

Mr. SKEEN. You had two bidders.

Mr. RUST. Two valid bids were submitted.

Mr. SKEEN. Then a panel went through and made the selection?

Mr. RUST. We had a panel made up of people like Dr. Harris, but also drawn from ERS, and ARS, and HHS and so forth. We have a very broad-based panel of technical experts from across the government sit in judgment on those two applicants.

COORDINATION OF FEDERAL SURVEY ACTIVITIES

Mr. SKEEN. How close is the cooperation and coordination between all the agencies in the federal government that do nutritional data survey? Is it on a day-by-day basis?

Mr. RUST. The answer is yes. For instance, we have a very close working relationship with the Centers for Disease Control. They have the health statistics agency under them, which is responsible for NHANES. I would say contact is certainly several times a week with them. We have a new mechanism, now required by the Nutrition Monitoring Act, which brings 22 federal agencies into a process of talking and working together. That has also helped us better coordinate survey-related activities.

Mr. SKEEN. Am I to assume that there is very little overlapping in the way that you do this, or is there a great deal of overlapping?

Mr. RUST. I have been in government too long to answer that one directly, Mr. Skeen. But I would say that the thing that saves us from too much overlapping in the surveys is that each one comes at it from a different point of view, and the point of view is critical.

Mr. SKEEN. That is escaping our understanding.

Mr. RUST. From the agricultural side, we need to know what are the changing patterns of what people are eating and buying, because it has implications for the agricultural system of this country.

Mr. SKEEN. Absolutely.

Mr. RUST. Where NHANES is looking at something very different, NHANES is trying to relate certain specific nutrients to health factors, and that is what they need to do for their mission. But if you stopped our survey work, you would find, I think, a very substantial void in data would develop that someone would have to fill. HNIS feeds information back into the agricultural sector of the economy in terms of what changes are occurring, what people are eating, and what they should be eating, and which way we would like them to go in terms of their diets.

To show you the value of it, Mr. Skeen, just the other day there was an article in The Washington Post that talked about some health factors, and it was interesting. It talked about 7 million cases of heart disease, and the number of people who died, how many people had coronary bypass and what that cost, 284,000 people at $30,000 per procedure.

When you talk about the cost of this particular survey, $14 million, if we could change the nutritional patterns of enough people, that you reduced that number by say just five or six hundred a year, and many of these people are on Medicare and Medicaid, you would probably have a savings to the government equal to the entire cost of the entire survey.

So what I am saying is that, in terms of the President's health initiatives and a lot of other related activities, our surveys play an important role.

Could the government get along without them? I think you would have to answer yes. But I think you would find that the other surveys would have to be modified to get this information.

TIMELINESS OF DATA RELEASE

Mr. SKEEN. Well, I think also one of the other elements in the question that has been presented to you today is the timeliness of these things. All those people that died of heart attacks, if the information comes out five or six years too late to make really significant adjustments, why I think we are denigrating the real purpose of what you are doing.

Mr. RUST. I came over to the Department of Agriculture last year, from the Social Security Administration. And one of the things that struck me and one of the things that my managers will tell you that I do is to press all of my divisions and branches to think in terms of setting specific goals and meeting those goals.

In a research organization you have a tendency to lose sight of that goal, because you want to get the data perfect. You want to analyze it and report it until it is perfect. And if that takes a few extra months, that may not bother you.

I agree with you 100 percent. I think the American people are giving us money to conduct this research, to conduct these surveys, and we have an obligation to get the data out as quickly as possible. And we have set goals. Ellen did not tell you today, but I have set specific goals for the data; that it be released to NTIS and through other channels, and the goal is within one year of the collection of the data.

Mr. SKEEN. Well, it appears that you have done a good job in accelerating that schedule.

Mr. RUST. Well, we are trying.

PRIVATE SECTOR USERS OF SURVEY DATA

Mr. SKEEN. How many private subscribers do you have for your information? Do you have a large number, small, modest amount? Give me some idea of about how much inclusion you have from the private sector for your information?

Mr. RUST. Most of our data is used by other government agencies.

Mr. SKEEN. And then it goes out in information.

Mr. RUST. But one of the areas where we go directly to the public is developing guidance for people on what to eat, the Dietary Guidelines for Americans, and the food guide pyramid, which Mr. Braley mentioned in introducing me. We give that material to a whole host of sources, private organizations, the Extension Service which carries it down through the land grant colleges, and so forth. So our findings are converted into a way that is useful directly to the general public, and we get it out just as quickly as we can.

Mr. SKEEN. You mentioned that. And we had exposure to that this weekend, as I alluded to earlier in a lot of new products which are coming out in response to nutritional information.

Mr. RUST. I am reminded that our principal non-governmental customers are academic researchers, the food industry itself, and state and local governments. And one way that we get it out to the general public is that we maintain and put more and more data on an electronic bulletin board, which can be accessed directly by anyone who has a PC. And a good bit of our data is available to be simply down-loaded.

Mr. SKEEN. That is one of the questions that I wanted to ask, about your electronic bulletin boards, how do you access this?

Mr. RUST. You can access it two ways. You can come in directly and get an ID number, if you have the right kind of modem on your personal computer. And also, there is Internet, which I believe was originally founded by the National Academy of Sciences. And if you are a subscriber to that, you can access our data base.

Mr. SKEEN. So you charge for the subscription of this service, or is it free?

Mr. RUST. I believe it is free.

Mr. SKEEN. Thank you very much for your responses.

And thank you, Mr. Chairman.

Mr. DURBIN. Mr. Peterson?

SCOPE OF THE SURVEY

Mr. PETERSON. Thank you, Mr. Chairman.

Just a couple of questions. Just to follow on with Mr. Skeen's comment, on the timeliness here. It seems that if you are going to avoid high cholesterol, you need to know where the problems are.

But my question is what is the construction of the survey, are you only looking at the supermarket exit, or are you going into the fast foods, the whole spectrum of American consumption, or just exactly how do you address that? Because it is a vast subject, it seems to me.

Mr. RUST. I am going to ask Ellen Harris to help me with that one, but let me start off.

The one that we have under way right now, the continuing survey.

Mr. PETERSON. How long is that, is that forever now, or how long is that contract?

Mr. RUST. I think that it depends on how long the Chairman is willing to fund it. But the way that we have been working it the last three cycles is we contract and do three full years of data collection. The contract which was signed in 1992 has a developmental year, which is ongoing right now.

The contractor, Westat Corporation of Rockville, is about to go into the field and do a pilot right now. They are testing the system, and getting the questionnaire finalized, and getting ready to go out into the field in January.

We will then do three full years of data collection, 1994, 1995, and 1996. Data will become available at the end of each of those years. We will be surveying about 15,000 to 16,000 families over the course of the three years. We inquire about individual intakes, what each member of the family eats both at home and outside of the home. Let me correct a previous statement. It is 15,000 individuals, rather than families. I am sorry.

Dr. HARRIS. First, as Mr. Rust said earlier in his testimony, we have three different surveys. We have a continuing survey, that looks at individual intake whereby individual people within a household are selected, and their dietary intake information is collected.

We have a household survey, whereby household food use information is collected. That is over a course of a week, and includes what foods come into the house and are used for food consumption of individuals.

Then we have a diet and health knowledge survey, which is a telephone follow-up to the continuing survey, whereby individuals who provided dietary intake information answer questions on diet and health knowledge. Questions there focus on attitude, people's knowledge of food labeling, and health issues.

Within the household survey, the household main food preparer is asked to keep records of the food that they purchase and bring into the home over a week. In the individual survey, individuals are selected. They may be adults and children and we ask them what they consumed the previous 24 hours.

Mr. Durbin had asked about dietary methodology in terms of the ways that you can collect information on what people consume. There is a 24 hour recall where you ask them to recall what they ate and drank over the course of a 24 hour period.

You can also do a diet record where they keep an ongoing tally of what they are consuming prospectively.

There is also another way where you can weigh people's food. Weigh the food, have them consume it, and then do measurements of their excretion of that food.

A survey based in the home or based where you have to get detailed information directly from the respondent, like children who may be consuming three-fourths of their food outside of the home, because they are participating in school breakfast or school lunch programs, can be very difficult.

So you have to use the best means currently available for collecting the information.

Mr. PETERSON. Are you doing all of those things?

Dr. HARRIS. We are doing what is termed the 24 hour recall, where we ask people to recall what they consumed 24 hours prior to the interview.

Mr. PETERSON. And that is the only kind of survey that you are doing?

Dr. HARRIS. For the household survey, we are doing a record where people write down over the course of seven days the foods that were purchased for the household.

RELEASE OF SURVEY DATA

Mr. PETERSON. I will let you off on that. Obviously, we could get into a lot of detail, and I do not want to do that.

Is the data then broken out and distributed based on age, ethnic group, and geographic considerations?

Dr. HARRIS. For the continuing survey, where you are looking at individuals, we have breakdowns by sex and age. For all of the surveys, there are other demographic characteristics that the data can be broken down into, such as region, degree of urbanization, and education level of the respondent.

USE OF REGIONAL CONTRACTORS

Mr. PETERSON. And my last question then. This is obviously a fairly large contract, an ongoing contract.

Was it ever discussed or even considered, or is it realistic to consider asking perhaps multiple universities to conduct the survey?

Dr. HARRIS. As Mr. Rust answered before, in terms of the number of bidders that we had, on this past contract, there are not a whole lot of people who can conduct this type of survey at the scale that is needed for a nationally representative sample.

The way that the RFP is written, universities have the opportunity to form a consortium and to submit a bid. But there are so many criteria built into the RFP. As with private organizations, it probably was too big of a contract for most universities to handle.

Mr. PETERSON. And that was really the point. It seems like with two bidders on a contract of that magnitude, that you are not getting much competition. And even after your technical review, you have no choice, which it seems to me is not in our best interest.

I would suggest that one should look at that from the standpoint of constructing bids based on maybe sectionalizing or something to make it of such a scope that you would increase your bidders, and therefore increase the potential for higher quality, more responsiveness, and cheaper operation. But that is only my observation. But it seems with just, what is it, $16 million?

Mr. RUST. It is about $14 million.

Mr. PETERSON. How much?

Mr. RUST. About $14 million over four years.

Mr. PETERSON. That with $14 million, you could get a lot of folks coming in, if that was handled a little differently.

Dr. HARRIS. Not being a sampling statistician, I cannot answer you in some respects. But it is sort of a Catch-22. Because you have many people who say our sample is not large enough for a national survey. It is something that all national surveys fight with and battle with in terms of how representative their samples are.

Mr. PETERSON. What I am saying though is if you have multiple contractors all operating under the same rules but doing it in different regions of the country and then have it be coordinated, you could actually have a larger sample, because perhaps the economy of scale here. And I do not know if that is true. But it is just that logic here prevails.

Dr. HARRIS. Through the nutrition monitoring system, we are trying to better coordinate the drawing of samples for the NHANES survey, and for our surveys. And also within that monitoring program, there are State and local representatives who also have needs that are not necessarily met by a national survey.

So one of the driving forces behind the nutrition monitoring program is to bring all of those parties together and determine how best to have a coordinated system.

Mr. RUST. If I could add, Mr. Peterson. I was disappointed frankly as a manager that we only got two bids on that contract. The size of it and the complexity were factors. You had to be able to run a system that can survey people in all parts of the United States, and be gathering data literally 365 days a year. It is a large and complicated task. Whether it could be regionalized, I do not know. But it would certainly be something that we would want to look at before we get to the next cycle. I would like to figure out a way to make this a much more competitive environment.

Mr. PETERSON. I think that it would make us more comfortable.

Mr. RUST. And it would make me more comfortable, too.

Mr. PETERSON. Then, of course, I think from that you might even find a greater improvement in data. Because now you are going to have contractors competing against contractors from a quality standpoint. They want their report to be more accurate and more substantial than maybe the one from Colorado or something like that. So that is just a consideration.

Mr. RUST. The critical element is to get them all to do it about the same way.

Mr. PETERSON. Well, that would be the oversight, and that is your job.

Mr. RUST. That is right.

Mr. PETERSON. And that is the point.

Thank you, Mr. Chairman.

COST OF THE CONTINUING SURVEY OF FOOD INTAKES BY INDIVIDUALS 1994–96

Mr. DURBIN. Thank you, Mr. Peterson.

Mr. Rust, do I understand that in the next survey there will be some 15,000 individuals questioned, is that what was said?

Mr. RUST. Between 15,000 and 16,500; yes, sir.

Mr. DURBIN. And the survey is going to cost $14 million?

Mr. RUST. Yes, sir.

Mr. DURBIN. So it is about $1000 per person?

Mr. RUST. Yes, sir.

Mr. DURBIN. Is that typical?

Mr. RUST. I understand from the contracts office that worked with us and supported us on this contract, that this is the first time to their knowledge that the Department has undertaken a survey through a fixed price contract. We went into tremendous detail about exactly what they are to do, and what response rates they are to get, and how they are to screen and so forth. We were very precise in this contract. Because we do not want to have the same problems that we have had in earlier surveys.

So my guess is that it may be somewhat of a more expensive contract certainly than we have done in the past. It is about twice what we paid for the last CSFII dollar-wise. And the sample then was about the same, and the numbers were about the same.

Mr. DURBIN. I understand that you are looking for a lot of different information through this survey. It is common in our business to pay about $50 a sample to get a survey of voters in our district on a whole wide range of different things, including personal family background and beliefs. What you are talking about is $1000 per person.

Can you tell me first, do you have a background in surveying?

Mr. RUST. I do not.

Mr. DURBIN. In nutrition?

Mr. RUST. No, sir.

Mr. DURBIN. What is your background?

Mr. RUST. I am a long time government manager. In my most recent management position, I was the Associate Commissioner of the Social Security Administration for the disability program, where we ran a large and elaborate program across the country.

Mr. DURBIN. Do you have anyone that works for you who is an expert on surveys?

Mr. RUST. Yes. I have quite a few.

Mr. DURBIN. Did they tell you that $1000 per person is a good price to pay for this survey?

Mr. RUST. I never asked them in quite that way. The discussions that we had on all of the surveys was what will it take to get quality information in a timely manner from the survey.

Mr. DURBIN. At $1000 a person, you should get some very good quality.

Ms. HARRIS. With every RFP, the government also has to develop a government cost estimate. For the CSFII contract, the technical staff along with Census Bureau staff, who we have joined with through an inter-agency agreement, came up with the cost for the survey. That $1000 per respondent incorporates costs such as screening individuals. That is going to a household and seeing if an individual within that household meets the selection criteria for the survey.

It incorporates costs for training interviewers for collecting food consumption information, which means that they have to know food, that they have to know the questionnaire that is composed of a number of questions that are submitted from our agency and from other agencies. And they have to know how best to record that information. So there are a number of costs built into the collection of the data per respondent.

Mr. DURBIN. How much do you pay each respondent for participating in the survey?

Ms. HARRIS. For the CSFII, OMB would not approve a cash incentive. For the last survey, respondents were given a $2 incentive and quite frankly, that was a bit absurd. It is not enough money to take up an individual's time. And we were asking for a $10 incentive this time. OMB is trying to discourage cash incentives and we were not allowed to offer one.

We were allowed to give a non-monetary incentive this time around. During our pilot, we are looking at how effective that approach may be. We are giving multi-colored lunch sacks as an incentive.

AGENCY MOVE TO WASHINGTON, D.C.

Mr. DURBIN. Let me switch to another topic. It is my understanding that you are moving from Hyattsville, Maryland to the District of Columbia. I also understand that your lease will expire in July of this year. Has the agency done any kind of a cost benefit analysis to determine whether this is a good move for your agency?

Mr. RUST. The answer is yes we have. Being in Hyattsville requires a great deal of time coming downtown to where the Department of Agriculture is located. We have factored in both the amount of time on the shuttles, the amount of time that senior staff spend driving back and forth to attend meetings in the District.

And then there are other factors. The building where we are right now, the space is inadequate for us. The layout of the building and the set-up of the building is really inadequate for the kind of research operation that we do.

The building is probably going to undergo very substantial rehabilitation. It is my understanding that even if we stayed in that location, that the cost that we are paying now or is being paid for us now is based on a ten or fifteen year old lease. Once that rehabilitation is done and that building is reoccupied, the cost there will be substantially higher.

So looking at all of the factors, first of all a better layout and a better environment for the staff to work in; and then secondly, bringing us closer to the other agencies that we work very closely with—the Food and Drug Administration, EPA, and the other agencies of the Department of Agriculture, we concluded that it made sense to be downtown because it would allow us to be more involved in policy.

Mr. DURBIN. You have about 100 employees?

Mr. RUST. About 115 full and part-time employees. And then a handful of others.

Mr. DURBIN. Can you tell me how many of these employees would come downtown during the ordinary course of business?

Mr. RUST. I guess that it would affect mostly the branch chiefs and the division chiefs, and then the people in the front office, which would probably be on a regular basis maybe having to come downtown every week or ten days. Probably fifteen people on a regular basis.

Mr. DURBIN. And what percentage of the employees at your agency live in Maryland?

Mr. RUST. I believe it is about 80 percent of them who live in Maryland.

Mr. DURBIN. I've been told it is 87 percent. What percentage of your employees have signed a petition asking not to be moved to the District of Columbia?

Mr. RUST. I do not know, Mr. Chairman. I have not seen the petition.

Mr. DURBIN. I've been told it is over half. I am not sitting here plugging away for Maryland like Steny Hoyer would and is doing, and like Barbara Mikulski might do, but it strikes me that to argue that 115 people have to move, because 10 or 15 have to come downtown on a regular basis really overlooks some basic questions as to the morale in the agency. You are asking a hundred people to make a pretty dramatic change in lifestyles, so that ten or fifteen do not have to drive downtown.

Mr. RUST. If I may, two things. I live in Maryland, and have commuted most of my life into downtown Washington or up to Baltimore where Social Security is headquartered. And I think that is a reasonable thing to ask employees to do. Hundreds of thousands of people live in Maryland and Virginia, and commute into the District every day to work. We are not moving the agency eighty miles. We are moving the agency six miles.

But more importantly than that, when you talk about morale you have to question the relevancy. When you sit out in Hyattsville and when you are that far from where policies are made and where the other agencies that you have to relate to are, I think that it diminishes the impact of the agency, and perhaps even the importance of the work we do. I am not sure that morale would not be better if we were located where the action is, which is down near the USDA headquarters, down near EPA, down near Food and Drug, and so forth, where the interplay would be greater, and the sense of accomplishment and the sense of the impact of our work would be greater.

I think that the aggregate effect of that on morale is something that you cannot measure at this time. But I think that it will be considerable.

Mr. DURBIN. But you are not moving to the USDA Headquarters facilities, are you?

Mr. RUST. No, sir. The General Services Administration has found us lease space. I would say it is 12 or 13 blocks from the USDA building.

Mr. DURBIN. I do not know if the argument about getting closer to the FDA is going to hold very well in this Subcommittee, since they are located in 35 different locations. I do not know how you get close to the FDA unless you hover over Washington.

Mr. RUST. The section we work with is the foods section. And they are located right behind the Humphrey building at the foot of Capitol Hill. So we would be substantially closer to the food component of FDA.

Mr. DURBIN. How much will the move cost?

Mr. RUST. The cost of the move to the Agency will be no more than $750,000. This amount will cover the costs not paid for by the General Services Administration (GSA), the purchase of new systems furniture and equipment for the employees, and a new telephone system.

Mr. DURBIN. Wouldn't it have been less expensive and disrupting to your employees to remain where you are?

Mr. RUST. It would appear at first glance that it would be less expensive and disruptive to HNIS employees to remain in this building. However, there are indirect and not so obvious costs and conditions that make this building less than a satisfactory location for our agency.

This building was built in the early 1960's before many building regulation were in place to protect the people from hazardous building materials like asbestos and lead in the drinking water. In addition the heating and cooling systems in the building do not always work properly. This has caused problems with the computer hardware overheating. The results of overheated hardware have been system failure and damage to the hardware which are very costly. Because of the limited space, and the arrangement of that space, it has been impossible for the agency to develop and implement a desirable space plan. Staff members that need to be located near each other to create quality products in a timely manner are scattered throughout the 3rd floor. In addition, there are some HNIS staff members on the 4th floor and in the basement of this building. Some employees that work in the same group sit far from each other. Clearly, more space and better space is needed.

In fulfilling the expectations of the Agency's mission, it is essential for HNIS to regularly interact with its Departmental leadership and other agencies in the conduct of our business. A location in downtown Washington, DC will facilitate communications and cooperation with the Environmental Protection Agency, the Food and Drug Administration, the Food and Nutrition Service, the Economic Research Service and other agencies who use our data or who are linked with us in the Nutrition Monitoring Program. Working in the District of Columbia closer to our customers will enable HNIS to better meet our agency's goals and objectives with much less down time due to travel.

Mr. DURBIN. Please submit for the record a copy of all cost analyses that were done to assist in the decision to move the agency from Hyattsville, Maryland to Washington, D.C.

Mr. RUST. I will submit for the record a comparison of the costs of HNIS's space requirements projected from the Generic Rental Rate Chart for Maryland, Virginia, and the District of Columbia.

I will also submit a summary of local travel, both reimbursed and on the USDA shuttle service, involving HNIS employees between Hyattsville and Washington, D.C.

Rental rates and local travel time and cost were the two areas the agency considered in making the decision to relocate into the District of Columbia.

[The information follows:]

CHANGING GEOGRAPHICAL LOCATION VIRGINIA OR MARYLAND

The current HNIS space package is for 36,635 square feet of space. Using the FY-93 Generic Rental Rate Chart (developed by the Department and GSA) below indicates that the annual rental rate would be: $802,358, Maryland; $1,184,871, Virginia; and $1,074,147, Washington, DC.

[Dollars per square foot]

Type space	Washington, DC	Maryland	Virginia
Office	28.30	20.94	30.83
Storage	20.07	14.97	21.58
Lab	46.86	35.96	55.19

[Dollars per Square Foot]

Type space	Washington, DC	Maryland	Virginia
ADP	42.28	34.49	48.71
Conference	35.49	25.05	36.69
Light industrial	19.39	16.26	26.61
Structrually cngd.	52.47	38.76	55.49

SUMMARY OF LOCAL TRAVEL FOR HNIS EMPLOYEES

Reimbursed Travel Expense

Using information from HNIS' SF-1164 (Claim for Reimbursement), an estimate of the local travel information is included in the following summary:

ESTIMATED TRAVEL FOR FISCAL YEAR 1992

Agency	Number of staff involved	Number of staff trips/months	Total trips	Travel cost	Staff years spent on travel
USDA	19	76	684	$2,565	0.35
Commerce	5	10	120	600	.06
OMB	3	6	54	270	.03
DHHS	25	200	1,800	4,500	.93
EPA	10	80	720	1,800	.37
Total	62	372	3,378	$9,735	1.74

Shuttle Service

The shuttle service, provided by APHIS, based on previous employee usage, estimates 1,400 HNIS employee trips for FY 1992. This amounts to another .36 staff years in travel time.

HNIS staff is presently spending approximately 2.1 staff years traveling between the Agency's headquarters in Hyattsville, Maryland and offices of other agencies located primarily in the District of Columbia. This travel time of 2.1 staff years, based on the median Agency salary of $50,000, will cost $105,000. The savings of staff time ($105,000) added to the savings recouped from travel reimbursement and rental payments to APHIS for shuttle service would offset any increase in the cost of office space in the District.

Mr. DURBIN. Thank you very much, Mr. Rust, for joining us today.

David A. Rust
Associate Administrator

Human Nutrition Information Service
U. S. Department of Agriculture

David A. Rust, has served as the Associate Administrator of the Human Nutrition Information Service (HNIS) since April 1992.

The Department of Agriculture promotes the health and well-being of Americans through improved nutrition. The Human Nutrition Information Service contributes to this mission through the conduct of national food consumption surveys, food composition research, and nutrition education programs. The Agency plays a primary role in the National Nutrition Monitoring and Related Research Program and in the development and promotion of the Dietary Guidelines for Americans.

HNIS serves the American public by conducting applied research in food and nutrition -- what foods we consume and what nutrients are in those foods, the factors that influence what we eat and how to make informed food choices.

Before coming to USDA, Mr Rust held a number of positions in the U.S. Department of Health & Human Services, most recently serving in several key positions at the Social Security Administration.

Mr. Rust is a graduate of the Catonsville Community College and Frostburg State University, Maryland, and has done graduate work at Towson State University, Maryland, and at the American University, Washington, D.C. He lives in Rockville, Maryland with his wife and two children.

Betty L. Warfield
Budget Officer
Human Nutrition Information Service

Betty Warfield was appointed Budget Officer in November 1992 for the Human Nutrition Information Service, after serving three years as Director of Finance and Administration for Citicorp Information Resources, Insurance Technology Division, New York. Insurance Technology Division was an extremely challenging organization, in that the subsidiary was a newly acquired company for Citicorp that required development and implementation of a financial control system as well as development of administrative plans and policies.

Ms. Warfield has over 15 years experience with the Federal Government; 14 years of that time with the Department of Defense (Department of the Army and Navy). During that time, she served as Resource Management Officer, and subsequently as Chief, Program and Budget for Kimbrough Army Hospital, Fort George G. Meade, MD. Her area of responsibility spanned eleven clinics as well as the financial operations of an entire hospital. She also has an extensive background in the financial operations of an environmental organization for the Department of the Army.

Ms. Warfield has received special awards for Civilian Service. She is a Notary Public for the State of Maryland, and an active member in the National Association for Female Executives. Ms. Warfield has an extensive portfolio of financial and administrative education.

Betty is married with four children.

ELLEN HARRIS

Dr. Ellen Harris is Director of the Nutrition Monitoring Division of the Human Nutrition Information Service (HNIS). As Division Director, she directs a national program of applied research in food and human nutrition to determine the nutritional adequacy of U.S. diets and the nutritive value of food. Prior to coming to HNIS in October 1991, Dr. Harris served as a Program Analyst with USDA's Food and Nutrition Service in the Office of Analysis and Evaluation; as a Congressional Fellow with the U.S. House of Representatives' Select Committee on Hunger; as an Assistant Professor in the Department of Nutrition and Food Sciences at Drexel University in Philadelphia; and as a WIC nutritionist in Houston, Texas.

Dr. Harris holds the degree of Doctor of Public Health from the University of Texas School of Public Health. She also has a M.S. degree from Texas Women's University and a B.S. from Antioch College. Dr. Harris' research interests include dietary quality within low-income households, Federal food assistance program evaluation and policy, sociocultural aspects of food habits and international nutrition.

In carrying out its mission, HNIS is the lead USDA agency in two critical areas. First the agency, in conjunction with the Department of Health and Human Services (DHHS), is responsible for updating and promoting the Dietary Guidelines for Americans, the most authoritative dietary guidance given by the Federal Government to the American people. By law, P.L. 101-445, the next update of the Dietary Guidelines for Americans will be released in 1995. Second, HNIS coordinates USDA activities under the National Nutrition Monitoring and Related Research Program (NNMRRP), a comprehensive effort spanning all of the nutrition monitoring activities of 22 Federal Departments and Agencies. This wide-ranging activity is mandated by P.L. 101-445, the National Nutrition Monitoring and Related Research Act of 1990.

The information HNIS collects, analyzes, and disseminates is essential to support the development of sound public policies by other agencies across the Department and the Federal Government. The policy formulation process for food assistance; food labeling; food safety; food formulation, production and marketing; and nutrition education and health promotion programs all benefit from the work done by HNIS.

Mr. Chairman, we have prepared a chart which visually displays the linkages between the work of HNIS and other Federal agencies, private sector organizations and the general public. I would ask the subcommittee's permission, Mr. Chairman, to insert this chart in the hearing record at this point in my testimony.

For Release Only by the
House Committee on Appropriations

HUMAN NUTRITION INFORMATION SERVICE

Statement of David A. Rust, Acting Administrator of the Human Nutrition Information Service (HNIS), before the Subcommittee on Agriculture, Rural Development, Food and Drug Administration, and Related Agencies.

Mr. Chairman and Members of the Committee:
I am David A. Rust, Acting Administrator of the Human Nutrition Information Service (HNIS). I am pleased to be here today to discuss HNIS's current activities and our plans for Fiscal Year 1994.

Mission of the Human Nutrition Information Service

HNIS is, as its name implies, an information service organization responsible for conducting applied research in three broad areas: (1) Food Consumption--what Americans buy and eat, (2) Food Composition--the nutrient content of foods, and (3) Nutrition Education--helping Americans make informed food choices. These activities enable HNIS to make a direct and ongoing contribution to the United States Department of Agriculture's (USDA) overarching mission of ensuring the health and well-being of all Americans through improved nutrition.

Our Mission Links Us with..

HNIS

Pesticide Data Program	AMS, EPA, FDA
Food Labeling support	FDA, FSIS
Survey Design, Survey Management	Census
Thrifty Food Plan, Food Stamp Program, School Lunch Program	FNS
Food Composition	ARS
Dietary Guidelines	DHHS, Private Sector
Nutrition Education	ES, FNS, DHHS, Private Sector
Nutrition Monitoring	DHHS, EPA, DOD, DOE, NMFS, AID, DVA, BLS, Census, 6 USDA agencies

HUMAN NUTRITION INFORMATION SERVICE

Organization Size and Location of the Agency

HNIS has a total of about 115 professional and support staff (full time and part time) in two operating components: the Nutrition Monitoring Division and the Nutrition Education Division.

The Nutrition Monitoring Division conducts surveys to obtain information on food consumption by households and individuals and is the world's foremost national resource for information on the composition and nutritive value of foods.

The Nutrition Education Division (NED) conducts research to determine the factors that influence dietary status and the most effective methods for improving the dietary status of the general public and at-risk groups. NED also determines how dietary guidance can best be communicated to the American public.

The work of the divisions is supported by small statistical, budget and finance, systems, and administrative units. HNIS is located in the Federal Building, Hyattsville, Maryland; and it has no field offices.

How the Agency is Doing with 1993 Funds

As we near the end of the second quarter, we are operating well within our Fiscal Year 1993 appropriation. There are two Fiscal Year 1993 issues that I would like to bring to the Subcommittee's attention:

1. When we formulated our Fiscal Year 1993 budget request we expected to spend between $2.8 and $3.0 million on the Continuing Survey of Food Intakes by Individuals (CSFII) contract. In September 1992, we entered into a fixed price contract with Westat Incorporated, Rockville, Maryland to conduct the CSFII 1994-1996. The developmental phase of this survey extends from September 1992 to December 1993. $1.1 million of Fiscal Year 1992 funds were used to fund this developmental work. The Office of the General Counsel determined that we could not expend Fiscal Year 1993 dollars for this contract. The basis of their decision was that Fiscal Year 1993 dollars were not needed to support this contract (bonafide need). As a result, funds for the data collection beginning in 1994 cannot be obligated in Fiscal Year 1993 as planned.

2. In the Fiscal Year 1993 budget request, the Administrator of HNIS asked this Subcommittee for $455,000 to cover the cost of moving our agency to a new location. The lease at our current location in Hyattsville, Maryland expires in July 1993 and we now expect to move into our new offices in the District of Columbia

at about that time. We estimate that no more that $750,000 will be needed to cover non-GSA moving expenses. Sufficient funds are available to cover these costs because funds originally intended for the CSFII 1994-1996 cannot be obligated in Fiscal Year 1993.

Current Activities

Mr. Chairman, I will discuss activities in our two major areas: nutrition monitoring; and, nutrition education.

Nutrition Monitoring. The agency monitors food intake and the nutrient content of the diets of the American population, and collects and publishes the most comprehensive data on the nutrient composition of foods. Major activities in progress include:

1. Implementing the requirements mandated in P.L. 101-445, the National Nutrition Monitoring and Related Research Act of 1990. USDA is committed to fulfilling the requirements of this legislation. We are working jointly with the DHHS, which shares joint responsibility for the National Nutrition Monitoring and Related Research Program. In accordance with P.L. 101-445, Federal coordination of monitoring activities is carried out under the auspices of the Interagency Board for Nutrition Monitoring and Related Research, co-chaired by the USDA Assistant Secretary for Food and Consumer Services and

the DHHS Assistant Secretary for Health. The Board consists of 22 Federal agencies that conduct surveys or other research activities related to nutrition monitoring. USDA and DHHS alternately provide the Executive Secretary to the Interagency Board. One recent accomplishment was the completion of the Ten-Year Comprehensive Plan for Nutrition Monitoring and Related Research. The Ten-Year Plan was formally transmitted to Congress in January 1993 and it addresses the objectives and activities needed over the next decade to meet the goal of a coordinated and comprehensive National Nutrition Monitoring Program.

Another requirement of P.L. 101-445 is the establishment of the nine-member National Nutrition Monitoring Advisory Council. The Council was established and held its first meeting in late February 1992, with two subsequent meetings later in the year. The Council issued its first report to the Secretaries of USDA and DHHS in December 1992. The Council's next meeting is scheduled for May 18-19, 1993.

2. Preparing for CSFII 1994-1996. A year of survey development has been planned for Fiscal Year 1993 including a pilot study of the data collection methods. Data collection for the full survey will begin in January 1994. In each of the three survey years, a nationally representative sample of individuals will be asked to provide, through in-person interviews, food intake information on two nonconsecutive days. About two weeks after the CSFII, selected individuals will be asked to participate in the Diet and Health Knowledge Survey (DHKS).

3. Analyzing and releasing the data from the CSFII 1989-1991, including the telephone follow-up Diet and Health Knowledge Survey (DHKS) that assesses consumer perceptions on diet/health and food safety issues. Data tapes from the 1989 survey phase were released in November 1992. The 1990 data are scheduled to be released in May 1993 with the final phase (1991) completed by the end of this calendar year. I would note, Mr. Chairman, that the data collection phase for CSFII 1991 was completed in May 1992. The agency has set a goal of releasing survey data in a more timely manner. You can see a steady improvement in the release of data from CSFII 1989-1991 and we are determined to release the data obtained in CSFII 1994-1996 even more efficiently after the completion of each yearly wave of data collection. In addition, HNIS is developing an

automated database management and on-line coding system to be used by future survey contractors to further improve data handling and timeliness.

4. Providing annual estimates of the nutrient content of the total U.S. food supply. This data series provides the only source of data on trends, since 1909, of the foods and nutrients available for consumption.

5. Continuing support to the Department's Pesticide Data Program. As one of four USDA agencies working on this program, HNIS is responsible for providing data on food consumption in a form that will allow the Federal Government to assess more accurately the population's exposure to certain pesticide residues. HNIS, with the cooperation of the Environmental Protection Agency and the Food and Drug Administration, is developing a Food Grouping System (FGS). When fully operational the FGS will enable us to convert more than 5,000 mixed food items consumed by individuals back into their basic agricultural components in a form that can be used to determine potential exposure to pesticide residue.

6. Maintaining and continually updating the National Nutrient Data Bank (NNDB) and the Survey Nutrient Data Base. HNIS maintains and updates the NNDB which is the most comprehensive resource for nutrient composition of foods in the world. Current analytical research on foods is focusing on the major contributors of fat, fatty acids, cholesterol and dietary fiber and for 26 nutrients

in the most frequently consumed foods as reported in USDA's food consumption surveys. HNIS also maintains the Survey Nutrient Data Base which is used in the CSFII and also by the National Center for Health Statistics (NCHS), DHHS, for their National Health and Nutrition Examination Survey (NHANES). An HNIS-NCHS interagency working group decides when food items should be added to the Survey Nutrient Data Base or when existing food descriptions should be updated.

7. Expanding our Nutrient Data Bank Electronic Bulletin Board to maintain and improve communications between HNIS and our data users. Our bulletin board is easily accessed by personal computer and provides up-to-date information about HNIS nutrient data, survey data releases, and other relevant topics. The data bank can also be accessed by way of the Internet System, run by the National Science Foundation, which makes the bulletin board available worldwide.

8. Publishing Agriculture Handbook No. 8--Composition of Foods, Raw, Processed, Prepared. "Handbook Eight" is made up of 21 sections each of which contains a table of nutrient data for a major food group. Ongoing revision is being done either by entire section, or by individual food items and these changes are published in annual supplements.

9. Planning for the 1996-1997 Household Food Consumption Survey. Early planning and development work with the Bureau of the Census is proceeding on schedule. The process involves input from the users so that the HFCS data will be of benefit to agencies across the Federal Government.

Nutrition Education. HNIS conducts research to determine the basis for dietary guidance policy and the most effective methods and strategies for improving the dietary status of Americans. Major activities include:

1. Research to assess the dietary status of the population. Over the past year, we have conducted studies on problem nutrients, food sources of nutrients, trends in the use of animal and vegetable products, food sufficiency, and food safety issues. Our research helps us and others in the nutrition/health community develop appropriately targeted programs and materials that will help Americans achieve a diet that maintains and even improves their health. The results of this work, along with methological studies, have been used to answer inquiries, have been presented at professional meetings and published, and have been used to develop our own educational material.

   A new focus of this work will be on the new food label as a tool for nutrition educators.

2. Establishing the research base for dietary guidance policy. The content of dietary guidance materials is based on research on bridging the gap between current American diets and dietary recommendations. For example, last year we published three reports on the research basis for the Food Guide Pyramid showing that established nutritional goals for vitamins, minerals, fats, calories and other food components could be achieved by following USDA's Food Guide. Menus and recipes, which are used in educational materials to show consumers practical ways of putting dietary guidance into practice, are developed and tested in our foods laboratory.
3. Conducting research to support development and updating of USDA's four family food plans-- thrifty, low-cost, moderate-cost, and liberal. The cost of these food plans is released monthly, and the cost of the thrifty food plan for June of each year is used as the basis for benefits in the Food Stamp Program for the following fiscal year.
4. Conducting research on the most effective methods of communicating dietary guidance to target audiences. To improve dietary behavior, we must give consumers information that is meaningful and useful to them. Various research techniques (such as focus groups and in-depth interviews) have been used to develop nutrition education materials for older adults, teenagers, and

adults with low literacy skills. The reactions of certain segments of the population to various graphic illustrations of our Food Guide have been presented and published. Work is ongoing on how best to communicate nutrition education to pregnant teenagers.

Developing dietary guidance materials designed to provide consumers with the practical information needed to improve their diets. Examples of publications released or soon to be released by the Agency are as follows:

- "The Food Guide Pyramid," Home and Garden Bulletin No. 252, 1992 -- a 32-page booklet for consumers that explains the pyramid.
- "Dietary Guidelines and Your Health: Health Educator's Teaching Kit," MP No. -1490, 1992-- a teaching kit with lesson plans and learning activities on healthy diet for health educators to use in teaching junior and high school students.
- "Making Healthy Food Choices," Home and Garden Bulletin No. 250-- a 17-page booklet on healthful diets for adults with low literacy skills.
- "Food Facts for Older Adults: Information on How to Use the Dietary Guidelines," Home and Garden Bulletin No. 251, (to be released in May, 1993)--a 68-page booklet on healthful diets for older adults.

Essential Fiscal Year 1994 Priorities

HNIS has identified the following six priority activities which we are currently planning to pursue in Fiscal Year 1994:

(1) CSFII 1994-1996 In September 1992, HNIS entered into a fixed price contract with Westat, Incorporated of Rockville, Maryland, to conduct the next three year cycle of the continuing survey. The total projected cost of the contract for the work currently planned is fourteen million dollars over four fiscal years. We are currently in the developmental phase of this contract and expect to begin the first full year of data collection in the second quarter of fiscal year 1994. The projected cost of the work to be funded in Fiscal Year 1994 is $4.2 million.

(2) Planning the Household Food Consumption Survey 1996-1997 (HFCS) (formerly the Nationwide Food Consumption Survey (NFCS)). Every 10 years since 1936, the USDA has conducted a major NFCS. In previous years, the NFCS gathered data on both household and individual consumption patterns. Now that individual food intake is measured by the CSFII, the HFCS 1996-1997 will focus exclusively on collecting household data. HNIS will continue working with the Bureau of the Census on planning for the HFCS.

(3) Continuing support for activities contained in the 10-Year Comprehensive Plan for Nutrition Monitoring. HNIS is responsible for 41 activities, 31 of those are shared responsibilities with another agency we serve as a contributing or collaborating organization for an additional 15 activities.

(4) Supporting, jointly with DHHS, the updating of the Dietary Guidelines for Americans, due to be completed in 1995.

(5) Using survey data and the developing Food Grouping System to better ascertain levels of exposure to pesticide residues.

(6) Modernizing the Nutrient Data Bank system and expanding food composition research.

In closing, Mr. Chairman, let me stress once again that HNIS plays an essential role in helping USDA meet its responsibility to promote the health and well-being of all Americans through improved nutrition. We are a small agency with an important mission. Fiscal Year 1994 will be a very productive year for the agency, and we are determined to deliver quality work in a timely manner to our customers at USDA, other federal agencies, private sector organizations and the general public.

Mr. Chairman, I will be happy to answer any questions you or other Committee members may have.

HUMAN NUTRITION INFORMATION SERVICE

PURPOSE STATEMENT

The Human Nutrition Information Service (HNIS) was established by the Secretary on October 1, 1981. The functions of this agency were formerly carried out within the Agricultural Research Service.

The Department of Agriculture promotes the health and well-being of Americans through improved nutrition. The Human Nutrition Information Service contributes to this mission through the conduct of national food consumption surveys, food composition research, and nutrition education programs. The Agency plays a primary role in the National Nutrition Monitoring and Related Research Program and in the development and promotion of the Dietary Guidelines for Americans.

HNIS serves the American public by conducting applied research in food and nutrition--what foods we consume and what nutrients are in those foods and how to make informed food choices.

The research and information produced by HNIS provides scientists, educators, policymakers, regulators, and health care professionals with the information needed to formulate strategies for:

* food assistance and nutrition intervention programs;
* national nutrition monitoring;
* food safety;
* development of nutrition information and education programs;
* research in nutrition and health; and
* food formulation, production, and marketing.

The Agency is located at Hyattsville, Maryland. As of September 30, 1992, there were 102 full-time permanent and 13 part-time permanent employees. A portion of the Agency's work is done via competitive contracts. These contracts are used for work that requires extensive human resources located throughout the country such as providing interviewers for nationwide surveys, or that requires specific technical expertise and equipment such as laboratory analyses of the nutrient composition of specific foods. Much of this work requires specialized technical skills that would be impractical for the agency to retain among its employees on a year-round basis.

HUMAN NUTRITION INFORMATION SERVICE

Available Funds and Staff-Years

1992 Actual and Estimated, 1993 and 1994

Item	1992 Actual		1993 Estimated		1994 Estimated	
	Amount	Staff-Years	Amount	Staff-Years	Amount	Staff-Years
Salaries and Expenses	$10,788,000	103	$10,788,000	110	$13,142,000[a]	110
Department of Health and Human Services	75,000		75,000		75,000	
Total, Human Nutrition Information Service	10,863,000	103	$10,863,000	110	13,217,000	110

[a]In FY 1993, $2.25 million in appropriated funds will lapse and be reappropriated for FY 1994 to be used for the Continuing Survey of Food Intakes by Individuals (CSFII), the purpose for which the funds were originally appropriated.

HUMAN NUTRITION INFORMATION SERVICE

Permanent Positions by Grade and Staff-Year Summary

1992 and Estimated 1993 and 1994

Grade	1992 Headquarters	1993 Headquarters	1994 Headquarters
SES 1	1	1	1
SES 2	1	1	1
GS/GM-15	4	4	4
GS/GM-14	8	8	8
GS/GM-13	22	22	22
GS-12	15	15	15
GS-11	23	23	23
GS-10	1	1	1
GS-9	9	11	11
GS-7	13	13	13
GS-6	3	3	3
GS-5	7	7	7
GS-4	5	5	5
GS-3	0	1	1
Total Permanent Positions.......	112	115	115
Unfilled Positions end-of year	-14	-13	-13
Total, Permanent Employment, end-of-year	98	102	102
Staff-Years	103	110	110

HUMAN NUTRITION INFORMATION SERVICE

CLASSIFICATION BY OBJECTS

1992 and Estimated 1993 and 1994

	1992	1993	1994
Personnel Compensation:			
Headquarters:			
11 Total personnel compensation..........	$ 4,159,879	$ 4,967,000	$ 5,072,000
12 Personnel benefits......	770,617	814,000	830,000
13 Benefits for former personnel.............	4,015	---	---
Total pers. comp. & benefits	4,934,511	5,781,000	5,902,000
Other Objects:			
21 Travel..................	75,892	60,000	60,000
22 Transportation of things.................	21,871	10,000	10,000
23.2 Rental payments to others.................	---	---	---
23.3 Communications, utilities, and misc. charges..........	153,098	107,000	107,000
24 Printing and reproduction...........	201,761	195,000	195,000
25.1 Consulting	1,133,429	750,000	6,450,000
25.2 Other services	3,151,485	1,417,000	233,000
26 Supplies and materials..	113,361	85,000	85,000
31 Equipment..............	917,490	133,000	100,000
Total other objects.......	5,768,387	2,757,000	7,240,000
Total direct obligations.....	10,702,898	8,538,000	13,142,000

Position Data:

	1992	1993	1994
Average Salary, ES positions.....	$92,200	$95,150	$95,150
Average Salary, GM/GS positions..	$41,411	$42,272	$42,554
Average Grade, GM/GS positions...	10.13	10.19	10.19

HUMAN NUTRITION INFORMATION SERVICE

The estimates include appropriation language for this item as follows (new language underscored; deleted matter enclosed in brackets):

Salaries and Expenses:

For necessary expenses to enable the Human Nutrition Information Service to perform applied research and demonstrations relating to human nutrition and consumer use and economics of food utilization, and nutrition monitoring, [$10,788,000] $10,892,000: Provided, That funds made available by P.L. 102-341 under this head shall remain available for obligation from October 1, 1993, through September 30, 1994, only for the purpose of expenses necessary to conduct the Continuing Survey of Food Intakes by Individuals: Provided further, That this appropriation shall be available for employment pursuant to the second sentence of section 706(a) of the Organic Act of 1944 (7 U.S.C. 2225).

HUMAN NUTRITION INFORMATION SERVICE

Appropriations Act, 1993	$10,788,000
Budget Allowance, 1994	13,142,000
Increase in Appropriation	+2,354,000

SUMMARY OF INCREASES AND DECREASES

(On basis of appropriation)

Item of Change	1993 Estimated	Pay Cost	Other Changes	1994 Estimated
Human Nutrition Information Service	$10,788,000	+$121,000	-$ 17,000	$10,892,000
Reappropriation			+2,250,000	+2,250,000
			2,233,000	13,142,000

In FY 1993, $2.25 million in appropriated funds will lapse and be reappropriated for FY 1994 to be used for the Continuing Survey of Food Intakes by Individuals (CSFII), the purpose for which the funds were originally appropriated.

PROJECT STATEMENT
(On basis of appropriation)

Project	Amount	Staff Years	Amount	Staff Years	Increase	Amount	Staff Years
Research, Analysis & Technical Assistance	$10,702,898	103	$ 8,538,000	110	+4,604,000	$13,142,000	110
Unobligated Balance	85,102	---	2,250,000	---	-2,250,000	---	---
Total, Appropriation	10,788,000	103	10,788,000	110	+2,354,000	13,142,000	110

EXPLANATION OF PROGRAM

Overview of Program Development. General authority for nutrition research and education comes from the mission mandated by Congress when the Department was established in 1862. The Organic Act of 1862 called for an institution, the "general design and duties of which shall be to acquire and diffuse among the people of the United States useful information on subjects connected to agriculture and rural development." Nutrition was subsequently specified as one such subject.

Early studies on food and nutrition were begun at the end of the last century by Dr. W.O. Atwater, the first director of USDA's Office of Experiment Stations. These small scale studies were aimed at helping the working class achieve good diets at low cost. The first food consumption survey of national scope was the "Consumer Purchase Study of 1936-37" conducted jointly by USDA and the U.S. Department of Labor. This study indicated that one-third of the nation's families had diets rated poor by nutrition standards. These findings added impetus to efforts to enrich flour and bread with iron and three B vitamins and to initiate school lunch programs and more vigorous nutrition education efforts.

The types of food eaten and the dietary status of the population have been measured subsequently through the decennial Nationwide Food Consumption Surveys (NFCS). The last NFCS was conducted in 1987-88. The results of these studies reflect changes over the years in the distribution and storage (refrigeration) of products, in the availability of convenience foods (mixes and ready-made products), in technology (more commercially frozen foods and new packaging), and in incomes and lifestyles (more working women). Having available up-to-date food consumption data is essential to understanding both the dietary status of the population and the safety of the food supply. In addition to the NFCS, the annual Continuing Survey of Food Intakes by Individuals (CSFII) updates NFCS findings and focuses on population groups at nutritional risk.

The Research and Marketing Act of 1946 explicity authorized research into problems of human nutrition and of the nutritive value of agriculture commodities. The role of USDA in conducting research in the fields of human nutrition, food consumption patterns, nutritive value of foods, and nutrition education activities was affirmed in the Food and Agriculture Act of 1977. Title XIV of this Act, "The National Agricultural Research, Extension, and Teaching Policy Act of 1977, "established USDA as the lead agency in the Federal Government for research, extension, and teaching in the food and agricultural sciences. Further, it directed that research into food and human nutrition be established as a separate and distinct mission of the Department. With this legislation, Congress supported USDA's traditional emphasis on the nutritional needs of normal, healthy individuals rather than the needs of individuals requiring clinical or therapeutic dietary support. This mission was reaffirmed in the Agriculture and Food Act of 1981 and the Food Security Act of 1985.

The National Nutrition Monitoring and Related Research Act of 1990 directed better coordination of nutrition monitoring government-wide and an expansion of activities in food consumption assessment, food composition research, and dietary guidance in order to strengthen national nutrition monitoring and foster nutrition education.

HNIS has been specified for leadership in providing the policy basis for Federal dietary guidance to the public for several years in conference reports accompanying the Agriculture, Rural Development, Food and Drug Administration, and Related Agencies Appropriations Bills.

HNIS was established on October 1, 1981, by the Secretary's Memorandum No. 1000-1 issued pursuant to Reorganization Plan No. 1 of 1953 (7 U.S.C. 2201). The functions of this agency were formerly carried out in the Agricultural Research Service. Currently the agency conducts the activities authorized under "Research Analysis and Technical Assistance" in sections 1451-1453 and 1589 of Public Law 99-198 (7 U.S.C. 3173 note and 3178a).

Agency Objectives. It is USDA policy to "promote optimal human health and well-being through improved nutrition" (Departmental Regulation 1020-4). HNIS implements this policy through three activities, including:

1) Nutrition Monitoring. Through the National Nutrition Monitoring and Related Research Program (NNMRRP), USDA proposes to strengthen nutrition monitoring by increasing efforts to measure the food and nutrition behavior of the general population and specific population subgroups, in order to better understand and target problem areas in food assistance, nutrition education, and food safety. HNIS's budget proposal for nutrition monitoring is $9.6 million for FY 1994, an increase of $4.6 million from FY 1993.

2) Food Consumption Research

The Continuing Survey of Food Intakes by Individuals (CSFII) 1994-1996 will be the third in a series of CSFII's conducted since 1985. A telephone follow-up survey, the Diet and Health Knowledge Survey (DHKS), initiated in CSFII 1989-1991 also will be conducted. The survey's target population consists of noninstitutionalized individuals in the 50 States and Washington, D.C. Approximately 45 percent of the sample will consist of individuals from low-income households. The number of CSFII respondents is expected to be between 15,000 and 16,500 over 3 years. The number of DHKS respondents is expected to be between 4,000 and 5,500 over 3 years.

CSFII 1994-1996 is designed to obtain 2 independent days of food intake data from designated individuals in the household in addition to sociodemographic, and diet and health-related questions. Data are used by policy-makers in formulating goals and policies for food and nutrition intervention programs. To improve the ability of these surveys to address the varied needs of Federal users, HNIS also created a Continuing Survey Users Group with representatives from several agencies that are major users of food consumption data. HNIS's budget proposal for Food Consumption Research remains at $1.8 million, unchanged from FY 1993.

3) Nutrition Education.

HNIS will continue its program in nutrition education designed to:

- o Help establish the standards for a healthful diet through activities such as the review of the Dietary Guidelines for Americans and updating of the Food Guide;
- o Assess how well Americans are currently following dietary recommendations and assess the factors that influence their dietary status. This is done through analysis of data from the National Nutrition Monitoring and Related Research Program as well as other sources and includes the development and testing of analytical methods; and
- o Develop and test materials/strategies that help consumers improve their diet. This includes conducting research on recipe development, basic communication and education research as well as the promotion and evaluation of educational materials and strategies. HNIS budget proposal for Nutrition Education for FY 1994 remains at $1.7 million, unchanged from FY 1993.

Program Level
(Dollars in Millions)

Program	1992 Actual	1993 Estimated	1994 Estimated
NUTRITION EDUCATION:			
Food Safety Activities	.3	.5	.5
Dietary Guidance and Education Programs	1.3	1.2	1.2
	1.6	1.7	1.7
NUTRITION MONITORING	7.0	7.2	7.4
Reappropriation		-2.2	+2.2
		5.0	9.6
NUTRITION RESEARCH	2.0	1.8	1.8
	10.6	8.5	13.1

JUSTIFICATION OF INCREASES AND DECREASES

An increase of $2,354,000, consisting of:

(1) A decrease of $17,000 for administrative efficiency

Need for Change. To promote the efficient use of resources for administrative purposes, in keeping with the President's Executive Order, total USDA baseline outlays for these activities will be reduced by 3 percent in FY 1994, 6 percent in FY 1995, 9 percent in FY 1996, and 14 percent in FY 1997.

Nature of Change. In order to achieve this savings, HNIS will closely monitor expenses, limit travel, training and other overhead to achieve required administrative efficiency.

(2) An increase of $121,000 which reflects the annualization of the fiscal year 1993 pay raise.

(3) Reappropriation of $2,250,000 in unobligated FY 1993 funds for FY 1994.

Need for Change. To extend the availability of 1993 appropriations for FY 1994 to make funds available for the CSFII.

Nature of Change. Background: CSFII 1994-96 is a major component of the National Nutrition Monitoring and Related Research Program (NNMRRP). The NNMRRP was established as a national priority following passage of the National Nutrition Monitoring and Related Research Act of 1990 (P.L. 101-445). The CSFII is responsive to NNMRRP requirments for the continuous collection, processing, and analysis of dietary status data. Original FY 1993 plans were to obligate funds for a year of survey development, including a pilot study of all survey operations, and the first year of nationwide data collection. This contract included an expanded survey development/testing and quality control period to meet GAO recommendations for improvement. After the Request for Contract had been released, the Office of the Inspector General, interpreting the Comptroller General's Decision B-241415, imposed a severable service requirement on CSFII 1994-96. As a result, funds for the data collection beginning in 1994 cannot be obligated in FY 1993 as planned. Reappropriation would make these funds available in FY 1994.

Human Nutrition Information Service
GEOGRAPHIC BREAKDOWN OF OBLIGATIONS AND STAFF-YEARS
1992 and Estimated 1993 and 1994

	1992		1993		1994	
Staff	Amount	Staff Years	Amount	Staff Years	Amount	Years
Maryland........	$10,702,898	103	$ 8,538,000	110	$13,142,000	110
Unobligated balance.......	85,102	--	+2,250,000	--	--	--
Total, Available or Estimate	10,788,000	103	10,788,000	110	13,142,000	110

HUMAN NUTRITION INFORMATION SERVICE

STATUS OF PROGRAM

The Human Nutrition Information Service (HNIS) is responsible for conducting applied research in food and nutrition--what foods Americans buy and eat, what nutrients are in the foods we eat, and how we can make informed food choices. HNIS research is used by policymakers to formulate research-based policies for nutrition and food intervention programs; consumer education including the Dietary Guidelines for Americans, which are the basis of Federal dietary guidance policy for the public; food fortification; food safety; and regulatory activities.

Current Activities carried out by HNIS include:

1. Food Consumption Research. Plan, coordinate, and report results of nationwide surveys of food consumption and dietary practices and behaviors by households and individuals, including the Household Food Consumption Survey, the Continuing Survey of Food Intakes by Individuals, and the Diet and Health Knowledge Survey. Develop, carry out, and report a program of research to improve food-consumption survey concepts and methods consistent with provisions of the National Nutrition Monitoring and Related Research Act of 1990.

2. Applied Research on the Nutrient Content of Foods. Direct research and gather data to determine the nutrient content of foods available to Americans, develop standard reference tables on the nutrient composition of foods, and maintain the National Nutrient Data Bank.

3. Applied Research on the Dietary Status of the U.S. Population. Provide research-based information for decision-making by Government policymakers, educators, and health professionals aimed at improving the nutritional quality of the American diet and supporting the Food Safety Data Initiative; maintain the historical series on the nutrient content of the U.S. food supply.

4. Nutrition Education Research. Develop dietary guidance concepts and techniques to help the American public make informed food choices.

5. Policy Coordination. Serve as lead USDA agency for the National Nutrition Monitoring and Related Research Program, for the development of the Dietary Guidelines for Americans--the basis for Federal dietary guidance policy, and for a number of Federal and Federal/private nutrition education activities such as the National Cholesterol Education Program. These activities are coordinated with the U.S. Department of Health and Human Services (DHHS) and other agencies.

Food Consumption Research

The Continuing Survey of Food Intakes by Individuals (CSFII) 1989-91 has been completed. Data collection for the 1991 CSFII, which began in April 1991, was completed in March 1992 for all members of 1,500 households in the general population and an additional 750 households in the low-income population. Over the three-year period the combined sample has targeted 6,700 households and 15,000 individuals. The survey was designed to obtain 3-day food intake data from all members of the household in addition to sociodemographic data and general questions on respondents' diet and health. Data tapes providing results from the 1989 CSFII have been made available for public distribution through the National Technical Information Service.

The Diet and Health Knowledge Survey (DHKS) was included in the 1989-91 CSFII as a telephone follow-up survey on the dietary knowledge and attitudes of survey participants. It was initiated to improve our understanding of factors that affect food choices and to obtain information on people's knowledge and attitudes about the concepts promoted by the Dietary Guidelines for Americans. This survey is significant in that it represents the first time that a nationwide survey will be used to study the relationship between individuals' actual dietary intakes and their attitudes about dietary behavior. Information from this survey will have a major effect on the design of nutrition education programs.

An extramural research project continued to determine guidelines needed for obtaining proxy information on food intake by children under 12 years of age and for food eaten by household members not at home at the time that the survey is conducted. Obtaining intake data for these groups is difficult, but the quality can be substantially improved by the participation of knowledgeable proxies.

Research on the Nutrient Content of Foods

The ongoing revision of Agriculture Handbook No. 8, "Composition of Foods," by publication sections continued with the AH-8-18, "Baked Products." This section contains data for 405 items. The items include bread, leavening agents, cakes, cookies, crackers, pies and muffins.

The National Nutrient Data Bank Bulletin Board was expanded to include Release 5 of the USDA Survey Nutrient Data Base and release 10 of the Standard Reference; the machine-readable version of Handbook No. 8. Since its inception in June 1989, the bulletin board has received over 5,000 calls from individuals representing academia, industry, the health professions, and the public. Arrangements have been made with the University of Maryland to make the bulletins and.data on the Bulletin Board available to users with access to the Internet system, which has already significantly expanded its availability nationally and internationally.

Extramural contracts were used for monitoring nutrient composition data. These included lipid components including fat, fatty acids, cholesterol, and plant sterols in selected foods; and total dietary fiber in selected foods. Key foods are being analyzed for vitamins, minerals, and proximates (protein, fat, carbohydrate, moisture). Studies were conducted on effects of cooking and baking individual foods and mixtures, on nutrient retention, and to fill knowledge gaps. Data obtained through these activities have been added to the National Nutrient Data Bank.

Research on the Dietary Status of the U.S. Population

The U.S. Food Supply Series, a historical series that dates from 1909, was updated. This series is the only source of data on trends in levels of foods and nutrients in the American diet since the beginning of this century. It reports quantities of foods available for consumption per capita per year, as estimated by USDA's Economic Research Service, and amounts of nutrients available per capita per day, as estimated by HNIS. The publication "Nutrient Content of the U.S. Food Supply, 1909-1988." was released by USDA. New data for 1989, 1990, and 1991 were added to the Food Supply Series database and results are being prepared for publication. Methodologies associated with the collection and reporting of this data have been reviewed and revised as appropriate. Selected results have also appeared in other Department publications and professional journals.

The results of several research studies that employed USDA food consumption survey data were disseminated via publications and presentations at professional meetings. Two papers at the First International Conference on Dietary Assessment Methods presented information on breaking down food mixtures into ingredients and on using graphical representations of multivariate assessments of dietary quality. A presentation at the annual American Agricultural Economics Association meeting examined two proxy variables used to estimate long-run food expenditures at home. An article evaluating a nutrition education program for Head Start parents was published in a peer-reviewed professional journal.

The cost of four USDA family food plans--thrifty, low-cost, moderate-cost, and liberal--was released monthly in FY 1992. An in-house study of the effects of new dietary recommendations and new food composition on the food plans was completed. It showed that the food plans as currently designed meet nutritional recommendations.

Pesticide Data Program

HNIS is one of four USDA agencies participating in the Pesticide Data Program (PDP), a program designed to provide actual residue and use data to help form the basis for conducting realistic risk assessments and setting pesticide tolerances. HNIS, with the cooperation of the Environmental Protection Agency and the Food and Drug Administration, is developing a Food Grouping System to translate data on foods as consumed into forms that can be linked with pesticide residue data. This system will provide intake data on food and commodities for EPA and other organizations to determine potential residue exposures for the total population and population subgroups, thereby enhancing risk assessments. Contract acquisition by the General Services Administration's Federal Office System Support Division is in progress with award anticipated in 1993.

Nutrition Education Research and Information

The Dietary Guidelines for Americans, jointly issued by the USDA and DHHS, represent Federal nutrition policy and are the basis for our nutrition guidance.

The third edition was released in November 1990. They are written for the general healthy population, but HNIS is also developing materials to meet the needs of special hard-to-reach population groups:

o A series of six brief factsheets for healthy older adults on using the Dietary Guidelines has been developed jointly with the National Institute on Aging (NIA) and is being designed for publication. It is anticipated that the series will be available in 1993 as a packet of factsheet-style leaflets in an attractive folder and will be distributed through the National Institute on Aging, Extension Service, HNIS, and other appropriate agencies.

o A manuscript for "Making Healthy Food Choices," a brief booklet on using the Dietary Guidelines for adults with low literacy skills, has been developed based on cooperative research previously conducted on adapting materials for this audience. This manuscript is also being designed for publication in 1993.

o A teacher's guide for secondary school health education teachers was done in cooperation with the Association for the Advancement of Health Education (AAHE). Design of the guide is under way and it will be jointly distributed by AAHE and HNIS in 1993.

A publication, The Food Guide Pyramid, was released which explains in detail to consumers how to follow USDA's food guide developed in the early 1980's. This publication includes the new pyramid graphic, which illustrates the Dietary Guidelines concept of variety, proportionality, and moderation. Fifty thousand copies of this publication and 100,000 posters are being distributed to nutrition professionals, extension home economists, teachers and consumers by HNIS. The pyramid graphic is being widely used by the media in newspaper and magazine articles, by the food industry on labels and in promotional materials, and by the schools in textbooks and curricula.

A condensed version of the 32 page "Food Guide Pyramid" booklet entitled, "The Food Guide Pyramid...Beyond the Basic 4," was developed by the Food Marketing Institute (FMI) in cooperation with USDA and DHHS. Twenty-five thousand copies each of a colored 8-panel brochure and a black-and-white reproducible are being distributed to nutrition professionals by HNIS. Through FMI, supermarkets throughout the nation will distribute the brochure to consumers.

A project to revise a set of seven bulletins on using the Dietary Guidelines, HG-232-1 through 7, "Dietary Guidelines and Your Diet," and develop one new overview bulletin is nearing completion. Revisions include updating nutrient data and scientific information and incorporating information specifically related to the third edition of the Dietary Guidelines. Revisions also consider previous nutrition education research studies to evaluate consumers' understanding and use of the bulletin series. Based on results of the focus groups, all eight bulletins have been prepared for printing and distribution as a set. In the past, these bulletins have been widely used by nutrition educators and incorporated into their programs in a number of ways.

A nutrition education research study sponsored by HNIS to assess nutrition education needs of pregnant teenagers is nearing completion. A prototype video has been developed based on a workshop with professionals who serve this clientele and a series of focus groups with pregnant teens. The prototype video and accompanying materials will be tested with the target audience--pregnant teens.

HNIS provides leadership for the USDA Dietary Guidance Working Group under the auspices of the Subcommittee for Human Nutrition. The Dietary Guidance Working Group continues to review all USDA publications that present dietary guidance information, including prospectuses and publication drafts. During the 1992 fiscal year approximately 19 drafts of publication and prospectuses were reviewed. The review process is intended to ensure that guidance conforms to the Dietary Guidelines and is consistent and supportive across USDA agencies and the Federal Government. The group, composed of representatives from ten USDA agencies that provide guidance to their clientele. The group has also been reviewing dietary guidance materials from DHHS. A Memorandum of Understanding is in final clearance by both Departments to establish the procedures by which the Secretaries of USDA and DHHS will carry out the requirements of the National Nutrition Monitoring and Related Research Act of 1990 for review and approval of dietary guidance for the general public.

Policy Coordination

As the USDA lead agency for the National Nutrition Monitoring and Related Research Program, HNIS worked with other agencies both inside and outside USDA to coordinate monitoring activities. HNIS, along with DHHS, provides Co-Executive Secretaries to the National Nutrition Monitoring Advisory Council. The Co-Executive Secretaries provide technical assistance and administrative service in the operation of the Council. HNIS provides liaison to the Executive Secretary for the Interagency Board on Nutrition Monitoring and Related Research (IBNMRR), which is cochaired by the USDA Assistant Secretary for Food and Consumer Services and the DHHS Assistant Secretary of Health. Through the activities of working groups of the IBNMRR, issues are being addressed on survey comparability, Federal and State information dissemination and exchange, and food composition. Implementation of the requirements defined in P.L. 101-445, the National Nutrition Monitoring and Related Research Act of 1990, is a major initiative within USDA in coordination with DHHS. As required by the law, USDA and DHHS have developed the Ten-Year Comprehensive Plan for Nutrition Monitoring and Related Research. The Plan lays out direction and activities in nutrition monitoring that the Federal government will take for the next decade.

HNIS will also be the lead for USDA, in coordination with DHHS, to contract with a scientific body to interpret available data and publish a report on the dietary, nutritional, and health-related status of the people of the United States. This scientific report is required by P.L. 101-445. HNIS further provides the USDA liaison to the National Cholesterol Education Campaign Coordinating Committee and the USDA member to the Working Group for the Year 2000 Nutrition Objectives, both of which are DHHS health promotion and disease prevention initiatives.

THURSDAY, APRIL 22, 1993.

OFFICE OF PUBLIC AFFAIRS

WITNESSES

ALI WEBB, DIRECTOR, OFFICE OF PUBLIC AFFAIRS

STEPHEN B. DEWHURST, BUDGET OFFICER, DEPARTMENT OF AGRICULTURE

Mr. DURBIN. Now we would like to call Ali Webb, Director of the Office of Public Affairs.

Welcome.

Ms. WEBB. Thank you.

Mr. DURBIN. Your statement will be made part of the record. If you'd like to summarize at this point, we will ask a few questions at the conclusion of your statement.

Please proceed.

Ms. WEBB. Thank you very much.

OPA MISSION

I am pleased to be here and appreciate the opportunity to come before the committee to talk about the Office of Public Affairs.

Unlike Mr. Hilty, I have only been in my job 5 weeks, so I don't have the benefit of a lot of historical knowledge about how things have worked at the United States Department of Agriculture. But I can shed some light on how we hope they are going to work in the future, particularly in the Office of Public Affairs.

As you know, the dissemination of information is part of the charter of the Department of Agriculture, and the Office of Public Affairs is the primary mechanism we have to get information out to the American public, the agricultural segment, as well as other interests that are served by the Department's programs. So our mission is fairly straightforward.

We have built over the years some information delivery systems to reach targeted audiences out in the communities. We use the traditional methods of press releases, as well as radio and television news feeds. We publish books, like the Yearbook of Agriculture, and we publish magazines.

We have a wide variety of tools throughout the Department. And our goal under Secretary Espy is to create a more coordinated, clearer communication of USDA's programs and policies to the American people in a cost-effective manner. And if we achieve that goal by the end of 4 years, I think we will have a very successful Office of Public Affairs.

Our budget request this year is basically a straight line request. We are going to figure out how to do more with what we have, should the committee fund us at that level. And I think we will get more product and better product for the same amount of money through the reorganization process.

So I would be glad to focus on any of the particular areas of public affairs.

[CLERK'S NOTE.—Ms. Webb's biography appears on pages 678 through 679. The prepared statement appears on pages 680 through 685. The budget justifications, which were received on April 28, 1993, appear on pages 686 through 700.]

Mr. DURBIN. Thank you very much.

OPA REORGANIZATION

Let me ask you about the reorganization of public affairs activities at the Department. There was a recent news article which suggested that you were going back to the drawing board in terms of reorganizing the far-flung public affairs structure of USDA. I take it from that statement, that there is a proposal on the table that has been shelved. Can you shed some light on what is going on here?

Ms. WEBB. Absolutely. As I said, I started five weeks ago, and was asked by the Secretary to evaluate several proposals that had been made in the first few weeks of his administration about what to do with Public Affairs. We took that information and basically began a process, using the reinventing government model of asking the Public Affairs employees at the Department to come up with the implementation of how we are going to reorganize. What is clear is that there is going to be a consolidation of functions.

We are looking for the duplication of services which occur across the agencies and duplication of personnel. The reorganization process is ongoing, so nothing's been shelved.

As described by the Secretary, we are trying to move into an implementation that invests, involves and empowers the employees of USDA who are actually doing the work. There has been a group meeting under my direction for the last four weeks. They have been doing extensive outreach to the public affairs' offices across the agencies. We hope to have some options for the Secretary within the next 10 days or so.

Mr. DURBIN. Your budget request for fiscal year 1994 does not reflect the Secretary's initiative to consolidate all public relations personnel from each agency into a single office at Headquarters. Can you tell us why?

Ms. WEBB. In line with the Secretary's consolidation efforts, I established a Working Group, which is composed of career public affairs people from several of the Department's public affairs offices, to develop streamlining recommendations which are to go forward to the Secretary for his consideration.

By the beginning of May, the Secretary will receive a set of recommendations from our Working Group, which was assembled 30 days ago. The Working Group has been looking at all public affairs functions.

The report will address the general themes that the Secretary laid down during his confirmation about public affairs functions at USDA. The Secretary has talked about consolidating public affairs functions in a central Department of Communications. What the

Working Group has been looking at is what functions should come in and which should stay with the agencies.

The Secretary has stressed that USDA must become more cost efficient, therefore, one of the goals of the Working Groups is to identify where cost savings can occur. Additionally, the report will make recommendations on new technology use for internal and external communication.

Mr. DURBIN. Thank you. I know you have been on board for only five weeks and I know you worked hard to prepare, but if there is a staff person with you that you would like to invite to come up to the table, we welcome that at the subcommittee.

Ms. WEBB. Thank you.

YEARBOOK OF AGRICULTURE

Mr. DURBIN. I want to ask you some specific questions about the Ag Yearbook.

Ms. WEBB. Oh, good.

Mr. SKEEN. Got a tab on it.

Ms. WEBB. Absolutely.

Mr. DURBIN. Under a law passed in 1968, Congress directed that your agency would publish or would provide a certain number of Yearbooks to the Senate, the House, and your own Department of Agriculture. All told, over half a million were to be provided under the statute. Over the years, that number has changed in terms of actual allocation, and instead of the 470,000 Agriculture Yearbooks given to Members of Congress for distribution, the most recent figure is closer to 232,000. I am trying to determine at this point, the status and future of the Ag Yearbook.

First let me tell you, I view it with some nostalgia, and not because I was raised on a farm, I might add. When I first came to Capitol Hill, 30 years ago, working in the office of a United States Senator, it was considered to be one of the great services his office would offer in providing these yearbooks, particularly in our agricultural State of Illinois.

These books were sought after. There are people still in America who have collections including every one of these yearbooks and they value them as many people would value a family treasure. I am going to try to take a look at this Ag Yearbook from a more cost-oriented perspective. How many yearbooks do you produce, and at what cost?

Ms. WEBB. We are directed by the Congress to produce 232,500 copies for their use.

The cost for the 1993 Yearbook on Nutrition is estimated at $453,000, which is roughly in line with the cost of previous yearbooks in the last ten years. That cost covers editing, writing and printing with printing being the largest component of cost. We estimate printing will be about $280,000 this year.

Mr. DURBIN. What is the cost per yearbook?

Ms. WEBB. Oh, that is a good question. I don't have a calculator.

Mr. DURBIN. Well, give me the rough figures, and we will just estimate it here.

Ms. WEBB. $453,000 in costs for 262,500 copies.

Mr. DURBIN. In preparation? And $280,000 for printing?

Ms. WEBB. Altogether $453,000. And the number is actually 232,250.

Mr. DURBIN. That is less than two dollars a book. Is that right?

Ms. WEBB. That is what we are directed to print.

Mr. DURBIN. I wonder if there is embedded in that cost some staff time that isn't allocated.

Ms. WEBB. That figure does not include the cost of the agencies to produce the manuscripts.

Mr. DURBIN. So this is the actual physical cost of production we are talking about?

Ms. WEBB. Correct.

Mr. DURBIN. If we were to step back and say to your contributors and authors, what is your time worth, then we are obviously dealing with a much larger figure?

Ms. WEBB. Yes, we would be dealing with a much larger figure, and I would welcome the participation and the help of the Subcommittee in figuring out if the yearbook is still meeting its original mission.

POPULARITY OF YEARBOOK

Mr. DURBIN. Well, let me just give you some examples.

We have asked in last year's testimony for some indication of the popularity of the yearbook. Now Members of Congress send these yearbooks out at no charge to their constituents, either upon request or where they think they might be useful, such as school libraries, farm organizations, different associations and the like.

But one indicator of popularity of the book is the general sales through the GPO. And it is interesting, when you look at the history of it, and we only have figures going back to 1948. It turns out that the biggest seller of all was the 1965 Yearbook entitled Consumers All. It looks like you sold about 125,000 copies through GPO, outside of the Congressional distribution network. I might say that it is interesting because this book tells you how to build a house. The 1972 book on landscaping was pretty popular and one on gardening did very well too.

But, starting in 1980, the bottom fell out of the Ag yearbook market. I'm sure this is not a reflection whatsoever on the fine contributions and the excellent articles, but for some reason the folks out there, the consuming public, have little or no interest in these books.

Ms. WEBB. Exactly.

YEARBOOK SALES

Mr. DURBIN. The 1965 yearbook sold 125,000 copies. The 1991 yearbook has sold 2,000 copies. I find the difference interesting. The books that sell the most tell folks how to build a house, how to landscape their home, what to do in the garden. They are how to books. These other books cover topics like Agriculture and the Constitution. Obviously people aren't interested.

The latest yearbook talks about agriculture and the environment. Its a very interesting book to me but, not to the folks who would be asked to put out a few bucks to buy it.

FUTURE OF YEARBOOK

So it comes down to the bottom line as to whether or not there is a future for this yearbook and whether we ought to step back, nostalgia notwithstanding, and say, I think the American people are telling us by and large they are not interested in this publication and we can no longer justify $453,000 and all of the embedded costs involved. Perhaps what we should do is ask, is there a future? If there is, what is it going to be? What are your thoughts on that?

Ms. WEBB. One of the first questions I raised was about the book publishing business that I found in the Office of Public Affairs. The Yearbook has a number of very strong supporters, many of whom are members of this committee and who believed that the Yearbook was a critical piece of work, the signature document for USDA.

In fact, this is our 101st year of production for the Yearbook. Some of the old Yearbooks on livestock diseases and climate issues that were a real help to the farmer are still on shelves out at the farm. But, what I would like to do is to ask Members of the Congress, who are our primary consumers of this information, to ask their constituents if this is the kind of information they want. I have a memo prepared that asks those kinds of questions.

Becausing we are producing the Yearbook, it appears to be for a congressional audience, who is requesting it because their constituents want it. I mean my biggest nightmare is to walk around here and open a closet somewhere and see a hundred thousand copies of the Yearbook of Agriculture.

We are going to print the Yearbook in soft cover this year to cut costs. That is about a $30,000 savings. Nutrition is this year's topic. We haven't picked a topic for next year for this very reason. We want to figure out whether this is the best information delivery system for this information, and if we are delivering the right information.

So I couldn't agree with your comments more.

LACK OF CONSUMER INTEREST

Mr. DURBIN. Well, I would just say, my guess is the nutrition book is not going to be a big seller, even though it is very important. I don't mean to diminish the importance of anything covered in the Yearbook. I think for those of us who are interested in the topic, it is well worth looking into and reading, and the source material is very good. But the consuming public out there, apparently, is not that interested in it.

Ms. WEBB. Yes.

Mr. DURBIN. They want books that tell them how to do things and help them do it. In the early history of the Department, there were many more farmers, and they really had a need for education and information. Things were changing quickly, and they had to keep up with it, and our U.S. Department of Agriculture was one of the few sources they had. Now we have television, government agencies like the Extension Service providing all sorts of information to producers and ranchers across the country.

I am going to ask the subcommittee to take a look at this topic with me and decide just where we go from here. I think it is time to ask tough questions even though they might challenge some, as we said, some pretty firmly held beliefs that this is part of America as is anything that we do at the Federal level.

The appropriation language states that not fewer than 232,250 copies of the Yearbook of Agriculture be available for use by the Senate and House of Representatives. How many copies does each representative receive for distribution?

Ms. WEBB. The Joint Committee on Printing determines how many copies of the Yearbook should be printed each year. For the 1992 Yearbook, each Member of the House was allotted 220 copies, and each Member of the Senate was allotted 240 copies.

Mr. DURBIN. Provide a table for the record showing the total cost associated with the production of the Yearbook of Agriculture for fiscal years 1988 through 1992.

Ms. WEBB. I will be glad to provide that information.

[The information follows:]

ANNUAL PRODUCTION COST OF THE YEARBOOK OF AGRICULTURE

Year:	Cost
1988	$490,871
1989	500,122
1990	463,990
1991	426,797
1992	360,761

Mr. DURBIN. Update the table that appears on pages 8 and 9 of last year's hearing record showing the number of Yearbooks sold to include additional sales in past years and sales of the 1992 Yearbook.

Ms. WEBB. I will be glad to update the table.

[The information follows:]

DEPARTMENT OF AGRICULTURE YEARBOOKS

Year:	Title of yearbook	GPO sales
1941	Climate and Man	([1])
1942	Keeping Livestock Healthy	([1])
1943–47	Science in Farming	([1])
1948	Grass	68,045
1949	Trees	123,324
1950–51	Crops in Peace and War	18,636
1952	Insects	93,138
1953	Plant Diseases	57,175
1954	Marketing	24,073
1955	Water	66,538
1956	Animal Diseases	74,747
1957	Soil	75,807
1958	Land	40,186
1959	Food	98,802
1960	Power to Produce	23,373
1961	Seeds	44,726
1962	After a Hundred Years (Centennial Edition)	27,757
1963	A Place to Live	29,805
1964	Farmer's World	23,374

DEPARTMENT OF AGRICULTURE YEARBOOKS—Continued

	Title of yearbook	GPO sales
1965	Consumers All	125,163
1966	Protecting Our Food	21,333
1967	Outdoors USA	93,945
1968	Science for Better Living	17,808
1969	Food for Us All	35,385
1970	Contours of Change	15,687
1971	A Good Life for More People	16,065
1972	Landscape for Living	76,103
1973	Handbook for the Home	43,189
1974	Shopper's Guide	31,362
1975	That We May Eat	20,047
1976	The Face of Rural America	17,306
1977	Gardening for Food and Fun	56,302
1978	Living on a Few Acres	55,461
1979	What's to Eat?	55,774
1980	Cutting Energy Costs	14,195
1981	Will There Be Enough Food?	7,056
1982	Food from Farm to Table	5,916
1983	Using Our Natural Resources	5,501
1984	Animal Health-Livestock and Pets	9,059
1985	U.S. Agriculture In A Global Economy	4,492
1986	Research For Tomorrow	4,196
1987	Our American Land	3,855
1988	Marketing U S. Agriculture	4,478
1989	Farm Management	5,381
1990	Americans In Agriculture, Portraits of Diversity	3,250
1991	Agriculture and the Environment	3,329
1992	New Crops, New Uses, New Markets: Industrial and Commercial Products from U S. Agriculture	2,374

[1] Not available

Sales figures for 1983 and prior years have not changed due to sales stocks being no longer available.

YEARBOOK OF AGRICULTURE

Mr. DURBIN. The Yearbook of Agriculture, as mandated by law, is to be "specially suited to interest and instruct the farmers of the country." How has the Yearbook met this mandate over the last ten years?

Ms. WEBB. The Yearbooks of the last 10 years have provided detailed, substantive, and readable information for farmers focusing on some of their key concerns. These include the topics of (1) natural resource management: "1983—Using Our Natural Resources," "1987—Our American Land," and "1991—Agriculture and the Environment;" (2) marketing skills and sales opportunities: "1985—U.S. Agriculture in a Global Economy," "1988—Marketing U.S. Agriculture," "1989—Farm Management," and "1992—New Crops, New Uses, New Markets;" (3) and specific relevant areas of scientific information: "1984—Animal Health," and "1986—Research for Tomorrow."

Mr. DURBIN. When you are deciding the topic and outline for the Yearbook do you seek input from the farm community as to what topic or information they would like to have?

Ms. WEBB. The Secretary of Agriculture chooses the topic for each Yearbook, taking into account suggestions from many sources including the Office of Public Affairs. The OPA staff looks for topics and chapters proposed by interested groups and individuals.

1993 YEARBOOK OF AGRICULTURE

Mr. DURBIN. What is the status and working outline for the 1993 Yearbook of Agriculture. When will it be available?

Ms. WEBB. The 1993 Yearbook on Nutrition has been planned, written, edited, and typeset. It awaits final clearance before going into production. We expect it to be available in the fall of this year. I will provide the working outline for the record.

[The information follows:]

NUTRITION
1993 Yearbook of Agriculture

TARGET READERS: Primary target is consumer or general reader. Yearbook will be appealing, convincing; it will help people learn more about nutrition and improve their eating habits. Secondary target includes professionals working in the nutrition field, agricultural producers, educators, students.

PURPOSE: Yearbook will offer nutrition guidance to help people make healthier food choices. It will also give general information on such aspects of nutrition as research, consumption, production, international picture, food safety, Government programs.

CONTENTS:

Front Matter

* Secretary's Introduction--Why is nutrition important to me? Solving hunger and enhancing health are basic to growth, learning, solving other problems of living. Include any other points of emphasis on Yearbook's content, nutrition generally.

* Editor's Preface--Lay out Yearbook structure and list credits

* Contents Page

PART I. What Do We Eat?

1. "A Glance at Our Nutrition Picture," by Jay H. Green, HNIS (Consumer quiz to attract people to the section's content--highlights questions related to consumer intake and knowledge)

2. "Diets of Americans: What We're Eating and How We Fare Nutritionally," by Cecilia Wilkinson Enns and Joanne Rosenthal Levine, HNIS (based on '87-'88 NFCS as presented in Chartbook)

3. "Why Do People Eat What They Eat? Factors Influencing Food Choices," by Joanne F. Guthrie, HNIS (Presents demographic variables and lifestyle issues)

4. "Consumers' Understanding of Diet and Health," by Linda Cleveland and Carole A. Davis, HNIS

5. "Money Value of Household Food, by Mary Hama," HNIS

PART II. What To Eat: How To Choose Food

1. "Dietary Guidance for the General Population," by Ann Shaw, Carol Davis, HNIS (Includes effects of various nutrients and food choices)

   --Sidebar: "Dietary Guidance for Special Groups," by Anne M. Shaw and Carol A. Davis, HNIS

   --Sidebar: "Should I Breastfeed My Baby? by Brenda Lisi," FNS

2. "Using the New Food Pyramid To Achieve a Healthy Diet," by Mary Clark, KS CES

3. "Using the New Nutrition Label To Make Choices," by Danielle Schor, FSIS, and Etta Saltos, ES (How to read and interpret food labels; how to use food labels in choosing a nutritious diet)

4. "Finding Vitamins and Minerals in Foods," by Lois H. Fulton, HNIS

5. "Separating Nutrition Information From Misinformation," by Myrtle Hogbin, HNIS

6. "Good Food Choices on a Limited Budget," by Suzanne J. Fundingsland, ES

7. "Bringing Nutrition to Life in New York's Schools," by Christine M. Olson and Patricia F. Thonney, Cornell Univ.

PART III. Safe Food Handling for Optimum Nutrition

1. "Food Safety at Home" by Susan Conley, FSIS, Elizabeth Andress, ES, and Mark Tamplin, FL (Safe food handling is a part of good nutrition. Includes education, specific target groups, meat and poultry hotline)

   --Sidebar: "Food Safety for the Immune-Compromised, Elderly, and Others with Special Needs

   --Sidebar: "Safe Food Handling for Children"

PART IV. The Cutting Edge of Nutrition Research

1. "A History of Nutrition Research (1894-1990)," by Gerald F. Combs, University of Southern Mississippi

2. "Recent Advances in Maternal and Infant Nutrition," by Nancy F. Butte, Children's Nutrition Research Center, Baylor College of Medicine

3. "Recent Advances in Nutrition: From Adolescence to Adulthood," by William W. Wong, Children's Nutrition Research Center, Baylor College of Medicine

4. "Nutrition and Cardiovascular Fitness," by F. W. Thye, VPI Blacksburg

5. "Maintaining a Strong Skeleton," by Connie M. Weaver, Purdue University

6. "Nutrition and a Robust Immune System," by Tim R. Kramer, ARS

7. "Energy Metabolism," by Joan M. Conway, ARS

8. "Bioavailability: How the Nutrients in Food Become Available to Our Bodies," by David S. Wilson, University of Nevada, and Andrew J. Clifford, University of California

9. "Nutrition, Brain Function, and Behavior," by James G. Penland, ARS

10. "Nutritional Needs of the Elderly," by Irwin H. Rosenberg, Human Nutrition Research Center on Aging, Tufts University

11. "Food Components That Contribute to Health: Analysis of Foods and Dissemination of Data," by Ruth Matthews, HNIS, and Gary Beecher, ARS

12. "Research Is Ongoing," by Lois Davis, CSRS

PART V. Domestic Food Assistance Programs

1. "Healthy Children Ready To Learn," by Stanley C. Garnett, FNS

2. "Food and Nutrition Service Programs Serving Special Populations," by Philip K. Cohen, FNS

3. "A Sturdy Safety Net--Food Stamps," by Richard G. Woods and Carol S. Stobaugh, FNS

4. "Helping Low-Income Americans with USDA Commodities," by Alberta C. Frost, FNS

5. "Gleaning To Feed Low-Income People," by Nancy Leidenfrost, ES

PART VI. International Nutrition: Focus on Developing Countries

1. "Nutritional Status of People in Developing Countries," by Arthur J. Dommen, ERS

2. "Composition of Diets in Nutrient-Deficient Countries," by Stacey Rosen and Linda Scott, ERS

3. "Dysfunctional Food Economies: The Case of the Republics of the Former USSR," by Bill Liefert, ERS

4. "The Role of Trade and Food Aid in Meeting Global Food Needs," by Gene A. Mathia, Nydia Rivera-Suarez, and Margaret Missiaen, ERS

5. "Prospects for Improving the Global Food Support System," by Cheryl Christensen, ERS, Dana Dalrymple, OICD, Carol Levin, OICD, and Roberta van Heaften, OICD

Mr. DURBIN. How does the topic of nutrition relate to the mandate that the Yearbook provide information of interest to the farmer?

Ms. WEBB. The topic of nutrition has definite implications for farmers, since it includes a discussion of recent and likely trends in the demand for various foods. Also, nutrition is of personal interest to most Americans including farmers; following good nutrition guidance will help improve farmers' health, longevity, and quality of life. The topic also reflects the broader mission of USDA which relates to feeding people.

USDA MATCHING AGREEMENTS

Mr. DURBIN. Under the Computer Matching and Privacy Protection Act of 1988 USDA has entered into three matching agreements to identify employees who may owe the Federal government money. Two of these agreements, one with the Postal Service and one with the Department of Defense, match the names of delinquent debtors against the payroll records of 850,000 postal employees and 10 million records maintained by the Defense Manpower Data Center. Both agreements were estimated to save the government $1 million and $1.5 million respectively. A third agreement entered into with the Department of Housing and Urban Development would give agencies and lenders access to the Credit Alert Interactive Voice Response System. Access would be used to prescreen direct loan and loan guarantee applicants for delinquency in paying a debt owed to or insured by the Federal government. The estimated savings from this agreement were not known at last year's hearing. Tell us the status of these agreements and what the actual costs and savings have been to date.

Ms. WEBB. For the record, I would like to reiterate that the agreement with the Department of Defense was estimated to save $2.5 million, instead of the reported $1.5 million. Collections under that program thus far, and the one with the Postal Service have totaled $727,155. Costs under the agreements, however have been $230,606, resulting in a net savings of $496,549. The projection currently for additional savings under the programs is estimated at $5.5 million. As for the Credit Alert Interactive Voice Response System—CAIVRS—USDA still has no savings to report, since the Department has not yet begun reporting CAIVRS delinquencies into the system or screening applicants against the system. USDA expects to activate the CAIVRS agreement in about 3 months.

Mr. DURBIN. Have you or do you plan to enter into any additional agreements?

Ms. WEBB. During the current fiscal year, USDA plans to enter into three additional matching programs for debt-collection or other purposes, all involving USDA's Food and Nutrition Service—FNS. One proposed program is a match between USDA's FNS, and all 50 States and three jurisdictions currently operating a food stamp program. Known as the "Disqualified Recipient System," the computer matching program will enable the Department to assist States in identifying individuals who have been disqualified from food stamp program participation. The program will ultimately allow States to assign the appropriate penalty period of ineligibility for persons found to have committed program fraud or other violations. The two other programs involving FNS will be conducted for debt-collection, salary-offset purposes with the Department of Defense and with the U.S. Postal Service—USPS. In addition this year, USDA intends to renew the existing agreements.

JOINT U.S./RUSSIA PUBLICATION ON SOIL AND WATER CONSERVATION

Mr. DURBIN. A cooperative agreement to develop a joint United States and Russia publication on soil and water conservation became void with the breakup of the Soviet Union. As I understand it there was to be 10 articles from each side and USDA has sent its completed articles to Moscow. What is the status of this issue? Will USDA publish its articles without Russia's input?

Ms. WEBB. The Office of Public Affairs has ten chapters from the Russian Academy of Agricultural Sciences after an extended delay following the breakup of the former Soviet Union. The Russian chapters are being reviewed by Soil Conservation Service specialists for any questions and clarifications that may be needed. After the articles have received editorial clearance, they will be submitted for final translation. Then, USDA will publish the articles with Russian chapters.

TRANSFERS FROM OTHER AGENCIES

Mr. DURBIN. Update the table that appears on page 10 of last year's hearing record showing reimbursements from other USDA agencies to include fiscal year 1992 actuals and fiscal year 1993 estimates.

Ms. WEBB. I will be glad to provide the requested information.

[The information follows:]

REIMBURSEMENTS TO OPA FROM OTHER USDA APPROPRIATIONS
(In thousands of dollars)

	1989	1990	1991	1992	1993	1994
Agricultural Cooperative Service	48	32	76	64	65	142
Agricultural Marketing Service	179	139	87	105	104	77
Agricultural Research Service	427	357	387	466	393	393
Agricultural Stabilization and Conservation Service	68	413	81	223	211	167
Animal and Plant Health Inspection Service	367	946	286	366	339	228
Cooperative State Research Service	105	31	103	110	109	109
Departmental Administration	109	99	134	77	75	71
Economics Management Staff	90	19	78	57	55	50
Economics Research Service	79	75	53	47	46	57
Extension Service	228	60	137	149	135	136
Farmers Home Administration	297	184	313	293	280	334
Federal Crop Insurance Corporation	5	9	3	82	80	79
Federal Grain Inspection Service	26	16	29	7	7	6
Food and Nutrition Service	236	406	231	428	405	527
Food Safety Inspection Service	262	126	199	204	199	193
Foreign Agricultural Service	180	258	205	183	175	194
Forest Service	940	439	977	1291	1262	1273
Graduate School	2	2	4	0	2	2
Human Nutrition Information Service	38	17	39	35	34	35
National Agricultural Library	79	15	52	50	49	55
National Agricultural Statistics Service	11	10	7	12	11	10
Office of Budget and Program Analysis	55	4	6	5	5	5
Office of Public Affairs	331	231	361	329	309	285
Office of the Inspector General	37	9	18	40	39	40
Office of International Cooperation and Development	9	10	9	6	7	7
Office of the General Counsel	4	17	8	8	7	6
Office of the Secretary	58	34	40	35	29	30
Office of Transportation	9	4	10	0	0	2
Packers and Stockyards Administration	10	4	4	11	11	12
Rural Electrification Administration	20	20	20	15	17	16
Science and Education Administration	11	8	7	0	0	0
Soil Conservation Service	351	513	578	436	402	436
World Agricultural Outlook Board	11	7	13	56	55	42
Non USDA	47	38	36	50	48	49
Total	4,729	4,552	4,591	5,240	4,965	5,068

PHOTO SERVICES REIMBURSEMENT

Mr. DURBIN. Reimbursement from other USDA agencies for photo services increased 23 percent in fiscal year 1992. What do you attribute this increase to?

Ms. WEBB. The 23 percent increase in fiscal year 1992 represents an increase in requests for services rather than a major increase in the cost of services.

EDUCATIONAL VIDEOS

Mr. DURBIN. The Video and Teleconference Division produces educational videos for the agencies use. One example of such is a tape entitled, "The WIC Connection," a training video to help WIC program staff enhance their capabilities related to substance abuse and screening. How much was reimbursed to OPA for educational videos?

Ms. WEBB. OPA receives no reimbursements to its appropriated funds for educational videos produced by the Video and Teleconference Division. Costs for such projects are billed directly to the requesting agency through the Division's working capital fund operation. The Video and Teleconference Division functions as the central facility serving needs of all 42 agencies and staff offices of USDA.

MEDIA SERVICES

Mr. DURBIN. Were any new media services provided in fiscal year 1992?

Ms. WEBB. The AgNewsFAX system, which enables news media to quickly obtain USDA news releases, and other news materials by fax machine was expanded by eight lines. The additional capacity has allowed us to offer this service to agricultural as well as consumer organizations, and others.

Mr. DURBIN. Were any previous services deleted? If so, what was the reason for deleting them?

Ms. WEBB. No previous services were deleted.

PRESS RELEASES

Mr. DURBIN. Please update the table that appears on page 12 of last year's hearing record showing the number of press releases issued by your office to include fiscal year 1992.

Ms. WEBB. I will be glad to update the table.

[The information follows:]

Number of News Releases Issued by the Office of Public Affairs

Calendar Years 1985–92:	*Amount*
1985	1,358
1986	1,300
1987	1,616
1988	1,720
1989	1,688
1990	1,693
1991	1,442
1992	1,366

NATIVE AMERICANS

Mr. DURBIN. How much of the intergovernmental affairs budget is spent towards liaison with Native Americans?

Ms. WEBB. For fiscal year 1993 total expenses for the Native American program within the Office of Intergovernmental Affairs are expected to be $182,000 or about 38 percent of the total operating budget of $468,000.

OPA STAFFING

Mr. DURBIN. Please provide a breakout of staff and total budget for each of the five offices within OPA for fiscal year 1992.

Ms. WEBB. I will be glad to provide the breakout.

[The information follows:]

OFFICE OF PUBLIC AFFAIRS AVAILABLE FUNDING AND STAFF YEARS, FISCAL YEAR 1992

Office of the Director.—Provides program direction, policy and oversight. Staff, 31; budget, $4,116,954.

Office of Intergovernmental Affairs.—USDA liaison for State and local government officials, including Indian Tribal Councils and the White House Office of Intergovernmental Relations. Staff, 6; budget, $468,000.

Office of Public Liaison.—Develops and maintains liaison with the food and agriculture industry, trade and consumer associations, groups, or other specialized interests seeking interaction with USDA. Staff, 5; budget, $302,102.

Office of Press and Media Relations.—Directs information programs targeted to radio, television and print media. Staff, 25; budget, $1,808,054.

Office of Publishing and Visual Communication.—Plans, produces and distributes all print and video information materials. OPVC provides centralized services for photography, printing, publishing, video production, teleconference, design, and exhibits. Staff, 60; budget, $2,697.890.

OBJECT CLASSES

Mr. DURBIN. In looking at the object class table in your explanatory notes, I noticed a significant change in object classes 22, 24, 25, 26, and 31. Would you briefly describe the reason for these changes?

Ms. WEBB. In fiscal year 1993, object class 2200, transportation of things, reflects an increase to cover anticipated relocation costs related to filling vacant positions. Object class 2400, printing and reproduction, also reflects a higher level in fiscal year 1993 to provide sufficient funds to cover increased costs, such as inflation and labor, that are anticipated to be included in the bids for the Yearbook. In fiscal year 1992 the amount of accepted bid was lower than the original estimate. The fiscal year 1992 object class 2500, other services, included money for one-time refurbishing of OPA spacing, including the Visitor's Center, which is not required in fiscal year 1993. Fiscal year 1992 object class 2600, supplies, and object class 3100, equipment, are at a higher level than fiscal year 1993 due to the purchase of hardware and associated software to upgrade and expand computer systems as part of OPA's technology modernization.

PHOTOGRAPHY EQUIPMENT

Mr. DURBIN. The Photography Division has ordered new equipment designed to convert photographs, transparencies, and negatives to digital images. It is anticipated that this will provide greater accessibility to USDA's photographic library as well as a cost savings to the agency. What was the cost to design and purchase this equipment and how much will it save the agency annually?

Ms. WEBB. The new digital photo library system was designed by the staff of the Photography Division based on the knowledge and experience of two recently employed managers. The equipment cost was $56,030. While actual savings are small, the benefit is our ability to distribute a picture with a story quickly, greatly enhancing our ability to provide needed information to the media. Our savings are based on our ability to produce effectively and efficiently digitized pictures with messages.

OUTLOOK 1992 CONFERENCE

Mr. DURBIN. What was the cost of providing 15 hours of live satellite coverage of the Outlook '92 Conference? Who were the recipients of this coverage?

Ms. WEBB. The total cost of providing live satellite coverage of Outlook '92 was $28,619. Viewers of this coverage included farmers and Land Grant University audiences as well as overflow crowds locally in Washington. One segment featured live interactive questions from farmers directed to the panelists. All of the callers were farmers who were watching at their own sites.

Mr. DURBIN. Mr. Skeen?

Mr. SKEEN. Thank you, Mr. Chairman. I appreciate the fact that you have been here five weeks, but I think that you have had a very instantaneous grasp of what you are doing. You sound very competent, and I appreciate that fact.

However, we have been talking about something that is traditional, and we tend to live with something that is traditional, to keep it going. I believe we fail to reexamine what is the use, what is the purpose. I think the Chairman's position is well taken. Maybe it is time we did a review.

TIMELY RESPONSE TO NEGATIVE NEWS

My major interest is a quick and accurate response to negative news media comments that are mostly erroneous insofar as nutritional values or harms. The fear mongering that goes on about nutritional products or nutritional problems in the United States is rampant. And I don't know of any official organization other than your Department which should have a quick and accurate response. And how do you feel about that?

Ms. WEBB. Well, I share with you your concern about quick and speedy response.

As you know, since he was sworn in, the Secretary has spent a great deal of time on the E. coli issue and the whole food safety issue. What we are trying to put together through the reorganization is a speedier and more accurate information collection as well as delivery system for the Secretary. We must help American consumers feel confident that their food supply is safe, and we must warn them when it is not. And, that is a primary responsibility of this Secretary and of this office.

MEDIA CONTACTS

Mr. SKEEN. Do you have the resources to respond quickly when some news media or media story comes out in general circulation? Do you respond directly to the people who author the stories and so forth?

Ms. WEBB. Absolutely. We have a staff of about 25 people engaged in that response mechanism, responding through various mediums. We have daily radio responses. We have television programming, trying to get to some of these issues. And we have a press operation that responds to reporters' questions.

Mr. SKEEN. Do you need more money for this operation or have you had the ability to survey what you need for that kind of response and contact?

Ms. WEBB. Well, I always hate to turn down any possibility of more funding.

Mr. SKEEN. Well, any agency does. If you do that, you are going to be a phenomenon.

Ms. WEBB. In the area of response to the press reports, I think we are putting together a terrific team to handle that kind of immediate response. We could use additional funding for more public education on food safety.

Mr. SKEEN. Absolutely.

Ms. WEBB. And that is a different program.

Mr. SKEEN. But you need a survey of what you have available to you now before you decide that you need more.

Ms. WEBB. Exactly. I think we are in good shape for the next fiscal year. I think we have tremendous tools. We need to harness them. I don't think they have been harnessed or used efficiently in the past.

Mr. SKEEN. Well, as an example, the alar scare was inexcusable, totally false information, totally inaccurate, and it absolutely devastated one sector of the agricultural production in this country. Agriculture operations are so fragile because of the few numbers that are involved in agricultural production today and the extreme cost. It can be devastating to the industry.

And it doesn't bode well for the future because lenders don't want to risk lending money to operators in agriculture because of this foolishness that goes on in the media. So I appreciate the fact that you have taken the responsibility and that you do have that response capability.

PROMOTING NEW AGRICULTURAL PRODUCTS

Also, promoting new agricultural products is very important. Have you had a chance to summarize some of the successes that USDA has had in promoting new agricultural products, things that come out of the Ag research groups?

Ms. WEBB. I met yesterday with the science and education administrators at USDA to talk about how we promote our agricultural research, which is leading to some kinds of exciting new products that will help farmers diversify crops and bring their income up, which is a stated goal of the Secretary.

What we are trying to build into the reorganization is better marketing-across-the Department and across-agencies. We haven't been really good at marketing, although some agencies do a terrific job of communicating about their products.

Mr. SKEEN. You talk about the research, but you don't talk about the product and its availability.

Ms. WEBB. We don't sell it very well.

NEW MILK PRODUCTS

Mr. SKEEN. That is correct. For instance, we went to the southern regional research facility in New Orleans where they have developed all these new products incorporating the use of milk. Of course, to many it doesn't sound too appetizing, but it needs a little marketing. For instance, milk fizz didn't sound too appetizing but the orange juice and milk mixture was very good. USDA should enhance the availability and the palatability of milk products to the general public, because it has been extremely slow.

DEFATTED PEANUTS

And peanuts versus defatted peanuts. I had no idea that this was a Department of Agriculture product and I enjoyed them. The problem is nobody knows where they came from and that they are defatted because the marketing has been just rather nebulous.

Ms. WEBB. Exactly. And we have a product, flavor-saver tomatoes, that came out of the biotechnology.

Mr. SKEEN. That is one of the Chairman's favorites.

Ms. WEBB. Must be why I remembered it.

But that product needs marketing. And we have the capacity to do that at USDA. We have to develop the will.

SOURCE OF GOOD NUTRITIONAL INFORMATION

Mr. SKEEN. But we need to establish ourselves as a market resource for good nutritional information and somebody or someplace that the public can rely on, notwithstanding what you may read in the amazement media. And I am not knocking them, because they have got a white page to fill every day, yet, food safety has been one of their favorite targets. And it is so easy to scare someone these days because we are so used to having good products, well-packaged, at a very convenient price.

I think the information service coming out of the Department of Agriculture is an extremely important part of USDA, and I appreciate the job that you are doing and the insights you are taking with it. Thank you.

Ms. WEBB. I appreciate that, thanks.

Mr. DURBIN. I want to just echo my colleague's statements. You can't pick up a publication, whether it is Reader's Digest or one of the supermarket tabloids, that doesn't jump all over U.S. Department of Agriculture research. We have to be much more aggressive. And I really hope, if you do nothing else while you are there, that you can get people thinking in the Department about being more aggressive about talking about the positive aspects of what the Department does.

Everybody just giggled their heads off when Ross Perot told his joke about the USDA employee crying because his farmer died. People weren't giggling when the E. coli problem broke out in the

State of Washington and USDA had to come to the rescue and try to find a way to make sure that families across America were protected from that sort of tragedy. That is, I assume, your major responsibility, the image and message of the Department. We want to work with you. We have some rather dim bulbs here in Congress who like to jump all over Ag research, and Mr. Skeen and I are trying to do our best to work on them as well.

Mr. SKEEN. Trying to up their wattage.

SALES PRICE OF YEARBOOK

Mr. DURBIN. We are trying. I am not sure we can do it.

Let me ask you one last question for the record. What do these Ag Yearbooks cost a person who contacts the Government Printing Office with a request to purchase one?

Ms. WEBB. I think they are $14.00 now.

Mr. DURBIN. $14.00?

Ms. WEBB. I believe that is the correct price. It has been going up, which may have something to do with its sales.

Mr. DURBIN. Provide a table showing the sales price for each fiscal year 1988 through 1992.

Ms. WEBB. I will be glad to provide the requested information.

[The information follows:]

SALES PRICES OF THE YEARBOOK OF AGRICULTURE

(As established by the Superintendent of Documents)

Year:	*Sales price*
1988	$9.50
1989	10.00
1990	10.00
1991	12.00
1992	14.00

Mr. DURBIN. Incidentally, back in 1965 it was $2 or $3, but I am sure the price of a stamp was pretty low at that point, too. We are probably talking about revenue in the range of $40,000 or $50,000 a year for the yearbook.

Ms. WEBB. You are absolutely right. This is not a hot seller.

Mr. DURBIN. That is what I need to know.

Thank you Mr. Skeen, and thank you, the panel, for your testimony. We will be back in touch with you.

Ms. WEBB. Thank you. Anything I can do to further your study of the yearbook, please let me know.

Mr. DURBIN. By the time you have been there 10 weeks, you are really going to be cooking.

[The biographical sketch and prepared statement follow:]

BIOGRAPHY:

ALI WEBB
DIRECTOR OF PUBLIC AFFAIRS, OFFICE OF PUBLIC AFFAIRS
U. S. DEPARTMENT OF AGRICULTURE

Aileen (Ali) Webb was appointed as director of public affairs for the U. S. Department of Agriculture on March 22, 1993, by Secretary of Agriculture Mike Espy. In this position, Ms. Webb is responsible for USDA's communications, public liaison and intergovernmental affairs operations. She is responsible for development and dissemination of information concerning USDA policies and programs to the news media; constituent organizations of farmers, consumers, environmentalists, etc.; commodity groups; and liaison with State agricultural departments, Indian Tribes and public groups.

Before joining USDA, Ms. Webb served as associate director for the League of Conservation Voters--a nonprofit, non-partisan national environmental organization--from September 1989 to January 1993. In that position she managed the organization's nationwide political and communications program and edited such publications as "Vote for the Earth and League of Conservation Voters' Guide to the Election."

During 1988 and 1989, Ms. Webb worked as a research fellow and teaching assistant at the Barone Center for Press, Politics and Public Policy at Harvard University's Kennedy School for Government at Cambridge, Massachusetts. She also taught a course on political communication at Emerson College in Boston during 1989.

From 1987 to 1988, she served as national press secretary for the "Dick Gephardt for President" campaign. She worked as press secretary for Los Angeles Mayor Tom Bradley from 1980 to 1987. Prior to this, she worked as a reporter for the "Eagle", a daily newspaper serving central Texas.

Ms. Webb, a native of California, holds a bachelors degree in journalism from Stanford University, and a master of public administration degree from Harvard University's Kennedy School of Government.

Ms. Webb's parents, Virginia and Richard Webb, raised her and two brothers in South Pasadena, California. Her grandparents, Ed and Eda Webb were active ranchers in San Joaquin Valley of California.

Ms. Webb and her husband, Keith Kehlbeck, reside in Silver Spring, Maryland.

OFFICE OF PUBLIC AFFAIRS

Statement of Ali Webb, Director of Public Affairs
before the Subcommittee on Agriculture, Rural Development,
Food and Drug Administration, and Related Agencies

Mr. Chairman and members of the Subcommittee, I am pleased to appear before you to discuss the fiscal year 1994 request for the Department of Agriculture's Office of Public Affairs.

Our mission is very straightforward. The Office of Public Affairs has the responsibility to communicate the policies, programs and activities of USDA to the public. The channels of communication, the medium and methods of information delivery, the role of media and interest groups are the challenging part of what we do with our budget dollars.

Under President Clinton's directive to "re-invent government", the Office of Public Affairs is a full participant in Secretary Espy's reorganization plans for USDA. In fact, I am confident that the Office of Public Affairs will lead the way to the new USDA created by Secretary Espy.

The Secretary's charge to the Office of Public Affairs is to create an office which communicates clearly and consistently with our audience in the most cost-effective way possible.

To that end, we are examining every channel and method of communication we now use, from the books we publish, like the Yearbook of Agriculture, to the television programming we produce three times a week and the range of information products in between. It is an exciting time of change as we begin to streamline the Department's communications structure.

In the middle of meeting the challenge of creating a new Office of Public Affairs, we are performing our mission every day. To coordinate the communications of 42 separate agencies and offices, the Office of Public Affairs has budgeted 156 staff years. Our staff works out of the main USDA headquarters in Washington, D.C.

The Office of Public Affairs has state of the art, sophisticated communications ability. In addition to the traditional delivery systems of the printed press release, we have the AGFAX system which allows us to reach out electronically to news organizations. We have production facilities for radio and television products which are competing in today's electronic world and global village.

One of the most interesting parts of the Office of Public Affairs is the Video and Teleconference Division which has pioneered the use of satellite technology in directly reaching consumer and farmer clientele and field staffs with critical information in all 50 states. For example, a national meeting of the Cooperative Extension system held via satellite originated from USDA's studio and included live guests from studios in Denver, CO., and Madison, WI. Presenters from all three sites were linked in the broadcast with live audio questions from viewers throughout the nation. Using satellite technology allows USDA to compete in the time sensitive information marketplace.

We have the capacity to send our information around the country and to bring together people from around the world through our teleconferencing facility. But, this is only one of the top notch service divisions at the Office of Public Affairs.

We use every medium available to communicate to our audiences. I say audiences because, as you know, the Department touches many people from the farmer in the field to the food stamp recipient to the child in the school cafeteria. The multiplicity of audiences require a variety of OPA services. We design our products to reach specific target audiences.

For example, some may get their news primarily from trade publications so we provide specific information to that information channel. Much of what we do at USDA is of interest to the general public and we communicate through traditional general interest sources like newspapers, radio and television news.

-- With "USDA Radio Newsline," we have a 24-hour radio service which carries five to ten current news items. Radio stations access the playback machines via telephone, recording the material for later use in their broadcasts. A number of agricultural networks of up to 150 affiliated stations each are regular users of the service.

-- With "USDA Television News Service" we provide news actualities. The items are distributed by satellite on Thursday evening and Saturday morning, and repeated Monday morning. Feature subjects are wide ranging and include topics such as marketing, consumer interests, rural development, nutrition, conservation, forestry, environment, economics, production agriculture and international trade.

-- In order to keep in step with changes and improvements in technology, our Photography Division can now convert photographs, transparencies, and negatives to digital images capable of being stored as digital files, and transmitted via modem to client agencies, the media, or to a satellite for greater media access.

These examples demonstrate that the Office of Public Affairs clearly has the technology to fulfill our interactive information mission. With a successful reorganization, we will use our technology even more effectively.

I invite the members of this Committee to come and visit the teleconferencing studio, design shop, news or television division to see first-hand the kind of communication tools we have at USDA. They belong to you, and your constituents. Although we use the media as a primary channel to reach the public, we also reach out to particular interest and trade groups as part of our public liaison function. A separate and very important unit under Public Affairs is Intergovernmental Affairs which is charged with coordination of our programs with local, state and tribal governments.

Fiscal Year 1994 Budget Request

The Office of Public Affairs is requesting $9.553 million for fiscal year 1994. This represents an increase of $160,000, or 1.7 percent over our fiscal year 1993 appropriation.

This increase is composed of $168,000 for annualization of the fiscal year 1993 pay raise and $49,000 for non-pay inflation; partially offset by a decrease of $56,000 for administrative efficiency and $1,000 for the FTS reduction.

We are actively engaged in a process to do more with what we now have. We fully expect that our reorganization efforts will allow us to enhance information delivery to the American public while reducing total costs. We will keep the Congress informed of these reorganization efforts within USDA.

This concludes my statement, Mr Chairman. I will be pleased to respond to any questions.

OFFICE OF PUBLIC AFFAIRS

Purpose Statement

The Office of Public Affairs (OPA) was established by the Secretary of Agriculture on October 1, 1989, under the Reorganization Plan 2 of 1953 (7 U.S.C. 2201).

The Office of Public Affairs provides leadership, expertise, and counsel for the development of public affairs strategies which are vital to the overall formulation, awareness, and acceptance of U.S. Department of Agriculture programs and policies. OPA serves as the principal USDA contact point for dissemination of consistent, timely information.

The two major programs are:

1. Public Affairs. Provides direction, leadership, and balance in the development and delivery of useful information through all media to the public on USDA's involvement in all areas of agriculture, including: research, educational and regulatory activities; nutrition, conservation and farm programs; forestry and international agriculture. It also serves as the focal point for liaison between the Department and the public, including the many associations and organizations representing America's food and fiber system, with emphasis on policy education and direction.

2. Intergovernmental Affairs. Directs and coordinates all programs involving the implementation of USDA policies and procedures applicable to the Department's intra and intergovernmental relations. Also, coordinates USDA's Native American and Alaskan Native assistance programs.

The Office of Public Affairs also provides centralized services financed through the Working Capital Fund in the areas of video and teleconference, and design and exhibits. Other centralized services are provided by the photography, printing, and publishing units. The agency is located in Washington, D.C. As of September 30, 1992, there were 138 full-time permanent employees and 6 other than full-time permanent employees.

OFFICE OF PUBLIC AFFAIRS

Available Funds and Staff-Years

1992 Actual and Estimated, 1993 and 1994

Item	1992 Actual Amount	1992 Actual Staff Years	1993 Estimated Amount	1993 Estimated Staff Years	1994 Estimated Amount	1994 Estimated Staff Years
Direct Appropriation...	$9,393,000	114	$9,393,000	127	$9,553,000	127
Obligations Under Other USDA Appropriations:						
Agency Photo Service...	695,879	--	574,000	--	572,000	--
Admin. Support to Working Capital Fund..	63,935	2	69,000	2	72,000	2
Total, Reimbursements..	759,814	2	643,000	2	644,000	2
Working Capital Fund:						
Video & Teleconference and Visual Design Services..............	4,479,874	23	4,322,000	27	4,424,000	27
Total, Working Capital Fund.................	4,479,874	23	4,322,000	27	4,424,000	27
Total, Other USDA Appropriations........	5,239,688	25	4,965,000	29	5,068,000	29
Total, Agriculture Appropriations........	14,632,688	139	14,358,000	156	14,621,000	156
Non-Federal Funds:						
Sale of Photos & Slides	10,885	--	10,000	--	10,000	--
Total, Office of Public Affairs...............	14,643,573	139	14,368,000	156	14,631,000	156

OFFICE OF PUBLIC AFFAIRS

Permanent Positions by Grade and Staff-Year Summary

1992 and Estimated 1993 and 1994

Grade	1992 Headquarters	1993 Headquarters	1994 Headquarters
ES-4	1	1	1
ES-2	3	3	3
ES-1	2	1	1
GS/GM-15	15	16	16
GS/GM-14	33	33	33
GS/GM-13	13	16	16
GS-12	20	20	20
GS-11	11	13	13
GS-9	13	17	17
GS-8	5	5	5
GS-7	15	16	16
GS-6	3	3	3
GS-5	6	6	6
GS-4	2	1	1
Upgraded Positions	5	5	5
Total Permanent Positions	147	156	156
Unfilled Positions end-of-year	-9	--	--
Total, Permanent Employment, end-of-year	138	156	156
Staff-Years: Ceiling	139	156	156

OFFICE OF PUBLIC AFFAIRS

CLASSIFICATION BY OBJECTS

1992 and Estimated 1993 and 1994

	1992	1993	1994
Personnel Compensation:			
Headquarters	$5,610,062	$6,509,000	$6,650,000
11 Total personnel compensation	5,610,062	6,509,000	6,650,000
12 Personnel Benefits..........	904,927	1,051,000	1,078,000
13 Benefits for former personnel.................	16,329	13,000	13,000
Total pers. comp & benefit....	6,531,318	7,573,000	7,741,000
Other Objects:			
21 Travel......................	69,182	75,000	75,000
22 Transportation of things....	2,103	11,000	11,000
23.3 Communications, utilities, and misc. charges.........	378,953	390,000	387,000
24 Printing....................	594,035	726,000	723,000
25 Other services.............	762,142	508,000	506,000
26 Supplies and materials......	234,296	97,000	97,000
31 Equipment..................	457,540	13,000	13,000
Total other objects...........	2,498,251	1,820,000	1,812,000
Total direct obligations............	9,029,569	9,393,000	9,553,000
Position Data:			
Average Salary, ES positions.....	$93,738	$97,720	$98,480
Average Salary, GM/GS position...	$46,737	$49,348	$50,472
Average Grade, GM/GS positions...	11.29	11.30	11.30

OFFICE OF PUBLIC AFFAIRS

The estimates include appropriation language for this item as follows (new language underscored; deleted matter enclosed in brackets):

Office of Public Affairs

[Public Affairs]

For necessary expenses to carry on services relating to the coordination of programs involving public affairs, and for the dissemination of agricultural information and the coordination of information, work and programs authorized by Congress in the Department, [$8,925,000] and for programs involving intergovernmental affairs, and liaison within the executive branch, $9,553,000 including employment pursuant to the second sentence of Section 706(a) of the Organic Act of 1944 (7 U.S.C. 2225), of which not to exceed $10,000 shall be available for employment under 5 U.S.C. 3109, and not to exceed $2,000,000 may be used for farmers' bulletins and not fewer than two hundred thirty-two thousand two hundred and fifty copies for the use of the Senate and House of Representatives of part 2 of the annual report of the Secretary (known as the Yearbook of Agriculture) as authorized by 44 U.S.C. 1301: Provided, that in the preparation of motion pictures or exhibits by the Department, this appropriation shall be available for employment pursuant to the second sentence of section 706(a) of the Organic Act of 1944 (7 U.S.C. 2225).

[Intergovernmental Affairs]

[For necessary expenses for programs involving intergovernmental affairs, and liaison within the executive branch, $468,000.]

This change proposes in the Fiscal Year 1994 Budget to merge amounts appropriated to two accounts into a single appropriation.

OFFICE OF PUBLIC AFFAIRS

Appropriations Act, 1993	$9,393,000
Budget Estimate, 1994	9,553,000
Increase in Appropriation	+160,000

SUMMARY OF INCREASES AND DECREASES
(On basis of appropriation)

Item of Change	1993 Estimated	Pay Cost	Other Changes	1994 Estimated
Public Affairs	$8,925,000	+$158,000	-$8,000	$9,075,000
Intergovernmental Affairs	468,000	+10,000	--	478,000
Total Available	9,393,000	+168,000	- 8,000	9,553,000

PROJECT STATEMENT
(On basis of appropriation)

Item of Change	1992 Actual Amount	1992 Actual Staff-Years	1993 Estimated Amount	1993 Estimated Staff-Years	Increase or Decrease	1994 Estimated Amount	1994 Estimated Staff-Years
Public Affairs	$8,570,281	108	$8,925,000	121	+$150,000(1)	$9,075,000	121
Intergov. Aff.	459,288	6	468,000	6	+10,000(2)	478,000	6
Unobligated Balance	363,431		--	--	--	--	--
Total Appropriation	9,393,000	114	9,393,000	127	+160,000	9,553,000	127

EXPLANATION OF PROGRAM

The appropriation for the Office of Public Affairs funds the activities established pursuant to the relevant sections of Secretary's Memorandum No. 1927, dated October 5, 1977, and the authority contained in 5 U.S.C. 301 and Reorganization Plan No. 2 of 1953 (7 U.S.C. 2201). The activities carried out are as follows:

--Public Affairs - Provides leadership, expertise, and counsel for the development of public affairs strategies which are vital to the overall formulation, awareness, and acceptance of U.S. Department of Agriculture programs and policies. Public Affairs serves as the principal USDA contact point for dissemination of consistent, timely information.

--Intergovernmental Affairs - Directs and coordinates programs involving the implementation of USDA policies and procedures applicable to the Department's intergovernmental affairs and relations with other Departments.

JUSTIFICATION OF INCREASES AND DECREASES

(1) A net increase of $150,000 for Public Affairs:

(a) An increase of $49,000, which reflects a 2.7 percent increase in non salary costs.

(b) An increase of $158,000, which reflects the annualization of the fiscal year 1993 pay raise.

(c) A decrease of $56,000 for administrative efficiency.

Need for change. To promote the efficient use of resources for administrative purposes, in keeping with the President's Executive Order, total USDA baseline outlays for these activities will be reduced by 3 percent in FY 1994, 6 percent in FY 1995, 9 percent in FY 1996 and 14 percent in FY 1997.

Nature of change. To achieve the desired reduction, OPA will monitor the level of information support products in printing and visual services, and conduct a review of administrative support service charges.

(d) A decrease of $1,000 for FTS 2000 funding.

This decrease reflects lower long distance telecommunications prices due to price redeterminations in the FTS 2000 contracts.

(2) An increase of $10,000 for Intergovernmental Affairs:

(a) An increase of $10,000 which reflects the annualization of the fiscal year 1993 pay raise.

GEOGRAPHIC BREAKDOWN OF OBLIGATIONS AND STAFF YEARS
1992, and estimated 1993 and 1994

	1992		1993		1994	
	Amount	Staff Years	Amount	Staff Years	Amount	Staff Years
Washington, D.C.	$9,029,569	114	$9,393,000	127	$9,553,000	127
Unobligated balance	363,431	--	--	--	--	--
Total, Available or Estimate.......	9,393,000	114	9,393,000	127	9,553,000	127

OFFICE OF PUBLIC AFFAIRS

STATUS OF PROGRAM

The Office of Public Affairs (OPA) provides useful information to the people of the United States, assuring that relevant USDA decision making processes are open to the effective expression of informed public viewpoints. To achieve that objective, OPA reports through the various media and sometimes directly to farmers, consumers, business interests, special groups, and the general public regarding the Department's programs, policies, and activities. The information arising from these programs is intended to provide basic information for the various publics served by USDA. The success of Department initiatives often depends on the effectiveness of public affairs programs in creating national public awareness, understanding, and acceptance.

Activities under this appropriation are carried out through two major program areas: Public Affairs and Intergovernmental Affairs.

PUBLIC AFFAIRS

Current Activities:

OPA serves as the Department's clearinghouse for providing the media with current information about USDA's programs and policies in the form of news releases, news features and photo features, background statements, speeches, report summaries, and similar materials. OPA maintains continuous liaison with reporters, writers, editors, radio/television broadcasters, producers and specialized journalists. OPA monitors the activities of associations and organizations to assure appropriate information is available to USDA officials, and assists in the preparation of briefing information for the White House and the Secretary. In fiscal year 1992, OPA released 1,329 of the above mentioned items for national distribution, with most of those materials available both on paper as well as through electronic dissemination and by facsimile to reach a broader section of the public with greater speed.

OPA also works closely with the agencies of the Department in providing feedback to top level officials on what the popular and trade press are saying about USDA programs, policies and actions, including preparing a daily book of news clippings and wire stories.

"AG a.m.," a daily news digest that summarizes articles and editorials from news wires, national newspapers, news magazines and other key periodicals dealing with agriculture, is electronically prepared each weekday, via facsimile and in hard copy for nationwide early morning distribution to Department officials.

Both formal and informal training on how to deal with the media is provided to Department officials upon request, and coordination is routinely provided for top staff involved in news conferences, media briefings, and individual interviews.

OPA continues to use new technology to disseminate information. It is the first Federal agency to use a FAX-on-demand system to allow reporters, using voice prompts on a telephone, to request and receive on their fax machine news releases, features, and backgrounders on specific subjects. The service, called AgNewsFAX, allows a reporter to call 24 hours a day, 7 days a week and receive faxes of releases. These news releases are listed by number, subject or date. Backgrounders on issues, information in Spanish, and other categories of information will be available in FY 1993. The service will be extended to organizations and other members of the public.

OPA continues to offer and expand its Computerized Information Delivery Service (CIDS) for accessing USDA information by news media, various electronic information services, agricultural organizations, and other publics. This information includes national and regional press releases, economic and statistical reports, market reports, export trade leads, agricultural research briefs, and other information released by USDA.

OPA provides publishing and visual communication production services for the Department. This includes taking an exhibit, publication, or video project from concept development through such stages as planning and schedule construction, text or script development, photography or video coordination and acquisition, editorial review, design, layout and typesetting, video editing or preparation of material for printing, and finally, printing or video post production. We enable the agencies to fulfill their mission to provide information to the public.

The OPA's Office of Publishing and Visual Communication (OPVC) has provided leadership for the Department and for the Federal Government in evaluation and testing of teleconferencing technology and methods over the past several years. As a viable alternative to the expense of travel, USDA has brought together a wide spectrum of teleconferencing tools, from audio only, to compressed video through telephone lines, to interactive teleconferencing with the use of satellite support.

OPVC also works with USDA agencies to provide a broad selection of training and education for the public. Education materials and resources range from publications to visitors centers to audio visual projects and broadcast materials.

A primary function in OPVC is the distribution or retrieval of information or materials for use by the public and by other agencies. Both functions, distribution and retrieval, become more complex as information expands, but new technology is enhancing our ability to serve the public faster, more comprehensively, and more cost effectively.

The OPVC is both the production resource and the repository of much of the material developed by the Department and held in trust for use by the public. Beyond first dissemination, protection of those resources for reuse is an important facet of our program capability, particularly in the area of still photography.

OPA serves as USDA's central coordinating unit for the increasing number of requests filed by news media and other publics for information under the Freedom of Information Act, and its amendments (Privacy Act and Computer Matching and Privacy Protection Act). Departmental regulations and guidelines are updated to conform with amendments to the law or new directives from the Department of Justice and Office of Management and Budget. A Data Integrity Board, required by the Computer Matching Act of 1988, has been established and is chaired by the Director of OPA.

OPA provides a variety of services, such as:

PUBLIC LIAISON (OPL)--Develops and maintains liaison with farm, trade and consumer associations, and with organizations representing women, minorities, educational interests and other specialized audiences. OPL provides information on Department policies and programs. They also plan and coordinate information and educational programs in cooperation with outside groups that want to play a role in informing and educating the public about USDA programs and services. OPL takes part in national and other significant meetings and conferences to provide information about USDA and its programs.

RADIO--"USDA Radio Newsline" provides 24-hour availability of five to ten news items, many with voice actualities, each no longer than 60 seconds. They are recorded and made available at 5 p.m. EST each weekday except holidays. Stations access the playback machines via telephone, recording the material for later use in their broadcasts. A number of agricultural networks with up to 150 affiliated stations each are regular users of the service.

In addition, four weekly series are offered on audio cassette with accompanying cue sheets and are distributed to approximately 900 radio stations and networks. The four include "Consumer Time," five programs featuring food, marketing, clothing, pest control, gardening and other topics; "Agri-Tape," five programs including USDA News Highlights and interviews on major issues; "Agriculture USA," a 13-1/2 minute documentary program covering a wide range of food and agricultural subjects aimed at the general public; and "News Feature Five," five features which include research findings and activities about a broad range of subjects.

Hispanic Information Service is a weekly tape service mailed to stations. Offered on both audio cassette and reel-to-reel tape, it contains at least five programs varying from 30 seconds to 8 minutes in length. It is voiced in Spanish with the content aimed at concerns of the Hispanic audience addressed by USDA. It is provided to approximately 230 stations.

TELEVISION--"USDA Television News Service" provides news actualities of Department policy officials and subject matter specialists, and features. The items are distributed by satellite (Galaxy 6) on Thursday evening and Saturday morning, and repeated Monday morning. Feature subjects are wide ranging and include topics such as marketing, consumer interests, rural development, nutrition, conservation, forestry, environment, economics, production agriculture and international trade.

"Agriculture Update," a 5-minute news format program is produced every other week, and provides information about agricultural production programs.

"Research News Features" are 2- to 3-minute programs produced on location and cover developments in agricultural research.

PHOTOGRAPHY--OPA maintains the centralized USDA Photo Library of captioned black and white prints and color slides. These images illustrate the programs and activities of USDA agencies and cover subjects relating to agriculture, including food production, distribution, nutrition, marketing, food safety and inspection, conservation, and research. OPA provides photographic research services and distributes photographs to the news media free of charge and to the public for a nominal fee covering the cost of reproduction.

PHOTOJOURNALISM--OPA works with USDA agencies to develop and distribute to national and regional media, picture stories and illustrated press releases to inform the public of USDA programs, activities, and services available.

AUDIOVISUAL PRESENTATIONS--OPA works with USDA agencies to produce and distribute narrated slide presentations on various agricultural topics and programs. These are available as slide sets or video cassettes to educational organizations, industry, and the public for a nominal fee which covers the cost of reproduction.

Selected Examples of Recent Progress:

1992 YEARBOOK OF AGRICULTURE--The 1992 Yearbook of Agriculture, "**NEW CROPS, NEW USES, NEW MARKETS:** Industrial and Commercial Products from U.S. Agriculture," describes industrial uses for new crops, as well as innovative uses for traditional crops and animal products. It covers scientific and technical breakthroughs, commercial and marketing advances, and the benefits of using these natural products for producers, consumers, rural communities, and the environment.

The 1992 Yearbook offers information about "Products from Nontraditional Crops"--such as, guayule, crambe, industrial rapeseed, and lesquerella. And it describes "New Products from Traditional Crops"--such as ink from soybeans, industrial oils from seed crops, medicine from plants and dairy products, and biodegradable plastic from corn starch. Special emphasis is given to renewable fuels, products for food industries, environmental benefits, and the farmer's viewpoint on growing new industrial crops.

This 300-page hardcover anthology, released in December 1992, is illustrated with photographs and charts. Its primary distribution is free through Members of Congress.

JOINT UNITED STATES/RUSSIA PUBLICATION ON SOIL AND WATER CONSERVATION--OPA coordinated the development of a joint United States/Russian publication on soil and water conservation which was scheduled for release in the fall of 1992. The cooperative agreement under which the publication was initiated with the former Soviet Union became null and void upon the dissolution of the USSR, and attempts to ascertain the status of the Russian contribution to the project have been unsuccessful. The USDA articles are complete and have been sent to Moscow; we are awaiting the Russian contributions, which are overdue. If the Russian articles do not arrive in early 1993, we will encourage the USDA Soil Conservation Service to publish its portion as a stand-alone. The publication will provide a broad array of information on conservation-related subjects including wind erosion control, irrigation, soil erosion control systems, drainage, and resource inventories. It will be used by technical and scientific specialists in State and Federal agencies, universities, and organizations throughout the United States and the former Soviet Union.

OUTLOOK '92 CONFERENCE--Live via satellite coverage was provided nationwide for 15 hours of the Outlook '92 Conference held in USDA's Jefferson Auditorium. Satellite coverage included keynote sessions, but the entire conference was telecast live on USDA's internal video network. Departmental employees in the downtown complex and the New York Avenue location could watch sessions in their own conference rooms without competing for limited auditorium seating. For the first time, live questions were included from the satellite viewing audience during one session. Favorable response to this coverage has prompted plans for complete coverage of the Outlook '93 Conference. Through satellite technology, farmers, economists and others can now actively participate in this annual event from their own homes or universities.

WORLD FOOD DAY--The Office of Public Liaison coordinated World Food Day activities as the lead agency for the Federal Government on this project. More than 15 Federal agencies and departments participated. USDA developed and distributed a government-wide calendar of events planned for the day, and produced a color poster on World Food Day for use throughout the government and private sector. USDA hosted the Federal Government's opening ceremony for World Food Day with activities honoring the 1992 World Fpod Prize winners.

TAKE PRIDE IN AMERICA (TPIA)--This is a national public awareness campaign to reduce and promote wise use of our Nation's resources by renewing a national stewardship ethic, encouraging an attitude of individual responsibility and creating pride in our communities. The U.S. Department of Agriculture's mission in this effort, which is carried out by the Office of Public Liaison, is to increase the public awareness of our stewardship of natural, cultural, historic, and agricultural resources.

During fiscal year 1992, the Office of Public Liaison planned and coordinated the USDA's Take Pride in America Honor Awards Program, which recognized 11 individuals and groups for contributing time and talent in achieving TPIA projects.

The Office of Public Liaison also coordinated and staffed the "Take Pride" exhibit during the Future Farmers of America National Convention at Kansas City, Missouri, attended by 23,000 FFA members. Also, the same exhibit was displayed during the annual conference of the National Association of Conservation Districts in Reno, Nevada.

VIDEOCONFERENCING--Major videoconferences this year included four national events on key food or agricultural initiatives. The first was a national training and informational conference on the "Food Pyramid" for nutrition education specialists. Then Secretary of Agriculture Edward Madigan hosted two Satellite Town Meetings with farmers in Texas and Ohio. In January, farmers from Hale County, Texas met with the

Secretary and key staff members to ask questions about farm programs and critical issues in a two-way video conference. Also, in conjunction with the Ohio Beef Expo in March, the Secretary again met via satellite with farmers at six Ohio sites to focus on agricultural issues. This was a one-video, two-way audio conference. Both events were pilot tests of this technology to quickly and efficiently impart information and obtain feedback from farmers. Farmer reaction was positive in both States. Finally, a training course on Total Quality Management primarily designed for meat graders of the Agricultural Marketing Service drew participation at 10 sites nationwide.

EDUCATIONAL VIDEOS--Major educational videos produced by the Video and Teleconference Division this year included: Timber Theft-Heeding the Warning Signs, a video designed to educate law enforcement officers and Forest Service staff about methods of theft detection and prevention in National Forests; The WIC Connection, a training video to help Women, Infants, and Children (WIC) program staff nationwide to enhance their capabilities related to substance abuse and screening; Determining and Verifying Eligibility-National School Lunch and Breakfast Programs, an informational video providing detailed training to school food authorities nationwide; ASCS County Committee, an educational video that demonstrates the key responsibilities and confidentiality required of citizens who serve in these important positions nationwide. Lifelines, an educational video produced last year for the Food and Nutrition Service, earned a Golden Eagle Award this year from the Council on International Theatrical Events (CINE) and merited "honorable mention" in the Gold Screen Awards presented by the National Association of Government Communicators.

AUDIOCONFERENCING--A new milestone was reached this year. Total number of audioconferences topped 10,000 since the service was begun in 1985. Last year, a total of 2,038 conferences were handled for USDA agencies.

USDA RADIO AND TV AWARDS--One of our Radio reporter/producers won a Silver medal from the International Radio Festival competition in New York for "The Bacteria Caper," a feature on food safety. One of our television reporter/producers won a Gold Screen Award from the National Association of Government Communicators for his television series on Iowa farming.

RADIO CASSETTE SERVICE--A variety of topics were featured on USDA Radio's AGRICULTURE USA documentary series. Examples of the programs include: "Food Safety Confusion", "The New School Lunch Program", "Reflections of the Soviet Food Production System", "Living on Less" and "Trade Talk Update".

RADIO NEWSLINE SERVICE--The number of news items on the daily service during fiscal year 1992 totalled 2,127. The number of calls to the service totalled 19,349, both about the same as fiscal year 1991.

TELEVISION NEWS SERVICE--The number of news and feature items transmitted via satellite during the fiscal year totalled 757, up slightly from last year. The features produced by USDA's Television News Service covered topics of interest to both the agricultural community and consumers. Stories included topics such as an Agricultural Research Service program to interest high school students in science, the unveiling of the food guide pyramid, food safety for children, sharing agricultural marketing expertise with Poland, a joint CIS-US research project on mapping groundwater supplies, using and protecting Pacific Yew trees and farmer's conservation efforts to protect the environment.

MEDIA LIAISON--The USDA broadcasting booth was exhibited at the National Association of Farm Broadcasters Convention in Kansas City in November 1991. Previously the booth was exhibited at the September 1991 annual conference of the Radio/Television News Directors Association Meeting in Denver, Colorado. The booth provides opportunities for Radio/TV News Program Directors to learn about USDA Radio/Television programming.

LASER DISC PROJECT--In fiscal year 1992 the Photography Division completed acquisition of imaging and authoring stations for laser discs. These are online and plans are underway for preparing materials for a second edition of the laser disc. This enables research of agricultural photography for and by the public and the media in a much more efficient and cost effective manner and offers access on a widespread basis through availability of the disc in libraries and other sources.

DIGITAL IMAGING--In order to keep in step with changes and improvements in technology Photography Division has designed and ordered equipment for converting photographs, transparencies, and negatives to digital images capable of being stored as digital files, transmitted via modem to client agencies, the media, or to a satellite for greater media access. The new equipment should be up and running early in fiscal year 1993. This can provide both greater accessibility to images in the USDA photographic library and also offers cost savings, since, now, the processing of film often can be eliminated as a step in the printing process.

CLIMATE CONTROLLED STORAGE--Construction has been completed on Photography Division's new climate controlled storage room. The new facility will give the Division archival approved storage for valuable original photography materials. This storage is available to all agencies photographic functions and provides centralized access for cross-agency and public utilization of materials.

GRAPHIC DESIGN--After a comparable slow start in the fiscal year a sizeable amount of visual requests were handled by the division including many sensitive issues. Highlights of accomplishments were: Dietary Guidelines and Food Pyramid, Spotted Owl and Timber-Cutting Material, Marketing Initiatives for Federal Crop Insurance, Scenic Byways and Special Places brochures, Universal Access for Handicapped People material, market development packages for Foreign Agriculture Service, numerous nutrition guides in various languages, hurricane, fire, drought, flood and disaster relief material, brochure packages for volunteers and human resources on the national forests, endangered and threatened species brochures, rural development material, food safety initiatives, Fire Coordination Center graphics, range management, minerals initiative, Passport in Time, and Smokey Bear materials.

EXHIBITS--Fiscal year 1992 was a record year for exhibits, displays and visitor centers. Highlights include: Wallowa-Whitman Visitor Center in Oregon, Big Horn Visitor Center in Wyoming, Mt. Rogers Visitor Center in Virginia, Mono Lake Visitor Center in California, the Research Center in Maryland, and the Milking Parlor at Beltsville.

Traveling and temporary exhibits include: Marketing Crop Insurance, Wildlife and Fisheries, Food Safety, Soil and Water Conservation, Nutrition, Water Quality, Engineering, Access Roads, Scientist of the Year, Beagle Brigade, America the Beautiful, Poultry Marketing, Recruitment exhibits, Cattle Diseases, Interpretive Trail displays, Old Growth Forest, FmHA Guaranteed Loans, Careers in Agriculture, Global Forestry, Resource Planning, Recreation in the National Forests and Scenic Rivers.

The following table provides workload data relating to the publications activity:

Publications Printed	FY 1991	FY 1992
Printing through main GPO or on contract	6,225	7,380
Miscellaneous orders placed through GPO's Rapid Response Center (RRC), GPO's Regional Printing Procurement Offices (RPPO), Federal Prison Industries (Unicor), and Commerce	2,050	1,699
Composition (In-House USDA)	1,280	996
Printing through USDA Duplicating Facility		
Miscellaneous orders placed through USDA Facility	128	143
Miscellaneous orders reviewed and cleared for printing in USDA Facility	871	1,059
Waivers for jobs not presented to OPA for clearance	4,337	4,295
Total Printing Orders	14,891	15,572

Popular Publications Distributed* (numbers in millions)	FY 1991	FY 1992
Total stock at start of year	2.38	2.170
New publications printed	.28	.005
Reprints and revisions printed	1.39	1.260
Total Available for distribution	4.05	3.435
Stock disposed of	.52	--
Stock at end of year	2.17	2.090
Total distributed	1.36	1.345

*Includes Farmer's Bulletins, Home and Garden Bulletins, Leaflets, Fact Sheets, and Yearbook Separates.

Publications Reviewed	FY 1991	FY 1992
New and Revised Manuscripts	433	371
Slight Revision and Reprints	124	86
Total Number of Reviews	557	457

Telephone Calls	FY 1992
Telephone calls for information/publications from Members of Congress.	10,073
Telephone calls handled by Visitors Information Center Staff.	59,800

INTERGOVERNMENTAL AFFAIRS

Current Activities:

The Office of Intergovernmental Affairs (OIA) maintains USDA liaison with The White House and State and local government officials including Indian Tribal Councils and the organizations representing these officials and councils. Specifically, the Office of Intergovernmental Affairs responds to inquiries and requests from State and local government officials either directly, or through the appropriate Government agency, as well as fax pertinent USDA news releases to these officials.

In the role of liaison, the Office of Intergovernmental Affairs seeks State and local officials' opinions regarding current and pending Federal actions which will affect agriculture and rural America.

Coordinates the notification process for "Disaster Designation" requests from Governors of the States.

In recognizing the long standing Federal Government policy regarding the government to government relationship with Indian Tribes, the Intergovernmental Affairs Office also maintains responsibility for directing and planning liaison with Native Americans with regard to delivery of USDA programs and services.

Selected Examples of Recent Progress:

OIA participated, when possible, in the annual regional meetings of the National Governors' Association, Council of State Governments, National Association of State Departments of Agriculture (NASDA), National Conference of State Legislatures, National Association of Counties, and National Association of Towns and Townships.

OIA received and disbursed, to appropriate agencies for their action, Western Governors Association and NASDA Resolutions. Their responses were sent back to OPA for consolidation and clearance by the Office of the General Counsel in time for NASDA's mid-year meeting and the Western Governors' Association annual meeting.

OIA submitted updated information to the Congressional Research Service on USDA programs which are beneficial to Native Americans. This report involved soliciting information from twelve separate agencies within USDA, and a detailed clearance process.

OIA has developed the Native American Working Group (NAWG) to coordinate and guide all USDA policies and programs regarding Native Americans. NAWG consists of senior USDA officials, and is responsible for providing advice and support to the Department in ensuring effective coordination and guidance of all USDA policies and programs regarding Native Americans. It has been responsible for the development of a number of outreach programs and other enhancements to agriculture program delivery to Native Americans.

A booklet called "Guide to USDA Programs for Native Americans" was released in the fall of 1992. It explains USDA programs available to Native Americans and provides guidance on how to participate in them. Over 14,000 copies were printed and are being distributed.

Through OIA, USDA has been represented at and participated in meetings of the Intertribal Agriculture Council, Intertribal Timber Council, the National Association of Food Distribution Programs on Indian Reservations, the Southwest Indian Agriculture Association, and others.

THURSDAY, APRIL 22, 1993.

OFFICE OF THE GENERAL COUNSEL

WITNESSES

J. MICHAEL KELLY, ACTING GENERAL COUNSEL
J. ROBERT FRANKS, DEPUTY GENERAL COUNSEL
WILLIAM PERRELLI, III, DIRECTOR, ADMINISTRATION AND RESOURCE MANAGEMENT
CHARLENE BUCKNER, BUDGET AND FINANCE ANALYST
STEPHEN B. DEWHURST, BUDGET OFFICER, DEPARTMENT OF AGRICULTURE

OPENING REMARKS

Mr. DURBIN. From the Office of the General Counsel we have J. Michael Kelly, the Acting General Counsel; J. Robert Franks, the Deputy General Counsel; William Perrelli, the Director of Administration and Resource Management; Charlene Buckner, the Budget and Finance Analyst; and Steve Dewhurst. Welcome.

Mr. SKEEN. I like to see Steve, change your seat over there.

Mr. DEWHURST. I didn't want to bother you, so I didn't move.

Mr. SKEEN. Steve, you are a joy to work with.

Mr. DURBIN. Mr. Kelly, we have your statement. If you would like to give us your closing argument here?

Mr. KELLY. I would, indeed—as long as Mr. Dewhurst is that far away and doesn't get to participate.

Mr. DURBIN. That is right. Hostile witness, huh?

You may proceed.

Mr. KELLY. Much of the time.

INTRODUCTION

Mr. Chairman, I am very pleased to be able to appear before this Subcommittee this morning to discuss the fiscal 1994 appropriations request for the Office of the General Counsel.

ORGANIZATION

As our statement indicates and you are aware, OGC is a full-service law office which provides all legal advice and services to the Secretary and all the offices and agencies of the Department. We provide these services principally through 11 divisions in Washington, D.C., and through 22 field offices around the country. We employ approximately 260 attorneys and about 146 support personnel.

STATUS OF FISCAL YEAR 1993

For fiscal year 1993, our appropriation is $24,554,000, which is the same amount which was appropriated for fiscal 1992. As you also know, we expect to receive approximately $1.1 million for providing legal services for the Department's user fee programs.

Our funding level for 1993 has caused us to continue a number of austerity measures which we had initially implemented in fiscal 1992.

Because of these efforts, it is clear that we will be able to continue operating for the balance of this fiscal year without any additional belt tightening or any other severe dislocation. I don't mean to minimize the effects of these measures we have implemented. We have had to delay promotions, cancel attorney recruitment, elect not to replace employees who leave—except in very rare circumstances—eliminate cash awards and bonuses, and reduce expenditures in some other areas. And because of that, it is fairly clear that employee morale has suffered, and we are somewhat less able to provide the level of service that we have traditionally been able to do.

FISCAL YEAR 1994 BUDGET REQUEST

For fiscal year 1994, we are requesting $25,045,000 in direct appropriations. This request represents a net increase of $491,000 over the fiscal 1993 appropriation. That increase principally reflects the cost of annualization of the fiscal 1993 pay raise.

We are a staff agency, Mr. Chairman, and we operate no prpgrams which are separately funded. Consequently, approximately 91 percent of our budget consists of funds for personnel compensation. We have no way to absorb cuts below the level of our 1994 request without placing a severe strain on the office and adversely affecting its ability to provide services for the Department.

CLOSING REMARKS

I hope this committee will be able to fully fund OGC at the level of the President's request so that we can maintain our current employment levels and our current levels of service to the Secretary and the Department.

[CLERK'S NOTE.—The Acting General Counsel's prepared statement appears on pages 747 through 756. The budget explanatory notes for the General Counsel's office were received by the Committee on April 28, 1993 and appear on pages 757 through 780.]

USER FEES

Mr. DURBIN. Mr. Kelly, your appropriation tells part of the story, but, we are concerned about the other parts, like the amounts the OGC receives from user fees. Can you tell us what you anticipate receiving from user fees this fiscal year and what you estimate for next year?

Mr. KELLY. Mr. Chairman, we hope this year to receive $1.107 million from the Department's user fee accounts.

Those programs run a fair gamut. They include the Perishable Agricultural Commodities Act program, other Agricultural Marketing Service programs, a half dozen research and promotion programs, Animal and Plant Health Inspection Service programs, Federal Grain Inspection Service programs, and a small program operated by ASCS.

If our estimates are correct, the amounts that we expect to receive in fiscal 1993 total $1.107 million. That figure for fiscal year 1994 would be $1.448 million. Now those are fairly soft figures, Mr. Chairman. Those figures are based on our estimates of the costs that we incur in providing legal services in support of those USDA programs.

It is interesting to note, Mr. Chairman, that the overall costs of those programs for the Department, which are charged to the user industries, exceed $300 million. So the OGC portion of that—for fiscal year 1993, $1.1 million, and for fiscal year 1994, $1.448 million—is less than half of 1 percent of what the Department is charging the industry users under those programs.

Mr. DURBIN. In past years the cost of legal services has not been included in determining the level of user fees. Have changes been made to the various user fee schedules to accommodate these costs? As I understand it some user fee programs would require legislation to raise the fee cap before the agency can take action.

Mr. KELLY. For fiscal year 1993, no changes were required or made to existing user fee schedules to recover the Department's legal costs. With respect to the commodity research and promotion programs administered by the Department's Agricultural Marketing Service, our legal costs have been included in the periodic billings submitted by AMS to the individual promotion boards. The Perishable Agricultural Commodities Act program is also administered by AMS. PACA license fees are currently at their statutory limit. In order to accommodate increased costs in administering the PACA program, including new costs for legal services, we understand that the agency will seek legislation to raise the fee cap.

Mr. DURBIN. What authority do you have to collect reimbursement for legal services provided to user fee accounts?

Mr. KELLY. The Department's authority to collect the costs of providing legal services to the user fee accounts is found in the legislation authorizing the various user fee programs. For example, Section 203 of the Agricultural Marketing Act of 1946, under which many of the Departments inspection and grading programs are conducted, provides authority to prescribe reasonable fees to cover the costs of providing the inspection services. Another example is found in section 3 of the Perishable Agricultural Commodities Act which authorizes the Secretary to establish license fees and to use the fees for all of the expenses necessary for the administration of that regulatory program. With respect to the numerous commodity research and promotion programs, the statutes authorizing these programs typically direct that the assessments prescribed by the promotion orders shall be used to fund authorized plans and projects and to reimburse the Department for the administrative costs incurred by the Department in carrying out its duties under those programs.

Mr. DURBIN. How are these accounts billed for services? Are they billed on an hourly basis or on a case-by-case basis?

Mr. KELLY. OGC maintains hourly time sheets for hours worked and expenses incurred in connection with all user fee programs. For AMS programs, OGC bills monthly based on hours worked, under an agreement which permits appropriate adjustments at the end of the fiscal year. For non-AMS programs, OGC bills on a quarterly basis, based upon estimates of hours to be worked under such programs.

Mr. DURBIN. For the record please list all the individual user fee programs involved, the amount of fees you have collected so far this fiscal year, the amount you expect to receive by the end of fiscal year 1993, and the amount you expect to receive in fiscal year 1994.

Mr. KELLY. I will provide for the record a list of the user fee programs involved, the amount of fees collected so far this fiscal year, the amount expected to be received by the end of fiscal year 1993 and the amount expected to be received in fiscal year 1994.

[The information follows:]

USER FEE PROGRAMS
FY 1993 STATUS AND FY 1994 ESTIMATES
AS OF DECEMBER 31, 1992

PROGRAM	FY 1993 COLLECTED AMOUNT	FY 1993 EXPECTED AMOUNT	FY 1994 ESTIMATED AMOUNT
Perishable Agricultural Commodities Act	$161,093	$ 321,000	$ 587,000
Agricultural Marketing Act	9,149	151,000	133,000
Tobacco Inspection Act	222	18,000	12,000
Cotton Standards Act	145	18,000	12,000
Plant Variety Protection Act	86	26,000	12,000
Dairy Production Stabilization Act	4,302	50,250	15,000
Egg Research and Consumer Information Act	256	37,000	12,000
Honey Research, Promotion and Consumer Information Act	0	17,250	12,000
Pork Promotion, Research and Consumer Information Act	1,332	15,300	12,000
Cotton Research and Promotion Act	0	17,250	12,000
Potato Research and Promotion Act	121	17,250	12,000
Beef Research & Information Act	905	15,300	15,000
Animal and Plant Health Inspection Services	51,844	207,000	325,000
United States Warehouse Act	5,833	23,000	34,000
United States Grain Standards Act	41,475	166,000	120,000
Watermelon Research & Promotion Act	82	300	9,000
Soybean Promotion, Research & Consumer Information Act	1,175	4,700	15,000
Mushroom Promotion, Research & Consumer Information Act	533	2,100	15,000
Lime Research, Promotion & Consumer Information Act	0	0	9,000
Pecan Promotion & Research Act	64	300	9,000
Organic Foods Production Act	0	0	37,000
Accredited Laboratories	0	0	29,000
	$278,617	$1,107,000	$1,448,000

Mr. DURBIN. From this list, tell us which programs were able to raise the fees without regulatory action, which programs require regulatory action, and which ones require legislative action as well as the status of each.

Mr. KELLY. It has not been necessary to raise fees for any of the programs to date, and no fee increases are expected this year with the exception of the Perishable Agricultural Commodities Act program. A fee increase will be necessary to offset increased program costs, including the costs of legal services, in administering the PACA. This will require legislation to increase the statutory fee cap. We understand this legislation has been drafted and will be presented to Congress later this year.

Mr. DURBIN. In fiscal year 1994, you project the amount to be reimbursed through user fees to increase by $341,000 to $1,448,000. How did you arrive at this increase? Is this increase built into the individual schedule?

Mr. KELLY. OGC surveyed the Washington headquarters staff and field office staff regarding the estimated staff years to be devoted to user fee programs during fiscal year 1994. Where possible, estimates for other costs such as travel were also provided. The estimated staff years spent on each user fee program was then multiplied by the average salary of an OGC attorney or support staff. OGC is not responsible for setting fee schedules for user fee programs. Agencies take into account all reimbursements, including reimbursements for OGC.

REIMBURSEMENTS

Mr. DURBIN. Now, in addition to user fees, you also collect money from other USDA agencies as reimbursements for your services. These reimbursements have increased from $253,000 in fiscal year 1991, to an estimated $2.2 million in fiscal year 1994. Is that correct?

Mr. KELLY. That is roughly correct, Mr. Chairman. Yes.

Mr. DURBIN. I take it your hourly rate has gone up pretty dramatically to have that kind of increase in the amount you receive from other agencies.

Mr. KELLY. Actually, the rate has not gone up at all, Mr. Chairman, or very modestly. What has gone up is the number of requests that we get from client agencies for the provision of additional kinds of services over and above what we are able to provide with our appropriated funds. Those are restricted to circumstances in which an agency has a need which is not presently being met and which can be distinguished from the purposes for which our appropriated funds are made available by the Congress.

Mr. DURBIN. Is this a fairly common practice in the Federal government, for the Office of General Counsel to charge the agencies, sub-agencies, within their Department for legal services?

Mr. KELLY. I can't say, Mr. Chairman. I know that it has been done for many years at USDA. While the practice has increased in the last several years within USDA, it is used, by and large, in circumstances where we did not initiate the arrangement. A client agency has come to us and said it has a need that has not been addressed, which OGC can address. And this need may be in a locus which is physically or geographically dissimilar from any place where OGC has attorneys but where the client needs some assistance. And, the other agency believes its appropriation is broad enough to permit it to pay for provision of that service.

Let me give you a couple of examples. We have attorneys stationed in four or five places—in cities where we otherwise do not have law offices—in the offices of Farmers Home Administration state directors in order to assist in the provision of particularized services for that agency.

If we find an attorney who is interested in this type of work, we try to accommodate their moving to one of these locations. We are about to employ an attorney in Boise, Idaho, to handle water rights adjudications within the State of Idaho. The State of Idaho has determined that in the Snake River watershed it will adjudicate various parties' claims to the use of water in that watershed through formal adjudications conducted by State hearing officers.

The Forest Service is a major presence in the State of Idaho and a major user of water. We have no choice but to represent the agency in those adjudications. We anticipate, if you can believe it, upwards of 15,000 USDA claims, which will be adjudicated in the State of Idaho in the next several years, and we have no choice but to attempt to provide the Forest Service with an attorney for that purpose.

That is clearly something that we have not identified in our appropriations request, and it is clearly a function where the Forest Service needs assistance and its appropriations are available.

So those are a couple of examples of the kinds of circumstances in which we are providing services on a reimbursable basis, Mr. Chairman.

Mr. DURBIN. So, if an agency requests assistance and you don't ordinarily have a lawyer in that location, your first question to that agency is, how are you going to pay for it?

Mr. KELLY. Well, not necessarily.

Our first question is, what is the lawyer for? If the lawyer is for the provision of legal services, which is clearly what OGC gets an appropriation to provide, then we are limited. We receive an appropriation which delimits the kind of services we can provide for the purposes the Congress has in mind when it provides that appropriation.

So only where there is a function that the agency has—or a need that the agency has—which is distinguishable from the kinds of services that we have told this committee—that we have told the Congress—we intend to provide with our appropriated monies, do we think that we can proceed on this kind of a reimbursable basis.

Mr. DURBIN. Who makes that determination?

Mr. KELLY. Well, the General Counsel, in consultation with the head of the agency that is making the request.

Mr. DURBIN. Can you give me an example of a request that you have turned down? An example where an agency came to you and said we need additional legal help, but can't afford to pay for it, and you said, well, we are not authorized to help you.

Mr. KELLY. The Forest Service has come to us with some requests for additional help that we simply cannot accommodate. Also, I believe, the Agricultural Stabilization and Conservation

Service wanted an additional attorney for procurement work that we were not able to provide. Likewise, we have been requested by several USDA agencies to provide additional legal services on a reimbusable basis for equal employment opportunity hearings, and we determined in those instances that we were not able to accommodate their requests.

We also have requests from the Forest Service for the employment of attorneys and support personnel in several locations where we simply are not going to be able to do it.

So we are not proceeding in any expeditious manner to enter into more of these reimbursable agreements, but we do take a hard look every time such a request is made.

Mr. DURBIN. Naturally this Subcommittee, as reflected in our Committee report last year, has some concerns about this practice. We are appropriating money to the Office of General Counsel, and yet you are reappropriating money from other agencies. It is very difficult many times for us to get a handle on what you are up to in the Office of General Counsel. And, conversely, I am sure, these agencies would complain that funds that might otherwise be used for some other purpose within their agency have to be diverted for legal services to the Office of General Counsel.

What authority do you have to charge for reimbursement of legal services provided to USDA agencies?

Mr. KELLY. We beleive that the authorities provided by the Economy Act—31 U.S.C. 1535—and under 7 U.S.C. 2263 and 31 U.S.C. 1534 authorize client agencies to enter into reimbursable agreements with OGC for the provision of legal services so long as such services are different from, or in addition to, legal services being provided from OGC's appropriations.

Mr. DURBIN. What agencies and programs are charged for your legal services? For the record provide a list of all agencies and programs from which you receive a reimbursement and the amount associated with each.

Mr. KELLY. I will provide for the record a list of all agencies and programs from which OGC receives reimbursement and the amount associated with each.

[The information follows:]

Agency and program	*Fiscal year 1993 estimated amount*
AMS: Affirmative and defensive marketing orders	$83,000
AMS-User Fees:	
Perishable Agricultural Commodities Act	321,000
Agricultural Marketing Act	151,000
Tobacco Inspection Act	18,000
Cotton Standards Act	18,000
Plant Variety Protection Act	26,000
Dairy Production Stabilization Act	50,250
Egg Research and Consumer Information Act	37,000
Honey Research, Promotion and Consumer Information Act	17,250
Pork Promotion, Research and Consumer Information Act	15,300
Cotton Research and Promotion Act	17,250
Potato Research and Promotion Act	17,250
Beef Research and Information Act	15,300
Watermelon Research and Promotion Act	300
Soybean Promotion, Research and Consumer Information Act	4,700
Mushroom Promotion, Research and Consumer Information Act	2,100

Agency and program	Fiscal year 1993 estimated amount
Pecan Promotion and Research Act	300
APHIS-User Fees: Animal and Plant Health Inspection Services	207,000
ASCS-User Fees: United States Warehouse Act	23,000
FGIS-User Fees: United States Grain Standards Act	166,000
FmHA: Bankruptcies, foreclosures and uniform commercial code matters	821,000
FS: Legislative Counseling Services, timber sales, timber theft, recreational issues and range management	1,122,000

Mr. DURBIN. How do you decide what agency and legal service provided will be required to pay for that service?

Mr. KELLY. Mr. Chairman, we do not require any agency to pay for legal services. As I mentioned previously, aside from the user fee reimbursements, legal services for which OGC receives reimbursements are provided to a client agency that requests additional or different legal services than we are currently providing or are able to provide. That agency must be able and willing to pay for those services. Only then do we consider entering into a reimbursable agreement to provide the services. Thus, the agency itself is the one to decide whether it needs and can pay for additional legal services, and the legal services involved are decided by agreement between OGC and the agency.

USE OF PRIVATE ATTORNEYS

Mr. DURBIN. Now one of the things that is happening, apparently, is that the Farmers Home Administration and others are starting to turn to private attorneys to supplement their needs. Is this a phenomena that is growing in the Department?

Mr. KELLY. Not to my knowledge, Mr. Chairman. There is a private attorney project which the Farmers Home Administration— which the Secretary of Agriculture is authorized to implement, with respect to foreclosures on single-family housing loans under the Housing Act of 1949. But that is a specific authorization recently granted to the Secretary of Agriculture. And when private attorneys are used for that purpose, they are selected by Farmers Home in consultation with our office and the Offices of the U.S. Attorneys.

Mr. DURBIN. Well, in this particular case, in 1991, Farmers Home was authorized to hire private counsel for judicial foreclosures and other legal actions related to single-family housing in a dozen states.

Mr. KELLY. That is correct.

Mr. DURBIN. Last year, Mr. Raul indicated that two other areas might be candidates for private counsel within Farmers Home, debt collection matters and bankruptcy. Are you saying in your testimony that that has not taken place, that Farmers Home is not using private attorneys for these purposes?

Mr. KELLY. No, they are not, Mr. Chairman.

Mr. Chairman, can I ask Bob Franks to respond to that?

Mr. DURBIN. Sure, of course.

Mr. FRANKS. Mr. Chairman, the pilot project that Mr. Kelly mentioned uses private attorneys for some bankruptcy work. The kinds of things that they are doing are primarily foreclosures but also a little bit of bankruptcy relating to single-family housing and some preparation of deeds, things like that.

I believe the references that Mr. Raul made last year were to areas where he thought, if we had authority, we might be able to get into. But we don't have authority to get into those, other than in the single-family housing area. I will provide a more detailed response for the record.

[The additional information follows:]

The Farmers Home Administration continues to use private counsel for foreclosures and other legal matters arising under section 502 of the Housing Act of 1949, the single family rural housing loan program. In fiscal year 1992, FmHA used private counsel under this program in 14 states to handle 1,534 foreclosures, 75 sales deed preparations, 35 repossessions of property, 69 bankruptcies, and 1 deficiency action. To my knowledge, this is the only USDA program in which the use of outside private counsel is specifically authorized.

KANSAS OFFICE MOVE

Mr. DURBIN. Do you know why your office in Kansas City, Missouri, was relocated?

Mr. FRANKS. Actually, it was relocated, a couple of years ago. That office has, basically, kind of moved back and forth between Kansas and Missouri. It was in Kansas City, Kansas, and Shawnee Mission, Kansas, at different times. It was in Kansas City, Missouri, at one point. I think about three years ago it moved across the Kansas/Missouri State line into what is Leawood, Kansas. It is right next to the ASCS Commodity Office. We have always considered it the Kansas City office.

This year we decided, rather than just call it the Kansas City, Missouri, office, we would call it the Leawood office. But it isn't a recent move. It is still the Kansas City office.

Mr. KELLY. We have just correctly identified it this year, Mr. Chairman.

Mr. DURBIN. All right.

Mr. KELLY. It moved three years ago, and nobody noticed.

FORECLOSURE SUSPENSION

Mr. DURBIN. On page seven of your statement you say that Secretary Espy has decided to suspend foreclosures involving Farmers Home Administration farmer program borrowers. Please describe this in further detail.

Mr. KELLY. Secretary Espy has been concerned about diffuse but persistent claims by farmers that they were not being treated fairly by Farmers Home Administration when it was servicing their delinquent loan accounts. Therefore, the Secretary, on March 5, 1993, announced that he would provide an opportunity for a review of each pending case in which foreclosure was about to take place. The agency has, accordingly, stopped all foreclosures in farmer program loan cases and has sent letters to the borrowers offering them 30 days in which to request a review of their case files to see whether the agency has in fact given them the loan servicing opportunities the law and regulations require. The agency has sent out 3,693 of these letters; the first mailing took place on March 31-April 1, and the last mailing was completed on April 20th.

The thirty days has not yet run—the time being measured from the date the farmer signs the receipt for the certified letter. But, thus far, a number of farmers have called a hot line the Secretary established to answer questions about the review, and 130 applications for review have been received. The Secretary is now in the process of appointing the team of reviewers to look at these files.

SIGNIFICANT REGULATORY CHANGES

Mr. DURBIN. In your statement you say that your office has been addressing some significant regulation changes in the areas of pesticide recordkeeping requirements, pine shoot beetles, biotechnology, and nutrition labelling. Would you briefly describe these changes and tell us what the impact of each has had on your workload?

Mr. KELLY. I will provide that information for the record.

[The information follows:]

PESTICIDE RECORDKEEPING REQUIREMENTS

Extensive legal services have been provided by OGC regarding implementation of the pesticide recordkeeping requirements in section 1491 of the Farm Bill of 1990. Those requirements provide for recordkeeping by certified applicators of federally restricted use pesticides, and for access to pesticide records by Federal or State officials, or by health professionals when needed to treat an individual who may have been exposed to such pesticides.

The Secretary of Agriculture is required to promulgate regulations implementing those requirements, which responsibility the Secretary has delegated to the Administrator of AMS. On May 12, 1992, the AMS published such proposed regulations for public comment, and a final rule was published in the Federal Register on April 9, 1993, with an effective date of May 10, 1993. Attorneys in OGC worked extensively with AMS to draft, review and clear such proposed and final regulations.

On April 22, 1992, the National Coalition Against the Misuse of Pesticides and others filed suit in the U.S. District court for the District of Columbia seeking, among other things, a preliminary injunction directing the Secretary and the Administrator to promulgate pesticide recordkeeping and access regulations within a certain time-frame. The motion for preliminary injunction was denied, and the complaint is now moot. However, the plaintiff has indicated that it intends to amend the complaint to challenge the legality of some of the regulations. An OGC attorney has worked extensively with the Department of Justice in defense of this suit.

We estimate that OGC has spent approximately .4 staff-years in providing legal services relating to the pesticide recordkeeping requirements.

PINE SHOOT BEETLE

This office provided significant legal services to the Animal and Plant Health Inspection Service (APHIS) regarding the pine shoot beetle. Such services have included giving legal advice, drafting and review and clearance of regulations, and reviewing and clearing numerous pieces of correspondence regarding those regulations. There has been considerable interest in this matter by members of Congress, state officials and the affected industry.

On November 19, 1992, APHIS issued an interim rule quarantining portions of Illinois Indiana, Michigan, New York, Ohio, and Pennsylvania and restricting interstate movement of regulated articles, such as pine nursery stock and Christmas trees and logs and lumber of fir, larch, pine and spruce with bark attached, because of the pine shoot beetle. On January 28, 1993, APHIS issued a second interim rule relieving restrictions on pine nursery stock. OGC has reviewed a third interim rule removing certain restrictions on logs and lumber, while adding additional articles to the list of regulated articles. This interim rule is currently under review by the Department. At the present time, APHIS is drafting a fourth interim rule which will add several counties to the quarantined areas.

A comprehensive final rule, addressing comments from the numerous interim rules, will be submitted to OGC for clearance at a future date. Any changes in the interim rules will be included in the final rule, which will be published in the Federal Register.

We estimate that OGC has spent approximately .1 staff-years in providing legal services relating to the pine shoot beetle matters.

Biotechnology

This office provided extensive legal services regarding biotechnology regulatory changes. Such services have included significant legal advice, drafting and review of complex and controversial regulations and notices, and review and clearance of numerous pieces of correspondence concerning such regulations. Under the Federal Plant Pest Act (FPPA) and regulations issued thereunder, APHIS regulates the introduction and importation, interstate movement, and release into the environment of regulated articles, i.e., genetically engineered organisms and products which are plant pests or which there is reason to believe are plant pests. The regulations set forth procedures for obtaining a permit for the release into the environment of regulated articles and for obtaining a limited permit for the importation or interstate movement of a regulated article.

APHIS received two petitions seeking determinations that genetically engineered plants do not present a plant pest risk and, therefore, are not regulated articles under the FPPA. In response to those petitions. APHIS published notices of proposed interpretive ruling concerning the regulatory status of Calgene, Inc.'s FLAVR SAVR® tomato, genetically modified to have a delayed ripening of the tomato fruit, and the Upjohn Company's ZW-20 squash, genetically modified to be resistant to the watermelon mosaic virus and the zucchini yellow mosaic virus.

A subsequent notice was published in the Federal Register announcing the issuance of an interpretive ruling that the FLAVR SAVR® tomato does not present a plant pest risk and is not a regulated article under the regulations contained in 7 CFR Part 340.

On November 6, 1992, APHIS published in the Federal Register a proposed rule to amend the regulations to provide for a notification process, in lieu of permits, for the introduction of certain genetically engineered plants. The proposed rule would also amend the regulations to provide for a petition process allowing for a determination that certain genetically engineered plants, which do not present a plant pest risk, are no longer considered regulated articles. APHIS issued a final rule on March 31, 1993, amending the regulations to provide for a notification process in lieu of permits for the introduction of certain genetically engineered plants and to provide for the petition process.

We estimate that OGC has spent approximately .75 staff-years in providing legal services relating to the biotechnology matters.

Nutrition Labelling

In January 1993, the Food Safety and Inspection Service (FSIS) published final nutrition labelling regulations under the Federal Meat Inspection Act and the Poultry Products Inspection Act for meat and poultry products. The final rule permits voluntary nutrition labelling on single-ingredient, raw meat and poultry products, and establishes mandatory nutrition labelling for all other meat and poultry products, with certain exemptions such as those for specified small businesses. There have been several issues raised regarding the regulations, including questions on the labelling format and the application of the regulations to menus at restaurants. It is likely that the regulations will be challenged by members of industry and consumer groups.

OGC has spent an extensive amount of time in assisting officials of FSIS and the Secretary's office in the drafting and review for legal sufficiency of the nutrition labelling and related rulemaking. In this connection, OGC has assisted in giving advice, reviewing and clearing numerous pieces of correspondence, and in resolving numerous, complex legal issues in connection with the rulemaking. Additionally, OGC participated in three rulemaking hearings concerning the exemptions for specified small businesses.

Until the effective date of the nutrition labelling regulations, OGC will continue to assist and advise FSIS in various ongoing aspects of the rulemaking. FSIS recently submitted to OGC for legal review and clearance a docket containing technical corrections and amendments to the final regulations, which OGC reviewed and cleared. OGC will also assist in the drafting and review of the final rule concerning use of "healthy" and similar terms on meat and poultry product labelling.

We estimate that OGC has spent approximately one staff-year in providing legal services relating to the nutrition labelling issues.

NORTH AMERICAN FREE TRADE AGREEMENT

Mr. DURBIN. Have you been involved with the negotiations on the North American Free Trade Agreement? In terms of dollars and staff, how much has been devoted to this issue?

Mr. KELLY. This office has been actively involved in the North American Free Trade Agreement (NAFTA) negotiations over the past two years. We have one staff attorney assigned to advise the Foreign Agricultural Service (FAS) in the NAFTA negotiations, and we estimate that he has spent approximately 25 percent of his time on that assignment over the past two years. Our staff attorney has participated directly in the negotiations as a key member of the U.S. delegation, and has travelled to Mexico and Canada with FAS and USTR negotiators. In addition, these negotiations have at times also required the involvement and attention of our Deputy Assistant General Counsel for International Affairs who has spent an estimated two person-months on NAFTA issues over the past two years.

FOOD STAMP PROGRAM

Mr. DURBIN. Last year Mr. Raul provided the Committee with information related to the funds and staff years dedicated to the Food Stamp program. Would you please update this information to include fiscal year 1992 actuals and fiscal year 1994 estimates?

Mr. KELLY. The five-year table that reflects the amount of funds and staff years for each year dedicated to the Food Stamp Program will be provided for the record.

[The information follows:]

FOOD STAMP PROGRAM—COST AND STAFF YEARS

	Fiscal year—				
	1990	1991	1992	1993	1994
Funds	$890,052	$910,534	$1,045,079	$1,077,843	$1,051,675
Staff years	16.30	16.45	16.42	15.96	15.96

Mr. DURBIN. You have stated that the 1990 Farm Bill would significantly impact your work related to quality control liability collection efforts. At last year's hearing the Committee was told that until the final regulation to implement the good cause waiver provisions and the proposed regulations to implement the administrative appeal procedures were final, the impact could not be measured. What is the status of these regulations and how has your workload been impacted?

Mr. KELLY. The good cause waiver provisions were published in final form September 28, 1992. The comment period for the proposed regulations to implement the administrative appeal procedures closed March 22, 1993. The final rule is being prepared and is expected to be completed and published in final form within the next several months. It is expected that QC billings and appeals for fiscal year 1992 will be underway this fall. We anticipate that the

QC administrative appeals and associated civil litigation will increase our workload significantly over the next two fiscal years in that 12 administrative cases are anticipated for fiscal year 1992 and a similar number for the following year. It is anticipated that these claims will be controversial and that substantial effort will be expended in defending the claims before the administrative law judges under the new appeal process. However, the overall workload in this area is anticipated to be more manageable due to the recent agreement between the Food and Nutrition Service (FNS) and 25 state welfare agencies to settle a backlog of 63 Food Stamp Program Quality Control (QC) claims for excess program errors in administration of the Food Stamp Program for fiscal years 1986 through 1991. FNS agreed to settle these outstanding QC claims in exchange for the states agreeing to invest approximately $45 million in programs designed to improve the accuracy of Food Stamp Program administration.

WORK ITEM MANAGEMENT SYSTEM

Mr. DURBIN. OGC implemented a pilot Work Item Management System for internal case tracking in the Washington, DC headquarters and San Francisco field offices in December, 1991 and the Atlanta field office in February, 1992. Does it perform as expected? What would be the cost to go nationwide with the system?

Mr. KELLY. The pilot Work Item Management System (WIMS) meets all of the requirements stated in OGC's "Functional Requirements Analysis for the Work Management System". Further fine tuning and system enhancements to improve system performance and create ad hoc reports will be necessary prior to any nationwide implementation.

The national reporting capabilities of our current pilot WIMS also met OGC's functional requirements; however, the communication costs of the dedicated phone lines to keep this portion of the pilot WIMS functional were too great so we have dropped this function temporarily. Without these phone lines being operational, OGC's national reporting requirements cannot be met.

To implement the WIMS nationwide, we estimate it will cost approximately $1,400,000. This includes software development costs estimated at $600,000 to develop conversion and specification tools for data migration, implementation of the WIMS software nationwide, and enhancements and modifications for ad hoc reports and system performance. This figure also includes $800,000 for computer hardware—specifically database servers—additional memory for the existing personal computer workstations, maintenance, communication lines, and modems to implement the database system nationwide.

LOCAL AREA NETWORKS

Mr. DURBIN. You were experiencing some technical problems last year with your local area networks interconnecting with the USDA local area networks. Has this problem been solved?

Mr. KELLY. This problem has not been fully solved. We have found a temporary solution by upgrading our Novell file server software in OGC Washington, DC headquarters that has enabled us to take advantage of higher processing speeds and additional memory requirements. But even with the enhancements we have made to date, due to the high number of LAN's interconnecting with the USDA LAN, we still experience slow performance on our personal computers and with regard to word processing and print sharing.

PENDING CASES

Mr. DURBIN. Please update the tables that appear on page 327 of last year's hearing record showing the number of new and pending civil and criminal cases as well as the dollar value related to pending cases to include fiscal year 1992.

Mr. KELLY. I will provide that for the record.

[The information follows:]

CIVIL AND CRIMINAL CASES

	New cases referred		Pending end of fiscal year	
	Civil	Criminal	Civil	Criminal
Fiscal year:				
1988	17,240	425	37,944	1,068
1989	13,537	444	34,488	976
1990	14,139	381	34,091	910
1991	15,493	367	33,811	792
1992	14,472	333	28,462	454

DEBT COLLECTION

	Pending cases	Dollar amount
September 30, 1988	30,103	$4,454,469,549
September 30, 1989	28,139	4,548,430,120
September 30, 1990	23,607	4,240,498,131
September 30, 1991	24,125	4,309,351,941
September 30, 1992	21,770	4,588,296,100

FEDERAL CROP INSURANCE

Mr. DURBIN. In your statement you state that, "The provisions of the Food, Agriculture, Conservation, and Trade Act of 1990 allowing private insurance companies to submit their private policies for reinsurance and subsidy significantly increased the OGC workload in this area." Would you describe this statement in more detail including specifically how much your workload has increased?

Mr. KELLY. The amendments to the Federal Crop Insurance Act by the Food, Agriculture, Conservation, and Trade Act of 1990 provided that private insurance companies could submit policies which they had developed to the Federal Crop Insurance Corporation (FCIC) for reinsurance and/or subsidy. If FCIC determined that the policies were properly rated and actuarially sound, the FCIC Board of Directors could approve the policies for reinsurance without regard to whether the policies were in conformance with the limitations established by the Federal Crop Insurance Act. To the extent the submitted policies provided insurance within the parameters of the

Federal Crop Insurance Act, the Board could also approve the policies for subsidy. The Office of the General Counsel's involvement in this process involves review of the private insurance companies submitted policies to determine what provisions of the policies are in accord with the provisions of the Federal Crop Insurance Act for subsidy purposes. The Office of the General Counsel also provides legal advice to the FCIC Board of Directors for their use in determining whether the policy should be reinsured. While only a few policies have been submitted for our review so far this fiscal year, we estimate that this review involves .1 staff year.

Mr. DURBIN. During last year's hearing, Mr. Raul told the Committee that OGC was the lead agency in connection with the establishment of a single crop insurance policy to be used nationwide, the publication of regulations reaffirming FCIC's preemption of state insurance regulations, and litigation involving the authority of FCIC to conduct a uniform national program. Please tell us the status of each of these initiatives.

Mr. KELLY. The Office of the General Counsel has cleared proposed regulations for the implementation of a single, nationwide policy for use of both FCIC contractors and reinsured companies. A final rule has been published affirming FCIC's preemption of state regulation of policies issued under the Federal Crop Insurance Act. Litigation brought by the State of Kansas pertaining to those regulations resulted in an opinion of the United States District Court for the District of Kansas in favor of FCIC. That decision is now before the United States Court of Appeals for the Tenth Circuit with oral argument scheduled for May 11th in Denver, Colorado. Litigation concerning states other than the State of Kansas awaits the outcome of the appeal before the Tenth Circuit.

Mr. DURBIN. What are the total annual resources expended by your office related to the Federal Crop Insurance Program?

Mr. KELLY. The Office of the General Counsel expends about 1.5 staff years each fiscal year supplying legal services to the Federal Crop Insurance Program.

PATENT APPLICATIONS

Mr. DURBIN. As in the past, please provide a list of applications for patent reviewed by your office for fiscal year 1992.

Mr. KELLY. I will provide that for the record.

[The information follows:]

Serial No: 07/936,991 Filed: 08/31/92
Title: BIOLOGICAL CONTROL OF WEEDS USING AAL-TOXIN
Inventors: ABBAS, BOYETTE, VESONDER

Serial No: 07/919,341 Filed: 07/23/92
Title: PROCESS TO ISOLATE 95% PROTEIN FROM JOJOBA
Inventors: ABBOTT, KLEIMAN, WANG, MONTGOMERY, WOLF

Serial No: 07/800,315 Filed: 11/29/91
Title: COPPER HYDROXIDE AS A REPELLENT
Inventors: AVERY, DECKER

Serial No: 07/792,508 Filed: 11/12/91
Title: CITRUS PROTEINS FOR USE IN FIELD DETECTION OF CITRUS BLIGHT USING IMMUNOLOGICAL TECHNIQUES
Inventors: BAUSHER

Serial No: 07/940,246 Filed: 08/28/92
Title: METHOD FOR PREPARATION AND USE OF 1A,24(S)-DIHYDROXY VITAMIN D2
Inventors: BISHOP, HORST, JONES, KOSZEWSKI, KNUTSON,

Serial No: 07/769,289 Filed: 10/01/91
Title: ANIONICALLY DYEABLE NON-FORMALDEHYDE CROSSLINKED CELLULOSIC MATERIALS AND PROCESSES FOR THEIR PRODUCTION
Inventors: BLANCHARD, REINHARDT, ANDREWS

Serial No: 07/883,749 Filed: 05/15/92
Title: CYTOTOXIC PROTEIN FROM THE YEAST PICHIA ACACIAE
Inventors: BOLEN, LIGON, HAYMAN, WORSHAM

Serial No: 07/803,664 Filed: 12/03/91
Title: WHIPPED TOPPING FORMULATION
Inventors: BOOKWALTER

Serial No: 07/839,000 Filed: 02/21/92
Title: PRESSURE AND DEPTH CONTROL FOR PLANTER
Inventors: CARTER

Serial No: 07/945,283 Filed: 09/11/92
Title: PSEUDORABIES VIRUS DELETION MUTANTS
Inventors: CHEUNG, WESLEY

Serial No: 07/939,764 Filed: 08/28/92
Title: COMPOST TOILET MIXING TOOL
Inventors: COOK

Serial No: 07/807,333 Filed: 12/16/91
Title: USE OF NATIVE ASPERGILLUS FLAVUS STRAINS TO PREVENT AFLATOXIN CONTAMINATION
Inventors: COTTY

Serial No: 07/911,864 Filed: 07/10/92
Title: AVIDIN AND HOMOLOGUES AS LARVICIDES AGAINST INSECT PESTS OF AGRONOMIC CROPS
Inventors: CZAPLA, KRAMER, MORGAN, OPPERT

Serial No: 07/826,750 Filed: 01/28/92
Title: SEX ATTRACTANT FOR MINT ROOT BORER
Inventors: DAVIS, MCDONOUGH

Serial No: 07/822,505 Filed: 01/17/92
Title: PROBIOTIC FOR CONTROL OF SALMONELLA
Inventors: DELOACH, CORRIER, HINTON

Serial No: 07/781,601 Filed: 10/23/91
Title: BIOCONTROL FORMULATIONS USING BACTERIAL ALGINATES AS GELLING AGENT
Inventors: DELUCCA, CONNICK, FRAVEL, LEWIS

Serial No: 07/950,346 Filed: 09/24/92
Title: LEPORIN A, AN ANTIINSECTAN FUNGAL METABOLITE
Inventors: DOWD, WICKLOW, GLOER

Serial No: 07/795,447 Filed: 11/21/91
Title: FACTICE FROM MIXTURES OF VEGETABLE OILS
Inventors: ERHAN, KLEIMAN

Serial No: 07/843,333 Filed: 02/28/92
Title: STARCH AND POLY(ETHYLENE-CO-ACRYLIC ACID) GELS
Inventors: FANTA, CHRISTIANSON

Serial No: 07/820,473 Filed: 01/14/92
Title: COTTON FIBER AND AIR FLOW CONTROL BARS
Inventors: GILLUM, HUGHS,

Serial No: 07/880,912 Filed: 05/12/92
Title: INDUSTRIAL ALKALINE PROTEASE FROM SHIPWORM BACTERIUM
Inventors: GRIFFIN, GREENE, COTTA

Serial No: 07/855,804 Filed: 03/23/92
Title: PLASMID-DNA BASED PROBES & A PROCEDURE FOR RAPID AND SPECIFIC DETECTION OF XANTHOMONAS CAMPESTRIS PV. CITRI
Inventors: HARTUNG, PRUVOST

Serial No: 07/901,439 Filed: 06/19/92
Title: SUPPRESSION OF GIOCLADIUM VIRENS PHYTOTOXIN PRODUCTION WITH STEROID INHIBITORS
Inventors: HOWELL, STIPANOVIC

Serial No: 07/908,284 Filed: 07/07/92
Title: GENE ACTIVATING ELEMENT
Inventors: HOWELL

Serial No: 07/815,996 Filed: 01/02/92
Title: AMYLODEXTRIN COMPOSITIONS AND METHOD THEREFOR
Inventors: INGLETT

Serial No: 07/909,263 Filed: 07/06/92
Title: PORTABLE WATER BAG
Inventors: JACKSON, PUTNAM

Serial No: 07/930,632 Filed: 08/17/92
Title: BIOLOGICAL CONTROL OF BLUE-MOLD AND GRAY-MOLD ON APPLE AND PEAR WITH SPOROBOLOMYCES ROSEUS
Inventors: JANISIEWICZ, BORS

Serial No: 07/857,060 Filed: 03/25/92
Title: METHOD OF REMOVING COLOR FROM KRAFT WOOD PULP
Inventors: JEFFRIES, GRABSKI, PATEL

Serial No: 07/902,164 Filed: 06/22/92
Title: MEROZOITE PROTEINS FOR USE IN DETECTION OF BABESIA EQUI IN HORSES USING IMMUNOLOGICAL TECHNIQUES
Inventors: KNOWLES, PERRYMAN

Serial No: 07/875,360 Filed: 04/29/92
Title: RADARIN ANTIINSECTAN METABOLITES
Inventors: LAAKSO, DOWD, GLOER, WICKLOW

Serial No: 07/876,819 Filed: 04/29/92
Title: MONOCLONAL ANTIBODIES AGAINST CHICKEN T-LYMPHOCYTES
Inventors: LILLEHOJ

Serial No: 07/947,867 Filed: 09/21/92
Title: HYDROPHOBIC EXTRACTED NEEM OIL
Inventors: LOCKE, LAREW, WALTER

Serial No: 07/866,968 Filed: 04/13/92
Title: INSECTICIDAL COMPOSITIONS DERIVED FROM NEEM OIL
Inventors: LOCKE, WALTER, LAREW

Serial No: 07/801,157 Filed: 12/02/91
Title: BAGGER RECEIVER BOX
Inventors: MARSHALL, WOLTHUIS, BROWN

Serial No: 07/885,052 Filed: 05/11/92
Title: COMPOSITION AND APPARATUS USEFUL FOR ATTRACTING AND CONTROLLING INSECT PESTS
Inventors: MCKIBBEN, SMITH, MCGOVERN

Serial No: 07/937,764 Filed: 09/01/92
Title: FUNGUS-BIOREGULATOR COMPOSITIONS AND METHODS FOR CONTROL OF PLANT-PARASITIC NEMATODES
Inventors: MEYER, HUETTEL

Serial No: 07/790,042 Filed: 11/12/91
Title: PROCESS FOR THE PREPARATION OF KETONES AND NOVEL INSECTICIDES PRODUCED THEREFROM
Inventors: MILLS, BROWN, MILLS JR

Serial No: 07/907,342 Filed: 07/01/92
Title: PROCESS FOR THE PREPARATION OF KETONES AND NOVEL INSECTICIDES PRODUCED THEREFROM
Inventors: MILLS, BROWN, MILLS JR

Serial No: 07/832,196 Filed: 02/06/92
Title: CHEMICAL PULPING PROCESS EMPLOYING SEPERATE ALKALI AND PEROXYMONOSULFATE TREATMENTS
Inventors: MINOR, SPRINGER

Serial No: 07/803,633 Filed: 12/10/91
Title: RECOMBINANT FOWLPOX VACCINE FOR PROTECTION AGAINST MAREK'S DISEASE
Inventors: NAZERIAN, LEE, LI

Serial No: 07/946,231 Filed: 09/18/92
Title: MAREK'S DISEASE VIRUS TEGUMENT GENES
Inventors: NAZERIAN, LEE, YANAGIDA

Serial No: 07/785,831 Filed: 10/31/91
Title: METHOD FOR REDUCING FECAL LEAKAGE AND CONTAMINATION DURING MEAT AND POULTRY PROCESSING
Inventors: NEAL, COOK

Serial No: 07/921,173 Filed: 07/29/92
Title: CHEMOSTAT DERIVED PROBIOTIC FOR CONTROL OF SALMONELLA
Inventors: NISBET, CORRIER, DELOACH

Serial No: 07/785,375 Filed: 10/30/91
Title: PRODUCTION OF EICOSAPENTAENOIC ACID FROM FILAMENTOUS FUNGI UTILIZING LACTOSE AS A PRIMARY CARBON SOURCE
Inventors: O'BRIEN, STINSON, WESSINGER, SOMKUTI

Serial No: 07/807,334 Filed: 12/16/91
Title: ATTACHED GROWTH BIOLOGICAL REACTOR
Inventors: O'BRIEN, HEILAND

Serial No: 07/945,761 Filed: 09/16/92
Title: HIGH ACTIVITY COCKROACH BAIT TRAY
Inventors: PATTERSON, KOEHLER, GOUGER

Serial No: 07/855,805 Filed: 03/23/92
Title: A METHOD OF RAPID FAT AND OIL SPLITTING USING A LIPASE CATALYST FOUND IN SEEDS
Inventors: PIAZZA, HAAS

Serial No: 07/877,507 Filed: 05/01/92
Title: NOVEL SUGAR ESTERS AS BIOLOGICAL PESTICIDES FROM NICOTIANA SPECIES
Inventors: PITTARELLI, BUTA, NEAL, LUSBY, WATERS

Serial No: 07/789,787 Filed: 11/08/91
Title: VACCINES FOR THE PROTECTION OF ANIMALS AGAINST HYPODERMOSIS
Inventors: PRUETT, FILES, KUHN, TEMEYER

Serial No: 07/883,434 Filed: 05/15/92
Title: SUPPRESSION OF HELICOVERPA ZEA AND SPODOPTERA FRUGIPERDA PREPUPAE AND PUPAE IN FRUITING CORN FIELDS USING A NEWLY DISCOVERED NEMATODE
Inventors: RAULSTON, PAIR, CABANILLAS

Serial No: 07/918,316 Filed: 07/17/92
Title: RECOMBINANT ORYZACYSTATIN COMPOSITION AND METHODS OF EXPRESSION AND PURIFICATION
Inventors: REECK, MING-SHUN, MUTHUKRISHNAM, KRAMER

Serial No: 07/936,423 Filed: 08/27/92
Title: PORTABLE INTRON AS VECTOR FOR GENE INSERTION
Inventors: REILLY, SILVA

Serial No: 07/770,258 Filed: 10/03/91
Title: ADJUSTABLE FLOW-MEASURING FLUME AND METERING GATE
Inventors: REPLOGLE

Serial No: 07/914,233 Filed: 07/13/92
Title: BIOCONTROL OF POST ROTS IN FRUITS
Inventors: ROBERTS

Serial No: 07/912,391 Filed: 07/13/92
Title: METHOD AND APPARATUS FOR IN SITU EVALUATION OF WOODEN MEMBERS
Inventors: ROSS, DEGROOT, GESKE, NELSON, MALINAUSKAS

Serial No: 07/857,146 Filed: 03/25/92
Title: METHOD AND APPARATUS FOR EVALUATING THE DRYING PROPERTIES OF UN-DRIED WOOD
Inventors: ROSS

Serial No: 07/913,565 Filed: 07/14/92
Title: ADHERENT STARCH GRANULES
Inventors: SHASHA, MCGUIRE

Serial No: 07/912,447 Filed: 07/13/92
Title: CAMPY-CEFEX SELECTIVE AND DIFFERENTIAL MEDIUM
Inventors: STERN, WOJTON, KWIATEK

Serial No: 07/848,775 Filed: 03/10/92
Title: ENZYMATIC PROCESSING OF MATERIALS CONTAINING CHROMIUM AND PROTEIN
Inventors: TAYLOR, MARMER, DIEFENDORF, BROWN

Serial No: 07/862,493 Filed: 04/02/92
Title: CONTROL OF FRUIT RIPENING THROUGH GENETIC CONTROL OF ACC SYNTHASE SYNTHESIS
Inventors: THEOLOGIS, SATO

Serial No: 07/925,685 Filed: 08/07/92
Title: A REPELLENT FOR ANTS
Inventors: VANDERMEER, BANKS, LOFGREN

Serial No: 07/908,844 Filed: 07/01/92
Title: TEMPERATURE ADAPTABLE TEXTILE FIBERS AND METHOD OF PREPARING SAME
Inventors: VIGO, ZIMMERMAN, BRUNO, DANNA

Serial No: 07/863,274 Filed: 04/03/92
Title: TEMPERATURE ADAPTABLE GLYOXAL-MODIFIED FIBERS AND METHOD OF PREPARING SAME
Inventors: VIGO, DANNA, BRUNO

Serial No: 07/949,180 Filed: 09/21/92
Title: NOVEL INSECTICIDAL COMPOSITIONS DERIVED FROM NEEM OIL AND NEEM WAX FRACTIONS
Inventors: WALTER, LOCKE, LAREW

Serial No: 07/818,748 Filed: 01/07/92
Title: NOVEL INSECTICIDAL COMPOSITIONS DERIVED FROM NEEM OIL AND NEEM WAX FRACTION
Inventors: WALTER, LOCKE, LAREW

Serial No: 07/937,634 Filed: 08/28/92
Title: OSIDATIVE BLEACHING OF WOOD PULP BY VANADIUM-SUBSTITUTED POLYOXOMETALATES
Inventors: WEINSTOCK, HILL

Serial No: 07/769,288 Filed: 10/01/91
Title: USE OF FREE AMINES FOR ENHANCEMENT OF POLYCARBOXYLIC ACID BASED CELLULOSE CROSSLINKING REACTIONS
Inventors: WELCH

Serial No: 07/770,806 Filed: 10/04/91
Title: APPARATUS AND METHOD FOR APPLYING MATERIAL TO AGRICULTURAL COMMODITIES
Inventors: WILSON, WISNIEWSKI

Serial No: 07/932,519 Filed: 08/20/92
Title: APPARATUS AND METHOD FOR APPLYING PROTECTIVE SUBSTANCES TO HARVESTED PRODUCE
Inventors: WILSON, WISNIEWSKI

Serial No: 07/791,691 Filed: 11/14/91
Title: PREPARATION OF SIMULATED MILK PROTEIN BY LOW TEMPERATURE MICROFILTRATION
Inventors: WOYCHIK

Serial No: 07/851,971 Filed: 03/17/92
Title: MAREK'S DISEASE VIRUS TEGUMENT GENES
Inventors: YANAGIDA, NAZARIAN, LEE

Serial No: 07/860,413 Filed: 03/30/92
Title: A NEW MATTER OF COMPOSITION AND METHOD FOR USING THE SAME AS PLANT BIOREGULATORS
Inventors: YOKOYAMA, KEITHLY, GAUSMAN

Serial No: 07/954,726 Filed: 09/30/92
Title: IN VITRO APPLICATIONS OF SUBSTITUTED BENZYLTRIAKYLAMINE BIOREGULATORY COMPOUNDS
Inventors: YOKOYAMA, KEITHLY, GAUSMAN

NEW AUTHORITIES

Mr. DURBIN. We know that every time a new authorization bill passes the authorities and workload of the Department change significantly. Please provide us with a list of all new authorities passed during the second session of the 102nd Congress and a brief description of any work effort OGC might have related to new authorities.

Mr. KELLY. I will provide that information for the record.

[The information follows:]

WIC Farmers' Market Nutrition Act of 1992
(Pub. L. 102-314)

SECTION	AUTHORITY	OGC WORK EFFORT
1-4	Authorizes grants for States for WIC Farmers' Market Nutrition Program.	Provide legal advice on implementation and administration; review implementing regulations.

Pacific Yew Act
(Pub. L. 102-335)

SECTION	AUTHORITY	OGC WORK EFFORT
[illegible]	Duty to provide for sustainable harvest and long-term conservation of Pacific yew.	Provide legal services related to implementing grants and agreements.
	Duty to assist research regarding Pacific yew.	Provide legal services related to implementing grants and agreements.
5	Negotiated sales of Pacific yew; use of receipts.	Provide legal services related to drafting and implementing guidelines for the disposal of Pacific yew, and the subsequent use of receipts generated.

Agriculture, Rural Development, Food and Drug Administration, and Related Agencies Appropriations Act, 1993 (Pub. L. No. 102-341)

SECTION	AUTHORITY	OGC WORK EFFORT
Titles I-V, Title VII	Various provisions throughout the Act.	Provide legal advice on the availability of funds for particular purposes and other general implementation questions.

Child Nutrition Amendments of 1992 (Pub. L. 102-342)

SECTION	AUTHORITY	OGC WORK EFFORT
Title II	Authorizes Breastfeeding Promotion Program.	Provide legal advice on implementation and administration.

The Second Dire Emergency Supplemental Appropriation Act, Fiscal Year 1992 (Pub. L. 102-368)

SECTION	AUTHORITY	OGC WORK EFFORT
Title XI	Provides for the implementation of Commodity Credit Corporation and Agricultural Stabilization and Conservation Service disaster assistance program provisions.	Review of implementing regulations, provide general advice and oral legal opinions.

Department of the Interior and Related Agencies Appropriations Act, 1993 (Pub. L. No. 102-381)

SECTION	AUTHORITY	OGC WORK EFFORT
Title II	Development and implementation of stewardship end-result contracts on six National Forests.	Assist in developing, and review proposed contracts for legal sufficiency.
	Authorizes the Forest Service to use Salvage Sale funds for timber sale preparation in specified circumstances.	Provide legal advice on the availability of funds for particular purposes and other general implementation questions.
Title II-III	Various provisions relating to the Forest Service.	Provide legal advice on the availability of funds for particular purposes and other general implementation questions.
322	Establish a notice and comment process for proposed Forest Service projects and activities implementing land and resource management plans.	Assist in drafting and legal review of implementing regulations.
	Modify existing administrative appeal procedures for Forest Service projects and activities implementing land and resource management plans.	Assist in drafting and legal review of implementing manual and handbook guidance; provide assistance in training of agency personnel in revised appeal procedures.

Federal Facility Compliance Act of 1992 (Pub. L. No. 102-386)

SECTION	AUTHORITY	OGC WORK EFFORT
§§102 and 103	Waives sovereign immunity for civil and administrative sanctions for violations of Federal, State or local solid or hazardous waste laws.	Provide counseling on the implications of this new Act; provide legal advice and representation in response to enforcement actions by environmental enforcement agencies.

Treasury, Postal Service, and General Government Appropriations Act, 1993 (Pub. L. 102-393)

SECTION	AUTHORITY	OGC WORK EFFORT
Alien Species Prevention and Enforcement Act of 1992, §(1)(b)(1)	Provides authority to enter into cooperative agreements with the State of Hawaii to enforce the Plant Quarantine Act, the Federal Plant Pest Act and the Terminal Inspection Act with regard to mail received in Hawaii.	Review proposed cooperative agreements, and correspondence, and render legal advice, as needed, regarding the Act, cooperative agreements, correspondence and any regulations that may be deemed necessary or desirable under the Acts.
Title VI	Various restrictions on use of appropriated funds.	Provide legal advice on restrictions on use of funds for employment of aliens, redecorating offices, etc.

Community Environmental Response
Facilitation Act
(Pub. L. No. 102-426)

SECTION	AUTHORITY	OGC WORK EFFORT
§§3 and 4	Requires identification of land on which no hazardous substances or petroleum products were stored, released or disposed of; addition to and clarification of covenant in deed requirements for sale or transfer of land by United States.	Provide legal advice on requirements for land transfers. Coordinate with other Federal agencies, including the Department of Interior, on the development of implementation policies for this new Act.

Rural Electrification Administration
Improvement Act of 1992
(Pub. L. 102-428)

SECTION	AUTHORITY	OGC WORK EFFORT
	Establishes a program providing for discounted prepayment of REA direct and insured loans.	Draft and review regulations and transaction documents and assist in closing transactions.

Freedom for Russia and Emerging Eurasian Democracies
and Open Markets Support Act of 1992
(Pub. L. 102-511)

SECTION	AUTHORITY	OGC WORK EFFORT
Title VII	Amends the authority to permit direct concessional credit sales, other credit sales and export promotion to emerging democracies.	Review of implementing regulations, provide oral legal opinions and general advice.

Children's Nutrition Assistance Act of 1992
(Pub. L. 102-512)

SECTION	AUTHORITY	OGC WORK EFFORT
Title II	Requires the Secretary to conduct bid solicitation on behalf of States for WIC infant formula rebates.	Provide legal advice on implementation and administration; review implementing regulations.

Housing and Community Development Act of 1992
(Pub. L. 102-550)

SECTION	AUTHORITY	OGC WORK EFFORT
702	Authorizes housing loans where land is owned by a community land trust.	Provide legal advice on interpretation and on implementing regulations.
703	Increases maximum income of borrowers eligible for guaranteed loans.	Provide legal advice on interpretation and on implementing regulations.
704	Adds tribal lands to definition of "remote rural areas".	Provide legal advice on interpretation and on implementing regulations.
705	Adds tribal lands and colonias to definition of "underserved areas".	Provide legal advice on interpretation and on implementing regulations.
706	Establishes a rural housing voucher program.	Provide legal advice on interpretation and on implementing regulations.
707-16	Changes numerous conditions to the making of rural rental housing loans and grants.	Provide legal advice on interpretation and on implementing regulations.

Amendments to the Food, Agriculture, Conservation, and Trade Act of 1990 to Improve Health Care Services and Educational Services through Telecommunications, and for Other Purposes
(Pub. L. 102-551)

SECTION	AUTHORITY	OGC WORK EFFORT
1	Authorizes grants to consortia for the provision of telecommunications services for health care and educational services.	Provide legal services on standard form grant agreement and on individual grant proposals.

An act to amend the United States Warehouse Act to provide for the use of electronic cotton warehouse receipts and for other purposes.
(Pub. L. 102-553)

SECTION	AUTHORITY	OGC WORK EFFORT
	Provides authority for the Secretary to institute a computer based type of negotiable instrument for the storage of cotton in warehouses licensed under the United States Warehouse Act.	Review and rewrite implementing regulations, provide general advice and participate in joint USDA industry meetings on establishment of the proposed system.

Agricultural Credit Improvement Act of 1992
(Pub. L. 102-554)

SECTION	AUTHORITY	OGC WORK EFFORT
2	Amends limit on aggregate indebtedness for farm ownership and down-payment loans.	Provide legal advice on regulation changes.
	Regulates interest rates and charges on certain guaranteed loans.	Provide legal advice on interpretation and on regulation changes.
5, 19	Provides for Federal-State partnerships for the provision of financial assistance to beginning farmers.	Provide legal advice on interpretation and on implementing regulations.

	Authorizes a new down-payment land acquisition loan program for beginning farmers.	Provide legal advice on interpretation and on implementing regulations.
8	Authorizes a new program to provide operating loans to beginning farmers.	Provide legal advice on interpretation and on implementing regulations.
	Authorizes a new program to encourage borrowers to obtain commercial credit and limits the number of years borrowers can receive FmHA credit.	Provide legal advice on interpretation and on implementing regulations.
10-13, 15	Changes loan application processing requirements for FmHA staff and county committees.	Provide legal advice on interpretation and on implementing regulations.
14	Establishes a new program to facilitate transferring direct borrowers to guaranteed loans.	Provide legal advice on interpretation and on implementing regulations.
16-17	Adds new preferences for sales of inventory property.	Provide legal advice on interpretation and on implementing regulations.
18	Authorizes a new "certified lender" program for guaranteed farm operating loans.	Provide legal advice on interpretation and on implementing regulations.
20	Requires targeting of farm operating and farm ownership funds to the new programs established in this Act.	Provide legal advice on interpretation and on implementing regulations.
21	Establishes target participation rates by gender for farmer program loans.	Provide legal advice on interpretation and on implementing regulations.
22	Changes certain conditions of mediation grants.	Provide legal advice on interpretation and on implementing regulations.

24	Adds definitions of areas where water and waste loans and grants can be made.	Provide legal advice on interpretation and on implementing regulations.

Small Business Research and Development Enhancement Act of 1992
(Pub. L. No. 102-564)

SECTION	AUTHORITY	OGC WORK EFFORT
Title I	Small Business Innovation Research Program.	Provide legal services related to implementation of the Small Business Innovation Program.

NEW LEGISLATION

Mr. DURBIN. Also, provide us a list of all new legislation that has had an impact on your work and tell us in both dollars and staff what the impact has been.

Mr. KELLY. I will provide that for the record.

[The information follows:]

MAJOR PROVISIONS OF NEW LEGISLATION ENACTED
OR MADE EFFECTIVE IN 1992 AND 1993

New Legislation	Impact of Legislation	Estimated Attorney Staff Years	Dollars
Children's Nutrition Assistance Act of 1992 (Pub. L. No. 102-512, Title I)	Provide legal advice on change in funding mechanism for homeless children demonstration project.	.05	$ 3,460
Older Americans Act Amendments of 1992 (Pub. L. No. 102-375, Section 310)	Provide legal advice on amendment to per meal rate of reimbursement for the Nutrition Program for the Elderly.	.05	3,460
Food, Agriculture, Conservation, and Trade Act Amendments of 1991 (Pub. L. No. 102-237)			
-Food Stamp Program	Review implementing regulations; provide general advice on new provisions.	.25	17,301
The Second Dire Emergency Supplemental Appropriations Act for Fiscal Year 1992 (Pub. L. 102-368)			
-Disaster Program	Review implementing regulations, provide general advice on new provisions.	.25	17,301
An Act to amend the United States Warehouse Act to provide for the use of electronic warehouse receipts (Pub. L. 102-553)	Review implementing regulations, provide general advice and oral legal opinions.	.20	13,841

Freedom Support Act (Pub. L. 102-511)	Review implementing regulations, provide general advice and oral and written legal opinions.	.50	34,602
Agricultural Credit Improvement Act of 1992 (Pub. L. 102-554	Review implementing regulations; provide general legal advice on new provisions.	3.00	207,612
Housing and Community Development Act of 1992 (Pub. L. 102-550)	Review implementing regulations; provide general legal advice on new provisions.	1.00	69,204
Rural Electrification Administration Act of 1992 (Pub. L. 102-428) § 2 - New REA Loan Prepayment Program	Draft and review implementing regulations and transaction documents and assist in closing transactions.	.50	34,602
The Energy Policy Act of 1992 (Pub. L. 102-486) Titles I, VII, XII, XXI provides for comprehensive changes in the electric utility industry	Review affected regulations, revise transaction documents to reflect industry-wide changes, provide general legal advice on implications for REA electric programs.	1.00	69,204

Forest Resources Conservation and Shortage Relief Act of 1990 (Pub. L. No 101-382)			
-Direct Export Restriction Program	Review a draft, comprehensive final regulation prohibiting export of unprocessed logs from federal lands in the West.	.75	51,903
-Indirect Export Restriction Program	Review materials developed to administer indirect export restriction program (e.g., handbook and manual sections).	.10	6,920
-Sourcing Area Establishment and Periodic Review Program	Prepare procedures for sourcing area adjudications and assist with sourcing area adjudications and review.	.20	13,841
-Civil Penalty Assessment Program	Review facts and assist with administrative prosecutions to enforce civil penalties.	.10	6,920
-Debarment Program	Review facts, procedures and proposed debarments.	.05	3,460
-Surplus species determination	Review proposed and final regulation re surplus species determination.	.05	3,460
Agriculture, Rural Development, Food and Drug Administration, and Related Agencies Appropriations Act, 1993 (Pub. L. No. 102-341)	Provide oral and written opinions.	.50	34,602

Small Business Research and Development Enhancement Act of 1992 (Pub. L. No. 102-331)	Provide general advice on new provisions.	.10	6,920
Department of the Interior and Related Agencies Appropriations Act, 1993 (Pub. L. No. 102-391)	Provide oral and written opinions.	.25	17,301
Treasury, Postal Service, and General Government Appropriations Act, 1993 (Pub. L. No. 102-393)	Provide oral opinions.	.05	3,460
Federal Facility Compliance Act of 1992 (Pub. L. No. 102-386)	Provide oral and written opinions; represent client agencies in enforcement actions taken by environmental enforcement agencies.	.10	6,920
Community Environmental Response Facilitation Act (Pub. L. No. 102-426)	Provide oral and written opinions. Coordinate with other Federal agencies, including the Department of Interior, on the development of implementation policies for this new Act.	.15	10,381
Pub. L. 102-551 establishes grant program for improving rural health care and educational services through tele-communications.	Draft and review implementing regulations and transaction documents and provide legal advice on program issues.	.25	17,301

LOCATION OF ATTORNEYS

Mr. DURBIN. For the record please provide a table showing the number of attorneys within the Office of the General Counsel and where they are located.

Mr. KELLY. I will provide for the record a table showing our attorneys by location as of March 19, 1993.

[The information follows:]

Attorney Locations and Positions

Washington, DC	143
Albuquerque, NM	4
Atlanta, GA	12
Chicago, IL	5
Columbus, OH	2
Denver, CO	12
Fresno, CA	1
Gainesville, FL	1
Greenwood, MS	1
Harrisburg, PA	7
Hato Rey, PR	2
Indianapolis, IN	1
Jackson, MS	3
Juneau, AK	3
Leawood, KS	8
Lincoln, NE	2
Little Rock, AR	7
Milwaukee, WI	7
Missoula, MT	6
Montgomery, AL	3
Mt. Holly, NJ	1
Ogden, UT	4
Portland, OR	12
Raleigh, NC	2
Richmond, VA	3
Sacramento, CA	1
San Francisco, CA	14
St. Paul, MN	1
Stevens Point, WI	1
Stillwater, OK	2
Temple, TX	5
Total	276

ATTORNEY HOURS WORKED

Mr. DURBIN. Please update the table that appears on page 322 of last year's hearing record showing attorney-hours worked by category to include fiscal year 1992.

Mr. KELLY. I will provide that for the record.

[The information follows:]

Attorney Hours Worked
Fiscal Years 1988 - 1992

Areas:	FY 1988	FY 1989	FY 1990	FY 1991	FY 1992
Administrative Cases	52,849	54,298.5	50,501.5	46,351.5	46,892
Civil Cases	112,413.5	118,953.5	119,104.5	121,716	131.865
Criminal Cases	4,730.5	4,702.5	3,764	3,595	8,253
Nonjudicial Foreclosures	5,904.5	5,923	5,076.5	5,997	6,326
Hearing Officer/Claims Adjudicator Cases	7,952.5	9,113	9,390	10,202	11,479
Regulations	22,509.5	21,103.5	22,047.5	22,579	20,574.5
Correspondence/Documents	80,482.5	85,013	86,878.5	94,781.5	102,117.5
Oral Opinions	43,644.5	44,211	44,962.5	47,092.5	55,236
Draft or Review Legislation, Legislative Reports, Testimony	4,486	5,689	5,886	6.961	6,234.5
Other	57,817.5	62,356.5	69,147	80,238	89,011
Total	392,790	411,363.5	416,758	439,513.5	477,988.5

Mr. DURBIN. Of the attorney-hours worked during fiscal year 1992, please provide us with a breakout of how much was spent for each USDA agency and what percentage this was of the total.

Mr. KELLY. I will provide that information for the record.

[Informaiton follows:]

ATTORNEY HOURS FOR FISCAL YEAR 1992

[By agency]

	Hours	Percent
Agricultural Marketing Service	33,459	7
Agricultural Stabilization and Conservation Service	19,119.5	4
Animal and Plant Health Inspection Service	33,459	7
Commodity Credit Corporation	9,560	2
Farmers Home Administration	129,057	27
Federal Crop Insurance Corporation	4,780	1
Food and Nutrition Service	23,899.5	5
Food Safety and Inspection Service	14,340	3
Foreign Agricultural Service	4,780	1
Forest Service	124,277	26
Packers and Stockyards Administration	9,560	2
Rural Electrification Administration	19,119.5	4
Soil Conservation Service	9,560	2
Other (includes OGC internal management and several UDSA agencies where time spent is less than 1%	43,018	9
Total	477,988.5	100

USER FEE ATTORNEY HOURS

Mr. DURBIN. For those agencies which you propose to collect or are already collecting a user fee reimbursement, please provide the attorney-hours spent during fiscal years 1991 through 1993.

Mr. KELLY. Our office did not keep records of attorney hours spent on user fee programs in FY 1991 because our office did not bill client agencies for legal services at that time. We believe, however, that the total hours spent would have approximated those reported for FY 1992. Our figures reflecting time spent on user fee programs in FY 1992 are based on existing work measurement data that in most cases was not user-fee program specific. The figures for the first five months of FY 1993 are based on actual hours spent during that time. The annual figures for FY 1993 are based on our estimate of hours to be worked.

[The information follows:]

ESTIMATED USER FEE ATTORNEY HOURS FOR FISCAL YEAR 1991–93

	Fiscal year—		
	1992	1993 (5 mos)	1993 (projected annual)
Agency:			
Agricultural Marketing Service	26,259	7,274	26,832
Animal and Plant Health Inspection Service	8,320	2,160	7,904
Federal Grain Inspection Service	6,656	54	6,864
Agricultural Stabilization and Conservation Service	936	59	956
Food Safety and Inspection Service	1,530	29	1,456

OTHER WORK SITES

Mr. DURBIN. Your statement mentions that services are provided through 11 Divisions in Washington, 22 field offices, and eight client host or other special work sites. Describe in further detail these client host or other special work sites.

Mr. KELLY. Five of the eight work sites mentioned involve attorneys who are located with Farmers Home Administration State Offices in Florida, Indiana, Minnesota, New Jersey, and Wisconsin. These attorneys are provided at the request of FmHA to meet the localized needs of those offices. Two of the eight sites involve attorneys who are located in the U.S. Attorney's offices in Fresno and Sacramento, California, handling marketing order compliance cases and timber theft cases, respectively. The attorney located in Greenwood, Mississippi, handles Perishable Agricultural Commodities Act cases for the Agricultural Marketing Service.

STAFF LEVELS

Mr. DURBIN. For the record, provide the Committee with a table showing the total OGC staff level and a breakout of this level between those funded through OGC's appropriation and those funded through reimbursement from other USDA appropriations for fiscal years 1990 through 1993.

Mr. KELLY. I will provide for the record a table showing a breakout of staff levels between those funded through appropriation and those funded through reimbursements.

[The information follows:]

OGC STAFF YEARS BY APPROPRIATION AND REIMBURSEMENTS—FISCAL YEAR 1990, 1991, 1992 ACTUALS AND FISCAL YEAR 1993 ESTIMATED

	Fiscal year—			
	1990	1991	1992	1993
Office of the General Counsel	363	372	381	352
Allocation from hazard waste management	0	5	7	7
Staff under other USDA appropriations:				
AMS			1	1
FmHA		1	4	11
FS		4	9	28
AMS—User fees				13
APHIS—User fees				4
FGIS—User fees				3
ASCS—User fees				1
Total, Other USDA appropriations	3	5	14	61
Total, Office of the General Counsel	366	382	402	420

Mr. DURBIN. Mr. Skeen?

Mr. SKEEN. I thank you.

DECISIONS ON REIMBURSABLES

Give me an example of how you make a decision on those that are constitutionally required to handle with no fee from the particular agency.

Mr. KELLY. I am sorry—I don't understand the question, Mr. Skeen.

Mr. SKEEN. Well, the Office of the General Counsel has certain basic responsibilities to the agencies, as I understand it.

Mr. KELLY. Certainly.

Mr. SKEEN. Do you charge for every case that you handle?

Mr. KELLY. No, we do not.

Mr. SKEEN. Well, give me an example. I am trying to get a line of delineation between the fee services and those that you handle on a regular basis without a fee.

Mr. KELLY. I understand. We receive an appropriation, as you well know, from the Congress each year, and that appropriation constitutes our principal funding.

Mr. SKEEN. Yes.

Mr. KELLY. If the Secretary's office or any agency of the Department asks us to perform an additional service which is distinguishable from the services for which we have sought and received an appropriation, which is not within the kinds of services that we normally perform or are expected to perform with those appropriations, then we think there is authority to enter into an agreement, a reimbursable agreement——

Mr. SKEEN. A contractual agreement?

Mr. KELLY. Essentially—with one of the Department's agencies to provide additional service on a reimbursable basis.

NUMBER OF ATTORNEYS

Mr. SKEEN. I see. How many attorneys do you have in the Office of the General Counsel?

Mr. KELLY. We have approximately 260 attorneys, and those are not quite equally divided—almost equally divided between Washington and the field offices.

Mr. SKEEN. That encompasses the whole group under the General Counsel?

Mr. KELLY. Yes, it does, Mr. Skeen.

ATTORNEY SALARIES

Mr. SKEEN. What are the salary scales, starting from the highest?

Mr. KELLY. Entry-level attorneys start at GS–11, and I believe that pay level is between $33,000 and $34,000 presently. The highest pay level is the highest pay level for the Senior Executive Service which is presently, I believe, up to $115,700.

LAWSUITS

Mr. SKEEN. How many lawsuits are you involved in now?

Mr. KELLY. We believe that there are about 40,000——

Mr. SKEEN. 40,000?

Mr. KELLY [continuing]. Cases presently involving the Department. The large bulk of those, of course, include Farmers Home foreclosures and bankruptcies and other litigation arising out of the Farmers Home lending programs.

But there are sizable numbers of cases that also arise out of the ASCS programs, the activities of the Forest Service, and both recipient and retailer lawsuits arising under the food and nutrition programs. So there is just a huge number of actions pending against the Department at any given time, Mr. Skeen.

Mr. SKEEN. That seems to be the same basis for the litigation in many of the agencies of the Federal Government. Are they increasing or decreasing?

Mr. KELLY. They are remaining about the same. Those numbers, roughly 40,000, have been true for several years.

ENDANGERED SPECIES ACT

Mr. SKEEN. I need to get an expression of how many lawsuits deal with the Endangered Species Act.

Mr. KELLY. Mr. Skeen, I would hesitate to give you a number. Certainly, there are a lot.

Mr. SKEEN. Quite a few.

Mr. KELLY. There are quite a few. And on no national forest in the Pacific Northwest, on no national forest anywhere in the West where there are sensitive or endangered or threatened species, it does seem to me that we are at least without one challenge to the implementation of a forest plan.

Mr. SKEEN. Just about everybody has a forestry problem.

Mr. KELLY. And this is clearly more critical in the Western States.

ENVIRONMENTAL ISSUES

Mr. SKEEN. How much of your litigation is involving environmental issues?

Mr. KELLY. I could supply a rough percentage of that for the record, if I could.

Mr. SKEEN. I would like a rough percentage on all those categories.

Mr. KELLY. Sure. I will provide the percentages for the record.

[The information follows:]

The Office of the General Counsel devotes substantial legal resources to environmental issues raised in litigation and administrative appeals. The Forest Service was a defendant in approximately 80 active cases in federal courts involving compliance with various environmental laws as of December 1992. About a quarter of these cases include specific claims alleging violation of the Endangered Species Act.

The National Forest System is home to 242 of the 749 plant and animal species listed as either threatened or endangered under the Endangered Species Act. National Forest System also provides habitat for 900 ESA "candidate" species. Regional Foresters have also identified 2,259 sensitive species that are managed to prevent listing under the Endangered Species Act.

The scope of a single challenge under the Endangered Species Act, the National Environmental Policy Act or the National Forest Management Act may be sweeping in effect. A single injunction in the Pacific Northwest halted new timber sales on portions of 17 National Forests in Washington, Oregon and California. The recently listed Mexican spotted owl will constrain management activities in a number of National Forests in Arizona, New Mexico, Utah and Colorado. Litigation involving standards to protect the Red-Cockaded Woodpecker affects 21 National Forests in the Southeast. The 1992 ESA listing of certain salmon stocks and concern for viability of other anadromous fish has triggered five lawsuits which have the potential for broad court orders affecting National Forest and other land usage.

As of March, 1993 the Forest Service had received 1216 administrative appeals of land management plans. Additionally, 3112 administrative appeals were filed during FY 92. These administrative appeals cover all program areas. While no specific records are kept of each individual allegation, virtually all of the appeals challenging projects and management activities on National Forest System Lands involve at least one allegation that environmental laws such as the National Environmental Policy Act, the National Forest Management Act or the Endangered Species Act have been violated.

AREAS OF LITIGATION

Mr. SKEEN. And which areas of litigation drive your expenditure of your appropriated funds?

Mr. KELLY. Oh, I would say the areas that arise under the Farmers Home Lending programs.

Mr. SKEEN. Farmers Home Lending programs?

Mr. KELLY. And the Forest Service activities.

OFFICE AUTOMATION

Mr. SKEEN. What is the condition of your database?

Mr. KELLY. Our database needs attention, Mr. Skeen.

Mr. SKEEN. This is a chronic problem. We take care of personnel, but we never worry about the database, and yet your personnel depends on the database.

Mr. KELLY. I am sure that is right. We started several years ago with a five-phased plan to upgrade OGC's database and to design and implement and put in place a work load item management system. That was, as I said——

Mr. SKEEN. Five years ago?

Mr. KELLY. Well, three or four years ago.

Mr. SKEEN. Okay.

Mr. KELLY. And that was a five-phased project. We got through phase two of the project before we, essentially, ran out of sufficient funds to continue. We have gone into a pilot use of the project in two field offices in Atlanta and San Francisco and in our Washington divisions.

Mr. SKEEN. Are you networked with all your field offices?

Mr. KELLY. We are networked with our regional offices.

Mr. SKEEN. Have you in principle, shut out improvements of your database because of lack of funding?

Mr. KELLY. We have done that, yes.

Mr. SKEEN. Have you asked for an increase in this year's appropriation?

Mr. KELLY. No, we have not asked for an appropriation for that——

Mr. SKEEN. Why not?

Mr. KELLY. We did ask for an increase, but it was denied.

Mr. SKEEN. At the Department level was it denied?

Mr. KELLY. No, it was denied in our final budget allowance from OMB. So it is not reflected in the request you have before you.

Mr. SKEEN. I don't see how they expect you to do your work if you don't have an adequate database. It makes it more difficult because you can't pick and shovel this work anymore.

Mr. KELLY. We look forward to the day when we would be able to have fully computerized records with respect to all lawsuits presently pending and all work items presently pending in our office nationwide, but I don't see it any time soon.

Mr. SKEEN. Without the database your costs are going to go up, I would assume, in handling the caseload that you have got.

Mr. KELLY. Not only is that a problem, but the fact is that the hardware that we presently have in place in many of our field offices and the Washington divisions is rapidly becoming obsolete.

Mr. SKEEN. Outmoded. If you gasp for just one year's gasping time with regard to data processing, you are getting behind the curve.

Mr. KELLY. Yes, that is right.

Mr. SKEEN. Thank you very much. I think we ought to put some more money in that database sometime.

Thank you, Mr. Chairman.

Mr. DURBIN. Thanks, Mr. Skeen.

Mr. Kelly and your panel, I appreciate your testimony.

Mr. KELLY. Thank you very much, Mr. Chairman.

OFFICE OF THE GENERAL COUNSEL

STATEMENT OF JAMES MICHAEL KELLY, ACTING GENERAL COUNSEL,

UNITED STATES DEPARTMENT OF AGRICULTURE

BEFORE THE

SUBCOMMITTEE ON AGRICULTURE, RURAL DEVELOPMENT,

FOOD AND DRUG ADMINISTRATION AND RELATED AGENCIES

INTRODUCTION

Mr. Chairman and members of the Subcommittee, I am pleased to appear before you today to discuss an overview of the Office of the General Counsel and our fiscal year 1994 appropriation request.

I am joined by Bob Franks, Deputy General Counsel; William Perrelli, Director, Administration and Resource Management; Charlene Buckner, our Finance and Budget Analyst; and of course, Mr. Dewhurst.

MISSION OF THE AGENCY

The Office of the General Counsel (OGC) is responsible for providing legal advice and services to the Secretary of Agriculture and other officials of the Department of Agriculture and for all programs, operations, and activities of the Department's 42 agencies, staff offices and corporations.

The mission of OGC is to determine legal policy, provide legal services, and direct the performance of all legal work for the Department throughout its Washington and field locations. The General Counsel is the principal legal advisor to the Secretary of Agriculture and is responsible for providing legal advice and representation for the Department.

SIZE

As of September 30, 1992, OGC had 406 employees of which 377 were permanent full-time employees and 29 were other employees. There were 178 permanent full-time employees and 9 other employees located in Washington, D.C., and 199 permanent full-time employees and 20 other employees in the field. Our full staffing levels are approximately 260 attorneys and 146 support staff.

ORGANIZATION

OGC's services are provided through 11 Divisions in Washington, 22 field offices, and 8 client host or other special work sites. The headquarters for OGC is located in Washington, D.C. The Office is directed by a General Counsel, a Deputy General Counsel, four Associate General Counsels, and 11 Assistant General Counsels, and a Director for Administration and Resource Management. We have attached an organizational chart for your information that shows the overall structure of the office.

The headquarters legal staff is divided into four areas: (1) Regulatory and Marketing; (2) International Affairs, Commodity Programs and Food Assistance Programs; (3) Community Development and Natural Resources; and (4) Legislation, Litigation, Research and Operations.

FIELD STRUCTURE

OGC has five regional offices, each headed by a Regional Attorney, and 17 branch offices headed by an Associate or Assistant Regional Attorney. The locations of these offices are listed on the attached organizational chart. Currently, OGC has 8 employees working in the offices of client agencies, U.S. Attorneys, or in other locations. These sites include Fresno and Sacramento, California; Mt. Holly, New Jersey; St. Paul, Minnesota; Stevens Point, Wisconsin; Gainesville, Florida; Greenwood, Mississippi; and Indianapolis, Indiana. We also expect shortly to have an attorney in Boise, Idaho.

OGC's field offices provide legal advice and services with respect to all matters arising from the administration of programs by agency field staff. A majority of the Department's litigation is completed at the field level through direct referrals to U.S. Attorneys, without involvement of the Washington office. OGC field-level legal services are provided primarily to the Agricultural Stabilization and Conservation

Service, Farmers Home Administration, and the Forest Service. Other Departmental agencies, including the Agricultural Marketing Service, Animal and Plant Health Inspection Service, Federal Crop Insurance Corporation, Food and Nutrition Service, Soil Conservation Service, and other agencies, also receive legal services from OGC field offices.

STATUS OF FY 1993 FUNDS

In fiscal year 1993, Congress appropriated $24,554,000, which is the same amount that was appropriated in fiscal year 1992. We also expect to receive approximately $1,107,000 for providing legal services to Department user fee programs. As you may recall, our budget request last year was reduced by this amount, with the reduction to be offset by reimbursements from the user fee programs. The amount of available funds for fiscal year 1993 has necessitated the continuation of certain austerity measures that were implemented in fiscal year 1992 and the implementation of some new measures. Some of the austerity measures include significant reductions in discretionary funding for travel, training, supplies, and equipment; delaying promotions for 120 days after approval; except in the case of emergencies, not replacing either legal or support staff as positions are vacated; reducing the use of automated legal research services; cancelling the attorney recruitment program; and eliminating cash awards and Senior Executive Service bonuses, rank awards and pay level adjustments. Continued implementation of OGC's database contract has also been suspended.

Through these initiatives, at the mid-year point in execution, we believe that OGC will be able to execute a balanced program for fiscal year 1993 without implementing any additional austerity measures. Every effort is being made to ensure that the current fiscal crunch will not unduly affect the quality of service we render to the Department or materially disrupt operations and morale within OGC.

CURRENT ACTIVITIES AND ISSUES

We understand that the Subcommittee would like us to address some of the current activities in which we are involved, as well as current issues. Much of OGC's workload is on-going in the sense that we continue to review regulations, prepare civil and criminal cases to be filed by the Department of Justice, defend against lawsuits filed against the Department, prosecute administrative cases, provide both formal and informal advice, and draft proposed legislation. While the names and issues change, the basic legal services we provide are essentially the same over time. However, I would like to highlight a few areas.

Because of changes in laws and changes required by court decisions, the Department is continuously amending its regulations. Some that we have been working on recently in the natural resources area and that are on-going include regulation changes relating to appeals of Forest Service decisions, land management planning regulations, cancellation of timber sales contracts for the protection of sensitive, threatened or endangered species, timber exports, and non-commercial use of National Forest System lands. In the regulatory area some of the significant regulation changes we have been addressing include those relating to pesticide recordkeeping requirements, pine shoot beetles, biotechnology, and various aspects of nutrition labelling. Extensive legal advice has been and will continue to be provided in connection with the Department's reappraisal of the meat and poultry inspection systems.

In the area of agricultural credit, we have been involved in developing regulations which implement new rural economic development programs, such as the Rural Electrification Administration's Distance Learning and Medical Link Program, and which revise existing programs, such as REA's Discounted Prepayment Program. We are also providing legal assistance in connection with development of the Farmers Home Administration beginning farmer operating loan and farm ownership downpayment loan programs.

Some pending litigation involves challenges to Department regulations. These cases involve labelling of mechanically separated meat and poultry, health labelling of meat, and Animal Welfare Act regulations. Other major litigation includes, of course, injunctions against timber sales because of the northern spotted owl, water rights adjudications, food stamp litigation, including the settlement of outstanding Quality Control claims against the states, and numerous bankruptcy matters.

The office also continues to provide legal services in connection with various international trade issues. These include questions arising in connection with agricultural provisions of the Uruguay Round of multilateral trade negotiations under the auspices of the General Agreement on Tariffs and Trade, the proposed North American Free Trade Agreement--which will also necessitate the drafting of legislation to implement various aspects of that proposal--and the United States-Canada Free-Trade Agreement.

Under the Clinton Administration, there undoubtedly will be new initiatives and actions that will likewise require OGC involvement. One example already is the decision by Secretary Espy to suspend foreclosures involving Farmers Home Administration farmer program borrowers. OGC has spent considerable time advising the Secretary's office and FmHA on the implementation of that initiative. We also expect to be heavily involved in Pacific Northwest wildlife and forestry issues.

With our appropriation essentially the same for the last two years and for the coming year, like most other agencies we have had to find ways to reduce spending. One of the issues arising from that relates to our contract to implement a standardized nationwide correspondence control and case tracking and reporting system. We have not been able to proceed beyond the installation of a pilot system in some of the Washington offices and 2 field offices. Since the current systems that most of our offices use to track their data have far surpassed their life expectancy, we will be faced shortly with a decision of replacing these obsolete systems with standalone database software applications and forgoing further implementation of the nationwide pilot system. We will be giving further consideration to this matter in the near future.

FY 1994 BUDGET REQUEST

For fiscal year 1994, OGC is requesting $25,045,000 in direct appropriations. This request represents a net increase of $491,000 over the fiscal year 1993 appropriation. Of the requested increase, $502,000 is for the annualization of the fiscal year 1993 pay raise. OGC's request was also increased by $55,000, which reflects a 2.7 percent increase for non-salary costs; however, that increase was offset by a $59,000 reduction, which reflects a 3 percent decrease for administrative purposes, in keeping with the President's Executive Order to promote the efficient use of resources. OGC's request was also reduced by $7,000 for FTS2000, due to anticipated lower price.

Mr. Chairman, we realize that in these times of huge federal deficits and tight budgets all agencies must tighten their belts and learn to provide more with less. It goes without saying that we are willing to do our part, and we have in fact adopted a number of cost-saving measures in both FY 1992 and FY 1993. However, the overall amount of legal work never seems to decrease, and Departmental agencies are continually seeking new or expanded legal services. We have worked directly with several of our client agencies to address their additional needs for more lawyers through reimbursable agreements. However, since OGC is a staff agency and 91 percent of our budget consists of funds for personnel compensation, we have no way to absorb cuts below our request without placing a severe strain on the office and adversely affecting daily operations. Therefore, the entire amount of our budget request is essential to maintain our current, existing staff and levels of service.

CLOSING

That concludes my statement, Mr. Chairman. We appreciate the support this Committee has given us in the past. I will be happy to answer any questions you and the Committee members may have at this time. Thank you.

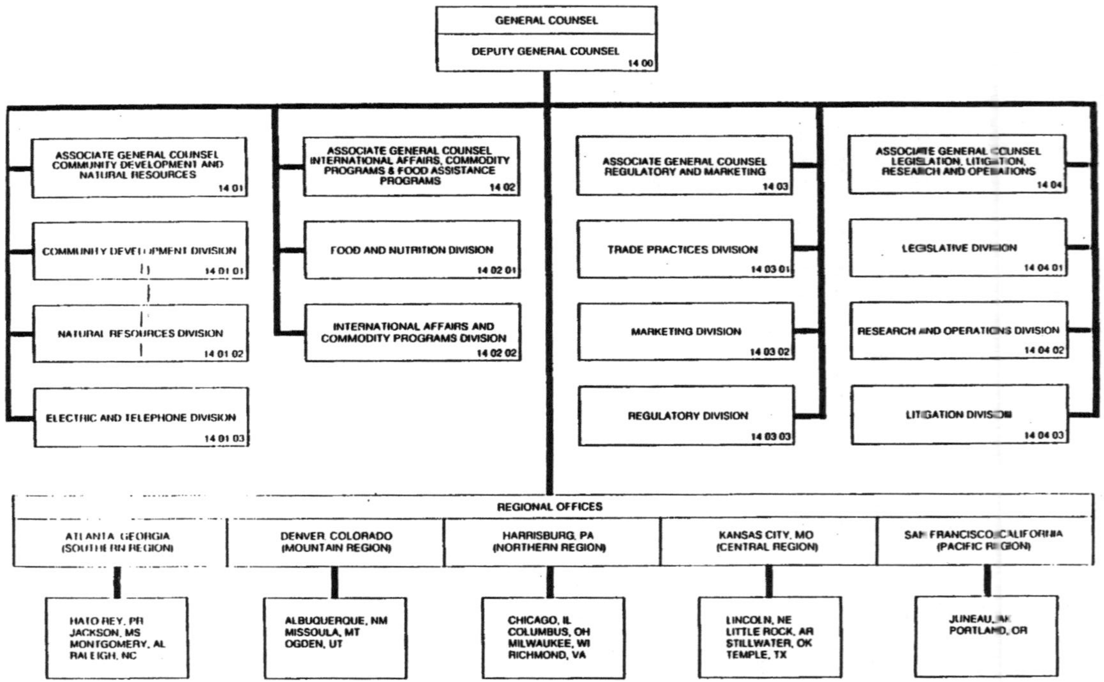

THE MISSION OF THE OFFICE OF THE GENERAL COUNSEL IS TO DETERMINE LEGAL POLICY AND DIRECT THE PERFORMANCE OF ALL LEGAL WORK BY THE DEPARTMENT

SUPERSEDES CHART DATED SEPTEMBER 20, 1988

OFFICE OF THE GENERAL COUNSEL

Purpose Statement

The Office of the General Counsel, which, prior to 1955, was known as the Office of the Solicitor, was established in 1910 (70 Stat. 742) as the law office of the Department of Agriculture.

The Office provides all essential and necessary legal advice and services for the Department's ongoing programs. The headquarters legal staff is divided into four sections: (1) Regulatory and Marketing; (2) International Affairs, Commodity Programs and Food Assistance Programs; (3) Community Development and Natural Resources; and (4) Legislation, Litigation, Research and Operations.

Geographic Location. The work of this office is carried out in Washington, D.C., and five regions which include 22 offices as follows:

Southern Region:
- Atlanta, Georgia
- Hato Rey, Puerto Rico
- Jackson, Mississippi
- Montgomery, Alabama
- Raleigh, North Carolina

Central Region:
- Leawood, Kansas
- Lincoln, Nebraska
- Little Rock, Arkansas
- Stillwater, Oklahoma
- Temple, Texas

Mountain Region:
- Denver, Colorado
- Albuquerque, New Mexico
- Missoula, Montana
- Ogden, Utah

Pacific Region:
- San Francisco, California
- Juneau, Alaska
- Portland, Oregon

Northern Region:
- Harrisburg, Pennsylvania
- Chicago, Illinois
- Columbus, Ohio
- Milwaukee, Wisconsin
- Richmond, Virginia

As of September 30, 1992, the office had 406 employees of which 377 were permanent full-time employees and 29 were other employees. There were 178 permanent full-time employees and 9 other employees located in Washington, D.C., and 199 permanent full-time employees and 20 other employees in the field.

6-2

OFFICE OF THE GENERAL COUNSEL

Available Funds and Staff-Years

1992 Actual and Estimated, 1993 and 1994

Item	1992 Actual		1993 Estimated		1994 Estimated	
	Amount	Staff-Years	Amount	Staff-Years	Amount	Staff-Years
Office of the General Counsel	$24,554,000	381	$24,554,000	352	$25,045,000	352
Allocation from:						
Hazardous Waste Management	595,007	7	513,000	7	492,000	7
Obliga- ons under other USDA appropriations:						
AMS	65,811	1	83,000	1	85,000	1
FmHA	360,286	4	821,000	11	810,000	11
FS	697,820	9	1,516,000	28	1,260,000	15
AMS-User Fees			711,000	13	926,000	13
APHIS-User Fees			207,000	4	325,000	4
FGIS-User Fees			166,000	3	123,000	3
ASCS-User Fees			23,000	1	34,000	1
FSIS-User Fees					40,000	1
Total, Other USDA Appropriations	1,123,917	14	3,527,000	61	3,603,000	49
Total, Office of the General Counsel	26,272,924	402	28,594,000	420	29,140,000	408

OFFICE OF THE GENERAL COUNSEL
Permanent Positions by Grade and Staff-Year Summary
1992 and Estimated 1993 and 1994

Grade	1992			1993			1994		
	Hdqrs	Field	Total	Hdqrs	Field	Total	Hdqrs	Field	Total
Executive Level IV	1	--	1	1	--	1	1	--	1
ES-6	2	--	2	2	--	2	2	--	2
ES-5	3	--	3	3	--	3	3	--	3
ES-4	6	1	7	6	1	7	7	1	8
ES-3	3	1	4	3	1	4	2	4	6
ES-2	--	3	3	--	3	3	1	0	1
ES-1	--	--	--	--	--	--	--	--	--
GS/GM-15	38	18	56	38	18	56	37	18	55
GS/GM-14	43	75	118	42	76	118	54	87	141
GS/GM-13	20	13	33	20	13	33	26	14	40
GS-12	17	14	31	19	14	33	17	5	22
GS-11	11	5	16	19	7	26	2	1	3
GS-10	--	--	--	--	--	--	1	--	1
GS- 9	8	13	21	8	14	22	5	13	18
GS- 8	10	9	19	10	9	19	10	8	18
GS- 7	9	20	29	9	21	30	11	24	35
GS- 6	9	17	26	9	17	26	8	15	23
GS- 5	3	22	25	3	22	25	4	20	24
GS- 4	4	7	11	4	8	12	1	6	7
GS- 3	--	--	--	--	--	--	--	--	--
GS- 2	--	--	--	--	--	--	--	--	--
Other Graded Positions	--	--	--	--	--	--	--	--	--
Ungraded Positions	--	--	--	--	--	--	--	--	--
Total Permanent Positions	187	218	405	196	224	420	192	216	408
Unfilled Positions, end-of-year..	-9	-19	-28	--	--	--	--	--	--
Total Permanent Employment, end-of-year..	178	199	377	196	224	420	192	216	408
Staff-Years Ceiling	187	215	402	196	224	420	192	216	408

OFFICE OF THE GENERAL COUNSEL

CLASSIFICATION BY OBJECTS

1992 and Estimated 1993 and 1994

	1992	1993	1994
Personnel Compensation:			
Headquarters	$10,057,487	$9,357,239	$ 9,546,079
Field	8,838,173	9,561,627	9,741,324
11 Total Personnel Compensation	18,895,660	18,918,866	19,287,403
12 Personnel Benefits	3,535,764	3,522,138	3,678,826
13 Benefits for former personnel	-0-	11,771	11,771
Total Pers. Comp. & Benefits	22,431,424	22,452,775	22,978,000
Other Objects:			
21 Travel	178,233	222,800	220,816
22 Transportation of things	7,035	10,000	7,000
23 Communications, utilities and other rent	669,018	729,828	697,411
24 Printing and reproduction ...	30,369	29,412	28,668
25 Other services	576,959	556,315	542,231
26 Supplies and materials	415,805	438,437	458,515
31 Equipment	215,660	114,433	112,359
43 Interest Penalty	1,271	- -	- -
44 Refunds	-1,774	- -	- -
Total Other Objects	2,092,576	2,101,225	2,067,000
Total Direct Obligations	24,524,000	24,554,000	25,045,000
Position Data:			
Average Salary, ES positions	$102,792	$105,785	$106,230
Average Salary, GM/GS positions	$44,058	$46,393	$48,084
Average Grade, GM/GS positions	11.27	11.23	11.48

OFFICE OF THE GENERAL COUNSEL

The estimates include appropriation language for this item as follows (new language underscored; deleted matter enclosed in brackets):

Office of the General Counsel:

For necessary expenses of the Office of the General Counsel, [$24,554,000]. $25,045,000

SALARIES AND EXPENSES

Appropriations Act, 1993	$24,554,000
Budget Request, 1994	25,045,000
Increase in Appropriation	+491,000

SUMMARY OF INCREASES AND DECREASES
(On basis of appropriation)

Item of Change	1993 Estimated	Pay Cost	Other Changes	1994 Estimated
Legal Services..	$24,554,000	+$502,000	-$11,000	$25,045,000

PROJECT STATEMENT
(On basis of appropriation)

Project	1992 Actual Amount	1992 Staff Years	1993 Estimated Amount	1993 Staff Years	Increase or Decrease	1994 Estimated Amount	1994 Staff Years
Legal Services	$24,524,000	381	$24,554,000	352	+491,000	$25,045,000	352
Unobligated balance	30,000						
Total, Appropriation	$24,554,000	381	$24,554,000	352	+491,000 (1)	$25,045,000	352

EXPLANATION OF PROGRAM

The General Counsel is the chief law officer of the Department and is responsible for providing legal services for all programs, operations, and activities of the Department. The General Counsel is assisted by a Deputy General Counsel and four Associate General Counsels, each of whom is responsible for a portion of the legal work of the Department. The functions of this Office are performed in the Washington office and five regions which include five regional and 17 branch offices. The Law Library was transferred from the National Agricultural Library to OGC in 1982.

The field offices handle legal work relating primarily to the activities of the Agricultural Stabilization and Conservation Service, Agricultural Marketing Service, Commodity Credit Corporation, Farmers Home Administration, Federal Crop Insurance Corporation, Forest Service, Rural Development Administration, Soil Conservation Service, and the Food and Nutrition Service. By delegation of the General Counsel, legal work relating to other programs and activities of the Department may be handled by a field office.

Legal Advice. The Office of the General Counsel issues both formal and informal opinions on legal questions arising in the administration of the Department's programs; prepares or reviews administrative rules and regulations applicable to the public; drafts proposed legislation; prepares or interprets contracts, mortgages, leases, deeds, and similar documents; prepares patent applications arising out of inventions by Department employees; and considers and determines claims by and against the United States arising out of the Department's activities.

Administrative Proceedings. The Department is represented by the General Counsel in administrative proceedings for the promulgation of rules having the force and effect of law and in quasi-judicial hearings held in connection with the administration of various USDA programs.

Civil Litigation. Civil litigation arising out of the Department's work is handled by the Department of Justice, with attorneys of the Office of the General Counsel assisting in the preparation and trial of such cases. The General Counsel represents the Secretary in administrative proceedings before the Interstate Commerce Commission involving freight rates on farm commodities and in appeals from the decisions of the Commission to the courts. By delegation, the Associate General Counsel for Legislation, Litigation, Research and Operations represents the Department in certain classes of cases before the United States Courts of Appeals.

Criminal Litigation. Criminal cases are reviewed for the purpose of referring them to the Department of Justice.

JUSTIFICATION OF INCREASES AND DECREASES

(1) An increase of $491,000 for the Office of the General Counsel consisting of:

(a) An increase of $55,000 which reflects a 2.7 percent increase in non-salary costs.

(b) An increase of $502,000 which reflects the annualization of the fiscal year 1993 pay raise.

(c) A decrease of $59,000 for administrative efficiency.

Need for Change. To promote the efficient use of resources for administrative purposes, in keeping with the President's Executive Order, total USDA baseline outlays for these activities will be reduced by 3 percent in FY 1994, 6 percent in FY 1995, 9 percent in FY 1996 and 14 percent in FY 1997.

Nature of Change. In order to achieve this savings, OGC will reduce supply purchases and printing and reproduction services. OGC will also closely monitor contractual services, utility and communication charges and reduce travel.

(d) A decrease of $7,000 for FTS 2000 funding.

This decrease reflects lower long distance telecommunications prices due to price redeterminations in the FTS 2000 contracts.

Office of the General Counsel
GEOGRAPHIC BREAKDOWN OF OBLIGATIONS AND STAFF-YEARS
1992 and Estimated 1993 and 1994

	1992		1993		1994	
	Amount	Staff Years	Amount	Staff Years	Amount	Staff Years
Alabama................	$ 276,139	6	$ 293,187	6	$ 298,294	6
Alaska.................	220,556	4	242,150	4	245,369	4
Arkansas...............	658,329	12	719,506	12	731,221	12
California.............	1,143,436	19	1,297,232	20	1,315,555	21
Colorado...............	861,809	15	910,726	15	924,329	15
District of Columbia...	13,548,629	178	12,892,079	151	13,203,701	149
Georgia................	1,343,225	25	1,317,732	24	1,339,831	24
Illinois...............	509,666	10	546,933	10	555,816	10
Kansas.................	817,294	14	863,864	14	876,523	14
Mississippi............	199,511	4	155,177	4	158,396	4
Montana................	466,049	8	435,650	8	442,645	8
Nebraska...............	199,210	4	202,579	4	205,798	4
New Mexico.............	255,515	5	317,867	5	322,974	5
North Carolina.........	184,965	4	188,702	4	191,921	4
Ohio...................	200,561	4	215,720	4	218,939	4
Oklahoma...............	261,715	5	237,781	4	241,000	4
Oregon.................	780,921	14	887,680	14	900,339	15
Pennsylvania...........	710,386	12	748,716	12	759,487	12
Puerto Rico............	214,980	5	184,319	4	187,538	4
Texas..................	579,417	12	690,145	12	700,916	12
Utah...................	331,882	6	362,558	6	367,665	6
Virginia...............	199,207	4	222,231	4	225,450	4
Wisconsin..............	560,598	11	621,466	11	631,293	11
Subtotal, Available or Estimate..........	24,524,000	381	24,554,000	352	25,045,000	352
Unobligated balance ...	30,000	--	--	--	--	--
Total, Available or Estimate..........	24,554,000	381	24,554,000	352	25,045,000	352

OFFICE OF THE GENERAL COUNSEL

STATUS OF PROGRAM

The Office of the General Counsel (OGC) serves as the legal advisor and counsel for the Secretary and the program agencies of the Department.

Current Activities: The Office provides legal services for all agencies of the Department. These services include, but are not limited to the following:

-- rendering opinions on legal questions;

-- preparing or reviewing rules and regulations;

-- preparing or interpreting contracts, mortgages, leases, deeds, and other documents;

-- preparing briefs and representing the Department in judicial proceedings and litigation;

-- representing departmental agencies in nonlitigation debt collection programs;

-- processing applications for patents for inventions by the Department's employees;

-- representing departmental agencies in state water rights adjudications;

-- considering and determining claims by and against the United States arising out of the Department's activities;

-- representing the Department in formal administrative proceedings;

-- assisting the Department of Justice (DOJ) in the preparation and trial of cases involving the Department; and

-- representing the Secretary of Agriculture and the Commodity Credit Corporation before the Interstate Commerce Commission, the Federal Maritime Commission, and the International Trade Commission.

Highlights of OGC's fiscal year 1992 operations are described below:

Selected Examples of Recent Progress:

ADMINISTRATION AND RESOURCE MANAGEMENT

The Office of the General Counsel (OGC) has implemented a Pilot Work Item Management System for internal case tracking in headquarters and two regional offices. Our two regional offices, San Francisco and Atlanta, have multiple workstations configured to access the Pilot System, and each of our eleven headquarter's divisions has one workstation for tracking and reporting purposes.

REGULATORY AND MARKETING

Meat and Poultry Products Inspection Acts: Approximately 185 criminal cases, civil injunction cases, civil seizure cases and claims collection cases were referred to DOJ or otherwise handled or disposed of with numerous successful criminal prosecutions. One of the most significant of those cases concerned the prosecution of Sandy Mac, a meat processing establishment in Pennsauken, New Jersey, and its three top officials. The plant and those officials were convicted of adulterating ham products with excessive water, falsifying USDA records, and offering money to USDA inspectors over a 12 year period. The Court imposed fines in the aggregate amount of $2 million against the defendants. It also sentenced the former president to two years in prison, and the other two officials to six months at a community treatment center. Four inspectors were convicted of bribery, and received prison sentences. All three of the officials were barred from any operational control of, or physical presence at, the plant for a 90 day period. During that period, separate Administrative Law Judge's decisions were obtained permanently barring those officials from operational control of, or physical presence at, the plant.

In addition, 22 administrative proceedings involving the withdrawal, suspension, or denial of Federal meat and poultry products inspection were litigated. One of the most notable of those cases concerned forcible assaults against a federal inspector by three plant officials at Murray Meat, a federal meat packing establishment in Salt Lake City, Utah. FSIS suspended inspection services pending an administrative action. An oral hearing was conducted to determine the validity of the suspension. The Administrative Law Judge issued an initial decision permanently removing one of the plant officials from the business. On appeal, the Judicial Officer issued a final decision permanently removing all three of the plant officials. Murray Meat cannot resume operations requiring Federal inspection until the three officials have been removed. OGC also assisted in defending the Secretary and other officials of the Department in 8 civil court actions. One of the most significant of those cases involves a lawsuit in the United States District Court for the District of Puerto Rico filed by Eurocaribe against USDA. The plaintiff seeks mandamus relief concerning USDA's alleged duty to require the retail establishments in Puerto Rico manufacturing sausage made with non-certified pork meat to comply with the federal meat inspection regulations for trichinae destruction. OGC filed a motion to dismiss, along with a lengthy brief, and plaintiff filed a reply. The case is pending a decision by the Court.

OGC also reviewed, revised, drafted, and cleared approximately 126 notices of proposed rulemaking or final rulemaking dockets, and drafted or reviewed numerous bills and reports concerning amendments to the Acts. In this regard, OGC provided substantial legal services in connection with three public hearings, and the review and clearance of a complex and voluminous final rulemaking docket, involving nutrition labeling of meat and poultry products. Another significant rulemaking docket reviewed and cleared by OGC concerned the exemption from inspection of meat and poultry pizzas, under legislation enacted in FY 1992. The legislation and implementing regulations involve very difficult, controversial issues. OGC also provided substantial legal services with respect to food safety legislation concerning pesticides and pesticide residues in food, final regulations on irradiation of poultry products, and proposed regulations concerning prior label approval.

Agricultural Marketing Act of 1946: OGC handled four criminal cases and two formal administrative proceedings seeking withdrawal of Federal meat and poultry grading and acceptance services. OGC is assisting in defending the Secretary and other officials of the Department in a civil court action brought in the United States District Court for the District of Colorado. The plaintiff seeks an injunction and a judgment declaring invalid USDA's implementation of a schedule or certification program permitting any certification of lamb which suggests quality grading without yield grading, or permitting a conflicting certification for lamb which has not been yield and quality graded. Following a hearing, the Court denied plaintiff's motion for a preliminary injunction and defendant's motion for summary judgment. The case is pending further proceedings on plaintiff's request for a permanent injunction and declaratory judgment. Additionally, OGC reviewed and cleared 13 notices of proposed rulemaking or final rulemaking dockets.

Animal and Plant Quarantine and related laws and Animal Damage Control:

OGC reviewed, or drafted and cleared about 277 notices of proposed rulemaking or final rulemaking dockets, and legal notices for publication in the Federal Register. OGC provided substantial legal assistance regarding regulations on genetically engineered plants, including interpretations and extensive proposed amendments to regulations which will substantially reduce regulatory burdens on the biotechnology industry and facilitate the marketing of such plants. Other such dockets included numerous proposed and final rules to implement APHIS user fee authority, a complete revision of the scrapie program based on negotiated rulemaking, a revision of the regulations and standards for accredited veterinarians, and substantial changes to the regulations governing the importation of fruits and vegetables and nursery stock into the United States. OGC also assisted in handling about 17 civil court actions which included defending the Secretary and other officials of the Department. OGC attorneys also handled approximately 535 administrative cases under the animal and plant quarantine and related laws during fiscal year 1992. Most of these cases sought the assessment of civil penalties, and OGC obtained approximately 201 decisions in civil penalty cases, assessing about $249,000. In addition, about 120 criminal cases and claims collection cases were referred to the DOJ or otherwise handled or disposed of during the fiscal year. Further, OGC reviewed over 300 pieces of correspondence and other documents, and rendered approximately 2150 oral legal opinions. OGC also performed substantial legal services with respect to proposed regulations regarding the importation of logs and other untreated wood products, lawsuits concerning the Salmonella enteritidis regulations and alleged unconstituted takings under those regulations, a lawsuit to enjoin the spraying of Bt in Washington and Oregon to eradicate the Asian Gypsy Moth, and a lawsuit to enjoin the Animal Damage Control Program for alleged violations of the Endangered Species Act. Further, OGC reviewed and/or drafted or redrafted and cleared 48 pieces of legislation and legislative reports concerning numerous matters, including legislation regarding inspection of mail, legislation to phase out importations of exotic birds that endanger the viability of the native population in the country of origin, and legislation regarding TB indemnity insurance programs for elk and other Cervidae.

Marketing Agreements and Orders: OGC attorneys devoted substantial legal resources to the milk and fruit and vegetable marketing order programs. There are 40 milk orders and 44 fruit and vegetable orders in effect. OGC attorneys reviewed and approved 200 rulemaking dockets, as well as many other documents relating to these orders. OGC also provided daily legal advice to client agencies in connection with a wide variety of matters arising under both the fruit and vegetable, and milk marketing order programs. OGC participates in all formal rulemaking proceedings as Department counsel. Several significant formal rulemaking hearings were conducted during the fiscal year concerning milk marketing orders. OGC attorneys represented the Department at these hearings and provided guidance in the evaluation of the record and preparation of Departmental decisions. The issues involved in these milk hearings included the review of Class I price differentials, Class II pricing, provisions for handling and pricing reconstituted milk, the uniform classification of milk uses, alternatives to the M-W price currently used in milk orders, and the establishment of a Class III-A pricing formula.

Substantial legal resources were also devoted to civil and administrative actions arising under the marketing order programs. These actions included civil forfeitures, injunctive actions, bankruptcy matters, and challenges to the legality of a variety of marketing order provisions. An important decision of the Ninth Circuit Court of Appeals upheld the Department's use of expedited rulemaking under the prorate provisions of the California citrus marketing orders.

Research and Promotion Programs: OGC provided substantial legal services to research and promotion programs administered by USDA under free-standing legislation. These include the promotion programs for milk, cotton, eggs, potatoes, honey, watermelons, beef, pork, soybeans, mushrooms, limes, pecans, wool and mohair. During the fiscal year OGC assisted in the preparation and issuance of final orders for limes, pecans, and cotton, and implementing regulations for most of the new or amended orders authorized by the most recent farm bill. In the litigation arena, OGC working with the Department of Justice defended against a series of injunctive actions brought to delay the producer referendum for the mushroom order.

Animal Welfare and Horse Protection Acts: OGC expended substantial resources in connection with the Animal Welfare and Horse Protection Act Programs. OGC attorneys serve as complaint counsel in administrative enforcement actions brought under these two statutes, and in FY 1992, OGC initiated 61 enforcement cases. OGC represented APHIS as trial counsel in 30 oral hearings conducted before the Department's administrative law judges and resolved over 160 administrative cases through trials on the merits, by negotiating consent decisions with the alleged violators or by other means.

Virus-Serum-Toxin Act: OGC reviewed and provided drafting assistance to APHIS in a number of rulemaking dockets concerning veterinary biologics during FY 1992. The dockets reviewed and approved by OGC included regulations implementing the Patent Term Restoration Act, regulations governing autogenous biologics, and rules specifying requirements applicable to the repackaging and labeling of individual dose veterinary vaccines for public use. In addition, substantial legal resources were devoted to litigation under the Virus-Serum-Toxin Act. These actions included an injunctive action against a licensed biological product manufacturer who attempted to ship a contaminated product. OGC also participated in successful defense of USDA's interpretation of the term "ship" under the Act. In that case, the federal district court held that the Department's interpretation of the term "ship" reasonably accommodated the policies of removing unsafe products from the market and decreasing the financial impact on manufacturers.

Grain Standards Act: OGC provided legal services to FGIS in connection with the agency's administration and enforcement of the United States Grain Standards Act. OGC reviewed and approved final rules revising the standards for wheat, soybeans, and sorghum; establishing new standards for canola; and establishing aflatoxin testing requirements for export corn. OGC also provided assistance to FGIS in connection with its implementation of the new official commercial inspection service, a more flexible, less costly grain inspection grading service.

Perishable Agricultural Commodities Act: During fiscal year 1992, 421 PACA reparation cases were referred to OGC for decision, and OGC staff rendered 320 opinions concerning contract disputes between members of the perishable agricultural commodities industry. In addition, OGC received 69 new administrative enforcement, 22 civil and 16 "responsibly connected" referrals. Seventy-one administrative cases and 22 civil cases were initiated during the fiscal year. At the end of the fiscal year, OGC had a reparation case inventory of 366 cases.

Packers and Stockyards Act: During fiscal year 1992, 95 administrative enforcement, 34 court actions and 9 reparation actions were initiated. Pursuant to section 1324 of the Food Security Act of 1985, OGC received seven applications regarding state central filing systems. At the end of the fiscal year, 23 enforcement actions and 15 court actions were under consideration by OGC, and 72 administrative enforcement, 23 civil and criminal matters, and 25 reparation cases were in litigation.

INTERNATIONAL AFFAIRS, COMMODITY PROGRAMS, AND FOOD ASSISTANCE PROGRAMS

Commodity Credit Corporation (CCC) and Agricultural Stabilization and Conservation Service (ASCS): OGC provided a significant amount of assistance in the final drafting of the Food, Agriculture, Conservation, and Trade Act Amendments of 1991. Subsequent to approval of this Act, OGC reviewed a substantial number of regulations which were used to administer ASCS and CCC programs authorized by that Act. OGC continued to provide legal advice on the administration of commodity price support and production adjustment programs authorized by the Agricultural Adjustment Act of 1938, the CCC Charter Act, and the Agricultural Act of 1949. Increased utilization of OGC resources for various conservation programs was necessary due to implementation of the Wetlands Reserve Program which required development of program documents and assistance in training programs involving ASCS personnel and programs involving private sector lenders, attorneys, and farm and environmental organizations. A significant amount of legal assistance was also provided to department officials in connection with the implementation of disaster assistance programs. Legal services were also required in connection with the Conservation Reserve Program, as well as payment limitation and disaster program litigation.

The table below summarizes litigation activity involving CCC and ASCS.

	FY 1991	FY 1992
Number of cases referred to Dept of Justice................	775	319
Total dollar value of cases filed by and against in millions............	$ 33	5.3
Number of cases pending in court or Justice Dept, end of year....................	2,529	1,690
Total dollar value of pending cases, end of year in millions.............	$ 153	135.3

Federal Crop Insurance Corporation (FCIC): OGC continued to draft and rewrite program regulations and contractual provisions to simplify and strengthen all aspects of the program ranging from producer participation to reinsurance and agency contractual relationships. Substantial resources have been required in an attempt to keep the program uniform across State lines in all delivery systems. The provisions of the Food, Agriculture, Conservation, and Trade Act of 1990 allowing private insurance companies to submit their private policies for reinsurance and subsidy significantly increased the OGC workload in this area.

Foreign Agricultural Service (FAS): Legal services provided by OGC in connection with international trade have continued to expand greatly. OGC attorneys have spent a considerable amount of time providing legal advice and participating in consultations as part of the U.S. negotiating team in connection with the Uruguay Round of multilateral trade negotiations under the auspices of the General Agreement on Tariffs and Trade (GATT). Documents filed by the United States Government with the dispute resolution panel of GATT in connection with the dispute with the European Community over its system of subsidization for oilseeds and oilseed products were prepared by attorneys in OGC.

OGC has actively participated in the successful conclusion of negotiations on the proposed North American Free Trade Agreement (NAFTA). OGC lawyers have not only been involved in the actual negotiations and drafting of proposed text of the treaty but also in evaluating the extent to which changes in U.S. domestic legislation will be required as part of the implementing legislation to be proposed to Congress.

Issues continue to arise under the U.S.-Canada Free-Trade Agreement (FTA) and increasingly involve agriculture. This has required commensurately increased involvement of OGC attorneys. OGC has been a principal participant in the efforts to resolve .ne continuing dispute with Canada concerning its compliance with the terms of the FTA in connection with exports of durum wheat to the United States. This dispute is only the fourth under the dispute settlement provisions (Chapter 18) of the FTA.

OGC has provided legal assistance to FAS with respect to implementing the provisions of the Food, Agriculture, Conservation, and Trade Act of 1990 which provide that the United States share agricultural expertise with emerging democracies. This assistance has included OGC's active participation in the negotiations to establish a model farm in St. Petersburg, Russia.

In the area of foreign assistance, OGC participated in the development and review of the Freedom Support Act of 1992 which provided a framework for assistance to the newly independent states of the former Soviet Union. This office also was closely involved in drafting a large number of agreements providing for the donation of agricultural commodities to these newly independent states as well as other countries.

Food Assistance Program: During fiscal year 1992, OGC worked closely with the Federal Trade Commission (FTC) in settling claims regarding questionable bidding practices for the contract to supply infant formula to the Supplemental Food Program for Women, Infants, and Children (WIC) in Puerto Rico against two of the three largest manufacturers of infant formula in the U.S. Under the settlement, the manufacturers will provide 3.6 million pounds of powdered infant formula to the WIC Program, which will use the formula to increase the number of eligible women, infants, and children it serves. OGC also drafted recently enacted legislation which encourages private sector participation in a national information campaign and education program to promote breastfeeding as the preferred method of infant nutrition and to foster wider public acceptance of breastfeeding.

Review of regulations was again a priority for OGC; OGC cleared for legal sufficiency 14 regulations concerning the Special Nutrition Programs. In the food stamp area, substantial time was devoted to the development of a pilot tax refund offset program. Under the program, the Internal Revenue Service (IRS) will offset tax refunds due to individuals who have received over-issuances of food stamps and have not repaid them.

Litigation involving the Department with respect to food assistance programs continues to be a significant element of work (89 open cases). There were 18 new court challenges to the domestic food assistance programs filed in FY 1992. Among other issues, the litigation challenged Food Stamp Program rules related to disaster relief, quality control claims, attribution of income to aliens, interest on debts owed to the federal government and treatment of payments to low income households as "energy assistance". In addition, 93 retailer/wholesaler enforcement judicial review cases were filed during fiscal year 1992.

OGC attorneys hosted a Food Stamp Program Civil Remedies Seminar as part of an effort to reduce Food Stamp Program retailer fraud and to encourage the use of the civil False Claims Act against retailers who fraudulently obtain payment from the U.S. Treasury. The seminar brought together various organizations involved in the Food Stamp Program's enforcement process.

COMMUNITY DEVELOPMENT AND NATURAL RESOURCES

Farmers Home Administration (FmHA), Farm Credit System Assistance Board, and Rural Development Administration (RDA) Programs: During fiscal year 1992, OGC provided legal assistance to FmHA and RDA in all their major areas of activity. These encompassed Farmer Program, Single- and Multi-Family Housing, Community Program and Business and Industry Loans. (In mid-year, the Community Program and Business and Industry Loans were moved to RDA.) These major areas of activity include more than 30 statutorily-separate loan and grant programs. The Community Development Division was involved in the task force working on the various aspects of actual establishment of RDA, which was created by the 1990 FACT Act. The Division also provided advice to the Department concerning the Secretary's statutory responsibilities as a member of the Board of Directors of the Farm Credit System Assistance Board. The Division's advice concerned both proposed and recently enacted legislation, proposed and final regulations, directives interpreting and implementing regulations, litigation, informal advice, and a variety of legal documents. During fiscal year 1992, the recorded work items in this area completed by the Community Development Division totaled 4,929. This amounts to an almost three percent increase over the work "items" closed in fiscal year 1991. Formally tracked "items" amounted to perhaps 60 percent of total Division workload.

Legislative work included advice to FmHA, and working with Congress on the 1991 Act making technical corrections to the 1990 FACT Act, the House bill dealing with farm loans to beginning farmers, and items relating to Appropriations Bills. The Division also dealt with a large volume of correspondence, including some congressional inquiries, especially relating to a tax issue regarding rural rental housing projects. Regulatory matters included a complete rewrite of the farmer program loan servicing regulations to implement the 1990 FACT Act. Other regulatory matters included revision of the guaranteed housing regulations, revisions of the conservation easement and inventory farm property sale priority regulations, and preparation of regulations establishing the Farms for the Future program as well as State review panels for rural development projects. For fiscal year 1992, the Division reviewed more than 500 separate regulatory proposals.

The Division also handled referrals from the Department of Justice (DOJ) of more than one hundred litigation cases during the year, and assisted DOJ in defending especially important cases involving a variety of claims against FmHA, including a number of issues arising from the implementation of the Agricultural Credit Act of 1987. This activity included work both at the trial court and the appellate levels. Informal legal advice consisted of verbal or written advice to the client on all aspects of administrative law and the laws and regulations governing the making of loans and grants, including the complicated arena of lender liability under CERCLA. Drafting work included drafting various loan agreements, guarantee and security forms, as well as proposals to be included in the Department's legislative package. The Community Development Division anticipates an increase in its workload for the future as more and more delinquent farm loans reach the judicial system; OGC field offices require its guidance on how to respond to issues arising out of implementation of the 1990 FACT Act; and the RDA becomes fully operational.

Rural Electrification and Telephone Programs: During fiscal year 1992, substantial legal services were required in connection with the loan and grant programs of the Rural Electrification Administration (REA) and the Rural Telephone Bank (RTB). REA approved insured loans totaling $662 million to 193 electric borrowers and 40 telephone borrowers and loan guarantees totaling approximately $185 million to 6 borrowers. In the telephone loan program, the Rural Telephone Bank made 29 loans totaling $185 million. In a newly available program, OGC negotiated and drafted agreements permitting borrowers to reprice certain REA guaranteed loans from the Federal Financing Bank. Fourteen of the transactions totaling $602 million were completed in FY 1992.

The legal services required in connection with REA and RTB lending programs included preparation of loan contracts, security instruments and related legal documents. OGC has undertaken the first major revision of the security instrument used in the electric loan program in over 20 years. The project involves not only updating many provisions of security instruments but also encompasses fundamental changes in the nature of the relationship between REA and its borrowers. The project has impacts on REA, its borrowers, private lenders and other groups. OGC also has undertaken to develop several new types of security instruments in the telephone program including a new form of common mortgage between REA, RTB, and private lenders.

OGC has drafted and reviewed a substantial number of significant new REA regulations during FY 1992. These include regulations providing for a new form of wholesale power contract between REA power supply borrowers and their members, regulations setting forth for the first time REA policy regarding lien accommodations and subordinations, and several regulations implementing rural economic development and distance learning and medical link loan and grant programs.

Legal services required in connection with financially-troubled REA borrowers continued at a high level during fiscal year 1992. During the year, eight borrowers with debt totaling $2.4 billion were either in workout or bankruptcy. The workouts involved a range of legal issues and required negotiations with borrowers, creditors, state regulatory bodies and others as well as litigation in a variety of forums. During the appraisal period, two of the bankruptcy cases, Colorado-Ute and New Hampshire Electric Cooperative, with outstanding Government debt of over $600 million, were resolved through the negotiation of consensual plans of reorganization. In both cases the Government's interests were protected. With the appointment of a trustee in bankruptcy in the case of Colorado-Ute, important program precedents were established which serve to discourage REA borrowers from attempting to shed federal debt through bankruptcy.

During fiscal year 1992, OGC was required to provide substantial legal services in litigation involving REA. Of particular significance is the issue of the right of REA to preempt rate jurisdiction of state regulatory bodies over certain financially troubled REA borrowers. Also of significance are several cases involving attempts by municipalities to condemn those portions of the borrowers electric systems and service rights that are most profitable. Such takings threaten to frustrate the purpose of the Rural Electrification Act, and REA, with OGC advice and assistance, is contesting the actions.

Forest Service (FS) Programs: In a climate of growing public concern on environmental issues, OGC provided significant legal counsel on land management planning, timber, minerals, wildlife, water, land status, recreation, grazing, and compliance with federal environmental and administrative laws. With regard to land management planning, OGC provided extensive advice on the development of 124 forest plans and on over 1,200 administrative appeals and 18 lawsuits challenging those plans filed to date. OGC's record in plan litigation is 13 wins and 4 losses. OGC provided national training on forest plan monitoring and evaluation and on wildlife issues, including Endangered Species Act compliance and biological diversity requirements. OGC has also provided advice on the development of revised land management planning and National Environmental Policy Act compliance regulations, and administrative appeal regulations.

With regard to timber, OGC provided substantial advice in response to numerous administrative appeals and significant litigation (70 pending cases) on the legality of decisions to offer individual timber sales under the National Environmental Policy Act, National Forest Management Act, Clean Water Act and Endangered Species Act. OGC also represented the Forest Service before the Comptroller General in approximately 25 bid protests challenging timber sale offerings. Extensive advice and services were provided on issues involving the contractual relationship with timber sale purchasers. These issues involve the Government's financial security, the Small Business Timber Set Aside Program, contract administration, including modifications, cancellations and defaults, timber theft, bid rigging, debt collection, bankruptcy, surety collection and revocation, suspensions and debarments and export restrictions. OGC represented or assisted the Department of Justice in representing the Forest Service in hundreds of cases involving timber sale purchasers filed in the Agriculture Board of Contract Appeals, U.S. Claims Court, U.S. District Courts, and U.S. Appellate Courts and in approximately 75 Forest Service debarment and/or suspension proceedings. Specifically, on defaulted timber sales, OGC worked closely with and continues to play a major role in assisting the Department of Justice in resolving litigation to recover damages from a large number of timber sale contracts defaulted in the early to mid-1980's. OGC also assisted the Forest Service in preparing submissions of 65 defaulted timber sale contracts for referral to the Department of the Treasury requesting that the surety companies who bonded defaulted contracts have their certificates of authority to do business with the government revoked for failure to pay the penal sums of the bonds. Important legal precedent also has been established in other defaulted timber sale contract cases, which has resulted in increased ability to collect damages and surety bonds. Training was provided to Forest Service personnel on debt collection, antitrust monitoring, timber theft, debarments, bid protests and the Contract Disputes Act.

OGC has provided counsel in the Forest Service's implementation of the Forest Resources Conservation and Shortage Relief Act of 1990, which prohibits the export of unprocessed federal timber and the purchase of unprocessed federal timber by a person who exports unprocessed private timber in the western United States. OGC has assisted the Forest Service in drafting interim rules implementing the exemptions, rules for new administrative processes required by the Act, and a proposed and final comprehensive rule on this Act of extraordinary complexity.

OGC has also worked closely with the Forest Service, the National Cancer Institute, and the United States Department of the Interior in developing the program to supply Pacific Yew bark needed for research and production of the promising anticancer drug taxol. OGC provided substantial assistance in the development and enactment of the Pacific Yew Act which was signed by the President in August of 1992. The Act provides substantial new authority for the Forest Service to finance and manage Pacific Yew efforts. The Act provides new authority for the Forest Service to negotiate sales of Pacific Yew bark, and to use the receipts to finance the administrative costs of the sales. OGC is assisting the Forest Service in implementing these new authorities.

In addition to litigation support involving challenges to recreation special use permits, OGC provided substantial advice and review on various aspects of recreation uses, including insurance, tort liability and fees. OGC also provided considerable assistance in the drafting of proposed regulations to govern group uses and distribution of printed material on the National Forest System and to simplify the application process of commercial special uses.

With regard to minerals, OGC provided extensive assistance in connection with sweeping legislative proposals to reform the statute governing the development of the vast majority of mineral deposits on federal lands. Substantial assistance was also provided in defending important mineral litigation and in responding to requests for legal advice arising through congressional oversight and from problems encountered in administering mineral development.

In the wildlife area, OGC provided substantial advice on complex questions concerning the Endangered Species Act and other wildlife laws. Significant litigation and questions arose from the national debate on the impact of national forest land management on the protection of species such as the spotted owl, the red-cockaded woodpecker, the Mount Graham red squirrel, the grizzly bear, and the marbled murrelet.

In the area of lands and associated real property matters, OGC continues to provide assistance to the Forest Service on a variety of complicated property law matters including takings under the 5th Amendment to the Constitution, issues related to rights of access over federal land, issues related to rights of mineral owners under deeds of severance, and Indian treaty rights. OGC provides instructors for national lands training and the Legal Education Institute of the Department of Justice. In the recent regulatory review process, amendments drafted by OGC to the Forest Service's special use regulations completed the entire amendatory process. Water rights and power regulation involve considerable legal services in adjudications of reserved water rights and licensing proceedings before the Federal Energy Regulatory Commission.

Land acquisitions and exchanges continue to require substantial legal resources. In FY 1992, the Forest Service obligated over $107.5 million in land acquisition funds for the acquisition of 166,781 acres of land. Land exchanges totaled over 90,000 acres.

There were several special projects dealing with the formulation of the Department's supplemental guidelines for the assessment of 5th Amendment takings required under Executive Order 12630. In addition, there were over 100 legislative proposals concerning national forest lands which involved OGC drafting services, review of testimony, and legislative clearances. Significant legislation was enacted affecting Forest Service programs including the "Energy Bill" amendments to the Alaska Native Claims Settlement

Act, several interstate land exchanges, and a new experimental forest in Hawaii.

OGC provided substantial assistance on other important issues relating to federal laws such as hazardous waste regulation and cleanup (including the Exxon Valdez oil spill), Native American treaty rights and religious freedom, use of herbicides and pesticides, and historic and archaeological resource protection. A national team of attorneys was established to assist USDA agencies in the pollution control area. In connection with the development of important regulations and policy statements, OGC provided substantial advice on compliance with federal administrative laws such as the Administrative Procedure Act, the Paperwork Reduction Act, the Freedom of Information Act, the Privacy Act, and executive orders and other authorities governing federal decision making. Substantial effort also was devoted to assisting the Forest Service in development and implementation of its administrative appeal processes.

During fiscal year 1992, the staff of the Natural Resources Division assisted in formulating, reviewing and providing legal advice on numerous written statements and legislative reports. OGC also drafted and reviewed numerous legislative proposals, including the National Forest System Lands Omnibus proposal, proposals to designate certain areas as wilderness, proposals for additions to the National Wild and Scenic Rivers System, and proposals concerning recreation and vendor fees. OGC accompanied Forest Service personnel at meetings with congressional staff members and mark-ups to provide legal assistance if needed.

A new Legislative Affairs section was created within the Natural Resources Division to provide enhanced legal assistance to the Forest Service in the wide range of legislative matters in which it is involved.

Soil Conservation Service (SCS) Programs: OGC provided legal counsel on range management, flood control and water resources projects, and natural resource protection; advice on the application of state and federal statutes to programs that affect approximately 3,000 soil and water conservation districts; the defense of lawsuits brought by parties challenging agency activities and the prosecution of claims on behalf of the agency. Additional legal review continues to be provided to SCS on activities related to development and implementation of conservation practices that meet the federal and state water quality requirements under the Clean Water Act.

There has been a considerable increase in OGC services to SCS concerning implementation of the conservation title of the Food Security Act of 1985 and the Food Agriculture Conservation and Trade Act of 1990 (FACT Act). FACT assigns specific responsibility to the SCS for assuring compliance by agricultural producers with the conservation compliance requirements, and the sodbuster and swampbuster proscriptions. By December 31, 1994, all agricultural producers will have to be in full compliance or risk loss of USDA subsidies and other benefits. In order to meet the statutory deadline, SCS to date has completed over 1.6 million conservation plans with at least 250,000 remaining yet to be done. The agency has made 1.63 million highly erodible land determinations with 2.8 million more to be done. The agency has completed 764,000 wetland determinations with 4.4 million to be done when the pending wetland guidelines are released.

LEGISLATION, LITIGATION, AND RESEARCH AND OPERATIONS

Legislation: During Fiscal Year 1992, the staff of the Legislative Division coordinated legal review of 533 legislative reports on pending bills and legislation proposed by agencies of the Department. The Legislative Division also coordinated the legal review of the written testimony of 310 Administration witnesses before Congressional Committees. The Division staff prepared or assisted in the preparation of drafts of bills or amendments on request for Members of Congress, Congressional Committees, and agencies within the Department. Technical assistance was provided to Members of Congress and Congressional Committees and advice was furnished to USDA legal and policy officials on the drafting, clearance, and presentation to Congress of legislation and ancillary legislative materials and on Congressional procedures. Effective in January, 1992, the Legislative Division was assigned responsibility for certifying to the Office of Management and Budget the compliance of all Department legislative proposals with the civil justice reform requirements of Executive Order 12778. The staff also coordinated legal review of legislative reports and Congressional testimony relating inter alia to: development of a national energy strategy; negotiation of a North American Free Trade Agreement; support for the democracies emerging from the former Soviet Union; environmental improvements at the U.S.-Mexico border and throughout Latin America; administration of the farm price support, conservation, and other programs under the Food, Agriculture, Conservation and Trade Act of 1990; improvements in the farm and rural credit programs of the Farmers Home Administration and Rural Electrification Administration; improvements in the food stamp and other nutrition programs of the Food and Nutrition Service including an initiative to promote breast feeding; water quality; pesticide safety; and numerous issues affecting management of National Forest ecosystems, including balanced administration of the resource and economic values of old growth timber, improved management of the Pacific yew tree as a source of the cancer drug taxol; mineral exploration and development, forest health and biodiversity, designations of wilderness and wild and scenic rivers, revision of the ski area permit fee system, and improvements in the administrative process for considering appeals of Forest Service decisions.

Litigation: OGC is responsible for the Department's position in cases on appeal. Staff attorneys assigned to the Litigation Division draft and review documents concerning cases in the United States Supreme Court, the United States Courts of Appeals, and State appellate tribunals. These attorneys brief and argue certain cases in the federal Circuit Courts and in State appellate courts. During fiscal year 1992 Litigation Division attorneys were assigned full responsibility for 21 appellate cases, and they obtained favorable results in 9 of the cases and unfavorable results in 1 of the cases. The other 11 appellate cases are awaiting briefing schedules, are fully briefed and argued, or are waiting to be scheduled for oral argument in the near future.

The appellate cases handled by Litigation Division attorneys involve diverse subjects and difficult factual and legal complications. The following cases illustrate the nature of the important issues addressed in the appellate litigation handled by the Division's attorneys.

William Dwaine Elliott v. APHIS, No. 92-1662 (4th Cir.), arose under the Horse Protection Act of 1970, 15 U.S.C. § 1821 et seq. APHIS alleged that Elliott had entered three horses in three horse shows while the horses were sore, in violation of the Act, which provides that "entering for the purpose of showing or exhibiting in any horse show or horse exhibition, any horse which is sore" is a violation. 15 U.S.C. § 1824(2)(B). Elliott argued that "entering" is a discrete, one-time event, that occurs at the time of clerical entry of the horse in the show. Because APHIS veterinarians found the horses to be sore at the pre-show examination rather than at the moment Elliott paid his entry fee, Elliott argued the horses were not sore when "entered." The Secretary found that "entering" is an ongoing process that begins with clerical sign-up of the horse, and includes all the pre-show requirements before the horse can be shown in the ring, including pre-show examination by the agency's veterinarians. Elliott is challenging the Secretary's conclusion in the Fourth Circuit.

In Christian Hanson and Evan Hanson v. Madigan, No. 92-1918 (7th Cir.), the District Court ruled against the Secretary, and he appealed for review by the Seventh Circuit. In the appellate litigation the Government seeks to have the Court of Appeals uphold the Secretary's position that the Hansons were not entitled to receive disaster assistance payments under the Disaster Assistance Act of 1988, 7 U.S.C.1521 note, Sec. 201-241, because their annual gross income exceeded the $2 million statutory ceiling on eligibility. The case pivots on significant statutory construction and evidentiary questions.

On September 18, 1992, the Ninth Circuit heard oral argument in Portland, Oregon, in James Joseph Hickey and Shannon Hansen v. USDA, No. 91-70169. The case involves challenges to the suspension by the Animal and Plant Health Inspection Service of a license as a dealer under the Animal Welfare Act and the denial of an application for a dealer's license by the suspended dealer's wife. The panel raised serious questions about the involvement of the applicant for a license in the violations found by the agency and about the standard of review which should be used by the Court.

In addition to actually litigating several important appellate cases, Litigation Division attorneys reviewed and made contributions to many of the briefs and arguments in other significant appellate cases involving the Department of Agriculture but handled by Justice Department attorneys. In this regard, Litigation Division attorneys have assisted in the Department of Justice's preparations to present the Government's position in U.S.A., U.S.D.A. v. Texas, S. Ct. No. 91-1729, a case which addresses the question of whether the Debt Collection Act of 1982 abrogated the Secretary's common-law right to collect interest on debts owed by the state under the Food Stamp Act. Litigation Division attorneys made important contributions to several other briefs filed by the Justice Department on behalf of the Secretary, and they will participate in the moot court preparations for the oral arguments.

Finally, but certainly of equal importance, OGC's appellate lawyers prepared the Department of Agriculture's recommendations to the Solicitor General on whether to appeal 78 adverse decisions of various trial courts during fiscal year 1992. In sum, Litigation Division attorneys were responsible for a total of 109 appellate cases during the past fiscal year.

Research and Operations: During fiscal year 1992, the Washington office received 98 new administrative claims filed under the Federal Tort Claims Act (FTCA) and 61 claims were open at the end of fiscal year 1992. Currently, 150 FTCA cases are in litigation. At the end of fiscal year 1992, there were approximately, 51 cases in litigation or administrative proceedings with "civil rights" implications relating to the Department's personnel policy, grant programs and direct assistance programs.

OGC attorneys provided representation for agencies of the Department in several appeals by Departmental employees of adverse actions before the Merit Systems Protection Board. Further, OGC attorneys provided representation for agencies of the Department in several administrative complaints, both individual and class, of employment discrimination by Departmental employees before the Equal Employment Opportunity Commission. Additionally, OGC attorneys rendered advisory opinions and reviewed proposed Departmental regulations as to enforcement of various civil rights statutes prohibiting discrimination in programs receiving Federal financial assistance from the Department. Legal services are also rendered in the areas of conflict of interest and conduct proscribed by regulations issued pursuant to executive order: budget and fiscal matters; property management; advisory committee acti. ties; internal reorganizations of the Department; and similar matters.

OGC was involved in reviewing for comment to the Office of Government Ethics, as well as coordinating Departmental implementation of the revised Standards of Ethical Conduct for Employees of the Executive Branch (5 C.F.R. Part 2635), Financial Disclosure (5 C.F.R. Parts 735, 2633, and 2634), and Ethics Training (5 C.F.R. Part 2638) regulations. It also has assisted the Office of Personnel in efforts to revise the Departmental employee conduct regulation (7 C.F.R. Part 0.735) in conjunction with the implementation of OGE's government-wide standards of ethical conduct. Continuing efforts were also made to collect more efficiently money owed to the Department. OGC reviewed for comment a Department of Justice draft revision to the Federal Claims Collection Standards, 4 C.F.R. Part 101 et. seq., (FCCS), as well as a draft Departmental regulation implementing the FCCS provisions concerning termination and settlement of agency claims. OGC also has been involved in litigation involving offsets taken against timber purchasers under the Debt Collection Act and concerning whether the provisions of that Act apply to offsets involving separate contracts.

OGC continued to counsel the science and education agencies of the Department regarding legal issues arising from the administration of the agricultural research, extension, and teaching programs. During fiscal year 1992, a significant portion of these issues continued to relate to the implementation of the research title of the 1990 FACT Act. In this vein, legal assistance included review of the final rules revising the administrative provisions for the National Competitive Research Initiative and the Special Research Grants Program; review of regulations establishing the administrative provisions for the Biotechnology Risk Assessment Research Grants Program; drafting charter documentation to establish and make fully operational the Alternative Agricultural Research and Commercialization Center and Board; and rendering legal opinions on the meaning and effect of various provisions of the FACT Act and related appropriations issues.

OGC provided legal advice to all agencies of the Department concerning the procurement of services, supplies, and construction. This assistance included drafting and reviewing regulations; reviewing solicitation documents; handling mistake-in-bid and protest matters; providing advice in pre-award and performance issues; and providing the assistance necessary to assert or defend contract claims. OGC received an increased number of requests for the review of Agriculture Property Management Regulations in fiscal year 1992 because the Department is revising and updating the Agriculture Property Management Regulations. The number of requests from contracting and leasing personnel involving matters of bankruptcy and organizational conflicts-of-interest, involving former employees of the Department continued to climb in fiscal year 1992. At the end of the fiscal year, staff attorneys in Research and Operations were responsible for 11 of the 125 cases pending before the Agriculture Board of Contract Appeals. The remaining cases were the responsibility of the field attorneys or attorneys in the Washington office supporting CCC program activities. In addition, Research and Operations attorneys were responsible for 8 acquisition-related cases in litigation in the Claims Court and Federal District Courts pending at the end of the fiscal year. Research and Operations attorneys also were assigned to 52 acquisition review teams that were active at the conclusion of fiscal year 1992. When compared to the previous fiscal year, this represents a more than 100 percent increase in this important area. The acquisition review teams are responsible for monitoring and approving the acquisitions of ADPE and related support services within the Department. There also was a significant increase in the requests for opinions relating to the funding of cost-reimbursable agreements, intra-agency transfers, and service contracts, particularly with regard to indefinite quantity acquisitions and acquisitions for studies. During fiscal year 1992, legal services were rendered with respect to 310 Freedom of Information Act (FOIA) appeals. Twelve FOIA cases were in litigation at the beginning of the fiscal year and 10 new cases were filed against the

Department in fiscal year 1992. Litigation support services were provided in 3 Privacy Act suits that were pending during the fiscal year. The Division also rendered substantial legal services in connection with computer matching programs to ferret out fraud, waste, and abuse.

Further, legal activities were performed pursuant to Executive Order 12088, and the Solid Waste Disposal Act, as amended by the Resource Conservation and Recovery Act, on behalf of the Agricultural Research Service. OGC also provided assistance with regard to legal issues relating to the establishment of the Rural Development Administration as well as the Alternative Agricultural Research and Commercialization Center and Board.

Under the direction of OGC, applications for patents were prepared on inventions by USDA employees and contractors with the objective of obtaining patent protection for the government. Sixty new inventions were reported to OGC during fiscal year 1992. Fifty-eight patent applications were prepared and submitted to the U.S. Patent Office during fiscal year 1992. Fifty-three patents were obtained, 16 applications were abandoned, and 14 cases were otherwise closed.

REGIONAL OFFICES

OGC currently has five regional and seventeen branch offices which provide legal services to numerous USDA agencies with field organizations, such as the Agricultural Marketing Service, Agricultural Stabilization and Conservation Service, Farmers Home Administration, Food and Nutrition Service, Forest Service and Soil Conservation Service. In addition, OGC has placed several employees with client agency personnel in locations where OGC does not maintain an office, in order to provide direct legal services where needed.

OGC's field offices provide legal advice and services on all matters within the scope of delegations of authority vesting extensive power to implement programs at the state and local level in agency field staff, and on litigation within delegations by the Attorney General to United States Attorneys. Work on this litigation is completed at the local level, without involvement of the Washington office or the Department of Justice. During fiscal year 1992, the Department had 48,387 cases in civil litigation. Ninety-six percent were the responsibility of OGC's 22 field offices. Compared to fiscal year 1991, we had a modest decrease in the backlog of these cases.

Some examples of successful litigation efforts include sensitive species litigation involving the northern goshawk and the Mexican spotted owl; the Forest Service's authority reasonably to condition access to national forest lands; and payment limitation litigation upholding the agency determinations regarding a large farm. In 1992 OGC coordinated the effort to achieve a negotiated settlement terminating the 19-year old Bernardi litigation. This extremely protracted and contentious litigation was originally filed in 1973 and concerned employment opportunities for women in the Forest Service's Pacific Southwest Region.

In addition to work on civil litigation, legal assistance during the year included work on cases before administrative law judges or boards including recovery of the cost of restoring an archeological resource damaged during a timber harvest operation; loan making and servicing; real estate transactions; violations of state and federal criminal laws including participation with the Forest Service in a Timber Theft Task Force that produced several indictments and a significant conviction; timber sale and procurement contracts; interpretations of state laws that affe.: federal jurisdiction and programs; application of federal regulations; assuring that local policy decisions were within the scope of delegated authorities and consistent with national policies; municipal financing practices required to meet federal laws and regulations; uses of national forests and their environmental consequences; the effect of state laws on federal lands; pre-litigation work including negotiations and/or settlements that avoid the need to litigate; and the direct handling of 8,138 nonjudicial foreclosure cases, an increase of 829 above fiscal year 1991.

New statutes enacted during the year, such as the Pacific Yew Management Act; amendments to the Food, Agriculture, Conservation and Trade Act; and provisions in Agriculture and Interior Appropriations Acts added to or revised agency authorities. This leads, in both initial and subsequent years, to increased field office legal work due to regulatory changes and questions on interpretations of new laws. Other laws, such as the National Environmental Policy; Endangered Species; Clean Water; Comprehensive Environmental Response, Compensation and Liability; National Forest Management; and Agricultural Credit Acts, though not revised, remain the source of substantial contentious litigation over a long period of years, increasing significantly OGC's workload.

Further progress was made during the fiscal year to increase the ability of the office to operate as a national law office. This has been enhanced through increased information exchange, reports, weekly conference calls, cross-servicing of cases among offices, and emphasis on training of client and OGC personnel. These efforts will continue in the future.

THURSDAY, APRIL 22, 1993.

DEPARTMENTAL ADMINISTRATION/OFFICE OF THE SECRETARY

WITNESSES

CHARLES R. HILTY, ASSISTANT SECRETARY FOR ADMINISTRATION
IRWIN T. DAVID, DEPUTY CHIEF FINANCIAL OFFICER
LARRY WILSON, DIRECTOR, OFFICE OF FINANCE AND MANAGEMENT
CONSTANCE D. GILLAM, BUDGET OFFICER, OFFICE OF FINANCE AND MANAGEMENT
STEPHEN B. DEWHURST, BUDGET OFFICER, DEPARTMENT OF AGRICULTURE

OPENING REMARKS

Mr. DURBIN. Welcome to this meeting of the Subcommittee on Agriculture and Related Agencies. This morning we will have testimony from the U.S. Department of Agriculture, Departmental Administration and Office of the Secretary. We are happy to welcome a friend of the subcommittee, Chuck Hilty, the Assistant Secretary for Administration. With him are Irwin David, the Deputy Chief Financial Officer; Larry Wilson, the Director of the Office of Finance and Management; Constance Gillam, the Budget Officer, and Steve Dewhurst. Thank you for joining us.

Mr. Hilty, we will include your entire statement in the record. If you would like to summarize it, highlight at this point, we welcome you to do so.

INTRODUCTORY STATEMENT

Mr. HILTY. Mr. Chairman, I would. And typically of someone who has been long in politics, I would like to digress just a little bit from the prepared statement. I would like to talk with you briefly this morning, Mr. Chairman, about Sally Farr.

Mrs. Farr is not mentioned in the prepared statement before you, but I think that she is someone that you should know. I hope the chance will come for you and some of your Subcommittee colleagues, as you travel about this country, to visit Mrs. Farr.

I would not identify the lady's age, because she is a lady and one never identifies age. Let's say that she is older than I. She is handicapped by multiple sclerosis, confined rather largely to a wheelchair.

EASY ACCESS PILOT PROJECT

I spent some time with her in her home last summer, in Sherman County, Kansas, near Goodland, Kansas. We were in her dining room, at her computer, where with the help of our USDA Easy Access pilot project in that county, she is managing 4,000 acres of Sherman County farmland, mostly from her home with the help of this computer program we are piloting in that county.

She has access to her files in the county office; she has, of course, access to her records at home. She can increasingly gain information from the county office, exchange information with the county office, and sharpen her own operation, while sitting in her wheelchair at her computer in her dining room. That is a project that we have had underway for about the last year and a half.

With great foresight, I placed two pilot projects of that sort in 1991. One was in Congressman Pat Roberts' district. He is now the Ranking Member of the House Agriculture Committee. And with even greater foresight, I placed the other pilot project in the district of Congressman Mike Espy, who has now moved on to some even greater involvement in agriculture.

The point I would like to make to you about Sally Farr and the Easy Access project there, is that this is the USDA program delivery structure of the future, the office of the future. We have several pilot projects of varying sorts that really are showing us ways in which we can clarify, simplify, and speed up all of our delivery of services to our farmers.

READER'S DIGEST ARTICLE

We recognize that is a prime responsibility of Departmental Administration. It is one of the main reasons that we have been created within the Department, to serve all the functions that come before us. I also cite that particular example of Sally Farr, Mr. Chairman, because a Reader's Digest article some months ago alluded to a USDA pilot project. It spoke of a place where we have a computer pilot project in the field, but someone who went there found boxes of three-by-five note cards and file cards for the Farmers Home Administration.

Mr. Chairman, I would like the record to show that when you go to that county, if you know what you are looking for, you will see the farms of the future and the farm service agencies of the future. The material alluded to in the Reader's Digest article was material that was part of an older record-keeping system used by Farmers Home. It was *not* part of the Easy Access project. Those 3-by-5 cards are what we are stepping away from. They are not what we are doing.

I hope that you will have a chance and the other Members of the subcommittee will have a chance to really take a look at what we are doing, how rapidly we are moving into the future, and what our capabilities are, as you also ask us what our needs may be.

ONE-STOP SHOPPING

This project and others like it are ones that really tie in to the point that Secretary Espy has made forcefully before this Committee when he appeared before you in February, before USDA employee groups, and to every other group he gets a chance to address. That is the theme that is alluded to in various points in our written testimony before you: the notion of "one-stop shopping," in all of our USDA field service offices, again, to clarify, simplify, and speed up delivery of our services, to exchange our information in one place and in one way for farmers all across the country. That is the heart of what we are about.

Those are the kinds of messages that we want to convey to you this morning and every other chance that comes before us.

So I close with that invitation for you to visit Sally Farr in her dining room, Mr. Chairman, I am sure that she would graciously concur in the invitation, even though I did not consult with her about it. I would like to respond to such questions as you may have or prepare for the record any broader responses that may seem indicated.

[CLERK'S NOTE.—Mr. David's biography appears on page 906. The Assistant Secretary's prepared statement appears on pages 907 through 918. The budget justifications appear on pages 919 through 1010.]

Mr. DURBIN. Thank you very much, Mr. Hilty. I understand from your testimony the message which you are delivering. Those of us on the Subcommittee are concerned about the critics of agriculture programs and agriculture research. They don't understand the importance of these activities and how much it means to the lives of so many people across this country. We are going to do our best in this Subcommittee, working with our colleagues, to get the other side of that message out. Your testimony today indicates that the message will also be coming from downtown. I hope we can be successful.

RENTAL PAYMENTS TO GSA

Let me ask you about a couple things on a more mundane or technical level and see if you can help me with them. It is my understanding that the USDA, quote, unquote, "rents its buildings from the GSA." It is also my understanding that your budget request is $50 million for rental payments for the next fiscal year, including retaining $5 million for non-recurring repairs.

It turns out that your landlord, GSA, is nowhere to be found when you have serious problems with the buildings downtown. I'm talking about major non-recurring repairs, not about ordinary maintenance, but major repairs. Now, we are also hearing that there may be a budget amendment asking for much more than $50 million. Can you tell me how your budget request of $50 million was arrived at, and whether you believe that there is going to be an additional request for funds for rental payments?

Mr. HILTY. The $50 million figure, Mr. Chairman, is a figure that has been set through the activities of this Subcommittee for more years than I have been occupying this position. It goes back well into the mid-1980s, at least. The figure fluctuates slightly from year to year. But as I reviewed the figures this morning, I find that it really has stabilized in the range of $49 million to $51 million, since about 1986.

The precise figure is set through the appropriations process, rather than being a percentage figure of what GSA would normally bill us for. GSA does own the buildings in the downtown Washington area, the Administration Building, the South Building, the Auditors Building and the Cotton Annex.

The broader question of that ownership came up during these hearings last year, and later on for the record I would like to refer to the responses I gave to Mr. McHugh, the Chairman of the day, on that question, and elaborate on the responses I provided then. I have been told that GSA is going to seek some higher figure from us, but I do not know whether that will be done, when it will be done, nor in what amount it may be done.

USDA has been provided also a Building Operations and Maintenance Fund, which has leveled out at about $25 million, and a Nonrecurring Repair Fund of about $5 million. Because the rentals have been capped and the Building Operations and Maintenance Funds have been provided more generously, and the Nonrecurring Repairs Fund exists, we do have more flexibility in our internal management of our buildings and we can respond much more rapidly to serious situations.

RESPONSE TO EMERGENCIES

I would like to cite one anecdote for you. On a Thursday morning last October, at 6:30, a.m., a massive fire broke out in the series of offices for the Administrator of the Rural Electrification Administration. While firemen were still in the building, we had repair teams already in place.

We had an emergency bank of telephones installed and in operation, so REA's national operations could continue, even while the fire inspectors were still in the building. We had remodeling plans prepared before the morning was done. And although that fire, which destroyed 10 working offices across the front of the South Building, occurred on Thursday morning, we had the Administrator and all his staff fully in place the next Monday morning, with suites fully rebuilt, rewired, new windows, new carpet, new paint, new furniture, and all the technical equipment reinstalled and up and running. That was an USDA project, not a GSA project. That was possible because we have the larger and more flexible management capability granted to the Building Operations Fund and the Nonrecurring Repair Funds.

The issues to us are highly important, that we retain that flexibility to operate and to maintain our buildings in this way. And we think that ultimately we will best be served by having ownership of the buildings as well.

I would like to have a chance to elaborate on that for the record in a more polished and orderly way, if I may?

GSA RENTAL RATES

Mr. DURBIN. Well, of course you will be given that opportunity, but last year's dialog between you and Mr. McHugh on the subject indicated that the General Services Administration has dramatically increased their rental estimates to USDA over the years. It's the OMB allowance that has not increased dramatically but has stayed in the range which you have already testified to.

There is also information, and I believe it has come through your testimony last year, about the amount that GSA pays for certain buildings occupied by USDA, as opposed to the USDA reimbursement. In every instance, the USDA is paying far more than the GSA pays for the same building.

We know that GSA has been lax in responding to needs for repairs, nonrecurring repairs, and I am trying to establish whether or not there is any rhyme or reason to the amount of money the USDA is being charged by GSA.

Mr. Dewhurst, are you familiar with any standards that are used by GSA in establishing rental rates?

Mr. DEWHURST. Yes, sir, under the system that has all Federal agencies pay rent to the GSA for office space, GSA sets those rates based on market value, irrespective of how much they paid for them or what the maintenance, they charge a market rate for that property.

It turns out, if I recall correctly, that the amount in the appropriation we give them each year is essentially about 40 percent of the market rate for the properties that the Department occupies. So essentially their position would be that we owe them something in excess of twice the amount of money we are actually paying them, based on the system that they are operating.

Mr. DURBIN. So their rate is based on market rate, as opposed to actual cost?

Mr. DEWHURST. Yes, sir.

Mr. HILTY. Mr. Chairman, it is what they call the Standard Level User Charge, and their rental estimates to USDA from 1984 through 1993 have increased from $69,402,000 in 1984, to the most recent rental estimate of $107,326,000 for fiscal 1993. The final OMB allowances that we received were, in 1984, that $69,402,000 that I alluded to as the GSA request. And then the fiscal 1993 OMB allowance in our request was $50,503,000, which is in line with the figures provided through the subcommittee.

GSA COSTS AND CHARGES

Mr. DURBIN. Provide the Committee with a list, similar to the one provided last year, of selected examples of rental costs GSA pays for some space it leases to USDA, the amount that GSA charges USDA for this space, and the percent these charges exceed the lease cost for fiscal year 1992.

Mr. HILTY. I will provide the record the table you request.

[The information follows:]

TABLE OF SELECTED EXAMPLES
OF SPACE ASSIGNMENTS
FROM THE GENERAL SERVICES ADMINISTRATION

This table identifies rental cost GSA pays for space it assigns to USDA, the amount that GSA charges USDA for the space, and the percent these charges exceed the lease cost for fiscal year 1992.

BUILDING LOCATION	GSA COST	USDA COST	% EXCEEDS
General Office Bldg. Rt. 44A Mansfield Center, CT	$101,324	$133,368	31%
34 Market Street Everett, MA	$30,013	$46,664	55%
Hunt Valley Prof. Bldg. 9 Schilling Rd. Lutherville, MD	$26,995	$33,409	23%
Tannesfield Plaza Mt. Holly, NJ	$91,614	$118,188	29%
Langley 1 Building 120 N. Langley Rd. Glen Burnie, MD	$19,676	$25,827	31%
Lewis Hall Annex Western MD College Westminister, MD	$66,370	$86,540	30%
3301 Galloway Philadelphia, PA	$23,585	$29,553	25%
Five Radnor Corp. Ctr. Matsonford Rd. Radnor, PA	$516,623	$591,083	14%
5700 Lake Worth Rd. Lake Worth, FL	$28,085	$33,262	18%
Woodward Building 1222 Woodward Ave. Orlando, FL	$73,853	$108,663	47%
3231 Ruckriegle Pkwy. Louisville, KY	$14,032	$20,475	45%
Simmons Building 1222 Buchanan Jackson, MS	$11,945	$14,477	21%

BUILDING LOCATION	GSA COST	USDA COST	% EXCEEDS
Angus Building 6301 E. Angus Dr. Raleigh, NC	$14,826	$19,126	29%
4841 Summer Ave. Bldg. Memphis, TN	$382,139	$458,214	19%
Willow Trace 830 Fesslers Pkwy. Nashville, TN	$12,119	$16,079	32%
Bolander Bldg. 251 Starkey St. St. Paul, MN	$29,382	$36,833	25%
Leawood Office Bldg. 8700 State Line Leawood, KS	$60,577	$91,730	51%
632 SW Van Buren Topeka, KS	$149,525	$177,580	18%
2113 Osuna Rd., NE Albuquerque, NM	$231,762	$287,814	24%
Hangar Craig/Moffat Airport Craig, CO	$3,720	$6,046	62%
Ag. Photo Lab 2222 W. 2300 St. Salt Lake City, UT	$1,023,479	$1,383,300	35%
.usk Airport Highway 20 .usk, WY	$7,378	$11,723	58%
Misner Building 1123 Big Horn Ave. Worland, WY	$14,183	$16,492	16%
2324 E. McDowell Rd. Phoenix, AZ	$439,686	$512,171	16%
4625 S. Wendler Dr. Tempe, AZ	$38,035	$44,990	18%
2121 Second St. Davis, CA	$320,908	$577,530	79%
1600 Tollhouse Rd. Clovis, CA	$369,584	$484,479	31%

BUILDING LOCATION	GSA COST	USDA COST	% EXCEEDS
1320 E. Olympic Blvd. Los Angeles, CA	$127,280	$153,649	20%
2245 Morello Ave. Pleasant Hill, CA	$204,427	$242,166	18%
21160 Box Spring Rd. Riverside, CA	$18,673	$22,447	20%
9580 Micron Ave. Sacramento, CA	$154,068	$264,644	71%
10845 Rancho Bernardo San Diego, CA	$255,268	$319,843	25%
1222 Monaco Ct. Stockton, CA	$55,699	$67,683	21%
194 W. Main St. Woodland, CA	$131,100	$188,562	43%
Palmer Bus. Plaza S. Bailey & W. Dahlia Palmer, AK	$22,914	$29,731	29%
Bus Barn 540 Oak St. Eugene, OR	$41,471	$57,071	37%
19501 SE Division St. Gresham, OR	$222,901	$330,710	48%
Nova Building 1329 NW 49th Dr. Pendleton, OR	$6,000	$7,918	31%
Forest Service Bldg. 853-57 Roosevelt Ave. E Enumclaw, WA	$152,702	$202,500	32%
Forest Service Bldg. 21905 64th Ave. Mountlake Terrace, WA	$426,541	$481,924	12%
Lynch Building W. Side Blacklake Blvd. Olympia, WA	$492,800	$579,851	17%
Goodway Building 4043 Roosevelt Way, NE Seattle, WA	$84,708	$109,599	29%

HEADQUARTERS COMPLEX RENTAL CHARGES

Mr. DURBIN. Also, provide a table showing the amount GSA charged USDA for the four buildings owned by GSA but occupied by USDA for fiscal year 1981 through fiscal year 1993.

Mr. HILTY. I will also provide for the record the table.

[The information follows:]

HEADQUARTERS COMPLEX RENTAL CHARGES—FISCAL YEARS 1981–93

	Administration Building	Agriculture Annex	South Building	Auditors Building
Fiscal year:				
1981	(1)	(1)	(1)	(1)
1982	(1)	(1)	(1)	(1)
1983	$1,859,496	$461,608	$14,225,076	$558,240
1984	2,077,284	520,032	14,320,032	651,480
1985	4,009,740	833,448	14,320,032	1,287,040
1986	4,045,437	−840,551	−14,150,346	1,287,040
1987	4,143,192	1,016,304	24,520,656	(2)
1988	4,873,616	1,195,652	28,146,984	(2)
1989	4,945,876	1,187,164	29,125,304	(2)
1990	4,890,931	1,208,180	29,677,452	2,266,420
1991	5,241,095	1,259,653	30,871,450	−2,375,556
1992	5,997,308	1,349,508	33,541,482	3,236,076
1993	6,083,882	1,428,235	35,498,557	3,652,898

[1] Prior to the creation of the rental payments to GSA appropriation for fiscal year 1983, agencies were individually charged for space and a departmental administration level is not available.

[2] The Auditors Building was vacated for renovation from 1987 until 1989.

FUND TRANSFERS

Mr. DURBIN. The fiscal year 1992 budget included transfers to the Soil Conservation Service, Farmers Home, and the National Agricultural Statistics Service. Why weren't these transfers included in fiscal year 1993?

Mr. HILTY. Agencies receive transfers of funds from this appropriation for the first two fiscal years following changes in space occupancy to allow sufficient time to program funding requirements into individual agency budgets. The transfers shown in last year's budget were primarily for space changes that occurred during fiscal year 1991.

STRATEGIC SPACE PLAN

Mr. DURBIN. In the Washington Metropolitan Area, USDA occupies space in 18 leased and four owned buildings. The Department is developing a Long Range Strategic Space Plan. When do you expect this plan to be completed?

Mr. HILTY. The Long Range Strategic Plan was completed in September 1991. However, the Plan is now being reviewed for updating to reflect the vision and plans of the new Secretary.

If the Department gains custody of the four Headquarters buildings in 1994 and retains GSA rental payments to finance the Strategic Space Plan, the plan could be completed by 2003.

GSA SPACE RENTAL ESTIMATES

Mr. DURBIN. What were GSA's estimates to USDA for the National Capital Region in fiscal years 1992, 1993, and 1994? Please break this out between leased and owned space.

Mr. HILTY. I will provide a table for the record to show these amounts.

[The information follows:]

GSA SPACE ESTIMATES

	Annual 1992	Annual 1993	Annual 1994
Owned	$44,124,374	$46,663,572	$47,828,213
Leased	21,815,961	20,923,746	21,734,057
Total	65,940,335	67,587,318	69,562,270

GSA BUILDING DELEGATION

Mr. DURBIN. What is the status of the delegation of authority you have with GSA?

Mr. HILTY. USDA has not reached an agreement with GSA to renew the delegation. USDA pursued with the GSA Administrator the concept of transferring title to the Headquarters buildings back to USDA. At this point no agreement has been reached.

RENTAL PAYMENTS AND GSA REPAIR COSTS

Mr. DURBIN. Update the two tables that appear on page 92 of last year's hearing record showing the amount of rental payments made to GSA and the amount spent by GSA for repairs to include fiscal year 1992.

Mr. HILTY. I will provide the information for the two tables for the record.

[The information follows:]

Rental payments to GSA—fiscal years 1985-92

Fiscal year	*Rental payments to GSA*
1985	$52,766,671
1986	47,751,006
1987	48,728,000
1988	45,857,311
1989	46,363,000
1990	44,788,846
1991	46,120,802
1992	45,679,002

Estimated costs of repair contracts awarded by GSA—fiscal year 1985-92

Administration Building	$3,720,518
Annex Building	875,000
Auditors Building—renovation	12,851,000
South Building	6,062,630
West Auditors Building—removed from the USDA inventory in 1988	680,000
Total estimate	24,189,148

STATUS OF HEADQUARTERS COMPLEX FACILITIES PROBLEMS

Mr. DURBIN. Mr. Hilty, at last year's hearing you testified that the four Headquarters Complex buildings were in serious trouble. The heating, ventilation, and cooling systems are incapable of providing the proper temperature, humidity or air quality to the employees. The systems are designed to return exhaust air down the main corridors, the same corridors the employees would use during emergencies. The electrical systems are inadequate for today's computer oriented workforce and power outages are common. The plumbing systems are so old that pipes are disintegrating within the walls. What has GSA done about these problem? Have you had any contact with GSA concerning these systems.

Mr. HILTY. Over the past year we have met with and written to the General Services Administration requesting priority consideration for correcting the serious life safety problems in the Headquarters complex. To date, GSA has refused to address these problems in USDA facilities because USDA has not paid the full amount of its rental billing.

BUILDING EVALUATION

Mr. DURBIN. GSA performs a building evaluation for all existing buildings every five years. An evaluation for the Administration and South Buildings was done in 1983 and an evaluation for the Annex building was done in 1989. When do you expect GSA to perform another evaluation?

Mr. HILTY. GSA has just recently begun building evaluations of the Administration Building and Annex Building. We were expecting a Prospectus Development Study to be done for the Agriculture South Building in FY 1993 but we now understand that this study has been deferred for at least another year. A post-occupancy evaluation of the Auditors Building was done in FY 1992, after the renovation project which was completed in FY 1990.

NON-RECURRING REPAIR REQUESTS

Mr. DURBIN. Please update the chart that appears on page 93 of last year's hearing record showing all requests for non-recurring repairs made to GSA, including the date, project, and cost estimates, and GSA's response to include any requests made in fiscal year 1992 or so far in fiscal year 1993.

Mr. HILTY. I will provide the updated table for the record.

[The information follows:]

Requests to GSA for Non-Recurring Repairs

Project	Estimated Cost	Request /Appeal	Reply Date	Action Date
Repair and Restore Hazardous Parapet Walls	$1,200,000	08/21/86 11/04/86 01/22/86	10/08/86 12/15/86 --	Denied Denied
Replace Deteriorated Rain Leaders	Unknown	11/04/86 12/29/86 03/23/87	11/24/86 01/21/87 04/27/87	Denied Denied Denied
Replace Defective Chiller No. 1	150,000	03/14/86 04/10/86 06/16/86	03/19/86 04/30/86 12/02/86	Denied Denied Denied
Remove Hazardous Asbestos Materials	$1,000,000(+)	10/17/86 11/21/86 01/22/86 04/23/87	-- -- 03/05/87 --	Request funding for immediate repairs
Replace Leaking Skylight	600,000	01/13/87 05/08/87	02/11/87 06/01/87	Completed 1991
Provide Emergency Power due to Power Lost in Fire	200,000	07/24/87	08/12/87	Denied
Repair Tunnel Leaks	Unknown	03/27/89	05/08/89	Denied
Replace Hazardous Transformers and Repair Vault 10	500,000	03/23/90	04/19/90	Accepted
Structural Leaks	Various	01/24/91	05/15/91	Being Programmed
Elevator for Gurney/Freight	500,000	07/09/92	08/24/92	Denied

USDA FUNDED REPAIRS

Mr. DURBIN. Provide a list of all non-recurring and recurring repairs that have been made using USDA funds and the cost of each for each year since fiscal year 1985. Differentiate between those that are non-recurring and those that are recurring repairs.

Mr. HILTY. I will provide a list of recurring and non-recurring repairs which USDA has accomplished for Fiscal Years 1985 through 1992. The nonrecurring repairs are identified for Fiscal Years 1988, the first year funds were authorized for non-recurring repairs, through 1992.

[The information follows:]

USDA Repair Program
Headquarters Complex

1985 PROJECTS

66,000	Remove Bird Excreta, Administration Building
15,974	Re-build 70 Ton Compressor, Administration Building
2,496	Seal Apron, Administration Building
34,000	Paint and Repair Windows, Administration Building
11,338	Elevator No.7 Door Replacement, Administration Building
20,600	Repair Flagstone on Terrace, Administration Building
12,500	AC Units for Elev. Penthouses, South Building
9,850	Conversion of Air Compressor, South Building
9,290	Install 25 Ton Cooling Tower, South Building
3,405	Re-finish Stage Floor, South Building
14,920	Paint Exterior Railings, South Building
23,900	Replace Elev. Cab #64, South Building
10,575	New HVAC System in 1601, South Building
167,410	Install Wall Guard System, South Building
2,986	Re-point Exterior Stairs, South Building
94,984	Removal of Abandoned Equipment, South Building
2,950	Flooring Repair, South Building
7,263	Exterior Door Locks, South Building
10,010	Repair Exterior Lights, Complex
99,688	Lighting Controls, Complex
39,987	New Lens Covers, Complex
221,600	New Induction Units, Complex
8,800	Asbestos Abatement, Annex Building

1986 PROJECTS

114,444	Replace Roof, Administration Building
202,777	Replace Chiller No. 2, Administration Building
24,414	Sound System, Patio, Administration Building
396,000	Mezzanine Renovations, Annex Building
318,000	Replace Roof, Phase I, South Building
136,000	Fitness Center Space Conversion, South Building
129,444	Parapet Wall Emergency Repairs, South Building
37,717	New Roof, Law Library, South Building
26,830	Jefferson Auditorium Ceiling, South Building
98,164	Removal of Abandoned Equipment, South Building
100,000	Renovate Restrooms, South Building
17,500	Fire Alarm System Repairs, South Building
4,500	Asbestos Removal, Annex Building
10,046	Renovate Restrooms, Auditors Building
8,896	Stairtreads, West Auditors Building
25,600	New Locks on All Mechanical Space, Complex
34,994	Asbestos Survey, Complex
50,000	Parking Lot Repairs, Complex

1987 PROJECTS

101,600 Repair Chiller No. 1, Administration Building
85,000 Computer Room, OIG, Administration Building
75,000 Repair Sprinkler System, Administration Building
57,360 Masonry Repairs, Annex Building
164,665 Replace Roof, Annex Building
9,752 Repair Window Screens, Annex Building
490,000 Waterproofing, Court 1, South Building
172,722 Replace Roofs, Phases II & III, South Building
72,200 Asbestos Abatement, Phase I, South Building
81,440 Replace Motor Control Centers, South Building
385,000 Law Library Space Conversion, South Building
6,232 Stair Repairs, South Building
100,000 Replace Electrical Panels, South Building

1988 PROJECTS

255,525 Replace Switchgear, Administration Building (N)
277,000 Masonry Restoration, Phase I, Administration Building (N)
162,000 Asbestos Abatement, Phase I, Administration Building (N)
45,095 Repair Cafeteria, Administration Building
23,000 Handicapped Modifications, Restrooms, Administration
6,000 Handicapped Ramp, Administration Building
12,000 Repair Sidewalks, Administration Building
14,975 Re-grout Apron, Administration Building
1,118,154 Restore Windows, Phase II, South Building (N)
174,000 Replace Bus Ducts, South Building (N)
136,594 Asbestos Abatement, Phase II, South Building (N)
71,100 Conference Facility Space Conversion, South Building
113,455 Conveyor, South Building
230,476 Replace Chiller, South Building
68,986 Handicapped Modifications to Restrooms, South Building
33,140 Replace Court 2 Security Booth, South Building
8,066 Replace Fire Alarm Printer, South Building
31,252 Vault High Voltage Breakers, Complex
16,626 Repair Security Stations, Complex

(N) - Non-Recurring Repairs

1989 PROJECTS

61,820 Limestone Repairs, South Building (N)
759,200 Restore Windows, Phase III, South Building (N)
593,000 Elevators 31, 32, 33, South Building
365,995 Masonry Restoration, Phase I, South Building
220,000 Elevator, Court 3, South Building
230,300 Temperature Controls, South Building
92,000 Restore Metal Work, South Building
249,000 Court Gates, South Building
469,000 Utility Mods. Court 3, South Building (N)
82,170 Chilled Water Riser, South Building

5,345 Elect. Repairs, Loading Dock, South Building
40,000 Repair Restroom Stall Doors, South Building
5,000 Loading Dock Ramp, South Building
266,000 Masonry Restoration, Phase II, Administration Building (N)
178,000 Asbestos Abatement, Phase II, Administration Building (N)
319,913 Panelboards and Feeders, Administration Building (N)
184,500 Temperature Controls, Administration Building
47,000 Concrete Repairs, Administration Building
12,000 Repair Stairs, Administration Building
13,000 Repair Restroom Accessories, Administration Building
75,000 Repair Concrete Curbing, Administration Building
28,000 Repair Entrance Gates, Administration Building
269,400 Utility Metering, Complex
113,750 Stairtread Replacement, Complex

1990 PROJECTS

347,000 Elevators 37 & 66, South Building (N)
1,236,350 Restore Windows, Phase IV, South Building (N)
930,000 Restore Masonry, Phase II, South Building
109,660 Asbestos Abatement, Phase III, South Building (N)
18,500 Ventilate Steam Station, South Building
2,011,483 Court 3 Sub-basement Space Conversion, South Building
15,000 Bird Proofing, Courts 1, 5, and 6, South Building
9,323 Repair Wall Guard System, South Building
369,525 Asbestos Abatement, Phase III, Administration Building (N)
258,000 Masonry Restoration, Phase III, Administration Building (N)
311,000 HVAC Modifications, Administration Building (N)
32,000 Repair Exit Doors, Administration Building
155,445 Asbestos Abatement, Phase I, Annex Building
112,000 Parking Lot Gates, Complex
1,207 Repair Flag Poles, Complex
1,088,700 Child Care Center Space Conversion, Auditors Building

(N) - Non-Recurring Repairs

1991 PROJECTS

217,000 HVAC Zoning, Administration Building
1,365,000 Wiring, Administration Building
34,700 Roof Repair, Administration Building
52,500 Emergency Lights, Administration Building (N)
472,274 Switchgear, East/West Wings, Administration Building (N)
33,086 Emergency Fire Repair, Administration Building
33,971 Bird Proof Netting, Administration Building
13,032 Bird Excrement Removal, Administration Building
22,500 Wall Protection, Administration Building
253,182 Masonry Repairs-Courts, South Building

459,600	Escalator, South Building
1,219,090	Windows, Court 1, South Building (N)
157,777	Handicapped Entrance, South Building (N)
572,572	Electrical Improvements, South Building (N)
130,000	Emergency Lights, South Building (N)
32,207	Repair Leaks, South Building
149,203	Roof Repairs, South Building
176,487	Replace Stair Treads, South Building
216,000	Lighting Retrofit, South Building
84,059	Replace Corridor Ceilings, South Building
57,454	Site drainage, Annex Building
27,938	Replace Ceilings, Annex Building
207,895	Loading Dock, Auditors Building
109,400	Wheelchair Lifts, Complex
884,829	Network Protectors, Complex
70,000	Fire Alarm Repairs, Complex
16,097	Switchgear Repairs, Complex

(N) - Non-Recurring Repairs

1992 PROJECTS

187,680	Asbestos Removal, Phase IV, South Building (N)
467,000	Replace Drains, South Building (N)
591,411	Training Center Space Conversion, South Building
137,777	Sub-basement Space Conversion, South Building
34,300	Upgrade Steam Station, South Building
87,240	HVAC Modifications, South Building
72,243	Resource Center for the Disabled, South Building
512,000	Winter Refrigeration, South Building (N)
124,447	Waterproofing Repairs, Court 2, South Building (N)
1,310,000	Windows and Masonry Repairs, Court 4, South Building (N)
446,000	Air Quality Improvements, South Building (N)
38,113	Emergency Cable Replacement in Vault, South Building
1,261,000	Windows, Administration Building (N)
52,709	Lighting Retrofit, Administration Building
91,837	5th Floor HVAC Improvements, Administration Building
504,000	Upgrade Vault 10, Administration Building
10,700	Upgrade Steam Station, Auditors Building
453,829	HVAC Improvements, Complex
39,201	Conference Rooms, Administration Building
54,500	Restore Railings, South Building
42,900	Winter Cooling, Administration Building
47,377	Install Street Lighting in Various Lots, Administration Building

(N) - Non-Recurring Repairs

MINOR REPAIRS

Mr. DURBIN. Also, provide a list of all minor repairs, those that cost under $10,000.

Mr. HILTY. I will provide a list of minor repairs for each fiscal year. Minor repairs are defined as those repairs less than $10,000 which are accomplished under our Operations and Maintenance Program.

[CLERK'S NOTE.—The document is too lengthy to be included in the record. It will be retained in Committee files.]

HISTORY OF GSA ESTIMATES

Mr. DURBIN. Update the table that appears on page 99 of last year's hearing record showing the amount GSA will charge USDA for rent, what the request to the Secretary was, what the Secretary's request to OMB was, and the OMB allowance to include fiscal year 1994.

Mr. HILTY. The table I will provide will outline the GSA estimates for the portion of space and related services that are paid from this central appropriation. These estimates will not include space and related costs from trust funds, revolving funds, reimbursements, or from Forest Service appropriations, since the Forest Service is funded in the Interior and Related Agencies Appropriation Act.

[The information follows:]

HISTORY OF GSA ESTIMATES AND REQUESTS

[In thousands of dollars]

	GSA rental estimate	Request to Secretary	Request to OMB	OMB allowance
Fiscal year.				
1984	69,402	69,402	69,402	69,402
1985	67,254	67,254	67,254	67,254
1986	77,193	69,092	69,092	59,500
1987	78,027	72,601	63,401	57,380
1988	92,647	70,319	57,380	56,407
1989	93,442	80,499	56,407	56,407
1990	93,993	94,573	50 659	50,659
1991	98,452	88,736	49,305	49,305
1992	105,136	93,057	53,052	51,598
1993	110,395	83,159	50,808	50,503
1994	132,742	54,104	50,503	50,503

NON-RECURRING REPAIRS

Mr. DURBIN. Under the delegation of authority that expired on October 1, 1989, GSA is responsible for all major non-recurring repairs. For the record, please list all major non-recurring repairs needed for the buildings in the D.C. complex and the cost of each.

Mr. HILTY. I will provide a list of the major non-recurring repairs needed for each building in the Headquarters Complex. The list has been compiled from both GSA's building evaluation reports and our own engineering studies of the buildings. USDA has prepared Master Plans which are comprehensive in identifying the repair needs of the buildings.

[The information follows:]

Major Non-Recurring Repair Needs
USDA Headquarter Complex
APRIL 1993

PROJECT	PRELIMINARY ESTIMATE
Administration Building	
Structural Repairs, Sub-Central Plant	62,500
Switchgear Replacement, Vault No. 10	315,000
Fire Safety Improvements	1,081,500
Improve Surface Drainage	120,750
Rehabilitate Parking Areas	472,500
Provide Service Elevator	525,000
Asbestos Abatement	1,575,000
Repair Existing HVAC System to Improve Operation	2,100,000
Install Storm Windows (Interior)	1,050,000
Replace Rain Leaders	525,000
Provide Energy Efficient Office Lighting	1,050,000
Replace HVAC System	6,300,000
Replace Mezzanine Service Floor	525,000
Modernize Restrooms, Modifications for Disabled	315,000
Auditors Building	
Site and Drainage Improvements	630,000
Exterior Masonry Restoration	525,000
Roof Repairs	210,000
Attic Mechanical Room Upgrade	315,000
HVAC Improvements	525,000
Elevator Improvements	840,000
Restoration of Clock Tower and Turret	525,000
Annex Building	
Space Conversion, 5th Floor Mezzanine	472,500
Space Conversion, Basement	472,500
Replace Basement Floor Slab	315,000
Fire Safety Improvements	210,000
Repair Existing HVAC System	315,000
Replace HVAC System	1,365,000
Upgrade Electrical Distribution System	945,000
Replace Windows	420,000
Plumbing System Repairs	63,000
Structural Repairs	126,000
Masonry Restoration	157,000
Disabled Access Improvements	210,000
Asbestos Abatement	105,000
General Renovation	630,000
Mid-Season Cooling System	168,000

PROJECT	PRELIMINARY ESTIMATE
South Building	
Penthouse Windows, Completion	210,000
Attic Space Conversion	3,000,000
Egress Security System	100,000
Utility System Improvements	750,000
Structural Repairs	525,000
Window Restoration, Courts 3, 5 and 6	3,900,000
Repair Masonry, Courts 1, 5 and 6	630,000
Upgrade Mail Handling Facility and Loading Dock	1,575,000
Replace Ceilings and Lighting	9,450,000
Install Condensate Drainage System	2,100,000
Provide Smoke and Heat Detector System	315,000
Provide Zoned Fire Alarm System	892,500
Replace Combustible Attic Insulation	2,835,000
Firestopping	525,000
Provide Ducted Exhaust System	1,470,000
Provide Fused Load Break Switches	1,207,500
Replace Switchgear 13,14, 15	367,500
Replace Distribution Panels	1,050,000
Redo Wire Closets	1,260,000
Replace Branch Circuit Panels	157,500
Redistribute Computer Power and Outlets	7,245,000
Replace Switchgear 2 and 17	1,000,000
Replace Breakers in Distribution Panels	315,000
Replace (14) Air Handling Units	367,500
Restore Secondary Water Flow	1,575,000
Provide Return Air System	2,625,000
Steam System Repairs	1,365,000
Chilled Water System Repairs	1,050,000
Remove Abandoned Piping	420,000
Roof Access Walkways	420,000
Central Drinking Water System	577,500
Replace Water System for Service Sinks	420,000
New Refrigeration System and Tunnel	7,560,000
Replace Roof, Wing 6 Attic	892,500
Replace Obsolete Induction Units	2,625,000
Waterproof Court 2	840,000
Air Quality Improvements	1,050,000
Replace Electrical Distribution System	39,375,000
Upgrade Toilet Rooms and Plumbing System	11,445,000
Parking Structure, Court No. 6	14,280,000
Replace Chilled Water Supply System	14,070,000
Replace HVAC System	23,205,000
Fire Protection Sprinklers	13,335,000
Asbestos Abatement	3,780,000
General Architectural Renovation	39,900,000

SOUTH BUILDING RENOVATION

Mr. DURBIN. The explanatory notes state that efforts will continue in fiscal year 1993 to keep the D.C. complex safe and operational until the proposed major renovation of the South Building is undertaken and accomplished. Is this a renovation that GSA plans to undertake?

Mr. HILTY. GSA initiated a Prospectus Development Study (PDS) for the South Building in 1986 and completed it in 1988. The PDS recommended a complete renovation, but USDA was advised by GSA that there would be no action taken to request funds from Congress because of the shortfall in USDA's rent payments to GSA. We were recently advised that a new PDS would be started in FY 1993, but have since learned that GSA has decided to defer the new PDS until at least FY 1994.

WINDOW RESTORATION

Mr. DURBIN. USDA has been undertaking a window restoration project since fiscal year 1988. What has been spent to date on this project and what are the estimates for the total job?

Mr. HILTY. The window restoration program for the Agriculture South Building is being accomplished in phases. I will provide a table showing the cost and number of windows included in each phase. GSA restored the windows on the south facade in 1987. USDA has completed the north, east, and west facades, and Courts 1 and 2. The Court 4 windows are now being restored under a contract awarded in fiscal year 1992. Total construction funds spent to date by USDA are $5,642,794. Three courts remain to be completed, at an estimated additional cost of $3.9 million.

The windows in the Administration Building are presently being restored under a contract awarded in Fiscal Year 1992 at a cost of $1,261,000.

[The information follows:]

WINDOW RESTORATION PROGRAM—SOUTH BUILDING

Fiscal year and location	Number of windows [1]	Cost
1988—E, W, and part N facades	700	$1,118,154
1989—Complete N facade	400	759,200
1990—Court 2	500	1,236,350
1991—Court 1	450	1,219,090
1992—Court 4	500	[2] 1,310,000
Construction costs to date		5,642,794

[1] Numbers of windows approximate

[2] Contract includes masonry repairs

CONTRACT WITH CERTIFIED INDUSTRIAL HYGIENE CONSULTANT

Mr. DURBIN. You have entered into a contract with a certified Industrial hygiene consultant to conduct air quality tests and report evaluations. What is the cost of this contract? How many tests have been performed? What were the results of these tests?

Mr. HILTY. The environmental testing contract was originally set up under our engineering program in fiscal year 1991, due to increasing concerns for environmental health and safety in our buildings. In fiscal year 1991, about 300 individual tests were done at a cost of about $13,500; in fiscal year 1992, about 1500 individual tests were done at a cost of about $76,000; and in fiscal year 1993 through March 1993 about 800 individual tests, a majority of which were more complex in testing requirements, have been done at a cost of about $61,500. The testing program includes such tests as asbestos material sampling, air quality tests for temperature and humidity, bacteria, carbon dioxide or other contaminants, and water quality tests for lead or other contaminants.

The testing results are used to evaluate the buildings environment and to take remedial action when the conditions warrant. Generally, the test results have showed systems were functioning marginally. Corrective actions in cases where threshold levels are approached or exceeded include increasing ventilation rates, where possible, cleaning, or replacement of systems.

NON-SALARY COSTS INCREASE AND ADMINISTRATIVE EFFICIENCY DECREASE

Mr. DURBIN. The 1994 appropriation for Building Operations and Maintenance includes a 2.7 percent increase or $569,000 in non-salary costs offset by a 3.0 percent decrease or $792,000 for administrative efficiency. Provide a specific breakout of how you arrived at these amounts.

Mr. HILTY. The 2.7% is the OMB estimate of inflation for non-pay costs. The $569,000 represents a 2.7% inflationary increase on non-salary obligations of $21,066,000 for the Building Operations and Maintenance account. This amount does not include the $50,503,000 originally requested for our GSA Rental Payments and non-recurring repair costs, which were calculated separately.

As part of the Administration's effort to assist in controlling the Federal deficit and in improving the administrative productivity of the Federal Government, each executive agency was required to reduce administrative expenses. This reduction was calculated as follows: Pay costs and inflation were added to the fiscal year 1993 appropriation. A 3 percent reduction was taken on the adjusted total. This reduction amounted to $792,000, which was applied to travel, communications and utilities, printing and reproduction, other services and supplies and materials.

SERVICE CONTRACT ACT OF 1965

Mr. DURBIN. As mandated in the Service Contract Act of 1965, you are required to account for an increase in labor costs annually as determined by the Department of Labor. What will these cost increases be for fiscal year 1994?

Mr. HILTY. The increase for labor costs is, as you say, determined by the Department of Labor. Therefore, USDA does not know at this time what those increases will be. Historically the increases have been about 8%, however due to the economic climate, the percent increases have been lower in the recent past. USDA recommended two major contracts for fiscal year 1993 and realized a reduced labor cost. We anticipate any increases over the next year will be small.

EMPLOYEES HANDLING BUILDING MAINTENANCE

Mr. DURBIN. How many employees do you have working to maintain the Headquarters Complex buildings?

Mr. HILTY. The total number of employees maintaining these buildings is 70 full-time Government employees and 253 full-time service contract personnel. In addition to our full-time employees, there are two architect-engineer professional services consulting firms with about 280 personnel, and construction contractors with about 290 personnel currently working on our construction projects. Most of these, however, are not working full-time on USDA projects.

FUNDS USED FOR BUILDING REPAIRS AND SALARIES

Mr. DURBIN. Of the total amount available for Building Operations and Maintenance, how much is used towards building repairs and how much is for salaries?

Mr. HILTY. During fiscal year 1992, $7,497,432 was used for building repairs and $4,370,904 was used for salaries. For fiscal year 1993, $9.8 million is planned for building repairs and $4.6 million is planned for salaries. For fiscal year 1994, $9.7 million is planned for building repairs and $4.7 million is planned for salaries.

FMHA PROCUREMENT AUTHORITY

Mr. DURBIN. Let me switch to another topic, if I might. Last year there was a $50,000 ADP procurement authority limit placed on Farmers Home in an effort to re-evaluate the Department's automatic data processing needs. What is the status of this limitation? Has their procurement authority been changed or reinstated in any way?

Mr. HILTY. It has been changed slightly, Mr. Chairman. We have raised it from $50,000 to $300,000, but that has been directed toward supplies and in-house maintenance activities, rather than authority to go out and make substantial purchases of new equipment or equipment outside our broader Department specifications.

In past years the Agriculture Stabilization and Conservation Service, and the Federal Crop Insurance Corporation have also had their delegated thresholds reduced because of problems in managing information systems. Although both agencies have been making progress, their full delegations have not yet been restored.

Each of these three agencies is proposed to become part of the Farm Service Agency. A key benefit of the proposed consolidation would be the opportunity to develop a cost effective single IRM system acquired under the Info Share umbrella for the Farm Service Agency, avoiding systems procurement problems encountered in the past.

Mr. DURBIN. The explanatory notes for Farmers Home include five pages of automation initiatives. Are each of these initiatives coordinated through your Office of Information Resources Management?

Mr. HILTY. Farmers Home Administration's automation initiatives described in the explanatory notes are fully coordinated within OIRM and the Info Share Program, covering the areas of IRM policy, planning and budgeting, telecommunications, security, review and standards, and information management, etc. OIRM reviewed and approved the agency's IRM plans. OIRM reviews and evaluates IRM plans and acquisition requests to ensure that they are in compliance with Departmental policy and procedures. Additionally, from a technical standpoint, they are reviewed to ensure that they effectively satisfy the problem to be solved from both an economy and efficiency perspective.

Mr. DURBIN. How are these initiatives coordinated with the agencies involved in the consolidation of offices into a single Farm Service Agency?

Mr. HILTY. IRM initiatives in ASCS, FmHA/RDA, SCS, FCIC and ES are currently being reviewed and evaluated as part of the Info Share program. Specifically, for the Farmers Home Administration several initiatives have been adopted and/or identified as short-term projects that are applicable to Info Share. Info Share managers and task team members are currently involved in every facet of the IRM programs for the five agencies. Info Share staff participate in the OIRM's Technical Review Process to ensure that all farm service related IRM resources are acquired under the Into Share umbrella. Creation of a Farm Service Agency (FSA) would present the opportunity for significant savings in IRM-related purchases and maintenance. We envision moving the FSA to a single IRM system as soon as possible after the FSA is established.

INFORMATION SHARING

Mr. DURBIN. Your request includes an increase of $384,000 for the Office of Information Resources Management to provide oversight and guidance to the planning, acquisition, and development efforts that promote information sharing among USDA computer systems. In order to provide this guidance, you propose to increase the staff of OIRM by only two staff years. Tell us in further detail how this money will be used.

Mr. HILTY. The Notes show a net increase of two staff years. This net increase is derived as follows: OIRM was reduced one staff year from the fiscal year 1993 level of 74 as part of the overall staff year reduction of 28 in Departmental Administration. Three staff years were then provided for development of USDA information sharing activities, the foundation of future integrated USDA information systems.

Of the total $384,000, $155,000 is for salaries and benefits for the three staff years. The remaining $215,000 will support training of USDA IRM staffs in the use of Information Engineering methodologies.

FCIC ADP PROCUREMENT

Mr. DURBIN. I understand that the Federal Crop Insurance Corporation was allowed to proceed with a $25,000,000 ADP equipment purchase in FY 1993. What justification did you use to allow them to proceed with this purchase in view of the fact that the Department was looking at the consolidation of offices including crop insurance?

Mr. HILTY. The General Accounting Office (GAO) recommended that FCIC not proceed with a nation-wide contract pending clarification of FCIC's future role and structure. FCIC management concurred and the CIC ADP equipment acquisition was canceled on March 1, 1993. USDA and GAO agreed that FCIC does have critical short term needs in support of crop risk management responsibilities of the Department. FCIC will satisfy these needs through existing government contracts, or contracts of limited scope. To be responsive to the many discussions about organizational changes, FCIC will select general purpose hardware and software that can support its short term requirements and the longer term needs of the Department, however it is structured. In particular, measures have been taken to assure that this equipment will be fully compatible with the directed consolidation of information systems procurements of the Farm Service agencies.

FCIC has refocused its internal efforts by limiting its procurements to those necessary to sustain operations. This action permits a two-thirds reduction in acquisition costs compared with the canceled acquisition. For long-term improvements, FCIC has reallocated staff to the Department to assist in the directed joint farm service agency information system initiative (Info Share).

USDA COMPUTER CAPABILITY

Mr. DURBIN. What is your evaluation of the computer capability within USDA in general? Do you feel that it is as it should be? Is it near state of the art? Is it approaching that? Is there a plan to bring it to that point?

Mr. HILTY. A three-part question.

Is it as it should be? No.

Near state of the art? In a few places, in very few places.

Are we moving in the right direction and is there a plan? Indeed there is.

IRM STRATEGIC PLAN

I would like to use the existence of that plan as an example of the transition from Administration to Administration, which, as you know, I do represent here in many ways today both symbolically and substantively. When Secretary Madigan left his office for the last time, the day before Inauguration Day, knowing that I was to serve as Acting Secretary until Mr. Espy's confirmation, he gave me two official documents to share with Mr. Espy as directly as possible, when he came to the Department after his confirmation.

One of the documents was a freshly delivered report dated that day to Secretary Madigan on food safety inspection concerns. He thought that was both timely and symbolic of the types of concerns that Mr. Espy soon would have, and he wanted that one delivered as an example of program concerns.

The other one that he asked me to give directly to Mr. Espy and talk with him a little bit about was the freshly completed IRM Strategic Plan for the Department of Agriculture, a long-range, five-year plan, bringing together with a clear central focus the IRM planning for the Department. And Mr. Madigan said that was particularly appropriate because it was one of the most important management documents of his tenure, and would be one of the most helpful things that he thought Secretary Espy should have and should understand early in his tenure.

Within that plan is a program that we call Info Share, which is referred to at several places in my written testimony. That is a plan that gives central authority to the Department to set technical specifications and procurement specifications for all major procurement activities involving agencies of the Department, but particularly the field service delivery agencies which so concern us.

There is a plan, it is well in place, it is beginning to move quite rapidly and it has found understanding and acceptance in many facets of the Department.

INTERNAL AUTOMATION

Mr. DURBIN. Mr. Hilty, when you were here last year you told the Committee about the Office of Personnel's two-year implementation plan for its internal automation replacement program. The program's goal is the placement of automated work stations at each employee's desk with standardization of equipment and software throughout the office. What is the status of this initiative?

Mr. HILTY. The Office of Personnel continues to struggle in the area of upgrading and automating systems that are essential for Department-wide communication, monitoring and oversight. Much of the existing equipment has come from excess property discarded by other agencies. The majority of office computers are at least one and in many cases two generations behind other office environments. Over 85% of the Office of Personnel employees are unable to communicate with the Agriculture agencies via computer. Even the simple exchange of data via a floppy diskette is difficult due to the mix of antiquated and modern equipment. The lack of printing and external communications capabilities affects the ability of analysts to acquire and analyze data, and perform a consultative and advisory role for USDA executive leadership and the agencies.

CROSS-SERVICING MORATORIUM

Mr. DURBIN. We recently had the opportunity to visit the National Finance Center, and you were kind enough to escort us on that trip. I have told the story far and wide about what I consider to be the success of that Center, and I hope that success will continue. They currently have a moratorium on expanding cross-service activities, activities to serve other government agencies. How long do you anticipate this moratorium to be in effect?

Mr. HILTY. I would not want to put a specific calendar date on it, Mr. Chairman. As you know from our very fruitful discussions down there, we think that we expanded very rapidly, that we served the Federal government quite well by having made those expansions, but that we now are at a place where we must limit those expansions to the increasing business that is generated from our current customers, rather than taking on new customers.

We find that it is time to strengthen some of our internal controls, some of our internal documentation, issues that you and Mr.

Skeen and several of us at this table discussed that day. We need to address some of our questions about modernizing some of our software there.

Therefore, I think it would be unwise of me today and perhaps unfair to those who follow me in this job, to set forth a specific timetable, but rather to say to you that we have responsive flexible new management in place at the Center. Those questions are being addressed.

At this very time yesterday, I was at the center, Mr. Chairman, talking with the Director about their preparations for some of these responses, giving further guidance on the ways in which we can strengthen our internal operation, so we can turn again to providing broader service for all parts of the Federal government. And I know that material I brought back for Dr. Wilson and Mr. David, about, even broader opportunities existing in New Orleans and at the Center, will be of keen interest to yourself and to Mr. Skeen.

We were truly glad to have you there and we hope that you will come back and bring some of your congressional friends with you.

CROSS-SERVICING

Mr. DURBIN. Please provide a list of all cross-servicing the National Finance Center performs.

Mr. HILTY. I will be glad to provide this information for the record.

[The information follows:]

NATIONAL FINANCE CENTER—CROSS-SERVICING CLIENTS, FY 1994

ACTION.
Appalachian Regional Commission.
Architect of the Capitol.
Commodity Futures Trading Commission.
Congressional Budget Office.
Copyright Royalty Tribunal.
Farm Credit Administration.
Farm Credit System Assistance Board.
Federal Communications Commission.
Federal Deposit Insurance Corporation.
Federal Emergency Management Agency.
Federal Employees Retirement System/Thrift Savings Plan.
Federal Mine Safety and Health Review Commission.
General Accounting Office.
John C. Stennis Center for Public Development.
Library of Congress.
Merit Systems Protection Board.
National Endowment for the Arts.
National Gallery of Art.
National Labor Relations Board.
National Park Service.
Occupational Safety and Health Review Commission.
Office of Government Ethics.
Office of Technology Assessments.
Small Business Administration.
Smithsonian Institution.
U.S. Commission on Civil Rights.
U.S. Court of Veterans Appeals.
U.S. Department of Commerce.
U.S. Department of Education.
U.S. Department of Housing and Urban Development.
U.S. Department of Justice.
U.S. Department of Labor.

U.S. Department of State.
U.S. Department of the Treasury.
U.S. Office of the Special Counsel.

Mr. DURBIN. Do you plan to reduce any of these services?

Mr. HILTY. USDA does not plan to reduce any cross-servicing services.

CONTAMINATION AT CCC SITES

Mr. DURBIN. Let me switch to another topic of concern that was raised yesterday by one of our public witnesses.

The EPA has identified a total of 32 former CCC grain storage sites where there is carbon tetrachloride contamination. CCC is conducting an alternative drinking water supply study at 12 of these sites with high contamination levels. Have any additional sites been identified by EPA beyond these 32?

Mr. HILTY. I cannot answer that personally. I would have to answer that for the record. I would say that it would not surprise me. The Hazardous Waste Management Fund that we have in our appropriation is only $16 million this year. Last year we did our best job in many, many years, of committing more fully than ever before the funds that were available to us through that appropriation and funds leftover from previous years.

We committed nearly 100 percent of the available funds. It is an account that I think needs strong attention, and ultimately will need more money than we are able to commit to it now.

I will have to provide for the record a more precise answer to your specific question, but I would like to have the opportunity to emphasize some things that we have been doing better, but things that we must broadly throughout the Department address even more aggressively, because there are hazardous waste management concerns that go beyond the questions that you cited about CCC.

[The information follows:]

As of January 1993, 75 sites have been identified by the EPA and/or State agencies as having carbon tetrachloride contamination in the groundwater. Since then, EPA has also informed us that Hilton, Kansas, has also been identified with a contamination level approaching 900 ppb.

The Safe Drinking Water Act (SDWA) maximum contaminant level (MCL) for carbon tetrachloride is 5 ppb. CCC has notified EPA that it will perform an alternate water supply for those sites with a carbon tetrachloride contamination of greater than or equal to 4 ppb. CCC established this 4 ppb trigger level as a quality assurance measure to help ensure compliance with the MCL.

Of the 75 sites, 34 reported carbon tetrachloride concentrations below the trigger level of 4 ppb; therefore, no further actions needed.

Another 34 sites have either been scheduled for an alternative water supply study or one has been completed. In addition to the alternate water supply study, five sites either have been scheduled for an extended site characterization study or one has been completed.

Seven additional sites have carbon tetrachloride contamination above the 4 ppb trigger level; however, an alternate water supply has not been scheduled pending EPA's comments on these seven sites.

DIRECTIVES ON ALTERNATE WATER SUPPLIES

Mr. DURBIN. While these studies are being completed, are the citizens located near these sites being provided with bottled water or instructions on how to avoid using contaminated water?

Mr. HILTY. Generally, the appropriate State authorities issue directives regarding whether and in what manner contaminated public or private wells may continue to be used. CCC works with these States to arrange for alternate water supplies if a threat to public health exists and action is needed to protect the citizens who may be affected. This could include interim actions, such as bottled water, or longer term solutions such as alternate water sources.

COST OF STUDIES

Mr. DURBIN. What is the cost of these studies? Is CCC paying the entire costs of these studies?

Mr. HILTY. Of the $3.0 million provided to the CCC in fiscal year 1993 from the USDA Hazardous Waste Management central account, $2.1 million is devoted to the cost of these studies. HWM has borne the entire cost of these studies.

ADVISORY COMMITTEES

Mr. DURBIN. Last year, this Subcommittee decided to cut the appropriation for advisory committees in half with the direction that the Department should decide which ones were important to continue and to eliminate those that weren't. Instead of eliminating some committees and fully funding others, the decision was made, by the Department, to fund all 42 at a reduced level. Can you tell us why that decision was made, as opposed to determining that perhaps some of these committees had out lived their usefulness?

Mr. HILTY. That decision, as you describe it, Mr. Chairman, was not a fully across-the-board decision. A number of the committees that were particularly active in fields of international trade and related topics were given a higher priority and were much more fully funded.

The other committees did receive less than half their requested allocation. Some of those committees then met less frequently. Fewer staff activities were assigned to them.

We now have underway in the Department an examination again of the committees, both discretionary and statutory. We have a working deadline of tomorrow for a first report, and a week from tomorrow for a final report. And when those internal reports are ready, Secretary Espy will be able in early or mid-May to report to the Congress which committees he would recommend for abandonment or for diminishment of activities.

PERSONNEL COMPENSATION

Mr. DURBIN. Mr. Hitly, on the object class table for advisory committees, you include a footnote next to Personnel Compensation which states that USDA agencies are allowed, under the Advisory Committee Act, to obligate funds for portions of salaries and benefits for staff-time devoted to the support of these committees. In addition to the funds allocated in this appropriation, provide a table showing the amount of funding, by agency, that has been allocated for advisory committees for fiscal year 1992, 1993 and 1994.

Mr. HILTY. Mr. Chairman, apparently the footnote in the budget is misleading. It was intended to explain why salaries and benefits are reported in an appropriation that has no staff years assigned to it. In addition to funding the direct activities of the committees, the central appropriation also funds the approximately 15 staff years utilized by USDA agencies in providing support to those committees. I am not aware of any agency that uses its own funds for this purpose. It would be a violation of law to do so. The only agencies with authority to finance advisory committee activities from their own funds are the Forest Service, which is funded from the Interior Appropriations Bill, and the Agricultural Marketing Service and the Commodity Credit Corporation, which finance advisory committees from user fees.

BREAKOUT OF FY 1994 FUNDS

Mr. DURBIN. Executive Order 12838, Termination and Limitation of Federal Advisory Committees, requires each agency to terminate at least one third or a minimum of seven discretionary advisory committees by the end of fiscal year 1993. As a result, your budget request did not include a breakout of funding levels in fiscal year 1994. When do you expect to make these decisions and submit to the Committee a list of those you plan to fund in 1994?

Mr. HILTY. The Department is currently reviewing all advisory committees to determine which committees provide essential advice and counsel and those that can be terminated to meet the requirement outlined in Executive Order 12838. A report that justifies the continued existence or poses termination of advisory committees will be prepared for the Secretary's review. Following the Secretary's review of the report, decisions on which committees to terminate will be made. The report will then be submitted to the OMB for review as required by E.O. 12838. After the final decisions have been made, funds will be allocated and an updated table of estimates will be provided to the Committee.

UNOBLIGATED BALANCE LAPSING

Mr. DURBIN. The budget reflects an unobligated balance lapsing in fiscal year 1992 of $225,494. Please explain this lapse of funds.

Mr. HILTY. This unobligated balance was due to unforeseen changes in the level of committee activities. The Global Climate Change Technical Advisory Committee, the Animal Health Science Research Advisory Committee, and the Advisory Council on National Sustainable Agriculture did not meet during fiscal year 1992 because of delays in approval of charters and/or appointment of committee members. Other advisory committees met less frequently, met for shorter periods, or had fewer members in attendance than planned.

POLICY ON TRAVEL

Mr. DURBIN. At last year's hearing you were developing a Department-wide policy on travel relating to Advisory Committees that was to result in substantial savings in travel costs. Was this policy ever developed? If so, what were the savings associated with it?

Mr. HILTY. The travel policy was not revised. An interagency group was charged with the task of reviewing existing travel policy to determine what changes were needed. Among the material the group reviewed was a survey in which agencies explained why they felt committee members should be reimbursed for travel expenses.

Basically, reimbursement of travel expenses results in broader representation and more participation. Further, this is the only compensation paid most committee members for the time and expertise they provide. Agencies preferred to undertake other cost containment measures, so that committee members could continue to be reimbursed for travel expenses. The group concurred with these findings and recommended that the travel policy not be changed.

ALTERNATIVE AGRICULTURE RESEARCH AND COMMERCIALIZATION CENTER ADVISORY COUNCIL

Mr. DURBIN. Who are the ten members of the Alternative Agriculture Research and Commercialization Center Advisory Council and how often do they plan to meet in fiscal year 1993?

Mr. HILTY. Because the Alternative Agriculture Research and Commercialization Center Advisory Council has not yet been chartered, members have not been appointed and meetings have not been planned.

COMMODITY DISTRIBUTION

Mr. DURBIN. The National Advisory Council on Commodity Distribution has recommended the discontinuation of commodity letter of credit sites. What was their reason for this recommendation?

Mr. HILTY. The commodity letter of credit sites were authorized as demonstration projects in school year 1982/1983, and have been reauthorized over the years. Basically, they operate as an alternate to the traditional commodity program, receiving commodity letters of credit rather than USDA donated commodities. The Council has expressed concerns about whether these sites are purchasing products of domestic origin, the timing of removing products from the market, the administrative feasibility of offering a national commodity letter of credit system and the practicality of having dual distribution systems in the States. The Council also has serious reservations about the buying power of individual schools and the ability to have the same impact on the market as USDA. Therefore, the Council saw no reason to continue these sites beyond their currently authorized time period.

RESEARCH AND EXTENSION USERS ADVISORY BOARD

Mr. DURBIN. The National Agricultural Research and Extension Users Advisory Board and the Joint Council heard presentations on the Endangered Species Act and agreed to write a paper on the potential implications of the Act to ranchers and farmers. Briefly, tell us what the conclusions of this paper are and submit a copy for the record.

Mr. HILTY. In its report, the Joint Council and Users Advisory Board recommended that Congress should make appropriate revisions to the Endangered Species Act, recognize the economic costs and other impacts of endangered species conservation efforts, and to integrate the consideration of these impacts into species listings and recovery planning. Specifically, the report recommended that the following provisions of the act be strengthened.

Species should be listed as threatened or endangered only after scientific evidence demonstrates to a reasonable degree that the population in question is declining to the point where protection is necessary for recovery. Population viability assessments should be conducted prior to the listing and should include an objective and quantitative evaluation of the prospects for survival.

An analysis of economic impact on human population, forestry, agriculture and natural resources should be done before a species is added to the list.

Suspected or alleged threats to population decline such as habitat modification, over-utilization, disease, and predation should be verified with scientific field investigations, that link the threats to specific commercial, urban, agricultural or forestry practices, or other identifiable relationships.

When critical habitat is designated for species' survival, agricultural and forest production, employment, and income from lands within the species range that are not critical to the species' survival should not be constrained.

Recovery plans should include a range of strategies that are each evaluated by biological and economic criteria, and include scientific evidence that recovery is biologically possible.

Listing decisions and recovery planning should be supported by sound, scientific information. In conjunction with studies on the individual species, research should include an analysis of how recovery strategies effect other organisms in the ecosystem. The approach of protecting ecosystems rather than individual species should be considered.

Once populations of a listed species attain a level sufficient to be considered recovered, the species should be removed as a listed species under the Act with adequate provisions to ensure the species does not later revert back to the list.

A copy of the full Position Statement will be provided for the record.

[The information follows:]

November 1992

WHITE PAPER

Reauthorization of the Endangered Species Act
of 1972, as Amended

POSITION STATEMENT
of the

National Agricultural Research and Extension Users Advisory Board
and the
Joint Council on Food and Agricultural Sciences

POSITION

The purpose of the Endangered Species Act is to identify species of plants and animals in danger of or threatened with extinction, provide protective measures to prevent extinction, and conserve the ecosystem upon which endangered and threatened species depend. Federal protection is provided to threatened and endangered species because of their aesthetic, ecological, educational, historical, recreational, and scientific value to the people of the United States.

Both the National Agricultural Research and Extension Users Advisory Board (Users Advisory Board) and the Joint Council on Food and Agricultural Sciences (Joint Council) endorse the purpose and rationale for conserving threatened and endangered species, and support the reauthorization, with modification, of the Endangered Species Act. However, as a consequence of valuing threatened and endangered species and implementing conservation programs to protect them, the human population is subjected to social and economic impacts. It is recommended that in regulating the Endangered Species Act, Congress make appropriate revisions to recognize the economic costs and other impacts of endangered species conservation efforts, and to integrate the consideration of these impacts into species listings and recovery planning.

RECOMMENDATIONS

The relevance of economic considerations to threatened and endangered species conservation is acknowledged in sections 4(b)(2) and 7(h)(i) of the Endangered Species Act. Section 4(b)(2) directs the Secretary (Interior or Commerce) to consider economic impacts when designating critical habitat. Section 7(h)(i) authorizes the Endangered Species Committee to grant an agency exemption to Section 7 constraints if the committee judges the "benefits" of agency action outweigh alternative actions. While the Act acknowledges the relevance of economic considerations, current provisions are cumbersome, imprecise, and not consistently applied. Major costs and constraints can be incurred before social and economic impacts are given full consideration. **The most effective means for ensuring full and balanced consideration of both biological and economic factors is for the Act to require that listing and recovery planning be founded on comprehensive, scientific, and objective information.** Specifically, it is recommended that the following provisions of the act be strengthened.

- Species should be listed as threatened or endangered only after scientific evidence demonstrates to a reasonable degree that the population in question is declining to the point where protection is likely necessary for recovery. Population viability assessments should be conducted prior to listing, and should include an objective and quantitative evaluation of the prospects for survival.

- An analysis of economic impact on human population, forestry, agriculture and natural resources should be done before a species is added to the list.

- Suspected or alleged threats to population decline such as habitat modification, over-utilization, disease, and predation should be verified with scientific field investigations, that link the threats to specific commercial, urban, agricultural or forestry practices, or other identifiable relationships.

- When critical habitat is designated for species' survival, agricultural and forest production, employment, and income from lands within the species range that are not critical to the species' survival should not be constrained.

- Recovery plans should include a range of recovery strategies that are each evaluated by biological and economic criteria, and include scientific evidence that recovery is biologically possible.

- Listing decisions and recovery planning should be supported by sound, scientific information. In conjunction with studies on the individual species, research should include an analysis of how recovery strategies effect other organisms in the ecosystem. The approach of protecting ecosystems rather than individual species should be considered.

- Once populations of a listed species attain a level sufficient to be considered recovered, the species should be removed as a listed species under the Act with adequate provisions to ensure the species does not later revert back to the list.

A greater emphasis on comprehensive and objective information in the listing and recovery process will provide a more appropriate balance among species' survival, human values, and impacts on people. A moderate shift of emphasis from protection "at all costs" to protection "at reasonable costs" is appropriate. Social and economic costs will be kept at reasonable and appropriate levels by listing only those species truly in danger of extinction or threatened to become endangered, by protecting only habitat critical for survival, and by evaluating the costs of alternative recovery strategies. In addition, the Department should request funds by which studies of the complex interactions between wild animal species and agricultural and forestry practices can be conducted, thereby providing a deeper understanding and thus, a more rational and appropriate approach to meeting the goals of the Act.

WELFARE SIMPLIFICATION

Mr. DURBIN. The Advisory Committee on Welfare Simplification and Coordination visited the Family Independence Program which provides cash to participants in lieu of food stamp coupons. What were the committees recommendations with regards to this initiative?

Mr. HILTY. The Committee was very impressed with the family-oriented design of the Family Independence Program (FIP). While in Seattle, Committee members spoke with program administrators and clients, all of whom expressed support for FIP. The Committee will incorporate its positive impressions into its July 1, 1993, report to Congress and the Federal agencies.

HUMAN NUTRITION BOARD OF SCIENTIFIC COUNSELORS

Mr. DURBIN. The Human Nutrition Board of Scientific Counselors held its annual meeting in March, 1992. Three resolutions were developed, adopted, and forwarded to the Secretary. These were: the need for enhanced nutrition monitoring; the need for evaluation of current nutrition education to improve nutrition programming in the Department; and support for ARS human nutrition research centers at Beltsville and San Francisco. Specifically what has been done with these recommendations?

Mr. HILTY. The resolutions of the Board regarding nutrition monitoring have been used to guide preparation of the "10-Year Comprehensive Plan for nutrition Monitoring and Related Research" approved by the Secretaries of Agriculture and Health and Human Services on January 14, 1993. The resolutions relating to evaluation of nutrition education have been used by the USDA agencies in their planning and program activities in fiscal year 1993. A feasibility study has been conducted for modernization of the Beltsville Center's facilities. The ARS continues to support the location of the Western Human Nutrition Research Center at the Presidio of San Francisco and has a request to that effect on record with the National Park Service. During fiscal year 1993, a Memorandum of Understanding between the University of California system and the Western Human Nutrition Research Center resulted in active collaborations with the University of California scientists at Davis, Berkeley, San Francisco, and Los Angeles.

JOINT COUNCIL

Mr. DURBIN. Please submit a copy, for the record, of the Joint Council on Food and Agricultural Sciences report, Fiscal Year 1994 Priorities for Research, Extension, and Higher Education: A Report to the Secretary of Agriculture.

Mr. HILTY. I will provide for the record a copy of the Joint Council on Food and Agricultural Sciences report, Fiscal Year 1994 Priorities for Research, Extension, and Higher Education.

[CLERKS NOTE.—The document is too lengthy to be included in the record and will be retained in Committee files.]

MEAT AND POULTRY INSPECTION

Mr. DURBIN. Please submit a copy of the recommendations made to the Food Safety and Inspection Service by the National Advisory Committee on Meat and Poultry Inspection as a result of the meeting that was held in September 1992.

Mr. HILTY. During the September 22 and 23, 1992 meeting of the National Advisory Committee on Meat and Poultry Inspection, Committee members considered several issues. Among them was the Microbiological Baseline Data Collection Program for Beef. The Committee members identified and discussed important variables such as the microbiological effects on carcasses sprayed with acetic acid, the collection of samples, and carcass sampling sites. The members were concerned about the variables that can bias the study and pointed out that pathogens on the carcass do not mean the same number of pathogens are on retail cuts such as steaks. The Committee also recommended that the Agency should establish baseline microbiological data on beef other than feed cattle. The Committee recommended that members provide input early in the agency processes, members will submit discussion topics, and the committee will provide general recommendations to the Agency. The Committee also suggested that the agency move toward greater use of risk analysis to decide what products and processes should be inspected or excluded from inspection.

A copy of the recommendation will be provided for the record.

[The information follows:]

MINUTES

THE NATIONAL ADVISORY COMMITTEE ON MEAT AND POULTRY INSPECTION
FAIRFAX, VIRGINIA

SEPTEMBER 22-23, 1992

Dr. H. Russell Cross called the meeting of the National Advisory Committee on Meat and Poultry Inspection (NACMPI) to order as scheduled on September 22, 1992, at The Holiday Inn Fair Oaks, Fairfax, Virginia.

Dr. Cross welcomed the members to the meeting, and each member introduced themselves highlighting backgrounds and professional interests. The agenda was introduced and approved by the Committee. (Attachment A) Committee members present were: Dr. Smith, Ms. Barr, Mr. Gill (substituting for Dr. Shank), Dr. Bonner, Dr. Carraway, Mr. Hodges, Dr. Hoes, Mr. Winslow, Mr. Gast, Mr. Emerling, Dr. Kastner, and Dr. Marshall. (Attachment B)

Mr. William West, Director, Budget and Finance Division, FSIS, updated members on the FSIS FY 1993 budget. Because of a reduced budget for FY 1993, the Agency will not be able to take on any new initiatives.

Dr. Cross updated the Committee on Appeals Procedures and Regulation Development Procedures at the headquarters level. He reported that currently the Agency is not planning any new activities in these two areas. One of the reasons for this is the President's order that prohibits adopting new regulations except those that are directly related to the health and safety of the consumer.

Dr. Norcross updated the Committee on: the safety of transgenic animals; Streamlined Inspection of Cattle (SIS Cattle); Campylobacter in poultry; and the Puerto Rico Study. He stated that the commercial marketing of transgenic animals is at least 10 years away and there is correlation between FDA and USDA policy on transgenic animals. The Committee was informed that the SIS cattle inspection proposal has been withdrawn.

Dr. Norcross stated that one of the benefits of the Puerto Rican study on poultry was that the Agency is very close to approving the use of trisodium phosphate to reduce pathogens on poultry.

Mr. Dennis informed the Committee that the small plant handbook is to be issued as a FSIS Directive.

Finally, Dr. Jim Harbottle, Assistant Deputy Administrator, Inspection Management Program, IO, updated the Committee on the HACCP initiative. He stated that the HACCP special team, will be disbanded in December, 1992, and that the HACCP operation task force is half-way through its task of developing a model for inspection.

Ms. Maggie Glavin, Deputy Administrator, Regulatory Programs, informed the Committee that the final rule on nutritional labeling is to be approved by November 9, 1992. The proposed nutritional regulation does not address heath claims or define "healthy." She indicated that Committee members could comment on the proposed regulation for label format, noting that FSIS and FDA had not agreed on a common format.

The Committee members discussed the merits of including stearic acid as part of the saturated fat on the label or excluding it since it does not affect serum cholesterol. Several Committee members felt that the educational component of the law was very important, and they wanted to know what FSIS plans were concerning this issue. Ms. Glavin replied that there will be a strong educational effort. Members also wanted to know if FSIS will determine the accuracy of the nutritional data bases. They were informed that the Agency position is that the processor is responsible for the accuracy of the data bases used to determine nutritional composition of the product. One member wanted to know if the raw product data can be extrapolated to processed product. His concern was that small processors would be extrapolating the data and could get caught in the dragnet.

Ms. Glavin continued to update the Committee on the proposed changes in the current FSIS label approval process. She stated that the Agency has two choices: 1) to do away with the current prior label approval process, or 2) to retain the current prior approval process with some modifications. Ms. Glavin stated that most of the comments are in favor of the current label approval process. Members of the Committee expressed that they also favor the current system, but they are concerned about the lengthy delays experienced in the approval of the labels. Members were also interested in knowing the impact of modifying the current approval process on the products that are exported.

Dr. Cross introduced Dr. Ann Marie McNamara, Director, Microbiology Division, Science and Technology, to present an overview of the Microbiological Baseline Data Collection Program for Beef. The study is to include both qualitative and quantitative data.

The Committee members discussed the variables such as carcasses sprayed with acetic acid, collection of samples, sampling sites which are critical variables that can effect the data. Several members were very concerned about the variables that can bias the study and pointed out that pathogens on the carcass does not mean that the same number of pathogens are on retail cuts such as steaks. They also recommended that the Agency should establish base-line microbiological data on beef other than fed cattle.

Committee members agreed that the study is important. However, they recommended that care should be taken regarding dissemination and interpretation of the data. Dr. Cross agreed with the Committee and added that one of the uses of the data could be to evaluate the effectiveness of the changes in the inspection system.

Dr. Cross initiated the dialogue on the structure, functions, and activities of this Advisory Committee. He emphasized that he wants the Committee to function in a constructive manner. He listed the following topics for the discussion: setting of the meeting agenda, type of agency support needed for the effective functioning of the Committee, the formation of subgroups to work on specific projects, and the publication of the work of subgroups in reputable journals. Finally, he reminded the Committee that any changes in the activities of the Committee would have to take into consideration the statutory requirements of the Federal Meat and Poultry Inspection Laws.

Some concerns were raised by Committee members in regard to the activities of the Committee such as: 1) most of the topics discussed were at the final stages of regulation development rather than the planning stage; 2) the meeting agenda did not include member recommended topics; 3) there is lack of continuous dialogue between the Agency and the Committee members; and 4) The Committee was not kept informed about the advice it provided to the Agency in the form of resolutions. Dr. Cross agreed with the concerns expressed by the Committee members and told the Committee that the Agency is in the process of developing a strategic plan for the future of the Agency.

The Committee and the Agency agreed to the following:

1) Members will have early input in the agency processes;
2) Members will submit topics for discussion; and
3) The committee will provide general recommendations to the agency.

The agenda of meetings will consist of topics suggested by the agency and Committee members. As necessary, FSIS will provide technical assistance to the members of NACMPI. It was also agreed that in the future the agenda items would be decided by a majority of the members.

Minutes

Two topics were recommended by the Committee for the next meeting. They were: the conflict between the European Community and United States of America, and the status of the pre-evisceration carcass wash.

Dr. Cross called the meeting to order at the appointed time on September 23, 1992. The same members of the Committee were present. Dr. Denton joined the group and was introduced. Mr. Andrew Burst, Foreign Agriculture Service, USDA, updated the Committee on the North American Free Trade Agreement (NAFTA). He reported that President Bush has formally notified Congress of his intention to sign the agreement. Congress has 90 days to act on it, and the agreement cannot be modified by Congress.

Mr. Burst stated that the NAFTA agreement contains approximately 1000 pages. It includes chapters on functional access, standards, dispute settlement, and rules of origin. The agricultural section of the NAFTA agreement has two chapters, market access, and sanitary and phyto-sanitary measures.

Members were informed that the market access part of the agreement requires among other things that the Mexican Government eliminate all non-tariff measures such as import licensing for corn and poultry; and the elimination of all tariffs on agricultural products. He also stated that the Mexican and the Canadian Governments have decided to exclude some products from the agreement. Examples of the products excluded between the two Governments are: poultry, dairy, and eggs. Mr. Burst also stated that the NAFTA bars using sanitary and phyto-sanitary requirements as trade barriers.

Each country has the basic right to maintain its standards and NAFTA allows all countries involved to enforce science-based, standards more stringent than those in the NAFTA. However, NAFTA promotes international standards such as CODEX. The objective of NAFTA is to promote the harmonizing of standards between the three countries. NAFTA requires that the three countries provide technical assistance to each other for promoting trade and inspection activities. There will be a transition period. If everything is approved and signed on schedule, the Agreement would be in effect January 1, 1994.

Committee members had several questions. What does harmonization and equivalency mean to each country? Does each country have the right to maintain its standards using international standards as base?

International standards do not cover all commodities. Many products are excluded from the agreement. The Committee was unanimous in recommending that the next meeting should include more discussion on the NAFTA.

Minutes

Ms. Carol Seymour, Director, Policy, Evaluation, and Planning Staff, talked about strategic planning in FSIS. The draft plan is to be published for public comments and finalized by spring, 1993. Committee members recommended that the agency plan for and study the organization of the Agency, requirements for human resources, and the quality of supervision. Members of this Committee wanted to be involved in the early stages of the planning.

Dr. Marvin Norcross, Deputy Administrator, Science and Technology, explained the preliminary thinking about how risk analysis might be done in FSIS. The Committee discussed the use of risk assessment in the inspection process. The Committee suggested that the agency move toward greater use of risk analysis to decide what products and processes should be inspected or should be excluded from the inspection.

Mr. Bill Dennis presented the evolutionary process the inspection activities have gone through in the 80-plus years ending with the role of Performance Based Inspection System (PBIS). The Committee members expressed the following opinions concerning the PBIS: (1) Individual inspection activities need to be checked. (2) Data gathering is not functioning well. (3) There is non-uniformity in application of inspection. An example of this is that most of the deficiencies noted by the inspectors are for the unscheduled tasks.

Dr. Cross stated that the Committee would discus- risk analysis and HACCP at its next meeting. The members discussed the next meeting and decided to meet again in late winter or early spring, 1993.

The meeting was opened for public comments. Mr. John Gould, AMI, expressed his desire that the plants should get feedback on the Microbiological Baseline Data Collection Program for Beef.

Being no other business, the Committee adjourned on schedule.

ATTACHMENT A

AGENDA - NATIONAL ADVISORY COMMITTEE ON MEAT AND POULTRY INSPECTION

September 22 and 23, 1992, Holiday Inn, Fair Oaks

SEPTEMBER 22, 1:00 P.M.

1.	Introductions, and Opening Comments	Dr. H. Russell Cross
2.	Review and Approval of Agenda	Dr. H. Russell Cross
3.	Questions/Comments from Committee Concerning Update Committee Papers on Items from Last Meeting	Dr. H. Russell Cross
4.	Microbiological Baseline Data Collection Program for Cattle, and Plans for Other Species	Dr. Ann McNamara
5.	Standards and Labeling Issues	Ms. Margaret Glavin
6.	Other Issues From the Committee; and/or Further Discussion of the Above Topics Left Unfinished	Committee

SEPTEMBER 23, 8:00 A.M.

7.	General Discussion of Issues Relevant to FSIS	Dr. H. Russell Cross and Committee
8.	North American Free Trade Agreement - Impact on Meat and Poultry	Representative from FAS
9.	Items From the Audience, Time Permitting	

FOREIGN ANIMAL AND POULTRY DISEASES

Mr. DURBIN. The Advisory Committee on Foreign Animal and Poultry Diseases met in June 1992 and made 12 comments or recommendations. What were they?

Mr. HILTY. The 12 recommendations made will be provided for the record.

[The information follows:]

(1) Privately—Owned Equine Quarantine Facilities.—The Committee recommended that the Administrator provide support to APHIS to enforce regulations in the operation and management of the facilities and that owners/operators of facilities be compelled to comply with the standards of USDA, APHIS quarantine facilities.

(2) Bovine Tuberculosis.—The Committee recommended that Tuberculosis be managed, controlled, and eradicated as an emergency animal disease by: (a) testing and quarantine of imported animals that may be infected with *Mycobacterium bovis (M. bovis)*; (b) development and use of testing methods and reagents to detect infection with *M. bovis*; (c) identification and control of cattle admitted for feeding and slaughter; (d) funding for complete depopulation; and (e) cooperative program with Mexican livestock producers and officials to implement a TB control and eradication program.

(3) Screwworms.—The Committee recommended that APHIS accelerate plans to develop a sterile screwworm fly plant in Panama and continue action to eradicate the outbreak of screwworms in Mexico and Central America, and information efforts be increased to inform livestock producers of eradication efforts.

(4) Bont Tick.—The Committee recommended that the Secretary of Agriculture support an internationally based region-wide Tropical Bont Tick Program.

(5) Harry S. Truman Animal Import Center (HSTAIC) Efficient Use.—The Committee recommended that APHIS modify the lottery system for use of the HSTAIC.

(6) Pharmaceutical Availability.—The Committee recommended that USDA support legislation in Congress that would provide veterinarians legal authority for extra-label use of animal drugs and use of human-label drugs in animals under FDA and USDA regulations.

(7) Student Training.—The Committee recommended that the Smith-Kilbourne Scholars Program be continued.

(8) Screen All Diseases/Animals.—The Committee recommended that USDA/APHIS revise animal quarantine procedures, seek advice and consult with knowledgeable people in the industry.

(9) United States/European Economic Community (EEC) Relationships.—The Committee recommended that USDA/APHIS initiate action to obtain legislation and/or recommendations to enhance movement of livestock, poultry, exotic animals and birds between the United States and the EEC.

(10) Consistent Foreign Animal Disease (FAD) Standards.—The Committee recommended that the Agency assure that FAD requirements be consistently applied at all points of entry.

(11) The Committee recommended that APHIS develop and complete an EIS for disease eradication efforts.

(12) User Fees.—The Committee recommended that the comments are from affected users, and the period be extended to 60 days for evaluation. Also, recommendation was made for user fees to be applied to compensate for inadequate Agency funding for the surveillance/detection and testing of foreign animal disease.

EMERGING DEMOCRACIES ADVISORY COMMITTEE

Mr. DURBIN. The explanatory notes state that starting in fiscal year 1993, the Emerging Democracies Advisory Committee will be funded entirely through the Commodity Credit Corporation. What authority allows you to fund the Committee this way?

Mr. HILTY. Section 1542(d) of the FACT Act of 1990, Public Law 101-624, provides both the authority for establishing the Emerging Democracies Advisory Committee and the use of Commodity Credit Corporation resources to finance its activities.

Mr. DURBIN. What was the funding level for this Committee in fiscal year 1992 and what will it be in fiscal year 1993?

Mr. HILTY. For fiscal year 1992, actual costs of the Emerging Democracies Advisory Committee totaled $12,958, which basically represents the start-up costs of the new committee. For fiscal year 1993, $50,000 is budgeted for the Committee as the full agenda of Committee activity begins.

REORGANIZATION PLAN

Mr. DURBIN. Do you anticipate the Secretary's reorganization plan to be submitted to Congress for consideration during this appropriation cycle?

Mr. HILTY. I can't speak directly for the Secretary on that. All of the activity that I have been involved in would suggest that is his hope. As you know, his reorganization plan involves not only appropriations but also changing some statutory authorities, and establishment of different Under Secretaryships, different reporting relationships for many of the key agencies.

Our offices and many of the other offices within the Department have been working vigorously toward addressing the statutory changes and the work that would be needed to carry out the headquarters-level reorganization that he spoke about before this Committee in mid-February.

So, I would say that it would be our hope and our expectation, that our preparations are directed toward being able to do that.

Mr. DURBIN. This is the last day of testimony before the Subcommittee. We will soon start our mark up in earnest, and it is pretty difficult to deal with the reorganization question, its impact on spending, and some other threshold decisions. Perhaps, we can have some informal consultation with you and the Secretary to determine the direction you are headed so that what we do might be complimentary as opposed to contradictory.

Mr. HILTY. Yes, we are prepared to do that. In our preparations we are trying to anticipate what the costs may be and we are asking ourselves a number of the "what if" questions so we can as quickly as possible suggest in what directions these allocations and appropriations must go.

NON-SALARY COSTS INCREASE AND ADMINISTRATIVE EFFICIENCY DECREASE

Mr. DURBIN. Your budget request is increased by $17,000 or 2.7 percent for non-salary costs and offset by a decrease of $18,000 or 3 percent for administrative efficiency. Would you provide a detailed summary of how these amounts were calculated?

Mr. DEWHURST. The $17,000 increase represents a 2.7% Inflationary Increase on nonpay obligations of $681,000. The 2.7% is the Administration's estimate of inflation for non-pay costs.

As part of the Administration's effort to assist in controlling the Federal deficit and in improving the administrative productivity of the Federal Government, each executive agency was required to reduce administrative expenses. For 1994, a 3 percent reduction from the 1993 base adjusted for inflation is required. This reduction was taken from travel and transportation, communications and utilities, printing and reproduction, other services and supplies and materials. The reduction of $18,000 represents a 3 percent reduction from the adjusted 1993 base of $614,000 for these object classes.

Mr. DURBIN. You propose an increase of $36,000 for non-salary costs offset by a decrease of $32,000 for administrative efficiency. Provide a complete breakout of how you arrived at these amounts, by office.

Mr. HILTY. The $36,000 increase represents a 2.7 percent inflation increase on non-salary obligations of $1,333,000. The 2.7 percent is the OMB estimate of inflation for non-salary costs.

As part of the Administration's effort to assist in controlling the Federal deficit and in improving the administrative productivity of the Federal Government, each executive agency was required to reduce administration expenses. For fiscal year 1994, a 3 percent reduction from the fiscal year 1993 base adjusted for inflation is required. This reduction was taken from transportation of things, communications and utilities, printing and reproduction, other services, and supplies and materials. The $32,000 represents a 3 percent reduction from the inflated fiscal year 1993 base of $1,065,000 for these object classes.

I will provide a breakout by office for the record.

[The information follows:]

OFFICE OF THE SECRETARY—INFLATION INCREASE AND ADMINISTRATIVE EFFICIENCY DECREASE

[Dollars in thousands]

Office	Inflation	Administrative efficiency
Immediate Office	$11	$-7
Deputy Secretary	3	-3
Administration	3	-3
Congressional Relations	5	-5
Economics	4	-4
Science and Education	2	-2
Marketing and Inspection Services	2	-2
International Affairs and Commodity Programs		
Natural Resources and Development	4	-4
Small Community and Rural Development		
Food and Consumer Services	2	-2
Total	36	-32

SECRETARY'S TRANSFER AUTHORITY

Mr. DURBIN. The budget for the Assistant Secretary for Administration and the Assistant Secretary for Marketing and Inspection Services in fiscal year 1993 were increased by $195,000 and two staff years and $130,000 and one staff year, respectively. These increases occurred through the Secretary's transfer authority. What was the reason for this transfer and where did it come from?

Mr. HILTY. The transfer to the Assistant Secretary for Administration is to fund the Deputy Chief Financial Officer and his secretary. The transfer to the Assistant Secretary for Marketing and Inspection Service is to fund a Deputy Assistant Secretary position. This Assistant Secretary is responsible for six USDA agencies and requires the additional Deputy Assistant Secretary to assist in dealing with the workload in this area. I am providing a table that identifies the source of funding. The staff years came from the Department's total allotment.

[The information follows:]

TRANSFERS TO THE OFFICE OF THE SECRETARY

[Fiscal year 1993]

Transfer from	Assistant Secretary for Administration	Assistant Secretary for Marketing and Inspection Service
Agricultural Research Service	$27,000	$19,000
Animal and Plant Health Inspection Service	28,000	19,000
Farmers Home Administration	28,000	19,000
Soil Conservation Service	28,000	18,000
Agricultural Stabilization and Conservation Service	28,000	18,000
Food Safety Inspection Service	28,000	19,000
Agricultural Marketing Service	28,000	18,000
Total	195,000	130,000

Mr. DURBIN. The $130,000 for one staff year transferred to the Office of the Assistant Secretary for Marketing and Inspection Services seems a little high. Tell us how this money is being spent.

Mr. HILTY. The $130,000 covers salary and benefits for an ES-4 Deputy Assistant Secretary position.

Mr. DURBIN. Provide a table showing all dollars and staff years that were transferred under this authority in fiscal year 1992, including who received transfers and where they were transferred from.

Mr. HILTY. The staff years came from the Department's total allotment. I will provide a table that shows who received the transfers and where they were transferred from for the record.

[The information follows:]

TRANSFERS USING AUTHORITY PROVIDED IN PUBLIC LAW 102-341

[Fiscal Year 1992]

Transfer from	Under Secy for Intl Affairs and Com Progs (.25 S/Y)	Asst Secy for Mktg and Insp Srvc (25 S/Y)	Asst Secy for Food and Cons Srvc (25 S/Y)	Dept Admin (4 25 S/Y)	Economic Research Srvc (2 S/Y)	World Agric Outlook Bd (1 S/Y)
Agricultural Research Service	$4,000	$5,000	$1,000	$46,000	$30,000	$12,000
Animal and Plant Health Inspection Service	4,000	5,000	1,000	46,000	30,000	12,000
Farmers Home Administration	5,000	4,000	1,000	46,000	30,000	12,000
Soil Conservation Service	4,000	4,000	2,000	45,000	30,000	13,000
Agricultural Stabilization and Conservation Service	4,000	4,000	2,000	46,000	30,000	12,000
Food Safety and Inspection Service	5,000	4,000	1,000	46,000	30,000	12,000
Forest Service	4,000	4,000	2,000	46,000	30,000	12,000
Total	30,000	30,000	10,000	321,000	210,000	85,000

HEALTH AND HUMAN SERVICES REIMBURSEMENT

Mr. DURBIN. Your budget for fiscal year 1992 reflects a reimbursement of $40,000 from Health and Human Services. What was this reimbursement for?

Mr. HILTY. This reimbursement was to help defray the costs for the evaluation research on graphic alternatives for conveying dietary guidance to all audiences of the general public, including children, low-income adults, and Spanish speaking-adults.

OSEC STAFFING

Mr. DURBIN. For the record, please provide a table showing the number of personnel assigned to the Office of the Secretary and each Under and Assistant Secretary's office for fiscal years 1990, 1991, and 1992 and estimates for fiscal years 1993 and 1994. Include in this table the number of personnel at each grade level.

Mr. HILTY. I will be happy to provide that information.

[The information follows:]

OFFICE OF THE SECRETARY
IMMEDIATE OFFICE
STAFFING FOR FISCAL YEARS 1990-1994

GRADE	ACTUAL 1990	ACTUAL 1991	ACTUAL 1992	ESTIMATE 1993	ESTIMATE 1994
EX-I	1	1	1	1	1
ES-6					6
ES-5		2			0
ES-4	1	0			1
ES-3	0	1	2		
ES-2	1		0	1	1
ES-1			1	0	0
GM-15				2	2
GM-14		1		0	0
GM-13		0		1	1
GS-12		2		2	2
GS-11	3	0	2	0	0
GS-10	0	1	0	0	0
GS-9	2		1	3	3
GS-8			1	2	2
GS-7			0	0	0
GS-6	1	0	0	0	0
WG-8	1	1	1	1	1
TOTAL	23	21	17	22	22

OFFICE OF THE SECRETARY
DEPUTY SECRETARY
STAFFING FOR FISCAL YEARS 1990-1994

GRADE	ACTUAL 1990	ACTUAL 1991	ACTUAL 1992	ESTIMATE 1993	ESTIMATE 1994
EX-II	1	1	1	1	1
ES-2	0	0	1	1	1
ES-1	1	1	0	0	0
GM-13			1	1	1
GS-12	1		0	0	0
GS-11	0		0	1	1
WG-7	0	1	1	0	0
WG-6	1	0	0	1	1
TOTAL	4	4	4	5	5

OFFICE OF THE SECRETARY
ASSISTANT SECRETARY FOR ADMINISTRATION
STAFFING FOR FISCAL YEARS 1990-1994

GRADE	ACTUAL 1990	ACTUAL 1991	ACTUAL 1992	ESTIMATE 1993	ESTIMATE 1994
EX-IV	1	1	1	1	1
ES-6	0	0	0		
ES-5	0	0	1		1
ES-4	0	1	0	0	0
ES-2	1	0	0	0	0
GM-14		0	0	1	1
GM-13	0	1	1	0	0
GS-12	0			2	2
GS-11	1	1		0	0
GS-10	0	0	1	2	2
GS-9	0	1	0	0	0
GS-8	1	0	0	0	0
GS-7	1	0	0	0	0
TOTAL	6	5	6	8	8

OFFICE OF THE SECRETARY
ASSISTANT SECRETARY FOR CONGRESSIONAL RELATIONS
STAFFING FOR FISCAL YEARS 1990-1994

GRADE	ACTUAL 1990	ACTUAL 1991	ACTUAL 1992	ESTIMATE 1993	ESTIMATE 1994
EX-IV	1	1	1	1	1
ES-6	-	-		-	1
GM-15					6
GM-14					2
GM-13		3	2	1	
GS-12		0	0	0	
GS-11		2	2	1	
GS-10			1		
GS-9	0	1	2	1	1
WG-7	1	1	1	1	1
TOTAL	15	14	15	15	15

OFFICE OF THE SECRETARY
ASSISTANT SECRETARY FOR ECONOMICS
STAFFING FOR FISCAL YEARS 1990-1994

GRADE	ACTUAL 1990	ACTUAL 1991	ACTUAL 1992	ESTIMATE 1993	ESTIMATE 1994
EX-IV	1	1	1	1	1
ES-6	0	1	1	1	1
ES-5	1	0	0	0	0
GM-13	0	0	0	1	1
GS-12	0		1	0	0
GS-11	2	2	0	1	1
GS-10	0	0	1	1	1
GS-9	1	1	1	0	0
TOTAL	5	5	5	5	5

OFFICE OF THE SECRETARY
ASSISTANT SECRETARY FOR SCIENCE AND EDUCATION
STAFFING FOR FISCAL YEARS 1990-1994

GRADE	ACTUAL 1990	ACTUAL 1991	ACTUAL 1992	ESTIMATE 1993	ESTIMATE 1994
EX-IV	1	1	1	1	1
ES-6					
GM-15			1		
GS-11	1	1	0	1	1
GS-9	1	1	1	1	1
TOTAL	5	5	4	5	5

OFFICE OF THE SECRETARY
ASSISTANT SECRETARY FOR MARKETING AND INSPECTION SERVICE
STAFFING FOR FISCAL YEARS 1990-1994

GRADE	ACTUAL 1990	ACTUAL 1991	ACTUAL 1992	ESTIMATE 1993	ESTIMATE 1994
EX-IV	1	1	1	1	1
ES-6	0	0	1	1	-
ES-5	0	1	0	0	
ES-3	1	0	0	1	
GM-15	0	0	1	1	1
GS-14	0	1	0	0	0
GS-13	1	0	0	0	0
GS-11	1	1	1	1	1
GS-10	1	1	1	1	1
TOTAL	5	5	5	6	6

OFFICE OF THE SECRETARY
UNDER SECRETARY FOR INTERNATIONAL AFFAIRS AND COMMODITY PROGRAMS
STAFFING FOR FISCAL YEARS 1990-1994

GRADE	ACTUAL 1990	ACTUAL 1991	ACTUAL 1992	ESTIMATE 1993	ESTIMATE 1994
EX-III	1	1	1	1	1
ES-6	2		0	0	0
ES-5	0	1	0	0	0
ES-3	1	0	0	0	0
ES-2	0	0		1	1
ES-1	0	0	0		
GM-12	1	1	0		
GS-11	0	0	0	1	1
GS-10	1	1	1	0	0
GS-9	0	0	1	0	0
GS-7	1	0	0	0	0
TOTAL	7	5	4	5	5

OFFICE OF THE SECRETARY
UNDER SECRETARY FOR SMALL COMMUNITY AND RURAL DEVELOPMENT
STAFFING FOR FISCAL YEARS 1990-1994

GRADE	ACTUAL 1990	ACTUAL 1991	ACTUAL 1992	ESTIMATE 1993	ESTIMATE 1994
EX-III	1	1	1	1	1
ES-6	2	2	1		
ES-3	0	0	0		1
ES-2	0	0	1	0	0
GM-14	1	0	0	0	0
GS-12	1	1	1	1	1
GS-11	0	0	1	0	0
GS-10	1	0	0	1	1
GS-9	1	1	0	0	0
TOTAL	7	5	5	5	5

OFFICE OF THE SECRETARY
ASSISTANT SECRETARY FOR NATURAL RESOURCES
STAFFING FOR FISCAL YEARS 1990-1994

GRADE	ACTUAL 1990	ACTUAL 1991	ACTUAL 1992	ESTIMATE 1993	ESTIMATE 1994
EX-IV	1	1	1	1	1
ES-6	0	0	1	1	1
ES-5	0	1	0	0	0
ES-3	1	0	0	0	0
GM-14	0	0	0	1	1
GM-13	1	0	1	0	0
GM-12	0	1	0	0	0
GS-11	0	0	1	1	1
GS-10	0	0			
GS-9	0	1	0	0	0
GS-8	1	1	0	0	0
TOTAL	4	5	5	5	5

OFFICE OF THE SECRETARY
ASSISTANT SECRETARY FOR FOOD AND CONSUMER SERVICES
STAFFING FOR FISCAL YEARS 1990-1994

GRADE	ACTUAL 1990	ACTUAL 1991	ACTUAL 1992	ESTIMATE 1993	ESTIMATE 1994
EX-IV	1	1	1	1	1
ES-5	0	0	0	-	1
ES-4	0	0	1		0
ES-3	0	1	0	0	0
ES-1	1	0	0	0	0
GM-15		1	-	1	1
GS-11			1		
GS-9	1	0	0	1	1
GS-8	0	1	1	0	0
TOTAL	5	5	5	5	5

REIMBURSABLE POSITIONS

Mr. DURBIN. Last year the Office of the Secretary had two temporary Special Assistants that were funded through reimbursements from a number of USDA agencies. One of those Assistants was the President's personal representative on agricultural issues and the second assistant taught and provided expertise on agricultural issues at the National War College. Are those two positions still in existence? If so, what is the cost associated with each?

Mr. HILTY. These positions still exist and are estimated to cost $276,000 in FY 1993 and $290,000 in FY 1994.

CONGRESSIONAL LIAISON

Mr. DURBIN. Update the table that appears on pages 19 and 20 of last year's hearing record to include fiscal year 1994.

Mr. HILTY. I will be happy to provide that information for the record.

[The information follows:]

USDA CONGRESSIONAL LIAISON
(Dollars in Thousands)

Agency	1992 Employment	1992 Staff Years	1993 Employment	1993 Staff Years	1994 Employment	1994 Staff Years
OSec:						
Professional	12	12.00	12	12.00	12	12.00
Clerical	3	3.00	3	3.00	3	3.00
Budget Authority	$1,231		$1,307		$1,333	
OIG:						
Professional	10	1.00	10	1.00	10	1.00
Clerical	0	0.00	0	0.00	0	0.00
Budget Authority	$52		$54		$54	
ARS:						
Professional	2	2.00	2	2.00	2	2.00
Clerical	1	1.00	1	1.00	1	1.00
Budget Authority	$150		$158		$164	
CSRS:						
Professional	1	0.80	1	0.80	1	0.80
Clerical	0	0.00	0	0.00	0	0.00
Budget Authority	$44		$49		$50	
FAS:						
Professional	2	2.00	2	1.00	2	2.00
Clerical	1	1.00	1	1.00	1	1.00
Budget Authority	$174		$120		$189	
ASCS:						
Professional	2	2.00	2	2.00	2	2.00
Clerical	1	1.00	1	1.00	1	1.00
Budget Authority	$161		$178		$182	
FCIC:						
Professional	3	1.50	3	1.50	3	1.50
Clerical	1	0.50	1	0.50	1	0.50
Budget Authority	$85		$87		$91	
REA:						
Professional	1	1.00	1	0.70	1	1.00
Clerical	1	0.50	1	0.50	1	0.50
Budget Authority	$70		$49		$74	
FmHA/RDA:						
Professional	7	5.50	7	5.50	7	5.50
Clerical	3	2.00	3	2.00	3	2.00
Budget Authority	$468		$485		$485	
SCS:						
Professional	4	2.90	4	2.40	5	5.00
Clerical	1	0.80	1	1.00	1	1.00
Budget Authority	$218		$223		$361	
APHIS:						
Professional	4	2.75	4	2.75	4	2.75
Clerical	1	0.25	1	0.25	1	0.25
Budget Authority	$145		$151		$157	
FGIS:						
Professional	2	0.20	3	0.40	2	0.20
Clerical	1	0.05	1	0.10	1	0.50
Budget Authority	$4		$10		$4	

Agency	1992 Employment	Staff Years	1993 Employment	Staff Years	1994 Employment	S
AMS:						
Professional	3	3.00	2	2.00	2	
Clerical	1	1.00	1	1.00	1	
Budget Authority	$355		$211		$211	
FSIS:						
Professional	3	3.00	3	3.00	3	
Clerical	1	1.00	2	2.00	2	
Budget Authority	$163		$188		$188	
FNS:						
Professional	4	6.00	5	4.50	5	
Clerical	2	2.00	2	2.00	2	
Budget Authority	$370		$400		$440	
HNIS:						
Professional	1	0.50	1	0.50	1	
Clerical	1	0.50	1	0.50	1	
Budget Authority	$40		$40		$40	
PSA:						
Professional	1	0.30	1	0.30	1	
Clerical	1	0.10	1	0.10	1	
Budget Authority	$39		$37		$37	
FS:						
Professional	1	1.00	1	1.00	1	
Clerical	1	0.50	1	0.50	1	
Budget Authority	$101		$105		$109	
TOTAL:						
Professional	63	47.45	64	43.35	64	
Clerical	21	15.20	22	16.45	22	
Budget Authority	$3,770		$3,852		$4,169	

APPROPRIATIONS AND STAFF YEARS TABLE

Mr. DURBIN. Please update the table that appears on pages 460 and 461 of last year's hearing record showing OBPA appropriations and staff years to include fiscal year 1992, fiscal year 1993, and fiscal year 1994 estimates.

Mr. DEWHURST. I will be happy to provide that information for the record.

[The information follows:]

OFFICE OF BUDGET AND PROGRAM ANALYSIS

[Dollar amounts in millions]

	Staff years	Appropriation
Year:		
1981	92	$3.9
1982	83	3.6
1983	79	3.6
1984	78	3.8
1985	76	3.8
1986	71	3.6
1987	68	3.8
1988	70	4.3
1989	74	4.4
1990	74	4.5
1991	71	5.0
1992	70	6.1
1993	76	5.8
1994	76	5.9

OBJECT CLASSIFICATION

Mr. DURBIN. Please provide an object class table for each Under Secretary's and Assistant Secretary's office for fiscal years 1991, 1992, 1993, and 1994.

Mr. HILTY. I will be happy to provide that information for the record.

[The information follows:]

OFFICE OF THE SECRETARY
IMMEDIATE OFFICE

CLASSIFICATION BY OBJECTS
Fiscal Years 1991, 1992 and Projected 1993 and 1994
(Dollars in Thousands)

Object Class	Title	1991 a/	1992	1993	1994
1100	Personnel Compensation	$1,016	$1,277	$1,582	$1,615
1200	Personnel Benefits	232	224	301	308
	Total	1,248	1,501	1,883	1,923
2100	Travel	48	57	85	85
2200	Transportation of Things	0	0	1	1
2300	Communications, Utilities and Rent	220	162	119	119
2400	Printing and Reproduction	160	81	41	41
2500	Other Services	109	131	116	118
2600	Supplies	64	22	37	37
3100	Equipment	7	6	0	0
	Total Other Objects	608	459	399	401
	Total Direct Obligations	1,856	1,960	2,282	2,324

a/ Actual obligations reflect adjustments that were not made before the books closed at the end of the fiscal year.

OFFICE OF THE SECRETARY
DEPUTY SECRETARY

CLASSIFICATION BY OBJECTS
Fiscal Years 1991, 1992 and Projected 1993 and 1994
(Dollars in Thousands)

Object Class	Title	1991	1992	1993	1994
1100	Personnel Compensation	$229	$308	$369	$377
1200	Personnel Benefits	57	62	78	80
	Total	286	370	447	457
2100	Travel	19	62	32	32
2200	Transportation of Things	0	0	0	0
2300	Communications, Utilities and Rent	12	10	20	20
2400	Printing and Reproduction	8	7	10	10
2500	Other Services	11	21	19	19
2600	Supplies	11	4	14	14
3100	Equipment	0	1	1	1
	Total Other Objects	61	105	96	96
	Total Direct Obligations	347	475	543	553

OFFICE OF THE SECRETARY
ADMINISTRATION

CLASSIFICATION BY OBJECTS
Fiscal Years 1991, 1992 and Projected 1993 and 1994
(Dollars in Thousands)

Object Class	Title	1991 a/	1992	1993	1994
1100	Personnel Compensation	$317	$373	$549	$563
1200	Personnel Benefits	81	90	115	118
	Total	398	463	664	681
2100	Travel	17	22	25	25
2200	Transportation of Things	0	0	1	1
2300	Communications, Utilities and Rent	18	20	26	26
2400	Printing and Reproduction	9	10	18	18
2500	Other Services	30	29	34	34
2600	Supplies	12	6	13	13
3100	Equipment	2	22	10	10
	Total Other Objects	88	109	127	127
	Total Direct Obligations	486	572	791	808

a/ Actual obligations reflect adjustments that were not made before the books closed at the end of the fiscal year.

OFFICE OF THE SECRETARY
CONGRESSIONAL RELATIONS

CLASSIFICATION BY OBJECTS
Fiscal Years 1991, 1992 and Projected 1993 and 1994
(Dollars in Thousands)

Object Class	Title	1991 a/	1992	1993	1994
1100	Personnel Compensation	$769	$906	$996	$1,018
1200	Personnel Benefits	164	175	204	208
	Total	933	1,081	1,200	1,226
2100	Travel	15	12	19	19
2200	Transportation of Things	0	0	0	0
2300	Communications, Utilities and Rent	36	43	25	25
2400	Printing and Reproduction	21	21	19	19
2500	Other Services	28	58	23	23
2600	Supplies	16	11	21	21
3100	Equipment	8	5	0	0
	Total Other Objects	124	150	107	107
	Total Direct Obligations	1,057	1,231	1,307	1,333

a/ Actual obligations reflect adjustments that were not made before the books closed at the end of the fiscal year.

OFFICE OF THE SECRETARY
ECONOMICS

CLASSIFICATION BY OBJECTS
Fiscal Years 1991, 1992 and Projected 1993 and 1994
(Dollars in Thousands)

Object Class	Title	1991 a/	1992	1993	1994
1100	Personnel Compensation	$347	$374	$369	$377
1200	Personnel Benefits	82	69	80	81
	Total	429	443	449	458
2100	Travel	30	16	24	24
2200	Transportation of Things	0	0	0	0
2300	Communications, Utilities and Rent	14	13	29	29
2400	Printing and Reproduction	8	8	14	14
2500	Other Services	9	38	32	32
2600	Supplies	10	8	26	26
3100	Equipment	0	16	6	6
	Total Other Objects	71	99	131	131
	Total Direct Obligations	500	542	580	589

a/ Actual obligations reflect adjustments that were not made before the books closed at the end of the fiscal year.

OFFICE OF THE SECRETARY
SCIENCE AND EDUCATION

CLASSIFICATION BY OBJECTS
Fiscal Years 1991, 1992 and Projected 1993 and 1994
(Dollars in Thousands)

Object Class	Title	1991	1992	1993	1994
1100	Personnel Compensation	$343	$294	$392	$400
1200	Personnel Benefits	71	56	81	82
	Total	414	350	473	482
2100	Travel	16	23	20	20
2200	Transportation of Things	0	0	0	0
2300	Communications, Utilities and Rent	11	12	18	18
2400	Printing and Reproduction	9	7	10	10
2500	Other Services	26	42	27	27
2600	Supplies	9	9	10	10
3100	Equipment	6	18	2	2
	Total Other Objects	77	111	87	87
	Total Direct Obligations	491	461	560	569

OFFICE OF THE SECRETARY
MARKETING AND INSPECTION SERVICES

CLASSIFICATION BY OBJECTS
Fiscal Years 1991, 1992 and Projected 1993 and 1994
(Dollars in Thousands)

Object Class	Title	1991 a/	1992	1993	1994
1100	Personnel Compensation	$336	$398	$491	$500
1200	Personnel Benefits	63	75	99	101
	Total	399	473	590	601
2100	Travel	11	16	18	18
2200	Transportation of Things	0	0	0	0
2300	Communications, Utilities and Rent	13	14	23	23
2400	Printing and Reproduction	14	7	16	16
2500	Other Services	16	23	21	21
2600	Supplies	5	8	12	12
3100	Equipment	2	10	0	0
	Total Other Objects	61	78	90	90
	Total Direct Obligations	460	551	680	691

a/ Actual obligations reflect adjustments that were not made before the books closed at the end of the fiscal year.

OFFICE OF THE SECRETARY
INTERNATIONAL AFFAIRS AND COMMODITY PROGRAMS

CLASSIFICATION BY OBJECTS
Fiscal Years 1991, 1992 and Projected 1993 and 1994
(Dollars in Thousands)

bject :lass	Title	1991 a/	1992	1993
1100	Personnel Compensation	$296	$360	$428
1200	Personnel Benefits	78	77	89
	Total	374	437	517
2100	Travel	4	10	5
2200	Transportation of Things	0	0	0
2300	Communications, Utilities and Rent	21	17	8
2400	Printing and Reproduction	10	9	8
2500	Other Services	17	46	8
2600	Supplies	9	9	5
3100	Equipment	22	0	0
	Total Other Objects	83	91	34
	Total Direct Obligations	457	528	551

Actual obligations reflect adjustments that were not made before the
sed at the end of the fiscal year.

OFFICE OF THE SECRETARY
SMALL COMMUNITY AND RURAL DEVELOPMENT

CLASSIFICATION BY OBJECTS
Fiscal Years 1991, 1992 and Projected 1993 and 1994
(Dollars in Thousands)

Object Class	Title	1991	1992	1993	1994
1100	Personnel Compensation	$373	$398	$440	$449
1200	Personnel Benefits	85	83	92	94
	Total	458	481	532	543
2100	Travel	3	11	3	3
2200	Transportation of Things		0		
2300	Communications, Utilities and Rent	17	16	12	12
2400	Printing and Reproduction	10	9	7	7
2500	Other Services	8	19	12	12
2600	Supplies	4	6	6	6
3100	Equipment	0	1	0	0
	Total Other Objects	51	62	40	40
	Total Direct Obligations	509	543	572	583

OFFICE OF THE SECRETARY
NATURAL RESOURCES AND ENVIRONMENT

CLASSIFICATION BY OBJECTS
Fiscal Years 1991, 1992 and Projected 1993 and 1994

Object Class	Title	1991	1992	1993	1994
1100	Personnel Compensation	$325	$311	$368	$380
1200	Personnel Benefits	63	65	76	79
	Total	388	376	444	459
2100	Travel		6	20	20
2200	Transportation of Things		0	1	1
2300	Communications, Utilities and Rent	14	13	28	28
2400	Printing and Reproduction	8	7	16	16
2500	Other Services	14	80	29	29
2600	Supplies	5	5	21	21
3100	Equipment	3	5	4	4
	Total Other Objects	50	116	119	119
	Total Direct Obligations	438	492	563	578

OFFICE OF THE SECRETARY
FOOD AND CONSUMER SERVICES

CLASSIFICATION BY OBJECTS
Fiscal Years 1991, 1992 and Projected 1993 and 1994
(Dollars in Thousands)

Object Class	Title	1991 a/	1992	1993	1994
1100	Personnel Compensation	$269	$359	$366	$376
1200	Personnel Benefits	53	64	73	75
	Total	322	423	439	451
2100	Travel	17	24	17	17
2200	Transportation of Things	0	1	0	0
2300	Communications, Utilities and Rent	18	18	27	27
2400	Printing and Reproduction	8	8	16	16
2500	Other Services	8	26	21	21
2600	Supplies	13	5	17	17
3100	Equipment	18	15	5	5
	Total Other Objects	82	97	103	103
	Total Direct Obligations	404	520	542	554

a/ Actual obligations reflect adjustments that were not made before the books closed at the end of the fiscal year.

TRAVEL EXPENSES

Mr. DURBIN. Travel expenses increased from $169,643 in fiscal year 1991 to $253,609 in fiscal year 1992 and are projected to increase further in fiscal year 1993. What is the reason for this?

Mr. HILTY. The cost of travel has increased as has the need for the Department's top policy officials and their staff to spend more time traveling—both foreign and domestic—in an effort to stay abreast of agricultural issues and problems as they occur. For example, foreign travel has increased due to the GATT negotiations and international concern for food safety issues. Domestic travel increased in response to natural disasters, the E. coli outbreak, the Timber Conference in the Pacific Northwest, and concerns about global water quality.

PRINTING COSTS

Mr. DURBIN. Printing costs increased form $23,053 in fiscal year 1991 to $143,392 in fiscal year 1992. Why was there such a large increase from one year to the next?

Mr. DEWHURST. The Office of Budget and Program Analysis' (OBPA) Fiscal Year 1991 and 1992 printing expenses were originally projected at $61,000 for each year. Due to the timing of the receipt of the actual bills from the Government Printing Office (GPO), only $23,053 had actually been charged to FY 1991 at the end of the fiscal year. Currently, we anticipate an additional $71,000 in printing expenses for FY 1991 for a total of $98,000.

Our FY 1992 printing costs are expected to be $143,392. This increased estimate along with the increased estimate for FY 1991 is based on actual GPO billings for FY 1990. The original FY 1990 printing estimate was $57,000. To date, actual FY 1990 printing costs are $96,000. Unfortunately, billings from the GPO run as much as two to three years after the actual service. This makes projections of printing expenses for the future tenuous at best. Each year, the majority of OBPA's printing expenses are for reports, laws, bills, Congressional Records, hearings, Federal Register listings and other documents and publications printed by GPO. The balance covers the OBPA cost for copier service.

SUPPLIES

Mr. DURBIN. Object class 26, "Supplies and Materials," is projected to almost double from $91,894 in fiscal year 1992 to $182,000 in both fiscal years 1993 and 1994. Tell us why.

Mr. HILTY. The Office of the Secretary was not fully staffed during fiscal year 1992. Several top policy positions were vacant for most of the year, and 14 positions were vacant at the end of the fiscal year. As a result, the consumption of supplies was significantly below previous levels, which averaged $159,000 for the three years prior to fiscal year 1992. As vacant positions are filled, it is anticipated that the need for office, ADP, and other supplies will approach average levels. In addition, slightly more than one-third of last year's obligations for equipment was for ADP and office equipment such as facsimile machines. Some additional ADP equipment is anticipated to be purchased this fiscal year. This equipment requires supplies of paper and other stock.

EQUIPMENT

Mr. DURBIN. On the same table, object class 31, "Equipment," is projected to decrease from $99,340 in fiscal year 1992 to $28,000 in fiscal years 1993 and 1994. Please explain this decrease.

Mr. HILTY. The Budget reflects the need to reduce or defer equipment purchases in order to absorb increased personnel costs.

UNOBLIGATED BALANCE

Mr. DURBIN. The budget reflects an unobligated balance of $858,734 at the end of fiscal year 1992. This represents almost 10 percent of the total amount appropriated. Why did this amount go unused?

Mr. HILTY. There were significant salary and benefit lapses associated with vacancies that were not filled during FY 1992. Some of these vacancies were at the Under and Assistant Secretary levels and remained vacant for most of the fiscal year.

RECEPTION FUND

Mr. DURBIN. Please list the utilization of funds available to the Secretary for official reception and representative expenses during fiscal year 1992 and the first two quarters of fiscal year 1993.

Mr. HILTY. I will be happy to provide that information for the record.

[The information follows:]

RECEPTION AND REPRESENTATION FUND

[Amounts rounded to nearest dollar]

Description	Fiscal year— 1992	Fiscal year— 1993 [1]
Breakfasts (includes congressional breakfasts, press interviews, award breakfasts)	$79	$73
Luncheons (includes luncheons for Chamber of Commerce, Treasury officials, members of agribusiness community, and a White House luncheon)	310	0
Receptions (includes press receptions, and other special receptions)	2,088	838
Supplies, refreshments, and other miscellaneous	366	188
Total	2,843	1,099

[1] Covers October 1, 1992 through April 26, 1993

Mr. DURBIN. Provide the same information for the Office of the Deputy Secretary.

Mr. HILTY. No funds were expended during FY 1992 or during the first two quarters of fiscal year 1993 by the Deputy Secretary for that purpose.

REGULATORY MORATORIUM

Mr. DURBIN. An automated process was expanded to improve the monitoring of regulatory activities under the President's regulatory reform initiative and regulatory moratorium. Is this moratorium still in effect under President Clinton?

Mr. DEWHURST. The regulatory moratorium is no longer in effect under the current Administration. However, on January 22, 1993, the Director of the Office of Management and Budget, Leon Panetta, directed Departments of Government to establish interim regulatory review procedures which would ensure that President Clinton's appointees have the opportunity to review and approve new regulations. Such procedures have been implemented at USDA.

EASY ACCESS

Mr. DURBIN. The Department initiated an Easy Access Program by which farmers, in cooperation with USDA employees, identify ways to improve service and then test these suggestions to determine their benefits and costs. Mr. Hilty, at last year's hearing you described eight pilot projects that were being tested. Would you update the Committee as to the status of each of these projects and tell us about any additional ones that were started in fiscal year 1992?

Mr. HILTY. The Easy Access pilot projects were concluded and a final report was sent to Secretary Madigan on October 20, 1992.

The Single PC pilot projects in Sherman County, Kansas and Bolivar County, Mississippi and the GIS project in Harrisonburg, Virginia are continuing as test sites for the new Info Share program. Lessons learned from the Single PC pilot project led to the formulation of the Info Share program, which will consolidate the development acquisition and management of USDA computer systems for the farm agencies.

A key wetlands certification form required of all farmers by ASCS was improved and is being implemented, reducing the time needed to complete this document.

Another pilot demonstrated the potential of Geographical Information Systems (GIS) in improving farm program operations in USDA field offices.

The Work Hours pilot resulted in the adjustment of field office hours to best benefit the farmer.

The Selectable 800 Telephone Service pilot project enabled producers to access farm service agency information more conveniently and quickly.

Pilot project work in the use of facsimile communications resulted in the installation of fax machines in collocated USDA field offices.

Our project evaluating video conferencing demonstrated the benefits of "Electronic town meetings" as a way to improve the flow of information between USDA agencies and their farm constituents.

The Smart Card pilot was not implemented due to projected high cost and marginal benefits.

Mr. DURBIN. Have any of these pilot projects been implemented nationwide as new programs?

Mr. HILTY. The lessons learned from the Single PC pilot project led to the formulation of the Info Share Program. Info Share, however, includes far more than the farm service and rural development agencies' field offices. Info Share includes all information technology requirements in all levels of those agencies. The new wetlands conservation form was implemented nationwide for the 1992 farm program. Facsimile equipment was acquired for collocated offices in fiscal year 1992.

PROCUREMENT PROTESTS

Mr. DURBIN. How many procurement protests do you have currently pending before the General Services Administration Board of Contract Appeals?

Mr. HILTY. As of April 23, 1993, USDA has no procurement protests pending before the General Services Administration Board of Contract Appeals.

TRANSFERS

Mr. DURBIN. The 1993 appropriations for Department Administration is adjusted to include a transfer of $700,000 and 10 staff years for the Agency Liaison Officer program and $84,000 and one staff year for the Equipment Management Information System upgrade. Where did these transfers come from and how long will they remain in this account?

Mr. HILTY. Transfers were made from USDA agency appropriations under authority provided to the Secretary of Agriculture in P.L. 102-341. I will provide for the record a table showing the source of these funds. The staff years were provided from within the Department's overall ceiling allocation. Fiscal year 1993 is the second year that the Secretary's transfer authority was used to fund these activities. The funding is made permanent in the fiscal year 1994 request.

[The information follows:]

TRANSFERS USING AUTHORITY PROVIDED IN P.L. 102-341—FISCAL YEAR 1993

[Dollars in thousands]

USDA agency	Agency liaison officers	Equipment management information system	Total
Agricultural Research Service	$100	$12	$112
Animal and Plant Health Inspection Service	100	12	112
Farmers Home Administration	100	12	112
Soil Conservation Service	100	12	112
Agricultural Stabilization and Conservation Service	100	12	112
Food Safety Inspection Service	100	12	112
Agricultural Marketing Service	100	12	112
Total	700	84	784

ALO OVERSIGHT AND COORDINATION

Mr. DURBIN. Briefly describe both initiatives and the accomplishments of each.

Mr. HILTY. The ALO program is designed to improve Departmental oversight and coordination of agency IRM planning and budgeting efforts. OIRM established a small staff of "agency liaison officers", each of which is assigned to two or more agencies. The ALO facilitates clear communication between the agencies and OIRM regarding IRM planning, budgeting, and information systems acquisition and implementation. The ALO provides knowledge of the agencies' activities to OIRM and provides Departmental input to the agencies. The program is an integral part of the Departmental oversight function. Specific accomplishments are included for the record.

[The information follows:]

ALO's reviewed the FY94 budget requests for selected major agencies and provided comments for use in budget presentations to the Deputy Secretary.

ALO's reviewed the FY94 long-range IRM plans for all USDA agencies and coordinated comments from other OIRM divisions in order to provide feedback to the agencies on the acceptability of their plans.

ALO's established an earlier due date for FY95 and subsequent IRM plans so that the plans can precede IRM budget preparation. The plans are due to OIRM on May 1, two and one half months earlier than previously required, and the ALO's have a goal of responding back to agencies within 30 days so that OIRM's response can guide agency IRM budget preparation.

ALO's have made significant changes to the OIRM requirements for OMB Circular A-11 IRM budgets for FY95. These changes will provide better information for USDA and meet OMB Circular A-11 requirements.

ALO's are in constant contact with Senior IRM Officials, in the agencies, as well as with other personnel in the agencies' IRM organizations. This frequency of contact gives OIRM much better information on agency activities than it had previously.

ALO's have been attending agency IRM Review Board meetings in the roles of observer and consultant. This gives OIRM a good picture of how the agencies make decisions about IRM initiatives that serve their programs and about their future direction in the IRM area.

ALO's are providing support to the Info Share initiative, which is the consolidated IRM program for the farm service agencies (ASCS, ES, FCIC, FmHA, and SCS).

OBJECT CLASS TABLES

Mr. DURBIN. For the record please provide a separate object class table for each office within Departmental Administration.

Mr. HILTY. I will provide for the record a separate object class table for each office within Departmental Administration.

[The information follows:]

Object Class Breakout
Direct Obligations

DEPARTMENTAL ADMINISTRATION
(Dollars in Thousands)

Object Class	1992 Actual	1993 Budget Est.	1994 President's Budget	Change from Current 1993 Est.
11.1	16,519	19,837	20,263	426
11.3	262	0	0	0
11.5	611	365	377	12
11.9	17,392	20,202	20,640	438
12.1	2,589	3,005	3,078	73
13.0	15	6	6	0
21.0	273	142	142	0
22.0	6	12	12	0
23.2	10	25	25	0
23.3	999	698	689	(9)
24.0	278	159	159	0
25.0	2,384	1,151	2,149	998
26.0	457	191	191	0
31.0	802	175	174	(1)
41.0	0	32	32	0
99.0	25,205	25,798	27,298	1,500

Object Class Breakout
Direct Obligations

OFFICE OF PERSONNEL
(Dollars in Thousands)

Object Class	1992 Actual	1993 Budget Est.	1994 President's Budget	Change from Current 1993 Est.
11.1	4,954	5,193	5,081	(112)
11.3	0	0	0	0
11.5	136	80	82	2
11.9	5,090	5,273	5,163	(110)
12.1	754	733	722	(11)
13.0	[illegible]	0	0	0
21.0	50	50	50	0
22.0	3	3	3	0
23.2	10	25	25	0
23.3	236	238	236	(2)
24.0	102	70	70	0
25.0	183	135	387	252
26.0	167	94	94	0
31.0	186	83	83	0
41.0	0	0	0	0
99.0	6,785	6,704	6,833	129

Object Class Breakout
Direct Obligations

OFFICE OF FINANCE AND MANAGEMENT
(Dollars in Thousands)

Object Class	1992 Actual	1993 Budget Est.	1994 President's Budget	Change from Current 1993 Est.
11.1	2,609	3,646	4,085	439
11.3	227	0	0	0
11.5	239	58	59	
11.9	3,075	3,704	4,144	440
12.1	442	562	633	71
13.0	0	0	0	0
21.0	28	15	15	0
22.0	0	.	.	0
23.2	0	0	0	0
23.3	175	27	20	(7)
24.0	41	0	0	0
25.0	382	34	242	208
26.0	79	6	6	0
31.0	122	22	21	(1)
41.0	0	0	0	0
99.0	4,344	4,371	5,082	711

Object Class Breakout
Direct Obligations

OFFICE OF OPERATIONS
(Dollars in Thousands)

Object Class	1992 Actual	1993 Budget Est.	1994 President's Budget	Change from Current 1993 Est.
11.1	2,027	2,474	2,360	(114)
11.3	7	0	0	0
11.5	127	135	138	3
11.9	2,161	2,609	2,498	(111)
12.1	352	414	397	(17)
13.0	2			0
21.0	74	9	9	0
22.0				0
23.2	0	0	0	0
23.3	147	54	53	(1)
24.0	22	13	13	0
25.0	225	32	226	194
26.0	69	20	20	0
31.0	58	20	20	0
41.0	0	0	0	0
99.0	3,111	3,173	3,239	66

Object Class Breakout
Direct Obligations

OFFICE OF INFORMATION RESOURCES MANAGEMENT
(Dollars in Thousands)

Object Class	1992 Actual	1993 Budget Est.	1994 President's Budget	Change from Current 1993 Est.
11.1	3,292	4,090	4,305	215
11.3	28	0	0	0
11.5	51	62	67	5
11.9	3,371	4,152	4,372	220
12.1	468	602	639	37
13.0	3	0	0	0
21.0	55	38	38	0
22.0	0	3	3	0
23.2	0	0	0	0
23.3	288	305	307	2
24.0	74	55	55	0
25.0	1,113	808	1,028	220
26.0	81	43	43	0
31.0	219	42	42	0
41.0	0	0	0	0
99.0	5,672	6,048	6,527	479

Object Class Breakout
Direct Obligations

OFFICE OF ADVOCACY AND ENTERPRISE
(Dollars in Thousands)

Object Class	1992 Actual	1993 Budget Est.	1994 President's Budget	Change from Current 1993 Est.
11.1	2,423	3,016	2,981	(35)
11.3	0	0	0	0
11.5	58	30	31	
11.9	2,481	3,046	3,012	(34)
12.1	413	486	470	(16)
13.0	6	5	5	0
21.0	60	25	25	0
22.0		2	2	0
23.2	0	0	0	0
23.3	82	26	25	(1)
24.0	28	13	13	0
25.0	370	42	170	128
26.0	37	16	16	0
31.0	187	6	6	0
41.0	0	32	32	0
99.0	3,665	3,699	3,776	77

Object Class Breakout
Direct Obligations

OFFICE OF ADMINISTRATIVE LAW JUDGES
(Dollars in Thousands)

Object Class	1992 Actual	1993 Budget Est.	1994 President's Budget	Change from Current 1993 Est.
11.1	1,031	1,235	1,263	28
11.3	0	0	0	0
11.5	0	0	0	0
11.9	1,031	1,235	1,263	28
12.1	132	180	187	7
13.0	0	0	0	0
21.0	2			0
22.0		2	2	0
23.2	0	0	0	0
23.3	60	38	38	0
24.0	11	8	8	0
25.0	111	100	98	(2)
26.0	24	12	12	0
31.0	30	2	2	0
41.0	0	0	0	0
99.0	1,402	1,578	1,611	33

Object Class Breakout
Direct Obligations

EMERGENCY PROGRAMS
(Dollars in Thousands)

Object Class	1992 Actual	1993 Budget Est.	1994 President's Budget	Change from Current 1993 Est.
11.1	183	183	187	.
11.3	0	0	0	0
11.5	0	0	0	0
11.9	183	183	187	
12.1	28	28	29	
13.0	0	0	0	0
21.0				0
22.0	0	0	0	0
23.2	0	0	0	0
23.3	10	10	10	0
24.0	0	0	0	0
25.0	0	0	0	0
26.0	0	0	0	0
31.0	0	0	0	0
41.0	0	0	0	0
99.0	225	225	230	5

RENTAL PAYMENTS TO OTHERS

Mr. DURBIN. Object Class 23.2, Rental Payments to Others, increases from $9,900 in fiscal year 1992 to $25,000 in fiscal years 1993 and 1994. What is the reason for this increase?

Mr. HILTY. That subobject class was obligated under the Office of Personnel. It pays for "1-800" telephone service for areas that are not covered by FTS 2000 intercity. We have a very far reaching field office system, and need such capability to communicate with our field level personnel staffs. These lines allow us to get policy and guidance out in an effective manner, plus we can hear back from the field their problems and questions. The increase over 1992 reflects anticipated use in 1993, however, there is no increase between fiscal year 1993 and 1994.

SUB-OBJECT CLASS BREAKOUT

Mr. DURBIN. The only increase in fiscal year 1994 from fiscal year 1993 is in Object Class 25, Other Services. Provide a sub-object class breakout for each fiscal year.

Mr. HILTY. I will provide that for the record.

[The information follows:]

DEPARTMENTAL ADMINISTRATION OBJECT CLASS 2500 BREAKOUT

Sub-object	Fiscal year—			
	1992	1993	1994	Increase
NFC Services	268,659	130,000	260,000	130,000
Repair Maintenance Agreements	133,679	65,000	150,000	85,000
Security Investigations	4,700	2,000	5,000	3,000
Computer Services	909,291	439,000	672,000	233,000
ADP Service Contracts	120,664	58,000	120,000	62,000
Federal Protective Services	68,325	33,000	69,000	36,000
Design Center Services	20,785	10,000	20,000	10,000
Video and Film Cntr. Services	42,817	21,000	43,000	22,000
Training, Tuition, etc	296,615	143,000	300,000	157,000
Agreements, Misc. Services	23,964	12,000	26,000	14,000
Reimbursable Details	20,477	10,000	40,000	30,000
Contact Services—Other Fed	333,947	161,000	300,000	139,000
Telephone Equipment	85,184	41,000	90,000	49,000
Equipment User/Fixed Ownership	53,205	26,000	55,000	29,000
Health Unit, Health Care	278	0	0	0
Recorder, Consultant Fees	915	0	0	0
Total subobjects	2,383,505	1,151,000	2,150,000	999,000

ORGANIZATIONAL STRUCTURE

Mr. DURBIN. The appropriation language proposes to include a separate budget activity for Emergency Programs. Where was this activity carried out in prior years?

Mr. HILTY. Emergency Programs was one of the functions assigned to the Office of Personnel.

MISSION OF USDA REGIONAL EMERGENCY STAFFS

Mr. DURBIN. Emergency Programs provides leadership, guidance, direction, and coordination to ten USDA Regional Emergency Staffs. Where are these staffs located and what is their mission?

Mr. HILTY. In the field, the Federal Emergency Management Agency (FEMA) is aligned according to the ten Standard Federal Regions. The Agencies within the Department, that operate on a regional structure, have their own regional alignments. To provide a Departmental match with FEMA, we have established ten USDA Regional Emergency Staffs with USDA personnel from within these ten Standard Federal Regions. These Staffs are comprised of USDA State personnel who, in addition to their normal activities, have a regional emergency responsibility with FEMA. These USDA personnel may be from anywhere within their respective Standard Federal Region. For example, in Region 10, we have representatives from six USDA Agencies and four different States. Our criteria is to have selected Agencies represented on the Staff, and their location within the Standard Federal Region is not of primary concern. The Regional Emergency Staff members operate from their normal work locations, and attend meetings at the FEMA Regional Offices when required.

EMERGENCY OPERATIONS HANDBOOK

Mr. DURBIN. The Emergency Operations Handbook for USDA State and County Emergency Boards was to be available for distribution this year. What is the status of this Handbook?

Mr. HILTY. The Interim Edition, Emergency Operations Handbook for USDA Emergency Personnel, was approved by the Secretary on March 5, 1993, and printed and disseminated to all USDA State and County Emergency Boards nationwide, shortly afterwards.

FIVE YEAR FUNDS AND STAFF YEARS

Mr. DURBIN. Provide a five year table showing the budget, in both dollars and staff, of each activity under Departmental Administration.

Mr. HILTY. I will be glade to provide that for the record.

[The information follows:]

APPROPRIATED AVAILABLE FUNDS AND STAFF YEARS—DEPARTMENTAL ADMINISTRATION

[Dollars in thousands]

Staff Office	Fiscal year— 1989 Funds	1989 SY	1990 Funds	1990 SY	1991 Funds	1991 SY	1992 Funds	1992 SY	1993 Funds	1993 SY	1994 [6] Funds	1994 [6] SY
OBPA [1]	4,389	78	n.a.	n.a.	n.a.	n a	n.a.	n a.	n a	n a.	n a.	n a.
OP	5,757	119	5,807	116	6,163	118	6,704	119	6,704	119	6,749	114
OFM	3,853	69	3,921	70	4,070	69	4,371	68	4,371	69	5,019	76
OO [2]	2,709	59	2,749	56	2,896	59	3,110	58	3,173	59	3,199	56
OIRM [3]	4,635	64	4,901	64	5,327	64	5,648	64	6,048	74	6,446	74
OAE	3,088	58	3,113	58	3,281	58	3,699	62	3,699	62	3,729	59
OALJ/JO	1,025	20	1,325	24	1,361	24	1,578	24	1,578	23	1,591	22
EP [4]	225	4	225	4	225	4	225	4	225	4	227	4

APPROPRIATED AVAILABLE FUNDS AND STAFF YEARS—DEPARTMENTAL ADMINISTRATION—Continued

[Dollars in thousands]

Staff Office	Fiscal year— 1989		1990		1991		1992		1993		1994 [6]	
	Funds	SY	Funds	SY	Funds	SY	Funds	SY	Funds	SY	Funds	SY
NCS [5]			2		50		50					
Total	25,681	471	22,043	392	25,160	399	25,385	399	25,798	410	26,960	405

[1] Since FY 1989 OBPA has been a separate appropriation.
[2] OO is adjusted for comparability from FY 1989–90 to reflect the transfer of $21,000 and 1 FTE from USDA for the Equipment Management Information System upgrade work in FY 1991–92
[3] OIRM is adjusted for comparability in FY 1988–90 to reflect the transfer of $300,000 and 5 FTE in FY 1991 and $700,000 and 10 FTE in FY 1992 for the Agency Liaison Officers work on IRM planning and oversight
[4] Emergency Programs has been removed from OP in FY 1988–92 for comparability with FY 1993
[5] National Communication System was a payment made by USDA to support a Nation-wide emergency preparadeness communications system under National Security Directive 205 FY 1992 was the last year this item was budgeted
[6] FY 1994 Total Funds reflect the FY 1994 Budget Amendment reductions

Mr. DURBIN. Your budget reflects a reimbursement from other USDA agencies of $1,500,000 in both fiscal years 1993 and 1994 for a Field Office System. Tell us what this is and where will this reimbursement come from?

Mr. HILTY. Funding in fiscal years 1993 and 1994 has been allocated to OIRM to support the Info Share program office for program planning and management, acquisition development. The funds are being reimbursed by the Agricultural Stabilization and Conservation Service, Farmers Home Administration, and the Soil Conservation Service from agency appropriations.

FOREIGN AGRICULTURAL SERVICE TRAINING

Mr. DURBIN. You also show a reimbursement of $245,000 in fiscal year 1992 for SES Training. Describe this in further detail.

Mr. HILTY. My apologies, Mr. Chairman the reimbursement labeled SES Training was actually for Foreign Agricultural Service (FAS) training. In FY 1992, the Office of Personnel planned, developed, coordinated and delivered six sessions of the Leadership Academy. The Leadership Academy is designed to augment the leadership, teamwork and communications skills of FAS managers, supervisors, and leaders. The $245,000 was expended to provide leadership education and training for 142 FAS employees. The cost of the training is exceptionally economical for FAS employees.

SENIOR EXECUTIVE SERVICE CANDIDATE DEVELOPMENT PROGRAM

Mr. DURBIN. In anticipation of large vacancies of SES positions over the next few years, the Department has initiated a Senior Executive Service Candidate Development Program. What is the cost of this program and where will these candidates work until positions become available?

Mr. HILTY. In FY 1992, the total cost of the program was approximately $435,000, including $102,000 from appropriated funds to cover SESCDP program development and management, and $333,000 for program implementation which was recovered through reimbursements from USDA agencies with candidates in the program.

USDA employees are expected to perform their regular work duties in addition to participating in the program. USDA agencies pay for the cost of SESCDP training for each of their employees accepted into the program. In some cases, USDA agencies are asked to place SESCDP candidates from external institutions into paid developmental assignments including salary, training and other related costs. A few candidates come from other Federal agencies and will remain in their current jobs with those agencies.

Three SESCDP program cycles are planned to establish an executive pool of up to 250 individuals. The opening conference for the first cycle was held in July 1992. For the first cycle, ninety individuals were competitively selected out of 1,120 applicants, from USDA, other government agencies, and the private sector. The quality and diversity of candidates in the first program are exceptional. Seventy of those selected are participating in a rigorous 6–18 month executive development program prior to Office of Personnel Management (OPM) senior executive certification.

The other 20 participants represent highly experienced, executive talent and have been proposed for immediate OPM certification through an innovative, accelerated, cost saving program. This accelerated program is the first of its kind in government. Nine of the 90 first cycle candidates already have been promoted into the SES, including one woman and four black males.

The opening conference for the second cycle will be held in May 1993. Applications were due in December 1992 and over 900 were received. The final selection of 90 SESCDP candidates from among these applicants will occur in May. The estimated cost of the second cycle is $467,000, of which $102,000 is appropriated funds and $365,000 reimbursed.

OP will continue to coordinate a continuing, smaller scale program beyond 1995.

WORK FORCE DIVERSITY/RECRUITMENT ACTIVITIES

Mr. DURBIN. The Department has established a USDA/1890 Outstanding Scholars Program with the goal of attracting and assisting students to careers in agriculture. The program provides full tuition, fees, books, and a personal computer and software for students pursuing a Bachelors degree from one of seventeen 1890 Historically Black Land-Grant Institutions in exchange for one year of service obligation for each year of support. The institution provides each student with room and board. How many students have been selected to participate in this program?

Mr. HILTY. Forty-three graduating high school senior students have been selected. Each student will be entering one of the seventeen 1890 Institutions this fall. As stated, this is a scholars program for outstanding students. Average high school Grade Point Average is 3.76, Scholastic Aptitude Test score is 1100, and American College Test score is 23. Sixteen USDA Agencies are participating, including the Office of the Secretary which will have one student. There will be a minimum of 2 scholars attending each of the 1890 Institutions. The scholars receive cooperative education appointments and must work for USDA for at least one year for every year of education.

USDA ROLE IN A CHEMICAL INCIDENT

Mr. DURBIN. The Department of Defense is planning to destroy all chemical and biological warfare weapons. What role does USDA play in this planning process?

Mr. HILTY. None, Mr. Chairman. USDA does have a role in being prepared to respond to emergencies that may occur as a result of destroying these weapons.

NATO DATABASE

Mr. DURBIN. The Department is establishing a database at the request of the NATO Food and Agriculture Planning Committee to be used to assess the impact of a disaster on agriculture. What is the cost of this database and when will it be complete? Are you receiving any funding from NATO? Who will use this database when it is complete?

Mr. HILTY. As of March 1993, the requirement for the US to establish a NATO emergency database has been put on hold, and it is believed that the requirement will be rescinded. It seems that the NATO nations, in light of the changing world environment, are reasonably convinced that the database is no longer required.

NORTH AMERICAN FREE TRADE AGREEMENT

Mr. DURBIN. With the possible ratification of the North American Free Trade Agreement, are you involved in negotiations regarding emergency preparedness with Mexico?

Mr. HILTY. No, we are not. The overall coordination of international emergency preparedness activities, such as NATO, Canada, and eventually with Mexico, is handled by the Federal Emergency Management Agency's Office of International Affairs.

INTERNAL MANAGEMENT STUDY OF MOTOR VEHICLES

Mr. DURBIN. The Department conducted an internal management study and cost comparison of rates of using GSA owned vehicles versus commercial lease vehicles. What were the results of this study?

Mr. HILTY. The study showed that using GSA owned vehicles is less costly in most cases than commercial lease vehicles. The internal management study of using GSA owned vehicles and commercial lease vehicles showed that the cost of USDA ownership and operation was the least costly means of providing vehicle transportation.

As part of the study, a cost model by vehicle type was developed that included direct and indirect operating and maintenance costs, annual depreciation and annual replacement cost increases based on actual ownership costs, GSA published rates, and commercial lease contract cost. I will provide a table of cost comparisons for the record.

[The information follows:]

AVERAGE COST PER MILE BY VEHICLE TYPE

Vehicle type	Commercial	GSA	USDA owned
Sedans	$.390	$.244	$.169
Station Wagons	.338	.261	.192
Lt. Truck 4x2	.637	.394	.285
Lt. Truck 4x4	.563	.397	.249
Medium Truck	.881	.648	.406
Heavy Truck	1.97	1.38	1.10

AIRCRAFT AND MOTOR VEHICLE MANAGEMENT

Mr. DURBIN. The Secretary has established an initiative to identify and make recommendation of needed improvement in the management of the Department's aircraft and motor vehicle fleet. When will this report be made available to the Secretary?

Mr. HILTY. This report was submitted to the Secretary on December 28, 1992. The report recommends improvements in Departmental oversight by establishing a central data system, encouraging energy and environmental efficiencies, coordinating an approach to research and development efforts, and eliminating policies which are impediments to good fleet management. The implementation of these recommendations has already begun.

DISTRIBUTION OF USDA VEHICLES

Mr. DURBIN. For the record, please provide a table showing the distribution of the Department's vehicles, by agency.

Mr. HILTY. I will provide for the record a table that shows the distribution of the Department's owned and domestically operated motor vehicle fleet as of October 1, 1992.

[The information follows:]

USDA domestically owned vehicles as of October 1, 1992 [1]

Agency:	*Number of vehicles*
Agricultural Marketing Service	62
Agricultural Research Service	3,242
Agricultural Stabilization and Conservation Service	8
Animal and Plant Health Inspection Service	3,023
Farmer's Home Administration	14
Federal Grain Inspection Service	1
Food Safety and Inspection Service	2
Forest Service	17,376
National Agricultural Statistics Service	17
Office of the Inspector General	18
Packers and Stockyards Administration	2
Soil Conservation Service	10,760
Total owned and operated vehicles	34,525

[1] This table includes 34,525 owned sedans, station wagons, light trucks (4×2 and 4×4), medium trucks, heavy trucks, buses, and ambulances. USDA also owns approximately 12,695 special purpose vehicles, including fire trucks, trash compactors, construction equipment, trailers, motorcycles, and snowmobiles. In foreign countries, USDA operates 403 vehicles. USDA also owns and loans to cooperators 25,468 pieces of fleet equipment and leases from GSA and commercial vendors about 7,000 vehicles.

DISTRIBUTION OF USDA AIRCRAFT

Mr. DURBIN. Also for the record, provide a similar table showing the Department's distribution of aircraft, by agency.

Mr. HILTY. I will provide for the record a table that reflects the distribution of the Department's owned and operated aircraft fleet as of October 1, 1992.

[The information follows:]

Distribution of owned and operated aircraft as of October 1, 1992 [1]

Agency:	Number of aircraft
Agricultural Research Service	8
Animal and Plant Health Inspection Service	21
Forest Service	45
Total owned and operated aircraft	74

[1] The Forest Service lends 241 aircraft to State Forestry organizations and 28 aircraft to museums. These organizations pay all costs associated with the aircraft. The Animal and Plant Health Inspection Service also leases on a year-round basis 8 aircraft and borrows 5 aircraft from cooperators. In addition, the Department acquires by contract charter, lease or rental $75.6 million in aircraft and aircraft services.

USDA AFFIRMATIVE PROCUREMENT PROGRAM PLAN

Mr. DURBIN. The explantory notes state that the USDA Affirmative Procurement Program Plan for Waste Reduction and the Recycling of Reusable Materials regulations will be implemented by June 1993. Please describe this in further detail.

Mr. HILTY. We remain on schedule for implementation by June 1993 of a USDA Affirmative Procurement Plan. "Buy recovered materials" will be the favored approach and will be widely promoted. While we have worked on this program, our staff has participated with the Office of Federal Procurement Policy and the Federal Recycling Council on several related efforts. Our personnel assisted OFPP in the preparation of the recent policy letter on the acquisition of environmentally-sound, energy-efficient products and services and products manufactured with recovered materials. That policy letter directs the implementation of its provisions in the Federal Acquisition Regulation. Our staff chaired a committee for OFPP and the Federal Recycling Council to prepare the case work for the FAR changes. This work is now ready for regulatory consideration. In addition, we have offered assistance and comments on the newly proposed Executive Order to replace the existing Federal Recycling Executive Order 12780. Our program must reflect the regulatory and Executive Order changes worked on by USDA Office of Operations staff members.

ON-SITE AND COMPLAINT INVESTIGATIONS

Mr. DURBIN. Did you conduct any on-site reviews and/or complaint investigations in fiscal year 1992? If so, please describe them.

Mr. HILTY. We conducted three on-site reviews and eleven on-site complaint investigations in fiscal year 1992.

In the Agricultural Stabilization and Conservation Service on-site reviews were conducted of the National Headquarters, the Kansas City Management Office, the Kansas City Commodity Office, the Kansas City Financial Management Office, and the Georgia Agricultural Stabilization and Conservation Service. The review included an assessment of both EEO and civil rights programs.

In the Agricultural Research Service on-site reviews were conducted of the Headquarters, the Beltsville Area Office and the Pacific West Area Office. The civil rights portion of the review was conducted to assist ARS in developing a civil rights program.

In the Forest Service EEO/Civil Rights Reviews were conducted at several sites throughout Region IX, including offices in Wisconsin, Minnesota, Missouri, West Virginia, Pennsylvania, Vermont, and New Hampshire.

I will provide a description of the eleven on-site complaint investigations for the record.

[The information follows:]

OAE FISCAL YEAR 1992 ON-SITE INVESTIGATIONS

Date started	Date completed	Program	Basis	City, state
7/27/92	7/31/92	Farm Operating Loan	Race	Colfax, Louisiana.
7/6/92	7/16/92	Rural Housing	Sex	Mullins, South Carolina.
8/23/92	9/5/92	Farm Operating Loan	Race	Belcher, Louisiana.
8/23/92	9/5/92	Farm Operating Loan	Race	Belcher, Louisiana.
8/23/92	9/5/92	Farm Operating Loan	Race	Belcher, Louisiana.
4/5/92	4/11/92	Farm Operating Loan	Race	Tillery, North Carolina.
4/5/92	4/11/92	Farm Operating Loan	Race	Halifax, North Carolina.
6/16/92	6/22/92	Farm Operating Loan	Age and marital status	Sondheimer, Louisiana.
3/30/92	4/03/92	County Election	Race	Baker County, Georgia.
6/22/92	6/26/92	Farm Operating Loan	Race	Monroe, Louisiana.
3/9/92	3/13/92	Emergency Loan	Race	Miami, Florida.

PROGRAM DISCRIMINATION

Mr. DURBIN. Please update the table that appears on page 42 of last year's hearing record showing the number of complaints of program discrimination you received and the number resolved to include fiscal year 1992 actuals.

Mr. HILTY. I will provide the table for the record.

[The information follows:]

TABLE OF PROGRAM COMPLAINTS FOR FISCAL YEARS 1982 THROUGH 1992

	Cases received	Cases resolved
Fiscal year:		
1982	373	[1] NA
1983	398	NA
1984	479	NA
1985	460	NA
1986	518	NA
1987	576	533
1988	578	537
1989	645	602
1990	651	681
1991	721	622
1992	794	791

[1] N/A—Through fiscal years 1982–1986, OAE did not have a tracking mechanism for cases resolved.

SUMMER INTERNS

Mr. DURBIN. What was the total number of summer interns you hired last year? How many were from 1980 Land Grant Institutions, how many were from the Hispanic Association of Colleges and Universities, how many were from American Indian Colleges, and how many were from other Colleges and Universities?

Mr. HILTY. USDA hired 1,400 Summer Interns last year. From this, 785 attended the 1890 Land Grant Institutions, 65 attended Hispanic Association Colleges and Universities, 20 attended American Indian Tribal Colleges, and 530 were from other colleges and universities. The Summer Intern program has proven to be an opportunity for USDA to "grow our own" work force and has demonstrated to the interns that USDA should be an "employer of choice" among groups that previously did not consider a career in USDA.

METRIC IMPLEMENTATION

Mr. DURBIN. What is the status of the Department's conversion to the metric system?

Mr. HILTY. As indicated in USDA's Annual Metrication Report to the Secretary of Commerce, we are pleased to report that the Department and its agencies are actively pursuing an effective and efficient process in conversion to the metric system. USDA agencies are working with contractors and other clientele to accomplish the conversion goal as efficiently and quickly as possible.

During fiscal year 1992, USDA completed and issued a Departmental Regulation which establishes policies and assigns responsibilities and authorities for implementation of the metric system of measurement within the Department.

DRUG-FREE WORKPLACE PROGRAM

Mr. DURBIN. Briefly describe the Department's Drug-Free Workplace Program.

Mr. HILTY. This program consists of employee counseling services, supervisory training, employee education, and drug testing. All aspects but drug testing were implemented in August of 1988. Drug testing was delayed until January of 1990 by litigation brought by the National Treasury Employees Union and the National Association of Agriculture Employees. To date, 1,581 employees have been randomly tested, 68 employees have volunteered for testing, and 160 job applicants have been tested. This testing resulted in four employees being found positive for illegal drug use. Reasonable suspicion and post accident testing will be implemented as soon as we receive approval of our implementing language from the Interagency Coordinating Group as required by the Office of National Drug Control Policy. Employees authorized to carry firearms, employees directly involved in drug interdiction duties, and employees with Secret security clearances will be added to our random testing program as soon as we receive approval from the Department of Justice. These additions will increase our number of random testing positions from 1,350 to 2,850.

CASH MANAGEMENT

Mr. DURBIN. How much interest costs to the Treasury was avoided from lockbox collections in fiscal year 1992?

Mr. HILTY. USDA collected $3.3 billion through the Department of the Treasury's (Treasury) Lockbox Network during Fiscal Year (FY) 1992. This represents about a 10 percent increase over FY 1991 collections through lockbox. Lockbox collections resulted in an interest avoidance to the Treasury of about $2.0 million.

The Deficit Reduction Act of 1984, requires agencies to use the most effective mechanisms in the movement of funds wherever feasible and in accordance with Treasury regulations. USDA has used lockboxes since the early 1980's.

USDA has 49 lockbox applications at four Treasury Network Lockbox Banks. USDA continues to evaluate cash flows for effective lockbox usage. USDA lockbox initiatives include the following collections and interest avoidance during FY 1992, which are provided for the record.

[The information follows:]

[Dollars in millions]

Agency	Lockbox collections	Interest avoided
Farmers Home Administration	$1,411	$.36
Forest Service	1,153	1.11
Office of Finance and Management	427	.23
Agricultural Stabilization and Conservation Service/Commodity Credit Corporation	236	.19
Federal Crop Insurance Corporation	29	.02
Food and Nutrition Service	21	.03
Total	3,277	1.94

BELTSVILLE SITE

Mr. DURBIN. Mr. Hilty, for the past two years we have been waiting for negotiations between the General Services Administration, the Washington Metropolitan Transit Authority, and USDA to resolve the sale of 75.3 acres of the ARS Beltsville site to the Authority. What is the status of this issue?

Mr. HILTY. On October 15, 1992, the General Services Administration (GSA) transferred 65.01 acres of the property to the Washington Metropolitan Area Transit Authority (WMATA), for which the ARS received a payment of $3.5 million. The remaining 10.30 acres is currently set aside as part of a remedial action plan to clean up contaminated soil at a 3-to-4 acre site known as the Biodegradable site. The 10.3 acres will be transferred to WMATA when the cleanup action has been satisfactorily completed and accepted by the State of Maryland and the EPA. A contract for the cleanup is underway and should be completed later this year. At that time, ARS will receive the remaining $1.5 million of the purchase price of $5.0 million, which is currently being held in escrow. In the interim, construction of the Green Line is proceeding concurrently with the cleanup of the Biodegradable site.

HISTORICALLY BLACK COLLEGES AND UNIVERSITIES

Mr. DURBIN. Please update the table that appears on page 53 of last year's hearing record showing the amount of funds USDA provides to Historically Black Colleges and Universities to include fiscal year 1992.

Mr. HILTY. I will provide the table for the record.

[The information follows:]

U.S. DEPARTMENT OF AGRICULTURE FUNDS PROVIDED TO ASSIST HISTORICALLY BLACK COLLEGES AND UNIVERSITIES

Program description	Fiscal year— 1990	1991	1992
Research and development	$30,441,291	$34,457,388	$34,749,401
Program evaluation	24,391,000	23,782,500	25,892,836
Training	255,610	376,493	666,606
Facilities and equipment	9,927,348	10,772,743	10,531,870
Fellowships, traineeships, recruitment, and IPA's	6,583,910	8,805,693	7,324,859
Student tuition, assistance, scholarships, and other aid	1,440,868	1,920,572	852,593
Total to HBCU's	73,040,027	80,115,389	80,018,165

PERFORMANCE OF COMMERCIAL ACTIVITIES (OMB CIRCULAR A-76)

Mr. DURBIN. How many A-76 reviews were completed by USDA during fiscal year 1992 and what are your plans for fiscal year 1993?

Mr. HILTY. USDA did not complete any A-76 reviews during fiscal year 1992, nor up to this date in fiscal year 1993. We do not anticipate that any studies will be completed through the balance of fiscal year 1993.

CFO ACT IMPLEMENTATION

Mr. DURBIN. You are requesting an increase of $616,000 and seven staff years to support additional requirements placed on the Department as a result of the Chief Financial Officers' Act. What is the total amount, in both dollars and staff, the Department is spending to comply with this Act?

Mr. HILTY. The only additional resources USDA has expended to comply with the Act are the costs associated with hiring a Deputy Chief Financial Officer, which is 2 FTE and $195,000.

USDA received no other additional resources to implement the CFO Act. USDA reallocated resources to implement the financial statement preparation and audit portions of the CFO Act. The chart below, provided for the record, details the staff years and funds reallocated for financial statement preparation and audit. We anticipate that the costs for financial statement preparation and audit will be reduced as we improve USDA's financial management information systems.

[The information follows:]

USDA CFO ACT IMPLEMENTATION—REALLOCATION OF RESOURCES FOR THE PREPARATION AND AUDIT OF FINANCIAL STATEMENTS

[Funds in thousands of dollars]

Agency	Amount	Staff years
Office of the Inspector General	$7,931	99
USDA Program Agencies	2,102	43
Departmental Administration	425	8
Total, USDA	10,458	150

Mr. DURBIN. How much in additional funding is needed to meet all the mandates of the Act and once they are met how much will be required to maintain it?

Mr. HILTY. In addition to the seven FTE's and $616,000 requested for fiscal year 1994, Departmental Administration will need an additional 25 FTE's and $1.88 million in future years to fully implement the provisions of the Act.

The CFO will also require the development, implementation, and maintenance of new financial management information systems in USDA. The cost of such systems are unknown at this time. We are currently developing a strategic plan for such financial management information systems.

WORKING CAPITAL FUND—MAP/AIMS

Mr. DURBIN. At last year's hearing you went into detail describing the Modernization of the Administrative Process and its software component the Administrative Integrated Management System. You anticipated Phase One, all administrative processes, accounting and information systems, to be complete by October 1996 with Phase Two, payroll and personnel, to follow. It is estimated that Phase One would cost approximately $40 million. Bring us up to date on the status of this project. Do you have cost estimates and a time frame for the second Phase?

Mr. HILTY. The Modernization of the Administrative Process (MAP) project began in 1989 with the goal of developing a single integrated administrative management system to replace the many stand-alone application systems that feed into the USDA National Finance Center in New Orleans. In June 1992 the USDA hired a contractor to perform an in-depth review of the MAP Project and its software component, the Administrative Integrated Management System (AIMS).

This review recommended that all software development efforts be stopped until a system design is completed and the data base is redesigned. It was also recommended that a project office be established in Washington to provide the drive and user coordination for the developmental efforts.

As a result of the review, virtually all actions related to Phase One of MAP were halted. In addition, a small project office was established in Washington, D.C. The Director of this office reports to the Assistant Secretary for Administration. The MAP Project Office is charged with providing direction, coordination, and support to Departmental Administration staff offices. A MAP Leadership Group—a steering committee—was formed to lead the renewed MAP effort. Along with the heads of the Departmental Staff Offices, the Deputy Chief Financial Officer, the Director of the Office of Budget and Program Analysis and a representative from the USDA Management Council also serve on this Leadership Group.

It is clear that the biggest payback will come from streamlining the paper intensive and duplicative processes we use to do our administrative work. Since August 1992, the efforts have been aimed at identifying processes that need to be streamlined prior to automation. In keeping with the requirements of the Chief Financial Officer's Act and the recommendations of the MAP Review, USDA is also focusing on strategies to do mid-range redesign of the National Finance Center's main frame data bases and improvement of their accounting system. We are also piloting efforts in the Personnel area to test a Department of Defense personnel system and a system being developed by the Forest Service under USDA Departmental leadership. In March, we began an intensive strategic planning initiative for the renewed MAP effort. We plan to publish a MAP Strategic Plan by August 1993, which will outline the goals, strategies and actions needed to achieve the MAP vision.

WORKING CAPITAL FUND—TRAINING CENTER

Mr. DURBIN. Approval was granted on January 12, 1993 for Working Capital Funds to be used to establish a Training Center. Would you describe this initiative in further detail including where the Center is located, how it is staffed, what type of training is provided to whom, and the cost to operate it?

Mr. HILTY. Mr. Chairman, we've been looking at the possibility of a Training Center to support headquarters personnel for some time. We were concerned that the costs we were incurring for renting commercial space for training were putting a strain on agency budgets. My personnel and finance staffs put together a proposal to establish a Training Center in the WCF. The proposal was sent to the Office of Management and Budget and approved by the Director, as required under 7 U.S.C. 2235, on January 12th of this year.

The Center is located in the 6th wing of the South Building in our headquarters building complex. It has "breakout" rooms that can be subdivided to accommodate more training sessions with smaller class sizes, and it has the capacity to conduct ADP training. Our priorities in supporting training in this facility include a focus on management of increasing workforce diversity, and development of the next generation of senior managers in the event of the expected large numbers of retirements among current senior managers in the years ahead. Specific programs include programs for incumbent senior executives, training for incumbent managers and supervisors, developmental programs for mid-level employees, automation training, secretarial and clerical support training, basic skills development programs, and program and mission-related training. Most of these programs will be presented by professional trainers and educators, whose services will be procured in conformance with regulations and procedures for procurement of such services. Some training will be performed by USDA agency experts with proficiency in training.

The estimates of operating costs and staff for the first full year of operation are $134,000 and 2 FTEs. Capital equipment costs are estimated at $173,000. These costs would be recovered through depreciation charges over the useful life of the equipment to users of the Center.

WORKING CAPITAL FUND—CENTRAL SUPPLY STORES

Mr. DURBIN. The explanatory notes mention that a feasibility study was commissioned to examine if USDA's self-service facility could be moved to a new location and if space alterations could be implemented to improve item accountability and enhance traffic flow. Would you be more specific and tell us what this self-service facility is, where it is located, and what problems it is experiencing?

Mr. HILTY. Certainly, Mr. Chairman. The self-service store provides over-the-counter, customer walk-in supply and materials services for approximately 12,000 employees located in the USDA headquarters complex. The supply store is located in the USDA South Building here in Washington.

A recent survey indicated that the present location is best suited for customer access. However, facility and automated inventory/distribution control upgrades are desirable for efficient customer support. We are pursuing these upgrades for the store in its present location.

WORKING CAPITAL FUND—CENTRAL SUPPLY FORMS

Mr. DURBIN. The transfer of publication inventories of the Forest Service, the Office of Public Affairs, and the Human Nutrition Information Service from GPO facilities will reduce costs for storage and distribution. Where will these publications be stored and how much will this save USDA?

Mr. HILTY. Publications previously stored by GPO for the Forest Service, Human Nutrition Information Service, and the Office of Public Affairs were absorbed into the USDA Consolidated Forms and Publications Distribution Center's inventories at the request of the Office of Public Affairs at no additional expense in operating costs.

We do not have the actual amount of cost savings. The Office of Public Affairs coordinated the storage arrangement with GPO.

WORKING CAPITAL FUND—DEPRECIATION CHARGES

Mr. DURBIN. Please update the table that appears on page 54 of last year's hearing record showing the Working Capital Fund depreciation charges to include fiscal year 1992 actuals and fiscal year 1994 estimates.

Mr. HILTY. I will do so.

[The information follows:]

1985	$3,147,000
1986	4,184,000
1987	6,675,000
1988	9,309,000
1989	11,345,000

1990	13,968,000
1991	17,384,000
1992	13,734,000
1993 [1]	14,545,000
1994 [1]	16,342,000

[1] Estimated charges.

WORKING CAPITAL FUND—INTERAGENCY REVIEW BOARD

Mr. DURBIN. An interagency advisory board was established in 1983 to provide recommendations to you on the operation and finances of Working Capital Fund activities. Who serves on this board and how often do they meet?

Mr. HILTY. Mr. Chairman, our WCF Interagency Review Board is comprised of eight members. Seven members serve 3-year terms, staggered to ensure continuity on the Board. These individuals are appointed by me from among senior managers in our agencies—usually deputy administrators for management or their organizational equivalent. The eighth member is a permanent representative from our Office of Budget and Program Analysis—either the Director or someone designated to serve on the Director's behalf.

The Board meets as often as I or the membership feel is necessary. This results in from 8 to 12 individual meetings each year. The number of meetings vary from year to year. However, every year, usually in mid-May, they hold a series of meetings to perform their annual review of WCF activity operations and budget requests.

Mr. DURBIN. With the increasing number of agencies outside USDA that are being served by the National Finance Center through cross-servicing agreements, will members from agencies outside USDA be allowed to participate on this board?

Mr. HILTY. From time to time we have considered this question. So far we have decided that this is an internal USDA management tool. The WCF Interagency Review Board is concerned with the oversight and management of the entire Departmental Working Capital Fund which funds 21 activity centers of which the National Finance Center is but one. Other mechanisms are in place to include representatives of cross-serviced agencies in coordinating the management and operation of the systems and services in which they participate. Therefore, we have no plans to include non-USDA agency representatives at this time.

WORKING CAPITAL FUND—EXECUTIVE SECRETARIAT

Mr. DURBIN. Now that the new Office of the Executive Secretariat has been in operation a full year, how has it improved the efficiency and control of executive correspondence?

Mr. HILTY. Mr. Chairman, establishing the new Office of the Executive Secretariat in the WCF has enabled us to develop and begin operation of a new automated mail-tracking program called the Executive Correspondence Tracking and Archival System, or ExecTrac. The new ExecTrac system replaced our old Hewlett-Packard 3000 mail tracking system that served the Department in the 1980's. So far, performance of ExecTrac exceeds our initial expectations. It allows us to monitor the whereabouts of all controlled correspondence as well as the timeliness of all agencies as they handle their respective correspondence responsibilities for the Secretary's mail. Also, each agency can monitor its own performance by producing a variety of reports from its correspondence control officers' workstations. The OES staff can query, retrieve, and collect pertinent data about correspondence much more quickly and thoroughly than was possible in the old system. Finally, the Exec-Trac system allows OES to scan all incoming and outgoing documents, thereby reducing staff time spent in file retrieval, maintaining clean replicas of original documents that would be available in the event of a misplaced original, and eliminating staff time making file copies at microfilm and walkup copier machines.

FTS 2000 VS WITS

Mr. DURBIN. As I understand it, all agencies were required to be using FTS 2000 telecommunications by the end of fiscal year 1992. Your explanatory notes state that the Telephone Services Operation Office assisted agencies in the successful transition to the Washington Interagency Telecommunications System (WITS). Please explain the difference.

Mr. HILTY. The use of FTS 2000 is mandated by GSA regulations for *inter-city,* or long distance, telecommunications.

The Washington Interagency Telecommunications System (WITS) is GSA's mandated, state-of-the-art digital telecommunications network designed for use by the Federal Government, in the Washington, D.C. metropolitan area, for *local service only.* Federal agencies on the WITS network, access the Federal Government's long distance network, either FTS 2000, Network "A", or "B", through the WITS switch. USDA agencies in the Washington, DC metropolitan area, are routed through Network "A", when dialing long distance numbers in the 48 contiguous states, Puerto Rico and the Virgin Islands.

FTS 2000

Mr. DURBIN. Included in all agencies' 1994 requests is a reduction for FTS 2000 funding. The reason for this is that contracts have been renegotiated at lower costs. Describe this in further detail.

Mr. HILTY. In 1992, there were two major price reductions that resulted in significant savings to the FTS 2000 customers. The first reduction took place on October 1, 1992, and the second price reduction took place on December 7, 1992. The October 1, 1992 price reductions were known as "Year 4 Pricing" which were built into the initial FTS 2000 contract. The December 7, 1992 price reductions were the result of Price Redetermination/Service Reallocation (PRSR). These PRSR reductions ranged from a 12% reduction for Exclusive Use Voice service to a 47.8% reduction in PSS dial services. This resulted in an overall across-the-board average reduction of approximately 20% in the cost of FTS 2000 services.

SIES USERS

Mr. DURBIN. How many employees are using the Standard Information Exchange System?

Mr. HILTY. Approximately 250 employees have been assigned an ID and use the full features of the Standard Information Exchange System (SIES). In addition, 14 agencies and staff offices have connected their own networks to SIES and use some of the services such as the gateway to FTS2000.

Additinally, there are four (4) staff offices with their own networks that bridge to the SIES network and share resources such as the X.400 gateway to AT&T FTS 2000. There are also ten (10) agencies that have their own network off of AT&T FTS 2000 connect to the SIES network through the X.400 gateway.

HWM-NATIONAL AGRICULTURAL LIBRARY

Mr. DURBIN. The explanatory notes show an allotment of $24,135 to the National Agricultural Library in fiscal year 1992. What was this for?

Mr. HILTY. The funding was for a contract for the cleanup of a leaking underground storage tank at the library facility.

HWM-RURAL DEVELOPMENT ADMINISTRATION ALLOTMENT

Mr. DURBIN. The notes also show an allotment of $300,000 in fiscal year 1994 to the Rural Development Administration. What is this for and is this the first allotment of many that will be made to the RDA?

Mr. HILTY. The $300,000 allotment to RDA for fiscal year 1994 is to investigate and if necessary to cleanup leaking underground storage tanks and hazardous wastes on property that is owned by RDA. HWM also investigates properties and have a potential to be acquired by RDA to determine the potential liability of the government. This is the first year of what we expect will be a continuing program for this type of work over the next several years. The needs of the program are anticipated to remain relatively stable as the funding is intended to be used primarily for investigations to avoid the large cleanup costs associated with the acquisition of severely contaminated property.

LEGAL SERVICES

Mr. DURBIN. The Office of General Counsel provides legal services in the administration of the CERCLA and RCRA programs. This amount was $269,000 in fiscal year 1991 and increased to $595,000 in fiscal year 1992. What had led to this increase? How are OGC services billed to this account?

Mr. HILTY. Between fiscal year 1991 and fiscal year 1992, the Office of the General Counsel experienced a substantial increase in requests for advice and representation of agencies on Comprehensive Environmental Response, Conservation Liability Act (CERCLA) and Resource Conservation Recovery Act (RCRA) matters. The increase in OGC's involvement is attributable to several factors.

First, in November of 1991, USDA's General Counsel took the initiative in establishing a National Pollution Control (NPC) Team within OGC. This Team is comprised of attorneys from OGC's regional offices, as well as attorneys representing various divisions within USDA. It is headed by a legal coordinator from the Natural

Resources Division. The NPC Team was established to address legal issues involving pollution control, primarily arising under CERCLA and RCRA, at a National level and to ensure that USDA client agencies take positions that are well considered and Nationally consistent.

The establishment of the NPC Team enables OGC to address CERCLA and RCRA issues more effectively, including the early identification of those issues which require legal attention. For example, the NPC Team attorneys identified a critical need for Department-wide training on CERCLA/RCRA issues to fulfill statutory responsibilities. Accordingly, the NPC Team attorneys participated in numerous client-sponsored training sessions and workshops in fiscal year 1992, including a comprehensive training session on CERCLA conducted by NPC Team attorneys for the Forest Service in fiscal year 1992.

Second, between fiscal year 1991 and 1992 USDA client agency requests for legal opinions, both formal and informal have more than doubled. Similarly, between the end of fiscal year 1991 and fiscal year 1992, the number of meetings with states, potentially responsible parties, and other Federal agencies, including EPA, have increased several fold. Also, OGC attorneys were frequently required to travel in connection with those meetings.

Third, the proportion of OGC's time spent on cases filed in federal courts also increased. Despite the relatively small number of cases, a fairly significant commitment of time and resources was required given the magnitude of potential liability in these matters, which can be in the many millions of dollars.

Fourth, enforcement of environmental laws against federal facilities has increased at both the state and Federal levels. This contributes to an increasing workload for OGC, as more advice was sought by client agencies. OGC is also experiencing an increase in other CERCLA/RCRA related activities, including required comments on regulations, representation of USDA interests in numerous meetings with EPA, DOJ, DOI, DOE, DOD, CEQ and OMB regarding a variety of government-wide hazardous waste issues, and the review and clearance of bills and testimony related to CERCLA and RCRA issues.

To answer the second part of your question, OGC has established an accounting code uniquely identifiable to CERCLA and RCRA efforts. When work is performed in support of the CERCLA and RCRA program, OGC personnel are instructed to utilize this accounting code as a system for more accurately determining the costs associated with the program. Reports are sent by OGC to the National Finance Center, where the CERCLA and RCRA account is charged.

UNOBLIGATED BALANCE

Mr. DURBIN. You show an unobligated balance of $2,190,065 at the end of fiscal year 1992. What is the reason for this carryover.

Mr. HILTY. HWM has made much progress in FY 1992 in achieving compliance with the Comprehensive Environmental Response, Conservation Liability Act and the Resource Conservation Recovery Act. We carefully monitored agency's progress on their cleanup projects and reallocated funding to ensure the most effective use of funds to achieve compliance with environmental laws. We also conducted oversight through internal accomplishment reports, budget issues and technical compliance items, and periodic reports to the Environmental Protection Agency. As a result of these efforts, we obligated 95 percent of the $39 million available and entered fiscal year 1993 with an unobligated balance of $2.2 million. Of the total amount, $1.5 million was attributable to an unavoidable delay in the award of a contract, which was subsequently awarded in the first quarter of FY 1993. The remaining amount was for a number of smaller contracts which were advertised but not awarded due to excessively high bids. These contracts have since been readvertised and are now under contract.

PILOT PROJECT

Mr. DURBIN. In fiscal year 1991, you entered into a $50,000 contract with the State of Vermont to conduct a pilot project to determine the amount of farm and household obsolete chemicals that required disposal and the procedures to collect and dispose of these chemicals through the State's Obsolete Pesticide Disposal Project. What were the results of this study?

Mr. HILTY. I am providing for the record a final report on this project.

[CLERK'S NOTE.—The document is too lengthy to include in the record and will be retained in committee files.]

IDENTIFIED CLEAN-UP SITES

Mr. DURBIN. Last year, you provided the Committee with a list of all sites that have been identified for cleanup, the total cost involved, and the expected completion dates. Please update this list.

Mr. HILTY. USDA agencies are currently being asked to update their project lists to reflect the current status of their programs. We will forward the list to the Committee as soon as it is completed.

FARM PROPERTIES

Mr. DURBIN. Farmers Home Administration is required by law to cleanup hazardous waste from property it acquires through foreclosure before the property can be resold. How many foreclosures in Farmers Home Inventory require cleanup action and what is the cost to comply with the law?

Mr. HILTY. The FmHA currently has 3,050 farm properties in inventory with 207 of these sites having hazardous waste or underground storage tank investigations or cleanup activities in progress. The estimated cost of this work is $5,730,000. Because the properties currently in inventory will not be reviewed until they are ready to be sold, it is expected that additional properties will require investigation and subsequent cleanup. Further, it is anticipated that 5 to 10 percent of the approximately 3,500 accounts with foreclosure actions pending will require actions to comply with CERCLA and RCRA.

PRELIMINARY ASSESSMENT

Mr. DURBIN. In fiscal year 1992 USDA agencies completed 48 preliminary assessments, six site investigations, and two remedial investigation/feasibility studies. All documents were sent to EPA and State agencies for their review and approval. Subsequent steps in the CERCLA process cannot proceed until approval is obtained. At this time last year only one preliminary assessment had been reviewed and approved. What is the status of the remaining actions?

Mr. HILTY. USDA agencies have received notice of review and evaluation by the Environmental Protection Agency (EPA) for 25 facilities since the last reporting period. Adding these sites to the number of sites previously evaluated by the EPA since the program was initiated brings the total to 45.

Mr. DURBIN. Have any additional assessments and/or investigations been sent to EPA or the States for review?

Mr. HILTY. Yes. As of the February 5, 1993, USDA had a total of 87 sites listed on the Federal Agency Hazardous Compliance Docket. Preliminary assessments for 61, six PA's have been reviewed and evaluated by the EPA. USDA agencies are currently on schedule for completing the remaining 26 PA's in accordance with established time frames.

RESOURCES REQUIRED

Mr. DURBIN. For the record, please provide a table showing the resources needed by USDA agencies to comply with requirements of the CERCLA and RCRA programs.

Mr. HILTY. I will be glad to provide this information for the record.

[The information follows:]

Enclosure 1

HAZARDOUS WASTE MANAGEMENT

AGRICULTURAL RESEARCH SERVICE

FISCAL YEAR 1994

FACILITY/LOCATION	INVESTIGATION	IMPLEMENTATION	PROBLEM AND/OR CORRECTIVE ACTION
Plum Island Animal Disease Center	$100,000	$700,000	UST removals and related activities, including remediation of contamination where necessary. A total of 42 tanks containing petroleum products. Work required to meet Federal and State requirements.
Clay Center, Nebraska		$308,000	Remediation of sites identified during SI.
East Lansing, Michigan		$140,000	Continuation of remediation work and monitoring at burial vault and other sites.
Subtotals	$100,000	$1,148,000	
	TOTAL	$1,248,000	

SOIL CONSERVATION SERVICE

ATTACHMENT 2

FY 1994 Submission for Hazardous Waste
(Budget authority in Thousands)

	FY 1994 (Budget)	FY 1995	FY 1996	FY 1997	FY 1998
		Planning Years			
I. Underground Storage Tanks (RCRA):					
A. FY 1994 Projects Requesting Planning Funds:	0				
B. FY 1994 Projects Requesting Funds for remedial Action:					
KINGSVILLE, TX PMC	35				
NACOGDOCHES, TX PMC	35				
TOTALS	70				
II. Abandoned Mines (CERCLA)					
None to report.					
III. OTHER RCRA					
A. FY 1994 Projects Requesting Planning Funds:					
B. FY 1994 Projects Requesting Funds for remedial Action:					
1. Improve pesticide storage facilities					
AMERICUS, GA PMC	40				
ABERDEEN, ID PMC	40				
BELTSVILLE, MD PMC	40				
TOTALS	120				
2. ELIMINATE WASTE PESTICIDE MIX AND RINSE WATER					
TUCSON, AZ PMC	45				
TOTALS	45				
Grand Total (all projects)	235				
Subtotal, FY 1993 Planning	0				
Subtotal, FY 1993 Remedial	235	0	0		

FOOD SAFETY AND INSPECTION SERVICE.

1994 Submission for Hazardous Waste	BY94
III. Other RCRA	
A. FY 1994 Projects Requesting Planning Funds:	
1. Lab Hazardous Waste Audits, Nationwide, FSIS	40,000
2. Investigations for Reduction of Haz Waste in Labs	200,000
Grand Total (All Projects)	240,000
Subtotal, FY 1994 Planning	240,000
Subtotal, FY 1994 Remedial	0

Enclosure 1

Rural Development Administration
FY 1994 Hazardous Waste Budget Request

The data for the Fiscal Year 1994 program budget request is based on anticipated needs.

Anticipated Needs by Project	Investigation	Implementation	Problem/Corrective Action
U.S. Army Corps of Engineers			
UST	$30,000.00	$20,000.00	Removal and Cleanup of UST's on acquired properties. Evaluate UST assessments ordered by lenders for loans with RDA loan guarantees.
Other CERCLA	$220,000.00	$30,000.00	Investigate, Cleanup, & Remediate hazardous wastes on acquired property, and evaluate hazardous waste assessments ordered by lenders for loans with RDA loan guarantees.
Totals	$250,000.00	$50,000.00	

ANIMAL AND PLANT HEALTH INSPECTION SERVICE

ENCLOSURE 2

FIVE YEAR HAZARDOUS WASTE MANAGEMENT PLAN

FY 1994 Submission for Hazardous Wastes (Budget Authority in thousands)	FY 1994 (Budget)
1) Remedial RCRA*	50.0
Varying locations, total	50.0
2) Remedial USTs**	0.0
Varying locations	0.0
UST Planning	0.0
Total	
Grand Total of all Projects	50.0

Attachment 1

Farmers Home Administration
FY 1994 Hazardous Waste Budget Request

The data for the Fiscal Year 1994 program budget request is based on the tentative resource levels for FY 1994 provided by OFM.

Anticipated Needs by Project	Investigation	Implementation	Problem/Corrective Action
U.S. Corps of Enginneers			
UST	$64,000.00	$189,000.00	Removal and Cleanup of UST's on acquired properties
Other CERCLA	$127,000.00	$383,000.00	Investigate, Cleanup, & Remediate Hazardous Wastes on acquired properties
TVA			
UST	$32,000.00	$94,500.00	Removal and Cleanup of UST's on acquired properties
Other CERCLA	$63,500.00	$191,500.00	Investigate, Cleanup, & Remediate Hazardous Wastes on acquired properties
National Contract			
UST	$32,000.00	$94,500.00	Removal and Cleanup of UST's on acquired properties
Other CERCLA	$63,500.00	$191,500.00	Investigate, Cleanup, & Remediate Hazardous Wastes on acquired properties
Totals	$382,000.00	$1,144,000.00	
Total UST's	$128,000.00	$378,000.00	
Total Other CERCLA	$254,000.00	$766,000.00	

HAZARDOUS WASTE MANAGEMENT
RESOURCE CONSERVATION AND RECOVERY ACT
FISCAL YEAR 1994

PROJECT NAME/FACILITY	Inv	Impl	PROBLEM AND/OR CORRECTIVE ACTION
Northern Region (R-1)			
LUST Cleanup Northern Region (01)	0.0	30.0	Final cleanup and monitoring of major LUST sites, Region-wide.
Pacific SW Region (R-5)			
Chuchupate LUST Cleanup Los Padres NF, Mt. Pinos RD	0.0	74.0	Ongoing cleanup of a site contaminated by a LUST
Harrison Gulch UST Shasta-Trinity NF	10.0	45.0	Investigation. Location and extent of contamination contingent on study results.
Various UST Sites Angeles NF	0.0	50.0	Cleanup of leaking UST's.
Pacific NW Region (R-6)			
Various UST Sites Wallowa-Whitman NF	0.0	35.0	Remove UST's.
Various UST Sites Umpqua NF	0.0	75.0	Remove UST's.
Hebo LUST	0.0	39.0	Complete cleanup of leaking UST.
Mapleton LUST	0.0	48.0	Complete cleanup of leaking UST.
Southern Region (R-8)			
Various UST Sites Region-wide (08)	0.0	80.0	Continued monitoring of LUST's.
Wakulla Fuel Cleanup	25.0	50.0	Cleanup of leaking gasoline UST.
Alaska Region (R-10)			
Kenai Lake WC Fuel Storage Tanks	0.0	30.0	Dispose/treat contaminated soils from LUST's.
Washington Office			
WO Project Support	0.0	27.0	WO project support and national program management.
TOTAL FY 1994 RCRA PROGRAM	35.0	583.0	(Total = $618.0)

HAZARDOUS WASTE MANAGEMENT
COMPREHENSIVE ENVIRONMENTAL RESPONSE, COMPENSATION, AND LIABILITY ACT
FISCAL YEAR 1994

PROJECT NAME/FACILITY	Inv	Impl	PROBLEM AND/OR CORRECTIVE ACTION
Northern Region (R-1) Discovery Program Northern Region (01)	200.0	0.0	Project discovery to determine which mineral impact sites may be appropriate for inclusion in CERCLA program.
Assessment/Inspection Program Northern Region (01)	100.0	0.0	Begin PA, SI, PRP searches and boundary surveys for sites identified as high priority during discovery program.
Coeur d'Alene River Watershed Idaho Panhandle NF	230.0	0.0	Prepare NRDA assessment report, economic analysis, and resource injury determination/quantification.
Clarkfork River Watershed Deerlodge NF	40.0	0.0	Prepare resource injury determination/quantification, draft NRDA plan, and economic analysis.
Region 1, CERCLA Total	570.0	0.0	
Rocky Mtn Region (R-2) Discovery Program Rocky Mountain Region (02)	200.0	0.0	Abandon mine discovery program with some PA/SI(s).
Assessment/Inspection Program Rocky Mountain Region (02)	150.0	0.0	Begin PA, SI, PRP searches at high priority sites identified during discovery program.
Bonanza Mining Area Rio Grande NF	200.0	0.0	Old mining area, remedial action.
Region 2, CERCLA Total	550.0	0.0	
Southwestern Region (R-3) Discovery Program Southwestern Region (03)	100.0	0.0	Region-wide discovery and onsite verification of mineral impact sites and HAZMAT disposal sites or dumps.

Continued...

PROJECT NAME/FACILITY	Inv	Impl	PROBLEM AND/OR CORRECTIVE ACTION
Assessment/Inspection Program Southwestern Region (03)	150.0	0.0	Begin PA, SI, PRP searches at high priority sites identified during discovery program.
Pecos CG's/Terrero Mine Site Santa Fe NF	0.0	575.0	Continued work on permanent solution for mine wastes used as road surfacing. Will be part of NPL site. Docketed site.
Lobo Canyon Dumpsite Cibola NF	0.0	100.0	Cleanup of FS pesticide dump.
Region 3, CERCLA Total	250.0	675.0	
Intermountain Region (R-4)			
Discovery Program Intermountain Region (04)	50.0	0.0	Region-wide discovery and onsite verification of mineral impact sites and HAZMAT disposal sites or dumps.
Region-wide post-treatment areas Intermountain Region (04)	0.0	50.0	Cleanup 10 Sites.
Assessment/Inspection Program Intermountain Region (04)	50.0	0.0	Begin PA, SI, PRP searches at high priority sites identified during the discovery program.
Blackbird Mine Salmon NF	800.0	0.0	NRDA
Buckskin Mine Humboldt NF	0.0	200.0	Cyanide barrel removal, tailings stabilization.
Rio Tinto Mine Humboldt NF	50.0	0.0	Work with state on remediation.
Gray Duan Mine Manti-LaSal NF	30.0	200.0	Removal assessment (EE/CA).
Missouri Mine Boise NF	50.0	0.0	Removal assessment (EE/CA).
Treasure Valley Mine Boise NF	50.0	0.0	Removal assessment (EE/CA).
Cinnabar Mine Payette NF	50.0	0.0	Site inspection for docketed site.

Continued...

PROJECT NAME/FACILITY	Inv	Impl	PROBLEM AND/OR CORRECTIVE ACTION
Stibnite Mine Payette NF	250.0	0.0	SI, Cost recovery, NRDA.
Fury-Grantsville Mine Toiyabe NF	0.0	75.0	Continuation of removal action started in FY 1993.
Region 4, CERCLA Total	1,380.0	525.0	
Pacific Southwest Region (R-5) Discovery Program Pacific Southwest Region	198.0	0.0	Identification and pre-screening of potential hazardous site.
Assessment/Inspection Program Pacific Southwest Region	150.0	0.0	PA, SI, PRP searches of high priority sites identified during discovery program.
Gibraltar Mine Los Padres NF	100.0	0.0	Site inspection.
Juniper Mine	100.0	0.0	Site inspection.
Black Bob Mine Los Padres NF, Mt. Pinos RD	50.0	0.0	Site investigation of hazardous materials.
Eel River AS Dump cleanup Mendocino NF, Covelo RD	0.0	70.0	Ongoing project. Admin/award contract to cleanup site, treat and dispose of contaminated soils, and treat any contaminated groundwater.
North Fork Sta Pesticide Bldng Sierra NF	0.0	175.0	Complete subsurface remediation.
Walker Mine Tailings Plumas NF	0.0	100.0	Stabilize tailings, create a wetland.
Region 5, CERCLA Total	598.0	345.0	

Continued...

PROJECT NAME/FACILITY	Inv	Impl	PROBLEM AND/OR CORRECTIVE ACTION
Pacific Northwest Region (R-6)			
Discovery Program Pacific Northwest Region	110.0	0.0	Identification and pre-screening of potential hazardous site.
White King/Lucky Lass Mines Fremont NF	328.0	0.0	A separate funding request for $6,800,000 has been made to USDA to begin remediation of this site.
Holden Mine	0.0	150.0	Complete slope stabilization, erosion control, and revegetation. Should complete project unless EPA requires additional work due to re-ranking. Should hear from EPA during FY 1993.
Shining Rock Mine cleanup	0.0	100.0	Remedial action for abandoned mine. PA/SI and interim removal action completed in FY 1991. EPA has deferred to state for action.
OKA Penta/Solvent cleanup's			
-- Eightmile Site "A" cleanup	0.0	50.0	Removal action for penta contaminated soils from an old post treatment site. PA/SI completed 91/92.
-- Eightmile Site "B" cleanup	0.0	50.0	Removal action for penta contaminated soils from an old post treatment site. PA/SI completed 91/92.
Lost Lake Site cleanup	0.0	75.0	Removal action for penta contaminated soils from an old post treatment site. This site is highest priority due to its proximity to groundwater. PA/SI completed in 91/92.
Tonasket RS Solvent cleanup	0.0	125.0	Removal action for solvent contaminated soils on the RS compound. This site is high priority due to its location in the community and its proximity to groundwater and wells. PA/SI completed in 91/92.

Continued...

PROJECT NAME/FACILITY	Inv	Impl	PROBLEM AND/OR CORRECTIVE ACTION
Stelico Work Center cleanups -- Site "A"	0.0	40.0	Removal action for penta/solvent contaminated soils next to a river. PA/SI completed in 91/92.
-- Site "B"	0.0	150.0	Removal Action for penta/solvent contaminated soils next to a river. PA/SI completed in 91/92.
Region 6, CERCLA Total	**438.0**	**740.0**	
Southern Region (R-8) Discovery Program Southern Region (08)	150.0	0.0	HAZMAT discovery and removal, Region-wide.
Assessment/Inspection Program Southern Region (08)	150.0	0.0	PA, SI, PRP searches of high priority sites identified during discovery program.
Columbia/Baker Dumps Apalachicola NF	250.0	0.0	RI/FS of confirmed contaminated sites.
Old Catahoula WC	0.0	30.0	Continue administration of cleanup.
Graham County/Swain County LF's Nantahala NF	30.0	0.0	Continue cost recovery activities.
Region 8, CERCLA Total	**580.0**	**30.0**	
Eastern Region (R-9) Discovery Program Eastern Region	150.0	0.0	ID/Discovery of potential CERCLA sites, Region-wide.
Assessment/Inspection Program Eastern Region	150.0	0.0	Begin PA, SI, PRP searches for high priority sites identified during discovery program.
Webb PCB site Wayne Hoosier NF	50.0	0.0	Investigation of PCB site. Dumped by individual with no resources to perform the cleanup.
DDT Disposal site Ottawa NF	70.0	0.0	Locate and evaluate site used for disposal of FS generated waste.

Continued...

PROJECT NAME/FACILITY	Inv	Impl	PROBLEM AND/OR CORRECTIVE ACTION
Branchville site Wayne Hoosier NF	0.0	105.0	Removal of DDT contaminated soil.
15 landfills (part 1) Chippewa NF	145.0		Continue PA/SIs on landfills.
Region 9, CERCLA Total	565.0	105.0	
Alaska Region (R-10) GRD mine/cannery sites Chugach National Forest	38.0	300.0	Removal action.
Discovery Program Alaska Region (10)	100.0	0.0	PA/SI activities.
Region 10, CERCLA Total	138.0	300.0	
Washington Office WO Project Support	120.0	0.0	WO project support and national program management

SUMMARY FY 1994 CERCLA PROGRAM

Investigation =	5,189.0	
Implementation =		2,720.0
Total =	$7,909.0	

COMMODITY CREDIT CORPORATION

Attachment # 2

Fiscal Year 1994 Submission for Hazardous Wastes a

	FY-1994
PROJECTS REQUESTING FUNDS FOR GROUNDWATER REMEDIATION ACTION	
FY 1994 REMEDIATION ACTIVITIES: Commodity Credit Corporation design and constructs an aquifer remediation system.	
1. Murdock	300,000
2. Utica	200,000
	$500,000
PLANNING: ALTERNATIVE WATER SUPPLY STUDY	
Site Investigation	
1. Hubbard	100,000
2. Clay Center	100,000
3. Adams	100,000
4. Humphrey	100,000
5. Agra	100,000
	$500,000
PLANNING: ALTERNATIVE WATER SUPPLY EFFORTS	
Provide alternative supply such as: Packed Tower Air Stripper, Activated Carbon Filters, etc.	
Sites dependentent of AWSS results.	$300,000
PLANNING: EXTENDED SITE CHARACTERIZATION	
1. Murdock	100,000
2 York	500,000
3. Aurora	80,000
4. Potwin	80,000
5. Utica	200,000
3. Bruno	700,000
3. Navarre	100,000
	$1,700,000
SUBTOTAL REMEDIATION:	500,000
SUBTOTAL PLANNING:	2,500,000
TOTAL	$3,000,000

Mr. DURBIN. Thank you very much. Mr. Skeen?
Mr. SKEEN. Thank you, Mr. Chairman.

RESTRUCTURING

Mr. Hilty, I want to apologize to you and your colleagues for being late, but I had to do a study on the 14th Street Bridge this morning and, boy, I tell you, what a mess. Talking about reorganization, wonder if we couldn't send some of the experts into the City of Washington or the District of Washington and get the traffic situation cleared up a little bit.

I notice that in your statement you talk about the restructuring. Would you agree with the bromide, that it costs money to save money?

Mr. HILTY. It does.

IRM ACTIVITIES

Mr. SKEEN. Are you working with the IRM in this restructuring and how is that going? I know this may be a little redundant and I apologize for that.

Mr. HILTY. Questions about IRM are never redundant, Mr. Skeen, because that is one of our finest tools and one of our areas of greatest opportunity. You weren't here at the very start because you were having your meditation period on the 14th Street Bridge, but I invited—

Mr. SKEEN. I am going to take up Buddhism.

Mr. HILTY. Well, I will be part of your group, because I have always respected you and I will respect you in your new role as well.

Mr. SKEEN. Contemplate our windshields.

Mr. HILTY. I extended an invitation to Chairman Durbin, that I would to you, to visit a lady named Sally Farr, in her dining room near Goodland, Kansas, Mrs. Farr is managing her 4,000 acres of farmland through use of a computer in her dining room linked to USDA offices in a county office in western Kansas.

We look on IRM as really our lodestone and our trip into the future. In the last week or so, we have been using in our discussions in USDA, the idea that IRM programs through USDA can be the REA of the 1990s. Just as REA really lit up the rural America that you and I remember from our youth.

Mr. SKEEN. Talking about data networking?

Mr. HILTY. Yes, data networking, communications.

Mr. SKEEN. Absolutely, you have already practiced a great deal of that in your financial center.

Mr. HILTY. Yes, yes. And we have much more that we can do. I would invite all of you to visit various test sites. Rockingham County, Virginia.

Mr. SKEEN. What was the lady's name?

Mr. HILTY. Sally Farr.

Mr. SKEEN. You think that she would welcome us?

Mr. HILTY. Well, she welcomed me, Mr. Skeen. She would certainly welcome a distinguished guy like you.

Mr. SKEEN. We might take you up on that.

Mr. HILTY. That is in your good friend Mr. Roberts' district, in the western part of his district.

Mr. SKEEN. We will take him along. Sally would love to see him, too, I think.

STATUS OF RESTRUCTURING

Let me ask you a question about this restructuring and consolidation. I am very interested in the official stance of USDA with regard to restructuring. I applaud you for thinking in terms of streamlining because it is a huge, huge organization. I understand, too, that you are going to start with the Washington office first. Yet, most of the publicity has been in regard to closing field offices. I am very wary of what may come out of that, but my stance has always been, if you're going to start restructuring and become or efficient, start with the head offices or the regional offices firste

How is that doing? And what is the cost increment involved in just the primary Department's restructure?

Mr. HILTY. How is it going? Clearly that is Secretary Espy's first focus. He set it forth when he appeared before this subcommittee in mid-February and said that Washington must be simplified and streamlined first.

His internal efforts since then have been direct and forceful, and we understand very clearly that is his primary first focus. He reiterated it when he appeared before the Senate earlier this week. And all of the plans that we are making are being directed towards the general restructuring ideas that he laid before this subcommittee and that he laid before other Congressional Members at a private breakfast in the Department late in January, looking towards changing assignments of Under Secretaries and Assistant Secretaries, realigning the responsibilities of the field service agencies, for a clearer definition and delivery of services to the farmers. That is moving rapidly.

It will depend, as I suggested in response earlier to Mr. Durbin, partly on necessary statutory change in assignment of some responsibilities and in the creation of some Under Secretaryships and other offices. But that is one that he hopes to have in place as rapidly as possible, so that his newly chosen, newly confirmed team of Assistant and Under secretaries will be able to work with the permanent structure.

Once that is achieved, then he hopes to move also to the questions of what necessary restructure may be needed elsewhere in the Department. But headquarters is his level of concentration.

COST SAVINGS

I do not have specific cost-saving figures to lay before you today, Mr. Skeen, because the final shape——

Mr. SKEEN. But you anticipate some savings in it.

Mr. HILTY. We do anticipate that there can be some savings through administrative consolidations.

WORK FORCE DIVERSITY

Mr. SKEEN. Appreciate that.

Let's talk about your Work Force Diversity. I know that is an ongoing program. What is the progress in that area?

Mr. HILTY. Okay.

Mr. SKEEN. The Equal Opportunity Program and some of the others, your work force diversity efforts.

Mr. HILTY. I would like to make a two-part response to that question, Mr. Skeen. Questions of that sort come to the heart of the activities of any Department of Federal Government. In the two-part response I would give to you, equal opportunity questions would be divided between the future, the present and the immediate past. The future clearly is in the hands of Secretary Espy, whose own record in that field is clear, whose intentions and determinations are quite clear.

SECRETARY ESPY'S CIVIL RIGHTS STATEMENT

I think the best way I could describe that is to share with you a few things from a statement that he made for all members of the Department of Agriculture within the last two weeks. I would like to take a couple of direct quotes from that, if I may.

"My goal is to make the Department of Agriculture a place where equal opportunity for all Americans is assured and where promoting civil rights is essential to employee and managerial success." This is a direct quote from Secretary Espy's civil rights statement.

I think a key phrase there, Mr. Skeen, is "managerial success." Because in putting it that way, Secretary Espy really does say to every manager within the Department, this is a high part of your portfolio and your effectiveness as a manager will be judged in great measure by your success as an advocate for and a manager of equal opportunity and civil rights.

It is a clear statement of secretarial intention and expectation, and it puts accountability where it must be, on managers.

Mr. SKEEN. There was a high consciousness level?

Mr. HILTY. There was a high consciousness level. He says later in this statement: "We will eliminate discrimination in our program delivery system, reach out to groups which have historically been neglected and insure that we are inclusive rather than exclusive in all aspects of our program delivery."

I think that is a highly significant statement within this broader statement, because it does identify one of the areas, perhaps *the* area, where USDA has historically been weakest in its delivery of services to its constituency across the country. Program delivery within USDA has been subject to discrimination in many areas of the country and many different types of programs, through many different agencies, and clearly the Secretary's statement says this will stop.

Then he concludes by saying: "This statement is a personal commitment to take the actions necessary to ensure implementation. Each employee at every level will be held personally accountable for her or his performance in ensuring equal opportunity and civil rights."

When he says "every level," he means truly that, his level, my level, my successor's level, and every level throughout the Department. So this is a clear and strong statement that identifies the areas of concern, that identifies the depth and the breadth of the commitment. So that is the future of this field within USDA .

WORK FORCE DIVERSITY INITIATIVES

Now if I could give the second part of my answer and talk about some things that we have underway now, three of which we have initiated within the last two years. One is a project that has been underway for the last five years. These involve our work with the 1890s Land Grant universities, our work with the Hispanic American colleges and universities, and our work with the Senior Executive Service Candidate Development Program.

1890 SCHOLARSHIP PROGRAM

We have established within the last year, and are selecting now, scholarship winners for the 1890 Scholarship Program. USDA will provide at least two full scholarships to each of these 17 universities fully in cooperation with each of the 1890s Land Grant universities.

This is the first scholarship program of its sort ever undertaken at the Federal level, and this is its first year. We will have at least 34 students each year entering this program. By four years from now, we will have 136 students on full scholarships at all of these 1890s universities, a program that will continue and will grow.

So that is a major commitment to bring bright young minority students into the academic ranks, eventually into employment of USDA.

Mr. SKEEN. Is there a follow-through on individual responsibilities amongst those individuals that are recipients of that program?

Mr. HILTY. Yes, sir, there is. There are employment arrangements with USDA so they would work with our various agencies during the summer and then as their careers sharpen, as they complete their academic education, there would be employment opportunities thereafter.

HISPANIC COLLEGES AND UNIVERSITIES

We have begun in the last 18 months, under the strong chairmanship of John Lee, who is the Administrator of Economic Research Service, a similar arrangement with the Hispanic American colleges and universities, a much more difficult thing to undertake, because we do not have the statutory relationship to those universities that we do with the less numerous 1890s Land Grant Universities.

But we have a number of innovative programs that we are starting to develop, as we have recognized both the needs and the opportunities to reach out to the universities with strong Hispanic American enrollments, several of which are in your State and in your district. Others, I believe, are in the district of Mr. Pastor, who also serves on this subcommittee.

SES CANDIDATE DEVELOPMENT

And then finally, we have underway a Senior Executive Candidate Development Program, selection of and training of the people most likely to be chosen for permanent Career Senior Executive opportunities in the Department from now into the future.

Our first class was selected last summer. Fifty-six percent of that class was white male compared to eighty-seven percent of the current Senior Executive Service at USDA that is white male. Five of the 20 persons selected for the fast track in that class were black. That is 25 percent of the people in the fast track, and a far higher percentage than we have of black employees now in the Senior Executive Service.

The second cycle of selection will be completed late next week and early the following week. The figures that we are generating now suggest that another highly qualified class, much more broadly representative of all of America, again will be chosen.

Those are four things I think are very, very promising for USDA: the working relationships with black universities, with Hispanic American universities, the scholarship program for minorities with the 1890s universities, and an invigorated, new approach to selecting future leadership of the Department in a more representative way. All those are highly promising. That is part of the present.

But there is a great, great distance to travel. The statement set out by Secretary Espy emphasizes that there is a great distance. It emphasizes the intensity of his commitment to see that we not only travel that distance, but we travel it a heck of a lot faster than we have ever traveled it before.

Mr. SKEEN. It is a strong dedication, I know, in the Department.

HAZARDOUS WASTE MANAGEMENT

Let's talk about hazardous waste and your commitment there. I understand you received $39 million in the 1992 budget in obligated funds. What are your plans for the expenditures in this category in 1993 and 1994?

Also, give me some idea how you coordinate with DOE, EPA and some of the other agencies.

Mr. HILTY. The $39 million, alas, has been reduced to $16 million in the budget that is before us. That represents a peeling back that was done as part of the appropriations process. The history behind that is that we had not spent as rapidly as we should have funds that had been allocated for those purposes in earlier years. So some money was peeled.

Mr. SKEEN. The authorization level is much greater than your appropriated request?

Mr. HILTY. Yes, yes. When we discovered that we were not spending as rapidly as we should, late in calendar 1991, and early in calendar 1992, we undertook a new and much more aggressive program. It began with quarterly, then monthly and then finally in the concluding days of that fiscal year, weekly reports from all of the agencies in the field about all the projects that had not been obligated.

So in the fiscal year that concluded September 30th, we obligated all save roughly $2 million of the approximately $39 million that was available. The great part of the money that was not obligated was because of a last minute dispute between local and State authorities in Texas involving a project that we were ready to commit for, but they could not define the terms that were acceptable to them. But because we had these large carry-overs from years before 1992, much less money was appropriated to us for fiscal year 1993. Hence, the $16 million that we are dealing with right now.

The aggressive approach that we have taken in reminding the agencies of their responsibilities to commit, to obligate and to spend the funds as rapidly as they are available, will continue. I would hope personally that chances would arise for those funds to grow again, because we have scattered needs all across the country of many kinds.

COORDINATION WITH DOE AND EPA

We do seek to coordinate with Energy, with EPA, and to be very, very responsive to the regulations that come down from them. And we find that our inventory of sites that we must be concerned with seems always to be growing, either as new law is written or as, in some cases, we acquire property through Farmers Home foreclosures, or other means that may be hazardous waste sites that we were not aware of.

HAZARDOUS WASTE PREVENTION

Mr. SKEEN. Let me ask you this. How much interest is there in your Department in preventative-type work in hazardous waste, as well as clean-up work? Is there a difference between the two obligations, and I know one is prospective and the other is retrospective?

Mr. HILTY. Yes, I think that interest has grown apace with the coming of environmental awareness all across the country. Many of the projects that we have, as you know, are ones that go back to disposal practices of the 1930s, 1940s and early 1950s. I think that we in the 1970s, 1980s and 1990s, have been as a society and as a Department, more aware of these concerns and have done what we could to prevent them.

I think that there is at every level of the Department a much greater awareness that we must stop all that we can now, while we fix what has been done before. But the point that you make that comes to my mind is that even through our hazardous waste management activities now, we might well undertake a hazardous waste management education thrust as well.

Mr. SKEEN. Thanks for your responses.

Thank you, Mr. Chairman.

Mr. DURBIN. Thank you, Mr. Skeen.

Mr. Pastor could not be with us today, but he has some questions that he would like answered for the record.

[The questions and responses follow:]

WORKFORCE DIVERSITY

Mr. PASTOR. What means have you developed to bolster workforce diversity goals within the Department of Agriculture at a time when you are looking to reduce the total number of employees within the Department?

RESPONSE. There are several examples. A year ago, we identified the probability that 40 percent of our Senior Executive Service employees would be retiring in the next few years. We selected and have begun training 90 candidates as replacements and are in the process of finalizing the selection of another 90 at the present time. Over 27 percent of the first group of candidates were women and 18.7 percent were minorities. This compares to our present Senior Executive Service workforce which is 9.5 percent women and 8.6 percent minority.

Most of the diversity in our workforce is in our younger employees at the lower grade levels so as we begin to plan for downsizing, we are planning to accomplish it primarily by attrition of older employees who are interested in retiring. We will be seeking ways to avoid use of reduction in force which has an adverse impact on younger employees. In cooperation with the Office of Personnel Management, we will be offering Optional Early Retirement to the maximum extent possible. For example, we recently obtained authority to offer Early Retirement to 351 employees in the Food and Nutrition Service.

Also, this is the first year of our USDA/1890 National Scholars Program. Forty-three top students have been selected for scholarships at these 17 Historically Black Land-Grant Institutions. This program should be a source of both quality and diversity for our future workforce.

Finally, although we anticipate the number of our summer interns to decline, we hope to increase the number of cooperative education students. Cooperative education students, unlike the summer interns, are more likely to enter our workforce.

Mr. PASTOR. In particular, what steps are you planning to take to help you achieve greater diversity in the Department's workforce in the near future? Are you planning to implement recruitment efforts and affirmative action initiatives to ensure the department's workforce becomes representative of the nation's population? And, how do you propose to enhance your outreach efforts and programs already in place at the post-secondary school level to foster minority interest in agricultural careers?

RESPONSE. We have several programs in effect to assist us in greater workforce diversity in the near future. We hope to reap the benefit of relationships we have been cultivating with the 1890 Historically Black Land-Grant Institutions for the past 4 years with the entry of more minority students into the permanent USDA workforce. Similarly, activities and partnerships with HACU will begin providing students for permanent employment within the next couple of years.

Some of our innovative programs with educational institutions include:

a. USDA/1890 National Scholars Program.—A program to provide full scholarships and a cooperative education appointment for 4 years to outstanding high school graduating seniors who go on to attend an 1890 Institution. The cooperating university provides room and board.

b. 1890 Liaison Officers.—Full-time USDA employees located on the campus of 17 Historically Black Colleges and Universities (1890 Historically Black Land Grant Institutions). A principal duty is recruitment.

c. Summer Intern Program.—Paid internship experiences with USDA agencies involving substantive work assignments for college students during the summer months. USDA obtained authorization to provide certain subsistence expenses for Cooperative Education and Summer Intern students working for the Forest Services.

d. Cooperative Education (Co-op Ed) in Residence Program.—Co-op Ed Students employed on campus who, after training, recruit fellow students to work at USDA.

e. Hispanic Serving Institution (HSI) Placement Officer Workshops.—Regional workshops with HSI Placement Officers to provide information about USDA student employment programs and career opportunities.

f. Summer-only Waiver for Cooperative Education Students.—A waiver granted by the Office of Personnel Management to permit the use of summer employment only as credit toward necessary hours of work experience before conversion to permanent employment upon graduation.

g. Partnerships in Education.—A policy authorizing administrative time for employees to teach, tutor, or provide USDA career information in schools throughout the country.

h. Intergovernmental Personnel Act (IPA).—An effort is being made to increase the use of Intergovernmental Personnel Act assignments between USDA agency staff and college and university faculty. The fifty percent matching required is waived for Historically Black Colleges and Universities.

We plan to enhance our outreach efforts and programs at post-secondary schools by expanding the National Scholars program to other education institutions, and by conducting a National Conference on "Getting More Minority Youths into Agriculture."

In addition, the Department is working vigorously to improve its diversity with respect to employees with disabilities. Some programs in this area include:

a. Operation Enable which is a program for recruitment, training, and retention of people with disabilities.

b. Sign Language Interpreter, a full-time sign language interpreter has been hired at the USDA headquarters complex to provide interpretive services for deaf employees.

c. Ceiling Exemption for Employment of People with Disabilities.—The Office of Management and Budget has granted exemptions for employment of people with disabilities within USDA for up to 2 years of employment under excepted appointing authorities.

Mr. DURBIN. Mr. Hilty and the panel, I want to thank you all for joining us. We will be in touch with you, as we start the mark up process, to discuss more of the details on reorganization and a few other aspects. Thank you very much for joining us today.

CLOSING REMARKS

Mr. HILTY. Mr. Chairman, could I make just a very brief concluding statement?

Mr. DURBIN. Certainly.

Mr. HILTY. I have appeared now before this subcommittee three years, before three different Chairmen. Mr. Whitten one year, and now Mr. McHugh was the Acting Chairman one year, and now yourself. I have had the unique opportunity to appear here representing two Secretaries, one Republican, one Democrat.

I have had the opportunity, as you know, and Mr. Skeen knows, of serving long on the staff of the committee where you began your congressional careers. So I have had the chance to participate in and prepare for hearings of this sort, both from that side of the podium and from this somewhat more focused and sometimes less comfortable side of the podium.

But I have found both sides to be uniquely educational. And having had the opportunity to prepare from both sides of the dais, I realize even more how important they are. Not only for the exchange of information from me to you, and the exchange of information from you to me, that comes through the range of your questions, but also for the preparation that we make, not only as Assistant Secretaries, but for senior staff such as Dr. Wilson, Mr. David and Mr. Dewhurst, the preparation that we make is equally important.

I have a heightened appreciation for that and a heightened appreciation for the role of staff preparation and member preparation. So the hearings serve far more purpose than just the dialog that we undertake today.

Thank you.

Mr. DURBIN. Thank you very much for your contribution and for all the people who have been with us in this first panel.

Thank you.

Mr. SKEEN. I will second that.

BIOGRAPHICAL SKETCH
IRWIN T. DAVID

Mr. Irwin T. David joined the Department of Agriculture as its first Deputy Chief Financial Officer (DCFO) on December 7, 1992.

As the DCFO, Mr. David is responsible for working with the Chief Financial Officer to implement the provisions of the Chief Financial Officers Act of 1990. The basic thrust of that Act is to provide financial and performance information to assist Departmental and Agency policy makers and managers in their decision making processes for both current operations and financial investments.

Mr. David, who is a CPA, spent most of his career with the public accounting firm of Touche Ross and Co. As a management consulting partner with the firm, he consulted with Federal, state, and local government agencies on financial management, computer systems, accounting and budgeting, and long-range planning activities. In addition, Mr. David was National Director of State and Local Government Services for Touche Ross and Co., and its successor firm, Deloitte and Touche. Since leaving Deloitte and Touche and just prior to joining USDA, Mr. David was Senior Vice President of Apogee Research Inc., a management consulting firm assisting Federal, state, and local governments in financial management areas.

Mr. David received his Bachelors Degree in Chemistry from the University of Illinois and a Masters Degree in Industrial Administration from Carnegie Institute of Technology. He is a CPA in Illinois and Washington, D.C. and is active in many professional organizations.

OFFICE OF THE SECRETARY
AND
DEPARTMENTAL ADMINISTRATION

Statement of Charles R. Hilty,
Assistant Secretary for Administration
Before the House Subcommittee on Agriculture,
Rural Development, Food and Drug Administration, and Related Agencies

Mr. Chairman and members of the Subcommittee, I am pleased to discuss the fiscal 1994 budget request for Department level and Department-wide USDA activities. I will be covering appropriations requests for Departmental Administration, GSA Rental Payments and Building Operations, Advisory Committees, Hazardous Waste Management, the Working Capital Fund, and the Office of the Secretary. With me today to ensure that you are fully informed and that all your questions are answered are Irwin T. David, the Deputy Chief Financial Officer, Larry Wilson, the Director of the Office of Finance and Management, and Connie Gillam, the Budget Officer for Departmental Administration, and Steve Dewhurst, the Department's Budget Officer.

DEPARTMENTAL MANAGEMENT

The Department is responsible for the broadest range of program activities of any civilian Federal department. We serve our "customers" through a diverse family of USDA's programs, touching all citizens--farmers, ranchers, producers, consumers, and children--daily in every state and county. These programs must be managed in an efficient, effective, and fair manner. It is the responsibility of the Departmental staff offices to help the Secretary, the Under and Assistant Secretaries, and agency policy officials make sure USDA's administrative management program meets these goals. The Departmental Administration staff activities are funded through the Departmental Administration and related appropriations. These activities cover policy related and operational areas ranging from human resources, civil rights, equal opportunity, financial management, information technology management to the operation of the physical facilities in the USDA headquarters complex.

Before I describe the current activities within Departmental Administration, I would like to take a moment to share with you some of the philosophy and emphasis Secretary Espy has brought to the Department, particularly as it affects Departmental Administration. Secretary Espy is interested in management improvement and has taken steps outlined in the 1994 budget request to guarantee continued proficient management at USDA. Secretary Espy is committed to the idea of "one stop shopping" for the customers of USDA. He does not want American farmers chasing all over the county or the State to obtain vital information from USDA. He does not want them buried in red tape and paperwork. This belief is reflected in initiatives such as the Info Share program, under the Office of Information Resources Management, which will consolidate three separate field office information systems to provide "one stop shopping" to farmers nationwide. Info Share is an example of programs under development at the Department where innovative new technologies and ideas are being invested to better serve our program recipients, provide accurate, timely and concise performance information to empower program decisionmakers at every level and reduce administrative costs. Departmental Administration has a large part to play in achieving those goals for the American farmer. I would like now to give you some of the details.

CURRENT ACTIVITIES

USDA's central **Office of Personnel**, or OP, the first personnel office in government, was established in 1925. It is the central policy, oversight and guidance office for all USDA agencies' personnel offices. OP also provides direct personnel support to the Office of the Secretary, Departmental Staff Offices, the General Counsel, and the Office of the Inspector General. For fiscal year 1993 about 26% of the Departmental Administration appropriation is used to fund OP's activities. OP's plans for fiscal year 1993 focus on expanding and improving the diversity of the USDA workforce, developing competent leadership for the future, and improving the quality and effectiveness of Departmental personnel systems and data bases.

The **Office of Finance and Management**, or OFM, provides central oversight and guidance within the Department for financial management systems, accounting, Federal assistance, management controls audit resolution, management and productivity improvement, occupational safety and health, and for management of the National Finance Center (NFC). The Director of OFM serves as the Department's Management Improvement Officer and Comptroller of the Working Capital Fund. OFM provides support to the Chief Financial Officer in carrying out provisions of the Chief Financial Officers Act. In addition, OFM provides budget, accounting and fiscal services for the Office of the Secretary and departmental staff offices. The Departmental Administration Budget Officer, Ms. Gillam, at the table with me today, is located in this staff office. Approximately 17% of the Departmental Administration appropriation funds OFM activities. Major initiatives for fiscal year 1993 are the implementation of the provisions of the Chief Financial Officers Act, the improvement of the central accounting and administrative systems, and strengthening accountability for USDA financial and management oversight and improvement efforts.

The **Office of Operations**, or OO, is the housekeeping organization within Departmental Administration. It provides Departmental policy oversight and guidance of management of real and personal property, procurement, contracts, transportation, supply, motor vehicles, aircraft, energy conservation and recycling programs. OO also is responsible for Department-wide information systems that monitor agency activities in these areas. OO provides agencies in the Washington, D.C. area with certain centralized administrative services, including headquarters facilities management, mail processing, acquisition and procurement services, distribution of supplies, forms, and publications, copy and reproduction services, shipping and receiving, imprest funds, warehouse services, and support of the Office of the Secretary. Funding OO's activities takes approximately 12% of the Departmental Administration appropriation. For fiscal year 1993, OO has established initiatives to assist USDA agencies in improving program accessibility to persons with disabilities and recycle reusable materials. In addition, OO is working to improve the efficiency and effectiveness of its operations through improvement in its organization structure and increased automation.

The **Office of Information Resources Management**, or OIRM, is our central information management and information technology systems planning, acquisition, and oversight arm. Through its data centers, it provides USDA agencies with direct ADP services. Twenty-three percent of the Departmental Administration appropriation supports OIRM's fiscal year 1993 activities. Two major efforts within OIRM merit special mention. The Agency Liaison Officer or ALO program is designed to improve Departmental oversight and coordination of agency IRM planning, budgeting, technology implementation and assessment, to provide a primary point of contact between the agencies and OIRM, and to provide an interface with OMB and other external oversight agencies. This critical oversight program is aimed specifically at guiding the development of USDA information systems to new levels of excellence in terms of program delivery and cost effectiveness. The USDA Info Share program I introduced earlier, is designed to promote "one stop shopping" by simultaneously reducing the amount of red tape and paperwork farmers face when doing business with USDA and improving public access, providing more accurate and timely performance data to program decisionmakers, and reducing the life cycle costs of the next generation of USDA information systems.

The **Office of Advocacy and Enterprise**, or OAE, is the Department's central civil rights and equal opportunity oversight office. OAE programs and activities account for approximately 14% of the Departmental Administration appropriation. During fiscal year 1993, OAE will continue to concentrate on eliminating discrimination in the delivery of USDA programs, improving the employment opportunities for minorities and women in USDA programs, and improving the Department's minority and small business procurement performance.

In the administrative law area, the **Office of Administrative Law Judges**, or OALJ, holds hearings and renders decisions on appeals of administrative decisions made in several USDA agency program operations. The **Judicial Officer**, or JO, renders final administrative decisions on appeals to the Secretary. OALJ and JO account for 6% of the Departmental Administration appropriation. Their main goal for fiscal year 1993 is to render fair and impartial decisions in a timely manner.

Emergency Programs, or EP, formerly part of the Office of Personnel, is a separate budget activity beginning in fiscal year 1993 to emphasize its importance as the Department's central contact point for emergency programs and emergency preparedness both within USDA as well as with other Federal, State and local agencies, and international agencies. This activity accounts for approximately 1% of the Departmental Administration appropriation. During fiscal year 1993, EP will develop plans and issue necessary guidelines and handbooks that will facilitate USDA agency planning, preparation for and response to disasters and emergency situations.

DEPARTMENTAL ADMINISTRATION BUDGET REQUEST

The budget request for Departmental Administration for FY 1994 is $27,298,000, an increase of $1.5 million above the fiscal year 1993 current estimate of $25,798,000. I know that in this era of deficit reduction and down-sizing of Federal programs it is difficult for this Committee to support budget increases, especially for staff organizations. However, I see compelling reasons to support this increase. Departmental staff offices are small, labor intensive activities. Over a third of this requested increase, $512,000, is for annualization of 1993 pay costs. The absorption of pay costs and inflation required in previous years makes it impossible to absorb further pay costs without harm to the oversight and operation of the Department's administrative management program activities.

The remaining $988,000 are primarily to strengthen financial management and financial systems to meet the requirements of the CFO Act and to expand Departmental information technology activities supporting farm service, research, natural resources, food safety and inspection programs, as well as other USDA agency programs providing direct services to consumers, farmers, ranchers, and other USDA clientele through the Info Share program.

The increase for financial management will be invested in improving USDA's financial management systems to provide modern, up-to-date systems that have the internal control mechanisms in place to prevent fraud, to assure that the award of loans, deficiency payments, and other forms of aid go to those that qualify and that program qualifications are upheld.

Farmers and all other USDA program recipients should be able to deal with a Department that is efficiently managed and responsive to their needs. They should not be overburdened with government forms and red tape. Other parts of the increase will be used to design and implement automated data systems under Info Share that are user friendly, integrate data bases, support requirements across several agencies, encourage one-stop shopping, and provide the Congress, the oversight agencies, and USDA management up to date data on the cost of our delivery of services, and measures of program success.

RENTAL PAYMENTS AND BUILDING OPERATIONS

The larger of these two appropriations, Rental Payments, finances a portion of the Department's payment to the General Services Administration for space rental and related costs. In fiscal year 1994, the Department requests $50,503,000 for Rental Payments to pay for its space, including $5 million for non-recurring repairs. The request provides that the funds for non-recurring repairs remain available until expended to accommodate the lengthy contracting process associated with these repairs and the extent of the work to be performed.

The Building Operations and Maintenance appropriation funds the Departmental staff and support services to operate and maintain the downtown Headquarters complex. For fiscal year 1994 the Building Operations and Maintenance request is $25,581,000, a net decrease of $119,000 from the fiscal year 1993 level of $25,700,000. This change reflects increases of $569,000 for non-salary inflation and $104,000 for annualization of the fiscal year 1993 pay raise which are offset by a decrease of $792,000 to meet deficit reduction targets.

ADVISORY COMMITTEES

In the fiscal year 1983 Appropriations Act, the Congress established a single appropriation for USDA Advisory Committees other than those funded from the Forest Service appropriation or user fees. The fiscal year 1994 USDA Advisory Committee request of $952,000 is the same level as that appropriated for Advisory Committees in fiscal year 1993. Executive Order 12838 calls for a one-third decrease in the number of advisory committees that are not mandated by legislation and justifications for continuation of all statutory and non-statutory committees. We are currently conducting the review that will accomplish the President's directive. Once the review is completed you will be provided a revised list of the committees proposed for funding during fiscal year 1994.

HAZARDOUS WASTE MANAGEMENT

USDA requests $16,000,000 for the Hazardous Waste Management program in fiscal year 1994. This level of funding will allow USDA's agencies to establish a minimum program level and to initiate cleanup activities at the most critical USDA sites with problems caused by past uncontrolled disposal practices.

The safe disposal of hazardous waste materials remains a serious challenge to the Nation. Past disposal methods often created serious environmental problems that now require costly corrective actions to remedy. The fiscal year 1994 budget continues USDA's program efforts to comply with the Comprehensive Environmental Response, Compensation and Liability Act and the Resource Conservation and Recovery Act.

Resources from the central hazardous waste management fund are allocated to the Departmental agencies according to priority needs. Funds are available until expended. Although there have been past problems in obligating funds in the year in which they were made available, we have improved oversight of the account to prevent this from recurring. For fiscal year 1992, we obligated over 95 percent of the $39 million available.

WORKING CAPITAL FUND

Our Departmental Working Capital Fund--WCF for short--was established in 1943. In the 50 years since its establishment, it has served as a financing mechanism for the acquisition of large-scale assets, such as mainframe computers, and for the provision of centrally-managed administrative services. The Fund allows users to take advantage of the economies of scale that come with centralized management. It also makes affordable to smaller USDA agencies services that would be much more expensive if those agencies had to provide them on their own. Further, the Fund provides the means to acquire and finance large scale procurement, recovering the costs through depreciation charges to users over the useful life of the asset acquired.

This year, the Fund supports 21 activities located in 6 Departmental staff offices--Finance and Management, Public Affairs, Information Resources Management, Operations, Personnel, and Executive Secretariat. Except for the National Finance Center in New Orleans, Louisiana; the National Computer Center/Mainframe office in Kansas City, Missouri; the National Computer Center/Network Management Services and Applications Design offices in Fort Collins, Colorado; and the Consolidated Forms and Publications Distribution Center in Landover, Maryland, which houses Central Supply Stores, Central Supply Forms, and Central Excess Property Operation warehousing activities, all other WCF activities are located in Washington, D.C..

The current estimate of fiscal year 1993 operating costs is approximately $174 million. Capital acquisition funds add another $19 million. The total operating cost figure reflects the growth in the volume of goods and services financed through the Fund over the past several years. The true measures of efficiency in the Fund -- unit costs of service -- show that this increased volume of service is being provided at a reduction in unit costs over the same period.

As an example, the payroll/personnel system operated by our National Finance Center and the IBM system mainframe computing operation in Kansas City are the two largest services supported by our Working Capital Fund. This year they will account for approximately 43 percent of estimated total costs. Efficiencies achieved in these areas, measured in the unit costs that users pay for service, will have a significant impact on total Fund productivity. We anticipate that the unit cost of payrolling an employee through our payroll/personnel system will be more than 13 percent below the FY 1990 level. Unit costs for computer processing services on IBM equipment at our National Computer Center, measured in dollars per central processing unit minute, will be reduced by about 32 percent over the same period.

At a time when the President is asking those of us overseeing administrative services to reduce costs, I am pleased with what has been accomplished through our WCF. Just as we have programs aimed at providing a responsive menu of services and "one stop shopping" to better serve farmers, WCF activities provide USDA and other federal agencies with responsive and extremely cost effective support services. I am committed to making further contributions to help achieve the President's cost reduction goals.

OFFICE OF THE SECRETARY

The offices of the Secretary provide policy oversight and guidance for the Department and maintain relationships with agricultural organizations and others in the development of USDA programs. OSEC also oversees special projects that are conducted at the behest of the Congress. These projects include short-term studies, investigations, and research on matters affecting the Department or its constituents.

OSEC currently is made up of the Secretary, Deputy Secretary, two Under and seven Assistant Secretaries and their staffs. Each OSEC office is financed from a separate appropriation--eleven separate appropriation accounts in all--most less than $600,000 and 6 FTE's. The restrictions placed on the flexibility of the Secretary to assign and redirect resources to meet top level USDA program oversight and direction needs or to meet an emergency limit his ability to establish priorities and shift resources necessary to meet the changing conditions of American agriculture. In the interest of efficiency and flexibility, we again ask that these accounts be combined into a single appropriation.

Thank you for the opportunity to speak today about our plans. I would be pleased to respond to your questions.

OFFICE OF THE SECRETARY

Purpose Statement

The Secretary of Agriculture, assisted by the Deputy Secretary, Under Secretaries and Assistant Secretaries, and members of their immediate staffs, directs and coordinates the work of the Department. This involves providing policy direction for all areas of the Department's responsibilities including research; educational and regulatory activities; nutrition, conservation and farm programs; and forestry and international agriculture. It also involves maintaining relationships with organizations and others in the development of programs, and maintaining liaison with the Executive Office of the President and members of Congress on all matters pertaining to Departmental policy.

The Board of Contract Appeals is a reimbursable activity in the Office of the Secretary. It is the authorized representative of the Secretary of Agriculture to make final administrative determinations for the Department of Agriculture in appeals handled under the Secretary's regulations.

The general authority of the Secretary to supervise and control the work of the Department is contained in the Organic Act (7 U.S.C. 2201-2202). The delegation of regulatory functions to the Department employees and authorization of appropriations to carry out these functions are contained in 7 U.S.C. 450c-450g.

The Secretary's staffs financed from this appropriation are located in Washington, D. C. As of September 30, 1992, there were 90 employees. Of this total, 83 were full-time permanent employees and 7 were other than full-time permanent employees.

1-2

OFFICE OF THE SECRETARY

Available Funds and Staff-Years

1992 Actual and Estimated, 1993 and 1994

Item	1992 Actual Amount	1992 Actual Staff Years	1993 Estimated Amount	1993 Estimated Staff Years	1994 Estimated Amount	1994 Estimated Staff Years
Direct Appropriation	$8,716,000	75	$8,971,000	86	$9,145,000	86
Obligations Under Other USDA /Appropriations:						
Board of Contract Appeals	1,031,096	10	1,243,000	10	1,257,000	10
Forest Service	43,244	1	79,000	1	85,000	1
Foreign Agricultural Service	168,136	--	138,000	--	145,000	--
Miscellaneous Reimbursements	15,555	--	138,000	--	145,000	--
Total, Other USDA Appropriations	1,258,031	11	1,598,000	11	1,632,000	11
Total, Agriculture Appropriations	9,974,031	11	10,569,000	11	10,777,000	11
Other Federal Funds:						
Health & Human Services	40,000	--	--	--	--	--
Total, Office of the Secretary	10,014,031	86	10,569,000	97	10,777,000	97

OFFICE OF THE SECRETARY

Permanent Positions by Grade and Staff-Year Summary

1992 and Estimated 1993 and 1994

Grade	1992 Headquarters	1993 Headquarters	1994 Headquarters
Executive Level I	1	1	1
Executive Level II	1	1	1
Executive Level III	2	2	2
Executive Level IV	7	7	7
ES-6	10	13	13
ES-5	1	2	2
ES-4	2	1	1
ES-3	2	4	4
ES-2	3	3	3
ES-1	1	1	1
CA-1	1	1	1
CA-2	1	1	1
CA-3	3	3	3
GS/GM-15	12	14	14
GS/GM-14	1	4	4
GS/GM-13	6	4	4
GS-12	4	6	6
GS-11	10	8	8
GS-10	7	7	7
GS-9	7	6	6
GS-8	4	4	4
GS-7	1	1	1
Ungraded Positions	3	3	3
Total Permanent Positions	90	97	97
Unfilled Positions end of year	-7	--	--
Total, Permanent Employment, end-of year	83	97	97
Staff-Years: Ceiling	86	97	97

OFFICE OF THE SECRETARY

CLASSIFICATION BY OBJECTS

1992 and Estimated 1993 and 1994

	1992	1993	1994
Personnel Compensation:			
Headquarters	$5,348,617	$6,350,000	$6,493,000
11 Total personnel compensation	5,348,617	6,350,000	6,493,000
12 Personnel Benefits..........	1,020,424	1,288,000	1,317,000
13 Benefits for former personnel.................	17,706	--	--
Total pers. comp & benefit........	6,386,747	7,638,000	7,810,000
Other Objects:			
21 Travel......................	253,609	268,000	268,000
22 Transportation of things....	1,461	3,000	3,000
23.3 Communications, utilities, and misc. charges.........	337,085	335,000	335,000
24 Printing....................	174,194	175,000	175,000
25 Other services..............	512,936	342,000	344,000
26 Supplies and materials......	91,894	182,000	182,000
31 Equipment...................	99,340	28,000	28,000
Total other objects...............	1,470,519	1,333,000	1,335,000
Total direct obligations............	7,857,266	8,971,000	9,145,000
Position Data:			
Average Salary, ES positions.....	$105,671	$109,471	$110,018
Average Salary, GM/GS position...	$54,996	$54,499	$55,043
Average Grade, GM/GS positions...	11.67	12.27	12.27

OFFICE OF THE SECRETARY

The estimate includes appropriation language for this item as follows: (new language underscored; deleted matter enclosed in brackets):

Office of the Secretary

For necessary expenses of the Office of the Secretary of Agriculture, and not to exceed [$50,000] $75,000 for employment under 5 U.S.C. 3109, $2,282,000] $9,145,000: Provided, That not to exceed [$8,000] $11,000 of this amount shall be available for official reception and representation expenses, not otherwise provided for, as determined by the Secretary: Provided further, That the Secretary may transfer salaries and expenses funds in this Act sufficient to finance a total of not to exceed 35 staff years between agencies of the Department of Agriculture to meet workload requirements.

[Office of the Deputy Secretary]

[For necessary expenses of the Office of the Deputy Secretary of Agriculture, including not to exceed $25,000 for employment under 5 U.S.C. 3109, $543,000: Provided, That not to exceed $3,000 of this amount shall be available for official reception and representation expenses, not otherwise provided for, as determined by the Deputy Secretary.]

[Office of the Assistant Secretary for Administration]

[For necessary expenses of the Office of the Assistant Secretary for Administration to carry out the programs funded in this Act, $596,000.]

[Office of the Assistant Secretary for Congressional Relations]

[For necessary expenses of the Office of the Assistant Secretary for Congressional Relations to carry out the programs funded in this Act, $1,307,000.]

[Office of the Assistant Secretary for Economics]

[For necessary expenses of the Office of the Assistant Secretary for Economics to carry out the programs funded in this Act, $580,000.]

[Office of the Assistant Secretary for Science and Education]

[For necessary salaries and expenses of the Office of the Assistant Secretary for Science and Education to administer the laws enacted by the Congress for the Agricultural Research Service, Cooperative State Research Service, Extension Service, and National Agricultural Library, $560,000.]

[Office of the Assistant Secretary for Marketing and Inspection Services]

[For necessary salaries and expenses of the Office of the Assistant Secretary for Marketing and Inspection Services to administer programs under the laws enacted by the Congress for the Animal and Plant Health Inspection Service, Food Safety and Inspection Service, Federal Grain Inspection Service, Agricultural Cooperative Service, Agricultural Marketing Service, and Packers and Stockyards Administration, $550,000.]

[Office of the Under Secretary for International Affairs and Commodity Programs]

[For necessary salaries and expenses of the Office of the Under Secretary for International Affairs and Commodity Programs to administer the laws enacted by Congress for the Agricultural Stabilization and Conservation Service, Office of International Cooperation and Development, Foreign Agricultural Service, and the Commodity Credit Corporation, $551,000.]

[Office of the Assistant Secretary for Natural Resources and Environment]

[For necessary salaries and expenses of the Office of the Assistant Secretary for Natural Resources and Environment to administer the laws enacted by the Congress for the Forest Service and the Soil Conservation Service, $563,000.]

[Office of the Under Secretary for Small Community and Rural Development]

[For necessary salaries and expenses of the Office of the Under Secretary for Small Community and Rural Development to administer programs under the laws enacted by the Congress for the Farmers Home Administration, Rural Development Administration, Rural Electrification Administration, and Federal Crop Insurance Corporation, $572,000.]

[Office of the Assistant Secretary for Food and Consumer Services]

[For necessary salaries and expenses of the Office of the Assistant Secretary for Food and Consumer Services to administer the laws enacted by the Congress for the Food and Nutrition Service and the Human Nutrition Information Service, $542,000.]

This change merges amounts appropriated to the Deputy Secretary and to Under and Assistant Secretaries with amounts appropriated to the Secretary of Agriculture for the operation of the offices within the Office of the Secretary to reestablish a single appropriation for that Office.

The fiscal year 1994 budget proposes to reestablish a single appropriation for these activities. The multiple accounts unduly restrict the discretion of the Secretary to organize the resources to carry out the Department's program in the most cost effective manner. The Secretary is charged with the responsibility and implementation of national agriculture policies enacted by the Congress. The Secretary has discussed his plan to reorganize the Department with the Congress. A single account will facilitate the implementaiton of a reorganization. The establishment of multiple appropriations limits his ability to establish priorities and shift resources necessary to meet the challenging conditions of America's agriculture.

OFFICE OF THE SECRETARY

Appropriations Act, 1993..	$ 8,646,000
Budget Estimate, 1994..	9,145,000
Increase in Appropriation..	+499,000

Adjustments in 1993		
Appropriations Act, 1993..............	$8,646,000	
Activities transferred from USDA Agencies a/..........................	+325,000	
Adjusted base for 1993............		8,971,000
Budget Estimate 1994.....................		9,145,000
Increase over adjusted 1993.............		+174,000

a/ Pursuant to the authority given to the Secretary in the Agriculture, Rural Development, Food and Drug Administration, and Related Agencies Appropriations Act, 1993 (P. L. 102-341) to transfer staff years and funding within USDA to meet workload requirements, 2 staff years and $195,000 were transferred to the Assistant Secretary for Administration and 1 staff year and $130,000 to the Assistant Secretary for Marketing and Inspection Services.

SUMMARY OF INCREASES AND DECREASES
(on basis of adjusted appropriation)

Item of Change	1993 Estimated	Pay Cost	Other Changes	1994 Estimated
Immediate Office of the Secretary	$2,282,000	+$40,000	+$2,000	$2,324,000
Office of the Deputy Secretary...	543,000	+10,000	-0-	553,000
Assistant Secretary for Administration.................	791,000	+17,000	-0-	808,000
Assistant Secretary for Congressional Relations........	1,307,000	+26,000	-0-	1,333,000
Assistant Secretary for Economics	580,000	+9,000	-0-	589,000
Assistant Secretary for Science and Education.................	560,000	+9,000	-0-	569,000
Assistant Secretary for Marketing and Inspection Services........	680,000	+11,000	-0-	691,000
Under Secretary for International Affairs and Commodity Programs.	551,000	+12,000	-0-	563,000
Assistant Secretary for Natural Resources and Environment......	563,000	+15,000	-0-	578,000
Under Secretary for Small Community and Rural Development...	572,000	+11,000	-0-	583,000
Assistant Secretary for Food and Consumer Services..............	542,000	+12,000	-0-	554,000
Total Available.........	8,971,000	+172,000	+2,000	9,145,000

PROJECT STATEMENT
(on basis of adjusted appropriation)

Item of Change	1992 Actual Amount	1992 Actual Staff-Years	1993 Estimated Amount	1993 Estimated Staff-Years	Increase or Decrease	1994 Estimated Amount	1994 Estimated Staff-Years
1. Secretary....	$1,960,139	17	$2,282,000	22	+$42,000	$2,324,000	22
2. Deputy Secretary....	474,416	4	543,000	5	+10,000	553,000	5
3. Under/Asst. Secretaries.:							
ADM.......	572,086	6	791,000	8	+17,000	808,000	8
CR.........	1,231,021	15	1,307,000	15	+26,000	1,333,000	15
ECON......	542,189	5	580,000	5	+9,000	589,000	5
S/E.......	461,022	4	560,000	5	+9,000	569,000	5
MIS.......	551,354	5	680,000	6	+11,000	691,000	6
IACP......	510,029	4	551,000	5	+12,000	563,000	5
NRE.......	492,021	5	563,000	5	+15,000	578,000	5
SCRD......	542,655	5	572,000	5	+11,000	583,000	5
FCS.......	520,334	5	542,000	5	+12,000	554,000	5
Total available or estimated...	7,857,266	75	8,971,000	86	+174,000	9,145,000	86
Unobligated balance.........	858,734	--	--	--	--	--	--
Total available or estimate....	8,716,000	75	8,971,000	86	+174,000(1)	9,145,000	86
Transfers:							
ADMIN..........	--	--	-195,000	-2			
MIS............	-30,000	-1	-130,000	-1			
IACP...........	-30,000	--	--	--			
FCS............	-10,000	--	--	--			
Total transfers from other USDA agencies..	-70,000	-1	-325,000	-3			
Total appropriations........	8,646,000	74	8,646,000	83			

Explanation of Program

The Office of the Secretary, Deputy Secretary, Under Secretaries, Assistant Secretaries, and their immediate staff, provide policy and guidance for the Department and maintain relationships with agricultural organizations and others in the development of farm programs.

The Office of the Secretary also oversees special projects that are conducted at the behest of the Congress. These projects include short-term studies, investigations, and research on matters affecting agriculture or the agricultural community. Usually, specific appropriations are provided to carry out these projects. Projects results are reported to the appropriate Congressional committees.

JUSTIFICATION OF INCREASES AND DECREASES

(1) A net increase of $174,000 consisting of:

(a) An increase of $36,000, which reflects a 2.7 percent increase in non-salary costs.

(b) An increase of $172,000, which reflects the annualization of the fiscal year 1993 pay raise.

(c) A decrease of $32,000 for administrative efficiency.

Need for Change. To promote the efficient use of resources for administrative purposes, in keeping with the President's Executive Order, total USDA baseline outlays for these activities will be reduced by 3 percent in FY 1994, 6 percent in FY 1995, 9 percent in FY 1996 and 14 in FY 1997.

Nature of Change. In order to achieve this savings, OSEC will reduce discretionary expenses such as--travel, training, printing and reproduction costs and telephone usage.

(d) A decrease of $2,000 for FTS funding.

This decrease reflects lower long distance telecommunications prices due to price redeterminations in the FTS 2000 contracts.

GEOGRAPHIC BREAKDOWN OF OBLIGATIONS AND STAFF YEARS
1992, and estimated 1993 and 1994

	1992		1993		1994	
	Amount	Staff Years	Amount	Staff Years	Amount	Staff Years
Washington, D.C.	$7,857,266	75	$8,971,000	86	$9,145,000	86
Unobligated balance	858,734	--	--	--	--	--
Total, Available or Estimate.......	8,716,000	75	8,971,000	86	9,145,000	86

DEPARTMENTAL ADMINISTRATION

Purpose Statement

Departmental Administration is comprised of the Staff Offices that report to the Assistant Secretary for Administration. These Offices provide staff support to the top policy officials of the Department and overall direction and coordination to the work of the Department. The Assistant Secretary for Administration has the responsibility for administering the following programs under authority contained in 7 U.S.C. 2202:

Departmental Administration. This appropriation funds the policy development and administrative operational activities associated with Departmentwide programs for human resource management, financial management, management improvement, occupational safety and health management, real and personal property management, procurement, contracting, motor vehicle and aircraft management, supply management, ADP and telecommunications management, civil rights, equal opportunity, special emphasis, small and disadvantaged business opportunities, emergency preparedness, and the regulatory hearings and administrative proceedings conducted by the Administrative Law Judges and the Judicial Officer.

Rental Payments and Building Operations and Maintenance. This account finances the appropriated portion of payments to the General Services Administration (GSA) for rental of leased space and related services. Funding is not provided for payments to GSA made by the Forest Service, since the Forest Service is funded in the Interior and Related Agencies Appropriations Act.

This account also finances operations, repair, improvement, and maintenance activities at the USDA Headquarters Complex. Since 1989 when the GSA delegation expired , USDA has been responsible for managing, operating, maintaining, repairing, and improving the Headquarters Complex, which encompasses 14.1 acres of ground and 4 buildings containing approximately 3 million square feet of space occupied by approximately 8,000 employees.

Not all administrative Staff Office activitites are financed from direct appropriations. The Staff Offices also provide central services that are financed under the Department's Working Capital Fund (7 U.S.C. 2235). Adetailed description of these activities is provided under the Purpose Statement of the Working Capital Fund.

Reimbursable Activities. Under the Economy Act, 31 U.S.C. 686, the Staff Offices also are reimbursed for services provided to USDA and non-USDA agencies. The following activities are financed through other reimbursements: travel and printing for the Administrative Law Judges, miscellaneous personnel details, selected short-term activities, as well as administrative, operational support to Working Capital Fund activities.

Geographic Location. The majority of the Staff Offices are located in Washington, D.C. Central services financed through the Working Capital Fund are provided by the National Finance Center located in New Orleans, Louisiana and by the Department's computer centers located in Kansas City, Missouri and Fort Collins, Colorado, and by other administrative service units located in the Washington Metropolitan area.

As of September 30, 1992, there were 2,341 employees, of which 2,221 were full-time and 120 were other than full-time permanent employees in the Staff Offices included under Departmental Administration. These employees were assigned as follows:

Location	Full-time permanent	Other	Total
Washington, D.C.	618	72	690
Field units	1,603	48	1,651
Total	2,221	120	2,341

DEPARTMENTAL ADMINISTRATION

Available Funds and Staff-Years

1992 Actual and Estimated, 1993 and 1994

Item	1992 Actual		1993 Estimated		1994 Estimated	
	Amount	Staff-Years	Amount	Staff-Years	Amount	Staff-Years
Direct Appropriations:						
Departmental Administration	$25,385,000	366	$25,798,000	410	$27,298,000	405
GSA Rental Payments	50,679,002	--	50,503,000	--	50,503,000	--
Building Ops. & Main.	25,700,000	87	25,700,000	87	25,581,000	86
Total, Direct	101,764,002	453	102,001,000	497	103,382,000	491
Reimbursements to Appropriations:						
Deptl. Administration:						
USDA Agencies:						
Field Office System	--	--	1,500,000	--	1,500,000	--
FmHA ADP/IRM	50,909	--	100,000	--	150,000	--
Office of Admin. Law Judges	39,714	--	49,000	--	52,000	--
SES Training	245,000	--	--	--	--	--
Target Center	418,724	2	400,000	4	368,000	4
Management Support Services provided to WCF Activities	4,579,264	73	4,748,219	71	4,967,000	71
Subtotal USDA agencies	5,333,611	75	6,797,219	75	7,037,000	75
Other Federal Agencies:						
Farm Credit Assistance	42,000	--	--	-	--	
Mine Safety Board	48,900	--	51,000	--	52,000	--
Court Vet. Appeals	45,000	--	68,000		69,000	--
Subtotal Other Fedl	135,900	--	119,000	--	121,000	--
Total Deptl. Admin	5,469,511	75	6,916,219	75	7,158,000	75
Building Ops. & Maint.						
Security Services	1,572,504	--	2,350,000	--	2,500,000	--
Other Bldg. Services	1,075,891	--	1,000,000	--	1,000,000	--
Subtotal, BOM	2,648,395	--	3,350,000	--	3,500,000	--
Total, Reimbursements	8,117,906	75	10,266,219	75	10,658,000	75
Working Capital Fund						
Supply and Other Central Services	18,010,000	195	19,527,000	206	19,856,000	203
OFM Finance Center	93,904,000	1,449	108,811,000	1,532	116,376,000	1,515
ADP Services	36,988,000	203	41,215,000	218	43,998,000	216
Purchase of Equipment	11,712,000	--	18,927,000	--	19,604,000	--
Subtotal, Working Capital Fund	160,614,000	1,847	188,480,000	1,956	199,834,000	1,934
Grand Total, Deptl Administration	270,495,906	2,375	300,165,219	2,528	313,257,000	2,500

DEPARTMENTAL ADMINISTRATION

Permanent Positions by Grade and Staff-Year Summary

1992 and Estimated 1993 and 1994

Grade	1992 HDQTRS	1992 FIELD	1992 TOTAL	1993 HDQTRS	1993 FIELD	1993 TOTAL	1994 HDQTRS	1994 FIELD	1994 TOTAL
ES-6.......	3	--	3	3	--	3	3	--	3
ES-5.......	4	2	6	4	2	6	4	2	6
ES-4.......	1	--	1	1	--	1	1	--	1
ES-2.......	--	1	1	1	1	2	1	1	2
ES-1.......	3	5	8	2	5	7	2	5	7
AL-3.......	4	--	4	5	--	5	5	--	5
AL-2.......	1	--	1	1	--	1	1	--	1
SL-2.......	--	--	--	1	--	1	1	--	1
SL-1.......	1	--	1	1	--	1	1	--	1
GS/GM-15...	34	14	48	38	15	53	38	15	53
GS/GM-14...	102	56	158	115	55	170	115	55	170
GS/GM-13...	142	106	248	165	116	281	159	116	275
GS-12......	59	222	281	73	253	326	71	253	324
GS-11......	42	216	258	37	231	268	37	231	268
GS-10......	2	11	13	3	12	15	3	12	15
GS-9.......	34	113	147	39	127	166	39	127	166
GS-8.......	12	37	49	16	37	53	16	37	53
GS-7.......	62	160	222	71	173	244	71	173	244
GS-6.......	33	170	203	37	172	209	37	172	209
GS-5.......	27	273	300	34	292	326	34	275	309
GS-4.......	38	103	141	49	103	152	46	103	149
GS-3.......	13	87	100	18	87	105	18	87	105
GS-2.......	3	3	6	2	3	5	2	3	5
Other Graded Positions	85	--	85	92	--	92	92	--	92
Ungraded Positions..	12	24	36	12	24	36	12	24	36
Total, Permanent Positions	717	1,603	2,320	820	1,708	2,528	809	1,691	2,500
Unfilled Positions.. end-of-year	--	--	--	--	--	--	--	--	--
Total Perm. Employment, end-of-year	717	1,603	2,320	820	1,708	2,528	809	1,691	2,500
Staff-Year Ceiling...	765	1,610	2,375	820	1,708	2,528	809	1,691	2,500

DEPARTMENTAL ADMINISTRATION

CLASSIFICATION BY OBJECTS

1992 and Estimated 1993 and 1994

	1992	1993	1994
Personnel Compensation:			
Headquarters	$17,392,344	$20,202,000	$20,640,000
11 Total personnel compensation	17,392,344	20,202,000	20,640,000
12 Personnel Benefits..........	2,588,920	3,005,000	3,078,000
13 Benefits for former personnel.................	14,885	6,000	6,000
Total pers. comp. & benefits..	19,996,149	23,213,000	23,724,000
Other Objects:			
21 Travel......................	273,446	142,000	142,000
22 Transportation of things....	6,361	12,000	12,000
23.2 Rental payments to others...	9,900	25,000	25,000
23.3 Communications, utilities, and misc. charges.........	999,095	698,000	689,000
24 Printing....................	278,266	159,000	159,000
25 Other services..............	2,383,030	1,151,000	2,150,000
26 Supplies and materials......	456,505	191,000	191,000
31 Equipment...................	802,248	175,000	174,000
41 Grants, Subsidies and Contributions.............	--	32,000	32,000
Total other objects...........	5,208,851	2,585,000	3,574,000
Total direct obligations............	25,205,000	25,798,000	27,298,000
Position Data:			
Average Salary, ES positions.....	$105,137	$108,526	$108,526
Average Salary, GM/GS position...	$41,339	$51,709	$52,852
Average Grade, GM/GS positions...	12.3	13.3	13.4

DEPARTMENTAL ADMINISTRATION

The estimates include appropriation language for this item as follows (new language underscored; deleted matter enclosed in brackets):

Departmental Administration

For Personnel, Finance and Management, Operations, Information Resources Management, Advocacy and Enterprise, Administrative Law Judges and Judicial Officer, and Emergency Programs, [25,014,000] 27,298,000 for Departmental Administration to provide for necessary expenses for management support services to offices of the Department of Agriculture and for general administration and emergency preparedness of the Department of Agriculture, repairs and alterations, and other miscellaneous supplies and expenses not otherwise provided for and necessary for the practical and efficient work of the Department of Agriculture, including employment pursuant to the second sentence of section 706(a) of the Organic Act of 1944 (7 U.S.C. 2225), of which not to exceed $10,000 is for employment under 5 U.S.C. 3109: Provided, That this appropriation shall be reimbursed from applicable appropriations in this Act for travel expenses incident to the holding of hearings as required by 5 U.S.C. 551-558.

This change proposes to include Emergency Programs as a separate budget activity to reflect the priority placed on emergency preparedness. This activity is the focal point of contact with the Federal Emergency Management Agency, all other Federal departments and agencies having emergency program responsibilities, and international agencies that deal with food and agriculture on an emergency basis. It provides oversight, coordination, and guidance to USDA agencies in their emergency planning, training, and activities.

DEPARTMENTAL ADMINISTRATION

Appropriations Act, 1993	$25,014,000
Budget Estimate, 1994	27,298,000
Increase in Appropriation	+2,284,000

Adjustments in 1993:		
Appropriations Act, 1993	$25,014,000	
Transfers from USDA agencies 1/	+784,000	
Adjusted Appropriations Act		25,798,000
Budget Estimate, 1994		27,298,000
Increase over adjusted 1993		+1,500,000

1/ Includes $700,000 and 10 staff years for the Agency Liaison Officer (ALO) Project to provide oversight and guidance to agencies' IRM activities and $84,000 and 1 staff year for the Equipment Management Information System (EMIS) upgrade transferred under authority provided by P.L. 102-341.

SUMMARY OF INCREASES AND DECREASES
(on basis of adjusted appropriation)

Item of Change	1993 Estimated	Pay Cost	Other Changes	1994 Estimated
Personnel	$6,704,000	+$132,000	-$3,000	$6,833,000
Finance and Management	4,371,000	+95,000	+616,000	5,082,000
Operations	3,173,000	+67,000	-1,000	3,239,000
Information Resources Management	6,048,000	+102,000	+377,000	6,527,000
Advocacy and Enterprise	3,699,000	+78,000	-1,000	3,776,000
Administrative Law Judges and Judicial Officer	1,578,000	+33,000	--	1,611,000
Emergency Programs	225,000	+5,000	--	230,000
Total Available	25,798,000	+512,000	+988,000	27,298,000

PROJECT STATEMENT
(on basis of adjusted appropriation)

Item of Change	1992 Actual Amount	1992 Actual Staff-Years	1993 Estimated Amount	1993 Estimated Staff-Years	Increase or Decrease	1994 Estimated Amount	1994 Estimated Staff-Years
Personnel	$6,785,744	112	$6,704,000	119	+$129,000(1)	$6,833,000	114
Finance and Management	4,343,700	62	4,371,000	69	+711,000(2)	5,082,000	76
Operations	3,111,468	53	3,173,000	59	+66,000(3)	3,239,000	55
Information Resources Management	5,671,850	64	6,048,000	74	+479,000(4)	6,527,000	76
Advocacy and Enterprise	3,665,130	51	3,699,000	62	+77,000(5)	3,776,000	59
Administrative Law Judges & Judicial Officer	1,401,936	20	1,578,000	23	+33,000(6)	1,611,000	21
Emergency Programs	225,172	4	225,000	4	+5,000(7)	230,000	4
Subtotal	25,205,000	366	25,798,000	410	+1,500,000	27,298,000	405
Unobligated balance	+180,000		--	--	--	--	--
Total available or estimate	25,385,000	366	25,798,000	410	+1,500,000	27,298,000	405
Transfers:							
ALO Project	-300,000	-5	-700,000	-10			
EMIS Project	-21,000	-1	-84,000	-1			
Total, Appropriation	25,064,000	360	25,014,000	399			

EXPLANATION OF PROGRAM

This appropriation provides for the following activities:

Personnel - This activity provides leadership, coordination and monitoring of the personnel management program in the Department and promulgates Departmental policies and procedures relating to all personnel functions. The Office of Personnel provides liaison with the Office of Personnel Management and sponsors innovations and change in personnel management. Operational services are provided to the Office of the Secretary, Office of the Inspector General, Office of the General Counsel, Office of Public Affairs, Office of Budget and Program Analysis, and the Departmental Administrative Staff Offices. Direction is provided to the Department's integrated payroll/personnel system that is utilized by a cross-section of Federal agencies. Equal Employment Opportunity under Title 7 of the Civil Rights Act of 1964 is provided to all USDA agencies.

Finance and Management - This activity provides Departmental leadership in developing and evaluating programs in finance, accounting, management control, Federal assistance, management and productivity improvement, metrication, audit follow-up and final action and occupational safety and health. The Director serves as the Department's management improvement officer and comptroller of the Working Capital Fund. OFM provides key staff support to the Department's Chief Financial Officer in implementing the CFO Act of 1990. Finance and Management also provides budget, accounting and fiscal operational services to the Office of the Secretary, the Departmental Administrative Staff Offices, Office of Public Affairs, and the Office of Budget and Program Analysis.

Operations - This activity provides USDA agencies leadership, oversight and policy development in the areas of real and personal property, procurement, contracts, supplies, motor vehicles and supply. Under an agreement with GSA, it operates and provides maintenance security and services to the Washington, D.C. building complex. The Office of Operations also provides procurement, contract, leasing, and other administrative services to the Office of the Secretary, Office of the General Counsel, Office of Public Affairs, the Office of Budget and Program Analysis, and the Departmental Staff Offices.

Information Resources Management - This activity develops, and disseminates Departmental standards, guidelines, rules, and regulations to implement approved Information Resources Management (IRM) principles, policies, and programs that improve the operational effectiveness of USDA's programs. It provides for Departmental long range IRM planning, guides the IRM planning of USDA agencies, monitors and oversees major agency and Departmental IRM programs. The Director serves as Departmental clearance officer for information collection. This activity provides telecommunications and ADP services to USDA agencies and staff offices through the National Computer Centers in Fort Collins, Colorado and Kansas City, Missouri. This activity also provides operational ADP services to the Office of the Secretary, Office of the General Counsel, Office of Public Affairs, the Office of Budget and Program Analysis, and the Departmental Administrative Staff Offices.

Advocacy and Enterprise - This activity provides overall policy and program guidance, leadership, coordination and direction for the Department's civil rights and equal opportunity programs; plans and coordinates the participation of women, minorities, and disabled persons, in Departmental programs; oversees direction and implementation of Sections 8 and 15 of the Small Business Act and oversees procurement to assure maximum participation of small and disadvantaged businesses; directs Departmental efforts to further the participation of minority colleges and universities in USDA programs; and directs and monitors USDA agencies compliance in promoting full and open competition in the Department's contracting process.

Administrative Law Judges/Judicial Officer - The Administrative Law Judges hold hearings in connection with prescribing new regulations and orders and on disciplinary complaints filed by the Department or on some petitions filed by private parties asking relief from actions of the Department. The Judicial Officer renders final administrative decisions in regulatory proceedings.

Emergency Programs This activity is the focal point of contact with the Federal Emergency Management Agency and all other Federal departments and agencies having emergency program responsibilities, and provides oversight, coordination, and guidance to USDA agencies in their emergency planning, training, and activities.

JUSTIFICATION OF INCREASES AND DECREASES

(1) A net increase of $129,000 for the Office of Personnel consists of:

(a) An increase of $19,000, which reflects a 2.7 percent increase in non-salary costs.

(b) An increase of $132,000, which reflects the annualization of the fiscal year 1993 pay raise.

(c) A decrease of $20,000, for administrative efficiency.

Need for change. To promote the efficient use of resources for administrative purposes, in keeping with the President's Executive Order, total USDA baseline outlays for these activities will be reduced by 3 percent in 1994, 6 percent in FY 1995, 9 percent in FY 1996, and 14 percent in FY 1997.

Nature of Change. In order to achieve this savings, OP will reduce discretionary expenses such as--travel, training, supply purchases, printing, and reproduction costs, and telephone usage.

(d) A decrease of $2,000 for FTS 2000 funding.

This decrease reflects lower long distance telecommunications prices due to price redeterminations in the FTS 2000 contracts.

(2) A net increase of $711,000 for the Office of Finance and Management consists of:

(a) An increase of 2,000, which reflects a 2.7 percent increase in non-salary costs.

(b) An increase of $95,000, which reflects the annualization of the fiscal year 1993 pay raise.

(c) A decrease of $2,000 for administrative efficiency.

Need for change. To promote the efficient use of resources for administrative purposes, in keeping with the President's Executive Order, total USDA baseline outlays for these activities will be reduced by 3 percent in 1994, 6 percent in FY 1995, 9 percent in FY 1996, and 14 percent in FY 1997.

Nature of Change. In order to achieve this savings, OFM will reduce discretionary expenses such as--travel, training, supply purchases, printing, and reproduction costs, and telephone usage.

(d) An increase of $616,000 and 7 staff years to strengthen Department-wide financial management and improve USDA financial systems.

Need for Change. Financial systems at USDA need large-scale remedial action to address GAO audit findings and concerns that placed this area in OMB's "high-risk" category. The Chief Financial Officers' Act (P.L. 101-976) places additional requirements on USDA to provide leadership and oversight of Departmental and agency fiscal operations.

Financial management programs at USDA involve huge sums of public funds entrusted to the Department. For example, USDA manages assets of over $146 billion, collects $20 billion and disburses $60 billion in a variety of programs. USDA manages a debt portfolio that constitutes over 40% of all debts owed to the Federal government.

USDA operates six different Nationwide financial management and program systems, numerous subsystems, as well as the systems at the National Finance Center in New Orleans. Each requires corrective actions and strengthened central oversight and coordination. In order to meet OMB requirements for financial systems plans for executive departments, additional resources are needed to closely analyze, monitor and improve accounting, financial information, and performance data of USDA agencies. The CFO Act mandates greater emphasis on the modernization and consolidation of financial systems, elimination of duplicative and unnecessary subsystems, and establishment of projects to bring systems into compliance with Federal standards. The added resources requested will enable OFM to begin work on revitalization of USDA financial management systems.

The CFO Act also requires executive departments to develop and submit Consolidated Financial Statements for audit. The recent findings of our Inspector General's audit revealed systemic problems. More resources are urgently needed to satisfy the legislative mandate.

Nature of Change. Funding requested will pay salaries and benefits for 7 positions and their related operating costs that will allow OFM to begin to address and remedy existing systemic financial management problems within USDA, correct deficiencies in preparation of financial statements for audit, and meet existing legislative and regulatory requirements under the CFO Act. Work will be concentrated in areas such as providing USDA agencies policy guidance and technical assistance in financial management planning, and supporting the CFO and Deputy CFO in their oversight and guidance of USDA's financial management systems and programs.

(3) A net increase of $66,000 for the Office of Operations consists of:

(a) An increase of $4,000, which reflects a 2.7 percent increase in non-salary costs.

(b) An increase of $67,000, which reflects the annualization of the fiscal year 1993 pay raise.

(c) A decrease of $4,000 for administrative efficiency.

Need for change. To promote the efficient use of resources for administrative purposes, in keeping with the President's Executive Order, total USDA baseline outlays for these activities will be reduced by 3 percent in 1994, 6 percent in FY 1995, 9 percent in FY 1996, and 14 percent in FY 1997.

Nature of Change. In order to achieve this savings, OO will reduce discretionary expenses such as--travel, training, supply purchases, printing, and reproduction costs, and telephone usage.

(d) A decrease of $1,000 for FTS 2000 funding.

This decrease reflects lower long distance telecommunications prices due to price redetermininations in the FTS 2000 contracts.

(4) A net increase of $479,000 and 2 staff years for the Office of Information Resources Management consists of:

(a) An increase of $38,000, which reflects a 2.7 percent increase in non-salary costs.

(b) An increase of $102,000, which reflects the annualization of the fiscal year 1993 pay raise.

(c) A decrease of $40,000 for administrative efficiency.

Need for change. To promote the efficient use of resources for administrative purposes, in keeping with the President's Executive Order, total USDA baseline outlays for these activities will be reduced by 3 percent in 1994, 6 percent in FY 1995, 9 percent in FY 1996, and 14 percent in FY 1997.

Nature of Change. In order to achieve this savings, OIRM will reduce discretionary expenses such as--travel, training, supply purchases, printing, and reproduction costs, and telephone usage.

(d) A decrease of $5,000 for FTS 2000 funding.

This decrease reflects lower long distance telecommunications prices due to price redetermininations in the FTS 2000 contracts.

(e) An increase of $384,000 and 2 staff years to provide oversight and guidance to the planning, acquisition and development efforts that promote information sharing among USDA computer systems.

Need for Change. Additional resources are needed for the development of information sharing systems within the Department. One such effort now underway which needs expanding in fiscal year 1994 is Info Share. Info Share will revolutionize service delivery to USDA's farm service clients by combining the elements of office automation tools, a shared corporate data base, a Geographic Information System (GIS), telecommunications, interoperability and connectivity, and remote management and maintenance to form the basis for IRM strategic systems that serve the public through USDA field offices of the proposed Farm Service Agency. An integrated information management environment is needed to serve both the constituent communities and provide vital information to Departmental and agency leadership.

A centralized, cooperative approach would result in lower operating costs due to:

- Reduced Design and Acquisition Costs. With OIRM providing leadership in the standardized design and acquisition functions for related agency systems, duplication of effort will be avoided. Additionally, agencies would be able to devote prime efforts to improving program service delivery.

- Combined Network Design and Implementation. By designing and implementing integrated systems instead of separate and incompatible agency networks as was previously planned, the many benefits of system interoperability can be realized at a lower cost.

- Reduced System Operation Costs. By centrally managing installation and implementation there will be less travel, more efficient installation scheduling and better coordination of resources. Managing the system after installation will require fewer resources. A consolidated, Nation-wide help desk will offer better service, reduce some training costs, and increase service coverage. Communications costs will be lower due to rates available for higher volumes over fewer lines.

Integrated network systems, such as Info Share, demonstrate that strong centralization of resources, improved exploitation of systems integration technologies, and thorough life cycle engineering are the means to improve service to clients, enhance management oversight and reduce costs.

Nature of Change. The additional resources will be used to pay salaries and benefits and operating costs for two staff years and for contract services to provide critical expertise to guide USDA integrated systems development to improve interagency information management, implement key requirements of the Farm Bill by easing the paper burden faced by farmers, and result in savings by eliminating current system incompatibilities and redundancies.

(5) A net increase of $77,000 for the Office of Advocacy and Enterprise consists of:

(a) An increase of $5,000, which reflects a 2.7 percent increase in non-salary costs.

(b) An increase of $78,000, which reflects the annualization of the fiscal year 1993 pay raise.

(c) A decrease of $5,000 for administrative efficiency.

Need for change. To promote the efficient use of resources for administrative purposes, in keeping with the President's Executive Order, total USDA baseline outlays for these activities will be reduced by 3 percent in 1994, 6 percent in FY 1995, 9 percent in FY 1996, and 14 percent in FY 1997.

Nature of Change. In order to achieve this savings, OAE will reduce discretionary expenses such as--travel, training, supply purchases, printing, and reproduction costs, and telephone usage.

(d) A decrease of $1,000 for FTS 2000 funding.

This decrease reflects lower long distance telecommunications prices due to price redetermininations in the FTS 2000 contracts.

(6) <u>A net increase of $33,000 for the Administrative Law Judges/Judicial Officer consists of:</u>

(a) <u>An increase of $2,000, which reflects a 2.7 percent increase in non-salary costs.</u>

(b) <u>An increase of $33,000, which reflects the annualization of the fiscal year 1993 pay raise.</u>

(c) <u>A decrease of $2,000 for administrative efficiency.</u>

<u>Need for change.</u> To promote the efficient use of resources for Administrative purposes, in keeping with the President's Executive Order, total USDA baseline outlays for these activities will be reduced by 3 percent in 1994, 6 percent in FY 1995, 9 percent in FY 1996, and 14 percent in FY 1997.

<u>Nature of Change</u>. In order to achieve this savings, OALJ will reduce discretionary expenses such as--travel, training, supply purchases, printing, and reproduction costs, and telephone usage.

(7) <u>An increase of $5,000 for the Director of Emergency Programs, which reflects the annualization of the fiscal year 1993 pay raise.</u>

<u>GEOGRAPHIC BREAKDOWN OF OBLIGATIONS AND STAFF YEARS</u>
<u>1992 and Estimated 1993 and 1994</u>

	1992		1993		1994	
	Amount	Staff-Years	Amount	Staff-Years	Amount	Staff-Years
Washington, D.C.	$25,205,000	366	$25,798,000	410	$27,298,000	405
Unobligated balance	180,000	--	--	--	--	--
Total, Available or Estimate	25,385,000	366	25,798,000	410	27,298,000	405

DEPARTMENTAL ADMINISTRATION

STATUS OF PROGRAM

OFFICE OF PERSONNEL

The Office of Personnel (OP) provides overall direction and leadership and promotes innovation for USDA human resources management programs and initiatives, including Work Force Diversity. OP provides leadership to and coordinates the Department's personnel management program in major functional areas such as: recruitment and employment, employee and labor relations, compensation and performance management, EEO counseling, EEO complaints management, training policy and executive development, personnel management information systems, payroll/personnel systems, and personnel management evaluations. Following consultation with cross serviced agencies, it establishes policy for the USDA payroll/personnel system which services 450,000 Federal employees. In addition, OP provides day-to-day operating personnel services to the Office of the Secretary and Departmental Staff Offices.

Current Activities:

1. Senior Executive Service Candidate Development Program (SESCDP). In July 1992, OP initiated an innovative Departmental program, to establish a high quality, diverse pool of senior executive candidates from which to fill vacancies created by expected high attrition in the SES in the mid-1990's. Ninety individuals were competitively selected out of 1,120 applicants from USDA, other government agencies, and the private sector. The quality and diversity of candidates in this first program is exceptional. Seventy of those selected are participating in a rigorous 6-18 month executive development program prior to OPM senior executive certification. The other 20 participants represent highly experienced executive talent and have been proposed for immediate OPM certification through an accelerated, cost-saving program. A second program will begin in March 1993.

2. Work Force Diversity - 1890/USDA Outstanding Scholars Program. In cooperation with the 1890 Historically Black Land-Grant Institutions, the Department established the USDA/1890 Outstanding Scholars Program to attract and assist outstanding students to careers in agriculture. The program will provide on an annual basis, full tuition, fees, books, and a personal computer and software for students pursuing a bachelors degree at one of the seventeen 1890 Historically Black Land-Grant Institutions. Each 1890 institution will provide a list of potential program participants for agencies to select from, as well as provide room and board for each scholar. USDA will require 1-year of service obligation for each year of financial support.

3. Modernization of the Administrative Process (MAP). The goal of USDA's MAP effort is to take specific and planned actions for eliminating or streamlining administrative regulations and processes that affect managers, employees, and the public. OP will be leading the USDA personnel community in the MAP process, which will create a modern role for personnel administration. A MAP steering committee for personnel has been formed, and "Change Teams" will design and implement new personnel processes for the short and long term. Process streamlining, integration, and automation will be the principal tools for MAP.

4. Ethics Program. To address the new Office of Government Ethics (OGE) regulations, OP submitted a comprehensive Department-wide ethics training plan to OGE. The plan covers initial training for over 110,000 employees, and annual training for 22,000 employees. The initial training will be accomplished in fiscal year 1993. OP also has reviewed the adequacy of agency resources devoted to the ethics program and established a USDA task force to implement the new Government-wide standards of conduct.

5. Human Resources Planning. OP initiated meetings with each agency personnel office in USDA to examine the personnel management program of the Department. Some of the issues discussed include: a) OP's Departmental responsibilities vs. agency personnel management responsibilities, b) work force diversity, c) automation of USDA personnel

processes, d) agency innovations in personnel management, e) mid-management training, f) EEO counseling, g) personnel management evaluations, and h) building professionalism in personnel administration. These meetings are identifying areas requiring greater Departmental leadership and USDA-wide action.

Selected Examples of Recent Progress:

1. Work Force Diversity - Student Programs. USDA is one of the leading Federal employers in the Cooperative Education, Presidential Management Intern, Stay-in-School, and Federal Junior Fellowship programs. OP coordinates USDA's summer intern program, which exposes college students to the fields of agriculture and natural resource management and focuses on attracting more women, minorities, and persons with disabilities into permanent positions at USDA. In 1992, USDA had over 1,400 participants with 850 summer interns from the 1890 Institutions, and about 100 students of Hispanic origin. OP employed the first "Coop-in-Residence" student in the Federal government in cooperation with the Hispanic Association of Colleges and Universities (HACU). The program provides educational guidance and employment for students majoring in human resources management or business administration programs.

2. Work Force Diversity - Individuals with Disabilities. In FY 1992, USDA agencies employed 187 new employees with disabilities using the ceiling exemption provided by the Office of Management and Budget for persons with targeted disabilities. OP recently obtained a 30-month extension of this ceiling exempt status. Overall, USDA employment of individuals with targeted disabilities was 1.12 percent of the permanent work force, which is only .02 percent below the Department's FY 1992 goal of 1.14 percent. OP, in cooperation with the agencies, completed two pilot sessions of "Operation Enable," a clerical and secretarial training program that attracts and retains qualified persons with disabilities. OP plans to expand the program to include more individuals and employees in technical positions. OP obtained authority to recruit a full-time sign language interpreter to perform interpretation, training, and outreach functions for Washington, D.C., area employees.

3. Personnel Leadership Forums. In May 1992, OP held the first USDA Personnel Leadership Forum, broadcast nation-wide to USDA teleconference sites. The forum covered "Managing for Peak Performance," and included remarks by a panel of subject matter experts, followed by employee call-in questions. The next Personnel Leadership Forum, to be held in December 1992, will cover "Retirement Planning." Another forum is planned on the subject of balancing family and work responsibilities.

4. Payroll/Personnel Systems Development. OP established the Agriculture Payroll/Personnel System Policy Advisory Council (APPSPAC) composed of the Directors of Personnel from each Department and agency serviced by the USDA payroll/personnel system. This group developed the first Agriculture Payroll/Personnel Systems. The plan prioritized essential enhancements to the payroll/personnel system Development Plan, which currently serves 450,000 employees. Resource requirements and cost-benefit assessments will be conducted to test the value and need for requested enhancements.

OFFICE OF FINANCE AND MANAGEMENT

The Office of Finance and Management (OFM) provides leadership, development, and evaluation of programs in finance, accounting, Federal assistance, management control, financial management systems, audit follow-up and final action, management and productivity improvement, metrication implementation, occupational safety and health; and for the management and operation of the National Finance Center (NFC). The Director serves as the Department's Management Improvement Officer and Comptroller of the Working Capital Fund. Also, OFM provides budget, accounting and fiscal services to the Office of the Secretary and Departmental Staff Offices.

Current Activities:

1. Drug Free Work Place. USDA continues to implement the drug testing component of the President's National Drug Control Strategy. Random, volunteer and applicant

testing throughout USDA began in January 1990. USDA's testing program includes all critical and sensitive testing designated positions at a rate of 33% per year.

2. Management Control. USDA is strengthening the Department's management control process by reviewing and closely monitoring high risk areas. Agencies with high risk areas include the Food and Nutrition Service, Farmers Home Administration, and the Federal Crop Insurance Corporation. OFM continues to provide assistance and monitoring in agency remedial action programs for these high risk areas. USDA has initiated the development and implementation of performance measures that will be utilized by USDA agencies within their financial statements.

3. Debt Management. During Fiscal Year 1992, Department of Agriculture agencies collected over $24.2 million from tax refund offset activities. This was an increase of about $15.2 million over Fiscal Year 1991 collections. The increase resulted from an increase in voluntary payments and in the number of claims referred for offset.

Selected Examples of Recent Progress:

1. Financial Statements. The consolidated statements included a statement of financial position, statement of operations, statement of cash flows, and a statement of reconciliation to budget reports. OFM prepared and submitted to the Office of Management and Budget, (OMB), preliminary Fiscal Year 1991 Consolidated Financial Statements for the Department prior to the statutory due date of March 31, 1992.

2. Cash Management. During Fiscal Year 1992, OFM led cash management initiatives resulted in avoided interest cost to the Treasury of approximately $38 million. This included:

-- $11.1 million from cash concentration system collection;

-- $17.9 million from electronic funds transfer collections and payments;

-- $5.1 million from warehousing payments;

-- $0.9 million from Direct Deposit/Electronic Funds Transfer for employee payments.

-- $1.8 million from electronic lockbox collection; and

-- $0.8 million from travel and charge card payments.

USDA interest penalties decreased by about one-third, from $1.2 million in FY 1991 to about $800,000 in FY 1992. USDA encourages the use of electronic remote personal computer entry to reduce paper, mail time, and keying errors. It began the use of remote personal computer inquiry to identify potential late purchase order payments for remedial action. The Office of Finance and Management also developed and issued a Prompt Payment Reference Guide.

OFFICE OF OPERATIONS

The Office of Operations (OO) provides Departmental policy, oversight, and guidance for the management of real and personal property, procurement, contracts, transportation, supply, motor vehicles, aircraft, and energy conservation. Certain centralized administrative services are also provided in Washington, D.C., including headquarters facilities management; mail processing; acquisition, warehousing, and distribution of forms, publications, and office supplies; reproduction and copying services; shipping and receiving; imprest fund; automated procurement; and administrative support to the Office of the Secretary.

Current Activities:

1. PCMI Recommendations to Improve Motor Vehicle Fleet Management. USDA is the lead agency for three President's Council on Management Improvement (PCMI) initiatives to

improve Federal motor vehicle fleet management. They are: 1) Develop guidelines to reduce the number of Government-owned fueling facilities considering environmental concerns, the availability of commercial alternatives and agency emergency requirements; 2) Determine vehicle acquisition standards to permit cost-effective consolidated procurements; and 3) Eliminate Congressionally imposed limits on acquisition of sedan/station wagon quantities. Interagency task forces have been formed for each initiative.

2. Aircraft and Motor Vehicles. The Secretary established an initiative to identify needed improvements in the management of USDA's aircraft and motor vehicle fleet. The initiative consists of six projects staffed by interagency teams made up of 13 agencies that will provide in-depth analysis, including: 1) roles and responsibilities; 2) information/data needs assessment; 3) systems requirements; 4) alternative fuel and energy conservation programs; 5) new technology; and 6) impediments to effective and efficient oversight of aircraft and motor vehicles. The project teams' findings and recommendations will be compiled into a final report for comment/concurrence and presentation to the Secretary.

3. Accommodations for the Disabled. In support of the report of the Secretary's Advisory Committee for Employees with Disabilities, OO is surveying all USDA buildings to determine their levels of accessibility. The results of the survey will be used to establish programs to improve the work-place environment and aid in the hiring of disabled persons.

4. USDA Recycling Program. The Department is implementing the Federal agency recycling provisions of E.O. 12780, signed October 31,1991. The Secretary appointed the Departmental Recycling Coordinator, and a Nation-wide USDA recycling organization is being assembled. The USDA Affirmative Procurement Plan for Waste Reduction and the Recycling of Reusable Materials regulation will be implemented by June 1993. This is a significant step towards changing USDA's buying habits to promote cost-effective waste reduction and recyclable materials product development, such as soybean based inks and alternative fuels.

5. PCMI Mail Management Initiative. The President's Council on Management Improvement tasked federal agencies to identify targets of opportunity which will result in postage savings of approximately $100,000,000 and strengthen agency mail programs by identifying cost-effective management practices and programs. USDA's Deputy Assistant Secretary for Administration chairs this initiative with the Office of Operations providing leadership to a task force representing large and small Executive Agencies.

Selected Examples of Recent Progress:

1. Improved Property Management. Negotiated with the Department of Defense to preserve our statutory authority to reuse DoD excess personal property in lieu of new procurements. In FY 1992, USDA obtained excess personal property valued at over $163 million.

2. Loan of Excess Personal Property to 1890 Land Grant Institutions. In concert with the joint USDA 1890 Institution Task Force, OO continued efforts to expand the acquisition and use of excess property by 1890 Land Grant Colleges and Tuskeegee University. In FY 1992, property valued at over $4 million was transferred to these institutions for specific agricultural research and extension service programs.

3. Alternative Fuels and Alternative Fuel Vehicles. Secretary's memorandum 5400-6 dated June 26, 1992 mandated the use of 10 percent ethanol-blended fuels in all owned and operated USDA motor vehicles if available at the same or lower prices than unleaded gasoline to reduce consumption of petroleum-based fuels and reduce air pollution. Also, USDA acquired 15 General Motors sedans designed to operate on a blend of 85 percent ethanol, to test the feasibility of this type of alternative fuel.

4. Real Property Activity. In accordance with E.O. 12512, the Department conducted 56 real property utilization surveys comprising more than 38,780 acres of land with a fair market value of over $141 million. The Office of Operations collaborated with

the Department's land holding agencies to report as excess to the General Services Administration 24.5 acres of land and improvements valued at over $364,000.

5. Customer Outreach Program. Published separate Departmental Property Management Guides for beginners, reviewers, utilization specialists and program managers. Inaugurated a Departmental training course for accountable Property Officers. Issued new regulations on managing materials, establishing new property replacement and use standards, and rules for controlling ADP software.

OFFICE OF INFORMATION RESOURCES MANAGEMENT

The Office of Information Resources Management (OIRM) provides policy guidance, leadership, coordination, and direction to the Department's information management and information technology activities in support of USDA program delivery. The office provides long-range IRM planning guidance, performs reviews of agency IRM programs, coordinates inter-agency IRM projects, and defines and implements standards to promote sharing of information. The office manages the voice and data telecommunications programs of the Department and operates the National Computer Center at Kansas City, Missouri and Fort Collins, Colorado.

Current Activities:

1. Agency Liaison Officer (ALO) Program. ALOs work with USDA agencies to integrate analysis of agency IRM budgets and plans through increased oversight, earlier planning, concentration on IRM components of cross-cutting issues, and detailed IRM budget reviews. This program was staffed in late fiscal year 1992/early fiscal year 1993, and commenced operations in fiscal year 1993.

2. USDA Telecommunications Long Range Plan. OIRM, with contractor support, is leading an interagency project team in formulating a comprehensive standards-based telecommunications strategy that will support USDA Business and Strategic Plans. The completion of this plan is scheduled for the third quarter of fiscal year 1993.

3. Easy Access Pilot Projects. Because of the success of the initial Easy Access pilot project, refinement and expansion will follow. New technologies and management techniques will be tested in an effort to provide better services to USDA clients. OIRM will continue to lead this effort for the Department in fiscal year 1993. For example, in fiscal year 1993 OIRM is working with the farm service agencies (ASCS, SCS and FmHA), to develop InfoShare, the framework for an integrated field office information system.

4. Telecommunications Standards and Policy. OIRM is currently engaged in a review of all departmental regulations to ensure they contain reference to available services and industry standards. A major goal is to rewrite all departmental directives for telecommunications policy to ensure that they are based on accepted industry and governmental standards.

5. Data Management. OIRM is establishing the foundation for a Data Management program to effectively and efficiently use information to support and accomplish the mission of USDA. OIRM will provide oversight for a Departmentwide, comprehensive, and cooperative program to improve information sharing, reduce paperwork, improve public service, and oversee the development of standards, guidelines, and policies for handling Departmental and agency data.

Selected Examples of Recent Progress:

1. EXECTRAC Implementation. OIRM provided program management leadership in the development of the Secretary's Controlled Correspondence system called EXECTRAC. This system was developed and implemented jointly by OIRM and an 8-A contractor, and provides up-to-the-minute-status on each piece of correspondence sent to the Secretary. EXECTRAC has significantly improved the response time for answering correspondence.

2. Easy Access Initiative. From the fall of 1991 through the summer of 1992, USDA tested several new technologies and management techniques to improve services to farmers and reduce the amount of red tape and paperwork farmers face when doing business with USDA. Seven pilot projects were implemented. The Easy Access Initiative has been so successful that two of the pilot projects have been implemented Department-wide.

3. Directives Automation and Reduction. OIRM designed and developed a Departmental Automated Directives System (DADS) from the previous paper-based Departmental Directives System that includes the Secretary's Memoranda and all Departmental regulations, manuals, or notices. DADS is an on-line text management system that is accessible Nation-wide by USDA employees. OIRM also initiated the first OIRM Directives Reduction Campaign which resulted in the elimination of 44 Departmental Directives.

4. Information Technology. The committee for Information Technology (INFOTECH) was established to provide a forum for U.S. Department of Agriculture agencies to receive and exchange up-to-date information on new and emerging technology and issues that have impact on systems for managing records, forms, and directives. INFOTECH facilitates sharing of expertise and keeping agencies informed of new and emerging technologies.

5. Computerized Information Delivery Service. OIRM led an interagency effort to define requirements and recompute the computer/data communications services contract for the dissemination of USDA time-sensitive and perishable reports to the public. When awarded in fiscal year 1995, the replacement contract is expected to reduce the costs to participating government agencies by approximately 20 percent.

OFFICE OF ADVOCACY AND ENTERPRISE

The Office of Advocacy and Enterprise (OAE) provides overall policy and program guidance, leadership, coordination and direction for the Department's civil rights and equal opportunity programs; plans and coordinates the participation of women, hispanics, blacks, native Americans, persons with disabilities, minority colleges and universities, etc., in departmental programs; oversees procurements to assure maximum participation of small and disadvantaged businesses in the procurement process; and directs and monitors agency compliance in promoting full and open competition in the Department's contracting process.

Current Activities:

1. Small and Disadvantaged Business Utilization (OSDBU). During FY 1992, OAE initiated monthly small business breakfast seminars to bring potential small business contractors together with USDA program officials to discuss issues that will help increase small business participation in USDA's contracting efforts. OSDBU also initiated, with the Small Business Administration, efforts to assist minority firms to become more competitive in filling USDA food commodity requirements. OSDBU's efforts resulted in an increased participation of 100 percent over FY 1991.

2. Equal Opportunity. A total of 650 complaints alleging discrimination in USDA programs and activities were processed in fiscal year 1992. OAE initiated its program investigations activity. During FY 1992, OAE conducted 11 on-sight investigations into alleged program discrimination.

3. Special Emphasis Outreach Program. USDA cannot retain senior black male employees. As part of its black male initiative, OAE sponsored USDA's first training seminar for senior-level black males. The training was designed to provide black male employees the necessary skills to effectively compete for USDA employment opportunities.

Selected Examples of Recent Progress:

1. Equal Opportunity. During FY 1992 USDA's minority employment increased from 16.6 percent to 17.0 percent, and female employment increased from 40.3 percent to 40.9 percent.

2. Equal Opportunity. OAE completed the implementation of the reorganization of Equal Opportunity Services. As a result, OAE's complaints closure increased from 195 in FY 1991 to 294 in FY 1992.

3. Small and Disadvantaged Business Utilization (OSDBU). OAE expanded its outreach to the small business community. During FY 1992, OAE sponsored an ADP subcontracting conference which had over 200 small, minority, and women-owned business participants and held a procurement symposium targeted at addressing the unique concerns of women who own businesses.

4. Special Emphasis Outreach Program. OAE provide USDA agency Heads with training on managing a diverse work force. The training provided insights to changes in the work force that are anticipated in the future and suggested ways to effectively manage these changes. OAE also provided training on the prevention of sexual harassment to all of USDA's Senior Executive Service employees.

OFFICE OF ADMINISTRATIVE LAW JUDGES/JUDICIAL OFFICER

The Office of Administrative Law Judges consists of five Judges, who conduct rulemaking and adjudicatory hearings throughout the United States in proceedings subject to the Administrative Procedure Act (APA), 5 U.S.C. 554 et seq. There are approximately 37 statutes administered by agencies within the Department of Agriculture requiring APA hearings. The Judges issue initial decisions and orders in adjudicatory proceedings, which become final decisions of the Secretary, unless appealed to the Secretary's Judicial Officer by a party to the proceedings. Final consent orders are issued by the Judges following hearings, or upon waiver of hearing. In addition, the Judges perform related duties consistent with their duties under the APA, such as the Chief Judge's performance of administrative duties and the conduct of appropriate, non-APA hearings.

The Judicial Officer serves as final deciding officer, in place of the Secretary, in quasi-judicial regulatory proceedings. These include appeals from Administrative Law Judges' initial decisions, and reparation proceedings under the Perishable Agricultural Commodities Act and the Packers and Stockyards Act, that under the APA do not require hearings before Administrative Law Judges. Any party to a proceeding may appeal Administrative Law Judges' initial decisions to the Judicial Officer. Oral argument is discretionary. The Judicial Officer also rules on matters arising in proceedings that are certified by the Administrative Law Judges.

The Office of the Hearing Clerk receives, files and serves pleadings, briefs, and decisions. It maintains the official records of the Department, including transcripts of adjudicatory and rulemaking hearings, and in the event of an appeal, certifies such records to the Court of Appeals or District Court for review.

The Hearing Clerk is responsible for publication of Agriculture Decisions, the official compilation of quasi-judicial and judicial decisions issued under regulatory laws administered by the Department. In addition to cases before the Administrative Law Judges, the Hearing Clerk processed the following in fiscal year 1992:

Perishable Agricultural Commodities Act:	
Reparation Cases	421
Packers and Stockyards Act Reparation Cases	7
Certification and Authentication of Documents	70
Certification of Administrative Records to Federal Courts	10
Board of Contracts Appeals:	
Scheduling/Canceling Reporting Service	38

The following table indicates the number of hearings held by Administrative Law Judges during the past 3 fiscal years, together with the number of initial decisions after hearings, initial decisions upon default, and final consent orders following hearing or upon waiver of hearing. At the end of fiscal year 1992, 111 cases were pending before the Judges, of which 50 were scheduled for hearings.

HEARINGS AND DISPOSITIONS
(Adjudicatory; Unless Otherwise Indicated)

	FY 1990		FY 1991		FY 1992	
TYPE OF PROCEEDING	Hearings	Disposit-ions	Hear-ings	Disposit-ions	Hear-ings	Disposit-ions
Agri. Marketing Agreement, 1937:						
Adjudicatory	4	17	2	22	--	11
Rule-Making	7	10	5	2	3	1
Inspection & Grading	--	4	--	--	--	1
Animal Plant Health Inspection Service Laws:						
Veterinary Accreditation	3	6	1	8	2	7
Animal Quarantine	4	70	7	69	1	72
Plant Quarantine	2	53	--	70	2	121
Animal Welfare Act	2	37	5	56	4	44
Beef Promotion Research Act	--	--	1	1	--	2
Debarment, Nonprocurement Suspension	--	--	2	--	--	2
Meat/Poultry Inspection	1	11	--	8	1	8
Forest Service Sourcing Area Applications	--	--	7	30	--	4
Grain Standards Act	--	--	--	4	--	--
Honey Research Promotion Consumer Information	--	--	--	1	--	--
Horse Protection Act	3	44	16	164	22	149
Inspection & Grading	--	--	--	3	--	--
Packers & Stockyards	8	140	3	101	3	81
Perishable Agricultural Commodities Act	5	46	5	88	4	61
Potato Research & Promotion Act	--	2	--	1	1	1
Tobacco Inspection/ Price Support (Rule)	2	2	2	2	--	--
TOTALS	41	442	56	630	43	565

EMERGENCY PROGRAMS

The Emergency Programs serves as the Department's focal point for coordinating emergency programs and is the primary contact with the Federal Emergency Management Agency and all other Federal Departments and Agencies having emergency programs responsibilities. EP establishes emergency programs policy and manages emergency activities of the Department to ensure that a structure is in place to assess the impact of a disaster on food production, processing, and storage facilities, and that food and assistance programs are available in the disaster impacted area. EP provides leadership, guidance, direction, and coordination to ten USDA Regional Emergency Staffs, Regional Emergency Management Teams, 50 State Emergency Boards, and approximately 2,800 County Emergency Boards. EP provides representation on NATO and other international committees dealing with emergency activities relating to food and agriculture.

Current Activities

1. Departmental Regulation 1800-1, Departmental Emergency Programs Responsibilities. In January 1992, EP initiated activities to update this regulation that assigns emergency responsibilities throughout the Department. The rewrite has been completed and concurrence obtained from all USDA Agencies. This regulation awaits the Secretary's signature. Upon signing of the regulation, it will be printed and disseminated nationwide.

2. Directory, USDA Emergency Personnel. This document lists USDA emergency personnel at national headquarters, regions, and States, as well as other Federal Departments and Agencies that impact USDA emergency programs. This document was updated, printed and distributed to all headquarters, regions and States involved in USDA emergency programs response.

3. Emergency Operations Handbook for USDA State and County Emergency Boards. In February 1992, EP initiated an effort to restructure and rewrite this Handbook to make it more useful to USDA regional, State and county personnel having emergency programs responsibilities. This Handbook should be ready for printing and distribution in the 2nd quarter of FY93.

4. NATO and USDA Data Bases. In 1992, EP initiated action, at the request of the NATO Food and Agriculture Planning Committee, to prepare a NATO agriculture data base for use in the event of a war or threat of war involving NATO. The USDA data base is being established to assist EP in preparing initial assessments of the impact of a disaster on agriculture related facilities. The data will be used to provide the Secretary and senior staff with a better initial insight to the possible agriculture related damage assessment.

WORKING CAPITAL FUND

Purpose Statement

The USDA Working Capital Fund (WCF) was established in legislation appropriating funds to the Department for FY 1944 and by 7 U.S.C. 2235. It is used to finance services provided to USDA and non-USDA agencies on a centralized basis. The costs of providing services to all WCF clients are recovered on the basis of the level of service each client receives. Services to non-USDA agencies reduce the share of fixed costs for WCF-supported services as the number of agencies sharing those costs expands.

Centrally managed operations provide efficient, economical services through economies of scale, extensive management attention, and high-level, regular fund control reviews. Users benefit from cost avoidances for administrative and support services. The Director, Office of Finance and Management (OFM), serves as WCF Comptroller, serving to monitor and supervise fund management activities. Five USDA agencies: OFM, the Office of Operations (OO), the Office of Public Affairs (OPA), the Office of Information Resources Management (OIRM), and the Office of the Executive Secretariat (OES) manage activities supported by the Fund. All are under the direct supervision of the Assistant Secretary for Administration except for OPA and OES activities. OPA activities are supervised by the Director, Office of Public Affairs, and OES activities are managed as a distinct activity under the Office of the Secretary.

OFM manages the National Finance Center (NFC), which provides financial and administrative management services to USDA agencies and more than 30 non-USDA entities.

OPA manages 2 WCF activities -- Video and Teleconferencing Services (V/T), and Design Center. V/T provides video production services to USDA agencies, and studio and production facilities for teleconferences in which USDA agencies participate. Design Center provides USDA agencies with exhibit design and visitor center support services.

OIRM manages 6 activity centers. Under the National Computer Center (NCC) umbrella organization there are three activity centers: NCC/Mainframe (NCC/MF), located in Kansas City, Missouri; NCC/Network Management Services (NCC/NMS), located in Fort Collins, Colorado; and NCC/Applications Design (NCC/AD), also in Fort Collins. These activities provide mainframe computing services, ADP training, and other ADP services; telecommunications services on behalf of USDA agencies; and systems and software development services to USDA agencies and non-USDA users. The Computer Services Unit provides ADP services to the Office of the Secretary and Departmental staff offices. The Telephone Services Operation is responsible for equipment and telephone system maintenance, as well as voice mail services. Local Area Network operates and maintains the local area network system serving the Headquarters buildings complex.

OO provides personal property management, mail and reproduction management, and executive support services through 10 activity centers. Central Supply-Stores and Central Supply-Forms provide centralized supply and forms management, as well as warehousing and inventory services. Central Excess Property Operation provides Departmental agencies with excess and surplus property disposition services in addition to furniture rehabilitation services. Central Mail Unit, Copier Service, Duplicating Unit, and Departmental Mailing List Service furnish USDA agencies with door-to-door mail pick up and delivery services, walk up and short order copier services, special order duplicating services, and updating and maintenance of the various Departmental mailing lists. Central Imprest Fund, Central Shipping and Receiving, and Agriculture Contract Automation System, offer a variety of executive support services to USDA agencies. Among these include cash disbursement for small purchases and travel, receipt and shipment of parcels, and maintenance of a procurement language software system.

The Office of the Executive Secretariat (OES) serves to improve correspondence management, tracking, and recordkeeping for the Department.

WORKING CAPITAL FUND

CLASSIFICATION BY OBJECTS

1992 and Estimated 1993 and 1994

	1992	1993	1994
Personnel Compensation:			
Headquarters	$6,317,000	$6,786,000	$7,265,000
Field	58,048,000	64,429,000	68,688,000
11 Total personnel compensation	64,365,000	71,215,000	75,953,000
12 Personnel benefits . . .	10,541,000	11,955,000	12,878,000
13 Benefits for former personnel	122,000	130,000	135,000
Total pers. comp. & benefits	75,028,000	83,300,000	88,966,000
Other Objects:			
21 Travel	1,276,000	1,468,000	1,504,000
22 Transportation of things	950,000	788,000	813,000
23.1 Building rental	4,065,000	5,654,000	5,726,000
23.2 Communications, utilities, and misc. charges	21,275,000	26,130,000	29,599,000
24 Printing and reproduction	1,277,000	1,237,000	1,278,000
25 Other services	40,723,000	46,715,000	47,520,000
26 Supplies and materials	6,630,000	7,284,000	8,006,000
31 Equipment	13,867,000	20,514,000	21,108,000
43 Interest	4,000	3,000	3,000
Total other objects	90,067,000	109,793,000	115,557,000
Total	165,095,000	193,093,000	204,523,000
Position Data:			
Average Salary, ES positions	$103,000	$107,000	$107,000
Average Salary, GM/GS positions	$26,000	$27,000	$28,000
Average Grade, GM/GS positions	8.2	8.4	8.4

WORKING CAPITAL FUND

Program Activity:

Current Estimate, 1993	$193,093,000
Budget Estimate, 1994	204,523,000
Increase Over 1993	11,430,000

SUMMARY OF INCREASES AND DECREASES (Program Activity)

Item of Change	1993 Estimated	Program Changes	1994 Estimated
1. Sup./ Cen. Svc	$19,527,000	+$329,000	$19,856,000
CS Stores	2,055,000	+43,000	2,098,000
CS Forms	3,761,000	+81,000	3,842,000
CEPO.	1,651,000	+29,000	1,680,000
CSR.	453,000	+42,000	495,000
Imp. Fund	281,000	-48,000	233,000
AGCAS	276,000	+8,000	284,000
Cent. Mail	3,473,000	+118,000	3,591,000
Dupl. Unit	1,342,000	+20,000	1,362,000
Cop. Svc.	4,062,000	+52,000	4,114,000
DMLS	195,000	+15,000	210,000
Ex. Secr.	1,788,000	+48,000	1,836,000
Tr. Ctr.	190,000	-79,000	111,000
2. Vid./Tel, and Visual Des. Svc.	4,337,000	+102,000	4,439,000
Vid./Tel.	1,705,000	+82,000	1,787,000
Des Center	2,632,000	+20,000	2,652,000
3. Finance & Mgt.	108,811,000	+7,565,000	116,376,000
4. ADP Svcs.	41,215,000	+2,783,000	43,998,000
NCC/Mainfr	32,300,000	+2,355,000	34,655,000
NCC/FTS	2,963,000	+330,000	3,293,000
NCC/AD	2,752,000	+227,000	2,979,000
CSU	1,245,000	+42,000	1,287,000
TSO	887,000	+53,000	940,000
LAN	1,068,000	-224,000	844,000
Rec. Op.	173,890,000	+10,779,000	184,669,000
Cap. Equip..	19,203,000	+651,000	19,854,000
Total	193,093,000	+11,430,000	204,523,000

PROJECT STATEMENT
(On basis of program activity)

Project	1992 Actual Amount	1992 Actual Staff-Years	1993 (Estimated) Amount	1993 (Estimated) Staff-Years	Increase or Decrease	1994 (Estimated) Amount	1994 (Estimated) Staff-Years
1. Sup./ Cen. Svc.	$18,010,000	195	$19,527,000	206	+$329,000	$19,856,000	203
CS Stores	2,438,000	7	2,055,000	8	+43,000	2,098,000	8
CS Forms	3,428,000	30	3,761,000	30	+81,000	3,842,000	29
CEPO	1,602,000	12	1,651,000	12	+29,000	1,680,000	12
CSR	363,000	1	453,000	1	+42,000	495,000	1
Imp. Fund	174,000	4	281,000	5	-48,000	233,000	5
AGCAS	185,000	2	276,000	2	+8,000	284,000	2
Cent. Mail	3,361,000	82	3,473,000	82	+118,000	3,591,000	81
Dupl. Unit	1,082,000	11	1,342,000	11	+20,000	1,362,000	11
Cop. Svc.	4,054,000	28	4,062,000	29	+52,000	4,114,000	28
DMLS	161,000	3	195,000	3	+15,000	210,000	3
Ex. Secr.	1,162,000	15	1,788,000	21	+48,000	1,836,000	21
Tr. Ctr./1	0	0	190,000	2	-79,000	111,000	2
2. Vid/Tel & Visual Des. Svc.	4,230,000	23	4,337,000	27	+102,000	4,439,000	27
Vid./Tel.	1,717,000	11	1,705,000	13	+82,000	1,787,000	13
Des. Ctr.	2,513,000	12	2,632,000	14	+20,000	2,652,000	14
3. Fin. and Mgt.	93,904,000	1,449	108,811,000	1,532	+7,565,000	116,376,000	1,515
4. ADP Svc	36,988,000	203	41,215,000	218	+2,783,000	43,998,000	216
NCC/MF	29,850,000	148	32,300,000	149	+2,355,000	34,655,000	147
NCC/FTS	2,430,000	24	2,963,000	23	+330,000	3,293,000	23
NCC/AD	1,920,000	20	2,752,000	36	+227,000	2,979,000	36
CSU	1,323,000	11	1,245,000	9	+42,000	1,287,000	9
TSO	683,000	0	887,000	1	+53,000	940,000	1
LAN	782,000	0	1,068,000	0	-224,000	844,000	0
Rec. Op.	153,132,000	1,870	173,890,000	1,983	+10,779,000	184,669,000	1,961
Cap. Eq.	11,963,000	0	19,203,000	0	+651,000	19,854,000	0
Total . .	165,095,000	1,870	193,093,000	1,983	+11,430,000	204,523,000	1,961

1/ Training Center (new WCF activity center) was approved by the Director, Office of Management and Budget January 12, 1993 (approval required under 7 U.S.C. 2235).

WORKING CAPITAL FUND

Explanation of Program

Authorized under Public Law 78-129, making appropriations to USDA for FY 1944 (7 U.S.C. 2235), the USDA Working Capital Fund finances services provided to USDA agencies on a centralized basis. Under the law, only activities approved by the Director of the Office of Management and Budget (OMB) may be carried out under the Fund. Centralization is recommended by the Department and approved by OMB when:

-- Centralization will result in cost savings due to:

- Economies of scale
- Reduced overhead
- Central cost-based management
- Coordination which avoids duplication of effort among agencies

-- Centralization offers other advantages such as:

- Improved services to agencies and to the public
- Availability of services to agencies which could not afford them except on a centralized basis
- Ability to replace equipment on a long-term basis through the use of depreciation charges to users

The Fund received an initial appropriation of $400,000 for FY 1944. Over the years, additional working capital has been made available through initial transfers into the Fund of activities meeting the above criteria and through Congressional authorizations to receive growth capital from serviced USDA agencies. WCF operations are financed by charging user agencies the actual costs of providing required services. The following are services financed through the Fund:

<u>Supply and Other Central Services.</u> The Office of Operations manages the following services under this category: (a) central supply, which provides for the acquisition, receipt, storage, issuance, packing, and shipment of office and other supplies, blank forms, and miscellaneous materials for the Department and other Government agencies; (b) central mail services, which include operation of the USDA mail processing, messenger, and automated mailing list services; (c) central excess property, which coordinates receipt, rehabilitation, and distribution of personal property for the Department and other Government agencies; (d) central shipping and receiving services; (e) central imprest fund, which provides cash advances for small purchases and travel; (f) automated contract system used by agencies and staff offices to prepare procurement documents; and (g) copier and duplicating services which provide duplicating, reproducing, binding, addressing and mailing, and short-order and walk-up copier stations for duplicating and xerographic production. The Office of the Executive Secretariat provides referral and correspondence control services for mail addressed to the Secretary, the immediate Office of the Secretary, and the Department. The Office of Personnel manages a Training Center that provides training facilities to agencies in the D.C. Metropolitan area.

FUNDING FROM NON-USDA AGENCIES
(On basis of program activity)

Project	1992 Actual Amount	1992 Actual Staff-Years	1993 (Estimated) Amount	1993 (Estimated) Staff-Years	Increase or Decrease	1994 (Estimated) Amount	1994 (Estimated) Staff-Years
1. Sup./ Cen. Svc.	$1,580,000	0	$1,909,000	0	+$214,000	$2,123,000	0
2. Vid/Tel & Visual. Des. Svc.	26,000	0	25,000	0	+0	25,000	0
3. Fin. & Mgt.	46,672,000	648	60,182,000	844	+6,973,000	67,155,000	805
4. ADP Svc	875,000	0	765,000	3	+90,000	855,000	3
Total . .	49,153,000	648	62,881,000	847	+7,277,000	70,158,000	808

Video and Teleconferencing, & Visual Design Services. These activities, managed by the Office of Public Affairs plan, design, and produce visual information materials, exhibits, art, and graphics materials for the Department and other Government agencies.

National Finance Center. This activity in the Office of Finance and Management designs, develops, implements, and operates centralized administrative systems for the Department. Centralized payroll, personnel, voucher and vendor payments, billings and collections, property management, accounting, and financial recordkeeping systems are currently provided. It also produces external financial reports to Treasury and other agencies, and internal management reports for Departmental agencies. In addition, the National Finance Center provides financial and accounting services to a number of other Federal Departments through "cross-servicing" agreements and serves as recordkeeper for the Thrift Savings Plan System under the Federal Employee Retirement System.

JUSTIFICATION OF INCREASES AND DECREASES

Centralized administrative services enable users to receive high-quality services at the lowest possible cost of operation. Services are operated in this manner in an effort to minimize unit costs for recurring operations. Expectations of progress in minimizing unit costs, as well as expected increases in demand for Fund-supported services among USDA agencies and existing non-USDA users serve as the basis for the FY 1993 revised and FY 1994 initial Working Capital Fund (WCF) cost estimates.

Centralized administrative services are subject to regular oversight consistent with both Administration management initiatives and Departmental productivity improvement activities. This oversight is undertaken to determine whether these activities should continue as centrally managed services and to offer Departmental management analyses of alternative operating methods. Enhanced productivity and cost-effectiveness result. The results of such oversight exercised in FY 1992 are reflected in the revised FY 1993 and initial FY 1994 cost estimates provided. As regular oversight is conducted, these estimates may be adjusted significantly, subject to review and approval by Departmental management.

The following is an explanation of program activity changes from FY 1993 to FY 1994 currently anticipated.

(1) An increase of $329,000 for recurring operations of Supply and Other Central Services consisting of:

Central Supply Stores	+$43,000
Central Supply Forms	+81,000
Central Excess Property	+29,000
Central Shipping and Receiving	+42,000
Central Imprest Fund	-48,000
Agriculture Contract Automation Service	+8,000
Central Mail Unit	+118,000
Duplicating Unit	+20,000
Copier Service	+52,000
Departmental Mailing List	+15,000
Office of the Executive Secretariat	+48,000
Training Center	-79,000
Total	+$329,000

Need for Change. Cost increases in this area are, for the most part, inflationary. The reduction in the Central Imprest Fund reflects lower estimates for supply and administrative management costs. The reduction in the Training Center represents the elimination of on-time start-up costs for opening of the Center (Note: Approval for WCF funding of a Training Center was granted by the Director, Office of Management and Budget, as required under 7 U.S.C. 2235, on January 12, 1993).

Nature of Change. Cost increases in excess of inflation are expected for Central Shipping and Receiving, Departmental Mailing List services. In Central Shipping and Receiving, non-inflationary increases are due to non-capitalized equipment acquisitions and maintenance charges. Non-inflationary cost increases in Departmental Mailing List services are due to increased depreciation costs on capitalized equipment.

(2) An increase of $102,000 for recurring operations of Video and Teleconferencing, and Visual Design Services consisting of:

Video and Teleconferencing Services	+$82,000
Design Services	+20,000
Total	+$102,000

Need for Change. Cost increases for Visual Design Services are expected to be less than inflation. Cost increases in Video and Teleconferencing are for enhancements in video production capability.

Nature of Change. Non-inflationary cost increases in Video and Teleconferencing Services reflect increases in depreciation on new equipment to improve reliability of service and contract support costs. All cost increases in Design Services are the result of personnel and other cost inflation with a slight offsetting reduction in depreciation costs.

(3) An increase of $7,565,000 for recurring operations of the National Finance Center (NFC).

Need for Change. Cost increases reflect demand increases among systems operated at the NFC. Fulfillment of prior service obligations to non-USDA users (primarily for Federal Employee Retirement System/Thrift Savings Plan services) will result in a significant increase in costs associated with services to non-USDA agencies (about 74 percent of the total cost increase of $7.5 million). Cost increases for core services to USDA agencies will be less than inflation.

Nature of Change. Non-inflationary cost increases at the NFC reflect costs for additional personnel, needed to meet increased non-USDA demand for services, and equipment expenses (purchase and rental of equipment, maintenance, software support, etc.) related to mainframe computer and other equipment needed to process expected increases in total workload volume. The most significant increases in workload volume will come in payroll/personnel services, which is a reflection of greater non-USDA activity, and Thrift Savings Plan recordkeeping and loan operations support.

(4) A net increase of $2,783,000 for recurring operations of ADP systems consisting of:

NCC/Mainframe	+$2,355,000
NCC/FTS-2000	+330,000
NCC/Applications Design	+227,000
Computer Services Unit	+42,000
Telephone Service Operations	+53,000
Local Area Network	-224,000
Total	+$2,783,000

Need for Change. Increases in demand estimates for mainframe computer services operated on IBM systems (13 percent), and telecommunications services such as electronic mail services (10 percent) are the principal reasons for ADP system cost increases. Users' increasing need for telecommunications and mainframe ADP support services require improvements in technological and management efficiency. The increases in total costs in mainframe and telecommunications services will result in lower unit operating costs.

Nature of Change. Increases in mainframe ADP services reflect increases in staffing levels to support mainframe operations, and increases in equipment rental costs and associated supply costs (e.g., software). There are partial offsetting reductions in depreciation on capitalized equipment.

(5) An expenditure of $19,854,000 for capital acquisitions in FY 1994 ($19,203,000 in FY 1993):

(a) Capital acquisitions for Supply and Other Central Services of $988,000.

Central Supply Stores	$0
Central Supply Forms	0
Central Excess Property	0
Central Shipping and Receiving	0
Central Imprest Fund	0
Agriculture Contract Automation Service	0
Central Mail Unit	30,000
Duplicating Unit	71,000
Copier Service	791,000
Departmental Mailing List	20,000
Office of the Executive Secretariat	76,000
Training Center	0
Total	$988,000

Need for Change. All expenditures will be in mail distribution and automation services, copier and duplicating services, and executive correspondence management and tracking.

Nature of Change. Acquisitions in copier/duplicating services will take advantages of newer technology in large and medium volume copiers and duplicating equipment. Acquisitions will assist these centers in responding to expected increases in demand for such services. Mail distribution services will obtain equipment to improve efficiency in distribution and take advantage of ADP technologies in maintaining mailing list data. The Office of the Executive Secretariat will procure equipment in an effort to improve tracking of executive correspondence and data storage capacity.

(b) Capital acquisitions for Video and Teleconferencing, and Visual Design Services of $250,000.

Video and Teleconferencing Services	$215,000
Visual Design Services	35,000
Total	$250,000

Need for Change. Most of the FY 1994 amount is in response to the need to improve the quality and reliability of services in video and teleconferencing services. Design services will realize improvements in production and graphics capabilities through its procurements.

Nature of Change. Acquisitions in video and teleconferencing services include network and teleconferencing equipment to improve those services and respond to expected increases in demand (approximately 5 percent in both video production requests and teleconferences). Further, production equipment upgrades (editing system, studio equipment, field video equipment) will improve the quality and reliability of service to USDA agencies. Purchase of plotter and printer equipment will enable the Design Center to improve the graphics and reproduction capabilities of its operations.

(c) Capital acquisitions for the National Finance Center of $13,130,000.

Need for Change. Purchases are needed for CPU upgrades to respond to increases in service demand, improve data telecommunications capabilities, and other ADP-related needs.

Nature of Change. Upgrading mainframe computer operations (CPU upgrade, associated software improvements) to respond to expected demand and avoid service interruptions will make up about half of total acquisitions. The remainder will be spent on telecommunications and video equipment, mail support, image processing equipment, and other ADP-related equipment.

(d) Capital acquisitions for ADP Services of $5,486,000.

NCC/Mainframe	$4,726,000
NCC/FTS-2000	403,000
NCC/Applications Design	0
Computer Services Unit	127,000
Telephone Service Operations	55,000
Local Area Network	175,000
Total	$5,486,000

Need for Change. Most of the FY 1994 amount (86 percent) will be devoted to mainframe computer services. Acquisitions in ADP Services will address mainframe equipment and support needs, personal computer and network equipment needs, and telecommunications support requirements.

Nature of Change. Mainframe computer and system operations will benefit from software acquisitions and direct access storage device equipment acquisitions, allowing users improved direct data access and more effective software applications use. Telecommunications and teleconferencing services will also be improved through related equipment acquisitions, allowing users to take advantage of enhancements in network and data communications technologies.

WORKING CAPITAL FUND

GEOGRAPHIC BREAKDOWN OF OBLIGATIONS AND STAFF-YEARS
1992 and Estimated 1993 and 1994

	1992		1993		1994	
	Amount	Staff Years	Amount	Staff Years	Amount	Staff Years
Louisiana	$102,406,000	1,441	$120,685,000	1,524	$128,774,000	1,507
Colorado	4,491,000	44	6,046,000	59	6,675,000	59
Missouri	30,428,000	148	37,017,000	149	39,381,000	147
Maryland	7,497,000	49	7,597,000	50	7,620,000	49
Dist. of Columbia	20,273,000	188	21,748,000	201	22,073,000	199
Total, Available or Estimate . .	165,095,000	1,870	193,093,000	1,983	204,523,000	1,961

WORKING CAPITAL FUND

STATUS OF PROGRAM

Current activities and selected examples of recent progress are outlined below:

SUPPLY AND OTHER CENTRAL SERVICES

Current Activities. Activity centers in this area managed by the Office of Operations (OO) continue to aggressively implement management reforms to hold down costs. Ongoing efforts are focused on two principal areas -- improvements in warehouse management and automated inventory management. Warehousing activities of Central Supply-Stores (except self-service store), Central Supply-Forms, and Central Excess Property Operation are physically consolidated at a single facility in Landover, Maryland. This holds down administrative support costs of these operations. Also, automation of the physical inventory for these activity centers provides a more accurate accounting and inventory of the stock items on hand in the warehouse facility. FY 1992 was the first full year of operation of the Office of the Executive Secretariat (OES), established to improve the efficiency and effectiveness of executive correspondence management. It is undertaking improvements in automation of correspondence management functions so that USDA can respond more effectively to inquiries and the information needs of the agricultural community.

Selected Examples of Recent Progress.

1. A feasibility study was commissioned to determine if the self-service facility could be moved to a new location and if space alterations could be implemented to improve item accountability and enhance traffic flow.

2. Established publication inventories for Forest Service, Office of Public Affairs, Government Printing Office (GPO), and Human Nutrition Information Service. The transfer, from GPO facilities in Laurel, Maryland, will reduce USDA agency costs for publication storage and distribution.

3. Agreements entered into with the Resolution Trust Corporation and the Small Business Administration will ensure full utilization of all available warehouse space, enabling all users to achieve economies of scale with regard to fixed costs of operations.

4. To meet the emergency needs of agencies for executive furniture, the Central Excess Property Operation established a small inventory of such furniture to respond to short turn around demands.

5. The domestic mail pre-sort program has saved over $1,000,000 in postage costs at USDA headquarters and the National Finance Center. International pre-sort saved over $57,000 in FY 1991 and realized savings at a comparable rate in FY 1992.

6. Executive correspondence deliveries were increased from 3 to 7 per day to ensure a 2-hour turn around time for such mail, as required under the Secretary's correspondence system.

7. Duplicating services uses 100 percent black soybean ink in its offset process to support use of renewable agricultural products. Of all ink used, 99 percent is black (few other colors are requested). A presentation on the use of black soybean ink was made to the Recycle Products Conference, resulting in significant interest among other governmental and private sector organizations in obtaining and using this product.

8. Installation of high-speed laser printing equipment for duplicating services saved approximately $45,000 (annual cost) in printing costs. A study was initiated to determine the economic feasibility of replacing a high-volume duplicator with the aim of increasing savings.

9. Initiated a copier operator program to train disabled persons from various local organizations. This enhanced the workers' employability, expanded the recruitment pool, and met or exceeded the intent of legislation. In conjunction with one of the vendors serving Copier Service, 16 persons with disabilities were trained.

10. Conducted both high and low copier volume tests on paper manufactured with 50 percent recycled materials. Conversion to recycled paper was done in the offset printing process.

11. Installed laser printing equipment for Departmental mailing list services that will allow offices to receive reports 3-4 days sooner and will save $24,000 - $30,000 annually in postage costs. Barcode printers were installed that would save an additional $4,000 per month if fully utilized. Limits on utilization are a function of agency use of the system. Laser printing use has achieved cost avoidances to users of 11 cents per page and enabled users to get information one week sooner.

12. Procurement actions were completed that will achieve maintenance cost avoidances of approximately $130,000.

13. The Central Excess Property Operation supplied furniture items for shipment to the U.S. Embassy in Moscow, Russia. Other furniture items are being held, per shipping instructions, for shipment to Kiev and Alma-Ata, Russia. These services were provided in support of the Foreign Agricultural Service.

14. The old Lektriever filing system was replaced with a mechanical mobile filing system that requires 50 percent less space while increasing capacity by 64 percent.

15. Automation of the OES operation was enhanced by providing each staff member a personal computer and training to aid in referring and tracking documents.

16. A new correspondence management system -- EXECTRAC -- has been designed and prototype work sessions completed. Training is being provided to all OES staff and all sub-Cabinet and agency correspondence officers on this system and OES policies and procedures. The EXECTRAC system will provide more storage and retrieval capacity than the old system operated on Hewlett-Packard (HP) 3000 minicomputer systems. The system will also allow OES to avoid using some manually-driven procedures necessary under the old HP system.

17. OES has completed preparation of a procedures manual, the first written document of its kind produced for use within a USDA executive secretariat office and for agency correspondence control officers that identifies accepted policies and procedures in handling OES-controlled mail.

VIDEO AND TELECONFERENCING & VISUAL DESIGN SERVICES

Current Activities. Desktop publishing and computer graphics remain two of the most rapidly expanding areas in visual design. Upgrading capabilities in these areas is a primary focus in Design Center. These technologies greatly enhance services in support of conferences, seminars, hearings, public meetings, interagency programs, and the like.

Expansion in teleconferencing service affords users promising cost efficiencies. This allows users to avoid higher costs of travel while maintaining contact between agency headquarters offices and field offices, agricultural program clients, and the general public.

Selected Examples of Recent Progress.

1. "Lifelines," a video feature produced for the Women, Infants, and Children (WIC) Program, earned a Golden Eagle Award from the Council on International Non-Theatrical

Events (CINE). This is the fifth such award earned by the Video and Teleconferencing Division for video production in the past three years.

2. Recent exhibits and publication efforts produced by the Design Center include the following:

- o Revised Food Guide Pyramid and related material.
- o Workforce Diversity publication series.
- o Global Research and Forestry Campaign.
- o Visitor Centers at: Hell's Canyon, Oregon; Chippewa Forest, Minnesota; Vista del Largo, California; Quake Lake, Montana; Ketchikan, Alaska; El Yunque, Puerto Rico
- o Exhibits for: Scientist of the Year (Agricultural Research Service), World International Forestry Conference, Minority Careers in Forestry (California)

3. New executive videoconferencing services were introduced to USDA agencies during an open house on June 18, 1992. The day-long open house included more than 50 participants representing 25 agencies and staff offices, and featured seven hours of continuous connection to another new compressed videoconferencing facility at Fort Collins, Colorado. With the new technologies of this center, USDA continues to lead the way as one of the few agencies having full-service capability for audioconferencing, compressed videoconferencing, and satellite videoconferencing.

NATIONAL FINANCE CENTER

Current Activities: Efforts are continuing to integrate many National Finance Center (NFC) administrative and financial management systems as part of USDA's "Modern Administrative Processing (MAP)" strategy. The Department has conducted a thorough review of the MAP strategy with the aim of developing and bringing on-line a system to benefit all USDA agencies. A MAP Project Office has been established to oversee development and implementation of the new MAP strategy. The software application element of this strategy is the "Administrative Integrated Management System (AIMS)," an integrated software package and system design which will simplify access to and operations making use of NFC's financial and administrative data. Simplified access and operation for agency users will mean improved service, enhanced system efficiency, and lower cost.

Selected Examples of Recent Progress:

1. Enhancements have been made to the process for salary payments through electronic funds transfer (EFT). The result is that inquiries and claims for non-receipt of checks are being reduced, receipt of payments for net pay and voluntary allotments are being expedited, and better service and satisfaction are being provided to employees electing to use EFT to receive salary payments.

2. Disaster recovery drills were completed successfully. Such drills are necessary to validate the effectiveness and efficiency of disaster recovery notification procedures and to determine the point at which recovery operations would commence at the Philadelphia Sungard Recovery Megacenter. A successful telecommunication connectivity test was conducted on June 6, 1992 at the Philadelphia facility.

3. NFC upgraded its central processing capabilities and increased its system capability by 34 percent, measured in instructions per second.

AUTOMATED DATA PROCESSING SERVICES

Current Activities: The technological and management environment for ADP services continues to change, and the Office of Information Resources Management (OIRM) continues to adapt itself to meet users changing needs. In 1991, OIRM reorganized mainframe operations, telecommunications support, and applications design services under an umbrella structure. The result has been a decrease in unit costs of service for ADP activities managed with WCF support by OIRM.

<u>Selected Examples of Recent Progress:</u>

1. In October 1991, NCC/Mainframe created all Departmental mailing lists and shared folders on FTS2000Mail. As agencies migrate onto this system, lists will be updated.

2. NCC successfully installed SUPERTRACS for Federal Crop Insurance Corporation (FCIC) re-insurance access. This will support approximately 30 FCIC re-insurance companies on the IBM systems.

3. NCC/Applications Development began processing hierarchy codes for the Forest Service so that reports can be prepared by units in the Forest Service regions.

4. NCC completed modifications to the Residue Violation Information System (RVIS) for the Food Safety Inspection Service (FSIS), added indexes, reoptimized the database, cleaned excess statistics from the system tables, and cleared the application's audit trail table. FSIS was assisted in loading data from its MARCIS system, implementing changes in the system's load process that will now reject laboratory results of specific residues for samples of the CAST project. RVIS data dictionary maintenance and cleanup was conducted, and the performance of report queries was reviewed.

5. NCC conducted tests on the Delinquent Loan System (DLS) for the Farmers Home Administration (FmHA). FmHA state and county offices will use the new DLS to query potential borrowers for previous delinquent loan balances. An estimated 300 or more concurrent users are expected to access the system when it becomes fully operational.

6. NCC has also been working with the Soil Conservation Service (SCS) to add state distributional data and publication information documenting data sources for SCS systems OIRM supports. NCC/Mainframe has also been working with SCS to install communications packages on SCS systems it supports.

7. NCC has continued to make progress with development of the Departmental Automated Directives System (DADS). All screens, macros, and reports were completed for departmental active and archive databases. NCC has been working with contractor support to convert documents to the system. The Animal and Plant Health Inspection Service (APHIS) -- the participating agency -- reviewed the DADS system in January 1992.

8. NCC placed in production Phase 1 of the Processed Commodity Inventory Management System (PCIMS) in November 1991. Phases 2 and 3 were put in production in February and April 1992, respectively.

9. The Computer Services Unit has delivered and configured personal computers for the Department's Office of Personnel in its ongoing office automation effort.

10. The Computer Services Unit has also supported efforts to convert the Points of Light System from minicomputer systems to microcomputer systems and to establish full motion compressed video services in USDA's South Building.

11. The Telephone Services Operation office assisted USDA agencies in the successful transition to the Washington Interagency Telecommunications System (WITS) at various locations in Maryland, Virginia, and Washington, D.C.

PROPOSED LANGUAGE CHANGES

RENTAL PAYMENTS AND BUILDING OPERATIONS AND MAINTENANCE

The estimates include appropriation language for this item as follows (new language underscored; deleted matter enclosed in brackets):

Rental Payments (USDA)

For payment of space rental and related costs pursuant to Public Law 102-142 for programs and activities of the Department of Agriculture which are included in this Act, $50,503,000 of which $5,000,000 shall be retained by the Department of Agriculture for non-recurring repairs as determined by the Department of Agriculture: Provided, That in the event an agency within the Department of Agriculture should require modification of space needs, the Secretary of Agriculture may transfer a share of that agency's appropriation made available by this Act to this appropriation, or may transfer a share of this appropriation to that agency's appropriation, but such transfers shall not exceed 10 percentum of the funds made available for space rental and related costs to or from this account.

Building Operations and Maintenance

For the operation, maintenance, and repair of Agriculture buildings [pursuant to the delegation of authority from the Administrator of General Services authorized by 40 U.S.C. 486,] [$26,482,000], $25,581,000.

This change proposes to delete reference to the delegation of authority from GSA to operate and maintain the buildings in the Headquarters complex. USDA has been operating without a delegation of authority since 1989. The change reflects the current state of affairs.

RENTAL PAYMENTS AND BUILDING OPERATIONS AND MAINTENANCE

Appropriations Act, 1993	$76,203,000
Budget Estimate, 1994	76,084,000
Decrease in Appropriation	-119,000

SUMMARY OF INCREASES AND DECREASES
(On basis of appropriation)

Item of Change	1993 Estimated	Pay Cost	Other Changes	1994 Estimated
Rental Payments to GSA	$50,503,000	--	--	$50,503,000
Building Operations and Maintenance	25,700,000	+$104,000	-$223,000	25,581,000
Total Available	76,203,000	+104,000	-$223,000	76,084,000

PROJECT STATEMENT
(On basis of appropriation)

Item of Change	1992 Actual Amount	1992 Actual Staff-Years	1993 Estimated Amount	1993 Estimated Staff-Years	Increase or Decrease	1994 Estimated Amount	1994 Estimated Staff-Years
1. Rental Payments	$50,679,002	--	$50,503,000	--	--	$50,503,000	--
2. Building Operations & Maintenance	25,700,000	87	25,700,000	87	-119,000 (1)	25,581,000	86
Total, available or estimate	76,379,002	87	76,203,000	87	-119,000 (1)	76,084,000	86
Transfer to:							
SCS	219,768	--	--	--			
FmHA	263,830	--	--	--			
NASS	40,400	--	--	--			
Total, Trans.	+523,998	--	--	--			
Total, Appropriation	76,903,000	87	76,203,000	87			

RENTAL PAYMENTS AND BUILDING OPERATIONS AND MAINTENANCE

CLASSIFICATION BY OBJECTS

1992 and Estimated 1993 and 1994

	1992	1993	1994
Personnel Compensation:			
Headquarters	$3,698,887	$3,935,000	$4,023,000
11 Total personnel compensation	3,698,887	3,935,000	4,023,000
12 Personnel Benefits..........	647,927	696,000	712,000
13 Benefits for former personnel.................	1,943	3,000	3,000
Total pers. comp & benefits...	4,348,757	4,634,000	4,738,000
Other Objects:			
21 Travel......................	13,658	12,000	12,000
22 Transportation of things....	5,216	5,000	5,000
23.1 Rental payments to GSA......	45,690,249	45,503,000	45,503,000
23.3 Communications, utilities, and misc. charges.......	5,362,261	5,428,000	5,365,000
24 Printing....................	25,657	25,000	25,000
25 Other services..............	19,695,001	19,466,000	19,311,000
26 Supplies and materials......	651,009	582,000	580,000
31 Equipment...................	430,489	344,000	342,000
32 Land and Structures.........	156,705	204,000	203,000
Total other objects.........	72,030,245	71,569,000	71,346,000
Total direct obligations...........	$76,379,002	$76,203,000	$76,084,000
Position Data:			
Average Salary, GM/GS position...	$37,880	$39,282	$41,128
Average Grade, GM/GS positions...	10.34	10.37	10.45

EXPLANATION OF PROGRAM

This appropriation provides funding for the following activities:

Rental Payments to GSA. The fiscal year 1983 Agriculture Appropriations Act (P.L. 97-370) consolidated most of the Department's rental payments to the General Services Administration (GSA) into a single appropriation. This activity does not provide funding to cover space costs incurred in other funding areas such as trust funds, the Working Capital Fund, and other non-appropriated funds. The amount in this account represents the appropriated portion of the total Departmental charges for rent payments to the GSA for all agencies and staff offices of the Department except the Forest Service. In addition, the appropriation provides for the retention of funds by USDA for non-recurring repairs.

Building Operations and Maintenance. On October 1, 1984, GSA delegated the operations and maintenance functions for the buildings in the D.C. complex to the Department. This activity provides Departmental staff and support services to operate, maintain, and repair the buildings in the D.C. complex. GSA retains responsibility for major non-recurring repairs. Since 1989 when the GSA delegation expired, USDA has been responsible for managing, operating, maintaining, repairing, and improving the Headquarters Complex, which encompasses 14.1 acres of ground and 4 buildings containing approximately 3 million square feet of space occupied by approximately 8,000 employees.

JUSTIFICATION OF INCREASES AND DECREASES

(1) A net decrease of $119,000 for building operations and maintenance composed of the following:

(a) An increase of $569,000 which reflects a 2.7 percent increase in non-salary costs.

(b) An increase of $104,000 for pay costs which reflects the annualization of the fiscal year 1993 pay raise.

(c) A decrease of $792,000 for administrative efficiency.

Need for Change. To promote the efficient use of resources for administrative purposes, in keeping with the President's Executive Order, total USDA baseline outlays for these activities will be reduced by 3 percent in FY 1994, 6 percent in FY 1995, 9 percent in FY 1996 and 14 percent in FY 1997.

Nature of Change. In order to achieve this savings, reductions will be made in discretionary expenses such as -- travel and transportation of persons, transportation of things, communications, utilities, printing and reproduction services, contracts for equipment maintenance, training, other services, supplies, and equipment purchases.

GEOGRAPHIC BREAKDOWN OF OBLIGATIONS AND STAFF YEARS
1992 and Estimated 1993 and 1994

	1992		1993		1994	
	Amount	Staff Years	Amount	Staff Years	Amount	Staff Years
Washington, D.C.	$76,379,002	87	$76,203,000	87	$76,084,000	86
Unobligated balance	--	--	--	--	--	--
Total, Available or Estimate	$76,379,002	87	$76,203,000	87	$76,084,000	86

STATUS OF PROGRAM

RENTAL PAYMENTS TO GSA

This account was established by the Agriculture, Rural Development and Related Agencies Appropriations Act of 1983 to finance the appropriated portion of the payment of the General Services Administration's fees for rental of leased space and related services to all USDA agencies except the Forest Service, which is funded in another appropriations bill.

Current Activities and Recent Progress:

1. GSA Controlled Space. USDA occupies nearly 4 million square feet in 18 leased buildings and 4 owned buildings in the Washington Metropolitan area. During fiscal year 1992 approximately 150,000 square feet of leased space was acquired. Pending space requests for expansion amount to nearly 77,000 square feet and replacement space will be required for over 300,000 square feet in fiscal year 1993. The Department is developing a Long Range Strategic Space Plan designed to reduce agency fragmentation and duplication of administrative support requirements.

BUILDING OPERATIONS AND MAINTENANCE

Since October 1, 1984, USDA has maintained and operated the Washington, D.C. Headquarters Complex. The four building complex, which is located on the south side of the Mall, is composed of historic buildings varying in age from 55 to 112 years. The complex is the focal point for carrying out USDA's mission.

Because these facilities were allowed to deteriorate under previous management strategies and funding limitations prior to fiscal year 1985, USDA began a maintenance program to repair, improve, and restore the facilities. During fiscal year 1992, approximately $10 million of USDA funds were used for repairs and improvements. A major effort was undertaken to upgrade mechanical and electrical systems and make the buildings accessible to the handicapped and disabled. In fiscal year 1993, USDA will continue implementing its long-range plan to correct the serious building deterioration. This effort will maintain or restore the integrity of the buildings in the Headquarters complex, and keep them safe and operational until the proposed major renovation of the South Building is undertaken and accomplished.

Current Activities and Recent Progress:

1. Window Restoration. USDA is continuing its program to restore approximately 4,600 windows in the South Building that had been allowed to deteriorate over 50 years. Contracts awarded in fiscal years 1988 and 1989 restored all the windows on the main facades of the building. The windows in Court 2 were restored in fiscal year 1990, and in Court 1 in fiscal year 1991. In fiscal year 1992, contracts were awarded to restore the windows and masonry in Court 4 of the South Building and the windows in the Administration Building. Construction will begin in November of fiscal year 1993. The restoration of the windows in Court 3 is scheduled to be awarded in fiscal year 1993.

2. Environmental Quality Program. The safety and health of the occupants of these buildings is a major concern. Activities in the area of environmental safety and health include:

a. Asbestos Abatement. Under the continuing asbestos abatement program, a major contract to abate asbestos in the South Building Phase IV was completed in fiscal year 1992. Phase V for the South Building is planned for award in fiscal year 1993.

b. Air Quality. A $446,000 contract to upgrade the air quality in a portion of the South Building was awarded in fiscal year 1992. Due to the increasing requests from agencies for evaluation of air quality in their environments, a contract has been set up with a certified industrial hygiene consultant to conduct tests and provide evaluation reports as needed. Numerous air quality environmental tests were done in fiscal year 1992, and remedial actions initiated as necessary. This contract will continue in fiscal year 1993.

3. Electrical Improvement Program. In fiscal year 1992, emphasis was placed on badly needed electrical repairs and improvements. In the Administration Building, replacement of the east and west vault switchgear and installation of an emergency lighting system were completed. A new wiring system is currently being installed. In fiscal year 1992, contracts for the upgrade of transformer vault 10 ($504,000) and a corridor lighting energy retrofit ($52,709) were awarded. In the South Building, replacement of network protectors and switchgears in vaults 4 and 5 is underway.

4. Accessibility for Disabled. Two major projects to provide accessibility for disabled persons were completed in December 1992: a) a new elevator entrance at Wing 1 of the South Building, and b) new wheelchair lifts located at the Television Studio, Training Center, Jefferson Auditorium, and Ceremonial Patio. In fiscal year 1992, a $72,243 contract was awarded and completed for the new TARGET Center, which is a technological resource and training center for persons with disabilities.

5. Masonry Restoration Program. The repair of the masonry in Courts 2 and 3 of the South Building was completed in fiscal year 1992. The repair of the masonry in Court 4 was combined with the window restoration of Court 4 into a single contract and was awarded in fiscal year 1992 for $1,310,000. The repair of Court 5 is planned for fiscal year 1993. Courts 1 and 6 are planned for future fiscal years.

ADVISORY COMMITTEES

Purpose Statement

The Federal Advisory Committee Act (P.L. 92-463) was passed in 1972 to recognize that committees and similar groups provide a useful and beneficial means of furnishing expert advice to officers of the Federal Government. The Assistant Secretary for Administration is the principal Department Officer responsible for performing functions and coordinating activities of the Act.

The Agriculture, Rural Development and Related Agencies Appropriations Act of 1983 consolidated all USDA advisory committee funds, except those in the Forest Service and those paid from user fees, in a separate appropriation.

ADVISORY COMMITTEES

Available Funds and Staff-Years

1992 Actual and Estimated, 1993 and 1994

Item	1992 Actual Amount	1992 Actual Staff-Years	1993 Estimated Amount	1993 Estimated Staff-Years	1994 Estimated Amount	1994 Estimated Staff Years
USDA Advisory Committees	$2,038,000	--	$952,000	--	$ 952,000	--
Total, Advisory Committees	2,038,000	--	952,000	--	952,000	--

ADVISORY COMMITTEES

CLASSIFICATION BY OBJECTS

1992 and Estimated 1993 and 1994

	1992	1993	1994
Personnel Compensation: a/			
11 Total personnel compensation	$715,625	$490,000	$502,000
12 Personnel Benefits..........	122,462	84,000	86,000
Total Pers. Comp & Benefits......	838,087	574,000	588,000
Other Objects:			
21 Travel......................	594,821	222,000	214,000
22 Transportation of things....	1,074	1,000	1,000
23.3 Communications, utilities, and other rent..............	48,338	10,000	10,000
24 Printing and reproduction...	43,630	31,000	30,000
25 Other services..............	246,964	95,000	92,000
26 Supplies and materials......	19,621	17,000	16,000
31 Equipment...................	396	2,000	1,000
41 Grants, Subsidies and Contributions..............	42,000	--	--
Total other objects..............	996,844	378,000	364,000
Total direct obligations............	1,834,931	952,000	952,000

a/ USDA agencies are allowed under the Advisory Committee Act to obligate funds for portions of salaries and benefits for staff-time devoted to the support of these committees.

ADVISORY COMMITTEES

The estimates include appropriation language for this item as follows:

> For necessary expenses for activities of advisory committees of the Department of Agriculture which are included in this Act, $952,000: *Provided*, That no other funds appropriated to the Department of Agriculture in this Act shall be available to the Department of Agriculture for support of such committees.

ADVISORY COMMITTEES

Appropriations Act, 1993.. $952,000
Budget Estimate, 1994... 952,000
Change in Appropriation... --

SUMMARY OF INCREASES AND DECREASES
(on basis of appropriation)

Item of Change	1993 Estimated	Program Changes	1994 Estimated
USDA Advisory Committees.........	$952,000	--	$952,000

PROJECT STATEMENT
(on basis of appropriation)

Item of Change	1992 Actual Amount	1992 Actual Staff-Years	1993 Estimated Amount	1993 Estimated Staff-Years	Increase or Decrease	1994 Estimated Amount	1994 Estimated Staff-Years
Advisory Committees....	$1,832,482	--	$952,000	--	--	$952,000	--
National Commission on Agriculture and Rural Develop..	2,449	--	--	--	--	--	--
Unobligated Balance Lapsing.......	225,494	--	--	--	--	--	--
Unobl. Balance Brought Forward	-22,425	--	--	--	--	--	--
Total, available or estimate.......	2,038,000	--	952,000	--	--	952,000	--
Total, Appropriation..	2,038,000	--					

EXPLANATION OF PROGRAM

The appropriation provides for financial support of all authorized Department of Agriculture advisory committee activities other than those included in the Forest Service or financed by user fees or other funds. The FY 1983 Agriculture, Rural Development and Related Agencies Appropriations Act provided a consolidated account for this purpose. The Federal Advisory Committee Act (P.L. 92-463) was passed in 1972 to recognize that committees and similar groups provide a useful and beneficial means of furnishing expert advice to officers of the Federal Government. In establishing the Act, Congress declared that: committees should be restricted in number to only those essential to provide the necessary expert advice in specialty areas; uniform standards and procedures should govern the establishment, operation, administration and duration of the committees; and Congress should be kept informed of the number and cost of committees.

Executive Order 12838, Termination and Limitation of Federal Advisory Committees, requires each agency to terminate at least one-third or a minimum of seven discretionary advisory committees by the end of fiscal year 1993. The Order further requires each agency to justify the continuation or termination of its statutory committees. The Department is currently reviewing its advisory committees to determine which should continue in effect and which should be proposed for termination. The Congress will be notified when these decisions are made.

JUSTIFICATION OF INCREASES AND DECREASES

(1) No net change is requested for advisory committees. Changes in funding requirements will be accomplished within the same level available in fiscal year 1993.

Estimates for the Department's Advisory Committees by major policy area follow.

USDA ADVISORY COMMITTEES

Policy Area and Committee Title	1992 Actual	1993 Estimate	1994 1/ Estimate
Office of the Secretary:			
Alternative Agriculture Research and Commercialization Center..........	--	$45,698	--
Food and Consumer Services:			
Nat'l Adv. Council on Maternal, Infant and Fetal Nutrition............................	$35,312	$8,000	--
Nat'l Adv. Council on Commodity Distribution.	60,583	26,600	--
Dietary Guidelines Advisory Committee.......	--	22,100	--
National Nutrition Monitoring Advisory Council....................................	61,807	19,900	--
Advisory Committee on Welfare Simplification and Coordination..........................	56,339	49,978	--
Total..................................	214,041	126,578	--
Science and Education:			
Nat'l Ag. Res. & Exten. Users Adv. Board....	247,425	100,030	--
National Arboretum Advisory Council..........	9,416	10,000	--
Human Nutrition Board of Scient. Counselors..	15,556	15,000	--
Science & Education Nat'l Res. Initiative....	17,217	14,000	--
Advisory Council for Nat'l Genetics Res......	17,557	15,000	--
Animal Health Science Research Adv.Board.....	14,261	6,500	--
Cooperative Forestry Res. Adv. Council.......	30,109	16,000	--
Committee of Nine............................	38,370	4,000	--
Agricultural Biotechnology Res. Adv. Comm....	151,476	40,000	--
Joint Council on Food and Agricultural Sciences....................................	245,789	100,000	--
Agricultural Science and Technology Review Board..............................	62,913	20,000	--
Advisory Council on National Sustainable Agriculture................................	21,470	14,000	--
Global Climate Change Technical Advisory Committee..................................	4,860	--	--
Total....................................	876,419	354,530	--
Marketing and Inspection Services:			
Federal Grain Inspection Svc. Adv. Comm.....	22,116	15,000	--
Nat'l Adv. Comm. on Meat & Poultry Insp.....	18,000	10,000	--
Nat'l Adv. Comm. on Microbiological Criteria for Foods..................................	47,125	41,249	--
Advisory Committees on:			
Foreign Animal and Poultry Diseases......	32,603	10,000	--
Gen. Conf. Comm. of the Nat'l Poultry Improvement Plan.......................	18,484	3,500	--
Nat'l Animal Damage Control Adv. Comm.......	52,093	10,000	--
National Organic Standards Board...........	118,083	45,646	--
Total..................................	308,504	135,395	--

Policy Area and Committee Title	1992 Actual	1993 Estimate	1994 1/ Estimate
International Affairs and Commodity Programs:			
Agricultural Policy Adv. Comm. for Trade...	16,906	14,848	
Agricultural Tech. Adv. Comm. for Trade:			
Cotton..................................	17,331	13,821	
Dairy Products..........................	17,331	13,821	
Fruits and Vegetables...................	17,331	13,821	
Grain and Feed..........................	18,403	14,847	
Livestock and Livestock Products........	20,308	14,847	
Oilseeds and Oilseed Products...........	17,331	13,821	
Poultry and Eggs........................	17,331	13,821	
Sweeteners..............................	15,620	13,821	
Tobacco.................................	17,844	13,821	
Processed Food..........................	17,331	13,821	
Agribusiness Promotion Council............	14,557	--	
Agricultural Adv. Comm. on Providing Advice to Emerging Democracies...........	12,958	--	--
Total.................................	220,582	155,110	--
Small Community and Rural Development:			
President's Council on Rural America.......	87,633	10,253	
National Commission on Agriculture and Rural Development........................	2,449	--	--
Total.................................	90,082	10,253	--
Economics:			
Nat'l Ag. Cost of Prod. Standards Review Bd.	31,042	24,273	
Departmental Administration:			
Citizen's Adv. Comm. on Equal Opportunity...	54,828	21,788	--
Committee Management Support...............	39,433	50,000	--
Total..................................	94,261	71,788	--
Reserved Contingency.......................	--	28,375	--
Total, Advisory Committees................	1,834,931	952,000	952,000

1/ Decisions have not been made on which committees will be active in fiscal year 1994 and the funding allocation to those committees. An updated table of committee estimates will be provided when deliberations are completed.

ADVISORY COMMITTEES

STATUS OF PROGRAM

The appropriation provides for direction and financial support of all authorized USDA Advisory Committee activities other than those included in the Forest Service and those financed from user fees. The Assistant Secretary for Administration is the Committee Management Officer and provides the policy guidance for the establishment and continuation of committees.

A table containing information on the authority and committee membership for each committee appears at the end of the committee activity descriptions.

OFFICE OF THE SECRETARY:

Alternative Agriculture Research and Commercialization Center (AARC)

The Alternative Agriculture Research and Commercialization Center Advisory Council advises the Alternative Agriculture Research and Commercialization Board and Regional Centers on all applications for assistance for projects commercializing new nonfood and nonfeed products using agricultural commodities.

In fiscal year 1993, the Council will make nonbinding recommendations on applications submitted; monitor the progress of ongoing projects, provide technical and business counseling, and provide technical and business counseling to entities that do not seek financial assistance but that are engaged in the commercialization of agriculture commodities.

FOOD AND CONSUMER SERVICES:

National Advisory Council on Maternal Infant and Fetal Nutrition

The purpose of this Council is to make a continuing study of the Special Supplemental Food Program for Women, Infants and Children (WIC) and related Programs such as the Commodity Supplemental Food Program (CSFP) to determine how these programs may be improved. The Council is required by law to report its recommendations for changes to the President and Congress every two years.

Nineteen Council members and thirty-six others attended the one Council meeting in fiscal year 1992. The focus of this meeting was to update the Council on activities within the Supplemental Food Programs so the Council could make recommendations at the 1994 Council meeting.

No meeting is scheduled in fiscal year 1993.

National Advisory Council on Commodity Distribution

This Council was established to advise the Secretary of Agriculture on the distribution of donated commodities to recipient agencies. It provides guidance on regulations and policy development on specifications.

The Council held two meetings in fiscal year 1992 in Washington, D.C. Twelve Council members attended the first meeting on February 10-13, 1992. During this meeting, the Council developed its formal recommendations for the annual report to the Congress. The report was distributed in September. The report contained recommendations regarding USDA specifications for beef purchases, and provided more processed commodities and nutritious commodities to help schools meet dietary guidelines and nutrition education initiatives. Other recommendations included considering ethnic and regional preferences, purchasing commodities, unitizing shipments of commodities, discontinuing the commodity letter of credit sites, issuing of the commodity foods newsletter, and providing guidance for States on State advisory councils.

The last meeting of the Council was held August 18-19, 1992. The Council discussed a number of issues which will be considered further in March 1993. At the March meeting, the Council will formulate recommendations for the next report to Congress.

Dietary Guidelines Advisory Committee

The purpose of this Committee is to advise the Secretaries of Agriculture and Health and Human Services if a review of Dietary Guidelines for Americans is currently warranted based on advances in scientific knowledge and to advise the Secretaries of any recommended revision to the Guidelines. They were last revised in 1990.

In fiscal year 1993, several public meetings will be held in anticipation of recommendations for revising the Guidelines in 1995.

National Nutrition Monitoring Advisory Council

The National Nutrition Monitoring Advisory Council provides scientific and technical advice on the development and implementation of the coordinated program and comprehensive plan for the nutrition monitoring and related research program, and to advise the Secretaries of Agriculture and Health and Human Services.

The Council met three times in fiscal year 1992, in Washington, D.C. The meeting dates were February 26-27, July 15-16, and September 24-25, 1992. The first meeting was devoted to orientation of the Council and updating them on the current activities in nutrition monitoring. The second meeting was held in conjunction with the quarterly meeting of the Interagency Board for Nutrition Monitoring and Related Research. At the third meeting, the Council invited two experts in nutrition monitoring from private industry and academia to address food composition data bases and monitoring high-risk population groups. The Council also finalized their report to the Secretaries of USDA and DHHS.

Two meetings are planned in Washington, D.C. in 1993. The Council plans to continue addressing identified areas of focus, to develop and implement a mechanism to monitor the Ten-Year Comprehensive Plan, and to develop their annual report of evaluation and recommendations to the Secretaries of USDA and DHHS.

Advisory Committee on Welfare Simplification and Coordination

The Welfare Simplification and Coordination Advisory Committee examines ways to better coordinate services to applicants and participants of the Food Stamp, Aid to Families with Dependent Children, Medicaid, and housing programs. The Committee will report its findings and recommendations to Congress and the Secretaries of Agriculture, Health and Human Services, and Housing and Urban Development by July 1, 1993.

The Committee met April 30-May 1, 1992, in Arlington, Virginia. It discussed identifying barriers to administration, examining reasons for different programs and policies, evaluating how different policies hinder the receipt of multiple benefits, recommending simplified programs and policies, and describing the major effects of simplified programs and policies. Representatives from FNS, HHS, and HUD briefed the Committee on key aspects of the Food Stamp Program, AFDC, Medicaid, and HUD housing programs.

The second meeting was held August 20 - 22, 1992, in Seattle, Washington. The Committee was briefed on the Community Caring Council of Cape Girardeau, Missouri, a non-profit corporation which promotes coordination and cooperation between social service providers, churches, the business community, and the educational system to empower families and individuals to become more self-sufficient. Committee members also visited the Family Independence Program (FIP), which provides incentives for employment and training and pays for child care expenses to help families move off welfare and become self-sufficient. The program provides cash to participants in lieu of food stamp coupons. The Committee formulated an initial set of basic principles on which to base its recommendations to Congress and discussed barriers to simplification and coordination.

The next meeting will be held January 7-9, 1993, in Charlotte, North Carolina to observe the Charlotte-Mecklenberg housing demonstration. The final meeting is scheduled for March 11-12, 1993, in Wilmington, Delaware. Members will observe a one-stop shopping case management system and will be briefed on Maryland's statewide Electronic Benefit Transfer System. The Committee expires July 1, 1993.

SCIENCE AND EDUCATION:

National Agricultural Research and Extension Users Advisory Board (UAB)

This statutory committee is composed of 21 citizens reporting directly to the Secretary, the President, and the Congress on policies, programs, and planning in the food and agricultural sciences.

At the meeting on October 21-23, 1991, the UAB and Joint Council reviewed research, teaching, and extension programs at the University of Arizona; research projects at the USDA Agriculture Research Service Western Area Laboratory; and research conducted by the U.S. Water Conservation Laboratory. The agenda focused on Water and Public Land issues. The UAB and Joint Council also heard presentations on the Endangered Species Act and agreed to write a white paper on the potential implications of the Act to ranchers and farmers. In a separate session, the Board conducted a strategic assessment and planning exercise to make decisions regarding methodology, so that a private sector advisory group can better identify and evaluate top priority areas of research and education. Eighteen UAB members attended the October meeting.

At the Washington, D.C. meeting on February 13-18, 1992, the UAB examined the President's fiscal year 1993 budget proposal for agricultural research, extension, and higher education; heard from agency heads, OMB, and College of Agriculture representatives about the proposed budget; and wrote its mandated budget report. At the conclusion of the meeting, UAB members briefed their U.S. Representatives and Senators on the Board's budget appraisal and program priority recommendations. Eighteen members attended this meeting.

Eighteen members attended the May 17-20, 1992, meeting in Ithaca, New York. The UAB learned about USDA agricultural biotechnology and food safety programs conducted by Cornell University and the USDA Agricultural Research Service. The focus of the twenty-eight presentations was on competitiveness, technology transfer, regulation and risk assessment. The UAB also heard a presentation on the role of the Board of Agriculture and held workgroup sessions to draft the UAB's 1992 July report.

Eighteen members attended the August 14-18, 1992 meeting in Anchorage and Fairbanks, Alaska. Field tours and presentations illustrated unique scientific, economic, and sociological conditions in subartic cultures. Special attention was paid to efforts made in rural economic development and resource development verses resource preservation because these are critical issues facing agriculture in general, but magnified in Alaska. At the business session the Board determined it would cancel the October 1992 and August 1993 meetings, hold the February and May 1993 meetings, and combine the budget report and priorities report. These decisions were necessary because of the budget constraints in fiscal year 1993.

The UAB Appraisal of the Proposed 1992 Budget for Food and Agricultural Sciences was distributed to three thousand people in April 1992. The Board's July report, Science and Education Issues: A midyear report of citizen concerns and recommendations for American agricultural research, teaching, and extension, was distributed to two thousand people in September 1992.

Two UAB meetings will be conducted in fiscal year 1993. At the February meeting the Board will appraise the proposed fiscal year 1994 budget for Science and Education. At the May meeting the Board will recommend program priorities for Science and Education in fiscal year 1995. The Board will combine this appraisal and priorities in one published report.

National Arboretum Advisory Council

This Council advises the Department on activities and long-range plans at the National Arboretum relating to tree and plant life research and education.

The annual meeting was held October 28-29, 1991, at the National Arboretum, Washington, D.C. with thirteen Council members in attendance. There was a review of existing research and education programs and long-range plans to meet the needs of the user community and general public. A written report containing ten major recommendations was presented to the Secretary of Agriculture on April 21, 1992. Recommendations were made to have the National Arboretum staff play an increased role in planning and coordinating national programs relating to woody landscape plants and to publish an annual report on current programs and accomplishments.

A meeting will be held in fiscal year 1993 to review and evaluate Arboretum programs and activities and to make additional recommendations on the scope and direction of research and education programs.

Human Nutrition Board of Scientific Counselors

The Board reviews research progress and educational activities of the USDA and reports to the Secretary on program direction, priorities, scope of activities, and quality of programs in human nutrition, research and education.

The annual meeting of the Board was held March 17-18, 1992, in Washington, D.C. Eight agencies of the USDA and liaison members from three other Departments reported. Three resolutions developed, adopted, and forwarded to the Secretary were: (1) the need for enhanced nutrition monitoring; (2) the need for evaluation of current nutrition education to improve nutrition programming in the Department; and (3) support for Agricultural Research Service human nutrition research centers at Beltsville, Maryland, and San Francisco, California. Nutrition

During 1993, the USDA is recognizing its centenary of human nutrition activities initiated by W.O. Atwater. One of the recognition events is a symposium in June examining the unique development of research, education, food consumption monitoring, and household food economics within the USDA. In conjunction with the symposium, the Board will be asked to hold a research planning meeting to provide guidance for future planning by the Department.

Science and Education National Research Initiative Advisory Committee

This Committee advises the Secretary of Agriculture concerning the administration of the Science and Education National Research Initiative (NRI) to assure that research is carried out on the highest priority areas with the widest participation by qualified scientists. Members are scientists drawn from government, industry, and academe and are representatives of the diverse food and agricultural system.

The Committee met on August 4, 1992, in Washington, D.C. with 12 members in attendance. The Committee discussed the NRI statement of purpose, the process involved in revision of the Request for Proposals and the ways in which the Committee will continue to function. The Committee made several suggestions relative to many issues, including individual committee members' plans to maintain contacts with program directors in areas of their expertise.

A second meeting of the Committee is planned for March 1993. Subcommittees will be appointed to develop agenda items and define steps to reach specific objectives including preparation of Request for Proposals, assessment of accomplishments of the program and possible changes in program objectives. Subcommittees will communicate by telephone and meet during the scheduled meetings of the full committee. No additional expenses will be incurred on behalf of the subcommittees.

Advisory Council for National Genetics Resources

This Council assesses national needs to identify high-priority programs for conserving, utilizing, and distributing plant genetic resources for the Secretary of Agriculture and officers of the National Association of State Universities and Land-Grant Colleges. The program's aim is to collect, preserve, and disseminate genetic material of importance to American food and agricultural production.

The Council held its first meeting on December 15-16, 1992, to address policy issues relating to intellectual property rights, exchange of genetic resources, and potential impact of the Convention on Biological Diversity on all aspects of the program. The Board will also address mode of linkage of the Council to the respective genetic resources communities.

Animal Health Science Research Advisory Board

This Board advises the Secretary of Agriculture on the implementation and priorities of animal health research authorized by the National Agricultural Research, Extension and Teaching Policy Act of 1977, as amended.

The Board did not meet during fiscal year 1992 because new Board members had not been appointed. The Board will meet in fiscal year 1993.

Cooperative Forestry Research Advisory Council (CFRAC)

The Council advises the Secretary of Agriculture on national and institutional administration of the McIntire-Stennis Cooperative Forestry Research Program. The Secretary annually receives a report from this Council concerning regional and national research planning and coordination of forestry research within the Federal and State agencies, forestry schools, and the forest industries.

Ten of the sixteen Council members met December 11-12, 1991, in Washington, D.C. Discussions at this meeting resulted in the formation of resolutions included in CFRAC's fiscal year 1992 annual report to the Secretary of Agriculture. On April 21, 1992, CFRAC's outgoing and incoming chairpersons met with the Deputy Secretary, to present the Report from the Cooperative Forestry Research Advisory Council to the Secretary of Agriculture. The long standing recommendation of the Council for attaining $25 million for the McIntire-Stennis program was reinforced. In addition, CFRAC recommended that the Secretary provide the leadership in establishing a National Forestry Research Council (NFRC), as recommended by the National Research Council (NRC) of the National Academy of Sciences.

One CFRAC meeting is planned for fiscal year 1993. During 1993, CFRAC will consider broadening to include all of forestry research support through USDA. This will involve cooperation between both USDA programs in forestry research, the CSRS McIntire-Stennis program and the Forest Service (FS) research program.

Committee of Nine

The Committee of Nine advises the Secretary of Agriculture in the conduct, management, and administration of cooperative regional research. The Committee develops and implements administrative procedures and recommends policies conducive to effective regional research; monitors the regional research program to insure adequate commitment and achievement by participants; reviews research priorities, and compares them with priorities in research projects in the regional program; and encourages development of agricultural research projects within or among regions to promote a sound and prosperous agricultural, rural life and welfare of the consumer.

Meetings were held December 5-6, 1991, in Baton Rouge, Louisiana, May 13-15, 1992, in Washington, D.C., and September 10-11, 1992, in St. Paul, Minnesota. In December, the Committee reviewed and made recommendations on new and revised Regional Research Fund proposals. In May, evaluation results were communicated to participating station directors and project administration advisers. In September, the Committee proposed a national research support project that would improve coordination among germplasm researchers, initiated a national planning project to analyze the regional project, continued the development of a mechanism for the emergence of a new national research project, and initiated a comprehensive revision of the regional research manual. The Committee evaluated and recommended approval of six National Research Support Projects. All members attended the meetings.

There are approximately 191 regional research projects. In fiscal year 1992, the Committee reviewed and took action on 79 regional research proposals including: 14 new proposals, 29 revisions, 19 extensions, and 11 deferrals or conditional approvals. There were six regional research proposal extensions denied.

In fiscal year 1993, only one meeting is scheduled for May 1993.

Agricultural Biotechnology Research Advisory Committee (ABRAC)

ABRAC advises the Secretary of Agriculture on policies, programs, operations, and activities associated with agricultural biotechnology research. It oversees the review of proposed research projects, evaluates the adequacy of draft proposals used by USDA in preparing environmental assessments of the above research projects, recommends necessary revisions to research guidelines and protocols, advises other Federal and State agencies on agricultural related research projects, and provides information to and maintains cognizance of Institutional Biosafety Committees (IBC's) to assure the availability of essential personnel to carry out oversight of agricultural related biotechnology functions.

There were three full ABRAC meetings and three ABRAC working group meeting in fiscal year 1992. The first full ABRAC meeting took place December 3-4, 1991, in Washington, D.C. It was attended by twenty-six visitors and four staff members, who finalized the Guidelines for Research Involving Planned introduction into the Environment of Genetically Modified Organisms.

The second ABRAC meeting was held March 11-13, 1992, in Arlington, Virginia. It was attended by forty-three visitors and six staff members. Half of this membership was new, so the meeting included background/orientation presentations. The major Committee action was the development of recommendations concerning the approval of an outdoor study of transgenic catfish in confined research ponds at Auburn University.

The final ABRAC meeting on August 26-27, 1992, in Arlington, Virginia was attended by 45 visitors and 5 staff members. The Committee heard (1) the report of the Risk Assessment Working Group, (2) plans for a meeting of its Working Group on Aquatic Biotechnology and Environmental Safety and (3) a briefing on potential societal issues associated with agricultural biotechnology research.

The ABRAC Classification and Confinement Working Group met on October 30-31, 1991 in Arlington, Virginia and December 2, 1992 in Washington, D.C. to finalize specific organism examples for the ABRAC research guidelines. The Classification/Confinement Working Group held their final meeting August 25, 1992 in Arlington, Virginia to review the scientific basis of proposed performance standards for field testing transgenic plants.

In fiscal year 1993, ABRAC will conduct one full committee meeting, tentatively scheduled for Research Triangle Park, North Carolina, and two or three small working group meetings.

Joint Council on Food and Agricultural Sciences

This statutory Council has the primary responsibility of bringing "about more effective research, extension, and teaching in the food and agriculture sciences in the United States by improving the planning and coordination of publicly and privately supported food and agriculture science activities and by relating Federal budget development and program management to these processes. The Council advises the Secretary and the Congress on priorities, policies, programs, planning, and coordination matters regarding the food and agriculture science and education system in the United States. Four meetings were held by the Joint Council in fiscal year 1992.

At the October 21-23, 1991 meeting, in Tucson, Arizona, the Joint Council and UAB held their combined annual meeting. Activities at this meeting are discussed under the National Agricultural Research and Extension Users Advisory Board.

At the January 29-31, 1992, meeting in Baton Rouge, Louisiana, the Council selected and ranked priorities for inclusion in its report, Fiscal Year 1994 Priorities for Research, Extension, and Higher Education: A Report to the Secretary of Agriculture. The Council also toured and reviewed programs at the Pennington Biomedical Research Center at Louisiana State University, heard presentations on planning and coordination of human nutrition research and on human nutrition information programs, and received a final draft of the Joint Council recommendations to the Secretary of Agriculture and Congress on the Endangered Species Act.

At the April 22-24, 1992 meeting in Washington, D.C., the Council selected 1992 Accomplishments for Research, Extension, and Higher Education, reviewed social issues and areas of emphasis for the 1992 Update of the Five Year Plan for Food and Agricultural Sciences, received a report on the Food Animal Integrated Research Initiative, and toured the Beltsville Agricultural Research Center, where the group received an update on human nutrition activities in science and education, including a proposed model for improving the planning and coordination of human research and education activities.

At the August 12-14, 1992 meeting in New Brunswick, New Jersey, the Council reviewed a draft of the 1991 Accomplishments Report and 1992 Update of the Five Year Plan for the Food and Agriculture Sciences; reviewed a report from the Organizing Committee on Human Nutrition; received an update on the Food and Agricultural Education Information System (FAEIS); toured the NABISCO headquarters and research facilities in East Hanover, New Jersey; received a proposal for evaluating the socio-economic and environmental impacts of research, extension, and higher education programs; heard presentations on sustaining agricultural and open space in the Northeast and on farming systems in an urbanized region; reviewed the public policy issues affecting agricultural in the Northeast; received a presentation and toured the Cook College/New Jersey Agriculture Experiment Station Centers for Advanced Food Technology (CAFT) and Agriculture Biotechnology.

During fiscal year 1992, the Council published the Fiscal Year 1994 Priorities for Research, Extension, and Higher Education: A Report to the Secretary of Agriculture, and the 1990 Accomplishments for Research, Extension, and Higher Education: A Report to the Secretary of Agricultural and the Nation.

For fiscal year 1993 the Council will meet twice.

Agricultural Science and Technology Review Board

The Agricultural Science and Technology Review Board which was authorized by the FACT Act of 1990, held its first meeting on September 24-25, 1992. The Board determined that it would meet twice in fiscal year 1993 to identify and assess current and emerging agricultural research and technology transfer initiatives, including emerging technologies from private industry and public institutions that would influence agricultural, natural resources, nutrition, and the broad social, economic, and health agricultural, natural resources, nutrition, and the broad social, economic, and health consequences on urban and rural communities. A report on these findings was made to the Secretary in December 1992.

Advisory Council on National Sustainable Agriculture

The Advisory Council on National Sustainable Agriculture is authorized by the FACT Act of 1990 to recommend projects that should receive funding, promote programs, coordinate research and extension activities, and establish general procedures for awarding and administering funds under the Sustainable Agricultural Research and Education program. The Council also considers recommendations for improving programs and facilitates cooperation and integration between sustainable agricultural, water quality, integrated pest management, food safety, and other related programs.

The Council was chartered in May 1992, and will hold its first meeting in fiscal year 1993. The Department is in the process of appointing members to the Council.

Global Climate Change Technical Advisory Committee (GCCTAC)

The Global Climate Change Technical Advisory Committee (GCCTAC) was established under Section 2404 of Title XXIV Global Climate Change provisions of the FACT Act of 1990. Its purpose is to advise the Secretary of Agricultural concerning research on the effects of global climate change on agricultural and forestry with specific emphasis on mitigation of negative effects of global climate change and actions for adaptation to global climate change and related phenomena.

This committee does not plan to meet in fiscal year 1993.

MARKETING AND INSPECTION SERVICES:

Federal Grain Inspection Service Advisory Committee

This Committee advises the Administrator of the Federal Grain Inspection Service (FGIS) on the implementation of the U.S. Grain Standards Act.

The Committee met twice in fiscal year 1992: once in Washington, D.C., and once in Manhattan, Kansas. One subcommittee met to make recommendations regarding alternatives to FGIS fee increases. Other issues addressed by the Committee were official commercial inspection, grain quality, standards and regulations, codex alimentarius activities, total quality marketing, financial management, aflatoxin issues, wheat protein, and research and technology.

One full committee meeting is scheduled for fiscal year 1993. One subcommittee is scheduled to review financial matters and fee structures.

National Advisory Committee on Meat and Poultry Inspection

The Secretary of Agriculture is required by Federal inspection laws to consult with this Committee prior to issuing product standards, labeling changes, or on matters affecting Federal and State inspection program activities. This Committee also reviews initiatives, helps develop standard descriptive terminology, and recommends when the regulatory policies need to be reexamined.

One meeting was held September 22-23, 1992, in Fairfax, Virginia. The Food Safety and Inspection Service (FSIS) received Committee recommendations and advice on such subjects as strategic planning and the risk assessment and analysis process. The Committee plans to meet three times within the next fiscal year.

National Advisory Committee on Microbiological Criteria for Foods

The National Advisory Committee on Microbiological Criteria for Foods is currently co-sponsored by the Food Safety and Inspection Service, the Food and Drug Administration, National Marine Fisheries Service and the U.S. Army Surgeon General's Office. The Committee provides advice on the development of microbiological criteria by which the safety and wholesomeness of the Nation's food supply can be assessed, including criteria for microorganisms that indicate whether foods have been processed using good manufacturing practices.

During fiscal year 1992 five meetings were held: November 4-6, 1991, in Chicago, Illinois, December 16-19, 1991, in Crystal City, Virginia, January 13-14, 1992, in Atlanta, Georgia, March 16-19, 1992, in Orlando, Florida, and September 28-30, 1992, in Washington, D.C. Two formal reports were presented to the Secretaries of Agriculture and Health and Human Services: (1) Hazard Analysis and Critical Control Point System and (2) Vacuum or Modified Atmosphere Packaging for Refrigerated Raw Fishery Products. The Committee provided its sponsors and those concerned with food safety with concrete recommendations that can be incorporated into food protection systems.

The Committee is scheduled to meet four to six times in fiscal year 1993 to complete deliberations on Hazard Analysis Critical Control Points Plans for Red Meat and Poultry, and scientific paper on Campylobacter, and develop consumer educational materials.

Advisory Committee on Foreign Animal and Poultry Diseases

This Committee advises the Secretary on the means to prevent, suppress, control, or eradicate an outbreak of foot-and-mouth disease (FMD) or other destructive foreign animal or poultry diseases should such diseases enter the United States. Committee duties involve advising and counseling on policy and regulatory action pertaining to dealing with an outbreak, changing practices in the production and marketing of animals, the importation of animals and animal products, and the handling and treatment of unusual, suspicious animal or poultry disease problems.

One Committee meeting was held June 2-4, 1992, in Key West, Florida, and attended by eighteen members. Topics of discussion included: Veterinary Services' basic organizational plans, animal disease research, the National Environmental Policy Act (NEPA), emergency plans for Emergency Preparedness and a Test Exercise, foreign animal disease (FAD) status of countries that are members of the European Community (EC), FAD training and diagnostic test development, progress in FAD research at Plum Island, revision of FAD emergency guidelines, import/export challenges and risk assessment in international trade, screwworm eradication in Mexico and Central America, USDA FAD strategic plan, and the world status of animal disease in 1990 and 1991.

Twelve comments or recommendations were made by the Committee. They addressed privately-owned equine quarantine facilities, bovine tuberculosis, Panama screwworm fly production plant, tropical bont tick program, the lottery system for use of Harry S Truman Animal Import Center (HSTAIC), USDA support of legal authority for extra-label use of animal drugs, Smith-Kilbourne Scholars Program, APHIS quarantine procedures, trade between the U.S. and the EC, and FAD requirements at points of entry. The Committee visited HSTAIC in Key West, Florida.

At least one meeting of the Committee will be held in fiscal year 1993 to receive recommendations on a number of subjects pertaining to preventing the introduction of foreign animal disease, strategies designed to contain incursions, risk assessment involving international trade, environmental issues, emergency preparedness, and animal import requirements.

General Conference Committee of the National Poultry Improvement Plan (NPIP)

The General Conference Committee represents cooperating State agencies and poultry industry members, and serves as liaison between the poultry industry and the U.S. Department of Agriculture on matters pertaining to poultry health.

In fiscal year 1992, two meetings of the General Conference Committee were held. The first meeting was held November 19-20, 1991, in Columbia, Maryland to plan for the forthcoming National Biennial Conference in June 1992. The draft proposed changes to the NPIP approved at the last Biennial Conference were reviewed to ensure that they reflected the intent of the delegates.

The second meeting was held June 29-July 2, 1992, in Colorado Springs, Colorado, in conjunction with the Biennial Conference of the NPIP. The Committee (1) rejected the inclusion of a Salmonella enteritidis control program for commercial pullets, 2) requested that the Secretary have the National Veterinary Services laboratory (NVSL) make Mycoplasma antigens and reagents available to the industry on a user fee basis, 3) requested funding at a level for 1994 to provide for a full-time veterinary coordinator, 4) and developed ten resolutions that were considered by delegates from thirty-one states present at the Biennial Conference. There is no meeting planned for fiscal year 1993.

National Animal Damage Control Advisory Committee (ADC)

This Committee provides advice to the Secretary on policies, program issues, and research needed to conduct the Animal Damage Control (ADC) program. Members represent a broad spectrum of agricultural, environmental and conservation groups, academia, and other interests.

The Committee met December 3-5, 1991, in Denver, Colorado. Issues discussed included distribution of Federal ADC funds to the States, insurance that ADC continues to provide wildlife damage control services, proper ranking of research activities, recruitment of non-Federal researchers in the process, and potentially expanded role of the 1080 Livestock Protection Collar.

The second meeting was held September 22-24, 1992, in Fort Collins, Colorado. Final recommendations were made to the Secretary of Agriculture covering topics discussed during the December 1991 meeting.

The committee plans one meeting during fiscal year 1993, tentatively scheduled to be held in conjunction with the North American Wildlife and Natural Resources Conference in March 1993, in Washington, D.C.

National Organic Standards Board

The National Organic Standards Board was established to provide recommendations to the Secretary on implementing the Organic Foods Production Act of 1990, which authorizes a national organic production program establishing national standards for the production and certification of organically produced foods.

During fiscal year 1992, three meetings were held: March 20-25, 1992, in Washington, D.C., July 7-10, 1992, in Fort Collins, Colorado, and September 27-30, 1992, in Augusta, Maine. The Board developed recommendations on topics such as organic farm planning, organic processing planning, dealing with emergency spray-drifting, evaluation applications for accreditation, harmonizing international organic standards, and a national list of approved and prohibited materials.

For fiscal year 1993 the Board will hold one meeting.

INTERNATIONAL AFFAIRS AND COMMODITY PROGRAMS:

Agricultural Policy Advisory Committee for Trade

Agricultural Technical Advisory Committees for Trade (10)

These advisory committees seek information and advice from representative elements of the private sector on negotiating objectives and bargaining positions before entering into a trade agreement, on the operation of any trade agreement once entered into, and on other matters arising in connection with the administration of United States trade policy.

The committees currently in existence are an Agricultural Policy Advisory Committee for Trade (APAC), and ten Agricultural Technical Advisory Committees for Trade (ATACs) in agricultural commodities (cotton, dairy products, fruits and vegetables, grain and feed, livestock and livestock products, oilseeds and products, poultry and eggs, sweeteners, tobacco and processed foods). The APAC provides advice regarding overall agricultural trade issues, and the ATACs provide detailed technical advice and information on their respective commodities. Each of these committees is composed of various agricultural interests such as farmers, farm and commodity organizations, processors, and traders, etc. The committees are reasonably limited in size with attention to representation from most aspects of the commodity trade and to minority and multi-sized entities.

During fiscal year 1992, some topics discussed in meetings were: 1) GATT Ministerial Meetings and the Uruguay Round of Multilateral Trade Negotiations generally, and the U.S. proposal for agricultural in the Uruguay Round, 2) U.S.-Canadian Free Trade Agreement, 3) North American Free Trade Agreement, 4) European Community trade in 1992, 5) Pending trade legislation, 6) The Long-Term Agricultural Trade Strategy, and other aspects of the Food, Agricultural Conservation and Trade Act of 1990, 7) Harmonized Tariff System conversion, 8) Various Section 301 cases and 9) other items of specific interest to the individual Committee members. All meetings were held in USDA facilities in Washington, D.C. The Agricultural Policy Advisory Committee met a total of seven times during the fiscal year. The Agricultural Technical Advisory Committees met six times during the fiscal year.

<u>Agribusiness Promotion Council</u>

The Agribusiness Promotion Council assists USDA in implementing the Caribbean Basin Initiative in furtherance of the Caribbean Basin Economic Recovery Act. The Council seeks to promote the sound economic development of the Caribbean Basin and further the good will and understanding between the people of the region and the United States. The Council met in Washington D.C. in October 1991, to review the status of activities relating to agribusiness development in the Caribbean Basin and to make recommendations to the Secretary of Agricultural on future activities.

During fiscal year 1992 members of the council participated in seminars and business missions in the region. The Council expired in December 1992.

<u>Agricultural Advisory Committee on Providing Advice to Emerging Democracies</u>

This committee provides information and advice useful to USDA in implementing the program to share agricultural expertise with emerging democracies. The Committee also advises USDA on ways to increase the involvement of the U.S. private sector in cooperative work with emerging democracies in food and rural business systems. During fiscal year 1992, the Committee held one meeting. The following topics were discussed: 1) the legislative mandate of the Emerging Democracies program and the role and approach of FAS as the supporting agency; 2) the past, present, and planned future activities under the Emerging Democracies program and unique problems in implementing the program; 3) technical assistance programs in the former Soviet Union; 4) the new program of credit guarantees for facilities authorized; and 5) the organization and basic function of the Advisory Committee.

Starting in fiscal year 1993, the Emerging Democracies Advisory Committee will be funded entirely through the Commodity Credit Corporation.

SMALL COMMUNITY AND RURAL DEVELOPMENT:

President's Council on Rural America

The President's Council on Rural America was established by Executive Order 12720 on July 16, 1990, to advise the President on how the Federal government can facilitate rural Americans' efforts to improve their quality of life and enhance their economy, as well as how to improve delivery of Federal services and utilize resources more effectively. This mission will be fulfilled by utilizing both council members and the general public. The two principal Council goals are: (1) To improve rural development program coordination among Federal agencies and begin active partnerships with states, localities and the private sector and (2) To adopt a strategic and comprehensive approach to rural development, while improving the effectiveness of the Federal rural development effort. Council participants will include state and local governments, and private sector organizations and individuals. Information topics will include: policy development and management, intergovernmental relations, attitudes as barriers to development, infrastructure community leadership, urban/rural linkages, environmental issues, human services, health, education, housing, technology transfer, trade development and tourism.

The full Council met three times in fiscal year 1992. Council meetings were held November 12-13, 1991, in Santa Fe, New Mexico, January 27-29, 1992, in Williamsburg, Virginia, and May 27-29, 1992, in Denver, Colorado. The Council's subcommittees held additional meetings to study issues such as economic development and infrastructure while gathering facts and utilizing expertise available from both the academic and private sectors. To gather public input, seven hearings were held in October and November of 1991 in Montgomery, Alabama; Sioux Falls, South Dakota; Springfield, Illinois; Huntington, West Virginia; Sacramento, California; Binghamton, New York; and Santa Fe, New Mexico.

The Council finalized its report in August 1992 and delivered it to the White House in October 1992. The Council expired on December 31, 1992.

ECONOMICS:

National Agricultural Cost of Production Standards Review Board

This Board reviews the adequacy, accuracy, and timeliness of the cost of production methodology used by the Department in determining specific cost of production estimates, reviews the adequacy of the parity formulae, advises the Secretary on such matters dealing with the cost of production of agricultural commodities and price support operations as the Secretary may request, and makes such recommendations to the Secretary as it deems appropriate, including ways in which the cost of production methodology and parity formulae can be improved.

The Board has customarily met twice each year to critique the survey design and questionnaires used to collect primary data from farmer respondents and to review current costs and returns concepts, procedures, and estimates. In addition, the Board has provided insight about the reasonableness of estimates prepared for farms of different types and sizes in various areas of the country.

The Board held one meeting in fiscal year 1992, July 27-28, 1992. Actions focused on reestablishing the Board's Charter, setting up procedures to identify eligible members representative of all types and characteristics of procedures.

Two meetings are planned for fiscal year 1993. The first meeting is planned for February 25-26, 1993. The agenda for this meeting includes discussions of USDA determination labor hours and wage rates for use in valuing labor used in producing crop and livestock commodities, estimation of machinery costs, and estimation of government commodity programs participation returns and costs. The Board will also hear discussion of results of the American Agricultural Economics Association's Task

Force on Commodity Costs and Returns Accounting Standards. The second meeting in fiscal year 1993 will most likely be held in July or August.

DEPARTMENTAL ADMINISTRATION:

Citizens Advisory Committee on Equal Opportunity

The Citizens Advisory Committee (CAC) on Equal Opportunity advises the Secretary on the effectiveness of Departmental civil rights and equal opportunity policies and practices and recommends changes that would strengthen the Departments's efforts in this area.

During fiscal year 1992, the Committee held eight meetings: two full committee meetings and six subcommittee meetings. The first full Committee meeting was held March 9-10, 1992, in Washington, D.C. to establish the Committee's fiscal year 1992 agenda.

Subcommittee meetings were held throughout the year to discuss how to explore and study USDA trade programs and their impact on minorities; how to use the 1890 Land-Grant Institutions and HACU as models to expand to other underrepresented groups; and how to evaluate employment practices and the delivery of programs by Farmers Home Administration.

The final full committee meeting was held September 14-16, 1992, in San Francisco, California. The meeting was convened to discuss the committee's fiscal year 1993 agenda and receive subcommittee reports. Other agenda activities included discussions on Departmental sexual harassment policy; the Department's Senior Executive Service Candidate Development Program; and updates on the status of the Committee's fiscal year 1993 budget. The committee established the Subcommittee on Farmers Home Administration (FmHA), the Subcommittee on Minority Outreach, and the Subcommittee on International Programs and Affects on Minority-Owned and Women-Owned Businesses.

The Committee submitted two reports to the Secretary during fiscal year 1992. The reports recommended operational improvements for the Employment Appeals Staff and improvements in the delivery of USDA programs and services to Hispanics and native Americans.

The Committee plans to hold its first fiscal year 1993 meeting in January 1993. Initial meetings of the Subcommittee on Minority Outreach and the Subcommittee on FmHA have been held. All subcommittees are in the process of setting fiscal year 1993 goals and establishing ways to coordinate their activities with the Office of Advocacy and Enterprise.

NATURAL RESOURCES AND ENVIRONMENT:

State Technical Committees

State Technical Committees assist the Secretary of Agriculture in the technical considerations relating to implementation of the Conservation provisions of the FACT Act of 1990. Each State Technical Committee will consist of ten to twenty members composed of professional resource managers who represent a variety of disciplines in the soil, water, wetland and wildlife sciences.

It is anticipated the State Technical Committees will be established in each state, the Caribbean area, and the Pacific Basin during fiscal year 1993. Each State Technical Committee is expected to meet at least once to provide information, analysis, and recommendations to those Federal agencies responsible for implementing a particular conservation provision. Committee recommendations will be made in writing and used by the Department in determining matters of fact, technical merit or scientific question.

Authority and Composition of USDA Advisory Committees

Committee Title	USDA Agency	Descrip. of Committee Authority Statutory (S)/Discretionary (D)	Committee Membership
OFFICE OF THE SECRETARY:			
Alternative Agriculture Research and Commercialization Center	OSEC	S 7 U.S.C. 5905(c)	10
FOOD AND CONSUMER SERVICES:			
National Advisory Council on Maternal, Infant and Fetal Nutrition	FNS	S 42 U.S.C. 1786	24
National Advisory Council on Commodity Distribution	FNS	S 42 U.S.C. 1786	14
Dietary Guidelines Advisory Committee	HNIS	D Departmental Regulation 1042-94	9
National Nutrition Monitoring Advisory Council	HNIS	S P.L. 101-445	
Advisory Committee on Welfare Simplification and Coordination	FNS	S 7 U.S.C. 2011	11
SCIENCE AND EDUCATION:			
National Agricultural Research and Extension Users Advisory Board	CSRS	S 7 U.S.C. 3123	21
National Arboretum Advisory Council	ARS	D Secretary's Memorandum 1702	23
Human Nutrition Board of Scientific Counselors	ARS	D Secretary's Memorandum 2030	13
Science and Education National Research Initiative Advisory Committee	CSRS	D Departmental Regulation 1043-5	17
Advisory Council for National Genetic Resources	ARS	S 7 U.S.C. 5843	
Animal Health Science Research Advisory Board	CSRS	S 7 U.S.C. 3194	12
Cooperative Forestry Research Advisory Council	CSRS	S 16 U.S.C. 582a-4	16
Committee of Nine	CSRS	S 7 U.S.C. 361c(c)3	9
Agricultural Biotechnology Research Advisory Committee	CSRS	D Departmental Regulation 1042-87	22

Committee Title	USDA Agency	Descrip. of Committee Authority Statutory (S)/Discretionary (D)	Committee Membership
Joint Council on Food and Agricultural Sciences	CSRS	S 7 U.S.C. 3122	21
Agricultural Science and Technology Review Board	CSRS	S 7 U.S.C. 3123(a)	11
Advisory Council on National Sustainable Agriculture	CSRS	S 7 U.S.C. 5812	28
Global Climate Change Technical Advisory Committee	ARS	S 7 U.S.C. 6703	Membership Not Determined
MARKETING AND INSPECTION SERVICES:			
Federal Grain Inspection Service Advisory Committee	FGIS	S 7 U.S.C. 87i	15
National Advisory Committee on Meat and Poultry Inspection	FSIS	S 21 U.S.C. 601	15
National Advisory Committee on Microbiological Criteria for Foods	FSIS	D Departmental Regulation 1043-28	26
Advisory Committee on Foreign Animal and Poultry Diseases	APHIS	D Secretary's Memorandum 1781	19
General Conference Committee of the National Poultry Improvement Plan	APHIS	D Secretary's Memorandum 1758	13
National Animal Damage Control Advisory Committee	APHIS	D Departmental Regulation 1043-27	20
National Organic Standards Board	AMS	S 7 U.S.C. 6518	14
INTERNATIONAL AFFAIRS AND COMMODITY PROGRAMS:			
Agricultural Policy Advisory Committee for Trade	FAS	D Secretary's Memorandum 1869	33
Ag. Tech. Adv. Comm. for Trade:			
Cotton	FAS	D Secretary's Memorandum 1868	14
Dairy Products	FAS	D Secretary's Memorandum 1868	19
Fruits and Vegeables	FAS	D Secretary's Memorandum 1868	12
Grain and Feed	FAS	D Secretary's Memorandum 1868	14
Livestock and Livestock Products	FAS	D Secretary's Memorandum 1868	10
Oilseeds and Oilseed Products	FAS	D Secretary's Memorandum 1868	10
Poultry and Eggs	FAS	D Secretary's Memorandum 1868	8
Sweeteners	FAS	D Secretary's Memorandum 1868	10
Tobacco	FAS	D Departmental Regulation 1042-82	9
Processed Foods	FAS	D Departmental Regulation 1042-68	12
Agribusiness Promotion Council	OICD	D Departmental Regulation 1043-11	20

Committee Title	USDA Agency	Descrip. of Committee Authority Statutory (S)/Discretionary (D)	Committee Membership
Agricultural Advisory Committee on Providing Advice to Emerging Democracies	FAS	S 7 U.S.C. 5622	20
SMALL COMMUNITY AND RURAL DEVELOPMENT:			
President's Council on Rural America	SCRD	S Executive Order 12720 July 16, 1990	19
ECONOMICS:			
National Agricultural Cost of Production Standards Review Board	ERS	S 7 U.S.C. 4101	11
DEPARTMENTAL ADMINISTRATION:			
Citizen's Advisory Committee on Equal Opportunity	DA	D Secretary's Memorandum 1960	20
NATURAL RESOURCES AND ENVIRONMENT			
Advisory Committee on Soil and Water Conservation	SCS	D 7 U.S.C. 5501	20
State Technical Committees	SCS	S 16 U.S.C. 3861-62	500-800

HAZARDOUS WASTE MANAGEMENT

Purpose Statement

This program is designed to promote facility compliance under the requirements of the Comprehensive Environmental Response, Compensation, and Liability Act (CERCLA) and the Resource Conservation Recovery Act (RCRA). These Acts require Federal agencies to meet the same standards for storage and disposition of hazardous wastes as private businesses. The funds provided for this program enable the Department to address problems posed by past uncontrolled hazardous waste disposal practices and to deal with the regulation of current hazardous substances.

A central fund has been established from which resources are allocated to USDA agencies according to priory of need. This approach permits the Department to correct compliance problems in a systematic manner.

HAZARDOUS WASTE MANAGEMENT

Available Funds and Staff-Years

1992 Actual and Estimated, 1993 and 1994

Item	1992 Actual Amount	1992 Actual Staff Years	1993 Estimated Amount	1993 Estimated Staff Years	1994 Estimated Amount	1994 Estimated Staff Years
Direct Appropriation...	$26,350,000	--	$16,000,000	--	$16,000,000	--
Deduct Allotments to Other Agencies:						
Commodity Credit Corporation......	-5,163,500	--	-3,000,000	--	-3,000,000	--
Forest Service.....	-10,696,000	--	-8,527,000	--	-8,527,000	--
Agricultural Research Service.	-5,209,691	--	-1,698,000	--	-1,248,000	--
Farmers Home Administration...	-4,000,000	--	-1,271,600	--	---	--
Soil Conservation Service..........	-245,000	--	-224,000	--	---	--
Farm Service Agency	---	--	---	--	-1,761,000	
Animal and Plant Health Inspection Service..........	-202,000	--	-149,000	--	-50,000	--
Office of the General Counsel..	-595,007	--	-513,000	--	-492,000	--
National Agricultural Library..........	-24,135	--	---	--	---	--
Food Safety and Inspection Svc...	-197,000	--	-120,000	--	-240,000	--
Departmental Admin.	-17,667	--	---	--	---	--
Rural Development Administration	...	--	---	--	-300,000	--
Total, Allotments....	-26,350,000	--	-15,502,600	--	-15,618,000	--
Reserve for Further Allocation...........	...	--	-497,400	--	-382,000	--
Total, HWM...........	0	--	0	--	0	--

HAZARDOUS WASTE MANAGEMENT

CLASSIFICATION BY OBJECTS

1992 and Estimated 1993 and 1994

	1992	1993	1994
Other Objects:			
21 Travel	317,000		---
22 Transportation of things	27,000		---
23.2 Rental payments to others	---		---
23.3 Communications, utilities, and misc. charges	95,000	---	---
24 Printing	15,000	---	---
25 Other services	34,555,573	18,190,065	16,000,000
26 Supplies and materials	377,000	---	---
31 Equipment	482,000	---	---
32 Lands and Structures	1,121,000	---	---
33 Investments and Loans	-1,000	---	
41 Grants, Subsidies and Contributions	10,000	---	
42 Insurance claims & Indemnities	1,000	---	---
43 Interest and Dividends	5,000	---	---
Total other objects	37,004,573	18,190,065	16,000,000
Total direct obligations	37,004,573	18,190,065	16,000,000

HAZARDOUS WASTE MANAGEMENT

The estimates include appropriation language for this item as follows:

Hazardous Waste Management

For necessary expenses of the Department of Agriculture to comply with the requirement of section 107g of the Comprehensive Environmental Response, Compensation, and Liability Act, as amended, 42 U.S.C. 9607g, and section 6001 of the Resource Conservation and Recovery Act, as amended, 42 U.S.C. 6961, $16,000,000 to remain available until expended: Provided, that appropriations and funds available herein to the Department of Agriculture for hazardous waste management may be transferred to any agency of the Department for its use in meeting all requirements pursuant to the above Acts on Federal and non-Federal lands.

HAZARDOUS WASTE MANAGEMENT

Appropriations Act, 1993	$16,000,000
Budget Request, 1994	16,000,000
Change in Appropriation	+ 0

PROJECT STATEMENT
(on basis of available funds)

	1992 Actual		1993 Estimated		Increase or Decrease	1994 Estimated	
	Amount	Staff-Years	Amount	Staff-Years		Amount	Staff-Years
Haz. Waste Mgmt	$37,004,573	---	$18,190,065	---	-$2,190,065	$16,000,000	---
Recovery of prior year obligation	-220,433	---	---	---	---	---	---
Unoblig. Bal. start of year.	-12,624,205	---	-2,190,065	---	+2,190,065	---	---
Unoblig. Bal. end of year...	+2,190,065	---	---	---	---	---	---
Appropriation..	26,350,000	---	16,000,000	---	---	16,000,000	---

Explanation of Program

This appropriation funds the Department's efforts to identify, assess, contain, and clean up hazardous waste sites in areas covered by programs of the Department or within Departmental jurisdiction. These responsibilities were imposed on all Federal agencies by the Comprehensive Environmental Response, Compensation and Liability Act (CERCLA) and the Resource Conservation and Recovery Act (RCRA).

Because the Department identified a number of hazardous waste sites requiring remedial action, a central fund was established in fiscal year 1988. Resources from this fund are allocated to Departmental agencies according to priority needs.

JUSTIFICATION OF INCREASES AND DECREASES

No increase is requested for this appropriation. The CERCLA and RCRA programs will be carried out within the level appropriated for fiscal year 1993.

Allocations to USDA agencies are shown below. The allocations for fiscal year 1994 are tentative, based on current program status.

Current and Proposed Allocation of Funds
for Hazardous Waste Management
(Dollars in Thousands)

USDA Agency	1993 Estimate	1994 Estimate
Agricultural Research Service	1,698	1,248
Animal and Plant Health Inspection Service	149	50
Commodity Credit Corporation	3,000	3,000
Farmers Home Administration	1,272	---
Farm Service Agency	---	1,761
Food Safety and Inspection Service	120	240
Forest Service	8,527	8,527
Office of the General Counsel	513	492
Soil Conservation Service	224	---
Rural Development Administration	---	300
Reserved for Further Allocation	497	382
Total Allocations	16,000	16,000

HAZARDOUS WASTE MANAGEMENT

STATUS OF PROGRAM

This program provides for facility compliance with the requirements of the Comprehensive Environmental Response, Compensation, and Liability Act (CERCLA) and the Resource Conservation Recovery Act (RCRA).

In August 1985, USDA initiated a Nation-wide survey to determine the overall scope of the problems associated with the past unregulated hazardous waste disposal practices and the current regulation of hazardous waste substances. USDA agencies identified and reported on facilities or sites in violation of applicable standards resulting in contamination of ground or surface water, as well as the release of hazardous substances. The initial survey identified a number of hazardous waste problems, which included improper handling of toxic chemicals at research facilities, inadequate storage of pesticides and other hazardous substances, and leaking underground storage tanks. Based on the potential magnitude of the costs of compliance, a central fund was created in fiscal year 1988 from which resources are reallocated to USDA agencies according to established need.

Current Activities:

CERCLA Program

Much of the activity under this program has been directed toward site discovery, preliminary assessments, and site investigations aimed at verifying and quantifying individual project and overall program requirements. This step in the CERCLA process is important because it establishes the basis for further actions, as the data gathered is used to determine the next phases that may be necessary. For example, the Forest Service has identified a number of serious problems associated with past mining activities and abandoned mining wastes and with permitted municipal landfills located on National Forest lands. The Farmers Home Administration also has identified the need to cleanup hazardous wastes on properties obtained through foreclosure. All of these problems are expected to continue in the near future. Efforts are underway to attempt to recover costs for some of this work from potential responsible parties (PRP's).

In fiscal year 1992, USDA agencies initiated investigations at over 140 CERCLA sites. They completed 58 preliminary assessments (PA's), 14 site investigations (SI's), and two remedial investigation/feasibility studies (RI/FS's). All of the documents associated with these assessments, investigations, and studies have been submitted to the Environmental Protection Agency (EPA) and the appropriate State agencies for their review and approval.

Cleanup activities were completed at 95 sites. Most cleanups involved emergency removal actions associated with illegal dumps and hazardous material spills. An example of several significant cleanups completed in fiscal year 1992 follows:

- **Spokane Mine, Black Hills NF - Custer, South Dakota:** A removal action was completed. Main items of work included covering old mine shafts, moving several small tailings piles, reshaping the site for drainage, applying line to the tailings, capping the site, and fencing and vegetating the area. The EPA has classified the site as "Site Evaluation Accomplished" with no further action required.

- **Yakima Agricultural Research Center:** Cleanup has been completed at this facility. Clean closure and post-closure monitoring has been approved. The site has been approved for removal from the National Priorities List.

- **Great Plains Research Laboratory, Fort Collins, Colorado:** Landfill reclamation at this facility has been completed. No further action is anticipated.

■ **Leslie Harmon Property, Mentor, Minnesota:** Investigation, removal, and proper disposal of waste agricultural chemicals was completed for this property.

RCRA Program

The activity under this program has been directed toward compliance with underground storage tank (UST) requirements. This included leak testing, monitoring tank removal, repair or replacement, and cleanup activities. USDA agencies made significant progress in this program this year by completing the following:

■ **Forest Service** removed a total of 225 tanks at 160 facility sites;

■ **Agricultural Research Service** removed tanks at 19 locations; and

■ **Soil Conservation Service (SCS)** removed UST's at 7 different locations throughout the country. Cleanup of contaminated soil was initiated at two sites where tanks leaked.

In addition to UST compliance, RCRA activities included the treatment and disposal of hazardous wastes. In fiscal year 1992, the Forest Service conducted site investigations and testing at five sites and began corrective actions at 63 other sites. Much of this effort involved old sanitary landfills or dumps that have been closed for several years and now pose a threat for the release of hazardous substances. In some cases site testing has proven negative; therefore, no further work will be needed. However, additional testing and/or corrective actions will be necessary at many sites. The Forest Service also faces another potentially serious problem related to small, local municipal landfills that have been permitted on National Forest lands. Leachate from these facilities is causing both soil and ground water contamination. In many cases where local communities do not have the resources to take necessary corrective action, the Forest Service will be held liable as manager of the lands.

Other agencies also were involved in RCRA cleanup activities during fiscal year 1992. For example, the SCS installed equipment to reduce or eliminate waste pesticides and rinse waters at locations in Idaho, Kansas, Kentucky, Michigan, and Mississippi. The SCS also completed improvements for handling waste pesticides at facilities in Kentucky, Louisiana and New Mexico.

OFFICE OF BUDGET AND PROGRAM ANALYSIS

Purpose Statement

The Office of Budget and Program Analysis coordinates the preparation of departmental budget estimates and legislative reports; administers systems for the allotment and apportionment of funds; provides policy, program and budgetary analysis of USDA programs and proposals; and provides staff assistance to USDA agencies in meeting their responsibilities for the development and review of regulations.

The Office of Budget and Program Analysis is located in Washington, D.C. As of September 30, 1992, there were 71 full-time permanent employees and one other than full-time permanent employee.

OFFICE OF BUDGET AND PROGRAM ANALYSIS

Available Funds and Staff-Years

1992 Actual and Estimated, 1993 and 1994

Item	1992 Actual Amount	1992 Actual Staff-Years	1993 Estimated Amount	1993 Estimated Staff-Years	1994 Estimated Amount	1994 Estimated Staff-Years
Direct Appropriation...	$6,149,000	70	$5,756,000	76	$5,853,000	76

OFFICE OF BUDGET AND PROGRAM ANALYSIS

Permanent Positions by Grade and Staff-Year Summary

1992 and Estimated 1993 and 1994

Grade	1992 Headquarters	1993 Headquarters	1994 Headquarters
ES-6	3	3	3
ES-5	2	2	2
GS/GM-15	8	8	8
GS/GM-14	19	20	20
GS/GM-13	17	18	18
GS-12	2	2	2
GS-11	4	3	3
GS-10	0	1	1
GS-9	4	3	3
GS-8	2	4	4
GS-7	7	6	6
GS-6	2	3	3
GS-5	2	2	2
GS-4	2	1	1
Total Permanent Positions	74	76	76
Unfilled Positions end-of-year	-3	0	0
Total, Permanent Employment, end-of-year	71	76	76
Staff-Years: Ceiling	70	76	76

OFFICE OF BUDGET AND PROGRAM ANALYSIS

CLASSIFICATION BY OBJECTS

1992 and Estimated 1993 and 1994

	1992	1993	1994
Personnel Compensation:			
Headquarters	$3,979,373	$4,420,000	$5,853,000
11 Total personnel compensation	3,979,373	4,420,000	4,505,000
12 Personnel benefits..........	546,730	650,000	663,000
13 Benefits for former personnel.................	0	5,000	5,000
Total pers. comp & benefits........	4,526,103	5,075,000	5,173,000
Other Objects:			
21 Travel......................	14,666	17,000	17,000
22 Transportation of things....	43	--	--
23.3 Communications, utilities, and misc. charges.........	79,546	87,000	87,000
24 Printing....................	143,392	61,000	61,000
25 Other services..............	369,168	289,000	288,000
26 Supplies and materials......	154,933	143,000	143,000
31 Equipment...................	726,197	84,000	84,000
Total other objects...........	1,487,945	681,000	680,000
Total direct obligations............	6,014,048	5,756,000	$5,853,000
Position Data:			
Average Salary, ES positions.....	$109,640	$113,649	$114,140
Average Salary, GM/GS position...	$52,787	$54,250	$55,413
Average Grade, GM/GS positions...	11.68	11.75	11.75

OFFICE OF BUDGET AND PROGRAM ANALYSIS

The estimates include appropriation language for this item as follows (new language underscored; deleted matter enclosed in brackets):

Office of Budget and Program Analysis

For necessary expenses of the Office of Budget and Program Analysis, including employment pursuant to the second sentence of section 706(a) of the Organic Act of 1944 (7 U.S.C. 2225), of which not to exceed $5,000 is for employment under 5 U.S.C. 3109, [$5,756,000] $5,853,000.

OFFICE OF BUDGET AND PROGRAM ANALYSIS

Appropriations Act, 1993	$5,756,000
Budget Estimate, 1994	5,853,000
Increase in Appropriation	+97,000

SUMMARY OF INCREASES AND DECREASES
(On basis of appropriation)

Item of Change	1993 Estimated	Pay Cost	Other Changes	1994 Estimated
Budget and Program Analysis	$5,756,000	+$98,000	-$1,000	$5,853,000

PROJECT STATEMENT
(On basis of appropriation)

	1992 Actual		1993 Estimated		Increase or Decrease	1994 Estimated	
	Amount	Staff-Years	Amount	Staff-Years		Amount	Staff-Years
Budget and Program Analysis	$6,014,048	70	$5,756,000	76	+$97,000(1)	$5,853,000	76
Unobligated Balance	134,952						
Total Appropriation	6,149,000	70	5,756,000	76	+97,000(1)	5,853,000	76

Explanation of Program

The Office of Budget and Program Analysis provides direction and administration of the Department's budgetary functions including development, presentation, and administration of the budget; reviews program and legislative proposals for program and budget and related implications; analyzes program and resource issues and alternatives, and prepares summaries of pertinent data to aid Departmental policy officials and agency program managers in the decision-making process; provides Department-wide coordination for and participation in the presentation of budget related matters to the Committees of the Congress, the press, and the public. The Office also provides Department-wide coordination of the preparation and processing of the legislative program and legislative reports; provides Department-wide coordination and processing of regulations; and aids the Secretary and other Departmental agency officials in making management decisions regarding the Department's programs and resources.

JUSTIFICATION OF INCREASES AND DECREASES

(1) A net increase of $97,000 consisting of:

(a) An increase of $17,000, which reflects a 2.7 percent increase in non-salary costs.

(b) An increase of $98,000, which reflects the annualization of the fiscal year 1993 pay raise.

(c) A decrease of $18,000 for administrative efficiency.

Need for Change. To promote the efficient use of resources for administrative purposes, in keeping with the President's Executive Order, total USDA baseline outlays for these activities will be reduced by 3 percent in FY 1994, 6 percent in FY 1995, 9 percent in FY 1996 and 14 percent in FY 1997.

Nature of Change. In order to achieve this savings, OBPA will reduce discretionary expenses such as--travel, training, supply purchases, printing and reproduction costs and telephone usage.

GEOGRAPHIC BREAKDOWN OF OBLIGATIONS AND STAFF YEARS
1992 and Estimated 1993 and 1994

	1992		1993		1994	
	Amount	Staff-Years	Amount	Staff-Years	Amount	Staff-Years
Washington, D.C.	$6,014,048	70	$5,756,000	76	$5,853,000	76
Unobligated balance	134,952	--	--	--	--	--
Total, Available or Estimate	6,149,000	70	5,756,000	76	5,853,000	76

OFFICE OF BUDGET AND PROGRAM ANALYSIS

STATUS OF PROGRAM

The Office of Budget and Program Analysis coordinates the preparation of departmental budget estimates and legislative reports; administers systems for the allotment and apportionment of funds; provides policy, program and budgetary analysis of USDA programs and proposals; and provides staff assistance to USDA agencies in meeting their responsibilities for the development and review of regulations.

In carrying out these responsibilities, OBPA assists the Secretary, Deputy Secretary, and other policy officials of the Department in the development, presentation, execution, and monitoring of the Department's budget. OBPA provides general oversight, review, and analytical studies related to alternative policy directions and resource levels. OBPA represents the Department at meetings and hearings with Congressional Committees, the Office of Management and Budget (OMB), the General Accounting Office (GAO), the Department of Treasury and others on matters related to the Department's budget.

Current Activities:

Development and Presentation of the USDA Budget

-- Reviews and analyzes agency budget estimates and develops alternatives and supporting data for the Secretary.

-- Consolidates materials for the budget submitted to OMB. Serves as liaison with OMB staff during their review of the Budget Estimates.

-- Prepares Department-wide budgetary statements and summaries.

-- Coordinates and prepares supporting justifications for budget requests to be presented to the Appropriations Committees.

-- Serves as liaison with the Appropriations Committees and their staffs for the purpose of scheduling hearings, reviewing transcripts, and answering questions concerning USDA programs.

-- Prepares and consolidates information requested by the appropriations, authorizing, and budget committees, and the Congressional Budget Office (CBO), including special budgetary analyses, reports, and appropriations hearings materials.

Management of USDA Funds and Staff-Years

-- Issues allotments and apportionments which allocate funds in accordance with laws, regulations, and the requirements of the Executive Branch and Congress.

-- Monitors and analyzes the Department's use of staff-year resources.

Program Analysis

-- Coordinates and/or conducts policy and program analyses and other reviews to assist agency and senior policy officials in formulating or implementing USDA policies and programs.

-- Reviews and analyzes legislation, regulations, and policy options to determine their impact on USDA programs and policy objectives.

-- Monitors ongoing studies with significant program or policy implications and periodically publishes USDA Study Agenda which provides the current status of each study.

Coordination of Regulatory Decisions

-- Reviews and assists in development of regulations and impact analyses used in regulatory decision making.

-- Maintains the Regulatory Tracking System to inform senior policy officials of the status of proposed regulations.

-- Coordinates and assists in preparation of the USDA portion of OMB's Regulatory Program and the Regulatory Agenda.

-- Maintains liaison with OMB, other Federal agencies and the Congress on the review of rules.

Coordination of Legislative Proposals and Reports

-- Coordinates and assists in the preparation of bills, resolutions, reports and other legislative material for submission to the Congress.

-- Compiles and produces the USDA Legislative Program which lists pending Administration proposals by subject area.

-- Maintains the Legislative Reports Tracking System to inform senior policy officials of the status of legislative proposals and reports.

Selected Examples of Recent Progress:

Automation. During FY 1992, a new officewide automated system was installed. This highly flexible ADP system has significantly upgraded the office's capacity to use automated tools, is expandable to meet future needs and facilitates greater automated communication and interaction with other organizations. The net effect is to significantly improve the office's ability to provide accurate and timely responses to requests for information and assistance.

Legislative Reports Tracking System. The Legislative Reports Tracking System continues to be a key element in OBPA's efforts to coordinate, monitor and provide information on the large volume of legislative reports, proposals, bills, and resolutions received by the Department. During the second session of the 102nd Congress, OBPA assisted in the preparation of approximately 800 legislative reports or proposals and monitored the intra-Department handling of about 8,000 bills, resolutions and other materials.

Regulatory Tracking System. An automated process was expanded to improve the capability to monitor and track Department-wide activity related to the preparation and review of regulations under the President's regulatory reform initiative and regulatory moratorium. The regulation preparation and review process was also revised pursuant to this initiative.

Major Legislation. During FY 1992, the Congress enacted and the President signed legislation authorizing payments to farmers who suffered 1990, 1991 or 1992 crop losses due to adverse weather conditions. OBPA prepared cost analyses which were used both within the Executive Branch and by the Congress during the legislative process.

Budget Summary. OBPA presented a series of technical, non-policy budget briefings for Congressional staff, the news media, special interest groups, and the general public when the Administration issued its FY 1993 budget proposals. These briefings were attended by over 100 Congressional staff and members of the press and were broadcast on USDA's closed circuit TV. OBPA also distributed about 2,000 copies of the Budget Summary document to Congressional Committees, the press, State governments, farm groups, and other people interested in USDA programs.

WITNESSES

INDEX

Economic Research Service

National Agricultural Statistics Service

World Agricultural Outlook Board

Food and Nutrition Service

Human Nutrition Information Service

Office of Public Affairs

Office of the General Counsel

Departmental Administration/Office of the Secretary

○

Lightning Source UK Ltd.
Milton Keynes UK
UKHW010632131218
333917UK00007B/163/P

9 780260 103086